THE BIG YELLOW BOOK OF GERMAN VERBS

555

FULLY CONJUGATED VERBS

Paul Listen, Ph.D. | Robert Di Donato, Ph.D.

Daniel Franklin

McGraw-Hill

New York Chicago San Francisco Lisbon London Madrid Mexico City Milan New Delhi San Juan Seoul Singapore Sydney Toronto

The McGraw·Hill Companies

Library of Congress Cataloging-in-Publication Data

Listen, Paul, 1961–
The big yellow book of German verbs : 555 fully conjugated verbs / Paul Listen, Robert Di Donato, Daniel Franklin.
p. cm.
Includes indexes.
ISBN 0-07-143300-7 (alk. paper)

1. German language—Verb. 2. German language—Self-instruction. I. Di Donato, Robert. II. Franklin, Daniel. III. Title.

PF3271.L57 2005
438.2'421—dc22 2005041598

3 4 5 6 7 8 9 10 11 12 13 14 15 16 VLP/VLP 0 9 8 7 6

ISBN 0-07-143300-7

Interior design by Village Typographers, Inc.

This book is printed on acid-free paper.

Contents

GERMAN TENSE PROFILES

THE BASICS OF CONJUGATION

A verb is the part of speech that expresses an action, mode of being, or occurrence, for example, *to run*, *to think*, *to live*, or in German, **laufen**, **denken**, **leben**. When used in a sentence, the verb is said to be inflected, meaning it may have endings or inflections. To conjugate a verb means to list all its different inflected forms in a specific and logical fashion.

German has more inflected forms than English. Compare the following two sentences.

Ich **laufe** jeden Tag.	*I run every day.*
Wir **laufen** jeden Tag.	*We run every day.*

Notice that English uses the same form (*run*) in both sentences, whereas German has two different forms (**laufe**, **laufen**). As you can see from the examples, the difference between the forms is the endings.

Endings are one of the ways inflected verbs can show the grammatical categories of person (***Person***), number (***Numerus*** or ***Zahl***), mood (***Modus***), and tense (***Tempus*** or ***Zeit***). This section provides an overview of these grammatical categories and the category of voice (***Genus***). The basics of German verb conjugation are also presented.

PERSON AND NUMBER

The grammatical categories of person and number are features of both nouns and verbs in German.

Number can be either singular or plural. A noun or pronoun is singular if it refers to a single person or thing, for example, *I*, *she*, *the house*, or *Mr. Smith*. A noun or pronoun is plural if it refers to more than one person or thing, for example, *we*, *they*, *orchids*, or *the Joneses*.

The verb in a German sentence agrees with the subject noun in that sentence. If the subject is singular, then the verb must be a singular form, too. If the subject is plural, the verb must be plural.

For convenience and efficiency, pronouns are used in the conjugation tables of this book. It is therefore important to understand the German pronouns, how they relate to person and number, and how they relate to other nouns.

German Pronouns

	NOMINATIVE	ACCUSATIVE	DATIVE	GENITIVE	
SINGULAR					
FIRST PERSON	ich	mich	mir	meiner	*I/me*
SECOND PERSON	du	dich	dir	deiner	*you* (familiar)
	Sie	Sie	Ihnen	Ihrer	*you* (formal)
THIRD PERSON	er	ihn	ihm	seiner	*he/him*
	sie	sie	ihr	ihrer	*she/her*
	es	es	ihm	seiner	*it*
PLURAL					
FIRST PERSON	wir	uns	uns	unser	*we/us*
SECOND PERSON	ihr	euch	euch	eurer	*you* (familiar)
	Sie	Sie	Ihnen	Ihrer	*you* (formal)
THIRD PERSON	sie	sie	ihnen	ihrer	*they/them*

Case is a characteristic of nouns and pronouns, as well as of the noun phrases they appear in. There are four cases in German: nominative, accusative, dative, and genitive.

The nominative case is used for the subject of a sentence, as well as for predicates involving verbs such as **sein** *to be* and **werden** *to become*. The accusative case is used for the direct object of a sentence (generally) and for the object of certain prepositions. The dative case is used for the indirect object of a sentence and for the object of certain verbs and prepositions. The genitive case is used to show possession or relation; it is also used for the object of certain verbs and prepositions. Genitive pronouns are not commonly used in modern German.

These tense profiles focus on nominative pronouns, since they are most relevant to the form of the verb in a sentence.

The category of person encompasses first person, second person, and third person. First person is the speaker or the speaker and others for whom he or she speaks. First person is expressed in the singular personal pronoun **ich** (*I*) and the plural personal pronoun **wir** (*we*). Second person is the hearer(s), or the person(s) to whom the speaker is talking, writing, or communicating, expressed in the personal pronouns **du**, **ihr**, and **Sie** (singular and plural) (*you*). Third person is anyone or anything other than the speaker and hearer. Thus, third person includes the subject pronouns **er**, **sie**, **es**, and **sie** (*he*, *she*, *it*, and *they*).

In the following table, the present tense of the verb **laufen** *to run* is shown in the format used in this book.

	SINGULAR	PLURAL
FIRST PERSON	ich lauf**e**	wir lauf**en**
SECOND PERSON	du läuf**st**	ihr lauf**t**
	Sie lauf**en**	Sie lauf**en**
THIRD PERSON	er/sie/es läuf**t**	sie lauf**en**

Each subject pronoun is paired with an inflected verb form, which shows the proper ending for agreement with that particular pronoun. (Some forms have an **ä** where others have an **a**. This is called "umlaut" or vowel change and is another way some verbs in German are inflected. This will be explained below.) The **du** and **ihr** forms are familiar; the **Sie** forms are formal.

An inflected verb is said to agree with the subject of its sentence, which means it has endings that are specific to the subject in both person (first, second, or third) and number (singular or plural).

Many sentences have subjects that are made up of more than pronouns, of course. It is important to understand how the subject pronouns used in the conjugation tables relate to nouns and other pronouns that might be used as the subject of a sentence.

Third person comprises all pronouns outside the first and second persons, as well as any common or proper noun. Unlike first and second person, third person frequently involves no pronouns at all. In the sentences below, the noun phrases used as subjects are all in the third person and would therefore require a third-person singular or third-person plural verb form.

Third-Person Singular

Sie lacht. — *She laughs.*
Unsere Mutter lacht. — *Our mother laughs.*

Third-Person Plural

Meine Freunde lachen. — *My friends laugh.*
Er und Bob lachen. — *He and Bob laugh.*

The last sentence above contains a compound subject, meaning more than one noun or pronoun is involved. If a sentence has a compound subject, the verb must be plural.

If a compound subject contains a first-person pronoun, the verb is first-person plural. If a compound subject contains a second-person pronoun, the verb is second-person plural unless the subject also contains a first-person pronoun. First person overrides second person.

First-Person Plural

Meine Freunde und ich kochen. — *My friends and I cook.*
Du und ich kochen. — *You and I cook.*

Second-Person Plural

Du und die Kinder kocht. — *You and the children cook.*
Sie und er kochen. — *You and he cook.*

MOOD AND TENSE

An inflected verb is said to be in one of three moods: indicative, subjunctive, or imperative. German uses the indicative mood to talk about things that the speaker perceives as real, true, or factual. The subjunctive mood is used for contingent, possible, hypothetical, and what-if expressions. It is also used to make requests more polite. German actually has two different kinds of subjunctive mood: subjunctive I and subjunctive II. The imperative mood is used for commands and instructions.

There are six basic tenses in German: present, simple past, future, present perfect, past perfect, and future perfect. Theses tenses combine with moods to make a total of 14 conjugation patterns (excluding the imperative).

Present	Present Perfect
Simple Past	Past Perfect
Future	Future Perfect
Present Subjunctive I	Past Subjunctive I
Present Subjunctive II	Past Subjunctive II
Future Subjunctive I	Future Perfect Subjunctive I
Future Subjunctive II	Future Perfect Subjunctive II

All German tenses are either indicative or subjunctive. "Simple past" is actually "simple past indicative"; the word "indicative" is usually omitted in tense names.

Inflections indicate agreement with the subject in person and number. They also show mood and tense.

VOICE

German has two voices: active and passive. In an active-voice sentence, the subject is the person or thing doing the action expressed by the verb. In a passive-voice sentence, the focus is on either the action itself or the person or thing being acted upon. The 555 conjugation tables in this book present only the active forms, since the passive forms can be easily derived from them. For details on formation and use of the passive, see pages 31–32.

THE GERMAN VERB

The Infinitive

Inflected forms are also known as finite forms. They are finite in that they are limited to a certain person and number. Forms that are not finite include infinitives and participles.

The basic German infinitive is made up of a stem and a suffix (**-n** or **-en**). By far, the more common suffix is **-en**.

bauen	**sammel**n
bringen	**tu**n
öffnen	**wander**n

These are actually present active infinitives; for other infinitive types, see pages 34–35.

Verb Classes

There are many ways to categorize German verbs. A common way, and one that is most useful for learning conjugations, is to divide them into classes based on their conjugation patterns. The names of these classes vary slightly from one approach to another. This book uses the terms "regular weak," "strong," "mixed," and "modal" to refer to four classes of verbs.

Regular Weak Verbs Regular weak verbs are often called simply "regular verbs" or "weak verbs." The great majority of German verbs belong to this class.

In some instances, the form of a German verb's infinitive provides a clue to its class. For example, all verbs ending in **-eln** or **-ern** are regular weak. All verbs ending in **-ieren** are regular weak, except for **frieren**, **verlieren**, and any prefixed verbs based on them. For all other German verbs, the form of the infinitive does not reliably indicate its class.

Regular weak verbs have **-te** as a marker of the simple past tense and the suffix **-(e)t** in the past participle. The stem stays the same in all forms. Once the infinitive of a regular weak verb is known, all other forms can be derived according to regular rules.

INFINITIVE	SIMPLE PAST TENSE (3 SG.)	PAST PARTICIPLE	ENGLISH
bauen	bau**te**	**ge**bau**t**	*to build*

For more details about regular weak verbs, see individual tense profiles beginning on page 7.

Strong Verbs Strong verbs are sometimes called "irregular strong verbs" or "irregular verbs" because the tenses differ from one another in significant and seemingly unpredictable ways. The stem vowel in the simple past tense is different from that of the present tense. Some strong verbs also change one or more stem consonants. Most have a sound change in the past participle as well. Strong verbs also have the suffix **-(e)n** in the past participle.

INFINITIVE	SIMPLE PAST TENSE (3SG.)	PAST PARTICIPLE	ENGLISH
ziehen	**zog**	gezog**en**	*to pull*

There are only about 200 strong verbs in German. For more details about strong verbs, see individual tense profiles beginning on page 7.

Mixed Verbs Mixed verbs are a small group of verbs that are like regular weak verbs in some ways, but like strong verbs in other ways. They are thus sometimes called "irregular mixed verbs" or "irregular weak verbs." Like regular weak verbs, mixed verbs have **-te** as a marker of the simple past tense, and the past participle ends in **-t**. Like strong verbs, however, mixed verbs have a stem or vowel change in the simple past.

INFINITIVE	SIMPLE PAST TENSE (3SG.)	PAST PARTICIPLE	ENGLISH
bringen	br**achte**	gebrach**t**	*to bring*

There are very few mixed verbs in German; the following is a list of them, grouped according to conjugation pattern.

brennen, kennen, nennen, rennen   senden, wenden   bringen, denken

For more details about mixed verbs, see individual tense profiles beginning on page 7.

Modal Verbs Modal verbs modify the main verb's meaning with respect to concepts such as ability, desire, intention, permission, and obligation. For example, consider the action expressed in the sentence **Herr Smith spricht Elbisch.** (*Mr. Smith speaks Elvish.*) Different attitudes toward the action of speaking Elvish can be supplied with the addition of the modal verbs, for example, **wollen** *to want (to)* and **können** *can.*

Herr Smith **will** Elbisch sprechen.	*Mr. Smith wants to speak Elvish.*
Herr Smith **kann** Elbisch sprechen.	*Mr. Smith can speak Elvish.*

There are six modal verbs in German.

dürfen, können, mögen, müssen, sollen, wollen

In their conjugations, modal verbs differ to some extent from other verb classes, although they share some patterns with other verbs. For more details about modal verbs, see individual tense profiles beginning on page 7. See also pages 30–31 for word order with modal verbs.

The Verbs *haben, sein, tun, werden,* and *wissen* The verbs **haben** *to have*, **sein** *to be*, **tun** *to do*, **werden** *to become*, and **wissen** *to know* do not fit neatly into any of the four classes described above. Their differences are explained in the tense profiles beginning on page 7.

A Note about Verb Class Some German verbs belong to more than one class. They are sometimes regular weak and sometimes strong, depending on meaning and context. Examples include **bleichen**, **glimmen**, and **schrecken**. A small number of verbs follow the patterns of one verb class in some tenses, but another verb class in other tenses; examples include **backen**, **hauen**, **mahlen**, and **schallen**. Details for these verbs are provided in their conjugation tables.

Principal Parts of the Verb

The infinitive of a verb is its entry word in most German dictionaries. This book presents verbs based on infinitives in alphabetical order. Three other verb forms are provided below the infinitive: the third-person singular, present tense form; the third-person singular, simple past tense form; and the past participle. These three forms plus the infinitive make up the four principal parts of the verb. All other forms of a German verb can be derived from these four forms (except for a few highly irregular verbs). Let verb No. 116, **brechen** *to break*, serve as an example.

brechen
bricht · brach · gebrochen

FORMS DERIVED FROM THE INFINITIVE **brechen**		FORMS DERIVED FROM THE PRESENT TENSE (3 SG.) **bricht**	FORMS DERIVED FROM THE SIMPLE PAST TENSE (3 SG.) **brach**	
PRESENT				
ich breche	wir brechen			
	ihr brecht	du brichst		
Sie brechen	Sie brechen			
	sie brechen	er/sie/es bricht		
SIMPLE PAST				
			ich brach	wir brachen
			du brachst	ihr bracht
			Sie brachen	Sie brachen
			er/sie/es brach	sie brachen
PRESENT SUBJUNCTIVE I				
ich breche	wir brechen			
du brechest	ihr brechet			
Sie brechen	Sie brechen			
er/sie/es breche	sie brechen			
PRESENT SUBJUNCTIVE II				
			ich bräche	wir brächen
			du brächest	ihr brächet
			Sie brächen	Sie brächen
			er/sie/es bräche	sie brächen
IMPERATIVE				
	brecht!	brich!		
brechen Sie!	brechen Sie!			

FUTURE
FUTURE SUBJUNCTIVE I
FUTURE SUBJUNCTIVE II } ... brechen (*all forms*)

***Infinitive:* brechen** The following tenses and forms can be derived from the infinitive (refer to the table above): the first-person singular, second-person singular formal, and all plural forms of the present indicative; all forms of the present subjunctive I; the plural familiar imperative; and the singular and plural formal imperative. The future, future subjunctive I, and future subjunctive II tenses use the infinitive **brechen** as the second component of all forms.

***Third-person Singular, Present Tense:* bricht** The second-person singular familiar of the present indicative and the singular familiar imperative can be derived from this principal part.

***Third-person Singular, Simple Past Tense:* brach** All other simple past tense forms, as well as all forms of the present subjunctive II, can be derived from this principal part. (A very few strong verbs have present subjunctive II forms that cannot be derived from the four principal parts. They must be individually learned.)

FORMS DERIVED FROM THE PAST PARTICIPLE **gebrochen**

PRESENT PERFECT
PAST PERFECT
FUTURE PERFECT
PAST SUBJUNCTIVE I
PAST SUBJUNCTIVE II
FUTURE PERFECT SUBJUNCTIVE I
FUTURE PERFECT SUBJUNCTIVE II
PASSIVE (*all tenses*) } ... gebrochen (*all forms*)

***Past Participle:* gebrochen** All other compound tenses, including all tenses of the passive voice, use the past participle as their second component.

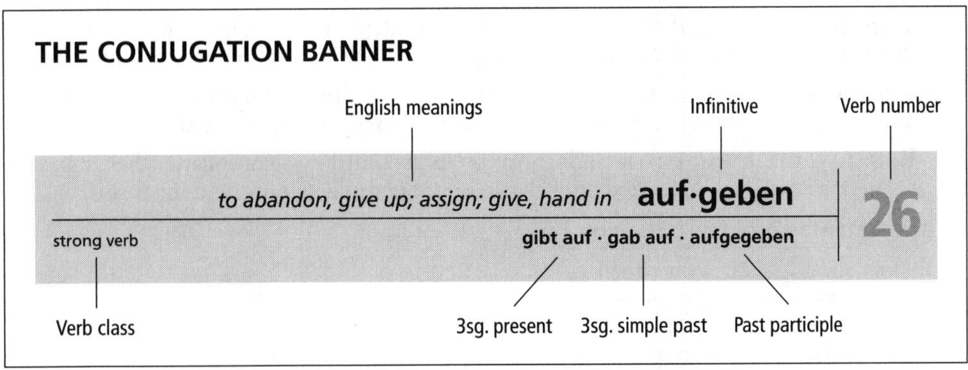

The Conjugation Banner

In the box above, the conjugation banner for the German verb **auf·geben** is shown. Many German verbs have prefixes that separate from the stem when conjugated in a main clause. Such verbs are indicated by a centerline dot between the prefix and the basic verb; in this instance, the separable prefix is **auf**. The third-person forms show the prefix separated from the basic verb as it would be in a sentence.

THE SIMPLE TENSES

German verb tenses can be grouped into simple and compound tenses. Generally speaking, a German verb in a simple tense does not need an auxiliary (helping) verb to be complete. By contrast, a verb in a compound tense requires an auxiliary verb.

There are four simple tenses in German.

Present (indicative)	(see below)
Simple past (indicative)	(see page 12)
Present subjunctive I	(see page 15)
Present subjunctive II	(see page 15)

The Present

In German, the present tense is usually called **Präsens** or **Gegenwart**. The present tense forms of German verbs are made up of a stem and an ending.

Regular Weak, Strong, and Mixed Verbs To form the present tense of all regular weak and mixed verbs, as well as most strong verbs, first take the infinitive and drop the ending; the result is the infinitive stem.

lachen *to laugh*	[drop **-en**]	>	**lach-**	jodeln *to yodel*	[drop **-n**]	>	**jodel-**
atmen *to breathe*	[drop **-en**]	>	**atm-**	singen *to sing*	[drop **-en**]	>	**sing-**
wandern *to hike*	[drop **-n**]	>	**wander-**	senden *to send*	[drop **-en**]	>	**send-**

Now add the present tense endings to the infinitive stem. The regular weak verb **lachen** and the strong verb **singen** show the basic endings for the present tense.

lachen *to laugh* (STEM **lach-**)	
ich lach**e**	wir lach**en**
du lach**st**	ihr lach**t**
Sie lach**en**	Sie lach**en**
er/sie/es lach**t**	sie lach**en**

singen *to sing* (STEM **sing-**)	
ich sing**e**	wir sing**en**
du sing**st**	ihr sing**t**
Sie sing**en**	Sie sing**en**
er/sie/es sing**t**	sie sing**en**

- The forms for **Sie**-singular, **wir**, **Sie**-plural, and **sie**-plural are *always the same in any given tense*. This is true for all verb classes.
- There are some minor adjustments that must be made to some of the endings for certain verbs. They are necessary when certain sounds at the end of the verb stem join with the

endings. It is best to think of these adjustments as adaptations instead of exceptions: The verb has to adapt to the ending by either adding or dropping certain letters/sounds.

The following five adjustment rules apply to verbs in the present tense in general. Special features of the present tense of each verb class are subsequently presented.

- **Rule 1.** If the infinitive stem ends in **-m** or **-n** preceded by a consonant other than **h, l, m, n,** or **r**, then **-e-** is inserted after the stem in the **du**, **er/sie/es**, and **ihr** forms.

atmen *to breathe* (STEM **atm-**)	
ich atme	wir atmen
du atm**est**	ihr atm**et**
Sie atmen	Sie atmen
er/sie/es atm**et**	sie atmen

Thus, for example, the third-person singular form for **atmen** is **atmet**, because the stem ends in **-m** preceded by the sound **t**. By contrast, although the stem for the verb **qualmen** also ends in **-m**, the **m** is preceded by the sound **l** and thus has the third-person singular form without **-e-** inserted: **qualmt**.

If the preceding **h** is part of a consonant cluster such as **ch**, **sch**, or **th**, the extra **-e-** is inserted. Thus, for example, the third-person singular form for **rechnen** is **rechnet**, because the stem ending in **-n** is preceded by the sound **ch** (a consonant cluster, not simple **h**).

- **Rule 2.** If the infinitive stem ends in **-s**, **-ß**, **x**, or **z**, then the **s** in the **-st** ending of the **du** form is omitted and the ending is simply **-t**. Examples include **rasen** (**du rast**), **fassen** (**du fasst**), **grüßen** (**du grüßt**), **feixen** (**du feixt**), and **sitzen** (**du sitzt**).

This rule does not apply to stems ending in **-sch**, for example, **kreischen** (**du kreischst**).

- **Rule 3.** If the infinitive stem ends in **-ie**, then the ending for the **Sie**-singular, **wir**, **Sie**-plural, and **sie**-plural forms is simply **-n**. The **ich** form has no extra **-e** added.

knien *to kneel* (STEM **knie-**)	
ich knie_	wir knie**n**
du kniest	ihr kniet
Sie knie**n**	Sie knie**n**
er/sie/es kniet	sie knie**n**

- **Rule 4.** If the infinitive stem ends in **-el** or **-er**, then the ending for the **Sie**-singular, **wir**, **Sie**-plural, and **sie**-plural forms is simply **-n**.

wandern *to hike* (STEM **wander-**)	
ich wandere	wir wander**n**
du wanderst	ihr wandert
Sie wander**n**	Sie wander**n**
er/sie/es wandert	sie wander**n**

- **Rule 5.** If the infinitive stem ends in **-el**, then the **e** of the stem is optionally dropped in the **ich** form. For example, it is correct to use either **jodle** or **jodele** for the first-person singular form of **jodeln**. The optional nature of this rule is shown in the conjugations by parentheses around the **e**: **jod(e)le**.

Special Features of Regular Weak Verbs and Mixed Verbs

Insertion of -e- In addition to the five rules above, the following rule applies to the present tense of all regular weak verbs and all mixed verbs. For verbs whose infinitive stem ends in **-d** or **-t**, it is necessary to insert **-e-** after the stem in the **du**, **er/sie/es**, and **ihr** forms.

retten *to rescue* (STEM **rett-**)	
ich rette	wir retten
du rett**est**	ihr rett**et**
Sie retten	Sie retten
er/sie/es rett**et**	sie retten

senden *to send* (STEM **send-**)	
ich sende	wir senden
du send**est**	ihr send**et**
Sie senden	Sie senden
er/sie/es send**et**	sie senden

Further examples include **berichten (berichtest, berichtet), reden (redest, redet), trösten (tröstest, tröstet), vermuten (vermutest, vermutet),** and **wenden (wendest, wendet).**

Special Features of Strong Verbs

In addition to the five rules above, the following rules apply to the present tense of strong verbs.

Stem Change Some strong verbs have vowel changes in the second- and third-person singular, present tense forms, as shown in the conjugations of **fahren** and **brechen.**

fahren *to drive* (STEM **fahr-**)	
ich fahre	wir fahren
du **fährst**	ihr fahrt
Sie fahren	Sie fahren
er/sie/es **fährt**	sie fahren

brechen *to break* (STEM **brech-**)	
ich breche	wir brechen
du **brichst**	ihr brecht
Sie brechen	Sie brechen
er/sie/es **bricht**	sie brechen

The following table shows the range of vowel changes with an example verb for each change.

	a → ä	au → äu	e → i	e → ie	ä → ie	o → ö	ö → i
INFINITIVE	fallen	laufen	nehmen	sehen	gebären	stoßen	löschen
PRESENT TENSE (2 SG.)	fällst	läufst	nimmst	siehst	gebierst	stößt	lischst
PRESENT TENSE (3 SG.)	fällt	läuft	nimmt	sieht	gebiert	stößt	lischt

Notice the stem consonant change in **nehmen**: the **h** is dropped and the **m** is doubled. Consonant changes apply to only a few verbs. To determine whether a verb's stem changes in the **du** and **er/sie/es** forms of the present tense, see the verb's conjugation table in this book.

Limited Insertion of -e- If the infinitive stem of a strong verb ends in **-d** or **-t**, then

- Insert **-e-** after the stem in the **du** and **er/sie/es** forms *only if those forms do not show the stem vowel change just described above.*
- Insert **-e-** after the stem in the **ihr** form, regardless of the stem vowel.

The following examples illustrate this rule. With the verb **reiten, -e-** is inserted in the **ihr** form, as well as in the **du** and **er/sie/es** forms. With the verb **halten, -e-** is inserted only in the **ihr** form.

reiten *to ride* (STEM **reit-**)	
ich reite	wir reiten
du reit**est**	ihr reit**et**
Sie reiten	Sie reiten
er/sie/es reit**et**	sie reiten

halten *to hold* (STEM **halt-**)	
ich halte	wir halten
du hältst	ihr halt**et**
Sie halten	Sie halten
er/sie/es hält	sie halten

If the vowel-changing stem ends in **-t**, the **er/sie/es** form does not add another **t**: **hält.**

Following are other verbs for which **-e-** is not added because of a vowel change.

	bersten	**braten**	**fechten**	**flechten**	**gelten**	**raten**	**treten**	**laden**
ich	bers**te**	bra**te**	fech**te**	flech**te**	gel**te**	ra**te**	tre**te**	la**de**
du	birst	brät**st**	ficht**st**	flicht**st**	gilt**st**	rät**st**	tritt**st**	läd**st**
er/sie/es	birst	brät	ficht	flicht	gilt	rät	tritt	läd**t**

- With **bersten,** the stem-ending **-st** is omitted: **bir~~st~~st → birst.**
- With **treten,** the stem-ending **-t** in the second- and third-person singular forms is doubled: **trittst, tritt.**

Modal Verbs The modal verbs are conjugated as follows in the present tense.

dürfen *to be allowed to* (STEM **dürf-**)	
ich darf	wir dürf**en**
du darf**st**	ihr dürf**t**
Sie dürf**en**	Sie dürf**en**
er/sie/es darf	sie dürf**en**

können *can, to be able to* (STEM **könn-**)	
ich kann	wir könn**en**
du kann**st**	ihr könn**t**
Sie könn**en**	Sie könn**en**
er/sie/es kann	sie könn**en**

mögen *to like (to)* (STEM **mög-**)	
ich mag	wir mög**en**
du mag**st**	ihr mög**t**
Sie mög**en**	Sie mög**en**
er/sie/es mag	sie mög**en**

müssen *must, to have to* (STEM **müss-**)	
ich muss	wir müss**en**
du muss**t**	ihr müss**t**
Sie müss**en**	Sie müss**en**
er/sie/es muss	sie müss**en**

sollen *should, to be supposed to* (STEM **soll-**)	
ich soll	wir soll**en**
du soll**st**	ihr soll**t**
Sie soll**en**	Sie soll**en**
er/sie/es soll	sie soll**en**

wollen *to want (to)* (STEM **woll-**)	
ich will	wir woll**en**
du will**st**	ihr woll**t**
Sie woll**en**	Sie woll**en**
er/sie/es will	sie woll**en**

- The first- and third-person singular forms have no endings.
- The stem vowel changes in the **ich**, **du**, and **er/sie/es** forms for all the modal verbs except **sollen**.
- The endings for the **Sie**, **wir**, **ihr**, and **sie**-plural forms are the same as the present tense endings of regular weak, strong, and mixed verbs.

The Verbs *haben, sein, tun, werden,* and *wissen* The verbs **haben**, **sein**, **werden**, and **wissen** are conjugated in the present tense as follows.

haben *to have* (STEM **hab-**)	
ich habe	wir haben
du hast	ihr habt
Sie haben	Sie haben
er/sie/es hat	sie haben

sein *to be, exist* (STEM **sei-**)	
ich bin	wir sind
du bist	ihr seid
Sie sind	Sie sind
er/sie/es ist	sie sind

werden *to become* (STEM **werd-**)	
ich werde	wir werden
du wirst	ihr werdet
Sie werden	Sie werden
er/sie/es wird	sie werden

wissen *to know* (STEM **wiss-**)	
ich weiß	wir wissen
du weißt	ihr wisst
Sie wissen	Sie wissen
er/sie/es weiß	sie wissen

- With **haben**, the **du** and **er/sie/es** forms do not have the **b** of the stem.
- **Sein** has a highly irregular conjugation.
- **Werden** is regular except in the **du** and **er/sie/es** forms.
- **Wissen** conjugates much like a modal verb: the **ich** and **er/sie/es** forms have no endings. The **ich**, **du**, and **er/sie/es** forms have the stem-vowel change **i** → **ei**. The **ss** becomes **ß** after the diphthong **ei** due to general spelling rules (see page 38).

In the present tense, **tun** conjugates like the regular weak verb **wandern** (see page 8); its stem is simply **tu-**.

Verbs with Prefixes

Separable Prefix Verbs German has many verbs that consist of a base verb and a complement that changes the meaning of the base verb. English has such verbs as well, for example, *to pick up*, *to stand up*. Unlike English, the German complement forms one word with the verb; it is considered a prefix of the verb and is joined to the base in the infinitive form.

abholen	*to pick up*
aufstehen	*to stand up*

Common separable prefixes include the following.

ab	bei	fort	nach	weg	zusammen
an	ein	her	nieder	weiter	zwischen
auf	empor	hin	vor	zu	
aus	entgegen	mit	vorbei	zurück	

When these verbs are conjugated in the simple tenses and are in a main clause, the prefix separates from the base verb and is placed at the end of the main clause.

Ich **hole** dich morgen am Bahnhof **ab**.	*I'll pick you up at the train station tomorrow.*

Inseparable Prefix Verbs Other German verbs have prefixes that do not separate from the base verb, for example, **besuchen**, **entwerten**, **erfinden**, **verlieren**. Common inseparable prefixes include the following.

be	ent	ge	zer
emp	er	ver	

Two-way Prefix Verbs Some verbs have prefixes that separate with some meanings and do not separate with others, for example, **übersetzen** (*to translate* as inseparable, *to set across* as separable). The most common of these prefixes are the following.

durch	über	unter	wider
hinter	um	voll	wieder

The presence of a separable or inseparable prefix has no direct impact on the form of the verb stem or endings; a base verb generally conjugates the same regardless of what prefix might be added to it. However, the two types of prefixes have differing effects on past participle formation (see pages 21–22). For more detailed information on German word order with separable prefix verbs, see the discussion of the sentence frame on pages 36–37.

In this book, separable prefix verbs are indicated by a centerline dot in the infinitive in the page banners: **ab·holen**, **auf·stehen**, **nieder·legen**, **vorbei·kommen**. To save space and avoid confusion in the conjugation tables, the prefix is not repeated eight times in each simple tense but is bracketed after the base verb forms as follows.

ich hole	wir holen	ab
du holst	ihr holt	
Sie holen	Sie holen	
er/sie/es holt	sie holen	

This paradigm is to be interpreted as follows.

ich hole ab	wir holen ab
du holst ab	ihr holt ab
Sie holen ab	Sie holen ab
er/sie/es holt ab	sie holen ab

Uses of the Present Tense

The present tense is used to talk about events that are currently happening, as well as ongoing, recurring, and habitual actions. The English translation varies, depending on context.

Die Katze **schläft** auf dem Sofa.	*The cat is asleep on the sofa.*
Julia **studiert** Jura.	*Julia is majoring in law.*
Ich **schlafe** auf einem Futon.	*I sleep on a futon.*

It can also express future events, especially when an adverb of time is included. English sometimes uses the present tense in such cases, but not as commonly as German.

Im Mai **reisen** wir nach Vancouver.	*We will travel to Vancouver in May.*
Morgen **bleibt** Silke zu Hause.	*Silke is staying home tomorrow.*
Wir **kaufen** nächstes Jahr ein Haus.	*We will buy a house next year.*

Actions that began in the past and continue to the present are expressed with the present tense plus a prepositional phrase with **seit** or plus the adverb **schon**.

Wie lange **seid** ihr schon da?	*How long have you been here?*
Wir **wohnen** seit einem Jahr hier.	*We've lived here for a year.*

German has only one present tense form, whereas English has three.

Niklas **spielt** Klavier.	*Niklas **is playing** the piano.*
	*Niklas **plays** the piano.*
	*Niklas **does play** the piano.*

The Simple Past

In German, the simple past tense is usually called **Präteritum** or **Imperfekt**. Other English names for the simple past include the "imperfect," "preterite," and "narrative past."

Regular Weak Verbs To form the simple past tense of regular weak verbs, add **-t-** and personal endings to the infinitive stem, as illustrated with the verb **lachen**. (To determine the infinitive stem, see page 7.)

lachen *to laugh* (STEM **lach-**)	
ich lach**te**	wir lach**ten**
du lach**test**	ihr lach**tet**
Sie lach**ten**	Sie lach**ten**
er/sie/es lach**te**	sie lach**ten**

The endings comprise the tense marker **-t-** followed by personal markers for the various persons and numbers, as follows.

-t-e	-t-en
-t-est	-t-et
-t-en	-t-en
-t-e	-t-en

There are minor adjustments that must be made to the conjugation of certain regular weak verbs in the simple past.

- Insert **-e-** after the stem in all forms where
  - The infinitive stem ends in **-d** or **-t**, or
  - The infinitive stem ends in **-m** or **-n** preceded by a consonant other than **l**, **m**, **n**, **r**, or simple **h**. (If the **h** is part of a consonant cluster such as **ch**, **sch**, or **th**, then the extra **-e-** is inserted.)

reden *to talk* (STEM **red-**)	
ich red**ete**	wir red**eten**
du red**etest**	ihr red**etet**
Sie red**eten**	Sie red**eten**
er/sie/es red**ete**	sie red**eten**

atmen *to breathe* (STEM **atm-**)	
ich atm**ete**	wir atm**eten**
du atm**etest**	ihr atm**etet**
Sie atm**eten**	Sie atm**eten**
er/sie/es atm**ete**	sie atm**eten**

Thus, for example, the third-person singular form for **rechnen** is **rechnete**. By contrast, although the stem for the verb **lernen**, for example, ends in **-n**, the **n** is preceded by the sound **r**, and thus the third-person singular form has no **-e-** inserted: **lernte**.

Strong Verbs The simple past tense of strong verbs shows a change in the vowel of the stem in all forms. Endings are added as illustrated by the verbs **beginnen** and **greifen**.

beginnen *to begin*	
ich begann	wir begann**en**
du begann**st**	ihr begann**t**
Sie begann**en**	Sie begann**en**
er/sie/es begann	sie begann**en**

greifen *to grasp*	
ich griff	wir griff**en**
du griff**st**	ihr griff**t**
Sie griff**en**	Sie griff**en**
er/sie/es griff	sie griff**en**

- The **ich** and **er/sie/es** forms are characterized by the lack of an ending; this is true for all strong verbs in the simple past. This form is sometimes called the simple past stem, since the simple past forms for all other persons can be derived from it.
- The verb **greifen** shows a consonant change: **f** → **ff**. Many strong verbs have a consonant change as well as a vowel change in the stem.
- There are minor adjustments that must be made to the endings of certain strong verbs in the simple past.
  - In the **du** form of strong verbs whose simple past stem ends in **-chs**, **-s**, **-ß**, **-z**, or sometimes **-sch**, **-e-** is inserted before the **-st** ending, for example, **du wuchsest**, **lasest**, **schlossest**, **aßest**, **schmolzest**, **wuschest**, but **du droschst**.

- If the simple past stem of a strong verb ends in **-d** or **-t**, **-e-** is inserted before the **-t** ending of the **ihr** form, for example, **ihr fochtet, hieltet, ludet, tratet, wandet.**

  For certain strong verbs, **-e-** is inserted before the **-st** ending of the **du** form as well, for example, **du fochtest, wandest,** but **du hieltst, ludst, tratst.** The **-e-** insertion rule applies only to certain verbs, and grammar authorities generally consider the insertion archaic. When in doubt, refer to the conjugation table of a particular verb.
- If the simple past stem of a strong verb ends in **-e**, the ending **-en** is reduced to **-n** to avoid two **e**s in a row; the verb **schreien** (**ich schrie**, but **wir schrien**) is an example.

- The changes in the simple past forms of strong verbs are not as unpredictable as they seem. They can be grouped into what are called "ablaut" patterns. (The German word **Ablaut** means simply "vowel change.") The verbs in each ablaut pattern have similar vowel changes, although the consonant changes, if any, may differ. English, too, has verbs with ablaut: *begin, began; speak, spoke.* These similarities help English speakers quickly grasp the German verb forms.

  The verb **greifen**, whose simple past tense forms are given above, shows the vowel change **ei → i** from the infinitive to the simple past. Although there are about 40 different ablaut patterns in all, the following patterns account for more than half of all strong verbs.

	a → u	**e → a**	**ei → i**	**ei → ie**	**ie → o**	**i → a**
INFINITIVE	f**a**hren	s**e**hen	b**ei**ßen	schr**ei**ben	b**ie**gen	tr**i**nken
SIMPLE PAST TENSE (3 SG.)	f**u**hr	s**a**h	b**i**ss	schr**ie**b	b**o**g	tr**a**nk

All ablaut patterns are represented in the conjugation tables of this book.

Mixed Verbs In the simple past tense, mixed verbs share aspects of both regular weak verbs and strong verbs. Like regular weak verbs, they have the tense marker **-t-**, but they also have a stem vowel change (and sometimes a consonant change), like strong verbs. The mixed verbs are conjugated according to four patterns.

bringen *to bring*

ich brach**te**	wir brach**ten**
du brach**test**	ihr brach**tet**
Sie brach**ten**	Sie brach**ten**
er/sie/es brach**te**	sie brach**ten**

denken *to think*

ich dach**te**	wir dach**ten**
du dach**test**	ihr dach**tet**
Sie dach**ten**	Sie dach**ten**
er/sie/es dach**te**	sie dach**ten**

kennen *to know*

ich kann**te**	wir kann**ten**
du kann**test**	ihr kann**tet**
Sie kann**ten**	Sie kann**ten**
er/sie/es kann**te**	sie kann**ten**

senden *to send*

ich sand**te**	wir sand**ten**
du sand**test**	ihr sand**tet**
Sie sand**ten**	Sie sand**ten**
er/sie/es sand**te**	sie sand**ten**

- The verbs **brennen, nennen,** and **rennen** conjugate like **kennen.** The verb **wenden** conjugates like **senden** (but it is sometimes conjugated as a regular weak verb: **wendete**).
- **Senden,** when it means *to broadcast,* is conjugated as a regular weak verb: **sendete.**

Modal Verbs The modal verbs are conjugated as follows in the simple past tense.

dürfen *to be allowed to*

ich durfte	wir durften
du durftest	ihr durftet
Sie durften	Sie durften
er/sie/es durfte	sie durften

können *can, to be able to*

ich konnte	wir konnten
du konntest	ihr konntet
Sie konnten	Sie konnten
er/sie/es konnte	sie konnten

mögen *to like (to)*

ich mochte	wir mochten
du mochtest	ihr mochtet
Sie mochten	Sie mochten
er/sie/es mochte	sie mochten

müssen *must, to have to*

ich musste	wir mussten
du musstest	ihr musstet
Sie mussten	Sie mussten
er/sie/es musste	sie mussten

sollen *should, to be supposed to*	
ich sollte	wir sollten
du solltest	ihr solltet
Sie sollten	Sie sollten
er/sie/es sollte	sie sollten

wollen *to want (to)*	
ich wollte	wir wollten
du wolltest	ihr wolltet
Sie wollten	Sie wollten
er/sie/es wollte	sie wollten

- As in other verb classes in the simple past, the first- and third-person singular forms of modal verbs are identical.
- There are no umlauts in the simple past tense in modal verbs.
- The simple past endings for the modal verbs are identical to those of regular weak and mixed verbs.

The Verbs *haben, sein, tun, werden,* and *wissen* The verbs **haben**, **sein**, **tun**, **werden**, and **wissen** are conjugated in the simple past tense as follows.

haben *to have*	
ich hatte	wir hatten
du hattest	ihr hattet
Sie hatten	Sie hatten
er/sie/es hatte	sie hatten

sein *to be, exist*	
ich war	wir waren
du warst	ihr wart
Sie waren	Sie waren
er/sie/es war	sie waren

tun *to do*	
ich tat	wir taten
du tat(e)st	ihr tatet
Sie taten	Sie taten
er/sie/es tat	sie taten

werden *to become*	
ich wurde	wir wurden
du wurdest	ihr wurdet
Sie wurden	Sie wurden
er/sie/es wurde	sie wurden

wissen *to know*	
ich wusste	wir wussten
du wusstest	ihr wusstet
Sie wussten	Sie wussten
er/sie/es wusste	sie wussten

- The **ich** form is identical to the **er/sie/es** form for all verbs in the simple past tense.
- Like regular weak and mixed verbs, **haben** and **wissen** have the tense marker **-t-** in the simple past.
- The verb **tun** is unique in that it has the tense marker **-t-**, but does not have the same endings as **haben** or **wissen** in the **ich** and **er/sie/es** forms.
- In many texts before 1900, the archaic form **ward** (not **wurde**) was used for the first- and third-person singular in the simple past tense of **werden**.

Uses of the Simple Past Tense

The simple past tense is used in structured texts such as fairy tales, connected discourse, written narratives, and reports that relate events that happened in the past, whether fact or fiction.

Der Mond **schien** hell.	*The moon was shining brightly.*
München **spielte** gestern gegen Köln.	*Munich played Cologne yesterday.*

The simple past is also used in conversational and spoken German with a few verbs to relate events that have already happened. These include **haben**, **sein**, and the modal verbs.

Warst du schon mal in Afrika?	*Have you ever been to Africa?*
Tanja **hatte** eine gute Idee.	*Tanja had a good idea.*
Ich **wollte** keinen Kaffee.	*I didn't want any coffee.*

The German simple past tense can translate in more than one way into English.

Der Mond **schien** hell.	*The moon* ***was shining*** *brightly.* *The moon* ***shone*** *brightly.*

The Present Subjunctive I

In German, the present subjunctive I tense is usually called **Konjunktiv I Präsens**, or simply **Konjunktiv Präsens**. Other English names include the "present subjunctive," "present subjunctive, primary," and "special subjunctive."

The present subjunctive I is formed by adding subjunctive endings to the infinitive stem.

lachen *to laugh* (STEM **lach-**)	
ich lach**e**	wir lach**en**
du lach**est**	ihr lach**et**
Sie lach**en**	Sie lach**en**
er/sie/es lach**e**	sie lach**en**

fahren *to drive* (STEM **fahr-**)	
ich fahr**e**	wir fahr**en**
du fahr**est**	ihr fahr**et**
Sie fahr**en**	Sie fahr**en**
er/sie/es fahr**e**	sie fahr**en**

- All present subjunctive I endings begin with **-e-**. The **ich** and **er/sie/es** endings are made up only of **-e**. This **-e-** is a characteristic feature of present subjunctive I.
- Endings are the same for all verbs except **sein**; some verbs, however, are adjusted as follows.
  - If the infinitive stem ends in **-ie**, all endings drop the characteristic **-e-**, since the stem already ends in **-e**, as shown with the verb **knien** below.
  - If the infinitive stem ends in **-el** or **-er**, all endings drop the characteristic **-e-** except in the **ich** and **er/sie/es** forms, as shown with the verb **wandern**.

knien *to kneel* (STEM **knie-**)	
ich knie	wir knie**n**
du knie**st**	ihr knie**t**
Sie knie**n**	Sie knie**n**
er/sie/es knie	sie knie**n**

wandern *to hike* (STEM **wander-**)	
ich wander**e**	wir wander**n**
du wander**st**	ihr wander**t**
Sie wander**n**	Sie wander**n**
er/sie/es wander**e**	sie wander**n**

- The verb **sein** has the following forms in the present subjunctive I.

sein *to be, exist* (STEM **sei-**)	
ich sei	wir sei**en**
du sei**est**	ihr sei**et**
Sie sei**en**	Sie sei**en**
er/sie/es sei	sie sei**en**

Uses of the Present Subjunctive I Tense

The present subjunctive I tense is used in standard and formal German for indirect speech that relates presently occurring action.

Laut Angaben **sei** er der Täter.	*According to sources, he is the perpetrator.*
Julia sagt, sie **habe** drei Gründe.	*Julia says she has three reasons.*

If the present subjunctive I form is indistinguishable from the present (indicative) tense form, then the present subjunctive II tense is used instead. Furthermore, in colloquial German, present subjunctive I is rarely used at all; present subjunctive II tends to be used for all indirect speech. See "Uses of the Present Subjunctive II Tense" on page 17.

The Present Subjunctive II

Because the form of this tense is based on the simple past form, it is called **Konjunktiv II Präteritum** or **Konjunktiv Imperfekt** in German and sometimes called "simple past subjunctive" or "past subjunctive" in English. This can be misleading, however, because the tense expresses time in the present. Other names in English include the "general subjunctive" and "present subjunctive, secondary."

Regular Weak Verbs For regular weak verbs, the present subjunctive II is identical to the simple past (indicative) (see page 12).

Strong Verbs For most strong verbs, the present subjunctive II is formed by adding subjunctive endings to the simple past stem. If the simple past stem vowel is **a**, **o**, or **u**, then an umlaut is added to the vowel.

halten *to hold* (SIMPLE PAST STEM **hielt-**)	
ich hielt**e**	wir hielt**en**
du hielt**est**	ihr hielt**et**
Sie hielt**en**	Sie hielt**en**
er/sie/es hielt**e**	sie hielt**en**

geben *to give* (SIMPLE PAST STEM **gab-**)	
ich gäb**e**	wir gäb**en**
du gäb**est**	ihr gäb**et**
Sie gäb**en**	Sie gäb**en**
er/sie/es gäb**e**	sie gäb**en**

- If the simple past stem of a strong verb ends in **-e**, the endings generally lose the beginning **-e-** so as not to have two **e**s in a row. For example, the simple past stem of the verb **schreien** is **schrie**, but the **ich** form of the present subjunctive II is more commonly **schrie** than **schriee**, although both are used.
- A few strong verbs have a stem vowel for the present subjunctive II that is different from that of the simple past stem. Others can take either of two stem vowels. Some of the more common verbs that follow these patterns are shown below, along with their first-/third-person singular forms.

INFINITIVE	SIMPLE PAST	PRESENT SUBJUNCTIVE II	ENGLISH
sterben	starb	stürbe	*to die*
verderben	verdarb	verdürbe	*to spoil*
werfen	warf	würfe	*to throw*
gelten	galt	gölte/gälte	*to be valid*
gewinnen	gewann	gewönne/gewänne	*to win*
helfen	half	hülfe/hälfe	*to help*
stehen	stand	stünde/stände	*to stand*

Note that these exceptional forms are avoided by modern speakers even in standard German; the **würde** + infinitive construction is used instead (see page 19).

Mixed Verbs Mixed verbs in the present subjunctive II share aspects of both regular weak verbs and strong verbs. Like regular weak verbs, they have the tense marker **-t-**, but some also have a stem vowel change or umlaut like strong verbs. Mixed verbs are conjugated according to four patterns.

bringen *to bring*	
ich brächte	wir brächten
du brächtest	ihr brächtet
Sie brächten	Sie brächten
er/sie/es brächte	sie brächten

denken *to think*	
ich dächte	wir dächten
du dächtest	ihr dächtet
Sie dächten	Sie dächten
er/sie/es dächte	sie dächten

kennen *to know*	
ich kennte	wir kennten
du kenntest	ihr kenntet
Sie kennten	Sie kennten
er/sie/es kennte	sie kennten

senden *to send*	
ich sendete	wir sendeten
du sendetest	ihr sendetet
Sie sendeten	Sie sendeten
er/sie/es sendete	sie sendeten

- The verbs **brennen**, **nennen**, and **rennen** conjugate like **kennen**. The verb **wenden** conjugates like **senden**.

Modal Verbs The present subjunctive II forms of the modal verbs are like those of the simple past, but with an umlaut added to the stem vowel, except for **sollen** and **wollen**, whose forms are identical to the simple past.

dürfen *to be allowed to*	
ich dürfte	wir dürften
du dürftest	ihr dürftet
Sie dürften	Sie dürften
er/sie/es dürfte	sie dürften

können *can, to be able to*	
ich könnte	wir könnten
du könntest	ihr könntet
Sie könnten	Sie könnten
er/sie/es könnte	sie könnten

mögen *to like (to)*	
ich möchte	wir möchten
du möchtest	ihr möchtet
Sie möchten	Sie möchten
er/sie/es möchte	sie möchten

müssen *must, to have to*	
ich müsste	wir müssten
du müsstest	ihr müsstet
Sie müssten	Sie müssten
er/sie/es müsste	sie müssten

sollen *should, to be supposed to*	
ich sollte	wir sollten
du solltest	ihr solltet
Sie sollten	Sie sollten
er/sie/es sollte	sie sollten

wollen *to want (to)*	
ich wollte	wir wollten
du wolltest	ihr wolltet
Sie wollten	Sie wollten
er/sie/es wollte	sie wollten

The Verbs *haben, sein, tun, werden,* and *wissen* In the present subjunctive II of the verbs **haben**, **sein**, **tun**, **werden**, and **wissen**, the forms are similar to those of the simple past, but with an umlaut added.

haben *to have*	
ich hätte	wir hätten
du hättest	ihr hättet
Sie hätten	Sie hätten
er/sie/es hätte	sie hätten

sein *to be, exist*	
ich wäre	wir wären
du wärest	ihr wäret
Sie wären	Sie wären
er/sie/es wäre	sie wären

tun *to do*	
ich täte	wir täten
du tätest	ihr tätet
Sie täten	Sie täten
er/sie/es täte	sie täten

werden *to become*	
ich würde	wir würden
du würdest	ihr würdet
Sie würden	Sie würden
er/sie/es würde	sie würden

wissen *to know*	
ich wüsste	wir wüssten
du wüsstest	ihr wüsstet
Sie wüssten	Sie wüssten
er/sie/es wüsste	sie wüssten

Uses of the Present Subjunctive II Tense

Irrealis The present subjunctive II can be used to describe present or future hypothetical or contrary-to-fact conditions or actions.

Wenn Uwe morgen **käme**, **wären** wir sehr glücklich. — *If Uwe were to come tomorrow, we'd be really happy.*

Lea tut, als ob sie den Grund nicht **wüsste**. — *Lea acts as though she doesn't know the reason.*

Wishes The present subjunctive II can be used to express wishes.

Wenn es nur nicht so kalt **wäre**! — *If only it weren't so cold!*

Ich wünschte, ich **könnte** gut malen. — *I wish I could paint well.*

Politeness Requests and questions can be made more polite with the use of the present subjunctive II. This applies especially to **haben**, **sein**, **wissen**, and the modal verbs.

Ich **hätte** gern ein Stück Käsekuchen. — *I would like a slice of cheesecake.*

Wüssten Sie, wie viel Uhr es ist? — *Would you know what time it is?*

Indirect Speech In standard and formal German, the present subjunctive II tense is used in place of present subjunctive I for indirect speech to relate presently occurring actions, but only if the present subjunctive I form is indistinguishable from the present (indicative) form.

Laut dem Bericht **kämen** sie aus Hamburg. — *According to the report, they come from Hamburg.*

Julia sagt, sie **hätten** drei Gründe. — *Julia says they have three reasons.*

In colloquial German, however, the present subjunctive II tense can be used for *all* indirect speech, even in instances when the present subjunctive I is used in formal German.

Leon meint, du **wärest** dafür zuständig.	*Leon says you're responsible for that.*
Julia sagt, sie **hätte** drei Gründe.	*Julia says she has three reasons.*

In colloquial German—and to some extent in standard German—the present subjunctive II tense is widely used only with a few common verbs, including **haben**, **kommen**, **sein**, **tun**, **werden**, **wissen**, and the modal verbs. For most verbs, spoken German tends to use the future subjunctive II tense but with a present meaning, more commonly known as the **würde** + infinitive construction. For details, see page 19.

THE COMPOUND TENSES

German compound tenses consist of a conjugated auxiliary verb plus a past participle and/or one or more infinitives. All compound tenses use the German sentence frame; see pages 36–38 for details. There are 10 compound tenses in German, four of which are indicative, although the word "indicative" is often omitted in referring to them; the other six tenses are subjunctive. The tenses are formed as follows.

Future Future Subjunctive I Future Subjunctive II	auxiliary **werden** + infinitive
Present Perfect Past Perfect Past Subjunctive I Past Subjunctive II	auxiliary **sein** or **haben** + past participle
Future Perfect Future Perfect Subjunctive I Future Perfect Subjunctive II	auxiliary **werden** + past participle + **sein** or **haben**

Future	(see below)	Past Subjunctive I	(see page 25)
Future Subjunctive I	(see page 19)	Past Subjunctive II	(see page 25)
Future Subjunctive II	(see page 19)	Future Perfect	(see page 26)
Present Perfect	(see page 20)	Future Perfect Subjunctive I	(see page 27)
Past Perfect	(see page 24)	Future Perfect Subjunctive II	(see page 28)

The Future

The future tense is usually called **Futur I** or simply **Zukunft** in German.

To form the future tense, combine the present tense of the verb **werden** with the infinitive of the main verb.

studieren *to study*	
ich werde studieren	wir werden studieren
du wirst studieren	ihr werdet studieren
Sie werden studieren	Sie werden studieren
er/sie/es wird studieren	sie werden studieren

Uses of the Future Tense

The future tense can be used to express future events, especially when no adverb of time is stated or when the future action is a stated intention.

Wir **werden** die Stadt Worms besichtigen.	*We are going to visit the city of Worms.*
Wirst du dabei sein?	*Will you be along?*
Ich **werde** das machen.	*I will/intend to do that.*

It can also express speculation or supposition about present events or actions, especially in combination with the adverb **wohl**.

Maria **wird wohl** im Büro sein.	*Maria is probably at the office.*

The Future Subjunctive I

The Future Subjunctive I is usually called **Konjunktiv Futur I** in German. Other names in English include "future subjunctive, primary" and simply "future subjunctive."

To form the future subjunctive I tense, adapt the future tense by using the auxiliary **werden** in its subjunctive I form.

sich vorbereiten *to prepare (oneself)*	
ich werde mich vorbereiten	wir werden uns vorbereiten
du werdest dich vorbereiten	ihr werdet euch vorbereiten
Sie werden sich vorbereiten	Sie werden sich vorbereiten
er/sie/es werde sich vorbereiten	sie werden sich vorbereiten

Uses of the Future Subjunctive I Tense

The future subjunctive I tense is used in standard and formal German for indirect speech relating to future events.

Laut Angaben **werde** Herr Wolf einen Plan vorlegen.	*According to sources, Mr. Wolf will submit a plan.*
Der Bürgermeister berichtete, dass er einen neuen Plan entwerfen **werde**.	*The mayor reported that he will devise a new plan.*

If the future subjunctive I form is indistinguishable from the future (indicative) tense form, then the future subjunctive II tense is used instead. Furthermore, in colloquial German, future subjunctive I is rarely used at all; future subjunctive II tends to be used instead.

The Future Subjunctive II

The future subjunctive II tense is usually called **Konjunktiv Futur II** in German. Other names in English include "future subjunctive, secondary" and "present conditional."

To form the future subjunctive II tense, adapt the future tense by using the auxiliary **werden** in its subjunctive II form.

sich vorbereiten *to prepare (oneself)*	
ich würde mich vorbereiten	wir würden uns vorbereiten
du würdest dich vorbereiten	ihr würdet euch vorbereiten
Sie würden sich vorbereiten	Sie würden sich vorbereiten
er/sie/es würde sich vorbereiten	sie würden sich vorbereiten

Uses of the Future Subjunctive II Tense

Using *würde* + Infinitive as a Substitute for the Present Subjunctive II Tense In modern spoken German, the compound tense future subjunctive II is very often used in place of the present subjunctive II, but with a present meaning.

Wenn Erich eine Königsschlange **kaufte**, **würfe** ihn seine Frau **aus**. Wenn Erich eine Königsschlange **kaufen würde**, **würde** ihn seine Frau **auswerfen**.	*If Erich bought a boa constrictor, his wife would throw him out.*

This substitution is almost always used with the verbs **helfen**, **sterben**, **verderben**, and **werfen**, because their present subjunctive II forms are felt to be archaic. However, it is generally not used with the verbs **haben**, **sein**, **werden**, and **wissen** and the modal verbs.

Wishes The future subjunctive II tense can also be used to express present wishes. This applies to verbs other than **haben**, **sein**, **wissen**, and the modal verbs, which use the present subjunctive II for such meanings.

Wenn es heute nur nicht **regnen würde**!	*If only it weren't raining today!*
Ich wünschte, ich **würde** ihn **verstehen**.	*I wish I understood him.*

Politeness Requests and questions can be made more polite with the use of the future subjunctive II tense. This applies to verbs other than **haben**, **sein**, **wissen**, and the modal verbs, which use the present subjunctive II for such meanings.

Würden Sie uns bitte **helfen**?	*Would you please help us?*
Ich **würde** gern **teilnehmen**.	*I would gladly participate.*

Indirect Speech In standard German, the future subjunctive II tense is also used for indirect speech to relate presently occurring or future actions, but only if two conditions are met: (1) the present subjunctive I form is indistinguishable from the present (indicative) form, and (2) the present subjunctive II form is indistinguishable from the simple past form. In the following example, these two conditions are met because the present indicative and present subjunctive I forms are identical (**wohnen**), and the simple past and present subjunctive II forms are identical (**wohnten**).

Laut dem Bericht **würden** sie in Hamburg **wohnen**.	*According to the report, they live in Hamburg.*

In colloquial German, the future subjunctive II tense can be used for practically any present or future indirect speech, especially for verbs other than **haben**, **sein**, **wissen**, and the modal verbs.

Leon meint, du **würdest** in Bonn **arbeiten**.	*Leon says you work in Bonn.*
Julia sagt, Sandra **würde** gut **malen**.	*Julia says Sandra paints well.*

The Present Perfect

In German, the present perfect is often called simply **Perfekt**. In English, it is sometimes called the "perfect tense" or "conversational past." The German present perfect tense is usually translated by the English simple past tense.

Wir **haben** den Film **gesehen**.	*We **saw** the film.*
Mein Vater **ist** nach Istanbul **geflogen**.	*My father **flew** to Istanbul.*
Wann **sind** Sie **angekommen**?	*When **did** you **arrive**?*

To form the present perfect tense, combine the present tense of the auxiliary verb **haben** or **sein** with the past participle of the main verb.

INFINITIVE	AUXILIARY	PAST PARTICIPLE	PRESENT PERFECT
sagen	hat	gesagt	hat gesagt
gehen	ist	gegangen	ist gegangen
senden	hat	gesandt	hat gesandt

In the following section, detailed rules for formation of the past participle are presented. These are followed by rules for choice of auxiliary.

THE PAST PARTICIPLE

The present perfect and other compound tenses typically use the past participle of the main verb. There are some exceptions that will be addressed below.

To form the past participle of most verbs, the general rule is to add the prefix **ge-** and the suffix **-t** or **-en** to the past participle stem. The suffix **-t** is used for regular weak and mixed verbs; **-en** is used for strong verbs.

	INFINITIVE	PAST PARTICIPLE STEM	PAST PARTICIPLE ELEMENTS	PAST PARTICIPLE
REGULAR WEAK VERBS (-t)	machen	mach-	**ge**-mach-**t**	gemacht
	reden	red-	**ge**-red-**et**	geredet
STRONG VERBS (-en)	schreiben	schrieb-	**ge**-schrieb-**en**	geschrieben
	stehen	stand-	**ge**-stand-**en**	gestanden
	schreien	schrie-	**ge**-schrie-**n**	geschrien
MIXED VERBS (-t)	kennen	kann-	**ge**-kann-**t**	gekannt

- For regular weak verbs, the past participle stem is the same as the stem of the infinitive. The past participle stems of strong and mixed verbs are usually different from their infinitive stems and must be learned.
- Insert **-e-** before the suffix **-t** for all regular weak verbs where
  - The past participle stem ends in **-d** or **-t** (for example, **geredet**), or
  - The past participle stem ends in **-m** or **-n** preceded by a consonant other than **l, m, n, r,** or simple **h** (for example, **gerechnet, geatmet**).
- Drop **-e-** from the suffix **-en** for all verbs whose past participle stem already ends in **-e** (for example, **geschrien**).
- Verbs borrowed from foreign languages that end in **-ieren** do not add the prefix **ge-**, but merely the suffix **-t**.

INFINITIVE	PAST PARTICIPLE STEM	PAST PARTICIPLE ELEMENTS	PAST PARTICIPLE
studieren	studier-	studier-**t**	studiert
informieren	informier-	informier-**t**	informiert

- The past participles of the modal verbs follow.

INFINITIVE	PAST PARTICIPLE	INFINITIVE	PAST PARTICIPLE
dürfen	gedurft	müssen	gemusst
können	gekonnt	sollen	gesollt
mögen	gemocht	wollen	gewollt

- As with regular weak verbs, the past participles of mixed verbs end in **-t**. The stems are identical to the simple past stems. Notice that for mixed verbs, no **-e-** is inserted even when the stem ends in **-d**.

INFINITIVE	PAST PARTICIPLE	INFINITIVE	PAST PARTICIPLE
brennen	gebrannt	senden	gesandt
kennen	gekannt	wenden	gewandt
nennen	genannt	bringen	gebracht
rennen	gerannt	denken	gedacht

- The past participles of the verbs **haben, sein, tun, werden,** and **wissen** follow.

INFINITIVE	PAST PARTICIPLE	INFINITIVE	PAST PARTICIPLE
haben	gehabt	werden	geworden
sein	gewesen	wissen	gewusst
tun	getan		

When used in a passive construction in a perfect tense, the past participle of **werden** is simply **worden**. For details on the passive voice, see pages 31–32.

Verbs with Prefixes

Some verbs are made up of a base verb with a prefix. Many prefixes look like prepositions, but some are particles or other words.

Verbs with Separable Prefixes To form the past participle of most verbs with a separable prefix, the general rule is to separate the prefix from the stem and insert the infix **-ge-** between them, then add the suffix **-t** or **-en**. (For exceptions to this rule, see "A Note About Prefixes" on page 22.)

	INFINITIVE	PAST PARTICIPLE STEM	PAST PARTICIPLE ELEMENTS	PAST PARTICIPLE
REGULAR WEAK VERBS	ausmachen	mach-	**aus-ge**-mach-**t**	ausgemacht
	einreden	red-	**ein-ge**-red-**et**	eingeredet
STRONG VERBS	vorschreiben	schrieb-	**vor-ge**-schrieb-**en**	vorgeschrieben
	aufstehen	stand-	**auf-ge**-stand-**en**	aufgestanden
	anschreien	schrie-	**an-ge**-schrie-**n**	angeschrien
MIXED VERBS	auskennen	kann-	**aus-ge**-kann-**t**	ausgekannt

Verbs with Inseparable Prefixes If the prefix is inseparable, then **-ge-** is not inserted at all; only the **-t/-en** suffix is added. Inseparable prefixes include **be-**, **emp-**, **ent-**, **er-**, **ge-**, **ver-**, and **zer-**.

	INFINITIVE	PAST PARTICIPLE STEM	PAST PARTICIPLE ELEMENTS	PAST PARTICIPLE
REGULAR WEAK VERBS	vermachen	mach-	**ver**-mach-**t**	vermacht
	bereden	red-	**be**-red-**et**	beredet
	zerstören	stör-	**zer**-stör-**t**	zerstört
STRONG VERBS	beschreiben	schrieb-	**be**-schrieb-**en**	beschrieben
	entstehen	stand-	**ent**-stand-**en**	entstanden
	gebären	bor-	**ge**-bor-**en**	geboren
MIXED VERBS	erkennen	kann-	**er**-kann-**t**	erkannt

Verbs with Two-way Prefixes Some verb prefixes can be separable or inseparable, depending on meaning. The pronunciation is also different: When inseparable, the prefix is unstressed; when the prefix is separable, it is stressed. Most common among these prefixes are **durch-**, **hinter-**, **über-**, **um-**, **unter-**, **voll-**, **wider-**, and **wieder-**.

INFINITIVE	MEANING	PAST PARTICIPLE STEM	PAST PARTICIPLE ELEMENTS	PAST PARTICIPLE
übersetzen	*to set across*	setz-	**über**-**ge**-setz-**t**	über**ge**setzt
übersetzen	*to translate*	setz-	**über**-setz-**t**	übersetzt
umschreiben	*to rewrite*	schrieb-	**um**-**ge**-schrieb-**en**	um**ge**schrieben
umschreiben	*to circumscribe*	schrieb-	**um**-schrieb-**en**	umschrieben

Prefixed Verbs in *-ieren* With prefixed verbs that are based on verbs borrowed from foreign languages and that end in **-ieren**, **-ge-** is not added to the past participle, no matter what prefix the verb has. These verbs simply add the suffix **-t** to the stem.

INFINITIVE	PAST PARTICIPLE STEM	PAST PARTICIPLE ELEMENTS	PAST PARTICIPLE
einstudieren	studier-	**ein**-studier-**t**	einstudiert
durchdiskutieren	diskutier-	**durch**-diskutier-**t**	durchdiskutiert

Verbs with a Compound Prefix Some verbs have multiple prefixes. Others have prefixes attached to verbs with multiple syllables. With verbs such as these, inseparable prefixes typically override separable ones. If any of the prefixes is inseparable on its own, then it can usually be assumed that neither prefix is separated and **-ge-** is not inserted. Otherwise, **-ge-** is inserted between the last prefix and the verb stem.

INFINITIVE	PAST PARTICIPLE STEM	PAST PARTICIPLE ELEMENTS	PAST PARTICIPLE
verabreden	red-	verab-red-et	verabredet
(The prefix **ver-** is inseparable, so neither prefix is separated and **-ge-** is not inserted.)			
voraussehen	seh-	voraus-**ge**-seh-en	vorausgesehen
(Both **vor-** and **aus-** are separable, so they separate and **-ge-** is inserted.)			
vor**ent**halten	halt-	vorent-halt-en	vorenthalten
(The prefix **ent-** is inseparable, so neither prefix is separated and **-ge-** is not inserted.)			

A Note About Prefixes It is important to recognize that some verbs whose prefixes separate in present or simple past tenses form their past participles *without* separating and without **-ge-**. These include prefixed **-ieren** verbs and verbs with compound prefixes containing a separable prefix followed by an inseparable one. A few examples follow.

INFINITIVE	PRESENT (3SG.)	PRESENT PERFECT (3SG.)
anbekommen	bekommt an	hat anbekommen
ausverkaufen	verkauft aus	hat ausverkauft
einstudieren	studiert ein	hat einstudiert
fortentwickeln	entwickelt fort	hat fortentwickelt
vorenthalten	enthält vor	hat vorenthalten
zuerkennen	erkennt zu	hat zuerkannt

Special Cases

With some multisyllabic verbs whose stress falls on the first syllable, **ge-** is prefixed, but with others **-ge-** is inserted. When the first syllable of such verbs is unstressed, **ge-** is generally not added at all.

INFINITIVE	PRESENT PERFECT (3SG.)
frühstücken	hat **ge**frühstückt
wehtun	hat weh**ge**tan
frohlocken	hat frohlockt

Refer to the conjugation tables or the German Verb Index at the end of this book for special cases.

THE PERFECT AUXILIARY: *haben* or *sein*?

All the perfect tenses use either **haben** or **sein** as auxiliary verbs, as illustrated with the examples of **jodeln** and **gehen**.

jodeln *to yodel* (AUXILIARY **haben**)

ich **habe** gejodelt	wir **haben** gejodelt
du **hast** gejodelt	ihr **habt** gejodelt
Sie **haben** gejodelt	Sie **haben** gejodelt
er/sie/es **hat** gejodelt	sie **haben** gejodelt

gehen *to go* (AUXILIARY **sein**)

ich **bin** gegangen	wir **sind** gegangen
du **bist** gegangen	ihr **seid** gegangen
Sie **sind** gegangen	Sie **sind** gegangen
er/sie/es **ist** gegangen	sie **sind** gegangen

Most verbs take **haben** as the auxiliary. The most useful rule of thumb is that if a verb has a direct object (that is, is transitive), it takes **haben**. The direct object can even be an accusative reflexive pronoun.

Arden **hat** den Film in Berkeley gesehen. — *Arden saw the film in Berkeley.*
Hast du dich gefreut? — *Were you happy?*

- However, in standard German, many intransitive verbs (verbs that cannot have direct objects) also take **haben**.

Mark **hat** geschlafen. — *Mark slept.*
Es **hat** geregnet. — *It rained.*

- Southern German, including that spoken in Austria and Switzerland, typically uses **sein** with intransitive verbs such as **liegen**, **sitzen**, and **stehen**.

The auxiliary **sein** is used much less frequently and is reserved for verbs of the following types.

- Verbs that describe movement from one point to another, such as **fahren** *to drive*, **gehen** *to go*, **laufen** *to run*, **reisen** *to travel*, **rennen** *to run*, **schwimmen** *to swim*, and **segeln** *to sail*.
- Verbs that describe a change of state, such as **einschlafen** *to go to sleep*, **sterben** *to die*, and **werden** *to become*.
- A small number of other verbs that must be learned individually; a few of the more common ones are **begegnen** *to encounter*, **bleiben** *to stay*, **geschehen** *to happen*, **misslingen** *to fail*, **passieren** *to happen*, and **sein** *to be*.

The verbs in the first category (verbs of movement) can also be used with the auxiliary **haben** in certain contexts where the focus is not on the motion from one point to another but on the activity itself, sometimes made apparent by the presence of a direct object. Compare the following sentences.

Erich ist nach Hawaii geflogen. — *Erich flew to Hawaii.*
Der Pilot hat den neuen 787 geflogen. — *The pilot flew the new 787.*

In this book, verbs that commonly take either **haben** or **sein** are presented with usage examples of both types.

Uses of the Present Perfect Tense

The present perfect tense is used in conversational German to relate events that have already taken place. Notice that the English translation is sometimes in the simple past and sometimes in the present perfect.

Maria **hat** mich in Seattle **besucht.**	*Maria visited me in Seattle.*
Wir **sind** nach Vancouver **gefahren.**	*We went to Vancouver.*
Ich **habe** noch nie so eine Wachtel **gesehen.**	*I've never seen a quail like that before.*

The verbs **haben**, **sein**, and **werden** and the modal verbs can be used in the present perfect tense to relate events that have already taken place, but in practice, speakers tend to prefer the simple past tense for those verbs. There is no real difference in meaning between the simple past and the present perfect; there is merely a difference of contexts in which the tenses are used. For uses of the simple past tense, see page 14.

The present perfect tense can also be used to describe future events that will happen before a second future event. Such meaning is often expressed using a compound sentence with **nachdem** *after*:

Nachdem Petra die Wäsche **gewaschen hat**, geht sie ins Café.	*After Petra has washed the laundry, she's going to a cafe.*

In such constructions, the earlier event is in the present perfect tense and the later event is in the present or future tense.

The Past Perfect

The past perfect tense is usually called **Plusquamperfekt** in German. Another name for it in English is the "pluperfect."

To form the past perfect tense, combine the simple past tense of the auxiliary verb **haben** or **sein** with the past participle of the main verb. The rules for choice of auxiliary are the same as for the present perfect tense.

jodeln *to yodel*

ich **hatte** gejodelt	wir **hatten** gejodelt
du **hattest** gejodelt	ihr **hattet** gejodelt
Sie **hatten** gejodelt	Sie **hatten** gejodelt
er/sie/es **hatte** gejodelt	sie **hatten** gejodelt

gehen *to go*

ich **war** gegangen	wir **waren** gegangen
du **warst** gegangen	ihr **wart** gegangen
Sie **waren** gegangen	Sie **waren** gegangen
er/sie/es **war** gegangen	sie **waren** gegangen

Uses of the Past Perfect Tense

The past perfect tense is used in German to relate past events that happened before other past events. Such meaning is often expressed using a compound sentence with **nachdem** *after* or **bevor** *before*.

Nachdem Petra die Wäsche **gewaschen hatte**, ist sie ins Café gegangen.	*After Petra had washed the laundry, she went to a cafe.*
Bevor wir meine Tante besuchten, **hatten** wir drei Tage in Berlin **verbracht.**	*Before we visited my aunt, we had spent three days in Berlin.*

In such constructions, the earlier event is in the past perfect tense and the later event is in the present perfect or simple past tense.

The Past Subjunctive I

In German, the past subjunctive I is often called **Konjunktiv Perfekt**. In English, it is sometimes called "perfect subjunctive" or "past subjunctive, primary."

To form the past subjunctive I tense, adapt the present perfect tense by using the auxiliary **haben** or **sein** in its subjunctive I form. The rules for choice of auxiliary are the same as for the present perfect tense.

jodeln *to yodel*	
ich **habe** gejodelt	wir **haben** gejodelt
du **habest** gejodelt	ihr **habet** gejodelt
Sie **haben** gejodelt	Sie **haben** gejodelt
er/sie/es **habe** gejodelt	sie **haben** gejodelt

gehen *to go*	
ich **sei** gegangen	wir **seien** gegangen
du **seiest** gegangen	ihr **seiet** gegangen
Sie **seien** gegangen	Sie **seien** gegangen
er/sie/es **sei** gegangen	sie **seien** gegangen

Uses of the Past Subjunctive I Tense

The past subjunctive I tense is used to render simple past, present perfect, and past perfect utterances into indirect speech. Note the correlations between direct speech and indirect speech.

DIRECT SPEECH

Columbus sagte: „Ich habe neues Land entdeckt."	*Columbus said, "I've discovered new land."*
Der Chef meint: „Dirk war dafür zuständig."	*The boss says, "Dirk was responsible for that."*
Lea sagte: „Ich hatte genug gehabt."	*Lea said, "I'd had enough."*

INDIRECT SPEECH

Columbus sagte, er **habe** neues Land **entdeckt**.	*Columbus said he has discovered new land.*
Der Chef meint, Dirk **sei** dafür zuständig **gewesen**.	*The boss says Dirk was responsible for that.*
Lea sagte, sie **habe** genug **gehabt**.	*Lea said that she'd had enough.*

As with other subjunctive I tenses, if the form is identical with the indicative form, then the subjunctive II is used instead. In colloquial German, the past subjunctive I tense is rarely used; the past subjunctive II tense tends to be used in such contexts instead. See "Uses of the Past Subjunctive II Tense" on page 26.

The Past Subjunctive II

In German, the past subjunctive II is often called **Konjunktiv Plusquamperfekt**. Other English names for it are "pluperfect subjunctive," "past perfect subjunctive," and "past subjunctive, secondary."

To form the past subjunctive II tense, adapt the present perfect tense by using the auxiliary **haben** or **sein** in its subjunctive II form. The rules for choice of auxiliary are the same as for the present perfect tense.

jodeln *to yodel*	
ich **hätte** gejodelt	wir **hätten** gejodelt
du **hättest** gejodelt	ihr **hättet** gejodelt
Sie **hätten** gejodelt	Sie **hätten** gejodelt
er/sie/es **hätte** gejodelt	sie **hätten** gejodelt

gehen *to go*

ich **wäre** gegangen	wir **wären** gegangen
du **wärest** gegangen	ihr **wäret** gegangen
Sie **wären** gegangen	Sie **wären** gegangen
er/sie/es **wäre** gegangen	sie **wären** gegangen

Uses of the Past Subjunctive II Tense

Irrealis The past subjunctive II tense can be used to describe past hypothetical or contrary-to-fact conditions or actions.

Wenn Uwe uns nicht **besucht hätte**, **wären** wir nicht nach Köln **gefahren**. — *If Uwe hadn't visited us, we wouldn't have gone to Cologne.*

Wishes The past subjunctive II tense can be used to express wishes about past events.

Wenn es nur nicht so kalt **gewesen wäre**! — *If only it hadn't been so cold!*
Ich wünschte, ich **hätte** den Film **gesehen**. — *I wish I had seen the film.*

Indirect Speech In standard and formal German, the past subjunctive II tense is also used for indirect speech relating past actions, but only if the past subjunctive I form is indistinguishable from the present perfect (indicative) form. In practice, this frequently happens when the third-person plural form of **haben** is used, but not with **sein**, since its past subjunctive I forms are unique.

DIRECT SPEECH

Im Bericht stand: „Die Männer wohnten früher in Hamburg." — *The report stated, "The men used to live in Hamburg."*

INDIRECT SPEECH

Laut dem Bericht **hätten** die Männer früher in Hamburg **gewohnt**. — *According to the report, the men used to live in Hamburg.*

In colloquial German, however, the past subjunctive II tense can be used for all past indirect speech, even in instances when the past subjunctive I tense is used in formal German. Such usage is strictly colloquial.

DIRECT SPEECH

Leon: „Dirk war dafür zuständig." — *Leon: "Dirk was responsible for that."*

INDIRECT SPEECH

Leon meint, Dirk **wäre** dafür zuständig **gewesen**. — *Leon says Dirk was responsible for that.*

The Future Perfect

In German, the future perfect is usually called **Futur II** or **vollendete Zukunft**.

For this tense, one must know the perfect infinitive of the main verb. The perfect infinitive consists of the past participle plus the auxiliary (**haben** or **sein**) in infinitive form. The rules for choice of **haben** or **sein** are the same as for the present perfect tense.

PERFECT INFINITIVE	ENGLISH
gesehen haben	*to have seen*
gekommen sein	*to have come*

To form the future perfect, combine the present tense of the auxiliary **werden** with the perfect infinitive.

sehen *to see*

ich **werde** gesehen haben	wir **werden** gesehen haben
du **wirst** gesehen haben	ihr **werdet** gesehen haben
Sie **werden** gesehen haben	Sie **werden** gesehen haben
er/sie/es **wird** gesehen haben	sie **werden** gesehen haben

kommen *to come*

ich **werde** gekommen sein	wir **werden** gekommen sein
du **wirst** gekommen sein	ihr **werdet** gekommen sein
Sie **werden** gekommen sein	Sie **werden** gekommen sein
er/sie/es **wird** gekommen sein	sie **werden** gekommen sein

Uses of the Future Perfect Tense

The future perfect tense can be used to express completion of events in the future. It is often used with a prepositional phrase with **bis** *by*.

Wir **werden** den Film bis den 15. März **gesehen haben**.	*We will have seen the film by March 15.*
Maria **wird** noch nicht **gekommen sein**.	*Maria will not yet have come.*

It can also express supposition about *past* events, when used in combination with the adverbs **schon** or **wohl**.

Robert **wird** den Grund wohl **verstanden haben**.	*Robert has probably understood the reason.*

The Future Perfect Subjunctive I

In German, the future perfect subjunctive I is usually called **Konjunktiv Futur II**. In English, it is also called "future perfect subjunctive, primary."

To form the future perfect subjunctive I, adapt the future perfect tense by using the auxiliary **werden** in its subjunctive I form. The rules for choice of **haben** or **sein** are the same for the future perfect subjunctive I as for the present perfect tense.

sehen *to see*

ich **werde** gesehen haben	wir **werden** gesehen haben
du **werdest** gesehen haben	ihr **werdet** gesehen haben
Sie **werden** gesehen haben	Sie **werden** gesehen haben
er/sie/es **werde** gesehen haben	sie **werden** gesehen haben

kommen *to come*

ich **werde** gekommen sein	wir **werden** gekommen sein
du **werdest** gekommen sein	ihr **werdet** gekommen sein
Sie **werden** gekommen sein	Sie **werden** gekommen sein
er/sie/es **werde** gekommen sein	sie **werden** gekommen sein

Uses of the Future Perfect Subjunctive I Tense

The future perfect subjunctive I tense is used to render future perfect utterances into indirect speech. Note the correlations between direct speech and indirect speech.

DIRECT SPEECH

Paul sagte, „Ich werde noch nicht gekommen sein."	*Paul said, "I will not yet have come."*
Lea fragte: „Wird Lars das bis Freitag gemacht haben?"	*Lea asked, "Will Lars have that done by Friday?"*

INDIRECT SPEECH

Paul sagte, er **werde** noch nicht **gekommen sein**.	*Paul said he will not yet have come.*
Lea fragte, ob Lars das bis Freitag **gemacht haben werde**.	*Lea asked whether Lars will have that done by Friday.*

As with other subjunctive I tenses, if the form is identical with the indicative form, then the subjunctive II is used instead. In colloquial German, the future perfect subjunctive I tense is very rarely used; instead, the future perfect subjunctive II tense tends to be used in such contexts. See "Uses of the Future Perfect Subjunctive II Tense" on page 28.

The Future Perfect Subjunctive II

The future perfect subjunctive II is often called **Konditional Perfekt** in German. In English, it is sometimes called the "perfect conditional," "past conditional," or "future perfect subjunctive, secondary."

To form the future perfect subjunctive II tense, adapt the future perfect tense by using the auxiliary **werden** in its subjunctive II form. The rules for choice of **haben** or **sein** are the same as for the present perfect tense.

sehen *to see*

ich **würde** gesehen haben	wir **würden** gesehen haben
du **würdest** gesehen haben	ihr **würdet** gesehen haben
Sie **würden** gesehen haben	Sie **würden** gesehen haben
er/sie/es **würde** gesehen haben	sie **würden** gesehen haben

kommen *to come*

ich **würde** gekommen sein	wir **würden** gekommen sein
du **würdest** gekommen sein	ihr **würdet** gekommen sein
Sie **würden** gekommen sein	Sie **würden** gekommen sein
er/sie/es **würde** gekommen sein	sie **würden** gekommen sein

Uses of the Future Perfect Subjunctive II Tense

Irrealis The future perfect subjunctive II tense can describe hypothetical or contrary-to-fact conditions or actions with a perspective from the future looking back.

Wenn das Projekt am Dienstag beginnen würde, **würde** Karin alles bis Freitag fertig **gemacht haben.** — *If the project were to begin on Tuesday, Karin would have finished everything by Friday.*

Indirect Speech In standard German, the future perfect subjunctive II tense is also used for indirect speech relating future perfect utterances, but only if the future perfect subjunctive I form is indistinguishable from the future perfect (indicative) form. In the example below, since subjunctive I **werden** is identical in form to indicative **werden**, the subjunctive II **würden** is used instead.

DIRECT SPEECH

„Sie werden bis Montag noch nicht gekommen sein." — *"They will not yet have come by Monday."*

INDIRECT SPEECH

Laut dem Bericht **würden** sie bis Montag noch nicht **gekommen sein.** — *According to the report, they will not yet have come by Monday.*

In colloquial German, however, the future perfect subjunctive II tense can be used to render all future perfect direct speech into indirect speech, even in instances when the future perfect subjunctive I is used in standard German.

STANDARD GERMAN

Leon meint, du **werdest** es **gesehen haben**. — *Leon says you will have seen it.*

COLLOQUIAL GERMAN

Leon meint, du **würdest** es **gesehen haben**. — *Leon says you will have seen it.*

As a Substitute for the Past Subjunctive II Tense In colloquial German, the future perfect subjunctive II tense is widely used as a substitute for the *past* subjunctive II tense in all of its functions. In such constructions, **würde** has no future meaning, but serves merely as a subjunctive auxiliary to the perfect infinitive.

STANDARD GERMAN

Jonas hätte dem Mann geholfen. — *Jonas would have helped the man.*

COLLOQUIAL GERMAN

Jonas **würde** dem Mann **geholfen haben**. — *Jonas would have helped the man.*

SPECIAL TYPES AND USES OF FINITE VERBS

REFLEXIVE VERBS

Many German verbs are used with reflexive pronouns. A reflexive pronoun is an accusative or dative pronoun that refers back to the subject of the sentence. For some verbs, use of the reflexive pronoun is obligatory; for others, it is optional. In English, the reflexive pronouns are formed with *-self* or *-selves.*

Ich habe **mich** verletzt. — *I've hurt **myself**.*

German uses reflexive pronouns much more than English. In German, the reflexive pronouns are as follows.

Reflexive Pronouns

		ACCUSATIVE	DATIVE	
SINGULAR	FIRST PERSON	mich	mir	*myself*
	SECOND PERSON	dich	dir	*yourself* (familiar)
		sich	sich	*yourself* (formal)
	THIRD PERSON	sich	sich	*himself/herself/itself*
PLURAL	FIRST PERSON	uns	uns	*ourselves*
	SECOND PERSON	euch	euch	*yourselves* (familiar)
		sich	sich	*yourselves* (formal)
	THIRD PERSON	sich	sich	*themselves*

- German has fewer different forms than English. All third-person forms are **sich**. Only first- and second-person singular distinguish between accusative and dative forms.

Types of Reflexive Verbs

Some German verbs are used only reflexively, that is, they always require a reflexive pronoun. Their English counterparts frequently do not use reflexives. An example is **sich beeilen** *to hurry*: **Ich beeile mich.** *I am hurrying.*

sich beeilen *to hurry*	
ich beeile mich	wir beeilen uns
du beeilst dich	ihr beeilt euch
Sie beeilen sich	Sie beeilen sich
er/sie/es beeilt sich	sie beeilen sich

Other verbs can be used reflexively or not, and the meaning changes based on reflexive or nonreflexive use. Examples include **(sich) ärgern** and **(sich) erinnern**.

NONREFLEXIVE USE

Max ärgert seine Schwester. — *Max is bothering his sister.*
Jens erinnert mich an Moritz Bleibtreu. — *Jens reminds me of Moritz Bleibtreu.*

REFLEXIVE USE

Warum haben Sie **sich** geärgert? — *Why were you upset?*
Ich erinnere **mich** an Opa nicht mehr. — *I can no longer remember Grandpa.*

Still other verbs can be used reflexively or not, without a change in the basic meaning of the verb. These include verbs such as **baden** and **verletzen.**

NONREFLEXIVE USE

Die Mutter badet das Kind. — *The mother is bathing the child.*
Der Hund hat den Briefträger verletzt. — *The dog has injured the letter carrier.*

REFLEXIVE USE

Lola badet **sich.** — *Lola is bathing.*
Das Kind hat **sich** verletzt. — *The child injured himself.*

Dative reflexive pronouns are used in some constructions, especially when a direct object is also present in the sentence. This is common for verbs relating to hygiene and body parts, although such use is not exclusive.

Ich wasche **mir** das Gesicht.	*I'm washing my face.*
Sie will **sich** die Hände waschen.	*She wants to wash her hands.*

Reciprocal Verbs A reciprocal verb is a particular type of reflexive verb. With a reciprocal verb, the reflexive relationship is mutual among the persons or things denoted by the subject. Examples include **sich ähneln**, **sich begrüßen**, **sich einigen**, and **sich gleichen**. This notion is often rendered in English with *each other*.

Die Zwillinge ähneln **sich** nicht.	*The twins do not resemble each other.*
Wir haben **uns** darüber geeinigt.	*We came to a (mutual) agreement about it.*

Some verbs have exclusively reciprocal meanings, while for others the reciprocity is optional.

DATIVE VERBS

In German, most transitive verbs have objects in the accusative case, but some German verbs require a dative object (for example, **danken**, **folgen**, and **gefallen**). These are often called "dative verbs" and are indicated in the conjugation tables by the descriptor "dative object."

Ich danke **Ihnen** für das Geschenk.	*I thank you for the gift.*
Folgen Sie **mir**.	*Follow me.*
Das Hemd gefällt **mir**.	*I like the shirt.* (lit., *The shirt pleases me.*)

GENITIVE VERBS

A few German verbs require a genitive object; examples are **bedürfen** and **gedenken**.

Die Patienten bedürfen **besserer Pflege**.	*The patients require better care.*
Heute gedenken wir **der Opfer**.	*Today we are remembering the victims.*

IMPERSONAL VERBS

Some German verbs use an impersonal subject, typically expressed with the subject pronoun **es**. Examples include weather phenomena, as well as other constructions.

Es schneit.	*It's snowing.*
Es gelingt ihm nicht.	*He's not succeeding in it.* (lit., *It is not successful for him.*)

MODAL VERBS AND *LASSEN*

Modal verbs and the verb **lassen** are typically used in sentences with other verbs to complete the meaning to be expressed. All examples below are in the third-person singular.

Simple Tenses When the sentence is in a simple tense, the modal verbs and the verb **lassen** take the place of the main verb in the present or simple past tense, and the main verb in its infinitive form then moves to the end of the main clause.

PRESENT	Uwe **lässt** ein Haus **bauen**.	*Uwe is having a house built.*
SIMPLE PAST	Jan **konnte** im Nebel nicht **sehen**.	*Jan couldn't see in the fog.*

Nonfuture Perfect Tenses In the present perfect, past perfect, and past subjunctive tenses, the infinitive of the modal verb or **lassen** is used instead of its perfect participle. It is placed at the end of the clause following the main verb's infinitive. This is called the "double infinitive" construction.

PRESENT PERFECT	Anja hat uns **besuchen wollen**.	*Anja wanted to visit us.*
PAST PERFECT	Tim hatte ein Haus **bauen lassen**.	*Tim had had a house built.*
PAST SUBJ. I	Max sagt, er habe das **machen müssen**.	*Max says he had to do that.*
PAST SUBJ. II	Lea hätte gestern **kommen können**.	*Lea could have come yesterday.*

Future Tenses The future tenses are formed in the same way, except that the future auxiliary **werden** is used.

FUTURE	Lea wird morgen **kommen können**.	*Lea will be able to come tomorrow.*
FUTURE SUBJ. I	Lisa sagt, sie werde **helfen können**.	*Lisa says she will be able to help.*
FUTURE SUBJ. II	Max würde es **machen lassen**.	*Max would have it done.*

Future Perfect Tenses A future perfect tense with a modal verb or **lassen** is rare. It is formed with the infinitive **haben**, followed by the main verb's present infinitive, followed by the infinitive of the modal verb or **lassen** at the end. The future auxiliary **werden** is conjugated.

FUT. PERF.	Max wird nicht **haben kommen können**.	*Max will not have been able to come.*
FUT. PERF. SUBJ. I	Tim werde ein Haus **haben bauen lassen**.	*Tim will have had a house built.*
FUT. PERF. SUBJ. II	Lea würde es **haben sehen können**.	*Lea would have been able to see it.*

An alternate form of the future perfect makes use of the perfect infinitive in place of **haben** + the present infinitive.

Maria wird nicht **gekommen sein können**. *Maria will not have been able to come.*

For the conjugation and usage examples of **lassen**, see verb No. 280. For usage examples of a modal verb + a main verb, see verb No. 458, **tun können**. For more details on word order, see the discussion of the sentence frame on pages 36–38.

OTHER DUAL-VERB CONSTRUCTIONS

A few other verbs are occasionally used in sentences with main verbs to complete a meaning to be expressed. Common among these are **gehen**, **hören**, **lernen**, and **sehen**. Unlike the modal verbs and **lassen**, these verbs do not use the double-infinitive construction in the perfect tenses.

SIMPLE TENSES	Ich **gehe** heute **einkaufen**.	*I'm going shopping today.*
PERFECT TENSES	Hast du Stephen **lachen gehört**?	*Did you hear Stephen laughing?*
FUTURE TENSES	Wir werden den neuen Studenten **kennen lernen**.	*We will meet the new student.*
FUTURE PERFECT TENSES	Er wird uns **kommen gesehen haben**.	*He will have seen us coming.*

For more details on word order, see the discussion of the sentence frame on pages 36–38.

THE PASSIVE VOICE

There are two voices in German: active and passive. The more common type of passive is the "true" or "processual" passive. Here, the focus is on a process. If the focus is on the resulting state, the form is called the "statal" passive.

The Processual Passive To form the processual passive, combine the auxiliary **werden** with the past participle of the main verb. In the following example, the past participle is **geliebt**.

PRESENT	Das Kaninchen wird geliebt.	*The bunny is loved.*
SIMPLE PAST	Das Kaninchen wurde geliebt.	*The bunny was loved.*
PRESENT SUBJUNCTIVE I	Das Kaninchen werde geliebt.	*The bunny is loved.*
PRESENT SUBJUNCTIVE II	Das Kaninchen würde geliebt.	*The bunny was/would be loved.*
FUTURE	Das Kaninchen wird geliebt werden.	*The bunny will be loved.*
FUTURE SUBJUNCTIVE I	Das Kaninchen werde geliebt werden.	*The bunny will be loved.*
FUTURE SUBJUNCTIVE II	Das Kaninchen würde geliebt werden.	*The bunny would be loved.*
PRESENT PERFECT	Das Kaninchen ist geliebt worden.	*The bunny has been loved.*
PAST PERFECT	Das Kaninchen war geliebt worden.	*The bunny had been loved.*
PAST SUBJUNCTIVE I	Das Kaninchen sei geliebt worden.	*The bunny has been loved.*
PAST SUBJUNCTIVE II	Das Kaninchen wäre geliebt worden.	*The bunny had been loved.*
FUTURE PERFECT	Das Kaninchen wird geliebt worden sein.	*The bunny will have been loved.*
FUTURE PERFECT SUBJUNCTIVE I	Das Kaninchen werde geliebt worden sein.	*The bunny will have been loved.*
FUTURE PERFECT SUBJUNCTIVE II	Das Kaninchen würde geliebt worden sein.	*The bunny would have been loved.*

The Statal Passive The statal passive is formed exactly like the processual passive, except that **sein** is used as the auxiliary instead of **werden**. The following examples set forth the pattern.

PRESENT	Es ist installiert.	*It is installed.*
SIMPLE PAST	Es war installiert.	*It was installed.*
FUTURE	Es wird installiert sein.	*It will be installed.*
PRESENT PERFECT	Es ist installiert gewesen.	*It has been installed.*

Main Verb + Modal Verb To form the (processual) passive with a modal verb added to a main verb, combine the modal verb with the passive infinitive. To form the passive infinitive, combine the past participle with the infinitive **werden**. In the following examples, the modal verb is **wollen** and the passive infinitive is **entdeckt werden**.

PRESENT	Er will entdeckt werden.	*He wants to be discovered.*
SIMPLE PAST	Er wollte entdeckt werden.	*He wanted to be discovered.*
FUTURE	Er wird entdeckt werden wollen.	*He will want to be discovered.*
PRESENT SUBJUNCTIVE I	Er wolle entdeckt werden.	*He wants to be discovered.*
PRESENT SUBJUNCTIVE II	Er wollte entdeckt werden.	*He wanted/would want to be discovered.*
FUTURE SUBJUNCTIVE I	Er werde entdeckt werden wollen.	*He will want to be discovered.*
FUTURE SUBJUNCTIVE II	Er würde entdeckt werden wollen.	*He would want to be discovered.*
PRESENT PERFECT	Er hat entdeckt werden wollen.	*He has wanted to be discovered.*
PAST PERFECT	Er hatte entdeckt werden wollen.	*He had wanted to be discovered.*
PAST SUBJUNCTIVE I	Er habe entdeckt werden wollen.	*He has wanted to be discovered.*
PAST SUBJUNCTIVE II	Er hätte entdeckt werden wollen.	*He would have wanted to be discovered.*

To form the statal passive with a modal verb added to a main verb, the process is the same as for processual passive, except that **sein** is used as the auxiliary instead of **werden**. The following examples set forth the pattern.

PRESENT	Es muss installiert sein.	*It must be installed.*
SIMPLE PAST	Es musste installiert sein.	*It had to be installed.*

Uses of the Passive Voice

Whereas the active voice focuses on the doer of the verb's action, the passive voice focuses on the object of the action or on the action itself. In the active voice, the doer of the action (also known as the "agent") is the subject of the sentence.

ACTIVE

Der Präsident hielt eine Rede über Globalerwärmung.	*The president gave a speech on global warming.*

In this sentence, the president is the agent. He is the one giving the speech, and therefore he is the subject. In a passive sentence, the subject is not the agent, but rather the thing acted on—in the following sentence, the speech.

PASSIVE

Eine Rede über Globalerwärmung wurde gehalten.	*A speech on global warming was given.*

The agent often disappears entirely from the sentence, since the focus is on something else. If the agent is expressed, the preposition **von** is used.

Ein wunderschönes Lied wurde **von** den Kindern gesungen.	*A wonderful song was sung by the children.*

Unlike English, German allows some sentences without objects (intransitive sentences) to be in the passive voice.

Auf der Party wurde viel getanzt.	*There was a lot of dancing at the party.*

THE IMPERATIVE MOOD

The imperative mood has several different forms in German, each of which corresponds to a different pronoun.

The Second-Person Imperative

The *du* Imperative To form the imperative for familiar singular **du**, remove the **-st** ending from the second-person singular, present tense form of the verb.

INFINITIVE	PRESENT TENSE **du** FORM	**du** IMPERATIVE	ENGLISH
kommen	kommst	Komm!	*Come!*

- If the verb is one of the strong verbs whose stem vowel has an umlaut in the **du** and **er/sie/es** forms but not in the infinitive, then the umlaut is dropped in the imperative.

INFINITIVE	PRESENT TENSE **du** FORM	**du** IMPERATIVE	ENGLISH
laufen	läufst	Lauf!	*Run!*

- With some verbs, the **du** imperative adds a final **-e**. The following rules apply.
  - *Always* add **-e** with the following verbs.
    - Verbs whose stems end in **-eln**, **-ern**, **-d**, or **-t**: **Jod(e)le! Wandere! Finde! Schalte!**
    - Verbs whose stems end in a consonant plus **-m** or **-n**: **Öffne! Rechne! Wappne!** This rule does not apply when the consonant preceding **-m** or **-n** is **l**, **m**, **n**, **r**, or simple **h**. (In these cases, the final **-e** is optional: **Qualm(e)! Komm(e)! Form(e)! Lehn(e)!**)
  - *Never* add **-e** with verbs whose stem vowel changes to **i** or **ie** in the **du** form of the present tense (**Friss! Gib!**), nor with verbs whose stem already ends in **-e** (**Knie!**).
  - *Optionally* add **-e** with all other verbs: **Glaub(e)! Plan(e)! Steh(e)! Stör(e)! Telefonier(e)! Tu(e)!**

  The verbs **haben**, **sein**, **werden**, **wissen**, and **wollen** do not follow the formation rules just outlined. For those verbs, the **du** imperative can be derived from the infinitive stem: **Hab(e)! Sei! Werde! Wisse! Wolle!**

The *ihr* Imperative To form the imperative for familiar plural **ihr**, simply remove the pronoun **ihr** from the second-person plural, present tense form of the verb.

Kommt morgen!	*Come tomorrow!*
Fragt euren Vater.	*Ask your father.*

The *Sie* Imperative To form the imperative for formal **Sie**, simply invert the pronoun and the second-person *Sie* form of the verb. The verb **sein** is irregular: **Seien Sie!**

Gehen Sie nach Hause.	*Go home.*
Bleiben Sie bitte etwas länger.	*Please stay a little longer.*

Uses of the Second-Person Imperative The second-person imperative is used to issue commands, orders, and directions. Whether the **du**, **ihr**, or **Sie** form is used, the imperative can be made more polite with the use of the particles **bitte**, **doch**, and **mal**.

Stehen Sie auf!	*Get up!*
Steh **mal** auf!	*Get up, won't you?*
Steht **bitte** auf.	*Please get up.*

The *wir* Imperative

To form the **wir** imperative, simply invert the pronoun and the first-person plural, present tense form of the verb.

Bleiben wir noch eine Stunde.	*Let's stay an hour longer.*

The **wir** imperative is used to make suggestions.

NONFINITE VERB FORMS

THE INFINITIVE

There are several types of German infinitives. The most common infinitive is the present active infinitive—the entry word for a verb in German dictionaries. The infinitives can be grouped broadly into active and passive. The more commonly used infinitives follow.

PRESENT ACTIVE INFINITIVE	sehen	*to see*
	sterben	*to die*
PERFECT ACTIVE INFINITIVE	gesehen haben	*to have seen*
	gestorben sein	*to have died*

The perfect infinitive is formed by combining the past participle with the auxiliary verb **haben** or **sein** in its present infinitive form.

PRESENT PASSIVE INFINITIVE	gesehen werden	*to be seen*
PERFECT PASSIVE INFINITIVE	gesehen worden sein	*to have been seen*

The present passive infinitive is formed by combining the past participle with the infinitive **werden**. The perfect passive infinitive consists of the past participle plus **worden sein**.

Uses of the Infinitives

The Present Active Infinitive The present infinitive is commonly used with modal verbs and in other dual-verb constructions.

Ich muss in die Bibliothek **gehen**. — *I have to go to the library.*
Hört ihr sie **singen**? — *Do you hear her singing?*

For more details of the use of the infinitive in these constructions, see pages 30–31.

The present infinitive is used with **werden** as a component of the future (indicative) and future subjunctive tenses.

Robert wird nicht mehr Auto **fahren**. — *Robert will no longer drive a car.*

The present infinitive is frequently used to give instructions to addressees of nonspecific social relationship to the speaker or author. This is common in recipes, in instructions for using equipment, and on public signs. The infinitive is placed at the end of the clause.

Das Wasser drei Minuten **sieden lassen**. — *Let the water boil for three minutes.*
Auf den Knopf **drücken**. — *Press the knob.*
Einfahrt **freihalten**! — *Do not block driveway!*

The Perfect Active Infinitive The perfect infinitive is used as a component of the future perfect tenses.

Ute wird den Brief nicht **gelesen haben**. — *Ute will not have read the letter.*

The perfect infinitive is also frequently used with modal verbs to make a subjective statement about an action in the past. Although the action expressed in the perfect infinitive is in the past, the tense of the modal verb need not be a past tense. Modality expressed in such usage is often one of speculation, assumption, or contention.

Sigrid kann ja auf der Party **gewesen sein**, denn sie war nicht zu Hause. — *Sigrid could possibly have been at the party, since she wasn't at home.*

The Present Passive Infinitive The present passive infinitive is commonly used with modal verbs in all tenses.

Die Hausaufgaben müssen **gemacht werden**. — *The homework must be done.*

The present passive infinitive is used with **werden** as a component of the future and future subjunctive tenses.

Der kleine Hund wird oft **übersehen werden**. — *The small dog will often be overlooked.*

The Perfect Passive Infinitive The perfect passive infinitive is used as a component of the future perfect passive tenses.

Der Brief wird noch nicht **gelesen worden sein**. — *The letter will not yet have been read.*

The perfect passive infinitive can also be used with modal verbs to make a subjective statement about an action in the past. Although the action expressed in the infinitive is in the past, the tense of the modal verb need not be a past tense.

Sigrid kann ja nicht auf der Party **gesehen worden sein**, denn sie war zu Hause.	*It is not possible that Sigrid was seen at the party, since she was at home.*

The Infinitival Clause

A common German construction is the **zu** infinitive, or infinitival clause. It consists of the particle **zu** and an infinitive form. With the present active infinitival clause, **zu** precedes the infinitive. If, however, the verb has a prefix that is separable in the simple tenses, the **zu** is inserted between the separable prefix and the verb stem.

PRESENT ACTIVE	zu verstehen	*to understand*
	zu reden	*to talk*
	auszuverkaufen	*to sell out*
	nachzudenken	*to think over*

The **zu** infinitive can also be used with a perfect infinitive, as well as with passive voice.

PERFECT ACTIVE	verstanden zu haben	*to have understood*
	aufgestanden zu sein	*to have stood up*
PRESENT PASSIVE	gesehen zu werden	*to be seen*
PERFECT PASSIVE	gelesen worden zu sein	*to have been read*

Uses of the Infinitival Clause

The infinitival clause is commonly used with modifying verbs, such as **brauchen** *to need*, **pflegen** *to tend*, and **scheinen** *to seem*.

Wir brauchen nicht **aufzustehen**.	*We don't need to stand up.*
Der Pfarrer pflegt monoton **zu reden**.	*The pastor tends to speak in a monotone.*
Bert scheint den Begriff **verstanden zu haben**.	*Bert seems to have understood the concept.*

Another common use of the infinitival clause is to express purpose (**um ... zu**), omission (**ohne ... zu**), or alternation (**statt/anstatt ... zu**).

Wir fahren mit dem Bus, **um** Geld **zu sparen**.	*We're going by bus in order to save money.*
Liesl ist ins Zimmer gekommen, **ohne zu klopfen**.	*Liesl came into the room without knocking.*
Warum gehst du nicht zu Fuß, **anstatt** mit dem Bus **zu fahren**?	*Why don't you walk instead of taking the bus?*

When a modal verb is added, the **zu** is inserted between the main verb and the modal verb.

Sie schläft jetzt ein, **um** morgen früh **aufstehen zu können**.	*She's going to sleep now in order to be able to get up early.*

The Verb *haben* or *sein* + *zu* Infinitive When used with **sein** or **haben**, the **zu** infinitive has the same general sense as a modal verb of obligation or necessity.

Die Sache **ist** noch **zu** klären.	*The matter has yet to be clarified.*
Wir **haben** die Hinweise **zu** beachten.	*We have to pay attention to the guidelines.*

THE PRESENT PARTICIPLE

To form the present participle, add **-d** to the present active infinitive.

lachen + d	→ lachend	*laughing*
schreien + d	→ schreiend	*screaming*

The present participle of the verbs **sein** and **tun** are irregular: **seiend, tuend.**

Uses of the Present Participle

Present participles are rarely used in German as verbs, but not infrequently as adjectives.

die lachende Kuh	*the laughing cow*
der schreiende Affe	*the screaming ape*

THE GERUNDIVE (*zu* + PRESENT PARTICIPLE)

To form the German gerundive, combine **zu** and the present participle. Placement of **zu** is the same as with the infinitival clause (see above).

PRESENT PARTICIPLE	GERUNDIVE
erledigend	zu erledigend
aufklärend	aufzuklärend

Uses of the Gerundive

The gerundive is used as an attributive, placed before the noun it modifies. It conveys a sense of necessity or obligation.

Die zu erledigende Arbeit ist noch nicht festgelegt.	*The work that is to be done is not yet decided.*

The gerundive is hardly ever used in spoken German, and it is used only infrequently in formal writing.

THE PAST PARTICIPLE

The past participle is the fourth principal part of the German verb. For details on formation of the past participle, see pages 20–23.

Uses of the Past Participle

The past participle is used in the following ways.

- To form perfect tenses (**sehen** *to see* ~ **gesehen**)

  Ich habe den Film **gesehen**. — *I've seen the film.*

- To form the passive voice (**streichen** *to cut, cancel* ~ **gestrichen**)

  Der Film wurde **gestrichen**. — *The film was cancelled.*

- As an adjective (**mischen** *to mix* ~ **gemischt**)

  Ich möchte den **gemischten** Salat. — *I'd like the mixed salad.*

- As an adjectival noun (**anstellen** *to employ* ~ **angestellt**)

  Dieser **Angestellte** verdient mehr als ich. — *This employee earns more than I.*

VERB PLACEMENT: OVERVIEW

The German sentence is characterized by the verb's fixed position in a sentence, while other constituents are transposable.

THE SENTENCE FRAME

The sentence is built around the sentence frame (**Satzklammer**). The frame is formed in a main clause by the conjugated verb in second position and other verbs or verbal complements in the end position. The positions are commonly called "fields."

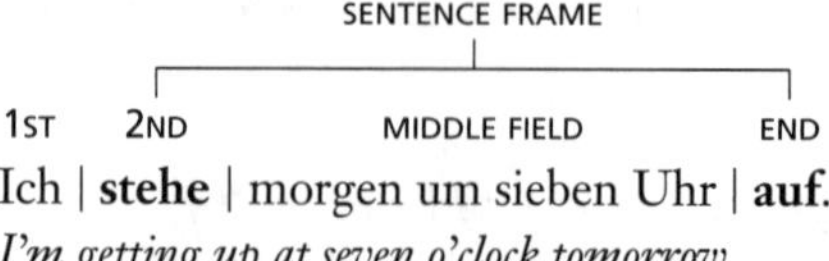

Ich | **stehe** | morgen um sieben Uhr | **auf**.

I'm getting up at seven o'clock tomorrow.

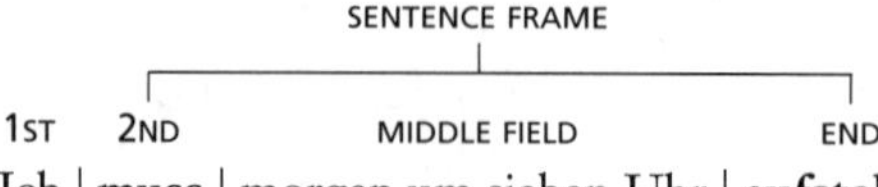

Ich | **muss** | morgen um sieben Uhr | **aufstehen**.

I have to get up at seven o'clock tomorrow.

If for reasons of emphasis or focus, the subject is displaced by another constituent in the first field, the subject then moves to the middle field, while the verb remains in the second field.

1ST	2ND	MIDDLE FIELD	END	
Ich	**stehe**	morgen um sieben Uhr	**auf.**	*I'm getting up at seven o'clock tomorrow.*
Morgen	**stehe**	ich um sieben Uhr	**auf.**	*Tomorrow I'm getting up at seven o'clock.*

Any number of complements can be added to the middle field, while the verb or complement retains its position in the end field.

Ich stehe morgen um sieben Uhr voller Energie auf. — *I'm getting up tomorrow at seven o'clock full of energy.*

Ich muss morgen um sieben Uhr voller Energie aufstehen. — *I have to get up tomorrow at seven o'clock full of energy.*

Compound Tenses The same rules apply to sentences with the perfect and other compound tenses.

Ich bin aufgestanden. — *I got up.*

Ich bin heute früh aufgestanden. — *I got up this morning.*

Ich bin heute früh um sieben Uhr aufgestanden. — *I got up this morning at seven o'clock.*

Ich bin heute früh um sieben Uhr voller Energie aufgestanden. — *I got up this morning at seven o'clock full of energy.*

Subordinate Word Order

Subordinate clauses are introduced by a subordinating conjunction, such as **dass** *that*, **ob** *whether*, **warum** *why*, and **weil** *because*.

Die Menschen glaubten, **dass** die Welt flach ist. — *People believed* ***that*** *the world is flat.*

The word order in these clauses is different from that of a main clause and is referred to as subordinate word order. Relative clauses, which are introduced by relative pronouns **der**, **die**, **das**, **den**, **dem**, and so forth, also have subordinate word order.

Der Mann, **der** oben im Baum steckt, ist Moritz. — *The man who is stuck up in the tree is Moritz.*

In clauses with subordinate word order, the sentence frame takes a different form: the conjugated verb is placed at the end of the clause.

SENTENCE FRAME

Ich weiß, warum er immer noch schläft.

I know why he's still sleeping.

Verbal prefixes are rejoined with the verb stem.

Ich hoffe, dass ich morgen um sieben Uhr aufstehe. — *I hope that I get up at seven o'clock tomorrow.*

In compound tenses, the conjugated verb comes after the nonfinite forms.

Ich weiß, warum er noch schlafen will. — *I know why he still wants to sleep.*

Ich hoffe, dass ich morgen um sieben Uhr aufstehen kann. — *I hope that I can get up at seven o'clock tomorrow.*

Er weiß, warum ich immer noch geschlafen habe. — *He knows why I was still sleeping.*

Ich hoffe, dass er heute um sechs Uhr aufgestanden ist. — *I hope that he got up at six o'clock today.*

Multiverb Complexes

In sentences containing several infinitives in a multiverb complex, the nonfinite verbs are all pushed to the end of the sentence.

Er baut ein neues Haus.	*He's building a new house.*
ADD **lassen**	ADD *have*
Er lässt ein neues Haus bauen.	*He's having a new house built.*
ADD **wollen**	ADD *want to*
Er will ein neues Haus bauen lassen.	*He wants to have a new house built.*

In corresponding subordinate clauses, the finite verb is placed at the very end of all the verbs.

Ich weiß, dass er ein neues Haus baut.	*I know he's building a new house.*
Ich weiß, dass er ein neues Haus bauen lässt.	*I know he's having a new house built.*
Ich weiß, dass er ein neues Haus bauen lassen will.	*I know he wants to have a new house built.*

However, if a multiverb complex with three or more verbs contains a form of **haben**, then **haben** comes before the rest of the verbal complex, whether in a main or subordinate clause.

Er wird ein neues Haus **haben bauen lassen**.	*He will have had a new house built.*
Ich weiß, warum sie es **hätte machen sollen**.	*I know why she should have done it.*

In subordinate clauses with such verbal complexes, the finite verb appears late in the clause, as shown by the position of **wird** in the following sentence in the future perfect tense.

Ich weiß, dass er ein neues Haus **wird haben bauen lassen**.	*I know he will have had a new house built.*

These constructions are not common.

SPELLING REFORM

Due to spelling reforms implemented by education and publishing authorities in German-speaking countries in 1999, older texts look different from modern ones. With respect to verbs, the differences are of two main types.

- Many verbs that were formerly compound verbs are now considered verbal complement + verb.

TRADITIONAL GERMAN	REVISED GERMAN
kennenlernen	kennen lernen
schwerfallen	schwer fallen

  One practical outcome of this reform is a change in the dictionary entry form. The two verbs above were previously listed under K and S, respectively. In the revised German, they appear under L and F, respectively, although dual entries are not uncommon.

- Due to spelling rule changes concerning the digraph **ß**, some verbs are now spelled with **ss** in some forms. The verb **essen**, for example, illustrates the revised rule for **ß**: Use **ss** after short vowels, but **ß** after long vowels and diphthongs.

TRADITIONAL GERMAN	REVISED GERMAN
ich esse, du ißt, er/sie/es ißt	ich esse, du isst, er/sie/es isst
ich aß, du aßest, er/sie/es aß	ich aß, du aßest, er/sie/es aß

555

FULLY CONJUGATED VERBS

Top 50 Verbs

The following 50 verbs have been selected for their high frequency and their use in many common idiomatic expressions. For each verb, a full page of example sentences and phrases providing guidance on correct usage immediately precedes or follows the conjugation table.

to turn (off) **ab·biegen** 1

strong verb **biegt ab · bog ab · abgebogen**

PRESENT

ich biege	wir biegen	ab
du biegst	ihr biegt	
Sie biegen	Sie biegen	
er/sie/es biegt	sie biegen	

SIMPLE PAST

ich bog	wir bogen	ab
du bogst	ihr bogt	
Sie bogen	Sie bogen	
er/sie/es bog	sie bogen	

FUTURE

ich werde	wir werden	abbiegen
du wirst	ihr werdet	
Sie werden	Sie werden	
er/sie/es wird	sie werden	

PRESENT SUBJUNCTIVE I

ich biege	wir biegen	ab
du biegest	ihr bieget	
Sie biegen	Sie biegen	
er/sie/es biege	sie biegen	

PRESENT SUBJUNCTIVE II

ich böge	wir bögen	ab
du bögest	ihr böget	
Sie bögen	Sie bögen	
er/sie/es böge	sie bögen	

FUTURE SUBJUNCTIVE I

ich werde	wir werden	abbiegen
du werdest	ihr werdet	
Sie werden	Sie werden	
er/sie/es werde	sie werden	

FUTURE SUBJUNCTIVE II

ich würde	wir würden	abbiegen
du würdest	ihr würdet	
Sie würden	Sie würden	
er/sie/es würde	sie würden	

PRESENT PERFECT

ich bin	wir sind	abgebogen
du bist	ihr seid	
Sie sind	Sie sind	
er/sie/es ist	sie sind	

PAST PERFECT

ich war	wir waren	abgebogen
du warst	ihr wart	
Sie waren	Sie waren	
er/sie/es war	sie waren	

FUTURE PERFECT

ich werde	wir werden	abgebogen sein
du wirst	ihr werdet	
Sie werden	Sie werden	
er/sie/es wird	sie werden	

PAST SUBJUNCTIVE I

ich sei	wir seien	abgebogen
du seiest	ihr seiet	
Sie seien	Sie seien	
er/sie/es sei	sie seien	

PAST SUBJUNCTIVE II

ich wäre	wir wären	abgebogen
du wärest	ihr wäret	
Sie wären	Sie wären	
er/sie/es wäre	sie wären	

FUTURE PERFECT SUBJUNCTIVE I

ich werde	wir werden	abgebogen sein
du werdest	ihr werdet	
Sie werden	Sie werden	
er/sie/es werde	sie werden	

FUTURE PERFECT SUBJUNCTIVE II

ich würde	wir würden	abgebogen sein
du würdest	ihr würdet	
Sie würden	Sie würden	
er/sie/es würde	sie würden	

COMMANDS bieg(e) ab! biegt ab! biegen Sie ab!

PRESENT PARTICIPLE abbiegend

Usage

Leider bin ich falsch abgebogen.	*Unfortunately, I took a wrong turn.*
Nach 100 Meter biegen Sie rechts ab.	*After 100 meters, you turn right.*
Das Auto biegt links nach Nordheim ab.	*The car is turning left toward Nordheim.*
Dann biegst du ab und fährst einen Umweg.	*Then you turn off and take a detour.*
Beim Schloss biegen wir ab zu den Ruinen.	*At the castle, we turn off toward the ruins.*
Mark biegt rechts ab und sieht da den Dom.	*Mark turns right and sees the cathedral there.*
Wir hätten eigentlich links abbiegen sollen.	*Actually, we should have turned left.*
Darf man hier abbiegen?	*Are you allowed to turn here?*

abbiegen (with **haben**) *to bend*

Dieser Draht lässt sich nicht leicht abbiegen.	*This wire does not easily bend.*
Gretl hat die Sache noch einmal abgebogen.	*Gretl just managed to stop things from going too far.*

RELATED VERBS *see* **biegen** (106)

2 ab·fahren *to depart, leave*

fährt ab · fuhr ab · abgefahren — strong verb

PRESENT			PRESENT PERFECT		
ich fahre	wir fahren	ab	ich bin	wir sind	abgefahren
du fährst	ihr fahrt		du bist	ihr seid	
Sie fahren	Sie fahren		Sie sind	Sie sind	
er/sie/es fährt	sie fahren		er/sie/es ist	sie sind	
SIMPLE PAST			**PAST PERFECT**		
ich fuhr	wir fuhren	ab	ich war	wir waren	abgefahren
du fuhrst	ihr fuhrt		du warst	ihr wart	
Sie fuhren	Sie fuhren		Sie waren	Sie waren	
er/sie/es fuhr	sie fuhren		er/sie/es war	sie waren	
FUTURE			**FUTURE PERFECT**		
ich werde	wir werden	abfahren	ich werde	wir werden	abgefahren sein
du wirst	ihr werdet		du wirst	ihr werdet	
Sie werden	Sie werden		Sie werden	Sie werden	
er/sie/es wird	sie werden		er/sie/es wird	sie werden	
PRESENT SUBJUNCTIVE I			**PAST SUBJUNCTIVE I**		
ich fahre	wir fahren	ab	ich sei	wir seien	abgefahren
du fahrest	ihr fahret		du seiest	ihr seiet	
Sie fahren	Sie fahren		Sie seien	Sie seien	
er/sie/es fahre	sie fahren		er/sie/es sei	sie seien	
PRESENT SUBJUNCTIVE II			**PAST SUBJUNCTIVE II**		
ich führe	wir führen	ab	ich wäre	wir wären	abgefahren
du führest	ihr führet		du wärest	ihr wäret	
Sie führen	Sie führen		Sie wären	Sie wären	
er/sie/es führe	sie führen		er/sie/es wäre	sie wären	
FUTURE SUBJUNCTIVE I			**FUTURE PERFECT SUBJUNCTIVE I**		
ich werde	wir werden	abfahren	ich werde	wir werden	abgefahren sein
du werdest	ihr werdet		du werdest	ihr werdet	
Sie werden	Sie werden		Sie werden	Sie werden	
er/sie/es werde	sie werden		er/sie/es werde	sie werden	
FUTURE SUBJUNCTIVE II			**FUTURE PERFECT SUBJUNCTIVE II**		
ich würde	wir würden	abfahren	ich würde	wir würden	abgefahren sein
du würdest	ihr würdet		du würdest	ihr würdet	
Sie würden	Sie würden		Sie würden	Sie würden	
er/sie/es würde	sie würden		er/sie/es würde	sie würden	

COMMANDS fahr(e) ab! fahrt ab! fahren Sie ab!

PRESENT PARTICIPLE abfahrend

Usage

Der Intercity nach Osnabrück war schon abgefahren.	*The Intercity to Osnabrück had already departed.*
Der Anschlusszug fährt von Gleis 12 ab.	*The connecting train departs from platform 12.*
Am frühen Morgen fuhren wir Richtung Hilo ab.	*In the early morning we departed for Hilo.*
Der Sonderzug nach Wien fährt am 9. Juli ab.	*The special train to Vienna departs on July 9.*
Wann fahrt ihr denn wieder ab?	*When are you leaving again?*
Kurz vor Mittag fuhr die Postkutsche ab.	*Just before noon, the stagecoach departed.*

abfahren (with **haben**) *to take away; wear out; cover*

Pflanzenabfälle werden einmal im Monat abgefahren.	*Plant debris is picked up once a month.*
Ungleich abgefahrene Reifen können Unfälle verursachen.	*Unevenly worn tires can cause accidents.*
Alle Strecken mussten von allen Teilnehmern abgefahren werden.	*Each stretch had to be covered by all participants.*

RELATED VERBS *see* **fahren** (177)

strong verb **gibt ab · gab ab · abgegeben**

PRESENT			PRESENT PERFECT		
ich gebe	wir geben	ab	ich habe	wir haben	abgegeben
du gibst	ihr gebt		du hast	ihr habt	
Sie geben	Sie geben		Sie haben	Sie haben	
er/sie/es gibt	sie geben		er/sie/es hat	sie haben	
SIMPLE PAST			PAST PERFECT		
ich gab	wir gaben	ab	ich hatte	wir hatten	abgegeben
du gabst	ihr gabt		du hattest	ihr hattet	
Sie gaben	Sie gaben		Sie hatten	Sie hatten	
er/sie/es gab	sie gaben		er/sie/es hatte	sie hatten	
FUTURE			FUTURE PERFECT		
ich werde	wir werden	abgeben	ich werde	wir werden	abgegeben haben
du wirst	ihr werdet		du wirst	ihr werdet	
Sie werden	Sie werden		Sie werden	Sie werden	
er/sie/es wird	sie werden		er/sie/es wird	sie werden	
PRESENT SUBJUNCTIVE I			PAST SUBJUNCTIVE I		
ich gebe	wir geben	ab	ich habe	wir haben	abgegeben
du gebest	ihr gebet		du habest	ihr habet	
Sie geben	Sie geben		Sie haben	Sie haben	
er/sie/es gebe	sie geben		er/sie/es habe	sie haben	
PRESENT SUBJUNCTIVE II			PAST SUBJUNCTIVE II		
ich gäbe	wir gäben	ab	ich hätte	wir hätten	abgegeben
du gäbest	ihr gäbet		du hättest	ihr hättet	
Sie gäben	Sie gäben		Sie hätten	Sie hätten	
er/sie/es gäbe	sie gäben		er/sie/es hätte	sie hätten	
FUTURE SUBJUNCTIVE I			FUTURE PERFECT SUBJUNCTIVE I		
ich werde	wir werden	abgeben	ich werde	wir werden	abgegeben haben
du werdest	ihr werdet		du werdest	ihr werdet	
Sie werden	Sie werden		Sie werden	Sie werden	
er/sie/es werde	sie werden		er/sie/es werde	sie werden	
FUTURE SUBJUNCTIVE II			FUTURE PERFECT SUBJUNCTIVE II		
ich würde	wir würden	abgeben	ich würde	wir würden	abgegeben haben
du würdest	ihr würdet		du würdest	ihr würdet	
Sie würden	Sie würden		Sie würden	Sie würden	
er/sie/es würde	sie würden		er/sie/es würde	sie würden	

COMMANDS gib ab! gebt ab! geben Sie ab!

PRESENT PARTICIPLE abgebend

Usage

Manfred Schmidt gibt den Direktionsposten ab. — *Manfred Schmidt is handing over the position of director.*
Etliche Brillen wurden beim Fundbüro abgegeben. — *Several pairs of glasses were turned in at the lost-and-found.*
Geben Sie Ihre Bewertung ab! — *Submit your evaluation!*
Jemand hat für Sie einen Brief abgegeben. — *Someone has left a letter for you.*
Gib deinen Mantel an der Garderobe ab. — *Leave your coat at the checkroom.*
Die Richter müssen ein faires Urteil abgeben. — *The judges must render a fair verdict.*
Schüsse wurden auf den Mann abgegeben. — *Shots were fired at the man.*
Solche Blumen können viel Pollen abgeben. — *Such flowers can produce a lot of pollen.*
Unser neuer Kamin gibt eine enorme Hitze ab. — *Our new fireplace radiates an enormous amount of heat.*

sich abgeben *to engage, bother*

Er gibt sich mit Tätigkeiten ab, die für die Arbeit nicht relevant sind. — *He engages in activities that are not relevant to work.*

RELATED VERBS *see* **geben** (206)

4

ab·holen *to fetch, pick up*

holt ab · holte ab · abgeholt regular weak verb

PRESENT

ich hole	wir holen	ab
du holst	ihr holt	
Sie holen	Sie holen	
er/sie/es holt	sie holen	

SIMPLE PAST

ich holte	wir holten	ab
du holtest	ihr holtet	
Sie holten	Sie holten	
er/sie/es holte	sie holten	

FUTURE

ich werde	wir werden	abholen
du wirst	ihr werdet	
Sie werden	Sie werden	
er/sie/es wird	sie werden	

PRESENT SUBJUNCTIVE I

ich hole	wir holen	ab
du holest	ihr holet	
Sie holen	Sie holen	
er/sie/es hole	sie holen	

PRESENT SUBJUNCTIVE II

ich holte	wir holten	ab
du holtest	ihr holtet	
Sie holten	Sie holten	
er/sie/es holte	sie holten	

FUTURE SUBJUNCTIVE I

ich werde	wir werden	abholen
du werdest	ihr werdet	
Sie werden	Sie werden	
er/sie/es werde	sie werden	

FUTURE SUBJUNCTIVE II

ich würde	wir würden	abholen
du würdest	ihr würdet	
Sie würden	Sie würden	
er/sie/es würde	sie würden	

PRESENT PERFECT

ich habe	wir haben	abgeholt
du hast	ihr habt	
Sie haben	Sie haben	
er/sie/es hat	sie haben	

PAST PERFECT

ich hatte	wir hatten	abgeholt
du hattest	ihr hattet	
Sie hatten	Sie hatten	
er/sie/es hatte	sie hatten	

FUTURE PERFECT

ich werde	wir werden	abgeholt haben
du wirst	ihr werdet	
Sie werden	Sie werden	
er/sie/es wird	sie werden	

PAST SUBJUNCTIVE I

ich habe	wir haben	abgeholt
du habest	ihr habet	
Sie haben	Sie haben	
er/sie/es habe	sie haben	

PAST SUBJUNCTIVE II

ich hätte	wir hätten	abgeholt
du hättest	ihr hättet	
Sie hätten	Sie hätten	
er/sie/es hätte	sie hätten	

FUTURE PERFECT SUBJUNCTIVE I

ich werde	wir werden	abgeholt haben
du werdest	ihr werdet	
Sie werden	Sie werden	
er/sie/es werde	sie werden	

FUTURE PERFECT SUBJUNCTIVE II

ich würde	wir würden	abgeholt haben
du würdest	ihr würdet	
Sie würden	Sie würden	
er/sie/es würde	sie würden	

COMMANDS hol(e) ab! holt ab! holen Sie ab!

PRESENT PARTICIPLE abholend

Usage

Maria hat uns vom Bahnhof abgeholt. — *Maria picked us up from the train station.*

Frau Kretschmer wollte ihre Tochter mit dem Auto von der Schule abholen. — *Mrs. Kretschmer wanted to pick up her daughter from school with the car.*

Die Besucher wurden von ihren Gastgebern am Flughafen abgeholt. — *The visitors were picked up at the airport by their hosts.*

Hol mich bitte ab! — *Please pick me up!*

Sie rief einen Wagen, der sie an der Tür abholte. — *She called for a car that picked her up at her door.*

Die Sektenanhänger glauben, dass ein Raumschiff sie in der Wüste abholen werde. — *The sect members believe a spaceship will pick them up in the desert.*

Ich habe mich mit dem Auto abholen lassen. — *I arranged to be picked up by car.*

Wir konnten die Theaterkarten an der Kasse abholen. — *We were able to pick up the theater tickets at the box office.*

Der Benutzer kann seine E-Mails durch den Web-Browser abholen. — *The user can get his e-mail through the Web browser.*

RELATED VERBS *see* **holen** (247)

regular weak verb **lehnt ab · lehnte ab · abgelehnt**

PRESENT

ich lehne	wir lehnen	ab
du lehnst	ihr lehnt	
Sie lehnen	Sie lehnen	
er/sie/es lehnt	sie lehnen	

SIMPLE PAST

ich lehnte	wir lehnten	ab
du lehntest	ihr lehntet	
Sie lehnten	Sie lehnten	
er/sie/es lehnte	sie lehnten	

FUTURE

ich werde	wir werden	ablehnen
du wirst	ihr werdet	
Sie werden	Sie werden	
er/sie/es wird	sie werden	

PRESENT SUBJUNCTIVE I

ich lehne	wir lehnen	ab
du lehnest	ihr lehnet	
Sie lehnen	Sie lehnen	
er/sie/es lehne	sie lehnen	

PRESENT SUBJUNCTIVE II

ich lehnte	wir lehnten	ab
du lehntest	ihr lehntet	
Sie lehnten	Sie lehnten	
er/sie/es lehnte	sie lehnten	

FUTURE SUBJUNCTIVE I

ich werde	wir werden	ablehnen
du werdest	ihr werdet	
Sie werden	Sie werden	
er/sie/es werde	sie werden	

FUTURE SUBJUNCTIVE II

ich würde	wir würden	ablehnen
du würdest	ihr würdet	
Sie würden	Sie würden	
er/sie/es würde	sie würden	

PRESENT PERFECT

ich habe	wir haben	abgelehnt
du hast	ihr habt	
Sie haben	Sie haben	
er/sie/es hat	sie haben	

PAST PERFECT

ich hatte	wir hatten	abgelehnt
du hattest	ihr hattet	
Sie hatten	Sie hatten	
er/sie/es hatte	sie hatten	

FUTURE PERFECT

ich werde	wir werden	abgelehnt haben
du wirst	ihr werdet	
Sie werden	Sie werden	
er/sie/es wird	sie werden	

PAST SUBJUNCTIVE I

ich habe	wir haben	abgelehnt
du habest	ihr habet	
Sie haben	Sie haben	
er/sie/es habe	sie haben	

PAST SUBJUNCTIVE II

ich hätte	wir hätten	abgelehnt
du hättest	ihr hättet	
Sie hätten	Sie hätten	
er/sie/es hätte	sie hätten	

FUTURE PERFECT SUBJUNCTIVE I

ich werde	wir werden	abgelehnt haben
du werdest	ihr werdet	
Sie werden	Sie werden	
er/sie/es werde	sie werden	

FUTURE PERFECT SUBJUNCTIVE II

ich würde	wir würden	abgelehnt haben
du würdest	ihr würdet	
Sie würden	Sie würden	
er/sie/es würde	sie würden	

COMMANDS lehn(e) ab! lehnt ab! lehnen Sie ab!

PRESENT PARTICIPLE ablehnend

Usage

Das Gericht hat ihren Antrag abgelehnt.	*The court rejected their petition.*
Herr Kunz muss Ihre Einladung leider ablehnen.	*Mr. Kunz must unfortunately decline your invitation.*
Dara lehnt es absolut ab, anders zu handeln.	*Dara absolutely refuses to act differently.*
Ich lehne jede Verantwortung dafür ab.	*I take no responsibility for that.*
Warum wird der Vorstand unseren Vorschlag ablehnen dürfen?	*Why will the board be allowed to turn down our proposal?*
Ihr Antrag ist abgelehnt worden.	*Your request has been denied.*
Sein eigenes Volk wird ihn ablehnen.	*His own people will reject him.*
Der Vermieter lehnte sämtliche Reparaturen kategorisch ab.	*The landlord categorically refused (to make) all repairs.*
Sie lehnt ärztliche Behandlung aus religiösen Gründen ab.	*She refuses medical treatment for religious reasons.*
Die Verlage haben seine ersten drei Romane abgelehnt.	*The publishers rejected his first three novels.*
Als Veganer lehnen sie alle tierischen Produkte ab.	*As vegans, they refuse (to eat) all animal products.*

RELATED VERBS *see* **lehnen** (284)

6 ab·nehmen *to lose weight; decrease; wane; remove, take off; take away*

nimmt ab · nahm ab · abgenommen strong verb

PRESENT

ich nehme	wir nehmen	ab
du nimmst	ihr nehmt	
Sie nehmen	Sie nehmen	
er/sie/es nimmt	sie nehmen	

PRESENT PERFECT

ich habe	wir haben	abgenommen
du hast	ihr habt	
Sie haben	Sie haben	
er/sie/es hat	sie haben	

SIMPLE PAST

ich nahm	wir nahmen	ab
du nahmst	ihr nahmt	
Sie nahmen	Sie nahmen	
er/sie/es nahm	sie nahmen	

PAST PERFECT

ich hatte	wir hatten	abgenommen
du hattest	ihr hattet	
Sie hatten	Sie hatten	
er/sie/es hatte	sie hatten	

FUTURE

ich werde	wir werden	abnehmen
du wirst	ihr werdet	
Sie werden	Sie werden	
er/sie/es wird	sie werden	

FUTURE PERFECT

ich werde	wir werden	abgenommen haben
du wirst	ihr werdet	
Sie werden	Sie werden	
er/sie/es wird	sie werden	

PRESENT SUBJUNCTIVE I

ich nehme	wir nehmen	ab
du nehmest	ihr nehmet	
Sie nehmen	Sie nehmen	
er/sie/es nehme	sie nehmen	

PAST SUBJUNCTIVE I

ich habe	wir haben	abgenommen
du habest	ihr habet	
Sie haben	Sie haben	
er/sie/es habe	sie haben	

PRESENT SUBJUNCTIVE II

ich nähme	wir nähmen	ab
du nähmest	ihr nähmet	
Sie nähmen	Sie nähmen	
er/sie/es nähme	sie nähmen	

PAST SUBJUNCTIVE II

ich hätte	wir hätten	abgenommen
du hättest	ihr hättet	
Sie hätten	Sie hätten	
er/sie/es hätte	sie hätten	

FUTURE SUBJUNCTIVE I

ich werde	wir werden	abnehmen
du werdest	ihr werdet	
Sie werden	Sie werden	
er/sie/es werde	sie werden	

FUTURE PERFECT SUBJUNCTIVE I

ich werde	wir werden	abgenommen haben
du werdest	ihr werdet	
Sie werden	Sie werden	
er/sie/es werde	sie werden	

FUTURE SUBJUNCTIVE II

ich würde	wir würden	abnehmen
du würdest	ihr würdet	
Sie würden	Sie würden	
er/sie/es würde	sie würden	

FUTURE PERFECT SUBJUNCTIVE II

ich würde	wir würden	abgenommen haben
du würdest	ihr würdet	
Sie würden	Sie würden	
er/sie/es würde	sie würden	

COMMANDS nimm ab! nehmt ab! nehmen Sie ab!

PRESENT PARTICIPLE abnehmend

Usage

Ich möchte abnehmen.	*I'd like to lose weight.*
Sie hat seit Oktober sehr viel abgenommen.	*She has lost a lot of weight since October.*
Die Anzahl der Beschäftigten nahm stark ab.	*The number of employed persons decreased considerably.*
Der Mond nimmt jetzt ab.	*The moon is waning now.*
Nehmen Sie bitte den Hut ab.	*Please remove your hat.*
Alexis hatte die Wäsche gerade von der Leine abgenommen.	*Alexis had just taken the laundry off the clothesline.*
Dann hat man ihr 500 ml Blut abgenommen.	*Then they took 500 ml of her blood.*
Heute nimmt der junge Priester zum ersten Mal die Beichte ab.	*The young priest is hearing confession for the first time today.*
Darf die Polizei meinen Führerschein abnehmen?	*Are the police allowed to take away my driver's license?*
Kannst du mir bitte die Pakete abnehmen?	*Can you please take the packages for me?*
Niemand wollte den Hörer abnehmen.	*Nobody wanted to pick up the phone.*

RELATED VERBS *see* **nehmen** (314)

regular weak verb **achtet · achtete · geachtet**

PRESENT

ich achte	wir achten
du achtest	ihr achtet
Sie achten	Sie achten
er/sie/es achtet	sie achten

SIMPLE PAST

ich achtete	wir achteten
du achtetest	ihr achtetet
Sie achteten	Sie achteten
er/sie/es achtete	sie achteten

FUTURE

ich werde	wir werden	achten
du wirst	ihr werdet	
Sie werden	Sie werden	
er/sie/es wird	sie werden	

PRESENT SUBJUNCTIVE I

ich achte	wir achten
du achtest	ihr achtet
Sie achten	Sie achten
er/sie/es achte	sie achten

PRESENT SUBJUNCTIVE II

ich achtete	wir achteten
du achtetest	ihr achtetet
Sie achteten	Sie achteten
er/sie/es achtete	sie achteten

FUTURE SUBJUNCTIVE I

ich werde	wir werden	achten
du werdest	ihr werdet	
Sie werden	Sie werden	
er/sie/es werde	sie werden	

FUTURE SUBJUNCTIVE II

ich würde	wir würden	achten
du würdest	ihr würdet	
Sie würden	Sie würden	
er/sie/es würde	sie würden	

PRESENT PERFECT

ich habe	wir haben	geachtet
du hast	ihr habt	
Sie haben	Sie haben	
er/sie/es hat	sie haben	

PAST PERFECT

ich hatte	wir hatten	geachtet
du hattest	ihr hattet	
Sie hatten	Sie hatten	
er/sie/es hatte	sie hatten	

FUTURE PERFECT

ich werde	wir werden	geachtet haben
du wirst	ihr werdet	
Sie werden	Sie werden	
er/sie/es wird	sie werden	

PAST SUBJUNCTIVE I

ich habe	wir haben	geachtet
du habest	ihr habet	
Sie haben	Sie haben	
er/sie/es habe	sie haben	

PAST SUBJUNCTIVE II

ich hätte	wir hätten	geachtet
du hättest	ihr hättet	
Sie hätten	Sie hätten	
er/sie/es hätte	sie hätten	

FUTURE PERFECT SUBJUNCTIVE I

ich werde	wir werden	geachtet haben
du werdest	ihr werdet	
Sie werden	Sie werden	
er/sie/es werde	sie werden	

FUTURE PERFECT SUBJUNCTIVE II

ich würde	wir würden	geachtet haben
du würdest	ihr würdet	
Sie würden	Sie würden	
er/sie/es würde	sie würden	

COMMANDS achte! achtet! achten Sie!

PRESENT PARTICIPLE achtend

Usage

Du brauchst nicht mehr auf Diät zu achten.	*You don't have to pay attention to your diet anymore.*
Es ist wichtig, auf die Gefühle anderer Menschen zu achten.	*It's important to consider the feelings of others.*
Dazu müssen wir die Gesetze des Landes achten.	*In addition, we must respect the laws of the land.*
Ich achte den Mut meiner Kollegen.	*I respect the courage of my colleagues.*
Warum achtetet ihr mich nicht?	*Why did you not respect me?*
Früher achteten sie Silber nicht.	*They used to not value silver at all.*
Achten Sie bitte auf Groß- und Kleinschreibung.	*Please pay attention to capitalization.*
Der Politiker achtete nicht auf die Zwischenrufe.	*The politician paid no attention to the heckling.*
Die Gäste haben auf Pünktlichkeit gar nicht geachtet.	*The guests paid no attention at all to punctuality.*
Damals hat Papa viel mehr auf Aussehen geachtet.	*In those days, Dad paid much more attention to looks.*
Aber der Ritter achtete auf die Worte der Frau nicht.	*But the knight paid no heed to the woman's words.*
Achten Sie bitte darauf, dass das richtige Programm auf Ihrem Computer aktiv ist.	*Please make sure that the correct program is running on your computer.*

RELATED VERBS begutachten, erachten, missachten, verachten; *see also* **beachten** (46), **beobachten** (72)

8 an·bieten *to offer*

bietet an · bot an · angeboten strong verb

PRESENT

ich biete	wir bieten	an
du bietest	ihr bietet	
Sie bieten	Sie bieten	
er/sie/es bietet	sie bieten	

PRESENT PERFECT

ich habe	wir haben	angeboten
du hast	ihr habt	
Sie haben	Sie haben	
er/sie/es hat	sie haben	

SIMPLE PAST

ich bot	wir boten	an
du bot(e)st	ihr botet	
Sie boten	Sie boten	
er/sie/es bot	sie boten	

PAST PERFECT

ich hatte	wir hatten	angeboten
du hattest	ihr hattet	
Sie hatten	Sie hatten	
er/sie/es hatte	sie hatten	

FUTURE

ich werde	wir werden	anbieten
du wirst	ihr werdet	
Sie werden	Sie werden	
er/sie/es wird	sie werden	

FUTURE PERFECT

ich werde	wir werden	angeboten haben
du wirst	ihr werdet	
Sie werden	Sie werden	
er/sie/es wird	sie werden	

PRESENT SUBJUNCTIVE I

ich biete	wir bieten	an
du bietest	ihr bietet	
Sie bieten	Sie bieten	
er/sie/es biete	sie bieten	

PAST SUBJUNCTIVE I

ich habe	wir haben	angeboten
du habest	ihr habet	
Sie haben	Sie haben	
er/sie/es habe	sie haben	

PRESENT SUBJUNCTIVE II

ich böte	wir böten	an
du bötest	ihr bötet	
Sie böten	Sie böten	
er/sie/es böte	sie böten	

PAST SUBJUNCTIVE II

ich hätte	wir hätten	angeboten
du hättest	ihr hättet	
Sie hätten	Sie hätten	
er/sie/es hätte	sie hätten	

FUTURE SUBJUNCTIVE I

ich werde	wir werden	anbieten
du werdest	ihr werdet	
Sie werden	Sie werden	
er/sie/es werde	sie werden	

FUTURE PERFECT SUBJUNCTIVE I

ich werde	wir werden	angeboten haben
du werdest	ihr werdet	
Sie werden	Sie werden	
er/sie/es werde	sie werden	

FUTURE SUBJUNCTIVE II

ich würde	wir würden	anbieten
du würdest	ihr würdet	
Sie würden	Sie würden	
er/sie/es würde	sie würden	

FUTURE PERFECT SUBJUNCTIVE II

ich würde	wir würden	angeboten haben
du würdest	ihr würdet	
Sie würden	Sie würden	
er/sie/es würde	sie würden	

COMMANDS biete an! bietet an! bieten Sie an!

PRESENT PARTICIPLE anbietend

Usage

Darf ich Ihnen meinen Platz anbieten?	*May I offer you my seat?*
Demnächst bietet die Bank ihre Dienste per Internet an.	*Soon the bank will offer its services via the Internet.*
Diese alte Brauerei bot früher mal zwölf Biersorten an.	*At one time, this old brewery offered 12 types of beer.*
An diesem Gymnasium wird Hebräisch angeboten.	*Hebrew is offered at this high school.*
Wir konnten ihm keine Lösung anbieten.	*We were unable to offer him a solution.*
In Deutschland wurde dem Dirigenten aber keine Stelle angeboten.	*However, the director was not offered a position in Germany.*
Wer bietet das an?	*Who makes that offer?*
Im Sommersemester sind keine Kurse angeboten worden.	*No courses were offered in the summer semester.*
Wir können es Ihnen zum günstigen Preis anbieten.	*We can offer it to you at a reasonable price.*

sich anbieten *to be a possibility, be an option*

Als Kompromiss böte sich an, die Texte ungekürzt zu veröffentlichen.	*A suitable compromise would be to publish the texts unabridged.*

RELATED VERBS *see* **bieten** (107)

PRESENT

ich ändere	wir ändern
du änderst	ihr ändert
Sie ändern	Sie ändern
er/sie/es ändert	sie ändern

SIMPLE PAST

ich änderte	wir änderten
du ändertest	ihr ändertet
Sie änderten	Sie änderten
er/sie/es änderte	sie änderten

FUTURE

ich werde	wir werden	ändern
du wirst	ihr werdet	
Sie werden	Sie werden	
er/sie/es wird	sie werden	

PRESENT SUBJUNCTIVE I

ich ändere	wir ändern
du änderst	ihr ändert
Sie ändern	Sie ändern
er/sie/es ändere	sie ändern

PRESENT SUBJUNCTIVE II

ich änderte	wir änderten
du ändertest	ihr ändertet
Sie änderten	Sie änderten
er/sie/es änderte	sie änderten

FUTURE SUBJUNCTIVE I

ich werde	wir werden	ändern
du werdest	ihr werdet	
Sie werden	Sie werden	
er/sie/es werde	sie werden	

FUTURE SUBJUNCTIVE II

ich würde	wir würden	ändern
du würdest	ihr würdet	
Sie würden	Sie würden	
er/sie/es würde	sie würden	

PRESENT PERFECT

ich habe	wir haben	geändert
du hast	ihr habt	
Sie haben	Sie haben	
er/sie/es hat	sie haben	

PAST PERFECT

ich hatte	wir hatten	geändert
du hattest	ihr hattet	
Sie hatten	Sie hatten	
er/sie/es hatte	sie hatten	

FUTURE PERFECT

ich werde	wir werden	geändert haben
du wirst	ihr werdet	
Sie werden	Sie werden	
er/sie/es wird	sie werden	

PAST SUBJUNCTIVE I

ich habe	wir haben	geändert
du habest	ihr habet	
Sie haben	Sie haben	
er/sie/es habe	sie haben	

PAST SUBJUNCTIVE II

ich hätte	wir hätten	geändert
du hättest	ihr hättet	
Sie hätten	Sie hätten	
er/sie/es hätte	sie hätten	

FUTURE PERFECT SUBJUNCTIVE I

ich werde	wir werden	geändert haben
du werdest	ihr werdet	
Sie werden	Sie werden	
er/sie/es werde	sie werden	

FUTURE PERFECT SUBJUNCTIVE II

ich würde	wir würden	geändert haben
du würdest	ihr würdet	
Sie würden	Sie würden	
er/sie/es würde	sie würden	

COMMANDS ändere! ändert! ändern Sie!

PRESENT PARTICIPLE ändernd

Usage

Dieser Titel kann nicht geändert werden. — *This title cannot be changed.*
Daran ist nichts zu ändern. — *Nothing about that can be changed.*
Klicken Sie hier, wenn sie Ihr Passwort ändern wollen. — *Click here if you want to change your password.*
Er hat sich entschlossen, sein Leben zu ändern. — *He has decided to change his life.*
Warum änderst du ständig deine Ansicht? — *Why are you constantly changing your opinion?*
Ich muss die Hose ändern lassen. — *I have to get the pants altered.*
Der Programmierer konnte das Programm nur schwer ändern. — *The programmer had difficulty modifying the program.*

sich ändern *to change*

Hat sich was auf dem Hof geändert? — *Has anything changed on the farm?*
Ich habe mich nicht ändern können. — *I have not been able to mend my ways.*
Meine Telefonnummer hat sich geändert. — *My telephone number has changed.*
Wird sich was ändern? — *Will anything change?*

RELATED VERBS ab·ändern, um·ändern; *see also* **verändern** (475)

10 an·fangen *to begin, start*

fängt an · fing an · angefangen strong verb

PRESENT

ich fange	wir fangen	an
du fängst	ihr fangt	
Sie fangen	Sie fangen	
er/sie/es fängt	sie fangen	

PRESENT PERFECT

ich habe	wir haben	angefangen
du hast	ihr habt	
Sie haben	Sie haben	
er/sie/es hat	sie haben	

SIMPLE PAST

ich fing	wir fingen	an
du fingst	ihr fingt	
Sie fingen	Sie fingen	
er/sie/es fing	sie fingen	

PAST PERFECT

ich hatte	wir hatten	angefangen
du hattest	ihr hattet	
Sie hatten	Sie hatten	
er/sie/es hatte	sie hatten	

FUTURE

ich werde	wir werden	anfangen
du wirst	ihr werdet	
Sie werden	Sie werden	
er/sie/es wird	sie werden	

FUTURE PERFECT

ich werde	wir werden	angefangen haben
du wirst	ihr werdet	
Sie werden	Sie werden	
er/sie/es wird	sie werden	

PRESENT SUBJUNCTIVE I

ich fange	wir fangen	an
du fangest	ihr fanget	
Sie fangen	Sie fangen	
er/sie/es fange	sie fangen	

PAST SUBJUNCTIVE I

ich habe	wir haben	angefangen
du habest	ihr habet	
Sie haben	Sie haben	
er/sie/es habe	sie haben	

PRESENT SUBJUNCTIVE II

ich finge	wir fingen	an
du fingest	ihr finget	
Sie fingen	Sie fingen	
er/sie/es finge	sie fingen	

PAST SUBJUNCTIVE II

ich hätte	wir hätten	angefangen
du hättest	ihr hättet	
Sie hätten	Sie hätten	
er/sie/es hätte	sie hätten	

FUTURE SUBJUNCTIVE I

ich werde	wir werden	anfangen
du werdest	ihr werdet	
Sie werden	Sie werden	
er/sie/es werde	sie werden	

FUTURE PERFECT SUBJUNCTIVE I

ich werde	wir werden	angefangen haben
du werdest	ihr werdet	
Sie werden	Sie werden	
er/sie/es werde	sie werden	

FUTURE SUBJUNCTIVE II

ich würde	wir würden	anfangen
du würdest	ihr würdet	
Sie würden	Sie würden	
er/sie/es würde	sie würden	

FUTURE PERFECT SUBJUNCTIVE II

ich würde	wir würden	angefangen haben
du würdest	ihr würdet	
Sie würden	Sie würden	
er/sie/es würde	sie würden	

COMMANDS fang(e) an! fangt an! fangen Sie an!

PRESENT PARTICIPLE anfangend

Usage

Heinz hat wieder angefangen zu rauchen.	*Heinz has started smoking again.*
Als es immer kälter wurde, fing das Kind an zu zittern.	*As it got colder and colder, the child began to shiver.*
Du kannst heute schon zu sparen anfangen.	*Even today you can begin saving.*
Warum hast du noch mal von vorne angefangen?	*Why did you start from the beginning again?*
Die Schule fängt an.	*School is starting.*
Fangen Sie bitte sofort an.	*Please begin immediately.*
So hat alles angefangen.	*It all started like this.*
Vor den Feiertagen will ich keine neuen Projekte anfangen.	*I don't want to start any new projects before the holidays.*
Wir wollten mit dem Geld ein Geschäft anfangen.	*We wanted to set up a business with the money.*
Peter hatte schon ein neues Buch angefangen.	*Peter had already started a new book.*
Ich konnte damit nichts anfangen. (*colloquial*)	*I didn't know what to do with that.*
Mit dem Menschen ist nichts anzufangen. (*colloquial*)	*That guy is impossible to deal with.*

RELATED VERBS *see* **fangen** (179)

regular weak verb **fasst an · fasste an · angefasst**

PRESENT			PRESENT PERFECT		
ich fasse	wir fassen	an	ich habe	wir haben	angefasst
du fasst	ihr fasst		du hast	ihr habt	
Sie fassen	Sie fassen		Sie haben	Sie haben	
er/sie/es fasst	sie fassen		er/sie/es hat	sie haben	
SIMPLE PAST			**PAST PERFECT**		
ich fasste	wir fassten	an	ich hatte	wir hatten	angefasst
du fasstest	ihr fasstet		du hattest	ihr hattet	
Sie fassten	Sie fassten		Sie hatten	Sie hatten	
er/sie/es fasste	sie fassten		er/sie/es hatte	sie hatten	
FUTURE			**FUTURE PERFECT**		
ich werde	wir werden	anfassen	ich werde	wir werden	angefasst haben
du wirst	ihr werdet		du wirst	ihr werdet	
Sie werden	Sie werden		Sie werden	Sie werden	
er/sie/es wird	sie werden		er/sie/es wird	sie werden	
PRESENT SUBJUNCTIVE I			**PAST SUBJUNCTIVE I**		
ich fasse	wir fassen	an	ich habe	wir haben	angefasst
du fassest	ihr fasset		du habest	ihr habet	
Sie fassen	Sie fassen		Sie haben	Sie haben	
er/sie/es fasse	sie fassen		er/sie/es habe	sie haben	
PRESENT SUBJUNCTIVE II			**PAST SUBJUNCTIVE II**		
ich fasste	wir fassten	an	ich hätte	wir hätten	angefasst
du fasstest	ihr fasstet		du hättest	ihr hättet	
Sie fassten	Sie fassten		Sie hätten	Sie hätten	
er/sie/es fasste	sie fassten		er/sie/es hätte	sie hätten	
FUTURE SUBJUNCTIVE I			**FUTURE PERFECT SUBJUNCTIVE I**		
ich werde	wir werden	anfassen	ich werde	wir werden	angefasst haben
du werdest	ihr werdet		du werdest	ihr werdet	
Sie werden	Sie werden		Sie werden	Sie werden	
er/sie/es werde	sie werden		er/sie/es werde	sie werden	
FUTURE SUBJUNCTIVE II			**FUTURE PERFECT SUBJUNCTIVE II**		
ich würde	wir würden	anfassen	ich würde	wir würden	angefasst haben
du würdest	ihr würdet		du würdest	ihr würdet	
Sie würden	Sie würden		Sie würden	Sie würden	
er/sie/es würde	sie würden		er/sie/es würde	sie würden	

COMMANDS fass(e) an! fasst an! fassen Sie an!

PRESENT PARTICIPLE anfassend

Usage

Die Katze lässt sich nicht gern anfassen.	*The cat doesn't like to be handled.*
Bitte nicht anfassen.	*Please do not touch.*
Unsere Mitarbeiter können jedes Problem anfassen.	*Our employees can tackle any problem.*
Wir haben die Website aktualisiert, ohne den Quelltext anzufassen.	*We updated the Web site without touching the source code.*
Der Bibliothekar fasste die alte Handschrift niemals mit bloßen Händen an.	*The librarian never handled the old manuscript with bare hands.*
Die Gefangenen werden nicht mit Glacéhandschuhen angefasst. (*figurative*)	*The prisoners are not being handled with kid gloves.*
Heinz schwört, nie wieder ein Klavier anzufassen.	*Heinz swears he'll never touch a piano again.*
Alles was du anfasst wird zu Gold.	*Everything you touch turns to gold.*

sich anfassen (wie) *to feel (like)*

Das Polster fasst sich wie Leder an.	*The upholstery feels like leather.*

RELATED VERBS *see* **fassen** (180)

12 an·kommen *to arrive*

kommt an · kam an · angekommen strong verb

PRESENT

ich komme	wir kommen	an
du kommst	ihr kommt	
Sie kommen	Sie kommen	
er/sie/es kommt	sie kommen	

PRESENT PERFECT

ich bin	wir sind	angekommen
du bist	ihr seid	
Sie sind	Sie sind	
er/sie/es ist	sie sind	

SIMPLE PAST

ich kam	wir kamen	an
du kamst	ihr kamt	
Sie kamen	Sie kamen	
er/sie/es kam	sie kamen	

PAST PERFECT

ich war	wir waren	angekommen
du warst	ihr wart	
Sie waren	Sie waren	
er/sie/es war	sie waren	

FUTURE

ich werde	wir werden	ankommen
du wirst	ihr werdet	
Sie werden	Sie werden	
er/sie/es wird	sie werden	

FUTURE PERFECT

ich werde	wir werden	angekommen sein
du wirst	ihr werdet	
Sie werden	Sie werden	
er/sie/es wird	sie werden	

PRESENT SUBJUNCTIVE I

ich komme	wir kommen	an
du kommest	ihr kommet	
Sie kommen	Sie kommen	
er/sie/es komme	sie kommen	

PAST SUBJUNCTIVE I

ich sei	wir seien	angekommen
du seiest	ihr seiet	
Sie seien	Sie seien	
er/sie/es sei	sie seien	

PRESENT SUBJUNCTIVE II

ich käme	wir kämen	an
du kämest	ihr kämet	
Sie kämen	Sie kämen	
er/sie/es käme	sie kämen	

PAST SUBJUNCTIVE II

ich wäre	wir wären	angekommen
du wärest	ihr wäret	
Sie wären	Sie wären	
er/sie/es wäre	sie wären	

FUTURE SUBJUNCTIVE I

ich werde	wir werden	ankommen
du werdest	ihr werdet	
Sie werden	Sie werden	
er/sie/es werde	sie werden	

FUTURE PERFECT SUBJUNCTIVE I

ich werde	wir werden	angekommen sein
du werdest	ihr werdet	
Sie werden	Sie werden	
er/sie/es werde	sie werden	

FUTURE SUBJUNCTIVE II

ich würde	wir würden	ankommen
du würdest	ihr würdet	
Sie würden	Sie würden	
er/sie/es würde	sie würden	

FUTURE PERFECT SUBJUNCTIVE II

ich würde	wir würden	angekommen sein
du würdest	ihr würdet	
Sie würden	Sie würden	
er/sie/es würde	sie würden	

COMMANDS komm(e) an! kommt an! kommen Sie an!

PRESENT PARTICIPLE ankommend

Usage

Dein Brief vom neunten ist erst heute angekommen.	*Your letter of the ninth arrived only today.*
Wann kommst du in Berlin an?	*When are you arriving in Berlin?*
Nimm doch eine Uhr mit, damit du pünktlich ankommst.	*Take a watch along so you'll arrive on time.*
Endlich war Ingrid mit ihrer Mutter angekommen.	*Finally, Ingrid had arrived with her mother.*
Die E-Mail ist nicht angekommen.	*The e-mail didn't come through.*
Die lange Reise kam ihn hart an.	*The long trip was difficult for him.*
Die Idee kam bei ihnen nicht gut an. (*colloquial*)	*The idea didn't go over well with them.*

ankommen gegen *to be able to cope with, deal with*

Die Demonstranten kamen nicht gegen die Blockade an.	*The demonstrators weren't able to cope with the blockade.*

ankommen auf *to depend on, be contingent on*

Es kommt darauf an, ob Carol am Projekt teilnimmt.	*It depends on whether Carol takes part in the project.*
Wenn es auf mich ankäme, würden wir morgen losfahren.	*If it were up to me, we would leave tomorrow.*

RELATED VERBS voran·kommen; *see also* **kommen** (265)

regular weak verb **macht an · machte an · angemacht**

PRESENT

ich mache	wir machen	an
du machst	ihr macht	
Sie machen	Sie machen	
er/sie/es macht	sie machen	

PRESENT PERFECT

ich habe	wir haben	angemacht
du hast	ihr habt	
Sie haben	Sie haben	
er/sie/es hat	sie haben	

SIMPLE PAST

ich machte	wir machten	an
du machtest	ihr machtet	
Sie machten	Sie machten	
er/sie/es machte	sie machten	

PAST PERFECT

ich hatte	wir hatten	angemacht
du hattest	ihr hattet	
Sie hatten	Sie hatten	
er/sie/es hatte	sie hatten	

FUTURE

ich werde	wir werden	anmachen
du wirst	ihr werdet	
Sie werden	Sie werden	
er/sie/es wird	sie werden	

FUTURE PERFECT

ich werde	wir werden	angemacht haben
du wirst	ihr werdet	
Sie werden	Sie werden	
er/sie/es wird	sie werden	

PRESENT SUBJUNCTIVE I

ich mache	wir machen	an
du machest	ihr machet	
Sie machen	Sie machen	
er/sie/es mache	sie machen	

PAST SUBJUNCTIVE I

ich habe	wir haben	angemacht
du habest	ihr habet	
Sie haben	Sie haben	
er/sie/es habe	sie haben	

PRESENT SUBJUNCTIVE II

ich machte	wir machten	an
du machtest	ihr machtet	
Sie machten	Sie machten	
er/sie/es machte	sie machten	

PAST SUBJUNCTIVE II

ich hätte	wir hätten	angemacht
du hättest	ihr hättet	
Sie hätten	Sie hätten	
er/sie/es hätte	sie hätten	

FUTURE SUBJUNCTIVE I

ich werde	wir werden	anmachen
du werdest	ihr werdet	
Sie werden	Sie werden	
er/sie/es werde	sie werden	

FUTURE PERFECT SUBJUNCTIVE I

ich werde	wir werden	angemacht haben
du werdest	ihr werdet	
Sie werden	Sie werden	
er/sie/es werde	sie werden	

FUTURE SUBJUNCTIVE II

ich würde	wir würden	anmachen
du würdest	ihr würdet	
Sie würden	Sie würden	
er/sie/es würde	sie würden	

FUTURE PERFECT SUBJUNCTIVE II

ich würde	wir würden	angemacht haben
du würdest	ihr würdet	
Sie würden	Sie würden	
er/sie/es würde	sie würden	

COMMANDS mach(e) an! macht an! machen Sie an!

PRESENT PARTICIPLE anmachend

Usage

Mach bitte den Fernseher an.	*Please turn on the television.*
Frühmorgens ist sie hinausgegangen, um Feuer anzumachen.	*Early in the morning, she went out to light a fire.*
Würdest du bitte das Radio anmachen?	*Would you please turn the radio on?*
Nachts muss die Heizung angemacht werden.	*The heat must be turned on at night.*
Ingo hat sofort Musik angemacht.	*Ingo immediately turned on some music.*
Am Ende der Stange wird ein Messer angemacht.	*A knife is attached to the end of the rod.*
Kopfsalat schmeckt besonders gut mit Öl und Essig angemacht.	*Lettuce tastes especially good dressed with oil and vinegar.*
Die Farbe soll 1 : 2 mit Wasser angemacht werden.	*The paint should be mixed with water at a ratio of 1 : 2.*
Der trockene Zement wird mit Wasser angemacht.	*The dry cement is mixed with water.*
Das Bindemittel ist vor dem Verarbeiten mit Wasser anzumachen.	*The adhesive is to be mixed with water before use.*

RELATED VERBS *see* **machen** (300)

14 an·melden *to announce; register, make an appointment; indicate, declare, express*

meldet an · meldete an · angemeldet regular weak verb

PRESENT			PRESENT PERFECT		
ich melde	wir melden	an	ich habe	wir haben	angemeldet
du meldest	ihr meldet		du hast	ihr habt	
Sie melden	Sie melden		Sie haben	Sie haben	
er/sie/es meldet	sie melden		er/sie/es hat	sie haben	
SIMPLE PAST			**PAST PERFECT**		
ich meldete	wir meldeten	an	ich hatte	wir hatten	angemeldet
du meldetest	ihr meldetet		du hattest	ihr hattet	
Sie meldeten	Sie meldeten		Sie hatten	Sie hatten	
er/sie/es meldete	sie meldeten		er/sie/es hatte	sie hatten	
FUTURE			**FUTURE PERFECT**		
ich werde	wir werden	anmelden	ich werde	wir werden	angemeldet haben
du wirst	ihr werdet		du wirst	ihr werdet	
Sie werden	Sie werden		Sie werden	Sie werden	
er/sie/es wird	sie werden		er/sie/es wird	sie werden	
PRESENT SUBJUNCTIVE I			**PAST SUBJUNCTIVE I**		
ich melde	wir melden	an	ich habe	wir haben	angemeldet
du meldest	ihr meldet		du habest	ihr habet	
Sie melden	Sie melden		Sie haben	Sie haben	
er/sie/es melde	sie melden		er/sie/es habe	sie haben	
PRESENT SUBJUNCTIVE II			**PAST SUBJUNCTIVE II**		
ich meldete	wir meldeten	an	ich hätte	wir hätten	angemeldet
du meldetest	ihr meldetet		du hättest	ihr hättet	
Sie meldeten	Sie meldeten		Sie hätten	Sie hätten	
er/sie/es meldete	sie meldeten		er/sie/es hätte	sie hätten	
FUTURE SUBJUNCTIVE I			**FUTURE PERFECT SUBJUNCTIVE I**		
ich werde	wir werden	anmelden	ich werde	wir werden	angemeldet haben
du werdest	ihr werdet		du werdest	ihr werdet	
Sie werden	Sie werden		Sie werden	Sie werden	
er/sie/es werde	sie werden		er/sie/es werde	sie werden	
FUTURE SUBJUNCTIVE II			**FUTURE PERFECT SUBJUNCTIVE II**		
ich würde	wir würden	anmelden	ich würde	wir würden	angemeldet haben
du würdest	ihr würdet		du würdest	ihr würdet	
Sie würden	Sie würden		Sie würden	Sie würden	
er/sie/es würde	sie würden		er/sie/es würde	sie würden	

COMMANDS melde an! meldet an! melden Sie an!

PRESENT PARTICIPLE anmeldend

Usage

Meine Tante Inge hat gerade ihren Besuch nächstes Wochenende angemeldet.	*My aunt Inge has just announced she will visit next weekend.*
Sind Sie angemeldet?	*Do you have an appointment?*
Persönliche Homepages dürfen hier nicht angemeldet werden.	*Personal home pages cannot be registered here.*
Dieser Markenname ist nicht angemeldet.	*This brand name is not registered.*
Jeder meldet hier an, wann er kommt.	*Everyone indicates here when he or she is coming.*
Die Firma hat Insolvenz angemeldet.	*The firm has declared bankruptcy.*
Der Hund meldet Besitzansprüche an seinem Spielzeug an.	*The dog declares ownership of his toy.*
Viele Experten haben Zweifel angemeldet.	*Many experts have expressed doubt.*

sich anmelden *to register (oneself)*

Haben Sie sich im Büro angemeldet?	*Did you register at the office?*
Ich möchte mich für das Seminar anmelden.	*I'd like to register for the seminar.*

RELATED VERBS *see* **melden** (305)

strong verb **nimmt an · nahm an · angenommen**

PRESENT			PRESENT PERFECT		
ich nehme	wir nehmen	an	ich habe	wir haben	angenommen
du nimmst	ihr nehmt		du hast	ihr habt	
Sie nehmen	Sie nehmen		Sie haben	Sie haben	
er/sie/es nimmt	sie nehmen		er/sie/es hat	sie haben	
SIMPLE PAST			**PAST PERFECT**		
ich nahm	wir nahmen	an	ich hatte	wir hatten	angenommen
du nahmst	ihr nahmt		du hattest	ihr hattet	
Sie nahmen	Sie nahmen		Sie hatten	Sie hatten	
er/sie/es nahm	sie nahmen		er/sie/es hatte	sie hatten	
FUTURE			**FUTURE PERFECT**		
ich werde	wir werden	annehmen	ich werde	wir werden	angenommen haben
du wirst	ihr werdet		du wirst	ihr werdet	
Sie werden	Sie werden		Sie werden	Sie werden	
er/sie/es wird	sie werden		er/sie/es wird	sie werden	
PRESENT SUBJUNCTIVE I			**PAST SUBJUNCTIVE I**		
ich nehme	wir nehmen	an	ich habe	wir haben	angenommen
du nehmest	ihr nehmet		du habest	ihr habet	
Sie nehmen	Sie nehmen		Sie haben	Sie haben	
er/sie/es nehme	sie nehmen		er/sie/es habe	sie haben	
PRESENT SUBJUNCTIVE II			**PAST SUBJUNCTIVE II**		
ich nähme	wir nähmen	an	ich hätte	wir hätten	angenommen
du nähmest	ihr nähmet		du hättest	ihr hättet	
Sie nähmen	Sie nähmen		Sie hätten	Sie hätten	
er/sie/es nähme	sie nähmen		er/sie/es hätte	sie hätten	
FUTURE SUBJUNCTIVE I			**FUTURE PERFECT SUBJUNCTIVE I**		
ich werde	wir werden	annehmen	ich werde	wir werden	angenommen haben
du werdest	ihr werdet		du werdest	ihr werdet	
Sie werden	Sie werden		Sie werden	Sie werden	
er/sie/es werde	sie werden		er/sie/es werde	sie werden	
FUTURE SUBJUNCTIVE II			**FUTURE PERFECT SUBJUNCTIVE II**		
ich würde	wir würden	annehmen	ich würde	wir würden	angenommen haben
du würdest	ihr würdet		du würdest	ihr würdet	
Sie würden	Sie würden		Sie würden	Sie würden	
er/sie/es würde	sie würden		er/sie/es würde	sie würden	

COMMANDS nimm an! nehmt an! nehmen Sie an!

PRESENT PARTICIPLE annehmend

Usage

Das können wir nicht annehmen.	*We cannot accept that.*
Das neue Wahlverfahren wurde gut angenommen.	*The new voting procedure was well received.*
Hast du die Stelle angenommen?	*Did you accept the position?*
Sie hätten den Auftrag nicht annehmen können.	*They wouldn't have been able to take on the task.*
Meinst du, Irene hätte es angenommen?	*Do you think Irene would have accepted it?*
Die Schule nimmt keine Schüler mehr an.	*The school isn't accepting any more students.*
Die Seuche nahm unerwartete Ausmaße an.	*The plague took on unexpected proportions.*
Die Schulden sind höher als angenommen.	*The debts are higher than assumed.*
Nehmen wir Folgendes an.	*Let's assume the following.*
Ich nehme an, dass du ein Handy hast.	*I assume you have a cell phone.*
Er hatte „Uwe Braun“ als Künstlernamen angenommen.	*He had assumed the stage name "Uwe Braun."*
Mit 60 zu 25 Stimmen wurde das Gesetz angenommen.	*The law was passed by a vote of 60 to 25.*

RELATED VERBS *see* **nehmen** (314)

16 an·rufen *to phone; appeal to; call out to*

ruft an · rief an · angerufen strong verb

PRESENT			PRESENT PERFECT		
ich rufe	wir rufen	an	ich habe	wir haben	angerufen
du rufst	ihr ruft		du hast	ihr habt	
Sie rufen	Sie rufen		Sie haben	Sie haben	
er/sie/es ruft	sie rufen		er/sie/es hat	sie haben	
SIMPLE PAST			**PAST PERFECT**		
ich rief	wir riefen	an	ich hatte	wir hatten	angerufen
du riefst	ihr rieft		du hattest	ihr hattet	
Sie riefen	Sie riefen		Sie hatten	Sie hatten	
er/sie/es rief	sie riefen		er/sie/es hatte	sie hatten	
FUTURE			**FUTURE PERFECT**		
ich werde	wir werden	anrufen	ich werde	wir werden	angerufen haben
du wirst	ihr werdet		du wirst	ihr werdet	
Sie werden	Sie werden		Sie werden	Sie werden	
er/sie/es wird	sie werden		er/sie/es wird	sie werden	
PRESENT SUBJUNCTIVE I			**PAST SUBJUNCTIVE I**		
ich rufe	wir rufen	an	ich habe	wir haben	angerufen
du rufest	ihr rufet		du habest	ihr habet	
Sie rufen	Sie rufen		Sie haben	Sie haben	
er/sie/es rufe	sie rufen		er/sie/es habe	sie haben	
PRESENT SUBJUNCTIVE II			**PAST SUBJUNCTIVE II**		
ich riefe	wir riefen	an	ich hätte	wir hätten	angerufen
du riefest	ihr riefet		du hättest	ihr hättet	
Sie riefen	Sie riefen		Sie hätten	Sie hätten	
er/sie/es riefe	sie riefen		er/sie/es hätte	sie hätten	
FUTURE SUBJUNCTIVE I			**FUTURE PERFECT SUBJUNCTIVE I**		
ich werde	wir werden	anrufen	ich werde	wir werden	angerufen haben
du werdest	ihr werdet		du werdest	ihr werdet	
Sie werden	Sie werden		Sie werden	Sie werden	
er/sie/es werde	sie werden		er/sie/es werde	sie werden	
FUTURE SUBJUNCTIVE II			**FUTURE PERFECT SUBJUNCTIVE II**		
ich würde	wir würden	anrufen	ich würde	wir würden	angerufen haben
du würdest	ihr würdet		du würdest	ihr würdet	
Sie würden	Sie würden		Sie würden	Sie würden	
er/sie/es würde	sie würden		er/sie/es würde	sie würden	

COMMANDS ruf(e) an! ruft an! rufen Sie an!

PRESENT PARTICIPLE anrufend

Usage

Rufst du mich morgen an?	*Will you call me tomorrow?*
Darf ich bei Ihnen anrufen?	*May I use your telephone?*
Der Arzt fragte, warum Frau Schuh so früh anriefe.	*The doctor asked why Mrs. Schuh was calling so early.*
Kannst du mich bei Gisela in Köln anrufen?	*Can you call me at Gisela's in Cologne?*
Rufen Sie bitte zu Hause an.	*Please phone home.*
Wenn sie nur anriefen!	*If only they would call!*
Basti hat schon dreimal angerufen.	*Basti has called three times already.*
Rufen Sie uns bitte unter (030) 12 34 56 an.	*Please call us at (030) 12 34 56.*
Alle Kollegen und Mitarbeiter wurden angerufen.	*All colleagues and co-workers were called.*
Sie sollte mal wieder ihre Mutter anrufen.	*She should call her mother again.*
Die sich streitenden Nachbarn riefen das Gericht an.	*The quarreling neighbors appealed to the courts.*
Der Pfarrer rief Gott um Gnade an.	*The pastor begged God for mercy.*

RELATED VERBS *see* **rufen** (347)

regular weak verb **schaut an · schaute an · angeschaut**

PRESENT			PRESENT PERFECT		
ich schaue	wir schauen	an	ich habe	wir haben	angeschaut
du schaust	ihr schaut		du hast	ihr habt	
Sie schauen	Sie schauen		Sie haben	Sie haben	
er/sie/es schaut	sie schauen		er/sie/es hat	sie haben	
SIMPLE PAST			PAST PERFECT		
ich schaute	wir schauten	an	ich hatte	wir hatten	angeschaut
du schautest	ihr schautet		du hattest	ihr hattet	
Sie schauten	Sie schauten		Sie hatten	Sie hatten	
er/sie/es schaute	sie schauten		er/sie/es hatte	sie hatten	
FUTURE			FUTURE PERFECT		
ich werde	wir werden	anschauen	ich werde	wir werden	angeschaut haben
du wirst	ihr werdet		du wirst	ihr werdet	
Sie werden	Sie werden		Sie werden	Sie werden	
er/sie/es wird	sie werden		er/sie/es wird	sie werden	
PRESENT SUBJUNCTIVE I			PAST SUBJUNCTIVE I		
ich schaue	wir schauen	an	ich habe	wir haben	angeschaut
du schauest	ihr schauet		du habest	ihr habet	
Sie schauen	Sie schauen		Sie haben	Sie haben	
er/sie/es schaue	sie schauen		er/sie/es habe	sie haben	
PRESENT SUBJUNCTIVE II			PAST SUBJUNCTIVE II		
ich schaute	wir schauten	an	ich hätte	wir hätten	angeschaut
du schautest	ihr schautet		du hättest	ihr hättet	
Sie schauten	Sie schauten		Sie hätten	Sie hätten	
er/sie/es schaute	sie schauten		er/sie/es hätte	sie hätten	
FUTURE SUBJUNCTIVE I			FUTURE PERFECT SUBJUNCTIVE I		
ich werde	wir werden	anschauen	ich werde	wir werden	angeschaut haben
du werdest	ihr werdet		du werdest	ihr werdet	
Sie werden	Sie werden		Sie werden	Sie werden	
er/sie/es werde	sie werden		er/sie/es werde	sie werden	
FUTURE SUBJUNCTIVE II			FUTURE PERFECT SUBJUNCTIVE II		
ich würde	wir würden	anschauen	ich würde	wir würden	angeschaut haben
du würdest	ihr würdet		du würdest	ihr würdet	
Sie würden	Sie würden		Sie würden	Sie würden	
er/sie/es würde	sie würden		er/sie/es würde	sie würden	

COMMANDS schau(e) an! schaut an! schauen Sie an!

PRESENT PARTICIPLE anschauend

Usage

Er hat den Film jetzt dreimal angeschaut.	*He has seen the film three times now.*
Sie schaute Herrn Kröger finster an.	*She looked menacingly at Mr. Kröger.*
Schaut an, was ich kann!	*Look what I can do!*
Abends wurden Dias angeschaut.	*In the evenings, we/they looked at slides.*
Schauen Sie mich nicht so an!	*Don't look at me that way!*
Schaust du nachts den Himmel an, so siehst du sie.	*If you look at the sky at night, you will see them.*
Wann kann ich mir das Auto mal anschauen?	*When can I have a look at the car?*
Eine alte Frau schaute mich an und flüsterte etwas.	*An old woman looked at me and whispered something.*
Wenn ich die Bilder anschaue, denke ich an dich.	*When I look at the pictures, I think of you.*
Die Touristen sollten Bilder von Matisse anschauen.	*The tourists were supposed to look at paintings by Matisse.*
Dann hat er mich ganz komisch angeschaut.	*Then he looked at me really funny.*
Diese Fotos können im neuen Format angeschaut werden.	*These photos can be viewed in the new format.*

RELATED VERBS *see* **schauen** (359)

18 **an·sehen** *to look at, watch; regard, consider; see*

sieht an · sah an · angesehen — strong verb

PRESENT

ich sehe	wir sehen	an
du siehst	ihr seht	
Sie sehen	Sie sehen	
er/sie/es sieht	sie sehen	

SIMPLE PAST

ich sah	wir sahen	an
du sahst	ihr saht	
Sie sahen	Sie sahen	
er/sie/es sah	sie sahen	

FUTURE

ich werde	wir werden	ansehen
du wirst	ihr werdet	
Sie werden	Sie werden	
er/sie/es wird	sie werden	

PRESENT SUBJUNCTIVE I

ich sehe	wir sehen	an
du sehest	ihr sehet	
Sie sehen	Sie sehen	
er/sie/es sehe	sie sehen	

PRESENT SUBJUNCTIVE II

ich sähe	wir sähen	an
du sähest	ihr sähet	
Sie sähen	Sie sähen	
er/sie/es sähe	sie sähen	

FUTURE SUBJUNCTIVE I

ich werde	wir werden	ansehen
du werdest	ihr werdet	
Sie werden	Sie werden	
er/sie/es werde	sie werden	

FUTURE SUBJUNCTIVE II

ich würde	wir würden	ansehen
du würdest	ihr würdet	
Sie würden	Sie würden	
er/sie/es würde	sie würden	

PRESENT PERFECT

ich habe	wir haben	angesehen
du hast	ihr habt	
Sie haben	Sie haben	
er/sie/es hat	sie haben	

PAST PERFECT

ich hatte	wir hatten	angesehen
du hattest	ihr hattet	
Sie hatten	Sie hatten	
er/sie/es hatte	sie hatten	

FUTURE PERFECT

ich werde	wir werden	angesehen haben
du wirst	ihr werdet	
Sie werden	Sie werden	
er/sie/es wird	sie werden	

PAST SUBJUNCTIVE I

ich habe	wir haben	angesehen
du habest	ihr habet	
Sie haben	Sie haben	
er/sie/es habe	sie haben	

PAST SUBJUNCTIVE II

ich hätte	wir hätten	angesehen
du hättest	ihr hättet	
Sie hätten	Sie hätten	
er/sie/es hätte	sie hätten	

FUTURE PERFECT SUBJUNCTIVE I

ich werde	wir werden	angesehen haben
du werdest	ihr werdet	
Sie werden	Sie werden	
er/sie/es werde	sie werden	

FUTURE PERFECT SUBJUNCTIVE II

ich würde	wir würden	angesehen haben
du würdest	ihr würdet	
Sie würden	Sie würden	
er/sie/es würde	sie würden	

COMMANDS sieh an! seht an! sehen Sie an!

PRESENT PARTICIPLE ansehend

Usage

Auf der Straße wird er immer argwöhnisch angesehen.	*On the street, people always eye him suspiciously.*
Er sah seinen Sohn verwundert an.	*He gazed in astonishment at his son.*
Das Kind sieht den Clown erstaunt an.	*The child looks at the clown with amazement.*
Man sieht ihr an, dass sie schwanger ist.	*You can tell by looking that she is pregnant.*
Jetzt wird sie die Menschen mit anderen Augen ansehen.	*Now she'll see people in a different light.*
Sieh dich nur an!	*Just look at yourself!*
Wir wollten uns das Spiel gemeinsam ansehen.	*We wanted to watch the game together.*
Ich sehe das als meine Pflicht an.	*I consider that my duty.*
Das Internat ist international hoch angesehen.	*The private school is internationally acclaimed.*
Die Forscher haben es als problematisch angesehen.	*The researchers considered it problematic.*

sich ansehen (wie) *to look (like), appear*

Es sah sich an, als wäre ihm schlecht.	*It looked as though he was ill.*

RELATED VERBS *see* **sehen** (397)

regular weak verb (dative object) **antwortet · antwortete · geantwortet**

PRESENT

ich antworte	wir antworten
du antwortest	ihr antwortet
Sie antworten	Sie antworten
er/sie/es antwortet	sie antworten

PRESENT PERFECT

ich habe	wir haben	geantwortet
du hast	ihr habt	
Sie haben	Sie haben	
er/sie/es hat	sie haben	

SIMPLE PAST

ich antwortete	wir antworteten
du antwortetest	ihr antwortetet
Sie antworteten	Sie antworteten
er/sie/es antwortete	sie antworteten

PAST PERFECT

ich hatte	wir hatten	geantwortet
du hattest	ihr hattet	
Sie hatten	Sie hatten	
er/sie/es hatte	sie hatten	

FUTURE

ich werde	wir werden	antworten
du wirst	ihr werdet	
Sie werden	Sie werden	
er/sie/es wird	sie werden	

FUTURE PERFECT

ich werde	wir werden	geantwortet haben
du wirst	ihr werdet	
Sie werden	Sie werden	
er/sie/es wird	sie werden	

PRESENT SUBJUNCTIVE I

ich antworte	wir antworten
du antwortest	ihr antwortet
Sie antworten	Sie antworten
er/sie/es antworte	sie antworten

PAST SUBJUNCTIVE I

ich habe	wir haben	geantwortet
du habest	ihr habet	
Sie haben	Sie haben	
er/sie/es habe	sie haben	

PRESENT SUBJUNCTIVE II

ich antwortete	wir antworteten
du antwortetest	ihr antwortetet
Sie antworteten	Sie antworteten
er/sie/es antwortete	sie antworteten

PAST SUBJUNCTIVE II

ich hätte	wir hätten	geantwortet
du hättest	ihr hättet	
Sie hätten	Sie hätten	
er/sie/es hätte	sie hätten	

FUTURE SUBJUNCTIVE I

ich werde	wir werden	antworten
du werdest	ihr werdet	
Sie werden	Sie werden	
er/sie/es werde	sie werden	

FUTURE PERFECT SUBJUNCTIVE I

ich werde	wir werden	geantwortet haben
du werdest	ihr werdet	
Sie werden	Sie werden	
er/sie/es werde	sie werden	

FUTURE SUBJUNCTIVE II

ich würde	wir würden	antworten
du würdest	ihr würdet	
Sie würden	Sie würden	
er/sie/es würde	sie würden	

FUTURE PERFECT SUBJUNCTIVE II

ich würde	wir würden	geantwortet haben
du würdest	ihr würdet	
Sie würden	Sie würden	
er/sie/es würde	sie würden	

COMMANDS antworte! antwortet! antworten Sie!

PRESENT PARTICIPLE antwortend

Usage

Wieso antworten Sie nicht?	*Why aren't you answering?*
Gerd hat auf den Brief von Karen geantwortet.	*Gerd answered the letter from Karen.*
Danke, dass du mir geantwortet hast.	*Thanks for answering me.*
Auf die letzte Frage antwortete Heinz: „Ja".	*Heinz answered "yes" to the last question.*
Der Lehrer hat der Studentin auf ihre Frage geantwortet.	*The teacher replied to the student's question.*
Bitte antworte uns.	*Please answer us.*
Antwortetest du dem Herrn?	*Did you answer the gentleman?*
Was sollen wir antworten?	*What should our answer be?*
„Aber ihr antwortetet nicht", sprach der Herr.	*"But ye answered not," spake the Lord.*
Wie antwortet man auf eine Anzeige?	*How does one reply to an ad?*
Ich musste auf seine Frage sofort antworten.	*I had to answer his question immediately.*
Heiko wird wohl noch nicht geantwortet haben.	*Heiko has probably not answered yet.*

RELATED VERBS beantworten, überantworten, verantworten

20 an·ziehen *to advance, increase; attract; draw up, pull at, tighten; take on*

zieht an · zog an · angezogen strong verb

PRESENT

ich ziehe	wir ziehen	an
du ziehst	ihr zieht	
Sie ziehen	Sie ziehen	
er/sie/es zieht	sie ziehen	

SIMPLE PAST

ich zog	wir zogen	an
du zogst	ihr zogt	
Sie zogen	Sie zogen	
er/sie/es zog	sie zogen	

FUTURE

ich werde	wir werden	anziehen
du wirst	ihr werdet	
Sie werden	Sie werden	
er/sie/es wird	sie werden	

PRESENT SUBJUNCTIVE I

ich ziehe	wir ziehen	an
du ziehest	ihr ziehet	
Sie ziehen	Sie ziehen	
er/sie/es ziehe	sie ziehen	

PRESENT SUBJUNCTIVE II

ich zöge	wir zögen	an
du zögest	ihr zöget	
Sie zögen	Sie zögen	
er/sie/es zöge	sie zögen	

FUTURE SUBJUNCTIVE I

ich werde	wir werden	anziehen
du werdest	ihr werdet	
Sie werden	Sie werden	
er/sie/es werde	sie werden	

FUTURE SUBJUNCTIVE II

ich würde	wir würden	anziehen
du würdest	ihr würdet	
Sie würden	Sie würden	
er/sie/es würde	sie würden	

PRESENT PERFECT

ich habe	wir haben	angezogen
du hast	ihr habt	
Sie haben	Sie haben	
er/sie/es hat	sie haben	

PAST PERFECT

ich hatte	wir hatten	angezogen
du hattest	ihr hattet	
Sie hatten	Sie hatten	
er/sie/es hatte	sie hatten	

FUTURE PERFECT

ich werde	wir werden	angezogen haben
du wirst	ihr werdet	
Sie werden	Sie werden	
er/sie/es wird	sie werden	

PAST SUBJUNCTIVE I

ich habe	wir haben	angezogen
du habest	ihr habet	
Sie haben	Sie haben	
er/sie/es habe	sie haben	

PAST SUBJUNCTIVE II

ich hätte	wir hätten	angezogen
du hättest	ihr hättet	
Sie hätten	Sie hätten	
er/sie/es hätte	sie hätten	

FUTURE PERFECT SUBJUNCTIVE I

ich werde	wir werden	angezogen haben
du werdest	ihr werdet	
Sie werden	Sie werden	
er/sie/es werde	sie werden	

FUTURE PERFECT SUBJUNCTIVE II

ich würde	wir würden	angezogen haben
du würdest	ihr würdet	
Sie würden	Sie würden	
er/sie/es würde	sie würden	

COMMANDS zieh(e) an! zieht an! ziehen Sie an!

PRESENT PARTICIPLE anziehend

Usage

Die Post zieht ihre Preise an.	*The post office is raising its prices.*
Die Wertpapiere hatten von 6 auf 7 Mio. Euro angezogen.	*The securities had advanced from 6 to 7 million euros.*
Die EU zieht immer mehr Länder an.	*The E.U. is attracting more and more countries.*
Beim nächsten Schritt muss man die Bolzen anziehen.	*In the next step, you must tighten the bolts.*
Die Wäsche hat einen leichten Geruch angezogen.	*The laundry has taken on a slight odor.*

sich anziehen *to dress; attract (each other)*

Zieh dir einen dicken Mantel an.	*Put on a heavy coat.*
Hast du dich warm angezogen?	*Did you dress warmly?*
Wieso zieht er sich schon an?	*Why is he getting dressed already?*
Gegensätze ziehen sich an.	*Opposites attract.*

anziehen (with **sein**) *to advance, move in, draw near*

Das Heer des Grafen Belderbusch zog an.	*The army of Count Belderbusch drew near.*

RELATED VERBS heran·ziehen; *see also* **ziehen** (549)

regular weak verb **zündet an · zündete an · angezündet**

PRESENT

ich zünde / wir zünden / du zündest / ihr zündet / Sie zünden / Sie zünden / er/sie/es zündet / sie zünden } an

ich zünde	wir zünden	an
du zündest	ihr zündet	
Sie zünden	Sie zünden	
er/sie/es zündet	sie zünden	

PRESENT PERFECT

ich habe	wir haben	angezündet
du hast	ihr habt	
Sie haben	Sie haben	
er/sie/es hat	sie haben	

SIMPLE PAST

ich zündete	wir zündeten	an
du zündetest	ihr zündetet	
Sie zündeten	Sie zündeten	
er/sie/es zündete	sie zündeten	

PAST PERFECT

ich hatte	wir hatten	angezündet
du hattest	ihr hattet	
Sie hatten	Sie hatten	
er/sie/es hatte	sie hatten	

FUTURE

ich werde	wir werden	anzünden
du wirst	ihr werdet	
Sie werden	Sie werden	
er/sie/es wird	sie werden	

FUTURE PERFECT

ich werde	wir werden	angezündet haben
du wirst	ihr werdet	
Sie werden	Sie werden	
er/sie/es wird	sie werden	

PRESENT SUBJUNCTIVE I

ich zünde	wir zünden	an
du zündest	ihr zündet	
Sie zünden	Sie zünden	
er/sie/es zünde	sie zünden	

PAST SUBJUNCTIVE I

ich habe	wir haben	angezündet
du habest	ihr habet	
Sie haben	Sie haben	
er/sie/es habe	sie haben	

PRESENT SUBJUNCTIVE II

ich zündete	wir zündeten	an
du zündetest	ihr zündetet	
Sie zündeten	Sie zündeten	
er/sie/es zündete	sie zündeten	

PAST SUBJUNCTIVE II

ich hätte	wir hätten	angezündet
du hättest	ihr hättet	
Sie hätten	Sie hätten	
er/sie/es hätte	sie hätten	

FUTURE SUBJUNCTIVE I

ich werde	wir werden	anzünden
du werdest	ihr werdet	
Sie werden	Sie werden	
er/sie/es werde	sie werden	

FUTURE PERFECT SUBJUNCTIVE I

ich werde	wir werden	angezündet haben
du werdest	ihr werdet	
Sie werden	Sie werden	
er/sie/es werde	sie werden	

FUTURE SUBJUNCTIVE II

ich würde	wir würden	anzünden
du würdest	ihr würdet	
Sie würden	Sie würden	
er/sie/es würde	sie würden	

FUTURE PERFECT SUBJUNCTIVE II

ich würde	wir würden	angezündet haben
du würdest	ihr würdet	
Sie würden	Sie würden	
er/sie/es würde	sie würden	

COMMANDS zünde an! zündet an! zünden Sie an!

PRESENT PARTICIPLE anzündend

Usage

Er schwieg und zündete eine Zigarette an.	*He fell silent and lit a cigarette.*
Könnten Sie diese Kerze anzünden?	*Could you light this candle?*
Zünde bitte den Grill an.	*Please light the grill.*
Sei vorsichtig, wenn du Feuerwerkskörper anzündest.	*Be careful when you set off fireworks.*
Nach einem guten Essen zündete Papa immer seine Pfeife an.	*After a good meal, Dad always lit his pipe.*
Liesl zündet ihre Zigaretten lieber mit Streichhölzern an.	*Liesl prefers to light her cigarettes with matches.*
An diesem Tag wird eine Fackel angezündet.	*On this day a torch is lit.*
Die Straßenlaternen sind angezündet.	*The streetlights are lit.*
Heute Nacht wurde ein Haus angezündet.	*A house was set on fire last night.*
Mehrere Autos waren in der Nacht angezündet worden.	*Several cars had been set on fire during the night.*
Ein Demonstrant zündete sich an.	*A demonstrator set himself on fire.*
Das Heer zündete die wehrlose Stadt an.	*The army set fire to the defenseless city.*

RELATED VERB zünden

arbeiten *to work, labor; function*

arbeitet · arbeitete · gearbeitet regular weak verb

MORE USAGE SENTENCES WITH arbeiten

Lassen Sie Ihr Geld für Sie arbeiten. — *Let your money work for you.*
Sie arbeitet gerade als Automechanikerin. — *She's currently working as an auto mechanic.*
Robert möchte bei einer Familie wohnen und auf ihrem Bauernhof arbeiten. — *Robert would like to live with a family and work on their farm.*
Der Durchschnittsarbeitnehmer arbeitet jetzt über 40 Stunden in der Woche. — *The average employee now works more than 40 hours per week.*
Mareika arbeitet seit drei Jahren freiberuflich als Webdesignerin. — *Mareika has worked as a freelance web designer for three years.*
Uwe arbeitet ehrenamtlich ein paar Stunden im Monat. — *Uwe does volunteer work a few hours a month.*
Mehr Frauen als Männer arbeiten in Teilzeitstellen. — *More women than men work at part-time jobs.*
Meine Mutter arbeitet gerade im Garten. — *My mother is working in the garden at the moment.*
Das Gerät arbeitet nach einem neuen Prinzip. — *The device functions according to a new principle.*
Der Teig kann nur an einem warmen Ort arbeiten. — *The dough will rise only in a warm location.*
Ein geschlagenes Ei mit einem Löffel in den Teig arbeiten. (*recipe*) — *Fold the beaten egg into the batter using a spoon.*
Diese Skulptur ist in Bronze gearbeitet. — *This sculpture is wrought in bronze.*

arbeiten an *to work on*

Wie oft arbeitest du an Hausaufgaben? — *How often do you work on homework?*
Vorher hatte sie an einem Buch gearbeitet. — *Before that, she'd worked on a book.*
Wir arbeiten daran. — *We're working on it.*

arbeiten für *to work for/toward*

Denis arbeitet für den Weltfrieden. — *Denis is working for world peace.*
Oliver und Yvonne arbeiten sehr hart für ihren Erfolg. — *Oliver and Yvonne are working very hard to be successful.*
Unser Ziel ist es, für Menschenrechte zu arbeiten. — *Our goal is to work for human rights.*

arbeiten gegen *to work against, work to prevent*

Wie können wir gegen Gewalt arbeiten? — *How can we work against violence?*
Anstatt gegeneinander zu arbeiten, sollten die Kinder miteinander arbeiten. — *Instead of working against each other, the children should work with each other.*

sich arbeiten *to work oneself*

Wie viele Arme arbeiten sich zu Tode? — *How many poor people work themselves to death?*
Hast du dich krank gearbeitet? — *Have you worked yourself sick?*
Arbeiten Sie sich nicht müde. — *Don't work to the point you're tired.*

es arbeitet sich (impersonal) *one works; working conditions are*

Es arbeitet sich an einem ergonomischen Schreibtisch viel effektiver. — *One works more effectively at an ergonomic desk.*
In einem ruhigen Raum arbeitet es sich konzentrierter. — *In a quiet space, you can concentrate more on your work.*
Hier arbeitet es sich besser. — *One can work better here.*

IDIOMATIC EXPRESSIONS

Warum arbeitet ihr für einen Hungerlohn? — *Why are you working for peanuts?*
Mein Großvater musste wie ein Ochse arbeiten. — *My grandfather had to work like an ox.*
Herr Schorlemer arbeitete den Nazis in die Hände. — *Mr. Schorlemer played into the hands of the Nazis.*
Ich arbeite gegen die Zeit. — *I'm working against the clock.*
Die Zeit arbeitet gegen uns. — *Time is working against us.*

regular weak verb **arbeitet · arbeitete · gearbeitet**

PRESENT

ich arbeite	wir arbeiten
du arbeitest	ihr arbeitet
Sie arbeiten	Sie arbeiten
er/sie/es arbeitet	sie arbeiten

SIMPLE PAST

ich arbeitete	wir arbeiteten
du arbeitetest	ihr arbeitetet
Sie arbeiteten	Sie arbeiteten
er/sie/es arbeitete	sie arbeiteten

FUTURE

ich werde	wir werden	arbeiten
du wirst	ihr werdet	
Sie werden	Sie werden	
er/sie/es wird	sie werden	

PRESENT SUBJUNCTIVE I

ich arbeite	wir arbeiten
du arbeitest	ihr arbeitet
Sie arbeiten	Sie arbeiten
er/sie/es arbeite	sie arbeiten

PRESENT SUBJUNCTIVE II

ich arbeitete	wir arbeiteten
du arbeitetest	ihr arbeitetet
Sie arbeiteten	Sie arbeiteten
er/sie/es arbeitete	sie arbeiteten

FUTURE SUBJUNCTIVE I

ich werde	wir werden	arbeiten
du werdest	ihr werdet	
Sie werden	Sie werden	
er/sie/es werde	sie werden	

FUTURE SUBJUNCTIVE II

ich würde	wir würden	arbeiten
du würdest	ihr würdet	
Sie würden	Sie würden	
er/sie/es würde	sie würden	

PRESENT PERFECT

ich habe	wir haben	gearbeitet
du hast	ihr habt	
Sie haben	Sie haben	
er/sie/es hat	sie haben	

PAST PERFECT

ich hatte	wir hatten	gearbeitet
du hattest	ihr hattet	
Sie hatten	Sie hatten	
er/sie/es hatte	sie hatten	

FUTURE PERFECT

ich werde	wir werden	gearbeitet haben
du wirst	ihr werdet	
Sie werden	Sie werden	
er/sie/es wird	sie werden	

PAST SUBJUNCTIVE I

ich habe	wir haben	gearbeitet
du habest	ihr habet	
Sie haben	Sie haben	
er/sie/es habe	sie haben	

PAST SUBJUNCTIVE II

ich hätte	wir hätten	gearbeitet
du hättest	ihr hättet	
Sie hätten	Sie hätten	
er/sie/es hätte	sie hätten	

FUTURE PERFECT SUBJUNCTIVE I

ich werde	wir werden	gearbeitet haben
du werdest	ihr werdet	
Sie werden	Sie werden	
er/sie/es werde	sie werden	

FUTURE PERFECT SUBJUNCTIVE II

ich würde	wir würden	gearbeitet haben
du würdest	ihr würdet	
Sie würden	Sie würden	
er/sie/es würde	sie würden	

COMMANDS arbeite! arbeitet! arbeiten Sie!

PRESENT PARTICIPLE arbeitend

Usage

Ich finde, dass Erich zu viel arbeitet.	*I think Erich works too much.*
Tante Inge arbeitete früher bei der Volksbank Dünen.	*Aunt Inge used to work at the Volksbank in Dünen.*
Arbeiten Sie noch bei Siemens, Herr Schimmerli?	*Do you still work for Siemens, Mr. Schimmerli?*
Dieser Bildhauer arbeitet in Holz und Stein.	*This sculptor works in wood and stone.*
Hier wird hart gearbeitet.	*People are working hard here.*
Möchten Sie zu Hause arbeiten?	*Would you like to work at home?*
Ich habe mit vielen Künstlern gearbeitet.	*I've worked with many artists.*
Würdest du als Modell arbeiten?	*Would you work as a model?*
Viele Studenten müssen während des Studiums arbeiten.	*Many students have to work while attending school.*

RELATED VERBS ab·arbeiten, auf·arbeiten, aus·arbeiten, bearbeiten, durch·arbeiten, ein·arbeiten, empor·arbeiten, entgegen·arbeiten, erarbeiten, handarbeiten, hoch·arbeiten, kurz·arbeiten, mit·arbeiten, nach·arbeiten, schwarz·arbeiten, überarbeiten, um·arbeiten, verarbeiten, vor·arbeiten, weiter·arbeiten, weiter·verarbeiten; *see also* **zusammen·arbeiten** (552)

23 ärgern *to annoy, irritate, upset*

ärgert · ärgerte · geärgert regular weak verb

PRESENT

ich ärgere	wir ärgern
du ärgerst	ihr ärgert
Sie ärgern	Sie ärgern
er/sie/es ärgert	sie ärgern

SIMPLE PAST

ich ärgerte	wir ärgerten
du ärgertest	ihr ärgertet
Sie ärgerten	Sie ärgerten
er/sie/es ärgerte	sie ärgerten

FUTURE

ich werde	wir werden	ärgern
du wirst	ihr werdet	
Sie werden	Sie werden	
er/sie/es wird	sie werden	

PRESENT SUBJUNCTIVE I

ich ärgere	wir ärgern
du ärgerst	ihr ärgert
Sie ärgern	Sie ärgern
er/sie/es ärgere	sie ärgern

PRESENT SUBJUNCTIVE II

ich ärgerte	wir ärgerten
du ärgertest	ihr ärgertet
Sie ärgerten	Sie ärgerten
er/sie/es ärgerte	sie ärgerten

FUTURE SUBJUNCTIVE I

ich werde	wir werden	ärgern
du werdest	ihr werdet	
Sie werden	Sie werden	
er/sie/es werde	sie werden	

FUTURE SUBJUNCTIVE II

ich würde	wir würden	ärgern
du würdest	ihr würdet	
Sie würden	Sie würden	
er/sie/es würde	sie würden	

PRESENT PERFECT

ich habe	wir haben	geärgert
du hast	ihr habt	
Sie haben	Sie haben	
er/sie/es hat	sie haben	

PAST PERFECT

ich hatte	wir hatten	geärgert
du hattest	ihr hattet	
Sie hatten	Sie hatten	
er/sie/es hatte	sie hatten	

FUTURE PERFECT

ich werde	wir werden	geärgert haben
du wirst	ihr werdet	
Sie werden	Sie werden	
er/sie/es wird	sie werden	

PAST SUBJUNCTIVE I

ich habe	wir haben	geärgert
du habest	ihr habet	
Sie haben	Sie haben	
er/sie/es habe	sie haben	

PAST SUBJUNCTIVE II

ich hätte	wir hätten	geärgert
du hättest	ihr hättet	
Sie hätten	Sie hätten	
er/sie/es hätte	sie hätten	

FUTURE PERFECT SUBJUNCTIVE I

ich werde	wir werden	geärgert haben
du werdest	ihr werdet	
Sie werden	Sie werden	
er/sie/es werde	sie werden	

FUTURE PERFECT SUBJUNCTIVE II

ich würde	wir würden	geärgert haben
du würdest	ihr würdet	
Sie würden	Sie würden	
er/sie/es würde	sie würden	

COMMANDS ärgere! ärgert! ärgern Sie!

PRESENT PARTICIPLE ärgernd

Usage

Es ärgert mich, dass er nicht mitkommt. — *It annoys me that he's not coming along.*
Mark, ärgere deine Schwester nicht! — *Mark, don't bother your sister!*
Nichts ärgert ihn mehr als Staus auf der Autobahn. — *Nothing irritates him more than traffic jams on the freeway.*
Jede Nacht ärgerten uns die Nachbarn. — *Every night the neighbors got on our nerves.*
Als Kind wurde ich oft von anderen Kindern geärgert. — *As a child, I was often teased by other children.*
Inge lässt sich von ihm ärgern. — *Inge lets him upset her.*

sich ärgern *to be angry/upset, get angry/upset*

Warum ärgerst du dich so? — *Why are you getting so upset?*
Thomas ärgerte sich über sich selbst. — *Thomas was angry with himself.*
Ich habe mich eben darüber geärgert. — *I just got irritated about it.*
Viele haben sich über solche Probleme geärgert. — *A lot of people have gotten upset about such problems.*
Ärgern Sie sich bitte nicht. — *Please don't get upset.*

RELATED VERB verärgern

regular weak verb **atmet · atmete · geatmet**

PRESENT

ich atme	wir atmen
du atmest	ihr atmet
Sie atmen	Sie atmen
er/sie/es atmet	sie atmen

SIMPLE PAST

ich atmete	wir atmeten
du atmetest	ihr atmetet
Sie atmeten	Sie atmeten
er/sie/es atmete	sie atmeten

FUTURE

ich werde	wir werden	atmen
du wirst	ihr werdet	
Sie werden	Sie werden	
er/sie/es wird	sie werden	

PRESENT SUBJUNCTIVE I

ich atme	wir atmen
du atmest	ihr atmet
Sie atmen	Sie atmen
er/sie/es atme	sie atmen

PRESENT SUBJUNCTIVE II

ich atmete	wir atmeten
du atmetest	ihr atmetet
Sie atmeten	Sie atmeten
er/sie/es atmete	sie atmeten

FUTURE SUBJUNCTIVE I

ich werde	wir werden	atmen
du werdest	ihr werdet	
Sie werden	Sie werden	
er/sie/es werde	sie werden	

FUTURE SUBJUNCTIVE II

ich würde	wir würden	atmen
du würdest	ihr würdet	
Sie würden	Sie würden	
er/sie/es würde	sie würden	

PRESENT PERFECT

ich habe	wir haben	geatmet
du hast	ihr habt	
Sie haben	Sie haben	
er/sie/es hat	sie haben	

PAST PERFECT

ich hatte	wir hatten	geatmet
du hattest	ihr hattet	
Sie hatten	Sie hatten	
er/sie/es hatte	sie hatten	

FUTURE PERFECT

ich werde	wir werden	geatmet haben
du wirst	ihr werdet	
Sie werden	Sie werden	
er/sie/es wird	sie werden	

PAST SUBJUNCTIVE I

ich habe	wir haben	geatmet
du habest	ihr habet	
Sie haben	Sie haben	
er/sie/es habe	sie haben	

PAST SUBJUNCTIVE II

ich hätte	wir hätten	geatmet
du hättest	ihr hättet	
Sie hätten	Sie hätten	
er/sie/es hätte	sie hätten	

FUTURE PERFECT SUBJUNCTIVE I

ich werde	wir werden	geatmet haben
du werdest	ihr werdet	
Sie werden	Sie werden	
er/sie/es werde	sie werden	

FUTURE PERFECT SUBJUNCTIVE II

ich würde	wir würden	geatmet haben
du würdest	ihr würdet	
Sie würden	Sie würden	
er/sie/es würde	sie würden	

COMMANDS atme! atmet! atmen Sie!

PRESENT PARTICIPLE atmend

Usage

Die meisten Menschen können nicht richtig atmen. — *Most people can't breathe properly.*
Atmet er eigentlich noch? — *Is he actually still breathing?*
Auf dem Land atmen Sie frische Luft. — *In the country you breathe fresh air.*
Der Mensch atmet nicht nur mit der Nase. — *Human beings don't breathe only with their noses.*
Atme doch nicht so laut! — *Don't breathe so loudly!*
Bei so einem Freifall muss per Maske geatmet werden. — *During such a free fall you have to breathe using a mask.*
1995 atmete ich zum ersten Mal Hamburger Luft. — *In 1995 I breathed Hamburg air for the first time.*
Maureen hat den ganzen Tag schwer geatmet. — *Maureen breathed heavily all day.*
Nach der Operation konnte er wieder richtig atmen. — *After the operation he could breathe properly again.*
Bei Hyperventilation merkt man einen Zwang tief zu atmen. — *With hyperventilation, one feels compelled to breathe deeply.*
In Gummistiefeln können die Füße nicht atmen. — *The feet can't breathe in rubber boots.*
Die schlechte Luft war kaum zu atmen. — *You could hardly breathe for the stale air.*

RELATED VERBS auf·atmen, aus·atmen, beatmen, durch·atmen

25 auf·fordern *to ask, call upon, demand; invite*

fordert auf · forderte auf · aufgefordert regular weak verb

PRESENT

ich fordere	wir fordern	auf
du forderst	ihr fordert	
Sie fordern	Sie fordern	
er/sie/es fordert	sie fordern	

PRESENT PERFECT

ich habe	wir haben	aufgefordert
du hast	ihr habt	
Sie haben	Sie haben	
er/sie/es hat	sie haben	

SIMPLE PAST

ich forderte	wir forderten	auf
du fordertest	ihr fordertet	
Sie forderten	Sie forderten	
er/sie/es forderte	sie forderten	

PAST PERFECT

ich hatte	wir hatten	aufgefordert
du hattest	ihr hattet	
Sie hatten	Sie hatten	
er/sie/es hatte	sie hatten	

FUTURE

ich werde	wir werden	auffordern
du wirst	ihr werdet	
Sie werden	Sie werden	
er/sie/es wird	sie werden	

FUTURE PERFECT

ich werde	wir werden	aufgefordert haben
du wirst	ihr werdet	
Sie werden	Sie werden	
er/sie/es wird	sie werden	

PRESENT SUBJUNCTIVE I

ich fordere	wir fordern	auf
du forderst	ihr fordert	
Sie fordern	Sie fordern	
er/sie/es fordere	sie fordern	

PAST SUBJUNCTIVE I

ich habe	wir haben	aufgefordert
du habest	ihr habet	
Sie haben	Sie haben	
er/sie/es habe	sie haben	

PRESENT SUBJUNCTIVE II

ich forderte	wir forderten	auf
du fordertest	ihr fordertet	
Sie forderten	Sie forderten	
er/sie/es forderte	sie forderten	

PAST SUBJUNCTIVE II

ich hätte	wir hätten	aufgefordert
du hättest	ihr hättet	
Sie hätten	Sie hätten	
er/sie/es hätte	sie hätten	

FUTURE SUBJUNCTIVE I

ich werde	wir werden	auffordern
du werdest	ihr werdet	
Sie werden	Sie werden	
er/sie/es werde	sie werden	

FUTURE PERFECT SUBJUNCTIVE I

ich werde	wir werden	aufgefordert haben
du werdest	ihr werdet	
Sie werden	Sie werden	
er/sie/es werde	sie werden	

FUTURE SUBJUNCTIVE II

ich würde	wir würden	auffordern
du würdest	ihr würdet	
Sie würden	Sie würden	
er/sie/es würde	sie würden	

FUTURE PERFECT SUBJUNCTIVE II

ich würde	wir würden	aufgefordert haben
du würdest	ihr würdet	
Sie würden	Sie würden	
er/sie/es würde	sie würden	

COMMANDS fordere auf! fordert auf! fordern Sie auf!

PRESENT PARTICIPLE auffordernd

Usage

Die UNO hat wiederholt aufgefordert, Truppen ins Gebiet zu schicken.	*The U.N. has repeatedly demanded that troops be sent into the region.*
Der Präsident forderte andere Länder auf, sich aus dem Konflikt herauszuhalten.	*The president called upon other nations to keep out of the conflict.*
Die Bürgerschaft wird aufgefordert, einen neuen Minister zu wählen.	*The citizenry is called upon to elect a new minister.*
Ich fordere dich zum Duell auf!	*I challenge you to a duel!*
Der Zwischenrufer wurde aufgefordert, den Hörsaal zu verlassen.	*The heckler was asked to leave the lecture hall.*
Die Behörden forderten die Firma auf, innerhalb sieben Wochen das Areal zu räumen.	*The authorities demanded that the firm clear the area within seven weeks.*
Alle Patienten werden dazu aufgefordert, noch mal mit ihren Ärzten darüber zu sprechen.	*All patients are asked to speak with their physicians about this again.*

RELATED VERBS *see* **fordern** (193)

strong verb **gibt auf · gab auf · aufgegeben**

PRESENT

ich gebe	wir geben	auf
du gibst	ihr gebt	
Sie geben	Sie geben	
er/sie/es gibt	sie geben	

SIMPLE PAST

ich gab	wir gaben	auf
du gabst	ihr gabt	
Sie gaben	Sie gaben	
er/sie/es gab	sie gaben	

FUTURE

ich werde	wir werden	aufgeben
du wirst	ihr werdet	
Sie werden	Sie werden	
er/sie/es wird	sie werden	

PRESENT SUBJUNCTIVE I

ich gebe	wir geben	auf
du gebest	ihr gebet	
Sie geben	Sie geben	
er/sie/es gebe	sie geben	

PRESENT SUBJUNCTIVE II

ich gäbe	wir gäben	auf
du gäbest	ihr gäbet	
Sie gäben	Sie gäben	
er/sie/es gäbe	sie gäben	

FUTURE SUBJUNCTIVE I

ich werde	wir werden	aufgeben
du werdest	ihr werdet	
Sie werden	Sie werden	
er/sie/es werde	sie werden	

FUTURE SUBJUNCTIVE II

ich würde	wir würden	aufgeben
du würdest	ihr würdet	
Sie würden	Sie würden	
er/sie/es würde	sie würden	

PRESENT PERFECT

ich habe	wir haben	aufgegeben
du hast	ihr habt	
Sie haben	Sie haben	
er/sie/es hat	sie haben	

PAST PERFECT

ich hatte	wir hatten	aufgegeben
du hattest	ihr hattet	
Sie hatten	Sie hatten	
er/sie/es hatte	sie hatten	

FUTURE PERFECT

ich werde	wir werden	aufgegeben haben
du wirst	ihr werdet	
Sie werden	Sie werden	
er/sie/es wird	sie werden	

PAST SUBJUNCTIVE I

ich habe	wir haben	aufgegeben
du habest	ihr habet	
Sie haben	Sie haben	
er/sie/es habe	sie haben	

PAST SUBJUNCTIVE II

ich hätte	wir hätten	aufgegeben
du hättest	ihr hättet	
Sie hätten	Sie hätten	
er/sie/es hätte	sie hätten	

FUTURE PERFECT SUBJUNCTIVE I

ich werde	wir werden	aufgegeben haben
du werdest	ihr werdet	
Sie werden	Sie werden	
er/sie/es werde	sie werden	

FUTURE PERFECT SUBJUNCTIVE II

ich würde	wir würden	aufgegeben haben
du würdest	ihr würdet	
Sie würden	Sie würden	
er/sie/es würde	sie würden	

COMMANDS gib auf! gebt auf! geben Sie auf!

PRESENT PARTICIPLE aufgebend

Usage

Gib doch nicht auf!	*Don't give up!*
Die Ärzte hatten jede Hoffnung aufgegeben.	*The doctors had abandoned all hope.*
Wir müssen die Vorstellung aufgeben, dass die Naturschätze der Erde unerschöpflich sind.	*We must abandon the notion that earth's natural resources are limitless.*
Es geht darum, ob die Mitglieder diesen Anspruch aufgeben.	*It is a question of whether the members will relinquish this claim.*
Ich hoffe, dass sie nicht aufgeben.	*I hope they don't give up.*
Der Lehrer hat ihnen nie was aufgegeben.	*The teacher never assigned them any homework.*
Monika hat in der Zeitung eine Annonce aufgegeben.	*Monika placed an ad in the newspaper.*
Man kann die Bestellung auch per Fax aufgeben.	*You can also place the order by fax.*
Wie viel Gepäck hast du aufzugeben?	*How much luggage do you have to check?*
Bei der Post kann man Briefe aufgeben.	*You can mail letters at the post office.*
Die beiden Freunde gaben einander oft Rätsel auf.	*The two friends often posed riddles to one another.*

RELATED VERBS *see* **geben** (206)

27 auf·heben *to balance out; keep; lift up; pick up; terminate*

hebt auf · hob auf · aufgehoben strong verb

PRESENT			PRESENT PERFECT		
ich hebe	wir heben	auf	ich habe	wir haben	aufgehoben
du hebst	ihr hebt		du hast	ihr habt	
Sie heben	Sie heben		Sie haben	Sie haben	
er/sie/es hebt	sie heben		er/sie/es hat	sie haben	

SIMPLE PAST			PAST PERFECT		
ich hob	wir hoben	auf	ich hatte	wir hatten	aufgehoben
du hobst	ihr hobt		du hattest	ihr hattet	
Sie hoben	Sie hoben		Sie hatten	Sie hatten	
er/sie/es hob	sie hoben		er/sie/es hatte	sie hatten	

FUTURE			FUTURE PERFECT		
ich werde	wir werden	aufheben	ich werde	wir werden	aufgehoben haben
du wirst	ihr werdet		du wirst	ihr werdet	
Sie werden	Sie werden		Sie werden	Sie werden	
er/sie/es wird	sie werden		er/sie/es wird	sie werden	

PRESENT SUBJUNCTIVE I			PAST SUBJUNCTIVE I		
ich hebe	wir heben	auf	ich habe	wir haben	aufgehoben
du hebest	ihr hebet		du habest	ihr habet	
Sie heben	Sie heben		Sie haben	Sie haben	
er/sie/es hebe	sie heben		er/sie/es habe	sie haben	

PRESENT SUBJUNCTIVE II			PAST SUBJUNCTIVE II		
ich höbe	wir höben	auf	ich hätte	wir hätten	aufgehoben
du höbest	ihr höbet		du hättest	ihr hättet	
Sie höben	Sie höben		Sie hätten	Sie hätten	
er/sie/es höbe	sie höben		er/sie/es hätte	sie hätten	

FUTURE SUBJUNCTIVE I			FUTURE PERFECT SUBJUNCTIVE I		
ich werde	wir werden	aufheben	ich werde	wir werden	aufgehoben haben
du werdest	ihr werdet		du werdest	ihr werdet	
Sie werden	Sie werden		Sie werden	Sie werden	
er/sie/es werde	sie werden		er/sie/es werde	sie werden	

FUTURE SUBJUNCTIVE II			FUTURE PERFECT SUBJUNCTIVE II		
ich würde	wir würden	aufheben	ich würde	wir würden	aufgehoben haben
du würdest	ihr würdet		du würdest	ihr würdet	
Sie würden	Sie würden		Sie würden	Sie würden	
er/sie/es würde	sie würden		er/sie/es würde	sie würden	

COMMANDS heb(e) auf! hebt auf! heben Sie auf!

PRESENT PARTICIPLE aufhebend

NOTE Archaic simple past **hub auf** and present subjunctive II **hübe auf** sometimes occur.

Usage

Die Werte heben sich gegenseitig auf.	*The values cancel each other out.*
Heben Sie bitte die Unterlagen bis zur nächsten Sitzung auf.	*Please keep the documents until the next session.*
Heb dein Passwort gut auf.	*Keep your password safe.*
Keiner konnte den Hammer aufheben.	*Nobody could pick up the hammer.*
Die Bundesregierung hebt die neuen Steuern auf.	*The federal government is repealing the new taxes.*
Der Minister will solche Vorschriften aufheben.	*The minister wants to lift such restrictions.*
Die beiden wollen den Vertrag aufheben.	*They both want to terminate the contract.*
Das heutige Urteil wurde sofort aufgehoben.	*Today's judgment was immediately voided.*
Mareike meint, sie müssten die Verlobung aufheben.	*Mareike thinks they have to break off the engagement.*
Nach langwieriger Diskussion hob man die Verordnung auf.	*After protracted discussion, the decree was revoked.*
Das Embargo muss aufgehoben werden.	*The embargo must be lifted.*

RELATED VERBS *see* **heben** (237)

regular weak verb **hört auf · hörte auf · aufgehört**

PRESENT			PRESENT PERFECT		
ich höre	wir hören	auf	ich habe	wir haben	aufgehört
du hörst	ihr hört		du hast	ihr habt	
Sie hören	Sie hören		Sie haben	Sie haben	
er/sie/es hört	sie hören		er/sie/es hat	sie haben	
SIMPLE PAST			**PAST PERFECT**		
ich hörte	wir hörten	auf	ich hatte	wir hatten	aufgehört
du hörtest	ihr hörtet		du hattest	ihr hattet	
Sie hörten	Sie hörten		Sie hatten	Sie hatten	
er/sie/es hörte	sie hörten		er/sie/es hatte	sie hatten	
FUTURE			**FUTURE PERFECT**		
ich werde	wir werden	aufhören	ich werde	wir werden	aufgehört haben
du wirst	ihr werdet		du wirst	ihr werdet	
Sie werden	Sie werden		Sie werden	Sie werden	
er/sie/es wird	sie werden		er/sie/es wird	sie werden	
PRESENT SUBJUNCTIVE I			**PAST SUBJUNCTIVE I**		
ich höre	wir hören	auf	ich habe	wir haben	aufgehört
du hörest	ihr höret		du habest	ihr habet	
Sie hören	Sie hören		Sie haben	Sie haben	
er/sie/es höre	sie hören		er/sie/es habe	sie haben	
PRESENT SUBJUNCTIVE II			**PAST SUBJUNCTIVE II**		
ich hörte	wir hörten	auf	ich hätte	wir hätten	aufgehört
du hörtest	ihr hörtet		du hättest	ihr hättet	
Sie hörten	Sie hörten		Sie hätten	Sie hätten	
er/sie/es hörte	sie hörten		er/sie/es hätte	sie hätten	
FUTURE SUBJUNCTIVE I			**FUTURE PERFECT SUBJUNCTIVE I**		
ich werde	wir werden	aufhören	ich werde	wir werden	aufgehört haben
du werdest	ihr werdet		du werdest	ihr werdet	
Sie werden	Sie werden		Sie werden	Sie werden	
er/sie/es werde	sie werden		er/sie/es werde	sie werden	
FUTURE SUBJUNCTIVE II			**FUTURE PERFECT SUBJUNCTIVE II**		
ich würde	wir würden	aufhören	ich würde	wir würden	aufgehört haben
du würdest	ihr würdet		du würdest	ihr würdet	
Sie würden	Sie würden		Sie würden	Sie würden	
er/sie/es würde	sie würden		er/sie/es würde	sie würden	

COMMANDS hör(e) auf! hört auf! hören Sie auf!

PRESENT PARTICIPLE aufhörend

Usage

Ute will nicht mit dem Rauchen aufhören.	*Ute doesn't want to stop smoking.*
Will sie auch mit ihrer Diät aufhören?	*Does she also want to stop dieting?*
Glücklicherweise wollte es nicht aufhören zu schneien.	*Fortunately, it wouldn't stop snowing.*
Das Baby hörte nicht auf zu weinen.	*The baby didn't stop crying.*
Der abgelegene Weiler hörte einfach auf zu existieren.	*The remote hamlet simply ceased to exist.*
Hör doch auf zu arbeiten!	*Stop working!*
Der Regen hörte plötzlich auf.	*The rain suddenly stopped.*
Ich hörte allmählich auf, sie täglich zu besuchen.	*I gradually discontinued my daily visits to her.*
Wenn ich mit dem Rauchen aufhörte, würde ich bestimmt zunehmen.	*If I stopped smoking, I'd surely gain weight.*
Wir liefen, bis der Weg aufhörte.	*We walked until the path ended.*
Hör bloß auf!	*Just stop it!*
Uwe wird endlich mit dem Trinken aufhören müssen.	*Uwe will ultimately have to give up drinking.*

RELATED VERBS *see* **hören** (248)

29 auf·passen *to beware, pay attention, watch over*

passt auf · passte auf · aufgepasst regular weak verb

PRESENT

ich passe	wir passen	auf
du passt	ihr passt	
Sie passen	Sie passen	
er/sie/es passt	sie passen	

PRESENT PERFECT

ich habe	wir haben	aufgepasst
du hast	ihr habt	
Sie haben	Sie haben	
er/sie/es hat	sie haben	

SIMPLE PAST

ich passte	wir passten	auf
du passtest	ihr passtet	
Sie passten	Sie passten	
er/sie/es passte	sie passten	

PAST PERFECT

ich hatte	wir hatten	aufgepasst
du hattest	ihr hattet	
Sie hatten	Sie hatten	
er/sie/es hatte	sie hatten	

FUTURE

ich werde	wir werden	aufpassen
du wirst	ihr werdet	
Sie werden	Sie werden	
er/sie/es wird	sie werden	

FUTURE PERFECT

ich werde	wir werden	aufgepasst haben
du wirst	ihr werdet	
Sie werden	Sie werden	
er/sie/es wird	sie werden	

PRESENT SUBJUNCTIVE I

ich passe	wir passen	auf
du passest	ihr passet	
Sie passen	Sie passen	
er/sie/es passe	sie passen	

PAST SUBJUNCTIVE I

ich habe	wir haben	aufgepasst
du habest	ihr habet	
Sie haben	Sie haben	
er/sie/es habe	sie haben	

PRESENT SUBJUNCTIVE II

ich passte	wir passten	auf
du passtest	ihr passtet	
Sie passten	Sie passten	
er/sie/es passte	sie passten	

PAST SUBJUNCTIVE II

ich hätte	wir hätten	aufgepasst
du hättest	ihr hättet	
Sie hätten	Sie hätten	
er/sie/es hätte	sie hätten	

FUTURE SUBJUNCTIVE I

ich werde	wir werden	aufpassen
du werdest	ihr werdet	
Sie werden	Sie werden	
er/sie/es werde	sie werden	

FUTURE PERFECT SUBJUNCTIVE I

ich werde	wir werden	aufgepasst haben
du werdest	ihr werdet	
Sie werden	Sie werden	
er/sie/es werde	sie werden	

FUTURE SUBJUNCTIVE II

ich würde	wir würden	aufpassen
du würdest	ihr würdet	
Sie würden	Sie würden	
er/sie/es würde	sie würden	

FUTURE PERFECT SUBJUNCTIVE II

ich würde	wir würden	aufgepasst haben
du würdest	ihr würdet	
Sie würden	Sie würden	
er/sie/es würde	sie würden	

COMMANDS pass(e) auf! passt auf! passen Sie auf!

PRESENT PARTICIPLE aufpassend

Usage

Aufgepasst!	*Beware!*
Besonders hier müssen Fußgänger beim Überqueren der Straße auf die Autos aufpassen.	*Especially here, pedestrians must watch out for cars when crossing the street.*
Wenn Sie nicht aufpassen, werden Sie die Prüfung nicht bestehen.	*If you don't pay attention, you won't pass the test.*
Der Fahrer hat nicht aufgepasst und den Hund überfahren.	*The driver wasn't paying attention and ran over the dog.*
Er passte genau auf, was gesagt wurde.	*He paid close attention to what was said.*
Kinder, warum habt ihr nicht besser aufgepasst?	*Children, why weren't you paying better attention?*
Die Polizei passte gut auf alles auf.	*The police kept a close eye on everything.*
Irene hat auf die Kinder aufgepasst, während wir im Kino waren.	*Irene looked after the children while we were at the movies.*
Passen Sie auf Ihre Gesundheit auf.	*Take care of your health.*

RELATED VERB passen

regular weak verb **räumt auf · räumte auf · aufgeräumt**

PRESENT

ich räume	wir räumen	auf
du räumst	ihr räumt	
Sie räumen	Sie räumen	
er/sie/es räumt	sie räumen	

PRESENT PERFECT

ich habe	wir haben	aufgeräumt
du hast	ihr habt	
Sie haben	Sie haben	
er/sie/es hat	sie haben	

SIMPLE PAST

ich räumte	wir räumten	auf
du räumtest	ihr räumtet	
Sie räumten	Sie räumten	
er/sie/es räumte	sie räumten	

PAST PERFECT

ich hatte	wir hatten	aufgeräumt
du hattest	ihr hattet	
Sie hatten	Sie hatten	
er/sie/es hatte	sie hatten	

FUTURE

ich werde	wir werden	aufräumen
du wirst	ihr werdet	
Sie werden	Sie werden	
er/sie/es wird	sie werden	

FUTURE PERFECT

ich werde	wir werden	aufgeräumt haben
du wirst	ihr werdet	
Sie werden	Sie werden	
er/sie/es wird	sie werden	

PRESENT SUBJUNCTIVE I

ich räume	wir räumen	auf
du räumest	ihr räumet	
Sie räumen	Sie räumen	
er/sie/es räume	sie räumen	

PAST SUBJUNCTIVE I

ich habe	wir haben	aufgeräumt
du habest	ihr habet	
Sie haben	Sie haben	
er/sie/es habe	sie haben	

PRESENT SUBJUNCTIVE II

ich räumte	wir räumten	auf
du räumtest	ihr räumtet	
Sie räumten	Sie räumten	
er/sie/es räumte	sie räumten	

PAST SUBJUNCTIVE II

ich hätte	wir hätten	aufgeräumt
du hättest	ihr hättet	
Sie hätten	Sie hätten	
er/sie/es hätte	sie hätten	

FUTURE SUBJUNCTIVE I

ich werde	wir werden	aufräumen
du werdest	ihr werdet	
Sie werden	Sie werden	
er/sie/es werde	sie werden	

FUTURE PERFECT SUBJUNCTIVE I

ich werde	wir werden	aufgeräumt haben
du werdest	ihr werdet	
Sie werden	Sie werden	
er/sie/es werde	sie werden	

FUTURE SUBJUNCTIVE II

ich würde	wir würden	aufräumen
du würdest	ihr würdet	
Sie würden	Sie würden	
er/sie/es würde	sie würden	

FUTURE PERFECT SUBJUNCTIVE II

ich würde	wir würden	aufgeräumt haben
du würdest	ihr würdet	
Sie würden	Sie würden	
er/sie/es würde	sie würden	

COMMANDS räum(e) auf! räumt auf! räumen Sie auf!

PRESENT PARTICIPLE aufräumend

Usage

Er hat die Festplatte zwar aufgeräumt, aber die falschen Dateien gelöscht.	*He cleaned off the hard drive but deleted the wrong files.*
Ihr Zimmer muss täglich aufgeräumt werden.	*Her room has to be cleaned daily.*
Entschuldigung, ich hätte das Zimmer aufräumen sollen.	*I'm sorry, I should have cleaned up the room.*
Ich wollte am Samstag meine Wohnung aufräumen.	*I wanted to straighten up my apartment on Saturday.*
Ich habe es gefunden, als ich endlich die Garage aufräumte.	*I found it when I finally straightened up the garage.*
Julia kocht und Jan räumt auf.	*Julia cooks and Jan tidies up.*
Mark räumte auf und ging nach Hause.	*Mark tidied up and went home.*
Kinder, räumt jetzt bitte auf!	*Children, please tidy up now!*
Wie oft räumen Sie auf?	*How often do you tidy up?*
Wollen wir den Tisch aufräumen?	*Shall we clear the table?*
Sie wollen mit diesem Vorurteil aufräumen.	*They want to do away with this prejudice.*
Kannst du bitte die Bücher aufräumen?	*Can you please put away the books?*

RELATED VERBS *see* **räumen** (330)

31 auf·regen *to upset; excite*

regt auf · regte auf · aufgeregt regular weak verb

PRESENT

ich rege	wir regen	auf
du regst	ihr regt	
Sie regen	Sie regen	
er/sie/es regt	sie regen	

SIMPLE PAST

ich regte	wir regten	auf
du regtest	ihr regtet	
Sie regten	Sie regten	
er/sie/es regte	sie regten	

FUTURE

ich werde	wir werden	aufregen
du wirst	ihr werdet	
Sie werden	Sie werden	
er/sie/es wird	sie werden	

PRESENT SUBJUNCTIVE I

ich rege	wir regen	auf
du regest	ihr reget	
Sie regen	Sie regen	
er/sie/es rege	sie regen	

PRESENT SUBJUNCTIVE II

ich regte	wir regten	auf
du regtest	ihr regtet	
Sie regten	Sie regten	
er/sie/es regte	sie regten	

FUTURE SUBJUNCTIVE I

ich werde	wir werden	aufregen
du werdest	ihr werdet	
Sie werden	Sie werden	
er/sie/es werde	sie werden	

FUTURE SUBJUNCTIVE II

ich würde	wir würden	aufregen
du würdest	ihr würdet	
Sie würden	Sie würden	
er/sie/es würde	sie würden	

PRESENT PERFECT

ich habe	wir haben	aufgeregt
du hast	ihr habt	
Sie haben	Sie haben	
er/sie/es hat	sie haben	

PAST PERFECT

ich hatte	wir hatten	aufgeregt
du hattest	ihr hattet	
Sie hatten	Sie hatten	
er/sie/es hatte	sie hatten	

FUTURE PERFECT

ich werde	wir werden	aufgeregt haben
du wirst	ihr werdet	
Sie werden	Sie werden	
er/sie/es wird	sie werden	

PAST SUBJUNCTIVE I

ich habe	wir haben	aufgeregt
du habest	ihr habet	
Sie haben	Sie haben	
er/sie/es habe	sie haben	

PAST SUBJUNCTIVE II

ich hätte	wir hätten	aufgeregt
du hättest	ihr hättet	
Sie hätten	Sie hätten	
er/sie/es hätte	sie hätten	

FUTURE PERFECT SUBJUNCTIVE I

ich werde	wir werden	aufgeregt haben
du werdest	ihr werdet	
Sie werden	Sie werden	
er/sie/es werde	sie werden	

FUTURE PERFECT SUBJUNCTIVE II

ich würde	wir würden	aufgeregt haben
du würdest	ihr würdet	
Sie würden	Sie würden	
er/sie/es würde	sie würden	

COMMANDS reg(e) auf! regt auf! regen Sie auf!

PRESENT PARTICIPLE aufregend

Usage

Nichts kann ihn aufregen. — *Nothing upsets him.*
Seine schroffen Worte regten mich auf. — *His blunt words upset me.*
So etwas regt mich immer auf. — *Something like that always upsets me.*
Du regst mich auf. — *You're getting on my nerves.*

sich aufregen *to get upset/excited*

Regen Sie sich darüber nicht auf. — *Don't get upset about that.*
Wie kannst du dich aufregen? Du hast gewonnen! — *How can you get upset? You won!*
Reg dich nicht so auf. — *Don't get so upset.*
Paul hat sich sehr aufgeregt. — *Paul got really excited.*
Wegen hohen Blutdrucks darf sie sich nicht aufregen. — *Because of high blood pressure she mustn't get excited.*
Wenn Papa sich aufregt, kriegt er einen Schluckauf. — *When Papa gets excited, he gets the hiccups.*

RELATED VERB regen

strong verb **steht auf · stand auf · aufgestanden**

PRESENT

ich stehe / wir stehen } auf
du stehst / ihr steht
Sie stehen / Sie stehen
er/sie/es steht / sie stehen

ich stehe	wir stehen	auf
du stehst	ihr steht	
Sie stehen	Sie stehen	
er/sie/es steht	sie stehen	

SIMPLE PAST

ich stand	wir standen	auf
du standst	ihr standet	
Sie standen	Sie standen	
er/sie/es stand	sie standen	

FUTURE

ich werde	wir werden	aufstehen
du wirst	ihr werdet	
Sie werden	Sie werden	
er/sie/es wird	sie werden	

PRESENT SUBJUNCTIVE I

ich stehe	wir stehen	auf
du stehest	ihr stehet	
Sie stehen	Sie stehen	
er/sie/es stehe	sie stehen	

PRESENT SUBJUNCTIVE II

ich stünde/stände	wir stünden/ständen	auf
du stündest/ständest	ihr stündet/ständet	
Sie stünden/ständen	Sie stünden/ständen	
er/sie/es stünde/stände	sie stünden/ständen	

FUTURE SUBJUNCTIVE I

ich werde	wir werden	aufstehen
du werdest	ihr werdet	
Sie werden	Sie werden	
er/sie/es werde	sie werden	

FUTURE SUBJUNCTIVE II

ich würde	wir würden	aufstehen
du würdest	ihr würdet	
Sie würden	Sie würden	
er/sie/es würde	sie würden	

PRESENT PERFECT

ich bin	wir sind	aufgestanden
du bist	ihr seid	
Sie sind	Sie sind	
er/sie/es ist	sie sind	

PAST PERFECT

ich war	wir waren	aufgestanden
du warst	ihr wart	
Sie waren	Sie waren	
er/sie/es war	sie waren	

FUTURE PERFECT

ich werde	wir werden	aufgestanden sein
du wirst	ihr werdet	
Sie werden	Sie werden	
er/sie/es wird	sie werden	

PAST SUBJUNCTIVE I

ich sei	wir seien	aufgestanden
du seiest	ihr seiet	
Sie seien	Sie seien	
er/sie/es sei	sie seien	

PAST SUBJUNCTIVE II

ich wäre	wir wären	aufgestanden
du wärest	ihr wäret	
Sie wären	Sie wären	
er/sie/es wäre	sie wären	

FUTURE PERFECT SUBJUNCTIVE I

ich werde	wir werden	aufgestanden sein
du werdest	ihr werdet	
Sie werden	Sie werden	
er/sie/es werde	sie werden	

FUTURE PERFECT SUBJUNCTIVE II

ich würde	wir würden	aufgestanden sein
du würdest	ihr würdet	
Sie würden	Sie würden	
er/sie/es würde	sie würden	

COMMANDS steh(e) auf! steht auf! stehen Sie auf!

PRESENT PARTICIPLE aufstehend

Usage

Ich stehe jetzt auf und hole die Post.	*I'll get up now and get the mail.*
Um wie viel Uhr stehst du morgens normalerweise auf?	*At what time do you normally get up in the morning?*
Amalie ist aufgestanden und hat sich angezogen.	*Amalie got up and got dressed.*
Mein Bruder behauptet, er sei um fünf Uhr aufgestanden.	*My brother claims he got up at five o'clock.*
Wenn ihr nicht gleich ins Bett geht, steht ihr bestimmt nicht zeitlich auf.	*If you don't go to bed right away, you'll definitely not get up on time.*
Um vier Uhr muss aufgestanden werden.	*One must get up at four o'clock.*
Wir wollen für den Frieden aufstehen.	*We want to stand up for peace.*
Er stand auf und verließ das Zimmer.	*He stood up and left the room.*
Das Volk ist gegen die Besatzungsmacht aufgestanden.	*The people have risen up against the occupying power.*

aufstehen (with **haben**) *to be open*

Die Autotür steht auf.	*The car door is open.*
Wie lange hat das Tor aufgestanden?	*How long was the gate open?*

RELATED VERBS *see* **stehen** (423)

33 auf·wachen *to awake, wake up*

wacht auf · wachte auf · aufgewacht regular weak verb

PRESENT

ich wache	wir wachen	auf
du wachst	ihr wacht	
Sie wachen	Sie wachen	
er/sie/es wacht	sie wachen	

SIMPLE PAST

ich wachte	wir wachten	auf
du wachtest	ihr wachtet	
Sie wachten	Sie wachten	
er/sie/es wachte	sie wachten	

FUTURE

ich werde	wir werden	aufwachen
du wirst	ihr werdet	
Sie werden	Sie werden	
er/sie/es wird	sie werden	

PRESENT SUBJUNCTIVE I

ich wache	wir wachen	auf
du wachest	ihr wachet	
Sie wachen	Sie wachen	
er/sie/es wache	sie wachen	

PRESENT SUBJUNCTIVE II

ich wachte	wir wachten	auf
du wachtest	ihr wachtet	
Sie wachten	Sie wachten	
er/sie/es wachte	sie wachten	

FUTURE SUBJUNCTIVE I

ich werde	wir werden	aufwachen
du werdest	ihr werdet	
Sie werden	Sie werden	
er/sie/es werde	sie werden	

FUTURE SUBJUNCTIVE II

ich würde	wir würden	aufwachen
du würdest	ihr würdet	
Sie würden	Sie würden	
er/sie/es würde	sie würden	

PRESENT PERFECT

ich bin	wir sind	aufgewacht
du bist	ihr seid	
Sie sind	Sie sind	
er/sie/es ist	sie sind	

PAST PERFECT

ich war	wir waren	aufgewacht
du warst	ihr wart	
Sie waren	Sie waren	
er/sie/es war	sie waren	

FUTURE PERFECT

ich werde	wir werden	aufgewacht sein
du wirst	ihr werdet	
Sie werden	Sie werden	
er/sie/es wird	sie werden	

PAST SUBJUNCTIVE I

ich sei	wir seien	aufgewacht
du seiest	ihr seiet	
Sie seien	Sie seien	
er/sie/es sei	sie seien	

PAST SUBJUNCTIVE II

ich wäre	wir wären	aufgewacht
du wärest	ihr wäret	
Sie wären	Sie wären	
er/sie/es wäre	sie wären	

FUTURE PERFECT SUBJUNCTIVE I

ich werde	wir werden	aufgewacht sein
du werdest	ihr werdet	
Sie werden	Sie werden	
er/sie/es werde	sie werden	

FUTURE PERFECT SUBJUNCTIVE II

ich würde	wir würden	aufgewacht sein
du würdest	ihr würdet	
Sie würden	Sie würden	
er/sie/es würde	sie würden	

COMMANDS wach(e) auf! wacht auf! wachen Sie auf!

PRESENT PARTICIPLE aufwachend

Usage

Oma Schmitz ist um fünf Uhr aufgewacht. — *Grandma Schmitz woke up at five o'clock.*

Ich wachte aus einem Traum auf. — *I awoke from a dream.*

Als Dennis eines Morgens letzte Woche aufwachte, entdeckte er eine Wunde am Kopf. — *As Dennis awoke one morning last week, he discovered a wound on his head.*

Nachdem Sie aufgewacht sind, können wir zusammen frühstücken. — *After you've woken up, we can eat breakfast together.*

Dornröschen ist aufgewacht. — *Sleeping Beauty has awakened.*

Mitten in der Nacht bin ich mit einem riesigen Durst aufgewacht. — *I woke up in the middle of the night extremely thirsty.*

Die Dorfbewohner waren noch nicht aufgewacht. — *The village residents hadn't yet awakened.*

Ich hätte Angst, dass ich nicht aufwachen würde. — *I'd be afraid I wouldn't wake up.*

Er sprach so leise, dass die Kinder nicht aufwachten. — *He spoke so softly that the children didn't wake up.*

Warum bist du so spät aufgewacht? — *Why did you wake up so late?*

RELATED VERB wachen

strong verb **gibt aus · gab aus · ausgegeben**

PRESENT			PRESENT PERFECT		
ich gebe	wir geben	aus	ich habe	wir haben	ausgegeben
du gibst	ihr gebt		du hast	ihr habt	
Sie geben	Sie geben		Sie haben	Sie haben	
er/sie/es gibt	sie geben		er/sie/es hat	sie haben	
SIMPLE PAST			**PAST PERFECT**		
ich gab	wir gaben	aus	ich hatte	wir hatten	ausgegeben
du gabst	ihr gabt		du hattest	ihr hattet	
Sie gaben	Sie gaben		Sie hatten	Sie hatten	
er/sie/es gab	sie gaben		er/sie/es hatte	sie hatten	
FUTURE			**FUTURE PERFECT**		
ich werde	wir werden	ausgeben	ich werde	wir werden	ausgegeben haben
du wirst	ihr werdet		du wirst	ihr werdet	
Sie werden	Sie werden		Sie werden	Sie werden	
er/sie/es wird	sie werden		er/sie/es wird	sie werden	
PRESENT SUBJUNCTIVE I			**PAST SUBJUNCTIVE I**		
ich gebe	wir geben	aus	ich habe	wir haben	ausgegeben
du gebest	ihr gebet		du habest	ihr habet	
Sie geben	Sie geben		Sie haben	Sie haben	
er/sie/es gebe	sie geben		er/sie/es habe	sie haben	
PRESENT SUBJUNCTIVE II			**PAST SUBJUNCTIVE II**		
ich gäbe	wir gäben	aus	ich hätte	wir hätten	ausgegeben
du gäbest	ihr gäbet		du hättest	ihr hättet	
Sie gäben	Sie gäben		Sie hätten	Sie hätten	
er/sie/es gäbe	sie gäben		er/sie/es hätte	sie hätten	
FUTURE SUBJUNCTIVE I			**FUTURE PERFECT SUBJUNCTIVE I**		
ich werde	wir werden	ausgeben	ich werde	wir werden	ausgegeben haben
du werdest	ihr werdet		du werdest	ihr werdet	
Sie werden	Sie werden		Sie werden	Sie werden	
er/sie/es werde	sie werden		er/sie/es werde	sie werden	
FUTURE SUBJUNCTIVE II			**FUTURE PERFECT SUBJUNCTIVE II**		
ich würde	wir würden	ausgeben	ich würde	wir würden	ausgegeben haben
du würdest	ihr würdet		du würdest	ihr würdet	
Sie würden	Sie würden		Sie würden	Sie würden	
er/sie/es würde	sie würden		er/sie/es würde	sie würden	

COMMANDS gib aus! gebt aus! geben Sie aus!

PRESENT PARTICIPLE ausgebend

Usage

2002 wurden in den USA mehrere Milliarden Dollar für Kino ausgegeben.	*In 2002 several billion dollars were spent on moviegoing in the U.S.A.*
Jörg hat vergessen, wofür er das ganze Geld ausgab.	*Jörg forgot where he spent all the money.*
Wenn du nicht so viel ausgegeben hättest, hättest du jetzt ein bisschen mehr.	*If you hadn't spent so much, you'd have a bit more now.*
Wir geben zu wenig Geld für Schulen aus.	*We spend too little money on schools.*
Die zur Verfügung stehenden Gelder werden an die einzelnen Universitäten ausgegeben.	*The monies available will be disbursed to the individual universities.*
Du mischst die Karten und ich gebe sie aus.	*You shuffle the cards and I'll deal them.*
Wenn ich die Entdeckung für eine Tatsache ausgegeben hätte, hätten mir viele Leute nicht geglaubt.	*If I'd declared the discovery to be a fact, a lot of people wouldn't have believed me.*
Das Programm gibt die Summe aus.	*The program outputs the sum.*
Er gibt sich für einen wohlhabenden Adligen aus.	*He pretends to be moneyed aristocracy.*

RELATED VERBS heraus·geben; *see also* **geben** (206)

35 aus·gehen *to go out; come out; start out, assume; come to an end*

geht aus · ging aus · ausgegangen

strong verb

PRESENT

ich gehe	wir gehen	aus
du gehst	ihr geht	
Sie gehen	Sie gehen	
er/sie/es geht	sie gehen	

PRESENT PERFECT

ich bin	wir sind	ausgegangen
du bist	ihr seid	
Sie sind	Sie sind	
er/sie/es ist	sie sind	

SIMPLE PAST

ich ging	wir gingen	aus
du gingst	ihr gingt	
Sie gingen	Sie gingen	
er/sie/es ging	sie gingen	

PAST PERFECT

ich war	wir waren	ausgegangen
du warst	ihr wart	
Sie waren	Sie waren	
er/sie/es war	sie waren	

FUTURE

ich werde	wir werden	ausgehen
du wirst	ihr werdet	
Sie werden	Sie werden	
er/sie/es wird	sie werden	

FUTURE PERFECT

ich werde	wir werden	ausgegangen sein
du wirst	ihr werdet	
Sie werden	Sie werden	
er/sie/es wird	sie werden	

PRESENT SUBJUNCTIVE I

ich gehe	wir gehen	aus
du gehest	ihr gehet	
Sie gehen	Sie gehen	
er/sie/es gehe	sie gehen	

PAST SUBJUNCTIVE I

ich sei	wir seien	ausgegangen
du seiest	ihr seiet	
Sie seien	Sie seien	
er/sie/es sei	sie seien	

PRESENT SUBJUNCTIVE II

ich ginge	wir gingen	aus
du gingest	ihr ginget	
Sie gingen	Sie gingen	
er/sie/es ginge	sie gingen	

PAST SUBJUNCTIVE II

ich wäre	wir wären	ausgegangen
du wärest	ihr wäret	
Sie wären	Sie wären	
er/sie/es wäre	sie wären	

FUTURE SUBJUNCTIVE I

ich werde	wir werden	ausgehen
du werdest	ihr werdet	
Sie werden	Sie werden	
er/sie/es werde	sie werden	

FUTURE PERFECT SUBJUNCTIVE I

ich werde	wir werden	ausgegangen sein
du werdest	ihr werdet	
Sie werden	Sie werden	
er/sie/es werde	sie werden	

FUTURE SUBJUNCTIVE II

ich würde	wir würden	ausgehen
du würdest	ihr würdet	
Sie würden	Sie würden	
er/sie/es würde	sie würden	

FUTURE PERFECT SUBJUNCTIVE II

ich würde	wir würden	ausgegangen sein
du würdest	ihr würdet	
Sie würden	Sie würden	
er/sie/es würde	sie würden	

COMMANDS geh(e) aus! geht aus! gehen Sie aus!

PRESENT PARTICIPLE ausgehend

Usage

Gehen Sie abends gern aus? — *Do you like to go out in the evening?*
Beatrice möchte nur einmal mit ihm ausgehen. — *Beatrice would like to go out with him just once.*
Amalie geht gern in Jeans aus. — *Amalie likes going out in jeans.*
Die Sache ist für uns schief ausgegangen. — *The affair turned out badly for us.*
Langsam gingen ihm die Haare aus. — *He gradually lost his hair.*
Ich bekomme 100 Euro, aber Erich geht leer aus. — *I'm getting 100 euros, but Erich comes away empty-handed.*

Ausgehend von einigen neuen wissenschaftlichen Erkenntnissen wollen wir heute zwei theoretische Fragen stellen. — *Based on some new scientific discoveries, we will pose two theoretical questions today.*
Ich gehe davon aus, dass er nicht mitkommt. — *I'm assuming he won't come along.*
Lasst das Feuer nicht ausgehen. — *Don't let the fire go out.*
Falls das Bier ausgeht, haben wir noch Wein. — *In case the beer runs out, we've still got wine.*
Während unserer Fahrt ist der Motor mehrmals ausgegangen. — *The engine died several times during our trip.*

RELATED VERBS *see* **gehen** (210)

regular weak verb **macht aus · machte aus · ausgemacht**

PRESENT

ich mache	wir machen	aus
du machst	ihr macht	
Sie machen	Sie machen	
er/sie/es macht	sie machen	

SIMPLE PAST

ich machte	wir machten	aus
du machtest	ihr machtet	
Sie machten	Sie machten	
er/sie/es machte	sie machten	

FUTURE

ich werde	wir werden	ausmachen
du wirst	ihr werdet	
Sie werden	Sie werden	
er/sie/es wird	sie werden	

PRESENT SUBJUNCTIVE I

ich mache	wir machen	aus
du machest	ihr machet	
Sie machen	Sie machen	
er/sie/es mache	sie machen	

PRESENT SUBJUNCTIVE II

ich machte	wir machten	aus
du machtest	ihr machtet	
Sie machten	Sie machten	
er/sie/es machte	sie machten	

FUTURE SUBJUNCTIVE I

ich werde	wir werden	ausmachen
du werdest	ihr werdet	
Sie werden	Sie werden	
er/sie/es werde	sie werden	

FUTURE SUBJUNCTIVE II

ich würde	wir würden	ausmachen
du würdest	ihr würdet	
Sie würden	Sie würden	
er/sie/es würde	sie würden	

PRESENT PERFECT

ich habe	wir haben	ausgemacht
du hast	ihr habt	
Sie haben	Sie haben	
er/sie/es hat	sie haben	

PAST PERFECT

ich hatte	wir hatten	ausgemacht
du hattest	ihr hattet	
Sie hatten	Sie hatten	
er/sie/es hatte	sie hatten	

FUTURE PERFECT

ich werde	wir werden	ausgemacht haben
du wirst	ihr werdet	
Sie werden	Sie werden	
er/sie/es wird	sie werden	

PAST SUBJUNCTIVE I

ich habe	wir haben	ausgemacht
du habest	ihr habet	
Sie haben	Sie haben	
er/sie/es habe	sie haben	

PAST SUBJUNCTIVE II

ich hätte	wir hätten	ausgemacht
du hättest	ihr hättet	
Sie hätten	Sie hätten	
er/sie/es hätte	sie hätten	

FUTURE PERFECT SUBJUNCTIVE I

ich werde	wir werden	ausgemacht haben
du werdest	ihr werdet	
Sie werden	Sie werden	
er/sie/es werde	sie werden	

FUTURE PERFECT SUBJUNCTIVE II

ich würde	wir würden	ausgemacht haben
du würdest	ihr würdet	
Sie würden	Sie würden	
er/sie/es würde	sie würden	

COMMANDS mach(e) aus! macht aus! machen Sie aus!

PRESENT PARTICIPLE ausmachend

Usage

Was habt ihr für das Wochenende ausgemacht? — *What have you arranged for the weekend?*
Frau Nari hat einen Termin beim Zahnarzt ausgemacht. — *Mrs. Nari made an appointment with the dentist.*
Damit können wir ausmachen, was wir unternehmen wollen. — *That way we can agree on what we want to do.*
Mach das Feuer aus, bevor du einschläfst. — *Put out the fire before you go to sleep.*
Würden Sie bitte das Licht ausmachen? — *Would you please turn out the light?*
Wer hat den Fernseher ausgemacht? — *Who turned off the television?*
Johann behauptet, dass er den Rechner ausgemacht habe. — *Johann maintains that he turned the computer off.*
Die Kosten können Tausende Euro ausmachen. — *The costs can amount to thousands of euros.*
Was macht eine glückliche Ehe aus? — *What constitutes a happy marriage?*
Es macht nichts aus, wie alt man aussieht. — *It makes no difference how old you look.*
Eine klare Tendenz lässt sich trotzdem ausmachen. — *A clear trend can nonetheless be discerned.*
Im düsteren Wald konnte er kein Tier ausmachen. — *He was unable to make out any animal in the gloomy forest.*

RELATED VERBS *see* **machen** (300)

37 aus·schalten *to switch off, turn off; eliminate, set aside*

schaltet aus · schaltete aus · ausgeschaltet regular weak verb

PRESENT

ich schalte	wir schalten	aus
du schaltest	ihr schaltet	
Sie schalten	Sie schalten	
er/sie/es schaltet	sie schalten	

SIMPLE PAST

ich schaltete	wir schalteten	aus
du schaltetest	ihr schaltetet	
Sie schalteten	Sie schalteten	
er/sie/es schaltete	sie schalteten	

FUTURE

ich werde	wir werden	ausschalten
du wirst	ihr werdet	
Sie werden	Sie werden	
er/sie/es wird	sie werden	

PRESENT SUBJUNCTIVE I

ich schalte	wir schalten	aus
du schaltest	ihr schaltet	
Sie schalten	Sie schalten	
er/sie/es schalte	sie schalten	

PRESENT SUBJUNCTIVE II

ich schaltete	wir schalteten	aus
du schaltetest	ihr schaltetet	
Sie schalteten	Sie schalteten	
er/sie/es schaltete	sie schalteten	

FUTURE SUBJUNCTIVE I

ich werde	wir werden	ausschalten
du werdest	ihr werdet	
Sie werden	Sie werden	
er/sie/es werde	sie werden	

FUTURE SUBJUNCTIVE II

ich würde	wir würden	ausschalten
du würdest	ihr würdet	
Sie würden	Sie würden	
er/sie/es würde	sie würden	

PRESENT PERFECT

ich habe	wir haben	ausgeschaltet
du hast	ihr habt	
Sie haben	Sie haben	
er/sie/es hat	sie haben	

PAST PERFECT

ich hatte	wir hatten	ausgeschaltet
du hattest	ihr hattet	
Sie hatten	Sie hatten	
er/sie/es hatte	sie hatten	

FUTURE PERFECT

ich werde	wir werden	ausgeschaltet haben
du wirst	ihr werdet	
Sie werden	Sie werden	
er/sie/es wird	sie werden	

PAST SUBJUNCTIVE I

ich habe	wir haben	ausgeschaltet
du habest	ihr habet	
Sie haben	Sie haben	
er/sie/es habe	sie haben	

PAST SUBJUNCTIVE II

ich hätte	wir hätten	ausgeschaltet
du hättest	ihr hättet	
Sie hätten	Sie hätten	
er/sie/es hätte	sie hätten	

FUTURE PERFECT SUBJUNCTIVE I

ich werde	wir werden	ausgeschaltet haben
du werdest	ihr werdet	
Sie werden	Sie werden	
er/sie/es werde	sie werden	

FUTURE PERFECT SUBJUNCTIVE II

ich würde	wir würden	ausgeschaltet haben
du würdest	ihr würdet	
Sie würden	Sie würden	
er/sie/es würde	sie würden	

COMMANDS schalte aus! schaltet aus! schalten Sie aus!

PRESENT PARTICIPLE ausschaltend

Usage

Ich empfehle, den Videorekorder auszuschalten.	*I recommend turning off the video recorder.*
Das Gerät kann per Fernbedienung ausgeschaltet werden.	*The device can be switched off via remote control.*
Man muss die Klimaanlage im Winter ausschalten.	*One must turn off the air conditioning in the winter.*
Sie sagten, die Kamera sei ja ausgeschaltet gewesen.	*They claimed the camera had been turned off.*
Der Fußballer konnte seinen Gegner ausschalten.	*The soccer player was able to shut down his opponent.*
Dem Bericht nach versuche man die Umweltorganisationen auszuschalten.	*According to the report, people are trying to eliminate the environmental organizations.*
Seine Kollegen hatten vor, ihn auszuschalten.	*His colleagues planned to exclude him.*
Wir dürfen den Verstand nicht ausschalten.	*We mustn't set reason aside.*
Dieses Unternehmen will die Konkurrenz ausschalten.	*This company wants to eliminate the competition.*

sich ausschalten *to switch/turn off*

Mein Rechner schaltet sich nicht aus.	*My computer won't shut down.*

RELATED VERBS *see* **schalten** (357)

strong verb **schließt aus · schloss aus · ausgeschlossen**

PRESENT

ich schließe	wir schließen	aus
du schließt	ihr schließt	
Sie schließen	Sie schließen	
er/sie/es schließt	sie schließen	

PRESENT PERFECT

ich habe	wir haben	ausgeschlossen
du hast	ihr habt	
Sie haben	Sie haben	
er/sie/es hat	sie haben	

SIMPLE PAST

ich schloss	wir schlossen	aus
du schlossest	ihr schlosst	
Sie schlossen	Sie schlossen	
er/sie/es schloss	sie schlossen	

PAST PERFECT

ich hatte	wir hatten	ausgeschlossen
du hattest	ihr hattet	
Sie hatten	Sie hatten	
er/sie/es hatte	sie hatten	

FUTURE

ich werde	wir werden	ausschließen
du wirst	ihr werdet	
Sie werden	Sie werden	
er/sie/es wird	sie werden	

FUTURE PERFECT

ich werde	wir werden	ausgeschlossen haben
du wirst	ihr werdet	
Sie werden	Sie werden	
er/sie/es wird	sie werden	

PRESENT SUBJUNCTIVE I

ich schließe	wir schließen	aus
du schließest	ihr schließet	
Sie schließen	Sie schließen	
er/sie/es schließe	sie schließen	

PAST SUBJUNCTIVE I

ich habe	wir haben	ausgeschlossen
du habest	ihr habet	
Sie haben	Sie haben	
er/sie/es habe	sie haben	

PRESENT SUBJUNCTIVE II

ich schlösse	wir schlössen	aus
du schlössest	ihr schlösset	
Sie schlössen	Sie schlössen	
er/sie/es schlösse	sie schlössen	

PAST SUBJUNCTIVE II

ich hätte	wir hätten	ausgeschlossen
du hättest	ihr hättet	
Sie hätten	Sie hätten	
er/sie/es hätte	sie hätten	

FUTURE SUBJUNCTIVE I

ich werde	wir werden	ausschließen
du werdest	ihr werdet	
Sie werden	Sie werden	
er/sie/es werde	sie werden	

FUTURE PERFECT SUBJUNCTIVE I

ich werde	wir werden	ausgeschlossen haben
du werdest	ihr werdet	
Sie werden	Sie werden	
er/sie/es werde	sie werden	

FUTURE SUBJUNCTIVE II

ich würde	wir würden	ausschließen
du würdest	ihr würdet	
Sie würden	Sie würden	
er/sie/es würde	sie würden	

FUTURE PERFECT SUBJUNCTIVE II

ich würde	wir würden	ausgeschlossen haben
du würdest	ihr würdet	
Sie würden	Sie würden	
er/sie/es würde	sie würden	

COMMANDS schließ(e) aus! schließt aus! schließen Sie aus!

PRESENT PARTICIPLE ausschließend

Usage

Die Polizei schließt nicht aus, dass es sich um Selbstmord handelte. — *The police aren't ruling out the possibility that it was suicide.*

Schüler werden bei solchen Verstößen aus der Schule ausgeschlossen. — *Students will be expelled for such infractions.*

Der neu gegründete Verein schließt alle Nichtgläubiger aus. — *The newly founded association refuses admittance to nonbelievers.*

Das Verfahren schließt ausländische Mitbewerber aus. — *The process excludes foreign competitors.*

Dies würde die Gefahr ausschließen, dass das Haus zusammenbricht. — *This would eliminate the danger of the house collapsing.*

Warum schließen Sie Kinder und Jugendliche aus? — *Why do you exclude children and youth?*

In diesem Fall ist Missbrauch nicht auszuschließen. — *In this case, abuse cannot be ruled out.*

Eine Weitergabe Ihrer persönlichen Angaben an Dritte schließen wir aus. — *We will not give your personal information to third parties.*

RELATED VERBS *see* **schließen** (375)

39 aus·sehen *to appear, look*

sieht aus · sah aus · ausgesehen

strong verb

PRESENT

ich sehe	wir sehen	aus
du siehst	ihr seht	
Sie sehen	Sie sehen	
er/sie/es sieht	sie sehen	

SIMPLE PAST

ich sah	wir sahen	aus
du sahst	ihr saht	
Sie sahen	Sie sahen	
er/sie/es sah	sie sahen	

FUTURE

ich werde	wir werden	aussehen
du wirst	ihr werdet	
Sie werden	Sie werden	
er/sie/es wird	sie werden	

PRESENT SUBJUNCTIVE I

ich sehe	wir sehen	aus
du sehest	ihr sehet	
Sie sehen	Sie sehen	
er/sie/es sehe	sie sehen	

PRESENT SUBJUNCTIVE II

ich sähe	wir sähen	aus
du sähest	ihr sähet	
Sie sähen	Sie sähen	
er/sie/es sähe	sie sähen	

FUTURE SUBJUNCTIVE I

ich werde	wir werden	aussehen
du werdest	ihr werdet	
Sie werden	Sie werden	
er/sie/es werde	sie werden	

FUTURE SUBJUNCTIVE II

ich würde	wir würden	aussehen
du würdest	ihr würdet	
Sie würden	Sie würden	
er/sie/es würde	sie würden	

PRESENT PERFECT

ich habe	wir haben	ausgesehen
du hast	ihr habt	
Sie haben	Sie haben	
er/sie/es hat	sie haben	

PAST PERFECT

ich hatte	wir hatten	ausgesehen
du hattest	ihr hattet	
Sie hatten	Sie hatten	
er/sie/es hatte	sie hatten	

FUTURE PERFECT

ich werde	wir werden	ausgesehen haben
du wirst	ihr werdet	
Sie werden	Sie werden	
er/sie/es wird	sie werden	

PAST SUBJUNCTIVE I

ich habe	wir haben	ausgesehen
du habest	ihr habet	
Sie haben	Sie haben	
er/sie/es habe	sie haben	

PAST SUBJUNCTIVE II

ich hätte	wir hätten	ausgesehen
du hättest	ihr hättet	
Sie hätten	Sie hätten	
er/sie/es hätte	sie hätten	

FUTURE PERFECT SUBJUNCTIVE I

ich werde	wir werden	ausgesehen haben
du werdest	ihr werdet	
Sie werden	Sie werden	
er/sie/es werde	sie werden	

FUTURE PERFECT SUBJUNCTIVE II

ich würde	wir würden	ausgesehen haben
du würdest	ihr würdet	
Sie würden	Sie würden	
er/sie/es würde	sie würden	

COMMANDS sieh aus! seht aus! sehen Sie aus!

PRESENT PARTICIPLE aussehend

Usage

Das sieht ja lecker aus.	*That looks really delicious.*
Es sah so aus, als ob wir eine Lösung gefunden hätten.	*It appeared as though we'd found a solution.*
So siehst du aus.	*This is how you look.*
Unser Haus hat vor dem Umbau besser ausgesehen!	*Our house looked better before the remodeling!*
Ich will einfach gut aussehen.	*I just want to look good.*
Wie schafft sie es jünger auszusehen?	*How does she manage to look younger?*
Wie sieht es bei dir aus? (*colloquial*)	*How are things with you?*
Wie seht ihr aus?	*What do you look like?*
Der Weihnachtsmann sah wie Papa aus.	*Santa Claus looked like Papa.*
Die Wachsfigur hat so echt ausgesehen, dass ich sie fast angesprochen habe.	*The wax figure looked so real that I almost spoke to it.*
Wie so eine Welt aussähe, beschreibt er in seinem Buch.	*He describes in his book what such a world would look like.*

RELATED VERBS voraus·sehen; *see also* **sehen** (397)

strong verb **spricht aus · sprach aus · ausgesprochen**

PRESENT

ich spreche	wir sprechen	aus
du sprichst	ihr sprecht	
Sie sprechen	Sie sprechen	
er/sie/es spricht	sie sprechen	

SIMPLE PAST

ich sprach	wir sprachen	aus
du sprachst	ihr spracht	
Sie sprachen	Sie sprachen	
er/sie/es sprach	sie sprachen	

FUTURE

ich werde	wir werden	aussprechen
du wirst	ihr werdet	
Sie werden	Sie werden	
er/sie/es wird	sie werden	

PRESENT SUBJUNCTIVE I

ich spreche	wir sprechen	aus
du sprechest	ihr sprechet	
Sie sprechen	Sie sprechen	
er/sie/es spreche	sie sprechen	

PRESENT SUBJUNCTIVE II

ich spräche	wir sprächen	aus
du sprächest	ihr sprächet	
Sie sprächen	Sie sprächen	
er/sie/es spräche	sie sprächen	

FUTURE SUBJUNCTIVE I

ich werde	wir werden	aussprechen
du werdest	ihr werdet	
Sie werden	Sie werden	
er/sie/es werde	sie werden	

FUTURE SUBJUNCTIVE II

ich würde	wir würden	aussprechen
du würdest	ihr würdet	
Sie würden	Sie würden	
er/sie/es würde	sie würden	

PRESENT PERFECT

ich habe	wir haben	ausgesprochen
du hast	ihr habt	
Sie haben	Sie haben	
er/sie/es hat	sie haben	

PAST PERFECT

ich hatte	wir hatten	ausgesprochen
du hattest	ihr hattet	
Sie hatten	Sie hatten	
er/sie/es hatte	sie hatten	

FUTURE PERFECT

ich werde	wir werden	ausgesprochen haben
du wirst	ihr werdet	
Sie werden	Sie werden	
er/sie/es wird	sie werden	

PAST SUBJUNCTIVE I

ich habe	wir haben	ausgesprochen
du habest	ihr habet	
Sie haben	Sie haben	
er/sie/es habe	sie haben	

PAST SUBJUNCTIVE II

ich hätte	wir hätten	ausgesprochen
du hättest	ihr hättet	
Sie hätten	Sie hätten	
er/sie/es hätte	sie hätten	

FUTURE PERFECT SUBJUNCTIVE I

ich werde	wir werden	ausgesprochen haben
du werdest	ihr werdet	
Sie werden	Sie werden	
er/sie/es werde	sie werden	

FUTURE PERFECT SUBJUNCTIVE II

ich würde	wir würden	ausgesprochen haben
du würdest	ihr würdet	
Sie würden	Sie würden	
er/sie/es würde	sie würden	

COMMANDS sprich aus! sprecht aus! sprechen Sie aus!

PRESENT PARTICIPLE aussprechend

Usage

Dort konnten sie ihre Gedanken aussprechen.	*There they were able to articulate their thoughts.*
Viele Politiker hatten diese Ansicht ausgesprochen.	*Many politicians had stated this view.*
Somit möchten wir unser Beileid aussprechen.	*And so we would like to offer our condolences.*
Ich kann das Wort nicht richtig aussprechen.	*I can't pronounce the word correctly.*
Fremdwörter spricht man oft falsch aus.	*Foreign words are often pronounced wrong.*
Der Lehrer hat mich nicht aussprechen lassen.	*The teacher didn't let me finish speaking.*
In diesem Land werden Freiheitsstrafen von bis zu sechs Jahren ausgesprochen.	*In this country, prison sentences of up to six years may be imposed.*

sich aussprechen *to state one's position; express oneself*

Irmgard spricht sich gegen Ölbohrung in der Barentssee aus.	*Irmgard is taking a position against oil drilling in the Bering Sea.*
Die ganze Zeit durfte ich mich nicht wirklich aussprechen.	*The whole time, I was not allowed to express myself.*

RELATED VERBS *see* **sprechen** (415)

41 aus·stellen *to display, exhibit; write out, issue*

stellt aus · stellte aus · ausgestellt regular weak verb

PRESENT

ich stelle	wir stellen	aus
du stellst	ihr stellt	
Sie stellen	Sie stellen	
er/sie/es stellt	sie stellen	

PRESENT PERFECT

ich habe	wir haben	ausgestellt
du hast	ihr habt	
Sie haben	Sie haben	
er/sie/es hat	sie haben	

SIMPLE PAST

ich stellte	wir stellten	aus
du stelltest	ihr stelltet	
Sie stellten	Sie stellten	
er/sie/es stellte	sie stellten	

PAST PERFECT

ich hatte	wir hatten	ausgestellt
du hattest	ihr hattet	
Sie hatten	Sie hatten	
er/sie/es hatte	sie hatten	

FUTURE

ich werde	wir werden	ausstellen
du wirst	ihr werdet	
Sie werden	Sie werden	
er/sie/es wird	sie werden	

FUTURE PERFECT

ich werde	wir werden	ausgestellt haben
du wirst	ihr werdet	
Sie werden	Sie werden	
er/sie/es wird	sie werden	

PRESENT SUBJUNCTIVE I

ich stelle	wir stellen	aus
du stellest	ihr stellet	
Sie stellen	Sie stellen	
er/sie/es stelle	sie stellen	

PAST SUBJUNCTIVE I

ich habe	wir haben	ausgestellt
du habest	ihr habet	
Sie haben	Sie haben	
er/sie/es habe	sie haben	

PRESENT SUBJUNCTIVE II

ich stellte	wir stellten	aus
du stelltest	ihr stelltet	
Sie stellten	Sie stellten	
er/sie/es stellte	sie stellten	

PAST SUBJUNCTIVE II

ich hätte	wir hätten	ausgestellt
du hättest	ihr hättet	
Sie hätten	Sie hätten	
er/sie/es hätte	sie hätten	

FUTURE SUBJUNCTIVE I

ich werde	wir werden	ausstellen
du werdest	ihr werdet	
Sie werden	Sie werden	
er/sie/es werde	sie werden	

FUTURE PERFECT SUBJUNCTIVE I

ich werde	wir werden	ausgestellt haben
du werdest	ihr werdet	
Sie werden	Sie werden	
er/sie/es werde	sie werden	

FUTURE SUBJUNCTIVE II

ich würde	wir würden	ausstellen
du würdest	ihr würdet	
Sie würden	Sie würden	
er/sie/es würde	sie würden	

FUTURE PERFECT SUBJUNCTIVE II

ich würde	wir würden	ausgestellt haben
du würdest	ihr würdet	
Sie würden	Sie würden	
er/sie/es würde	sie würden	

COMMANDS stell(e) aus! stellt aus! stellen Sie aus!

PRESENT PARTICIPLE ausstellend

Usage

Der Künstler möchte seine Werke ausstellen.	*The artist would like to exhibit his work.*
Die folgenden Bilder wurden auf der Konferenz ausgestellt.	*The following pictures were displayed at the conference.*
In der Leibnizstraße steht die Galerie, in der ich meine Fotos ausstelle.	*The gallery where I'm exhibiting my photos is on Leibniz Street.*
Denjenigen Ausstellern, die auf der letzten Messe nicht ausstellten, wird keine Ermäßigung mehr gewährt.	*Those exhibitors who didn't exhibit at the last trade fair no longer receive a discount.*
Bereits als Kind stellte Karin ihre Skulpturen aus.	*Even as a child, Karin exhibited her sculptures.*
Wenn du einen Scheck ausstellen möchtest, trag bitte meinen Namen als Empfänger ein.	*If you would like to make out a check, please put my name down as payee.*
Manche Bescheinigungen können von der Botschaft ausgestellt werden.	*Some certificates can be issued by the embassy.*
Die Behörden stellten ihm einen provisorischen Pass aus.	*The authorities issued him a provisional passport.*

RELATED VERBS heraus·stellen; *see also* **stellen** (426)

strong verb **zieht aus · zog aus · ausgezogen**

PRESENT

ich ziehe	wir ziehen	aus
du ziehst	ihr zieht	
Sie ziehen	Sie ziehen	
er/sie/es zieht	sie ziehen	

SIMPLE PAST

ich zog	wir zogen	aus
du zogst	ihr zogt	
Sie zogen	Sie zogen	
er/sie/es zog	sie zogen	

FUTURE

ich werde	wir werden	ausziehen
du wirst	ihr werdet	
Sie werden	Sie werden	
er/sie/es wird	sie werden	

PRESENT SUBJUNCTIVE I

ich ziehe	wir ziehen	aus
du ziehest	ihr ziehet	
Sie ziehen	Sie ziehen	
er/sie/es ziehe	sie ziehen	

PRESENT SUBJUNCTIVE II

ich zöge	wir zögen	aus
du zögest	ihr zöget	
Sie zögen	Sie zögen	
er/sie/es zöge	sie zögen	

FUTURE SUBJUNCTIVE I

ich werde	wir werden	ausziehen
du werdest	ihr werdet	
Sie werden	Sie werden	
er/sie/es werde	sie werden	

FUTURE SUBJUNCTIVE II

ich würde	wir würden	ausziehen
du würdest	ihr würdet	
Sie würden	Sie würden	
er/sie/es würde	sie würden	

PRESENT PERFECT

ich habe	wir haben	ausgezogen
du hast	ihr habt	
Sie haben	Sie haben	
er/sie/es hat	sie haben	

PAST PERFECT

ich hatte	wir hatten	ausgezogen
du hattest	ihr hattet	
Sie hatten	Sie hatten	
er/sie/es hatte	sie hatten	

FUTURE PERFECT

ich werde	wir werden	ausgezogen haben
du wirst	ihr werdet	
Sie werden	Sie werden	
er/sie/es wird	sie werden	

PAST SUBJUNCTIVE I

ich habe	wir haben	ausgezogen
du habest	ihr habet	
Sie haben	Sie haben	
er/sie/es habe	sie haben	

PAST SUBJUNCTIVE II

ich hätte	wir hätten	ausgezogen
du hättest	ihr hättet	
Sie hätten	Sie hätten	
er/sie/es hätte	sie hätten	

FUTURE PERFECT SUBJUNCTIVE I

ich werde	wir werden	ausgezogen haben
du werdest	ihr werdet	
Sie werden	Sie werden	
er/sie/es werde	sie werden	

FUTURE PERFECT SUBJUNCTIVE II

ich würde	wir würden	ausgezogen haben
du würdest	ihr würdet	
Sie würden	Sie würden	
er/sie/es würde	sie würden	

COMMANDS zieh(e) aus! zieht aus! ziehen Sie aus!

PRESENT PARTICIPLE ausziehend

Usage

Ich musste mir neulich einen Zahn ausziehen lassen. — *I recently had to have a tooth pulled.*
Könnten Sie bitte dem Kind die Jacke ausziehen? — *Could you please remove the child's jacket?*

sich ausziehen *to undress, take off*

Wollte er sich wirklich ausziehen? — *Did he really want to undress?*
Zieht euch bitte die Schuhe aus. — *Please take off your shoes.*

ausziehen (with **sein**) *to move (house); set out*

Aus der Wohnung in der Grimmstraße war ich gerade ausgezogen. — *I had just moved from the apartment on Grimm Street.*
Dirk musste ausziehen, weil er die Miete nicht mehr zahlen konnte. — *Dirk had to move out because he could no longer pay the rent.*
Sie zogen aus, um das Gelobte Land zu finden. — *They set out to find the Promised Land.*

RELATED VERBS hinaus·ziehen; *see also* **ziehen** (549)

43 backen *to bake*

backt/bäckt · backte/buk · gebacken regular weak verb/strong verb

PRESENT

ich backe	wir backen
du backst/bäckst	ihr backt
Sie backen	Sie backen
er/sie/es backt/bäckt	sie backen

SIMPLE PAST

ich backte/buk	wir backten/buken
du backtest/bukst	ihr backtet/bukt
Sie backten/buken	Sie backten/buken
er/sie/es backte/buk	sie backten/buken

FUTURE

ich werde	wir werden	backen
du wirst	ihr werdet	
Sie werden	Sie werden	
er/sie/es wird	sie werden	

PRESENT SUBJUNCTIVE I

ich backe	wir backen
du backest	ihr backet
Sie backen	Sie backen
er/sie/es backe	sie backen

PRESENT SUBJUNCTIVE II

ich backte/büke	wir backten/büken
du backtest/bükest	ihr backtet/büket
Sie backten/büken	Sie backten/büken
er/sie/es backte/büke	sie backten/büken

FUTURE SUBJUNCTIVE I

ich werde	wir werden	backen
du werdest	ihr werdet	
Sie werden	Sie werden	
er/sie/es werde	sie werden	

FUTURE SUBJUNCTIVE II

ich würde	wir würden	backen
du würdest	ihr würdet	
Sie würden	Sie würden	
er/sie/es würde	sie würden	

COMMANDS back(e)! backt! backen Sie!

PRESENT PARTICIPLE backend

PRESENT PERFECT

ich habe	wir haben	gebacken
du hast	ihr habt	
Sie haben	Sie haben	
er/sie/es hat	sie haben	

PAST PERFECT

ich hatte	wir hatten	gebacken
du hattest	ihr hattet	
Sie hatten	Sie hatten	
er/sie/es hatte	sie hatten	

FUTURE PERFECT

ich werde	wir werden	gebacken haben
du wirst	ihr werdet	
Sie werden	Sie werden	
er/sie/es wird	sie werden	

PAST SUBJUNCTIVE I

ich habe	wir haben	gebacken
du habest	ihr habet	
Sie haben	Sie haben	
er/sie/es habe	sie haben	

PAST SUBJUNCTIVE II

ich hätte	wir hätten	gebacken
du hättest	ihr hättet	
Sie hätten	Sie hätten	
er/sie/es hätte	sie hätten	

FUTURE PERFECT SUBJUNCTIVE I

ich werde	wir werden	gebacken haben
du werdest	ihr werdet	
Sie werden	Sie werden	
er/sie/es werde	sie werden	

FUTURE PERFECT SUBJUNCTIVE II

ich würde	wir würden	gebacken haben
du würdest	ihr würdet	
Sie würden	Sie würden	
er/sie/es würde	sie würden	

Usage

Volker hat uns eine leckere Torte gebacken.	*Volker baked us a delicious tart.*
Samstags backt Mutti oft Brot.	*Mom often bakes bread on Saturdays.*
Die Schüler backen heute Pizza.	*The students are making pizza today.*
Ein Bäcker hätte damals andere Brotsorten gebacken.	*A baker in those days would have baked different kinds of bread.*
Die Kinder backten Plätzchen und Kuchen.	*The children baked cookies and cakes.*
Den ganzen Tag wurde gebacken und gekocht.	*There was baking and cooking all day long.*
Wir backen regionale Spezialitäten für Sie.	*We'll bake regional specialties for you.*
Was für einen Kuchen hast du ihm gebacken?	*What kind of cake did you bake for him?*
Die Brötchen, die du gebacken hast, sind alle.	*The rolls you baked are gone.*
Ich backe gern Brot aus frisch gemahlenem Mehl.	*I like to bake bread from freshly milled wheat.*
Die alte Frau buk Hänsel und Gretel einen Lebkuchen.	*The old woman baked Hänsel and Gretel a gingerbread cake.*

RELATED VERBS ab·backen, an·backen, auf·backen, aus·backen, durch·backen, überbacken, verbacken

regular weak verb **badet · badete · gebadet**

PRESENT

ich bade	wir baden
du badest	ihr badet
Sie baden	Sie baden
er/sie/es badet	sie baden

SIMPLE PAST

ich badete	wir badeten
du badetest	ihr badetet
Sie badeten	Sie badeten
er/sie/es badete	sie badeten

FUTURE

ich werde	wir werden	baden
du wirst	ihr werdet	
Sie werden	Sie werden	
er/sie/es wird	sie werden	

PRESENT SUBJUNCTIVE I

ich bade	wir baden
du badest	ihr badet
Sie baden	Sie baden
er/sie/es bade	sie baden

PRESENT SUBJUNCTIVE II

ich badete	wir badeten
du badetest	ihr badetet
Sie badeten	Sie badeten
er/sie/es badete	sie badeten

FUTURE SUBJUNCTIVE I

ich werde	wir werden	baden
du werdest	ihr werdet	
Sie werden	Sie werden	
er/sie/es werde	sie werden	

FUTURE SUBJUNCTIVE II

ich würde	wir würden	baden
du würdest	ihr würdet	
Sie würden	Sie würden	
er/sie/es würde	sie würden	

PRESENT PERFECT

ich habe	wir haben	gebadet
du hast	ihr habt	
Sie haben	Sie haben	
er/sie/es hat	sie haben	

PAST PERFECT

ich hatte	wir hatten	gebadet
du hattest	ihr hattet	
Sie hatten	Sie hatten	
er/sie/es hatte	sie hatten	

FUTURE PERFECT

ich werde	wir werden	gebadet haben
du wirst	ihr werdet	
Sie werden	Sie werden	
er/sie/es wird	sie werden	

PAST SUBJUNCTIVE I

ich habe	wir haben	gebadet
du habest	ihr habet	
Sie haben	Sie haben	
er/sie/es habe	sie haben	

PAST SUBJUNCTIVE II

ich hätte	wir hätten	gebadet
du hättest	ihr hättet	
Sie hätten	Sie hätten	
er/sie/es hätte	sie hätten	

FUTURE PERFECT SUBJUNCTIVE I

ich werde	wir werden	gebadet haben
du werdest	ihr werdet	
Sie werden	Sie werden	
er/sie/es werde	sie werden	

FUTURE PERFECT SUBJUNCTIVE II

ich würde	wir würden	gebadet haben
du würdest	ihr würdet	
Sie würden	Sie würden	
er/sie/es würde	sie würden	

COMMANDS bade! badet! baden Sie!

PRESENT PARTICIPLE badend

Usage

Er durfte mit einer offenen Wunde nicht baden.	*He was not permitted to bathe with an open wound.*
Ich habe mir die Füße erst warm dann kalt gebadet.	*I bathed my feet first in warm water, then in cold.*
Nachdem er sich gebadet hat, macht er einen Spaziergang.	*After he takes a bath, he takes a walk.*
Erwin, bade bitte den Hund!	*Erwin, please give the dog a bath!*
Die Hebamme hat das Baby gebadet.	*The midwife gave the baby a bath.*
Erst sieben Tage nach der Operation kann gebadet werden.	*There is to be no bathing until seven days after the operation.*
Die Sonne badete ihn in Licht.	*The sun bathed him in light.*
Wollt ihr baden gehen?	*Do you want to go swimming?*
Auch im Winter kann man dort baden.	*Even in the winter you can swim there.*
Wir waren in Schweiß gebadet.	*We were soaked in sweat.*
Er badete sich im Blut des Drachens.	*He wallowed in the dragon's blood.*

45 **bauen** *to build; cultivate*

baut · baute · gebaut regular weak verb

PRESENT

ich baue	wir bauen
du baust	ihr baut
Sie bauen	Sie bauen
er/sie/es baut	sie bauen

PRESENT PERFECT

ich habe	wir haben	gebaut
du hast	ihr habt	
Sie haben	Sie haben	
er/sie/es hat	sie haben	

SIMPLE PAST

ich baute	wir bauten
du bautest	ihr bautet
Sie bauten	Sie bauten
er/sie/es baute	sie bauten

PAST PERFECT

ich hatte	wir hatten	gebaut
du hattest	ihr hattet	
Sie hatten	Sie hatten	
er/sie/es hatte	sie hatten	

FUTURE

ich werde	wir werden	bauen
du wirst	ihr werdet	
Sie werden	Sie werden	
er/sie/es wird	sie werden	

FUTURE PERFECT

ich werde	wir werden	gebaut haben
du wirst	ihr werdet	
Sie werden	Sie werden	
er/sie/es wird	sie werden	

PRESENT SUBJUNCTIVE I

ich baue	wir bauen
du bauest	ihr bauet
Sie bauen	Sie bauen
er/sie/es baue	sie bauen

PAST SUBJUNCTIVE I

ich habe	wir haben	gebaut
du habest	ihr habet	
Sie haben	Sie haben	
er/sie/es habe	sie haben	

PRESENT SUBJUNCTIVE II

ich baute	wir bauten
du bautest	ihr bautet
Sie bauten	Sie bauten
er/sie/es baute	sie bauten

PAST SUBJUNCTIVE II

ich hätte	wir hätten	gebaut
du hättest	ihr hättet	
Sie hätten	Sie hätten	
er/sie/es hätte	sie hätten	

FUTURE SUBJUNCTIVE I

ich werde	wir werden	bauen
du werdest	ihr werdet	
Sie werden	Sie werden	
er/sie/es werde	sie werden	

FUTURE PERFECT SUBJUNCTIVE I

ich werde	wir werden	gebaut haben
du werdest	ihr werdet	
Sie werden	Sie werden	
er/sie/es werde	sie werden	

FUTURE SUBJUNCTIVE II

ich würde	wir würden	bauen
du würdest	ihr würdet	
Sie würden	Sie würden	
er/sie/es würde	sie würden	

FUTURE PERFECT SUBJUNCTIVE II

ich würde	wir würden	gebaut haben
du würdest	ihr würdet	
Sie würden	Sie würden	
er/sie/es würde	sie würden	

COMMANDS bau(e)! baut! bauen Sie!

PRESENT PARTICIPLE bauend

Usage

Familie Fricke möchte ein neues Haus bauen. — *The Fricke family would like to build a new house.*

Ich habe diesen Esstisch selbst gebaut. — *I built this dining room table myself.*

Der Plan, einen Sportplatz zu bauen, entstand letztes Jahr. — *Plans to construct a playing field were drawn up last year.*

Die Stadt will hier bauen, aber die Landwirte wollen es nicht. — *The city wants to build here, but the farmers don't want that.*

Die meisten Produkte wurden aus Holz gebaut. — *Most products were constructed of wood.*

Als Kind hat Ernst Modellflugzeuge gebaut. — *As a child, Ernst built model airplanes.*

Wenn du ein Haus baust, achte auf die Kleinigkeiten! — *When you build a house, pay attention to detail!*

Die Kinder bauten Wagen aus alten Kisten. — *The children built wagons from old crates.*

In diesem Tal können Weizen und Gerste gebaut werden. — *Wheat and barley can be cultivated in this valley.*

RELATED VERBS ab·bauen, an·bauen, auf·bauen, aus·bauen, bebauen, ein·bauen, erbauen, nach·bauen, über·bauen, überbauen, um·bauen, umbauen, unterbauen, verbauen, vor·bauen, wiederauf·bauen, zu·bauen, zusammen·bauen

regular weak verb **beachtet · beachtete · beachtet**

PRESENT

ich beachte	wir beachten
du beachtest	ihr beachtet
Sie beachten	Sie beachten
er/sie/es beachtet	sie beachten

SIMPLE PAST

ich beachtete	wir beachteten
du beachtetest	ihr beachtetet
Sie beachteten	Sie beachteten
er/sie/es beachtete	sie beachteten

FUTURE

ich werde	wir werden	beachten
du wirst	ihr werdet	
Sie werden	Sie werden	
er/sie/es wird	sie werden	

PRESENT SUBJUNCTIVE I

ich beachte	wir beachten
du beachtest	ihr beachtet
Sie beachten	Sie beachten
er/sie/es beachte	sie beachten

PRESENT SUBJUNCTIVE II

ich beachtete	wir beachteten
du beachtetest	ihr beachtetet
Sie beachteten	Sie beachteten
er/sie/es beachtete	sie beachteten

FUTURE SUBJUNCTIVE I

ich werde	wir werden	beachten
du werdest	ihr werdet	
Sie werden	Sie werden	
er/sie/es werde	sie werden	

FUTURE SUBJUNCTIVE II

ich würde	wir würden	beachten
du würdest	ihr würdet	
Sie würden	Sie würden	
er/sie/es würde	sie würden	

PRESENT PERFECT

ich habe	wir haben	beachtet
du hast	ihr habt	
Sie haben	Sie haben	
er/sie/es hat	sie haben	

PAST PERFECT

ich hatte	wir hatten	beachtet
du hattest	ihr hattet	
Sie hatten	Sie hatten	
er/sie/es hatte	sie hatten	

FUTURE PERFECT

ich werde	wir werden	beachtet haben
du wirst	ihr werdet	
Sie werden	Sie werden	
er/sie/es wird	sie werden	

PAST SUBJUNCTIVE I

ich habe	wir haben	beachtet
du habest	ihr habet	
Sie haben	Sie haben	
er/sie/es habe	sie haben	

PAST SUBJUNCTIVE II

ich hätte	wir hätten	beachtet
du hättest	ihr hättet	
Sie hätten	Sie hätten	
er/sie/es hätte	sie hätten	

FUTURE PERFECT SUBJUNCTIVE I

ich werde	wir werden	beachtet haben
du werdest	ihr werdet	
Sie werden	Sie werden	
er/sie/es werde	sie werden	

FUTURE PERFECT SUBJUNCTIVE II

ich würde	wir würden	beachtet haben
du würdest	ihr würdet	
Sie würden	Sie würden	
er/sie/es würde	sie würden	

COMMANDS beachte! beachtet! beachten Sie!

PRESENT PARTICIPLE beachtend

Usage

Beachten Sie bitte die Regeln und Vorschriften.	*Please obey the rules and regulations.*
Man sollte die Hinweise unbedingt beachten.	*You should follow the instructions no matter what.*
Sowohl der Arbeitnehmer als auch der Arbeitgeber müssen alle örtlichen Verordnungen beachten.	*Both employer and employee must observe all local ordinances.*
Kursteilnehmer werden gebeten, die folgenden Regeln zu beachten.	*Course participants are asked to note the following rules.*
Bitte beachten Sie, dass wir keine Garantie für die Richtigkeit der Angaben übernehmen können.	*Please note that we do not guarantee the accuracy of the information.*
Er beachtete kaum die Frau in der Ecke.	*He hardly took notice of the woman in the corner.*
Warum beachtest du mich nicht?	*Why don't you pay attention to me?*
Leider hatten sie die Sturmwarnungen nicht beachtet.	*Unfortunately, they hadn't paid attention to the storm warnings.*
Beachten Sie bitte die Lautsprecheransagen.	*Please pay attention to the public announcements.*

RELATED VERBS *see* **achten** (7)

47 # beantragen *to apply for; propose, call for*

beantragt · beantragte · beantragt regular weak verb

PRESENT		PRESENT PERFECT		
ich beantrage	wir beantragen	ich habe	wir haben	beantragt
du beantragst	ihr beantragt	du hast	ihr habt	
Sie beantragen	Sie beantragen	Sie haben	Sie haben	
er/sie/es beantragt	sie beantragen	er/sie/es hat	sie haben	

SIMPLE PAST		PAST PERFECT		
ich beantragte	wir beantragten	ich hatte	wir hatten	beantragt
du beantragtest	ihr beantragtet	du hattest	ihr hattet	
Sie beantragten	Sie beantragten	Sie hatten	Sie hatten	
er/sie/es beantragte	sie beantragten	er/sie/es hatte	sie hatten	

FUTURE			FUTURE PERFECT		
ich werde	wir werden	beantragen	ich werde	wir werden	beantragt haben
du wirst	ihr werdet		du wirst	ihr werdet	
Sie werden	Sie werden		Sie werden	Sie werden	
er/sie/es wird	sie werden		er/sie/es wird	sie werden	

PRESENT SUBJUNCTIVE I		PAST SUBJUNCTIVE I		
ich beantrage	wir beantragen	ich habe	wir haben	beantragt
du beantragest	ihr beantraget	du habest	ihr habet	
Sie beantragen	Sie beantragen	Sie haben	Sie haben	
er/sie/es beantrage	sie beantragen	er/sie/es habe	sie haben	

PRESENT SUBJUNCTIVE II		PAST SUBJUNCTIVE II		
ich beantragte	wir beantragten	ich hätte	wir hätten	beantragt
du beantragtest	ihr beantragtet	du hättest	ihr hättet	
Sie beantragten	Sie beantragten	Sie hätten	Sie hätten	
er/sie/es beantragte	sie beantragten	er/sie/es hätte	sie hätten	

FUTURE SUBJUNCTIVE I			FUTURE PERFECT SUBJUNCTIVE I		
ich werde	wir werden	beantragen	ich werde	wir werden	beantragt haben
du werdest	ihr werdet		du werdest	ihr werdet	
Sie werden	Sie werden		Sie werden	Sie werden	
er/sie/es werde	sie werden		er/sie/es werde	sie werden	

FUTURE SUBJUNCTIVE II			FUTURE PERFECT SUBJUNCTIVE II		
ich würde	wir würden	beantragen	ich würde	wir würden	beantragt haben
du würdest	ihr würdet		du würdest	ihr würdet	
Sie würden	Sie würden		Sie würden	Sie würden	
er/sie/es würde	sie würden		er/sie/es würde	sie würden	

COMMANDS beantrag(e)! beantragt! beantragen Sie!

PRESENT PARTICIPLE beantragend

Usage

Möchten Sie eine Kreditkarte beantragen?	*Would you like to apply for a credit card?*
Ich beantrage hiermit die Mitgliedschaft im Verein.	*I hereby apply for membership in the association.*
Es ist nicht erforderlich, eine neue Lizenz zu beantragen.	*It is not necessary to apply for a new license.*
Bei wem hast du das Visum beantragt?	*With whom did you apply for the visa?*
Beantragen Sie Arbeitslosengeld?	*Are you applying for unemployment?*
Der Vater durfte das Sorgerecht für den Sohn nicht beantragen.	*The father was not allowed to apply for custody of the son.*
Vor Beginn muss man bei den Behörden eine Erlaubnis beantragen.	*Before beginning, you must seek permission from the authorities.*
Die Verteidigung hat Freispruch beantragt.	*The defense moved for acquittal.*
Die Regierung beantragt, die Frist um ein Jahr zu verlängern.	*The government proposes extending the term by one year.*
Die neuen Maßnahmen wurden vom Stadtrat beantragt.	*The new measures were proposed by the city council.*

regular weak verb **bedeutet · bedeutete · bedeutet**

PRESENT

ich bedeute	wir bedeuten
du bedeutest	ihr bedeutet
Sie bedeuten	Sie bedeuten
er/sie/es bedeutet	sie bedeuten

SIMPLE PAST

ich bedeutete	wir bedeuteten
du bedeutetest	ihr bedeutetet
Sie bedeuteten	Sie bedeuteten
er/sie/es bedeutete	sie bedeuteten

FUTURE

ich werde	wir werden	bedeuten
du wirst	ihr werdet	
Sie werden	Sie werden	
er/sie/es wird	sie werden	

PRESENT SUBJUNCTIVE I

ich bedeute	wir bedeuten
du bedeutest	ihr bedeutet
Sie bedeuten	Sie bedeuten
er/sie/es bedeute	sie bedeuten

PRESENT SUBJUNCTIVE II

ich bedeutete	wir bedeuteten
du bedeutetest	ihr bedeutetet
Sie bedeuteten	Sie bedeuteten
er/sie/es bedeutete	sie bedeuteten

FUTURE SUBJUNCTIVE I

ich werde	wir werden	bedeuten
du werdest	ihr werdet	
Sie werden	Sie werden	
er/sie/es werde	sie werden	

FUTURE SUBJUNCTIVE II

ich würde	wir würden	bedeuten
du würdest	ihr würdet	
Sie würden	Sie würden	
er/sie/es würde	sie würden	

PRESENT PERFECT

ich habe	wir haben	bedeutet
du hast	ihr habt	
Sie haben	Sie haben	
er/sie/es hat	sie haben	

PAST PERFECT

ich hatte	wir hatten	bedeutet
du hattest	ihr hattet	
Sie hatten	Sie hatten	
er/sie/es hatte	sie hatten	

FUTURE PERFECT

ich werde	wir werden	bedeutet haben
du wirst	ihr werdet	
Sie werden	Sie werden	
er/sie/es wird	sie werden	

PAST SUBJUNCTIVE I

ich habe	wir haben	bedeutet
du habest	ihr habet	
Sie haben	Sie haben	
er/sie/es habe	sie haben	

PAST SUBJUNCTIVE II

ich hätte	wir hätten	bedeutet
du hättest	ihr hättet	
Sie hätten	Sie hätten	
er/sie/es hätte	sie hätten	

FUTURE PERFECT SUBJUNCTIVE I

ich werde	wir werden	bedeutet haben
du werdest	ihr werdet	
Sie werden	Sie werden	
er/sie/es werde	sie werden	

FUTURE PERFECT SUBJUNCTIVE II

ich würde	wir würden	bedeutet haben
du würdest	ihr würdet	
Sie würden	Sie würden	
er/sie/es würde	sie würden	

COMMANDS bedeute! bedeutet! bedeuten Sie!

PRESENT PARTICIPLE bedeutend

Usage

Das hat nichts zu bedeuten.	*That is of no importance.*
Was bedeutet „Management by Objectives“?	*What does “management by objectives” mean?*
„Bedeute ich dir noch etwas?“	*“Do I still mean anything to you?”*
„Ja, du bedeutest mir viel.“	*“Yes, you mean a lot to me.”*
Der Unfall bedeutet das Ende ihrer Karriere.	*The accident means the end of her career.*
Die weiße Taube bedeutet Frieden.	*The white dove signifies peace.*
Diese Entscheidung bedeutet, dass alle Gelder gekürzt werden.	*This decision means that all funds will be cut back.*
Ein positives Ergebnis bedeutet nicht unbedingt, dass die Person infiziert ist.	*A positive result doesn't necessarily mean that the person is infected.*
Was das ihm bedeutet, ist nicht klar.	*What that means to him is not clear.*
Die Invasion bedeutete den Tod der ganzen Bevölkerung.	*The invasion meant the death of the entire population.*

RELATED VERB deuten

49 **bedienen** *to serve, wait on; operate, work*

bedient · bediente · bedient regular weak verb

PRESENT

ich bediene	wir bedienen
du bedienst	ihr bedient
Sie bedienen	Sie bedienen
er/sie/es bedient	sie bedienen

PRESENT PERFECT

ich habe	wir haben	bedient
du hast	ihr habt	
Sie haben	Sie haben	
er/sie/es hat	sie haben	

SIMPLE PAST

ich bediente	wir bedienten
du bedientest	ihr bedientet
Sie bedienten	Sie bedienten
er/sie/es bediente	sie bedienten

PAST PERFECT

ich hatte	wir hatten	bedient
du hattest	ihr hattet	
Sie hatten	Sie hatten	
er/sie/es hatte	sie hatten	

FUTURE

ich werde	wir werden	bedienen
du wirst	ihr werdet	
Sie werden	Sie werden	
er/sie/es wird	sie werden	

FUTURE PERFECT

ich werde	wir werden	bedient haben
du wirst	ihr werdet	
Sie werden	Sie werden	
er/sie/es wird	sie werden	

PRESENT SUBJUNCTIVE I

ich bediene	wir bedienen
du bedienest	ihr bedienet
Sie bedienen	Sie bedienen
er/sie/es bediene	sie bedienen

PAST SUBJUNCTIVE I

ich habe	wir haben	bedient
du habest	ihr habet	
Sie haben	Sie haben	
er/sie/es habe	sie haben	

PRESENT SUBJUNCTIVE II

ich bediente	wir bedienten
du bedientest	ihr bedientet
Sie bedienten	Sie bedienten
er/sie/es bediente	sie bedienten

PAST SUBJUNCTIVE II

ich hätte	wir hätten	bedient
du hättest	ihr hättet	
Sie hätten	Sie hätten	
er/sie/es hätte	sie hätten	

FUTURE SUBJUNCTIVE I

ich werde	wir werden	bedienen
du werdest	ihr werdet	
Sie werden	Sie werden	
er/sie/es werde	sie werden	

FUTURE PERFECT SUBJUNCTIVE I

ich werde	wir werden	bedient haben
du werdest	ihr werdet	
Sie werden	Sie werden	
er/sie/es werde	sie werden	

FUTURE SUBJUNCTIVE II

ich würde	wir würden	bedienen
du würdest	ihr würdet	
Sie würden	Sie würden	
er/sie/es würde	sie würden	

FUTURE PERFECT SUBJUNCTIVE II

ich würde	wir würden	bedient haben
du würdest	ihr würdet	
Sie würden	Sie würden	
er/sie/es würde	sie würden	

COMMANDS bedien(e)! bedient! bedienen Sie!

PRESENT PARTICIPLE bedienend

Usage

Diese Firma bedient Kunden via Satellit.	*This company serves customers via satellite.*
Wir bedienen Sie von Montag bis Freitag, von 8 bis 17 Uhr.	*We're open for business Monday through Friday from 8 to 5.*
Eine nette Verkäuferin hat mich gestern bedient.	*A nice saleswoman waited on me yesterday.*
In den meisten Fast-Food-Restaurants wird nicht am Tisch bedient.	*In most fast-food restaurants, you're not served at the table.*
Ohne Frames kann das Programm nicht bedient werden.	*Without frames, the program can't be used.*
Um das Gerät zu bedienen, braucht man Münzen.	*You need coins to operate the machine.*

sich bedienen + genitive *to help oneself to; make use of*

Bedient euch!	*Help yourselves!*
Er bediente sich eines neu entwickelten Systems.	*He made use of a newly developed system.*
Warum muss er sich einer feindlichen Rhetorik bedienen?	*Why does he have to use hostile rhetoric?*

RELATED VERBS *see* **dienen** (123)

regular weak verb **bedingt · bedingte · bedingt**

PRESENT

ich bedinge	wir bedingen
du bedingst	ihr bedingt
Sie bedingen	Sie bedingen
er/sie/es bedingt	sie bedingen

SIMPLE PAST

ich bedingte	wir bedingten
du bedingtest	ihr bedingtet
Sie bedingten	Sie bedingten
er/sie/es bedingte	sie bedingten

FUTURE

ich werde	wir werden	bedingen
du wirst	ihr werdet	
Sie werden	Sie werden	
er/sie/es wird	sie werden	

PRESENT SUBJUNCTIVE I

ich bedinge	wir bedingen
du bedingest	ihr bedinget
Sie bedingen	Sie bedingen
er/sie/es bedinge	sie bedingen

PRESENT SUBJUNCTIVE II

ich bedingte	wir bedingten
du bedingtest	ihr bedingtet
Sie bedingten	Sie bedingten
er/sie/es bedingte	sie bedingten

FUTURE SUBJUNCTIVE I

ich werde	wir werden	bedingen
du werdest	ihr werdet	
Sie werden	Sie werden	
er/sie/es werde	sie werden	

FUTURE SUBJUNCTIVE II

ich würde	wir würden	bedingen
du würdest	ihr würdet	
Sie würden	Sie würden	
er/sie/es würde	sie würden	

PRESENT PERFECT

ich habe	wir haben	bedingt
du hast	ihr habt	
Sie haben	Sie haben	
er/sie/es hat	sie haben	

PAST PERFECT

ich hatte	wir hatten	bedingt
du hattest	ihr hattet	
Sie hatten	Sie hatten	
er/sie/es hatte	sie hatten	

FUTURE PERFECT

ich werde	wir werden	bedingt haben
du wirst	ihr werdet	
Sie werden	Sie werden	
er/sie/es wird	sie werden	

PAST SUBJUNCTIVE I

ich habe	wir haben	bedingt
du habest	ihr habet	
Sie haben	Sie haben	
er/sie/es habe	sie haben	

PAST SUBJUNCTIVE II

ich hätte	wir hätten	bedingt
du hättest	ihr hättet	
Sie hätten	Sie hätten	
er/sie/es hätte	sie hätten	

FUTURE PERFECT SUBJUNCTIVE I

ich werde	wir werden	bedingt haben
du werdest	ihr werdet	
Sie werden	Sie werden	
er/sie/es werde	sie werden	

FUTURE PERFECT SUBJUNCTIVE II

ich würde	wir würden	bedingt haben
du würdest	ihr würdet	
Sie würden	Sie würden	
er/sie/es würde	sie würden	

COMMANDS beding(e)! bedingt! bedingen Sie!

PRESENT PARTICIPLE bedingend

Usage

Yin und Yang bedingen sich gegenseitig. — *Yin and yang are mutually dependent.*

Das würde bedingen, dass eine rege Auseinandersetzung stattfindet. — *This would indicate that a lively discussion is taking place.*

Die Lage der Kontinente ist zum Teil durch die Kontinentaldrift bedingt. — *The location of the continents is determined in part by continental drift.*

Die neuen Vorschriften bedingen die veränderten Geschäftsstrategien. — *The new regulations determine the modified business strategies.*

Subjekt und Objekt sind wechselseitig bedingt. — *Subject and object are reciprocally determined.*

Diese Lösung würde bedingen, dass die Vorlage überarbeitet werden müsste. — *This solution would require reworking the original.*

sich bedingen *to stipulate (for oneself)* (**NOTE** The strong verb **bedingen, bedang, bedungen** is rare.)

Die Tagelöhner bedangen sich zwei Pausen am Tag. — *The day laborers stipulated two breaks per day.*

RELATED VERBS aus·bedingen, dingen

51 sich beeilen *to hurry, quicken*

beeilt sich · beeilte sich · sich beeilt regular weak verb

PRESENT

ich beeile mich	wir beeilen uns
du beeilst dich	ihr beeilt euch
Sie beeilen sich	Sie beeilen sich
er/sie/es beeilt sich	sie beeilen sich

SIMPLE PAST

ich beeilte mich	wir beeilten uns
du beeiltest dich	ihr beeiltet euch
Sie beeilten sich	Sie beeilten sich
er/sie/es beeilte sich	sie beeilten sich

FUTURE

ich werde mich	wir werden uns	beeilen
du wirst dich	ihr werdet euch	
Sie werden sich	Sie werden sich	
er/sie/es wird sich	sie werden sich	

PRESENT SUBJUNCTIVE I

ich beeile mich	wir beeilen uns
du beeilest dich	ihr beeilet euch
Sie beeilen sich	Sie beeilen sich
er/sie/es beeile sich	sie beeilen sich

PRESENT SUBJUNCTIVE II

ich beeilte mich	wir beeilten uns
du beeiltest dich	ihr beeiltet euch
Sie beeilten sich	Sie beeilten sich
er/sie/es beeilte sich	sie beeilten sich

FUTURE SUBJUNCTIVE I

ich werde mich	wir werden uns	beeilen
du werdest dich	ihr werdet euch	
Sie werden sich	Sie werden sich	
er/sie/es werde sich	sie werden sich	

FUTURE SUBJUNCTIVE II

ich würde mich	wir würden uns	beeilen
du würdest dich	ihr würdet euch	
Sie würden sich	Sie würden sich	
er/sie/es würde sich	sie würden sich	

PRESENT PERFECT

ich habe mich	wir haben uns	beeilt
du hast dich	ihr habt euch	
Sie haben sich	Sie haben sich	
er/sie/es hat sich	sie haben sich	

PAST PERFECT

ich hatte mich	wir hatten uns	beeilt
du hattest dich	ihr hattet euch	
Sie hatten sich	Sie hatten sich	
er/sie/es hatte sich	sie hatten sich	

FUTURE PERFECT

ich werde mich	wir werden uns	beeilt haben
du wirst dich	ihr werdet euch	
Sie werden sich	Sie werden sich	
er/sie/es wird sich	sie werden sich	

PAST SUBJUNCTIVE I

ich habe mich	wir haben uns	beeilt
du habest dich	ihr habet euch	
Sie haben sich	Sie haben sich	
er/sie/es habe sich	sie haben sich	

PAST SUBJUNCTIVE II

ich hätte mich	wir hätten uns	beeilt
du hättest dich	ihr hättet euch	
Sie hätten sich	Sie hätten sich	
er/sie/es hätte sich	sie hätten sich	

FUTURE PERFECT SUBJUNCTIVE I

ich werde mich	wir werden uns	beeilt haben
du werdest dich	ihr werdet euch	
Sie werden sich	Sie werden sich	
er/sie/es werde sich	sie werden sich	

FUTURE PERFECT SUBJUNCTIVE II

ich würde mich	wir würden uns	beeilt haben
du würdest dich	ihr würdet euch	
Sie würden sich	Sie würden sich	
er/sie/es würde sich	sie würden sich	

COMMANDS beeil(e) dich! beeilt euch! beeilen Sie sich!

PRESENT PARTICIPLE sich beeilend

Usage

Als es anfing zu regnen beeilten wir uns bei der Arbeit.	*When it started to rain, we hurried with our work.*
Es ist gut, dass ihr euch so beeilt habt.	*It's good that you hurried so much.*
Ich musste mich nicht beeilen, weil der Termin noch nicht festgelegt war.	*I didn't have to hurry because the deadline hadn't been set yet.*
Er müsste sich wirklich beeilen, um den Zug zu erreichen.	*He'd really have to hurry to catch the train.*
Sie werden sich beeilen müssen, denn es ist schon acht Uhr.	*You'll have to hurry, because it's already eight o'clock.*
Weil sie sich nicht beeilt hat, ist sie zu spät angekommen.	*Because she didn't hurry, she arrived too late.*
Warum haben sich die Studenten nicht beeilt?	*Why didn't the students hurry?*
Wir hätten uns nicht beeilen müssen, wenn du früher aufgestanden wärest.	*We wouldn't have had to hurry if you'd gotten up sooner.*
Norbert scheint sich beeilen zu wollen.	*Norbert appears to want to hurry.*
Könnten Sie sich bitte etwas beeilen?	*Could you please quicken the pace a bit?*

RELATED VERB eilen

regular weak verb **beeinflusst · beeinflusste · beeinflusst**

PRESENT

ich beeinflusse	wir beeinflussen
du beeinflusst	ihr beeinflusst
Sie beeinflussen	Sie beeinflussen
er/sie/es beeinflusst	sie beeinflussen

PRESENT PERFECT

ich habe	wir haben	beeinflusst
du hast	ihr habt	
Sie haben	Sie haben	
er/sie/es hat	sie haben	

SIMPLE PAST

ich beeinflusste	wir beeinflussten
du beeinflusstest	ihr beeinflusstet
Sie beeinflussten	Sie beeinflussten
er/sie/es beeinflusste	sie beeinflussten

PAST PERFECT

ich hatte	wir hatten	beeinflusst
du hattest	ihr hattet	
Sie hatten	Sie hatten	
er/sie/es hatte	sie hatten	

FUTURE

ich werde	wir werden	beeinflussen
du wirst	ihr werdet	
Sie werden	Sie werden	
er/sie/es wird	sie werden	

FUTURE PERFECT

ich werde	wir werden	beeinflusst haben
du wirst	ihr werdet	
Sie werden	Sie werden	
er/sie/es wird	sie werden	

PRESENT SUBJUNCTIVE I

ich beeinflusse	wir beeinflussen
du beeinflussest	ihr beeinflusset
Sie beeinflussen	Sie beeinflussen
er/sie/es beeinflusse	sie beeinflussen

PAST SUBJUNCTIVE I

ich habe	wir haben	beeinflusst
du habest	ihr habet	
Sie haben	Sie haben	
er/sie/es habe	sie haben	

PRESENT SUBJUNCTIVE II

ich beeinflusste	wir beeinflussten
du beeinflusstest	ihr beeinflusstet
Sie beeinflussten	Sie beeinflussten
er/sie/es beeinflusste	sie beeinflussten

PAST SUBJUNCTIVE II

ich hätte	wir hätten	beeinflusst
du hättest	ihr hättet	
Sie hätten	Sie hätten	
er/sie/es hätte	sie hätten	

FUTURE SUBJUNCTIVE I

ich werde	wir werden	beeinflussen
du werdest	ihr werdet	
Sie werden	Sie werden	
er/sie/es werde	sie werden	

FUTURE PERFECT SUBJUNCTIVE I

ich werde	wir werden	beeinflusst haben
du werdest	ihr werdet	
Sie werden	Sie werden	
er/sie/es werde	sie werden	

FUTURE SUBJUNCTIVE II

ich würde	wir würden	beeinflussen
du würdest	ihr würdet	
Sie würden	Sie würden	
er/sie/es würde	sie würden	

FUTURE PERFECT SUBJUNCTIVE II

ich würde	wir würden	beeinflusst haben
du würdest	ihr würdet	
Sie würden	Sie würden	
er/sie/es würde	sie würden	

COMMANDS beeinfluss(e)! beeinflusst! beeinflussen Sie!

PRESENT PARTICIPLE beeinflussend

Usage

Meine Eltern haben mich sehr beeinflusst.	*My parents have greatly influenced me.*
Kann der Mensch das Wetter beeinflussen?	*Can humans have an effect on the weather?*
Der Mond beeinflusst die Gezeiten.	*The moon influences the tides.*
Ihre Kultur wurde durch das Christentum stark beeinflusst.	*Their culture was strongly influenced by Christianity.*
Sein Verhalten wird dadurch positiv beeinflusst.	*This is having a positive effect on his behavior.*
Gewisse Proteine beeinflussen die Produktion von Hormonen.	*Certain proteins affect hormone production.*
Das globale Wetter wurde von El Niño beeinflusst.	*El Niño had an impact on global weather.*
Man beeinflusst andere, nur insofern sich andere beeinflussen lassen.	*One influences others only to the extent that they allow themselves to be influenced.*
Sind Sie leicht zu beeinflussen?	*Are you easy to influence?*
Die Diskussion scheint, seine Entscheidung doch beeinflusst zu haben.	*The discussion appears to have influenced his decision, after all.*
Wärest du von ihnen beeinflusst worden?	*Would you have been influenced by them?*

53 befehlen *to command, dictate, order; commend, entrust*

befiehlt · befahl · befohlen strong verb

PRESENT

ich befehle	wir befehlen
du befiehlst	ihr befehlt
Sie befehlen	Sie befehlen
er/sie/es befiehlt	sie befehlen

SIMPLE PAST

ich befahl	wir befahlen
du befahlst	ihr befahlt
Sie befahlen	Sie befahlen
er/sie/es befahl	sie befahlen

FUTURE

ich werde	wir werden	befehlen
du wirst	ihr werdet	
Sie werden	Sie werden	
er/sie/es wird	sie werden	

PRESENT SUBJUNCTIVE I

ich befehle	wir befehlen
du befehlest	ihr befehlet
Sie befehlen	Sie befehlen
er/sie/es befehle	sie befehlen

PRESENT SUBJUNCTIVE II

ich beföhle/befähle	wir beföhlen/befählen
du beföhlest/befählest	ihr beföhlet/befählet
Sie beföhlen/befählen	Sie beföhlen/befählen
er/sie/es beföhle/befähle	sie beföhlen/befählen

FUTURE SUBJUNCTIVE I

ich werde	wir werden	befehlen
du werdest	ihr werdet	
Sie werden	Sie werden	
er/sie/es werde	sie werden	

FUTURE SUBJUNCTIVE II

ich würde	wir würden	befehlen
du würdest	ihr würdet	
Sie würden	Sie würden	
er/sie/es würde	sie würden	

PRESENT PERFECT

ich habe	wir haben	befohlen
du hast	ihr habt	
Sie haben	Sie haben	
er/sie/es hat	sie haben	

PAST PERFECT

ich hatte	wir hatten	befohlen
du hattest	ihr hattet	
Sie hatten	Sie hatten	
er/sie/es hatte	sie hatten	

FUTURE PERFECT

ich werde	wir werden	befohlen haben
du wirst	ihr werdet	
Sie werden	Sie werden	
er/sie/es wird	sie werden	

PAST SUBJUNCTIVE I

ich habe	wir haben	befohlen
du habest	ihr habet	
Sie haben	Sie haben	
er/sie/es habe	sie haben	

PAST SUBJUNCTIVE II

ich hätte	wir hätten	befohlen
du hättest	ihr hättet	
Sie hätten	Sie hätten	
er/sie/es hätte	sie hätten	

FUTURE PERFECT SUBJUNCTIVE I

ich werde	wir werden	befohlen haben
du werdest	ihr werdet	
Sie werden	Sie werden	
er/sie/es werde	sie werden	

FUTURE PERFECT SUBJUNCTIVE II

ich würde	wir würden	befohlen haben
du würdest	ihr würdet	
Sie würden	Sie würden	
er/sie/es würde	sie würden	

COMMANDS befiehl! befehlt! befehlen Sie!

PRESENT PARTICIPLE befehlend

Usage

Der Offizier befahl ihm, an Bord zu kommen.	*The officer ordered him to come aboard.*
Gott hat uns befohlen, den Armen zu helfen.	*God has commanded us to help the poor.*
Die Truppen verlassen das Gebiet, so wie es das Gesetz befiehlt.	*The troops are leaving the area, as the law dictates.*
Der Prophet hat seinen Anhängern befohlen, täglich zu beten.	*The prophet has instructed his followers to pray daily.*
Wenn der König seinen Untertanen beföhle, höhere Steuern zu zahlen, könnte es zum Aufstand kommen.	*If the king were to order his subjects to pay higher taxes, there could be an uprising.*
Selbst wenn der Leutnant mir befehlen würde mitzumachen, würde ich es nicht tun.	*Even if the lieutenant ordered me to participate, I wouldn't do it.*
Eure Hoheit, ich tat, wie Ihr es befahlt.	*Your Highness, I did as ye commanded it.*
Ich befehle euch Gott.	*I commend you to God.*
Der Papst hatte dem Erzbischof ein bedingtes Legat befohlen.	*The pope had entrusted the archbishop with a contingent bequest.*

RELATED VERBS an·befehlen; *see also* **empfehlen** (142)

strong verb **befindet · befand · befunden**

PRESENT

ich befinde	wir befinden
du befindest	ihr befindet
Sie befinden	Sie befinden
er/sie/es befindet	sie befinden

SIMPLE PAST

ich befand	wir befanden
du befandst	ihr befandet
Sie befanden	Sie befanden
er/sie/es befand	sie befanden

FUTURE

ich werde	wir werden	befinden
du wirst	ihr werdet	
Sie werden	Sie werden	
er/sie/es wird	sie werden	

PRESENT SUBJUNCTIVE I

ich befinde	wir befinden
du befindest	ihr befindet
Sie befinden	Sie befinden
er/sie/es befinde	sie befinden

PRESENT SUBJUNCTIVE II

ich befände	wir befänden
du befändest	ihr befändet
Sie befänden	Sie befänden
er/sie/es befände	sie befänden

FUTURE SUBJUNCTIVE I

ich werde	wir werden	befinden
du werdest	ihr werdet	
Sie werden	Sie werden	
er/sie/es werde	sie werden	

FUTURE SUBJUNCTIVE II

ich würde	wir würden	befinden
du würdest	ihr würdet	
Sie würden	Sie würden	
er/sie/es würde	sie würden	

PRESENT PERFECT

ich habe	wir haben	befunden
du hast	ihr habt	
Sie haben	Sie haben	
er/sie/es hat	sie haben	

PAST PERFECT

ich hatte	wir hatten	befunden
du hattest	ihr hattet	
Sie hatten	Sie hatten	
er/sie/es hatte	sie hatten	

FUTURE PERFECT

ich werde	wir werden	befunden haben
du wirst	ihr werdet	
Sie werden	Sie werden	
er/sie/es wird	sie werden	

PAST SUBJUNCTIVE I

ich habe	wir haben	befunden
du habest	ihr habet	
Sie haben	Sie haben	
er/sie/es habe	sie haben	

PAST SUBJUNCTIVE II

ich hätte	wir hätten	befunden
du hättest	ihr hättet	
Sie hätten	Sie hätten	
er/sie/es hätte	sie hätten	

FUTURE PERFECT SUBJUNCTIVE I

ich werde	wir werden	befunden haben
du werdest	ihr werdet	
Sie werden	Sie werden	
er/sie/es werde	sie werden	

FUTURE PERFECT SUBJUNCTIVE II

ich würde	wir würden	befunden haben
du würdest	ihr würdet	
Sie würden	Sie würden	
er/sie/es würde	sie würden	

COMMANDS befinde! befindet! befinden Sie!

PRESENT PARTICIPLE befindend

Usage

Er wurde der Steuerhinterziehung schuldig befunden.	*He was found guilty of tax evasion.*
Das Projekt wird vom Stadtrat für gut befunden.	*The project is deemed to be a good one by the city council.*

sich befinden *to be, be located*

Unter den Teilnehmern befand sich ein Herr aus Hildesheim namens Norbert Hüppe.	*Among the participants, there was a gentleman from Hildesheim by the name of Norbert Hüppe.*
Der Sprecher behauptet, dass sich die Firma in einer schwierigen Lage befinde.	*The spokesperson maintains that the company is in a difficult position.*
Wo befindet sich der Eingang?	*Where is the entrance located?*
Ein ähnliches Werk befindet sich im Kunstmuseum Basel.	*A similar piece is located in the Basel Art Museum.*
Plötzlich habe ich mich in einer anderen Dimension befunden.	*Suddenly I found myself in another dimension.*
Heute befindet sich der Chef in bester Laune.	*The boss is in a very good mood today.*

RELATED VERBS *see* **finden** (186)

55 **befreien** *to free, liberate; release; excuse, exempt*

befreit · befreite · befreit regular weak verb

PRESENT

ich befreie	wir befreien
du befreist	ihr befreit
Sie befreien	Sie befreien
er/sie/es befreit	sie befreien

SIMPLE PAST

ich befreite	wir befreiten
du befreitest	ihr befreitet
Sie befreiten	Sie befreiten
er/sie/es befreite	sie befreiten

FUTURE

ich werde	wir werden	befreien
du wirst	ihr werdet	
Sie werden	Sie werden	
er/sie/es wird	sie werden	

PRESENT SUBJUNCTIVE I

ich befreie	wir befreien
du befreiest	ihr befreiet
Sie befreien	Sie befreien
er/sie/es befreie	sie befreien

PRESENT SUBJUNCTIVE II

ich befreite	wir befreiten
du befreitest	ihr befreitet
Sie befreiten	Sie befreiten
er/sie/es befreite	sie befreiten

FUTURE SUBJUNCTIVE I

ich werde	wir werden	befreien
du werdest	ihr werdet	
Sie werden	Sie werden	
er/sie/es werde	sie werden	

FUTURE SUBJUNCTIVE II

ich würde	wir würden	befreien
du würdest	ihr würdet	
Sie würden	Sie würden	
er/sie/es würde	sie würden	

COMMANDS befrei(e)! befreit! befreien Sie!

PRESENT PARTICIPLE befreiend

PRESENT PERFECT

ich habe	wir haben	befreit
du hast	ihr habt	
Sie haben	Sie haben	
er/sie/es hat	sie haben	

PAST PERFECT

ich hatte	wir hatten	befreit
du hattest	ihr hattet	
Sie hatten	Sie hatten	
er/sie/es hatte	sie hatten	

FUTURE PERFECT

ich werde	wir werden	befreit haben
du wirst	ihr werdet	
Sie werden	Sie werden	
er/sie/es wird	sie werden	

PAST SUBJUNCTIVE I

ich habe	wir haben	befreit
du habest	ihr habet	
Sie haben	Sie haben	
er/sie/es habe	sie haben	

PAST SUBJUNCTIVE II

ich hätte	wir hätten	befreit
du hättest	ihr hättet	
Sie hätten	Sie hätten	
er/sie/es hätte	sie hätten	

FUTURE PERFECT SUBJUNCTIVE I

ich werde	wir werden	befreit haben
du werdest	ihr werdet	
Sie werden	Sie werden	
er/sie/es werde	sie werden	

FUTURE PERFECT SUBJUNCTIVE II

ich würde	wir würden	befreit haben
du würdest	ihr würdet	
Sie würden	Sie würden	
er/sie/es würde	sie würden	

Usage

Bertram konnte das leidende Tier von der eisernen Falle nicht befreien. — *Bertram couldn't rescue the suffering animal from the iron trap.*

1945 wurde das Konzentrationslager befreit. — *In 1945 the concentration camp was liberated.*

Befreie dein inneres Selbst! — *Liberate your inner self!*

Wir mussten uns von ihm befreien. — *We had to free ourselves from him.*

Im Rehazentrum ist sie endlich von ihrer Drogensucht befreit worden. — *In the rehab center, she was finally freed from her addiction.*

Wussten Sie, dass Sie deswegen vom Dienst befreit werden können? — *Did you know that you can be relieved of duty for that?*

Viele Eigentümer werden dadurch von allen gesetzlichen Pflichten befreit. — *Many owners will be thereby released from all legal obligations.*

Alle Schüler wurden an diesem besonderen Tag von der Schule befreit. — *All pupils were excused from school on this special day.*

RELATED VERB freien

regular weak verb (dative object) **begegnet · begegnete · begegnet**

PRESENT		PRESENT PERFECT		
ich begegne	wir begegnen	ich bin	wir sind	begegnet
du begegnest	ihr begegnet	du bist	ihr seid	
Sie begegnen	Sie begegnen	Sie sind	Sie sind	
er/sie/es begegnet	sie begegnen	er/sie/es ist	sie sind	

SIMPLE PAST		PAST PERFECT		
ich begegnete	wir begegneten	ich war	wir waren	begegnet
du begegnetest	ihr begegnetet	du warst	ihr wart	
Sie begegneten	Sie begegneten	Sie waren	Sie waren	
er/sie/es begegnete	sie begegneten	er/sie/es war	sie waren	

FUTURE			FUTURE PERFECT		
ich werde	wir werden	begegnen	ich werde	wir werden	begegnet sein
du wirst	ihr werdet		du wirst	ihr werdet	
Sie werden	Sie werden		Sie werden	Sie werden	
er/sie/es wird	sie werden		er/sie/es wird	sie werden	

PRESENT SUBJUNCTIVE I		PAST SUBJUNCTIVE I		
ich begegne	wir begegnen	ich sei	wir seien	begegnet
du begegnest	ihr begegnet	du seiest	ihr seiet	
Sie begegnen	Sie begegnen	Sie seien	Sie seien	
er/sie/es begegne	sie begegnen	er/sie/es sei	sie seien	

PRESENT SUBJUNCTIVE II		PAST SUBJUNCTIVE II		
ich begegnete	wir begegneten	ich wäre	wir wären	begegnet
du begegnetest	ihr begegnetet	du wärest	ihr wäret	
Sie begegneten	Sie begegneten	Sie wären	Sie wären	
er/sie/es begegnete	sie begegneten	er/sie/es wäre	sie wären	

FUTURE SUBJUNCTIVE I			FUTURE PERFECT SUBJUNCTIVE I		
ich werde	wir werden	begegnen	ich werde	wir werden	begegnet sein
du werdest	ihr werdet		du werdest	ihr werdet	
Sie werden	Sie werden		Sie werden	Sie werden	
er/sie/es werde	sie werden		er/sie/es werde	sie werden	

FUTURE SUBJUNCTIVE II			FUTURE PERFECT SUBJUNCTIVE II		
ich würde	wir würden	begegnen	ich würde	wir würden	begegnet sein
du würdest	ihr würdet		du würdest	ihr würdet	
Sie würden	Sie würden		Sie würden	Sie würden	
er/sie/es würde	sie würden		er/sie/es würde	sie würden	

COMMANDS begegne! begegnet! begegnen Sie!

PRESENT PARTICIPLE begegnend

Usage

Wie Rotkäppchen in den dunklen Wald kam, begegnete ihm ein hungriger Wolf.	*As Little Red Riding Hood entered the dark forest, she encountered a hungry wolf.*
Im Jahr 1794 begegnete Goethe Schiller in Jena.	*In the year 1794, Goethe met Schiller in Jena.*
Im Hotel Excelsior sind wir einem jungen Mann aus Istanbul begegnet.	*In the Excelsior Hotel, we met a young man from Istanbul.*
Seine Augen begegnen dem ängstlichen Blick des verletzten Hundes.	*His eyes meet the fearful gaze of the injured dog.*
Im jedem Vorkommnis, das uns im täglichen Leben begegnet, finden wir neue geistige Kraft.	*In every occurrence that befalls us in daily life, we find new spiritual energy.*
Wer seinem Vorgesetzten grob begegnet, wird umgehend entlassen.	*Whoever treats his superior rudely will be immediately dismissed.*
Die Polizistin hat erklärt, wie derartigen Gefahren zu begegnen ist.	*The policewoman explained how to counter dangers of this sort.*

RELATED VERB wieder·begegnen

57 beginnen *to begin, start; undertake*

beginnt · begann · begonnen strong verb

PRESENT

ich beginne	wir beginnen
du beginnst	ihr beginnt
Sie beginnen	Sie beginnen
er/sie/es beginnt	sie beginnen

PRESENT PERFECT

ich habe	wir haben	begonnen
du hast	ihr habt	
Sie haben	Sie haben	
er/sie/es hat	sie haben	

SIMPLE PAST

ich begann	wir begannen
du begannst	ihr begannt
Sie begannen	Sie begannen
er/sie/es begann	sie begannen

PAST PERFECT

ich hatte	wir hatten	begonnen
du hattest	ihr hattet	
Sie hatten	Sie hatten	
er/sie/es hatte	sie hatten	

FUTURE

ich werde	wir werden	beginnen
du wirst	ihr werdet	
Sie werden	Sie werden	
er/sie/es wird	sie werden	

FUTURE PERFECT

ich werde	wir werden	begonnen haben
du wirst	ihr werdet	
Sie werden	Sie werden	
er/sie/es wird	sie werden	

PRESENT SUBJUNCTIVE I

ich beginne	wir beginnen
du beginnest	ihr beginnet
Sie beginnen	Sie beginnen
er/sie/es beginne	sie beginnen

PAST SUBJUNCTIVE I

ich habe	wir haben	begonnen
du habest	ihr habet	
Sie haben	Sie haben	
er/sie/es habe	sie haben	

PRESENT SUBJUNCTIVE II

ich begänne/begönne	wir begännen/begönnen
du begännest/begönnest	ihr begännet/begönnet
Sie begännen/begönnen	Sie begännen/begönnen
er/sie/es begänne/begönne	sie begännen/begönnen

PAST SUBJUNCTIVE II

ich hätte	wir hätten	begonnen
du hättest	ihr hättet	
Sie hätten	Sie hätten	
er/sie/es hätte	sie hätten	

FUTURE SUBJUNCTIVE I

ich werde	wir werden	beginnen
du werdest	ihr werdet	
Sie werden	Sie werden	
er/sie/es werde	sie werden	

FUTURE PERFECT SUBJUNCTIVE I

ich werde	wir werden	begonnen haben
du werdest	ihr werdet	
Sie werden	Sie werden	
er/sie/es werde	sie werden	

FUTURE SUBJUNCTIVE II

ich würde	wir würden	beginnen
du würdest	ihr würdet	
Sie würden	Sie würden	
er/sie/es würde	sie würden	

FUTURE PERFECT SUBJUNCTIVE II

ich würde	wir würden	begonnen haben
du würdest	ihr würdet	
Sie würden	Sie würden	
er/sie/es würde	sie würden	

COMMANDS beginn(e)! beginnt! beginnen Sie!

PRESENT PARTICIPLE beginnend

Usage

Wann beginnt die Vorstellung?	*When does the presentation begin?*
Der Unterricht hat nicht pünktlich begonnen, weil der Lehrer sich verspätet hatte.	*Class didn't begin on time because the instructor was delayed.*
Die Debatte über dieses Thema begann mit einer Frage an Ilse Schleiermacher.	*The debate on this topic began with a question to Ilse Schleiermacher.*
Der Arbeitstag des Präsidenten beginnt oft vor fünf Uhr frühmorgens.	*The president's workday often begins before five o'clock in the morning.*
Wann hat das neue Jahrtausend wirklich begonnen?	*When did the new millennium really begin?*
Im Juni beginnen die Rosen zu blühen.	*Roses start blooming in June.*
Meine kleine Schwester wollte gestern mit einer neuen Diät beginnen.	*My little sister wanted to start a new diet yesterday.*
Die Teilnehmer haben das Projekt im September letzten Jahres begonnen.	*The participants undertook the project in September of last year.*
Wann beginnen wir?	*When do we start?*

regular weak verb **begleitet · begleitete · begleitet**

PRESENT

ich begleite	wir begleiten
du begleitest	ihr begleitet
Sie begleiten	Sie begleiten
er/sie/es begleitet	sie begleiten

SIMPLE PAST

ich begleitete	wir begleiteten
du begleitetest	ihr begleitetet
Sie begleiteten	Sie begleiteten
er/sie/es begleitete	sie begleiteten

FUTURE

ich werde	wir werden	begleiten
du wirst	ihr werdet	
Sie werden	Sie werden	
er/sie/es wird	sie werden	

PRESENT SUBJUNCTIVE I

ich begleite	wir begleiten
du begleitest	ihr begleitet
Sie begleiten	Sie begleiten
er/sie/es begleite	sie begleiten

PRESENT SUBJUNCTIVE II

ich begleitete	wir begleiteten
du begleitetest	ihr begleitetet
Sie begleiteten	Sie begleiteten
er/sie/es begleitete	sie begleiteten

FUTURE SUBJUNCTIVE I

ich werde	wir werden	begleiten
du werdest	ihr werdet	
Sie werden	Sie werden	
er/sie/es werde	sie werden	

FUTURE SUBJUNCTIVE II

ich würde	wir würden	begleiten
du würdest	ihr würdet	
Sie würden	Sie würden	
er/sie/es würde	sie würden	

PRESENT PERFECT

ich habe	wir haben	begleitet
du hast	ihr habt	
Sie haben	Sie haben	
er/sie/es hat	sie haben	

PAST PERFECT

ich hatte	wir hatten	begleitet
du hattest	ihr hattet	
Sie hatten	Sie hatten	
er/sie/es hatte	sie hatten	

FUTURE PERFECT

ich werde	wir werden	begleitet haben
du wirst	ihr werdet	
Sie werden	Sie werden	
er/sie/es wird	sie werden	

PAST SUBJUNCTIVE I

ich habe	wir haben	begleitet
du habest	ihr habet	
Sie haben	Sie haben	
er/sie/es habe	sie haben	

PAST SUBJUNCTIVE II

ich hätte	wir hätten	begleitet
du hättest	ihr hättet	
Sie hätten	Sie hätten	
er/sie/es hätte	sie hätten	

FUTURE PERFECT SUBJUNCTIVE I

ich werde	wir werden	begleitet haben
du werdest	ihr werdet	
Sie werden	Sie werden	
er/sie/es werde	sie werden	

FUTURE PERFECT SUBJUNCTIVE II

ich würde	wir würden	begleitet haben
du würdest	ihr würdet	
Sie würden	Sie würden	
er/sie/es würde	sie würden	

COMMANDS begleite! begleitet! begleiten Sie!

PRESENT PARTICIPLE begleitend

Usage

Friedrich Gummersheimer wird die Vokalisten am Klavier begleiten. — *Friedrich Gummersheimer will accompany the vocalists on the piano.*

Die psychologischen Symptome werden oft von physischen Beschwerden begleitet. — *The psychological symptoms are often accompanied by physical complaints.*

Ein diplomierter Zoologe begleitete die begeisterten Tiergartenbesucher. — *A trained zoologist accompanied the enthusiastic zoo visitors.*

Die Exerzitiengruppe wird von Frau Umbreit begleitet. — *The exercise group is accompanied by Mrs. Umbreit.*

Wir begleiten Sie auf einer Reise durch Afrika. — *We'll accompany you on a trip through Africa.*

Die ältere Frau wurde vom Krankenhauspersonal nach Hause begleitet. — *The elderly woman was escorted home by hospital personnel.*

Dieser Verdacht hatte den Heinrich durch sein ganzes Leben begleitet. — *This suspicion had dogged Henry his whole life.*

Der Portier begleitete sie zum Zimmer. — *The doorman escorted them to the room.*

RELATED VERBS heim·begleiten, zurück·begleiten

59

begründen *to substantiate, supply evidence for; found, establish, start*

begründet · begründete · begründet regular weak verb

PRESENT

ich begründe	wir begründen
du begründest	ihr begründet
Sie begründen	Sie begründen
er/sie/es begründet	sie begründen

PRESENT PERFECT

ich habe	wir haben	begründet
du hast	ihr habt	
Sie haben	Sie haben	
er/sie/es hat	sie haben	

SIMPLE PAST

ich begründete	wir begründeten
du begründetest	ihr begründetet
Sie begründeten	Sie begründeten
er/sie/es begründete	sie begründeten

PAST PERFECT

ich hatte	wir hatten	begründet
du hattest	ihr hattet	
Sie hatten	Sie hatten	
er/sie/es hatte	sie hatten	

FUTURE

ich werde	wir werden	begründen
du wirst	ihr werdet	
Sie werden	Sie werden	
er/sie/es wird	sie werden	

FUTURE PERFECT

ich werde	wir werden	begründet haben
du wirst	ihr werdet	
Sie werden	Sie werden	
er/sie/es wird	sie werden	

PRESENT SUBJUNCTIVE I

ich begründe	wir begründen
du begründest	ihr begründet
Sie begründen	Sie begründen
er/sie/es begründe	sie begründen

PAST SUBJUNCTIVE I

ich habe	wir haben	begründet
du habest	ihr habet	
Sie haben	Sie haben	
er/sie/es habe	sie haben	

PRESENT SUBJUNCTIVE II

ich begründete	wir begründeten
du begründetest	ihr begründetet
Sie begründeten	Sie begründeten
er/sie/es begründete	sie begründeten

PAST SUBJUNCTIVE II

ich hätte	wir hätten	begründet
du hättest	ihr hättet	
Sie hätten	Sie hätten	
er/sie/es hätte	sie hätten	

FUTURE SUBJUNCTIVE I

ich werde	wir werden	begründen
du werdest	ihr werdet	
Sie werden	Sie werden	
er/sie/es werde	sie werden	

FUTURE PERFECT SUBJUNCTIVE I

ich werde	wir werden	begründet haben
du werdest	ihr werdet	
Sie werden	Sie werden	
er/sie/es werde	sie werden	

FUTURE SUBJUNCTIVE II

ich würde	wir würden	begründen
du würdest	ihr würdet	
Sie würden	Sie würden	
er/sie/es würde	sie würden	

FUTURE PERFECT SUBJUNCTIVE II

ich würde	wir würden	begründet haben
du würdest	ihr würdet	
Sie würden	Sie würden	
er/sie/es würde	sie würden	

COMMANDS begründe! begründet! begründen Sie!

PRESENT PARTICIPLE begründend

Usage

Begründen Sie Ihre Meinung. — *Support your opinion.*

Die Streikteilnehmer versuchten vergeblich, ihre Aktion zu begründen. — *The strikers tried unsuccessfully to justify their action.*

Begründet, dass diese die einzige mögliche Lösung der Gleichung auf Seite 12 ist. — *Prove that this is the only possible solution to the equation on page 12.*

Alle guten Forscher müssen ihre Vorgehensweise objektiv begründen können. — *All good researchers must be able to justify their methodology objectively.*

Die extreme Maßnahme wurde mit einem fragwürdigen Argument begründet. — *The extreme measure was justified with a dubious argument.*

Wann wollen Sie eine Familie begründen? — *When do you want to start a family?*

sich begründen *to be based/founded*

Ihre Meinung begründet sich auf ihrer Angst. — *Her opinion is based on her fear.*

RELATED VERBS *see* **gründen** (227)

to greet, hail, welcome **begrüßen** 60

regular weak verb **begrüßt · begrüßte · begrüßt**

PRESENT

ich begrüße	wir begrüßen
du begrüßt	ihr begrüßt
Sie begrüßen	Sie begrüßen
er/sie/es begrüßt	sie begrüßen

SIMPLE PAST

ich begrüßte	wir begrüßten
du begrüßtest	ihr begrüßtet
Sie begrüßten	Sie begrüßten
er/sie/es begrüßte	sie begrüßten

FUTURE

ich werde	wir werden	begrüßen
du wirst	ihr werdet	
Sie werden	Sie werden	
er/sie/es wird	sie werden	

PRESENT SUBJUNCTIVE I

ich begrüße	wir begrüßen
du begrüßest	ihr begrüßet
Sie begrüßen	Sie begrüßen
er/sie/es begrüße	sie begrüßen

PRESENT SUBJUNCTIVE II

ich begrüßte	wir begrüßten
du begrüßtest	ihr begrüßtet
Sie begrüßten	Sie begrüßten
er/sie/es begrüßte	sie begrüßten

FUTURE SUBJUNCTIVE I

ich werde	wir werden	begrüßen
du werdest	ihr werdet	
Sie werden	Sie werden	
er/sie/es werde	sie werden	

FUTURE SUBJUNCTIVE II

ich würde	wir würden	begrüßen
du würdest	ihr würdet	
Sie würden	Sie würden	
er/sie/es würde	sie würden	

PRESENT PERFECT

ich habe	wir haben	begrüßt
du hast	ihr habt	
Sie haben	Sie haben	
er/sie/es hat	sie haben	

PAST PERFECT

ich hatte	wir hatten	begrüßt
du hattest	ihr hattet	
Sie hatten	Sie hatten	
er/sie/es hatte	sie hatten	

FUTURE PERFECT

ich werde	wir werden	begrüßt haben
du wirst	ihr werdet	
Sie werden	Sie werden	
er/sie/es wird	sie werden	

PAST SUBJUNCTIVE I

ich habe	wir haben	begrüßt
du habest	ihr habet	
Sie haben	Sie haben	
er/sie/es habe	sie haben	

PAST SUBJUNCTIVE II

ich hätte	wir hätten	begrüßt
du hättest	ihr hättet	
Sie hätten	Sie hätten	
er/sie/es hätte	sie hätten	

FUTURE PERFECT SUBJUNCTIVE I

ich werde	wir werden	begrüßt haben
du werdest	ihr werdet	
Sie werden	Sie werden	
er/sie/es werde	sie werden	

FUTURE PERFECT SUBJUNCTIVE II

ich würde	wir würden	begrüßt haben
du würdest	ihr würdet	
Sie würden	Sie würden	
er/sie/es würde	sie würden	

COMMANDS begrüß(e)! begrüßt! begrüßen Sie!

PRESENT PARTICIPLE begrüßend

Usage

Er begrüßte den Morgen voller Hoffnung.	*He greeted the morning full of hope.*
Die Vereinsvorsitzende begrüßte die vielen Gäste aus den USA.	*The association president greeted the many guests from the U.S.A.*
Unsere Söhne begrüßten den ersten Schneefall mit Freude.	*Our sons greeted the first snowfall with delight.*
In diesem Land wird oft mit einem Kuss begrüßt.	*In this country one is often greeted with a kiss.*
Es freut uns, Sie bei uns begrüßen zu dürfen.	*It pleases us to be able to welcome you in our home.*
Ich darf Sie im Namen der ganzen Gemeinde recht herzlich begrüßen.	*I have the pleasure of cordially welcoming you on behalf of the entire community.*
Alle Mitglieder begrüßten eine Diskussion der Transitionsstrategie.	*All members welcomed a discussion of the transition strategy.*
Die Einwohner der Stadt begrüßen den Vorschlag der Kommission.	*The city's residents welcome the commission's suggestion.*
Wir begrüßen es sehr, dass Sie am Projekt mitarbeiten.	*We warmly welcome your cooperation on the project.*

RELATED VERBS *see* **grüßen** (228)

61 behalten *to keep, retain; remember; maintain*

behält · behielt · behalten strong verb

PRESENT

ich behalte	wir behalten
du behältst	ihr behaltet
Sie behalten	Sie behalten
er/sie/es behält	sie behalten

SIMPLE PAST

ich behielt	wir behielten
du behieltst	ihr behieltet
Sie behielten	Sie behielten
er/sie/es behielt	sie behielten

FUTURE

ich werde	wir werden	behalten
du wirst	ihr werdet	
Sie werden	Sie werden	
er/sie/es wird	sie werden	

PRESENT SUBJUNCTIVE I

ich behalte	wir behalten
du behaltest	ihr behaltet
Sie behalten	Sie behalten
er/sie/es behalte	sie behalten

PRESENT SUBJUNCTIVE II

ich behielte	wir behielten
du behieltest	ihr behieltet
Sie behielten	Sie behielten
er/sie/es behielte	sie behielten

FUTURE SUBJUNCTIVE I

ich werde	wir werden	behalten
du werdest	ihr werdet	
Sie werden	Sie werden	
er/sie/es werde	sie werden	

FUTURE SUBJUNCTIVE II

ich würde	wir würden	behalten
du würdest	ihr würdet	
Sie würden	Sie würden	
er/sie/es würde	sie würden	

PRESENT PERFECT

ich habe	wir haben	behalten
du hast	ihr habt	
Sie haben	Sie haben	
er/sie/es hat	sie haben	

PAST PERFECT

ich hatte	wir hatten	behalten
du hattest	ihr hattet	
Sie hatten	Sie hatten	
er/sie/es hatte	sie hatten	

FUTURE PERFECT

ich werde	wir werden	behalten haben
du wirst	ihr werdet	
Sie werden	Sie werden	
er/sie/es wird	sie werden	

PAST SUBJUNCTIVE I

ich habe	wir haben	behalten
du habest	ihr habet	
Sie haben	Sie haben	
er/sie/es habe	sie haben	

PAST SUBJUNCTIVE II

ich hätte	wir hätten	behalten
du hättest	ihr hättet	
Sie hätten	Sie hätten	
er/sie/es hätte	sie hätten	

FUTURE PERFECT SUBJUNCTIVE I

ich werde	wir werden	behalten haben
du werdest	ihr werdet	
Sie werden	Sie werden	
er/sie/es werde	sie werden	

FUTURE PERFECT SUBJUNCTIVE II

ich würde	wir würden	behalten haben
du würdest	ihr würdet	
Sie würden	Sie würden	
er/sie/es würde	sie würden	

COMMANDS behalte! behaltet! behalten Sie!

PRESENT PARTICIPLE behaltend

Usage

Mein Großvater hat das Bild zum Andenken behalten. *My grandfather kept the picture as a memento.*

Jahre lang behielt Ingrid die Sache für sich. *For years Ingrid kept the matter to herself.*

Während ihrer schweren Krankheit konnte meine Großmutter die Nahrung bei sich nicht behalten. *During her difficult illness, my grandmother was unable to keep food down.*

Möchtest du mich als Freund behalten? *Would you like to remain my friend?*

Ihre Mutter hatte von der Krankheit einen Gehirnschaden behalten. *Her mother had been left with brain damage from the disease.*

Der Bewerber dürfte nur einen Besitz behalten. *The applicant would be permitted to retain only one piece of property.*

Das behalte ich nicht im Kopf. *I will forget that.*

Maximilian behält Telefonnummern sehr gut. *Maximilian easily remembers telephone numbers.*

Das Metall behält seinen Glanz auch beim Regen. *This metal maintains its luster even in the rain.*

Anton hat sie immer lieb behalten. *Anton was always fond of her.*

RELATED VERBS ab·behalten, bei·behalten, ein·behalten, vor·behalten, zurück·behalten; *see also* **halten** (231) regular weak verb **behandelt · behandelte · behandelt**

PRESENT

ich behand(e)le	wir behandeln
du behandelst	ihr behandelt
Sie behandeln	Sie behandeln
er/sie/es behandelt	sie behandeln

SIMPLE PAST

ich behandelte	wir behandelten
du behandeltest	ihr behandeltet
Sie behandelten	Sie behandelten
er/sie/es behandelte	sie behandelten

FUTURE

ich werde	wir werden	behandeln
du wirst	ihr werdet	
Sie werden	Sie werden	
er/sie/es wird	sie werden	

PRESENT SUBJUNCTIVE I

ich behand(e)le	wir behandeln
du behandelst	ihr behandelt
Sie behandeln	Sie behandeln
er/sie/es behand(e)le	sie behandeln

PRESENT SUBJUNCTIVE II

ich behandelte	wir behandelten
du behandeltest	ihr behandeltet
Sie behandelten	Sie behandelten
er/sie/es behandelte	sie behandelten

FUTURE SUBJUNCTIVE I

ich werde	wir werden	behandeln
du werdest	ihr werdet	
Sie werden	Sie werden	
er/sie/es werde	sie werden	

FUTURE SUBJUNCTIVE II

ich würde	wir würden	behandeln
du würdest	ihr würdet	
Sie würden	Sie würden	
er/sie/es würde	sie würden	

PRESENT PERFECT

ich habe	wir haben	behandelt
du hast	ihr habt	
Sie haben	Sie haben	
er/sie/es hat	sie haben	

PAST PERFECT

ich hatte	wir hatten	behandelt
du hattest	ihr hattet	
Sie hatten	Sie hatten	
er/sie/es hatte	sie hatten	

FUTURE PERFECT

ich werde	wir werden	behandelt haben
du wirst	ihr werdet	
Sie werden	Sie werden	
er/sie/es wird	sie werden	

PAST SUBJUNCTIVE I

ich habe	wir haben	behandelt
du habest	ihr habet	
Sie haben	Sie haben	
er/sie/es habe	sie haben	

PAST SUBJUNCTIVE II

ich hätte	wir hätten	behandelt
du hättest	ihr hättet	
Sie hätten	Sie hätten	
er/sie/es hätte	sie hätten	

FUTURE PERFECT SUBJUNCTIVE I

ich werde	wir werden	behandelt haben
du werdest	ihr werdet	
Sie werden	Sie werden	
er/sie/es werde	sie werden	

FUTURE PERFECT SUBJUNCTIVE II

ich würde	wir würden	behandelt haben
du würdest	ihr würdet	
Sie würden	Sie würden	
er/sie/es würde	sie würden	

COMMANDS behand(e)le! behandelt! behandeln Sie!

PRESENT PARTICIPLE behandelnd

Usage

Man darf den Rechner nicht wie einen Menschen behandeln. — *You can't treat the computer like a human being.*

Behandle ihn genau so wie du von ihm behandelt werden willst. — *Treat him exactly the same way you want to be treated by him.*

Viele Geisteskrankheiten können psychotherapeutisch behandelt werden. — *Many mental disorders can be treated with psychotherapy.*

Der Arzt behandelt täglich 10 bis 12 Patienten. — *The physician treats 10 to 12 patients daily.*

Mein Papa lässt sich nicht ärztlich behandeln. — *My dad is not receiving medical attention.*

Tante Inge wird wegen Lungenentzündung behandelt. — *Aunt Inge is being treated for pneumonia.*

Der Zeitungsartikel behandelt das Thema Datenbankprogrammierung. — *The newspaper article deals with the topic of database programming.*

Die Lehrer an dieser Grundschule verstehen es, Schüler vernünftig zu behandeln. — *The teachers at this grade school understand how to handle pupils sensibly.*

RELATED VERBS nach behandeln, vor·behandeln; *see also* **handeln** (232)

63 behaupten *to maintain; retain possession of; assert, contend*

behauptet · behauptete · behauptet regular weak verb

PRESENT

ich behaupte	wir behaupten
du behauptest	ihr behauptet
Sie behaupten	Sie behaupten
er/sie/es behauptet	sie behaupten

SIMPLE PAST

ich behauptete	wir behaupteten
du behauptetest	ihr behauptetet
Sie behaupteten	Sie behaupteten
er/sie/es behauptete	sie behaupteten

FUTURE

ich werde	wir werden	behaupten
du wirst	ihr werdet	
Sie werden	Sie werden	
er/sie/es wird	sie werden	

PRESENT SUBJUNCTIVE I

ich behaupte	wir behaupten
du behauptest	ihr behauptet
Sie behaupten	Sie behaupten
er/sie/es behaupte	sie behaupten

PRESENT SUBJUNCTIVE II

ich behauptete	wir behaupteten
du behauptetest	ihr behauptetet
Sie behaupteten	Sie behaupteten
er/sie/es behauptete	sie behaupteten

FUTURE SUBJUNCTIVE I

ich werde	wir werden	behaupten
du werdest	ihr werdet	
Sie werden	Sie werden	
er/sie/es werde	sie werden	

FUTURE SUBJUNCTIVE II

ich würde	wir würden	behaupten
du würdest	ihr würdet	
Sie würden	Sie würden	
er/sie/es würde	sie würden	

PRESENT PERFECT

ich habe	wir haben	behauptet
du hast	ihr habt	
Sie haben	Sie haben	
er/sie/es hat	sie haben	

PAST PERFECT

ich hatte	wir hatten	behauptet
du hattest	ihr hattet	
Sie hatten	Sie hatten	
er/sie/es hatte	sie hatten	

FUTURE PERFECT

ich werde	wir werden	behauptet haben
du wirst	ihr werdet	
Sie werden	Sie werden	
er/sie/es wird	sie werden	

PAST SUBJUNCTIVE I

ich habe	wir haben	behauptet
du habest	ihr habet	
Sie haben	Sie haben	
er/sie/es habe	sie haben	

PAST SUBJUNCTIVE II

ich hätte	wir hätten	behauptet
du hättest	ihr hättet	
Sie hätten	Sie hätten	
er/sie/es hätte	sie hätten	

FUTURE PERFECT SUBJUNCTIVE I

ich werde	wir werden	behauptet haben
du werdest	ihr werdet	
Sie werden	Sie werden	
er/sie/es werde	sie werden	

FUTURE PERFECT SUBJUNCTIVE II

ich würde	wir würden	behauptet haben
du würdest	ihr würdet	
Sie würden	Sie würden	
er/sie/es würde	sie würden	

COMMANDS behaupte! behauptet! behaupten Sie!

PRESENT PARTICIPLE behauptend

Usage

Ich habe immer behauptet, dass er eines Tages einen großen Durchbruch macht.
I always maintained that he would achieve a major breakthrough one day.

Es ist nicht zu viel behauptet, dass das Dorf in wenigen Jahren nicht mehr existieren wird.
It's not overstating the case to say that the village won't exist in a few years.

Falls Dritte entgegenstehende Rechte behaupten, wird der Kunde die Firma schriftlich informieren.
In case third parties assert contradictory rights, the customer will inform the company in writing.

Marx behauptet, dass die Geschichte aller bisherigen Gesellschaft die Geschichte von Klassenkämpfen sei.
Marx contends that the history of all hitherto existing society is the history of class struggles.

sich behaupten *to hold one's own, stand one's ground*

Die Soldaten konnten sich trotz der neuen Waffentechnik nicht behaupten.
The soldiers were unable to stand their ground in spite of the new weapons technology.

Die Preise behaupteten sich.
The prices remained steady.

Behaupte dich!
Stand up for yourself!

regular weak verb

behindert · behinderte · behindert

PRESENT

ich behindere	wir behindern
du behinderst	ihr behindert
Sie behindern	Sie behindern
er/sie/es behindert	sie behindern

SIMPLE PAST

ich behinderte	wir behinderten
du behindertest	ihr behindertet
Sie behinderten	Sie behinderten
er/sie/es behinderte	sie behinderten

FUTURE

ich werde	wir werden	behindern
du wirst	ihr werdet	
Sie werden	Sie werden	
er/sie/es wird	sie werden	

PRESENT SUBJUNCTIVE I

ich behindere	wir behindern
du behinderst	ihr behindert
Sie behindern	Sie behindern
er/sie/es behindere	sie behindern

PRESENT SUBJUNCTIVE II

ich behinderte	wir behinderten
du behindertest	ihr behindertet
Sie behinderten	Sie behinderten
er/sie/es behinderte	sie behinderten

FUTURE SUBJUNCTIVE I

ich werde	wir werden	behindern
du werdest	ihr werdet	
Sie werden	Sie werden	
er/sie/es werde	sie werden	

FUTURE SUBJUNCTIVE II

ich würde	wir würden	behindern
du würdest	ihr würdet	
Sie würden	Sie würden	
er/sie/es würde	sie würden	

PRESENT PERFECT

ich habe	wir haben	behindert
du hast	ihr habt	
Sie haben	Sie haben	
er/sie/es hat	sie haben	

PAST PERFECT

ich hatte	wir hatten	behindert
du hattest	ihr hattet	
Sie hatten	Sie hatten	
er/sie/es hatte	sie hatten	

FUTURE PERFECT

ich werde	wir werden	behindert haben
du wirst	ihr werdet	
Sie werden	Sie werden	
er/sie/es wird	sie werden	

PAST SUBJUNCTIVE I

ich habe	wir haben	behindert
du habest	ihr habet	
Sie haben	Sie haben	
er/sie/es habe	sie haben	

PAST SUBJUNCTIVE II

ich hätte	wir hätten	behindert
du hättest	ihr hättet	
Sie hätten	Sie hätten	
er/sie/es hätte	sie hätten	

FUTURE PERFECT SUBJUNCTIVE I

ich werde	wir werden	behindert haben
du werdest	ihr werdet	
Sie werden	Sie werden	
er/sie/es werde	sie werden	

FUTURE PERFECT SUBJUNCTIVE II

ich würde	wir würden	behindert haben
du würdest	ihr würdet	
Sie würden	Sie würden	
er/sie/es würde	sie würden	

COMMANDS behindere! behindert! behindern Sie!

PRESENT PARTICIPLE behindernd

Usage

Radfahrer dürfen den Verkehrsfluss nicht behindern.	*Bicyclists are not permitted to obstruct the flow of traffic.*
Hohe Ölpreise behinderten den zu erwartenden wirtschaftlichen Aufschwung.	*High oil prices hampered the expected economic upswing.*
Der Beamte ist in der Ausführung seiner täglichen Aufgaben behindert worden.	*The official was hindered from carrying out his daily duties.*
Glatte Straßen behinderten den Verkehr.	*Slick streets hampered the traffic.*
Kalte Getränke können die Verdauung behindern.	*Cold drinks can impede digestion.*
In diesem Fall hat Rauschgiftmissbrauch die gesunde kognitive Entwicklung behindert.	*In this case, drug abuse hindered healthy cognitive development.*
Sprachbarrieren behindern die Kommunikation zwischen den Völkern.	*Language barriers impede communication between peoples.*
Ein Streit zwischen den Parteien behinderte die Verhandlungen über Gesundheitsreform.	*A conflict between the parties hobbled talks on health care reform.*

RELATED VERBS hindern; *see also* **verhindern** (490)

65 beißen *to bite, sting*

beißt · biss · gebissen strong verb

PRESENT

ich beiße	wir beißen
du beißt	ihr beißt
Sie beißen	Sie beißen
er/sie/es beißt	sie beißen

SIMPLE PAST

ich biss	wir bissen
du bissest	ihr bisst
Sie bissen	Sie bissen
er/sie/es biss	sie bissen

FUTURE

ich werde	wir werden	beißen
du wirst	ihr werdet	
Sie werden	Sie werden	
er/sie/es wird	sie werden	

PRESENT SUBJUNCTIVE I

ich beiße	wir beißen
du beißest	ihr beißet
Sie beißen	Sie beißen
er/sie/es beiße	sie beißen

PRESENT SUBJUNCTIVE II

ich bisse	wir bissen
du bissest	ihr bisset
Sie bissen	Sie bissen
er/sie/es bisse	sie bissen

FUTURE SUBJUNCTIVE I

ich werde	wir werden	beißen
du werdest	ihr werdet	
Sie werden	Sie werden	
er/sie/es werde	sie werden	

FUTURE SUBJUNCTIVE II

ich würde	wir würden	beißen
du würdest	ihr würdet	
Sie würden	Sie würden	
er/sie/es würde	sie würden	

PRESENT PERFECT

ich habe	wir haben	gebissen
du hast	ihr habt	
Sie haben	Sie haben	
er/sie/es hat	sie haben	

PAST PERFECT

ich hatte	wir hatten	gebissen
du hattest	ihr hattet	
Sie hatten	Sie hatten	
er/sie/es hatte	sie hatten	

FUTURE PERFECT

ich werde	wir werden	gebissen haben
du wirst	ihr werdet	
Sie werden	Sie werden	
er/sie/es wird	sie werden	

PAST SUBJUNCTIVE I

ich habe	wir haben	gebissen
du habest	ihr habet	
Sie haben	Sie haben	
er/sie/es habe	sie haben	

PAST SUBJUNCTIVE II

ich hätte	wir hätten	gebissen
du hättest	ihr hättet	
Sie hätten	Sie hätten	
er/sie/es hätte	sie hätten	

FUTURE PERFECT SUBJUNCTIVE I

ich werde	wir werden	gebissen haben
du werdest	ihr werdet	
Sie werden	Sie werden	
er/sie/es werde	sie werden	

FUTURE PERFECT SUBJUNCTIVE II

ich würde	wir würden	gebissen haben
du würdest	ihr würdet	
Sie würden	Sie würden	
er/sie/es würde	sie würden	

COMMANDS beiß(e)! beißt! beißen Sie!

PRESENT PARTICIPLE beißend

Usage

Als Kind biss sie ständig die Fingernägel.	*As a child she was constantly biting her fingernails.*
Beißt Ihr Hund?	*Does your dog bite?*
Mein Kater beißt mir in den Fuß, wenn er spielen will.	*My cat bites me on the foot when he wants to play.*
Im Wald kann man von einer Zecke gebissen werden.	*In the woods you can get bitten by a tick.*
So ein lieber Hund würde doch niemanden beißen!	*Such a sweet dog wouldn't bite anyone!*
Ich musste mir auf die Zunge beißen, um nicht zu lachen.	*I had to bite my tongue to keep from laughing.*
Der Nachbarshund soll ein 4-jähriges Mädchen gebissen haben.	*The neighbors' dog is said to have bitten a four-year-old girl.*
Er bellt, aber er beißt nicht.	*He barks, but he doesn't bite.*
Bist du schon mal von einem Pferd gebissen worden?	*Have you ever been bitten by a horse?*
Dieses Kindershampoo beißt nicht in den Augen.	*This shampoo for kids doesn't sting the eyes.*
Ein riesiger Stechrochen hat auf den Köder gebissen.	*A huge stingray took the bait.*

RELATED VERBS an·beißen, auf·beißen, aus·beißen, durch·beißen, durchbeißen, verbeißen, zu·beißen

strong verb **bekommt · bekam · bekommen**

PRESENT

ich bekomme	wir bekommen
du bekommst	ihr bekommt
Sie bekommen	Sie bekommen
er/sie/es bekommt	sie bekommen

SIMPLE PAST

ich bekam	wir bekamen
du bekamst	ihr bekamt
Sie bekamen	Sie bekamen
er/sie/es bekam	sie bekamen

FUTURE

ich werde	wir werden	bekommen
du wirst	ihr werdet	
Sie werden	Sie werden	
er/sie/es wird	sie werden	

PRESENT SUBJUNCTIVE I

ich bekomme	wir bekommen
du bekommest	ihr bekommet
Sie bekommen	Sie bekommen
er/sie/es bekomme	sie bekommen

PRESENT SUBJUNCTIVE II

ich bekäme	wir bekämen
du bekämest	ihr bekämet
Sie bekämen	Sie bekämen
er/sie/es bekäme	sie bekämen

FUTURE SUBJUNCTIVE I

ich werde	wir werden	bekommen
du werdest	ihr werdet	
Sie werden	Sie werden	
er/sie/es werde	sie werden	

FUTURE SUBJUNCTIVE II

ich würde	wir würden	bekommen
du würdest	ihr würdet	
Sie würden	Sie würden	
er/sie/es würde	sie würden	

PRESENT PERFECT

ich habe	wir haben	bekommen
du hast	ihr habt	
Sie haben	Sie haben	
er/sie/es hat	sie haben	

PAST PERFECT

ich hatte	wir hatten	bekommen
du hattest	ihr hattet	
Sie hatten	Sie hatten	
er/sie/es hatte	sie hatten	

FUTURE PERFECT

ich werde	wir werden	bekommen haben
du wirst	ihr werdet	
Sie werden	Sie werden	
er/sie/es wird	sie werden	

PAST SUBJUNCTIVE I

ich habe	wir haben	bekommen
du habest	ihr habet	
Sie haben	Sie haben	
er/sie/es habe	sie haben	

PAST SUBJUNCTIVE II

ich hätte	wir hätten	bekommen
du hättest	ihr hättet	
Sie hätten	Sie hätten	
er/sie/es hätte	sie hätten	

FUTURE PERFECT SUBJUNCTIVE I

ich werde	wir werden	bekommen haben
du werdest	ihr werdet	
Sie werden	Sie werden	
er/sie/es werde	sie werden	

FUTURE PERFECT SUBJUNCTIVE II

ich würde	wir würden	bekommen haben
du würdest	ihr würdet	
Sie würden	Sie würden	
er/sie/es würde	sie würden	

COMMANDS bekomm(e)! bekommt! bekommen Sie!

PRESENT PARTICIPLE bekommend

Usage

Wo bekommt man das Passwort?	*Where do you get the password?*
Bürgermeister Kister bekommt jetzt breitgefächerte Unterstützung für seine Pläne.	*Mayor Kister is now receiving widespread support for his plans.*
Somit bekommen Sie einen Eindruck von den Leistungen unserer Organisation.	*In this way you can get an idea of the services offered by our organization.*
Wie kann ich diese Leistungen bekommen?	*How can I obtain these services?*
Sabine bekam monatlich 307 Euro Kindergeld.	*Sabine received 307 euros a month for child support.*
In der letzten Wahl hätte ich bestimmt mehr Stimmen als er bekommen, wenn ich kandidiert hätte.	*In the last election I would have definitely received more votes than he if I had run for office.*
WAP-fähige Handys bekommt man jetzt überall.	*WAP-enabled cell phones are available everywhere now.*
Sie bekommt ein Kind.	*She's going to have a baby.*

RELATED VERBS ab·bekommen, an·bekommen, mit·bekommen, frei·bekommen, her·bekommen, weg·bekommen, wieder·bekommen, zurück·bekommen, zusammen·bekommen; *see also* **kommen** (265)

TOP 50 VERB ☞

bekommen *to get, receive, obtain*

bekommt · bekam · bekommen strong verb

MORE USAGE SENTENCES WITH bekommen

Bekommen Sie schon? — *Are you being helped?* (in a store)
Was bekommen Sie? — *Can I help you?/What would you like?* (in a restaurant)/ *How much is that?*

bekommen (with **sein**) *to agree with, suit*

Die zuckerbeladene Torte ist mir schlecht bekommen. — *The cake loaded with sugar didn't agree with me.*
Mein Kater ist sensibel: ein kalter Fußboden bekommt ihm nicht. — *My cat is sensitive: A cold floor doesn't suit him.*
Wohl bekomme es Ihnen! (*formal toast*) — *To your health!*

bekommen (with **zu** + infinitive) *to have the opportunity/chance to*

Wir werden es nächste Woche zu sehen bekommen. — *We will have a chance to see it next week.*
In Zürich bekommt man echte Sprüngli-Pralinen zu kaufen. — *In Zurich, you'll have an opportunity to buy genuine Sprüngli pralines.*
Kann man am Flughafen etwas zu essen bekommen? — *Can you get something to eat at the airport?*

bekommen (with past participle)

Woher hast du das Fahrrad geliehen bekommen? — *Where did you borrow the bicycle?*
Ich habe die CD geschenkt bekommen. — *I received the CD as a gift.*
Bekommt man die Sauerstoffmaske von der Krankenkasse bezahlt? — *Do you get the oxygen mask paid by your health insurance?*

IDIOMATIC EXPRESSIONS

Das Kind hat Angst bekommen. — *The child became afraid.*
Maria hat Lust bekommen, nach Tasmanien zu reisen. — *Maria has gotten the urge to travel to Tasmania.*
Der Patient bekommt wieder Hunger. — *The patient is getting hungry again.*
Ich bekomme noch zehn Euro von dir. — *You still owe me ten euros.*
Wann bekommen Sie das Projekt fertig? — *When will you get the project finished?*
Wenn ich das schon höre, bekomme ich Gänsehaut. — *When I so much as hear that, I get goose bumps.*
Studierende werden bis Freitag Bescheid bekommen, ob sie einen Wohnheimplatz erhalten haben. — *Students will be informed by Friday whether they've been assigned a dormitory room.*
Mein Sohn hat einen Ausschlag im Gesicht bekommen. — *My son's face has broken out in a rash.*
Lars hat wegen schlechter Noten von seinen Eltern Ärger bekommen. — *Lars got into trouble with his parents because of poor grades.*
Heute haben wir den ersten Schnee des Jahres bekommen. — *We got the first snow of the year today.*
Werner und Edwina bekommen jetzt kalte Füße und machen nicht mehr mit. — *Werner and Edwina are getting cold feet now and aren't going to participate any more.*
Wir haben das Problem endlich in den Griff bekommen. — *We've finally gotten a handle on the problem.*
Wie viel Urlaub bekommen Sie im Jahr? — *How much vacation do you get in a year?*
In Italien bekam Goethe die Anregung für seine *Römischen Elegien.* — *In Italy, Goethe got the inspiration for his* Roman Elegies.
Ernst bekommt einen Knoten in der Zunge, wenn er „Schokoladenladen" ausspricht. — *Ernst gets tongue-tied when he pronounces "chocolate shop."*
Die Bürger bekamen Wind vom Vorhaben des Stadtrats. — *The citizens got wind of the city council's plan.*
Der Pirat hat Land in Sicht bekommen. — *The pirate sighted land.*
Der Fußballspieler hat einen Schnupfen bekommen. — *The soccer player has caught a cold.*
Dafür muss man schriftliche Einwilligung bekommen. — *You have to get written consent for that.*
Christian hat den Mut bekommen, mit seinem Vater darüber zu reden. — *Christian has mustered up the courage to talk with his father about it.*

regular weak verb **beleidigt · beleidigte · beleidigt**

PRESENT

ich beleidige	wir beleidigen
du beleidigst	ihr beleidigt
Sie beleidigen	Sie beleidigen
er/sie/es beleidigt	sie beleidigen

SIMPLE PAST

ich beleidigte	wir beleidigten
du beleidigtest	ihr beleidigtet
Sie beleidigten	Sie beleidigten
er/sie/es beleidigte	sie beleidigten

FUTURE

ich werde	wir werden	beleidigen
du wirst	ihr werdet	
Sie werden	Sie werden	
er/sie/es wird	sie werden	

PRESENT SUBJUNCTIVE I

ich beleidige	wir beleidigen
du beleidigest	ihr beleidiget
Sie beleidigen	Sie beleidigen
er/sie/es beleidige	sie beleidigen

PRESENT SUBJUNCTIVE II

ich beleidigte	wir beleidigten
du beleidigtest	ihr beleidigtet
Sie beleidigten	Sie beleidigten
er/sie/es beleidigte	sie beleidigten

FUTURE SUBJUNCTIVE I

ich werde	wir werden	beleidigen
du werdest	ihr werdet	
Sie werden	Sie werden	
er/sie/es werde	sie werden	

FUTURE SUBJUNCTIVE II

ich würde	wir würden	beleidigen
du würdest	ihr würdet	
Sie würden	Sie würden	
er/sie/es würde	sie würden	

PRESENT PERFECT

ich habe	wir haben	beleidigt
du hast	ihr habt	
Sie haben	Sie haben	
er/sie/es hat	sie haben	

PAST PERFECT

ich hatte	wir hatten	beleidigt
du hattest	ihr hattet	
Sie hatten	Sie hatten	
er/sie/es hatte	sie hatten	

FUTURE PERFECT

ich werde	wir werden	beleidigt haben
du wirst	ihr werdet	
Sie werden	Sie werden	
er/sie/es wird	sie werden	

PAST SUBJUNCTIVE I

ich habe	wir haben	beleidigt
du habest	ihr habet	
Sie haben	Sie haben	
er/sie/es habe	sie haben	

PAST SUBJUNCTIVE II

ich hätte	wir hätten	beleidigt
du hättest	ihr hättet	
Sie hätten	Sie hätten	
er/sie/es hätte	sie hätten	

FUTURE PERFECT SUBJUNCTIVE I

ich werde	wir werden	beleidigt haben
du werdest	ihr werdet	
Sie werden	Sie werden	
er/sie/es werde	sie werden	

FUTURE PERFECT SUBJUNCTIVE II

ich würde	wir würden	beleidigt haben
du würdest	ihr würdet	
Sie würden	Sie würden	
er/sie/es würde	sie würden	

COMMANDS beleidig(e)! beleidigt! beleidigen Sie!

PRESENT PARTICIPLE beleidigend

Usage

Ich wollte dich nicht beleidigen.	*I didn't mean to offend you.*
Seine unbesonnenen Worte beleidigten Ingrid.	*His thoughtless words offended Ingrid.*
Es ist weit angenehmer, zu beleidigen und später um Verzeihung zu bitten, als beleidigt zu werden und Verzeihung zu gewähren. (NIETZSCHE)	*It is much more agreeable to offend and later ask forgiveness than to be offended and grant forgiveness.*
Wieso beleidigst du ihn dauernd?	*Why do you constantly insult him?*
Die Parteimitglieder beleidigten sich gegenseitig.	*The party members insulted one another.*
Erich hatte anonyme Emails verschickt, um die anderen Schüler zu beleidigen.	*Erich had sent anonymous e-mails to insult the other pupils.*
Sünde beleidigt Gott.	*Sin is an affront to God.*
Manni hat seine Freundin mit seiner Äußerung beleidigt.	*Manni offended his girlfriend with his comment.*
Der Gast muss ein Bisschen von allem probieren, um den Gastgeber nicht zu beleidigen.	*The guest must try a little of everything so as not to offend the host.*
Der Dialekt des Übersetzers beleidigt mein Ohr.	*The translator's dialect offends my ear.*

68 bellen *to bark, yap*

bellt · bellte · gebellt

regular weak verb

PRESENT

ich belle	wir bellen
du bellst	ihr bellt
Sie bellen	Sie bellen
er/sie/es bellt	sie bellen

SIMPLE PAST

ich bellte	wir bellten
du belltest	ihr belltet
Sie bellten	Sie bellten
er/sie/es bellte	sie bellten

FUTURE

ich werde	wir werden	bellen
du wirst	ihr werdet	
Sie werden	Sie werden	
er/sie/es wird	sie werden	

PRESENT SUBJUNCTIVE I

ich belle	wir bellen
du bellest	ihr bellet
Sie bellen	Sie bellen
er/sie/es belle	sie bellen

PRESENT SUBJUNCTIVE II

ich bellte	wir bellten
du belltest	ihr belltet
Sie bellten	Sie bellten
er/sie/es bellte	sie bellten

FUTURE SUBJUNCTIVE I

ich werde	wir werden	bellen
du werdest	ihr werdet	
Sie werden	Sie werden	
er/sie/es werde	sie werden	

FUTURE SUBJUNCTIVE II

ich würde	wir würden	bellen
du würdest	ihr würdet	
Sie würden	Sie würden	
er/sie/es würde	sie würden	

PRESENT PERFECT

ich habe	wir haben	gebellt
du hast	ihr habt	
Sie haben	Sie haben	
er/sie/es hat	sie haben	

PAST PERFECT

ich hatte	wir hatten	gebellt
du hattest	ihr hattet	
Sie hatten	Sie hatten	
er/sie/es hatte	sie hatten	

FUTURE PERFECT

ich werde	wir werden	gebellt haben
du wirst	ihr werdet	
Sie werden	Sie werden	
er/sie/es wird	sie werden	

PAST SUBJUNCTIVE I

ich habe	wir haben	gebellt
du habest	ihr habet	
Sie haben	Sie haben	
er/sie/es habe	sie haben	

PAST SUBJUNCTIVE II

ich hätte	wir hätten	gebellt
du hättest	ihr hättet	
Sie hätten	Sie hätten	
er/sie/es hätte	sie hätten	

FUTURE PERFECT SUBJUNCTIVE I

ich werde	wir werden	gebellt haben
du werdest	ihr werdet	
Sie werden	Sie werden	
er/sie/es werde	sie werden	

FUTURE PERFECT SUBJUNCTIVE II

ich würde	wir würden	gebellt haben
du würdest	ihr würdet	
Sie würden	Sie würden	
er/sie/es würde	sie würden	

COMMANDS bell(e)! bellt! bellen Sie!

PRESENT PARTICIPLE bellend

Usage

Max bellt immer, wenn er Sirenen hört. — *Max always barks when he hears sirens.*

Unser Hund hat die ganze Nacht gebellt. — *Our dog barked the whole night.*

Wie kann ich meinem Hund das unnötige Bellen abgewöhnen? — *How can I get my dog to stop barking unnecessarily?*

Der Basenji ist ein Hund, der nicht bellt sondern „jodelt". — *The basenji is a dog that doesn't bark but rather "yodels."*

Hunde, die bellen, beißen nicht. (PROVERB) — *Barking dogs don't bite.*

Der Hauptmann bellte Befehle und verlangte Gehorsam. — *The captain barked orders and demanded obedience.*

bellen (as a strong verb [*bellen, billt, boll, gebollen*]—archaic) *to bark*

Es boll ein Hund. (JEAN PAUL) — *There was a dog barking.*

Doch immer kläfft es hinterher / Und billt aus allen Kräften. (GOETHE) — *But it always yaps behind us / And barks with all its might.*

RELATED VERBS an·bellen, verbellen

regular weak verb **bemerkt · bemerkte · bemerkt**

PRESENT

ich bemerke	wir bemerken
du bemerkst	ihr bemerkt
Sie bemerken	Sie bemerken
er/sie/es bemerkt	sie bemerken

SIMPLE PAST

ich bemerkte	wir bemerkten
du bemerktest	ihr bemerktet
Sie bemerkten	Sie bemerkten
er/sie/es bemerkte	sie bemerkten

FUTURE

ich werde	wir werden	bemerken
du wirst	ihr werdet	
Sie werden	Sie werden	
er/sie/es wird	sie werden	

PRESENT SUBJUNCTIVE I

ich bemerke	wir bemerken
du bemerkest	ihr bemerket
Sie bemerken	Sie bemerken
er/sie/es bemerke	sie bemerken

PRESENT SUBJUNCTIVE II

ich bemerkte	wir bemerkten
du bemerktest	ihr bemerktet
Sie bemerkten	Sie bemerkten
er/sie/es bemerkte	sie bemerkten

FUTURE SUBJUNCTIVE I

ich werde	wir werden	bemerken
du werdest	ihr werdet	
Sie werden	Sie werden	
er/sie/es werde	sie werden	

FUTURE SUBJUNCTIVE II

ich würde	wir würden	bemerken
du würdest	ihr würdet	
Sie würden	Sie würden	
er/sie/es würde	sie würden	

PRESENT PERFECT

ich habe	wir haben	bemerkt
du hast	ihr habt	
Sie haben	Sie haben	
er/sie/es hat	sie haben	

PAST PERFECT

ich hatte	wir hatten	bemerkt
du hattest	ihr hattet	
Sie hatten	Sie hatten	
er/sie/es hatte	sie hatten	

FUTURE PERFECT

ich werde	wir werden	bemerkt haben
du wirst	ihr werdet	
Sie werden	Sie werden	
er/sie/es wird	sie werden	

PAST SUBJUNCTIVE I

ich habe	wir haben	bemerkt
du habest	ihr habet	
Sie haben	Sie haben	
er/sie/es habe	sie haben	

PAST SUBJUNCTIVE II

ich hätte	wir hätten	bemerkt
du hättest	ihr hättet	
Sie hätten	Sie hätten	
er/sie/es hätte	sie hätten	

FUTURE PERFECT SUBJUNCTIVE I

ich werde	wir werden	bemerkt haben
du werdest	ihr werdet	
Sie werden	Sie werden	
er/sie/es werde	sie werden	

FUTURE PERFECT SUBJUNCTIVE II

ich würde	wir würden	bemerkt haben
du würdest	ihr würdet	
Sie würden	Sie würden	
er/sie/es würde	sie würden	

COMMANDS bemerk(e)! bemerkt! bemerken Sie!

PRESENT PARTICIPLE bemerkend

Usage

Ich bemerke, dass die Schmerzen jetzt etwas geringer sind.	*I am noticing that there is somewhat less pain now.*
Was soll ich machen, wenn ich solche Symptome bei meinem Mann bemerke?	*What should I do if I observe such symptoms in my husband?*
Bemerken Sie, wie sich Ihr Gemütszustand auf die Dauer ändert.	*Observe how your frame of mind changes over time.*
Plötzlich bemerkte die Prinzessin den bösen Zauberer.	*Suddenly the princess caught sight of the evil magician.*
Zu spät hat er bemerkt, dass der Tank leer war.	*He realized too late that the tank was empty.*
Danach war immer noch keine Verbesserung zu bemerken.	*Afterwards, there was still no noticeable improvement.*
Wenn ich die Uhrzeit bemerkt hätte, wäre ich mitgekommen.	*If I had noticed the time, I would have come along.*
Es ist zu bemerken, dass zu viel Salz ungesund ist.	*It should be noted that too much salt is unhealthy.*
„Solche Ressourcen sind uns nützlich“, bemerkte der Projektleiter.	*“Such resources are useful to us,” remarked the project leader.*

RELATED VERBS *see* **merken** (306)

70 sich bemühen *to endeavor, make an effort; concern oneself; bother*

bemüht sich · bemühte sich · sich bemüht regular weak verb

PRESENT

ich bemühe mich	wir bemühen uns
du bemühst dich	ihr bemüht euch
Sie bemühen sich	Sie bemühen sich
er/sie/es bemüht sich	sie bemühen sich

SIMPLE PAST

ich bemühte mich	wir bemühten uns
du bemühtest dich	ihr bemühtet euch
Sie bemühten sich	Sie bemühten sich
er/sie/es bemühte sich	sie bemühten sich

FUTURE

ich werde mich	wir werden uns	bemühen
du wirst dich	ihr werdet euch	
Sie werden sich	Sie werden sich	
er/sie/es wird sich	sie werden sich	

PRESENT SUBJUNCTIVE I

ich bemühe mich	wir bemühen uns
du bemühest dich	ihr bemühet euch
Sie bemühen sich	Sie bemühen sich
er/sie/es bemühe sich	sie bemühen sich

PRESENT SUBJUNCTIVE II

ich bemühte mich	wir bemühten uns
du bemühtest dich	ihr bemühtet euch
Sie bemühten sich	Sie bemühten sich
er/sie/es bemühte sich	sie bemühten sich

FUTURE SUBJUNCTIVE I

ich werde mich	wir werden uns	bemühen
du werdest dich	ihr werdet euch	
Sie werden sich	Sie werden sich	
er/sie/es werde sich	sie werden sich	

FUTURE SUBJUNCTIVE II

ich würde mich	wir würden uns	bemühen
du würdest dich	ihr würdet euch	
Sie würden sich	Sie würden sich	
er/sie/es würde sich	sie würden sich	

PRESENT PERFECT

ich habe mich	wir haben uns	bemüht
du hast dich	ihr habt euch	
Sie haben sich	Sie haben sich	
er/sie/es hat sich	sie haben sich	

PAST PERFECT

ich hatte mich	wir hatten uns	bemüht
du hattest dich	ihr hattet euch	
Sie hatten sich	Sie hatten sich	
er/sie/es hatte sich	sie hatten sich	

FUTURE PERFECT

ich werde mich	wir werden uns	bemüht haben
du wirst dich	ihr werdet euch	
Sie werden sich	Sie werden sich	
er/sie/es wird sich	sie werden sich	

PAST SUBJUNCTIVE I

ich habe mich	wir haben uns	bemüht
du habest dich	ihr habet euch	
Sie haben sich	Sie haben sich	
er/sie/es habe sich	sie haben sich	

PAST SUBJUNCTIVE II

ich hätte mich	wir hätten uns	bemüht
du hättest dich	ihr hättet euch	
Sie hätten sich	Sie hätten sich	
er/sie/es hätte sich	sie hätten sich	

FUTURE PERFECT SUBJUNCTIVE I

ich werde mich	wir werden uns	bemüht haben
du werdest dich	ihr werdet euch	
Sie werden sich	Sie werden sich	
er/sie/es werde sich	sie werden sich	

FUTURE PERFECT SUBJUNCTIVE II

ich würde mich	wir würden uns	bemüht haben
du würdest dich	ihr würdet euch	
Sie würden sich	Sie würden sich	
er/sie/es würde sich	sie würden sich	

COMMANDS bemüh(e) dich! bemüht euch! bemühen Sie sich!

PRESENT PARTICIPLE sich bemühend

Usage

Ich bemühe mich um gute Beziehungen zu meinen Kollegen. — *I strive for good relationships with my coworkers.*

Aus diesem Grunde bemühen wir uns, eine harmonische Atmosphäre anzubieten. — *For this reason we make every effort to provide a harmonious atmosphere.*

Ich werde mich bemühen, deinen Brief bald zu beantworten. — *I will endeavor to answer your letter soon.*

Auf der Reise bemühte sich Papa um die Unterkunft, Mama um die Mahlzeiten. — *On the trip, Dad concerned himself with lodging, Mom with the meals.*

Anke wird sich wohl nicht bemühen, auf meine Email zu antworten. — *Anke will probably not bother to answer my e-mail.*

bemühen *to trouble*

Darf ich Sie nochmal bemühen? — *Might I trouble you again?*

RELATED VERB mühen

regular weak verb **benutzt · benutzte · benutzt**

PRESENT

ich benutze	wir benutzen
du benutzt	ihr benutzt
Sie benutzen	Sie benutzen
er/sie/es benutzt	sie benutzen

SIMPLE PAST

ich benutzte	wir benutzten
du benutztest	ihr benutztet
Sie benutzten	Sie benutzten
er/sie/es benutzte	sie benutzten

FUTURE

ich werde	wir werden	benutzen
du wirst	ihr werdet	
Sie werden	Sie werden	
er/sie/es wird	sie werden	

PRESENT SUBJUNCTIVE I

ich benutze	wir benutzen
du benutzest	ihr benutzet
Sie benutzen	Sie benutzen
er/sie/es benutze	sie benutzen

PRESENT SUBJUNCTIVE II

ich benutzte	wir benutzten
du benutztest	ihr benutztet
Sie benutzten	Sie benutzten
er/sie/es benutzte	sie benutzten

FUTURE SUBJUNCTIVE I

ich werde	wir werden	benutzen
du werdest	ihr werdet	
Sie werden	Sie werden	
er/sie/es werde	sie werden	

FUTURE SUBJUNCTIVE II

ich würde	wir würden	benutzen
du würdest	ihr würdet	
Sie würden	Sie würden	
er/sie/es würde	sie würden	

PRESENT PERFECT

ich habe	wir haben	benutzt
du hast	ihr habt	
Sie haben	Sie haben	
er/sie/es hat	sie haben	

PAST PERFECT

ich hatte	wir hatten	benutzt
du hattest	ihr hattet	
Sie hatten	Sie hatten	
er/sie/es hatte	sie hatten	

FUTURE PERFECT

ich werde	wir werden	benutzt haben
du wirst	ihr werdet	
Sie werden	Sie werden	
er/sie/es wird	sie werden	

PAST SUBJUNCTIVE I

ich habe	wir haben	benutzt
du habest	ihr habet	
Sie haben	Sie haben	
er/sie/es habe	sie haben	

PAST SUBJUNCTIVE II

ich hätte	wir hätten	benutzt
du hättest	ihr hättet	
Sie hätten	Sie hätten	
er/sie/es hätte	sie hätten	

FUTURE PERFECT SUBJUNCTIVE I

ich werde	wir werden	benutzt haben
du werdest	ihr werdet	
Sie werden	Sie werden	
er/sie/es werde	sie werden	

FUTURE PERFECT SUBJUNCTIVE II

ich würde	wir würden	benutzt haben
du würdest	ihr würdet	
Sie würden	Sie würden	
er/sie/es würde	sie würden	

COMMANDS benutz(e)! benutzt! benutzen Sie!

PRESENT PARTICIPLE benutzend

Usage

Das Militär benutzt innovative Kommunikationssysteme.	*The military utilizes innovative communications systems.*
Bitte benutzen Sie einen Browser, der Frames unterstützt.	*Please use a browser that supports frames.*
Unsere Systeme benutzen nur die neueste Software.	*Our systems employ only the latest software.*
Wie benutze ich dieses Programm?	*How do I use this program?*
Hast du Stoff- oder Einwegwindeln benutzt?	*Did you use cloth diapers or disposables?*
Benutze einen Kopfhörer!	*Use headphones!*
Diese Künstlerin benutzte oft Wasserfarben.	*This artist often utilized watercolors.*
Fußgänger dürfen den Radweg nicht benutzen.	*Pedestrians are not allowed to use the bike path.*
Das sind die Verfahren, die benutzt werden können.	*Those are the processes that can be employed.*
Benutzen Sie bitte einen Bleistift.	*Please use a lead pencil.*
Ausländische Studenten durften ein Wörterbuch benutzen.	*Foreign students were allowed to consult a dictionary.*

RELATED VERBS mit·benutzen; *see also* **nutzen** (316)

72 beobachten *to observe, watch; comply with*

beobachtet · beobachtete · beobachtet — regular weak verb

PRESENT

ich beobachte	wir beobachten
du beobachtest	ihr beobachtet
Sie beobachten	Sie beobachten
er/sie/es beobachtet	sie beobachten

PRESENT PERFECT

ich habe	wir haben	beobachtet
du hast	ihr habt	
Sie haben	Sie haben	
er/sie/es hat	sie haben	

SIMPLE PAST

ich beobachtete	wir beobachteten
du beobachtetest	ihr beobachtetet
Sie beobachteten	Sie beobachteten
er/sie/es beobachtete	sie beobachteten

PAST PERFECT

ich hatte	wir hatten	beobachtet
du hattest	ihr hattet	
Sie hatten	Sie hatten	
er/sie/es hatte	sie hatten	

FUTURE

ich werde	wir werden	beobachten
du wirst	ihr werdet	
Sie werden	Sie werden	
er/sie/es wird	sie werden	

FUTURE PERFECT

ich werde	wir werden	beobachtet haben
du wirst	ihr werdet	
Sie werden	Sie werden	
er/sie/es wird	sie werden	

PRESENT SUBJUNCTIVE I

ich beobachte	wir beobachten
du beobachtest	ihr beobachtet
Sie beobachten	Sie beobachten
er/sie/es beobachte	sie beobachten

PAST SUBJUNCTIVE I

ich habe	wir haben	beobachtet
du habest	ihr habet	
Sie haben	Sie haben	
er/sie/es habe	sie haben	

PRESENT SUBJUNCTIVE II

ich beobachtete	wir beobachteten
du beobachtetest	ihr beobachtetet
Sie beobachteten	Sie beobachteten
er/sie/es beobachtete	sie beobachteten

PAST SUBJUNCTIVE II

ich hätte	wir hätten	beobachtet
du hättest	ihr hättet	
Sie hätten	Sie hätten	
er/sie/es hätte	sie hätten	

FUTURE SUBJUNCTIVE I

ich werde	wir werden	beobachten
du werdest	ihr werdet	
Sie werden	Sie werden	
er/sie/es werde	sie werden	

FUTURE PERFECT SUBJUNCTIVE I

ich werde	wir werden	beobachtet haben
du werdest	ihr werdet	
Sie werden	Sie werden	
er/sie/es werde	sie werden	

FUTURE SUBJUNCTIVE II

ich würde	wir würden	beobachten
du würdest	ihr würdet	
Sie würden	Sie würden	
er/sie/es würde	sie würden	

FUTURE PERFECT SUBJUNCTIVE II

ich würde	wir würden	beobachtet haben
du würdest	ihr würdet	
Sie würden	Sie würden	
er/sie/es würde	sie würden	

COMMANDS beobachte! beobachtet! beobachten Sie!

PRESENT PARTICIPLE beobachtend

Usage

Der Planet Mars kann mit einem Amateurteleskop beobachtet werden. — *The planet Mars can be viewed using an amateur telescope.*

Der Knabe saß am Ufer und beobachtete die vorbeischwimmenden Fische. — *The boy sat on the bank and watched the fish swim by.*

Charles Darwin hat einzigartige Tierarten in den Galápagos beobachtet. — *Charles Darwin observed unique animal species in the Galapagos.*

Auf unserer Alaskareise konnten wir das Polarlicht beobachten. — *On our Alaska trip we were able to see the aurora borealis.*

Liesl beobachtet gerne Vögel. — *Liesl likes watching birds.*

Wir beobachteten, wie Anja ins Auto stieg und davon fuhr. — *We watched Anja get into the car and drive away.*

In diesem Fall muss man unbedingt alle Vorschriften genau beobachten. — *In this case, one must carefully comply with all regulations.*

RELATED VERBS *see* **achten** (7)

strong verb **berät · beriet · beraten**

PRESENT

ich berate	wir beraten
du berätst	ihr beratet
Sie beraten	Sie beraten
er/sie/es berät	sie beraten

SIMPLE PAST

ich beriet	wir berieten
du berietst	ihr berietet
Sie berieten	Sie berieten
er/sie/es beriet	sie berieten

FUTURE

ich werde	wir werden	beraten
du wirst	ihr werdet	
Sie werden	Sie werden	
er/sie/es wird	sie werden	

PRESENT SUBJUNCTIVE I

ich berate	wir beraten
du beratest	ihr beratet
Sie beraten	Sie beraten
er/sie/es berate	sie beraten

PRESENT SUBJUNCTIVE II

ich beriete	wir berieten
du berietest	ihr berietet
Sie berieten	Sie berieten
er/sie/es beriete	sie berieten

FUTURE SUBJUNCTIVE I

ich werde	wir werden	beraten
du werdest	ihr werdet	
Sie werden	Sie werden	
er/sie/es werde	sie werden	

FUTURE SUBJUNCTIVE II

ich würde	wir würden	beraten
du würdest	ihr würdet	
Sie würden	Sie würden	
er/sie/es würde	sie würden	

PRESENT PERFECT

ich habe	wir haben	beraten
du hast	ihr habt	
Sie haben	Sie haben	
er/sie/es hat	sie haben	

PAST PERFECT

ich hatte	wir hatten	beraten
du hattest	ihr hattet	
Sie hatten	Sie hatten	
er/sie/es hatte	sie hatten	

FUTURE PERFECT

ich werde	wir werden	beraten haben
du wirst	ihr werdet	
Sie werden	Sie werden	
er/sie/es wird	sie werden	

PAST SUBJUNCTIVE I

ich habe	wir haben	beraten
du habest	ihr habet	
Sie haben	Sie haben	
er/sie/es habe	sie haben	

PAST SUBJUNCTIVE II

ich hätte	wir hätten	beraten
du hättest	ihr hättet	
Sie hätten	Sie hätten	
er/sie/es hätte	sie hätten	

FUTURE PERFECT SUBJUNCTIVE I

ich werde	wir werden	beraten haben
du werdest	ihr werdet	
Sie werden	Sie werden	
er/sie/es werde	sie werden	

FUTURE PERFECT SUBJUNCTIVE II

ich würde	wir würden	beraten haben
du würdest	ihr würdet	
Sie würden	Sie würden	
er/sie/es würde	sie würden	

COMMANDS berate! beratet! beraten Sie!

PRESENT PARTICIPLE beratend

Usage

Frau Schmidtbauer berät Arbeitgeber im Arbeitsrecht.	*Mrs. Schmidtbauer advises employers in labor law.*
Die Firma hat uns im Bereich Webdesign und Internetmarketing beraten.	*The firm provided consulting services to us in Web design and Internet marketing.*
Astrologen beraten den Popstar täglich.	*Astrologists advise the pop star daily.*
Der Diätetiker beriet in Fragen zu Bulimie.	*The nutritionist gave advice on questions about bulimia.*
Ich sollte mich von einem Facharzt beraten lassen.	*I was supposed to get advice from a medical specialist.*
Lassen Sie sich von uns beraten!	*Let us advise you.*
Berätst du gerne deine Freunde?	*Do you like giving your friends advice?*
Wir beraten Sie fachkundig.	*We will provide professional advice.*
Nächste Woche wird das Kabinett über den Plan des Kanzlers beraten.	*Next week the cabinet will discuss the chancellor's plan.*
Es wurde berichtet, dass das Parlament über den Haushalt berate.	*It was reported that the parliament is conferring on the budget.*

RELATED VERBS vor·beraten; *see also* **raten** (329)

74 bereiten *to make ready, prepare; give, bring*

bereitet · bereitete · bereitet regular weak verb

PRESENT

ich bereite	wir bereiten
du bereitest	ihr bereitet
Sie bereiten	Sie bereiten
er/sie/es bereitet	sie bereiten

SIMPLE PAST

ich bereitete	wir bereiteten
du bereitetest	ihr bereitetet
Sie bereiteten	Sie bereiteten
er/sie/es bereitete	sie bereiteten

FUTURE

ich werde	wir werden	bereiten
du wirst	ihr werdet	
Sie werden	Sie werden	
er/sie/es wird	sie werden	

PRESENT SUBJUNCTIVE I

ich bereite	wir bereiten
du bereitest	ihr bereitet
Sie bereiten	Sie bereiten
er/sie/es bereite	sie bereiten

PRESENT SUBJUNCTIVE II

ich bereitete	wir bereiteten
du bereitetest	ihr bereitetet
Sie bereiteten	Sie bereiteten
er/sie/es bereitete	sie bereiteten

FUTURE SUBJUNCTIVE I

ich werde	wir werden	bereiten
du werdest	ihr werdet	
Sie werden	Sie werden	
er/sie/es werde	sie werden	

FUTURE SUBJUNCTIVE II

ich würde	wir würden	bereiten
du würdest	ihr würdet	
Sie würden	Sie würden	
er/sie/es würde	sie würden	

PRESENT PERFECT

ich habe	wir haben	bereitet
du hast	ihr habt	
Sie haben	Sie haben	
er/sie/es hat	sie haben	

PAST PERFECT

ich hatte	wir hatten	bereitet
du hattest	ihr hattet	
Sie hatten	Sie hatten	
er/sie/es hatte	sie hatten	

FUTURE PERFECT

ich werde	wir werden	bereitet haben
du wirst	ihr werdet	
Sie werden	Sie werden	
er/sie/es wird	sie werden	

PAST SUBJUNCTIVE I

ich habe	wir haben	bereitet
du habest	ihr habet	
Sie haben	Sie haben	
er/sie/es habe	sie haben	

PAST SUBJUNCTIVE II

ich hätte	wir hätten	bereitet
du hättest	ihr hättet	
Sie hätten	Sie hätten	
er/sie/es hätte	sie hätten	

FUTURE PERFECT SUBJUNCTIVE I

ich werde	wir werden	bereitet haben
du werdest	ihr werdet	
Sie werden	Sie werden	
er/sie/es werde	sie werden	

FUTURE PERFECT SUBJUNCTIVE II

ich würde	wir würden	bereitet haben
du würdest	ihr würdet	
Sie würden	Sie würden	
er/sie/es würde	sie würden	

COMMANDS bereite! bereitet! bereiten Sie!

PRESENT PARTICIPLE bereitend

Usage

Der erste menschliche Gedanke bereitet, ... mit anderen dialogieren zu können. (Johann Herder)
The first human thought prepares one for communication with others.

Ich bin früher aufgestanden, um uns ein kleines Frühstück zu bereiten.
I got up earlier to fix us a small breakfast.

Und wenn ich hingehe, euch die Stätte zu bereiten, so will ich wiederkommen und euch zu mir nehmen. (Johannes 14,3)
And if I go and prepare a place for you, I will come again and receive you unto myself. (John 14:3)

Die jetzige Krise bereitet den Boden für neue Aufstände.
The current crisis is preparing the way for new uprisings.

Ihr Besuch hat mir so eine Freude bereitet!
Her visit brought me such joy!

Das Computersystem bereitet uns eine Menge Probleme.
The computer system is causing us a lot of problems.

Zu viel Fernsehen bereitet Erziehern große Sorgen.
Too much television causes educators great concern.

Sein Dilemma bereitete ihm Kopfzerbrechen.
His dilemma was puzzling to him.

Der Plan bereitet nun unerwartete Schwierigkeiten.
The plan is now posing unexpected difficulties.

RELATED VERBS auf·bereiten, nach·bereiten, zu·bereiten; *see also* **vor·bereiten** (508)

strong verb **birgt · barg · geborgen**

PRESENT

ich berge	wir bergen
du birgst	ihr bergt
Sie bergen	Sie bergen
er/sie/es birgt	sie bergen

SIMPLE PAST

ich barg	wir bargen
du bargst	ihr bargt
Sie bargen	Sie bargen
er/sie/es barg	sie bargen

FUTURE

ich werde	wir werden	bergen
du wirst	ihr werdet	
Sie werden	Sie werden	
er/sie/es wird	sie werden	

PRESENT SUBJUNCTIVE I

ich berge	wir bergen
du bergest	ihr berget
Sie bergen	Sie bergen
er/sie/es berge	sie bergen

PRESENT SUBJUNCTIVE II

ich bärge	wir bärgen
du bärgest	ihr bärget
Sie bärgen	Sie bärgen
er/sie/es bärge	sie bärgen

FUTURE SUBJUNCTIVE I

ich werde	wir werden	bergen
du werdest	ihr werdet	
Sie werden	Sie werden	
er/sie/es werde	sie werden	

FUTURE SUBJUNCTIVE II

ich würde	wir würden	bergen
du würdest	ihr würdet	
Sie würden	Sie würden	
er/sie/es würde	sie würden	

PRESENT PERFECT

ich habe	wir haben	geborgen
du hast	ihr habt	
Sie haben	Sie haben	
er/sie/es hat	sie haben	

PAST PERFECT

ich hatte	wir hatten	geborgen
du hattest	ihr hattet	
Sie hatten	Sie hatten	
er/sie/es hatte	sie hatten	

FUTURE PERFECT

ich werde	wir werden	geborgen haben
du wirst	ihr werdet	
Sie werden	Sie werden	
er/sie/es wird	sie werden	

PAST SUBJUNCTIVE I

ich habe	wir haben	geborgen
du habest	ihr habet	
Sie haben	Sie haben	
er/sie/es habe	sie haben	

PAST SUBJUNCTIVE II

ich hätte	wir hätten	geborgen
du hättest	ihr hättet	
Sie hätten	Sie hätten	
er/sie/es hätte	sie hätten	

FUTURE PERFECT SUBJUNCTIVE I

ich werde	wir werden	geborgen haben
du werdest	ihr werdet	
Sie werden	Sie werden	
er/sie/es werde	sie werden	

FUTURE PERFECT SUBJUNCTIVE II

ich würde	wir würden	geborgen haben
du würdest	ihr würdet	
Sie würden	Sie würden	
er/sie/es würde	sie würden	

COMMANDS birg! bergt! bergen Sie!

PRESENT PARTICIPLE bergend

Usage

Mehr als siebentausend Verletzte wurden am darauffolgenden Tag geborgen. — *More than 7,000 people with injuries were rescued on the following day.*

Die Küstenwache konnte die Tiefseetaucher ins Boot bergen. — *The coast guard was able to bring the deep sea divers to safety in the boat.*

Die Archäologen bergen Funde außerhalb der Stadt. — *The archeologists are recovering finds outside the city.*

Keine Überlebenden wurden aus den Trümmern geborgen. — *No survivors were rescued from the wreckage.*

Dieses Tal birgt viele Sehenswürdigkeiten und historische Denkmäler. — *This valley contains many sights and historic monuments.*

Solche Maßnahmen könnten neue Sicherheitsrisiken bergen. — *Such measures could involve new security risks.*

Mein Sohn, was birgst du so bang dein Gesicht? (Goethe) — *My son, why do you hide your face in such fear?*

RELATED VERB verbergen

76 berichten *to report; advise, inform*

berichtet · berichtete · berichtet regular weak verb

PRESENT

ich berichte	wir berichten
du berichtest	ihr berichtet
Sie berichten	Sie berichten
er/sie/es berichtet	sie berichten

PRESENT PERFECT

ich habe	wir haben	berichtet
du hast	ihr habt	
Sie haben	Sie haben	
er/sie/es hat	sie haben	

SIMPLE PAST

ich berichtete	wir berichteten
du berichtetest	ihr berichtetet
Sie berichteten	Sie berichteten
er/sie/es berichtete	sie berichteten

PAST PERFECT

ich hatte	wir hatten	berichtet
du hattest	ihr hattet	
Sie hatten	Sie hatten	
er/sie/es hatte	sie hatten	

FUTURE

ich werde	wir werden	berichten
du wirst	ihr werdet	
Sie werden	Sie werden	
er/sie/es wird	sie werden	

FUTURE PERFECT

ich werde	wir werden	berichtet haben
du wirst	ihr werdet	
Sie werden	Sie werden	
er/sie/es wird	sie werden	

PRESENT SUBJUNCTIVE I

ich berichte	wir berichten
du berichtest	ihr berichtet
Sie berichten	Sie berichten
er/sie/es berichte	sie berichten

PAST SUBJUNCTIVE I

ich habe	wir haben	berichtet
du habest	ihr habet	
Sie haben	Sie haben	
er/sie/es habe	sie haben	

PRESENT SUBJUNCTIVE II

ich berichtete	wir berichteten
du berichtetest	ihr berichtetet
Sie berichteten	Sie berichteten
er/sie/es berichtete	sie berichteten

PAST SUBJUNCTIVE II

ich hätte	wir hätten	berichtet
du hättest	ihr hättet	
Sie hätten	Sie hätten	
er/sie/es hätte	sie hätten	

FUTURE SUBJUNCTIVE I

ich werde	wir werden	berichten
du werdest	ihr werdet	
Sie werden	Sie werden	
er/sie/es werde	sie werden	

FUTURE PERFECT SUBJUNCTIVE I

ich werde	wir werden	berichtet haben
du werdest	ihr werdet	
Sie werden	Sie werden	
er/sie/es werde	sie werden	

FUTURE SUBJUNCTIVE II

ich würde	wir würden	berichten
du würdest	ihr würdet	
Sie würden	Sie würden	
er/sie/es würde	sie würden	

FUTURE PERFECT SUBJUNCTIVE II

ich würde	wir würden	berichtet haben
du würdest	ihr würdet	
Sie würden	Sie würden	
er/sie/es würde	sie würden	

COMMANDS berichte! berichtet! berichten Sie!

PRESENT PARTICIPLE berichtend

Usage

Die Polizei berichtet von einem weiteren Mord. — *The police are reporting another murder.*

Augenzeugen berichteten über die Ereignisse des Tages. — *Witnesses reported on the events of the day.*

Die Anthropologen und Biologen haben aus erster Hand über ihre Erlebnisse am Amazonas berichtet. — *The anthropologists and biologists gave a firsthand account of their experiences on the Amazon.*

Die Wissenschaftler in Kiel berichten über globale Klimaänderungen. — *The scientists in Kiel are reporting on global climate changes.*

Amerikanische Zeitungen berichten sehr selten über Geschehnisse in Deutschland. — *American newspapers very seldom report on events in Germany.*

Die Journalistin berichtet aus Moskau. — *The journalist is reporting from Moscow.*

Wir haben nichts Neues zu berichten. — *We have nothing new to report.*

Es wird berichtet, dass der Inhaber ermordet worden sei. — *It is reported that the owner has been murdered.*

Die Ortszeitung berichtet über Steuerhinterziehung. — *The local paper is reporting on tax evasion.*

Neulich wurde über Rauschgiftmissbrauch berichtet. — *Recently there was a report on drug abuse.*

RELATED VERBS richten; *see also* **ein·richten** (135), **unterrichten** (470)

strong verb **birst · barst · geborsten**

PRESENT

ich berste	wir bersten
du birst	ihr berstet
Sie bersten	Sie bersten
er/sie/es birst	sie bersten

SIMPLE PAST

ich barst	wir barsten
du barstest	ihr barstet
Sie barsten	Sie barsten
er/sie/es barst	sie barsten

FUTURE

ich werde	wir werden	bersten
du wirst	ihr werdet	
Sie werden	Sie werden	
er/sie/es wird	sie werden	

PRESENT SUBJUNCTIVE I

ich berste	wir bersten
du berstest	ihr berstet
Sie bersten	Sie bersten
er/sie/es berste	sie bersten

PRESENT SUBJUNCTIVE II

ich bärste	wir bärsten
du bärstest	ihr bärstet
Sie bärsten	Sie bärsten
er/sie/es bärste	sie bärsten

FUTURE SUBJUNCTIVE I

ich werde	wir werden	bersten
du werdest	ihr werdet	
Sie werden	Sie werden	
er/sie/es werde	sie werden	

FUTURE SUBJUNCTIVE II

ich würde	wir würden	bersten
du würdest	ihr würdet	
Sie würden	Sie würden	
er/sie/es würde	sie würden	

PRESENT PERFECT

ich bin	wir sind	geborsten
du bist	ihr seid	
Sie sind	Sie sind	
er/sie/es ist	sie sind	

PAST PERFECT

ich war	wir waren	geborsten
du warst	ihr wart	
Sie waren	Sie waren	
er/sie/es war	sie waren	

FUTURE PERFECT

ich werde	wir werden	geborsten sein
du wirst	ihr werdet	
Sie werden	Sie werden	
er/sie/es wird	sie werden	

PAST SUBJUNCTIVE I

ich sei	wir seien	geborsten
du seiest	ihr seiet	
Sie seien	Sie seien	
er/sie/es sei	sie seien	

PAST SUBJUNCTIVE II

ich wäre	wir wären	geborsten
du wärest	ihr wäret	
Sie wären	Sie wären	
er/sie/es wäre	sie wären	

FUTURE PERFECT SUBJUNCTIVE I

ich werde	wir werden	geborsten sein
du werdest	ihr werdet	
Sie werden	Sie werden	
er/sie/es werde	sie werden	

FUTURE PERFECT SUBJUNCTIVE II

ich würde	wir würden	geborsten sein
du würdest	ihr würdet	
Sie würden	Sie würden	
er/sie/es würde	sie würden	

COMMANDS birst! berstet! bersten Sie!

PRESENT PARTICIPLE berstend

Usage

Der Porzellantopf ist durch die zu große Hitze geborsten. — *The porcelain pot burst because of the excessive heat.*
Erichs Schlafzimmerfenster barst durch die Explosion. — *Erich's bedroom window shattered from the explosion.*
Ein altes Wasserrohr war in der heutigen Nacht geborsten. — *An old water pipe had burst last night.*
Die Blasen sind geborsten. — *The bubbles burst.*
Wenn der Tank wegen des hohen Drucks birst, entsteht keine magnetische Emission. — *If the tank bursts due to high pressure, no magnetic emission occurs.*
Der sonst feste Deich drohte an diesem Tag zu bersten. — *The dike, which was otherwise sound, threatened to give way on this particular day.*

Die Zuschauer barsten vor Lachen. — *The audience burst out laughing.*
Ihr Herz birst vor Freude. — *Her heart is bursting with joy.*
Das Schiff wurde gerammt und barst in drei Teile. — *The ship was rammed and broke into three pieces.*
Das Lokal an der Ecke war zum Bersten voll. — *The corner bar was full to bursting.*
… als wär' die Erde mitten entzwei geborsten … (SCHILLER) — *… as though the earth had burst asunder …*

RELATED VERB zerbersten

78 berücksichtigen *to take into consideration, allow for, bear in mind*

berücksichtigt · berücksichtigte · berücksichtigt regular weak verb

PRESENT

ich berücksichtige	wir berücksichtigen
du berücksichtigst	ihr berücksichtigt
Sie berücksichtigen	Sie berücksichtigen
er/sie/es berücksichtigt	sie berücksichtigen

PRESENT PERFECT

ich habe	wir haben	berücksichtigt
du hast	ihr habt	
Sie haben	Sie haben	
er/sie/es hat	sie haben	

SIMPLE PAST

ich berücksichtigte	wir berücksichtigten
du berücksichtigtest	ihr berücksichtigtet
Sie berücksichtigten	Sie berücksichtigten
er/sie/es berücksichtigte	sie berücksichtigten

PAST PERFECT

ich hatte	wir hatten	berücksichtigt
du hattest	ihr hattet	
Sie hatten	Sie hatten	
er/sie/es hatte	sie hatten	

FUTURE

ich werde	wir werden	berücksichtigen
du wirst	ihr werdet	
Sie werden	Sie werden	
er/sie/es wird	sie werden	

FUTURE PERFECT

ich werde	wir werden	berücksichtigt haben
du wirst	ihr werdet	
Sie werden	Sie werden	
er/sie/es wird	sie werden	

PRESENT SUBJUNCTIVE I

ich berücksichtige	wir berücksichtigen
du berücksichtigest	ihr berücksichtiget
Sie berücksichtigen	Sie berücksichtigen
er/sie/es berücksichtige	sie berücksichtigen

PAST SUBJUNCTIVE I

ich habe	wir haben	berücksichtigt
du habest	ihr habet	
Sie haben	Sie haben	
er/sie/es habe	sie haben	

PRESENT SUBJUNCTIVE II

ich berücksichtigte	wir berücksichtigten
du berücksichtigtest	ihr berücksichtigtet
Sie berücksichtigten	Sie berücksichtigten
er/sie/es berücksichtigte	sie berücksichtigten

PAST SUBJUNCTIVE II

ich hätte	wir hätten	berücksichtigt
du hättest	ihr hättet	
Sie hätten	Sie hätten	
er/sie/es hätte	sie hätten	

FUTURE SUBJUNCTIVE I

ich werde	wir werden	berücksichtigen
du werdest	ihr werdet	
Sie werden	Sie werden	
er/sie/es werde	sie werden	

FUTURE PERFECT SUBJUNCTIVE I

ich werde	wir werden	berücksichtigt haben
du werdest	ihr werdet	
Sie werden	Sie werden	
er/sie/es werde	sie werden	

FUTURE SUBJUNCTIVE II

ich würde	wir würden	berücksichtigen
du würdest	ihr würdet	
Sie würden	Sie würden	
er/sie/es würde	sie würden	

FUTURE PERFECT SUBJUNCTIVE II

ich würde	wir würden	berücksichtigt haben
du würdest	ihr würdet	
Sie würden	Sie würden	
er/sie/es würde	sie würden	

COMMANDS berücksichtig(e)! berücksichtigt! berücksichtigen Sie!

PRESENT PARTICIPLE berücksichtigend

Usage

Herrn Sterners Bedürfnisse werden dieses Jahr nicht mehr berücksichtigt.
Mr. Sterner's needs are no longer being considered this year.

Die Produzenten wollten die Interessen der Konsumenten berücksichtigen.
The producers wanted to consider the consumers' interests.

Jochens Leistungen der letzten drei Jahre wurden nicht berücksichtigt.
Jochen's accomplishments of the past three years were not considered.

Man muss enorm hohe Startup-Kosten berücksichtigen.
You must allow for enormously high start-up costs.

Könnten wir hier die Behinderten in unserer Stadt vielleicht berücksichtigen?
Could we perhaps take the handicapped people of our city into consideration here?

Bei der Planung berücksichtigen wir auch die Notwendigkeit einer neuen Perspektive.
As we plan, we are also allowing for the necessity of a new perspective.

Die Armen sind besonders zu berücksichtigen.
The poor should especially be kept in mind.

Dabei muss berücksichtigt werden, dass eine entsprechende Ausbildung möglich ist.
At the same time it must be kept in mind that relevant training is possible.

strong verb **beruft · berief · berufen**

PRESENT

ich berufe | wir berufen
du berufst | ihr beruft
Sie berufen | Sie berufen
er/sie/es beruft | sie berufen

SIMPLE PAST

ich berief | wir beriefen
du beriefst | ihr berieft
Sie beriefen | Sie beriefen
er/sie/es berief | sie beriefen

FUTURE

ich werde | wir werden
du wirst | ihr werdet
Sie werden | Sie werden
er/sie/es wird | sie werden
} berufen

PRESENT SUBJUNCTIVE I

ich berufe | wir berufen
du berufest | ihr berufet
Sie berufen | Sie berufen
er/sie/es berufe | sie berufen

PRESENT SUBJUNCTIVE II

ich beriefe | wir beriefen
du beriefest | ihr beriefet
Sie beriefen | Sie beriefen
er/sie/es beriefe | sie beriefen

FUTURE SUBJUNCTIVE I

ich werde | wir werden
du werdest | ihr werdet
Sie werden | Sie werden
er/sie/es werde | sie werden
} berufen

FUTURE SUBJUNCTIVE II

ich würde | wir würden
du würdest | ihr würdet
Sie würden | Sie würden
er/sie/es würde | sie würden
} berufen

PRESENT PERFECT

ich habe | wir haben
du hast | ihr habt
Sie haben | Sie haben
er/sie/es hat | sie haben
} berufen

PAST PERFECT

ich hatte | wir hatten
du hattest | ihr hattet
Sie hatten | Sie hatten
er/sie/es hatte | sie hatten
} berufen

FUTURE PERFECT

ich werde | wir werden
du wirst | ihr werdet
Sie werden | Sie werden
er/sie/es wird | sie werden
} berufen haben

PAST SUBJUNCTIVE I

ich habe | wir haben
du habest | ihr habet
Sie haben | Sie haben
er/sie/es habe | sie haben
} berufen

PAST SUBJUNCTIVE II

ich hätte | wir hätten
du hättest | ihr hättet
Sie hätten | Sie hätten
er/sie/es hätte | sie hätten
} berufen

FUTURE PERFECT SUBJUNCTIVE I

ich werde | wir werden
du werdest | ihr werdet
Sie werden | Sie werden
er/sie/es werde | sie werden
} berufen haben

FUTURE PERFECT SUBJUNCTIVE II

ich würde | wir würden
du würdest | ihr würdet
Sie würden | Sie würden
er/sie/es würde | sie würden
} berufen haben

COMMANDS beruf(e)! beruft! berufen Sie!

PRESENT PARTICIPLE berufend

Usage

Voriges Jahr berief man ihn ins Ausland. — *The previous year he was summoned abroad.*

Der Minister hat den Senat zu einer außerordentlichen Sitzung berufen. — *The minister convened a special session of the senate.*

In der darauffolgenden Woche berief die Kommission drei von ihnen in den neuen Vorstand. — *In the following week, the commission appointed three of them to the new board of directors.*

1847 wurde ein neuer Erzbischof berufen. — *In 1847 a new archbishop was appointed.*

sich berufen auf *to quote; rely on; appeal to*

Ich berufe mich auf verlässliche Quellen. — *I am quoting reliable sources.*

Der Anwalt der Angeklagten berief sich später auf Artikel 15 der Verordnung. — *The defendants' attorney later cited article 15 of the ordinance.*

Sie berufen sich auf die Verfassung. — *They're appealing to the constitution.*

Falls Sie sich an den Präsidenten um Hilfe wenden, können Sie sich auf mich berufen. — *In case you turn to the president for help, you can mention my name.*

RELATED VERBS ab·berufen, ein·berufen; *see also* **rufen** (347)

80 beruhigen *to calm, quiet*

beruhigt · beruhigte · beruhigt regular weak verb

PRESENT

ich beruhige	wir beruhigen
du beruhigst	ihr beruhigt
Sie beruhigen	Sie beruhigen
er/sie/es beruhigt	sie beruhigen

SIMPLE PAST

ich beruhigte	wir beruhigten
du beruhigtest	ihr beruhigtet
Sie beruhigten	Sie beruhigten
er/sie/es beruhigte	sie beruhigten

FUTURE

ich werde	wir werden	beruhigen
du wirst	ihr werdet	
Sie werden	Sie werden	
er/sie/es wird	sie werden	

PRESENT SUBJUNCTIVE I

ich beruhige	wir beruhigen
du beruhigest	ihr beruhiget
Sie beruhigen	Sie beruhigen
er/sie/es beruhige	sie beruhigen

PRESENT SUBJUNCTIVE II

ich beruhigte	wir beruhigten
du beruhigtest	ihr beruhigtet
Sie beruhigten	Sie beruhigten
er/sie/es beruhigte	sie beruhigten

FUTURE SUBJUNCTIVE I

ich werde	wir werden	beruhigen
du werdest	ihr werdet	
Sie werden	Sie werden	
er/sie/es werde	sie werden	

FUTURE SUBJUNCTIVE II

ich würde	wir würden	beruhigen
du würdest	ihr würdet	
Sie würden	Sie würden	
er/sie/es würde	sie würden	

PRESENT PERFECT

ich habe	wir haben	beruhigt
du hast	ihr habt	
Sie haben	Sie haben	
er/sie/es hat	sie haben	

PAST PERFECT

ich hatte	wir hatten	beruhigt
du hattest	ihr hattet	
Sie hatten	Sie hatten	
er/sie/es hatte	sie hatten	

FUTURE PERFECT

ich werde	wir werden	beruhigt haben
du wirst	ihr werdet	
Sie werden	Sie werden	
er/sie/es wird	sie werden	

PAST SUBJUNCTIVE I

ich habe	wir haben	beruhigt
du habest	ihr habet	
Sie haben	Sie haben	
er/sie/es habe	sie haben	

PAST SUBJUNCTIVE II

ich hätte	wir hätten	beruhigt
du hättest	ihr hättet	
Sie hätten	Sie hätten	
er/sie/es hätte	sie hätten	

FUTURE PERFECT SUBJUNCTIVE I

ich werde	wir werden	beruhigt haben
du werdest	ihr werdet	
Sie werden	Sie werden	
er/sie/es werde	sie werden	

FUTURE PERFECT SUBJUNCTIVE II

ich würde	wir würden	beruhigt haben
du würdest	ihr würdet	
Sie würden	Sie würden	
er/sie/es würde	sie würden	

COMMANDS beruhig(e)! beruhigt! beruhigen Sie!

PRESENT PARTICIPLE beruhigend

Usage

Grete hat den bellenden Hund beruhigt. — *Grete quieted down the barking dog.*

Die Ärzte versuchten ihn zu beruhigen. — *The doctors tried to calm him.*

Freiherr Brenkermann konnte seine Frau nach dem Tod ihrer dänischen Dogge nicht beruhigen. — *Baron Brenkermann was unable to soothe his wife after the death of her Great Dane.*

Das Baby weinte, und die Eltern beruhigten es. — *The baby was crying, and the parents quieted it.*

Der neue Wirtschaftsminister konnte seine Kritiker nicht beruhigen. — *The new economics minister couldn't silence his critics.*

Der Politiker musste das Publikum erstmal beruhigen. — *The politician first had to placate the public.*

sich beruhigen *to calm oneself*

Beruhigen Sie sich! — *Calm yourself!/Settle down!*

Es dauerte einige Stunden, bis er sich beruhigt hatte. — *It took him a few hours to calm down.*

Dara trinkt jetzt Kräutertee und beruhigt sich langsam. — *Dara is drinking some herbal tea now and calming herself down.*

Die Einzelhandelpreise beruhigen sich. — *Retail prices are leveling out.*

regular weak verb **beschädigt · beschädigte · beschädigt**

PRESENT

ich beschädige	wir beschädigen
du beschädigst	ihr beschädigt
Sie beschädigen	Sie beschädigen
er/sie/es beschädigt	sie beschädigen

SIMPLE PAST

ich beschädigte	wir beschädigten
du beschädigtest	ihr beschädigtet
Sie beschädigten	Sie beschädigten
er/sie/es beschädigte	sie beschädigten

FUTURE

ich werde	wir werden	beschädigen
du wirst	ihr werdet	
Sie werden	Sie werden	
er/sie/es wird	sie werden	

PRESENT SUBJUNCTIVE I

ich beschädige	wir beschädigen
du beschädigest	ihr beschädiget
Sie beschädigen	Sie beschädigen
er/sie/es beschädige	sie beschädigen

PRESENT SUBJUNCTIVE II

ich beschädigte	wir beschädigten
du beschädigtest	ihr beschädigtet
Sie beschädigten	Sie beschädigten
er/sie/es beschädigte	sie beschädigten

FUTURE SUBJUNCTIVE I

ich werde	wir werden	beschädigen
du werdest	ihr werdet	
Sie werden	Sie werden	
er/sie/es werde	sie werden	

FUTURE SUBJUNCTIVE II

ich würde	wir würden	beschädigen
du würdest	ihr würdet	
Sie würden	Sie würden	
er/sie/es würde	sie würden	

PRESENT PERFECT

ich habe	wir haben	beschädigt
du hast	ihr habt	
Sie haben	Sie haben	
er/sie/es hat	sie haben	

PAST PERFECT

ich hatte	wir hatten	beschädigt
du hattest	ihr hattet	
Sie hatten	Sie hatten	
er/sie/es hatte	sie hatten	

FUTURE PERFECT

ich werde	wir werden	beschädigt haben
du wirst	ihr werdet	
Sie werden	Sie werden	
er/sie/es wird	sie werden	

PAST SUBJUNCTIVE I

ich habe	wir haben	beschädigt
du habest	ihr habet	
Sie haben	Sie haben	
er/sie/es habe	sie haben	

PAST SUBJUNCTIVE II

ich hätte	wir hätten	beschädigt
du hättest	ihr hättet	
Sie hätten	Sie hätten	
er/sie/es hätte	sie hätten	

FUTURE PERFECT SUBJUNCTIVE I

ich werde	wir werden	beschädigt haben
du werdest	ihr werdet	
Sie werden	Sie werden	
er/sie/es werde	sie werden	

FUTURE PERFECT SUBJUNCTIVE II

ich würde	wir würden	beschädigt haben
du würdest	ihr würdet	
Sie würden	Sie würden	
er/sie/es würde	sie würden	

COMMANDS beschädig(e)! beschädigt! beschädigen Sie!

PRESENT PARTICIPLE beschädigend

Usage

Die Waren, die Sie mir geschickt haben, wurden beim Transport beschädigt. — *The goods that you sent me were damaged in shipment.*

Zum Glück waren keine Knochen beschädigt worden. — *Luckily, there had been no bone damage.*

Die Randalierer haben Fenster eingeworfen und mehrere Autos beschädigt. — *The rioters broke windows and damaged several cars.*

Unsere Installation könnte vielleicht beschädigt sein. — *Our installation might perhaps be flawed.*

Dabei wurden mehrere Häuser von der Lava zerstört oder beschädigt. — *In the process, several houses were destroyed or damaged by the lava.*

Die niedrigen Temperaturen haben das Obst beschädigt. — *The low temperatures damaged the fruit.*

Die Überschwemmung hat die Straßen leicht beschädigt. — *The flood has damaged the streets somewhat.*

Wie sind die Dateien beschädigt worden? — *How were the files damaged?*

Nur so hätte man garantieren können, dass keine Instrumente beschädigt werden. — *This would have been the only way to guarantee that no instruments would be damaged.*

RELATED VERB schädigen

beschäftigen *to occupy, engage*

beschäftigt · beschäftigte · beschäftigt regular weak verb

PRESENT

ich beschäftige	wir beschäftigen
du beschäftigst	ihr beschäftigt
Sie beschäftigen	Sie beschäftigen
er/sie/es beschäftigt	sie beschäftigen

PRESENT PERFECT

ich habe	wir haben	beschäftigt
du hast	ihr habt	
Sie haben	Sie haben	
er/sie/es hat	sie haben	

SIMPLE PAST

ich beschäftigte	wir beschäftigten
du beschäftigtest	ihr beschäftigtet
Sie beschäftigten	Sie beschäftigten
er/sie/es beschäftigte	sie beschäftigten

PAST PERFECT

ich hatte	wir hatten	beschäftigt
du hattest	ihr hattet	
Sie hatten	Sie hatten	
er/sie/es hatte	sie hatten	

FUTURE

ich werde	wir werden	beschäftigen
du wirst	ihr werdet	
Sie werden	Sie werden	
er/sie/es wird	sie werden	

FUTURE PERFECT

ich werde	wir werden	beschäftigt haben
du wirst	ihr werdet	
Sie werden	Sie werden	
er/sie/es wird	sie werden	

PRESENT SUBJUNCTIVE I

ich beschäftige	wir beschäftigen
du beschäftigest	ihr beschäftiget
Sie beschäftigen	Sie beschäftigen
er/sie/es beschäftige	sie beschäftigen

PAST SUBJUNCTIVE I

ich habe	wir haben	beschäftigt
du habest	ihr habet	
Sie haben	Sie haben	
er/sie/es habe	sie haben	

PRESENT SUBJUNCTIVE II

ich beschäftigte	wir beschäftigten
du beschäftigtest	ihr beschäftigtet
Sie beschäftigten	Sie beschäftigten
er/sie/es beschäftigte	sie beschäftigten

PAST SUBJUNCTIVE II

ich hätte	wir hätten	beschäftigt
du hättest	ihr hättet	
Sie hätten	Sie hätten	
er/sie/es hätte	sie hätten	

FUTURE SUBJUNCTIVE I

ich werde	wir werden	beschäftigen
du werdest	ihr werdet	
Sie werden	Sie werden	
er/sie/es werde	sie werden	

FUTURE PERFECT SUBJUNCTIVE I

ich werde	wir werden	beschäftigt haben
du werdest	ihr werdet	
Sie werden	Sie werden	
er/sie/es werde	sie werden	

FUTURE SUBJUNCTIVE II

ich würde	wir würden	beschäftigen
du würdest	ihr würdet	
Sie würden	Sie würden	
er/sie/es würde	sie würden	

FUTURE PERFECT SUBJUNCTIVE II

ich würde	wir würden	beschäftigt haben
du würdest	ihr würdet	
Sie würden	Sie würden	
er/sie/es würde	sie würden	

COMMANDS beschäftig(e)! beschäftigt! beschäftigen Sie!

PRESENT PARTICIPLE beschäftigend

Usage

Dieses Problem beschäftigt uns Biologen sehr. — *We biologists are much occupied with this problem.*

Firma Adelsleben beschäftigt zur Zeit 236 Mitarbeiter. — *The Adelsleben Company employs 236 workers at the moment.*

Was beschäftigt dich so? — *What's on your mind?*

sich beschäftigen *to occupy oneself*

Herr Richardson beschäftigt sich mit der Frage der Einbürgerung. — *Mr. Richardson is occupied with the question of naturalization.*

Es gibt viele Themen, womit sich der Sprachwissenschaftler beschäftigen kann. — *There are many topics that can engage a linguist.*

Danach habe ich mich mit der Genealogie beschäftigt. — *After that I devoted myself to genealogy.*

Meister Eckhart beschäftigte sich mit der Frage, wie der Mensch zu Gott kommt. — *Master Eckhart was preoccupied with the question of how a human being comes to God.*

Dieses Buch beschäftigt sich mit der Kryptographie als mathematische Wissenschaft. — *This book deals with cryptography as mathematical science.*

strong verb **beschließt · beschloss · beschlossen**

PRESENT

ich beschließe	wir beschließen
du beschließt	ihr beschließt
Sie beschließen	Sie beschließen
er/sie/es beschließt	sie beschließen

SIMPLE PAST

ich beschloss	wir beschlossen
du beschlossest	ihr beschlosst
Sie beschlossen	Sie beschlossen
er/sie/es beschloss	sie beschlossen

FUTURE

ich werde	wir werden	beschließen
du wirst	ihr werdet	
Sie werden	Sie werden	
er/sie/es wird	sie werden	

PRESENT SUBJUNCTIVE I

ich beschließe	wir beschließen
du beschließest	ihr beschließet
Sie beschließen	Sie beschließen
er/sie/es beschließe	sie beschließen

PRESENT SUBJUNCTIVE II

ich beschlösse	wir beschlössen
du beschlössest	ihr beschlösset
Sie beschlössen	Sie beschlössen
er/sie/es beschlösse	sie beschlössen

FUTURE SUBJUNCTIVE I

ich werde	wir werden	beschließen
du werdest	ihr werdet	
Sie werden	Sie werden	
er/sie/es werde	sie werden	

FUTURE SUBJUNCTIVE II

ich würde	wir würden	beschließen
du würdest	ihr würdet	
Sie würden	Sie würden	
er/sie/es würde	sie würden	

PRESENT PERFECT

ich habe	wir haben	beschlossen
du hast	ihr habt	
Sie haben	Sie haben	
er/sie/es hat	sie haben	

PAST PERFECT

ich hatte	wir hatten	beschlossen
du hattest	ihr hattet	
Sie hatten	Sie hatten	
er/sie/es hatte	sie hatten	

FUTURE PERFECT

ich werde	wir werden	beschlossen haben
du wirst	ihr werdet	
Sie werden	Sie werden	
er/sie/es wird	sie werden	

PAST SUBJUNCTIVE I

ich habe	wir haben	beschlossen
du habest	ihr habet	
Sie haben	Sie haben	
er/sie/es habe	sie haben	

PAST SUBJUNCTIVE II

ich hätte	wir hätten	beschlossen
du hättest	ihr hättet	
Sie hätten	Sie hätten	
er/sie/es hätte	sie hätten	

FUTURE PERFECT SUBJUNCTIVE I

ich werde	wir werden	beschlossen haben
du werdest	ihr werdet	
Sie werden	Sie werden	
er/sie/es werde	sie werden	

FUTURE PERFECT SUBJUNCTIVE II

ich würde	wir würden	beschlossen haben
du würdest	ihr würdet	
Sie würden	Sie würden	
er/sie/es würde	sie würden	

COMMANDS beschließ(e)! beschließt! beschließen Sie!

PRESENT PARTICIPLE beschließend

Usage

Wir haben beschlossen, doch nicht mitzukommen. — *We decided not to come along after all.*

Der Vorstand beschloss eine Etatkürzung. — *The board of directors decided on a budget cut.*

Meine Kusinen haben beschlossen, die Safari abzubrechen. — *My cousins decided to discontinue the safari.*

Der Bundestag beschloss gestern ein ähnliches Gesetz. — *The Bundestag passed a similar law yesterday.*

Der UN-Sicherheitsrat hat neulich beschlossen, mehr Truppen einzusetzen. — *The U.N. Security Council has recently decided to send more troops into action.*

Die Versammlung hat den Streik beschlossen. — *The assembly has resolved to strike.*

Nach kurzer Debatte beschloss das Parlament die Aufhebung des kontroversen Gesetzes. — *After a brief debate the parliament decided to rescind the controversial law.*

Die Änderungen wurden einstimmig beschlossen. — *The amendments were unanimously passed.*

Professorin Richardson beschloss den Vortrag mit Hegels Worten: „Die Wahrheit ist das Ganze." — *Professor Richardson ended the talk with Hegel's words: "Truth is everything."*

RELATED VERBS *see* **schließen** (375)

84

beschreiben *to describe; write on*

beschreibt · beschrieb · beschrieben strong verb

PRESENT

ich beschreibe	wir beschreiben
du beschreibst	ihr beschreibt
Sie beschreiben	Sie beschreiben
er/sie/es beschreibt	sie beschreiben

SIMPLE PAST

ich beschrieb	wir beschrieben
du beschriebst	ihr beschriebt
Sie beschrieben	Sie beschrieben
er/sie/es beschrieb	sie beschrieben

FUTURE

ich werde	wir werden	beschreiben
du wirst	ihr werdet	
Sie werden	Sie werden	
er/sie/es wird	sie werden	

PRESENT SUBJUNCTIVE I

ich beschreibe	wir beschreiben
du beschreibest	ihr beschreibet
Sie beschreiben	Sie beschreiben
er/sie/es beschreibe	sie beschreiben

PRESENT SUBJUNCTIVE II

ich beschriebe	wir beschrieben
du beschriebest	ihr beschriebet
Sie beschrieben	Sie beschrieben
er/sie/es beschriebe	sie beschrieben

FUTURE SUBJUNCTIVE I

ich werde	wir werden	beschreiben
du werdest	ihr werdet	
Sie werden	Sie werden	
er/sie/es werde	sie werden	

FUTURE SUBJUNCTIVE II

ich würde	wir würden	beschreiben
du würdest	ihr würdet	
Sie würden	Sie würden	
er/sie/es würde	sie würden	

PRESENT PERFECT

ich habe	wir haben	beschrieben
du hast	ihr habt	
Sie haben	Sie haben	
er/sie/es hat	sie haben	

PAST PERFECT

ich hatte	wir hatten	beschrieben
du hattest	ihr hattet	
Sie hatten	Sie hatten	
er/sie/es hatte	sie hatten	

FUTURE PERFECT

ich werde	wir werden	beschrieben haben
du wirst	ihr werdet	
Sie werden	Sie werden	
er/sie/es wird	sie werden	

PAST SUBJUNCTIVE I

ich habe	wir haben	beschrieben
du habest	ihr habet	
Sie haben	Sie haben	
er/sie/es habe	sie haben	

PAST SUBJUNCTIVE II

ich hätte	wir hätten	beschrieben
du hättest	ihr hättet	
Sie hätten	Sie hätten	
er/sie/es hätte	sie hätten	

FUTURE PERFECT SUBJUNCTIVE I

ich werde	wir werden	beschrieben haben
du werdest	ihr werdet	
Sie werden	Sie werden	
er/sie/es werde	sie werden	

FUTURE PERFECT SUBJUNCTIVE II

ich würde	wir würden	beschrieben haben
du würdest	ihr würdet	
Sie würden	Sie würden	
er/sie/es würde	sie würden	

COMMANDS beschreib(e)! beschreibt! beschreiben Sie!

PRESENT PARTICIPLE beschreibend

Usage

Beschreiben Sie bitte Ihre Erfahrungen.	*Please describe your experiences.*
Das ist ein Prosawerk, das den Bauernaufstand beschreibt.	*That is a work of prose that describes the peasant revolt.*
Was ich hier beschreibe ist in sich selbst nicht kontrovers.	*What I describe here is in and of itself not controversial.*
Hoffmann war einer der Vorläufer des Realismus, indem seine Werke die Alltagswelt sehr genau beschrieben.	*Hoffmann was a precursor of realism in that his works described the everyday world very exactingly.*
Der Pfad zur Oberflächenstruktur wird durch Transformationalgrammatik beschrieben.	*The path to surface structure is described in transformational grammar.*
Die Naturalisten beschrieben den Zustand des Proletariats.	*The naturalists described the condition of the proletariat.*
Ich kann dir nicht beschreiben, wie ich mich auf dieses Wochenende freue.	*I can't tell you how much I am looking forward to this weekend.*
Das Blatt darf nur einseitig beschrieben werden.	*You are to write on only one side of the paper.*
Hiermit beschreibt man eine CD.	*With this you can write to a CD.*

RELATED VERBS um·beschreiben; *see also* **schreiben** (385)

regular weak verb **beschwert · beschwerte · beschwert**

PRESENT

ich beschwere	wir beschweren
du beschwerst	ihr beschwert
Sie beschweren	Sie beschweren
er/sie/es beschwert	sie beschweren

SIMPLE PAST

ich beschwerte	wir beschwerten
du beschwertest	ihr beschwertet
Sie beschwerten	Sie beschwerten
er/sie/es beschwerte	sie beschwerten

FUTURE

ich werde	wir werden	beschweren
du wirst	ihr werdet	
Sie werden	Sie werden	
er/sie/es wird	sie werden	

PRESENT SUBJUNCTIVE I

ich beschwere	wir beschweren
du beschwerest	ihr beschweret
Sie beschweren	Sie beschweren
er/sie/es beschwere	sie beschweren

PRESENT SUBJUNCTIVE II

ich beschwerte	wir beschwerten
du beschwertest	ihr beschwertet
Sie beschwerten	Sie beschwerten
er/sie/es beschwerte	sie beschwerten

FUTURE SUBJUNCTIVE I

ich werde	wir werden	beschweren
du werdest	ihr werdet	
Sie werden	Sie werden	
er/sie/es werde	sie werden	

FUTURE SUBJUNCTIVE II

ich würde	wir würden	beschweren
du würdest	ihr würdet	
Sie würden	Sie würden	
er/sie/es würde	sie würden	

PRESENT PERFECT

ich habe	wir haben	beschwert
du hast	ihr habt	
Sie haben	Sie haben	
er/sie/es hat	sie haben	

PAST PERFECT

ich hatte	wir hatten	beschwert
du hattest	ihr hattet	
Sie hatten	Sie hatten	
er/sie/es hatte	sie hatten	

FUTURE PERFECT

ich werde	wir werden	beschwert haben
du wirst	ihr werdet	
Sie werden	Sie werden	
er/sie/es wird	sie werden	

PAST SUBJUNCTIVE I

ich habe	wir haben	beschwert
du habest	ihr habet	
Sie haben	Sie haben	
er/sie/es habe	sie haben	

PAST SUBJUNCTIVE II

ich hätte	wir hätten	beschwert
du hättest	ihr hättet	
Sie hätten	Sie hätten	
er/sie/es hätte	sie hätten	

FUTURE PERFECT SUBJUNCTIVE I

ich werde	wir werden	beschwert haben
du werdest	ihr werdet	
Sie werden	Sie werden	
er/sie/es werde	sie werden	

FUTURE PERFECT SUBJUNCTIVE II

ich würde	wir würden	beschwert haben
du würdest	ihr würdet	
Sie würden	Sie würden	
er/sie/es würde	sie würden	

COMMANDS beschwer(e)! beschwert! beschweren Sie!

PRESENT PARTICIPLE beschwerend

Usage

Das Mittagessen beschwert uns den Magen. — *Lunch is sitting heavy on our stomachs.*

Diese Entwicklung hat uns sehr beschwert. — *This development weighed on us heavily.*

Überflüssige Details beschwerten den Aufsatz, der sonst gut geschrieben war. — *Excessive details only encumbered the essay, which was otherwise well written.*

sich beschweren *to complain*

Warum beschwerst du dich nicht? — *Why don't you complain?*

Beatrice beschwert sich wieder, dass etwas mit dem Computer nicht stimmt. — *Beatrice is complaining again that something's not right with the computer.*

„Es ist aber zu warm hier", beschwerte sich Peter. — *"But it's too warm here," Peter grumbled.*

Gestern hat Maria sich über den ständigen Lärm im Keller beschwert. — *Yesterday Maria complained about the constant noise in the basement.*

Herr Leitner beschwert sich täglich bei dem Hausmeister. — *Mr. Leitner complains to the building superintendent daily.*

Ich kann mich nicht beschweren. — *I can't complain.*

besichtigen *to inspect, examine; go sightseeing in*

besichtigt · besichtigte · besichtigt regular weak verb

PRESENT

ich besichtige	wir besichtigen
du besichtigst	ihr besichtigt
Sie besichtigen	Sie besichtigen
er/sie/es besichtigt	sie besichtigen

PRESENT PERFECT

ich habe	wir haben	besichtigt
du hast	ihr habt	
Sie haben	Sie haben	
er/sie/es hat	sie haben	

SIMPLE PAST

ich besichtigte	wir besichtigten
du besichtigtest	ihr besichtigtet
Sie besichtigten	Sie besichtigten
er/sie/es besichtigte	sie besichtigten

PAST PERFECT

ich hatte	wir hatten	besichtigt
du hattest	ihr hattet	
Sie hatten	Sie hatten	
er/sie/es hatte	sie hatten	

FUTURE

ich werde	wir werden	besichtigen
du wirst	ihr werdet	
Sie werden	Sie werden	
er/sie/es wird	sie werden	

FUTURE PERFECT

ich werde	wir werden	besichtigt haben
du wirst	ihr werdet	
Sie werden	Sie werden	
er/sie/es wird	sie werden	

PRESENT SUBJUNCTIVE I

ich besichtige	wir besichtigen
du besichtigest	ihr besichtiget
Sie besichtigen	Sie besichtigen
er/sie/es besichtige	sie besichtigen

PAST SUBJUNCTIVE I

ich habe	wir haben	besichtigt
du habest	ihr habet	
Sie haben	Sie haben	
er/sie/es habe	sie haben	

PRESENT SUBJUNCTIVE II

ich besichtigte	wir besichtigten
du besichtigtest	ihr besichtigtet
Sie besichtigten	Sie besichtigten
er/sie/es besichtigte	sie besichtigten

PAST SUBJUNCTIVE II

ich hätte	wir hätten	besichtigt
du hättest	ihr hättet	
Sie hätten	Sie hätten	
er/sie/es hätte	sie hätten	

FUTURE SUBJUNCTIVE I

ich werde	wir werden	besichtigen
du werdest	ihr werdet	
Sie werden	Sie werden	
er/sie/es werde	sie werden	

FUTURE PERFECT SUBJUNCTIVE I

ich werde	wir werden	besichtigt haben
du werdest	ihr werdet	
Sie werden	Sie werden	
er/sie/es werde	sie werden	

FUTURE SUBJUNCTIVE II

ich würde	wir würden	besichtigen
du würdest	ihr würdet	
Sie würden	Sie würden	
er/sie/es würde	sie würden	

FUTURE PERFECT SUBJUNCTIVE II

ich würde	wir würden	besichtigt haben
du würdest	ihr würdet	
Sie würden	Sie würden	
er/sie/es würde	sie würden	

COMMANDS besichtig(e)! besichtigt! besichtigen Sie!

PRESENT PARTICIPLE besichtigend

Usage

Herr und Frau Keister möchten gern die Residenz in Ansbach besichtigen. — *Mr. and Mrs. Keister would like very much to see the residence in Ansbach.*

Regina und ihr Mann wollten die Altbauwohnung in der Innenstadt nicht besichtigen. — *Regina and her husband didn't want to look at the old apartment in the inner city.*

General Dessaix besichtigte regelmäßig seine Truppen. — *General Dessaix inspected his troops regularly.*

Frau Fricke hat die neuen Produkte im Lagerraum in Kassel besichtigt. — *Mrs. Fricke examined the new products in the warehouse in Kassel.*

Besichtigt meine Website! — *Visit my Web site!*

Hätte es nicht geregnet, so hätten sie den Schlossgarten besichten können. — *Had it not rained, they would have been able to see the palace garden.*

Wollen wir Schloss Sanssouci auch besichtigen? — *Do we want to tour Sanssouci Palace, too?*

Meine Mutter und ich haben vor einigen Jahren die mittelalterliche Stadt Rothenburg besichtigt. — *My mother and I went sightseeing in the medieval city of Rothenburg a few years ago.*

Rund 2 Mio. Personen besichtigen den Vulkan jedes Jahr. — *Around two million people visit the volcano every year.*

strong verb **besitzt · besaß · besessen**

PRESENT

ich besitze	wir besitzen
du besitzt	ihr besitzt
Sie besitzen	Sie besitzen
er/sie/es besitzt	sie besitzen

SIMPLE PAST

ich besaß	wir besaßen
du besaßest	ihr besaßt
Sie besaßen	Sie besaßen
er/sie/es besaß	sie besaßen

FUTURE

ich werde	wir werden	besitzen
du wirst	ihr werdet	
Sie werden	Sie werden	
er/sie/es wird	sie werden	

PRESENT SUBJUNCTIVE I

ich besitze	wir besitzen
du besitzest	ihr besitzet
Sie besitzen	Sie besitzen
er/sie/es besitze	sie besitzen

PRESENT SUBJUNCTIVE II

ich besäße	wir besäßen
du besäßest	ihr besäßet
Sie besäßen	Sie besäßen
er/sie/es besäße	sie besäßen

FUTURE SUBJUNCTIVE I

ich werde	wir werden	besitzen
du werdest	ihr werdet	
Sie werden	Sie werden	
er/sie/es werde	sie werden	

FUTURE SUBJUNCTIVE II

ich würde	wir würden	besitzen
du würdest	ihr würdet	
Sie würden	Sie würden	
er/sie/es würde	sie würden	

PRESENT PERFECT

ich habe	wir haben	besessen
du hast	ihr habt	
Sie haben	Sie haben	
er/sie/es hat	sie haben	

PAST PERFECT

ich hatte	wir hatten	besessen
du hattest	ihr hattet	
Sie hatten	Sie hatten	
er/sie/es hatte	sie hatten	

FUTURE PERFECT

ich werde	wir werden	besessen haben
du wirst	ihr werdet	
Sie werden	Sie werden	
er/sie/es wird	sie werden	

PAST SUBJUNCTIVE I

ich habe	wir haben	besessen
du habest	ihr habet	
Sie haben	Sie haben	
er/sie/es habe	sie haben	

PAST SUBJUNCTIVE II

ich hätte	wir hätten	besessen
du hättest	ihr hättet	
Sie hätten	Sie hätten	
er/sie/es hätte	sie hätten	

FUTURE PERFECT SUBJUNCTIVE I

ich werde	wir werden	besessen haben
du werdest	ihr werdet	
Sie werden	Sie werden	
er/sie/es werde	sie werden	

FUTURE PERFECT SUBJUNCTIVE II

ich würde	wir würden	besessen haben
du würdest	ihr würdet	
Sie würden	Sie würden	
er/sie/es würde	sie würden	

COMMANDS besitz(e)! besitzt! besitzen Sie!

PRESENT PARTICIPLE besitzend

Usage

Die Grafen besaßen Güter sowohl in Westfalen als auch in Böhmen. — *The counts owned estates in Bohemia as well as in Westphalia.*

Besitzen Sie solche Fähigkeiten? — *Do you possess such abilities?*

Der Mensch besitzt ein Langzeit- und ein Kurzzeitgedächtnis. — *The human being possesses a long-term and a short-term memory.*

Wie viele Schuhen besitzt du? — *How many shoes do you own?*

Unser Großvater hat uns alles hinterlassen, was er besessen hatte. — *Our grandfather left us everything he'd owned.*

Der Milliardär besitzt sogar eine Insel im Pazifik. — *The billionaire even owns an island in the Pacific.*

Der Sammler Herr Smith besitzt genau 7234 Bücher und 973 CDs. — *The collector Mr. Smith owns exactly 7,234 books and 973 CDs.*

Diese unsinnige Idee besaß ihn und beherrschte sein ganzes Leben. — *This absurd idea possessed him and dictated his entire life.*

RELATED VERBS *see* **sitzen (406)**

88 besorgen *to look after; attend to; get, procure*

besorgt · besorgte · besorgt regular weak verb

PRESENT

ich besorge	wir besorgen
du besorgst	ihr besorgt
Sie besorgen	Sie besorgen
er/sie/es besorgt	sie besorgen

SIMPLE PAST

ich besorgte	wir besorgten
du besorgtest	ihr besorgtet
Sie besorgten	Sie besorgten
er/sie/es besorgte	sie besorgten

FUTURE

ich werde	wir werden	besorgen
du wirst	ihr werdet	
Sie werden	Sie werden	
er/sie/es wird	sie werden	

PRESENT SUBJUNCTIVE I

ich besorge	wir besorgen
du besorgest	ihr besorget
Sie besorgen	Sie besorgen
er/sie/es besorge	sie besorgen

PRESENT SUBJUNCTIVE II

ich besorgte	wir besorgten
du besorgtest	ihr besorgtet
Sie besorgten	Sie besorgten
er/sie/es besorgte	sie besorgten

FUTURE SUBJUNCTIVE I

ich werde	wir werden	besorgen
du werdest	ihr werdet	
Sie werden	Sie werden	
er/sie/es werde	sie werden	

FUTURE SUBJUNCTIVE II

ich würde	wir würden	besorgen
du würdest	ihr würdet	
Sie würden	Sie würden	
er/sie/es würde	sie würden	

PRESENT PERFECT

ich habe	wir haben	besorgt
du hast	ihr habt	
Sie haben	Sie haben	
er/sie/es hat	sie haben	

PAST PERFECT

ich hatte	wir hatten	besorgt
du hattest	ihr hattet	
Sie hatten	Sie hatten	
er/sie/es hatte	sie hatten	

FUTURE PERFECT

ich werde	wir werden	besorgt haben
du wirst	ihr werdet	
Sie werden	Sie werden	
er/sie/es wird	sie werden	

PAST SUBJUNCTIVE I

ich habe	wir haben	besorgt
du habest	ihr habet	
Sie haben	Sie haben	
er/sie/es habe	sie haben	

PAST SUBJUNCTIVE II

ich hätte	wir hätten	besorgt
du hättest	ihr hättet	
Sie hätten	Sie hätten	
er/sie/es hätte	sie hätten	

FUTURE PERFECT SUBJUNCTIVE I

ich werde	wir werden	besorgt haben
du werdest	ihr werdet	
Sie werden	Sie werden	
er/sie/es werde	sie werden	

FUTURE PERFECT SUBJUNCTIVE II

ich würde	wir würden	besorgt haben
du würdest	ihr würdet	
Sie würden	Sie würden	
er/sie/es würde	sie würden	

COMMANDS besorg(e)! besorgt! besorgen Sie!

PRESENT PARTICIPLE besorgend

Usage

Kannst du die Kinder besorgen?	*Can you look after the children?*
Tante Inge besorgt noch den Haushalt.	*Aunt Inge still keeps house.*
Ich besorge die Einladungen.	*I'll get the invitations.*
Meine Freundin Monika hat die Eintrittskarten schon heute Morgen besorgt.	*My friend Monika got the tickets this morning already.*
Ingrid muss noch ein paar Kleinigkeiten besorgen.	*Ingrid still has to get a few small items.*
Am Bahnhof haben wir uns einen Stadtplan besorgt.	*We got a city map at the train station.*
Wir werden wohl das Ersatzteil bei Firma Rössler besorgen können.	*We will likely be able to procure the replacement part from the Rössler Company.*
Der Portier hat mir ein Taxi besorgt.	*The doorman got me a taxi.*
Demnächst besorge ich mir einen neuen CD-Spieler.	*I'm going to get myself a new CD player soon.*
Was du heute kannst besorgen, das verschiebe nicht auf morgen. (PROVERB)	*Don't put off until tomorrow what you can do today.*

RELATED VERBS *see* **sorgen** (408)

regular weak verb **bestätigt · bestätigte · bestätigt**

PRESENT

ich bestätige	wir bestätigen
du bestätigst	ihr bestätigt
Sie bestätigen	Sie bestätigen
er/sie/es bestätigt	sie bestätigen

SIMPLE PAST

ich bestätigte	wir bestätigten
du bestätigtest	ihr bestätigtet
Sie bestätigten	Sie bestätigten
er/sie/es bestätigte	sie bestätigten

FUTURE

ich werde	wir werden	bestätigen
du wirst	ihr werdet	
Sie werden	Sie werden	
er/sie/es wird	sie werden	

PRESENT SUBJUNCTIVE I

ich bestätige	wir bestätigen
du bestätigest	ihr bestätiget
Sie bestätigen	Sie bestätigen
er/sie/es bestätige	sie bestätigen

PRESENT SUBJUNCTIVE II

ich bestätigte	wir bestätigten
du bestätigtest	ihr bestätigtet
Sie bestätigten	Sie bestätigten
er/sie/es bestätigte	sie bestätigten

FUTURE SUBJUNCTIVE I

ich werde	wir werden	bestätigen
du werdest	ihr werdet	
Sie werden	Sie werden	
er/sie/es werde	sie werden	

FUTURE SUBJUNCTIVE II

ich würde	wir würden	bestätigen
du würdest	ihr würdet	
Sie würden	Sie würden	
er/sie/es würde	sie würden	

PRESENT PERFECT

ich habe	wir haben	bestätigt
du hast	ihr habt	
Sie haben	Sie haben	
er/sie/es hat	sie haben	

PAST PERFECT

ich hatte	wir hatten	bestätigt
du hattest	ihr hattet	
Sie hatten	Sie hatten	
er/sie/es hatte	sie hatten	

FUTURE PERFECT

ich werde	wir werden	bestätigt haben
du wirst	ihr werdet	
Sie werden	Sie werden	
er/sie/es wird	sie werden	

PAST SUBJUNCTIVE I

ich habe	wir haben	bestätigt
du habest	ihr habet	
Sie haben	Sie haben	
er/sie/es habe	sie haben	

PAST SUBJUNCTIVE II

ich hätte	wir hätten	bestätigt
du hättest	ihr hättet	
Sie hätten	Sie hätten	
er/sie/es hätte	sie hätten	

FUTURE PERFECT SUBJUNCTIVE I

ich werde	wir werden	bestätigt haben
du werdest	ihr werdet	
Sie werden	Sie werden	
er/sie/es werde	sie werden	

FUTURE PERFECT SUBJUNCTIVE II

ich würde	wir würden	bestätigt haben
du würdest	ihr würdet	
Sie würden	Sie würden	
er/sie/es würde	sie würden	

COMMANDS bestätig(e)! bestätigt! bestätigen Sie!

PRESENT PARTICIPLE bestätigend

Usage

Ich kann nur bestätigen, was du sagst.	*I can only confirm what you're saying.*
Die Untersuchungen haben unsere früheren Vermutungen bestätigt.	*Research has verified our earlier suppositions.*
Der Pressesprecher wollte nichts bestätigen oder dementieren.	*The press spokesman didn't want to confirm or deny anything.*
In einem Fernsehinterview bestätigte der CEO die Entscheidung des Vorstands.	*The CEO confirmed the board's decision in a TV interview.*
Hiermit bestätigen wir die Entgegennahme der Waren bzw. Dienstleistungen.	*This is to acknowledge receipt of the goods or services.*
Der Stadtrat muss den Entschluss dann bestätigen.	*The city council must then validate the decision.*
Deine Antwort hat mir bestätigt, dass du es bist.	*Your answer has confirmed to me that you are the one.*

sich bestätigen *to prove true, be confirmed; prove oneself*

Die Annahme hat sich bestätigt.	*The assumption has been confirmed.*
David hat sich als guter Lehrer bestätigt.	*David has proved himself (to be) a good teacher.*

bestehen *to undergo, endure, pass; exist, persist; consist, be composed; insist*

besteht · bestand · bestanden strong verb

PRESENT

ich bestehe	wir bestehen
du bestehst	ihr besteht
Sie bestehen	Sie bestehen
er/sie/es besteht	sie bestehen

SIMPLE PAST

ich bestand	wir bestanden
du bestandst	ihr bestandet
Sie bestanden	Sie bestanden
er/sie/es bestand	sie bestanden

FUTURE

ich werde	wir werden	bestehen
du wirst	ihr werdet	
Sie werden	Sie werden	
er/sie/es wird	sie werden	

PRESENT SUBJUNCTIVE I

ich bestehe	wir bestehen
du bestehest	ihr bestehet
Sie bestehen	Sie bestehen
er/sie/es bestehe	sie bestehen

PRESENT SUBJUNCTIVE II

ich bestünde/bestände	wir bestünden/beständen
du bestündest/beständest	ihr bestündet/beständet
Sie bestünden/beständen	Sie bestünden/beständen
er/sie/es bestünde/bestände	sie bestünden/beständen

FUTURE SUBJUNCTIVE I

ich werde	wir werden	bestehen
du werdest	ihr werdet	
Sie werden	Sie werden	
er/sie/es werde	sie werden	

FUTURE SUBJUNCTIVE II

ich würde	wir würden	bestehen
du würdest	ihr würdet	
Sie würden	Sie würden	
er/sie/es würde	sie würden	

PRESENT PERFECT

ich habe	wir haben	bestanden
du hast	ihr habt	
Sie haben	Sie haben	
er/sie/es hat	sie haben	

PAST PERFECT

ich hatte	wir hatten	bestanden
du hattest	ihr hattet	
Sie hatten	Sie hatten	
er/sie/es hatte	sie hatten	

FUTURE PERFECT

ich werde	wir werden	bestanden haben
du wirst	ihr werdet	
Sie werden	Sie werden	
er/sie/es wird	sie werden	

PAST SUBJUNCTIVE I

ich habe	wir haben	bestanden
du habest	ihr habet	
Sie haben	Sie haben	
er/sie/es habe	sie haben	

PAST SUBJUNCTIVE II

ich hätte	wir hätten	bestanden
du hättest	ihr hättet	
Sie hätten	Sie hätten	
er/sie/es hätte	sie hätten	

FUTURE PERFECT SUBJUNCTIVE I

ich werde	wir werden	bestanden haben
du werdest	ihr werdet	
Sie werden	Sie werden	
er/sie/es werde	sie werden	

FUTURE PERFECT SUBJUNCTIVE II

ich würde	wir würden	bestanden haben
du würdest	ihr würdet	
Sie würden	Sie würden	
er/sie/es würde	sie würden	

COMMANDS besteh(e)! besteht! bestehen Sie!

PRESENT PARTICIPLE bestehend

Usage

Hast du die Prüfung bestanden?	*Did you pass the test?*
Der Protagonist des Romans musste viel bestehen.	*The novel's protagonist had to endure a lot.*
Besteht ein Zusammenhang zwischen Arbeitslosigkeit und gesellschaftlicher Ausgrenzung?	*Does a connection exist between unemployment and social exclusion?*
Große Einkommensunterschiede bestehen immer noch.	*Great differences in income still persist.*
Unser Verein besteht seit 1866.	*Our club has been in existence since 1866.*
Über diese Frage besteht jedoch Klarheit.	*On this question, however, there is clarity.*
Die Komödie besteht aus drei Akten.	*The comedy consists of three acts.*
Unsere Aufgabe besteht darin, möglichst viele Beispiele zu sammeln.	*Our assignment entails collecting as many examples as possible.*
Die Salbe besteht aus Olivenöl, Rosmarin, Johanniskraut, Arnika und Teebaumöl.	*The salve consists of olive oil, rosemary, St. John's wort, arnica, and tea tree oil.*
Er besteht auf seinem Recht auf Selbstverteidigung.	*He insists on his right to self-defense.*

RELATED VERBS fort·bestehen; *see also* **stehen** (423)

regular weak verb

bestellt · bestellte · bestellt

PRESENT

ich bestelle	wir bestellen
du bestellst	ihr bestellt
Sie bestellen	Sie bestellen
er/sie/es bestellt	sie bestellen

SIMPLE PAST

ich bestellte	wir bestellten
du bestelltest	ihr bestelltet
Sie bestellten	Sie bestellten
er/sie/es bestellte	sie bestellten

FUTURE

ich werde	wir werden	bestellen
du wirst	ihr werdet	
Sie werden	Sie werden	
er/sie/es wird	sie werden	

PRESENT SUBJUNCTIVE I

ich bestelle	wir bestellen
du bestellest	ihr bestellet
Sie bestellen	Sie bestellen
er/sie/es bestelle	sie bestellen

PRESENT SUBJUNCTIVE II

ich bestellte	wir bestellten
du bestelltest	ihr bestelltet
Sie bestellten	Sie bestellten
er/sie/es bestellte	sie bestellten

FUTURE SUBJUNCTIVE I

ich werde	wir werden	bestellen
du werdest	ihr werdet	
Sie werden	Sie werden	
er/sie/es werde	sie werden	

FUTURE SUBJUNCTIVE II

ich würde	wir würden	bestellen
du würdest	ihr würdet	
Sie würden	Sie würden	
er/sie/es würde	sie würden	

PRESENT PERFECT

ich habe	wir haben	bestellt
du hast	ihr habt	
Sie haben	Sie haben	
er/sie/es hat	sie haben	

PAST PERFECT

ich hatte	wir hatten	bestellt
du hattest	ihr hattet	
Sie hatten	Sie hatten	
er/sie/es hatte	sie hatten	

FUTURE PERFECT

ich werde	wir werden	bestellt haben
du wirst	ihr werdet	
Sie werden	Sie werden	
er/sie/es wird	sie werden	

PAST SUBJUNCTIVE I

ich habe	wir haben	bestellt
du habest	ihr habet	
Sie haben	Sie haben	
er/sie/es habe	sie haben	

PAST SUBJUNCTIVE II

ich hätte	wir hätten	bestellt
du hättest	ihr hättet	
Sie hätten	Sie hätten	
er/sie/es hätte	sie hätten	

FUTURE PERFECT SUBJUNCTIVE I

ich werde	wir werden	bestellt haben
du werdest	ihr werdet	
Sie werden	Sie werden	
er/sie/es werde	sie werden	

FUTURE PERFECT SUBJUNCTIVE II

ich würde	wir würden	bestellt haben
du würdest	ihr würdet	
Sie würden	Sie würden	
er/sie/es würde	sie würden	

COMMANDS bestell(e)! bestellt! bestellen Sie!

PRESENT PARTICIPLE bestellend

Usage

Manfred hätte ein Glas Wein bestellt.	*Manfred would have ordered a glass of wine.*
Kann man online bestellen?	*Can you order online?*
Warum bestellst du so viele Sachen?	*Why are you ordering so many things?*
Wir möchten einen Tisch für vier Personen bestellen.	*We would like to reserve a table for four.*
Der Notarzt wurde bestellt.	*An emergency medic was called.*
Unser Papagei ist um zehn Uhr zum Tierarzt bestellt.	*Our parrot has an appointment with the veterinarian at ten o'clock.*
Haben Sie die Blumen für die Hochzeit bestellt?	*Have you arranged for flowers for the wedding?*
Mein Neffe ist zum Erben bestellt worden.	*My nephew has been designated as heir.*
Eure Majestät, ich habe Euren Brief bestellt.	*Your Majesty, I have delivered your letter.*
Ich soll dir Grüße von ihm bestellen.	*I'm supposed to tell you he says hello.*
Der König hatte sie zu sich bestellt.	*The king had summoned them.*

RELATED VERBS ab·bestellen, ein·bestellen, nach·bestellen, um·bestellen, vor·bestellen; *see also* **stellen** (426)

92 bestimmen *to determine, fix; intend; designate*

bestimmt · bestimmte · bestimmt regular weak verb

PRESENT

ich bestimme	wir bestimmen
du bestimmst	ihr bestimmt
Sie bestimmen	Sie bestimmen
er/sie/es bestimmt	sie bestimmen

SIMPLE PAST

ich bestimmte	wir bestimmten
du bestimmtest	ihr bestimmtet
Sie bestimmten	Sie bestimmten
er/sie/es bestimmte	sie bestimmten

FUTURE

ich werde	wir werden	bestimmen
du wirst	ihr werdet	
Sie werden	Sie werden	
er/sie/es wird	sie werden	

PRESENT SUBJUNCTIVE I

ich bestimme	wir bestimmen
du bestimmest	ihr bestimmet
Sie bestimmen	Sie bestimmen
er/sie/es bestimme	sie bestimmen

PRESENT SUBJUNCTIVE II

ich bestimmte	wir bestimmten
du bestimmtest	ihr bestimmtet
Sie bestimmten	Sie bestimmten
er/sie/es bestimmte	sie bestimmten

FUTURE SUBJUNCTIVE I

ich werde	wir werden	bestimmen
du werdest	ihr werdet	
Sie werden	Sie werden	
er/sie/es werde	sie werden	

FUTURE SUBJUNCTIVE II

ich würde	wir würden	bestimmen
du würdest	ihr würdet	
Sie würden	Sie würden	
er/sie/es würde	sie würden	

PRESENT PERFECT

ich habe	wir haben	bestimmt
du hast	ihr habt	
Sie haben	Sie haben	
er/sie/es hat	sie haben	

PAST PERFECT

ich hatte	wir hatten	bestimmt
du hattest	ihr hattet	
Sie hatten	Sie hatten	
er/sie/es hatte	sie hatten	

FUTURE PERFECT

ich werde	wir werden	bestimmt haben
du wirst	ihr werdet	
Sie werden	Sie werden	
er/sie/es wird	sie werden	

PAST SUBJUNCTIVE I

ich habe	wir haben	bestimmt
du habest	ihr habet	
Sie haben	Sie haben	
er/sie/es habe	sie haben	

PAST SUBJUNCTIVE II

ich hätte	wir hätten	bestimmt
du hättest	ihr hättet	
Sie hätten	Sie hätten	
er/sie/es hätte	sie hätten	

FUTURE PERFECT SUBJUNCTIVE I

ich werde	wir werden	bestimmt haben
du werdest	ihr werdet	
Sie werden	Sie werden	
er/sie/es werde	sie werden	

FUTURE PERFECT SUBJUNCTIVE II

ich würde	wir würden	bestimmt haben
du würdest	ihr würdet	
Sie würden	Sie würden	
er/sie/es würde	sie würden	

COMMANDS bestimm(e)! bestimmt! bestimmen Sie!

PRESENT PARTICIPLE bestimmend

Usage

Ernst hat den Ort bestimmt.	*Ernst determined the location.*
Der Käufer bestimmt die Art des Versands.	*The buyer determines the method of shipping.*
Die Amtsdauer wird durch das Gesetz bestimmt.	*The term of office is fixed by law.*
Wer kann das Ausmaß des Projekts bestimmen?	*Who can determine the scope of the project?*
Als Freiberufler bestimme ich meine Arbeitszeiten.	*As a freelancer, I set my own working hours.*
Dieser Sessel ist für mein Wohnzimmer bestimmt.	*This chair is destined for my living room.*
Heiner Ulrich wurde vom Vorstand zum Vorsitzenden bestimmt.	*Heiner Ulrich was appointed chair by the board.*
Meeresströmungen bestimmen das globale Klima.	*Ocean currents determine global climate.*

sich bestimmen *to be determined, be influenced*

Der Gesamtbetrag bestimmt sich in den meisten Fällen nach den Umzugskosten.	*The grand total is determined in most cases by the moving expenses.*

RELATED VERBS mit·bestimmen, vor·bestimmen; *see also* **stimmen** (428)

regular weak verb **besucht · besuchte · besucht**

PRESENT

ich besuche	wir besuchen
du besuchst	ihr besucht
Sie besuchen	Sie besuchen
er/sie/es besucht	sie besuchen

SIMPLE PAST

ich besuchte	wir besuchten
du besuchtest	ihr besuchtet
Sie besuchten	Sie besuchten
er/sie/es besuchte	sie besuchten

FUTURE

ich werde	wir werden	besuchen
du wirst	ihr werdet	
Sie werden	Sie werden	
er/sie/es wird	sie werden	

PRESENT SUBJUNCTIVE I

ich besuche	wir besuchen
du besuchest	ihr besuchet
Sie besuchen	Sie besuchen
er/sie/es besuche	sie besuchen

PRESENT SUBJUNCTIVE II

ich besuchte	wir besuchten
du besuchtest	ihr besuchtet
Sie besuchten	Sie besuchten
er/sie/es besuchte	sie besuchten

FUTURE SUBJUNCTIVE I

ich werde	wir werden	besuchen
du werdest	ihr werdet	
Sie werden	Sie werden	
er/sie/es werde	sie werden	

FUTURE SUBJUNCTIVE II

ich würde	wir würden	besuchen
du würdest	ihr würdet	
Sie würden	Sie würden	
er/sie/es würde	sie würden	

PRESENT PERFECT

ich habe	wir haben	besucht
du hast	ihr habt	
Sie haben	Sie haben	
er/sie/es hat	sie haben	

PAST PERFECT

ich hatte	wir hatten	besucht
du hattest	ihr hattet	
Sie hatten	Sie hatten	
er/sie/es hatte	sie hatten	

FUTURE PERFECT

ich werde	wir werden	besucht haben
du wirst	ihr werdet	
Sie werden	Sie werden	
er/sie/es wird	sie werden	

PAST SUBJUNCTIVE I

ich habe	wir haben	besucht
du habest	ihr habet	
Sie haben	Sie haben	
er/sie/es habe	sie haben	

PAST SUBJUNCTIVE II

ich hätte	wir hätten	besucht
du hättest	ihr hättet	
Sie hätten	Sie hätten	
er/sie/es hätte	sie hätten	

FUTURE PERFECT SUBJUNCTIVE I

ich werde	wir werden	besucht haben
du werdest	ihr werdet	
Sie werden	Sie werden	
er/sie/es werde	sie werden	

FUTURE PERFECT SUBJUNCTIVE II

ich würde	wir würden	besucht haben
du würdest	ihr würdet	
Sie würden	Sie würden	
er/sie/es würde	sie würden	

COMMANDS besuch(e)! besucht! besuchen Sie!

PRESENT PARTICIPLE besuchend

Usage

Ich möchte Maria besuchen. — *I'd like to visit Maria.*

Mark hat seine Tante im Altersheim besucht. — *Mark visited his aunt in the nursing home.*

Liedmeiers hätten gerne ihre Freunde in Bielefeld besucht, aber sie hatten keine Zeit. — *The Liedmeiers would have liked to visit their friends in Bielefeld, but they didn't have the time.*

Frau Fritsch wollte ihre Bekannte Frau Neumann am Samstagnachmittag besuchen. — *Mrs. Fritsch wanted to call on her acquaintance Mrs. Neumann on Saturday afternoon.*

Besuchst du meine Website? — *Will you visit my Web site?*

Wie lange besuchst du schon diese Hochschule? — *How long have you been attending this college?*

Dagmar durfte die Kunstakademie in Hamburg nicht besuchen. — *Dagmar wasn't allowed to attend the art academy in Hamburg.*

Letztes Jahr habe ich einen Kurs am Community College besucht. — *Last year I took a course at the community college.*

Der Zoo ist gut besucht. — *The zoo is heavily patronized.*

RELATED VERBS *see* **suchen** (440)

94 beteiligen *to give a share*

beteiligt · beteiligte · beteiligt

regular weak verb

PRESENT

ich beteilige	wir beteiligen
du beteiligst	ihr beteiligt
Sie beteiligen	Sie beteiligen
er/sie/es beteiligt	sie beteiligen

SIMPLE PAST

ich beteiligte	wir beteiligten
du beteiligtest	ihr beteiligtet
Sie beteiligten	Sie beteiligten
er/sie/es beteiligte	sie beteiligten

FUTURE

ich werde	wir werden	beteiligen
du wirst	ihr werdet	
Sie werden	Sie werden	
er/sie/es wird	sie werden	

PRESENT SUBJUNCTIVE I

ich beteilige	wir beteiligen
du beteiligest	ihr beteiliget
Sie beteiligen	Sie beteiligen
er/sie/es beteilige	sie beteiligen

PRESENT SUBJUNCTIVE II

ich beteiligte	wir beteiligten
du beteiligtest	ihr beteiligtet
Sie beteiligten	Sie beteiligten
er/sie/es beteiligte	sie beteiligten

FUTURE SUBJUNCTIVE I

ich werde	wir werden	beteiligen
du werdest	ihr werdet	
Sie werden	Sie werden	
er/sie/es werde	sie werden	

FUTURE SUBJUNCTIVE II

ich würde	wir würden	beteiligen
du würdest	ihr würdet	
Sie würden	Sie würden	
er/sie/es würde	sie würden	

PRESENT PERFECT

ich habe	wir haben	beteiligt
du hast	ihr habt	
Sie haben	Sie haben	
er/sie/es hat	sie haben	

PAST PERFECT

ich hatte	wir hatten	beteiligt
du hattest	ihr hattet	
Sie hatten	Sie hatten	
er/sie/es hatte	sie hatten	

FUTURE PERFECT

ich werde	wir werden	beteiligt haben
du wirst	ihr werdet	
Sie werden	Sie werden	
er/sie/es wird	sie werden	

PAST SUBJUNCTIVE I

ich habe	wir haben	beteiligt
du habest	ihr habet	
Sie haben	Sie haben	
er/sie/es habe	sie haben	

PAST SUBJUNCTIVE II

ich hätte	wir hätten	beteiligt
du hättest	ihr hättet	
Sie hätten	Sie hätten	
er/sie/es hätte	sie hätten	

FUTURE PERFECT SUBJUNCTIVE I

ich werde	wir werden	beteiligt haben
du werdest	ihr werdet	
Sie werden	Sie werden	
er/sie/es werde	sie werden	

FUTURE PERFECT SUBJUNCTIVE II

ich würde	wir würden	beteiligt haben
du würdest	ihr würdet	
Sie würden	Sie würden	
er/sie/es würde	sie würden	

COMMANDS beteilig(e)! beteiligt! beteiligen Sie!

PRESENT PARTICIPLE beteiligend

Usage

Ihr Mann wollte sie nicht am Lottogewinn beteiligen. — *Her husband didn't want to give her a share of the lottery winnings.*

Die jüngste Sohn wurde vom Vater nicht an der Erbschaft beteiligt. — *The youngest son didn't get a share of the father's inheritance.*

sich beteiligen *to be involved, take part, participate*

Beteiligen Sie sich an diesem Projekt? — *Are you involved in this project?*

Etwa 4 000 Personen haben sich daran beteiligt. — *About 4,000 people took part in it.*

Studierende können sich an internationalen Austauschprogrammen beteiligen. — *Students can participate in international exchange programs.*

Dem Bericht nach habe sich Frau Ostrowski gestern an diesem Verbrechen beteiligt. — *According to the report, Mrs. Ostrowski was a party to this crime yesterday.*

Das ist eine Veranstaltung, an der sich keine Schüler beteiligen dürfen. — *That is an event in which students are not allowed to participate.*

regular weak verb **betet · betete · gebetet**

PRESENT

ich bete	wir beten
du betest	ihr betet
Sie beten	Sie beten
er/sie/es betet	sie beten

SIMPLE PAST

ich betete	wir beteten
du betetest	ihr betetet
Sie beteten	Sie beteten
er/sie/es betete	sie beteten

FUTURE

ich werde	wir werden	beten
du wirst	ihr werdet	
Sie werden	Sie werden	
er/sie/es wird	sie werden	

PRESENT SUBJUNCTIVE I

ich bete	wir beten
du betest	ihr betet
Sie beten	Sie beten
er/sie/es bete	sie beten

PRESENT SUBJUNCTIVE II

ich betete	wir beteten
du betetest	ihr betetet
Sie beteten	Sie beteten
er/sie/es betete	sie beteten

FUTURE SUBJUNCTIVE I

ich werde	wir werden	beten
du werdest	ihr werdet	
Sie werden	Sie werden	
er/sie/es werde	sie werden	

FUTURE SUBJUNCTIVE II

ich würde	wir würden	beten
du würdest	ihr würdet	
Sie würden	Sie würden	
er/sie/es würde	sie würden	

PRESENT PERFECT

ich habe	wir haben	gebetet
du hast	ihr habt	
Sie haben	Sie haben	
er/sie/es hat	sie haben	

PAST PERFECT

ich hatte	wir hatten	gebetet
du hattest	ihr hattet	
Sie hatten	Sie hatten	
er/sie/es hatte	sie hatten	

FUTURE PERFECT

ich werde	wir werden	gebetet haben
du wirst	ihr werdet	
Sie werden	Sie werden	
er/sie/es wird	sie werden	

PAST SUBJUNCTIVE I

ich habe	wir haben	gebetet
du habest	ihr habet	
Sie haben	Sie haben	
er/sie/es habe	sie haben	

PAST SUBJUNCTIVE II

ich hätte	wir hätten	gebetet
du hättest	ihr hättet	
Sie hätten	Sie hätten	
er/sie/es hätte	sie hätten	

FUTURE PERFECT SUBJUNCTIVE I

ich werde	wir werden	gebetet haben
du werdest	ihr werdet	
Sie werden	Sie werden	
er/sie/es werde	sie werden	

FUTURE PERFECT SUBJUNCTIVE II

ich würde	wir würden	gebetet haben
du würdest	ihr würdet	
Sie würden	Sie würden	
er/sie/es würde	sie würden	

COMMANDS bete! betet! beten Sie!

PRESENT PARTICIPLE betend

Usage

Ich bete für Sie.	*I will pray for you.*
Es wird oft in festgelegten Formeln gebetet.	*People often pray using established formulas.*
Lasset uns beten. (*archaic*)	*Let us pray.*
Wenn aber du betest, so ... bete zu deinem Vater im Verborgenen. (MATTHÄUS 6,6)	*When thou prayest, ... pray to thy Father, which is in secret.* (MATTHEW 6:6)
Er betet und fastet.	*He prays and fasts.*
Im Parlament wird vor Beginn der Sitzung gebetet.	*In Parliament, they pray before the beginning of the session.*
Wir beten für Regen.	*We're praying for rain.*
Jeden Morgen betet sie am Grabmal ihrer Mutter.	*Each morning she prays at her mother's grave.*
Das Vaterunser wird gebetet.	*The Lord's Prayer is being recited.*
Früher betete man viel mehr auf Latein.	*People used to pray more in Latin.*

RELATED VERBS an·beten, erbeten, vor·beten

96 betonen *to stress, emphasize*

betont · betonte · betont

regular weak verb

PRESENT

ich betone	wir betonen
du betonst	ihr betont
Sie betonen	Sie betonen
er/sie/es betont	sie betonen

SIMPLE PAST

ich betonte	wir betonten
du betontest	ihr betontet
Sie betonten	Sie betonten
er/sie/es betonte	sie betonten

FUTURE

ich werde	wir werden	betonen
du wirst	ihr werdet	
Sie werden	Sie werden	
er/sie/es wird	sie werden	

PRESENT SUBJUNCTIVE I

ich betone	wir betonen
du betonest	ihr betonet
Sie betonen	Sie betonen
er/sie/es betone	sie betonen

PRESENT SUBJUNCTIVE II

ich betonte	wir betonten
du betontest	ihr betontet
Sie betonten	Sie betonten
er/sie/es betonte	sie betonten

FUTURE SUBJUNCTIVE I

ich werde	wir werden	betonen
du werdest	ihr werdet	
Sie werden	Sie werden	
er/sie/es werde	sie werden	

FUTURE SUBJUNCTIVE II

ich würde	wir würden	betonen
du würdest	ihr würdet	
Sie würden	Sie würden	
er/sie/es würde	sie würden	

PRESENT PERFECT

ich habe	wir haben	betont
du hast	ihr habt	
Sie haben	Sie haben	
er/sie/es hat	sie haben	

PAST PERFECT

ich hatte	wir hatten	betont
du hattest	ihr hattet	
Sie hatten	Sie hatten	
er/sie/es hatte	sie hatten	

FUTURE PERFECT

ich werde	wir werden	betont haben
du wirst	ihr werdet	
Sie werden	Sie werden	
er/sie/es wird	sie werden	

PAST SUBJUNCTIVE I

ich habe	wir haben	betont
du habest	ihr habet	
Sie haben	Sie haben	
er/sie/es habe	sie haben	

PAST SUBJUNCTIVE II

ich hätte	wir hätten	betont
du hättest	ihr hättet	
Sie hätten	Sie hätten	
er/sie/es hätte	sie hätten	

FUTURE PERFECT SUBJUNCTIVE I

ich werde	wir werden	betont haben
du werdest	ihr werdet	
Sie werden	Sie werden	
er/sie/es werde	sie werden	

FUTURE PERFECT SUBJUNCTIVE II

ich würde	wir würden	betont haben
du würdest	ihr würdet	
Sie würden	Sie würden	
er/sie/es würde	sie würden	

COMMANDS beton(e)! betont! betonen Sie!

PRESENT PARTICIPLE betonend

Usage

Die Treue wird unter ihnen stark betont. — *Loyalty is strongly emphasized among them.*

Der Redner betonte häufig einen ganz anderen Punkt. — *The speaker frequently stressed a completely different point.*

Bernhard hat das Wort „vielleicht“ besonders betont. — *Bernhard especially emphasized the word “perhaps.”*

Im Wort „betonen“ wird die erste Silbe nicht betont. — *In the word “betonen” the first syllable is not stressed.*

Wir können nicht genug betonen, dass diese Anschaffung völlig überflüssig ist. — *We cannot stress enough that this acquisition is completely unnecessary.*

Es ist allerdings zu betonen, dass solche Ideologien gefährlich sind. — *However, it is to be emphasized that such ideologies are dangerous.*

Die Vorstandsvorsitzende betonte: „Wir haben keinen Grund daran zu zweifeln.“ — *The chair of the board stressed, “We have no reason to doubt this.”*

Die Mystiker betonten Einheit mit Gott. — *The mystics emphasized unity with God.*

In seiner Rede wurde die Rolle der UNO betont. — *In his speech the role of the U.N. was stressed.*

RELATED VERB überbetonen

PRESENT

ich betrage	wir betragen
du beträgst	ihr betragt
Sie betragen	Sie betragen
er/sie/es beträgt	sie betragen

SIMPLE PAST

ich betrug	wir betrugen
du betrugst	ihr betrugt
Sie betrugen	Sie betrugen
er/sie/es betrug	sie betrugen

FUTURE

ich werde	wir werden	betragen
du wirst	ihr werdet	
Sie werden	Sie werden	
er/sie/es wird	sie werden	

PRESENT SUBJUNCTIVE I

ich betrage	wir betragen
du betragest	ihr betraget
Sie betragen	Sie betragen
er/sie/es betrage	sie betragen

PRESENT SUBJUNCTIVE II

ich betrüge	wir betrügen
du betrügest	ihr betrüget
Sie betrügen	Sie betrügen
er/sie/es betrüge	sie betrügen

FUTURE SUBJUNCTIVE I

ich werde	wir werden	betragen
du werdest	ihr werdet	
Sie werden	Sie werden	
er/sie/es werde	sie werden	

FUTURE SUBJUNCTIVE II

ich würde	wir würden	betragen
du würdest	ihr würdet	
Sie würden	Sie würden	
er/sie/es würde	sie würden	

PRESENT PERFECT

ich habe	wir haben	betragen
du hast	ihr habt	
Sie haben	Sie haben	
er/sie/es hat	sie haben	

PAST PERFECT

ich hatte	wir hatten	betragen
du hattest	ihr hattet	
Sie hatten	Sie hatten	
er/sie/es hatte	sie hatten	

FUTURE PERFECT

ich werde	wir werden	betragen haben
du wirst	ihr werdet	
Sie werden	Sie werden	
er/sie/es wird	sie werden	

PAST SUBJUNCTIVE I

ich habe	wir haben	betragen
du habest	ihr habet	
Sie haben	Sie haben	
er/sie/es habe	sie haben	

PAST SUBJUNCTIVE II

ich hätte	wir hätten	betragen
du hättest	ihr hättet	
Sie hätten	Sie hätten	
er/sie/es hätte	sie hätten	

FUTURE PERFECT SUBJUNCTIVE I

ich werde	wir werden	betragen haben
du werdest	ihr werdet	
Sie werden	Sie werden	
er/sie/es werde	sie werden	

FUTURE PERFECT SUBJUNCTIVE II

ich würde	wir würden	betragen haben
du würdest	ihr würdet	
Sie würden	Sie würden	
er/sie/es würde	sie würden	

COMMANDS betrag(e)! betragt! betragen Sie!

PRESENT PARTICIPLE betragend

Usage

Insgesamt betragen die Sanierungskosten etwa 25 000 Euro. — *The total restoration costs come to about 25,000 euros.*

Das Durchschnittsalter der Teilnehmer betrug 34 Jahre. — *The average age of the participants was 34 years.*

Die Entfernung zwischen diesen Sternen beträgt 12,5 Lichtjahre. — *The distance between these stars is 12.5 light years.*

Die Sturmschäden haben 73 Mio Euro betragen. — *The storm damage came to 73 million euros.*

Glücklicherweise wird der Zuschlag höchstens 10 % des Gesamtbetrags betragen. — *Fortunately the surcharge will amount to at most 10% of the total.*

Mit Steuer betrüge der Preis mehr als €200 [200 Euro]. — *With tax, the price would be more than 200 euros.*

sich betragen *to act, behave*

Ich habe mich nicht ganz ordentlich betragen. — *I haven't behaved quite properly.*

Christian beträgt sich ihr gegenüber relativ manierlich. — *Christian is relatively well mannered around her.*

RELATED VERBS *see* **tragen** (446)

98 betrügen *to deceive; defraud; be unfaithful to*

betrügt · betrog · betrogen strong verb

PRESENT

ich betrüge	wir betrügen
du betrügst	ihr betrügt
Sie betrügen	Sie betrügen
er/sie/es betrügt	sie betrügen

SIMPLE PAST

ich betrog	wir betrogen
du betrogst	ihr betrogt
Sie betrogen	Sie betrogen
er/sie/es betrog	sie betrogen

FUTURE

ich werde	wir werden	betrügen
du wirst	ihr werdet	
Sie werden	Sie werden	
er/sie/es wird	sie werden	

PRESENT SUBJUNCTIVE I

ich betrüge	wir betrügen
du betrügest	ihr betrüget
Sie betrügen	Sie betrügen
er/sie/es betrüge	sie betrügen

PRESENT SUBJUNCTIVE II

ich betröge	wir betrögen
du betrögest	ihr betröget
Sie betrögen	Sie betrögen
er/sie/es betröge	sie betrögen

FUTURE SUBJUNCTIVE I

ich werde	wir werden	betrügen
du werdest	ihr werdet	
Sie werden	Sie werden	
er/sie/es werde	sie werden	

FUTURE SUBJUNCTIVE II

ich würde	wir würden	betrügen
du würdest	ihr würdet	
Sie würden	Sie würden	
er/sie/es würde	sie würden	

PRESENT PERFECT

ich habe	wir haben	betrogen
du hast	ihr habt	
Sie haben	Sie haben	
er/sie/es hat	sie haben	

PAST PERFECT

ich hatte	wir hatten	betrogen
du hattest	ihr hattet	
Sie hatten	Sie hatten	
er/sie/es hatte	sie hatten	

FUTURE PERFECT

ich werde	wir werden	betrogen haben
du wirst	ihr werdet	
Sie werden	Sie werden	
er/sie/es wird	sie werden	

PAST SUBJUNCTIVE I

ich habe	wir haben	betrogen
du habest	ihr habet	
Sie haben	Sie haben	
er/sie/es habe	sie haben	

PAST SUBJUNCTIVE II

ich hätte	wir hätten	betrogen
du hättest	ihr hättet	
Sie hätten	Sie hätten	
er/sie/es hätte	sie hätten	

FUTURE PERFECT SUBJUNCTIVE I

ich werde	wir werden	betrogen haben
du werdest	ihr werdet	
Sie werden	Sie werden	
er/sie/es werde	sie werden	

FUTURE PERFECT SUBJUNCTIVE II

ich würde	wir würden	betrogen haben
du würdest	ihr würdet	
Sie würden	Sie würden	
er/sie/es würde	sie würden	

COMMANDS betrüg(e)! betrügt! betrügen Sie!

PRESENT PARTICIPLE betrügend

Usage

Das Publikum wurde betrogen.	*The public was deceived.*
Herr Mannheimer hat seine Kollegen betrogen und belogen.	*Mr. Mannheimer deceived and lied to his colleagues.*
Lasst euch nicht betrügen!	*Don't be fooled!*
Ich würde dich nie betrügen.	*I would never deceive you.*
Die Kunden werden von der Firma betrogen.	*The customers are being cheated by the firm.*
Der Stadtrat will die Bürger betrügen.	*The city council wants to deceive the citizens.*
Du betrügst dich selbst.	*You are deceiving yourself.*
Franke scheint, die Steuerbehörden diesmal wirklich betrogen zu haben.	*Franke really seems to have defrauded the tax authorities this time.*
Ich danke dir, Albert, dass du mich betrogen hast. (GOETHE)	*I thank you, Albert, for deceiving me.*
Er betrog seine Frau.	*He was unfaithful to his wife.*

RELATED VERBS *see* **trügen** (456)

strong verb **bewegt · bewog · bewogen**

PRESENT

ich bewege	wir bewegen
du bewegst	ihr bewegt
Sie bewegen	Sie bewegen
er/sie/es bewegt	sie bewegen

SIMPLE PAST

ich bewog	wir bewogen
du bewogst	ihr bewogt
Sie bewogen	Sie bewogen
er/sie/es bewog	sie bewogen

FUTURE

ich werde	wir werden	bewegen
du wirst	ihr werdet	
Sie werden	Sie werden	
er/sie/es wird	sie werden	

PRESENT SUBJUNCTIVE I

ich bewege	wir bewegen
du bewegest	ihr beweget
Sie bewegen	Sie bewegen
er/sie/es bewege	sie bewegen

PRESENT SUBJUNCTIVE II

ich bewöge	wir bewögen
du bewögest	ihr bewöget
Sie bewögen	Sie bewögen
er/sie/es bewöge	sie bewögen

FUTURE SUBJUNCTIVE I

ich werde	wir werden	bewegen
du werdest	ihr werdet	
Sie werden	Sie werden	
er/sie/es werde	sie werden	

FUTURE SUBJUNCTIVE II

ich würde	wir würden	bewegen
du würdest	ihr würdet	
Sie würden	Sie würden	
er/sie/es würde	sie würden	

PRESENT PERFECT

ich habe	wir haben	bewogen
du hast	ihr habt	
Sie haben	Sie haben	
er/sie/es hat	sie haben	

PAST PERFECT

ich hatte	wir hatten	bewogen
du hattest	ihr hattet	
Sie hatten	Sie hatten	
er/sie/es hatte	sie hatten	

FUTURE PERFECT

ich werde	wir werden	bewogen haben
du wirst	ihr werdet	
Sie werden	Sie werden	
er/sie/es wird	sie werden	

PAST SUBJUNCTIVE I

ich habe	wir haben	bewogen
du habest	ihr habet	
Sie haben	Sie haben	
er/sie/es habe	sie haben	

PAST SUBJUNCTIVE II

ich hätte	wir hätten	bewogen
du hättest	ihr hättet	
Sie hätten	Sie hätten	
er/sie/es hätte	sie hätten	

FUTURE PERFECT SUBJUNCTIVE I

ich werde	wir werden	bewogen haben
du werdest	ihr werdet	
Sie werden	Sie werden	
er/sie/es werde	sie werden	

FUTURE PERFECT SUBJUNCTIVE II

ich würde	wir würden	bewogen haben
du würdest	ihr würdet	
Sie würden	Sie würden	
er/sie/es würde	sie würden	

COMMANDS beweg(e)! bewegt! bewegen Sie!

PRESENT PARTICIPLE bewegend

Usage

Seine Angst vor den Nazis bewog ihn, 1933 Deutschland zu verlassen. — *His fear of the Nazis caused him to leave Germany in 1933.*

Amalie lässt sich nicht bewegen, die Arbeitsstelle zu kündigen. — *Amalie won't be persuaded to quit the job.*

Das Bauernvolk wurde durch Drohungen des Bischofs bewogen, den Zehnten zu geben. — *The peasants were induced to tithe by the bishop's threats.*

Die Rede der Bundesrätin hat die Mitglieder zu dieser Entscheidung bewogen. — *The senator's speech led the members to this decision.*

Was bewegt dich dazu, dein Arbeitszimmer so üppig einzurichten? — *What prompts you to furnish your home office so luxuriously?*

Solche Ereignisse bewegen einen, sich politisch zu engagieren. — *Such events prompt people to get politically involved.*

Ich fühlte mich bewogen, Frau Schumanski im Krankenhaus zu besuchen. — *I felt moved to visit Mrs. Schumanski in the hospital.*

100 bewegen[2] *to move, stir; occupy one's mind*

bewegt · bewegte · bewegt

regular weak verb

PRESENT

ich bewege	wir bewegen
du bewegst	ihr bewegt
Sie bewegen	Sie bewegen
er/sie/es bewegt	sie bewegen

SIMPLE PAST

ich bewegte	wir bewegten
du bewegtest	ihr bewegtet
Sie bewegten	Sie bewegten
er/sie/es bewegte	sie bewegten

FUTURE

ich werde	wir werden	bewegen
du wirst	ihr werdet	
Sie werden	Sie werden	
er/sie/es wird	sie werden	

PRESENT SUBJUNCTIVE I

ich bewege	wir bewegen
du bewegest	ihr beweget
Sie bewegen	Sie bewegen
er/sie/es bewege	sie bewegen

PRESENT SUBJUNCTIVE II

ich bewegte	wir bewegten
du bewegtest	ihr bewegtet
Sie bewegten	Sie bewegten
er/sie/es bewegte	sie bewegten

FUTURE SUBJUNCTIVE I

ich werde	wir werden	bewegen
du werdest	ihr werdet	
Sie werden	Sie werden	
er/sie/es werde	sie werden	

FUTURE SUBJUNCTIVE II

ich würde	wir würden	bewegen
du würdest	ihr würdet	
Sie würden	Sie würden	
er/sie/es würde	sie würden	

PRESENT PERFECT

ich habe	wir haben	bewegt
du hast	ihr habt	
Sie haben	Sie haben	
er/sie/es hat	sie haben	

PAST PERFECT

ich hatte	wir hatten	bewegt
du hattest	ihr hattet	
Sie hatten	Sie hatten	
er/sie/es hatte	sie hatten	

FUTURE PERFECT

ich werde	wir werden	bewegt haben
du wirst	ihr werdet	
Sie werden	Sie werden	
er/sie/es wird	sie werden	

PAST SUBJUNCTIVE I

ich habe	wir haben	bewegt
du habest	ihr habet	
Sie haben	Sie haben	
er/sie/es habe	sie haben	

PAST SUBJUNCTIVE II

ich hätte	wir hätten	bewegt
du hättest	ihr hättet	
Sie hätten	Sie hätten	
er/sie/es hätte	sie hätten	

FUTURE PERFECT SUBJUNCTIVE I

ich werde	wir werden	bewegt haben
du werdest	ihr werdet	
Sie werden	Sie werden	
er/sie/es werde	sie werden	

FUTURE PERFECT SUBJUNCTIVE II

ich würde	wir würden	bewegt haben
du würdest	ihr würdet	
Sie würden	Sie würden	
er/sie/es würde	sie würden	

COMMANDS beweg(e)! bewegt! bewegen Sie!

PRESENT PARTICIPLE bewegend

Usage

Bewegen Sie jetzt die Arme vorwärts. — *Now move your arms forward.*

Was hat dich so tief bewegt? — *What stirred you so deeply?*

Unser Hund Max lag auf der Terrasse und ließ sich nicht bewegen. — *Our dog Max lay on the patio and wouldn't be budged.*

Diese Vorstellung bewegt mich seit dem Tod meines Vaters. — *This idea has occupied my mind since my father's death.*

sich bewegen *to move; exercise*

Er lag da und bewegte sich nicht. — *He lay there and didn't move.*

Beweg dich nicht vom Fleck. — *Don't move from that spot.*

Nach der Operation konnte sich meine Mutter nur langsam bewegen. — *After the operation, my mother was only able to move slowly.*

Mein Arzt sagt, dass ich mich mehr bewegen muss. — *My doctor says I have to get more exercise.*

RELATED VERB zu·bewegen

strong verb **beweist · bewies · bewiesen**

PRESENT		
ich beweise	wir beweisen	
du beweist	ihr beweist	
Sie beweisen	Sie beweisen	
er/sie/es beweist	sie beweisen	

SIMPLE PAST		
ich bewies	wir bewiesen	
du bewiesest	ihr bewiest	
Sie bewiesen	Sie bewiesen	
er/sie/es bewies	sie bewiesen	

FUTURE		
ich werde	wir werden	beweisen
du wirst	ihr werdet	
Sie werden	Sie werden	
er/sie/es wird	sie werden	

PRESENT SUBJUNCTIVE I		
ich beweise	wir beweisen	
du beweisest	ihr beweiset	
Sie beweisen	Sie beweisen	
er/sie/es beweise	sie beweisen	

PRESENT SUBJUNCTIVE II		
ich bewiese	wir bewiesen	
du bewiesest	ihr bewieset	
Sie bewiesen	Sie bewiesen	
er/sie/es bewiese	sie bewiesen	

FUTURE SUBJUNCTIVE I		
ich werde	wir werden	beweisen
du werdest	ihr werdet	
Sie werden	Sie werden	
er/sie/es werde	sie werden	

FUTURE SUBJUNCTIVE II		
ich würde	wir würden	beweisen
du würdest	ihr würdet	
Sie würden	Sie würden	
er/sie/es würde	sie würden	

PRESENT PERFECT		
ich habe	wir haben	bewiesen
du hast	ihr habt	
Sie haben	Sie haben	
er/sie/es hat	sie haben	

PAST PERFECT		
ich hatte	wir hatten	bewiesen
du hattest	ihr hattet	
Sie hatten	Sie hatten	
er/sie/es hatte	sie hatten	

FUTURE PERFECT		
ich werde	wir werden	bewiesen haben
du wirst	ihr werdet	
Sie werden	Sie werden	
er/sie/es wird	sie werden	

PAST SUBJUNCTIVE I		
ich habe	wir haben	bewiesen
du habest	ihr habet	
Sie haben	Sie haben	
er/sie/es habe	sie haben	

PAST SUBJUNCTIVE II		
ich hätte	wir hätten	bewiesen
du hättest	ihr hättet	
Sie hätten	Sie hätten	
er/sie/es hätte	sie hätten	

FUTURE PERFECT SUBJUNCTIVE I		
ich werde	wir werden	bewiesen haben
du werdest	ihr werdet	
Sie werden	Sie werden	
er/sie/es werde	sie werden	

FUTURE PERFECT SUBJUNCTIVE II		
ich würde	wir würden	bewiesen haben
du würdest	ihr würdet	
Sie würden	Sie würden	
er/sie/es würde	sie würden	

COMMANDS beweis(e)! beweist! beweisen Sie!

PRESENT PARTICIPLE beweisend

Usage

Wie kann ich euch denn beweisen, dass ich es alleine machen kann? — *How can I prove to you that I can do it by myself?*

Danach hat er gerade das Gegenteil bewiesen. — *After that he proved exactly the opposite.*

Sein Handeln hat uns bewiesen, dass er die Sache ernst nimmt. — *His actions showed us that he takes the matter seriously.*

Die scharfe Kritik beweist, dass das Thema doch noch relevant ist. — *The sharp criticism is evidence that the topic is indeed still relevant.*

Das beweist nichts. — *That proves nothing.*

sich beweisen *to be proved*

Die Behauptung hat sich bewiesen. — *The claim has been proved.*

Der Händler hat sich schließlich als Betrüger bewiesen. — *The dealer turned out to be a fraud.*

RELATED VERBS *see* **weisen** (526)

102 sich bewerben *to apply; compete*

bewirbt sich · bewarb sich · sich beworben strong verb

PRESENT

ich bewerbe mich	wir bewerben uns
du bewirbst dich	ihr bewerbt euch
Sie bewerben sich	Sie bewerben sich
er/sie/es bewirbt sich	sie bewerben sich

PRESENT PERFECT

ich habe mich	wir haben uns	beworben
du hast dich	ihr habt euch	
Sie haben sich	Sie haben sich	
er/sie/es hat sich	sie haben sich	

SIMPLE PAST

ich bewarb mich	wir bewarben uns
du bewarbst dich	ihr bewarbt euch
Sie bewarben sich	Sie bewarben sich
er/sie/es bewarb sich	sie bewarben sich

PAST PERFECT

ich hatte mich	wir hatten uns	beworben
du hattest dich	ihr hattet euch	
Sie hatten sich	Sie hatten sich	
er/sie/es hatte sich	sie hatten sich	

FUTURE

ich werde mich	wir werden uns	bewerben
du wirst dich	ihr werdet euch	
Sie werden sich	Sie werden sich	
er/sie/es wird sich	sie werden sich	

FUTURE PERFECT

ich werde mich	wir werden uns	beworben haben
du wirst dich	ihr werdet euch	
Sie werden sich	Sie werden sich	
er/sie/es wird sich	sie werden sich	

PRESENT SUBJUNCTIVE I

ich bewerbe mich	wir bewerben uns
du bewerbest dich	ihr bewerbet euch
Sie bewerben sich	Sie bewerben sich
er/sie/es bewerbe sich	sie bewerben sich

PAST SUBJUNCTIVE I

ich habe mich	wir haben uns	beworben
du habest dich	ihr habet euch	
Sie haben sich	Sie haben sich	
er/sie/es habe sich	sie haben sich	

PRESENT SUBJUNCTIVE II

ich bewürbe mich	wir bewürben uns
du bewürbest dich	ihr bewürbet euch
Sie bewürben sich	Sie bewürben sich
er/sie/es bewürbe sich	sie bewürben sich

PAST SUBJUNCTIVE II

ich hätte mich	wir hätten uns	beworben
du hättest dich	ihr hättet euch	
Sie hätten sich	Sie hätten sich	
er/sie/es hätte sich	sie hätten sich	

FUTURE SUBJUNCTIVE I

ich werde mich	wir werden uns	bewerben
du werdest dich	ihr werdet euch	
Sie werden sich	Sie werden sich	
er/sie/es werde sich	sie werden sich	

FUTURE PERFECT SUBJUNCTIVE I

ich werde mich	wir werden uns	beworben haben
du werdest dich	ihr werdet euch	
Sie werden sich	Sie werden sich	
er/sie/es werde sich	sie werden sich	

FUTURE SUBJUNCTIVE II

ich würde mich	wir würden uns	bewerben
du würdest dich	ihr würdet euch	
Sie würden sich	Sie würden sich	
er/sie/es würde sich	sie würden sich	

FUTURE PERFECT SUBJUNCTIVE II

ich würde mich	wir würden uns	beworben haben
du würdest dich	ihr würdet euch	
Sie würden sich	Sie würden sich	
er/sie/es würde sich	sie würden sich	

COMMANDS bewirb dich! bewerbt euch! bewerben Sie sich!

PRESENT PARTICIPLE sich bewerbend

Usage

Ich habe mich um eine Stelle als Posaunist beworben.	*I applied for a position as trombonist.*
Warum bewirbst du dich doch nicht bei der Firma Schmidt?	*Why don't you apply at the Schmidt Company?*
Studierende sollten sich rechtzeitig um Wohnheimplätze bewerben.	*Students should apply for dormitory housing in a timely manner.*
Hiermit bewerbe ich mich um einen Ausbildungsplatz als Bäckerin.	*Herewith I am applying for an apprenticeship as baker.*
Angelika möchte sich um ein Fulbright-Stipendium bewerben.	*Angelika would like to apply for a Fulbright Fellowship.*
Insgesamt bewerben sich siebzehn Unternehmen um die neuen Aufträge.	*A total of 17 enterprises are competing for the new contracts.*
Der Prinz bewarb sich um die schöne Königstochter. (*archaic*)	*The prince proposed to the king's beautiful daughter.*

RELATED VERBS *see* **werben** (528)

regular weak verb **bezahlt · bezahlte · bezahlt**

PRESENT

ich bezahle	wir bezahlen
du bezahlst	ihr bezahlt
Sie bezahlen	Sie bezahlen
er/sie/es bezahlt	sie bezahlen

SIMPLE PAST

ich bezahlte	wir bezahlten
du bezahltest	ihr bezahltet
Sie bezahlten	Sie bezahlten
er/sie/es bezahlte	sie bezahlten

FUTURE

ich werde	wir werden	bezahlen
du wirst	ihr werdet	
Sie werden	Sie werden	
er/sie/es wird	sie werden	

PRESENT SUBJUNCTIVE I

ich bezahle	wir bezahlen
du bezahlest	ihr bezahlet
Sie bezahlen	Sie bezahlen
er/sie/es bezahle	sie bezahlen

PRESENT SUBJUNCTIVE II

ich bezahlte	wir bezahlten
du bezahltest	ihr bezahltet
Sie bezahlten	Sie bezahlten
er/sie/es bezahlte	sie bezahlten

FUTURE SUBJUNCTIVE I

ich werde	wir werden	bezahlen
du werdest	ihr werdet	
Sie werden	Sie werden	
er/sie/es werde	sie werden	

FUTURE SUBJUNCTIVE II

ich würde	wir würden	bezahlen
du würdest	ihr würdet	
Sie würden	Sie würden	
er/sie/es würde	sie würden	

PRESENT PERFECT

ich habe	wir haben	bezahlt
du hast	ihr habt	
Sie haben	Sie haben	
er/sie/es hat	sie haben	

PAST PERFECT

ich hatte	wir hatten	bezahlt
du hattest	ihr hattet	
Sie hatten	Sie hatten	
er/sie/es hatte	sie hatten	

FUTURE PERFECT

ich werde	wir werden	bezahlt haben
du wirst	ihr werdet	
Sie werden	Sie werden	
er/sie/es wird	sie werden	

PAST SUBJUNCTIVE I

ich habe	wir haben	bezahlt
du habest	ihr habet	
Sie haben	Sie haben	
er/sie/es habe	sie haben	

PAST SUBJUNCTIVE II

ich hätte	wir hätten	bezahlt
du hättest	ihr hättet	
Sie hätten	Sie hätten	
er/sie/es hätte	sie hätten	

FUTURE PERFECT SUBJUNCTIVE I

ich werde	wir werden	bezahlt haben
du werdest	ihr werdet	
Sie werden	Sie werden	
er/sie/es werde	sie werden	

FUTURE PERFECT SUBJUNCTIVE II

ich würde	wir würden	bezahlt haben
du würdest	ihr würdet	
Sie würden	Sie würden	
er/sie/es würde	sie würden	

COMMANDS bezahl(e)! bezahlt! bezahlen Sie!

PRESENT PARTICIPLE bezahlend

Usage

Die wohlhabende Kundin hat die Rechnung mit einem 500 Euro-Schein bezahlt.	*The wealthy customer paid with a 500-euro bill.*
Den Restbetrag kann man bei Ankunft per Kreditkarte bezahlen.	*The balance can be paid by credit card upon arrival.*
Kann ich bar bezahlen?	*Can I pay cash?*
In Europa bezahlt man häufig per Überweisung.	*In Europe people frequently pay by electronic bank transfer.*
Die Miete ist am ersten des Monats zu bezahlen.	*The rent is due on the first of the month.*
Mitarbeiter müssen für Wochenendarbeit bezahlt werden.	*Employees must be remunerated for weekend work.*
Wer kann das schon bezahlen?	*Who can afford that?*
Das Rentensystem ist nicht mehr zu bezahlen.	*The pension system can no longer be afforded.*
Ich möchte bezahlen! *(idiomatic)*	*Check, please!*

RELATED VERBS ab·bezahlen, an·bezahlen, aus·bezahlen, überbezahlen, unterbezahlen, vor·bezahlen; *see also* **zahlen** (543)

bezeichnen *to mark, indicate; designate; denote; refer to*

bezeichnet · bezeichnete · bezeichnet regular weak verb

PRESENT

ich bezeichne	wir bezeichnen
du bezeichnest	ihr bezeichnet
Sie bezeichnen	Sie bezeichnen
er/sie/es bezeichnet	sie bezeichnen

SIMPLE PAST

ich bezeichnete	wir bezeichneten
du bezeichnetest	ihr bezeichnetet
Sie bezeichneten	Sie bezeichneten
er/sie/es bezeichnete	sie bezeichneten

FUTURE

ich werde	wir werden	bezeichnen
du wirst	ihr werdet	
Sie werden	Sie werden	
er/sie/es wird	sie werden	

PRESENT SUBJUNCTIVE I

ich bezeichne	wir bezeichnen
du bezeichnest	ihr bezeichnet
Sie bezeichnen	Sie bezeichnen
er/sie/es bezeichne	sie bezeichnen

PRESENT SUBJUNCTIVE II

ich bezeichnete	wir bezeichneten
du bezeichnetest	ihr bezeichnetet
Sie bezeichneten	Sie bezeichneten
er/sie/es bezeichnete	sie bezeichneten

FUTURE SUBJUNCTIVE I

ich werde	wir werden	bezeichnen
du werdest	ihr werdet	
Sie werden	Sie werden	
er/sie/es werde	sie werden	

FUTURE SUBJUNCTIVE II

ich würde	wir würden	bezeichnen
du würdest	ihr würdet	
Sie würden	Sie würden	
er/sie/es würde	sie würden	

PRESENT PERFECT

ich habe	wir haben	bezeichnet
du hast	ihr habt	
Sie haben	Sie haben	
er/sie/es hat	sie haben	

PAST PERFECT

ich hatte	wir hatten	bezeichnet
du hattest	ihr hattet	
Sie hatten	Sie hatten	
er/sie/es hatte	sie hatten	

FUTURE PERFECT

ich werde	wir werden	bezeichnet haben
du wirst	ihr werdet	
Sie werden	Sie werden	
er/sie/es wird	sie werden	

PAST SUBJUNCTIVE I

ich habe	wir haben	bezeichnet
du habest	ihr habet	
Sie haben	Sie haben	
er/sie/es habe	sie haben	

PAST SUBJUNCTIVE II

ich hätte	wir hätten	bezeichnet
du hättest	ihr hättet	
Sie hätten	Sie hätten	
er/sie/es hätte	sie hätten	

FUTURE PERFECT SUBJUNCTIVE I

ich werde	wir werden	bezeichnet haben
du werdest	ihr werdet	
Sie werden	Sie werden	
er/sie/es werde	sie werden	

FUTURE PERFECT SUBJUNCTIVE II

ich würde	wir würden	bezeichnet haben
du würdest	ihr würdet	
Sie würden	Sie würden	
er/sie/es würde	sie würden	

COMMANDS bezeichne! bezeichnet! bezeichnen Sie!

PRESENT PARTICIPLE bezeichnend

Usage

Der blaue Stern bezeichnet den relevanten Ort auf der Landkarte. — *The blue star indicates the relevant location on the map.*

Schilder bezeichnen die ganze Route. — *Signs mark the entire route.*

Literaturwissenschaftler bezeichneten das Werk als grundsätzlich heroisch. — *Literary scholars described the work as fundamentally heroic.*

Diese HTML-Elemente werden als „Tags" bezeichnet. — *These HTML elements are known as "tags."*

Die Firma bezeichnete ihren Umsatz im dritten Quartal als „anständig". — *The firm characterized its revenue in the third quarter as "respectable."*

Ich bezeichne mich als Optimist. — *I consider myself an optimist.*

Die Farbe Orange wird als warme Farbe bezeichnet. — *Orange is referred to as a warm color.*

Mehrere Minister haben den Angriff als einen Fehler bezeichnet. — *Several ministers referred to the attack as a mistake.*

RELATED VERBS *see* **zeichnen** (545)

strong verb **bezieht · bezog · bezogen**

PRESENT

ich beziehe	wir beziehen
du beziehst	ihr bezieht
Sie beziehen	Sie beziehen
er/sie/es bezieht	sie beziehen

PRESENT PERFECT

ich habe	wir haben	bezogen
du hast	ihr habt	
Sie haben	Sie haben	
er/sie/es hat	sie haben	

SIMPLE PAST

ich bezog	wir bezogen
du bezogst	ihr bezogt
Sie bezogen	Sie bezogen
er/sie/es bezog	sie bezogen

PAST PERFECT

ich hatte	wir hatten	bezogen
du hattest	ihr hattet	
Sie hatten	Sie hatten	
er/sie/es hatte	sie hatten	

FUTURE

ich werde	wir werden	beziehen
du wirst	ihr werdet	
Sie werden	Sie werden	
er/sie/es wird	sie werden	

FUTURE PERFECT

ich werde	wir werden	bezogen haben
du wirst	ihr werdet	
Sie werden	Sie werden	
er/sie/es wird	sie werden	

PRESENT SUBJUNCTIVE I

ich beziehe	wir beziehen
du beziehest	ihr beziehet
Sie beziehen	Sie beziehen
er/sie/es beziehe	sie beziehen

PAST SUBJUNCTIVE I

ich habe	wir haben	bezogen
du habest	ihr habet	
Sie haben	Sie haben	
er/sie/es habe	sie haben	

PRESENT SUBJUNCTIVE II

ich bezöge	wir bezögen
du bezögest	ihr bezöget
Sie bezögen	Sie bezögen
er/sie/es bezöge	sie bezögen

PAST SUBJUNCTIVE II

ich hätte	wir hätten	bezogen
du hättest	ihr hättet	
Sie hätten	Sie hätten	
er/sie/es hätte	sie hätten	

FUTURE SUBJUNCTIVE I

ich werde	wir werden	beziehen
du werdest	ihr werdet	
Sie werden	Sie werden	
er/sie/es werde	sie werden	

FUTURE PERFECT SUBJUNCTIVE I

ich werde	wir werden	bezogen haben
du werdest	ihr werdet	
Sie werden	Sie werden	
er/sie/es werde	sie werden	

FUTURE SUBJUNCTIVE II

ich würde	wir würden	beziehen
du würdest	ihr würdet	
Sie würden	Sie würden	
er/sie/es würde	sie würden	

FUTURE PERFECT SUBJUNCTIVE II

ich würde	wir würden	bezogen haben
du würdest	ihr würdet	
Sie würden	Sie würden	
er/sie/es würde	sie würden	

COMMANDS bezieh(e)! bezieht! beziehen Sie!

PRESENT PARTICIPLE beziehend

Usage

Hans pflegt, solche Situationen auf seine eigenen Probleme zu beziehen. — *Hans tends to relate such situations to his own problems.*

Jeden Morgen muss Frau Sauberhaus alle Betten in ihrem Haus frisch beziehen. — *Every morning, Mrs. Sauberhaus has to put clean sheets on the beds in her house.*

Familie Birnenbaum hat ein neues Haus bezogen. — *The Birnenbaum family has moved into a new house.*

Wir beziehen unsere Waren direkt von den Herstellern. — *Our products are supplied directly from the manufacturers.*

Mein Großvater bezieht die Lokalzeitung schon seit 1947. — *My grandfather has subscribed to the local newspaper since 1947.*

sich beziehen *to relate, refer*

Ich möchte mich auf einen ganz anderen Punkt beziehen. — *I'd like to refer to a completely different point.*

Worauf bezieht sich dieser Textausschnitt? — *What does this text excerpt refer to?*

RELATED VERBS ein·beziehen, zurück·beziehen; *see also* **ziehen** (549)

biegen *to bend, curve; wind*

biegt · bog · gebogen

strong verb

PRESENT

ich biege	wir biegen
du biegst	ihr biegt
Sie biegen	Sie biegen
er/sie/es biegt	sie biegen

SIMPLE PAST

ich bog	wir bogen
du bogst	ihr bogt
Sie bogen	Sie bogen
er/sie/es bog	sie bogen

FUTURE

ich werde	wir werden	biegen
du wirst	ihr werdet	
Sie werden	Sie werden	
er/sie/es wird	sie werden	

PRESENT SUBJUNCTIVE I

ich biege	wir biegen
du biegest	ihr bieget
Sie biegen	Sie biegen
er/sie/es biege	sie biegen

PRESENT SUBJUNCTIVE II

ich böge	wir bögen
du bögest	ihr böget
Sie bögen	Sie bögen
er/sie/es böge	sie bögen

FUTURE SUBJUNCTIVE I

ich werde	wir werden	biegen
du werdest	ihr werdet	
Sie werden	Sie werden	
er/sie/es werde	sie werden	

FUTURE SUBJUNCTIVE II

ich würde	wir würden	biegen
du würdest	ihr würdet	
Sie würden	Sie würden	
er/sie/es würde	sie würden	

PRESENT PERFECT

ich habe	wir haben	gebogen
du hast	ihr habt	
Sie haben	Sie haben	
er/sie/es hat	sie haben	

PAST PERFECT

ich hatte	wir hatten	gebogen
du hattest	ihr hattet	
Sie hatten	Sie hatten	
er/sie/es hatte	sie hatten	

FUTURE PERFECT

ich werde	wir werden	gebogen haben
du wirst	ihr werdet	
Sie werden	Sie werden	
er/sie/es wird	sie werden	

PAST SUBJUNCTIVE I

ich habe	wir haben	gebogen
du habest	ihr habet	
Sie haben	Sie haben	
er/sie/es habe	sie haben	

PAST SUBJUNCTIVE II

ich hätte	wir hätten	gebogen
du hättest	ihr hättet	
Sie hätten	Sie hätten	
er/sie/es hätte	sie hätten	

FUTURE PERFECT SUBJUNCTIVE I

ich werde	wir werden	gebogen haben
du werdest	ihr werdet	
Sie werden	Sie werden	
er/sie/es werde	sie werden	

FUTURE PERFECT SUBJUNCTIVE II

ich würde	wir würden	gebogen haben
du würdest	ihr würdet	
Sie würden	Sie würden	
er/sie/es würde	sie würden	

COMMANDS bieg(e)! biegt! biegen Sie!

PRESENT PARTICIPLE biegend

Usage

Biegen Sie bitte den linken Arm nach hinten. — *Please bend your left arm back.*
Aluminium ist leicht zu biegen. — *Aluminum is easy to bend.*
Kannst du die Stange wieder gerade biegen? — *Can you bend the rod back straight?*
Die Regierung biegt die Wahrheit und täuscht uns. — *The government is bending the truth and deceiving us.*

sich biegen *to bend, curve*

Die Kiefer biegen sich im Wind. — *The pines are bending in the wind.*
Die Äste bogen sich unter der Last der Äpfel. — *The limbs sagged under the weight of the apples.*
Die Zuschauer bogen sich vor Lachen. (*idiomatic*) — *The audience doubled over laughing.*

biegen (with **sein**) *to bend, turn*

Der Waldpfad biegt nach rechts. — *The forest path curves to the right.*
Das Auto war gerade um die Ecke gebogen. — *The car had just turned the corner.*

RELATED VERBS auf·biegen, aus·biegen, durch·biegen, ein·biegen, um·biegen, verbiegen; *see also* **ab·biegen** (1)

strong verb **bietet · bot · geboten**

PRESENT

ich biete	wir bieten
du bietest	ihr bietet
Sie bieten	Sie bieten
er/sie/es bietet	sie bieten

SIMPLE PAST

ich bot	wir boten
du bot(e)st	ihr botet
Sie boten	Sie boten
er/sie/es bot	sie boten

FUTURE

ich werde	wir werden	bieten
du wirst	ihr werdet	
Sie werden	Sie werden	
er/sie/es wird	sie werden	

PRESENT SUBJUNCTIVE I

ich biete	wir bieten
du bietest	ihr bietet
Sie bieten	Sie bieten
er/sie/es biete	sie bieten

PRESENT SUBJUNCTIVE II

ich böte	wir böten
du bötest	ihr bötet
Sie böten	Sie böten
er/sie/es böte	sie böten

FUTURE SUBJUNCTIVE I

ich werde	wir werden	bieten
du werdest	ihr werdet	
Sie werden	Sie werden	
er/sie/es werde	sie werden	

FUTURE SUBJUNCTIVE II

ich würde	wir würden	bieten
du würdest	ihr würdet	
Sie würden	Sie würden	
er/sie/es würde	sie würden	

PRESENT PERFECT

ich habe	wir haben	geboten
du hast	ihr habt	
Sie haben	Sie haben	
er/sie/es hat	sie haben	

PAST PERFECT

ich hatte	wir hatten	geboten
du hattest	ihr hattet	
Sie hatten	Sie hatten	
er/sie/es hatte	sie hatten	

FUTURE PERFECT

ich werde	wir werden	geboten haben
du wirst	ihr werdet	
Sie werden	Sie werden	
er/sie/es wird	sie werden	

PAST SUBJUNCTIVE I

ich habe	wir haben	geboten
du habest	ihr habet	
Sie haben	Sie haben	
er/sie/es habe	sie haben	

PAST SUBJUNCTIVE II

ich hätte	wir hätten	geboten
du hättest	ihr hättet	
Sie hätten	Sie hätten	
er/sie/es hätte	sie hätten	

FUTURE PERFECT SUBJUNCTIVE I

ich werde	wir werden	geboten haben
du werdest	ihr werdet	
Sie werden	Sie werden	
er/sie/es werde	sie werden	

FUTURE PERFECT SUBJUNCTIVE II

ich würde	wir würden	geboten haben
du würdest	ihr würdet	
Sie würden	Sie würden	
er/sie/es würde	sie würden	

COMMANDS biete! bietet! bieten Sie!

PRESENT PARTICIPLE bietend

Usage

Dieser Autor hat den Lesern eine spannende Erzählung geboten.	*This author has offered readers an exciting narrative.*
Sabines Vorschlag bietet mehr Probleme als Lösungen.	*Sabine's suggestion presents more problems than solutions.*
Ich biete Ihnen die Möglichkeit, reich zu werden.	*I am offering you the opportunity to get rich.*
Die Inflationsrate bietet Grund zur Sorge.	*The inflation rate gives reason for concern.*
Alle Gästezimmer bieten einen Ausblick auf die Gärten.	*All guest rooms offer a view of the gardens.*
Herr Smith möchte auf diese wertvolle Erstausgabe bieten.	*Mr. Smith would like to bid on this valuable first edition.*

sich bieten *to arise, occur, exist*

Diese Gelegenheit bietet sich relativ selten.	*This opportunity arises relatively rarely.*
Dazu bietet sich ein Sommerprogramm für ausländische Studierende.	*In addition there is a summer program for foreign students.*

RELATED VERBS auf·bieten, entbieten, erbieten, gebieten, überbieten, unterbieten; *see also* **an·bieten** (8), **verbieten** (477)

108 binden *to bind, tie; compel, oblige; be binding; retain*

bindet · band · gebunden strong verb

PRESENT

ich binde	wir binden
du bindest	ihr bindet
Sie binden	Sie binden
er/sie/es bindet	sie binden

SIMPLE PAST

ich band	wir banden
du band(e)st	ihr bandet
Sie banden	Sie banden
er/sie/es band	sie banden

FUTURE

ich werde	wir werden	binden
du wirst	ihr werdet	
Sie werden	Sie werden	
er/sie/es wird	sie werden	

PRESENT SUBJUNCTIVE I

ich binde	wir binden
du bindest	ihr bindet
Sie binden	Sie binden
er/sie/es binde	sie binden

PRESENT SUBJUNCTIVE II

ich bände	wir bänden
du bändest	ihr bändet
Sie bänden	Sie bänden
er/sie/es bände	sie bänden

FUTURE SUBJUNCTIVE I

ich werde	wir werden	binden
du werdest	ihr werdet	
Sie werden	Sie werden	
er/sie/es werde	sie werden	

FUTURE SUBJUNCTIVE II

ich würde	wir würden	binden
du würdest	ihr würdet	
Sie würden	Sie würden	
er/sie/es würde	sie würden	

PRESENT PERFECT

ich habe	wir haben	gebunden
du hast	ihr habt	
Sie haben	Sie haben	
er/sie/es hat	sie haben	

PAST PERFECT

ich hatte	wir hatten	gebunden
du hattest	ihr hattet	
Sie hatten	Sie hatten	
er/sie/es hatte	sie hatten	

FUTURE PERFECT

ich werde	wir werden	gebunden haben
du wirst	ihr werdet	
Sie werden	Sie werden	
er/sie/es wird	sie werden	

PAST SUBJUNCTIVE I

ich habe	wir haben	gebunden
du habest	ihr habet	
Sie haben	Sie haben	
er/sie/es habe	sie haben	

PAST SUBJUNCTIVE II

ich hätte	wir hätten	gebunden
du hättest	ihr hättet	
Sie hätten	Sie hätten	
er/sie/es hätte	sie hätten	

FUTURE PERFECT SUBJUNCTIVE I

ich werde	wir werden	gebunden haben
du werdest	ihr werdet	
Sie werden	Sie werden	
er/sie/es werde	sie werden	

FUTURE PERFECT SUBJUNCTIVE II

ich würde	wir würden	gebunden haben
du würdest	ihr würdet	
Sie würden	Sie würden	
er/sie/es würde	sie würden	

COMMANDS binde! bindet! binden Sie!

PRESENT PARTICIPLE bindend

Usage

Früher musste der Bauer die Getreidegarben binden und zum Trocknen aufstellen.	*The farmer used to have to bind the grain into sheaves and stand it up to dry.*
Die Opfer wurden an einen Pfosten gebunden.	*The victims were tied to a post.*
Manchmal binden die Peptide an Fängermoleküle.	*Sometimes the peptides bind to receptor molecules.*
Sein Beruf bindet ihn an diese Stadt.	*His career ties him to this city.*
Warum bindet man Bücher in Leder?	*Why are books bound in leather?*
Der Gefangene wurde an Händen und Füßen gebunden.	*The prisoner's hands and feet were tied.*
Der Minister fühlt sich nicht mehr an sein Versprechen gebunden, die Steuern zu senken.	*The minister no longer feels bound by his promise to lower taxes.*
Wie können wir unsere produktivsten Mitarbeiter am besten binden?	*How can we best retain our most productive employees?*

RELATED VERBS ab·binden, an·binden, auf·binden, ein·binden, entbinden, um·binden, unterbinden, zu·binden; *see also* **verbinden** (478)

strong verb **bittet · bat · gebeten**

PRESENT

ich bitte	wir bitten
du bittest	ihr bittet
Sie bitten	Sie bitten
er/sie/es bittet	sie bitten

SIMPLE PAST

ich bat	wir baten
du bat(e)st	ihr batet
Sie baten	Sie baten
er/sie/es bat	sie baten

FUTURE

ich werde	wir werden	bitten
du wirst	ihr werdet	
Sie werden	Sie werden	
er/sie/es wird	sie werden	

PRESENT SUBJUNCTIVE I

ich bitte	wir bitten
du bittest	ihr bittet
Sie bitten	Sie bitten
er/sie/es bitte	sie bitten

PRESENT SUBJUNCTIVE II

ich bäte	wir bäten
du bätest	ihr bätet
Sie bäten	Sie bäten
er/sie/es bäte	sie bäten

FUTURE SUBJUNCTIVE I

ich werde	wir werden	bitten
du werdest	ihr werdet	
Sie werden	Sie werden	
er/sie/es werde	sie werden	

FUTURE SUBJUNCTIVE II

ich würde	wir würden	bitten
du würdest	ihr würdet	
Sie würden	Sie würden	
er/sie/es würde	sie würden	

PRESENT PERFECT

ich habe	wir haben	gebeten
du hast	ihr habt	
Sie haben	Sie haben	
er/sie/es hat	sie haben	

PAST PERFECT

ich hatte	wir hatten	gebeten
du hattest	ihr hattet	
Sie hatten	Sie hatten	
er/sie/es hatte	sie hatten	

FUTURE PERFECT

ich werde	wir werden	gebeten haben
du wirst	ihr werdet	
Sie werden	Sie werden	
er/sie/es wird	sie werden	

PAST SUBJUNCTIVE I

ich habe	wir haben	gebeten
du habest	ihr habet	
Sie haben	Sie haben	
er/sie/es habe	sie haben	

PAST SUBJUNCTIVE II

ich hätte	wir hätten	gebeten
du hättest	ihr hättet	
Sie hätten	Sie hätten	
er/sie/es hätte	sie hätten	

FUTURE PERFECT SUBJUNCTIVE I

ich werde	wir werden	gebeten haben
du werdest	ihr werdet	
Sie werden	Sie werden	
er/sie/es werde	sie werden	

FUTURE PERFECT SUBJUNCTIVE II

ich würde	wir würden	gebeten haben
du würdest	ihr würdet	
Sie würden	Sie würden	
er/sie/es würde	sie würden	

COMMANDS bitte! bittet! bitten Sie!

PRESENT PARTICIPLE bittend

Usage

Ihr Freund bat sie in einem Brief darum, das Geschenk zurückzugeben.	*In a letter, her boyfriend asked her to return the gift.*
Inge will um Hilfe bitten.	*Inge wants to request help.*
Der Schriftsteller bittet den Verleger um mehr Zeit.	*The writer is asking the publisher for more time.*
Bitten Sie beim Anwalt um einen Termin.	*Request an appointment with the lawyer.*
Hast du um Verzeihung gebeten?	*Have you asked for forgiveness?*
Wir bitten Sie folgende Hinweise zu beachten.	*We ask that you follow the instructions below.*
Bitten Sie ihn doch einfach mitzukommen!	*Why don't you just ask him to come along?*
Wer hat um einen Bleistift gebeten?	*Who was asking for a pencil?*
Der Bürgermeister lässt bitten.	*The mayor requests your presence.*
Sandra hat einen Freund zu sich nach Hause gebeten.	*Sandra invited a friend to her home.*
Ich bitte dich!	*I'm pleading with you!*

RELATED VERBS ab·bitten, aus·bitten, erbitten, verbitten

110 blasen *to blow; play*

bläst · blies · geblasen strong verb

PRESENT		PRESENT PERFECT		
ich blase	wir blasen	ich habe	wir haben	geblasen
du bläst	ihr blast	du hast	ihr habt	
Sie blasen	Sie blasen	Sie haben	Sie haben	
er/sie/es bläst	sie blasen	er/sie/es hat	sie haben	

SIMPLE PAST		PAST PERFECT		
ich blies	wir bliesen	ich hatte	wir hatten	geblasen
du bliesest	ihr bliest	du hattest	ihr hattet	
Sie bliesen	Sie bliesen	Sie hatten	Sie hatten	
er/sie/es blies	sie bliesen	er/sie/es hatte	sie hatten	

FUTURE			FUTURE PERFECT		
ich werde	wir werden	blasen	ich werde	wir werden	geblasen haben
du wirst	ihr werdet		du wirst	ihr werdet	
Sie werden	Sie werden		Sie werden	Sie werden	
er/sie/es wird	sie werden		er/sie/es wird	sie werden	

PRESENT SUBJUNCTIVE I		PAST SUBJUNCTIVE I		
ich blase	wir blasen	ich habe	wir haben	geblasen
du blasest	ihr blaset	du habest	ihr habet	
Sie blasen	Sie blasen	Sie haben	Sie haben	
er/sie/es blase	sie blasen	er/sie/es habe	sie haben	

PRESENT SUBJUNCTIVE II		PAST SUBJUNCTIVE II		
ich bliese	wir bliesen	ich hätte	wir hätten	geblasen
du bliesest	ihr blieset	du hättest	ihr hättet	
Sie bliesen	Sie bliesen	Sie hätten	Sie hätten	
er/sie/es bliese	sie bliesen	er/sie/es hätte	sie hätten	

FUTURE SUBJUNCTIVE I			FUTURE PERFECT SUBJUNCTIVE I		
ich werde	wir werden	blasen	ich werde	wir werden	geblasen haben
du werdest	ihr werdet		du werdest	ihr werdet	
Sie werden	Sie werden		Sie werden	Sie werden	
er/sie/es werde	sie werden		er/sie/es werde	sie werden	

FUTURE SUBJUNCTIVE II			FUTURE PERFECT SUBJUNCTIVE II		
ich würde	wir würden	blasen	ich würde	wir würden	geblasen haben
du würdest	ihr würdet		du würdest	ihr würdet	
Sie würden	Sie würden		Sie würden	Sie würden	
er/sie/es würde	sie würden		er/sie/es würde	sie würden	

COMMANDS blas(e)! blast! blasen Sie!

PRESENT PARTICIPLE blasend

Usage

Herr Pförtner kann sogar Glas blasen.	*Mr. Pförtner even knows how to blow glass.*
Grete hat die Brotkrümel vom Küchentisch geblasen.	*Grete blew the breadcrumbs off the kitchen table.*
Eine leichte Brise bläst durch die Palmen.	*A light breeze is blowing through the palms.*
Eiskalt blies der Nordwind nachts durch die Ruinen der mittelalterlichen Burg.	*During the night, the icy north wind blew through the ruins of the medieval castle.*
Warum blasen Sie den Rauch in diese Richtung?	*Why are you blowing smoke in this direction?*
Der starke Wind blies unaufhaltsam durch alle Ritzen der alten Waldhütte.	*The strong wind blew incessantly through the cracks of the old cabin in the woods.*
Heinz kann Rauchringe blasen.	*Heinz knows how to blow smoke rings.*
Der Soldat nahm sein Horn und blies zum Angriff.	*The soldier took his horn and sounded the charge.*
Hört ihr die Hörner blasen?	*Do you hear the horns playing?*

RELATED VERBS ab·blasen, an·blasen, auf·blasen, aus·blasen, durch·blasen, ein·blasen, umblasen, um·blasen strong verb **bleibt · blieb · geblieben**

PRESENT

ich bleibe	wir bleiben
du bleibst	ihr bleibt
Sie bleiben	Sie bleiben
er/sie/es bleibt	sie bleiben

SIMPLE PAST

ich blieb	wir blieben
du bliebst	ihr bliebt
Sie blieben	Sie blieben
er/sie/es blieb	sie blieben

FUTURE

ich werde	wir werden	bleiben
du wirst	ihr werdet	
Sie werden	Sie werden	
er/sie/es wird	sie werden	

PRESENT SUBJUNCTIVE I

ich bleibe	wir bleiben
du bleibest	ihr bleibet
Sie bleiben	Sie bleiben
er/sie/es bleibe	sie bleiben

PRESENT SUBJUNCTIVE II

ich bliebe	wir blieben
du bliebest	ihr bliebet
Sie blieben	Sie blieben
er/sie/es bliebe	sie blieben

FUTURE SUBJUNCTIVE I

ich werde	wir werden	bleiben
du werdest	ihr werdet	
Sie werden	Sie werden	
er/sie/es werde	sie werden	

FUTURE SUBJUNCTIVE II

ich würde	wir würden	bleiben
du würdest	ihr würdet	
Sie würden	Sie würden	
er/sie/es würde	sie würden	

PRESENT PERFECT

ich bin	wir sind	geblieben
du bist	ihr seid	
Sie sind	Sie sind	
er/sie/es ist	sie sind	

PAST PERFECT

ich war	wir waren	geblieben
du warst	ihr wart	
Sie waren	Sie waren	
er/sie/es war	sie waren	

FUTURE PERFECT

ich werde	wir werden	geblieben sein
du wirst	ihr werdet	
Sie werden	Sie werden	
er/sie/es wird	sie werden	

PAST SUBJUNCTIVE I

ich sei	wir seien	geblieben
du seiest	ihr seiet	
Sie seien	Sie seien	
er/sie/es sei	sie seien	

PAST SUBJUNCTIVE II

ich wäre	wir wären	geblieben
du wärest	ihr wäret	
Sie wären	Sie wären	
er/sie/es wäre	sie wären	

FUTURE PERFECT SUBJUNCTIVE I

ich werde	wir werden	geblieben sein
du werdest	ihr werdet	
Sie werden	Sie werden	
er/sie/es werde	sie werden	

FUTURE PERFECT SUBJUNCTIVE II

ich würde	wir würden	geblieben sein
du würdest	ihr würdet	
Sie würden	Sie würden	
er/sie/es würde	sie würden	

COMMANDS bleib(e)! bleibt! bleiben Sie!

PRESENT PARTICIPLE bleibend

Usage

Der Verfasser des Werks bleibt immer noch anonym.	*The author of the work still remains anonymous.*
Am Sonntag bin ich zu Hause geblieben.	*I stayed home on Sunday.*
Auch nach dem Krieg blieben sie feste Freunde.	*Even after the war they remained good friends.*
Es bleibt also dem engagierten Bürger ein schwieriges Dilemma.	*Thus, the involved citizen is left with a difficult dilemma.*
Moritz ist ledig geblieben.	*Moritz remained single.*
Heinz raucht seit 30 Jahren und er bleibt bei der selben Marke.	*Heinz has smoked for thirty years and he's sticking with the same brand.*
Bleib ruhig, mein Kind.	*Keep calm, my child.*
Bleiben Sie bitte am Apparat.	*Please stay on the line.* (telephone)

RELATED VERBS aus·bleiben, dabei·bleiben, unterbleiben, verbleiben

TOP 50 VERB ☞

bleiben *to remain, stay; keep*

bleibt · blieb · geblieben strong verb

bleiben + infinitive

Bleiben Sie bitte sitzen! — *Please stay seated!*
Der Schlüssel war im Schloss stecken geblieben. — *The key had gotten stuck in the lock.*
Bleibt bitte stehen, damit ich ein Foto machen kann. — *Please remain standing so I can take a picture.*
Das Baby will nicht liegen bleiben. — *The baby doesn't want to stay lying down.*
Die staatlichen Theatersubventionen werden einige Zeit bestehen bleiben. — *The governmental theater subsidies will stay in effect for some time.*
Die Erfahrung ist in Herrn Ludwigs Gedächtnis haften geblieben. — *The experience persisted in Mr. Ludwig's memory.*

bleiben zu + infinitive

Es bleibt noch zu klären, ob der Autor das machen will. — *We must still clarify whether the author will do that.*
Es bleibt zu hoffen, dass jemand uns findet. — *We can only hope that someone finds us.*

bleiben lassen *to refrain from doing, stop doing*

Das lasst ihr lieber bleiben. — *You'd best not do that.*
Du solltest das Rauchen bleiben lassen. — *You should stop smoking.*

bleiben + past participle

Bleiben Sie gelassen und schonen Sie Ihre Nerven. — *Remain calm and spare your nerves.*
Seine Werke sind von Kritikern unbeachtet geblieben. — *His works have escaped the notice of critics.*
Frau Schöters Verdienste bleiben uns unvergessen. — *Mrs. Schöter's accomplishments will not be forgotten by us.*
Der sekundäre Handlungsstrang bleibt den Zuschauern verborgen. — *The secondary plot line remains hidden from the audience.*
Wichtige Fragen bleiben noch unbeantwortet. — *Important questions remain unanswered.*

bleiben + adverb/adjective

Wie lange seid ihr dort geblieben? — *How long did you stay there?*
Ich habe eine neue Telefonnummer, aber meine Email-Adresse bleibt gleich. — *I have a new telephone number, but my e-mail address remains the same.*
Wie lange blieb die Tür offen? — *How long did the door remain open?*
Papa sagt, du sollst mit mir hier bleiben. — *Daddy says you're supposed to stay here with me.*
Das Paar blieb einander immer treu. — *The couple remained forever loyal to each other.*
Wir hatten einen Riesenhunger und nichts blieb übrig. — *We were ravenous and nothing was left over.*

bleiben + prepositional complement

Bleibst du mit deinen Eltern in Verbindung? — *Do you keep in touch with your parents?*
Das Gerät darf nicht länger als zwei Stunden in Betrieb bleiben. — *The device cannot remain in operation longer than two hours.*

IDIOMATIC EXPRESSIONS

Bleiben Sie bitte bei der Sache! — *Please don't change the subject!*
Erich bleibt immer auf dem Laufenden. — *Erich is always well informed.*
Es blieb uns keine andere Möglichkeit. — *We were left with no other option.*
Die Sache bleibt unter uns. — *The matter is strictly between us.*
Es bleibt dabei! — *Agreed!*
Wo ist er geblieben? — *What has happened with him?*
1944 ist sein Großvater im Krieg geblieben. (*euphemism*) — *In 1944, his grandfather died in the war.*

regular weak verb **bleicht · bleichte · gebleicht**

PRESENT		PRESENT PERFECT		
ich bleiche	wir bleichen	ich habe	wir haben	gebleicht
du bleichst	ihr bleicht	du hast	ihr habt	
Sie bleichen	Sie bleichen	Sie haben	Sie haben	
er/sie/es bleicht	sie bleichen	er/sie/es hat	sie haben	

SIMPLE PAST		PAST PERFECT		
ich bleichte	wir bleichten	ich hatte	wir hatten	gebleicht
du bleichtest	ihr bleichtet	du hattest	ihr hattet	
Sie bleichten	Sie bleichten	Sie hatten	Sie hatten	
er/sie/es bleichte	sie bleichten	er/sie/es hatte	sie hatten	

FUTURE			FUTURE PERFECT		
ich werde	wir werden	bleichen	ich werde	wir werden	gebleicht haben
du wirst	ihr werdet		du wirst	ihr werdet	
Sie werden	Sie werden		Sie werden	Sie werden	
er/sie/es wird	sie werden		er/sie/es wird	sie werden	

PRESENT SUBJUNCTIVE I		PAST SUBJUNCTIVE I		
ich bleiche	wir bleichen	ich habe	wir haben	gebleicht
du bleichest	ihr bleichet	du habest	ihr habet	
Sie bleichen	Sie bleichen	Sie haben	Sie haben	
er/sie/es bleiche	sie bleichen	er/sie/es habe	sie haben	

PRESENT SUBJUNCTIVE II		PAST SUBJUNCTIVE II		
ich bleichte	wir bleichten	ich hätte	wir hätten	gebleicht
du bleichtest	ihr bleichtet	du hättest	ihr hättet	
Sie bleichten	Sie bleichten	Sie hätten	Sie hätten	
er/sie/es bleichte	sie bleichten	er/sie/es hätte	sie hätten	

FUTURE SUBJUNCTIVE I			FUTURE PERFECT SUBJUNCTIVE I		
ich werde	wir werden	bleichen	ich werde	wir werden	gebleicht haben
du werdest	ihr werdet		du werdest	ihr werdet	
Sie werden	Sie werden		Sie werden	Sie werden	
er/sie/es werde	sie werden		er/sie/es werde	sie werden	

FUTURE SUBJUNCTIVE II			FUTURE PERFECT SUBJUNCTIVE II		
ich würde	wir würden	bleichen	ich würde	wir würden	gebleicht haben
du würdest	ihr würdet		du würdest	ihr würdet	
Sie würden	Sie würden		Sie würden	Sie würden	
er/sie/es würde	sie würden		er/sie/es würde	sie würden	

COMMANDS bleich(e)! bleicht! bleichen Sie!

PRESENT PARTICIPLE bleichend

Usage

Ach je, die Susanne hat sich die Haare gebleicht!	*Oh no, Susanne has bleached her hair!*
Wie kann man die Wäsche chlorfrei bleichen?	*How can you bleach clothing without chlorine?*
Bleichst du dir die Haare?	*Do you bleach your hair?*
Roland bleichte sich den Bart.	*Roland bleached his beard.*
Angelika lässt sich die Zähne bleichen.	*Angelika is having her teeth whitened.*
Die Endivie wird vor der Ernte gebleicht.	*Endive is lightened in color before harvest.*

bleichen (with **sein**) *fade* (**NOTE** The archaic strong past tense forms **blich** and **geblichen** are sometimes found.)

Das rote Tuch blich allmählich in der Sonne und wurde fast gelb.	*The red towel gradually faded in the sun and turned almost yellow.*
Der alte Schenkelknochen ist geblichen.	*The old thighbone has turned white.*

RELATED VERBS ab·bleichen, aus·bleichen, erbleichen, verbleichen

113 blühen *to bloom, blossom; prosper, thrive; be in store*

blüht · blühte · geblüht regular weak verb

PRESENT

ich blühe	wir blühen
du blühst	ihr blüht
Sie blühen	Sie blühen
er/sie/es blüht	sie blühen

PRESENT PERFECT

ich habe	wir haben	geblüht
du hast	ihr habt	
Sie haben	Sie haben	
er/sie/es hat	sie haben	

SIMPLE PAST

ich blühte	wir blühten
du blühtest	ihr blühtet
Sie blühten	Sie blühten
er/sie/es blühte	sie blühten

PAST PERFECT

ich hatte	wir hatten	geblüht
du hattest	ihr hattet	
Sie hatten	Sie hatten	
er/sie/es hatte	sie hatten	

FUTURE

ich werde	wir werden	blühen
du wirst	ihr werdet	
Sie werden	Sie werden	
er/sie/es wird	sie werden	

FUTURE PERFECT

ich werde	wir werden	geblüht haben
du wirst	ihr werdet	
Sie werden	Sie werden	
er/sie/es wird	sie werden	

PRESENT SUBJUNCTIVE I

ich blühe	wir blühen
du blühest	ihr blühet
Sie blühen	Sie blühen
er/sie/es blühe	sie blühen

PAST SUBJUNCTIVE I

ich habe	wir haben	geblüht
du habest	ihr habet	
Sie haben	Sie haben	
er/sie/es habe	sie haben	

PRESENT SUBJUNCTIVE II

ich blühte	wir blühten
du blühtest	ihr blühtet
Sie blühten	Sie blühten
er/sie/es blühte	sie blühten

PAST SUBJUNCTIVE II

ich hätte	wir hätten	geblüht
du hättest	ihr hättet	
Sie hätten	Sie hätten	
er/sie/es hätte	sie hätten	

FUTURE SUBJUNCTIVE I

ich werde	wir werden	blühen
du werdest	ihr werdet	
Sie werden	Sie werden	
er/sie/es werde	sie werden	

FUTURE PERFECT SUBJUNCTIVE I

ich werde	wir werden	geblüht haben
du werdest	ihr werdet	
Sie werden	Sie werden	
er/sie/es werde	sie werden	

FUTURE SUBJUNCTIVE II

ich würde	wir würden	blühen
du würdest	ihr würdet	
Sie würden	Sie würden	
er/sie/es würde	sie würden	

FUTURE PERFECT SUBJUNCTIVE II

ich würde	wir würden	geblüht haben
du würdest	ihr würdet	
Sie würden	Sie würden	
er/sie/es würde	sie würden	

COMMANDS blüh(e)! blüht! blühen Sie!

PRESENT PARTICIPLE blühend

Usage

Die Mondblume blüht hauptsächlich in der Nacht.	*The moonflower blooms primarily at night.*
Unsere Kirschbäume haben schon im März geblüht.	*Our cherry trees were already blossoming in March.*
Mein Rosenbusch blühte das ganze Jahr durch.	*My rosebush bloomed the whole year through.*
Wann beginnen die Blumen zu blühen?	*When do the flowers begin blooming?*
Wie bringt man Seerosen zum Blühen?	*How do you get water lilies to bloom?*
Drei Monate lang blühten die Orchideen auf dem Fenstersims.	*For three months, the orchids on the windowsill were in bloom.*
Bei uns blühen die Geranien noch.	*At our place, the geraniums are still blooming.*
Sein Kamingeschäft blüht aufgrund der hohen Ölpreise.	*His fireplace business is thriving because of high oil prices.*
Wenn die Wirtschaft blüht, gibt man mehr aus.	*When the economy prospers, people spend more money.*
Ich habe schon erfahren, was mir blüht.	*I've already found out what lies in store for me.*
Wie freut es mich, dass du mir ewig blühst. (Bettine von Arnim)	*How happy it makes me that you bloom eternally for me.*

RELATED VERBS ab·blühen, auf·blühen, aus·blühen, erblühen, verblühen

strong verb **brät · briet · gebraten**

PRESENT

ich brate	wir braten
du brätst	ihr bratet
Sie braten	Sie braten
er/sie/es brät	sie braten

SIMPLE PAST

ich briet	wir brieten
du brietst	ihr brietet
Sie brieten	Sie brieten
er/sie/es briet	sie brieten

FUTURE

ich werde	wir werden	braten
du wirst	ihr werdet	
Sie werden	Sie werden	
er/sie/es wird	sie werden	

PRESENT SUBJUNCTIVE I

ich brate	wir braten
du bratest	ihr bratet
Sie braten	Sie braten
er/sie/es brate	sie braten

PRESENT SUBJUNCTIVE II

ich briete	wir brieten
du brietest	ihr brietet
Sie brieten	Sie brieten
er/sie/es briete	sie brieten

FUTURE SUBJUNCTIVE I

ich werde	wir werden	braten
du werdest	ihr werdet	
Sie werden	Sie werden	
er/sie/es werde	sie werden	

FUTURE SUBJUNCTIVE II

ich würde	wir würden	braten
du würdest	ihr würdet	
Sie würden	Sie würden	
er/sie/es würde	sie würden	

PRESENT PERFECT

ich habe	wir haben	gebraten
du hast	ihr habt	
Sie haben	Sie haben	
er/sie/es hat	sie haben	

PAST PERFECT

ich hatte	wir hatten	gebraten
du hattest	ihr hattet	
Sie hatten	Sie hatten	
er/sie/es hatte	sie hatten	

FUTURE PERFECT

ich werde	wir werden	gebraten haben
du wirst	ihr werdet	
Sie werden	Sie werden	
er/sie/es wird	sie werden	

PAST SUBJUNCTIVE I

ich habe	wir haben	gebraten
du habest	ihr habet	
Sie haben	Sie haben	
er/sie/es habe	sie haben	

PAST SUBJUNCTIVE II

ich hätte	wir hätten	gebraten
du hättest	ihr hättet	
Sie hätten	Sie hätten	
er/sie/es hätte	sie hätten	

FUTURE PERFECT SUBJUNCTIVE I

ich werde	wir werden	gebraten haben
du werdest	ihr werdet	
Sie werden	Sie werden	
er/sie/es werde	sie werden	

FUTURE PERFECT SUBJUNCTIVE II

ich würde	wir würden	gebraten haben
du würdest	ihr würdet	
Sie würden	Sie würden	
er/sie/es würde	sie würden	

COMMANDS brate! bratet! braten Sie!

PRESENT PARTICIPLE bratend

Usage

„Wie lange brätst du Schweineschnitzel?" — *"How long do you fry pork cutlets?"*
„Ich brate sie zwölf bis fünfzehn Minuten." — *"I fry them twelve to fifteen minutes."*

In Pflanzenöl auf beiden Seiten braten. (RECIPE) — *Fry in vegetable oil on both sides.*

Die Zucchini in Olivenöl leicht braten. — *Sauté the zucchini in olive oil.*

Der Bauernknecht briet einen Hasen an einem Spieß. — *The farmhand roasted a rabbit on a spit.*

„Der Fisch schmeckt gut. Haben Sie ihn gebraten oder gedünstet?" — *"The fish tastes good. Did you grill it or steam it?"*

„Ich habe ihn erstmal kurz gebraten und dann gedünstet." — *"First I grilled it, then I steamed it."*

Heinz machte das Lagerfeuer an und briet ein Fisch in einer Pfanne. — *Heinz made a campfire and pan-fried a fish.*

RELATED VERBS an·braten, aus·braten, durch·braten, verbraten

115 **brauchen** *to need, require*

braucht · brauchte · gebraucht regular weak verb

MORE USAGE SENTENCES WITH brauchen

Jans Eltern brauchen ein neues Auto.	*Jan's parents need a new car.*
„Was braucht ihr noch für den Kuchen?"	*"What do you still need for the cake?"*
„Wir brauchen Eier und Milch."	*"We need eggs and milk."*
Herr Schmidt braucht einen Stock, um beim Gehen das Gleichgewicht zu halten.	*Mr. Schmidt needs a cane to keep his balance when he walks.*
Für welchen Zweck brauchte man ein Pilzmesser? Zum Pflücken von Pilzen natürlich!	*For what purpose would one need a mushroom knife? To harvest mushrooms, of course!*
Eine Erklärung der Umstände wird dringend gebraucht.	*An explanation of the circumstances is urgently needed.*
Du brauchst dich nicht zu schämen.	*You don't need to be ashamed.*
Der Arzt hat gesagt, ich brauche dringend Ruhe.	*The doctor said I absolutely must get some rest.*
Das Gefühl, auf dem Hof nicht mehr gebraucht zu werden, konnte Opa nicht gut verkraften.	*Grandpa couldn't cope well with the feeling that he was no longer needed on the farm.*
Bürgermeister Vogler braucht jetzt Unterstützung für seine Pläne.	*Mayor Vogler needs support for his plans now.*
Brauchst du Hilfe?	*Do you need help?*

brauchen zu + infinitive *to need to, have to*

Sie brauchen sich nicht zu rechtfertigen.	*You don't have to justify yourself.*
Was Lars davon hält, braucht dich nicht zu kümmern.	*What Lars thinks about it doesn't need to concern you.*
Sag ihm bitte, dass er heute nicht zu arbeiten braucht.	*Please tell him he doesn't have to work today.*
Man brauchte kein Prophet zu sein, um das kommen zu sehen.	*You didn't have to be a prophet to see that coming.*
Es braucht dir nicht Leid zu tun, dass du das gesagt hast.	*You need not be sorry for saying that.*

brauchen + time duration *to take*

Wie lange braucht der Bus bis Hildesheim?	*How long does the bus to Hildesheim take?*
Es brauchte eine Weile, bis ich meinem Freund den Grund erklären konnte.	*It took me a while to explain the reason to my friend.*
Aber Ihr brauchtet wohl auch nur wenig Zeit zur Entschließung? (GOETHE)	*But you also probably took very little time to decide.*

es braucht + genitive case (elevated style) *there is a need*

Es braucht eines Theologen, um von wissenschaftlichen Erkenntnissen theologische Wechselbeziehungen herzuleiten.	*A theologian is needed to derive theological correlations from scientific knowledge.*
Es braucht keines Beweises mehr, dass das jetzige System auf die Dauer nicht funktionsfähig bleibt.	*There is no need for further proof that the current system will not remain functional in the long term.*

IDIOMATIC EXPRESSIONS

Sie brauchen es nur zu sagen.	*You only need mention it.*
Eine erfolgreiche Firma braucht manchmal frisches Blut.	*A successful company sometimes needs new blood.*
Der Hund braucht eine feste Hand.	*The dog requires a firm hand.*
Gut Ding braucht Weile. (PROVERB)	*Good things take time.*

regular weak verb **braucht · brauchte · gebraucht**

PRESENT

ich brauche	wir brauchen
du brauchst	ihr braucht
Sie brauchen	Sie brauchen
er/sie/es braucht	sie brauchen

PRESENT PERFECT

ich habe	wir haben	gebraucht
du hast	ihr habt	
Sie haben	Sie haben	
er/sie/es hat	sie haben	

SIMPLE PAST

ich brauchte	wir brauchten
du brauchtest	ihr brauchtet
Sie brauchten	Sie brauchten
er/sie/es brauchte	sie brauchten

PAST PERFECT

ich hatte	wir hatten	gebraucht
du hattest	ihr hattet	
Sie hatten	Sie hatten	
er/sie/es hatte	sie hatten	

FUTURE

ich werde	wir werden	brauchen
du wirst	ihr werdet	
Sie werden	Sie werden	
er/sie/es wird	sie werden	

FUTURE PERFECT

ich werde	wir werden	gebraucht haben
du wirst	ihr werdet	
Sie werden	Sie werden	
er/sie/es wird	sie werden	

PRESENT SUBJUNCTIVE I

ich brauche	wir brauchen
du brauchest	ihr brauchet
Sie brauchen	Sie brauchen
er/sie/es brauche	sie brauchen

PAST SUBJUNCTIVE I

ich habe	wir haben	gebraucht
du habest	ihr habet	
Sie haben	Sie haben	
er/sie/es habe	sie haben	

PRESENT SUBJUNCTIVE II

ich brauchte	wir brauchten
du brauchtest	ihr brauchtet
Sie brauchten	Sie brauchten
er/sie/es brauchte	sie brauchten

PAST SUBJUNCTIVE II

ich hätte	wir hätten	gebraucht
du hättest	ihr hättet	
Sie hätten	Sie hätten	
er/sie/es hätte	sie hätten	

FUTURE SUBJUNCTIVE I

ich werde	wir werden	brauchen
du werdest	ihr werdet	
Sie werden	Sie werden	
er/sie/es werde	sie werden	

FUTURE PERFECT SUBJUNCTIVE I

ich werde	wir werden	gebraucht haben
du werdest	ihr werdet	
Sie werden	Sie werden	
er/sie/es werde	sie werden	

FUTURE SUBJUNCTIVE II

ich würde	wir würden	brauchen
du würdest	ihr würdet	
Sie würden	Sie würden	
er/sie/es würde	sie würden	

FUTURE PERFECT SUBJUNCTIVE II

ich würde	wir würden	gebraucht haben
du würdest	ihr würdet	
Sie würden	Sie würden	
er/sie/es würde	sie würden	

COMMANDS brauch(e)! braucht! brauchen Sie!

PRESENT PARTICIPLE brauchend

Usage

Unser neuer Kühlschrank braucht sehr wenig Strom.	*Our new refrigerator requires very little electricity.*
Ich brauche mehr Zeit.	*I need more time.*
Sie braucht einen Steuerberater.	*She needs a tax advisor.*
Frau Merkel hat ein starkes Bedürfnis, von anderen gebraucht zu werden.	*Mrs. Merkel has a strong need to be needed by others.*
Das kann ich nicht brauchen.	*That's of no use to me.*
Alles, was Sie brauchen, finden Sie hier.	*You'll find everything you need here.*
Meine Zimmerpflanze braucht wenig Sonne.	*My houseplant requires little sunlight.*
Wie viele Stimmen braucht der Kandidat noch?	*How many votes does the candidate still need?*
Ich brauche unbedingt Urlaub!	*I really need a vacation!*
Welche Größe brauchen Sie?	*What size do you need?*

RELATED VERBS ab·brauchen, auf·brauchen, missbrauchen; *see also* **gebrauchen** (207), **verbrauchen** (479)

brechen *to break, breach, crack, rupture*

bricht · brach · gebrochen strong verb

PRESENT		PRESENT PERFECT		
ich breche	wir brechen	ich habe	wir haben	gebrochen
du brichst	ihr brecht	du hast	ihr habt	
Sie brechen	Sie brechen	Sie haben	Sie haben	
er/sie/es bricht	sie brechen	er/sie/es hat	sie haben	

SIMPLE PAST		PAST PERFECT		
ich brach	wir brachen	ich hatte	wir hatten	gebrochen
du brachst	ihr bracht	du hattest	ihr hattet	
Sie brachen	Sie brachen	Sie hatten	Sie hatten	
er/sie/es brach	sie brachen	er/sie/es hatte	sie hatten	

FUTURE			FUTURE PERFECT		
ich werde	wir werden	brechen	ich werde	wir werden	gebrochen haben
du wirst	ihr werdet		du wirst	ihr werdet	
Sie werden	Sie werden		Sie werden	Sie werden	
er/sie/es wird	sie werden		er/sie/es wird	sie werden	

PRESENT SUBJUNCTIVE I		PAST SUBJUNCTIVE I		
ich breche	wir brechen	ich habe	wir haben	gebrochen
du brechest	ihr brechet	du habest	ihr habet	
Sie brechen	Sie brechen	Sie haben	Sie haben	
er/sie/es breche	sie brechen	er/sie/es habe	sie haben	

PRESENT SUBJUNCTIVE II		PAST SUBJUNCTIVE II		
ich bräche	wir brächen	ich hätte	wir hätten	gebrochen
du brächest	ihr brächet	du hättest	ihr hättet	
Sie brächen	Sie brächen	Sie hätten	Sie hätten	
er/sie/es bräche	sie brächen	er/sie/es hätte	sie hätten	

FUTURE SUBJUNCTIVE I			FUTURE PERFECT SUBJUNCTIVE I		
ich werde	wir werden	brechen	ich werde	wir werden	gebrochen haben
du werdest	ihr werdet		du werdest	ihr werdet	
Sie werden	Sie werden		Sie werden	Sie werden	
er/sie/es werde	sie werden		er/sie/es werde	sie werden	

FUTURE SUBJUNCTIVE II			FUTURE PERFECT SUBJUNCTIVE II		
ich würde	wir würden	brechen	ich würde	wir würden	gebrochen haben
du würdest	ihr würdet		du würdest	ihr würdet	
Sie würden	Sie würden		Sie würden	Sie würden	
er/sie/es würde	sie würden		er/sie/es würde	sie würden	

COMMANDS brich! brecht! brechen Sie!

PRESENT PARTICIPLE brechend

Usage

Es brach ihr das Herz, als er sie eines Herbstmorgens verließ. — *It broke her heart when he left her one autumn morning.*

Der Soldat hat dem Gefangenen den Arm gebrochen. — *The soldier has broken the prisoner's arm.*

Der Junge hat den Stock gebrochen. — *The boy broke the stick.*

Diese Athleten hoffen, den Weltrekord zu brechen. — *These athletes hope to break the world record.*

brechen (with sein) *to break, breach, crack, rupture*

Die Sonnenstrahlen waren endlich durch die Wolken gebrochen, als wir am späten Nachmittag eintrafen. — *The rays of sun had finally breached the clouds as we arrived in the late afternoon.*

sich brechen *to break*

Die 10-Meter-Wellen brechen sich explosiv an den Felsen. — *The 10-meter waves break explosively against the rocks.*

RELATED VERBS ab·brechen, an·brechen, auf·brechen, aus·brechen, durchbrechen, durch·brechen, ein·brechen, entzwei·brechen, erbrechen, gebrechen, um·brechen, verbrechen, zerbrechen; *see also* **unterbrechen** (467)

PRESENT

ich brenne	wir brennen
du brennst	ihr brennt
Sie brennen	Sie brennen
er/sie/es brennt	sie brennen

SIMPLE PAST

ich brannte	wir brannten
du branntest	ihr branntet
Sie brannten	Sie brannten
er/sie/es brannte	sie brannten

FUTURE

ich werde	wir werden	brennen
du wirst	ihr werdet	
Sie werden	Sie werden	
er/sie/es wird	sie werden	

PRESENT SUBJUNCTIVE I

ich brenne	wir brennen
du brennest	ihr brennet
Sie brennen	Sie brennen
er/sie/es brenne	sie brennen

PRESENT SUBJUNCTIVE II

ich brennte	wir brennten
du brenntest	ihr brenntet
Sie brennten	Sie brennten
er/sie/es brennte	sie brennten

FUTURE SUBJUNCTIVE I

ich werde	wir werden	brennen
du werdest	ihr werdet	
Sie werden	Sie werden	
er/sie/es werde	sie werden	

FUTURE SUBJUNCTIVE II

ich würde	wir würden	brennen
du würdest	ihr würdet	
Sie würden	Sie würden	
er/sie/es würde	sie würden	

PRESENT PERFECT

ich habe	wir haben	gebrannt
du hast	ihr habt	
Sie haben	Sie haben	
er/sie/es hat	sie haben	

PAST PERFECT

ich hatte	wir hatten	gebrannt
du hattest	ihr hattet	
Sie hatten	Sie hatten	
er/sie/es hatte	sie hatten	

FUTURE PERFECT

ich werde	wir werden	gebrannt haben
du wirst	ihr werdet	
Sie werden	Sie werden	
er/sie/es wird	sie werden	

PAST SUBJUNCTIVE I

ich habe	wir haben	gebrannt
du habest	ihr habet	
Sie haben	Sie haben	
er/sie/es habe	sie haben	

PAST SUBJUNCTIVE II

ich hätte	wir hätten	gebrannt
du hättest	ihr hättet	
Sie hätten	Sie hätten	
er/sie/es hätte	sie hätten	

FUTURE PERFECT SUBJUNCTIVE I

ich werde	wir werden	gebrannt haben
du werdest	ihr werdet	
Sie werden	Sie werden	
er/sie/es werde	sie werden	

FUTURE PERFECT SUBJUNCTIVE II

ich würde	wir würden	gebrannt haben
du würdest	ihr würdet	
Sie würden	Sie würden	
er/sie/es würde	sie würden	

COMMANDS brenn(e)! brennt! brennen Sie!

PRESENT PARTICIPLE brennend

Usage

Der Regenwald brennt und wir sehen einfach zu.	*The rainforest is burning and we're just watching.*
Jetzt brennen mir die Augen.	*Now my eyes are burning.*
Brennt Diesel so schnell wie Benzin?	*Does diesel burn as quickly as gasoline?*
Destillerie Douglas & Cie hatte Whiskey schon seit 1877 gebrannt.	*The distillery Douglas & Co. had been distilling whiskey since 1877.*
Tondachziegel werden in einem großen Ofen gebrannt.	*Clay roofing shingles are baked in a large oven.*
Nach einigen Tagen werden die Kaffeebohnen gebrannt.	*After a few days, the coffee beans are roasted.*
Vier Öllampen haben im Zimmer gebrannt.	*Four oil lamps were burning in the room.*
Wenn alle LEDs brennen, ist das Gerät defekt.	*If all LEDs are lit, the device is defective.*
Kein Licht brannte mehr in den Häusern. (BETTINA VON ARNIM)	*The lights were no longer burning in the houses.*
„Papa, das Haus brennt!" schrie Anna.	*"Papa, the house is on fire!" screamed Anna.*

RELATED VERBS ab·brennen, an·brennen, auf·brennen, aus·brennen, durch·brennen, ein·brennen, nieder·brennen, verbrennen

118 **bringen** *to bring; take; yield; present; put*

bringt · brachte · gebracht — mixed verb

MORE USAGE SENTENCES WITH bringen

Lars hat mich nach Hause gebracht. — *Lars brought me home.*

Das Wasser zum Kochen bringen. — *Bring the water to a boil.*

Alle Schiffspassagiere waren an Land in Sicherheit gebracht worden. — *All the ship's passengers had been brought ashore to safety.*

Am 12. September 1833 brachte Elisabeth Kleist geb. Schmidt ein Kind zur Welt. — *On September 12, 1833, Elisabeth Kleist née Schmidt brought a child into the world.*

Neue Tatsachen sind ans Licht gebracht worden. — *New facts have been brought to light.*

Ingrid wollte das Thema Abtreibung nicht ins Gespräch bringen. — *Ingrid didn't want to bring the topic of abortion up for discussion.*

Der Parteivorsteher muss zur Vernunft gebracht werden. — *The party chairman must be brought to his senses.*

Wie viel Zinsen bringen €1 000 zu 2 % in 12 Monaten? — *How much interest does 1,000 euros yield at 2% over 12 months?*

IDIOMATIC EXPRESSIONS

Gesellschaftlich engagierte Schriftsteller hatten die Möglichkeit, ihre Ideen zum Ausdruck zu bringen. — *Socially engaged writers had an opportunity to express their ideas.*

Ich habe es immer noch nicht fertig gebracht, den Dachboden zu räumen. — *I've still not managed to clear out the attic.*

Als Flötistin hat sie es im Beruf weit gebracht. — *She's done well in her career as flautist.*

Die Mitarbeiter werden um einen gerechten Lohn gebracht. — *The employees are being denied a fair wage.*

Amalie fiel es leicht, ihre Gedanken zu Papier zu bringen. — *It was easy for Amalie to put her thoughts on paper.*

Jack the Ripper sollte fünf Frauen ums Leben gebracht haben. — *Jack the Ripper was said to have taken the lives of five women.*

Du hast mich auf eine tolle Idee gebracht! — *You've given me a great idea!*

Was dann passierte, brachte Dieter aus der Fassung. — *What happened then disconcerted Dieter greatly.*

Die Wirtschaftskrise brachte viele Familien an den Bettelstab. — *The economic crisis reduced many families to poverty.*

Soweit ich in Erfahrung gebracht habe, wird die alte Serie durch eine neue abgelöst. — *As far as I can ascertain, the old series is being replaced by a new one.*

2003 wurde das Thema zum ersten Mal zur Sprache gebracht. — *In 2003, the topic was broached for the first time.*

Ich bringe die beiden Namen immer durcheinander. — *I always confuse the two names.*

Thorsten hat das Projekt auf die Beine gebracht. — *Thorsten has gotten the project going.*

In dem Fall muss man halt ein Bauernopfer bringen. — *In that case, you just have to sacrifice a pawn.*

Die Firma hat ein neues Produkt auf den Markt gebracht. — *The firm has launched a new product on the market.*

Meine kleine Schwester hat meine Briefmarkensammlung durcheinander gebracht. — *My little sister made a mess of my stamp collection.*

Das Geschäft hat schon einen Gewinn gebracht. — *The business has already shown a profit.*

Die Menschen haben die Umwelt aus dem Gleichgewicht gebracht. — *Humans have thrown the environment out of balance.*

Der Lehrer wollte uns mittelalterliche Dichtung nahe bringen. — *The teacher wanted to make medieval poetry accessible to us.*

Die Geschäftsleitung hat mir diese Richtlinien zur Kenntnis gebracht. — *Management has made me aware of these guidelines.*

Kein Journalist hätte gewagt, das Skandal an die Öffentlichkeit zu bringen. — *No journalist would have dared make the scandal public.*

mixed verb **bringt · brachte · gebracht**

PRESENT

ich bringe	wir bringen
du bringst	ihr bringt
Sie bringen	Sie bringen
er/sie/es bringt	sie bringen

SIMPLE PAST

ich brachte	wir brachten
du brachtest	ihr brachtet
Sie brachten	Sie brachten
er/sie/es brachte	sie brachten

FUTURE

ich werde	wir werden	bringen
du wirst	ihr werdet	
Sie werden	Sie werden	
er/sie/es wird	sie werden	

PRESENT SUBJUNCTIVE I

ich bringe	wir bringen
du bringest	ihr bringet
Sie bringen	Sie bringen
er/sie/es bringe	sie bringen

PRESENT SUBJUNCTIVE II

ich brächte	wir brächten
du brächtest	ihr brächtet
Sie brächten	Sie brächten
er/sie/es brächte	sie brächten

FUTURE SUBJUNCTIVE I

ich werde	wir werden	bringen
du werdest	ihr werdet	
Sie werden	Sie werden	
er/sie/es werde	sie werden	

FUTURE SUBJUNCTIVE II

ich würde	wir würden	bringen
du würdest	ihr würdet	
Sie würden	Sie würden	
er/sie/es würde	sie würden	

PRESENT PERFECT

ich habe	wir haben	gebracht
du hast	ihr habt	
Sie haben	Sie haben	
er/sie/es hat	sie haben	

PAST PERFECT

ich hatte	wir hatten	gebracht
du hattest	ihr hattet	
Sie hatten	Sie hatten	
er/sie/es hatte	sie hatten	

FUTURE PERFECT

ich werde	wir werden	gebracht haben
du wirst	ihr werdet	
Sie werden	Sie werden	
er/sie/es wird	sie werden	

PAST SUBJUNCTIVE I

ich habe	wir haben	gebracht
du habest	ihr habet	
Sie haben	Sie haben	
er/sie/es habe	sie haben	

PAST SUBJUNCTIVE II

ich hätte	wir hätten	gebracht
du hättest	ihr hättet	
Sie hätten	Sie hätten	
er/sie/es hätte	sie hätten	

FUTURE PERFECT SUBJUNCTIVE I

ich werde	wir werden	gebracht haben
du werdest	ihr werdet	
Sie werden	Sie werden	
er/sie/es werde	sie werden	

FUTURE PERFECT SUBJUNCTIVE II

ich würde	wir würden	gebracht haben
du würdest	ihr würdet	
Sie würden	Sie würden	
er/sie/es würde	sie würden	

COMMANDS bring(e)! bringt! bringen Sie!

PRESENT PARTICIPLE bringend

Usage

Hans, bringst du mir bitte die Zeitung? — *Hans, would you please bring me the paper?*

Solche Kontrapositionen bringen andere Überlegungen ins Spiel. — *Such contrapositions bring other considerations into play.*

Das Stadttheater bringt nur traditionelle Stücke auf die Bühne. — *The municipal theater brings only traditional plays to the stage.*

Der Dichter hat die Macht, das Fantastische ins Alltägliche zu bringen. — *The poet has the power to bring the fantastical into the everyday.*

Heinz hat sie zum Bahnhof gebracht. — *Heinz took her to the train station.*

Diese Entwicklungen bringen neue Probleme mit sich. — *These developments present new problems.*

Die Mutter hat ihre Kinder ins Bett gebracht. — *The mother put her children to bed.*

RELATED VERBS ab·bringen, an·bringen, auf·bringen, aus·bringen, bei·bringen, durch·bringen, ein·bringen, erbringen, fort·bringen, hinterbringen, mit·bringen, nach·bringen, überbringen, um·bringen, unter·bringen, vor·bringen, weg·bringen, wieder·bringen, zu·bringen; *see also* **verbringen** (480)

119 buchen *to book, reserve; enter* (bookkeeping)

bucht · buchte · gebucht regular weak verb

PRESENT

ich buche	wir buchen
du buchst	ihr bucht
Sie buchen	Sie buchen
er/sie/es bucht	sie buchen

SIMPLE PAST

ich buchte	wir buchten
du buchtest	ihr buchtet
Sie buchten	Sie buchten
er/sie/es buchte	sie buchten

FUTURE

ich werde	wir werden	buchen
du wirst	ihr werdet	
Sie werden	Sie werden	
er/sie/es wird	sie werden	

PRESENT SUBJUNCTIVE I

ich buche	wir buchen
du buchest	ihr buchet
Sie buchen	Sie buchen
er/sie/es buche	sie buchen

PRESENT SUBJUNCTIVE II

ich buchte	wir buchten
du buchtest	ihr buchtet
Sie buchten	Sie buchten
er/sie/es buchte	sie buchten

FUTURE SUBJUNCTIVE I

ich werde	wir werden	buchen
du werdest	ihr werdet	
Sie werden	Sie werden	
er/sie/es werde	sie werden	

FUTURE SUBJUNCTIVE II

ich würde	wir würden	buchen
du würdest	ihr würdet	
Sie würden	Sie würden	
er/sie/es würde	sie würden	

COMMANDS buch(e)! bucht! buchen Sie!

PRESENT PARTICIPLE buchend

PRESENT PERFECT

ich habe	wir haben	gebucht
du hast	ihr habt	
Sie haben	Sie haben	
er/sie/es hat	sie haben	

PAST PERFECT

ich hatte	wir hatten	gebucht
du hattest	ihr hattet	
Sie hatten	Sie hatten	
er/sie/es hatte	sie hatten	

FUTURE PERFECT

ich werde	wir werden	gebucht haben
du wirst	ihr werdet	
Sie werden	Sie werden	
er/sie/es wird	sie werden	

PAST SUBJUNCTIVE I

ich habe	wir haben	gebucht
du habest	ihr habet	
Sie haben	Sie haben	
er/sie/es habe	sie haben	

PAST SUBJUNCTIVE II

ich hätte	wir hätten	gebucht
du hättest	ihr hättet	
Sie hätten	Sie hätten	
er/sie/es hätte	sie hätten	

FUTURE PERFECT SUBJUNCTIVE I

ich werde	wir werden	gebucht haben
du werdest	ihr werdet	
Sie werden	Sie werden	
er/sie/es werde	sie werden	

FUTURE PERFECT SUBJUNCTIVE II

ich würde	wir würden	gebucht haben
du würdest	ihr würdet	
Sie würden	Sie würden	
er/sie/es würde	sie würden	

Usage

„Hast du deinen Flug nach Tasmanien schon gebucht, Maria?“ — *“Have you already booked your flight to Tasmania, Maria?”*

„Gebucht, ja, aber noch nicht bezahlt.“ — *“Booked yes, but not yet paid for.”*

Aufenthalte von mehr als zwei Tagen müssten im Voraus gebucht werden. — *Stays of more than two days would have to be booked in advance.*

Guten Tag, ich möchte eine Tour buchen. — *Hello, I'd like to book a tour.*

Sie können Ihren Platz im Workshop über das Internet buchen. — *You can reserve your place in the workshop over the Internet.*

Buchst du immer Vollpension? — *Do you always book full board?*

An deiner Stelle würde ich den Rückflug noch nicht buchen. — *If I were you, I wouldn't book the return flight yet.*

Heute muss ich die Rechnungen buchen. — *Today I must enter the invoices.*

RELATED VERBS aus·buchen, überbuchen, um·buchen

regular weak verb (dative object) **dankt · dankte · gedankt**

PRESENT

ich danke	wir danken
du dankst	ihr dankt
Sie danken	Sie danken
er/sie/es dankt	sie danken

SIMPLE PAST

ich dankte	wir dankten
du danktest	ihr danktet
Sie dankten	Sie dankten
er/sie/es dankte	sie dankten

FUTURE

ich werde	wir werden	danken
du wirst	ihr werdet	
Sie werden	Sie werden	
er/sie/es wird	sie werden	

PRESENT SUBJUNCTIVE I

ich danke	wir danken
du dankest	ihr danket
Sie danken	Sie danken
er/sie/es danke	sie danken

PRESENT SUBJUNCTIVE II

ich dankte	wir dankten
du danktest	ihr danktet
Sie dankten	Sie dankten
er/sie/es dankte	sie dankten

FUTURE SUBJUNCTIVE I

ich werde	wir werden	danken
du werdest	ihr werdet	
Sie werden	Sie werden	
er/sie/es werde	sie werden	

FUTURE SUBJUNCTIVE II

ich würde	wir würden	danken
du würdest	ihr würdet	
Sie würden	Sie würden	
er/sie/es würde	sie würden	

PRESENT PERFECT

ich habe	wir haben	gedankt
du hast	ihr habt	
Sie haben	Sie haben	
er/sie/es hat	sie haben	

PAST PERFECT

ich hatte	wir hatten	gedankt
du hattest	ihr hattet	
Sie hatten	Sie hatten	
er/sie/es hatte	sie hatten	

FUTURE PERFECT

ich werde	wir werden	gedankt haben
du wirst	ihr werdet	
Sie werden	Sie werden	
er/sie/es wird	sie werden	

PAST SUBJUNCTIVE I

ich habe	wir haben	gedankt
du habest	ihr habet	
Sie haben	Sie haben	
er/sie/es habe	sie haben	

PAST SUBJUNCTIVE II

ich hätte	wir hätten	gedankt
du hättest	ihr hättet	
Sie hätten	Sie hätten	
er/sie/es hätte	sie hätten	

FUTURE PERFECT SUBJUNCTIVE I

ich werde	wir werden	gedankt haben
du werdest	ihr werdet	
Sie werden	Sie werden	
er/sie/es werde	sie werden	

FUTURE PERFECT SUBJUNCTIVE II

ich würde	wir würden	gedankt haben
du würdest	ihr würdet	
Sie würden	Sie würden	
er/sie/es würde	sie würden	

COMMANDS dank(e)! dankt! danken Sie!

PRESENT PARTICIPLE dankend

Usage

Ich möchte allen danken, die mir geholfen haben.	*I'd like to thank everyone who helped me.*
Anton dankte seinen Kollegen und verabschiedete sich.	*Anton thanked his colleagues and said good-bye.*
Wir danken Ihnen für Ihr Verständnis.	*We thank you for your understanding.*
Die Reisegruppe hat ihrem Reiseleiter mit einer Flasche Wein gedankt.	*The tour group thanked their guide with a bottle of wine.*
Deborah lässt danken.	*Deborah sends her thanks.*
Ich danke dir mein Leben.	*I owe you my life.*
„Möchtest du etwas essen?"	*"Would you like something to eat?"*
„Danke, ich habe schon gegessen."	*"No thanks, I've already eaten."*
Ihnen allen sei herzlich gedankt!	*Heartfelt thanks to you all!*
Wie kann ich euch jemals danken?	*How can I ever thank you?*
Nichts zu danken.	*Don't mention it.*

RELATED VERBS ab·danken, bedanken, verdanken

121 dauern *to last, endure; take (time); feel sorry for*

dauert · dauerte · gedauert regular weak verb

PRESENT

ich dauere	wir dauern
du dauerst	ihr dauert
Sie dauern	Sie dauern
er/sie/es dauert	sie dauern

SIMPLE PAST

ich dauerte	wir dauerten
du dauertest	ihr dauertet
Sie dauerten	Sie dauerten
er/sie/es dauerte	sie dauerten

FUTURE

ich werde	wir werden	dauern
du wirst	ihr werdet	
Sie werden	Sie werden	
er/sie/es wird	sie werden	

PRESENT SUBJUNCTIVE I

ich dauere	wir dauern
du dauerst	ihr dauert
Sie dauern	Sie dauern
er/sie/es dauere	sie dauern

PRESENT SUBJUNCTIVE II

ich dauerte	wir dauerten
du dauertest	ihr dauertet
Sie dauerten	Sie dauerten
er/sie/es dauerte	sie dauerten

FUTURE SUBJUNCTIVE I

ich werde	wir werden	dauern
du werdest	ihr werdet	
Sie werden	Sie werden	
er/sie/es werde	sie werden	

FUTURE SUBJUNCTIVE II

ich würde	wir würden	dauern
du würdest	ihr würdet	
Sie würden	Sie würden	
er/sie/es würde	sie würden	

PRESENT PERFECT

ich habe	wir haben	gedauert
du hast	ihr habt	
Sie haben	Sie haben	
er/sie/es hat	sie haben	

PAST PERFECT

ich hatte	wir hatten	gedauert
du hattest	ihr hattet	
Sie hatten	Sie hatten	
er/sie/es hatte	sie hatten	

FUTURE PERFECT

ich werde	wir werden	gedauert haben
du wirst	ihr werdet	
Sie werden	Sie werden	
er/sie/es wird	sie werden	

PAST SUBJUNCTIVE I

ich habe	wir haben	gedauert
du habest	ihr habet	
Sie haben	Sie haben	
er/sie/es habe	sie haben	

PAST SUBJUNCTIVE II

ich hätte	wir hätten	gedauert
du hättest	ihr hättet	
Sie hätten	Sie hätten	
er/sie/es hätte	sie hätten	

FUTURE PERFECT SUBJUNCTIVE I

ich werde	wir werden	gedauert haben
du werdest	ihr werdet	
Sie werden	Sie werden	
er/sie/es werde	sie werden	

FUTURE PERFECT SUBJUNCTIVE II

ich würde	wir würden	gedauert haben
du würdest	ihr würdet	
Sie würden	Sie würden	
er/sie/es würde	sie würden	

COMMANDS dauere! dauert! dauern Sie!

PRESENT PARTICIPLE dauernd

Usage

Der Investiturstreit dauerte bis 1122.	*The Conflict of Investitures lasted until 1122.*
Die Ehe dauerte bis zu seinem Tod.	*The marriage lasted until his death.*
Das Semester dauert 15 Wochen.	*The semester lasts 15 weeks.*
Ihre Beziehung wird bestimmt dauern.	*Their relationship will surely endure.*
Es hat lange gedauert.	*It lasted/took a long time.*
Wenn es nur nicht so lange dauern würde!	*If only it wouldn't last so long!*
Der Dreißigjährige Krieg dauerte von 1618 bis 1648.	*The Thirty Years' War lasted from 1618 to 1648.*
Wie lange dauert es, bis er nach Hause kommt?	*How long will it be before he comes home?*
Zusendung kann einige Wochen dauern.	*Shipping can take a few weeks.*
Die Dürre dauerte ungefähr 10 Jahre und viele Oklahomaner zogen nach Kalifornien.	*The drought lasted about 10 years, and many Oklahomans moved to California.*
Du dauerst mich, du allerliebstes Kind. (GÜNTHER)	*I am sorry for you, dearest child.*

RELATED VERBS an·dauern, aus·dauern, bedauern, fort·dauern, überdauern

PRESENT

ich denke	wir denken
du denkst	ihr denkt
Sie denken	Sie denken
er/sie/es denkt	sie denken

SIMPLE PAST

ich dachte	wir dachten
du dachtest	ihr dachtet
Sie dachten	Sie dachten
er/sie/es dachte	sie dachten

FUTURE

ich werde	wir werden	denken
du wirst	ihr werdet	
Sie werden	Sie werden	
er/sie/es wird	sie werden	

PRESENT SUBJUNCTIVE I

ich denke	wir denken
du denkest	ihr denket
Sie denken	Sie denken
er/sie/es denke	sie denken

PRESENT SUBJUNCTIVE II

ich dächte	wir dächten
du dächtest	ihr dächtet
Sie dächten	Sie dächten
er/sie/es dächte	sie dächten

FUTURE SUBJUNCTIVE I

ich werde	wir werden	denken
du werdest	ihr werdet	
Sie werden	Sie werden	
er/sie/es werde	sie werden	

FUTURE SUBJUNCTIVE II

ich würde	wir würden	denken
du würdest	ihr würdet	
Sie würden	Sie würden	
er/sie/es würde	sie würden	

PRESENT PERFECT

ich habe	wir haben	gedacht
du hast	ihr habt	
Sie haben	Sie haben	
er/sie/es hat	sie haben	

PAST PERFECT

ich hatte	wir hatten	gedacht
du hattest	ihr hattet	
Sie hatten	Sie hatten	
er/sie/es hatte	sie hatten	

FUTURE PERFECT

ich werde	wir werden	gedacht haben
du wirst	ihr werdet	
Sie werden	Sie werden	
er/sie/es wird	sie werden	

PAST SUBJUNCTIVE I

ich habe	wir haben	gedacht
du habest	ihr habet	
Sie haben	Sie haben	
er/sie/es habe	sie haben	

PAST SUBJUNCTIVE II

ich hätte	wir hätten	gedacht
du hättest	ihr hättet	
Sie hätten	Sie hätten	
er/sie/es hätte	sie hätten	

FUTURE PERFECT SUBJUNCTIVE I

ich werde	wir werden	gedacht haben
du werdest	ihr werdet	
Sie werden	Sie werden	
er/sie/es werde	sie werden	

FUTURE PERFECT SUBJUNCTIVE II

ich würde	wir würden	gedacht haben
du würdest	ihr würdet	
Sie würden	Sie würden	
er/sie/es würde	sie würden	

COMMANDS denk(e)! denkt! denken Sie!

PRESENT PARTICIPLE denkend

Usage

Eigentlich dachte ich, dass wir alle beitragen.	*Actually, I thought we would all contribute.*
Rudi, denk doch nicht so viel!	*Rudi, just don't think so much!*
Diese Regel kann als Einfluss von dem Lateinischen gedacht werden.	*One can conceive of this rule as influence from the Latin.*
Habt ihr das zu Ende gedacht?	*Have you thought that through?*
Herr Unger denkt und handelt stets pragmatisch.	*Mr. Unger always thinks and acts pragmatically.*
Kannst du nicht selbstständig denken?	*Can't you think for yourself?*
Man weiß nie, was er denkt.	*You never know what he's thinking.*
Wer hätte gedacht, dass es so schwer ist, eine Lösung zu finden?	*Who would have thought it would be so hard to find a solution?*

RELATED VERBS aus·denken, bedenken, durchdenken, durch·denken, erdenken, gedenken, überdenken, um·denken, verdenken, weg·denken, zu·denken, zurück·denken; *see also* **nach·denken** (313)

TOP 50 VERB ☞

122 denken *to think, conceive; believe; bear in mind*

denkt · dachte · gedacht mixed verb

denken an + accusative *to think about/of; bear in mind, remember*

„Woran denken Sie?" — *"What are you thinking about?"*
„Ich denke an meinen Vater." — *"I'm thinking about my father."*
Astrid denkt nur an sich selbst. — *Astrid is thinking only of herself.*
Denkst du oft an mich? — *Do you think of me often?*
Susanne denkt nur noch an Sofie. — *Susanne is thinking only of Sofie.*
Denkt daran, dass Manfred auch mitkommen will. — *Bear in mind that Manfred also wants to come along.*
Denken Sie daran, mich anzurufen. — *Don't forget to call me.*
Die Melodie lässt an Schuberts „Das Wandern" denken. — *The melody reminds one of Schubert's "Das Wandern."*

denken über + accusative *to think about*

Was denken Sie über die Wahlergebnisse? — *What do you think about the election results?*
Erich denkt zu viel darüber. — *Erich thinks too much about that.*
Was denkst du darüber? — *What do you think about that?*

denken von *to think of*

Was denkt sie von mir? — *What does she think of me?*
Wie niedrig Sie von Menschenwürde denken! (SCHILLER) — *Such a low opinion you have of the worthiness of man!*

denken + genitive *to think of* (poetic)

Es ist der erste Mai, und ich denke deiner, du schöne Ilse. (HEINE) — *It is the first of May and I think of you, beautiful Ilse.*

sich denken *to imagine, conceive, mean*

Ich kann mir denken, dass so was nicht leicht ist. — *I can imagine that something like that isn't easy.*
Frau Arnhem dachte sich nichts dabei. — *Mrs. Arnhem didn't think anything of it.*
Ich habe mir nichts Schlimmes dabei gedacht. — *I didn't mean anything bad by it.*
Ich hätte mir gleich denken können, dass er es nicht ernst meint. — *I should have known that he isn't serious about it.*

bei sich denken *to think to oneself*

Erich dachte bei sich: „Vielleicht klappt's doch noch." — *Erich thought to himself, "Maybe it'll work yet."*

für etwas/jemanden gedacht sein *to be intended for something/someone*

Das Gerät war für einen anderen Zweck gedacht. — *The device was intended for another purpose.*

IDIOMATIC EXPRESSIONS

Wir müssen um die Ecke denken, um dieses Problem zu lösen. — *We have to think outside the box to solve this problem.*
Erst denken, dann handeln. — *Think before you act.*
Das hat mir zu denken gegeben. — *That has made me wonder.*
Es lässt sich denken, dass sie die Adresse vergessen hat. — *It's conceivable that she forgot the address.*
Ich denke schon. — *I think so.*
Solange ich denken kann, hatte Heinz einen Bart. — *Heinz has had a beard as long as I can remember.*
Daran ist nicht zu denken. — *That's not possible.*
Der Mensch denkt, Gott lenkt. (PROVERB) — *Man proposes, God disposes.*

regular weak verb (dative object) **dient · diente · gedient**

PRESENT

ich diene	wir dienen
du dienst	ihr dient
Sie dienen	Sie dienen
er/sie/es dient	sie dienen

SIMPLE PAST

ich diente	wir dienten
du dientest	ihr dientet
Sie dienten	Sie dienten
er/sie/es diente	sie dienten

FUTURE

ich werde	wir werden	dienen
du wirst	ihr werdet	
Sie werden	Sie werden	
er/sie/es wird	sie werden	

PRESENT SUBJUNCTIVE I

ich diene	wir dienen
du dienest	ihr dienet
Sie dienen	Sie dienen
er/sie/es diene	sie dienen

PRESENT SUBJUNCTIVE II

ich diente	wir dienten
du dientest	ihr dientet
Sie dienten	Sie dienten
er/sie/es diente	sie dienten

FUTURE SUBJUNCTIVE I

ich werde	wir werden	dienen
du werdest	ihr werdet	
Sie werden	Sie werden	
er/sie/es werde	sie werden	

FUTURE SUBJUNCTIVE II

ich würde	wir würden	dienen
du würdest	ihr würdet	
Sie würden	Sie würden	
er/sie/es würde	sie würden	

PRESENT PERFECT

ich habe	wir haben	gedient
du hast	ihr habt	
Sie haben	Sie haben	
er/sie/es hat	sie haben	

PAST PERFECT

ich hatte	wir hatten	gedient
du hattest	ihr hattet	
Sie hatten	Sie hatten	
er/sie/es hatte	sie hatten	

FUTURE PERFECT

ich werde	wir werden	gedient haben
du wirst	ihr werdet	
Sie werden	Sie werden	
er/sie/es wird	sie werden	

PAST SUBJUNCTIVE I

ich habe	wir haben	gedient
du habest	ihr habet	
Sie haben	Sie haben	
er/sie/es habe	sie haben	

PAST SUBJUNCTIVE II

ich hätte	wir hätten	gedient
du hättest	ihr hättet	
Sie hätten	Sie hätten	
er/sie/es hätte	sie hätten	

FUTURE PERFECT SUBJUNCTIVE I

ich werde	wir werden	gedient haben
du werdest	ihr werdet	
Sie werden	Sie werden	
er/sie/es werde	sie werden	

FUTURE PERFECT SUBJUNCTIVE II

ich würde	wir würden	gedient haben
du würdest	ihr würdet	
Sie würden	Sie würden	
er/sie/es würde	sie würden	

COMMANDS dien(e)! dient! dienen Sie!

PRESENT PARTICIPLE dienend

Usage

Wilhelm Meisters Lehrjahre dient als gutes Beispiel für einen Bildungsroman. — Wilhelm Meisters Lehrjahre *serves as a good example of a* bildungsroman.

Christian hat zwei Jahre bei der Bundeswehr gedient. — *Christian served in the federal army for two years.*

Das Geld dient einem guten Zweck. — *The money serves a good purpose.*

Dieser Streit diente als Hintergrund für die politischen Geschehnisse des 12. Jahrhunderts. — *This conflict served as a backdrop for the political events of the twelfth century.*

Die treuen Untertanen dienten ihrem König. — *The loyal subjects served their king.*

Hannas Vater soll als Arzt in Entwicklungsländern gedient haben. — *Hanna's father is said to have served as a doctor in developing countries.*

Mit bloßen Worten ist ihnen nicht gedient. — *Mere words are of no use to them.*

Andere Theaterstücke hatten dazu gedient, Geschichten aus der Bibel zu schildern. — *Other plays had been useful for depicting stories from the Bible.*

Womit können wir Ihnen dienen? (*idiomatic*) — *How can we help you?*

RELATED VERBS an·dienen; *see also* **bedienen** (49), **verdienen** (482)

124 diskutieren *to discuss, debate; talk*

diskutiert · diskutierte · diskutiert regular weak verb

PRESENT

ich diskutiere	wir diskutieren
du diskutierst	ihr diskutiert
Sie diskutieren	Sie diskutieren
er/sie/es diskutiert	sie diskutieren

SIMPLE PAST

ich diskutierte	wir diskutierten
du diskutiertest	ihr diskutiertet
Sie diskutierten	Sie diskutierten
er/sie/es diskutierte	sie diskutierten

FUTURE

ich werde	wir werden	diskutieren
du wirst	ihr werdet	
Sie werden	Sie werden	
er/sie/es wird	sie werden	

PRESENT SUBJUNCTIVE I

ich diskutiere	wir diskutieren
du diskutierest	ihr diskutieret
Sie diskutieren	Sie diskutieren
er/sie/es diskutiere	sie diskutieren

PRESENT SUBJUNCTIVE II

ich diskutierte	wir diskutierten
du diskutiertest	ihr diskutiertet
Sie diskutierten	Sie diskutierten
er/sie/es diskutierte	sie diskutierten

FUTURE SUBJUNCTIVE I

ich werde	wir werden	diskutieren
du werdest	ihr werdet	
Sie werden	Sie werden	
er/sie/es werde	sie werden	

FUTURE SUBJUNCTIVE II

ich würde	wir würden	diskutieren
du würdest	ihr würdet	
Sie würden	Sie würden	
er/sie/es würde	sie würden	

PRESENT PERFECT

ich habe	wir haben	diskutiert
du hast	ihr habt	
Sie haben	Sie haben	
er/sie/es hat	sie haben	

PAST PERFECT

ich hatte	wir hatten	diskutiert
du hattest	ihr hattet	
Sie hatten	Sie hatten	
er/sie/es hatte	sie hatten	

FUTURE PERFECT

ich werde	wir werden	diskutiert haben
du wirst	ihr werdet	
Sie werden	Sie werden	
er/sie/es wird	sie werden	

PAST SUBJUNCTIVE I

ich habe	wir haben	diskutiert
du habest	ihr habet	
Sie haben	Sie haben	
er/sie/es habe	sie haben	

PAST SUBJUNCTIVE II

ich hätte	wir hätten	diskutiert
du hättest	ihr hättet	
Sie hätten	Sie hätten	
er/sie/es hätte	sie hätten	

FUTURE PERFECT SUBJUNCTIVE I

ich werde	wir werden	diskutiert haben
du werdest	ihr werdet	
Sie werden	Sie werden	
er/sie/es werde	sie werden	

FUTURE PERFECT SUBJUNCTIVE II

ich würde	wir würden	diskutiert haben
du würdest	ihr würdet	
Sie würden	Sie würden	
er/sie/es würde	sie würden	

COMMANDS diskutier(e)! diskutiert! diskutieren Sie!

PRESENT PARTICIPLE diskutierend

Usage

Wir haben das Problem ausführlich diskutiert.	*We thoroughly discussed the problem.*
Condillac diskutiert menschliche Sprache in Hinsicht auf spontane Gesten.	*Condillac discusses human language relative to spontaneous gestures.*
Es ist notwendig, die neuen Entwicklungen gemeinsam zu diskutieren.	*It is necessary to discuss the new developments together.*
Letzte Woche wurde über einen Artikel aus *Der Spiegel* diskutiert.	*Last week an article from* Der Spiegel *was discussed.*
Die Ursachen des Terrorismus müssen diskutiert werden.	*The causes of terrorism must be discussed.*
Die Rolle der NATO wurde heute im Parlament diskutiert.	*The role of NATO was discussed in Parliament today.*
Die Politiker haben das Thema stundenlang diskutiert.	*The politicians debated the topic for hours.*
In unserem Chat wird über klassische Musik diskutiert.	*In our chat room, we talk about classical music.*
In einem Radiointerview diskutierte der CEO seinen Rücktritt.	*In a radio interview, the CEO talked about his resignation.*

RELATED VERBS aus·diskutieren, durch·diskutieren, weg·diskutieren

regular weak verb **dreht · drehte · gedreht**

PRESENT

ich drehe	wir drehen
du drehst	ihr dreht
Sie drehen	Sie drehen
er/sie/es dreht	sie drehen

SIMPLE PAST

ich drehte	wir drehten
du drehtest	ihr drehtet
Sie drehten	Sie drehten
er/sie/es drehte	sie drehten

FUTURE

ich werde	wir werden	drehen
du wirst	ihr werdet	
Sie werden	Sie werden	
er/sie/es wird	sie werden	

PRESENT SUBJUNCTIVE I

ich drehe	wir drehen
du drehest	ihr drehet
Sie drehen	Sie drehen
er/sie/es drehe	sie drehen

PRESENT SUBJUNCTIVE II

ich drehte	wir drehten
du drehtest	ihr drehtet
Sie drehten	Sie drehten
er/sie/es drehte	sie drehten

FUTURE SUBJUNCTIVE I

ich werde	wir werden	drehen
du werdest	ihr werdet	
Sie werden	Sie werden	
er/sie/es werde	sie werden	

FUTURE SUBJUNCTIVE II

ich würde	wir würden	drehen
du würdest	ihr würdet	
Sie würden	Sie würden	
er/sie/es würde	sie würden	

PRESENT PERFECT

ich habe	wir haben	gedreht
du hast	ihr habt	
Sie haben	Sie haben	
er/sie/es hat	sie haben	

PAST PERFECT

ich hatte	wir hatten	gedreht
du hattest	ihr hattet	
Sie hatten	Sie hatten	
er/sie/es hatte	sie hatten	

FUTURE PERFECT

ich werde	wir werden	gedreht haben
du wirst	ihr werdet	
Sie werden	Sie werden	
er/sie/es wird	sie werden	

PAST SUBJUNCTIVE I

ich habe	wir haben	gedreht
du habest	ihr habet	
Sie haben	Sie haben	
er/sie/es habe	sie haben	

PAST SUBJUNCTIVE II

ich hätte	wir hätten	gedreht
du hättest	ihr hättet	
Sie hätten	Sie hätten	
er/sie/es hätte	sie hätten	

FUTURE PERFECT SUBJUNCTIVE I

ich werde	wir werden	gedreht haben
du werdest	ihr werdet	
Sie werden	Sie werden	
er/sie/es werde	sie werden	

FUTURE PERFECT SUBJUNCTIVE II

ich würde	wir würden	gedreht haben
du würdest	ihr würdet	
Sie würden	Sie würden	
er/sie/es würde	sie würden	

COMMANDS dreh(e)! dreht! drehen Sie!

PRESENT PARTICIPLE drehend

Usage

Du drehst die Schraube doch im Gegenuhrzeigersinn. — *But you are turning the screw counterclockwise.*
Er kann seinen Fuß nicht nach außen drehen. — *He is unable to rotate his foot outward.*
Kannst du Makisushi drehen? — *Can you roll makizushi?*
Früher hat Heinz seine Zigaretten selbst gedreht. — *Heinz used to roll his own cigarettes.*
Doris Dörrie drehte den Film in Japan. — *Doris Dörrie shot the film in Japan.*

sich drehen *to turn, rotate, roll, revolve, spin, orbit*

Der Türschlüssel dreht sich schwer. — *The door key is hard to turn.*
Diese Festplatte dreht sich mit 7.200 U/min. — *This hard drive spins at 7,200 rpm.*
Die Erde dreht sich um die Sonne. — *The earth orbits the sun.*
Vier Jahre drehten sie sich im Kreis, weil sie kein Ziel im Sinn hatten. (*idiomatic*) — *For four years, they spun their wheels because they had no goal in mind.*

RELATED VERBS ab·drehen, an·drehen, auf·drehen, aus·drehen, durch·drehen, ein·drehen, hoch·drehen, überdrehen, um·drehen, verdrehen, weg·drehen, zu·drehen, zurück·drehen

126 dreschen *to thresh*

drischt · drosch/drasch · gedroschen strong verb

PRESENT

ich dresche	wir dreschen
du drischst	ihr drescht
Sie dreschen	Sie dreschen
er/sie/es drischt	sie dreschen

SIMPLE PAST

ich drosch/drasch	wir droschen/draschen
du droschst/draschst	ihr droscht/drascht
Sie droschen/draschen	Sie droschen/draschen
er/sie/es drosch/drasch	sie droschen/draschen

FUTURE

ich werde	wir werden	dreschen
du wirst	ihr werdet	
Sie werden	Sie werden	
er/sie/es wird	sie werden	

PRESENT SUBJUNCTIVE I

ich dresche	wir dreschen
du dreschest	ihr dreschet
Sie dreschen	Sie dreschen
er/sie/es dresche	sie dreschen

PRESENT SUBJUNCTIVE II

ich drösche/dräsche	wir dröschen/dräschen
du dröschest/dräschest	ihr dröschet/dräschet
Sie dröschen/dräschen	Sie dröschen/dräschen
er/sie/es drösche/dräsche	sie dröschen/dräschen

FUTURE SUBJUNCTIVE I

ich werde	wir werden	dreschen
du werdest	ihr werdet	
Sie werden	Sie werden	
er/sie/es werde	sie werden	

FUTURE SUBJUNCTIVE II

ich würde	wir würden	dreschen
du würdest	ihr würdet	
Sie würden	Sie würden	
er/sie/es würde	sie würden	

PRESENT PERFECT

ich habe	wir haben	gedroschen
du hast	ihr habt	
Sie haben	Sie haben	
er/sie/es hat	sie haben	

PAST PERFECT

ich hatte	wir hatten	gedroschen
du hattest	ihr hattet	
Sie hatten	Sie hatten	
er/sie/es hatte	sie hatten	

FUTURE PERFECT

ich werde	wir werden	gedroschen haben
du wirst	ihr werdet	
Sie werden	Sie werden	
er/sie/es wird	sie werden	

PAST SUBJUNCTIVE I

ich habe	wir haben	gedroschen
du habest	ihr habet	
Sie haben	Sie haben	
er/sie/es habe	sie haben	

PAST SUBJUNCTIVE II

ich hätte	wir hätten	gedroschen
du hättest	ihr hättet	
Sie hätten	Sie hätten	
er/sie/es hätte	sie hätten	

FUTURE PERFECT SUBJUNCTIVE I

ich werde	wir werden	gedroschen haben
du werdest	ihr werdet	
Sie werden	Sie werden	
er/sie/es werde	sie werden	

FUTURE PERFECT SUBJUNCTIVE II

ich würde	wir würden	gedroschen haben
du würdest	ihr würdet	
Sie würden	Sie würden	
er/sie/es würde	sie würden	

COMMANDS drisch! drescht! dreschen Sie!

PRESENT PARTICIPLE dreschend

Usage

Im August muss das Getreide gedroschen werden.	*In August the grain must be threshed.*
Wenn es regnet, können wir die Weizen nicht dreschen.	*If it rains, we can't thresh the wheat.*
Wir denken, morgen zu dreschen.	*We intend to thresh tomorrow.*
Ein Drescher ist jemand, der drischt.	*A thresher is someone who threshes.*
Opa, drischst du gerne?	*Grandpa, do you like threshing?*
Franz-Josef drischt mit einem modernen Mähdrescher.	*Franz-Josef threshes with a modern combine.*
Sein Vater drosch das Getreide mit einem Dreschflegel.	*His father threshed grain with a threshing flail.*
Mein Vater fing immer frühmorgens an zu dreschen.	*My father always began threshing early in the morning.*
Rolf drosch den Ball aus 13 Metern in dic Maschen.	*Rolf slammed the ball into the net from 13 meters out.*
Der Glücksspieler drosch mit der Faust auf den Tisch.	*The gambler banged his fist on the table.*

RELATED VERB aus·dreschen

strong verb **dringt · drang · gedrungen**

PRESENT

ich dringe	wir dringen
du dringst	ihr dringt
Sie dringen	Sie dringen
er/sie/es dringt	sie dringen

SIMPLE PAST

ich drang	wir drangen
du drangst	ihr drangt
Sie drangen	Sie drangen
er/sie/es drang	sie drangen

FUTURE

ich werde	wir werden	dringen
du wirst	ihr werdet	
Sie werden	Sie werden	
er/sie/es wird	sie werden	

PRESENT SUBJUNCTIVE I

ich dringe	wir dringen
du dringest	ihr dringet
Sie dringen	Sie dringen
er/sie/es dringe	sie dringen

PRESENT SUBJUNCTIVE II

ich dränge	wir drängen
du drängest	ihr dränget
Sie drängen	Sie drängen
er/sie/es dränge	sie drängen

FUTURE SUBJUNCTIVE I

ich werde	wir werden	dringen
du werdest	ihr werdet	
Sie werden	Sie werden	
er/sie/es werde	sie werden	

FUTURE SUBJUNCTIVE II

ich würde	wir würden	dringen
du würdest	ihr würdet	
Sie würden	Sie würden	
er/sie/es würde	sie würden	

PRESENT PERFECT

ich bin	wir sind	gedrungen
du bist	ihr seid	
Sie sind	Sie sind	
er/sie/es ist	sie sind	

PAST PERFECT

ich war	wir waren	gedrungen
du warst	ihr wart	
Sie waren	Sie waren	
er/sie/es war	sie waren	

FUTURE PERFECT

ich werde	wir werden	gedrungen sein
du wirst	ihr werdet	
Sie werden	Sie werden	
er/sie/es wird	sie werden	

PAST SUBJUNCTIVE I

ich sei	wir seien	gedrungen
du seiest	ihr seiet	
Sie seien	Sie seien	
er/sie/es sei	sie seien	

PAST SUBJUNCTIVE II

ich wäre	wir wären	gedrungen
du wärest	ihr wäret	
Sie wären	Sie wären	
er/sie/es wäre	sie wären	

FUTURE PERFECT SUBJUNCTIVE I

ich werde	wir werden	gedrungen sein
du werdest	ihr werdet	
Sie werden	Sie werden	
er/sie/es werde	sie werden	

FUTURE PERFECT SUBJUNCTIVE II

ich würde	wir würden	gedrungen sein
du würdest	ihr würdet	
Sie würden	Sie würden	
er/sie/es würde	sie würden	

COMMANDS dring(e)! dringt! dringen Sie!

PRESENT PARTICIPLE dringend

Usage

Diese Substanzen dringen langsam durch die Haut. — *These substances slowly penetrate the skin.*

Die Nachricht ist an die Öffentlichkeit gedrungen. — *The news has reached the public.*

Sein Ruf drang weit ins Ausland. — *His reputation spread far abroad.*

Das Gelächter drang durch den Hörsaal. — *The laughter spread through the auditorium.*

Ein leises Echo ist durch den Wald bis zu unserem Zelt gedrungen. — *A soft echo swept through the forest as far as our tent.*

Ein abscheulicher Geruch drang mir in die Nase. — *A disgusting smell reached my nose.*

dringen (with **haben**) *to entreat, beg, urge*

Die Politiker haben auf ein Ende des Waffenembargos gedrungen. — *The politicians urged an end to the weapons embargo.*

Die Vorstandsmitglieder dringen auf eine schnelle Entscheidung. — *The board members are pushing for a quick decision.*

RELATED VERBS an·dringen, durch·dringen, durchdringen, ein·dringen, vor·dringen

128 drucken *to print*

druckt · druckte · gedruckt regular weak verb

PRESENT

ich drucke	wir drucken
du druckst	ihr druckt
Sie drucken	Sie drucken
er/sie/es druckt	sie drucken

SIMPLE PAST

ich druckte	wir druckten
du drucktest	ihr drucktet
Sie druckten	Sie druckten
er/sie/es druckte	sie druckten

FUTURE

ich werde	wir werden	drucken
du wirst	ihr werdet	
Sie werden	Sie werden	
er/sie/es wird	sie werden	

PRESENT SUBJUNCTIVE I

ich drucke	wir drucken
du druckest	ihr drucket
Sie drucken	Sie drucken
er/sie/es drucke	sie drucken

PRESENT SUBJUNCTIVE II

ich druckte	wir druckten
du drucktest	ihr drucktet
Sie druckten	Sie druckten
er/sie/es druckte	sie druckten

FUTURE SUBJUNCTIVE I

ich werde	wir werden	drucken
du werdest	ihr werdet	
Sie werden	Sie werden	
er/sie/es werde	sie werden	

FUTURE SUBJUNCTIVE II

ich würde	wir würden	drucken
du würdest	ihr würdet	
Sie würden	Sie würden	
er/sie/es würde	sie würden	

PRESENT PERFECT

ich habe	wir haben	gedruckt
du hast	ihr habt	
Sie haben	Sie haben	
er/sie/es hat	sie haben	

PAST PERFECT

ich hatte	wir hatten	gedruckt
du hattest	ihr hattet	
Sie hatten	Sie hatten	
er/sie/es hatte	sie hatten	

FUTURE PERFECT

ich werde	wir werden	gedruckt haben
du wirst	ihr werdet	
Sie werden	Sie werden	
er/sie/es wird	sie werden	

PAST SUBJUNCTIVE I

ich habe	wir haben	gedruckt
du habest	ihr habet	
Sie haben	Sie haben	
er/sie/es habe	sie haben	

PAST SUBJUNCTIVE II

ich hätte	wir hätten	gedruckt
du hättest	ihr hättet	
Sie hätten	Sie hätten	
er/sie/es hätte	sie hätten	

FUTURE PERFECT SUBJUNCTIVE I

ich werde	wir werden	gedruckt haben
du werdest	ihr werdet	
Sie werden	Sie werden	
er/sie/es werde	sie werden	

FUTURE PERFECT SUBJUNCTIVE II

ich würde	wir würden	gedruckt haben
du würdest	ihr würdet	
Sie würden	Sie würden	
er/sie/es würde	sie würden	

COMMANDS druck(e)! druckt! drucken Sie!

PRESENT PARTICIPLE druckend

Usage

Wie druckt man Bilder mit diesem Drucker? — *How do you print pictures with this printer?*

Gutenberg druckte Bücher schon in der Mitte des 15. Jahrhunderts. — *Gutenberg printed books as early as the middle of the fifteenth century.*

Bücher, die vor 1500 gedruckt wurden, nennt man Inkunabeln. — *Books printed before the year 1500 are called incunabula.*

Kann man das genau so drucken, wie es am Bildschirm angezeigt wird? — *Can you print that exactly the way it appears on the screen?*

Die erste Reihe müsste in den 60er Jahren in kleiner Auflage gedruckt worden sein. — *The first series must have been printed in a small edition in the 1960s.*

In diesem Text werden Schlüsselwörter fett gedruckt. — *Key words are printed boldface in this text.*

Nicht alle Leserbriefe werden gedruckt. — *Not all letters to the editor get printed.*

RELATED VERBS ab·drucken, an·drucken, auf·drucken, aus·drucken, bedrucken, beeindrucken, ein·drucken, nach·drucken, überdrucken, um·drucken, verdrucken, vor·drucken

PRESENT

ich drücke	wir drücken
du drückst	ihr drückt
Sie drücken	Sie drücken
er/sie/es drückt	sie drücken

SIMPLE PAST

ich drückte	wir drückten
du drücktest	ihr drücktet
Sie drückten	Sie drückten
er/sie/es drückte	sie drückten

FUTURE

ich werde	wir werden	drücken
du wirst	ihr werdet	
Sie werden	Sie werden	
er/sie/es wird	sie werden	

PRESENT SUBJUNCTIVE I

ich drücke	wir drücken
du drückest	ihr drücket
Sie drücken	Sie drücken
er/sie/es drücke	sie drücken

PRESENT SUBJUNCTIVE II

ich drückte	wir drückten
du drücktest	ihr drücktet
Sie drückten	Sie drückten
er/sie/es drückte	sie drückten

FUTURE SUBJUNCTIVE I

ich werde	wir werden	drücken
du werdest	ihr werdet	
Sie werden	Sie werden	
er/sie/es werde	sie werden	

FUTURE SUBJUNCTIVE II

ich würde	wir würden	drücken
du würdest	ihr würdet	
Sie würden	Sie würden	
er/sie/es würde	sie würden	

PRESENT PERFECT

ich habe	wir haben	gedrückt
du hast	ihr habt	
Sie haben	Sie haben	
er/sie/es hat	sie haben	

PAST PERFECT

ich hatte	wir hatten	gedrückt
du hattest	ihr hattet	
Sie hatten	Sie hatten	
er/sie/es hatte	sie hatten	

FUTURE PERFECT

ich werde	wir werden	gedrückt haben
du wirst	ihr werdet	
Sie werden	Sie werden	
er/sie/es wird	sie werden	

PAST SUBJUNCTIVE I

ich habe	wir haben	gedrückt
du habest	ihr habet	
Sie haben	Sie haben	
er/sie/es habe	sie haben	

PAST SUBJUNCTIVE II

ich hätte	wir hätten	gedrückt
du hättest	ihr hättet	
Sie hätten	Sie hätten	
er/sie/es hätte	sie hätten	

FUTURE PERFECT SUBJUNCTIVE I

ich werde	wir werden	gedrückt haben
du werdest	ihr werdet	
Sie werden	Sie werden	
er/sie/es werde	sie werden	

FUTURE PERFECT SUBJUNCTIVE II

ich würde	wir würden	gedrückt haben
du würdest	ihr würdet	
Sie würden	Sie würden	
er/sie/es würde	sie würden	

COMMANDS drück(e)! drückt! drücken Sie!

PRESENT PARTICIPLE drückend

Usage

Tragen Sie die gefragten Angaben ein und drücken Sie dann auf ENTER.	*Enter the information requested and then press* ENTER.
Das Kind hat sein Gesicht ins Kissen gedrückt.	*The child pressed his face into the pillow.*
Ich habe auf den Knopf gedrückt, aber nichts passiert.	*I pushed the button but nothing is happening.*
Ein Stempel wurde in meinen Pass gedrückt.	*A stamp was imprinted on my passport.*
Ein kleines „P" wird in die Vorderseite der Münze gedrückt.	*A small "P" is pressed into the obverse side of the coin.*
Wie drückst du die Zahnpasta aus der Tube?	*How do you squeeze toothpaste from the tube?*
Ernst hat ihre Hand zärtlich gedrückt.	*Ernst tenderly squeezed her hand.*
Drück nicht so fest!	*Don't squeeze so hard!*
Der Gedanke drückte schwer auf meinen Sohn.	*The thought weighed heavily on my son.*

RELATED VERBS ab·drücken, an·drücken, auf·drücken, aus·drücken, bedrücken, durch·drücken, ein·drücken, erdrücken, nieder·drücken, unterdrücken, verdrücken, weg·drücken, zerdrücken, zu·drücken, zusammen·drücken

130 dürfen *may, might, to be allowed to, be permitted to*

darf · durfte · gedurft modal verb

PRESENT

ich darf	wir dürfen
du darfst	ihr dürft
Sie dürfen	Sie dürfen
er/sie/es darf	sie dürfen

SIMPLE PAST

ich durfte	wir durften
du durftest	ihr durftet
Sie durften	Sie durften
er/sie/es durfte	sie durften

FUTURE

ich werde	wir werden	dürfen
du wirst	ihr werdet	
Sie werden	Sie werden	
er/sie/es wird	sie werden	

PRESENT SUBJUNCTIVE I

ich dürfe	wir dürfen
du dürfest	ihr dürfet
Sie dürfen	Sie dürfen
er/sie/es dürfe	sie dürfen

PRESENT SUBJUNCTIVE II

ich dürfte	wir dürften
du dürftest	ihr dürftet
Sie dürften	Sie dürften
er/sie/es dürfte	sie dürften

FUTURE SUBJUNCTIVE I

ich werde	wir werden	dürfen
du werdest	ihr werdet	
Sie werden	Sie werden	
er/sie/es werde	sie werden	

FUTURE SUBJUNCTIVE II

ich würde	wir würden	dürfen
du würdest	ihr würdet	
Sie würden	Sie würden	
er/sie/es würde	sie würden	

PRESENT PERFECT

ich habe	wir haben	gedurft
du hast	ihr habt	
Sie haben	Sie haben	
er/sie/es hat	sie haben	

PAST PERFECT

ich hatte	wir hatten	gedurft
du hattest	ihr hattet	
Sie hatten	Sie hatten	
er/sie/es hatte	sie hatten	

FUTURE PERFECT

ich werde	wir werden	gedurft haben
du wirst	ihr werdet	
Sie werden	Sie werden	
er/sie/es wird	sie werden	

PAST SUBJUNCTIVE I

ich habe	wir haben	gedurft
du habest	ihr habet	
Sie haben	Sie haben	
er/sie/es habe	sie haben	

PAST SUBJUNCTIVE II

ich hätte	wir hätten	gedurft
du hättest	ihr hättet	
Sie hätten	Sie hätten	
er/sie/es hätte	sie hätten	

FUTURE PERFECT SUBJUNCTIVE I

ich werde	wir werden	gedurft haben
du werdest	ihr werdet	
Sie werden	Sie werden	
er/sie/es werde	sie werden	

FUTURE PERFECT SUBJUNCTIVE II

ich würde	wir würden	gedurft haben
du würdest	ihr würdet	
Sie würden	Sie würden	
er/sie/es würde	sie würden	

COMMANDS —

PRESENT PARTICIPLE dürfend

Usage

Darf ich rauchen?	*May I smoke?*
Dürften wir hier übernachten?	*Might we spend the night here?*
Wir durften nicht über die Grenze gehen.	*We weren't allowed to cross the border.*
In den USA darf man mit sechzehn Jahren Auto fahren.	*In the U.S. you are permitted to drive when you are 16 years old.*
Was darf ich für Sie tun?	*What may I do for you?*

dürfen (present subjunctive II + infinitive; to express likelihood, presumption)

Das dürfte kein Problem sein.	*That will not likely be a problem.*
Diese Kirche dürfte vor 1500 gebaut worden sein.	*This church was probably built before 1500.*

dürfen (double infinitive)

Ich hätte das nicht machen dürfen.	*I would not have been permitted to do that.*

RELATED VERBS bedürfen, zurück·dürfen

regular weak verb **ehrt · ehrte · geehrt**

PRESENT

ich ehre	wir ehren
du ehrst	ihr ehrt
Sie ehren	Sie ehren
er/sie/es ehrt	sie ehren

SIMPLE PAST

ich ehrte	wir ehrten
du ehrtest	ihr ehrtet
Sie ehrten	Sie ehrten
er/sie/es ehrte	sie ehrten

FUTURE

ich werde	wir werden	ehren
du wirst	ihr werdet	
Sie werden	Sie werden	
er/sie/es wird	sie werden	

PRESENT SUBJUNCTIVE I

ich ehre	wir ehren
du ehrest	ihr ehret
Sie ehren	Sie ehren
er/sie/es ehre	sie ehren

PRESENT SUBJUNCTIVE II

ich ehrte	wir ehrten
du ehrtest	ihr ehrtet
Sie ehrten	Sie ehrten
er/sie/es ehrte	sie ehrten

FUTURE SUBJUNCTIVE I

ich werde	wir werden	ehren
du werdest	ihr werdet	
Sie werden	Sie werden	
er/sie/es werde	sie werden	

FUTURE SUBJUNCTIVE II

ich würde	wir würden	ehren
du würdest	ihr würdet	
Sie würden	Sie würden	
er/sie/es würde	sie würden	

PRESENT PERFECT

ich habe	wir haben	geehrt
du hast	ihr habt	
Sie haben	Sie haben	
er/sie/es hat	sie haben	

PAST PERFECT

ich hatte	wir hatten	geehrt
du hattest	ihr hattet	
Sie hatten	Sie hatten	
er/sie/es hatte	sie hatten	

FUTURE PERFECT

ich werde	wir werden	geehrt haben
du wirst	ihr werdet	
Sie werden	Sie werden	
er/sie/es wird	sie werden	

PAST SUBJUNCTIVE I

ich habe	wir haben	geehrt
du habest	ihr habet	
Sie haben	Sie haben	
er/sie/es habe	sie haben	

PAST SUBJUNCTIVE II

ich hätte	wir hätten	geehrt
du hättest	ihr hättet	
Sie hätten	Sie hätten	
er/sie/es hätte	sie hätten	

FUTURE PERFECT SUBJUNCTIVE I

ich werde	wir werden	geehrt haben
du werdest	ihr werdet	
Sie werden	Sie werden	
er/sie/es werde	sie werden	

FUTURE PERFECT SUBJUNCTIVE II

ich würde	wir würden	geehrt haben
du würdest	ihr würdet	
Sie würden	Sie würden	
er/sie/es würde	sie würden	

COMMANDS ehr(e)! ehrt! ehren Sie!

PRESENT PARTICIPLE ehrend

Usage

Der Minister ehrt die Nationalmannschaft für ihre Leistungen.	*The minister honors the national team for their accomplishments.*
Ehre deinen Vater und deine Mutter. (2. MOSE 20,12)	*Honor thy father and thy mother.* (EXODUS 20:12)
Der alternde Schauspieler wurde für sein Lebenswerk geehrt.	*The aging actor was honored for his life's work.*
Man hat den Schriftsteller durch einen Preis geehrt.	*The writer was honored with a prize.*
Bürgermeister Hüppe ehrt die Bürger der Stadt.	*Mayor Hüppe is honoring the citizens of the city.*
Die heilige Elisabeth war für ihre Wunderheilungen bekannt und wird von vielen geehrt.	*St. Elizabeth was known for her miraculous healings and is revered by many.*
Die Statue ehrt das Andenken der vielen Opfer dieser Katastrophe.	*The statue does honor to the memory of the many victims of this catastrophe.*
An diesem Ort ehrte der Stamm seine Ahnen.	*The tribe paid respects to their ancestors at this location.*

RELATED VERBS beehren, entehren, verehren

132 ein·fallen *to collapse, give way; invade, overrun; occur to, strike*

fällt ein · fiel ein · eingefallen strong verb (dative object)

PRESENT

ich falle	wir fallen	ein
du fällst	ihr fallt	
Sie fallen	Sie fallen	
er/sie/es fällt	sie fallen	

SIMPLE PAST

ich fiel	wir fielen	ein
du fielst	ihr fielt	
Sie fielen	Sie fielen	
er/sie/es fiel	sie fielen	

FUTURE

ich werde	wir werden	einfallen
du wirst	ihr werdet	
Sie werden	Sie werden	
er/sie/es wird	sie werden	

PRESENT SUBJUNCTIVE I

ich falle	wir fallen	ein
du fallest	ihr fallet	
Sie fallen	Sie fallen	
er/sie/es falle	sie fallen	

PRESENT SUBJUNCTIVE II

ich fiele	wir fielen	ein
du fielest	ihr fielet	
Sie fielen	Sie fielen	
er/sie/es fiele	sie fielen	

FUTURE SUBJUNCTIVE I

ich werde	wir werden	einfallen
du werdest	ihr werdet	
Sie werden	Sie werden	
er/sie/es werde	sie werden	

FUTURE SUBJUNCTIVE II

ich würde	wir würden	einfallen
du würdest	ihr würdet	
Sie würden	Sie würden	
er/sie/es würde	sie würden	

PRESENT PERFECT

ich bin	wir sind	eingefallen
du bist	ihr seid	
Sie sind	Sie sind	
er/sie/es ist	sie sind	

PAST PERFECT

ich war	wir waren	eingefallen
du warst	ihr wart	
Sie waren	Sie waren	
er/sie/es war	sie waren	

FUTURE PERFECT

ich werde	wir werden	eingefallen sein
du wirst	ihr werdet	
Sie werden	Sie werden	
er/sie/es wird	sie werden	

PAST SUBJUNCTIVE I

ich sei	wir seien	eingefallen
du seiest	ihr seiet	
Sie seien	Sie seien	
er/sie/es sei	sie seien	

PAST SUBJUNCTIVE II

ich wäre	wir wären	eingefallen
du wärest	ihr wäret	
Sie wären	Sie wären	
er/sie/es wäre	sie wären	

FUTURE PERFECT SUBJUNCTIVE I

ich werde	wir werden	eingefallen sein
du werdest	ihr werdet	
Sie werden	Sie werden	
er/sie/es werde	sie werden	

FUTURE PERFECT SUBJUNCTIVE II

ich würde	wir würden	eingefallen sein
du würdest	ihr würdet	
Sie würden	Sie würden	
er/sie/es würde	sie würden	

COMMANDS fall(e) ein! fallt ein! fallen Sie ein!

PRESENT PARTICIPLE einfallend

Usage

Nach dem Brand ist das Haus eingefallen.	*After the fire the house collapsed.*
Ein päpstliches Heer war in Thüringen eingefallen.	*A papal army had invaded Thuringia.*
Die Heuschrecken fielen mehrmals in das landwirtschaftliche Gebiet ein.	*Grasshoppers overran the agricultural area several times.*
795 fielen die Wikinger auf die Insel ein.	*In 795, the Vikings overran the island.*
Eine neue Arbeitsmethode ist mir gerade eingefallen.	*A new method of working has just occurred to me.*
Plötzlich fiel ihm eine Idee ein.	*Suddenly an idea struck him.*
Es würde mir nie einfallen, Lebensmittel über das Internet einzukaufen.	*I would never think to shop for groceries over the Internet.*
Eine Erklärung wird mir schon einfallen.	*An explanation will come to me yet.*
Mir fällt spontan nichts ein.	*Nothing occurs to me at the moment.*
Was fällt dir denn überhaupt ein? (*idiomatic*)	*What do you think you're doing?*

RELATED VERBS *see* **fallen** (178)

regular weak verb **kauft ein · kaufte ein · eingekauft**

PRESENT			PRESENT PERFECT		
ich kaufe	wir kaufen	ein	ich habe	wir haben	eingekauft
du kaufst	ihr kauft		du hast	ihr habt	
Sie kaufen	Sie kaufen		Sie haben	Sie haben	
er/sie/es kauft	sie kaufen		er/sie/es hat	sie haben	
SIMPLE PAST			**PAST PERFECT**		
ich kaufte	wir kauften	ein	ich hatte	wir hatten	eingekauft
du kauftest	ihr kauftet		du hattest	ihr hattet	
Sie kauften	Sie kauften		Sie hatten	Sie hatten	
er/sie/es kaufte	sie kauften		er/sie/es hatte	sie hatten	
FUTURE			**FUTURE PERFECT**		
ich werde	wir werden	einkaufen	ich werde	wir werden	eingekauft haben
du wirst	ihr werdet		du wirst	ihr werdet	
Sie werden	Sie werden		Sie werden	Sie werden	
er/sie/es wird	sie werden		er/sie/es wird	sie werden	
PRESENT SUBJUNCTIVE I			**PAST SUBJUNCTIVE I**		
ich kaufe	wir kaufen	ein	ich habe	wir haben	eingekauft
du kaufest	ihr kaufet		du habest	ihr habet	
Sie kaufen	Sie kaufen		Sie haben	Sie haben	
er/sie/es kaufe	sie kaufen		er/sie/es habe	sie haben	
PRESENT SUBJUNCTIVE II			**PAST SUBJUNCTIVE II**		
ich kaufte	wir kauften	ein	ich hätte	wir hätten	eingekauft
du kauftest	ihr kauftet		du hättest	ihr hättet	
Sie kauften	Sie kauften		Sie hätten	Sie hätten	
er/sie/es kaufte	sie kauften		er/sie/es hätte	sie hätten	
FUTURE SUBJUNCTIVE I			**FUTURE PERFECT SUBJUNCTIVE I**		
ich werde	wir werden	einkaufen	ich werde	wir werden	eingekauft haben
du werdest	ihr werdet		du werdest	ihr werdet	
Sie werden	Sie werden		Sie werden	Sie werden	
er/sie/es werde	sie werden		er/sie/es werde	sie werden	
FUTURE SUBJUNCTIVE II			**FUTURE PERFECT SUBJUNCTIVE II**		
ich würde	wir würden	einkaufen	ich würde	wir würden	eingekauft haben
du würdest	ihr würdet		du würdest	ihr würdet	
Sie würden	Sie würden		Sie würden	Sie würden	
er/sie/es würde	sie würden		er/sie/es würde	sie würden	

COMMANDS kauf(e) ein! kauft ein! kaufen Sie ein!

PRESENT PARTICIPLE einkaufend

Usage

Ich habe Lebensmittel gerade eingekauft. — *I've just shopped for groceries.*
Wie oft gehst du einkaufen? — *How often do you go shopping?*
Ernst kauft so gut wie immer Bioprodukte ein. — *Ernst almost always purchases organic products.*

„Hast du heute bei Wernermann eingekauft?" — *"Did you shop at Wernermann's today?"*
„Ja, ich kaufe oft dort ein." — *"Yes, I shop there often."*

Die Kletterausrüstung kann auch online eingekauft werden. — *The spelunking equipment can also be purchased online.*
Die Fußballmannschaft kauft drei neue Spieler ein. — *The soccer team is signing three new players.*
Frau Eschermann kauft lieber bargeldlos ein. — *Mrs. Eschermann prefers making purchases without cash.*

sich einkaufen *to buy into*

Der Unternehmer kauft sich in ein neues Geschäft ein. — *The entrepreneur is buying into a new business.*

RELATED VERBS *see* **kaufen** (253)

134 ein·laden *to invite; treat, pay for; load*

lädt ein · lud ein · eingeladen — strong verb

PRESENT

ich lade	wir laden	ein
du lädst	ihr ladet	
Sie laden	Sie laden	
er/sie/es lädt	sie laden	

SIMPLE PAST

ich lud	wir luden	ein
du ludst	ihr ludet	
Sie luden	Sie luden	
er/sie/es lud	sie luden	

FUTURE

ich werde	wir werden	einladen
du wirst	ihr werdet	
Sie werden	Sie werden	
er/sie/es wird	sie werden	

PRESENT SUBJUNCTIVE I

ich lade	wir laden	ein
du ladest	ihr ladet	
Sie laden	Sie laden	
er/sie/es lade	sie laden	

PRESENT SUBJUNCTIVE II

ich lüde	wir lüden	ein
du lüdest	ihr lüdet	
Sie lüden	Sie lüden	
er/sie/es lüde	sie lüden	

FUTURE SUBJUNCTIVE I

ich werde	wir werden	einladen
du werdest	ihr werdet	
Sie werden	Sie werden	
er/sie/es werde	sie werden	

FUTURE SUBJUNCTIVE II

ich würde	wir würden	einladen
du würdest	ihr würdet	
Sie würden	Sie würden	
er/sie/es würde	sie würden	

PRESENT PERFECT

ich habe	wir haben	eingeladen
du hast	ihr habt	
Sie haben	Sie haben	
er/sie/es hat	sie haben	

PAST PERFECT

ich hatte	wir hatten	eingeladen
du hattest	ihr hattet	
Sie hatten	Sie hatten	
er/sie/es hatte	sie hatten	

FUTURE PERFECT

ich werde	wir werden	eingeladen haben
du wirst	ihr werdet	
Sie werden	Sie werden	
er/sie/es wird	sie werden	

PAST SUBJUNCTIVE I

ich habe	wir haben	eingeladen
du habest	ihr habet	
Sie haben	Sie haben	
er/sie/es habe	sie haben	

PAST SUBJUNCTIVE II

ich hätte	wir hätten	eingeladen
du hättest	ihr hättet	
Sie hätten	Sie hätten	
er/sie/es hätte	sie hätten	

FUTURE PERFECT SUBJUNCTIVE I

ich werde	wir werden	eingeladen haben
du werdest	ihr werdet	
Sie werden	Sie werden	
er/sie/es werde	sie werden	

FUTURE PERFECT SUBJUNCTIVE II

ich würde	wir würden	eingeladen haben
du würdest	ihr würdet	
Sie würden	Sie würden	
er/sie/es würde	sie würden	

COMMANDS lade ein! ladet ein! laden Sie ein!

PRESENT PARTICIPLE einladend

Usage

Danach wurden sie zu einer Hochzeit in Worms eingeladen.	*After that they were invited to a wedding in Worms.*
Ich habe einige Freunde zu mir eingeladen.	*I've invited some friends to my place.*
Sie sind herzlich eingeladen!	*You are cordially invited!*
Ladet ihr Stefan und Erich ein?	*Are you inviting Stefan and Erich?*
Er sagt, dass er Manfred sowieso nicht eingeladen hätte.	*He says that he wouldn't have invited Manfred anyway.*
Wir möchten euch für Samstag zum Kaffee einladen.	*We'd like to invite you to coffee on Saturday.*
Obwohl meine Schwester nicht eingeladen wurde, kommt sie mit.	*Even though my sister wasn't invited, she's coming along.*
Der König lud viele Gäste zum Hoffest ein.	*The king invited many guests to the court festival.*
Heute Abend lade ich dich zu einem Bier ein.	*This evening I'll treat you to a beer.*
Man kann die Daten direkt in Tabellen einladen.	*You can load the data directly into tables.*

RELATED VERBS *see* **laden** (278)

regular weak verb **richtet ein · richtete ein · eingerichtet**

PRESENT

ich richte	wir richten	ein
du richtest	ihr richtet	
Sie richten	Sie richten	
er/sie/es richtet	sie richten	

PRESENT PERFECT

ich habe	wir haben	eingerichtet
du hast	ihr habt	
Sie haben	Sie haben	
er/sie/es hat	sie haben	

SIMPLE PAST

ich richtete	wir richteten	ein
du richtetest	ihr richtetet	
Sie richteten	Sie richteten	
er/sie/es richtete	sie richteten	

PAST PERFECT

ich hatte	wir hatten	eingerichtet
du hattest	ihr hattet	
Sie hatten	Sie hatten	
er/sie/es hatte	sie hatten	

FUTURE

ich werde	wir werden	einrichten
du wirst	ihr werdet	
Sie werden	Sie werden	
er/sie/es wird	sie werden	

FUTURE PERFECT

ich werde	wir werden	eingerichtet haben
du wirst	ihr werdet	
Sie werden	Sie werden	
er/sie/es wird	sie werden	

PRESENT SUBJUNCTIVE I

ich richte	wir richten	ein
du richtest	ihr richtet	
Sie richten	Sie richten	
er/sie/es richte	sie richten	

PAST SUBJUNCTIVE I

ich habe	wir haben	eingerichtet
du habest	ihr habet	
Sie haben	Sie haben	
er/sie/es habe	sie haben	

PRESENT SUBJUNCTIVE II

ich richtete	wir richteten	ein
du richtetest	ihr richtetet	
Sie richteten	Sie richteten	
er/sie/es richtete	sie richteten	

PAST SUBJUNCTIVE II

ich hätte	wir hätten	eingerichtet
du hättest	ihr hättet	
Sie hätten	Sie hätten	
er/sie/es hätte	sie hätten	

FUTURE SUBJUNCTIVE I

ich werde	wir werden	einrichten
du werdest	ihr werdet	
Sie werden	Sie werden	
er/sie/es werde	sie werden	

FUTURE PERFECT SUBJUNCTIVE I

ich werde	wir werden	eingerichtet haben
du werdest	ihr werdet	
Sie werden	Sie werden	
er/sie/es werde	sie werden	

FUTURE SUBJUNCTIVE II

ich würde	wir würden	einrichten
du würdest	ihr würdet	
Sie würden	Sie würden	
er/sie/es würde	sie würden	

FUTURE PERFECT SUBJUNCTIVE II

ich würde	wir würden	eingerichtet haben
du würdest	ihr würdet	
Sie würden	Sie würden	
er/sie/es würde	sie würden	

COMMANDS richte ein! richtet ein! richten Sie ein!

PRESENT PARTICIPLE einrichtend

Usage

Die Mitglieder richteten letztes Jahr einen neuen Verein ein. *The members organized a new association last year.*

Wir haben das Boot für sechs Personen eingerichtet. *We equipped the boat for six persons.*

Lars richtet sein Wohnheimzimmer ganz komfortabel ein. *Lars is furnishing his dorm room quite comfortably.*

Ein wissenschaftlicher Beirat wurde vom Vorstand eingerichtet. *A scientific advisory committee was established by the board.*

Wie kann ich ein neues Konto einrichten? *How can I set up a new account?*

sich einrichten *to adapt, accommodate; set oneself up, establish oneself*

Meine Schwester hat sich auf die schwierigen Lebensumstände eingerichtet. *My sister has adapted to the difficult circumstances of life.*

Du hast dich hier schön eingerichtet. *You have set up a nice place here.*

RELATED VERBS richten; *see also* **berichten** (76), **unterrichten** (470)

136 ein·schalten *to insert; switch on, engage; bring into*

schaltet ein · schaltete ein · eingeschaltet regular weak verb

PRESENT

ich schalte	wir schalten	ein
du schaltest	ihr schaltet	
Sie schalten	Sie schalten	
er/sie/es schaltet	sie schalten	

SIMPLE PAST

ich schaltete	wir schalteten	ein
du schaltetest	ihr schaltetet	
Sie schalteten	Sie schalteten	
er/sie/es schaltete	sie schalteten	

FUTURE

ich werde	wir werden	einschalten
du wirst	ihr werdet	
Sie werden	Sie werden	
er/sie/es wird	sie werden	

PRESENT SUBJUNCTIVE I

ich schalte	wir schalten	ein
du schaltest	ihr schaltet	
Sie schalten	Sie schalten	
er/sie/es schalte	sie schalten	

PRESENT SUBJUNCTIVE II

ich schaltete	wir schalteten	ein
du schaltetest	ihr schaltetet	
Sie schalteten	Sie schalteten	
er/sie/es schaltete	sie schalteten	

FUTURE SUBJUNCTIVE I

ich werde	wir werden	einschalten
du werdest	ihr werdet	
Sie werden	Sie werden	
er/sie/es werde	sie werden	

FUTURE SUBJUNCTIVE II

ich würde	wir würden	einschalten
du würdest	ihr würdet	
Sie würden	Sie würden	
er/sie/es würde	sie würden	

PRESENT PERFECT

ich habe	wir haben	eingeschaltet
du hast	ihr habt	
Sie haben	Sie haben	
er/sie/es hat	sie haben	

PAST PERFECT

ich hatte	wir hatten	eingeschaltet
du hattest	ihr hattet	
Sie hatten	Sie hatten	
er/sie/es hatte	sie hatten	

FUTURE PERFECT

ich werde	wir werden	eingeschaltet haben
du wirst	ihr werdet	
Sie werden	Sie werden	
er/sie/es wird	sie werden	

PAST SUBJUNCTIVE I

ich habe	wir haben	eingeschaltet
du habest	ihr habet	
Sie haben	Sie haben	
er/sie/es habe	sie haben	

PAST SUBJUNCTIVE II

ich hätte	wir hätten	eingeschaltet
du hättest	ihr hättet	
Sie hätten	Sie hätten	
er/sie/es hätte	sie hätten	

FUTURE PERFECT SUBJUNCTIVE I

ich werde	wir werden	eingeschaltet haben
du werdest	ihr werdet	
Sie werden	Sie werden	
er/sie/es werde	sie werden	

FUTURE PERFECT SUBJUNCTIVE II

ich würde	wir würden	eingeschaltet haben
du würdest	ihr würdet	
Sie würden	Sie würden	
er/sie/es würde	sie würden	

COMMANDS schalte ein! schaltet ein! schalten Sie ein!

PRESENT PARTICIPLE einschaltend

Usage

Wir schalteten mehr Werbung ein. — *We inserted more advertising.*
Schalte bitte den Empfänger ein. — *Please switch on the receiver.*
Schalten Sie bitte die Nachrichten ein. — *Please turn on the news.*
Der Kapitän hat den Autopiloten eingeschaltet. — *The captain engaged the autopilot.*
Man kann die Videokamera per Fernbedienung einschalten. — *You can turn on the video camera by remote control.*
Die Polizei wurde in die Sache eingeschaltet. — *The police were brought into the matter.*

sich einschalten *to switch on; intervene; join in*

Der Motor schaltet sich automatisch ein. — *The engine switches on automatically.*
Wann schaltest du dich endlich in den Streit ein? — *When will you finally intervene in the conflict?*
Herr Biedermann wollte sich nicht ins Gespräch einschalten. — *Mr. Biedermann didn't want to join in the conversation.*

RELATED VERBS *see* **schalten** (357)

137 ein·setzen *to insert, put in place, install, appoint; begin*

regular weak verb — **setzt ein · setzte ein · eingesetzt**

PRESENT

ich setze	wir setzen	ein
du setzt	ihr setzt	
Sie setzen	Sie setzen	
er/sie/es setzt	sie setzen	

PRESENT PERFECT

ich habe	wir haben	eingesetzt
du hast	ihr habt	
Sie haben	Sie haben	
er/sie/es hat	sie haben	

SIMPLE PAST

ich setzte	wir setzten	ein
du setztest	ihr setztet	
Sie setzten	Sie setzten	
er/sie/es setzte	sie setzten	

PAST PERFECT

ich hatte	wir hatten	eingesetzt
du hattest	ihr hattet	
Sie hatten	Sie hatten	
er/sie/es hatte	sie hatten	

FUTURE

ich werde	wir werden	einsetzen
du wirst	ihr werdet	
Sie werden	Sie werden	
er/sie/es wird	sie werden	

FUTURE PERFECT

ich werde	wir werden	eingesetzt haben
du wirst	ihr werdet	
Sie werden	Sie werden	
er/sie/es wird	sie werden	

PRESENT SUBJUNCTIVE I

ich setze	wir setzen	ein
du setzest	ihr setzet	
Sie setzen	Sie setzen	
er/sie/es setze	sie setzen	

PAST SUBJUNCTIVE I

ich habe	wir haben	eingesetzt
du habest	ihr habet	
Sie haben	Sie haben	
er/sie/es habe	sie haben	

PRESENT SUBJUNCTIVE II

ich setzte	wir setzten	ein
du setztest	ihr setztet	
Sie setzten	Sie setzten	
er/sie/es setzte	sie setzten	

PAST SUBJUNCTIVE II

ich hätte	wir hätten	eingesetzt
du hättest	ihr hättet	
Sie hätten	Sie hätten	
er/sie/es hätte	sie hätten	

FUTURE SUBJUNCTIVE I

ich werde	wir werden	einsetzen
du werdest	ihr werdet	
Sie werden	Sie werden	
er/sie/es werde	sie werden	

FUTURE PERFECT SUBJUNCTIVE I

ich werde	wir werden	eingesetzt haben
du werdest	ihr werdet	
Sie werden	Sie werden	
er/sie/es werde	sie werden	

FUTURE SUBJUNCTIVE II

ich würde	wir würden	einsetzen
du würdest	ihr würdet	
Sie würden	Sie würden	
er/sie/es würde	sie würden	

FUTURE PERFECT SUBJUNCTIVE II

ich würde	wir würden	eingesetzt haben
du würdest	ihr würdet	
Sie würden	Sie würden	
er/sie/es würde	sie würden	

COMMANDS setz(e) ein! setzt ein! setzen Sie ein!

PRESENT PARTICIPLE einsetzend

Usage

Setzen Sie den richtigen Wert ein. — *Please insert the correct value.*
Im Notfall setzen wir Kampfhubschrauber ein. — *In an emergency, we'll put attack helicopters in place.*
Sie wollten die neuen Offiziere nicht sofort einsetzen. — *They didn't want to install the new officers immediately.*
Zwölf Soldaten wurden in Bussayah eingesetzt. — *Twelve soldiers were inserted in Bussayah.*
Bis zu acht Spieler können eingesetzt werden. — *Up to eight players can be sent in.*
Alle zwei Jahre wird ein neuer Vorsitzender eingesetzt. — *A new chair is appointed every two years.*
Ich wollte sonnenbaden, aber ein Gewitter setzt gerade ein. — *I wanted to go sunbathing, but a storm is just beginning.*

sich einsetzen für *to support, stand up for*

Der Minister hat sich für den Friedensplan eingesetzt. — *The minister supported the peace plan.*
Auf jeden Fall setze ich mich für dich ein. — *In any case, I'll stand up for you.*
Bernd setzt sich mit aller Kraft dafür ein, die Lebensbedingungen der Armen zu verbessern. — *Bernd is doing all he can to improve the living conditions of the poor.*

RELATED VERBS *see* **setzen** (400)

138 ein·steigen *to board, climb in, get in*

steigt ein · stieg ein · eingestiegen strong verb

PRESENT

ich steige	wir steigen	ein
du steigst	ihr steigt	
Sie steigen	Sie steigen	
er/sie/es steigt	sie steigen	

PRESENT PERFECT

ich bin	wir sind	eingestiegen
du bist	ihr seid	
Sie sind	Sie sind	
er/sie/es ist	sie sind	

SIMPLE PAST

ich stieg	wir stiegen	ein
du stiegst	ihr stiegt	
Sie stiegen	Sie stiegen	
er/sie/es stieg	sie stiegen	

PAST PERFECT

ich war	wir waren	eingestiegen
du warst	ihr wart	
Sie waren	Sie waren	
er/sie/es war	sie waren	

FUTURE

ich werde	wir werden	einsteigen
du wirst	ihr werdet	
Sie werden	Sie werden	
er/sie/es wird	sie werden	

FUTURE PERFECT

ich werde	wir werden	eingestiegen sein
du wirst	ihr werdet	
Sie werden	Sie werden	
er/sie/es wird	sie werden	

PRESENT SUBJUNCTIVE I

ich steige	wir steigen	ein
du steigest	ihr steiget	
Sie steigen	Sie steigen	
er/sie/es steige	sie steigen	

PAST SUBJUNCTIVE I

ich sei	wir seien	eingestiegen
du seiest	ihr seiet	
Sie seien	Sie seien	
er/sie/es sei	sie seien	

PRESENT SUBJUNCTIVE II

ich stiege	wir stiegen	ein
du stiegest	ihr stieget	
Sie stiegen	Sie stiegen	
er/sie/es stiege	sie stiegen	

PAST SUBJUNCTIVE II

ich wäre	wir wären	eingestiegen
du wärest	ihr wäret	
Sie wären	Sie wären	
er/sie/es wäre	sie wären	

FUTURE SUBJUNCTIVE I

ich werde	wir werden	einsteigen
du werdest	ihr werdet	
Sie werden	Sie werden	
er/sie/es werde	sie werden	

FUTURE PERFECT SUBJUNCTIVE I

ich werde	wir werden	eingestiegen sein
du werdest	ihr werdet	
Sie werden	Sie werden	
er/sie/es werde	sie werden	

FUTURE SUBJUNCTIVE II

ich würde	wir würden	einsteigen
du würdest	ihr würdet	
Sie würden	Sie würden	
er/sie/es würde	sie würden	

FUTURE PERFECT SUBJUNCTIVE II

ich würde	wir würden	eingestiegen sein
du würdest	ihr würdet	
Sie würden	Sie würden	
er/sie/es würde	sie würden	

COMMANDS steig(e) ein! steigt ein! steigen Sie ein!

PRESENT PARTICIPLE einsteigend

Usage

Als ich in den Zug einstieg, habe ich mir das rechte Fußgelenk verstaucht. — *As I was boarding the train, I sprained my right ankle.*

Drei kleine Kinder waren in Schladen eingestiegen. — *Three small children had boarded in Schladen.*

Steig mal ins Auto ein. — *Get in the car.*

Wann dürfen wir ins Flugzeug einsteigen? — *When are we allowed to board the plane?*

Oma Schmitz stieg ängstlich in den Seitenwagen des Motorrads ein. — *Grandma Schmitz apprehensively climbed into the motorcycle sidecar.*

Muss man vorne einsteigen? — *Do you have to board at the front?*

Tante Marga sagte neulich, dass Onkel Ferdinand ins Musikgeschäft eingestiegen sei. — *Aunt Marga said recently that Uncle Ferdinand had gotten into the music business.*

Ich möchte in die Politik einsteigen. — *I'd like to get into politics.*

Wie kann man in den Chat einsteigen? — *How do you enter the chat room?*

RELATED VERBS *see* **steigen** (425)

regular weak verb **stellt ein · stellte ein · eingestellt**

PRESENT

ich stelle	wir stellen	ein
du stellst	ihr stellt	
Sie stellen	Sie stellen	
er/sie/es stellt	sie stellen	

PRESENT PERFECT

ich habe	wir haben	eingestellt
du hast	ihr habt	
Sie haben	Sie haben	
er/sie/es hat	sie haben	

SIMPLE PAST

ich stellte	wir stellten	ein
du stelltest	ihr stelltet	
Sie stellten	Sie stellten	
er/sie/es stellte	sie stellten	

PAST PERFECT

ich hatte	wir hatten	eingestellt
du hattest	ihr hattet	
Sie hatten	Sie hatten	
er/sie/es hatte	sie hatten	

FUTURE

ich werde	wir werden	einstellen
du wirst	ihr werdet	
Sie werden	Sie werden	
er/sie/es wird	sie werden	

FUTURE PERFECT

ich werde	wir werden	eingestellt haben
du wirst	ihr werdet	
Sie werden	Sie werden	
er/sie/es wird	sie werden	

PRESENT SUBJUNCTIVE I

ich stelle	wir stellen	ein
du stellest	ihr stellet	
Sie stellen	Sie stellen	
er/sie/es stelle	sie stellen	

PAST SUBJUNCTIVE I

ich habe	wir haben	eingestellt
du habest	ihr habet	
Sie haben	Sie haben	
er/sie/es habe	sie haben	

PRESENT SUBJUNCTIVE II

ich stellte	wir stellten	ein
du stelltest	ihr stelltet	
Sie stellten	Sie stellten	
er/sie/es stellte	sie stellten	

PAST SUBJUNCTIVE II

ich hätte	wir hätten	eingestellt
du hättest	ihr hättet	
Sie hätten	Sie hätten	
er/sie/es hätte	sie hätten	

FUTURE SUBJUNCTIVE I

ich werde	wir werden	einstellen
du werdest	ihr werdet	
Sie werden	Sie werden	
er/sie/es werde	sie werden	

FUTURE PERFECT SUBJUNCTIVE I

ich werde	wir werden	eingestellt haben
du werdest	ihr werdet	
Sie werden	Sie werden	
er/sie/es werde	sie werden	

FUTURE SUBJUNCTIVE II

ich würde	wir würden	einstellen
du würdest	ihr würdet	
Sie würden	Sie würden	
er/sie/es würde	sie würden	

FUTURE PERFECT SUBJUNCTIVE II

ich würde	wir würden	eingestellt haben
du würdest	ihr würdet	
Sie würden	Sie würden	
er/sie/es würde	sie würden	

COMMANDS stell(e) ein! stellt ein! stellen Sie ein!

PRESENT PARTICIPLE einstellend

Usage

Stell das Buch ins Regal ein. — *Put the book on the bookshelf.*

Im Juni wurde Pawel als Assistent eingestellt. — *In June Pavel was hired as an assistant.*

Wie stellt man den Bildschirm ein? — *How do you adjust the screen?*

Hast du die Papiergröße richtig eingestellt? — *Did you adjust the paper size correctly?*

Mit dem neuen Baby hat er jetzt einen sehr guten Grund, das Rauchen einzustellen. — *With the new baby, he now has a very good reason to stop smoking.*

sich einstellen *to appear, present oneself*

Bei vielen Patienten stellen sich die Symptome schon nach zwei Tagen ein. — *With many patients, the symptoms appear after only two days.*

sich einstellen auf *to adapt to, set one's mind to*

Frau Schlund stellt sich langsam auf das Leben ohne ihren Mann ein. — *Mrs. Schlund is slowly adapting to life without her husband.*

RELATED VERBS *see* **stellen** (426)

140 ein·ziehen *to draw in, absorb, draft; retract, recall; collect*

zieht ein · zog ein · eingezogen strong verb

PRESENT

ich ziehe	wir ziehen	ein
du ziehst	ihr zieht	
Sie ziehen	Sie ziehen	
er/sie/es zieht	sie ziehen	

PRESENT PERFECT

ich habe	wir haben	eingezogen
du hast	ihr habt	
Sie haben	Sie haben	
er/sie/es hat	sie haben	

SIMPLE PAST

ich zog	wir zogen	ein
du zogst	ihr zogt	
Sie zogen	Sie zogen	
er/sie/es zog	sie zogen	

PAST PERFECT

ich hatte	wir hatten	eingezogen
du hattest	ihr hattet	
Sie hatten	Sie hatten	
er/sie/es hatte	sie hatten	

FUTURE

ich werde	wir werden	einziehen
du wirst	ihr werdet	
Sie werden	Sie werden	
er/sie/es wird	sie werden	

FUTURE PERFECT

ich werde	wir werden	eingezogen haben
du wirst	ihr werdet	
Sie werden	Sie werden	
er/sie/es wird	sie werden	

PRESENT SUBJUNCTIVE I

ich ziehe	wir ziehen	ein
du ziehest	ihr ziehet	
Sie ziehen	Sie ziehen	
er/sie/es ziehe	sie ziehen	

PAST SUBJUNCTIVE I

ich habe	wir haben	eingezogen
du habest	ihr habet	
Sie haben	Sie haben	
er/sie/es habe	sie haben	

PRESENT SUBJUNCTIVE II

ich zöge	wir zögen	ein
du zögest	ihr zöget	
Sie zögen	Sie zögen	
er/sie/es zöge	sie zögen	

PAST SUBJUNCTIVE II

ich hätte	wir hätten	eingezogen
du hättest	ihr hättet	
Sie hätten	Sie hätten	
er/sie/es hätte	sie hätten	

FUTURE SUBJUNCTIVE I

ich werde	wir werden	einziehen
du werdest	ihr werdet	
Sie werden	Sie werden	
er/sie/es werde	sie werden	

FUTURE PERFECT SUBJUNCTIVE I

ich werde	wir werden	eingezogen haben
du werdest	ihr werdet	
Sie werden	Sie werden	
er/sie/es werde	sie werden	

FUTURE SUBJUNCTIVE II

ich würde	wir würden	einziehen
du würdest	ihr würdet	
Sie würden	Sie würden	
er/sie/es würde	sie würden	

FUTURE PERFECT SUBJUNCTIVE II

ich würde	wir würden	eingezogen haben
du würdest	ihr würdet	
Sie würden	Sie würden	
er/sie/es würde	sie würden	

COMMANDS zieh(e) ein! zieht ein! ziehen Sie ein!

PRESENT PARTICIPLE einziehend

Usage

Der Schwamm zieht das Wasser ein. — *The sponge is absorbing the water.*

Sein Großvater wurde 1918 zur Reichswehr eingezogen. — *His grandfather was drafted into the imperial army in 1918.*

Die Räder werden eingezogen und die Radkästen geschlossen. — *The wheels are retracted and the wheel housing is closed.*

Die Firma zieht die defekten Produkte ein. — *The firm is recalling the defective products.*

Wir ziehen jetzt alle ausstehenden Rechnungen ein. — *We are now collecting all outstanding accounts.*

Fahrscheine werden im Zug eingezogen werden. — *Tickets will be collected on the train.*

einziehen (with **sein**) *to enter, move in; soak in, absorb*

Wann ziehst du in die neue Wohnung ein? — *When are you moving into the new apartment?*

Unsere Mannschaft ist ins Endspiel eingezogen. — *Our team has moved into the finals.*

Diese Hautcreme zieht schnell ein. — *This skin cream absorbs quickly.*

RELATED VERBS *see* **ziehen** (549)

strong verb **empfängt · empfing · empfangen**

PRESENT

ich empfange	wir empfangen
du empfängst	ihr empfangt
Sie empfangen	Sie empfangen
er/sie/es empfängt	sie empfangen

SIMPLE PAST

ich empfing	wir empfingen
du empfingst	ihr empfingt
Sie empfingen	Sie empfingen
er/sie/es empfing	sie empfingen

FUTURE

ich werde	wir werden	empfangen
du wirst	ihr werdet	
Sie werden	Sie werden	
er/sie/es wird	sie werden	

PRESENT SUBJUNCTIVE I

ich empfange	wir empfangen
du empfangest	ihr empfanget
Sie empfangen	Sie empfangen
er/sie/es empfange	sie empfangen

PRESENT SUBJUNCTIVE II

ich empfinge	wir empfingen
du empfingest	ihr empfinget
Sie empfingen	Sie empfingen
er/sie/es empfinge	sie empfingen

FUTURE SUBJUNCTIVE I

ich werde	wir werden	empfangen
du werdest	ihr werdet	
Sie werden	Sie werden	
er/sie/es werde	sie werden	

FUTURE SUBJUNCTIVE II

ich würde	wir würden	empfangen
du würdest	ihr würdet	
Sie würden	Sie würden	
er/sie/es würde	sie würden	

PRESENT PERFECT

ich habe	wir haben	empfangen
du hast	ihr habt	
Sie haben	Sie haben	
er/sie/es hat	sie haben	

PAST PERFECT

ich hatte	wir hatten	empfangen
du hattest	ihr hattet	
Sie hatten	Sie hatten	
er/sie/es hatte	sie hatten	

FUTURE PERFECT

ich werde	wir werden	empfangen haben
du wirst	ihr werdet	
Sie werden	Sie werden	
er/sie/es wird	sie werden	

PAST SUBJUNCTIVE I

ich habe	wir haben	empfangen
du habest	ihr habet	
Sie haben	Sie haben	
er/sie/es habe	sie haben	

PAST SUBJUNCTIVE II

ich hätte	wir hätten	empfangen
du hättest	ihr hättet	
Sie hätten	Sie hätten	
er/sie/es hätte	sie hätten	

FUTURE PERFECT SUBJUNCTIVE I

ich werde	wir werden	empfangen haben
du werdest	ihr werdet	
Sie werden	Sie werden	
er/sie/es werde	sie werden	

FUTURE PERFECT SUBJUNCTIVE II

ich würde	wir würden	empfangen haben
du würdest	ihr würdet	
Sie würden	Sie würden	
er/sie/es würde	sie würden	

COMMANDS empfang(e)! empfangt! empfangen Sie!

PRESENT PARTICIPLE empfangend

Usage

Auf welcher Frequenz empfängst du die Radiosendung? — *At what frequency do you receive the radio transmission?*

Die Bürger und Bürgerinnen der Stadt wurden am Abend von Freiherrn Erpermann empfangen. — *The city's citizens were greeted by Baron Erpermann in the evening.*

Kann man diesen Fernsehsender auch über das Internet empfangen? — *Can you receive this television station over the Internet, too?*

Der Pförtner empfing die Gäste an der Tür. — *The doorman greeted the guests at the door.*

Wir wurden bei der Ankunft mit einer Flasche Sekt empfangen. — *We were greeted with a bottle of sparkling wine upon arrival.*

Die Küstenwache hat ein Notsignal empfangen. — *The coast guard has received a distress signal.*

Das Gerät empfängt GPS-Koordinaten und sendet Signale aus. — *The device receives GPS coordinates and transmits signals.*

Lea empfing und gebar einen Sohn. (1. MOSE 29,32) — *Leah conceived and bore a son.* (GENESIS 29:32)

RELATED VERBS *see* **fangen** (179)

empfehlen *to recommend; commend*

empfiehlt · empfahl · empfohlen strong verb

PRESENT

ich empfehle	wir empfehlen
du empfiehlst	ihr empfehlt
Sie empfehlen	Sie empfehlen
er/sie/es empfiehlt	sie empfehlen

SIMPLE PAST

ich empfahl	wir empfahlen
du empfahlst	ihr empfahlt
Sie empfahlen	Sie empfahlen
er/sie/es empfahl	sie empfahlen

FUTURE

ich werde	wir werden	empfehlen
du wirst	ihr werdet	
Sie werden	Sie werden	
er/sie/es wird	sie werden	

PRESENT SUBJUNCTIVE I

ich empfehle	wir empfehlen
du empfehlest	ihr empfehlet
Sie empfehlen	Sie empfehlen
er/sie/es empfehle	sie empfehlen

PRESENT SUBJUNCTIVE II

ich empföhle/empfähle	wir empföhlen/empfählen
du empföhlest/empfählest	ihr empföhlet/empfählet
Sie empföhlen/empfählen	Sie empföhlen/empfählen
er/sie/es empföhle/empfähle	sie empföhlen/empfählen

FUTURE SUBJUNCTIVE I

ich werde	wir werden	empfehlen
du werdest	ihr werdet	
Sie werden	Sie werden	
er/sie/es werde	sie werden	

FUTURE SUBJUNCTIVE II

ich würde	wir würden	empfehlen
du würdest	ihr würdet	
Sie würden	Sie würden	
er/sie/es würde	sie würden	

PRESENT PERFECT

ich habe	wir haben	empfohlen
du hast	ihr habt	
Sie haben	Sie haben	
er/sie/es hat	sie haben	

PAST PERFECT

ich hatte	wir hatten	empfohlen
du hattest	ihr hattet	
Sie hatten	Sie hatten	
er/sie/es hatte	sie hatten	

FUTURE PERFECT

ich werde	wir werden	empfohlen haben
du wirst	ihr werdet	
Sie werden	Sie werden	
er/sie/es wird	sie werden	

PAST SUBJUNCTIVE I

ich habe	wir haben	empfohlen
du habest	ihr habet	
Sie haben	Sie haben	
er/sie/es habe	sie haben	

PAST SUBJUNCTIVE II

ich hätte	wir hätten	empfohlen
du hättest	ihr hättet	
Sie hätten	Sie hätten	
er/sie/es hätte	sie hätten	

FUTURE PERFECT SUBJUNCTIVE I

ich werde	wir werden	empfohlen haben
du werdest	ihr werdet	
Sie werden	Sie werden	
er/sie/es werde	sie werden	

FUTURE PERFECT SUBJUNCTIVE II

ich würde	wir würden	empfohlen haben
du würdest	ihr würdet	
Sie würden	Sie würden	
er/sie/es würde	sie würden	

COMMANDS empfiehl! empfehlt! empfehlen Sie!

PRESENT PARTICIPLE empfehlend

Usage

Mein Arzt empfahl therapeutische Massage für schmerzhafte Muskeln.	*My physician recommended therapeutic massage for sore muscles.*
Die Weltgesundheitsorganisation empfiehlt Impfung gegen Pocken.	*The World Health Organization is recommending immunization against smallpox.*
„Markus, was empfiehlst du als Beilage?“	*“Markus, what do you recommend as a side dish?”*
„Als Beilage empfehle ich entweder den Gurkensalat oder den Rotkohl.“	*“As a side dish, I recommend either the cucumber salad or the red cabbage.”*
Sie empfahl ihn Gott. (*archaic*)	*She commended him to God.*

sich empfehlen *to take leave; be recommended, be advisable*

Der Reiter empfahl sich und ritt weg.	*The rider bade farewell and rode away.*
Da das Reiseziel beliebt ist, empfiehlt es sich, die Zimmer mehrere Monate im Voraus zu buchen.	*Since this travel destination is popular, it is advisable to book rooms several months in advance.*

RELATED VERBS an·empfehlen; *see also* **befehlen** (53)

regular weak verb **entdeckt · entdeckte · entdeckt**

PRESENT

ich entdecke	wir entdecken
du entdeckst	ihr entdeckt
Sie entdecken	Sie entdecken
er/sie/es entdeckt	sie entdecken

SIMPLE PAST

ich entdeckte	wir entdeckten
du entdecktest	ihr entdecktet
Sie entdeckten	Sie entdeckten
er/sie/es entdeckte	sie entdeckten

FUTURE

ich werde	wir werden	entdecken
du wirst	ihr werdet	
Sie werden	Sie werden	
er/sie/es wird	sie werden	

PRESENT SUBJUNCTIVE I

ich entdecke	wir entdecken
du entdeckest	ihr entdecket
Sie entdecken	Sie entdecken
er/sie/es entdecke	sie entdecken

PRESENT SUBJUNCTIVE II

ich entdeckte	wir entdeckten
du entdecktest	ihr entdecktet
Sie entdeckten	Sie entdeckten
er/sie/es entdeckte	sie entdeckten

FUTURE SUBJUNCTIVE I

ich werde	wir werden	entdecken
du werdest	ihr werdet	
Sie werden	Sie werden	
er/sie/es werde	sie werden	

FUTURE SUBJUNCTIVE II

ich würde	wir würden	entdecken
du würdest	ihr würdet	
Sie würden	Sie würden	
er/sie/es würde	sie würden	

PRESENT PERFECT

ich habe	wir haben	entdeckt
du hast	ihr habt	
Sie haben	Sie haben	
er/sie/es hat	sie haben	

PAST PERFECT

ich hatte	wir hatten	entdeckt
du hattest	ihr hattet	
Sie hatten	Sie hatten	
er/sie/es hatte	sie hatten	

FUTURE PERFECT

ich werde	wir werden	entdeckt haben
du wirst	ihr werdet	
Sie werden	Sie werden	
er/sie/es wird	sie werden	

PAST SUBJUNCTIVE I

ich habe	wir haben	entdeckt
du habest	ihr habet	
Sie haben	Sie haben	
er/sie/es habe	sie haben	

PAST SUBJUNCTIVE II

ich hätte	wir hätten	entdeckt
du hättest	ihr hättet	
Sie hätten	Sie hätten	
er/sie/es hätte	sie hätten	

FUTURE PERFECT SUBJUNCTIVE I

ich werde	wir werden	entdeckt haben
du werdest	ihr werdet	
Sie werden	Sie werden	
er/sie/es werde	sie werden	

FUTURE PERFECT SUBJUNCTIVE II

ich würde	wir würden	entdeckt haben
du würdest	ihr würdet	
Sie würden	Sie würden	
er/sie/es würde	sie würden	

COMMANDS entdeck(e)! entdeckt! entdecken Sie!

PRESENT PARTICIPLE entdeckend

Usage

In welchem Jahr wurde der Planet Pluto entdeckt?	*In what year was the planet Pluto discovered?*
Wir müssen solche Missetaten entdecken und an die Öffentlichkeit bringen.	*We must expose such misdeeds and bring them to public attention.*
Neue Beweise seiner Mitschuld sind vor kurzem in archivalischen Materialien entdeckt worden.	*New evidence of his complicity has recently been uncovered in archival materials.*
Mein Vetter hat letztes Jahr in Brasilien eine bisher unbekannte Orchideen-Art entdeckt.	*My cousin discovered a previously unknown orchid variety in Brazil last year.*
Auf der täglichen Autofahrt vom Büro nach Hause habe ich heute eine kürzere Route entdeckt.	*During my daily car trip home from the office today I discovered a shorter route.*
Was machst du, wenn du ein Haar in deiner Suppe entdeckst?	*What do you do when you spot a hair in your soup?*
Während meines Studiums habe ich mein Interesse an klassischer Musik entdeckt.	*During my studies I discovered my interest in classical music.*

RELATED VERBS decken, wieder·entdecken

144 enthalten *to hold, comprise, include, contain*

enthält · enthielt · enthalten strong verb

PRESENT

ich enthalte	wir enthalten
du enthältst	ihr enthaltet
Sie enthalten	Sie enthalten
er/sie/es enthält	sie enthalten

SIMPLE PAST

ich enthielt	wir enthielten
du enthieltst	ihr enthieltet
Sie enthielten	Sie enthielten
er/sie/es enthielt	sie enthielten

FUTURE

ich werde	wir werden	enthalten
du wirst	ihr werdet	
Sie werden	Sie werden	
er/sie/es wird	sie werden	

PRESENT SUBJUNCTIVE I

ich enthalte	wir enthalten
du enthaltest	ihr enthaltet
Sie enthalten	Sie enthalten
er/sie/es enthalte	sie enthalten

PRESENT SUBJUNCTIVE II

ich enthielte	wir enthielten
du enthieltest	ihr enthieltet
Sie enthielten	Sie enthielten
er/sie/es enthielte	sie enthielten

FUTURE SUBJUNCTIVE I

ich werde	wir werden	enthalten
du werdest	ihr werdet	
Sie werden	Sie werden	
er/sie/es werde	sie werden	

FUTURE SUBJUNCTIVE II

ich würde	wir würden	enthalten
du würdest	ihr würdet	
Sie würden	Sie würden	
er/sie/es würde	sie würden	

PRESENT PERFECT

ich habe	wir haben	enthalten
du hast	ihr habt	
Sie haben	Sie haben	
er/sie/es hat	sie haben	

PAST PERFECT

ich hatte	wir hatten	enthalten
du hattest	ihr hattet	
Sie hatten	Sie hatten	
er/sie/es hatte	sie hatten	

FUTURE PERFECT

ich werde	wir werden	enthalten haben
du wirst	ihr werdet	
Sie werden	Sie werden	
er/sie/es wird	sie werden	

PAST SUBJUNCTIVE I

ich habe	wir haben	enthalten
du habest	ihr habet	
Sie haben	Sie haben	
er/sie/es habe	sie haben	

PAST SUBJUNCTIVE II

ich hätte	wir hätten	enthalten
du hättest	ihr hättet	
Sie hätten	Sie hätten	
er/sie/es hätte	sie hätten	

FUTURE PERFECT SUBJUNCTIVE I

ich werde	wir werden	enthalten haben
du werdest	ihr werdet	
Sie werden	Sie werden	
er/sie/es werde	sie werden	

FUTURE PERFECT SUBJUNCTIVE II

ich würde	wir würden	enthalten haben
du würdest	ihr würdet	
Sie würden	Sie würden	
er/sie/es würde	sie würden	

COMMANDS enthalte! enthaltet! enthalten Sie!

PRESENT PARTICIPLE enthaltend

Usage

Das Pulver enthält ätzende Substanzen.	*The powder contains corrosive substances.*
Ihre Email enthielt einen Virus.	*Your e-mail contained a virus.*
Vollkornbrötchen enthalten gesunde Ballaststoffe.	*Whole grain rolls contain healthy fiber.*
Der Preis enthält Steuern und Versicherung.	*The price includes taxes and insurance.*
Mein Aufsatz hat zu viele typographische Fehler enthalten.	*My essay contained too many typographical errors.*
Die Sammlung enthält Briefe, Handschriften und andere Dokumente.	*The collection holds letters, manuscripts, and other documents.*
Laut Polizeiangaben habe der Safe Diamanten enthalten.	*According to police reports, the safe contained diamonds.*

sich enthalten *to abstain, refrain*

Ich enthalte mich von Süßigkeiten.	*I am abstaining from sweets.*
Warum enthältst du dich des Kommentars?	*Why are you refraining from comment?*

RELATED VERBS vor·enthalten; *see also* **halten** (231)

strong verb **entlässt · entließ · entlassen**

PRESENT

ich entlasse	wir entlassen
du entlässt	ihr entlasst
Sie entlassen	Sie entlassen
er/sie/es entlässt	sie entlassen

PRESENT PERFECT

ich habe	wir haben	entlassen
du hast	ihr habt	
Sie haben	Sie haben	
er/sie/es hat	sie haben	

SIMPLE PAST

ich entließ	wir entließen
du entließest	ihr entließt
Sie entließen	Sie entließen
er/sie/es entließ	sie entließen

PAST PERFECT

ich hatte	wir hatten	entlassen
du hattest	ihr hattet	
Sie hatten	Sie hatten	
er/sie/es hatte	sie hatten	

FUTURE

ich werde	wir werden	entlassen
du wirst	ihr werdet	
Sie werden	Sie werden	
er/sie/es wird	sie werden	

FUTURE PERFECT

ich werde	wir werden	entlassen haben
du wirst	ihr werdet	
Sie werden	Sie werden	
er/sie/es wird	sie werden	

PRESENT SUBJUNCTIVE I

ich entlasse	wir entlassen
du entlassest	ihr entlasset
Sie entlassen	Sie entlassen
er/sie/es entlasse	sie entlassen

PAST SUBJUNCTIVE I

ich habe	wir haben	entlassen
du habest	ihr habet	
Sie haben	Sie haben	
er/sie/es habe	sie haben	

PRESENT SUBJUNCTIVE II

ich entließe	wir entließen
du entließest	ihr entließet
Sie entließen	Sie entließen
er/sie/es entließe	sie entließen

PAST SUBJUNCTIVE II

ich hätte	wir hätten	entlassen
du hättest	ihr hättet	
Sie hätten	Sie hätten	
er/sie/es hätte	sie hätten	

FUTURE SUBJUNCTIVE I

ich werde	wir werden	entlassen
du werdest	ihr werdet	
Sie werden	Sie werden	
er/sie/es werde	sie werden	

FUTURE PERFECT SUBJUNCTIVE I

ich werde	wir werden	entlassen haben
du werdest	ihr werdet	
Sie werden	Sie werden	
er/sie/es werde	sie werden	

FUTURE SUBJUNCTIVE II

ich würde	wir würden	entlassen
du würdest	ihr würdet	
Sie würden	Sie würden	
er/sie/es würde	sie würden	

FUTURE PERFECT SUBJUNCTIVE II

ich würde	wir würden	entlassen haben
du würdest	ihr würdet	
Sie würden	Sie würden	
er/sie/es würde	sie würden	

COMMANDS entlass(e)! entlasst! entlassen Sie!

PRESENT PARTICIPLE entlassend

Usage

Drogemeyer hat letzte Woche 150 Mitarbeiter entlassen müssen. — *Drogemeyer had to lay off 150 employees last week.*
Ich habe Angst davor, entlassen zu werden. — *I'm afraid of being laid off.*
Sebastian wurde aus der Bundeswehr entlassen. — *Sebastian was discharged from the army.*
Die Lehrerin hat Maximilian vorzeitig aus dem Unterricht entlassen. — *The teacher dismissed Maximilian from class early.*
Unser Vermieter entlässt uns aus dem Mietsvertrag. — *Our landlord is letting us out of the lease.*
Zwölf Gefangene werden entlassen. — *Twelve prisoners are being released.*
Nach einem Jahr hat man mich entlassen. — *After one year they let me go.*
Wann wird mein Vater aus dem Krankenhaus entlassen? — *When is my father being released from the hospital?*
Diese Entscheidung entlässt uns nicht aus der Verantwortung, bestehende Programme zu finanzieren. — *This decision does not release us from the responsibility of financing existing programs.*

RELATED VERBS *see* **lassen** (280)

146 entscheiden *to decide, determine; settle* (legally)

entscheidet · entschied · entschieden strong verb

PRESENT

ich entscheide	wir entscheiden
du entscheidest	ihr entscheidet
Sie entscheiden	Sie entscheiden
er/sie/es entscheidet	sie entscheiden

PRESENT PERFECT

ich habe	wir haben	entschieden
du hast	ihr habt	
Sie haben	Sie haben	
er/sie/es hat	sie haben	

SIMPLE PAST

ich entschied	wir entschieden
du entschiedst	ihr entschiedet
Sie entschieden	Sie entschieden
er/sie/es entschied	sie entschieden

PAST PERFECT

ich hatte	wir hatten	entschieden
du hattest	ihr hattet	
Sie hatten	Sie hatten	
er/sie/es hatte	sie hatten	

FUTURE

ich werde	wir werden	entscheiden
du wirst	ihr werdet	
Sie werden	Sie werden	
er/sie/es wird	sie werden	

FUTURE PERFECT

ich werde	wir werden	entschieden haben
du wirst	ihr werdet	
Sie werden	Sie werden	
er/sie/es wird	sie werden	

PRESENT SUBJUNCTIVE I

ich entscheide	wir entscheiden
du entscheidest	ihr entscheidet
Sie entscheiden	Sie entscheiden
er/sie/es entscheide	sie entscheiden

PAST SUBJUNCTIVE I

ich habe	wir haben	entschieden
du habest	ihr habet	
Sie haben	Sie haben	
er/sie/es habe	sie haben	

PRESENT SUBJUNCTIVE II

ich entschiede	wir entschieden
du entschiedest	ihr entschiedet
Sie entschieden	Sie entschieden
er/sie/es entschiede	sie entschieden

PAST SUBJUNCTIVE II

ich hätte	wir hätten	entschieden
du hättest	ihr hättet	
Sie hätten	Sie hätten	
er/sie/es hätte	sie hätten	

FUTURE SUBJUNCTIVE I

ich werde	wir werden	entscheiden
du werdest	ihr werdet	
Sie werden	Sie werden	
er/sie/es werde	sie werden	

FUTURE PERFECT SUBJUNCTIVE I

ich werde	wir werden	entschieden haben
du werdest	ihr werdet	
Sie werden	Sie werden	
er/sie/es werde	sie werden	

FUTURE SUBJUNCTIVE II

ich würde	wir würden	entscheiden
du würdest	ihr würdet	
Sie würden	Sie würden	
er/sie/es würde	sie würden	

FUTURE PERFECT SUBJUNCTIVE II

ich würde	wir würden	entschieden haben
du würdest	ihr würdet	
Sie würden	Sie würden	
er/sie/es würde	sie würden	

COMMANDS entscheide! entscheidet! entscheiden Sie!

PRESENT PARTICIPLE entscheidend

Usage

Ich lasse dich entscheiden, wo wir essen sollten. — *I'll let you decide where we should eat.*
Der Richter entschied zugunsten von Greenpeace. — *The judge decided in favor of Greenpeace.*
Das Wetter hat den Spielausgang entschieden. — *The weather determined the outcome of the game.*
Die Angelegenheit wurde vor Gericht entschieden. — *The matter was settled in court.*

sich entscheiden *to decide, make up one's mind*

Anselmus stand vor dem Problem, sich zu entscheiden, ob er Veronika oder Elisabeth wählen sollte. — *Anselmus was faced with the problem of deciding whether he should choose Veronika or Elisabeth.*
Du musst dich jetzt entscheiden. — *You have to make up your mind now.*
Ich habe mich gerade entschieden, mit dem Auto dahinzufahren. — *I have just decided to go there by car.*
Tim scheint sich nicht entscheiden zu können. — *Tim doesn't seem to be able to make up his mind.*

RELATED VERBS vor·entscheiden; *see also* **scheiden** (360) strong verb **entschließt sich · entschloss sich · sich entschlossen**

PRESENT

ich entschließe mich	wir entschließen uns
du entschließt dich	ihr entschließt euch
Sie entschließen sich	Sie entschließen sich
er/sie/es entschließt sich	sie entschließen sich

PRESENT PERFECT

ich habe mich	wir haben uns	entschlossen
du hast dich	ihr habt euch	
Sie haben sich	Sie haben sich	
er/sie/es hat sich	sie haben sich	

SIMPLE PAST

ich entschloss mich	wir entschlossen uns
du entschlossest dich	ihr entschlosst euch
Sie entschlossen sich	Sie entschlossen sich
er/sie/es entschloss sich	sie entschlossen sich

PAST PERFECT

ich hatte mich	wir hatten uns	entschlossen
du hattest dich	ihr hattet euch	
Sie hatten sich	Sie hatten sich	
er/sie/es hatte sich	sie hatten sich	

FUTURE

ich werde mich	wir werden uns	entschließen
du wirst dich	ihr werdet euch	
Sie werden sich	Sie werden sich	
er/sie/es wird sich	sie werden sich	

FUTURE PERFECT

ich werde mich	wir werden uns	entschlossen haben
du wirst dich	ihr werdet euch	
Sie werden sich	Sie werden sich	
er/sie/es wird sich	sie werden sich	

PRESENT SUBJUNCTIVE I

ich entschließe mich	wir entschließen uns
du entschließest dich	ihr entschließet euch
Sie entschließen sich	Sie entschließen sich
er/sie/es entschließe sich	sie entschließen sich

PAST SUBJUNCTIVE I

ich habe mich	wir haben uns	entschlossen
du habest dich	ihr habet euch	
Sie haben sich	Sie haben sich	
er/sie/es habe sich	sie haben sich	

PRESENT SUBJUNCTIVE II

ich entschlösse mich	wir entschlössen uns
du entschlössest dich	ihr entschlösset euch
Sie entschlössen sich	Sie entschlössen sich
er/sie/es entschlösse sich	sie entschlössen sich

PAST SUBJUNCTIVE II

ich hätte mich	wir hätten uns	entschlossen
du hättest dich	ihr hättet euch	
Sie hätten sich	Sie hätten sich	
er/sie/es hätte sich	sie hätten sich	

FUTURE SUBJUNCTIVE I

ich werde mich	wir werden uns	entschließen
du werdest dich	ihr werdet euch	
Sie werden sich	Sie werden sich	
er/sie/es werde sich	sie werden sich	

FUTURE PERFECT SUBJUNCTIVE I

ich werde mich	wir werden uns	entschlossen haben
du werdest dich	ihr werdet euch	
Sie werden sich	Sie werden sich	
er/sie/es werde sich	sie werden sich	

FUTURE SUBJUNCTIVE II

ich würde mich	wir würden uns	entschließen
du würdest dich	ihr würdet euch	
Sie würden sich	Sie würden sich	
er/sie/es würde sich	sie würden sich	

FUTURE PERFECT SUBJUNCTIVE II

ich würde mich	wir würden uns	entschlossen haben
du würdest dich	ihr würdet euch	
Sie würden sich	Sie würden sich	
er/sie/es würde sich	sie würden sich	

COMMANDS entschließ(e) dich! entschließt euch! entschließen Sie sich!

PRESENT PARTICIPLE sich entschließend

Usage

Wir haben uns entschlossen, seine asozialen Tendenzen zu diskutieren.	*We have decided to discuss his asocial tendencies.*
Wegen des Wetters entschloss er sich nach Hause zurückzufahren.	*Because of the weather he made up his mind to go back home.*
Die Kinder entschlossen sich zu einem monatlichen Besuch bei ihrer Tante.	*The children resolved to visit their aunt once a month.*
Sie hat Langeweile und hat sich zu einer Veränderung entschlossen.	*She is bored and has decided to make a change.*
Danach entschließt er sich in Deutschland zu bleiben.	*After that, he decides to stay in Germany.*
Nach langem Nachdenken habe ich mich endlich entschlossen, mich um die Stelle zu bewerben.	*After lengthy consideration, I have finally made up my mind to apply for the position.*
Nach dem Meeting hat sie sich anders entschlossen.	*After the meeting, she changed her mind.*

RELATED VERBS *see* **schließen** (375)

148 entschuldigen *to excuse, pardon; justify*

entschuldigt · entschuldigte · entschuldigt regular weak verb

PRESENT

ich entschuldige	wir entschuldigen
du entschuldigst	ihr entschuldigt
Sie entschuldigen	Sie entschuldigen
er/sie/es entschuldigt	sie entschuldigen

SIMPLE PAST

ich entschuldigte	wir entschuldigten
du entschuldigtest	ihr entschuldigtet
Sie entschuldigten	Sie entschuldigten
er/sie/es entschuldigte	sie entschuldigten

FUTURE

ich werde	wir werden	entschuldigen
du wirst	ihr werdet	
Sie werden	Sie werden	
er/sie/es wird	sie werden	

PRESENT SUBJUNCTIVE I

ich entschuldige	wir entschuldigen
du entschuldigest	ihr entschuldiget
Sie entschuldigen	Sie entschuldigen
er/sie/es entschuldige	sie entschuldigen

PRESENT SUBJUNCTIVE II

ich entschuldigte	wir entschuldigten
du entschuldigtest	ihr entschuldigtet
Sie entschuldigten	Sie entschuldigten
er/sie/es entschuldigte	sie entschuldigten

FUTURE SUBJUNCTIVE I

ich werde	wir werden	entschuldigen
du werdest	ihr werdet	
Sie werden	Sie werden	
er/sie/es werde	sie werden	

FUTURE SUBJUNCTIVE II

ich würde	wir würden	entschuldigen
du würdest	ihr würdet	
Sie würden	Sie würden	
er/sie/es würde	sie würden	

PRESENT PERFECT

ich habe	wir haben	entschuldigt
du hast	ihr habt	
Sie haben	Sie haben	
er/sie/es hat	sie haben	

PAST PERFECT

ich hatte	wir hatten	entschuldigt
du hattest	ihr hattet	
Sie hatten	Sie hatten	
er/sie/es hatte	sie hatten	

FUTURE PERFECT

ich werde	wir werden	entschuldigt haben
du wirst	ihr werdet	
Sie werden	Sie werden	
er/sie/es wird	sie werden	

PAST SUBJUNCTIVE I

ich habe	wir haben	entschuldigt
du habest	ihr habet	
Sie haben	Sie haben	
er/sie/es habe	sie haben	

PAST SUBJUNCTIVE II

ich hätte	wir hätten	entschuldigt
du hättest	ihr hättet	
Sie hätten	Sie hätten	
er/sie/es hätte	sie hätten	

FUTURE PERFECT SUBJUNCTIVE I

ich werde	wir werden	entschuldigt haben
du werdest	ihr werdet	
Sie werden	Sie werden	
er/sie/es werde	sie werden	

FUTURE PERFECT SUBJUNCTIVE II

ich würde	wir würden	entschuldigt haben
du würdest	ihr würdet	
Sie würden	Sie würden	
er/sie/es würde	sie würden	

COMMANDS entschuldig(e)! entschuldigt! entschuldigen Sie!

PRESENT PARTICIPLE entschuldigend

Usage

Entschuldigen Sie mich. — *Excuse me.*

Entschuldigt, wenn ich störe, aber wisst ihr, wo der Kellerschlüssel steckt? — *Pardon me for interrupting, but do you know where the basement key is?*

Dieter bleibt zu Hause und wird in der Schule entschuldigt. — *Dieter is staying home and is excused from school.*

Sep versuchte seine Taten zu entschuldigen. — *Sep tried to justify his actions.*

sich entschuldigen *to apologize, excuse oneself*

Bernd hat sich gestern bei Frau Dormagen für den Unfall entschuldigt. — *Bernd apologized to Mrs. Dormagen yesterday for the accident.*

Ich möchte mich entschuldigen. — *I'd like to apologize.*

Tante Grete hat sich bei mir endlich entschuldigt. — *Aunt Grete finally apologized to me.*

Alex entschuldigte sich vom Abendbrot und ging in sein Zimmer. — *Alex excused himself from dinner and went to his room.*

strong verb (dative object) **entspricht · entsprach · entsprochen**

PRESENT

ich entspreche	wir entsprechen
du entsprichst	ihr entsprecht
Sie entsprechen	Sie entsprechen
er/sie/es entspricht	sie entsprechen

SIMPLE PAST

ich entsprach	wir entsprachen
du entsprachst	ihr entspracht
Sie entsprachen	Sie entsprachen
er/sie/es entsprach	sie entsprachen

FUTURE

ich werde	wir werden	entsprechen
du wirst	ihr werdet	
Sie werden	Sie werden	
er/sie/es wird	sie werden	

PRESENT SUBJUNCTIVE I

ich entspreche	wir entsprechen
du entsprechest	ihr entsprechet
Sie entsprechen	Sie entsprechen
er/sie/es entspreche	sie entsprechen

PRESENT SUBJUNCTIVE II

ich entspräche	wir entsprächen
du entsprächest	ihr entsprächet
Sie entsprächen	Sie entsprächen
er/sie/es entspräche	sie entsprächen

FUTURE SUBJUNCTIVE I

ich werde	wir werden	entsprechen
du werdest	ihr werdet	
Sie werden	Sie werden	
er/sie/es werde	sie werden	

FUTURE SUBJUNCTIVE II

ich würde	wir würden	entsprechen
du würdest	ihr würdet	
Sie würden	Sie würden	
er/sie/es würde	sie würden	

PRESENT PERFECT

ich habe	wir haben	entsprochen
du hast	ihr habt	
Sie haben	Sie haben	
er/sie/es hat	sie haben	

PAST PERFECT

ich hatte	wir hatten	entsprochen
du hattest	ihr hattet	
Sie hatten	Sie hatten	
er/sie/es hatte	sie hatten	

FUTURE PERFECT

ich werde	wir werden	entsprochen haben
du wirst	ihr werdet	
Sie werden	Sie werden	
er/sie/es wird	sie werden	

PAST SUBJUNCTIVE I

ich habe	wir haben	entsprochen
du habest	ihr habet	
Sie haben	Sie haben	
er/sie/es habe	sie haben	

PAST SUBJUNCTIVE II

ich hätte	wir hätten	entsprochen
du hättest	ihr hättet	
Sie hätten	Sie hätten	
er/sie/es hätte	sie hätten	

FUTURE PERFECT SUBJUNCTIVE I

ich werde	wir werden	entsprochen haben
du werdest	ihr werdet	
Sie werden	Sie werden	
er/sie/es werde	sie werden	

FUTURE PERFECT SUBJUNCTIVE II

ich würde	wir würden	entsprochen haben
du würdest	ihr würdet	
Sie würden	Sie würden	
er/sie/es würde	sie würden	

COMMANDS entsprich! entsprecht! entsprechen Sie!

PRESENT PARTICIPLE entsprechend

Usage

Die Leistung des Produkts entspricht nicht unseren Erwartungen.	*The product's performance doesn't meet our expectations.*
Werners Aussage entsprach den Tatsachen nicht.	*Werner's statement wasn't consistent with the facts.*
Die Papiergröße 2 entspricht dem Standardformat DIN A4.	*Paper size 2 corresponds to the standard DIN A4 format.*
Howard behauptet, dass das Angebot in diesem Fall der Nachfrage entspreche.	*Howard maintains that in this case supply does meet demand.*
Diese Münze aus dem Jahr 1733 hat in Größe und Form dem heutigen US-amerikanischen Quarter entsprochen.	*This coin from the year 1733 had the same size and shape as the present-day U.S. American quarter.*
Dieser diplomatische Schritt entspricht der Meinung der meisten Bürger des Landes.	*This diplomatic move is consistent with the opinion of most of the country's citizens.*
Der neue Paragraph 7 entspricht dem Gesetz.	*The new paragraph 7 is consistent with the law.*

RELATED VERBS *see* **sprechen** (415)

150 entstehen *to originate, arise, ensue, emerge, be created*

entsteht · entstand · entstanden strong verb

PRESENT

ich entstehe	wir entstehen
du entstehst	ihr entsteht
Sie entstehen	Sie entstehen
er/sie/es entsteht	sie entstehen

SIMPLE PAST

ich entstand	wir entstanden
du entstandst	ihr entstandet
Sie entstanden	Sie entstanden
er/sie/es entstand	sie entstanden

FUTURE

ich werde	wir werden	entstehen
du wirst	ihr werdet	
Sie werden	Sie werden	
er/sie/es wird	sie werden	

PRESENT SUBJUNCTIVE I

ich entstehe	wir entstehen
du entstehest	ihr entstehet
Sie entstehen	Sie entstehen
er/sie/es entstehe	sie entstehen

PRESENT SUBJUNCTIVE II

ich entstünde/entstände	wir entstünden/entständen
du entstündest/entständest	ihr entstündet/entständet
Sie entstünden/entständen	Sie entstünden/entständen
er/sie/es entstünde/entstände	sie entstünden/entständen

FUTURE SUBJUNCTIVE I

ich werde	wir werden	entstehen
du werdest	ihr werdet	
Sie werden	Sie werden	
er/sie/es werde	sie werden	

FUTURE SUBJUNCTIVE II

ich würde	wir würden	entstehen
du würdest	ihr würdet	
Sie würden	Sie würden	
er/sie/es würde	sie würden	

PRESENT PERFECT

ich bin	wir sind	entstanden
du bist	ihr seid	
Sie sind	Sie sind	
er/sie/es ist	sie sind	

PAST PERFECT

ich war	wir waren	entstanden
du warst	ihr wart	
Sie waren	Sie waren	
er/sie/es war	sie waren	

FUTURE PERFECT

ich werde	wir werden	entstanden sein
du wirst	ihr werdet	
Sie werden	Sie werden	
er/sie/es wird	sie werden	

PAST SUBJUNCTIVE I

ich sei	wir seien	entstanden
du seiest	ihr seiet	
Sie seien	Sie seien	
er/sie/es sei	sie seien	

PAST SUBJUNCTIVE II

ich wäre	wir wären	entstanden
du wärest	ihr wäret	
Sie wären	Sie wären	
er/sie/es wäre	sie wären	

FUTURE PERFECT SUBJUNCTIVE I

ich werde	wir werden	entstanden sein
du werdest	ihr werdet	
Sie werden	Sie werden	
er/sie/es werde	sie werden	

FUTURE PERFECT SUBJUNCTIVE II

ich würde	wir würden	entstanden sein
du würdest	ihr würdet	
Sie würden	Sie würden	
er/sie/es würde	sie würden	

COMMANDS entsteh(e)! entsteht! entstehen Sie!

PRESENT PARTICIPLE entstehend

Usage

Ein großer Aufruhr entstand. — *A great tumult ensued.*

Das Unternehmen ist aus dem Zusammenschluss mehrerer kleinerer Firmen entstanden. — *The enterprise resulted from the merger of several smaller firms.*

Es wird allgemein gesagt, dass Jazz in New Orleans entstanden sei. — *It is generally said that jazz originated in New Orleans.*

Der Begriff „Rosinenbomber" entstand 1948 während der sowjetischen Blockade von Berlin. — *The term "Raisin Bomber" arose in 1948 during the Soviet blockade of Berlin.*

Alte Viren mutieren und neue Viren entstehen. — *Old viruses mutate and new viruses are formed.*

Meine erste Komposition ist 1979 entstanden. — *My first composition was created in 1979.*

Der Grammatikfehler war entstanden, bevor der Text in den Satz ging. — *The grammatical mistake surfaced before the text was typeset.*

Vögel sind aus Reptilien entstanden. — *Birds have their origin in reptiles.*

Dem Käufer entstehen keine Gebühren. — *The buyer incurs no fees.*

RELATED VERBS *see* **stehen** (423)

to disappoint **enttäuschen**

regular weak verb

enttäuscht · enttäuschte · enttäuscht

PRESENT

ich enttäusche	wir enttäuschen
du enttäuschst	ihr enttäuscht
Sie enttäuschen	Sie enttäuschen
er/sie/es enttäuscht	sie enttäuschen

SIMPLE PAST

ich enttäuschte	wir enttäuschten
du enttäuschtest	ihr enttäuschtet
Sie enttäuschten	Sie enttäuschten
er/sie/es enttäuschte	sie enttäuschten

FUTURE

ich werde	wir werden	enttäuschen
du wirst	ihr werdet	
Sie werden	Sie werden	
er/sie/es wird	sie werden	

PRESENT SUBJUNCTIVE I

ich enttäusche	wir enttäuschen
du enttäuschest	ihr enttäuschet
Sie enttäuschen	Sie enttäuschen
er/sie/es enttäusche	sie enttäuschen

PRESENT SUBJUNCTIVE II

ich enttäuschte	wir enttäuschten
du enttäuschtest	ihr enttäuschtet
Sie enttäuschten	Sie enttäuschten
er/sie/es enttäuschte	sie enttäuschten

FUTURE SUBJUNCTIVE I

ich werde	wir werden	enttäuschen
du werdest	ihr werdet	
Sie werden	Sie werden	
er/sie/es werde	sie werden	

FUTURE SUBJUNCTIVE II

ich würde	wir würden	enttäuschen
du würdest	ihr würdet	
Sie würden	Sie würden	
er/sie/es würde	sie würden	

PRESENT PERFECT

ich habe	wir haben	enttäuscht
du hast	ihr habt	
Sie haben	Sie haben	
er/sie/es hat	sie haben	

PAST PERFECT

ich hatte	wir hatten	enttäuscht
du hattest	ihr hattet	
Sie hatten	Sie hatten	
er/sie/es hatte	sie hatten	

FUTURE PERFECT

ich werde	wir werden	enttäuscht haben
du wirst	ihr werdet	
Sie werden	Sie werden	
er/sie/es wird	sie werden	

PAST SUBJUNCTIVE I

ich habe	wir haben	enttäuscht
du habest	ihr habet	
Sie haben	Sie haben	
er/sie/es habe	sie haben	

PAST SUBJUNCTIVE II

ich hätte	wir hätten	enttäuscht
du hättest	ihr hättet	
Sie hätten	Sie hätten	
er/sie/es hätte	sie hätten	

FUTURE PERFECT SUBJUNCTIVE I

ich werde	wir werden	enttäuscht haben
du werdest	ihr werdet	
Sie werden	Sie werden	
er/sie/es werde	sie werden	

FUTURE PERFECT SUBJUNCTIVE II

ich würde	wir würden	enttäuscht haben
du würdest	ihr würdet	
Sie würden	Sie würden	
er/sie/es würde	sie würden	

COMMANDS enttäusch(e)! enttäuscht! enttäuschen Sie!

PRESENT PARTICIPLE enttäuschend

Usage

Die Lesererwartungen wurden nicht enttäuscht.	*The reader's expectations were not disappointed.*
Du enttäuschst mich sehr.	*You really disappoint me.*
Der Quartalumsatz hat Investoren enttäuscht.	*Quarterly revenue disappointed investors.*
Habe ich Sie enttäuscht?	*Have I disappointed you?*
Die Uraufführung der Oper enttäuschte die Kritiker.	*The premiere of the opera disappointed the critics.*
Leider muss ich dich enttäuschen.	*Unfortunately I have to disappoint you.*
Die Fans sind von der Schlussszene des Films enttäuscht worden.	*The fans were disappointed by the closing scene of the film.*
Um die Kinder nicht zu enttäuschen, sind sie trotz des Wetters hingefahren.	*In order not to disappoint the children, they went in spite of the weather.*
Das Hotel enttäuschte uns wegen der schmutzigen Matratzen.	*The hotel disappointed us because of the dirty mattresses.*

RELATED VERB täuschen

152 entwickeln *to develop*

entwickelt · entwickelte · entwickelt regular weak verb

PRESENT

ich entwick(e)le	wir entwickeln
du entwickelst	ihr entwickelt
Sie entwickeln	Sie entwickeln
er/sie/es entwickelt	sie entwickeln

SIMPLE PAST

ich entwickelte	wir entwickelten
du entwickeltest	ihr entwickeltet
Sie entwickelten	Sie entwickelten
er/sie/es entwickelte	sie entwickelten

FUTURE

ich werde	wir werden	entwickeln
du wirst	ihr werdet	
Sie werden	Sie werden	
er/sie/es wird	sie werden	

PRESENT SUBJUNCTIVE I

ich entwick(e)le	wir entwickeln
du entwickelst	ihr entwickelt
Sie entwickeln	Sie entwickeln
er/sie/es entwick(e)le	sie entwickeln

PRESENT SUBJUNCTIVE II

ich entwickelte	wir entwickelten
du entwickeltest	ihr entwickeltet
Sie entwickelten	Sie entwickelten
er/sie/es entwickelte	sie entwickelten

FUTURE SUBJUNCTIVE I

ich werde	wir werden	entwickeln
du werdest	ihr werdet	
Sie werden	Sie werden	
er/sie/es werde	sie werden	

FUTURE SUBJUNCTIVE II

ich würde	wir würden	entwickeln
du würdest	ihr würdet	
Sie würden	Sie würden	
er/sie/es würde	sie würden	

PRESENT PERFECT

ich habe	wir haben	entwickelt
du hast	ihr habt	
Sie haben	Sie haben	
er/sie/es hat	sie haben	

PAST PERFECT

ich hatte	wir hatten	entwickelt
du hattest	ihr hattet	
Sie hatten	Sie hatten	
er/sie/es hatte	sie hatten	

FUTURE PERFECT

ich werde	wir werden	entwickelt haben
du wirst	ihr werdet	
Sie werden	Sie werden	
er/sie/es wird	sie werden	

PAST SUBJUNCTIVE I

ich habe	wir haben	entwickelt
du habest	ihr habet	
Sie haben	Sie haben	
er/sie/es habe	sie haben	

PAST SUBJUNCTIVE II

ich hätte	wir hätten	entwickelt
du hättest	ihr hättet	
Sie hätten	Sie hätten	
er/sie/es hätte	sie hätten	

FUTURE PERFECT SUBJUNCTIVE I

ich werde	wir werden	entwickelt haben
du werdest	ihr werdet	
Sie werden	Sie werden	
er/sie/es werde	sie werden	

FUTURE PERFECT SUBJUNCTIVE II

ich würde	wir würden	entwickelt haben
du würdest	ihr würdet	
Sie würden	Sie würden	
er/sie/es würde	sie würden	

COMMANDS entwick(e)le! entwickelt! entwickeln Sie!

PRESENT PARTICIPLE entwickelnd

Usage

Ich entwickle Werkzeuge für Elektrotechnik. — *I develop tools for electrotechnology.*

Immer mehr Bakterien entwickeln Resistenzen gegen bestehende Antibiotika. — *An increasing number of bacteria are developing resistance to existing antibiotics.*

Das Ziel ist es, mehr Verständnis für Behinderte zu entwickeln. — *The goal is to develop greater understanding of the handicapped.*

Forscher haben ein neues Medikament entwickelt. — *Researchers have developed a new medicine.*

Ich möchte den Film entwickeln lassen. — *I'd like to get the film developed.*

sich entwickeln *to develop, evolve, grow*

Dieser Kunststil entwickelt sich seit der Mitte der 90er Jahre in eine völlig neue Richtung. — *This style of art has been evolving in a completely new direction since the mid-90s.*

Anschließend entwickelten sich zwei parallele Bewegungen in der früh nachmittelalterlichen Zeit. — *Subsequently, two parallel movements developed in the early postmedieval period.*

RELATED VERBS aus·entwickeln, fort·entwickeln, weiter·entwickeln, wickeln, zurück·entwickeln

regular weak verb **ereignet sich · ereignete sich · sich ereignet**

PRESENT

ich ereigne mich	wir ereignen uns
du ereignest dich	ihr ereignet euch
Sie ereignen sich	Sie ereignen sich
er/sie/es ereignet sich	sie ereignen sich

PRESENT PERFECT

ich habe mich	wir haben uns	ereignet
du hast dich	ihr habt euch	
Sie haben sich	Sie haben sich	
er/sie/es hat sich	sie haben sich	

SIMPLE PAST

ich ereignete mich	wir ereigneten uns
du ereignetest dich	ihr ereignetet euch
Sie ereigneten sich	Sie ereigneten sich
er/sie/es ereignete sich	sie ereigneten sich

PAST PERFECT

ich hatte mich	wir hatten uns	ereignet
du hattest dich	ihr hattet euch	
Sie hatten sich	Sie hatten sich	
er/sie/es hatte sich	sie hatten sich	

FUTURE

ich werde mich	wir werden uns	ereignen
du wirst dich	ihr werdet euch	
Sie werden sich	Sie werden sich	
er/sie/es wird sich	sie werden sich	

FUTURE PERFECT

ich werde mich	wir werden uns	ereignet haben
du wirst dich	ihr werdet euch	
Sie werden sich	Sie werden sich	
er/sie/es wird sich	sie werden sich	

PRESENT SUBJUNCTIVE I

ich ereigne mich	wir ereignen uns
du ereignest dich	ihr ereignet euch
Sie ereignen sich	Sie ereignen sich
er/sie/es ereigne sich	sie ereignen sich

PAST SUBJUNCTIVE I

ich habe mich	wir haben uns	ereignet
du habest dich	ihr habet euch	
Sie haben sich	Sie haben sich	
er/sie/es habe sich	sie haben sich	

PRESENT SUBJUNCTIVE II

ich ereignete mich	wir ereigneten uns
du ereignetest dich	ihr ereignetet euch
Sie ereigneten sich	Sie ereigneten sich
er/sie/es ereignete sich	sie ereigneten sich

PAST SUBJUNCTIVE II

ich hätte mich	wir hätten uns	ereignet
du hättest dich	ihr hättet euch	
Sie hätten sich	Sie hätten sich	
er/sie/es hätte sich	sie hätten sich	

FUTURE SUBJUNCTIVE I

ich werde mich	wir werden uns	ereignen
du werdest dich	ihr werdet euch	
Sie werden sich	Sie werden sich	
er/sie/es werde sich	sie werden sich	

FUTURE PERFECT SUBJUNCTIVE I

ich werde mich	wir werden uns	ereignet haben
du werdest dich	ihr werdet euch	
Sie werden sich	Sie werden sich	
er/sie/es werde sich	sie werden sich	

FUTURE SUBJUNCTIVE II

ich würde mich	wir würden uns	ereignen
du würdest dich	ihr würdet euch	
Sie würden sich	Sie würden sich	
er/sie/es würde sich	sie würden sich	

FUTURE PERFECT SUBJUNCTIVE II

ich würde mich	wir würden uns	ereignet haben
du würdest dich	ihr würdet euch	
Sie würden sich	Sie würden sich	
er/sie/es würde sich	sie würden sich	

COMMANDS ereigne dich! ereignet euch! ereignen Sie sich!

PRESENT PARTICIPLE sich ereignend

Usage

In Europa ereignet sich jedes Jahr mehr als eine Million Verkehrsunfälle. — *More than a million traffic accidents occur each year in Europe.*

1883 ereignete sich ein Vulkanausbruch auf der Insel Krakatau. — *In 1883, a volcanic eruption took place on the island of Krakatau.*

Der Polizeisprecher hat berichtet, der Mord habe sich vor Mitternacht ereignet. — *The police spokesman reported that the murder happened before midnight.*

Etwas Interessantes hat sich heute Nachmittag bei mir im Büro ereignet. — *Something interesting happened this afternoon at my office.*

Seit dem Fall der Berliner Mauer hat sich viel ereignet. — *Since the fall of the Berlin Wall, a lot has happened.*

Man wusste nicht genau, was sich ereignet hatte. — *People didn't know exactly what had occurred.*

Der Vorfall ereignete sich am 25. Juli 2005 um 5.30 Uhr. — *The incident occurred on July 25, 2005 at 5:30 A.M.*

Eine nukleare Katastrophe ereignete sich im April 1986 in Tschernobyl in der Ukraine. — *A nuclear catastrophe took place in April 1986 in Chernobyl in Ukraine.*

RELATED VERB eignen

154 erfahren *to learn, discover; experience, undergo*

erfährt · erfuhr · erfahren strong verb

PRESENT

ich erfahre	wir erfahren
du erfährst	ihr erfahrt
Sie erfahren	Sie erfahren
er/sie/es erfährt	sie erfahren

SIMPLE PAST

ich erfuhr	wir erfuhren
du erfuhrst	ihr erfuhrt
Sie erfuhren	Sie erfuhren
er/sie/es erfuhr	sie erfuhren

FUTURE

ich werde	wir werden	erfahren
du wirst	ihr werdet	
Sie werden	Sie werden	
er/sie/es wird	sie werden	

PRESENT SUBJUNCTIVE I

ich erfahre	wir erfahren
du erfahrest	ihr erfahret
Sie erfahren	Sie erfahren
er/sie/es erfahre	sie erfahren

PRESENT SUBJUNCTIVE II

ich erführe	wir erführen
du erführest	ihr erführet
Sie erführen	Sie erführen
er/sie/es erführe	sie erführen

FUTURE SUBJUNCTIVE I

ich werde	wir werden	erfahren
du werdest	ihr werdet	
Sie werden	Sie werden	
er/sie/es werde	sie werden	

FUTURE SUBJUNCTIVE II

ich würde	wir würden	erfahren
du würdest	ihr würdet	
Sie würden	Sie würden	
er/sie/es würde	sie würden	

PRESENT PERFECT

ich habe	wir haben	erfahren
du hast	ihr habt	
Sie haben	Sie haben	
er/sie/es hat	sie haben	

PAST PERFECT

ich hatte	wir hatten	erfahren
du hattest	ihr hattet	
Sie hatten	Sie hatten	
er/sie/es hatte	sie hatten	

FUTURE PERFECT

ich werde	wir werden	erfahren haben
du wirst	ihr werdet	
Sie werden	Sie werden	
er/sie/es wird	sie werden	

PAST SUBJUNCTIVE I

ich habe	wir haben	erfahren
du habest	ihr habet	
Sie haben	Sie haben	
er/sie/es habe	sie haben	

PAST SUBJUNCTIVE II

ich hätte	wir hätten	erfahren
du hättest	ihr hättet	
Sie hätten	Sie hätten	
er/sie/es hätte	sie hätten	

FUTURE PERFECT SUBJUNCTIVE I

ich werde	wir werden	erfahren haben
du werdest	ihr werdet	
Sie werden	Sie werden	
er/sie/es werde	sie werden	

FUTURE PERFECT SUBJUNCTIVE II

ich würde	wir würden	erfahren haben
du würdest	ihr würdet	
Sie würden	Sie würden	
er/sie/es würde	sie würden	

COMMANDS erfahr(e)! erfahrt! erfahren Sie!

PRESENT PARTICIPLE erfahrend

Usage

Ich habe gerade erfahren, dass mein Onkel im Krankenhaus liegt. — *I've just learned that my uncle is in the hospital.*

Der kritische Leser erfährt in diesem Werk sowohl heroische als auch höfische Aspekte. — *The critical reader will discover heroic as well as courtly aspects in this work.*

Wie es funktioniert erfahren Sie hier. — *You will learn here how it works.*

Der Romantiker sehnt sich nach einer Welt, in der man das Unendliche erfahren kann. — *The romantic yearns for a world in which one can experience the infinite.*

Gregor erfuhr eine Verwandlung in einen Käfer. — *Gregor underwent a transformation into a beetle.*

Dieser Tritt ins Phantastische, den der Held oft erfährt, ist nicht rational zu erklären. — *This step into the fantastical that the hero often experiences can't be rationally explained.*

Das historische Gebäude hat 1999 eine Restaurierung erfahren. — *The historic building underwent restoration in 1999.*

RELATED VERBS *see* **fahren** (177)

strong verb **erfindet · erfand · erfunden**

PRESENT

ich erfinde	wir erfinden
du erfindest	ihr erfindet
Sie erfinden	Sie erfinden
er/sie/es erfindet	sie erfinden

SIMPLE PAST

ich erfand	wir erfanden
du erfandst	ihr erfandet
Sie erfanden	Sie erfanden
er/sie/es erfand	sie erfanden

FUTURE

ich werde	wir werden	erfinden
du wirst	ihr werdet	
Sie werden	Sie werden	
er/sie/es wird	sie werden	

PRESENT SUBJUNCTIVE I

ich erfinde	wir erfinden
du erfindest	ihr erfindet
Sie erfinden	Sie erfinden
er/sie/es erfinde	sie erfinden

PRESENT SUBJUNCTIVE II

ich erfände	wir erfänden
du erfändest	ihr erfändet
Sie erfänden	Sie erfänden
er/sie/es erfände	sie erfänden

FUTURE SUBJUNCTIVE I

ich werde	wir werden	erfinden
du werdest	ihr werdet	
Sie werden	Sie werden	
er/sie/es werde	sie werden	

FUTURE SUBJUNCTIVE II

ich würde	wir würden	erfinden
du würdest	ihr würdet	
Sie würden	Sie würden	
er/sie/es würde	sie würden	

PRESENT PERFECT

ich habe	wir haben	erfunden
du hast	ihr habt	
Sie haben	Sie haben	
er/sie/es hat	sie haben	

PAST PERFECT

ich hatte	wir hatten	erfunden
du hattest	ihr hattet	
Sie hatten	Sie hatten	
er/sie/es hatte	sie hatten	

FUTURE PERFECT

ich werde	wir werden	erfunden haben
du wirst	ihr werdet	
Sie werden	Sie werden	
er/sie/es wird	sie werden	

PAST SUBJUNCTIVE I

ich habe	wir haben	erfunden
du habest	ihr habet	
Sie haben	Sie haben	
er/sie/es habe	sie haben	

PAST SUBJUNCTIVE II

ich hätte	wir hätten	erfunden
du hättest	ihr hättet	
Sie hätten	Sie hätten	
er/sie/es hätte	sie hätten	

FUTURE PERFECT SUBJUNCTIVE I

ich werde	wir werden	erfunden haben
du werdest	ihr werdet	
Sie werden	Sie werden	
er/sie/es werde	sie werden	

FUTURE PERFECT SUBJUNCTIVE II

ich würde	wir würden	erfunden haben
du würdest	ihr würdet	
Sie würden	Sie würden	
er/sie/es würde	sie würden	

COMMANDS erfinde! erfindet! erfinden Sie!

PRESENT PARTICIPLE erfindend

Usage

Der Mensch musste Sprache erfinden, weil er Mensch war, und er wurde Mensch, weil er Sprache erfunden hatte.	*Humans had to invent language because they were human, and they became human because they had invented language.*
Wer hat den Transistor erfunden?	*Who invented the transistor?*
Wo wurde das Mountainbike erfunden?	*Where was the mountain bike invented?*
Das Stereoskop wurde 1832 von Sir Charles Wheatstone erfunden.	*The stereoscope was invented in 1832 by Sir Charles Wheatstone.*
Wir wollen das Rad nicht neu erfinden. (*idiomatic*)	*We don't want to reinvent the wheel.*
Warum musst du immer solche unwahrscheinlichen Erklärungen erfinden?	*Why must you always contrive such improbable explanations?*
Manni erfand eine Ausrede.	*Manni made up an excuse.*
Diese Geschichte wurde frei erfunden.	*This story was completely fabricated.*
Er sagt, dass Serena die ganze Sache erfunden habe.	*He says that Serena fabricated the whole thing.*

RELATED VERBS *see* **finden** (186)

156 erfüllen *to fill; fulfill, perform*

erfüllt · erfüllte · erfüllt

regular weak verb

PRESENT

ich erfülle	wir erfüllen
du erfüllst	ihr erfüllt
Sie erfüllen	Sie erfüllen
er/sie/es erfüllt	sie erfüllen

SIMPLE PAST

ich erfüllte	wir erfüllten
du erfülltest	ihr erfülltet
Sie erfüllten	Sie erfüllten
er/sie/es erfüllte	sie erfüllten

FUTURE

ich werde	wir werden	erfüllen
du wirst	ihr werdet	
Sie werden	Sie werden	
er/sie/es wird	sie werden	

PRESENT SUBJUNCTIVE I

ich erfülle	wir erfüllen
du erfüllest	ihr erfüllet
Sie erfüllen	Sie erfüllen
er/sie/es erfülle	sie erfüllen

PRESENT SUBJUNCTIVE II

ich erfüllte	wir erfüllten
du erfülltest	ihr erfülltet
Sie erfüllten	Sie erfüllten
er/sie/es erfüllte	sie erfüllten

FUTURE SUBJUNCTIVE I

ich werde	wir werden	erfüllen
du werdest	ihr werdet	
Sie werden	Sie werden	
er/sie/es werde	sie werden	

FUTURE SUBJUNCTIVE II

ich würde	wir würden	erfüllen
du würdest	ihr würdet	
Sie würden	Sie würden	
er/sie/es würde	sie würden	

PRESENT PERFECT

ich habe	wir haben	erfüllt
du hast	ihr habt	
Sie haben	Sie haben	
er/sie/es hat	sie haben	

PAST PERFECT

ich hatte	wir hatten	erfüllt
du hattest	ihr hattet	
Sie hatten	Sie hatten	
er/sie/es hatte	sie hatten	

FUTURE PERFECT

ich werde	wir werden	erfüllt haben
du wirst	ihr werdet	
Sie werden	Sie werden	
er/sie/es wird	sie werden	

PAST SUBJUNCTIVE I

ich habe	wir haben	erfüllt
du habest	ihr habet	
Sie haben	Sie haben	
er/sie/es habe	sie haben	

PAST SUBJUNCTIVE II

ich hätte	wir hätten	erfüllt
du hättest	ihr hättet	
Sie hätten	Sie hätten	
er/sie/es hätte	sie hätten	

FUTURE PERFECT SUBJUNCTIVE I

ich werde	wir werden	erfüllt haben
du werdest	ihr werdet	
Sie werden	Sie werden	
er/sie/es werde	sie werden	

FUTURE PERFECT SUBJUNCTIVE II

ich würde	wir würden	erfüllt haben
du würdest	ihr würdet	
Sie würden	Sie würden	
er/sie/es würde	sie würden	

COMMANDS erfüll(e)! erfüllt! erfüllen Sie!

PRESENT PARTICIPLE erfüllend

Usage

Der Geruch frisch gebackenen Brotes erfüllte die Küche meiner Großmutter. — *The aroma of freshly baked bread filled my grandmother's kitchen.*

Seine Missetaten erfüllten uns mit Ekel. — *His crimes filled us with disgust.*

Die Digitalkamera hat meine Erwartungen erfüllt. — *The digital camera has fulfilled my expectations.*

Alle Quoten wurden im dritten Quartal erfüllt. — *All quotas were fulfilled in the third quarter.*

Sie müssen die folgenden Voraussetzungen erfüllen, um angenommen zu werden. — *You must fulfill the following prerequisites in order to be accepted.*

Der Soldat erfüllte seinen Schwur. — *The soldier carried out his oath.*

sich erfüllen *to become reality, come true*

Sein Traum einer Eigentumswohnung erfüllte sich dieses Jahr. — *His dream of owning a home became a reality this year.*

RELATED VERBS übererfüllen; *see also* **füllen** (201)

157 erhalten

to receive, obtain; save, preserve; keep, support

strong verb

erhält · erhielt · erhalten

PRESENT

ich erhalte	wir erhalten
du erhältst	ihr erhaltet
Sie erhalten	Sie erhalten
er/sie/es erhält	sie erhalten

SIMPLE PAST

ich erhielt	wir erhielten
du erhieltst	ihr erhieltet
Sie erhielten	Sie erhielten
er/sie/es erhielt	sie erhielten

FUTURE

ich werde	wir werden	erhalten
du wirst	ihr werdet	
Sie werden	Sie werden	
er/sie/es wird	sie werden	

PRESENT SUBJUNCTIVE I

ich erhalte	wir erhalten
du erhaltest	ihr erhaltet
Sie erhalten	Sie erhalten
er/sie/es erhalte	sie erhalten

PRESENT SUBJUNCTIVE II

ich erhielte	wir erhielten
du erhieltest	ihr erhieltet
Sie erhielten	Sie erhielten
er/sie/es erhielte	sie erhielten

FUTURE SUBJUNCTIVE I

ich werde	wir werden	erhalten
du werdest	ihr werdet	
Sie werden	Sie werden	
er/sie/es werde	sie werden	

FUTURE SUBJUNCTIVE II

ich würde	wir würden	erhalten
du würdest	ihr würdet	
Sie würden	Sie würden	
er/sie/es würde	sie würden	

PRESENT PERFECT

ich habe	wir haben	erhalten
du hast	ihr habt	
Sie haben	Sie haben	
er/sie/es hat	sie haben	

PAST PERFECT

ich hatte	wir hatten	erhalten
du hattest	ihr hattet	
Sie hatten	Sie hatten	
er/sie/es hatte	sie hatten	

FUTURE PERFECT

ich werde	wir werden	erhalten haben
du wirst	ihr werdet	
Sie werden	Sie werden	
er/sie/es wird	sie werden	

PAST SUBJUNCTIVE I

ich habe	wir haben	erhalten
du habest	ihr habet	
Sie haben	Sie haben	
er/sie/es habe	sie haben	

PAST SUBJUNCTIVE II

ich hätte	wir hätten	erhalten
du hättest	ihr hättet	
Sie hätten	Sie hätten	
er/sie/es hätte	sie hätten	

FUTURE PERFECT SUBJUNCTIVE I

ich werde	wir werden	erhalten haben
du werdest	ihr werdet	
Sie werden	Sie werden	
er/sie/es werde	sie werden	

FUTURE PERFECT SUBJUNCTIVE II

ich würde	wir würden	erhalten haben
du würdest	ihr würdet	
Sie würden	Sie würden	
er/sie/es würde	sie würden	

COMMANDS erhalte! erhaltet! erhalten Sie!

PRESENT PARTICIPLE erhaltend

Usage

Herders Schrift „Abhandlung über den Ursprung der Sprache“ erhielt einen Preis. — *Herder's manuscript "Treatise on the Origin of Language" received an award.*

Ich habe wertvolle Anregungen von den Kursteilnehmern erhalten. — *I received valuable suggestions from the course participants.*

Wir erhielten eine Genehmigung von den Soldaten, über die Grenze zu fahren. — *We obtained permission from the soldiers to drive across the border.*

Sarah hätte eine Arbeitserlaubnis erhalten können. — *Sarah could have obtained a work permit.*

Gott erhalte den König! (*formulaic*) — *God save the king!*

Die Dorfbewohner haben diese Tradition bis heute erhalten. — *The village inhabitants have preserved this tradition up to today.*

Kann Manfred eine Familie erhalten? — *Can Manfred support a family?*

Die Eigentümer wollten das alte Haus in gutem Zustand erhalten. — *The owners wanted to keep the old house in good condition.*

RELATED VERBS aufrecht·erhalten, wieder·erhalten, zurück·erhalten; *see also* **halten** (231)

158 erhöhen *to raise, increase; enhance*

erhöht · erhöhte · erhöht regular weak verb

PRESENT

ich erhöhe	wir erhöhen
du erhöhst	ihr erhöht
Sie erhöhen	Sie erhöhen
er/sie/es erhöht	sie erhöhen

SIMPLE PAST

ich erhöhte	wir erhöhten
du erhöhtest	ihr erhöhtet
Sie erhöhten	Sie erhöhten
er/sie/es erhöhte	sie erhöhten

FUTURE

ich werde	wir werden	erhöhen
du wirst	ihr werdet	
Sie werden	Sie werden	
er/sie/es wird	sie werden	

PRESENT SUBJUNCTIVE I

ich erhöhe	wir erhöhen
du erhöhest	ihr erhöhet
Sie erhöhen	Sie erhöhen
er/sie/es erhöhe	sie erhöhen

PRESENT SUBJUNCTIVE II

ich erhöhte	wir erhöhten
du erhöhtest	ihr erhöhtet
Sie erhöhten	Sie erhöhten
er/sie/es erhöhte	sie erhöhten

FUTURE SUBJUNCTIVE I

ich werde	wir werden	erhöhen
du werdest	ihr werdet	
Sie werden	Sie werden	
er/sie/es werde	sie werden	

FUTURE SUBJUNCTIVE II

ich würde	wir würden	erhöhen
du würdest	ihr würdet	
Sie würden	Sie würden	
er/sie/es würde	sie würden	

PRESENT PERFECT

ich habe	wir haben	erhöht
du hast	ihr habt	
Sie haben	Sie haben	
er/sie/es hat	sie haben	

PAST PERFECT

ich hatte	wir hatten	erhöht
du hattest	ihr hattet	
Sie hatten	Sie hatten	
er/sie/es hatte	sie hatten	

FUTURE PERFECT

ich werde	wir werden	erhöht haben
du wirst	ihr werdet	
Sie werden	Sie werden	
er/sie/es wird	sie werden	

PAST SUBJUNCTIVE I

ich habe	wir haben	erhöht
du habest	ihr habet	
Sie haben	Sie haben	
er/sie/es habe	sie haben	

PAST SUBJUNCTIVE II

ich hätte	wir hätten	erhöht
du hättest	ihr hättet	
Sie hätten	Sie hätten	
er/sie/es hätte	sie hätten	

FUTURE PERFECT SUBJUNCTIVE I

ich werde	wir werden	erhöht haben
du werdest	ihr werdet	
Sie werden	Sie werden	
er/sie/es werde	sie werden	

FUTURE PERFECT SUBJUNCTIVE II

ich würde	wir würden	erhöht haben
du würdest	ihr würdet	
Sie würden	Sie würden	
er/sie/es würde	sie würden	

COMMANDS erhöh(e)! erhöht! erhöhen Sie!

PRESENT PARTICIPLE erhöhend

Usage

Im Mittelalter wurde die römische Stadtmauer um 10 Zoll erhöht. — *In the Middle Ages, the Roman city wall was raised 10 inches.*

Zu viel Stress erhöht die Anfälligkeit für Entzündungen. — *Too much stress increases susceptibility to inflammation.*

Yoga erhöht das Wohlbefinden. — *Yoga increases one's sense of well-being.*

Die Qualität des Produkts soll wesentlich erhöht worden sein. — *The product's quality is supposed to have been significantly enhanced.*

Wie kann die Intensität des Erdbeeraromas künstlich erhöht werden? — *How can the intensity of strawberry flavor be artificially enhanced?*

sich erhöhen *to rise, increase*

Benzinpreise erhöhen sich. — *Gasoline prices are rising.*

Dadurch erhöht sich die Wahrscheinlichkeit, dass ein Spieler ausscheidet. — *The probability thereby increases that a player will be eliminated.*

RELATED VERB höhen

regular weak verb **erholt sich · erholte sich · sich erholt**

PRESENT

ich erhole mich	wir erholen uns
du erholst dich	ihr erholt euch
Sie erholen sich	Sie erholen sich
er/sie/es erholt sich	sie erholen sich

PRESENT PERFECT

ich habe mich	wir haben uns	erholt
du hast dich	ihr habt euch	
Sie haben sich	Sie haben sich	
er/sie/es hat sich	sie haben sich	

SIMPLE PAST

ich erholte mich	wir erholten uns
du erholtest dich	ihr erholtet euch
Sie erholten sich	Sie erholten sich
er/sie/es erholte sich	sie erholten sich

PAST PERFECT

ich hatte mich	wir hatten uns	erholt
du hattest dich	ihr hattet euch	
Sie hatten sich	Sie hatten sich	
er/sie/es hatte sich	sie hatten sich	

FUTURE

ich werde mich	wir werden uns	erholen
du wirst dich	ihr werdet euch	
Sie werden sich	Sie werden sich	
er/sie/es wird sich	sie werden sich	

FUTURE PERFECT

ich werde mich	wir werden uns	erholt haben
du wirst dich	ihr werdet euch	
Sie werden sich	Sie werden sich	
er/sie/es wird sich	sie werden sich	

PRESENT SUBJUNCTIVE I

ich erhole mich	wir erholen uns
du erholest dich	ihr erholet euch
Sie erholen sich	Sie erholen sich
er/sie/es erhole sich	sie erholen sich

PAST SUBJUNCTIVE I

ich habe mich	wir haben uns	erholt
du habest dich	ihr habet euch	
Sie haben sich	Sie haben sich	
er/sie/es habe sich	sie haben sich	

PRESENT SUBJUNCTIVE II

ich erholte mich	wir erholten uns
du erholtest dich	ihr erholtet euch
Sie erholten sich	Sie erholten sich
er/sie/es erholte sich	sie erholten sich

PAST SUBJUNCTIVE II

ich hätte mich	wir hätten uns	erholt
du hättest dich	ihr hättet euch	
Sie hätten sich	Sie hätten sich	
er/sie/es hätte sich	sie hätten sich	

FUTURE SUBJUNCTIVE I

ich werde mich	wir werden uns	erholen
du werdest dich	ihr werdet euch	
Sie werden sich	Sie werden sich	
er/sie/es werde sich	sie werden sich	

FUTURE PERFECT SUBJUNCTIVE I

ich werde mich	wir werden uns	erholt haben
du werdest dich	ihr werdet euch	
Sie werden sich	Sie werden sich	
er/sie/es werde sich	sie werden sich	

FUTURE SUBJUNCTIVE II

ich würde mich	wir würden uns	erholen
du würdest dich	ihr würdet euch	
Sie würden sich	Sie würden sich	
er/sie/es würde sich	sie würden sich	

FUTURE PERFECT SUBJUNCTIVE II

ich würde mich	wir würden uns	erholt haben
du würdest dich	ihr würdet euch	
Sie würden sich	Sie würden sich	
er/sie/es würde sich	sie würden sich	

COMMANDS erhol(e) dich! erholt euch! erholen Sie sich!

PRESENT PARTICIPLE sich erholend

Usage

Karl musste sich von einer schweren Krankheit erholen.	*Karl had to recover from a serious illness.*
Die Wirtschaft hat sich langsam erholt.	*The economy has slowly recovered.*
Die Börse wird sich von Verlusten erholen.	*The stock market will recover from its losses.*
Am Samstag erholt Elisabeth sich von der stressigen Woche mit Fitnesstraining und Yoga.	*On Saturday, Elisabeth recuperates from the stressful week with fitness training and yoga.*
Die Großmutter aß den Kuchen und trank den Wein und erholte sich wieder. (Grimm)	*Grandmother ate the cake and drank the wine and recuperated again.*
Wie erholst du dich in deiner Freizeit?	*How do you relax in your free time?*
Sie können sich bei uns auf dem Land erholen und die Natur genießen.	*You can relax with us in the country and enjoy nature.*
Wir haben uns auf einer ehemaligen Zuckerplantage auf Hawaii erholt.	*We relaxed at a former sugar plantation in Hawaii.*

RELATED VERBS *see* **holen** (247)

160 erinnern *to remind*

erinnert · erinnerte · erinnert — regular weak verb

PRESENT

ich erinnere	wir erinnern
du erinnerst	ihr erinnert
Sie erinnern	Sie erinnern
er/sie/es erinnert	sie erinnern

SIMPLE PAST

ich erinnerte	wir erinnerten
du erinnertest	ihr erinnertet
Sie erinnerten	Sie erinnerten
er/sie/es erinnerte	sie erinnerten

FUTURE

ich werde	wir werden	erinnern
du wirst	ihr werdet	
Sie werden	Sie werden	
er/sie/es wird	sie werden	

PRESENT SUBJUNCTIVE I

ich erinnere	wir erinnern
du erinnerst	ihr erinnert
Sie erinnern	Sie erinnern
er/sie/es erinnere	sie erinnern

PRESENT SUBJUNCTIVE II

ich erinnerte	wir erinnerten
du erinnertest	ihr erinnertet
Sie erinnerten	Sie erinnerten
er/sie/es erinnerte	sie erinnerten

FUTURE SUBJUNCTIVE I

ich werde	wir werden	erinnern
du werdest	ihr werdet	
Sie werden	Sie werden	
er/sie/es werde	sie werden	

FUTURE SUBJUNCTIVE II

ich würde	wir würden	erinnern
du würdest	ihr würdet	
Sie würden	Sie würden	
er/sie/es würde	sie würden	

PRESENT PERFECT

ich habe	wir haben	erinnert
du hast	ihr habt	
Sie haben	Sie haben	
er/sie/es hat	sie haben	

PAST PERFECT

ich hatte	wir hatten	erinnert
du hattest	ihr hattet	
Sie hatten	Sie hatten	
er/sie/es hatte	sie hatten	

FUTURE PERFECT

ich werde	wir werden	erinnert haben
du wirst	ihr werdet	
Sie werden	Sie werden	
er/sie/es wird	sie werden	

PAST SUBJUNCTIVE I

ich habe	wir haben	erinnert
du habest	ihr habet	
Sie haben	Sie haben	
er/sie/es habe	sie haben	

PAST SUBJUNCTIVE II

ich hätte	wir hätten	erinnert
du hättest	ihr hättet	
Sie hätten	Sie hätten	
er/sie/es hätte	sie hätten	

FUTURE PERFECT SUBJUNCTIVE I

ich werde	wir werden	erinnert haben
du werdest	ihr werdet	
Sie werden	Sie werden	
er/sie/es werde	sie werden	

FUTURE PERFECT SUBJUNCTIVE II

ich würde	wir würden	erinnert haben
du würdest	ihr würdet	
Sie würden	Sie würden	
er/sie/es würde	sie würden	

COMMANDS erinnere! erinnert! erinnern Sie!

PRESENT PARTICIPLE erinnernd

Usage

Du erinnerst mich an meine Mutter. — *You remind me of my mother.*
Bestimmte Orte erinnern Ruprecht an seine Kindheit. — *Certain places remind Ruprecht of his childhood.*
Ich will nicht daran erinnert werden. — *I don't want to be reminded of that.*
Die Gedächtniskirche erinnert an den Zweiten Krieg. — *The Memorial Church is a reminder of the Second World War.*

Herr Gimmler hat uns an den Termin erinnert. — *Mr. Gimmler reminded us of the appointment.*

sich erinnern *to remember*

Frau Küstermann erinnert sich an die Bombenangriffe. — *Mrs. Küstermann remembers the bombing attacks.*
Ich kann mich an meine Schulzeit erinnern. — *I can remember my school days.*
Meine Großtante erinnerte sich an den Ersten Weltkrieg. — *My great aunt remembered the First World War.*
Soweit ich mich erinnern kann, war der Blumenladen an dieser Ecke. — *As far as I remember, the florist was on this corner.*

RELATED VERB zurück·erinnern

regular weak verb **erkältet · erkältete · erkältet**

PRESENT

ich erkälte	wir erkälten
du erkältest	ihr erkältet
Sie erkälten	Sie erkälten
er/sie/es erkältet	sie erkälten

SIMPLE PAST

ich erkältete	wir erkälteten
du erkältetest	ihr erkältetet
Sie erkälteten	Sie erkälteten
er/sie/es erkältete	sie erkälteten

FUTURE

ich werde	wir werden	erkälten
du wirst	ihr werdet	
Sie werden	Sie werden	
er/sie/es wird	sie werden	

PRESENT SUBJUNCTIVE I

ich erkälte	wir erkälten
du erkältest	ihr erkältet
Sie erkälten	Sie erkälten
er/sie/es erkälte	sie erkälten

PRESENT SUBJUNCTIVE II

ich erkältete	wir erkälteten
du erkältetest	ihr erkältetet
Sie erkälteten	Sie erkälteten
er/sie/es erkältete	sie erkälteten

FUTURE SUBJUNCTIVE I

ich werde	wir werden	erkälten
du werdest	ihr werdet	
Sie werden	Sie werden	
er/sie/es werde	sie werden	

FUTURE SUBJUNCTIVE II

ich würde	wir würden	erkälten
du würdest	ihr würdet	
Sie würden	Sie würden	
er/sie/es würde	sie würden	

PRESENT PERFECT

ich habe	wir haben	erkältet
du hast	ihr habt	
Sie haben	Sie haben	
er/sie/es hat	sie haben	

PAST PERFECT

ich hatte	wir hatten	erkältet
du hattest	ihr hattet	
Sie hatten	Sie hatten	
er/sie/es hatte	sie hatten	

FUTURE PERFECT

ich werde	wir werden	erkältet haben
du wirst	ihr werdet	
Sie werden	Sie werden	
er/sie/es wird	sie werden	

PAST SUBJUNCTIVE I

ich habe	wir haben	erkältet
du habest	ihr habet	
Sie haben	Sie haben	
er/sie/es habe	sie haben	

PAST SUBJUNCTIVE II

ich hätte	wir hätten	erkältet
du hättest	ihr hättet	
Sie hätten	Sie hätten	
er/sie/es hätte	sie hätten	

FUTURE PERFECT SUBJUNCTIVE I

ich werde	wir werden	erkältet haben
du werdest	ihr werdet	
Sie werden	Sie werden	
er/sie/es werde	sie werden	

FUTURE PERFECT SUBJUNCTIVE II

ich würde	wir würden	erkältet haben
du würdest	ihr würdet	
Sie würden	Sie würden	
er/sie/es würde	sie würden	

COMMANDS erkälte! erkältet! erkälten Sie!

PRESENT PARTICIPLE erkältend

Usage

Das Eiswasser hat ihm den Magen erkältet. — *The ice water chilled his stomach.*

sich erkälten *to catch (a) cold*

Ich habe mich während der Reise erkältet. — *I caught a cold during the trip.*
Pass auf, dass du dich nicht erkältest. — *Be careful that you don't catch cold.*
Kinder erkälten sich häufiger als Erwachsene. — *Children catch cold more frequently than adults.*
Amalie hat sich stark erkältet. — *Amalie has caught a severe cold.*

„Wie oft erkältest du dich?" — *"How often do you catch cold?"*
„Ich erkälte mich zweimal im Jahr." — *"I catch cold twice a year."*

Wenn ihr euch erkältet habt, solltet ihr vielleicht zu Hause bleiben. — *If you have caught cold, perhaps you should stay at home.*
Alle meine Kolleginnen und Kollegen haben sich erkältet! — *All my coworkers have a cold!*

RELATED VERB kälten

162 erkennen *to perceive, recognize, identify; be cognizant of; impose sentence*

erkennt · erkannte · erkannt mixed verb

PRESENT

ich erkenne	wir erkennen
du erkennst	ihr erkennt
Sie erkennen	Sie erkennen
er/sie/es erkennt	sie erkennen

SIMPLE PAST

ich erkannte	wir erkannten
du erkanntest	ihr erkanntet
Sie erkannten	Sie erkannten
er/sie/es erkannte	sie erkannten

FUTURE

ich werde	wir werden	erkennen
du wirst	ihr werdet	
Sie werden	Sie werden	
er/sie/es wird	sie werden	

PRESENT SUBJUNCTIVE I

ich erkenne	wir erkennen
du erkennest	ihr erkennet
Sie erkennen	Sie erkennen
er/sie/es erkenne	sie erkennen

PRESENT SUBJUNCTIVE II

ich erkennte	wir erkennten
du erkenntest	ihr erkenntet
Sie erkennten	Sie erkennten
er/sie/es erkennte	sie erkennten

FUTURE SUBJUNCTIVE I

ich werde	wir werden	erkennen
du werdest	ihr werdet	
Sie werden	Sie werden	
er/sie/es werde	sie werden	

FUTURE SUBJUNCTIVE II

ich würde	wir würden	erkennen
du würdest	ihr würdet	
Sie würden	Sie würden	
er/sie/es würde	sie würden	

PRESENT PERFECT

ich habe	wir haben	erkannt
du hast	ihr habt	
Sie haben	Sie haben	
er/sie/es hat	sie haben	

PAST PERFECT

ich hatte	wir hatten	erkannt
du hattest	ihr hattet	
Sie hatten	Sie hatten	
er/sie/es hatte	sie hatten	

FUTURE PERFECT

ich werde	wir werden	erkannt haben
du wirst	ihr werdet	
Sie werden	Sie werden	
er/sie/es wird	sie werden	

PAST SUBJUNCTIVE I

ich habe	wir haben	erkannt
du habest	ihr habet	
Sie haben	Sie haben	
er/sie/es habe	sie haben	

PAST SUBJUNCTIVE II

ich hätte	wir hätten	erkannt
du hättest	ihr hättet	
Sie hätten	Sie hätten	
er/sie/es hätte	sie hätten	

FUTURE PERFECT SUBJUNCTIVE I

ich werde	wir werden	erkannt haben
du werdest	ihr werdet	
Sie werden	Sie werden	
er/sie/es werde	sie werden	

FUTURE PERFECT SUBJUNCTIVE II

ich würde	wir würden	erkannt haben
du würdest	ihr würdet	
Sie würden	Sie würden	
er/sie/es würde	sie würden	

COMMANDS erkenn(e)! erkennt! erkennen Sie!

PRESENT PARTICIPLE erkennend

Usage

In diesem Augenblick des Zweifelns erkennt Kai die richtige Entscheidung.	*In this moment of doubt, Kai perceives the correct decision.*
„Erkennst du mich nicht?"	*"Don't you recognize me?"*
„Nein, ich erkenne dich nicht."	*"No, I don't recognize you."*
Es fällt mir nicht schwer zu erkennen, ob jemand lügt.	*It's not difficult for me to recognize whether someone is lying.*
Ich konnte das Dorf nicht erkennen.	*I was unable to recognize the village.*
Gregor hat Steve an seinem Lachen erkannt.	*Gregor recognized Steve by his laugh.*
Der Philosoph hat in dieser Erklärung die Besonderheiten des anaphorischen Bezugs erkannt.	*In this explanation, the philosopher has identified the peculiarities of anaphoric reference.*
Der Junge erkennt seine eigenen Fehler nicht.	*The boy is not cognizant of his own faults.*
Das Gericht kann nur auf Geldstrafe erkennen.	*The court can only impose a sentence of a monetary fine.*

RELATED VERBS ab·erkennen, an·erkennen, wieder·erkennen, zu·erkennen; *see also* **kennen** (256)

regular weak verb **erklärt · erklärte · erklärt**

PRESENT

ich erkläre	wir erklären
du erklärst	ihr erklärt
Sie erklären	Sie erklären
er/sie/es erklärt	sie erklären

SIMPLE PAST

ich erklärte	wir erklärten
du erklärtest	ihr erklärtet
Sie erklärten	Sie erklärten
er/sie/es erklärte	sie erklärten

FUTURE

ich werde	wir werden	erklären
du wirst	ihr werdet	
Sie werden	Sie werden	
er/sie/es wird	sie werden	

PRESENT SUBJUNCTIVE I

ich erkläre	wir erklären
du erklärest	ihr erkläret
Sie erklären	Sie erklären
er/sie/es erkläre	sie erklären

PRESENT SUBJUNCTIVE II

ich erklärte	wir erklärten
du erklärtest	ihr erklärtet
Sie erklärten	Sie erklärten
er/sie/es erklärte	sie erklärten

FUTURE SUBJUNCTIVE I

ich werde	wir werden	erklären
du werdest	ihr werdet	
Sie werden	Sie werden	
er/sie/es werde	sie werden	

FUTURE SUBJUNCTIVE II

ich würde	wir würden	erklären
du würdest	ihr würdet	
Sie würden	Sie würden	
er/sie/es würde	sie würden	

PRESENT PERFECT

ich habe	wir haben	erklärt
du hast	ihr habt	
Sie haben	Sie haben	
er/sie/es hat	sie haben	

PAST PERFECT

ich hatte	wir hatten	erklärt
du hattest	ihr hattet	
Sie hatten	Sie hatten	
er/sie/es hatte	sie hatten	

FUTURE PERFECT

ich werde	wir werden	erklärt haben
du wirst	ihr werdet	
Sie werden	Sie werden	
er/sie/es wird	sie werden	

PAST SUBJUNCTIVE I

ich habe	wir haben	erklärt
du habest	ihr habet	
Sie haben	Sie haben	
er/sie/es habe	sie haben	

PAST SUBJUNCTIVE II

ich hätte	wir hätten	erklärt
du hättest	ihr hättet	
Sie hätten	Sie hätten	
er/sie/es hätte	sie hätten	

FUTURE PERFECT SUBJUNCTIVE I

ich werde	wir werden	erklärt haben
du werdest	ihr werdet	
Sie werden	Sie werden	
er/sie/es werde	sie werden	

FUTURE PERFECT SUBJUNCTIVE II

ich würde	wir würden	erklärt haben
du würdest	ihr würdet	
Sie würden	Sie würden	
er/sie/es würde	sie würden	

COMMANDS erklär(e)! erklärt! erklären Sie!

PRESENT PARTICIPLE erklärend

Usage

Erklär mir bitte mal, was das bedeutet.	*Please explain to me what that means.*
Der Wissenschaftler versucht, gegensätzliche Phänomene anhand einer einzigen Regel zu erklären.	*The scientist is trying to explain conflicting phenomena using a single rule.*
Würden Sie das Bild bitte erklären?	*Would you please comment on the picture?*
Wie erklärt ihr das?	*How do you explain that?*
Sein Benehmen muss auch moralisch erklärt werden.	*His behavior must also be explained in moral terms.*
Du brauchst mir nicht zu erklären, was der Trend gerade ist.	*You don't have to explain to me what the current trend is.*
Später erklärte er, dass er keinen Fehler gemacht habe.	*He later declared that he hadn't made a mistake.*
Die Orthodoxie des 19. Jahrhunderts erklärte einen göttlichen Unterricht als Ursprung der menschlichen Sprache.	*Nineteenth-century orthodoxy proclaimed divine instruction as the origin of human language.*
Ernst erklärte sich bereit, das Projekt zu leiten.	*Ernst declared himself ready to lead the project.*

RELATED VERB klären

164 erlauben *to allow, permit*

erlaubt · erlaubte · erlaubt

regular weak verb

PRESENT

ich erlaube	wir erlauben
du erlaubst	ihr erlaubt
Sie erlauben	Sie erlauben
er/sie/es erlaubt	sie erlauben

SIMPLE PAST

ich erlaubte	wir erlaubten
du erlaubtest	ihr erlaubtet
Sie erlaubten	Sie erlaubten
er/sie/es erlaubte	sie erlaubten

FUTURE

ich werde	wir werden	erlauben
du wirst	ihr werdet	
Sie werden	Sie werden	
er/sie/es wird	sie werden	

PRESENT SUBJUNCTIVE I

ich erlaube	wir erlauben
du erlaubest	ihr erlaubet
Sie erlauben	Sie erlauben
er/sie/es erlaube	sie erlauben

PRESENT SUBJUNCTIVE II

ich erlaubte	wir erlaubten
du erlaubtest	ihr erlaubtet
Sie erlaubten	Sie erlaubten
er/sie/es erlaubte	sie erlaubten

FUTURE SUBJUNCTIVE I

ich werde	wir werden	erlauben
du werdest	ihr werdet	
Sie werden	Sie werden	
er/sie/es werde	sie werden	

FUTURE SUBJUNCTIVE II

ich würde	wir würden	erlauben
du würdest	ihr würdet	
Sie würden	Sie würden	
er/sie/es würde	sie würden	

PRESENT PERFECT

ich habe	wir haben	erlaubt
du hast	ihr habt	
Sie haben	Sie haben	
er/sie/es hat	sie haben	

PAST PERFECT

ich hatte	wir hatten	erlaubt
du hattest	ihr hattet	
Sie hatten	Sie hatten	
er/sie/es hatte	sie hatten	

FUTURE PERFECT

ich werde	wir werden	erlaubt haben
du wirst	ihr werdet	
Sie werden	Sie werden	
er/sie/es wird	sie werden	

PAST SUBJUNCTIVE I

ich habe	wir haben	erlaubt
du habest	ihr habet	
Sie haben	Sie haben	
er/sie/es habe	sie haben	

PAST SUBJUNCTIVE II

ich hätte	wir hätten	erlaubt
du hättest	ihr hättet	
Sie hätten	Sie hätten	
er/sie/es hätte	sie hätten	

FUTURE PERFECT SUBJUNCTIVE I

ich werde	wir werden	erlaubt haben
du werdest	ihr werdet	
Sie werden	Sie werden	
er/sie/es werde	sie werden	

FUTURE PERFECT SUBJUNCTIVE II

ich würde	wir würden	erlaubt haben
du würdest	ihr würdet	
Sie würden	Sie würden	
er/sie/es würde	sie würden	

COMMANDS erlaub(e)! erlaubt! erlauben Sie!

PRESENT PARTICIPLE erlaubend

Usage

Dem Leser wird nicht erlaubt, mehr über den Protagonisten zu erfahren. — *The reader is not permitted to learn more about the protagonist.*

Erlauben Sie mir bitte eine Bemerkung. — *Please allow me a comment.*

Ihr Vertrag erlaubt maximal 1 000 Emails pro Tag. — *Your contract permits a maximum of 1,000 e-mails per day.*

Das ist absolut nicht erlaubt! — *That is absolutely not allowed!*

Eine neue Theorie erlaubt eine exaktere Deutung der Situation. — *A new theory allows a more exact interpretation of the situation.*

Das Parken ist vor dem Laden nicht erlaubt. — *Parking is not permitted in front of the shop.*

sich erlauben *to allow oneself, indulge in*

Opa Friedrichsen erlaubte sich selten ein Glas Wein oder Bier. — *Grandpa Friedrichsen seldom allowed himself a glass of wine or beer.*

Ich erlaube mir ab und zu ein Stück New Yorker Käsekuchen. — *I indulge in a slice of New York cheesecake now and then.*

regular weak verb **erlebt · erlebte · erlebt**

PRESENT

ich erlebe	wir erleben
du erlebst	ihr erlebt
Sie erleben	Sie erleben
er/sie/es erlebt	sie erleben

SIMPLE PAST

ich erlebte	wir erlebten
du erlebtest	ihr erlebtet
Sie erlebten	Sie erlebten
er/sie/es erlebte	sie erlebten

FUTURE

ich werde	wir werden	erleben
du wirst	ihr werdet	
Sie werden	Sie werden	
er/sie/es wird	sie werden	

PRESENT SUBJUNCTIVE I

ich erlebe	wir erleben
du erlebest	ihr erlebet
Sie erleben	Sie erleben
er/sie/es erlebe	sie erleben

PRESENT SUBJUNCTIVE II

ich erlebte	wir erlebten
du erlebtest	ihr erlebtet
Sie erlebten	Sie erlebten
er/sie/es erlebte	sie erlebten

FUTURE SUBJUNCTIVE I

ich werde	wir werden	erleben
du werdest	ihr werdet	
Sie werden	Sie werden	
er/sie/es werde	sie werden	

FUTURE SUBJUNCTIVE II

ich würde	wir würden	erleben
du würdest	ihr würdet	
Sie würden	Sie würden	
er/sie/es würde	sie würden	

PRESENT PERFECT

ich habe	wir haben	erlebt
du hast	ihr habt	
Sie haben	Sie haben	
er/sie/es hat	sie haben	

PAST PERFECT

ich hatte	wir hatten	erlebt
du hattest	ihr hattet	
Sie hatten	Sie hatten	
er/sie/es hatte	sie hatten	

FUTURE PERFECT

ich werde	wir werden	erlebt haben
du wirst	ihr werdet	
Sie werden	Sie werden	
er/sie/es wird	sie werden	

PAST SUBJUNCTIVE I

ich habe	wir haben	erlebt
du habest	ihr habet	
Sie haben	Sie haben	
er/sie/es habe	sie haben	

PAST SUBJUNCTIVE II

ich hätte	wir hätten	erlebt
du hättest	ihr hättet	
Sie hätten	Sie hätten	
er/sie/es hätte	sie hätten	

FUTURE PERFECT SUBJUNCTIVE I

ich werde	wir werden	erlebt haben
du werdest	ihr werdet	
Sie werden	Sie werden	
er/sie/es werde	sie werden	

FUTURE PERFECT SUBJUNCTIVE II

ich würde	wir würden	erlebt haben
du würdest	ihr würdet	
Sie würden	Sie würden	
er/sie/es würde	sie würden	

COMMANDS erleb(e)! erlebt! erleben Sie!

PRESENT PARTICIPLE erlebend

Usage

Nach dem Deutsch-Französischen Krieg (1870–71) erlebte Deutschland einen ökonomischen Aufschwung. — *After the Franco-Prussian War (1870–71), Germany experienced an economic upswing.*

Manfred erlebt jeden Tag neue Abenteuer. — *Manfred experiences new adventures every day.*

In den Nationalparks kann man die Wunder der Natur aus erster Hand erleben. — *In the national parks, you can experience the wonders of nature firsthand.*

Im Krieg erlebt der Mensch unmenschliche Dinge. — *In war, a human experiences inhuman things.*

Mein Großvater hat den Zweiten Weltkrieg erlebt. — *My grandfather lived through the Second World War.*

Die Familie hofft, eines Tages den Frieden zu erleben. — *The family hopes to live to see peace some day.*

He, Finger weg von der Schokolade, sonst kannst du was erleben! (*colloquial idiomatic*) — *Hey, keep your hands off the chocolate or you're gonna get it!*

sich erleben *to perceive/see oneself*

Opfer erleben sich oft als unmächtig. — *Victims often perceive themselves as powerless.*

RELATED VERBS mit·erleben; nach·erleben; *see also* **leben** (282)

166 erledigen *to deal with, attend to, set right, handle, settle, complete, do*

erledigt · erledigte · erledigt regular weak verb

PRESENT

ich erledige	wir erledigen
du erledigst	ihr erledigt
Sie erledigen	Sie erledigen
er/sie/es erledigt	sie erledigen

SIMPLE PAST

ich erledigte	wir erledigten
du erledigtest	ihr erledigtet
Sie erledigten	Sie erledigten
er/sie/es erledigte	sie erledigten

FUTURE

ich werde	wir werden	erledigen
du wirst	ihr werdet	
Sie werden	Sie werden	
er/sie/es wird	sie werden	

PRESENT SUBJUNCTIVE I

ich erledige	wir erledigen
du erledigest	ihr erlediget
Sie erledigen	Sie erledigen
er/sie/es erledige	sie erledigen

PRESENT SUBJUNCTIVE II

ich erledigte	wir erledigten
du erledigtest	ihr erledigtet
Sie erledigten	Sie erledigten
er/sie/es erledigte	sie erledigten

FUTURE SUBJUNCTIVE I

ich werde	wir werden	erledigen
du werdest	ihr werdet	
Sie werden	Sie werden	
er/sie/es werde	sie werden	

FUTURE SUBJUNCTIVE II

ich würde	wir würden	erledigen
du würdest	ihr würdet	
Sie würden	Sie würden	
er/sie/es würde	sie würden	

PRESENT PERFECT

ich habe	wir haben	erledigt
du hast	ihr habt	
Sie haben	Sie haben	
er/sie/es hat	sie haben	

PAST PERFECT

ich hatte	wir hatten	erledigt
du hattest	ihr hattet	
Sie hatten	Sie hatten	
er/sie/es hatte	sie hatten	

FUTURE PERFECT

ich werde	wir werden	erledigt haben
du wirst	ihr werdet	
Sie werden	Sie werden	
er/sie/es wird	sie werden	

PAST SUBJUNCTIVE I

ich habe	wir haben	erledigt
du habest	ihr habet	
Sie haben	Sie haben	
er/sie/es habe	sie haben	

PAST SUBJUNCTIVE II

ich hätte	wir hätten	erledigt
du hättest	ihr hättet	
Sie hätten	Sie hätten	
er/sie/es hätte	sie hätten	

FUTURE PERFECT SUBJUNCTIVE I

ich werde	wir werden	erledigt haben
du werdest	ihr werdet	
Sie werden	Sie werden	
er/sie/es werde	sie werden	

FUTURE PERFECT SUBJUNCTIVE II

ich würde	wir würden	erledigt haben
du würdest	ihr würdet	
Sie würden	Sie würden	
er/sie/es würde	sie würden	

COMMANDS erledig(e)! erledigt! erledigen Sie!

PRESENT PARTICIPLE erledigend

Usage

Erstmal sind einige Formalitäten zu erledigen.	*First there are some formalities to deal with.*
Maria hat noch einiges im Büro erledigt, dann ist sie nach Hause gekommen.	*Maria attended to a few more things at the office, then she came home.*
Was kann man alles per Email erledigen?	*What all can you get done via e-mail?*
Wir wollten die Sache ein für alle mal erledigen.	*We wanted to settle the matter once and for all.*
Insgesamt müssen fünf Aufgaben erledigt werden.	*Five tasks must be completed in all.*
Die Touristen erledigten ein paar Visaformalitäten in der Botschaft.	*The tourists took care of a few visa formalities at the embassy.*
Müssen die Schüler viele Hausaufgaben erledigen?	*Do the pupils have to do a lot of homework?*
Ich erledige ein paar Einkäufe heute Nachmittag.	*I'm doing some shopping this afternoon.*
Wann erledigst du das?	*When will you take care of that?*

sich erledigen *to settle itself, resolve itself*

Das Problem wird sich von selbst erledigen.	*The problem will resolve itself.*

strong verb **erlischt · erlosch · erloschen**

PRESENT

ich erlösche	wir erlöschen
du erlischst	ihr erlöscht
Sie erlöschen	Sie erlöschen
er/sie/es erlischt	sie erlöschen

SIMPLE PAST

ich erlosch	wir erloschen
du erloschst	ihr erloscht
Sie erloschen	Sie erloschen
er/sie/es erlosch	sie erloschen

FUTURE

ich werde	wir werden	erlöschen
du wirst	ihr werdet	
Sie werden	Sie werden	
er/sie/es wird	sie werden	

PRESENT SUBJUNCTIVE I

ich erlösche	wir erlöschen
du erlöschest	ihr erlöschet
Sie erlöschen	Sie erlöschen
er/sie/es erlösche	sie erlöschen

PRESENT SUBJUNCTIVE II

ich erlösche	wir erlöschen
du erlöschest	ihr erlöschet
Sie erlöschen	Sie erlöschen
er/sie/es erlösche	sie erlöschen

FUTURE SUBJUNCTIVE I

ich werde	wir werden	erlöschen
du werdest	ihr werdet	
Sie werden	Sie werden	
er/sie/es werde	sie werden	

FUTURE SUBJUNCTIVE II

ich würde	wir würden	erlöschen
du würdest	ihr würdet	
Sie würden	Sie würden	
er/sie/es würde	sie würden	

PRESENT PERFECT

ich bin	wir sind	erloschen
du bist	ihr seid	
Sie sind	Sie sind	
er/sie/es ist	sie sind	

PAST PERFECT

ich war	wir waren	erloschen
du warst	ihr wart	
Sie waren	Sie waren	
er/sie/es war	sie waren	

FUTURE PERFECT

ich werde	wir werden	erloschen sein
du wirst	ihr werdet	
Sie werden	Sie werden	
er/sie/es wird	sie werden	

PAST SUBJUNCTIVE I

ich sei	wir seien	erloschen
du seiest	ihr seiet	
Sie seien	Sie seien	
er/sie/es sei	sie seien	

PAST SUBJUNCTIVE II

ich wäre	wir wären	erloschen
du wärest	ihr wäret	
Sie wären	Sie wären	
er/sie/es wäre	sie wären	

FUTURE PERFECT SUBJUNCTIVE I

ich werde	wir werden	erloschen sein
du werdest	ihr werdet	
Sie werden	Sie werden	
er/sie/es werde	sie werden	

FUTURE PERFECT SUBJUNCTIVE II

ich würde	wir würden	erloschen sein
du würdest	ihr würdet	
Sie würden	Sie würden	
er/sie/es würde	sie würden	

COMMANDS erlisch! erlöscht! erlöschen Sie!

PRESENT PARTICIPLE erlöschend

Usage

Liesl zündete eine Kerze an, aber die schwache Flamme erlosch sofort. — *Liesl lit a candle, but the weak flame went out immediately.*

Meine Leidenschaft für Science-Fiction ist schon lange erloschen. — *My passion for science fiction has long since died out.*

Das adlige Geschlecht Billerbeck in Brandenburg ist vor langer Zeit erloschen. — *The aristocratic house of Billerbeck in Brandenburg died out a long time ago.*

Das Rückgaberecht erlischt bei Öffnung der Verpackung. — *The right to return is invalidated by opening the package.*

Die Zimmerreservierung erlischt nach drei Tagen automatisch, wenn Zahlung nicht empfangen wird. — *The room reservation automatically expires after three days if payment is not received.*

Sein Anspruch auf Arbeitslosengeld erlischt nächsten Monat. — *His entitlement to unemployment compensation lapses next month.*

RELATED VERBS *see* **löschen** (297)

168 **eröffnen** *to open, start; unseal; inaugurate; reveal, disclose*

eröffnet · eröffnete · eröffnet regular weak verb

PRESENT

ich eröffne	wir eröffnen
du eröffnest	ihr eröffnet
Sie eröffnen	Sie eröffnen
er/sie/es eröffnet	sie eröffnen

SIMPLE PAST

ich eröffnete	wir eröffneten
du eröffnetest	ihr eröffnetet
Sie eröffneten	Sie eröffneten
er/sie/es eröffnete	sie eröffneten

FUTURE

ich werde	wir werden	eröffnen
du wirst	ihr werdet	
Sie werden	Sie werden	
er/sie/es wird	sie werden	

PRESENT SUBJUNCTIVE I

ich eröffne	wir eröffnen
du eröffnest	ihr eröffnet
Sie eröffnen	Sie eröffnen
er/sie/es eröffne	sie eröffnen

PRESENT SUBJUNCTIVE II

ich eröffnete	wir eröffneten
du eröffnetest	ihr eröffnetet
Sie eröffneten	Sie eröffneten
er/sie/es eröffnete	sie eröffneten

FUTURE SUBJUNCTIVE I

ich werde	wir werden	eröffnen
du werdest	ihr werdet	
Sie werden	Sie werden	
er/sie/es werde	sie werden	

FUTURE SUBJUNCTIVE II

ich würde	wir würden	eröffnen
du würdest	ihr würdet	
Sie würden	Sie würden	
er/sie/es würde	sie würden	

PRESENT PERFECT

ich habe	wir haben	eröffnet
du hast	ihr habt	
Sie haben	Sie haben	
er/sie/es hat	sie haben	

PAST PERFECT

ich hatte	wir hatten	eröffnet
du hattest	ihr hattet	
Sie hatten	Sie hatten	
er/sie/es hatte	sie hatten	

FUTURE PERFECT

ich werde	wir werden	eröffnet haben
du wirst	ihr werdet	
Sie werden	Sie werden	
er/sie/es wird	sie werden	

PAST SUBJUNCTIVE I

ich habe	wir haben	eröffnet
du habest	ihr habet	
Sie haben	Sie haben	
er/sie/es habe	sie haben	

PAST SUBJUNCTIVE II

ich hätte	wir hätten	eröffnet
du hättest	ihr hättet	
Sie hätten	Sie hätten	
er/sie/es hätte	sie hätten	

FUTURE PERFECT SUBJUNCTIVE I

ich werde	wir werden	eröffnet haben
du werdest	ihr werdet	
Sie werden	Sie werden	
er/sie/es werde	sie werden	

FUTURE PERFECT SUBJUNCTIVE II

ich würde	wir würden	eröffnet haben
du würdest	ihr würdet	
Sie würden	Sie würden	
er/sie/es würde	sie würden	

COMMANDS eröffne! eröffnet! eröffnen Sie!

PRESENT PARTICIPLE eröffnend

Usage

Ein kleiner Blumenladen wird nächste Woche in der Hauptstraße eröffnet.
A small flower shop is being opened on Main Street next week.

Der archäologische Befund eröffnet völlig neue Forschungsmöglichkeiten.
The archeological find opens up completely new research opportunities.

Unsere Mannschaft eröffnete das Spiel mit einer starken Offensive.
Our team started the game with a strong offense.

Die Orchestersaison wurde mit einer Fete vor dem Rathaus eröffnet.
The orchestra season was inaugurated with a party in front of city hall.

Jürg hat mir neulich eröffnet, dass er homosexuell ist.
Jürg recently disclosed to me that he is homosexual.

sich eröffnen *to present/open oneself*

Nachdem ich das Buch gelesen hatte, eröffnete sich mir eine alternative Denkweise.
After I'd read the book, an alternate way of thinking presented itself to me.

RELATED VERBS wieder·eröffnen; *see also* **öffnen** (317)

regular weak verb **erreicht · erreichte · erreicht**

PRESENT

ich erreiche	wir erreichen
du erreichst	ihr erreicht
Sie erreichen	Sie erreichen
er/sie/es erreicht	sie erreichen

SIMPLE PAST

ich erreichte	wir erreichten
du erreichtest	ihr erreichtet
Sie erreichten	Sie erreichten
er/sie/es erreichte	sie erreichten

FUTURE

ich werde	wir werden	erreichen
du wirst	ihr werdet	
Sie werden	Sie werden	
er/sie/es wird	sie werden	

PRESENT SUBJUNCTIVE I

ich erreiche	wir erreichen
du erreichest	ihr erreichet
Sie erreichen	Sie erreichen
er/sie/es erreiche	sie erreichen

PRESENT SUBJUNCTIVE II

ich erreichte	wir erreichten
du erreichtest	ihr erreichtet
Sie erreichten	Sie erreichten
er/sie/es erreichte	sie erreichten

FUTURE SUBJUNCTIVE I

ich werde	wir werden	erreichen
du werdest	ihr werdet	
Sie werden	Sie werden	
er/sie/es werde	sie werden	

FUTURE SUBJUNCTIVE II

ich würde	wir würden	erreichen
du würdest	ihr würdet	
Sie würden	Sie würden	
er/sie/es würde	sie würden	

PRESENT PERFECT

ich habe	wir haben	erreicht
du hast	ihr habt	
Sie haben	Sie haben	
er/sie/es hat	sie haben	

PAST PERFECT

ich hatte	wir hatten	erreicht
du hattest	ihr hattet	
Sie hatten	Sie hatten	
er/sie/es hatte	sie hatten	

FUTURE PERFECT

ich werde	wir werden	erreicht haben
du wirst	ihr werdet	
Sie werden	Sie werden	
er/sie/es wird	sie werden	

PAST SUBJUNCTIVE I

ich habe	wir haben	erreicht
du habest	ihr habet	
Sie haben	Sie haben	
er/sie/es habe	sie haben	

PAST SUBJUNCTIVE II

ich hätte	wir hätten	erreicht
du hättest	ihr hättet	
Sie hätten	Sie hätten	
er/sie/es hätte	sie hätten	

FUTURE PERFECT SUBJUNCTIVE I

ich werde	wir werden	erreicht haben
du werdest	ihr werdet	
Sie werden	Sie werden	
er/sie/es werde	sie werden	

FUTURE PERFECT SUBJUNCTIVE II

ich würde	wir würden	erreicht haben
du würdest	ihr würdet	
Sie würden	Sie würden	
er/sie/es würde	sie würden	

COMMANDS erreich(e)! erreicht! erreichen Sie!

PRESENT PARTICIPLE erreichend

Usage

Ich konnte dich nicht erreichen. — *I was unable to reach you.*

Tante Thusnelde hatte ihr achtes Lebensjahr gerade erreicht, als das 20. Jahrhundert begann. — *Aunt Thusnelde had just turned eight years old when the twentieth century began.*

Sie können mich unter der Telefonnummer 12345 erreichen. — *You can reach me on the telephone at 12345.*

Mit diesem Schritt werde ich meine Ziele erreicht haben. — *With this step, I will have finally achieved my aims.*

Ein Trancezustand lässt sich durch Hypnose erreichen. — *A state of trance can be achieved through hypnosis.*

Wie kann man ein gesundes Körpergewicht erreichen? — *How can you attain a healthy body weight?*

Meine Damen und Herren, in wenigen Minuten erreichen wir Hildesheim. — *Ladies and gentlemen, in a few minutes we will reach Hildesheim.*

Herr Schiller erreichte sein Büro um neun Uhr. — *Mr. Schiller arrived at his office at nine o'clock.*

Habt ihr das Denkmal am Ende des Pfades erreicht? — *Did you get to the memorial at the end of the path?*

RELATED VERBS *see* **reichen** (338)

170 erscheinen *to appear; be published, come out; seem*

erscheint · erschien · erschienen strong verb

PRESENT		PRESENT PERFECT		
ich erscheine	wir erscheinen	ich bin	wir sind	erschienen
du erscheinst	ihr erscheint	du bist	ihr seid	
Sie erscheinen	Sie erscheinen	Sie sind	Sie sind	
er/sie/es erscheint	sie erscheinen	er/sie/es ist	sie sind	

SIMPLE PAST		PAST PERFECT		
ich erschien	wir erschienen	ich war	wir waren	erschienen
du erschienst	ihr erschient	du warst	ihr wart	
Sie erschienen	Sie erschienen	Sie waren	Sie waren	
er/sie/es erschien	sie erschienen	er/sie/es war	sie waren	

FUTURE			FUTURE PERFECT		
ich werde	wir werden	erscheinen	ich werde	wir werden	erschienen sein
du wirst	ihr werdet		du wirst	ihr werdet	
Sie werden	Sie werden		Sie werden	Sie werden	
er/sie/es wird	sie werden		er/sie/es wird	sie werden	

PRESENT SUBJUNCTIVE I		PAST SUBJUNCTIVE I		
ich erscheine	wir erscheinen	ich sei	wir seien	erschienen
du erscheinest	ihr erscheinet	du seiest	ihr seiet	
Sie erscheinen	Sie erscheinen	Sie seien	Sie seien	
er/sie/es erscheine	sie erscheinen	er/sie/es sei	sie seien	

PRESENT SUBJUNCTIVE II		PAST SUBJUNCTIVE II		
ich erschiene	wir erschienen	ich wäre	wir wären	erschienen
du erschienest	ihr erschienet	du wärest	ihr wäret	
Sie erschienen	Sie erschienen	Sie wären	Sie wären	
er/sie/es erschiene	sie erschienen	er/sie/es wäre	sie wären	

FUTURE SUBJUNCTIVE I			FUTURE PERFECT SUBJUNCTIVE I		
ich werde	wir werden	erscheinen	ich werde	wir werden	erschienen sein
du werdest	ihr werdet		du werdest	ihr werdet	
Sie werden	Sie werden		Sie werden	Sie werden	
er/sie/es werde	sie werden		er/sie/es werde	sie werden	

FUTURE SUBJUNCTIVE II			FUTURE PERFECT SUBJUNCTIVE II		
ich würde	wir würden	erscheinen	ich würde	wir würden	erschienen sein
du würdest	ihr würdet		du würdest	ihr würdet	
Sie würden	Sie würden		Sie würden	Sie würden	
er/sie/es würde	sie würden		er/sie/es würde	sie würden	

COMMANDS erschein(e)! erscheint! erscheinen Sie!

PRESENT PARTICIPLE erscheinend

Usage

Ein Papagei mit einer grünen Sonnenbrille erschien in meinem Traum.	*A parrot with green sunglasses appeared in my dream.*
Halderdorfs Buch war 1967 im Erstdruck erschienen.	*Halderdorf's book had appeared in its first printing in 1967.*
Upton Sinclairs *The Jungle* erschien 1906 bei Doubleday.	*Upton Sinclair's* The Jungle *was published in 1906 by Doubleday.*
Wann erscheint Ihr nächstes Album?	*When will your next album come out?*
Die Grande Sonate in A erschien 1810.	*The Grand Sonata in A appeared in 1810.*
Die Großmutter erscheint gegen Ende des Spieles mit einem geheimnisvollen Paket in der Tasche.	*The grandmother makes an appearance near the end of the play with a mysterious package in her purse.*
Die Version 3.0 der Software ist erschienen.	*Version 3.0 of the software has come out.*
Seine Erklärung erschien uns plausibel.	*His explanation seemed plausible to us.*
Diese Folge mag als paradox erscheinen.	*This consequence may seem paradoxical.*

RELATED VERBS *see* **scheinen** (361)

strong verb **erschrickt · erschrak · erschrocken**

PRESENT

ich erschrecke	wir erschrecken
du erschrickst	ihr erschreckt
Sie erschrecken	Sie erschrecken
er/sie/es erschrickt	sie erschrecken

SIMPLE PAST

ich erschrak	wir erschraken
du erschrakst	ihr erschrakt
Sie erschraken	Sie erschraken
er/sie/es erschrak	sie erschraken

FUTURE

ich werde	wir werden	erschrecken
du wirst	ihr werdet	
Sie werden	Sie werden	
er/sie/es wird	sie werden	

PRESENT SUBJUNCTIVE I

ich erschrecke	wir erschrecken
du erschreckest	ihr erschrecket
Sie erschrecken	Sie erschrecken
er/sie/es erschrecke	sie erschrecken

PRESENT SUBJUNCTIVE II

ich erschräke	wir erschräken
du erschräkest	ihr erschräket
Sie erschräken	Sie erschräken
er/sie/es erschräke	sie erschräken

FUTURE SUBJUNCTIVE I

ich werde	wir werden	erschrecken
du werdest	ihr werdet	
Sie werden	Sie werden	
er/sie/es werde	sie werden	

FUTURE SUBJUNCTIVE II

ich würde	wir würden	erschrecken
du würdest	ihr würdet	
Sie würden	Sie würden	
er/sie/es würde	sie würden	

PRESENT PERFECT

ich bin	wir sind	erschrocken
du bist	ihr seid	
Sie sind	Sie sind	
er/sie/es ist	sie sind	

PAST PERFECT

ich war	wir waren	erschrocken
du warst	ihr wart	
Sie waren	Sie waren	
er/sie/es war	sie waren	

FUTURE PERFECT

ich werde	wir werden	erschrocken sein
du wirst	ihr werdet	
Sie werden	Sie werden	
er/sie/es wird	sie werden	

PAST SUBJUNCTIVE I

ich sei	wir seien	erschrocken
du seiest	ihr seiet	
Sie seien	Sie seien	
er/sie/es sei	sie seien	

PAST SUBJUNCTIVE II

ich wäre	wir wären	erschrocken
du wärest	ihr wäret	
Sie wären	Sie wären	
er/sie/es wäre	sie wären	

FUTURE PERFECT SUBJUNCTIVE I

ich werde	wir werden	erschrocken sein
du werdest	ihr werdet	
Sie werden	Sie werden	
er/sie/es werde	sie werden	

FUTURE PERFECT SUBJUNCTIVE II

ich würde	wir würden	erschrocken sein
du würdest	ihr würdet	
Sie würden	Sie würden	
er/sie/es würde	sie würden	

COMMANDS erschrick! erschreckt! erschrecken Sie!

PRESENT PARTICIPLE erschreckend

Usage

Die Katze ist vor dem Klang der Glocke erschrocken. — *The cat was frightened at the sound of the chimes.*

Ein Donnerschlag krachte in der Nacht und Emil erschrak. — *A thunderclap crashed in the night and Emil was scared.*

Seit dem Vorfall erschrickt mein Kind immer, wenn er allein in seinem Zimmer ist. — *Ever since the incident, my child becomes frightened when he is alone in his room.*

Da erschrak die Königin und ward grün vor Neid. (GRIMM) — *The queen was shocked and turned green with envy.*

Erschrecken Sie bitte nicht, wenn Sie meine chaotische Wohnung sehen. — *Please don't be alarmed when you see my messy apartment.*

Ehrlich gesagt bin ich etwas erschrocken. — *To be honest, I am somewhat alarmed.*

Die Vögel sahen ihn, erschraken und flogen weg. — *The birds saw him, were alarmed, and flew away.*

NOTE When it means "to frighten," **erschrecken** is conjugated as a regular weak verb and takes the auxiliary **haben**.

Der Schrei hat mich erschreckt. — *The scream scared me.*

RELATED VERBS *see* **schrecken** (384)

172 erwähnen *to mention, make reference to*

erwähnt · erwähnte · erwähnt regular weak verb

PRESENT

ich erwähne	wir erwähnen
du erwähnst	ihr erwähnt
Sie erwähnen	Sie erwähnen
er/sie/es erwähnt	sie erwähnen

SIMPLE PAST

ich erwähnte	wir erwähnten
du erwähntest	ihr erwähntet
Sie erwähnten	Sie erwähnten
er/sie/es erwähnte	sie erwähnten

FUTURE

ich werde	wir werden	erwähnen
du wirst	ihr werdet	
Sie werden	Sie werden	
er/sie/es wird	sie werden	

PRESENT SUBJUNCTIVE I

ich erwähne	wir erwähnen
du erwähnest	ihr erwähnet
Sie erwähnen	Sie erwähnen
er/sie/es erwähne	sie erwähnen

PRESENT SUBJUNCTIVE II

ich erwähnte	wir erwähnten
du erwähntest	ihr erwähntet
Sie erwähnten	Sie erwähnten
er/sie/es erwähnte	sie erwähnten

FUTURE SUBJUNCTIVE I

ich werde	wir werden	erwähnen
du werdest	ihr werdet	
Sie werden	Sie werden	
er/sie/es werde	sie werden	

FUTURE SUBJUNCTIVE II

ich würde	wir würden	erwähnen
du würdest	ihr würdet	
Sie würden	Sie würden	
er/sie/es würde	sie würden	

PRESENT PERFECT

ich habe	wir haben	erwähnt
du hast	ihr habt	
Sie haben	Sie haben	
er/sie/es hat	sie haben	

PAST PERFECT

ich hatte	wir hatten	erwähnt
du hattest	ihr hattet	
Sie hatten	Sie hatten	
er/sie/es hatte	sie hatten	

FUTURE PERFECT

ich werde	wir werden	erwähnt haben
du wirst	ihr werdet	
Sie werden	Sie werden	
er/sie/es wird	sie werden	

PAST SUBJUNCTIVE I

ich habe	wir haben	erwähnt
du habest	ihr habet	
Sie haben	Sie haben	
er/sie/es habe	sie haben	

PAST SUBJUNCTIVE II

ich hätte	wir hätten	erwähnt
du hättest	ihr hättet	
Sie hätten	Sie hätten	
er/sie/es hätte	sie hätten	

FUTURE PERFECT SUBJUNCTIVE I

ich werde	wir werden	erwähnt haben
du werdest	ihr werdet	
Sie werden	Sie werden	
er/sie/es werde	sie werden	

FUTURE PERFECT SUBJUNCTIVE II

ich würde	wir würden	erwähnt haben
du würdest	ihr würdet	
Sie würden	Sie würden	
er/sie/es würde	sie würden	

COMMANDS erwähn(e)! erwähnt! erwähnen Sie!

PRESENT PARTICIPLE erwähnend

Usage

Sein Name wird im Bericht erwähnt. — *His name is mentioned in the report.*

„Haben Sie die Tatsache erwähnt, dass das Geld nicht ausreicht?" — *"Did you mention the fact that the money won't last?"*

„Ja, ich erwähne das immer wieder, aber er glaubt es mir nicht." — *"Yes, I mention that again and again, but he doesn't believe me."*

Habe ich bereits erwähnt, dass Melanie schwanger ist? — *Have I already mentioned that Melanie is pregnant?*

Herr Leitner erwähnte einmal einen Mann in seinem Dorf, der Polnisch und Tschechisch konnte. — *Mr. Leitner once made reference to a man in his village who could speak Polish and Czech.*

Die hier angewandten Methoden zur Untersuchung wurden in Kapitel 7 erwähnt. — *The research methods applied here were mentioned in chapter 7.*

Ich brauche nicht zu erwähnen, dass es meiner Meinung nach völlig sinnlos ist. — *I don't have to mention that it is completely senseless in my opinion.*

RELATED VERB wähnen

regular weak verb **erwartet · erwartete · erwartet**

PRESENT

ich erwarte	wir erwarten
du erwartest	ihr erwartet
Sie erwarten	Sie erwarten
er/sie/es erwartet	sie erwarten

SIMPLE PAST

ich erwartete	wir erwarteten
du erwartetest	ihr erwartetet
Sie erwarteten	Sie erwarteten
er/sie/es erwartete	sie erwarteten

FUTURE

ich werde	wir werden	erwarten
du wirst	ihr werdet	
Sie werden	Sie werden	
er/sie/es wird	sie werden	

PRESENT SUBJUNCTIVE I

ich erwarte	wir erwarten
du erwartest	ihr erwartet
Sie erwarten	Sie erwarten
er/sie/es erwarte	sie erwarten

PRESENT SUBJUNCTIVE II

ich erwartete	wir erwarteten
du erwartetest	ihr erwartetet
Sie erwarteten	Sie erwarteten
er/sie/es erwartete	sie erwarteten

FUTURE SUBJUNCTIVE I

ich werde	wir werden	erwarten
du werdest	ihr werdet	
Sie werden	Sie werden	
er/sie/es werde	sie werden	

FUTURE SUBJUNCTIVE II

ich würde	wir würden	erwarten
du würdest	ihr würdet	
Sie würden	Sie würden	
er/sie/es würde	sie würden	

PRESENT PERFECT

ich habe	wir haben	erwartet
du hast	ihr habt	
Sie haben	Sie haben	
er/sie/es hat	sie haben	

PAST PERFECT

ich hatte	wir hatten	erwartet
du hattest	ihr hattet	
Sie hatten	Sie hatten	
er/sie/es hatte	sie hatten	

FUTURE PERFECT

ich werde	wir werden	erwartet haben
du wirst	ihr werdet	
Sie werden	Sie werden	
er/sie/es wird	sie werden	

PAST SUBJUNCTIVE I

ich habe	wir haben	erwartet
du habest	ihr habet	
Sie haben	Sie haben	
er/sie/es habe	sie haben	

PAST SUBJUNCTIVE II

ich hätte	wir hätten	erwartet
du hättest	ihr hättet	
Sie hätten	Sie hätten	
er/sie/es hätte	sie hätten	

FUTURE PERFECT SUBJUNCTIVE I

ich werde	wir werden	erwartet haben
du werdest	ihr werdet	
Sie werden	Sie werden	
er/sie/es werde	sie werden	

FUTURE PERFECT SUBJUNCTIVE II

ich würde	wir würden	erwartet haben
du würdest	ihr würdet	
Sie würden	Sie würden	
er/sie/es würde	sie würden	

COMMANDS erwarte! erwartet! erwarten Sie!

PRESENT PARTICIPLE erwartend

Usage

„Was erwarten Sie von mir?" — *"What do you expect from me?"*
„Ich erwarte, dass Sie ehrlich sind." — *"I expect you to be honest."*

Der professionelle Sportler erwartet von sich selbst zu jeder Zeit maximale Leistung. — *The professional athlete expects maximum performance of himself at all times.*

„Wann erwartet ihr eure Gäste?" — *"When do you expect your guests?"*
„Wir erwarten sie um halb acht Uhr." — *"We expect them at seven thirty."*

Es ist nicht zu erwarten, dass sie es allein schafft. — *She can't be expected to accomplish it alone.*
Ihre Schwester erwartet eine heiße Diskussion darüber. — *Her sister is anticipating a heated discussion of that.*
Die Familie erwartet das Urteil des Militärgerichts. — *The family is awaiting the military court's decision.*
Viel Spaß erwartet uns bei Spielpark Gandersheim. — *Lots of fun awaits us at Gandersheim Amusement Park.*
Neuere Studien lassen für die Zukunft wesentlich bessere therapeutische Möglichkeiten erwarten. — *Recent studies lead us to expect significantly better therapeutic options for the future.*

RELATED VERBS *see* **warten** (518)

174 erzählen *to tell, narrate, recount*

erzählt · erzählte · erzählt — regular weak verb

PRESENT

ich erzähle	wir erzählen
du erzählst	ihr erzählt
Sie erzählen	Sie erzählen
er/sie/es erzählt	sie erzählen

PRESENT PERFECT

ich habe	wir haben	erzählt
du hast	ihr habt	
Sie haben	Sie haben	
er/sie/es hat	sie haben	

SIMPLE PAST

ich erzählte	wir erzählten
du erzähltest	ihr erzähltet
Sie erzählten	Sie erzählten
er/sie/es erzählte	sie erzählten

PAST PERFECT

ich hatte	wir hatten	erzählt
du hattest	ihr hattet	
Sie hatten	Sie hatten	
er/sie/es hatte	sie hatten	

FUTURE

ich werde	wir werden	erzählen
du wirst	ihr werdet	
Sie werden	Sie werden	
er/sie/es wird	sie werden	

FUTURE PERFECT

ich werde	wir werden	erzählt haben
du wirst	ihr werdet	
Sie werden	Sie werden	
er/sie/es wird	sie werden	

PRESENT SUBJUNCTIVE I

ich erzähle	wir erzählen
du erzählest	ihr erzählet
Sie erzählen	Sie erzählen
er/sie/es erzähle	sie erzählen

PAST SUBJUNCTIVE I

ich habe	wir haben	erzählt
du habest	ihr habet	
Sie haben	Sie haben	
er/sie/es habe	sie haben	

PRESENT SUBJUNCTIVE II

ich erzählte	wir erzählten
du erzähltest	ihr erzähltet
Sie erzählten	Sie erzählten
er/sie/es erzählte	sie erzählten

PAST SUBJUNCTIVE II

ich hätte	wir hätten	erzählt
du hättest	ihr hättet	
Sie hätten	Sie hätten	
er/sie/es hätte	sie hätten	

FUTURE SUBJUNCTIVE I

ich werde	wir werden	erzählen
du werdest	ihr werdet	
Sie werden	Sie werden	
er/sie/es werde	sie werden	

FUTURE PERFECT SUBJUNCTIVE I

ich werde	wir werden	erzählt haben
du werdest	ihr werdet	
Sie werden	Sie werden	
er/sie/es werde	sie werden	

FUTURE SUBJUNCTIVE II

ich würde	wir würden	erzählen
du würdest	ihr würdet	
Sie würden	Sie würden	
er/sie/es würde	sie würden	

FUTURE PERFECT SUBJUNCTIVE II

ich würde	wir würden	erzählt haben
du würdest	ihr würdet	
Sie würden	Sie würden	
er/sie/es würde	sie würden	

COMMANDS erzähl(e)! erzählt! erzählen Sie!

PRESENT PARTICIPLE erzählend

Usage

Erzähl schon!	*Do tell!*
Oma Josephine hat uns Kindern immer von ihrer Heimat in Böhmen erzählt.	*Grandma Josephine always told us children about her home in Bohemia.*
Herr Bodmeier erzählt seinen Enkelkindern gern Märchen.	*Mr. Bodmeier likes to narrate fairy tales to his grandchildren.*
Nach dem Abendessen erzählte Herr Hüppe, wie er den Krieg überlebte.	*After dinner, Mr. Hüppe recounted how he lived through the war.*
Ich erzähle euch morgen, was passiert ist.	*I'll tell you tomorrow what happened.*
Irmgard kann sehr gut Geschichten erzählen.	*Irmgard is very good at telling stories.*
Papa, erzählst du mir bitte eine Geschichte?	*Papa, will you please tell me a story?*
Goethes Ballade „Erlkönig" erzählt von dem Tod eines Jungen in den Armen seines Vaters.	*Goethe's ballad "Earl King" tells of a boy's death in his father's arms.*
Es gibt nicht viel zu erzählen.	*There's not much to tell.*

RELATED VERBS nach·erzählen, weiter·erzählen, wieder·erzählen; *see also* **zählen** (544)

strong verb **isst · aß · gegessen**

PRESENT		PRESENT PERFECT		
ich esse	wir essen	ich habe	wir haben	gegessen
du isst	ihr esst	du hast	ihr habt	
Sie essen	Sie essen	Sie haben	Sie haben	
er/sie/es isst	sie essen	er/sie/es hat	sie haben	

SIMPLE PAST		PAST PERFECT		
ich aß	wir aßen	ich hatte	wir hatten	gegessen
du aßest	ihr aßt	du hattest	ihr hattet	
Sie aßen	Sie aßen	Sie hatten	Sie hatten	
er/sie/es aß	sie aßen	er/sie/es hatte	sie hatten	

FUTURE			FUTURE PERFECT		
ich werde	wir werden	essen	ich werde	wir werden	gegessen haben
du wirst	ihr werdet		du wirst	ihr werdet	
Sie werden	Sie werden		Sie werden	Sie werden	
er/sie/es wird	sie werden		er/sie/es wird	sie werden	

PRESENT SUBJUNCTIVE I		PAST SUBJUNCTIVE I		
ich esse	wir essen	ich habe	wir haben	gegessen
du essest	ihr esset	du habest	ihr habet	
Sie essen	Sie essen	Sie haben	Sie haben	
er/sie/es esse	sie essen	er/sie/es habe	sie haben	

PRESENT SUBJUNCTIVE II		PAST SUBJUNCTIVE II		
ich äße	wir äßen	ich hätte	wir hätten	gegessen
du äßest	ihr äßet	du hättest	ihr hättet	
Sie äßen	Sie äßen	Sie hätten	Sie hätten	
er/sie/es äße	sie äßen	er/sie/es hätte	sie hätten	

FUTURE SUBJUNCTIVE I			FUTURE PERFECT SUBJUNCTIVE I		
ich werde	wir werden	essen	ich werde	wir werden	gegessen haben
du werdest	ihr werdet		du werdest	ihr werdet	
Sie werden	Sie werden		Sie werden	Sie werden	
er/sie/es werde	sie werden		er/sie/es werde	sie werden	

FUTURE SUBJUNCTIVE II			FUTURE PERFECT SUBJUNCTIVE II		
ich würde	wir würden	essen	ich würde	wir würden	gegessen haben
du würdest	ihr würdet		du würdest	ihr würdet	
Sie würden	Sie würden		Sie würden	Sie würden	
er/sie/es würde	sie würden		er/sie/es würde	sie würden	

COMMANDS iss! esst! essen Sie!

PRESENT PARTICIPLE essend

Usage

Morgens esse ich nur ein Butterbrot mit Marmelade.	*In the morning, I eat only buttered bread with jam.*
Ich nehme nicht ab, ich esse zu gern.	*I'm not losing weight—I like eating too much.*
„Esst ihr oft in der Mensa?"	*"Do you often eat in the cafeteria?"*
„Nein, wir essen meistens zu Hause."	*"No, we mostly eat at home."*
Wenn du Käse äßest, wärst du kein Veganer mehr.	*If you ate cheese, you'd no longer be a vegan.*
Die Amerikaner essen ihre Pommes frites mit Ketchup anstatt Majonäse.	*The Americans eat their French fries with ketchup instead of mayonnaise.*
Isst du gern Makisushi mit Thunfisch?	*Do you like to eat makizushi with tuna?*
Wohin gehen wir heute Abend essen?	*Where shall we go to eat this evening?*
Wird dort mit den Fingern gegessen?	*Do people eat with their fingers there?*

RELATED VERBS ab·essen, an·essen, auf·essen, aus·essen, durch·essen, mit·essen, überessen, über·essen, weg·essen

TOP 50 VERB ☞

essen *to eat, take a meal*

isst · aß · gegessen strong verb

MORE USAGE SENTENCES WITH essen

Darf ich Ihnen etwas zu essen anbieten?	*May I offer you something to eat?*
Der hungrige Mann aß schnell und gierig.	*The hungry man ate quickly and greedily.*
Der Wirt gab dem Reisenden zu essen und trinken.	*The innkeeper gave the traveler something to eat and drink.*
Es ist gesund, viel Obst und Gemüse zu essen.	*Eating lots of fruits and vegetables is healthy.*
Essen wir das eine Stück und heben das andere auf.	*Let's eat one piece and save the other.*
Esst den Teller leer, Kinder, sonst gibt's keinen Nachtisch!	*Clean your plates, children, or there'll be no dessert!*
Hast du dich an Spaghetti nicht satt gegessen?	*Haven't you eaten your fill of spaghetti?*
Ich habe mich satt gegessen.	*I ate my fill.*
Ich esse Sushi mit Stäbchen.	*I eat sushi with chopsticks.*
Ich hatte keine Lust etwas zu essen.	*I didn't feel like eating anything.*
In Mallorca haben Jost und Irene abends bei Kerzenlicht gegessen.	*In Mallorca, Jost and Irene ate by candlelight in the evenings.*
Lars hat mehr auf den Teller getan, als er essen konnte.	*Lars put more on his plate than he could eat.*
Man kann den Fisch roh essen.	*You can eat the fish raw.*
Manfred darf nur koscher essen.	*Manfred can only eat kosher.*
Möchtest du rustikal essen?	*Would you like to eat country style?*
Nach der Katastrophe hatten wir tagelang wenig zu essen.	*After the catastrophe, we had little to eat for days.*
Schmidts essen nur sehr selten auswärts.	*The Schmidts eat out only very rarely.*
Wir haben auf Kosten der Firma gegessen.	*We ate on the company's expense account.*
Bis 19 Uhr wird Heinz noch nicht haben essen können.	*By 7 P.M., Heinz won't yet have been able to eat.*
Ich esse gern Tofu-Wurst mit Gemüse.	*I'm fond of tofu hot dogs with vegetables.*

essen von *to eat (some) of*

Aber von dem Baum der Erkenntnis des Guten und Bösen sollst du nicht essen. (1. MOSE 2,17)	*But of the tree of the knowledge of good and evil, thou shalt not eat of it.* (GENESIS 2:17)
Wer hat von dem Kuchen gegessen?	*Who ate some of the cake?*

sich essen lassen *to be edible*

Arugulasamen lassen sich ja essen.	*Arugula seeds are indeed edible.*

IDIOMATIC EXPRESSIONS

Habt ihr in Ungarn gut gegessen?	*Did you have good food in Hungary?*
Das kranke Kind isst schlecht.	*The sick child has a poor appetite.*
Zu Mittag essen viele Deutsche warm.	*Many Germans eat a hot lunch.*
Zu Abend essen sie oft kalt.	*For dinner they often eat a cold meal.*
Wes Brot ich ess', des Lied ich sing'. (PROVERB)	*He who pays the piper calls the tune.*
Man ist was man isst. (PROVERB)	*You are what you eat.*

PRESENT

ich existiere	wir existieren
du existierst	ihr existiert
Sie existieren	Sie existieren
er/sie/es existiert	sie existieren

SIMPLE PAST

ich existierte	wir existierten
du existiertest	ihr existiertet
Sie existierten	Sie existierten
er/sie/es existierte	sie existierten

FUTURE

ich werde	wir werden	existieren
du wirst	ihr werdet	
Sie werden	Sie werden	
er/sie/es wird	sie werden	

PRESENT SUBJUNCTIVE I

ich existiere	wir existieren
du existierest	ihr existieret
Sie existieren	Sie existieren
er/sie/es existiere	sie existieren

PRESENT SUBJUNCTIVE II

ich existierte	wir existierten
du existiertest	ihr existiertet
Sie existierten	Sie existierten
er/sie/es existierte	sie existierten

FUTURE SUBJUNCTIVE I

ich werde	wir werden	existieren
du werdest	ihr werdet	
Sie werden	Sie werden	
er/sie/es werde	sie werden	

FUTURE SUBJUNCTIVE II

ich würde	wir würden	existieren
du würdest	ihr würdet	
Sie würden	Sie würden	
er/sie/es würde	sie würden	

PRESENT PERFECT

ich habe	wir haben	existiert
du hast	ihr habt	
Sie haben	Sie haben	
er/sie/es hat	sie haben	

PAST PERFECT

ich hatte	wir hatten	existiert
du hattest	ihr hattet	
Sie hatten	Sie hatten	
er/sie/es hatte	sie hatten	

FUTURE PERFECT

ich werde	wir werden	existiert haben
du wirst	ihr werdet	
Sie werden	Sie werden	
er/sie/es wird	sie werden	

PAST SUBJUNCTIVE I

ich habe	wir haben	existiert
du habest	ihr habet	
Sie haben	Sie haben	
er/sie/es habe	sie haben	

PAST SUBJUNCTIVE II

ich hätte	wir hätten	existiert
du hättest	ihr hättet	
Sie hätten	Sie hätten	
er/sie/es hätte	sie hätten	

FUTURE PERFECT SUBJUNCTIVE I

ich werde	wir werden	existiert haben
du werdest	ihr werdet	
Sie werden	Sie werden	
er/sie/es werde	sie werden	

FUTURE PERFECT SUBJUNCTIVE II

ich würde	wir würden	existiert haben
du würdest	ihr würdet	
Sie würden	Sie würden	
er/sie/es würde	sie würden	

COMMANDS existier(e)! existiert! existieren Sie!

PRESENT PARTICIPLE existierend

Usage

Seit 1681 existieren die Dronten nicht mehr.	*Dodo birds haven't existed since 1681.*
Diese Figuren existieren nur in seiner Fantasie.	*These figures exist only in his imagination.*
Die höfischen und epischen Werke existierten gleichzeitig miteinander.	*The courtly and epic works existed together at the same time.*
Ihre Diskussion im Philosophieseminar geht um die Frage, ob Gott existiere.	*Their discussion in the philosophy seminar has to do with whether God exists.*
Das Dorf existiert nicht mehr.	*The village no longer exists.*
Existieren andere Lebewesen im Weltall?	*Do other living beings exist in the universe?*
Erich meint, dass der Yeti wirklich existiert.	*Erich thinks that the yeti really exists.*
In Australien existieren drei Zeitzonen.	*In Australia there are three time zones.*
Das Problem scheint nicht mehr zu existieren.	*The problem seems no longer to exist.*
Diese Seite existiert nicht mehr. Sie werden auf unsere Startseite umgeleitet.	*This page doen't exist anymore. You are being rerouted to our home page.*

fahren *to drive, go, travel, ride; move hurriedly; convey, carry*

fährt · fuhr · gefahren strong verb

MORE USAGE SENTENCES WITH fahren

An der Ampel fährt man nach links. *At the light you turn left.*
In Großbritannien fährt man links. *In Great Britain, you drive on the left.*
Als Kind ist Opa oft mit der Kutsche gefahren. *As a child, Grandpa often traveled by carriage.*
Das Schiff fährt unter der Flagge der Bahamas. *The ship sails under the flag of the Bahamas.*
Die LKWs fahren mit Diesel. *The trucks run on diesel.*
Erich fährt nie schneller als 140 Stundenkilometer. *Erich never drives faster than 140 kilometers per hour.*
„Fahren Sie gern Ski?" *"Do you like to ski?"*
„Nein, aber ich fahre gern Skateboard." *"No, but I like to skateboard."*
Gehst du zu Fuß oder fährst du? *Are you walking or driving/riding?*
Ich fahre diese Strecke jeden Morgen. *I drive this route every morning.*
Ich fahre mit dem Bus zur Universität. *I take a bus to the university.*
Im Sommer fuhren sie gerne ins Grüne. *In the summer, they liked to drive into the country.*
In den USA darf man mit 16 Auto fahren. *In the U.S., you can drive a car at 16.*
Oma fährt nur im zweiten Gang. *Grandma only drives in second gear.*
Sabine wird 18 und lernt jetzt Auto fahren. *Sabine is turning 18 and is learning to drive a car.*
Yvonne ist bei Rot über die Kreuzung gefahren. *Yvonne drove through the intersection on red.*

fahren + direct object (with **haben**) *to drive; run; convey, carry, haul*

Schuhmacher hat im Rennen die beste Zeit gefahren. *Schuhmacher drove the best time in the race.*
Herr Liedmeyer fährt seine Tochter jeden Nachmittag zum Spielplatz. *Mr. Liedmeyer drives his daughter to the playground every afternoon.*
Wenn sich das Wetter hält, fährt der Bauer morgen Heu. *If the weather holds, the farmer will haul hay tomorrow.*
Als ich auf dem Bauernhof war, habe ich den Traktor gefahren. *When I was on the farm, I drove the tractor.*

fahren (with **sein**) *to run, jump, leap, go*

Ein Schauer fuhr ihm über den Rücken. *A shiver ran down his spine.*
Er fuhr mit der Hand über seine Stirn. *He ran his hand across his forehead.*
Die Katze ist plötzlich in die Höhe gefahren. *The cat suddenly shot up.*
Sara fuhr erschrocken aus dem Bett. *Sara leapt from bed terrified.*

sich fahren *to drive*

Mein neuer Mercedes fährt sich superb. *My new Mercedes drives superbly.*
Es fährt sich auf Sand nicht leicht. *It's not easy to drive on sand.*

fahren + infinitive *to go, drive (to do something)*

Wollen wir dieses Wochenende campen fahren? *Shall we go camping this weekend?*
Wir sind mit Oma aufs Land spazieren gefahren. *We went for a drive with Grandma in the country.*
Fahren Sie jetzt essen? *Are you going to go eat now?*

IDIOMATIC EXPRESSIONS

Alkoholisierter Taxifahrer fährt sein Taxi zu Bruch (NEWS HEADLINE) *Drunk taxi driver smashes up his taxi*
Ingrids Mutter ist aus der Haut gefahren. *Ingrid's mother has lost her patience.*
Fahrt wohl, ihr Trauten! (*archaic*) *Farewell, ye beloved!*
In dem Fall müsste man alle Hoffnung fahren lassen. *In that case, you'd have to abandon all hope.*
Fahren wir? *Shall we go?*
Was ist in sie gefahren? *What's gotten into her?*

strong verb **fährt · fuhr · gefahren**

PRESENT

ich fahre	wir fahren
du fährst	ihr fahrt
Sie fahren	Sie fahren
er/sie/es fährt	sie fahren

SIMPLE PAST

ich fuhr	wir fuhren
du fuhrst	ihr fuhrt
Sie fuhren	Sie fuhren
er/sie/es fuhr	sie fuhren

FUTURE

ich werde	wir werden	fahren
du wirst	ihr werdet	
Sie werden	Sie werden	
er/sie/es wird	sie werden	

PRESENT SUBJUNCTIVE I

ich fahre	wir fahren
du fahrest	ihr fahret
Sie fahren	Sie fahren
er/sie/es fahre	sie fahren

PRESENT SUBJUNCTIVE II

ich führe	wir führen
du führest	ihr führet
Sie führen	Sie führen
er/sie/es führe	sie führen

FUTURE SUBJUNCTIVE I

ich werde	wir werden	fahren
du werdest	ihr werdet	
Sie werden	Sie werden	
er/sie/es werde	sie werden	

FUTURE SUBJUNCTIVE II

ich würde	wir würden	fahren
du würdest	ihr würdet	
Sie würden	Sie würden	
er/sie/es würde	sie würden	

COMMANDS fahr(e)! fahrt! fahren Sie!

PRESENT PARTICIPLE fahrend

PRESENT PERFECT

ich bin	wir sind	gefahren
du bist	ihr seid	
Sie sind	Sie sind	
er/sie/es ist	sie sind	

PAST PERFECT

ich war	wir waren	gefahren
du warst	ihr wart	
Sie waren	Sie waren	
er/sie/es war	sie waren	

FUTURE PERFECT

ich werde	wir werden	gefahren sein
du wirst	ihr werdet	
Sie werden	Sie werden	
er/sie/es wird	sie werden	

PAST SUBJUNCTIVE I

ich sei	wir seien	gefahren
du seiest	ihr seiet	
Sie seien	Sie seien	
er/sie/es sei	sie seien	

PAST SUBJUNCTIVE II

ich wäre	wir wären	gefahren
du wärest	ihr wäret	
Sie wären	Sie wären	
er/sie/es wäre	sie wären	

FUTURE PERFECT SUBJUNCTIVE I

ich werde	wir werden	gefahren sein
du werdest	ihr werdet	
Sie werden	Sie werden	
er/sie/es werde	sie werden	

FUTURE PERFECT SUBJUNCTIVE II

ich würde	wir würden	gefahren sein
du würdest	ihr würdet	
Sie würden	Sie würden	
er/sie/es würde	sie würden	

Usage

Am nächsten Tag sind wir nach Yosemite gefahren. — *The next day we drove to Yosemite.*
Ich fahre in die Stadt. Fährst du mit? — *I'm going into town. Do you want to ride along?*
Dirk, Maja, Horst und Birgit fuhren drei Stunden durch die Wüste. — *Dirk, Maja, Horst, and Birgit drove for three hours through the desert.*
Fährt dieser Bus nach Wolfenbüttel? — *Does this bus go to Wolfenbüttel?*
Wie sind Sie nach Lettland gefahren? — *How did you travel to Latvia?*

RELATED VERBS an·fahren, auf·fahren, aus·fahren, befahren, durchfahren, durch·fahren, ein·fahren, empor·fahren, entfahren, entgegen·fahren, fest·fahren, fort·fahren, heim·fahren, herunter·fahren, hin·fahren, hoch·fahren, los·fahren, mit·fahren, nach·fahren, schwarz·fahren, tot·fahren, überfahren, über·fahren, umfahren, um·fahren, verfahren, vorbei·fahren, vor·fahren, weg·fahren, weiter·fahren, widerfahren, zu·fahren, zurück·fahren, zusammen·fahren; *see also* **ab·fahren** (2), **erfahren** (154)

fallen *to fall; be captured; be killed (in action); decline, drop*

fällt · fiel · gefallen strong verb

PRESENT

ich falle	wir fallen
du fällst	ihr fallt
Sie fallen	Sie fallen
er/sie/es fällt	sie fallen

SIMPLE PAST

ich fiel	wir fielen
du fielst	ihr fielt
Sie fielen	Sie fielen
er/sie/es fiel	sie fielen

FUTURE

ich werde	wir werden	fallen
du wirst	ihr werdet	
Sie werden	Sie werden	
er/sie/es wird	sie werden	

PRESENT SUBJUNCTIVE I

ich falle	wir fallen
du fallest	ihr fallet
Sie fallen	Sie fallen
er/sie/es falle	sie fallen

PRESENT SUBJUNCTIVE II

ich fiele	wir fielen
du fielest	ihr fielet
Sie fielen	Sie fielen
er/sie/es fiele	sie fielen

FUTURE SUBJUNCTIVE I

ich werde	wir werden	fallen
du werdest	ihr werdet	
Sie werden	Sie werden	
er/sie/es werde	sie werden	

FUTURE SUBJUNCTIVE II

ich würde	wir würden	fallen
du würdest	ihr würdet	
Sie würden	Sie würden	
er/sie/es würde	sie würden	

PRESENT PERFECT

ich bin	wir sind	gefallen
du bist	ihr seid	
Sie sind	Sie sind	
er/sie/es ist	sie sind	

PAST PERFECT

ich war	wir waren	gefallen
du warst	ihr wart	
Sie waren	Sie waren	
er/sie/es war	sie waren	

FUTURE PERFECT

ich werde	wir werden	gefallen sein
du wirst	ihr werdet	
Sie werden	Sie werden	
er/sie/es wird	sie werden	

PAST SUBJUNCTIVE I

ich sei	wir seien	gefallen
du seiest	ihr seiet	
Sie seien	Sie seien	
er/sie/es sei	sie seien	

PAST SUBJUNCTIVE II

ich wäre	wir wären	gefallen
du wärest	ihr wäret	
Sie wären	Sie wären	
er/sie/es wäre	sie wären	

FUTURE PERFECT SUBJUNCTIVE I

ich werde	wir werden	gefallen sein
du werdest	ihr werdet	
Sie werden	Sie werden	
er/sie/es werde	sie werden	

FUTURE PERFECT SUBJUNCTIVE II

ich würde	wir würden	gefallen sein
du würdest	ihr würdet	
Sie würden	Sie würden	
er/sie/es würde	sie würden	

COMMANDS fall(e)! fallt! fallen Sie!

PRESENT PARTICIPLE fallend

Usage

Heute Morgen ist der erste Schnee des Jahres gefallen.	*This morning the first snow of the year fell.*
Lass die Vase nicht fallen!	*Don't drop the vase!*
Das Licht fällt ihm ins Gesicht.	*The light is falling on his face.*
Clemens Rössler fiel im Jahr 1800 in der Schlacht bei Marengo in Italien.	*Clemens Rössler was killed in action in the year 1800 in the Battle of Marengo in Italy.*
Wann werden die Benzinpreise endlich fallen?	*When will gasoline prices finally drop?*
Die Aktie fiel um 6% auf €25,30.	*The stock declined 6% to €25.30.*

fallen with verbal complements

Algebra ist mir in der Schule nicht schwer gefallen.	*Algebra was not difficult for me in school.*
Es fällt Mark leicht Termine einzuhalten.	*It's easy for Mark to keep appointments.*

RELATED VERBS ab·fallen, an·fallen, auf·fallen, aus·fallen, befallen, daneben·fallen, durch·fallen, entfallen, fort·fallen, hin·fallen, missfallen, nieder·fallen, überfallen, über·fallen, um·fallen, verfallen, vor·fallen, weg·fallen, zerfallen, zu·fallen, zurück·fallen, zusammen·fallen; *see also* **ein·fallen** (132), **gefallen** (209)

strong verb **fängt · fing · gefangen**

PRESENT

ich fange	wir fangen
du fängst	ihr fangt
Sie fangen	Sie fangen
er/sie/es fängt	sie fangen

SIMPLE PAST

ich fing	wir fingen
du fingst	ihr fingt
Sie fingen	Sie fingen
er/sie/es fing	sie fingen

FUTURE

ich werde	wir werden	fangen
du wirst	ihr werdet	
Sie werden	Sie werden	
er/sie/es wird	sie werden	

PRESENT SUBJUNCTIVE I

ich fange	wir fangen
du fangest	ihr fanget
Sie fangen	Sie fangen
er/sie/es fange	sie fangen

PRESENT SUBJUNCTIVE II

ich finge	wir fingen
du fingest	ihr finget
Sie fingen	Sie fingen
er/sie/es finge	sie fingen

FUTURE SUBJUNCTIVE I

ich werde	wir werden	fangen
du werdest	ihr werdet	
Sie werden	Sie werden	
er/sie/es werde	sie werden	

FUTURE SUBJUNCTIVE II

ich würde	wir würden	fangen
du würdest	ihr würdet	
Sie würden	Sie würden	
er/sie/es würde	sie würden	

PRESENT PERFECT

ich habe	wir haben	gefangen
du hast	ihr habt	
Sie haben	Sie haben	
er/sie/es hat	sie haben	

PAST PERFECT

ich hatte	wir hatten	gefangen
du hattest	ihr hattet	
Sie hatten	Sie hatten	
er/sie/es hatte	sie hatten	

FUTURE PERFECT

ich werde	wir werden	gefangen haben
du wirst	ihr werdet	
Sie werden	Sie werden	
er/sie/es wird	sie werden	

PAST SUBJUNCTIVE I

ich habe	wir haben	gefangen
du habest	ihr habet	
Sie haben	Sie haben	
er/sie/es habe	sie haben	

PAST SUBJUNCTIVE II

ich hätte	wir hätten	gefangen
du hättest	ihr hättet	
Sie hätten	Sie hätten	
er/sie/es hätte	sie hätten	

FUTURE PERFECT SUBJUNCTIVE I

ich werde	wir werden	gefangen haben
du werdest	ihr werdet	
Sie werden	Sie werden	
er/sie/es werde	sie werden	

FUTURE PERFECT SUBJUNCTIVE II

ich würde	wir würden	gefangen haben
du würdest	ihr würdet	
Sie würden	Sie würden	
er/sie/es würde	sie würden	

COMMANDS fang(e)! fangt! fangen Sie!

PRESENT PARTICIPLE fangend

Usage

Unser Kater Dominik fängt nie Mäuse. — *Our tomcat Dominik never catches mice.*
Fang den Ball! — *Catch the ball!*
Die drei Bankräuber wurden heute früh gefangen. — *The three bank robbers were captured this morning.*
Herr O'Shaunessy fängt kanadische Biber, um ihre Felle zu verkaufen. — *Mr. O'Shaunessy traps Canadian beavers to sell the pelts.*
Der Feind wird gefangen und in ein Lager geschickt. — *The enemy is taken prisoner and sent to a camp.*
Das Fett wurde zu heiß und die Pfanne hat Feuer gefangen. — *The fat became too hot and the pan caught fire.*

sich fangen *to become caught/trapped; gain one's composure*

Die Kuh hat sich im Zaun gefangen. — *The cow got caught in the fence.*
Endlich hat Reinhard sich wieder gefangen. — *Finally Reinhard regained his composure.*

RELATED VERBS ab·fangen, auf·fangen, ein·fangen, umfangen, unterfangen, verfangen; *see also* **an·fangen** (10), **empfangen** (141)

180 fassen

to grasp, take hold of; apprehend; express; hold, accommodate, embrace; understand; pass

fasst · fasste · gefasst — regular weak verb

PRESENT

ich fasse	wir fassen
du fasst	ihr fasst
Sie fassen	Sie fassen
er/sie/es fasst	sie fassen

PRESENT PERFECT

ich habe	wir haben	gefasst
du hast	ihr habt	
Sie haben	Sie haben	
er/sie/es hat	sie haben	

SIMPLE PAST

ich fasste	wir fassten
du fasstest	ihr fasstet
Sie fassten	Sie fassten
er/sie/es fasste	sie fassten

PAST PERFECT

ich hatte	wir hatten	gefasst
du hattest	ihr hattet	
Sie hatten	Sie hatten	
er/sie/es hatte	sie hatten	

FUTURE

ich werde	wir werden	fassen
du wirst	ihr werdet	
Sie werden	Sie werden	
er/sie/es wird	sie werden	

FUTURE PERFECT

ich werde	wir werden	gefasst haben
du wirst	ihr werdet	
Sie werden	Sie werden	
er/sie/es wird	sie werden	

PRESENT SUBJUNCTIVE I

ich fasse	wir fassen
du fassest	ihr fasset
Sie fassen	Sie fassen
er/sie/es fasse	sie fassen

PAST SUBJUNCTIVE I

ich habe	wir haben	gefasst
du habest	ihr habet	
Sie haben	Sie haben	
er/sie/es habe	sie haben	

PRESENT SUBJUNCTIVE II

ich fasste	wir fassten
du fasstest	ihr fasstet
Sie fassten	Sie fassten
er/sie/es fasste	sie fassten

PAST SUBJUNCTIVE II

ich hätte	wir hätten	gefasst
du hättest	ihr hättet	
Sie hätten	Sie hätten	
er/sie/es hätte	sie hätten	

FUTURE SUBJUNCTIVE I

ich werde	wir werden	fassen
du werdest	ihr werdet	
Sie werden	Sie werden	
er/sie/es werde	sie werden	

FUTURE PERFECT SUBJUNCTIVE I

ich werde	wir werden	gefasst haben
du werdest	ihr werdet	
Sie werden	Sie werden	
er/sie/es werde	sie werden	

FUTURE SUBJUNCTIVE II

ich würde	wir würden	fassen
du würdest	ihr würdet	
Sie würden	Sie würden	
er/sie/es würde	sie würden	

FUTURE PERFECT SUBJUNCTIVE II

ich würde	wir würden	gefasst haben
du würdest	ihr würdet	
Sie würden	Sie würden	
er/sie/es würde	sie würden	

COMMANDS fass(e)! fasst! fassen Sie!

PRESENT PARTICIPLE fassend

Usage

Fassen Sie den Ball mit der linken Hand. — *Grasp the ball with your left hand.*

Der Fremde fasste sie am Hals als wollte er sie würgen. — *The stranger took hold of her neck as though he wanted to strangle her.*

Fass! (*command to dog*) — *Attack!*

War der Verbrecher schon gefasst worden? — *Had the criminal already been apprehended?*

Der Schriftführer soll das Gespräch in grammatisch richtiges Deutsch fassen. — *The secretary is supposed to put the conversation into grammatically correct German.*

Die Krüge müssen mindestens zwei Liter fassen. — *The jugs must hold at least two liters.*

Der Bus fasst 50 Passagiere mit Gepäck. — *The bus accommodates 50 passengers with luggage.*

Ich konnte nicht fassen, was ich dort gesehen habe. — *I couldn't understand what I saw there.*

Der Stadtrat hat letztes Jahr mehrere Beschlüsse gefasst. — *The city council passed several resolutions last year.*

RELATED VERBS ab·fassen, auf·fassen, befassen, ein·fassen, erfassen, nach·fassen, umfassen, um·fassen, unter·fassen, verfassen, zu·fassen; *see also* **an·fassen** (11), **zusammen·fassen** (553) regular weak verb (dative object) **fehlt · fehlte · gefehlt**

PRESENT

ich fehle	wir fehlen
du fehlst	ihr fehlt
Sie fehlen	Sie fehlen
er/sie/es fehlt	sie fehlen

SIMPLE PAST

ich fehlte	wir fehlten
du fehltest	ihr fehltet
Sie fehlten	Sie fehlten
er/sie/es fehlte	sie fehlten

FUTURE

ich werde	wir werden	fehlen
du wirst	ihr werdet	
Sie werden	Sie werden	
er/sie/es wird	sie werden	

PRESENT SUBJUNCTIVE I

ich fehle	wir fehlen
du fehlest	ihr fehlet
Sie fehlen	Sie fehlen
er/sie/es fehle	sie fehlen

PRESENT SUBJUNCTIVE II

ich fehlte	wir fehlten
du fehltest	ihr fehltet
Sie fehlten	Sie fehlten
er/sie/es fehlte	sie fehlten

FUTURE SUBJUNCTIVE I

ich werde	wir werden	fehlen
du werdest	ihr werdet	
Sie werden	Sie werden	
er/sie/es werde	sie werden	

FUTURE SUBJUNCTIVE II

ich würde	wir würden	fehlen
du würdest	ihr würdet	
Sie würden	Sie würden	
er/sie/es würde	sie würden	

PRESENT PERFECT

ich habe	wir haben	gefehlt
du hast	ihr habt	
Sie haben	Sie haben	
er/sie/es hat	sie haben	

PAST PERFECT

ich hatte	wir hatten	gefehlt
du hattest	ihr hattet	
Sie hatten	Sie hatten	
er/sie/es hatte	sie hatten	

FUTURE PERFECT

ich werde	wir werden	gefehlt haben
du wirst	ihr werdet	
Sie werden	Sie werden	
er/sie/es wird	sie werden	

PAST SUBJUNCTIVE I

ich habe	wir haben	gefehlt
du habest	ihr habet	
Sie haben	Sie haben	
er/sie/es habe	sie haben	

PAST SUBJUNCTIVE II

ich hätte	wir hätten	gefehlt
du hättest	ihr hättet	
Sie hätten	Sie hätten	
er/sie/es hätte	sie hätten	

FUTURE PERFECT SUBJUNCTIVE I

ich werde	wir werden	gefehlt haben
du werdest	ihr werdet	
Sie werden	Sie werden	
er/sie/es werde	sie werden	

FUTURE PERFECT SUBJUNCTIVE II

ich würde	wir würden	gefehlt haben
du würdest	ihr würdet	
Sie würden	Sie würden	
er/sie/es würde	sie würden	

COMMANDS fehl(e)! fehlt! fehlen Sie!

PRESENT PARTICIPLE fehlend

Usage

Du fehlst mir.	*I miss you.*
Barbara wollte die Tür aufmachen, aber die Türklinke fehlte.	*Barbara wanted to open the door, but the doorknob was missing.*
Pläne für eine Implementierung fehlen noch.	*Implementation plans are still lacking.*
Es fehlt dem Politiker nicht an Charisma.	*The politician is not wanting in charisma.*
Warum hat Hans ein paar Tage in der Schule unentschuldigt gefehlt?	*Why was Hans absent from school a few days without an excuse?*
Es fehlt ihnen an Geld.	*They are short of money.*
Frau Klepsch fehlt auf dem Bild.	*Mrs. Klepsch is missing from the picture.*
Vielen großen Unternehmen fehlt eine langfristige Perspektive.	*Many large companies lack a long-range perspective.*
Jetzt fehlen uns nur noch die Gabeln.	*Now all we need are the forks.*

RELATED VERB verfehlen

feiern *to celebrate, commemorate*

feiert · feierte · gefeiert

regular weak verb

PRESENT

ich feiere	wir feiern
du feierst	ihr feiert
Sie feiern	Sie feiern
er/sie/es feiert	sie feiern

SIMPLE PAST

ich feierte	wir feierten
du feiertest	ihr feiertet
Sie feierten	Sie feierten
er/sie/es feierte	sie feierten

FUTURE

ich werde	wir werden	feiern
du wirst	ihr werdet	
Sie werden	Sie werden	
er/sie/es wird	sie werden	

PRESENT SUBJUNCTIVE I

ich feiere	wir feiern
du feierst	ihr feiert
Sie feiern	Sie feiern
er/sie/es feiere	sie feiern

PRESENT SUBJUNCTIVE II

ich feierte	wir feierten
du feiertest	ihr feiertet
Sie feierten	Sie feierten
er/sie/es feierte	sie feierten

FUTURE SUBJUNCTIVE I

ich werde	wir werden	feiern
du werdest	ihr werdet	
Sie werden	Sie werden	
er/sie/es werde	sie werden	

FUTURE SUBJUNCTIVE II

ich würde	wir würden	feiern
du würdest	ihr würdet	
Sie würden	Sie würden	
er/sie/es würde	sie würden	

PRESENT PERFECT

ich habe	wir haben	gefeiert
du hast	ihr habt	
Sie haben	Sie haben	
er/sie/es hat	sie haben	

PAST PERFECT

ich hatte	wir hatten	gefeiert
du hattest	ihr hattet	
Sie hatten	Sie hatten	
er/sie/es hatte	sie hatten	

FUTURE PERFECT

ich werde	wir werden	gefeiert haben
du wirst	ihr werdet	
Sie werden	Sie werden	
er/sie/es wird	sie werden	

PAST SUBJUNCTIVE I

ich habe	wir haben	gefeiert
du habest	ihr habet	
Sie haben	Sie haben	
er/sie/es habe	sie haben	

PAST SUBJUNCTIVE II

ich hätte	wir hätten	gefeiert
du hättest	ihr hättet	
Sie hätten	Sie hätten	
er/sie/es hätte	sie hätten	

FUTURE PERFECT SUBJUNCTIVE I

ich werde	wir werden	gefeiert haben
du werdest	ihr werdet	
Sie werden	Sie werden	
er/sie/es werde	sie werden	

FUTURE PERFECT SUBJUNCTIVE II

ich würde	wir würden	gefeiert haben
du würdest	ihr würdet	
Sie würden	Sie würden	
er/sie/es würde	sie würden	

COMMANDS feiere! feiert! feiern Sie!

PRESENT PARTICIPLE feiernd

Usage

Franz-Josef und Inge feiern dieses Jahr ihre silberne Hochzeit.	*Franz-Josef and Inge are celebrating their silver wedding anniversary this year.*
Die Stadt feierte 1995 das 5-jährige Bestehen ihrer Partnerschaft mit dem Verein.	*In 1995, the city commemorated the fifth anniversary of its partnership with the association.*
Wir haben bis zwei Uhr morgens gefeiert.	*We celebrated until two in the morning.*
Unsere Mannschaft feiert den Sieg.	*Our team is celebrating the victory.*
Wie wird Ostern bei Ihnen gefeiert?	*How is Easter celebrated where you're from?*
Wir feiern jedes Jahr den Tag, an dem wir uns kennen gelernt haben.	*Every year we commemorate the day we met.*
Wie feierst du Geburtstag?	*How do you celebrate your birthday?*
Der ehemalige General wird als Held gefeiert.	*The former general is celebrated as a hero.*
Dirk hat zu viel gefeiert und hat einen Kater. (*colloquial*)	*Dirk partied too much and has a hangover.*

RELATED VERBS nach·feiern, vor·feiern

regular weak verb **feixt · feixte · gefeixt**

PRESENT

ich feixe	wir feixen
du feixt	ihr feixt
Sie feixen	Sie feixen
er/sie/es feixt	sie feixen

SIMPLE PAST

ich feixte	wir feixten
du feixtest	ihr feixtet
Sie feixten	Sie feixten
er/sie/es feixte	sie feixten

FUTURE

ich werde	wir werden	feixen
du wirst	ihr werdet	
Sie werden	Sie werden	
er/sie/es wird	sie werden	

PRESENT SUBJUNCTIVE I

ich feixe	wir feixen
du feixest	ihr feixet
Sie feixen	Sie feixen
er/sie/es feixe	sie feixen

PRESENT SUBJUNCTIVE II

ich feixte	wir feixten
du feixtest	ihr feixtet
Sie feixten	Sie feixten
er/sie/es feixte	sie feixten

FUTURE SUBJUNCTIVE I

ich werde	wir werden	feixen
du werdest	ihr werdet	
Sie werden	Sie werden	
er/sie/es werde	sie werden	

FUTURE SUBJUNCTIVE II

ich würde	wir würden	feixen
du würdest	ihr würdet	
Sie würden	Sie würden	
er/sie/es würde	sie würden	

COMMANDS feix(e)! feixt! feixen Sie!

PRESENT PARTICIPLE feixend

PRESENT PERFECT

ich habe	wir haben	gefeixt
du hast	ihr habt	
Sie haben	Sie haben	
er/sie/es hat	sie haben	

PAST PERFECT

ich hatte	wir hatten	gefeixt
du hattest	ihr hattet	
Sie hatten	Sie hatten	
er/sie/es hatte	sie hatten	

FUTURE PERFECT

ich werde	wir werden	gefeixt haben
du wirst	ihr werdet	
Sie werden	Sie werden	
er/sie/es wird	sie werden	

PAST SUBJUNCTIVE I

ich habe	wir haben	gefeixt
du habest	ihr habet	
Sie haben	Sie haben	
er/sie/es habe	sie haben	

PAST SUBJUNCTIVE II

ich hätte	wir hätten	gefeixt
du hättest	ihr hättet	
Sie hätten	Sie hätten	
er/sie/es hätte	sie hätten	

FUTURE PERFECT SUBJUNCTIVE I

ich werde	wir werden	gefeixt haben
du werdest	ihr werdet	
Sie werden	Sie werden	
er/sie/es werde	sie werden	

FUTURE PERFECT SUBJUNCTIVE II

ich würde	wir würden	gefeixt haben
du würdest	ihr würdet	
Sie würden	Sie würden	
er/sie/es würde	sie würden	

Usage

„Das habe ich mir gedacht!" feixte der Knabe. — *"I thought so!" grinned the boy.*

Warum feixt du so? — *Why are you grinning like that?*

Jörg sieht ihn an und feixt innerlich. — *Jörg is watching him and grinning to himself.*

Während der Rede wurde gekichert und gefeixt. — *During the speech, people chuckled and grinned.*

Die Jugendlichen feixten und lachten, von der drohenden Gefahr nichts ahnend. — *The young people grinned and laughed, unaware of the imminent danger.*

Die wenigen Leute auf der Straße, die Häuser, selbst die Droschkenpferde schauten mich höhnisch an und feixten. (Hermann Schmitz) — *The few people on the street, the houses, even the hackneys looked at me with smirks of derision.*

184 fest·halten *to hold tight, keep, maintain; detain, capture*

hält fest · hielt fest · festgehalten

strong verb

PRESENT

ich halte	wir halten	fest
du hältst	ihr haltet	
Sie halten	Sie halten	
er/sie/es hält	sie halten	

SIMPLE PAST

ich hielt	wir hielten	fest
du hieltst	ihr hieltet	
Sie hielten	Sie hielten	
er/sie/es hielt	sie hielten	

FUTURE

ich werde	wir werden	festhalten
du wirst	ihr werdet	
Sie werden	Sie werden	
er/sie/es wird	sie werden	

PRESENT SUBJUNCTIVE I

ich halte	wir halten	fest
du haltest	ihr haltet	
Sie halten	Sie halten	
er/sie/es halte	sie halten	

PRESENT SUBJUNCTIVE II

ich hielte	wir hielten	fest
du hieltest	ihr hieltet	
Sie hielten	Sie hielten	
er/sie/es hielte	sie hielten	

FUTURE SUBJUNCTIVE I

ich werde	wir werden	festhalten
du werdest	ihr werdet	
Sie werden	Sie werden	
er/sie/es werde	sie werden	

FUTURE SUBJUNCTIVE II

ich würde	wir würden	festhalten
du würdest	ihr würdet	
Sie würden	Sie würden	
er/sie/es würde	sie würden	

PRESENT PERFECT

ich habe	wir haben	festgehalten
du hast	ihr habt	
Sie haben	Sie haben	
er/sie/es hat	sie haben	

PAST PERFECT

ich hatte	wir hatten	festgehalten
du hattest	ihr hattet	
Sie hatten	Sie hatten	
er/sie/es hatte	sie hatten	

FUTURE PERFECT

ich werde	wir werden	festgehalten haben
du wirst	ihr werdet	
Sie werden	Sie werden	
er/sie/es wird	sie werden	

PAST SUBJUNCTIVE I

ich habe	wir haben	festgehalten
du habest	ihr habet	
Sie haben	Sie haben	
er/sie/es habe	sie haben	

PAST SUBJUNCTIVE II

ich hätte	wir hätten	festgehalten
du hättest	ihr hättet	
Sie hätten	Sie hätten	
er/sie/es hätte	sie hätten	

FUTURE PERFECT SUBJUNCTIVE I

ich werde	wir werden	festgehalten haben
du werdest	ihr werdet	
Sie werden	Sie werden	
er/sie/es werde	sie werden	

FUTURE PERFECT SUBJUNCTIVE II

ich würde	wir würden	festgehalten haben
du würdest	ihr würdet	
Sie würden	Sie würden	
er/sie/es würde	sie würden	

COMMANDS halte fest! haltet fest! halten Sie fest!

PRESENT PARTICIPLE festhaltend

Usage

Elisabeth konnte den großen Hund nicht an der Leine festhalten.	*Elisabeth was unable to hold the large dog on the leash.*
Halt mal fest, Karen!	*Hold tight, Karen!*
Viele Dorfbewohner halten an dieser alten Tradition fest.	*Many villagers keep to this old tradition.*
Wir müssen den folgenden Punkt im Gedächtnis festhalten.	*We must keep the following point in mind.*
Der Vorstand hält an seiner Strategie fest.	*The board is maintaining its strategy.*
Die Verdächtigen wurden 14 Stunden am Flughafen festgehalten.	*The suspects were detained at the airport for 14 hours.*
Der glückliche Augenblick wurde im Bild festgehalten.	*The happy moment was captured in a photograph.*

sich festhalten an *to hold fast to, cling to*

Mir wurde schwindelig und ich musste mich am Baum festhalten.	*I got dizzy and had to cling to a tree.*

RELATED VERBS *see* **halten** (231)

to establish, ascertain, determine; state; observe, realize; locate; secure **fest·stellen** **185**

regular weak verb **stellt fest · stellte fest · festgestellt**

PRESENT

ich stelle	wir stellen	fest
du stellst	ihr stellt	
Sie stellen	Sie stellen	
er/sie/es stellt	sie stellen	

SIMPLE PAST

ich stellte	wir stellten	fest
du stelltest	ihr stelltet	
Sie stellten	Sie stellten	
er/sie/es stellte	sie stellten	

FUTURE

ich werde	wir werden	feststellen
du wirst	ihr werdet	
Sie werden	Sie werden	
er/sie/es wird	sie werden	

PRESENT SUBJUNCTIVE I

ich stelle	wir stellen	fest
du stellest	ihr stellet	
Sie stellen	Sie stellen	
er/sie/es stelle	sie stellen	

PRESENT SUBJUNCTIVE II

ich stellte	wir stellten	fest
du stelltest	ihr stelltet	
Sie stellten	Sie stellten	
er/sie/es stellte	sie stellten	

FUTURE SUBJUNCTIVE I

ich werde	wir werden	feststellen
du werdest	ihr werdet	
Sie werden	Sie werden	
er/sie/es werde	sie werden	

FUTURE SUBJUNCTIVE II

ich würde	wir würden	feststellen
du würdest	ihr würdet	
Sie würden	Sie würden	
er/sie/es würde	sie würden	

PRESENT PERFECT

ich habe	wir haben	festgestellt
du hast	ihr habt	
Sie haben	Sie haben	
er/sie/es hat	sie haben	

PAST PERFECT

ich hatte	wir hatten	festgestellt
du hattest	ihr hattet	
Sie hatten	Sie hatten	
er/sie/es hatte	sie hatten	

FUTURE PERFECT

ich werde	wir werden	festgestellt haben
du wirst	ihr werdet	
Sie werden	Sie werden	
er/sie/es wird	sie werden	

PAST SUBJUNCTIVE I

ich habe	wir haben	festgestellt
du habest	ihr habet	
Sie haben	Sie haben	
er/sie/es habe	sie haben	

PAST SUBJUNCTIVE II

ich hätte	wir hätten	festgestellt
du hättest	ihr hättet	
Sie hätten	Sie hätten	
er/sie/es hätte	sie hätten	

FUTURE PERFECT SUBJUNCTIVE I

ich werde	wir werden	festgestellt haben
du werdest	ihr werdet	
Sie werden	Sie werden	
er/sie/es werde	sie werden	

FUTURE PERFECT SUBJUNCTIVE II

ich würde	wir würden	festgestellt haben
du würdest	ihr würdet	
Sie würden	Sie würden	
er/sie/es würde	sie würden	

COMMANDS stell(e) fest! stellt fest! stellen Sie fest!

PRESENT PARTICIPLE feststellend

Usage

Smith konnte jetzt in einer Studie (2002:155) den Grund dafür feststellen.	*Smith has now been able to establish the reason for this in a study (2002:155).*
Durch seine Methoden können die Lesererwartungen festgestellt werden.	*Using his methods, the reader's expectations can be ascertained.*
Wir haben festgestellt, dass unser System schwere Defizite aufweist.	*We have determined that our system exhibits serious deficiencies.*
Ich muss feststellen, der Truppeneinsatz ist politisch kontraproduktiv.	*I am obliged to state that the troop deployment is politically counterproductive.*
Diese Wirkung—wie wir bereits festgestellt haben—lässt nach einiger Zeit nach.	*This effect—as we have already observed—diminishes after some time.*
Archäologen haben die alten Mauerreste mithilfe von Röntgenstrahlen festgestellt.	*Archeologists located the remains of the old wall with the help of X-rays.*
Dann kann man den Gurt feststellen.	*Then one can secure the strap.*

RELATED VERBS *see* **stellen** (426)

finden *to find, discover, come across; think, consider*

findet · fand · gefunden strong verb

MORE USAGE SENTENCES WITH finden

Nach dem Krieg konnten Bert und Regina nicht zueinander finden. — *After the war, Bert and Regina were unable to find each other.*

Ohne seinen Hund konnte der Sehbehinderte nicht nach Hause finden. — *Without his dog, the visually impaired man was unable to find his way home.*

Wir müssen eine Erklärung finden. — *We have to find a solution.*

Hast du eine Stellung gefunden? — *Have you found a job?*

Der Bischof findet Unterstützung für seine Pläne. — *The bishop is encountering support for his plans.*

Heinz fand seine Vermutungen bestätigt. — *Heinz found his conjectures confirmed.*

Ich finde, der Fotograf sollte mindestens 100 Fotos machen. — *I think the photographer should take at least 100 pictures.*

Wie findest du sein neues Hemd? — *What do you think of his new shirt?*

Heinz findet es schade, dass wir nicht alle mitfahren können. — *Heinz thinks it's too bad that we can't all come along.*

Wir finden sein Benehmen unangemessen. — *We consider his behavior inappropriate.*

Ehrlich gesagt finde ich deinen Vorschlag unpraktisch. — *To be honest, I consider your suggestion impractical.*

Und wenn du ihn fändest, würdest du ihn vergebens gefunden haben. (HEINRICH ZSCHOKKE) — *And if you were to find him, you would have found him for naught.*

Wer sucht, der findet. — *He who seeks will find.*

Keine Massenvernichtungswaffen wurden gefunden. — *No weapons of mass destruction were found.*

Gefunden: schwarz-weißer Kater, 12. Februar in der Innenstadt am Marktplatz (NOTICE) — *Found: black and white tomcat, February 12 in the city center on the market square*

sich finden *to show up, be found*

Deine Brille wird sich bestimmt finden. — *Your glasses will surely show up.*

Es findet sich keiner, der die Kosten trägt. — *There's nobody to cover the expenses.*

Es wird sich finden, ob sie das Projekt erfolgreich abschließen können. — *It remains to be seen whether they can successfully complete the project.*

Es wird sich schon finden. — *It will work out alright.*

Die neue Mutter muss sich in ihre Rolle finden. — *The new mother must come to terms with her role.*

IDIOMATIC EXPRESSIONS

Auch ein blindes Huhn findet mal ein Korn. (PROVERB) — *Given enough time, even a blind chicken finds the corn.*

Sie fiel in die Tiefe und fand ihren Tod in dem Meere. (GUSTAV SCHWAB) — *She fell into the deep and met her death in the sea.*

Seine Initiative hat in der Presse keine Erwähnung gefunden. — *His initiative was not mentioned in the press.*

Laut Breitbach hätten die Interessen der Anwohner keine Berücksichtigung gefunden. — *According to Breitbach, the residents' interests were not considered.*

Ingrid fand Gefallen an ihrer Arbeit als Beraterin. — *Ingrid enjoyed her work as advisor.*

Was findest du an ihr? — *What do you see in her?*

Lars findet keine Anerkennung für seine Bemühungen. — *Lars receives no recognition for his efforts.*

Habt ihr Freunde gefunden? — *Have you made friends?*

Finde zu dir selbst; erlebe dein inneres Kind. — *Come to terms with yourself; experience your inner child.*

Frau Anrum fand kein Gehör beim Stadtrat. — *Mrs. Anrum was met with no response from the city council.*

strong verb **findet · fand · gefunden**

PRESENT		
ich finde	wir finden	
du findest	ihr findet	
Sie finden	Sie finden	
er/sie/es findet	sie finden	

SIMPLE PAST		
ich fand	wir fanden	
du fandst	ihr fandet	
Sie fanden	Sie fanden	
er/sie/es fand	sie fanden	

FUTURE		
ich werde	wir werden	finden
du wirst	ihr werdet	
Sie werden	Sie werden	
er/sie/es wird	sie werden	

PRESENT SUBJUNCTIVE I		
ich finde	wir finden	
du findest	ihr findet	
Sie finden	Sie finden	
er/sie/es finde	sie finden	

PRESENT SUBJUNCTIVE II		
ich fände	wir fänden	
du fändest	ihr fändet	
Sie fänden	Sie fänden	
er/sie/es fände	sie fänden	

FUTURE SUBJUNCTIVE I		
ich werde	wir werden	finden
du werdest	ihr werdet	
Sie werden	Sie werden	
er/sie/es werde	sie werden	

FUTURE SUBJUNCTIVE II		
ich würde	wir würden	finden
du würdest	ihr würdet	
Sie würden	Sie würden	
er/sie/es würde	sie würden	

PRESENT PERFECT		
ich habe	wir haben	gefunden
du hast	ihr habt	
Sie haben	Sie haben	
er/sie/es hat	sie haben	

PAST PERFECT		
ich hatte	wir hatten	gefunden
du hattest	ihr hattet	
Sie hatten	Sie hatten	
er/sie/es hatte	sie hatten	

FUTURE PERFECT		
ich werde	wir werden	gefunden haben
du wirst	ihr werdet	
Sie werden	Sie werden	
er/sie/es wird	sie werden	

PAST SUBJUNCTIVE I		
ich habe	wir haben	gefunden
du habest	ihr habet	
Sie haben	Sie haben	
er/sie/es habe	sie haben	

PAST SUBJUNCTIVE II		
ich hätte	wir hätten	gefunden
du hättest	ihr hättet	
Sie hätten	Sie hätten	
er/sie/es hätte	sie hätten	

FUTURE PERFECT SUBJUNCTIVE I		
ich werde	wir werden	gefunden haben
du werdest	ihr werdet	
Sie werden	Sie werden	
er/sie/es werde	sie werden	

FUTURE PERFECT SUBJUNCTIVE II		
ich würde	wir würden	gefunden haben
du würdest	ihr würdet	
Sie würden	Sie würden	
er/sie/es würde	sie würden	

COMMANDS finde! findet! finden Sie!

PRESENT PARTICIPLE findend

Usage

Ich habe heute 10 Euro auf der Straße gefunden!	*I found 10 euros on the street today!*
Hoffentlich finden wir Mamas Ohrringe.	*Let's hope we find Mama's earrings.*
Beim Stöbern im Dachboden fand er eines Tages eine Kiste voller Briefe.	*While rummaging in the attic one day, he came across a box full of letters.*
Der Hund konnte nicht zurück zu seinem Herrchen finden.	*The dog couldn't find his way back to his master.*
In Wien fanden die Werke des jungen Musikers Anklang beim Publikum.	*In Vienna, the young musician's works found favor with the public.*
Die Socke ist nicht zu finden.	*The sock cannot be found.*

RELATED VERBS ab·finden, auf·finden, durch·finden, ein·finden, empfinden, heim·finden, heraus·finden, mit-empfinden, nach-empfinden, vor·finden, wieder·finden, zurecht·finden, zurück·finden, zusammen·finden; *see also* **befinden** (54), **erfinden** (155), **statt·finden** (420)

187 **flechten** *to braid, plait; weave, interweave; wind*

flicht · flocht · geflochten — strong verb

PRESENT

ich flechte	wir flechten
du flichtst	ihr flechtet
Sie flechten	Sie flechten
er/sie/es flicht	sie flechten

PRESENT PERFECT

ich habe	wir haben	geflochten
du hast	ihr habt	
Sie haben	Sie haben	
er/sie/es hat	sie haben	

SIMPLE PAST

ich flocht	wir flochten
du flochtest	ihr flochtet
Sie flochten	Sie flochten
er/sie/es flocht	sie flochten

PAST PERFECT

ich hatte	wir hatten	geflochten
du hattest	ihr hattet	
Sie hatten	Sie hatten	
er/sie/es hatte	sie hatten	

FUTURE

ich werde	wir werden	flechten
du wirst	ihr werdet	
Sie werden	Sie werden	
er/sie/es wird	sie werden	

FUTURE PERFECT

ich werde	wir werden	geflochten haben
du wirst	ihr werdet	
Sie werden	Sie werden	
er/sie/es wird	sie werden	

PRESENT SUBJUNCTIVE I

ich flechte	wir flechten
du flechtest	ihr flechtet
Sie flechten	Sie flechten
er/sie/es flechte	sie flechten

PAST SUBJUNCTIVE I

ich habe	wir haben	geflochten
du habest	ihr habet	
Sie haben	Sie haben	
er/sie/es habe	sie haben	

PRESENT SUBJUNCTIVE II

ich flöchte	wir flöchten
du flöchtest	ihr flöchtet
Sie flöchten	Sie flöchten
er/sie/es flöchte	sie flöchten

PAST SUBJUNCTIVE II

ich hätte	wir hätten	geflochten
du hättest	ihr hättet	
Sie hätten	Sie hätten	
er/sie/es hätte	sie hätten	

FUTURE SUBJUNCTIVE I

ich werde	wir werden	flechten
du werdest	ihr werdet	
Sie werden	Sie werden	
er/sie/es werde	sie werden	

FUTURE PERFECT SUBJUNCTIVE I

ich werde	wir werden	geflochten haben
du werdest	ihr werdet	
Sie werden	Sie werden	
er/sie/es werde	sie werden	

FUTURE SUBJUNCTIVE II

ich würde	wir würden	flechten
du würdest	ihr würdet	
Sie würden	Sie würden	
er/sie/es würde	sie würden	

FUTURE PERFECT SUBJUNCTIVE II

ich würde	wir würden	geflochten haben
du würdest	ihr würdet	
Sie würden	Sie würden	
er/sie/es würde	sie würden	

COMMANDS flicht! flechtet! flechten Sie!

PRESENT PARTICIPLE flechtend

Usage

„Ich flechte den Pferdeschweif.“	*“I'm braiding the horse's tail.”*
„Flichtst du auch die Pferdemähne?“	*“Are you going to braid the mane, too?”*
Brigitte befestigte eine Feder an einem Band und flocht sie dann ins Haar.	*Brigitte attached a feather to a cord and then braided it into her hair.*
Jedes Jahr flicht Tante Bärbel einen Adventkranz aus Tannenzweigen.	*Every year, Aunt Bärbel weaves an advent wreath out of fir twigs.*
Die Frauen flochten einen Korb.	*The women wove a basket.*
Die Fee flocht eine Leiter aus Seide.	*The fairy wove a ladder from silk.*
Die Männer versuchten Dächer aus Palmwedeln zu flechten.	*The men tried weaving roofs out of palm fronds.*
Die junge Frau hat ihr Haar zu einem Zopf geflochten.	*The young woman wound her hair in a bun.*

RELATED VERBS durch·flechten, durchflechten, ein·flechten, entflechten (*also occurs with regular weak finite forms*), umflechten, verflechten

PRESENT

ich fliege	wir fliegen
du fliegst	ihr fliegt
Sie fliegen	Sie fliegen
er/sie/es fliegt	sie fliegen

SIMPLE PAST

ich flog	wir flogen
du flogst	ihr flogt
Sie flogen	Sie flogen
er/sie/es flog	sie flogen

FUTURE

ich werde	wir werden	fliegen
du wirst	ihr werdet	
Sie werden	Sie werden	
er/sie/es wird	sie werden	

PRESENT SUBJUNCTIVE I

ich fliege	wir fliegen
du fliegest	ihr flieget
Sie fliegen	Sie fliegen
er/sie/es fliege	sie fliegen

PRESENT SUBJUNCTIVE II

ich flöge	wir flögen
du flögest	ihr flöget
Sie flögen	Sie flögen
er/sie/es flöge	sie flögen

FUTURE SUBJUNCTIVE I

ich werde	wir werden	fliegen
du werdest	ihr werdet	
Sie werden	Sie werden	
er/sie/es werde	sie werden	

FUTURE SUBJUNCTIVE II

ich würde	wir würden	fliegen
du würdest	ihr würdet	
Sie würden	Sie würden	
er/sie/es würde	sie würden	

PRESENT PERFECT

ich bin	wir sind	geflogen
du bist	ihr seid	
Sie sind	Sie sind	
er/sie/es ist	sie sind	

PAST PERFECT

ich war	wir waren	geflogen
du warst	ihr wart	
Sie waren	Sie waren	
er/sie/es war	sie waren	

FUTURE PERFECT

ich werde	wir werden	geflogen sein
du wirst	ihr werdet	
Sie werden	Sie werden	
er/sie/es wird	sie werden	

PAST SUBJUNCTIVE I

ich sei	wir seien	geflogen
du seiest	ihr seiet	
Sie seien	Sie seien	
er/sie/es sei	sie seien	

PAST SUBJUNCTIVE II

ich wäre	wir wären	geflogen
du wärest	ihr wäret	
Sie wären	Sie wären	
er/sie/es wäre	sie wären	

FUTURE PERFECT SUBJUNCTIVE I

ich werde	wir werden	geflogen sein
du werdest	ihr werdet	
Sie werden	Sie werden	
er/sie/es werde	sie werden	

FUTURE PERFECT SUBJUNCTIVE II

ich würde	wir würden	geflogen sein
du würdest	ihr würdet	
Sie würden	Sie würden	
er/sie/es würde	sie würden	

COMMANDS flieg(e)! fliegt! fliegen Sie!

PRESENT PARTICIPLE fliegend

Usage

„Fährst du mit der Bahn oder fliegst du?“
„Ich fliege.“

“Are you going by train or flying?”
“I'm flying.”

Der Bube hatte die Arme ausgestreckt als ob er flöge. — *The boy had outstretched arms as though he were flying.*

Es war als flöge Angela auf einem Zauberteppich. — *It was as if Angela were flying on a magic carpet.*

Die Papiere flogen aus dem Fenster. — *The papers flew out the window.*

fliegen (with **haben**) *to pilot, fly*

Der Pilot hat letzte Woche zum ersten Mal ein Düsenflugzeug geflogen. — *The pilot flew a jet airplane for the first time last week.*

sich fliegen *to fly*

Das neue Flugzeug fliegt sich leichter als das alte. — *The new airplane is easier to fly than the old one.*

RELATED VERBS ab·fliegen, an·fliegen, auf·fliegen, aus·fliegen, befliegen, durch·fliegen, durchfliegen, ein·fliegen, entfliegen, überfliegen, umfliegen, verfliegen, weg·fliegen, zu·fliegen, zurück·fliegen

189 fliehen *to flee, retreat*

flieht · floh · geflohen strong verb

PRESENT

ich fliehe	wir fliehen
du fliehst	ihr flieht
Sie fliehen	Sie fliehen
er/sie/es flieht	sie fliehen

SIMPLE PAST

ich floh	wir flohen
du flohst	ihr floht
Sie flohen	Sie flohen
er/sie/es floh	sie flohen

FUTURE

ich werde	wir werden	fliehen
du wirst	ihr werdet	
Sie werden	Sie werden	
er/sie/es wird	sie werden	

PRESENT SUBJUNCTIVE I

ich fliehe	wir fliehen
du fliehest	ihr fliehet
Sie fliehen	Sie fliehen
er/sie/es fliehe	sie fliehen

PRESENT SUBJUNCTIVE II

ich flöhe	wir flöhen
du flöhest	ihr flöhet
Sie flöhen	Sie flöhen
er/sie/es flöhe	sie flöhen

FUTURE SUBJUNCTIVE I

ich werde	wir werden	fliehen
du werdest	ihr werdet	
Sie werden	Sie werden	
er/sie/es werde	sie werden	

FUTURE SUBJUNCTIVE II

ich würde	wir würden	fliehen
du würdest	ihr würdet	
Sie würden	Sie würden	
er/sie/es würde	sie würden	

PRESENT PERFECT

ich bin	wir sind	geflohen
du bist	ihr seid	
Sie sind	Sie sind	
er/sie/es ist	sie sind	

PAST PERFECT

ich war	wir waren	geflohen
du warst	ihr wart	
Sie waren	Sie waren	
er/sie/es war	sie waren	

FUTURE PERFECT

ich werde	wir werden	geflohen sein
du wirst	ihr werdet	
Sie werden	Sie werden	
er/sie/es wird	sie werden	

PAST SUBJUNCTIVE I

ich sei	wir seien	geflohen
du seiest	ihr seiet	
Sie seien	Sie seien	
er/sie/es sei	sie seien	

PAST SUBJUNCTIVE II

ich wäre	wir wären	geflohen
du wärest	ihr wäret	
Sie wären	Sie wären	
er/sie/es wäre	sie wären	

FUTURE PERFECT SUBJUNCTIVE I

ich werde	wir werden	geflohen sein
du werdest	ihr werdet	
Sie werden	Sie werden	
er/sie/es werde	sie werden	

FUTURE PERFECT SUBJUNCTIVE II

ich würde	wir würden	geflohen sein
du würdest	ihr würdet	
Sie würden	Sie würden	
er/sie/es würde	sie würden	

COMMANDS flieh(e)! flieht! fliehen Sie!

PRESENT PARTICIPLE fliehend

Usage

Über 500 000 Menschen sind vor dem Bürgerkrieg ins Grenzgebiet geflohen. — *More than 500,000 people have fled from the civil war into the border region.*

Die Nazi-Verbrecher flohen nach Argentinien. — *The Nazi criminals fled to Argentina.*

Der Täter könnte ins Ausland geflohen sein. — *The perpetrator could have fled abroad.*

Margarete flieht in eine Traumwelt, um ihre Lebensumstände vergessen zu können. — *Margarete retreats into a world of dreams in order to be able to forget her life circumstances.*

„Ach, wie schnell die Tage fliehen." (Klingemann) — *"Oh, how quickly the days slip by."*

fliehen (with **haben**) *to flee; shun, avoid*

Unsere Familie hat die gefährliche Situation in der Stadt geflohen. — *Our family has fled the dangerous situation in the city.*

Dirk flieht den Lärm der Großstadt und zieht aufs Land. — *Dirk is escaping the noise of the big city and moving to the country.*

RELATED VERB entfliehen

strong verb **fließt · floss · geflossen**

PRESENT

ich fließe	wir fließen
du fließt	ihr fließt
Sie fließen	Sie fließen
er/sie/es fließt	sie fließen

SIMPLE PAST

ich floss	wir flossen
du flossest	ihr flosst
Sie flossen	Sie flossen
er/sie/es floss	sie flossen

FUTURE

ich werde	wir werden	fließen
du wirst	ihr werdet	
Sie werden	Sie werden	
er/sie/es wird	sie werden	

PRESENT SUBJUNCTIVE I

ich fließe	wir fließen
du fließest	ihr fließet
Sie fließen	Sie fließen
er/sie/es fließe	sie fließen

PRESENT SUBJUNCTIVE II

ich flösse	wir flössen
du flössest	ihr flösset
Sie flössen	Sie flössen
er/sie/es flösse	sie flössen

FUTURE SUBJUNCTIVE I

ich werde	wir werden	fließen
du werdest	ihr werdet	
Sie werden	Sie werden	
er/sie/es werde	sie werden	

FUTURE SUBJUNCTIVE II

ich würde	wir würden	fließen
du würdest	ihr würdet	
Sie würden	Sie würden	
er/sie/es würde	sie würden	

PRESENT PERFECT

ich bin	wir sind	geflossen
du bist	ihr seid	
Sie sind	Sie sind	
er/sie/es ist	sie sind	

PAST PERFECT

ich war	wir waren	geflossen
du warst	ihr wart	
Sie waren	Sie waren	
er/sie/es war	sie waren	

FUTURE PERFECT

ich werde	wir werden	geflossen sein
du wirst	ihr werdet	
Sie werden	Sie werden	
er/sie/es wird	sie werden	

PAST SUBJUNCTIVE I

ich sei	wir seien	geflossen
du seiest	ihr seiet	
Sie seien	Sie seien	
er/sie/es sei	sie seien	

PAST SUBJUNCTIVE II

ich wäre	wir wären	geflossen
du wärest	ihr wäret	
Sie wären	Sie wären	
er/sie/es wäre	sie wären	

FUTURE PERFECT SUBJUNCTIVE I

ich werde	wir werden	geflossen sein
du werdest	ihr werdet	
Sie werden	Sie werden	
er/sie/es werde	sie werden	

FUTURE PERFECT SUBJUNCTIVE II

ich würde	wir würden	geflossen sein
du würdest	ihr würdet	
Sie würden	Sie würden	
er/sie/es würde	sie würden	

COMMANDS fließ(e)! fließt! fließen Sie!

PRESENT PARTICIPLE fließend

Usage

Ein kleiner Bach floss leise neben der verkommenen Hütte.	*A small stream flowed quietly alongside the crumbling cabin.*
Die Chi-Energie fließt durch alle Räume des Hauses.	*The chi energy flows through all rooms of the house.*
Die Weser und die Elbe fließen in die Nordsee.	*The Weser and the Elbe flow into the North Sea.*
Das Geld fließt in die Börse.	*The money is flowing into the stock market.*
Als sich das Paar trennte, flossen die Tränen.	*As the couple parted, tears flowed.*
Der Strom fließt nicht mehr.	*The electricity isn't flowing anymore.*
Das Bier war auf Bernhards Fete reichlich geflossen.	*The beer had flowed plentifully at Bernhard's party.*
Nach einem Rohrbruch ist Wasser durch die Straßen geflossen.	*After a pipe rupture, water poured through the streets.*
Blut floss ihm aus den Ohren.	*Blood streamed from his ears.*

RELATED VERBS ab·fließen, aus·fließen, durch·fließen, durchfließen, ein·fließen, über·fließen, umfließen, verfließen, vorbei·fließen, weg·fließen, zerfließen, zu·fließen, zurück·fließen, zusammen·fließen

191 fluchen *to curse, swear*

flucht · fluchte · geflucht regular weak verb

PRESENT

ich fluche	wir fluchen
du fluchst	ihr flucht
Sie fluchen	Sie fluchen
er/sie/es flucht	sie fluchen

SIMPLE PAST

ich fluchte	wir fluchten
du fluchtest	ihr fluchtet
Sie fluchten	Sie fluchten
er/sie/es fluchte	sie fluchten

FUTURE

ich werde	wir werden	fluchen
du wirst	ihr werdet	
Sie werden	Sie werden	
er/sie/es wird	sie werden	

PRESENT SUBJUNCTIVE I

ich fluche	wir fluchen
du fluchest	ihr fluchet
Sie fluchen	Sie fluchen
er/sie/es fluche	sie fluchen

PRESENT SUBJUNCTIVE II

ich fluchte	wir fluchten
du fluchtest	ihr fluchtet
Sie fluchten	Sie fluchten
er/sie/es fluchte	sie fluchten

FUTURE SUBJUNCTIVE I

ich werde	wir werden	fluchen
du werdest	ihr werdet	
Sie werden	Sie werden	
er/sie/es werde	sie werden	

FUTURE SUBJUNCTIVE II

ich würde	wir würden	fluchen
du würdest	ihr würdet	
Sie würden	Sie würden	
er/sie/es würde	sie würden	

PRESENT PERFECT

ich habe	wir haben	geflucht
du hast	ihr habt	
Sie haben	Sie haben	
er/sie/es hat	sie haben	

PAST PERFECT

ich hatte	wir hatten	geflucht
du hattest	ihr hattet	
Sie hatten	Sie hatten	
er/sie/es hatte	sie hatten	

FUTURE PERFECT

ich werde	wir werden	geflucht haben
du wirst	ihr werdet	
Sie werden	Sie werden	
er/sie/es wird	sie werden	

PAST SUBJUNCTIVE I

ich habe	wir haben	geflucht
du habest	ihr habet	
Sie haben	Sie haben	
er/sie/es habe	sie haben	

PAST SUBJUNCTIVE II

ich hätte	wir hätten	geflucht
du hättest	ihr hättet	
Sie hätten	Sie hätten	
er/sie/es hätte	sie hätten	

FUTURE PERFECT SUBJUNCTIVE I

ich werde	wir werden	geflucht haben
du werdest	ihr werdet	
Sie werden	Sie werden	
er/sie/es werde	sie werden	

FUTURE PERFECT SUBJUNCTIVE II

ich würde	wir würden	geflucht haben
du würdest	ihr würdet	
Sie würden	Sie würden	
er/sie/es würde	sie würden	

COMMANDS fluch(e)! flucht! fluchen Sie!

PRESENT PARTICIPLE fluchend

Usage

Fluch doch nicht so laut.	*Don't swear so loudly.*
Ich habe den ganzen Tag darüber geflucht, dass ich am Sonntag arbeiten musste.	*I was cursing all day long about the fact that I had to work on Sunday.*
Herr Beiermann fluchte zitternd auf die Kälte.	*Shivering, Mr. Beiermann cursed the cold.*
Flucht ihr auf andere Autofahrer?	*Do you curse at other drivers?*
Tut mir Leid, dass ich auf dich geflucht habe.	*I'm sorry I swore at you.*
Mein Opa Eriksen konnte auf Dänisch fluchen.	*My grandpa Eriksen could curse in Danish.*
Du sollst nicht fluchen.	*You shouldn't swear.*
Wir haben über den Stau geflucht.	*We cursed about the traffic jam.*
Frau Sperling flucht auf den Euro.	*Mrs. Sperling curses the euro.*
Fluche mir, wie du dem Bruder fluchtest! (HEBBEL)	*Curse me as you cursed your brother!*
Paula flucht wie ein Rohrspatz. (*idiomatic*)	*Paula swears like a reed bunting.*
Tod, Euch sei geflucht! (*archaic*)	*Death, may You be cursed!*

RELATED VERB verfluchen

regular weak verb (dative object) **folgt · folgte · gefolgt**

PRESENT

ich folge	wir folgen
du folgst	ihr folgt
Sie folgen	Sie folgen
er/sie/es folgt	sie folgen

SIMPLE PAST

ich folgte	wir folgten
du folgtest	ihr folgtet
Sie folgten	Sie folgten
er/sie/es folgte	sie folgten

FUTURE

ich werde	wir werden	folgen
du wirst	ihr werdet	
Sie werden	Sie werden	
er/sie/es wird	sie werden	

PRESENT SUBJUNCTIVE I

ich folge	wir folgen
du folgest	ihr folget
Sie folgen	Sie folgen
er/sie/es folge	sie folgen

PRESENT SUBJUNCTIVE II

ich folgte	wir folgten
du folgtest	ihr folgtet
Sie folgten	Sie folgten
er/sie/es folgte	sie folgten

FUTURE SUBJUNCTIVE I

ich werde	wir werden	folgen
du werdest	ihr werdet	
Sie werden	Sie werden	
er/sie/es werde	sie werden	

FUTURE SUBJUNCTIVE II

ich würde	wir würden	folgen
du würdest	ihr würdet	
Sie würden	Sie würden	
er/sie/es würde	sie würden	

PRESENT PERFECT

ich bin	wir sind	gefolgt
du bist	ihr seid	
Sie sind	Sie sind	
er/sie/es ist	sie sind	

PAST PERFECT

ich war	wir waren	gefolgt
du warst	ihr wart	
Sie waren	Sie waren	
er/sie/es war	sie waren	

FUTURE PERFECT

ich werde	wir werden	gefolgt sein
du wirst	ihr werdet	
Sie werden	Sie werden	
er/sie/es wird	sie werden	

PAST SUBJUNCTIVE I

ich sei	wir seien	gefolgt
du seiest	ihr seiet	
Sie seien	Sie seien	
er/sie/es sei	sie seien	

PAST SUBJUNCTIVE II

ich wäre	wir wären	gefolgt
du wärest	ihr wäret	
Sie wären	Sie wären	
er/sie/es wäre	sie wären	

FUTURE PERFECT SUBJUNCTIVE I

ich werde	wir werden	gefolgt sein
du werdest	ihr werdet	
Sie werden	Sie werden	
er/sie/es werde	sie werden	

FUTURE PERFECT SUBJUNCTIVE II

ich würde	wir würden	gefolgt sein
du würdest	ihr würdet	
Sie würden	Sie würden	
er/sie/es würde	sie würden	

COMMANDS folg(e)! folgt! folgen Sie!

PRESENT PARTICIPLE folgend

Usage

Thomas ist seiner Schwester Christine in den Wald gefolgt.	*Thomas followed his sister Christine into the forest.*
Folgen Sie mir bitte.	*Please follow me.*
Das Gesetz lautet wie folgt.	*The law reads as follows.*
Der Herzog dankte ab und Chaos folgte.	*The duke abdicated and chaos ensued.*
Was folgt daraus für die Nichtversicherten?	*What will the consequences of this be for those who have no insurance?*
Ludwig der Fromme folgte seinem Vater Karl dem Großen auf dem Thron.	*Louis the Pious succeeded his father, Charlemagne, on the throne.*

folgen (with **haben**) *to obey; adhere/conform to*

Max und Moritz haben dem Lehrer nicht gefolgt.	*Max and Moritz didn't obey the teacher.*
Dieser Text folgt den neuen Rechtschreibregeln.	*This text conforms to the new spelling rules.*

RELATED VERBS aus·folgen, befolgen, erfolgen, nach·folgen, verfolgen, zurück·verfolgen

193 fordern *to demand, ask for; summon; claim*

fordert · forderte · gefordert — regular weak verb

PRESENT

ich fordere	wir fordern
du forderst	ihr fordert
Sie fordern	Sie fordern
er/sie/es fordert	sie fordern

SIMPLE PAST

ich forderte	wir forderten
du fordertest	ihr fordertet
Sie forderten	Sie forderten
er/sie/es forderte	sie forderten

FUTURE

ich werde	wir werden	fordern
du wirst	ihr werdet	
Sie werden	Sie werden	
er/sie/es wird	sie werden	

PRESENT SUBJUNCTIVE I

ich fordere	wir fordern
du forderst	ihr fordert
Sie fordern	Sie fordern
er/sie/es fordere	sie fordern

PRESENT SUBJUNCTIVE II

ich forderte	wir forderten
du fordertest	ihr fordertet
Sie forderten	Sie forderten
er/sie/es forderte	sie forderten

FUTURE SUBJUNCTIVE I

ich werde	wir werden	fordern
du werdest	ihr werdet	
Sie werden	Sie werden	
er/sie/es werde	sie werden	

FUTURE SUBJUNCTIVE II

ich würde	wir würden	fordern
du würdest	ihr würdet	
Sie würden	Sie würden	
er/sie/es würde	sie würden	

PRESENT PERFECT

ich habe	wir haben	gefordert
du hast	ihr habt	
Sie haben	Sie haben	
er/sie/es hat	sie haben	

PAST PERFECT

ich hatte	wir hatten	gefordert
du hattest	ihr hattet	
Sie hatten	Sie hatten	
er/sie/es hatte	sie hatten	

FUTURE PERFECT

ich werde	wir werden	gefordert haben
du wirst	ihr werdet	
Sie werden	Sie werden	
er/sie/es wird	sie werden	

PAST SUBJUNCTIVE I

ich habe	wir haben	gefordert
du habest	ihr habet	
Sie haben	Sie haben	
er/sie/es habe	sie haben	

PAST SUBJUNCTIVE II

ich hätte	wir hätten	gefordert
du hättest	ihr hättet	
Sie hätten	Sie hätten	
er/sie/es hätte	sie hätten	

FUTURE PERFECT SUBJUNCTIVE I

ich werde	wir werden	gefordert haben
du werdest	ihr werdet	
Sie werden	Sie werden	
er/sie/es werde	sie werden	

FUTURE PERFECT SUBJUNCTIVE II

ich würde	wir würden	gefordert haben
du würdest	ihr würdet	
Sie würden	Sie würden	
er/sie/es würde	sie würden	

COMMANDS fordere! fordert! fordern Sie!

PRESENT PARTICIPLE fordernd

Usage

Die Gewerkschaften fordern einen gerechten Lohn.	*The unions are demanding just wages.*
Die Opfer fordern 5 Millionen Schadenersatz.	*The victims are asking for five million in compensation.*
Welche Partei fordert ein Klonverbot?	*Which party is demanding a ban on cloning?*
Wir fordern ein einfaches Steuersystem.	*We demand a simple tax system.*
Die Bürger forderten ein Verbot genetisch modifizierter Organismen.	*The citizens demanded a prohibition on genetically modified organisms.*
Ich fordere Gleichberechtigung.	*I demand equal rights.*
Was fordern Sie von ihm?	*What do you demand of him?*
Unsere Nachbarin wurde vor Gericht gefordert.	*Our neighbor was summoned to court.*
Laut WFP-Statisken fordert der Hunger jeden Tag 24 000 Menschenleben.	*According to WFP statistics, hunger claims 24,000 human lives every day.*

RELATED VERBS ab·fordern, an·fordern, ein·fordern, erfordern, heraus·fordern, nach·fordern, überfordern, wieder·fordern, zurück·fordern; *see also* **auf·fordern** (25)

regular weak verb **fragt · fragte · gefragt**

PRESENT

ich frage	wir fragen
du fragst	ihr fragt
Sie fragen	Sie fragen
er/sie/es fragt	sie fragen

PRESENT PERFECT

ich habe	wir haben	gefragt
du hast	ihr habt	
Sie haben	Sie haben	
er/sie/es hat	sie haben	

SIMPLE PAST

ich fragte	wir fragten
du fragtest	ihr fragtet
Sie fragten	Sie fragten
er/sie/es fragte	sie fragten

PAST PERFECT

ich hatte	wir hatten	gefragt
du hattest	ihr hattet	
Sie hatten	Sie hatten	
er/sie/es hatte	sie hatten	

FUTURE

ich werde	wir werden	fragen
du wirst	ihr werdet	
Sie werden	Sie werden	
er/sie/es wird	sie werden	

FUTURE PERFECT

ich werde	wir werden	gefragt haben
du wirst	ihr werdet	
Sie werden	Sie werden	
er/sie/es wird	sie werden	

PRESENT SUBJUNCTIVE I

ich frage	wir fragen
du fragest	ihr fraget
Sie fragen	Sie fragen
er/sie/es frage	sie fragen

PAST SUBJUNCTIVE I

ich habe	wir haben	gefragt
du habest	ihr habet	
Sie haben	Sie haben	
er/sie/es habe	sie haben	

PRESENT SUBJUNCTIVE II

ich fragte	wir fragten
du fragtest	ihr fragtet
Sie fragten	Sie fragten
er/sie/es fragte	sie fragten

PAST SUBJUNCTIVE II

ich hätte	wir hätten	gefragt
du hättest	ihr hättet	
Sie hätten	Sie hätten	
er/sie/es hätte	sie hätten	

FUTURE SUBJUNCTIVE I

ich werde	wir werden	fragen
du werdest	ihr werdet	
Sie werden	Sie werden	
er/sie/es werde	sie werden	

FUTURE PERFECT SUBJUNCTIVE I

ich werde	wir werden	gefragt haben
du werdest	ihr werdet	
Sie werden	Sie werden	
er/sie/es werde	sie werden	

FUTURE SUBJUNCTIVE II

ich würde	wir würden	fragen
du würdest	ihr würdet	
Sie würden	Sie würden	
er/sie/es würde	sie würden	

FUTURE PERFECT SUBJUNCTIVE II

ich würde	wir würden	gefragt haben
du würdest	ihr würdet	
Sie würden	Sie würden	
er/sie/es würde	sie würden	

COMMANDS frag(e)! fragt! fragen Sie!

PRESENT PARTICIPLE fragend

Usage

Frag mich bloß nicht!	*Just don't ask me!*
„Bist du immer noch da?" fragte Tine ungeduldig.	*"Are you still there?" asked Tina impatiently.*
Irma fragt nur, ob Manni bereit ist, diese Verantwortung zu übernehmen.	*Irma is only questioning whether Manni is prepared to take over this responsibility.*
Fragen Sie bitte am nächsten Schalter.	*Please inquire at the next window.*
„Wann ist endlich Schluss?" fragte sie hartnäckig.	*"When will it finally end?" she persisted in asking.*
Der Polizist fragte uns, was passiert ist.	*The policeman asked us what happened.*
Er fragte stockend: „Kommt er morgen?"	*He asked hesitantly, "Will he come tomorrow?"*
Jost hat das Geschäft gekauft, ohne andere um Rat zu fragen.	*Jost bought the business without asking others for advice.*

RELATED VERBS ab·fragen, an·fragen, aus·fragen, befragen, durch·fragen, erfragen, hinterfragen, nach·fragen, überfragen

TOP 50 VERB ☞

194 fragen *to ask, inquire, question*

fragt · fragte · gefragt regular weak verb

MORE USAGE SENTENCES WITH **fragen**

Fragen Sie jemand anderen.	*Ask someone else.*
Ich frage mal ganz naiv, ob euer Vorhaben überhaupt machbar ist.	*I'm asking quite simply whether your plan is even doable.*
Was machen Sie beruflich, wenn ich fragen darf?	*What do you do careerwise, if you don't mind my asking?*
Wir haben ihn ganz gezielt gefragt, was er vorhat.	*We asked him specifically what he has in mind.*
Man hat wiederholt gefragt, was los war.	*They asked repeatedly what the matter was.*
Du fragst mich zu viel.	*I don't know either.*
Du kannst ihn ruhig fragen.	*Don't hesitate to ask him.*
Es muss gefragt werden, ob der Mensch dadurch wirklich gesünder wird.	*The question must be asked whether humans are really healthier because of this.*
Ich bin nicht gefragt worden, ob ich zustimme.	*I wasn't asked whether I agree.*
Uwe scheint nicht fragen zu wollen.	*Uwe doesn't appear to want to ask.*
Es wurde nicht gefragt, wie viel der Plan kostet.	*Nobody asked how much the plan costs.*
In der Pressekonferenz fragten die Reporter, ob der militärische Einsatz notwendig ist.	*At the press conference, reporters asked whether the military intervention was necessary.*
Danke, dass du fragst.	*Thanks for asking.*

sich fragen *to ask oneself, wonder; be a question, be questionable*

Ich frage mich warum.	*I wonder why.*
Es fragt sich natürlich, wie groß der Andrang eigentlich sein wird.	*Of course, the question is how big the crowd will actually be.*
Nach einigen Jahren begann er sich selbst zu fragen, woher das Geld kam.	*After a few years, he began wondering where the money was coming from.*

fragen nach *to ask for/about, inquire about, question*

Sollten wir nach dem Weg fragen?	*Should we ask for directions?*
Ich frage nach dem Preis.	*I'll inquire about the price.*
Ein Philosoph fragt nach dem Sinn des Lebens.	*A philosopher inquires into the meaning of life.*
Ich wurde von einer älteren Dame nach der Uhrzeit gefragt.	*I was asked for the time by an older lady.*
Warum fragst du mich nach meiner Tante?	*Why are you asking about my aunt?*
Man fragte mich nach meiner Meinung.	*I was asked for my opinion.*

fragen um *to ask for*

Der Urheber muss um Erlaubnis fragen.	*The author must ask for permission.*

fragen wegen *to ask about, inquire pertaining to*

Der Reporter fragte den Politiker wegen des Haushaltsdefizits.	*The reporter asked the politician about the budget deficit.*
Die Kinder fragen Oma wegen ihrer Kindheit in Transsylvanien.	*The children are asking Grandma about her childhood in Transylvania.*

gefragt sein *to be in demand, be requested*

Lederjacken werden jetzt sehr gefragt.	*Leather jackets are in great demand now.*

IDIOMATIC EXPRESSIONS

Frag nicht so dumm.	*Don't ask such a silly question.*
Hänsl fragt einem ein Loch in den Bauch.	*Hänsl doesn't stop asking questions.*
Wer viel fragt, erhält viel Antwort. (PROVERB)	*He who asks many questions gets many answers.*

strong verb **frisst · fraß · gefressen**

PRESENT

ich fresse	wir fressen
du frisst	ihr fresst
Sie fressen	Sie fressen
er/sie/es frisst	sie fressen

SIMPLE PAST

ich fraß	wir fraßen
du fraßest	ihr fraßt
Sie fraßen	Sie fraßen
er/sie/es fraß	sie fraßen

FUTURE

ich werde	wir werden	fressen
du wirst	ihr werdet	
Sie werden	Sie werden	
er/sie/es wird	sie werden	

PRESENT SUBJUNCTIVE I

ich fresse	wir fressen
du fressest	ihr fresset
Sie fressen	Sie fressen
er/sie/es fresse	sie fressen

PRESENT SUBJUNCTIVE II

ich fräße	wir fräßen
du fräßest	ihr fräßet
Sie fräßen	Sie fräßen
er/sie/es fräße	sie fräßen

FUTURE SUBJUNCTIVE I

ich werde	wir werden	fressen
du werdest	ihr werdet	
Sie werden	Sie werden	
er/sie/es werde	sie werden	

FUTURE SUBJUNCTIVE II

ich würde	wir würden	fressen
du würdest	ihr würdet	
Sie würden	Sie würden	
er/sie/es würde	sie würden	

PRESENT PERFECT

ich habe	wir haben	gefressen
du hast	ihr habt	
Sie haben	Sie haben	
er/sie/es hat	sie haben	

PAST PERFECT

ich hatte	wir hatten	gefressen
du hattest	ihr hattet	
Sie hatten	Sie hatten	
er/sie/es hatte	sie hatten	

FUTURE PERFECT

ich werde	wir werden	gefressen haben
du wirst	ihr werdet	
Sie werden	Sie werden	
er/sie/es wird	sie werden	

PAST SUBJUNCTIVE I

ich habe	wir haben	gefressen
du habest	ihr habet	
Sie haben	Sie haben	
er/sie/es habe	sie haben	

PAST SUBJUNCTIVE II

ich hätte	wir hätten	gefressen
du hättest	ihr hättet	
Sie hätten	Sie hätten	
er/sie/es hätte	sie hätten	

FUTURE PERFECT SUBJUNCTIVE I

ich werde	wir werden	gefressen haben
du werdest	ihr werdet	
Sie werden	Sie werden	
er/sie/es werde	sie werden	

FUTURE PERFECT SUBJUNCTIVE II

ich würde	wir würden	gefressen haben
du würdest	ihr würdet	
Sie würden	Sie würden	
er/sie/es würde	sie würden	

COMMANDS friss! fresst! fressen Sie!

PRESENT PARTICIPLE fressend

Usage

Die Vögel in unserem Garten fressen gern Hirsesamen. — *The birds in our yard like to eat millet seed.*
Sein Hund Maxl frisst lieber Katzenfutter. — *His dog, Maxl, prefers eating cat food.*
Rex, friss nicht so laut! — *Rex, don't eat so noisily!*
Die Raupe fraß an vielen Blättern. — *The caterpillar nibbled on many leaves.*
Motten hatten ein Loch in seine Jacke gefressen. — *Moths had eaten a hole in his jacket.*
Kinder, ihr fresst wie Schweine! — *Children, you're eating like pigs!*
Ich gebe zu, ich habe den ganzen Kuchen gefressen. — *I admit I devoured the whole cake.*
Der Wolf könnte die Großmutter gefressen haben und sie wäre noch zu retten. (GRIMM) — *The wolf could have eaten Grandmother, and she might yet be rescued.*

sich fressen *to penetrate, eat into*

Die Säuren haben sich durch die alten Bücher gefressen. — *The acids have eaten through the old books.*

RELATED VERBS ab·fressen, an·fressen, auf·fressen, aus·fressen, durch·fressen, ein·fressen, überfressen, verfressen, weg·fressen, zerfressen

196

freuen *to make glad, delight*

freut · freute · gefreut regular weak verb

PRESENT		PRESENT PERFECT		
ich freue	wir freuen	ich habe	wir haben	gefreut
du freust	ihr freut	du hast	ihr habt	
Sie freuen	Sie freuen	Sie haben	Sie haben	
er/sie/es freut	sie freuen	er/sie/es hat	sie haben	

SIMPLE PAST		PAST PERFECT		
ich freute	wir freuten	ich hatte	wir hatten	gefreut
du freutest	ihr freutet	du hattest	ihr hattet	
Sie freuten	Sie freuten	Sie hatten	Sie hatten	
er/sie/es freute	sie freuten	er/sie/es hatte	sie hatten	

FUTURE			FUTURE PERFECT		
ich werde	wir werden	freuen	ich werde	wir werden	gefreut haben
du wirst	ihr werdet		du wirst	ihr werdet	
Sie werden	Sie werden		Sie werden	Sie werden	
er/sie/es wird	sie werden		er/sie/es wird	sie werden	

PRESENT SUBJUNCTIVE I		PAST SUBJUNCTIVE I		
ich freue	wir freuen	ich habe	wir haben	gefreut
du freuest	ihr freuet	du habest	ihr habet	
Sie freuen	Sie freuen	Sie haben	Sie haben	
er/sie/es freue	sie freuen	er/sie/es habe	sie haben	

PRESENT SUBJUNCTIVE II		PAST SUBJUNCTIVE II		
ich freute	wir freuten	ich hätte	wir hätten	gefreut
du freutest	ihr freutet	du hättest	ihr hättet	
Sie freuten	Sie freuten	Sie hätten	Sie hätten	
er/sie/es freute	sie freuten	er/sie/es hätte	sie hätten	

FUTURE SUBJUNCTIVE I			FUTURE PERFECT SUBJUNCTIVE I		
ich werde	wir werden	freuen	ich werde	wir werden	gefreut haben
du werdest	ihr werdet		du werdest	ihr werdet	
Sie werden	Sie werden		Sie werden	Sie werden	
er/sie/es werde	sie werden		er/sie/es werde	sie werden	

FUTURE SUBJUNCTIVE II			FUTURE PERFECT SUBJUNCTIVE II		
ich würde	wir würden	freuen	ich würde	wir würden	gefreut haben
du würdest	ihr würdet		du würdest	ihr würdet	
Sie würden	Sie würden		Sie würden	Sie würden	
er/sie/es würde	sie würden		er/sie/es würde	sie würden	

COMMANDS freu(e)! freut! freuen Sie!

PRESENT PARTICIPLE freuend

Usage

Freut mich. (*idiomatic*) — *Glad to meet you.*
Es freute ihn sehr, dass Manni mitkommen wollte. — *He was delighted that Manni wanted to come along.*
Die Nachricht hat uns sehr gefreut. — *The news made us very happy.*

sich freuen auf *to look forward to*

Ich freue mich auf euren Anruf. — *I'm looking forward to your phone call.*
Hätten Sie sich darauf gefreut? — *Would you have looked forward to that?*

sich freuen über *to be happy about*

Hast du dich darüber gefreut? — *Were you happy about that?*
Die Snowboarder freuen sich über den Schnee. — *The snowboarders are happy about the snow.*

sich freuen + genitive (archaic) *to rejoice in, be happy about*

Und sie freute sich des schönen Meeres. (SCHILLER) — *And she rejoiced in the beautiful ocean.*

RELATED VERB erfreuen

strong verb **friert · fror · gefroren**

PRESENT		PRESENT PERFECT		
ich friere	wir frieren	ich habe	wir haben	gefroren
du frierst	ihr friert	du hast	ihr habt	
Sie frieren	Sie frieren	Sie haben	Sie haben	
er/sie/es friert	sie frieren	er/sie/es hat	sie haben	

SIMPLE PAST		PAST PERFECT		
ich fror	wir froren	ich hatte	wir hatten	gefroren
du frorst	ihr frort	du hattest	ihr hattet	
Sie froren	Sie froren	Sie hatten	Sie hatten	
er/sie/es fror	sie froren	er/sie/es hatte	sie hatten	

FUTURE			FUTURE PERFECT		
ich werde	wir werden	frieren	ich werde	wir werden	gefroren haben
du wirst	ihr werdet		du wirst	ihr werdet	
Sie werden	Sie werden		Sie werden	Sie werden	
er/sie/es wird	sie werden		er/sie/es wird	sie werden	

PRESENT SUBJUNCTIVE I		PAST SUBJUNCTIVE I		
ich friere	wir frieren	ich habe	wir haben	gefroren
du frierest	ihr frieret	du habest	ihr habet	
Sie frieren	Sie frieren	Sie haben	Sie haben	
er/sie/es friere	sie frieren	er/sie/es habe	sie haben	

PRESENT SUBJUNCTIVE II		PAST SUBJUNCTIVE II		
ich fröre	wir frören	ich hätte	wir hätten	gefroren
du frörest	ihr fröret	du hättest	ihr hättet	
Sie frören	Sie frören	Sie hätten	Sie hätten	
er/sie/es fröre	sie frören	er/sie/es hätte	sie hätten	

FUTURE SUBJUNCTIVE I			FUTURE PERFECT SUBJUNCTIVE I		
ich werde	wir werden	frieren	ich werde	wir werden	gefroren haben
du werdest	ihr werdet		du werdest	ihr werdet	
Sie werden	Sie werden		Sie werden	Sie werden	
er/sie/es werde	sie werden		er/sie/es werde	sie werden	

FUTURE SUBJUNCTIVE II			FUTURE PERFECT SUBJUNCTIVE II		
ich würde	wir würden	frieren	ich würde	wir würden	gefroren haben
du würdest	ihr würdet		du würdest	ihr würdet	
Sie würden	Sie würden		Sie würden	Sie würden	
er/sie/es würde	sie würden		er/sie/es würde	sie würden	

COMMANDS frier(e)! friert! frieren Sie!

PRESENT PARTICIPLE frierend

Usage

Tagsüber war es warm in der Wüste, aber nachts hat es gefroren.	*During the day it was warm in the desert, but at night it froze.*
Tante Gerlinde friert leicht und muss sich immer warm anziehen.	*Aunt Gerlinde chills easily and always has to dress warmly.*
Wir mussten im Nationalpark im Freien schlafen und haben richtig gefroren.	*We had to sleep out in the open in the national park and really froze.*
Bernhard fror am ganzen Leib.	*Bernhard was freezing all over.*

frieren (with sein) *to freeze*

Das Wasser in der Pfütze ist in der Nacht gefroren.	*The water in the puddle froze during the night.*
Es war so kalt, dass der Schlauch steif gefroren war.	*It was so cold that the hose had frozen stiff.*

RELATED VERBS ab·frieren, an·frieren, aus·frieren, durch·frieren, ein·frieren, erfrieren, gefrieren, überfrieren, zu·frieren

198 frühstücken *to eat breakfast*

frühstückt · frühstückte · gefrühstückt regular weak verb

PRESENT

ich frühstücke	wir frühstücken
du frühstückst	ihr frühstückt
Sie frühstücken	Sie frühstücken
er/sie/es frühstückt	sie frühstücken

PRESENT PERFECT

ich habe	wir haben	gefrühstückt
du hast	ihr habt	
Sie haben	Sie haben	
er/sie/es hat	sie haben	

SIMPLE PAST

ich frühstückte	wir frühstückten
du frühstücktest	ihr frühstücktet
Sie frühstückten	Sie frühstückten
er/sie/es frühstückte	sie frühstückten

PAST PERFECT

ich hatte	wir hatten	gefrühstückt
du hattest	ihr hattet	
Sie hatten	Sie hatten	
er/sie/es hatte	sie hatten	

FUTURE

ich werde	wir werden	frühstücken
du wirst	ihr werdet	
Sie werden	Sie werden	
er/sie/es wird	sie werden	

FUTURE PERFECT

ich werde	wir werden	gefrühstückt haben
du wirst	ihr werdet	
Sie werden	Sie werden	
er/sie/es wird	sie werden	

PRESENT SUBJUNCTIVE I

ich frühstücke	wir frühstücken
du frühstückest	ihr frühstücket
Sie frühstücken	Sie frühstücken
er/sie/es frühstücke	sie frühstücken

PAST SUBJUNCTIVE I

ich habe	wir haben	gefrühstückt
du habest	ihr habet	
Sie haben	Sie haben	
er/sie/es habe	sie haben	

PRESENT SUBJUNCTIVE II

ich frühstückte	wir frühstückten
du frühstücktest	ihr frühstücktet
Sie frühstückten	Sie frühstückten
er/sie/es frühstückte	sie frühstückten

PAST SUBJUNCTIVE II

ich hätte	wir hätten	gefrühstückt
du hättest	ihr hättet	
Sie hätten	Sie hätten	
er/sie/es hätte	sie hätten	

FUTURE SUBJUNCTIVE I

ich werde	wir werden	frühstücken
du werdest	ihr werdet	
Sie werden	Sie werden	
er/sie/es werde	sie werden	

FUTURE PERFECT SUBJUNCTIVE I

ich werde	wir werden	gefrühstückt haben
du werdest	ihr werdet	
Sie werden	Sie werden	
er/sie/es werde	sie werden	

FUTURE SUBJUNCTIVE II

ich würde	wir würden	frühstücken
du würdest	ihr würdet	
Sie würden	Sie würden	
er/sie/es würde	sie würden	

FUTURE PERFECT SUBJUNCTIVE II

ich würde	wir würden	gefrühstückt haben
du würdest	ihr würdet	
Sie würden	Sie würden	
er/sie/es würde	sie würden	

COMMANDS frühstück(e)! frühstückt! frühstücken Sie!

PRESENT PARTICIPLE frühstückend

Usage

Herr Tolzmann frühstückt um sieben Uhr.	*Mr. Tolzmann eats breakfast at seven o'clock.*
Am Sonntag haben wir schön gefrühstückt und sind dann spazieren gegangen.	*On Sunday, we had a nice breakfast, then went for a walk.*
Ich frühstücke nicht.	*I don't eat breakfast.*
Wann können wir frühstücken?	*When can we eat breakfast?*
Karen möchte mit uns frühstücken.	*Karen would like to have breakfast with us.*
Hast du keine Zeit zu frühstücken?	*Don't you have time to eat breakfast?*
Wenn ich frühstücken würde, würde ich Müsli essen.	*If I did eat breakfast, I'd eat muesli.*
Um wie viel Uhr wird gefrühstückt?	*What time is breakfast?*
Frühstückst du zu Hause oder im Büro?	*Do you eat breakfast at home or at the office?*
Irene fährt ins Büro ohne zu frühstücken.	*Irene goes to the office without eating breakfast.*
Heute habe ich Roggenbrot und ein Ei gefrühstückt.	*Today I had rye bread and an egg for breakfast.*

RELATED VERB stücken

regular weak verb **fühlt · fühlte · gefühlt**

PRESENT

ich fühle	wir fühlen
du fühlst	ihr fühlt
Sie fühlen	Sie fühlen
er/sie/es fühlt	sie fühlen

SIMPLE PAST

ich fühlte	wir fühlten
du fühltest	ihr fühltet
Sie fühlten	Sie fühlten
er/sie/es fühlte	sie fühlten

FUTURE

ich werde	wir werden	fühlen
du wirst	ihr werdet	
Sie werden	Sie werden	
er/sie/es wird	sie werden	

PRESENT SUBJUNCTIVE I

ich fühle	wir fühlen
du fühlest	ihr fühlet
Sie fühlen	Sie fühlen
er/sie/es fühle	sie fühlen

PRESENT SUBJUNCTIVE II

ich fühlte	wir fühlten
du fühltest	ihr fühltet
Sie fühlten	Sie fühlten
er/sie/es fühlte	sie fühlten

FUTURE SUBJUNCTIVE I

ich werde	wir werden	fühlen
du werdest	ihr werdet	
Sie werden	Sie werden	
er/sie/es werde	sie werden	

FUTURE SUBJUNCTIVE II

ich würde	wir würden	fühlen
du würdest	ihr würdet	
Sie würden	Sie würden	
er/sie/es würde	sie würden	

PRESENT PERFECT

ich habe	wir haben	gefühlt
du hast	ihr habt	
Sie haben	Sie haben	
er/sie/es hat	sie haben	

PAST PERFECT

ich hatte	wir hatten	gefühlt
du hattest	ihr hattet	
Sie hatten	Sie hatten	
er/sie/es hatte	sie hatten	

FUTURE PERFECT

ich werde	wir werden	gefühlt haben
du wirst	ihr werdet	
Sie werden	Sie werden	
er/sie/es wird	sie werden	

PAST SUBJUNCTIVE I

ich habe	wir haben	gefühlt
du habest	ihr habet	
Sie haben	Sie haben	
er/sie/es habe	sie haben	

PAST SUBJUNCTIVE II

ich hätte	wir hätten	gefühlt
du hättest	ihr hättet	
Sie hätten	Sie hätten	
er/sie/es hätte	sie hätten	

FUTURE PERFECT SUBJUNCTIVE I

ich werde	wir werden	gefühlt haben
du werdest	ihr werdet	
Sie werden	Sie werden	
er/sie/es werde	sie werden	

FUTURE PERFECT SUBJUNCTIVE II

ich würde	wir würden	gefühlt haben
du würdest	ihr würdet	
Sie würden	Sie würden	
er/sie/es würde	sie würden	

COMMANDS fühl(e)! fühlt! fühlen Sie!

PRESENT PARTICIPLE fühlend

Usage

Fühlt ihr Mitleid mit einem verletzten Tier?	*Do you feel pity for an injured animal?*
Stefan beugte sich über sie und fühlte nach ihrem Puls.	*Stefan leaned over her and felt for her pulse.*
Was denken und fühlen Tiere?	*What do animals think and feel?*
Gretchen fühlte die Wärme des Feuers und schlief ein.	*Gretchen felt the warmth of the fire and fell asleep.*
Meine Beine waren zwar gebrochen, aber wegen der Anästhesie fühlte ich keine Schmerzen.	*My legs were in fact broken, but because of the anesthetic I wasn't aware of any pain.*

sich fühlen *to feel*

Fühlst du dich nicht wohl?	*Do you not feel well?*
In den Armen seines Vaters fühlte sich der Junge sicher.	*In his father's arms, the boy felt secure.*
Ich fühle mich gar nicht schuldig.	*I don't feel guilty at all.*
Fühlen Sie sich verpflichtet, den anderen zu helfen?	*Do you feel obligated to help the others?*
Fühlen Sie sich wie zu Hause. (*idiomatic*)	*Make yourself at home.*

RELATED VERBS ab·fühlen, an·fühlen, befühlen, durch·fühlen, ein·fühlen, mit·fühlen, nach·fühlen, vor·fühlen

200 führen *to conduct, lead; take, carry; handle, manage*

führt · führte · geführt regular weak verb

PRESENT		PRESENT PERFECT		
ich führe	wir führen	ich habe	wir haben	geführt
du führst	ihr führt	du hast	ihr habt	
Sie führen	Sie führen	Sie haben	Sie haben	
er/sie/es führt	sie führen	er/sie/es hat	sie haben	

SIMPLE PAST		PAST PERFECT		
ich führte	wir führten	ich hatte	wir hatten	geführt
du führtest	ihr führtet	du hattest	ihr hattet	
Sie führten	Sie führten	Sie hatten	Sie hatten	
er/sie/es führte	sie führten	er/sie/es hatte	sie hatten	

FUTURE			FUTURE PERFECT		
ich werde	wir werden	führen	ich werde	wir werden	geführt haben
du wirst	ihr werdet		du wirst	ihr werdet	
Sie werden	Sie werden		Sie werden	Sie werden	
er/sie/es wird	sie werden		er/sie/es wird	sie werden	

PRESENT SUBJUNCTIVE I		PAST SUBJUNCTIVE I		
ich führe	wir führen	ich habe	wir haben	geführt
du führest	ihr führet	du habest	ihr habet	
Sie führen	Sie führen	Sie haben	Sie haben	
er/sie/es führe	sie führen	er/sie/es habe	sie haben	

PRESENT SUBJUNCTIVE II		PAST SUBJUNCTIVE II		
ich führte	wir führten	ich hätte	wir hätten	geführt
du führtest	ihr führtet	du hättest	ihr hättet	
Sie führten	Sie führten	Sie hätten	Sie hätten	
er/sie/es führte	sie führten	er/sie/es hätte	sie hätten	

FUTURE SUBJUNCTIVE I			FUTURE PERFECT SUBJUNCTIVE I		
ich werde	wir werden	führen	ich werde	wir werden	geführt haben
du werdest	ihr werdet		du werdest	ihr werdet	
Sie werden	Sie werden		Sie werden	Sie werden	
er/sie/es werde	sie werden		er/sie/es werde	sie werden	

FUTURE SUBJUNCTIVE II			FUTURE PERFECT SUBJUNCTIVE II		
ich würde	wir würden	führen	ich würde	wir würden	geführt haben
du würdest	ihr würdet		du würdest	ihr würdet	
Sie würden	Sie würden		Sie würden	Sie würden	
er/sie/es würde	sie würden		er/sie/es würde	sie würden	

COMMANDS führ(e)! führt! führen Sie!

PRESENT PARTICIPLE führend

Usage

Unser Lehrer hat uns durch das Museum geführt.	*Our teacher led us through the museum.*
Das Land führt Krieg gegen schwächere Gegner.	*The country conducts war against weaker adversaries.*
Wohin führt dieser Weg?	*Where will this path lead?*
Nicolaus hat unsere Diskussion geführt.	*Nicolaus led our discussion.*
Die Maßnahmen führten zu einem unerwarteten Ergebnis.	*The measures led to an unexpected result.*
Ich habe meine Großmutter über die Straße geführt.	*I led my grandmother across the street.*
Führe uns nicht in Versuchung. (MATTHÄUS 6,13)	*Lead us not into temptation.* (MATTHEW 6:13)
Manuela, ich führe den Hund jetzt spazieren.	*Manuela, I'm taking the dog for a walk now.*
„Führen Sie zweiäugige Spiegelreflexkameras?"	*"Do you carry double lens reflex cameras?"*
„Nein, wir führen nur noch die einäugigen Kameras."	*"No, we now carry only the single lens cameras."*

RELATED VERBS ab·führen, an·führen, auf·führen, aus·führen, durch·führen, ein·führen, entführen, fort·führen, heim·führen, herbei·führen, irre·führen, mit·führen, nasführen, über·führen, überführen, urauf·führen, verführen, vollführen, vor·führen, weg·führen, weiter·führen, zu·führen, zurück·führen, zusammen·führen

regular weak verb **füllt · füllte · gefüllt**

PRESENT

ich fülle	wir füllen
du füllst	ihr füllt
Sie füllen	Sie füllen
er/sie/es füllt	sie füllen

SIMPLE PAST

ich füllte	wir füllten
du fülltest	ihr fülltet
Sie füllten	Sie füllten
er/sie/es füllte	sie füllten

FUTURE

ich werde	wir werden	füllen
du wirst	ihr werdet	
Sie werden	Sie werden	
er/sie/es wird	sie werden	

PRESENT SUBJUNCTIVE I

ich fülle	wir füllen
du füllest	ihr füllet
Sie füllen	Sie füllen
er/sie/es fülle	sie füllen

PRESENT SUBJUNCTIVE II

ich füllte	wir füllten
du fülltest	ihr fülltet
Sie füllten	Sie füllten
er/sie/es füllte	sie füllten

FUTURE SUBJUNCTIVE I

ich werde	wir werden	füllen
du werdest	ihr werdet	
Sie werden	Sie werden	
er/sie/es werde	sie werden	

FUTURE SUBJUNCTIVE II

ich würde	wir würden	füllen
du würdest	ihr würdet	
Sie würden	Sie würden	
er/sie/es würde	sie würden	

PRESENT PERFECT

ich habe	wir haben	gefüllt
du hast	ihr habt	
Sie haben	Sie haben	
er/sie/es hat	sie haben	

PAST PERFECT

ich hatte	wir hatten	gefüllt
du hattest	ihr hattet	
Sie hatten	Sie hatten	
er/sie/es hatte	sie hatten	

FUTURE PERFECT

ich werde	wir werden	gefüllt haben
du wirst	ihr werdet	
Sie werden	Sie werden	
er/sie/es wird	sie werden	

PAST SUBJUNCTIVE I

ich habe	wir haben	gefüllt
du habest	ihr habet	
Sie haben	Sie haben	
er/sie/es habe	sie haben	

PAST SUBJUNCTIVE II

ich hätte	wir hätten	gefüllt
du hättest	ihr hättet	
Sie hätten	Sie hätten	
er/sie/es hätte	sie hätten	

FUTURE PERFECT SUBJUNCTIVE I

ich werde	wir werden	gefüllt haben
du werdest	ihr werdet	
Sie werden	Sie werden	
er/sie/es werde	sie werden	

FUTURE PERFECT SUBJUNCTIVE II

ich würde	wir würden	gefüllt haben
du würdest	ihr würdet	
Sie würden	Sie würden	
er/sie/es würde	sie würden	

COMMANDS füll(e)! füllt! füllen Sie!

PRESENT PARTICIPLE füllend

Usage

Seine Werke füllen zwanzig Bände.	*His works fill 20 volumes.*
Bei der Uraufführung haben fast 2 000 Menschen das Theater gefüllt.	*At the premiere, almost 2,000 people filled the theater.*
Stefan musste sich einen Zahn füllen lassen.	*Stefan had to have a tooth filled.*
Fülle bitte das Glas mit Wasser.	*Please fill the glass with water.*
Wie füllt man diese Ballons?	*How do you inflate these balloons?*
Teddybären werden mit Baumwollwatte gefüllt.	*Teddy bears are stuffed with cotton wadding.*

sich füllen *to fill*

Der Hörsaal füllte sich langsam mit Studenten.	*The auditorium slowly filled with students.*
Die Wunde darf sich nicht mit Blut füllen.	*The wound should not be allowed to fill with blood.*
Das Haus füllte sich zum Ersticken. (Droste-Hülshoff)	*The house got so full you could suffocate.*

RELATED VERBS ab·füllen, an·füllen, auf·füllen, aus·füllen, ein·füllen, nach·füllen, überfüllen, um·füllen; see *also* **erfüllen** (156)

funktionieren *to function, operate, work*

funktioniert · funktionierte · funktioniert regular weak verb

PRESENT

ich funktioniere	wir funktionieren
du funktionierst	ihr funktioniert
Sie funktionieren	Sie funktionieren
er/sie/es funktioniert	sie funktionieren

SIMPLE PAST

ich funktionierte	wir funktionierten
du funktioniertest	ihr funktioniertet
Sie funktionierten	Sie funktionierten
er/sie/es funktionierte	sie funktionierten

FUTURE

ich werde	wir werden	funktionieren
du wirst	ihr werdet	
Sie werden	Sie werden	
er/sie/es wird	sie werden	

PRESENT SUBJUNCTIVE I

ich funktioniere	wir funktionieren
du funktionierest	ihr funktionieret
Sie funktionieren	Sie funktionieren
er/sie/es funktioniere	sie funktionieren

PRESENT SUBJUNCTIVE II

ich funktionierte	wir funktionierten
du funktioniertest	ihr funktioniertet
Sie funktionierten	Sie funktionierten
er/sie/es funktionierte	sie funktionierten

FUTURE SUBJUNCTIVE I

ich werde	wir werden	funktionieren
du werdest	ihr werdet	
Sie werden	Sie werden	
er/sie/es werde	sie werden	

FUTURE SUBJUNCTIVE II

ich würde	wir würden	funktionieren
du würdest	ihr würdet	
Sie würden	Sie würden	
er/sie/es würde	sie würden	

PRESENT PERFECT

ich habe	wir haben	funktioniert
du hast	ihr habt	
Sie haben	Sie haben	
er/sie/es hat	sie haben	

PAST PERFECT

ich hatte	wir hatten	funktioniert
du hattest	ihr hattet	
Sie hatten	Sie hatten	
er/sie/es hatte	sie hatten	

FUTURE PERFECT

ich werde	wir werden	funktioniert haben
du wirst	ihr werdet	
Sie werden	Sie werden	
er/sie/es wird	sie werden	

PAST SUBJUNCTIVE I

ich habe	wir haben	funktioniert
du habest	ihr habet	
Sie haben	Sie haben	
er/sie/es habe	sie haben	

PAST SUBJUNCTIVE II

ich hätte	wir hätten	funktioniert
du hättest	ihr hättet	
Sie hätten	Sie hätten	
er/sie/es hätte	sie hätten	

FUTURE PERFECT SUBJUNCTIVE I

ich werde	wir werden	funktioniert haben
du werdest	ihr werdet	
Sie werden	Sie werden	
er/sie/es werde	sie werden	

FUTURE PERFECT SUBJUNCTIVE II

ich würde	wir würden	funktioniert haben
du würdest	ihr würdet	
Sie würden	Sie würden	
er/sie/es würde	sie würden	

COMMANDS funktionier(e)! funktioniert! funktionieren Sie!

PRESENT PARTICIPLE funktionierend

Usage

Mein Fernseher funktioniert doch nicht mehr.	*My television doesn't work anymore.*
Der linke Blinker funktionierte nicht richtig.	*The left turn signal didn't function properly.*
Warum funktionieren der Drucker und der Scanner nicht gleichzeitig?	*Why won't the printer and the scanner operate at the same time?*
Bertrands neuer DVD-Spieler funktioniert seit mehreren Tagen problemlos.	*Bertrand's new DVD player has been functioning without problems for several days.*
Wie soll das funktionieren?	*How is that supposed to work?*
Sein Immunsystem hat endlich etwas besser funktioniert.	*His immune system finally functioned somewhat better.*
Das System scheint wieder zu funktionieren.	*The system seems to be working again.*
Wie funktioniert eigentlich ein Luftentfeuchter?	*How exactly does a dehumidifier work?*
Meine ergonomische Tastatur funktionierte ausgezeichnet, bis ich sie eines Tages mit Kaffee getränkt habe.	*My ergonomic keyboard worked great until I gave it a soaking with coffee one day.*

RELATED VERB um·funktionieren

PRESENT

ich fürchte	wir fürchten
du fürchtest	ihr fürchtet
Sie fürchten	Sie fürchten
er/sie/es fürchtet	sie fürchten

SIMPLE PAST

ich fürchtete	wir fürchteten
du fürchtetest	ihr fürchtetet
Sie fürchteten	Sie fürchteten
er/sie/es fürchtete	sie fürchteten

FUTURE

ich werde	wir werden	fürchten
du wirst	ihr werdet	
Sie werden	Sie werden	
er/sie/es wird	sie werden	

PRESENT SUBJUNCTIVE I

ich fürchte	wir fürchten
du fürchtest	ihr fürchtet
Sie fürchten	Sie fürchten
er/sie/es fürchte	sie fürchten

PRESENT SUBJUNCTIVE II

ich fürchtete	wir fürchteten
du fürchtetest	ihr fürchtetet
Sie fürchteten	Sie fürchteten
er/sie/es fürchtete	sie fürchteten

FUTURE SUBJUNCTIVE I

ich werde	wir werden	fürchten
du werdest	ihr werdet	
Sie werden	Sie werden	
er/sie/es werde	sie werden	

FUTURE SUBJUNCTIVE II

ich würde	wir würden	fürchten
du würdest	ihr würdet	
Sie würden	Sie würden	
er/sie/es würde	sie würden	

PRESENT PERFECT

ich habe	wir haben	gefürchtet
du hast	ihr habt	
Sie haben	Sie haben	
er/sie/es hat	sie haben	

PAST PERFECT

ich hatte	wir hatten	gefürchtet
du hattest	ihr hattet	
Sie hatten	Sie hatten	
er/sie/es hatte	sie hatten	

FUTURE PERFECT

ich werde	wir werden	gefürchtet haben
du wirst	ihr werdet	
Sie werden	Sie werden	
er/sie/es wird	sie werden	

PAST SUBJUNCTIVE I

ich habe	wir haben	gefürchtet
du habest	ihr habet	
Sie haben	Sie haben	
er/sie/es habe	sie haben	

PAST SUBJUNCTIVE II

ich hätte	wir hätten	gefürchtet
du hättest	ihr hättet	
Sie hätten	Sie hätten	
er/sie/es hätte	sie hätten	

FUTURE PERFECT SUBJUNCTIVE I

ich werde	wir werden	gefürchtet haben
du werdest	ihr werdet	
Sie werden	Sie werden	
er/sie/es werde	sie werden	

FUTURE PERFECT SUBJUNCTIVE II

ich würde	wir würden	gefürchtet haben
du würdest	ihr würdet	
Sie würden	Sie würden	
er/sie/es würde	sie würden	

COMMANDS fürchte! fürchtet! fürchten Sie!

PRESENT PARTICIPLE fürchtend

Usage

Experten fürchten, dass das Virus sich bald auf Menschen überträgt. — *Experts fear that the virus will soon spread to humans.*

Wir haben allen Grund zu fürchten, dass mehr Arbeiter entlassen werden. — *We have every reason to fear that more workers will be laid off.*

Ich fürchte den Tag, an dem mein Onkel stirbt. — *I dread the day my uncle dies.*

Fürchtest du den Tod? — *Do you fear death?*

Die Inselbewohner fürchteten die Vulkanausbrüche. — *The island's inhabitants were in awe of the volcanic eruptions.*

sich fürchten *to fear, be afraid*

Maximilian fürchtet sich vor niemandem. — *Maximilian fears no one.*

Fürchtetest du dich vor großen Hunden, als du Kind warst? — *Were you afraid of large dogs when you were a child?*

RELATED VERB befürchten

204 gären *to ferment; seethe*

gärt · gor/gärte · gegoren/gegärt — strong verb or regular weak verb

PRESENT

ich gäre	wir gären
du gärst	ihr gärt
Sie gären	Sie gären
er/sie/es gärt	sie gären

SIMPLE PAST

ich gor/gärte	wir goren/gärten
du gorst/gärtest	ihr gort/gärtet
Sie goren/gärten	Sie goren/gärten
er/sie/es gor/gärte	sie goren/gärten

FUTURE

ich werde	wir werden	gären
du wirst	ihr werdet	
Sie werden	Sie werden	
er/sie/es wird	sie werden	

PRESENT SUBJUNCTIVE I

ich gäre	wir gären
du gärest	ihr gäret
Sie gären	Sie gären
er/sie/es gäre	sie gären

PRESENT SUBJUNCTIVE II

ich göre/gärte	wir gören/gärten
du görest/gärtest	ihr göret/gärtet
Sie gören/gärten	Sie gören/gärten
er/sie/es göre/gärte	sie gören/gärten

FUTURE SUBJUNCTIVE I

ich werde	wir werden	gären
du werdest	ihr werdet	
Sie werden	Sie werden	
er/sie/es werde	sie werden	

FUTURE SUBJUNCTIVE II

ich würde	wir würden	gären
du würdest	ihr würdet	
Sie würden	Sie würden	
er/sie/es würde	sie würden	

PRESENT PERFECT

ich habe	wir haben	gegoren/gegärt
du hast	ihr habt	
Sie haben	Sie haben	
er/sie/es hat	sie haben	

PAST PERFECT

ich hatte	wir hatten	gegoren/gegärt
du hattest	ihr hattet	
Sie hatten	Sie hatten	
er/sie/es hatte	sie hatten	

FUTURE PERFECT

ich werde	wir werden	gegoren haben
du wirst	ihr werdet	OR
Sie werden	Sie werden	gegärt haben
er/sie/es wird	sie werden	

PAST SUBJUNCTIVE I

ich habe	wir haben	gegoren/gegärt
du habest	ihr habet	
Sie haben	Sie haben	
er/sie/es habe	sie haben	

PAST SUBJUNCTIVE II

ich hätte	wir hätten	gegoren/gegärt
du hättest	ihr hättet	
Sie hätten	Sie hätten	
er/sie/es hätte	sie hätten	

FUTURE PERFECT SUBJUNCTIVE I

ich werde	wir werden	gegoren haben
du werdest	ihr werdet	OR
Sie werden	Sie werden	gegärt haben
er/sie/es werde	sie werden	

FUTURE PERFECT SUBJUNCTIVE II

ich würde	wir würden	gegoren haben
du würdest	ihr würdet	OR
Sie würden	Sie würden	gegärt haben
er/sie/es würde	sie würden	

COMMANDS gär(e)! gärt! gären Sie!

PRESENT PARTICIPLE gärend

NOTE Figurative meanings of **gären** tend to use **haben** as auxiliary and also use regular weak forms: **gärte, gegärt**.

Usage

Die von Hand gelesenen Trauben goren sechs bis sieben Wochen in Behältnissen. — *The handpicked grapes fermented for six to seven weeks in tanks.*

Diese Idee hatte schon lange in mir gegärt. — *This idea had been fermenting in my mind for a long time.*

Lange gärte der Unmut unter den Bauern, weil die Herrscher ihnen Unrecht getan hatten. — *Unrest simmered a long time among the peasants because the rulers had done them wrong.*

gären (with **sein**) *to ferment*

Die reifen Früchte sind in der heißen Sonne schnell gegoren. — *The ripe fruits quickly fermented in the hot sun.*

Der Saft ist gegoren, bevor sie ihn austrinken konnten. — *The juice fermented before they could drink it all.*

Wenn Teeblätter gären, werden sie dunkler. — *When tea leaves ferment, they become darker.*

RELATED VERBS aus·gären, nach·gären, vergären

strong verb **gebärt/gebiert · gebar · geboren**

PRESENT

ich gebäre	wir gebären
du gebärst/gebierst	ihr gebärt
Sie gebären	Sie gebären
er/sie/es gebärt/gebiert	sie gebären

PRESENT PERFECT

ich habe	wir haben	geboren
du hast	ihr habt	
Sie haben	Sie haben	
er/sie/es hat	sie haben	

SIMPLE PAST

ich gebar	wir gebaren
du gebarst	ihr gebart
Sie gebaren	Sie gebaren
er/sie/es gebar	sie gebaren

PAST PERFECT

ich hatte	wir hatten	geboren
du hattest	ihr hattet	
Sie hatten	Sie hatten	
er/sie/es hatte	sie hatten	

FUTURE

ich werde	wir werden	gebären
du wirst	ihr werdet	
Sie werden	Sie werden	
er/sie/es wird	sie werden	

FUTURE PERFECT

ich werde	wir werden	geboren haben
du wirst	ihr werdet	
Sie werden	Sie werden	
er/sie/es wird	sie werden	

PRESENT SUBJUNCTIVE I

ich gebäre	wir gebären
du gebärest	ihr gebäret
Sie gebären	Sie gebären
er/sie/es gebäre	sie gebären

PAST SUBJUNCTIVE I

ich habe	wir haben	geboren
du habest	ihr habet	
Sie haben	Sie haben	
er/sie/es habe	sie haben	

PRESENT SUBJUNCTIVE II

ich gebäre	wir gebären
du gebärest	ihr gebäret
Sie gebären	Sie gebären
er/sie/es gebäre	sie gebären

PAST SUBJUNCTIVE II

ich hätte	wir hätten	geboren
du hättest	ihr hättet	
Sie hätten	Sie hätten	
er/sie/es hätte	sie hätten	

FUTURE SUBJUNCTIVE I

ich werde	wir werden	gebären
du werdest	ihr werdet	
Sie werden	Sie werden	
er/sie/es werde	sie werden	

FUTURE PERFECT SUBJUNCTIVE I

ich werde	wir werden	geboren haben
du werdest	ihr werdet	
Sie werden	Sie werden	
er/sie/es werde	sie werden	

FUTURE SUBJUNCTIVE II

ich würde	wir würden	gebären
du würdest	ihr würdet	
Sie würden	Sie würden	
er/sie/es würde	sie würden	

FUTURE PERFECT SUBJUNCTIVE II

ich würde	wir würden	geboren haben
du würdest	ihr würdet	
Sie würden	Sie würden	
er/sie/es würde	sie würden	

COMMANDS gebär(e)/gebier! gebärt! gebären Sie!

PRESENT PARTICIPLE gebärend

NOTE Forms with a vowel change in the second- and third-person singular of the present tense (**gebierst, gebiert**) are increasingly archaic; contemporary usage prefers **gebärst, gebärt**.

Usage

Alle paar Jahre gebären diese Mutterschafe Zwillinge.	*Every few years these ewes bear twins.*
Hagar gebar dem Abram einen Sohn. (1. Mose 16,15)	*Hagar bore Abram a son.* (Genesis 16:15)
Ich werde keine Kinder mehr gebären.	*I won't bear any more children.*
Die Frau hat ihr zwölftes Kind geboren.	*The woman has given birth to her twelfth child.*
Karoline möchte nicht in einem Krankenhaus gebären.	*Karoline doesn't want to give birth in a hospital.*
Ludwig van Beethoven wurde 1770 in Bonn geboren.	*Ludwig van Beethoven was born in 1770 in Bonn.*
Fünf Ferkel waren schon geboren worden.	*Five piglets had already been born.*
Unsere Kuh gebärt jedes Jahr ein Kalb.	*Our cow produces a calf every year.*

geboren sein (statal passive) *to be born*

„Wann bist du geboren?"	*"When were you born?"* (lit., *"When are you born?"*)
„Ich bin 1961 geboren."	*"I was born in 1961."*

geben *to give, confer; grant; emit; yield; provide*

gibt · gab · gegeben strong verb

sich geben *to pretend to be; abate, subside*

Zugleich gibt sich Frau Wolff als anständige Bürgerin. — *At the same time, Frau Wolff pretends to be an upstanding citizen.*

Herr Täuscher gibt sich als Immobilienmakler. — *Mr. Täuscher passes himself off as a real estate agent.*

Der Regen hat sich gegeben. — *The rain subsided.*

Anfangs hatte ich Angst, das hat sich aber gegeben. — *In the beginning I was afraid, but that has passed.*

sich geben + past participle or adverb

Die Soldaten gaben sich am nächsten Tag gefangen. — *The soldiers surrendered the next day.*

Die beiden Firmen haben heute ihre Fusion bekannt gegeben. — *The two firms announced their merger today.*

Nach sieben Runden gab er sich endlich geschlagen. — *After seven rounds, he finally admitted defeat.*

Larissa gibt sich irgendwie mit ihrer Lage zufrieden. — *Larissa somehow puts up with her situation.*

es gibt *there is, there are*

In anderen Werken gibt es ähnliche Themen. — *In other works, there are similar themes.*

Es gab damals noch keine Straßenbahn. — *In those days, there was no streetcar yet.*

Früher hat es an dieser Ecke eine Apotheke gegeben. — *There used to be a pharmacy on this corner.*

Es gibt uns noch! — *We're still around!*

Wenn sich meine Eltern nicht kennen gelernt hätten, dann gäbe es mich nicht. — *If my parents had not met, I wouldn't be here.*

geben zu + infinitive

Das gibt zu denken. — *It makes you think.*

Der Beamte gab mir zu wissen, dass mein Pass nicht gültig ist. — *The official let me know that my passport wasn't valid.*

Ich gebe Ihnen zu bedenken, dass die Gelder nicht direkt auszuzahlen sind. — *I would have you consider that the monies are not to be paid out directly.*

IDIOMATIC EXPRESSIONS

Das gibt keinen Sinn. — *That makes no sense.*

Das gibt's nicht! — *That's impossible!*

Der Preis dürfte den Ausschlag gegeben haben. — *The price was probably the decisive factor.*

Gebt ihr mir die Schuld an allem? — *Are you blaming me for everything?*

Habt ihr eine Zusage gegeben? — *Have you accepted the offer?*

Ich gebe dir Recht. — *I admit you're correct.*

Katharina gab keinen Laut von sich. — *Katharina didn't utter a peep.*

Leo gibt ein schlechtes Beispiel. — *Leo sets a bad example.*

Man muss auf einen missmutigen Hund Acht geben. — *One should pay heed to an ill-tempered dog.*

Marias 50. Geburtstag gibt Anlass zu feiern! — *Maria's fiftieth birthday is an occasion to celebrate!*

Monika gibt montags und mittwochs Unterricht. — *Monika teaches on Mondays and Wednesdays.*

Sechs mal zwei gibt zwölf. — *Six times two is twelve.*

Sein Buch hat mir die Anregung gegeben, einen Dokumentarfilm zu drehen. — *His book inspired me to shoot a documentary film.*

Was es nicht alles gibt! — *What a wonder!*

Wir haben uns die größte Mühe gegeben, alle erforderlichen Einzelheiten zu regeln. — *We've taken great pains to settle all necessary details.*

Das Projekt wurde bei uns in Auftrag gegeben. — *The project was commissioned by us.*

Zur Begrüßung gibt man sich die Hand. — *To greet someone, you shake hands.*

strong verb **gibt · gab · gegeben**

PRESENT		PRESENT PERFECT		
ich gebe	wir geben	ich habe	wir haben	gegeben
du gibst	ihr gebt	du hast	ihr habt	
Sie geben	Sie geben	Sie haben	Sie haben	
er/sie/es gibt	sie geben	er/sie/es hat	sie haben	

SIMPLE PAST		PAST PERFECT		
ich gab	wir gaben	ich hatte	wir hatten	gegeben
du gabst	ihr gabt	du hattest	ihr hattet	
Sie gaben	Sie gaben	Sie hatten	Sie hatten	
er/sie/es gab	sie gaben	er/sie/es hatte	sie hatten	

FUTURE			FUTURE PERFECT		
ich werde	wir werden	geben	ich werde	wir werden	gegeben haben
du wirst	ihr werdet		du wirst	ihr werdet	
Sie werden	Sie werden		Sie werden	Sie werden	
er/sie/es wird	sie werden		er/sie/es wird	sie werden	

PRESENT SUBJUNCTIVE I		PAST SUBJUNCTIVE I		
ich gebe	wir geben	ich habe	wir haben	gegeben
du gebest	ihr gebet	du habest	ihr habet	
Sie geben	Sie geben	Sie haben	Sie haben	
er/sie/es gebe	sie geben	er/sie/es habe	sie haben	

PRESENT SUBJUNCTIVE II		PAST SUBJUNCTIVE II		
ich gäbe	wir gäben	ich hätte	wir hätten	gegeben
du gäbest	ihr gäbet	du hättest	ihr hättet	
Sie gäben	Sie gäben	Sie hätten	Sie hätten	
er/sie/es gäbe	sie gäben	er/sie/es hätte	sie hätten	

FUTURE SUBJUNCTIVE I			FUTURE PERFECT SUBJUNCTIVE I		
ich werde	wir werden	geben	ich werde	wir werden	gegeben haben
du werdest	ihr werdet		du werdest	ihr werdet	
Sie werden	Sie werden		Sie werden	Sie werden	
er/sie/es werde	sie werden		er/sie/es werde	sie werden	

FUTURE SUBJUNCTIVE II			FUTURE PERFECT SUBJUNCTIVE II		
ich würde	wir würden	geben	ich würde	wir würden	gegeben haben
du würdest	ihr würdet		du würdest	ihr würdet	
Sie würden	Sie würden		Sie würden	Sie würden	
er/sie/es würde	sie würden		er/sie/es würde	sie würden	

COMMANDS gib! gebt! geben Sie!

PRESENT PARTICIPLE gebend

Usage

Gib mir einen Kuss!	*Give me a kiss!*
Könntest du mir einen Rat geben?	*Could you give me some advice?*
Dietrich hat mir sein Wort gegeben, dass er es macht.	*Dietrich gave me his word that he'll do it.*
Eine ambivalente Wirklichkeit gibt dem Dichter schöpferische Kraft.	*An ambivalent reality confers creative power on the poet.*
Hier wird nicht versucht, eine Erklärung der Unterschiede zu geben.	*No attempt will be made here to provide an explanation of the differences.*
Die Behörden haben für den Plan grünes Licht gegeben.	*The authorities have given the go-ahead for the plan.*
Gott gebe dir einen guten Tag! (ARCHAIC GREETING)	*May God grant you a good day!*

RELATED VERBS an·geben, begeben, bei·geben, durch·geben, ein·geben, ergeben, fort·begeben, frei·geben, heim·begeben, her·geben, hin·geben, kund·geben, mit·geben, nach·geben, preis·geben, übergeben, umgeben, vergeben, vor·geben, weg·geben, weiter·geben, wieder·geben, zu·geben, zurück·begeben, zurück·geben; *see also* **ab·geben** (3), **auf·geben** (26), **aus·geben** (34)

207 gebrauchen *to use, employ*

gebraucht · gebrauchte · gebraucht regular weak verb

PRESENT

ich gebrauche	wir gebrauchen
du gebrauchst	ihr gebraucht
Sie gebrauchen	Sie gebrauchen
er/sie/es gebraucht	sie gebrauchen

SIMPLE PAST

ich gebrauchte	wir gebrauchten
du gebrauchtest	ihr gebrauchtet
Sie gebrauchten	Sie gebrauchten
er/sie/es gebrauchte	sie gebrauchten

FUTURE

ich werde	wir werden	gebrauchen
du wirst	ihr werdet	
Sie werden	Sie werden	
er/sie/es wird	sie werden	

PRESENT SUBJUNCTIVE I

ich gebrauche	wir gebrauchen
du gebrauchest	ihr gebrauchet
Sie gebrauchen	Sie gebrauchen
er/sie/es gebrauche	sie gebrauchen

PRESENT SUBJUNCTIVE II

ich gebrauchte	wir gebrauchten
du gebrauchtest	ihr gebrauchtet
Sie gebrauchten	Sie gebrauchten
er/sie/es gebrauchte	sie gebrauchten

FUTURE SUBJUNCTIVE I

ich werde	wir werden	gebrauchen
du werdest	ihr werdet	
Sie werden	Sie werden	
er/sie/es werde	sie werden	

FUTURE SUBJUNCTIVE II

ich würde	wir würden	gebrauchen
du würdest	ihr würdet	
Sie würden	Sie würden	
er/sie/es würde	sie würden	

PRESENT PERFECT

ich habe	wir haben	gebraucht
du hast	ihr habt	
Sie haben	Sie haben	
er/sie/es hat	sie haben	

PAST PERFECT

ich hatte	wir hatten	gebraucht
du hattest	ihr hattet	
Sie hatten	Sie hatten	
er/sie/es hatte	sie hatten	

FUTURE PERFECT

ich werde	wir werden	gebraucht haben
du wirst	ihr werdet	
Sie werden	Sie werden	
er/sie/es wird	sie werden	

PAST SUBJUNCTIVE I

ich habe	wir haben	gebraucht
du habest	ihr habet	
Sie haben	Sie haben	
er/sie/es habe	sie haben	

PAST SUBJUNCTIVE II

ich hätte	wir hätten	gebraucht
du hättest	ihr hättet	
Sie hätten	Sie hätten	
er/sie/es hätte	sie hätten	

FUTURE PERFECT SUBJUNCTIVE I

ich werde	wir werden	gebraucht haben
du werdest	ihr werdet	
Sie werden	Sie werden	
er/sie/es werde	sie werden	

FUTURE PERFECT SUBJUNCTIVE II

ich würde	wir würden	gebraucht haben
du würdest	ihr würdet	
Sie würden	Sie würden	
er/sie/es würde	sie würden	

COMMANDS gebrauch(e)! gebraucht! gebrauchen Sie!

PRESENT PARTICIPLE gebrauchend

Usage

Diese Tücher sind mehrfach zu gebrauchen. — *These towels can be used over and over.*
Frau Zähringer gebraucht oft Fremdwörter. — *Frau Zähringer often uses foreign words.*
Wann gebraucht man Konjunktiv? — *When do you use the subjunctive?*
Zu Hause gebrauchen sie ihre Muttersprache. — *At home, they use their native language.*
Ungewöhnliche Methoden wurden gebraucht. — *Unusual methods were employed.*
Gebrauchst du Schimpfwörter? — *Do you use bad language?*
Ich gebrauche das Fünf-Gewürze-Pulver, wenn ich chinesisch koche. — *I use the five-spice powder when I cook Chinese.*
Wie oft gebrauchen Sie das Internet? — *How often do you use the Internet?*
Der Einbrecher hatte einen Hammer gebraucht, um ins Haus zu gelangen. — *The intruder had used a hammer to gain entry to the house.*
Ich könnte jetzt eine Massage gut gebrauchen. (*colloquial*) — *I could really use a massage now.*

RELATED VERBS *see* **brauchen** (115)

PRESENT

ich gedeihe	wir gedeihen
du gedeihst	ihr gedeiht
Sie gedeihen	Sie gedeihen
er/sie/es gedeiht	sie gedeihen

SIMPLE PAST

ich gedieh	wir gediehen
du gediehst	ihr gedieht
Sie gediehen	Sie gediehen
er/sie/es gedieh	sie gediehen

FUTURE

ich werde	wir werden	gedeihen
du wirst	ihr werdet	
Sie werden	Sie werden	
er/sie/es wird	sie werden	

PRESENT SUBJUNCTIVE I

ich gedeihe	wir gedeihen
du gedeihest	ihr gedeihet
Sie gedeihen	Sie gedeihen
er/sie/es gedeihe	sie gedeihen

PRESENT SUBJUNCTIVE II

ich gediehe	wir gediehen
du gediehest	ihr gediehet
Sie gediehen	Sie gediehen
er/sie/es gediehe	sie gediehen

FUTURE SUBJUNCTIVE I

ich werde	wir werden	gedeihen
du werdest	ihr werdet	
Sie werden	Sie werden	
er/sie/es werde	sie werden	

FUTURE SUBJUNCTIVE II

ich würde	wir würden	gedeihen
du würdest	ihr würdet	
Sie würden	Sie würden	
er/sie/es würde	sie würden	

PRESENT PERFECT

ich bin	wir sind	gediehen
du bist	ihr seid	
Sie sind	Sie sind	
er/sie/es ist	sie sind	

PAST PERFECT

ich war	wir waren	gediehen
du warst	ihr wart	
Sie waren	Sie waren	
er/sie/es war	sie waren	

FUTURE PERFECT

ich werde	wir werden	gediehen sein
du wirst	ihr werdet	
Sie werden	Sie werden	
er/sie/es wird	sie werden	

PAST SUBJUNCTIVE I

ich sei	wir seien	gediehen
du seiest	ihr seiet	
Sie seien	Sie seien	
er/sie/es sei	sie seien	

PAST SUBJUNCTIVE II

ich wäre	wir wären	gediehen
du wärest	ihr wäret	
Sie wären	Sie wären	
er/sie/es wäre	sie wären	

FUTURE PERFECT SUBJUNCTIVE I

ich werde	wir werden	gediehen sein
du werdest	ihr werdet	
Sie werden	Sie werden	
er/sie/es werde	sie werden	

FUTURE PERFECT SUBJUNCTIVE II

ich würde	wir würden	gediehen sein
du würdest	ihr würdet	
Sie würden	Sie würden	
er/sie/es würde	sie würden	

COMMANDS gedeih(e)! gedeiht! gedeihen Sie!

PRESENT PARTICIPLE gedeihend

Usage

Basilikum gedeiht gut in Töpfen. — *Basilicum grows well in pots.*

Sogar Zitronenbäume gedeihen auf dieser Insel. — *Even lemon trees grow on this island.*

Blaugrüne Algen gediehen im warmen Wasser. — *Blue-green algae thrived in the warm water.*

Okrapflanzen gedeihen bei Temperaturen über 30 Grad Celsius. — *Okra plants flourish at temperatures above 30 degrees Celsius.*

Ihre Kinder gedeihen trotz der ärmlichen Lebensverhältnisse. — *Her children are flourishing despite the poor living conditions.*

Die Hafenstadt gedieh unter der Herrschaft der Griechen. — *The seaport city prospered under Greek rule.*

Meine Arbeit ist einen Schritt weiter gediehen. — *My work has progressed a step further.*

Wie weit ist euer Projekt gediehen? — *How far has your project progressed?*

Die Diskussionen über Umweltschutz sind nicht weit gediehen. — *Not much headway has been made in the discussions on environmental protection.*

209 gefallen *to be pleasing*

gefällt · gefiel · gefallen strong verb (dative object)

PRESENT

ich gefalle	wir gefallen
du gefällst	ihr gefallt
Sie gefallen	Sie gefallen
er/sie/es gefällt	sie gefallen

SIMPLE PAST

ich gefiel	wir gefielen
du gefielst	ihr gefielt
Sie gefielen	Sie gefielen
er/sie/es gefiel	sie gefielen

FUTURE

ich werde	wir werden	gefallen
du wirst	ihr werdet	
Sie werden	Sie werden	
er/sie/es wird	sie werden	

PRESENT SUBJUNCTIVE I

ich gefalle	wir gefallen
du gefallest	ihr gefallet
Sie gefallen	Sie gefallen
er/sie/es gefalle	sie gefallen

PRESENT SUBJUNCTIVE II

ich gefiele	wir gefielen
du gefielest	ihr gefielet
Sie gefielen	Sie gefielen
er/sie/es gefiele	sie gefielen

FUTURE SUBJUNCTIVE I

ich werde	wir werden	gefallen
du werdest	ihr werdet	
Sie werden	Sie werden	
er/sie/es werde	sie werden	

FUTURE SUBJUNCTIVE II

ich würde	wir würden	gefallen
du würdest	ihr würdet	
Sie würden	Sie würden	
er/sie/es würde	sie würden	

PRESENT PERFECT

ich habe	wir haben	gefallen
du hast	ihr habt	
Sie haben	Sie haben	
er/sie/es hat	sie haben	

PAST PERFECT

ich hatte	wir hatten	gefallen
du hattest	ihr hattet	
Sie hatten	Sie hatten	
er/sie/es hatte	sie hatten	

FUTURE PERFECT

ich werde	wir werden	gefallen haben
du wirst	ihr werdet	
Sie werden	Sie werden	
er/sie/es wird	sie werden	

PAST SUBJUNCTIVE I

ich habe	wir haben	gefallen
du habest	ihr habet	
Sie haben	Sie haben	
er/sie/es habe	sie haben	

PAST SUBJUNCTIVE II

ich hätte	wir hätten	gefallen
du hättest	ihr hättet	
Sie hätten	Sie hätten	
er/sie/es hätte	sie hätten	

FUTURE PERFECT SUBJUNCTIVE I

ich werde	wir werden	gefallen haben
du werdest	ihr werdet	
Sie werden	Sie werden	
er/sie/es werde	sie werden	

FUTURE PERFECT SUBJUNCTIVE II

ich würde	wir würden	gefallen haben
du würdest	ihr würdet	
Sie würden	Sie würden	
er/sie/es würde	sie würden	

COMMANDS gefall(e)! gefallt! gefallen Sie!

PRESENT PARTICIPLE gefallend

NOTE The subject of the English sentence is a dative object in the equivalent German sentence.

Usage

Diese Farbe gefällt mir nicht.	*I don't like this color.*
Hat der Film dir gefallen?	*Did you like the film?*
Es gefiel Hans, wie das Eichhörnchen die Nuss aß.	*Hans liked how the squirrel ate the nut.*
Hip-Hop-Musik gefällt ihr sehr.	*She likes hip-hop music a lot.*
Was hat euch an der Reise am meisten gefallen?	*What pleased you all most about the trip?*

sich gefallen *to imagine/fancy oneself*

Jan gefällt sich in der Rolle eines großen Staatsmannes. *Jan fancies himself a great statesman.*

sich gefallen lassen (colloquial) *to put up with, stand for*

Sie braucht sich diese Behandlung nicht gefallen zu lassen. *She doesn't need to put up with this treatment.*

RELATED VERBS *see* **fallen** (178)

strong verb **geht · ging · gegangen**

PRESENT

ich gehe	wir gehen
du gehst	ihr geht
Sie gehen	Sie gehen
er/sie/es geht	sie gehen

SIMPLE PAST

ich ging	wir gingen
du gingst	ihr gingt
Sie gingen	Sie gingen
er/sie/es ging	sie gingen

FUTURE

ich werde	wir werden	gehen
du wirst	ihr werdet	
Sie werden	Sie werden	
er/sie/es wird	sie werden	

PRESENT SUBJUNCTIVE I

ich gehe	wir gehen
du gehest	ihr gehet
Sie gehen	Sie gehen
er/sie/es gehe	sie gehen

PRESENT SUBJUNCTIVE II

ich ginge	wir gingen
du gingest	ihr ginget
Sie gingen	Sie gingen
er/sie/es ginge	sie gingen

FUTURE SUBJUNCTIVE I

ich werde	wir werden	gehen
du werdest	ihr werdet	
Sie werden	Sie werden	
er/sie/es werde	sie werden	

FUTURE SUBJUNCTIVE II

ich würde	wir würden	gehen
du würdest	ihr würdet	
Sie würden	Sie würden	
er/sie/es würde	sie würden	

PRESENT PERFECT

ich bin	wir sind	gegangen
du bist	ihr seid	
Sie sind	Sie sind	
er/sie/es ist	sie sind	

PAST PERFECT

ich war	wir waren	gegangen
du warst	ihr wart	
Sie waren	Sie waren	
er/sie/es war	sie waren	

FUTURE PERFECT

ich werde	wir werden	gegangen sein
du wirst	ihr werdet	
Sie werden	Sie werden	
er/sie/es wird	sie werden	

PAST SUBJUNCTIVE I

ich sei	wir seien	gegangen
du seiest	ihr seiet	
Sie seien	Sie seien	
er/sie/es sei	sie seien	

PAST SUBJUNCTIVE II

ich wäre	wir wären	gegangen
du wärest	ihr wäret	
Sie wären	Sie wären	
er/sie/es wäre	sie wären	

FUTURE PERFECT SUBJUNCTIVE I

ich werde	wir werden	gegangen sein
du werdest	ihr werdet	
Sie werden	Sie werden	
er/sie/es werde	sie werden	

FUTURE PERFECT SUBJUNCTIVE II

ich würde	wir würden	gegangen sein
du würdest	ihr würdet	
Sie würden	Sie würden	
er/sie/es würde	sie würden	

COMMANDS geh(e)! geht! gehen Sie!

PRESENT PARTICIPLE gehend

Usage

Wann bist du in die Kneipe gegangen?	*When did you go to the pub?*
Gehst du heute Abend ins Kino?	*Are you going to the movies this evening?*
Gehen Sie bis zur Ecke und dann gehen Sie nach links.	*Go as far as the corner, then turn left.*
Um wie viel Uhr geht ihr ins Bett?	*When do you all go to bed?*
Als wir knapp 100 Meter gegangen waren, begann es zu schneien.	*When we'd gone barely 100 meters, it began to snow.*
Gehst du zu Fuß zur Schule oder fährst du mit dem Bus?	*Do you walk to school or do you take the bus?*

RELATED VERBS ab·gehen, an·gehen, auf·gehen, begehen, daneben·gehen, durch·gehen, ein·gehen, einher·gehen, entgegen·gehen, entgehen, entlang·gehen, entzwei·gehen, ergehen, fehl·gehen, fort·gehen, hervor·gehen, hin·gehen, hintergehen, hoch·gehen, irre·gehen, los·gehen, mit·gehen, nach·gehen, nieder·gehen, sicher·gehen, über·gehen, übergehen, um·gehen, umgehen, unter·gehen, vergehen, voran·gehen, vorbei·gehen, vor·gehen, vorher·gehen, vorüber·gehen, weg·gehen, weiter·gehen, zergehen, zu·gehen, zurück·gehen, zusammen·gehen; *see also* **aus·gehen** (35)

TOP 50 VERB ☞

gehen *to go, walk, move; go away, leave; work, function*

geht · ging · gegangen strong verb

MORE USAGE SENTENCES WITH gehen

Ich lasse dich nicht gehen. *I will not let you go.*
Morgen gehen Inge und ich zu Regina. *Tomorrow Inge and I are going to Regina's.*
Wohin hätte ich gehen sollen? *Where should I have gone?*
Monika ging drei Schritte und stand vor dem Fenster. *Monika took three steps and stood in front of the window.*
Geh nach Hause! *Go home!*
Wann geht der Zug nach Osnabrück? *When does the train for Osnabrück leave?*
Nun bist du wirklich zu weit gegangen, Birgit! *This time you've really gone too far, Birgit!*

sich gehen *to walk*

Auf dem Eis geht es sich schlecht. *It's hard to walk on the ice.*

es geht (jemandem) um etwas *to be a matter of something (for someone)*

Mir geht es um die Wahrung des Scheins. *For me, it is a matter of keeping up appearances.*
Es geht ihnen nicht um Ethik sondern um Geld. *For them, it's not a matter of ethics, but rather of money.*

gehen *to work, function*

Die Fernbedienung geht nicht mehr. *The remote control doesn't work anymore.*
Das geht nicht. *That won't work.*

gehen + infinitive *to go (do something)*

Wir gehen schwimmen, kommt ihr mit? *We're going swimming; do you want to come along?*
Maria ist bei Hertie einkaufen gegangen. *Maria went shopping at Hertie.*

IDIOMATIC EXPRESSIONS

Alle Fenster meiner Wohnung gehen nach Süden. *All the windows in my apartment face south.*
Trent will mit 50 in den Ruhestand gehen. *Trent wants to retire at 50.*
Yvonne geht mir auf die Nerven. *Yvonne is getting on my nerves.*
Uwe geht mit mir einig, dass das Thema nicht hergehört. *Uwe agrees with me that the topic doesn't belong here.*
Das Geschäft geht gut. *Business is doing well.*
Das Lied geht mir nicht aus dem Kopf. *I can't get that song out of my head.*
Wie geht die Melodie wieder? *How does the melody go again?*
Der Soldat ging in Deckung hinter einem Pkw. *The soldier took cover behind a car.*
Die Gewinne multinationaler Konzerne gehen in die Milliarden. *The profits of multinational corporations run into the billions.*
Es ging mir genau so wie dir. *The exact same thing happened to me as to you.*
Es wird spät, ich muss jetzt an die Arbeit gehen. *It's getting late; I have to get to work now.*
Ganze Dörfer gingen im Tsunami zugrunde. *Entire villages perished in the tsunami.*
Gestern war Erich krank, aber heute geht es ihm besser. *Yesterday Erich was sick, but today he's doing better.*
Herr Schnurrbusch geht auf die 90. *Mr. Schnurrbusch is approaching 90.*
Marias Wunsch ging in Erfüllung. *Maria's wish came true.*
Mein Ring ist verloren gegangen. *My ring has disappeared.*
Seit der Scheidung lässt er sich gehen. *Since the divorce, he's let himself go.*
Sieglinde geht mir immer aus dem Weg. *Sieglinde always avoids me.*
Wenn es nach mir ginge, würden wir alle daran teilnehmen dürfen. *If it were up to me, we'd all be allowed to participate.*

„Wie geht es dir denn?" „Es geht mir gut, und dir?" *"So how are you doing?" "I'm doing fine, and you?"*
„Wie war die Prüfung?" „Es ging so." *"How was the exam?" "It could have been worse."*
Wer sucht, der geht leicht selber verloren. (Nietzsche) *He who seeks becomes easily lost himself.*

regular weak verb (dative object) **gehört · gehörte · gehört**

PRESENT

ich gehöre	wir gehören
du gehörst	ihr gehört
Sie gehören	Sie gehören
er/sie/es gehört	sie gehören

SIMPLE PAST

ich gehörte	wir gehörten
du gehörtest	ihr gehörtet
Sie gehörten	Sie gehörten
er/sie/es gehörte	sie gehörten

FUTURE

ich werde	wir werden	gehören
du wirst	ihr werdet	
Sie werden	Sie werden	
er/sie/es wird	sie werden	

PRESENT SUBJUNCTIVE I

ich gehöre	wir gehören
du gehörest	ihr gehöret
Sie gehören	Sie gehören
er/sie/es gehöre	sie gehören

PRESENT SUBJUNCTIVE II

ich gehörte	wir gehörten
du gehörtest	ihr gehörtet
Sie gehörten	Sie gehörten
er/sie/es gehörte	sie gehörten

FUTURE SUBJUNCTIVE I

ich werde	wir werden	gehören
du werdest	ihr werdet	
Sie werden	Sie werden	
er/sie/es werde	sie werden	

FUTURE SUBJUNCTIVE II

ich würde	wir würden	gehören
du würdest	ihr würdet	
Sie würden	Sie würden	
er/sie/es würde	sie würden	

PRESENT PERFECT

ich habe	wir haben	gehört
du hast	ihr habt	
Sie haben	Sie haben	
er/sie/es hat	sie haben	

PAST PERFECT

ich hatte	wir hatten	gehört
du hattest	ihr hattet	
Sie hatten	Sie hatten	
er/sie/es hatte	sie hatten	

FUTURE PERFECT

ich werde	wir werden	gehört haben
du wirst	ihr werdet	
Sie werden	Sie werden	
er/sie/es wird	sie werden	

PAST SUBJUNCTIVE I

ich habe	wir haben	gehört
du habest	ihr habet	
Sie haben	Sie haben	
er/sie/es habe	sie haben	

PAST SUBJUNCTIVE II

ich hätte	wir hätten	gehört
du hättest	ihr hättet	
Sie hätten	Sie hätten	
er/sie/es hätte	sie hätten	

FUTURE PERFECT SUBJUNCTIVE I

ich werde	wir werden	gehört haben
du werdest	ihr werdet	
Sie werden	Sie werden	
er/sie/es werde	sie werden	

FUTURE PERFECT SUBJUNCTIVE II

ich würde	wir würden	gehört haben
du würdest	ihr würdet	
Sie würden	Sie würden	
er/sie/es würde	sie würden	

COMMANDS gehör(e)! gehört! gehören Sie!

PRESENT PARTICIPLE gehörend

Usage

Wem gehören die roten Socken?	*To whom do the red socks belong?*
Der neue Mercedes gehört meinem Onkel Heinz.	*The new Mercedes belongs to my Uncle Heinz.*
Du gehörst mir!	*You belong to me!*
Wenn das Geschäft mir gehörte, würde so etwas nie passieren.	*If the business belonged to me, nothing like that would ever happen.*
Wohin gehören die Gabeln und Messer?	*Where do the forks and knives belong?*
Dieses Gut gehört seit vielen Jahren einem Grafen.	*This estate has belonged to a count for many years.*
Du gabest hin die Seligkeit, gehörst uns nun in Ewigkeit! (Heine)	*You relinquished blessedness and now belong to us in eternity!*
Ingrids Dachshund gehört ihr nicht sondern umgekehrt!	*Ingrid's dachshund doesn't belong to her; it's rather the other way around!*

RELATED VERBS an·gehören, her·gehören, zu·gehören, zusammen·gehören; *see also* **hören** (248)

TOP 50 VERB ☞

gehören *to belong, be owned; pertain*

gehört · gehörte · gehört regular weak verb (dative object)

MORE USAGE SENTENCES WITH gehören

Mein Herz gehört dir, mein Schatz.	*My heart belongs to you, my sweetheart.*
„Der Ball gehört doch mir!" schrie das Kind.	*"But the ball belongs to me!" screamed the child.*
Gehört das Auto Ihnen allein oder Ihnen beiden gemeinsam?	*Does the car belong to you alone or to both of you?*
Das Handtuch gehört an den Haken da.	*The towel belongs on the hook there.*
Das große Haus an der Ecke gehörte früher dem Apotheker Schmidthammer.	*The large house on the corner was formerly owned by the pharmacist Schmidthammer.*
Dem Konzern gehören Immobilien in der ganzen Welt.	*The company owns real estate all around the world.*
Meine persönlichen Interessen und Neigungen gehören der Musik.	*My personal interests and proclivities pertain to music.*

sich gehören *to be appropriate/suitable/proper*

Solches Benehmen gehört sich nicht.	*Such behavior isn't appropriate.*

gehören in *to belong in, go in; pertain to*

Das Skateboard gehört nicht ins Haus.	*The skateboard doesn't belong in the house.*
Diese Vorstellung gehört ins Reich der Fabel.	*That notion belongs in the world of make-believe.*
Moni sagt, du würdest ins Irrenhaus gehören.	*Moni says you belong in the loony bin.*
Es ist schon Mitternacht, Kinder, ihr gehört ins Bett!	*It's already midnight, children; you belong in bed!*
Stell die Stehlampe bitte dahin, aber die Tischlampe gehört ins Schlafzimmer.	*Please put the floor lamp there, but the table lamp goes in the bedroom.*
Thorstens Theorie gehört nicht in diesen Zusammenhang.	*Thorsten's theory isn't relevant in this context.*

gehören zu *to be among; be part of, be; be required*

Zu seinen Schülern gehörten Gräfin Anna Maria von Zichy und Ludwig van Beethoven.	*Among his pupils were Countess Anna Maria von Zichy and Ludwig van Beethoven.*
Baumann gehörte zu den besten Athleten Deutschlands.	*Baumann was among the best athletes in Germany.*
Seit 1855 gehört die Insel zu Japan.	*Since 1855 the island has been part of Japan.*
Diese Siedlung gehörte bis 1973 zur Gemeinde Obersdorf.	*This development was part of the town of Obersdorf until 1973.*
Seine schöpferischen Werke gehörten zur zweiten Garnitur.	*His creative works were second-rate.*
Wale und Delfine gehören zu den Säugetieren.	*Whales and dolphins are mammals.*
Es gehört zum Allgemeinwissen, dass die Erde nicht flach ist.	*It is general knowledge that the earth is not flat.*
Dazu gehören Geduld und Ausdauer.	*That requires patience and tenacity.*

IDIOMATIC EXPRESSIONS

Es gehört nicht zum guten Ton, über Anwesende in der dritten Person zu reden.	*It's not polite to talk about those present in the third person.*
Es gehört einiges dazu, einen Roman zu schreiben.	*It takes a bit of doing to write a novel.*
Das gehört nicht zur Sache.	*That's beside the point.*
Zu den Pommes frites gehört einfach Majonäse.	*Mayonnaise is a must with french fries.*

strong verb (impersonal) (dative object) **gelingt · gelang · gelungen**

PRESENT		PRESENT PERFECT	
er/sie/es gelingt	sie gelingen	er/sie/es ist gelungen	sie sind gelungen

SIMPLE PAST		PAST PERFECT	
er/sie/es gelang	sie gelangen	er/sie/es war gelungen	sie waren gelungen

FUTURE		FUTURE PERFECT	
er/sie/es wird gelingen	sie werden gelingen	er/sie/es wird gelungen sein	sie werden gelungen sein

PRESENT SUBJUNCTIVE I		PAST SUBJUNCTIVE I	
er/sie/es gelinge	sie gelingen	er/sie/es sei gelungen	sie seien gelungen

PRESENT SUBJUNCTIVE II		PAST SUBJUNCTIVE II	
er/sie/es gelänge	sie gelängen	er/sie/es wäre gelungen	sie wären gelungen

FUTURE SUBJUNCTIVE I		FUTURE PERFECT SUBJUNCTIVE I	
er/sie/es werde gelingen	sie werden gelingen	er/sie/es werde gelungen sein	sie werden gelungen sein

FUTURE SUBJUNCTIVE II		FUTURE PERFECT SUBJUNCTIVE II	
er/sie/es würde gelingen	sie würden gelingen	er/sie/es würde gelungen sein	sie würden gelungen sein

COMMANDS —

PRESENT PARTICIPLE gelingend

NOTE Generally speaking, **gelingen** is an impersonal verb and appears only in the third person, whereas the English verbs *succeed* and *manage* are personal verbs. For this reason, the subject of the English sentence is a dative object in the equivalent German sentence.

Usage

1996 gelang es Wissenschaftlern, ein Schaf zu klonen.	*In 1996, scientists succeeded in cloning a sheep.*
Die Torte ist mir gut gelungen.	*My cake was a success.*
Nachdem es ihnen gelungen war, mich zu überzeugen, wollten sie nicht mehr mitmachen.	*After they had succeeded in convincing me, they no longer wanted to participate.*
Der Versuch scheint gelungen zu sein.	*The attempt appears to have been successful.*
Wenn es uns gelänge, mehr Arbeitsplätze zu schaffen, würden wir einen wirtschaftlichen Aufschwung erleben.	*If we could manage to create more jobs, we would experience an economic boom.*
Dem verzweifelten Kandidaten ist es gelungen, die Aufmerksamkeit der Wählerschaft auf weniger kontroverse Themen zu lenken.	*The desperate candidate managed to draw his constituents' attention to less controversial topics.*
Es gelingt ihr nicht, die Tür aufzumachen.	*She tries but cannot open the door.*

RELATED VERB *see* **misslingen** (309)

213 gelten *to be valid, hold true; matter; be effective; apply to; be considered as*

gilt · galt · gegolten strong verb

PRESENT

ich gelte	wir gelten
du giltst	ihr geltet
Sie gelten	Sie gelten
er/sie/es gilt	sie gelten

SIMPLE PAST

ich galt	wir galten
du galt(e)st	ihr galtet
Sie galten	Sie galten
er/sie/es galt	sie galten

FUTURE

ich werde	wir werden	gelten
du wirst	ihr werdet	
Sie werden	Sie werden	
er/sie/es wird	sie werden	

PRESENT SUBJUNCTIVE I

ich gelte	wir gelten
du geltest	ihr geltet
Sie gelten	Sie gelten
er/sie/es gelte	sie gelten

PRESENT SUBJUNCTIVE II

ich gölte/gälte	wir gölten/gälten
du göltest/gältest	ihr göltet/gältet
Sie gölten/gälten	Sie gölten/gälten
er/sie/es gölte/gälte	sie gölten/gälten

FUTURE SUBJUNCTIVE I

ich werde	wir werden	gelten
du werdest	ihr werdet	
Sie werden	Sie werden	
er/sie/es werde	sie werden	

FUTURE SUBJUNCTIVE II

ich würde	wir würden	gelten
du würdest	ihr würdet	
Sie würden	Sie würden	
er/sie/es würde	sie würden	

PRESENT PERFECT

ich habe	wir haben	gegolten
du hast	ihr habt	
Sie haben	Sie haben	
er/sie/es hat	sie haben	

PAST PERFECT

ich hatte	wir hatten	gegolten
du hattest	ihr hattet	
Sie hatten	Sie hatten	
er/sie/es hatte	sie hatten	

FUTURE PERFECT

ich werde	wir werden	gegolten haben
du wirst	ihr werdet	
Sie werden	Sie werden	
er/sie/es wird	sie werden	

PAST SUBJUNCTIVE I

ich habe	wir haben	gegolten
du habest	ihr habet	
Sie haben	Sie haben	
er/sie/es habe	sie haben	

PAST SUBJUNCTIVE II

ich hätte	wir hätten	gegolten
du hättest	ihr hättet	
Sie hätten	Sie hätten	
er/sie/es hätte	sie hätten	

FUTURE PERFECT SUBJUNCTIVE I

ich werde	wir werden	gegolten haben
du werdest	ihr werdet	
Sie werden	Sie werden	
er/sie/es werde	sie werden	

FUTURE PERFECT SUBJUNCTIVE II

ich würde	wir würden	gegolten haben
du würdest	ihr würdet	
Sie würden	Sie würden	
er/sie/es würde	sie würden	

COMMANDS gilt! geltet! gelten Sie!

PRESENT PARTICIPLE geltend

Usage

Der Ausweis gilt bis Januar 2010.	*The ID is valid until January 2010.*
Das, was du gestern gesagt hast, gilt nicht mehr!	*What you said yesterday no longer holds true!*
Es gilt, einen neuen Weg zu finden.	*What matters is that a new way is found.*
Der Verbot gilt bis Ende nächsten Monats.	*The prohibition is effective until the end of next month.*
Die Buhrufe galten doch nicht dir!	*The booing wasn't meant for you at all!*
Das galt für Mozarts Schüler genau so wie es heute für Musikschüler gilt.	*This applied to Mozart's pupils just as it applies to music students today.*
Der folgende Hinweis gilt allen Reisenden.	*The following instruction applies to all travelers.*
Bernd gilt als der Intelligente der Gruppe.	*Bernd is considered the intelligent one of the group.*
Das Werk gilt immer noch als problematisch für Literaturwissenschaftler.	*The work is still considered problematic for literary scholars.*
Du giltst für klug. (GRILLPARZER)	*You're considered to be smart.*

RELATED VERBS ab·gelten, entgelten, vergelten

214 genesen

to get well, recover, convalesce **genesen**

strong verb **genest · genas · genesen**

PRESENT

ich genese	wir genesen
du genest	ihr genest
Sie genesen	Sie genesen
er/sie/es genest	sie genesen

SIMPLE PAST

ich genas	wir genasen
du genasest	ihr genast
Sie genasen	Sie genasen
er/sie/es genas	sie genasen

FUTURE

ich werde	wir werden	genesen
du wirst	ihr werdet	
Sie werden	Sie werden	
er/sie/es wird	sie werden	

PRESENT SUBJUNCTIVE I

ich genese	wir genesen
du genesest	ihr geneset
Sie genesen	Sie genesen
er/sie/es genese	sie genesen

PRESENT SUBJUNCTIVE II

ich genäse	wir genäsen
du genäsest	ihr genäset
Sie genäsen	Sie genäsen
er/sie/es genäse	sie genäsen

FUTURE SUBJUNCTIVE I

ich werde	wir werden	genesen
du werdest	ihr werdet	
Sie werden	Sie werden	
er/sie/es werde	sie werden	

FUTURE SUBJUNCTIVE II

ich würde	wir würden	genesen
du würdest	ihr würdet	
Sie würden	Sie würden	
er/sie/es würde	sie würden	

PRESENT PERFECT

ich bin	wir sind	genesen
du bist	ihr seid	
Sie sind	Sie sind	
er/sie/es ist	sie sind	

PAST PERFECT

ich war	wir waren	genesen
du warst	ihr wart	
Sie waren	Sie waren	
er/sie/es war	sie waren	

FUTURE PERFECT

ich werde	wir werden	genesen sein
du wirst	ihr werdet	
Sie werden	Sie werden	
er/sie/es wird	sie werden	

PAST SUBJUNCTIVE I

ich sei	wir seien	genesen
du seiest	ihr seiet	
Sie seien	Sie seien	
er/sie/es sei	sie seien	

PAST SUBJUNCTIVE II

ich wäre	wir wären	genesen
du wärest	ihr wäret	
Sie wären	Sie wären	
er/sie/es wäre	sie wären	

FUTURE PERFECT SUBJUNCTIVE I

ich werde	wir werden	genesen sein
du werdest	ihr werdet	
Sie werden	Sie werden	
er/sie/es werde	sie werden	

FUTURE PERFECT SUBJUNCTIVE II

ich würde	wir würden	genesen sein
du würdest	ihr würdet	
Sie würden	Sie würden	
er/sie/es würde	sie würden	

COMMANDS genes(e)! genest! genesen Sie!

PRESENT PARTICIPLE genesend

Usage

Der Patient ist nach zehn Monaten nicht genesen.	*The patient did not recover after ten months.*
Versprichst du mir, ich soll genesen in diesem Wust von Raserei? (Goethe)	*Are you promising me that I will get well in this mad confusion?*
Kaiser, wollt Ihr das Leben haben, so tut mir Sicherheit, dass ich genese. (Grimm)	*Emperor, if ye would live, then assure me that I shall get well.*
Tante Marga konnte nach der Operation zu Hause genesen.	*Aunt Marga was able to convalesce at home after the operation.*
Der Junge genas ziemlich schnell.	*The boy recovered rather quickly.*
Er scheint nicht genesen zu wollen.	*He doesn't seem to want to get well.*
Die Patienten würden schneller genesen, wenn sie nicht arbeiten müssten.	*The patients would recover more quickly if they didn't have to work.*
Anke ist noch nicht ganz genesen.	*Anke hasn't yet completely recovered.*
Manfred ließ sich die Weisheitszähne ziehen und muss jetzt genesen.	*Manfred had his wisdom teeth pulled and now has to recover.*

215 genießen *to enjoy, savor*

genießt · genoss · genossen strong verb

PRESENT

ich genieße	wir genießen
du genießt	ihr genießt
Sie genießen	Sie genießen
er/sie/es genießt	sie genießen

SIMPLE PAST

ich genoss	wir genossen
du genossest	ihr genosst
Sie genossen	Sie genossen
er/sie/es genoss	sie genossen

FUTURE

ich werde	wir werden	genießen
du wirst	ihr werdet	
Sie werden	Sie werden	
er/sie/es wird	sie werden	

PRESENT SUBJUNCTIVE I

ich genieße	wir genießen
du genießest	ihr genießet
Sie genießen	Sie genießen
er/sie/es genieße	sie genießen

PRESENT SUBJUNCTIVE II

ich genösse	wir genössen
du genössest	ihr genösset
Sie genössen	Sie genössen
er/sie/es genösse	sie genössen

FUTURE SUBJUNCTIVE I

ich werde	wir werden	genießen
du werdest	ihr werdet	
Sie werden	Sie werden	
er/sie/es werde	sie werden	

FUTURE SUBJUNCTIVE II

ich würde	wir würden	genießen
du würdest	ihr würdet	
Sie würden	Sie würden	
er/sie/es würde	sie würden	

PRESENT PERFECT

ich habe	wir haben	genossen
du hast	ihr habt	
Sie haben	Sie haben	
er/sie/es hat	sie haben	

PAST PERFECT

ich hatte	wir hatten	genossen
du hattest	ihr hattet	
Sie hatten	Sie hatten	
er/sie/es hatte	sie hatten	

FUTURE PERFECT

ich werde	wir werden	genossen haben
du wirst	ihr werdet	
Sie werden	Sie werden	
er/sie/es wird	sie werden	

PAST SUBJUNCTIVE I

ich habe	wir haben	genossen
du habest	ihr habet	
Sie haben	Sie haben	
er/sie/es habe	sie haben	

PAST SUBJUNCTIVE II

ich hätte	wir hätten	genossen
du hättest	ihr hättet	
Sie hätten	Sie hätten	
er/sie/es hätte	sie hätten	

FUTURE PERFECT SUBJUNCTIVE I

ich werde	wir werden	genossen haben
du werdest	ihr werdet	
Sie werden	Sie werden	
er/sie/es werde	sie werden	

FUTURE PERFECT SUBJUNCTIVE II

ich würde	wir würden	genossen haben
du würdest	ihr würdet	
Sie würden	Sie würden	
er/sie/es würde	sie würden	

COMMANDS genieß(e)! genießt! genießen Sie!

PRESENT PARTICIPLE genießend

Usage

Ich genieße die langen, warmen Sommertage. — *I savor the long, warm summer days.*

Ab und zu genießen wir ein Glas Wein. — *Once in a while, we enjoy a glass of wine.*

Habt ihr den Abend genossen? — *Did you enjoy the evening?*

Wir genossen den Flug in erster Klasse. — *We enjoyed the flight in first class.*

Brenda genoss es, am Strand zu liegen. — *Brenda enjoyed lying on the beach.*

Genieß das Leben! — *Enjoy life!*

Das Institut für Umweltschutz genießt einen guten Ruf im Ausland. — *The Institute for Environmental Protection enjoys a good reputation abroad.*

Meine Eltern haben die vierzehn Tage in Vancouver sehr genossen. — *My parents really enjoyed the 14 days in Vancouver.*

Genießt du auch klassische Musik? — *Do you enjoy classical music, too?*

Ich konnte den Nachtisch nicht genießen. — *I couldn't enjoy the dessert.*

Sandra wird den Film bestimmt genießen. — *Sandra will definitely enjoy the film.*

Der Hund genoss das kühle Wasser. — *The dog enjoyed the cool water.*

strong verb **gerät · geriet · geraten**

PRESENT

ich gerate	wir geraten
du gerätst	ihr geratet
Sie geraten	Sie geraten
er/sie/es gerät	sie geraten

SIMPLE PAST

ich geriet	wir gerieten
du gerietst	ihr gerietet
Sie gerieten	Sie gerieten
er/sie/es geriet	sie gerieten

FUTURE

ich werde	wir werden	geraten
du wirst	ihr werdet	
Sie werden	Sie werden	
er/sie/es wird	sie werden	

PRESENT SUBJUNCTIVE I

ich gerate	wir geraten
du geratest	ihr geratet
Sie geraten	Sie geraten
er/sie/es gerate	sie geraten

PRESENT SUBJUNCTIVE II

ich geriete	wir gerieten
du gerietest	ihr gerietet
Sie gerieten	Sie gerieten
er/sie/es geriete	sie gerieten

FUTURE SUBJUNCTIVE I

ich werde	wir werden	geraten
du werdest	ihr werdet	
Sie werden	Sie werden	
er/sie/es werde	sie werden	

FUTURE SUBJUNCTIVE II

ich würde	wir würden	geraten
du würdest	ihr würdet	
Sie würden	Sie würden	
er/sie/es würde	sie würden	

PRESENT PERFECT

ich bin	wir sind	geraten
du bist	ihr seid	
Sie sind	Sie sind	
er/sie/es ist	sie sind	

PAST PERFECT

ich war	wir waren	geraten
du warst	ihr wart	
Sie waren	Sie waren	
er/sie/es war	sie waren	

FUTURE PERFECT

ich werde	wir werden	geraten sein
du wirst	ihr werdet	
Sie werden	Sie werden	
er/sie/es wird	sie werden	

PAST SUBJUNCTIVE I

ich sei	wir seien	geraten
du seiest	ihr seiet	
Sie seien	Sie seien	
er/sie/es sei	sie seien	

PAST SUBJUNCTIVE II

ich wäre	wir wären	geraten
du wärest	ihr wäret	
Sie wären	Sie wären	
er/sie/es wäre	sie wären	

FUTURE PERFECT SUBJUNCTIVE I

ich werde	wir werden	geraten sein
du werdest	ihr werdet	
Sie werden	Sie werden	
er/sie/es werde	sie werden	

FUTURE PERFECT SUBJUNCTIVE II

ich würde	wir würden	geraten sein
du würdest	ihr würdet	
Sie würden	Sie würden	
er/sie/es würde	sie würden	

COMMANDS gerate! geratet! geraten Sie!

PRESENT PARTICIPLE geratend

Usage

In Wien geriet der junge Musiker in finanzielle Schwierigkeiten. — *In Vienna, the young musician fell into financial difficulties.*
Mein Sohn war unter den Einfluss einer Sekte geraten. — *My son had come under the influence of a sect.*
Das Mädchen geriet in Verlegenheit. — *The girl became embarrassed.*
Die Kinder gerieten in Streit über den Ball. — *The children got into a fight over the ball.*
Warum ist der Dirigent immer in Wut geraten? — *Why did the conductor always become angry?*
Der Politiker ist in die Kritik geraten. — *The politician has come under criticism.*
Vorgestern geriet das Haus an der Ecke in Brand. — *The house on the corner caught fire the day before yesterday.*

Passt gut auf, sonst geratet ihr ins Gefängnis! — *Watch out, or else you'll land in prison!*
Ich gerate in Panik, wenn ich zum Zahnarzt muss. — *I panic when I have to go to the dentist.*
Der Mangokuchen ist uns gut geraten. — *The mango cake turned out well for us.*
Das Passwort war in die falschen Hände geraten. — *The password had fallen into the wrong hands.*

RELATED VERBS *see* **raten** (329)

217 geschehen *to happen, take place, occur*

geschieht · geschah · geschehen strong verb

PRESENT

ich geschehe	wir geschehen
du geschiehst	ihr gescheht
Sie geschehen	Sie geschehen
er/sie/es geschieht	sie geschehen

SIMPLE PAST

ich geschah	wir geschahen
du geschahst	ihr geschaht
Sie geschahen	Sie geschahen
er/sie/es geschah	sie geschahen

FUTURE

ich werde	wir werden	geschehen
du wirst	ihr werdet	
Sie werden	Sie werden	
er/sie/es wird	sie werden	

PRESENT SUBJUNCTIVE I

ich geschehe	wir geschehen
du geschehest	ihr geschehet
Sie geschehen	Sie geschehen
er/sie/es geschehe	sie geschehen

PRESENT SUBJUNCTIVE II

ich geschähe	wir geschähen
du geschähest	ihr geschähet
Sie geschähen	Sie geschähen
er/sie/es geschähe	sie geschähen

FUTURE SUBJUNCTIVE I

ich werde	wir werden	geschehen
du werdest	ihr werdet	
Sie werden	Sie werden	
er/sie/es werde	sie werden	

FUTURE SUBJUNCTIVE II

ich würde	wir würden	geschehen
du würdest	ihr würdet	
Sie würden	Sie würden	
er/sie/es würde	sie würden	

PRESENT PERFECT

ich bin	wir sind	geschehen
du bist	ihr seid	
Sie sind	Sie sind	
er/sie/es ist	sie sind	

PAST PERFECT

ich war	wir waren	geschehen
du warst	ihr wart	
Sie waren	Sie waren	
er/sie/es war	sie waren	

FUTURE PERFECT

ich werde	wir werden	geschehen sein
du wirst	ihr werdet	
Sie werden	Sie werden	
er/sie/es wird	sie werden	

PAST SUBJUNCTIVE I

ich sei	wir seien	geschehen
du seiest	ihr seiet	
Sie seien	Sie seien	
er/sie/es sei	sie seien	

PAST SUBJUNCTIVE II

ich wäre	wir wären	geschehen
du wärest	ihr wäret	
Sie wären	Sie wären	
er/sie/es wäre	sie wären	

FUTURE PERFECT SUBJUNCTIVE I

ich werde	wir werden	geschehen sein
du werdest	ihr werdet	
Sie werden	Sie werden	
er/sie/es werde	sie werden	

FUTURE PERFECT SUBJUNCTIVE II

ich würde	wir würden	geschehen sein
du würdest	ihr würdet	
Sie würden	Sie würden	
er/sie/es würde	sie würden	

COMMANDS —

PRESENT PARTICIPLE geschehend

Usage

Was ist hier geschehen?	*What has happened here?*
In der Zwischenzeit kann viel geschehen.	*A lot can happen in the meantime.*
Die Behörden wussten nicht, was mit dem Atommüll geschehen soll.	*The authorities didn't know what should happen with the nuclear waste.*
Was geschah vor dem Urknall?	*What took place before the Big Bang?*
Die Entlassung der Häftlinge geschah kurz vor dem Ende des Krieges.	*The prisoners' release occurred just prior to the end of the war.*
Was geschieht, wenn wir einfach nichts machen?	*What will happen if we simply do nothing?*
Der Hauptgeschäftsführer behauptet, es geschehe ohne seine Zustimmung.	*The CEO claims it is happening without his consent.*

um jemanden geschehen sein *to be all over for someone; be lost/ruined*

Es war um mich geschehen.	*It was all over for me.*

strong verb **gewinnt · gewann · gewonnen**

PRESENT

ich gewinne	wir gewinnen
du gewinnst	ihr gewinnt
Sie gewinnen	Sie gewinnen
er/sie/es gewinnt	sie gewinnen

SIMPLE PAST

ich gewann	wir gewannen
du gewannst	ihr gewannt
Sie gewannen	Sie gewannen
er/sie/es gewann	sie gewannen

FUTURE

ich werde	wir werden	gewinnen
du wirst	ihr werdet	
Sie werden	Sie werden	
er/sie/es wird	sie werden	

PRESENT SUBJUNCTIVE I

ich gewinne	wir gewinnen
du gewinnest	ihr gewinnet
Sie gewinnen	Sie gewinnen
er/sie/es gewinne	sie gewinnen

PRESENT SUBJUNCTIVE II

ich gewönne/gewänne	wir gewönnen/gewännen
du gewönnest/gewännest	ihr gewönnet/gewännet
Sie gewönnen/gewännen	Sie gewönnen/gewännen
er/sie/es gewönne/gewänne	sie gewönnen/gewännen

FUTURE SUBJUNCTIVE I

ich werde	wir werden	gewinnen
du werdest	ihr werdet	
Sie werden	Sie werden	
er/sie/es werde	sie werden	

FUTURE SUBJUNCTIVE II

ich würde	wir würden	gewinnen
du würdest	ihr würdet	
Sie würden	Sie würden	
er/sie/es würde	sie würden	

PRESENT PERFECT

ich habe	wir haben	gewonnen
du hast	ihr habt	
Sie haben	Sie haben	
er/sie/es hat	sie haben	

PAST PERFECT

ich hatte	wir hatten	gewonnen
du hattest	ihr hattet	
Sie hatten	Sie hatten	
er/sie/es hatte	sie hatten	

FUTURE PERFECT

ich werde	wir werden	gewonnen haben
du wirst	ihr werdet	
Sie werden	Sie werden	
er/sie/es wird	sie werden	

PAST SUBJUNCTIVE I

ich habe	wir haben	gewonnen
du habest	ihr habet	
Sie haben	Sie haben	
er/sie/es habe	sie haben	

PAST SUBJUNCTIVE II

ich hätte	wir hätten	gewonnen
du hättest	ihr hättet	
Sie hätten	Sie hätten	
er/sie/es hätte	sie hätten	

FUTURE PERFECT SUBJUNCTIVE I

ich werde	wir werden	gewonnen haben
du werdest	ihr werdet	
Sie werden	Sie werden	
er/sie/es werde	sie werden	

FUTURE PERFECT SUBJUNCTIVE II

ich würde	wir würden	gewonnen haben
du würdest	ihr würdet	
Sie würden	Sie würden	
er/sie/es würde	sie würden	

COMMANDS gewinn(e)! gewinnt! gewinnen Sie!

PRESENT PARTICIPLE gewinnend

Usage

Wer hat dieses Jahr die besten Chancen, die Tour de France zu gewinnen?	*Who has the best chance of winning the Tour de France this year?*
Monika muss viel üben, wenn sie gewinnen will.	*Monika must practice a lot if she wants to win.*
Unsere Mannschaft gewann mit 5:3.	*Our team won 5 to 3.*
Hast du neue Einsichten gewonnen?	*Have you gained any new insights?*
Nach der Beweisführung von Anthropologen gewann die Theorie an Anerkennung.	*After the presentation of evidence by anthropologists, the theory gained recognition.*
Ich wollte etwas Zeit gewinnen.	*I wanted to gain some time.*
Stefan und Thomas gewannen schnell ihre Sympathie.	*Stefan and Thomas quickly earned her sympathy.*
Das Trinkwasser wird aus einem See gewonnen.	*The drinking water is obtained from a lake.*
Mineralien werden aus dem Boden gewonnen.	*Minerals are extracted from the soil.*
Neues Land ist in der Nähe von Groningen gewonnen worden.	*New land has been reclaimed in the vicinity of Groningen.*

RELATED VERBS ab-gewinnen, wieder-gewinnen, zurück-gewinnen

gewöhnen *to accustom, familiarize*

gewöhnt · gewöhnte · gewöhnt regular weak verb

PRESENT

ich gewöhne	wir gewöhnen
du gewöhnst	ihr gewöhnt
Sie gewöhnen	Sie gewöhnen
er/sie/es gewöhnt	sie gewöhnen

SIMPLE PAST

ich gewöhnte	wir gewöhnten
du gewöhntest	ihr gewöhntet
Sie gewöhnten	Sie gewöhnten
er/sie/es gewöhnte	sie gewöhnten

FUTURE

ich werde	wir werden	gewöhnen
du wirst	ihr werdet	
Sie werden	Sie werden	
er/sie/es wird	sie werden	

PRESENT SUBJUNCTIVE I

ich gewöhne	wir gewöhnen
du gewöhnest	ihr gewöhnet
Sie gewöhnen	Sie gewöhnen
er/sie/es gewöhne	sie gewöhnen

PRESENT SUBJUNCTIVE II

ich gewöhnte	wir gewöhnten
du gewöhntest	ihr gewöhntet
Sie gewöhnten	Sie gewöhnten
er/sie/es gewöhnte	sie gewöhnten

FUTURE SUBJUNCTIVE I

ich werde	wir werden	gewöhnen
du werdest	ihr werdet	
Sie werden	Sie werden	
er/sie/es werde	sie werden	

FUTURE SUBJUNCTIVE II

ich würde	wir würden	gewöhnen
du würdest	ihr würdet	
Sie würden	Sie würden	
er/sie/es würde	sie würden	

PRESENT PERFECT

ich habe	wir haben	gewöhnt
du hast	ihr habt	
Sie haben	Sie haben	
er/sie/es hat	sie haben	

PAST PERFECT

ich hatte	wir hatten	gewöhnt
du hattest	ihr hattet	
Sie hatten	Sie hatten	
er/sie/es hatte	sie hatten	

FUTURE PERFECT

ich werde	wir werden	gewöhnt haben
du wirst	ihr werdet	
Sie werden	Sie werden	
er/sie/es wird	sie werden	

PAST SUBJUNCTIVE I

ich habe	wir haben	gewöhnt
du habest	ihr habet	
Sie haben	Sie haben	
er/sie/es habe	sie haben	

PAST SUBJUNCTIVE II

ich hätte	wir hätten	gewöhnt
du hättest	ihr hättet	
Sie hätten	Sie hätten	
er/sie/es hätte	sie hätten	

FUTURE PERFECT SUBJUNCTIVE I

ich werde	wir werden	gewöhnt haben
du werdest	ihr werdet	
Sie werden	Sie werden	
er/sie/es werde	sie werden	

FUTURE PERFECT SUBJUNCTIVE II

ich würde	wir würden	gewöhnt haben
du würdest	ihr würdet	
Sie würden	Sie würden	
er/sie/es würde	sie würden	

COMMANDS gewöhn(e)! gewöhnt! gewöhnen Sie!

PRESENT PARTICIPLE gewöhnend

Usage

Sie sollten das Baby an eine Routine gewöhnen. — *You should accustom the baby to a routine.*

Wir wollen den Hund daran gewöhnen, dass er draußen schläft. — *We want to get the dog used to sleeping outside.*

sich gewöhnen an *to get used to, become familiar with*

Die Katze gewöhnt sich langsam an ihr neues Zuhause. — *The cat will slowly get used to its new home.*

Wir müssen uns daran gewöhnen, dass der Supermarkt ziemlich weit entfernt ist. — *We have to become accustomed to the supermarket's being rather far away.*

Ich gewöhne mich endlich an die täglichen Temperaturschwankungen in der Wüste. — *I am finally becoming accustomed to the daily temperature fluctuations in the desert.*

Emilie konnte sich an das Trinkwasser nicht gewöhnen. — *Emilie couldn't get used to the drinking water.*

Bald hatte sich die neue Mutter an das Leben mit einem Baby gewöhnt. — *Soon the new mother had gotten used to life with a baby.*

RELATED VERBS ab-gewöhnen, an-gewöhnen, ein-gewöhnen

PRESENT

ich gieße	wir gießen
du gießt	ihr gießt
Sie gießen	Sie gießen
er/sie/es gießt	sie gießen

SIMPLE PAST

ich goss	wir gossen
du gossest	ihr gosst
Sie gossen	Sie gossen
er/sie/es goss	sie gossen

FUTURE

ich werde	wir werden	gießen
du wirst	ihr werdet	
Sie werden	Sie werden	
er/sie/es wird	sie werden	

PRESENT SUBJUNCTIVE I

ich gieße	wir gießen
du gießest	ihr gießet
Sie gießen	Sie gießen
er/sie/es gieße	sie gießen

PRESENT SUBJUNCTIVE II

ich gösse	wir gössen
du gössest	ihr gösset
Sie gössen	Sie gössen
er/sie/es gösse	sie gössen

FUTURE SUBJUNCTIVE I

ich werde	wir werden	gießen
du werdest	ihr werdet	
Sie werden	Sie werden	
er/sie/es werde	sie werden	

FUTURE SUBJUNCTIVE II

ich würde	wir würden	gießen
du würdest	ihr würdet	
Sie würden	Sie würden	
er/sie/es würde	sie würden	

PRESENT PERFECT

ich habe	wir haben	gegossen
du hast	ihr habt	
Sie haben	Sie haben	
er/sie/es hat	sie haben	

PAST PERFECT

ich hatte	wir hatten	gegossen
du hattest	ihr hattet	
Sie hatten	Sie hatten	
er/sie/es hatte	sie hatten	

FUTURE PERFECT

ich werde	wir werden	gegossen haben
du wirst	ihr werdet	
Sie werden	Sie werden	
er/sie/es wird	sie werden	

PAST SUBJUNCTIVE I

ich habe	wir haben	gegossen
du habest	ihr habet	
Sie haben	Sie haben	
er/sie/es habe	sie haben	

PAST SUBJUNCTIVE II

ich hätte	wir hätten	gegossen
du hättest	ihr hättet	
Sie hätten	Sie hätten	
er/sie/es hätte	sie hätten	

FUTURE PERFECT SUBJUNCTIVE I

ich werde	wir werden	gegossen haben
du werdest	ihr werdet	
Sie werden	Sie werden	
er/sie/es werde	sie werden	

FUTURE PERFECT SUBJUNCTIVE II

ich würde	wir würden	gegossen haben
du würdest	ihr würdet	
Sie würden	Sie würden	
er/sie/es würde	sie würden	

COMMANDS gieß(e)! gießt! gießen Sie!

PRESENT PARTICIPLE gießend

Usage

Das Fundament wurde vorgestern gegossen.	*The foundation was poured the day before yesterday.*
Gieß mal die Schüssel voll.	*Please fill the bowl with water.*
Inge gießt jeden Morgen ihre Blumen im Garten.	*Inge waters her flowers every morning in the garden.*
Der Junge goss das Wasser aus der Schüssel auf den Boden.	*The boy poured the water from the bowl onto the floor.*
Spielsoldaten werden aus Zinn gegossen.	*Toy soldiers are cast from tin.*
Gutenberg gebrauchte eine Legierung aus Blei, Zinn und Antimon, um die Drucktypen zu gießen.	*Gutenberg used an alloy of lead, tin, and antimony to cast his printing type.*
Wir gießen Kerzen aus Bienenwachs.	*We mold candles from beeswax.*

sich gießen (impersonal) *to pour*

Aus der Tasse gießt es sich nicht gut.	*This cup doesn't pour very well.*

RELATED VERBS ab·gießen, an·gießen, auf·gießen, aus·gießen, begießen, durch·gießen, ein·gießen, ergießen, nach·gießen, über·gießen, übergießen, um·gießen, vergießen, weg·gießen, zu·gießen

221 **glauben** *to believe, think, imagine; trust*

glaubt · glaubte · geglaubt regular weak verb

MORE USAGE SENTENCES WITH glauben

Ich glaube dir aufs Wort.	*I'll take your word for it.*
„Hat die Vorlesung schon begonnen?" „Ich glaube, ja."	*"Did the lecture already begin?" "I believe so."*
„Ist Melanie heute krank?" „Ich glaube, nein."	*"Is Melanie sick today?" "I don't believe so."*
Du glaubst gar nicht, wie schwer es ist.	*You have no idea how heavy it is.*
Er gibt uns zu glauben, dass der Krieg gerecht ist.	*He wants to make us believe the war is just.*
Es ist nicht zu glauben, wie kalt es geworden ist.	*It's incredible how cold it's gotten.*
Der Manager glaubt mit Recht, dass Kundenbindung schwieriger als Kundenerwerbung sei.	*The manager rightly believes that retaining customers is more difficult than attracting them.*
Opa sagte immer, man könnte nicht alles glauben, was in der Zeitung steht.	*Grandpa always said you can't believe everything you read in the newspaper.*
Das ist die Wahrheit, ob du es glaubst oder nicht.	*That's the truth, believe it or not.*
Jost glaubte seine Schwester zu sehen.	*Jost thought he saw his sister.*
Wir glauben fest, dass Weltfrieden möglich ist.	*We firmly believe world peace is possible.*
Maria, es ist kaum zu glauben, dass wir uns seit 23 Jahren kennen.	*Maria, it's hard to believe we've known each other for 23 years.*
Das will ich nicht glauben!	*I don't want to believe that!*
Irrtümlicherweise glaubte Sebastian, dass sein Reisepass gültig ist.	*Sebastian erroneously believed his passport was valid.*
Ihm ist nicht zu glauben.	*He can't be believed.*
Man glaubt, dass er an den russischen Feldzügen teilnahm.	*It is believed that he took part in the Russian campaigns.*
Die Wissenschaftler glaubten, den Ursprung der menschlichen Sprache gefunden zu haben.	*The scientists believed they had found the origin of human language.*
Der Leser weiß nicht, was zu glauben: was ist wirklich und was ist unwirklich?	*The reader doesn't know what to believe: what is real and what is unreal?*
Oh, daß du mich hörtest, daß du mir glaubtest vor meinem Tode! (HOFMANNSTHAL)	*Oh, that you would hear me, that you would believe me before my death!*

glauben an *to believe in, have faith/trust in*

Glaubt ihr an Gott?	*Do you believe in God?*
Du musst an dich selbst glauben.	*You have to have faith in yourself.*
Glaubst du an Außerirdische?	*Do you believe in extraterrestrials?*
Früher glaubten Menschen daran, dass die Bodenschätze der Erde unerschöpflich sind.	*Humans used to trust that the earth's natural resources were inexhaustible.*
Glauben Sie nicht an die Zukunft der menschlichen Zivilisation?	*Do you not have faith in the future of human civilization?*
Ich glaube nicht mehr an ihn, seitdem er uns belogen hat.	*I no longer have faith in him since he lied to us.*
Ich glaube an Wunder.	*I believe in miracles.*
Glaubst du etwa noch an den Weihnachtsmann?	*I'll bet you still believe in Santa Claus.*

glauben + direct object + adjective *to believe/think something/someone to be*

Dieter glaubt sich sicher.	*Dieter thinks he is safe.*
Der Mann wurde vermisst und die Polizei glaubte ihn tot.	*The man was missing, and police believed him dead.*
Ortwins Eltern glaubten ihn längst in Hannover.	*Ortwin's parents believed he had been in Hanover a long time already.*
Wir glaubten uns zu zwei. (GOETHE)	*We believed we were two.*
Das Liebespaar hatte sich beim Rendezvous am Strand unbeobachtet geglaubt.	*The lovebirds had thought they were not being watched during their rendezvous on the beach.*

regular weak verb **glaubt · glaubte · geglaubt**

PRESENT

ich glaube	wir glauben
du glaubst	ihr glaubt
Sie glauben	Sie glauben
er/sie/es glaubt	sie glauben

SIMPLE PAST

ich glaubte	wir glaubten
du glaubtest	ihr glaubtet
Sie glaubten	Sie glaubten
er/sie/es glaubte	sie glaubten

FUTURE

ich werde	wir werden	glauben
du wirst	ihr werdet	
Sie werden	Sie werden	
er/sie/es wird	sie werden	

PRESENT SUBJUNCTIVE I

ich glaube	wir glauben
du glaubest	ihr glaubet
Sie glauben	Sie glauben
er/sie/es glaube	sie glauben

PRESENT SUBJUNCTIVE II

ich glaubte	wir glaubten
du glaubtest	ihr glaubtet
Sie glaubten	Sie glaubten
er/sie/es glaubte	sie glaubten

FUTURE SUBJUNCTIVE I

ich werde	wir werden	glauben
du werdest	ihr werdet	
Sie werden	Sie werden	
er/sie/es werde	sie werden	

FUTURE SUBJUNCTIVE II

ich würde	wir würden	glauben
du würdest	ihr würdet	
Sie würden	Sie würden	
er/sie/es würde	sie würden	

PRESENT PERFECT

ich habe	wir haben	geglaubt
du hast	ihr habt	
Sie haben	Sie haben	
er/sie/es hat	sie haben	

PAST PERFECT

ich hatte	wir hatten	geglaubt
du hattest	ihr hattet	
Sie hatten	Sie hatten	
er/sie/es hatte	sie hatten	

FUTURE PERFECT

ich werde	wir werden	geglaubt haben
du wirst	ihr werdet	
Sie werden	Sie werden	
er/sie/es wird	sie werden	

PAST SUBJUNCTIVE I

ich habe	wir haben	geglaubt
du habest	ihr habet	
Sie haben	Sie haben	
er/sie/es habe	sie haben	

PAST SUBJUNCTIVE II

ich hätte	wir hätten	geglaubt
du hättest	ihr hättet	
Sie hätten	Sie hätten	
er/sie/es hätte	sie hätten	

FUTURE PERFECT SUBJUNCTIVE I

ich werde	wir werden	geglaubt haben
du werdest	ihr werdet	
Sie werden	Sie werden	
er/sie/es werde	sie werden	

FUTURE PERFECT SUBJUNCTIVE II

ich würde	wir würden	geglaubt haben
du würdest	ihr würdet	
Sie würden	Sie würden	
er/sie/es würde	sie würden	

COMMANDS glaub(e)! glaubt! glauben Sie!

PRESENT PARTICIPLE glaubend

Usage

Mit Lucas Howard glaubten sie, einen neuen Geschäftsführer gefunden zu haben. — *They believed they had found in Lucas Howard a new executive officer.*

Kaum jemand hätte geglaubt, dass der ältere Mann das Rennen gewinnen würde. — *Hardly anyone would have imagined that the older man would win the race.*

Ich glaube nicht, dass Berta auf die Fete kommt. — *I don't think Berta is coming to the party.*

Glaubst du, du bist der einzige, dem es nicht gefällt? — *Do you think you're the only one who doesn't like it?*

Man könnte glauben, der Typ würde hier wohnen, aber er ist nur zu Besuch. — *You might think the guy lived here, but he's only visiting.*

Langsam glaubte Norbert, dass sein Hund ihn absichtlich ärgerte. — *Norbert slowly began to think that his dog was irritating him intentionally.*

Warum glauben Sie mir nicht? — *Why don't you believe me?*

Jutta glaubt ihm jedes Wort. — *Jutta believes his every word.*

Du scheinst nicht mehr zu glauben, dass das vermisste Känguru gefunden wird. — *You seem no longer to believe that the missing kangaroo will be found.*

222 gleichen *to be equal to; resemble; be comparable to*

gleicht · glich · geglichen strong verb (dative object)

PRESENT

ich gleiche	wir gleichen
du gleichst	ihr gleicht
Sie gleichen	Sie gleichen
er/sie/es gleicht	sie gleichen

SIMPLE PAST

ich glich	wir glichen
du glichst	ihr glicht
Sie glichen	Sie glichen
er/sie/es glich	sie glichen

FUTURE

ich werde	wir werden	gleichen
du wirst	ihr werdet	
Sie werden	Sie werden	
er/sie/es wird	sie werden	

PRESENT SUBJUNCTIVE I

ich gleiche	wir gleichen
du gleichest	ihr gleichet
Sie gleichen	Sie gleichen
er/sie/es gleiche	sie gleichen

PRESENT SUBJUNCTIVE II

ich gliche	wir glichen
du glichest	ihr glichet
Sie glichen	Sie glichen
er/sie/es gliche	sie glichen

FUTURE SUBJUNCTIVE I

ich werde	wir werden	gleichen
du werdest	ihr werdet	
Sie werden	Sie werden	
er/sie/es werde	sie werden	

FUTURE SUBJUNCTIVE II

ich würde	wir würden	gleichen
du würdest	ihr würdet	
Sie würden	Sie würden	
er/sie/es würde	sie würden	

PRESENT PERFECT

ich habe	wir haben	geglichen
du hast	ihr habt	
Sie haben	Sie haben	
er/sie/es hat	sie haben	

PAST PERFECT

ich hatte	wir hatten	geglichen
du hattest	ihr hattet	
Sie hatten	Sie hatten	
er/sie/es hatte	sie hatten	

FUTURE PERFECT

ich werde	wir werden	geglichen haben
du wirst	ihr werdet	
Sie werden	Sie werden	
er/sie/es wird	sie werden	

PAST SUBJUNCTIVE I

ich habe	wir haben	geglichen
du habest	ihr habet	
Sie haben	Sie haben	
er/sie/es habe	sie haben	

PAST SUBJUNCTIVE II

ich hätte	wir hätten	geglichen
du hättest	ihr hättet	
Sie hätten	Sie hätten	
er/sie/es hätte	sie hätten	

FUTURE PERFECT SUBJUNCTIVE I

ich werde	wir werden	geglichen haben
du werdest	ihr werdet	
Sie werden	Sie werden	
er/sie/es werde	sie werden	

FUTURE PERFECT SUBJUNCTIVE II

ich würde	wir würden	geglichen haben
du würdest	ihr würdet	
Sie würden	Sie würden	
er/sie/es würde	sie würden	

COMMANDS gleich(e)! gleicht! gleichen Sie!

PRESENT PARTICIPLE gleichend

Usage

Er behauptet, kein Stück gleiche dem anderen. — *He claims no two pieces are the same.*

Der eine Soldat glich dem anderen, nur ein einziger war etwas verschieden. (Grimm) — *Each soldier was the same as every other, but one was somewhat different.*

Die Theorien glichen sich in ihren Annahmen und Aussagen. — *The theories were equivalent in their assumptions and propositions.*

Die Bühnendekoration der zweiten Szene glich einem Bauernhof des 19. Jahrhunderts. — *The stage set in the second scene resembled a nineteenth-century farmyard.*

Seine Fagottsonate hat eher einem Duo für Fagott und Klavier geglichen. — *His bassoon sonata rather resembled a duet for bassoon and piano.*

Der Vorschlag des Vorsitzenden gleicht inhaltlich dem Entwurf des Rats. — *The chair's suggestion is comparable in substance to the council's proposal.*

Tine und Line gleichen sich aufs Haar. (*idiomatic*) — *Tine and Line are the spitting image of each other.*

RELATED VERBS ab·gleichen, an·gleichen, aus·gleichen, begleichen; *see also* **vergleichen** (485)

PRESENT		PRESENT PERFECT		
ich gleite	wir gleiten	ich bin	wir sind	geglitten
du gleitest	ihr gleitet	du bist	ihr seid	
Sie gleiten	Sie gleiten	Sie sind	Sie sind	
er/sie/es gleitet	sie gleiten	er/sie/es ist	sie sind	

SIMPLE PAST		PAST PERFECT		
ich glitt	wir glitten	ich war	wir waren	geglitten
du glittst	ihr glittet	du warst	ihr wart	
Sie glitten	Sie glitten	Sie waren	Sie waren	
er/sie/es glitt	sie glitten	er/sie/es war	sie waren	

FUTURE			FUTURE PERFECT		
ich werde	wir werden	gleiten	ich werde	wir werden	geglitten sein
du wirst	ihr werdet		du wirst	ihr werdet	
Sie werden	Sie werden		Sie werden	Sie werden	
er/sie/es wird	sie werden		er/sie/es wird	sie werden	

PRESENT SUBJUNCTIVE I		PAST SUBJUNCTIVE I		
ich gleite	wir gleiten	ich sei	wir seien	geglitten
du gleitest	ihr gleitet	du seiest	ihr seiet	
Sie gleiten	Sie gleiten	Sie seien	Sie seien	
er/sie/es gleite	sie gleiten	er/sie/es sei	sie seien	

PRESENT SUBJUNCTIVE II		PAST SUBJUNCTIVE II		
ich glitte	wir glitten	ich wäre	wir wären	geglitten
du glittest	ihr glittet	du wärest	ihr wäret	
Sie glitten	Sie glitten	Sie wären	Sie wären	
er/sie/es glitte	sie glitten	er/sie/es wäre	sie wären	

FUTURE SUBJUNCTIVE I			FUTURE PERFECT SUBJUNCTIVE I		
ich werde	wir werden	gleiten	ich werde	wir werden	geglitten sein
du werdest	ihr werdet		du werdest	ihr werdet	
Sie werden	Sie werden		Sie werden	Sie werden	
er/sie/es werde	sie werden		er/sie/es werde	sie werden	

FUTURE SUBJUNCTIVE II			FUTURE PERFECT SUBJUNCTIVE II		
ich würde	wir würden	gleiten	ich würde	wir würden	geglitten sein
du würdest	ihr würdet		du würdest	ihr würdet	
Sie würden	Sie würden		Sie würden	Sie würden	
er/sie/es würde	sie würden		er/sie/es würde	sie würden	

COMMANDS gleite! gleitet! gleiten Sie!

PRESENT PARTICIPLE gleitend

Usage

Am späten Nachmittag glitten wir den Kanal abwärts bis nach Bergeshövede.	*In the late afternoon, we glided down the canal as far as Bergeshövede.*
Die Schlittschuhläufer gleiten auf dem zugefrorenen See.	*The ice skaters are gliding on the frozen lake.*
Weiße Schwäne gleiten über den stillen Teich.	*White swans are gliding across the still pond.*
Der Heißluftballon glitt ruhig zu Boden.	*The hot-air balloon glided serenely to the ground.*
Liesls Tasche ist plötzlich von ihrer Schulter auf den Bürgersteig geglitten.	*Liesl's purse suddenly slid off her shoulder onto the sidewalk.*
Der schlafende Herr glitt langsam aus seinem Sitz auf den Fußboden.	*The sleeping gentleman slowly slipped from his seat onto the floor.*
Die scharfen Augen des Detektivs glitten über die Szene im Zimmer.	*The detective's sharp eyes swept over the scene in the room.*
Das Krokodil glitt leise durch das Wasser.	*The crocodile glided quietly through the water.*

RELATED VERBS ab·gleiten, aus·gleiten, entgleiten, zurück·gleiten

224 glimmen *to glimmer, smolder, glow*

glimmt · glomm/glimmte · geglommen/geglimmt strong verb or regular weak verb

PRESENT

ich glimme	wir glimmen
du glimmst	ihr glimmt
Sie glimmen	Sie glimmen
er/sie/es glimmt	sie glimmen

SIMPLE PAST

ich glomm/glimmte	wir glommen/glimmten
du glommst/glimmtest	ihr glommt/glimmtet
Sie glommen/glimmten	Sie glommen/glimmten
er/sie/es glomm/glimmte	sie glommen/glimmten

FUTURE

ich werde	wir werden	glimmen
du wirst	ihr werdet	
Sie werden	Sie werden	
er/sie/es wird	sie werden	

PRESENT SUBJUNCTIVE I

ich glimme	wir glimmen
du glimmest	ihr glimmet
Sie glimmen	Sie glimmen
er/sie/es glimme	sie glimmen

PRESENT SUBJUNCTIVE II

ich glömme/glimmte	wir glömmen/glimmten
du glömmest/glimmtest	ihr glömmet/glimmtet
Sie glömmen/glimmten	Sie glömmen/glimmten
er/sie/es glömme/glimmte	sie glömmen/glimmten

FUTURE SUBJUNCTIVE I

ich werde	wir werden	glimmen
du werdest	ihr werdet	
Sie werden	Sie werden	
er/sie/es werde	sie werden	

FUTURE SUBJUNCTIVE II

ich würde	wir würden	glimmen
du würdest	ihr würdet	
Sie würden	Sie würden	
er/sie/es würde	sie würden	

PRESENT PERFECT

ich habe	wir haben	geglommen/geglimmt
du hast	ihr habt	
Sie haben	Sie haben	
er/sie/es hat	sie haben	

PAST PERFECT

ich hatte	wir hatten	geglommen/geglimmt
du hattest	ihr hattet	
Sie hatten	Sie hatten	
er/sie/es hatte	sie hatten	

FUTURE PERFECT

ich werde	wir werden	geglommen haben
du wirst	ihr werdet	OR
Sie werden	Sie werden	geglimmt haben
er/sie/es wird	sie werden	

PAST SUBJUNCTIVE I

ich habe	wir haben	geglommen/geglimmt
du habest	ihr habet	
Sie haben	Sie haben	
er/sie/es habe	sie haben	

PAST SUBJUNCTIVE II

ich hätte	wir hätten	geglommen/geglimmt
du hättest	ihr hättet	
Sie hätten	Sie hätten	
er/sie/es hätte	sie hätten	

FUTURE PERFECT SUBJUNCTIVE I

ich werde	wir werden	geglommen haben
du werdest	ihr werdet	OR
Sie werden	Sie werden	geglimmt haben
er/sie/es werde	sie werden	

FUTURE PERFECT SUBJUNCTIVE II

ich würde	wir würden	geglommen haben
du würdest	ihr würdet	OR
Sie würden	Sie würden	geglimmt haben
er/sie/es würde	sie würden	

COMMANDS glimm(e)! glimmt! glimmen Sie!

PRESENT PARTICIPLE glimmend

Usage

Ein Funke Hoffnung glimmt in ihren Augen.	*A spark of hope glimmers in their eyes.*
Unser Lagerfeuer glomm nur noch schwach.	*Our campfire smoldered but feebly.*
Die schneebedeckten Gipfeln glommen rot im Sonnenuntergang.	*The snow-covered peaks glowed red in the sunset.*
In der Ferne glommen gespenstische Lichter in dem leer stehenden Schloss.	*In the distance, ghostly lights glowed in the empty castle.*
Mutti, wie glimmen die Leuchtkäfer?	*Mommy, how do fireflies glow?*

NOTE Regular weak forms of **glimmen** also occur.

Unter der Asche haben die heißen Kohlen noch geglimmt.	*Under the ashes, the hot coals still smoldered.*
Eine kubanische Zigarre glimmte merklich hell im sonst dunklen Zimmer.	*A Cuban cigar glowed noticeably brightly in the otherwise dark room.*

RELATED VERBS auf·glimmen, verglimmen

PRESENT

ich grabe	wir graben
du gräbst	ihr grabt
Sie graben	Sie graben
er/sie/es gräbt	sie graben

SIMPLE PAST

ich grub	wir gruben
du grubst	ihr grubt
Sie gruben	Sie gruben
er/sie/es grub	sie gruben

FUTURE

ich werde	wir werden	graben
du wirst	ihr werdet	
Sie werden	Sie werden	
er/sie/es wird	sie werden	

PRESENT SUBJUNCTIVE I

ich grabe	wir graben
du grabest	ihr grabet
Sie graben	Sie graben
er/sie/es grabe	sie graben

PRESENT SUBJUNCTIVE II

ich grübe	wir grüben
du grübest	ihr grübet
Sie grüben	Sie grüben
er/sie/es grübe	sie grüben

FUTURE SUBJUNCTIVE I

ich werde	wir werden	graben
du werdest	ihr werdet	
Sie werden	Sie werden	
er/sie/es werde	sie werden	

FUTURE SUBJUNCTIVE II

ich würde	wir würden	graben
du würdest	ihr würdet	
Sie würden	Sie würden	
er/sie/es würde	sie würden	

PRESENT PERFECT

ich habe	wir haben	gegraben
du hast	ihr habt	
Sie haben	Sie haben	
er/sie/es hat	sie haben	

PAST PERFECT

ich hatte	wir hatten	gegraben
du hattest	ihr hattet	
Sie hatten	Sie hatten	
er/sie/es hatte	sie hatten	

FUTURE PERFECT

ich werde	wir werden	gegraben haben
du wirst	ihr werdet	
Sie werden	Sie werden	
er/sie/es wird	sie werden	

PAST SUBJUNCTIVE I

ich habe	wir haben	gegraben
du habest	ihr habet	
Sie haben	Sie haben	
er/sie/es habe	sie haben	

PAST SUBJUNCTIVE II

ich hätte	wir hätten	gegraben
du hättest	ihr hättet	
Sie hätten	Sie hätten	
er/sie/es hätte	sie hätten	

FUTURE PERFECT SUBJUNCTIVE I

ich werde	wir werden	gegraben haben
du werdest	ihr werdet	
Sie werden	Sie werden	
er/sie/es werde	sie werden	

FUTURE PERFECT SUBJUNCTIVE II

ich würde	wir würden	gegraben haben
du würdest	ihr würdet	
Sie würden	Sie würden	
er/sie/es würde	sie würden	

COMMANDS grab(e)! grabt! graben Sie!

PRESENT PARTICIPLE grabend

Usage

Heinrich Schliemann war wohl der erste Archäologe, der bei Troja grub. — *Heinrich Schliemann was probably the first archeologist to excavate at Troy.*

Ein Wasserbrunnen war im späten 18. Jahrhundert hier gegraben worden. — *A water well had been dug here in the late eighteenth century.*

Wer andern eine Grube gräbt, fällt selbst hinein. (PROVERB) — *He who digs a hole for others will fall in himself.*

Der schüchterne Junge grub seine Hände in seine Hosentaschen. — *The shy boy dug his hands into his trouser pockets.*

sich graben *to dig*

Die Regenwürmer graben sich durch die verfaulten Blätter und Erde. — *The earthworms tunnel their way through the decomposing leaves and soil.*

RELATED VERBS ab·graben, auf·graben, aus·graben, begraben, durch·graben, ein·graben, um·graben, unter·graben, untergraben, vergraben

greifen *to grasp, seize, catch hold (of); reach; resort to*

greift · griff · gegriffen strong verb

PRESENT

ich greife	wir greifen
du greifst	ihr greift
Sie greifen	Sie greifen
er/sie/es greift	sie greifen

SIMPLE PAST

ich griff	wir griffen
du griffst	ihr grifft
Sie griffen	Sie griffen
er/sie/es griff	sie griffen

FUTURE

ich werde	wir werden	greifen
du wirst	ihr werdet	
Sie werden	Sie werden	
er/sie/es wird	sie werden	

PRESENT SUBJUNCTIVE I

ich greife	wir greifen
du greifest	ihr greifet
Sie greifen	Sie greifen
er/sie/es greife	sie greifen

PRESENT SUBJUNCTIVE II

ich griffe	wir griffen
du griffest	ihr griffet
Sie griffen	Sie griffen
er/sie/es griffe	sie griffen

FUTURE SUBJUNCTIVE I

ich werde	wir werden	greifen
du werdest	ihr werdet	
Sie werden	Sie werden	
er/sie/es werde	sie werden	

FUTURE SUBJUNCTIVE II

ich würde	wir würden	greifen
du würdest	ihr würdet	
Sie würden	Sie würden	
er/sie/es würde	sie würden	

PRESENT PERFECT

ich habe	wir haben	gegriffen
du hast	ihr habt	
Sie haben	Sie haben	
er/sie/es hat	sie haben	

PAST PERFECT

ich hatte	wir hatten	gegriffen
du hattest	ihr hattet	
Sie hatten	Sie hatten	
er/sie/es hatte	sie hatten	

FUTURE PERFECT

ich werde	wir werden	gegriffen haben
du wirst	ihr werdet	
Sie werden	Sie werden	
er/sie/es wird	sie werden	

PAST SUBJUNCTIVE I

ich habe	wir haben	gegriffen
du habest	ihr habet	
Sie haben	Sie haben	
er/sie/es habe	sie haben	

PAST SUBJUNCTIVE II

ich hätte	wir hätten	gegriffen
du hättest	ihr hättet	
Sie hätten	Sie hätten	
er/sie/es hätte	sie hätten	

FUTURE PERFECT SUBJUNCTIVE I

ich werde	wir werden	gegriffen haben
du werdest	ihr werdet	
Sie werden	Sie werden	
er/sie/es werde	sie werden	

FUTURE PERFECT SUBJUNCTIVE II

ich würde	wir würden	gegriffen haben
du würdest	ihr würdet	
Sie würden	Sie würden	
er/sie/es würde	sie würden	

COMMANDS greif(e)! greift! greifen Sie!

PRESENT PARTICIPLE greifend

Usage

Greifen Sie die Zange mit der rechten Hand. — *Grasp the pliers with your right hand.*

Der weltberühmte Klaviervirtuose griff energisch und inspiriert in die Tasten. — *The world-famous piano virtuoso struck the keys with energy and inspiration.*

In den letzten Wochen habe ich zu oft ins Portemonnaie greifen müssen. (*idiomatic*) — *During the last few weeks, I've had to reach for my wallet too often.*

Wenn ich nervös bin, greife ich zur Zigarette. — *When I'm nervous, I reach for a cigarette.*

Eckhard greift leider zur Lüge. — *Eckhard, unfortunately, is resorting to lying.*

Wir haben zu extremen Maßnahmen gegriffen. — *We resorted to extreme measures.*

greifen um sich *to spread*

Die Flammen griffen schnell um sich. — *The flames spread quickly.*

RELATED VERBS ab·greifen, an·greifen, auf·greifen, aus·greifen, begreifen, daneben·greifen, durch·greifen, ein·begreifen, ein·greifen, ergreifen, über·greifen, um·greifen, umgreifen, vergreifen, vor·greifen, zu·greifen, zurück·greifen

regular weak verb **gründet · gründete · gegründet**

PRESENT

ich gründe	wir gründen
du gründest	ihr gründet
Sie gründen	Sie gründen
er/sie/es gründet	sie gründen

SIMPLE PAST

ich gründete	wir gründeten
du gründetest	ihr gründetet
Sie gründeten	Sie gründeten
er/sie/es gründete	sie gründeten

FUTURE

ich werde	wir werden	gründen
du wirst	ihr werdet	
Sie werden	Sie werden	
er/sie/es wird	sie werden	

PRESENT SUBJUNCTIVE I

ich gründe	wir gründen
du gründest	ihr gründet
Sie gründen	Sie gründen
er/sie/es gründe	sie gründen

PRESENT SUBJUNCTIVE II

ich gründete	wir gründeten
du gründetest	ihr gründetet
Sie gründeten	Sie gründeten
er/sie/es gründete	sie gründeten

FUTURE SUBJUNCTIVE I

ich werde	wir werden	gründen
du werdest	ihr werdet	
Sie werden	Sie werden	
er/sie/es werde	sie werden	

FUTURE SUBJUNCTIVE II

ich würde	wir würden	gründen
du würdest	ihr würdet	
Sie würden	Sie würden	
er/sie/es würde	sie würden	

PRESENT PERFECT

ich habe	wir haben	gegründet
du hast	ihr habt	
Sie haben	Sie haben	
er/sie/es hat	sie haben	

PAST PERFECT

ich hatte	wir hatten	gegründet
du hattest	ihr hattet	
Sie hatten	Sie hatten	
er/sie/es hatte	sie hatten	

FUTURE PERFECT

ich werde	wir werden	gegründet haben
du wirst	ihr werdet	
Sie werden	Sie werden	
er/sie/es wird	sie werden	

PAST SUBJUNCTIVE I

ich habe	wir haben	gegründet
du habest	ihr habet	
Sie haben	Sie haben	
er/sie/es habe	sie haben	

PAST SUBJUNCTIVE II

ich hätte	wir hätten	gegründet
du hättest	ihr hättet	
Sie hätten	Sie hätten	
er/sie/es hätte	sie hätten	

FUTURE PERFECT SUBJUNCTIVE I

ich werde	wir werden	gegründet haben
du werdest	ihr werdet	
Sie werden	Sie werden	
er/sie/es werde	sie werden	

FUTURE PERFECT SUBJUNCTIVE II

ich würde	wir würden	gegründet haben
du würdest	ihr würdet	
Sie würden	Sie würden	
er/sie/es würde	sie würden	

COMMANDS gründe! gründet! gründen Sie!

PRESENT PARTICIPLE gründend

Usage

Der SC Hörstel wurde 1921 als Fußballverein gegründet. — *The Hörstel SC was founded in 1921 as a soccer club.*

Vor zwei Jahren habe ich mich entschlossen, meine eigene Firma zu gründen. — *Two years ago, I decided to establish my own company.*

Unser Nachbar Robert hat mit seinen Freunden eine Rockband gegründet. — *Our neighbor Robert started a rock band with his friends.*

Wir möchten eine Familie gründen. — *We'd like to start a family.*

Der Chef gründete seine Entscheidung auf die gegenwärtigen Verhältnisse. — *The boss based his decision on current conditions.*

Stille Wasser gründen tief. (PROVERB) — *Still waters run deep.*

sich gründen *to be based, rest*

Die Doktrin vom Präventivkrieg gründet sich nicht auf aufgeklärte Vernunft sondern auf Angst und Paranoia. — *The doctrine of preventive war is based not on enlightened reason, but on fear and paranoia.*

RELATED VERBS ergründen, um·gründen; *see also* **begründen** (59)

228 grüßen *to greet, say hello (to), salute*

grüßt · grüßte · gegrüßt regular weak verb

PRESENT

ich grüße	wir grüßen
du grüßt	ihr grüßt
Sie grüßen	Sie grüßen
er/sie/es grüßt	sie grüßen

PRESENT PERFECT

ich habe	wir haben	gegrüßt
du hast	ihr habt	
Sie haben	Sie haben	
er/sie/es hat	sie haben	

SIMPLE PAST

ich grüßte	wir grüßten
du grüßtest	ihr grüßtet
Sie grüßten	Sie grüßten
er/sie/es grüßte	sie grüßten

PAST PERFECT

ich hatte	wir hatten	gegrüßt
du hattest	ihr hattet	
Sie hatten	Sie hatten	
er/sie/es hatte	sie hatten	

FUTURE

ich werde	wir werden	grüßen
du wirst	ihr werdet	
Sie werden	Sie werden	
er/sie/es wird	sie werden	

FUTURE PERFECT

ich werde	wir werden	gegrüßt haben
du wirst	ihr werdet	
Sie werden	Sie werden	
er/sie/es wird	sie werden	

PRESENT SUBJUNCTIVE I

ich grüße	wir grüßen
du grüßest	ihr grüßet
Sie grüßen	Sie grüßen
er/sie/es grüße	sie grüßen

PAST SUBJUNCTIVE I

ich habe	wir haben	gegrüßt
du habest	ihr habet	
Sie haben	Sie haben	
er/sie/es habe	sie haben	

PRESENT SUBJUNCTIVE II

ich grüßte	wir grüßten
du grüßtest	ihr grüßtet
Sie grüßten	Sie grüßten
er/sie/es grüßte	sie grüßten

PAST SUBJUNCTIVE II

ich hätte	wir hätten	gegrüßt
du hättest	ihr hättet	
Sie hätten	Sie hätten	
er/sie/es hätte	sie hätten	

FUTURE SUBJUNCTIVE I

ich werde	wir werden	grüßen
du werdest	ihr werdet	
Sie werden	Sie werden	
er/sie/es werde	sie werden	

FUTURE PERFECT SUBJUNCTIVE I

ich werde	wir werden	gegrüßt haben
du werdest	ihr werdet	
Sie werden	Sie werden	
er/sie/es werde	sie werden	

FUTURE SUBJUNCTIVE II

ich würde	wir würden	grüßen
du würdest	ihr würdet	
Sie würden	Sie würden	
er/sie/es würde	sie würden	

FUTURE PERFECT SUBJUNCTIVE II

ich würde	wir würden	gegrüßt haben
du würdest	ihr würdet	
Sie würden	Sie würden	
er/sie/es würde	sie würden	

COMMANDS grüß(e)! grüßt! grüßen Sie!

PRESENT PARTICIPLE grüßend

Usage

Der freundliche Bürgermeister grüßte die Besucher aus Waltham Abbey. — *The friendly mayor greeted the visitors from Waltham Abbey.*

Grüß mal deinen Mann von mir. — *Give your husband my regards.*

Sie grüßen einander in zwei verschiedenen Sprachen, ohne ein Wort zu verstehen. — *They greet each other in two different languages without understanding a word.*

Wir grüßen uns jeden Morgen, aber ich weiß seinen Namen nicht. — *We greet one another every morning, but I don't know his name.*

grüßen lassen *to send one's greetings/regards*

Papa lässt grüßen. — *Papa said to say hello.*

sich grüßen mit *to greet, say hello (to)*

Habt ihr euch mit Tante Bärbel gegrüßt? — *Did you say hello to Aunt Bärbel?*

RELATED VERBS wieder·grüßen; *see also* **begrüßen** (60)

regular weak verb **guckt · guckte · geguckt**

PRESENT		PRESENT PERFECT		
ich gucke	wir gucken	ich habe	wir haben	geguckt
du guckst	ihr guckt	du hast	ihr habt	
Sie gucken	Sie gucken	Sie haben	Sie haben	
er/sie/es guckt	sie gucken	er/sie/es hat	sie haben	

SIMPLE PAST		PAST PERFECT		
ich guckte	wir guckten	ich hatte	wir hatten	geguckt
du gucktest	ihr gucktet	du hattest	ihr hattet	
Sie guckten	Sie guckten	Sie hatten	Sie hatten	
er/sie/es guckte	sie guckten	er/sie/es hatte	sie hatten	

FUTURE			FUTURE PERFECT		
ich werde	wir werden	gucken	ich werde	wir werden	geguckt haben
du wirst	ihr werdet		du wirst	ihr werdet	
Sie werden	Sie werden		Sie werden	Sie werden	
er/sie/es wird	sie werden		er/sie/es wird	sie werden	

PRESENT SUBJUNCTIVE I		PAST SUBJUNCTIVE I		
ich gucke	wir gucken	ich habe	wir haben	geguckt
du guckest	ihr gucket	du habest	ihr habet	
Sie gucken	Sie gucken	Sie haben	Sie haben	
er/sie/es gucke	sie gucken	er/sie/es habe	sie haben	

PRESENT SUBJUNCTIVE II		PAST SUBJUNCTIVE II		
ich guckte	wir guckten	ich hätte	wir hätten	geguckt
du gucktest	ihr gucktet	du hättest	ihr hättet	
Sie guckten	Sie guckten	Sie hätten	Sie hätten	
er/sie/es guckte	sie guckten	er/sie/es hätte	sie hätten	

FUTURE SUBJUNCTIVE I			FUTURE PERFECT SUBJUNCTIVE I		
ich werde	wir werden	gucken	ich werde	wir werden	geguckt haben
du werdest	ihr werdet		du werdest	ihr werdet	
Sie werden	Sie werden		Sie werden	Sie werden	
er/sie/es werde	sie werden		er/sie/es werde	sie werden	

FUTURE SUBJUNCTIVE II			FUTURE PERFECT SUBJUNCTIVE II		
ich würde	wir würden	gucken	ich würde	wir würden	geguckt haben
du würdest	ihr würdet		du würdest	ihr würdet	
Sie würden	Sie würden		Sie würden	Sie würden	
er/sie/es würde	sie würden		er/sie/es würde	sie würden	

COMMANDS guck(e)! guckt! gucken Sie!

PRESENT PARTICIPLE guckend

Usage (colloquial)

Als Kind habe ich immer neugierig in den Ofen geguckt, wenn Mama einen Kuchen gebacken hat. — *As a child, I always peeked with curiosity in the oven whenever Mama baked a cake.*

Guck mal! — *Look!*

Die Schulkinder durften dem Bildhauer bei der Arbeit über die Schulter gucken. — *The schoolchildren were allowed to watch over the sculptor's shoulders while he worked.*

„Hast du beim Trödelmarkt etwas gekauft?" — *"Did you buy anything at the flea market?"*
„Nein, ich habe nur geguckt." — *"No, I just looked."*

Heute Abend wollen wir einen Film gucken. — *We want to watch a movie this evening.*

Guckst du gern Fußball? — *Do you like to watch soccer?*

Ich gucke nur noch Nachrichtensendungen. — *I only watch news programs anymore.*

Mal gucken. (*idiomatic*) — *We'll (wait and) see (what happens).*

RELATED VERBS ab·gucken, an·gucken, auf·gucken, aus·gucken, begucken, durch·gucken, um·gucken, vergucken, vor·gucken, zu·gucken

haben *to have, possess, bear*

hat · hatte · gehabt irregular verb (perfect auxiliary)

MORE USAGE SENTENCES WITH haben

„Wo ist bloß meine Tasche?“ „Ich habe keine Ahnung.“ — *“Where on earth is my purse?” “I haven't the faintest idea.”*
Mit zwei Jobs hat sie es wirklich schwer. — *With two jobs, things are really rough for her.*
Ich habe nichts dagegen. — *I have nothing against that.*
Maria hat Fernweh und will wegfahren. — *Maria has wanderlust and wants to travel.*
Das Baby hat hohes Fieber. — *The baby has a high fever.*
Der gelbe VW hatte Vorfahrt. — *The yellow VW had the right-of-way.*
„Willst du ins Kino?“ „Leider habe ich keine Zeit.“ — *“Do you want to go to a movie?” “Unfortunately, I have no time.”*
Haben Sie bitte etwas Geduld. — *Please have a little patience.*

sich haben *to be; act up, make a scene* (colloquial)

Damit hat es sich! — *There it is!/That's the end of that!*
Hab' dich nicht so! — *Don't be like that!*

haben zu + infinitive *must, to have to, be obligated to*

Sie haben diese Regelungen zu beachten. — *You must observe these rules.*
Auf einer Baustelle hat man Lärm zu erwarten. — *On a construction site, you have to expect noise.*

IDIOMATIC EXPRESSIONS

Manfred hat Anspruch auf Entschädigung. — *Manfred is entitled to compensation.*
Das hat zu Folge, dass Kursteilnehmer sich wohl fühlen. — *As a consequence, course participants feel at ease.*
Wer hat Schuld daran? — *Whose fault is that?*
Lars sagte, er hätte Liesl gern. — *Lars said he's fond of Liesl.*
Ich hätte gern das Schweinekotelett mit Pommes. — *I'd like the pork cutlet with fries.*
Maxl hat Durst. — *Maxl is thirsty.*
Heute haben wir schönes Wetter, nicht? — *It's beautiful weather today, isn't it?*
Bei der Ein- und Ausreise hat man einen Pass nötig. — *When entering and leaving, you need a passport.*
Da hast du es! — *There, you see!/I told you so!*
Wir haben heute den dritten Mai. — *Today is the third of May.*
Das hat nicht viel auf sich. — *That is of little consequence.*
Das hat etwas für sich. — *There's something to be said for that.*
Woher hast du das? — *Where did you get that?*
Gott habe ihn selig. — *God rest his soul.*
Liesl hat viel von ihrer Mutter. — *Liesl takes after her mother.*
Man hat, was man hat. (PROVERB) — *Something is better than nothing.*
Das hat Zeit. — *There's no hurry.*
Ich kann es nicht haben, wenn er so daherredet. — *I can't stand it when he blabbers like that.*
Maria hat zu tun. — *Maria is busy.*
Ein Modell mit Vorderradantrieb ist nicht zu haben. — *A model with front-wheel drive is not available.*
Du hast Recht, deine Katze ist wählerisch. — *You're right; your cat is finicky.*
Habt Acht vor dem nächtlichen Heer! (WAGNER) — *Beware the nocturnal host!*
Serene hatte ihn lieb. — *Serene loved him.*
Gehen wir, ich habe es eilig. — *Let's go; I'm in a hurry.*
Wir hatten Hunger, aber nichts zu essen. — *We were hungry but had nothing to eat.*
Diese Software hat das so an sich. — *That's just the way this software is.*
Sie haben es gemütlich warm in Ihrer Hütte. — *You are cozy and warm in your cabin.*

COLLOQUIALISMS

Was habe ich denn davon? — *What's in it for me?*
Ich habe dich satt! — *I'm fed up with you!*
Was hast du denn? — *What's the matter?*
Du hast einen Vogel. — *You're crazy.*
Du hast mir nichts zu sagen! — *You can't tell me what to do.*

PRESENT		PRESENT PERFECT		
ich habe	wir haben	ich habe	wir haben	gehabt
du hast	ihr habt	du hast	ihr habt	
Sie haben	Sie haben	Sie haben	Sie haben	
er/sie/es hat	sie haben	er/sie/es hat	sie haben	

SIMPLE PAST		PAST PERFECT		
ich hatte	wir hatten	ich hatte	wir hatten	gehabt
du hattest	ihr hattet	du hattest	ihr hattet	
Sie hatten	Sie hatten	Sie hatten	Sie hatten	
er/sie/es hatte	sie hatten	er/sie/es hatte	sie hatten	

FUTURE			FUTURE PERFECT		
ich werde	wir werden	haben	ich werde	wir werden	gehabt haben
du wirst	ihr werdet		du wirst	ihr werdet	
Sie werden	Sie werden		Sie werden	Sie werden	
er/sie/es wird	sie werden		er/sie/es wird	sie werden	

PRESENT SUBJUNCTIVE I		PAST SUBJUNCTIVE I		
ich habe	wir haben	ich habe	wir haben	gehabt
du habest	ihr habet	du habest	ihr habet	
Sie haben	Sie haben	Sie haben	Sie haben	
er/sie/es habe	sie haben	er/sie/es habe	sie haben	

PRESENT SUBJUNCTIVE II		PAST SUBJUNCTIVE II		
ich hätte	wir hätten	ich hätte	wir hätten	gehabt
du hättest	ihr hättet	du hättest	ihr hättet	
Sie hätten	Sie hätten	Sie hätten	Sie hätten	
er/sie/es hätte	sie hätten	er/sie/es hätte	sie hätten	

FUTURE SUBJUNCTIVE I			FUTURE PERFECT SUBJUNCTIVE I		
ich werde	wir werden	haben	ich werde	wir werden	gehabt haben
du werdest	ihr werdet		du werdest	ihr werdet	
Sie werden	Sie werden		Sie werden	Sie werden	
er/sie/es werde	sie werden		er/sie/es werde	sie werden	

FUTURE SUBJUNCTIVE II			FUTURE PERFECT SUBJUNCTIVE II		
ich würde	wir würden	haben	ich würde	wir würden	gehabt haben
du würdest	ihr würdet		du würdest	ihr würdet	
Sie würden	Sie würden		Sie würden	Sie würden	
er/sie/es würde	sie würden		er/sie/es würde	sie würden	

COMMANDS hab(e)! habt! haben Sie!

PRESENT PARTICIPLE habend

Usage

Onkel Heinz hatte früher einen Mercedes.	*Uncle Heinz used to have a Mercedes.*
Der jüngste Sohn der Familie hat in der Tat ein photographisches Gedächtnis.	*The youngest son in the family in fact possesses a photographic memory.*
Ich habe drei Schwestern.	*I have three sisters.*
Hast du nicht eine neue Chefin?	*Don't you have a new boss?*
Monika hat bestimmt einen guten Vorschlag.	*Monika will surely have a good suggestion.*
Sie haben das Recht auf einen Anwalt.	*You have the right to an attorney.*
„Ihr habt es gut, Kinder", sagte der Großvater.	*"You have it good, children," said the grandfather.*
Unser Haus hat zwölf Zimmer.	*Our house has twelve rooms.*
Könnte ich bitte ein Glas Wasser haben?	*Could I please have a glass of water?*
Haben Sie einen Ausweis?	*Do you have identification?*
Wir haben noch viel vor uns.	*We still have a lot to do.*

RELATED VERBS ab·haben, an·haben, auf·haben, beisammen·haben, gut·haben, inne·haben, los·haben, teil·haben, über·haben, vor·haben, wahr·haben, weg·haben, wieder·haben

231 halten

to hold, keep; detain, constrain; observe; think, consider; stop; last, endure

hält · hielt · gehalten strong verb

PRESENT

ich halte	wir halten
du hältst	ihr haltet
Sie halten	Sie halten
er/sie/es hält	sie halten

PRESENT PERFECT

ich habe	wir haben	gehalten
du hast	ihr habt	
Sie haben	Sie haben	
er/sie/es hat	sie haben	

SIMPLE PAST

ich hielt	wir hielten
du hieltst	ihr hieltet
Sie hielten	Sie hielten
er/sie/es hielt	sie hielten

PAST PERFECT

ich hatte	wir hatten	gehalten
du hattest	ihr hattet	
Sie hatten	Sie hatten	
er/sie/es hatte	sie hatten	

FUTURE

ich werde	wir werden	halten
du wirst	ihr werdet	
Sie werden	Sie werden	
er/sie/es wird	sie werden	

FUTURE PERFECT

ich werde	wir werden	gehalten haben
du wirst	ihr werdet	
Sie werden	Sie werden	
er/sie/es wird	sie werden	

PRESENT SUBJUNCTIVE I

ich halte	wir halten
du haltest	ihr haltet
Sie halten	Sie halten
er/sie/es halte	sie halten

PAST SUBJUNCTIVE I

ich habe	wir haben	gehalten
du habest	ihr habet	
Sie haben	Sie haben	
er/sie/es habe	sie haben	

PRESENT SUBJUNCTIVE II

ich hielte	wir hielten
du hieltest	ihr hieltet
Sie hielten	Sie hielten
er/sie/es hielte	sie hielten

PAST SUBJUNCTIVE II

ich hätte	wir hätten	gehalten
du hättest	ihr hättet	
Sie hätten	Sie hätten	
er/sie/es hätte	sie hätten	

FUTURE SUBJUNCTIVE I

ich werde	wir werden	halten
du werdest	ihr werdet	
Sie werden	Sie werden	
er/sie/es werde	sie werden	

FUTURE PERFECT SUBJUNCTIVE I

ich werde	wir werden	gehalten haben
du werdest	ihr werdet	
Sie werden	Sie werden	
er/sie/es werde	sie werden	

FUTURE SUBJUNCTIVE II

ich würde	wir würden	halten
du würdest	ihr würdet	
Sie würden	Sie würden	
er/sie/es würde	sie würden	

FUTURE PERFECT SUBJUNCTIVE II

ich würde	wir würden	gehalten haben
du würdest	ihr würdet	
Sie würden	Sie würden	
er/sie/es würde	sie würden	

COMMANDS halte! haltet! halten Sie!

PRESENT PARTICIPLE haltend

Usage

Der kleine Dackel konnte nicht Schritt halten.	*The little dachshund couldn't keep pace.*
Wie könntest du das Essen warm halten?	*How could you keep the food warm?*
Die Präsidentin hat ihr Wort gehalten.	*The president kept her word.*
Wir wollen den Ort geheim halten.	*We want to keep the location a secret.*
Ich habe viel Tee getrunken, um mich wach zu halten.	*I drank a lot of tea to keep awake.*
Dreißig Soldaten wurden gefangen gehalten.	*Thirty soldiers were held prisoner.*
Mein Vater hält nicht viel von dieser Idee.	*My father doesn't think much of this idea.*
Regina hielt seine Äußerung für unnötig.	*Regina considered his comment unnecessary.*
Halten Sie bitte hier!	*Please stop here!*

RELATED VERBS ab·halten, an·halten, auf·halten, aus·halten, bereit·halten, durch·halten, ein·halten, entgegen·halten, frei·halten, her·halten, hoch·halten, inne·halten, mit·halten, nieder·halten, stand·halten, still·halten, vor·halten, zu·halten, zurück·halten, zusammen·halten; *see also* **behalten** (61), **enthalten** (144), **erhalten** (157), **fest·halten** (184), **unterhalten** (468), **verhalten** (487)

regular weak verb **handelt · handelte · gehandelt**

PRESENT		PRESENT PERFECT		
ich hand(e)le	wir handeln	ich habe	wir haben	gehandelt
du handelst	ihr handelt	du hast	ihr habt	
Sie handeln	Sie handeln	Sie haben	Sie haben	
er/sie/es handelt	sie handeln	er/sie/es hat	sie haben	

SIMPLE PAST		PAST PERFECT		
ich handelte	wir handelten	ich hatte	wir hatten	gehandelt
du handeltest	ihr handeltet	du hattest	ihr hattet	
Sie handelten	Sie handelten	Sie hatten	Sie hatten	
er/sie/es handelte	sie handelten	er/sie/es hatte	sie hatten	

FUTURE			FUTURE PERFECT		
ich werde	wir werden	handeln	ich werde	wir werden	gehandelt haben
du wirst	ihr werdet		du wirst	ihr werdet	
Sie werden	Sie werden		Sie werden	Sie werden	
er/sie/es wird	sie werden		er/sie/es wird	sie werden	

PRESENT SUBJUNCTIVE I		PAST SUBJUNCTIVE I		
ich hand(e)le	wir handeln	ich habe	wir haben	gehandelt
du handelst	ihr handelt	du habest	ihr habet	
Sie handeln	Sie handeln	Sie haben	Sie haben	
er/sie/es hand(e)le	sie handeln	er/sie/es habe	sie haben	

PRESENT SUBJUNCTIVE II		PAST SUBJUNCTIVE II		
ich handelte	wir handelten	ich hätte	wir hätten	gehandelt
du handeltest	ihr handeltet	du hättest	ihr hättet	
Sie handelten	Sie handelten	Sie hätten	Sie hätten	
er/sie/es handelte	sie handelten	er/sie/es hätte	sie hätten	

FUTURE SUBJUNCTIVE I			FUTURE PERFECT SUBJUNCTIVE I		
ich werde	wir werden	handeln	ich werde	wir werden	gehandelt haben
du werdest	ihr werdet		du werdest	ihr werdet	
Sie werden	Sie werden		Sie werden	Sie werden	
er/sie/es werde	sie werden		er/sie/es werde	sie werden	

FUTURE SUBJUNCTIVE II			FUTURE PERFECT SUBJUNCTIVE II		
ich würde	wir würden	handeln	ich würde	wir würden	gehandelt haben
du würdest	ihr würdet		du würdest	ihr würdet	
Sie würden	Sie würden		Sie würden	Sie würden	
er/sie/es würde	sie würden		er/sie/es würde	sie würden	

COMMANDS hand(e)le! handelt! handeln Sie!

PRESENT PARTICIPLE handelnd

Usage

Die Firma handelt mit vielen ausländischen Unternehmen. *The firm trades with many foreign companies.*
Wir handeln fair und effizient. *We deal fairly and efficiently.*
Oliver hat um den Preis gehandelt. *Oliver bargained over the price.*
Meine Damen und Herren, Sie müssen sofort handeln! *Ladies and gentlemen, you must act immediately!*
Jeder Mitarbeiter muss als Firmenvertreter handeln können. *Every employee must be able to act as the company's representative.*

handeln von *to deal with, be about*

Der Roman handelt von einer alleinerziehenden Mutter. *The novel deals with a single mother.*

sich handeln um *to be a question/matter of*

Mit diesem Gemälde handelt es sich um eine Fälschung. *This painting is a case of forgery.*

RELATED VERBS ab·handeln, aus·handeln, ein·handeln, entgegen·handeln, misshandeln, unterhandeln, zuwider·handeln; *see also* **behandeln** (62), **verhandeln** (488)

233 hängen[1] *to hang, be suspended; cling, be caught*

hängt · hing · gehangen strong verb

PRESENT

ich hänge	wir hängen
du hängst	ihr hängt
Sie hängen	Sie hängen
er/sie/es hängt	sie hängen

SIMPLE PAST

ich hing	wir hingen
du hingst	ihr hingt
Sie hingen	Sie hingen
er/sie/es hing	sie hingen

FUTURE

ich werde	wir werden	hängen
du wirst	ihr werdet	
Sie werden	Sie werden	
er/sie/es wird	sie werden	

PRESENT SUBJUNCTIVE I

ich hänge	wir hängen
du hängest	ihr hänget
Sie hängen	Sie hängen
er/sie/es hänge	sie hängen

PRESENT SUBJUNCTIVE II

ich hinge	wir hingen
du hingest	ihr hinget
Sie hingen	Sie hingen
er/sie/es hinge	sie hingen

FUTURE SUBJUNCTIVE I

ich werde	wir werden	hängen
du werdest	ihr werdet	
Sie werden	Sie werden	
er/sie/es werde	sie werden	

FUTURE SUBJUNCTIVE II

ich würde	wir würden	hängen
du würdest	ihr würdet	
Sie würden	Sie würden	
er/sie/es würde	sie würden	

PRESENT PERFECT

ich habe	wir haben	gehangen
du hast	ihr habt	
Sie haben	Sie haben	
er/sie/es hat	sie haben	

PAST PERFECT

ich hatte	wir hatten	gehangen
du hattest	ihr hattet	
Sie hatten	Sie hatten	
er/sie/es hatte	sie hatten	

FUTURE PERFECT

ich werde	wir werden	gehangen haben
du wirst	ihr werdet	
Sie werden	Sie werden	
er/sie/es wird	sie werden	

PAST SUBJUNCTIVE I

ich habe	wir haben	gehangen
du habest	ihr habet	
Sie haben	Sie haben	
er/sie/es habe	sie haben	

PAST SUBJUNCTIVE II

ich hätte	wir hätten	gehangen
du hättest	ihr hättet	
Sie hätten	Sie hätten	
er/sie/es hätte	sie hätten	

FUTURE PERFECT SUBJUNCTIVE I

ich werde	wir werden	gehangen haben
du werdest	ihr werdet	
Sie werden	Sie werden	
er/sie/es werde	sie werden	

FUTURE PERFECT SUBJUNCTIVE II

ich würde	wir würden	gehangen haben
du würdest	ihr würdet	
Sie würden	Sie würden	
er/sie/es würde	sie würden	

COMMANDS häng(e)! hängt! hängen Sie!

PRESENT PARTICIPLE hängend

Usage

Das Handtuch hängt am Haken hinter der Tür. — *The towel is hanging on a hook behind the door.*

Die Lampe hing von der Decke. — *The lamp was suspended from the ceiling.*

Ein Ölgemälde von meinem Ururgroßvater hing bis 1940 über dem Ofen in der Küche meiner Großmutter. — *An oil painting of my great-great-grandfather hung over the oven in my grandmother's kitchen until 1940.*

Am Baum hingen tausende von reifen Aprikosen. — *Thousands of ripe apricots hung on the tree.*

Ein Poster hängt an der Wand über meinem Bett. — *A poster hangs on the wall above my bed.*

Es wäre schöner, wenn etwas von Rembrandt an meiner Wand hinge. — *It would be nicer if something by Rembrandt hung on my wall.*

Ein dünner Nebel hat über dem Sumpf gehangen. — *A thin fog hung over the swamp.*

Witwe Nägeli, die sonst keine Verwandten hatte, hing an ihrem Kater Georg. — *The widow Nägeli, who had no relatives, clung to her cat, Georg.*

Eine Plastiktüte hängt im Baum und flattert im Wind. — *A plastic bag is caught in the tree and flutters in the wind.*

RELATED VERBS ab·hängen, an·hängen, aus·hängen, durch·hängen, über·hängen, umhängen, zusammen·hängen

regular weak verb **hängt · hängte · gehängt**

PRESENT

ich hänge	wir hängen
du hängst	ihr hängt
Sie hängen	Sie hängen
er/sie/es hängt	sie hängen

PRESENT PERFECT

ich habe	wir haben	gehängt
du hast	ihr habt	
Sie haben	Sie haben	
er/sie/es hat	sie haben	

SIMPLE PAST

ich hängte	wir hängten
du hängtest	ihr hängtet
Sie hängten	Sie hängten
er/sie/es hängte	sie hängten

PAST PERFECT

ich hatte	wir hatten	gehängt
du hattest	ihr hattet	
Sie hatten	Sie hatten	
er/sie/es hatte	sie hatten	

FUTURE

ich werde	wir werden	hängen
du wirst	ihr werdet	
Sie werden	Sie werden	
er/sie/es wird	sie werden	

FUTURE PERFECT

ich werde	wir werden	gehängt haben
du wirst	ihr werdet	
Sie werden	Sie werden	
er/sie/es wird	sie werden	

PRESENT SUBJUNCTIVE I

ich hänge	wir hängen
du hängest	ihr hänget
Sie hängen	Sie hängen
er/sie/es hänge	sie hängen

PAST SUBJUNCTIVE I

ich habe	wir haben	gehängt
du habest	ihr habet	
Sie haben	Sie haben	
er/sie/es habe	sie haben	

PRESENT SUBJUNCTIVE II

ich hängte	wir hängten
du hängtest	ihr hängtet
Sie hängten	Sie hängten
er/sie/es hängte	sie hängten

PAST SUBJUNCTIVE II

ich hätte	wir hätten	gehängt
du hättest	ihr hättet	
Sie hätten	Sie hätten	
er/sie/es hätte	sie hätten	

FUTURE SUBJUNCTIVE I

ich werde	wir werden	hängen
du werdest	ihr werdet	
Sie werden	Sie werden	
er/sie/es werde	sie werden	

FUTURE PERFECT SUBJUNCTIVE I

ich werde	wir werden	gehängt haben
du werdest	ihr werdet	
Sie werden	Sie werden	
er/sie/es werde	sie werden	

FUTURE SUBJUNCTIVE II

ich würde	wir würden	hängen
du würdest	ihr würdet	
Sie würden	Sie würden	
er/sie/es würde	sie würden	

FUTURE PERFECT SUBJUNCTIVE II

ich würde	wir würden	gehängt haben
du würdest	ihr würdet	
Sie würden	Sie würden	
er/sie/es würde	sie würden	

COMMANDS häng(e)! hängt! hängen Sie!

PRESENT PARTICIPLE hängend

Usage

Gabriele hat das Handtuch an den Haken gehängt. — *Gabriele hung the towel on the hook.*
Hängen Sie das Bild bitte über den Schreibtisch. — *Please hang the picture over the desk.*
Möchtest du ein Poster über das Bett hängen? — *Would you like to hang a poster over the bed?*
Kalender werden an die Wand gehängt. — *Calendars are hung on the wall.*
Dann hängte er ihr eine Perlenkette um den Hals. — *Then he draped a pearl necklace around her neck.*
Vergewaltiger werden in diesem Land gehängt. — *Rapists are hanged in this country.*
Ingo hat Plüschwürfel vom Rückblickspiegel gehängt. — *Ingo has hung fuzzy dice from the rearview mirror.*
Du könntest das Plakat ans schwarze Brett hängen. — *You could hang the poster on the bulletin board.*

sich hängen *to hang oneself*

Eines Abends nach dem Abendessen hat sie sich gehängt. — *One evening after dinner, she hanged herself.*

RELATED VERBS ab·hängen, an·hängen, auf·hängen, aus·hängen, behängen, ein·hängen, erhängen, über·hängen, überhängen, um·hängen, umhängen, verhängen, vor·hängen, weg·hängen, zu·hängen

235 hassen *to hate, detest, abhor*

hasst · hasste · gehasst regular weak verb

PRESENT		PRESENT PERFECT		
ich hasse	wir hassen	ich habe	wir haben	gehasst
du hasst	ihr hasst	du hast	ihr habt	
Sie hassen	Sie hassen	Sie haben	Sie haben	
er/sie/es hasst	sie hassen	er/sie/es hat	sie haben	

SIMPLE PAST		PAST PERFECT		
ich hasste	wir hassten	ich hatte	wir hatten	gehasst
du hasstest	ihr hasstet	du hattest	ihr hattet	
Sie hassten	Sie hassten	Sie hatten	Sie hatten	
er/sie/es hasste	sie hassten	er/sie/es hatte	sie hatten	

FUTURE			FUTURE PERFECT		
ich werde	wir werden	hassen	ich werde	wir werden	gehasst haben
du wirst	ihr werdet		du wirst	ihr werdet	
Sie werden	Sie werden		Sie werden	Sie werden	
er/sie/es wird	sie werden		er/sie/es wird	sie werden	

PRESENT SUBJUNCTIVE I		PAST SUBJUNCTIVE I		
ich hasse	wir hassen	ich habe	wir haben	gehasst
du hassest	ihr hasset	du habest	ihr habet	
Sie hassen	Sie hassen	Sie haben	Sie haben	
er/sie/es hasse	sie hassen	er/sie/es habe	sie haben	

PRESENT SUBJUNCTIVE II		PAST SUBJUNCTIVE II		
ich hasste	wir hassten	ich hätte	wir hätten	gehasst
du hasstest	ihr hasstet	du hättest	ihr hättet	
Sie hassten	Sie hassten	Sie hätten	Sie hätten	
er/sie/es hasste	sie hassten	er/sie/es hätte	sie hätten	

FUTURE SUBJUNCTIVE I			FUTURE PERFECT SUBJUNCTIVE I		
ich werde	wir werden	hassen	ich werde	wir werden	gehasst haben
du werdest	ihr werdet		du werdest	ihr werdet	
Sie werden	Sie werden		Sie werden	Sie werden	
er/sie/es werde	sie werden		er/sie/es werde	sie werden	

FUTURE SUBJUNCTIVE II			FUTURE PERFECT SUBJUNCTIVE II		
ich würde	wir würden	hassen	ich würde	wir würden	gehasst haben
du würdest	ihr würdet		du würdest	ihr würdet	
Sie würden	Sie würden		Sie würden	Sie würden	
er/sie/es würde	sie würden		er/sie/es würde	sie würden	

COMMANDS hass(e)! hasst! hassen Sie!

PRESENT PARTICIPLE hassend

Usage

Stephanie hasst Geburtstage. — *Stephanie abhors birthdays.*
Die Therapeutin berichtete, dass Jürg seinen Vater hasse und seine Mutter verehre. — *The therapist reported that Jürg hates his father and adores his mother.*
Die alten Männer hassten einander. — *The old men detested one another.*
Warum wird Dirk von anderen so gehasst? — *Why is Dirk so hated by others?*
Ich hasse es, wenn du Recht hast. — *I hate it when you're right.*
Hasst du Spinat? — *Do you hate spinach?*
Marga scheint ihre Stiefmutter zu hassen. — *Marga seems to hate her stepmother.*
Sie haben es nicht verdient, gehasst zu werden. — *You don't deserve to be hated.*
Anja hasste ihn, da er alles besser konnte als sie. — *Anja detested him, because he could do everything better than she could.*

So einen lieben Hund kann keiner hassen. — *Nobody can hate such a sweet dog.*
Nach einigen Jahren begann er sich selbst zu hassen. — *After a few years, he began to hate himself.*
Sterben lehrt mich dein Meineid, aber nicht hassen. (Schiller) — *Your treachery bids me to die, but not to hate.*

regular weak verb/strong verb **haut · haute/hieb · gehauen**

PRESENT

ich haue	wir hauen
du haust	ihr haut
Sie hauen	Sie hauen
er/sie/es haut	sie hauen

SIMPLE PAST

ich haute/hieb	wir hauten/hieben
du hautest/hiebst	ihr hautet/hiebt
Sie hauten/hieben	Sie hauten/hieben
er/sie/es haute/hieb	sie hauten/hieben

FUTURE

ich werde	wir werden	hauen
du wirst	ihr werdet	
Sie werden	Sie werden	
er/sie/es wird	sie werden	

PRESENT SUBJUNCTIVE I

ich haue	wir hauen
du hauest	ihr hauet
Sie hauen	Sie hauen
er/sie/es haue	sie hauen

PRESENT SUBJUNCTIVE II

ich haute/hiebe	wir hauten/hieben
du hautest/hiebest	ihr hautet/hiebet
Sie hauten/hieben	Sie hauten/hieben
er/sie/es haute/hiebe	sie hauten/hieben

FUTURE SUBJUNCTIVE I

ich werde	wir werden	hauen
du werdest	ihr werdet	
Sie werden	Sie werden	
er/sie/es werde	sie werden	

FUTURE SUBJUNCTIVE II

ich würde	wir würden	hauen
du würdest	ihr würdet	
Sie würden	Sie würden	
er/sie/es würde	sie würden	

PRESENT PERFECT

ich habe	wir haben	gehauen
du hast	ihr habt	
Sie haben	Sie haben	
er/sie/es hat	sie haben	

PAST PERFECT

ich hatte	wir hatten	gehauen
du hattest	ihr hattet	
Sie hatten	Sie hatten	
er/sie/es hatte	sie hatten	

FUTURE PERFECT

ich werde	wir werden	gehauen haben
du wirst	ihr werdet	
Sie werden	Sie werden	
er/sie/es wird	sie werden	

PAST SUBJUNCTIVE I

ich habe	wir haben	gehauen
du habest	ihr habet	
Sie haben	Sie haben	
er/sie/es habe	sie haben	

PAST SUBJUNCTIVE II

ich hätte	wir hätten	gehauen
du hättest	ihr hättet	
Sie hätten	Sie hätten	
er/sie/es hätte	sie hätten	

FUTURE PERFECT SUBJUNCTIVE I

ich werde	wir werden	gehauen haben
du werdest	ihr werdet	
Sie werden	Sie werden	
er/sie/es werde	sie werden	

FUTURE PERFECT SUBJUNCTIVE II

ich würde	wir würden	gehauen haben
du würdest	ihr würdet	
Sie würden	Sie würden	
er/sie/es würde	sie würden	

COMMANDS hau(e)! haut! hauen Sie!

PRESENT PARTICIPLE hauend

NOTE In standard German, the regular weak simple past (**haute**) is generally used with the meanings "chop, cut down, carve," whereas the strong simple past (**hieb**) is generally reserved for the meanings "whip, hit, beat, strike" and typically involves a weapon. However, colloquial German frequently uses the regular weak simple past for all meanings. Either way, the perfect participle is generally strong (**gehauen**).

Usage

Wer hat denn ein Loch in meine Sandburg gehauen?	*Who chopped a hole in my sand castle?*
Als Kind haute ich einmal eine Skulptur aus Stein.	*As a child, I once carved a sculpture from stone.*
Tobias haut Köpfe aus Eichenholz.	*Tobias carves heads from oak wood.*
Der Junge hatte sich einen Nagel in den linken Zeigefinger gehauen.	*The boy had slammed a nail in his left index finger.*
Michael hieb mit dem Messer auf den Gegner.	*Michael struck at the opponent with a knife.*
Der Kämpfer hieb ihn mit einer Axt in den Arm.	*The warrior struck him in the arm with an ax.*
Parzival konnte Gawan nicht vom Pferd hauen.	*Parsifal was unable to knock Gawain from his horse.*

RELATED VERBS ab·hauen, an·hauen, auf·hauen, aus·hauen, behauen, daneben·hauen, nieder·hauen, um·hauen, verhauen, zerhauen

237 **heben** *to raise, lift, heave; boost, enhance*

hebt · hob · gehoben strong verb

PRESENT

ich hebe	wir heben
du hebst	ihr hebt
Sie heben	Sie heben
er/sie/es hebt	sie heben

SIMPLE PAST

ich hob	wir hoben
du hobst	ihr hobt
Sie hoben	Sie hoben
er/sie/es hob	sie hoben

FUTURE

ich werde	wir werden	heben
du wirst	ihr werdet	
Sie werden	Sie werden	
er/sie/es wird	sie werden	

PRESENT SUBJUNCTIVE I

ich hebe	wir heben
du hebest	ihr hebet
Sie heben	Sie heben
er/sie/es hebe	sie heben

PRESENT SUBJUNCTIVE II

ich höbe	wir höben
du höbest	ihr höbet
Sie höben	Sie höben
er/sie/es höbe	sie höben

FUTURE SUBJUNCTIVE I

ich werde	wir werden	heben
du werdest	ihr werdet	
Sie werden	Sie werden	
er/sie/es werde	sie werden	

FUTURE SUBJUNCTIVE II

ich würde	wir würden	heben
du würdest	ihr würdet	
Sie würden	Sie würden	
er/sie/es würde	sie würden	

PRESENT PERFECT

ich habe	wir haben	gehoben
du hast	ihr habt	
Sie haben	Sie haben	
er/sie/es hat	sie haben	

PAST PERFECT

ich hatte	wir hatten	gehoben
du hattest	ihr hattet	
Sie hatten	Sie hatten	
er/sie/es hatte	sie hatten	

FUTURE PERFECT

ich werde	wir werden	gehoben haben
du wirst	ihr werdet	
Sie werden	Sie werden	
er/sie/es wird	sie werden	

PAST SUBJUNCTIVE I

ich habe	wir haben	gehoben
du habest	ihr habet	
Sie haben	Sie haben	
er/sie/es habe	sie haben	

PAST SUBJUNCTIVE II

ich hätte	wir hätten	gehoben
du hättest	ihr hättet	
Sie hätten	Sie hätten	
er/sie/es hätte	sie hätten	

FUTURE PERFECT SUBJUNCTIVE I

ich werde	wir werden	gehoben haben
du werdest	ihr werdet	
Sie werden	Sie werden	
er/sie/es werde	sie werden	

FUTURE PERFECT SUBJUNCTIVE II

ich würde	wir würden	gehoben haben
du würdest	ihr würdet	
Sie würden	Sie würden	
er/sie/es würde	sie würden	

COMMANDS heb(e)! hebt! heben Sie!

PRESENT PARTICIPLE hebend

NOTE Archaic simple past **hub** and present subjunctive II **hübe** sometimes occur.

Usage

Lukas hat gerade 200 Kilo gehoben.	*Lukas just lifted 200 kilos.*
Der schwache Hund konnte seinen Kopf nicht heben.	*The weak dog wasn't able to raise his head.*
Heben Sie die rechte Hand.	*Raise your right hand.*
Der Fußballspieler hob den Ball über seinen Kopf.	*The soccer player raised the ball above his head.*
Ein Erfolg hebt die Moral.	*A success will boost morale.*
Er verspricht, dass dieses System die Leistung des Motors hebe.	*He promises this system will enhance the motor's performance.*

sich heben *to raise, lift*

Die Rakete hob sich in die Luft.	*The rocket lifted into the air.*
Ihre Stimmung hebt sich.	*Their mood is improving.*

RELATED VERBS ab·heben, an·heben, aus·heben, beheben, entheben, erheben, hervor·heben, hoch·heben, überheben, verheben; *see also* **auf·heben** (27) regular weak verb **heiratet · heiratete · geheiratet**

PRESENT

ich heirate	wir heiraten
du heiratest	ihr heiratet
Sie heiraten	Sie heiraten
er/sie/es heiratet	sie heiraten

SIMPLE PAST

ich heiratete	wir heirateten
du heiratetest	ihr heiratetet
Sie heirateten	Sie heirateten
er/sie/es heiratete	sie heirateten

FUTURE

ich werde	wir werden	heiraten
du wirst	ihr werdet	
Sie werden	Sie werden	
er/sie/es wird	sie werden	

PRESENT SUBJUNCTIVE I

ich heirate	wir heiraten
du heiratest	ihr heiratet
Sie heiraten	Sie heiraten
er/sie/es heirate	sie heiraten

PRESENT SUBJUNCTIVE II

ich heiratete	wir heirateten
du heiratetest	ihr heiratetet
Sie heirateten	Sie heirateten
er/sie/es heiratete	sie heirateten

FUTURE SUBJUNCTIVE I

ich werde	wir werden	heiraten
du werdest	ihr werdet	
Sie werden	Sie werden	
er/sie/es werde	sie werden	

FUTURE SUBJUNCTIVE II

ich würde	wir würden	heiraten
du würdest	ihr würdet	
Sie würden	Sie würden	
er/sie/es würde	sie würden	

PRESENT PERFECT

ich habe	wir haben	geheiratet
du hast	ihr habt	
Sie haben	Sie haben	
er/sie/es hat	sie haben	

PAST PERFECT

ich hatte	wir hatten	geheiratet
du hattest	ihr hattet	
Sie hatten	Sie hatten	
er/sie/es hatte	sie hatten	

FUTURE PERFECT

ich werde	wir werden	geheiratet haben
du wirst	ihr werdet	
Sie werden	Sie werden	
er/sie/es wird	sie werden	

PAST SUBJUNCTIVE I

ich habe	wir haben	geheiratet
du habest	ihr habet	
Sie haben	Sie haben	
er/sie/es habe	sie haben	

PAST SUBJUNCTIVE II

ich hätte	wir hätten	geheiratet
du hättest	ihr hättet	
Sie hätten	Sie hätten	
er/sie/es hätte	sie hätten	

FUTURE PERFECT SUBJUNCTIVE I

ich werde	wir werden	geheiratet haben
du werdest	ihr werdet	
Sie werden	Sie werden	
er/sie/es werde	sie werden	

FUTURE PERFECT SUBJUNCTIVE II

ich würde	wir würden	geheiratet haben
du würdest	ihr würdet	
Sie würden	Sie würden	
er/sie/es würde	sie würden	

COMMANDS heirate! heiratet! heiraten Sie!

PRESENT PARTICIPLE heiratend

Usage

Wolfgang Amadeus Mozart heiratete Konstanze Weber im Jahr 1782. — *Wolfgang Amadeus Mozart married Konstanze Weber in the year 1782.*

Damals heiratete man schon mit 18 Jahren. — *Back then, people used to get married at 18 years of age.*

In Dänemark durften gleichgeschlechtliche Paare schon 1989 heiraten. — *In Denmark same-sex couples were allowed to wed as early as 1989.*

Martin heiratete Alexander letztes Jahr in Toronto. — *Martin married Alexander last year in Toronto.*

Ich möchte dich heiraten. — *I'd like to marry you.*

Melanie hat ihren ersten Freund Uwe geheiratet. — *Melanie married her first boyfriend, Uwe.*

Warum heiratest du nicht? — *Why don't you get married?*

Nach dem Tod seiner ersten Frau hatte Herr Brenker Katharina Groß geheiratet. — *After the death of his first wife, Mr. Brenker had married Katharina Groß.*

Wann heiratet ihr? — *When are you getting married?*

Alfrieda hat ihn aus Liebe geheiratet. — *Alfrieda married him for love.*

RELATED VERBS ein·heiraten; *see also* **verheiraten** (489)

heißen *to be called/named; command, order; mean, signify*

heißt · hieß · geheißen strong verb

OTHER USAGE SENTENCES WITH heißen

Wie heißen Sie? — *What is your name?*
Ich heiße Laufkötter, Marie Laufkötter. — *My name is Laufkötter, Marie Laufkötter.*
Der Bischof hieß die Männer gehen. — *The bishop commanded the men to go.*
Dann bleibe ich bei dir so lange, bis du mich selber wieder fort gehen hießest. (GERSTÄCKER) — *Then I will stay with you until you yourself would command me to leave again.*
Was soll das denn heißen? — *What's the meaning of that?*
Ich kenne den Namen nicht, aber das will nicht viel heißen, da ich nichts von Rapmusik weiß. — *I don't know that name, but that doesn't mean anything, since I know nothing about rap music.*
Ich bin noch nicht fertig, aber das soll nicht heißen, dass du auf mich wartest. — *I'm not finished yet, but that doesn't mean you should wait for me.*
Was heißt eigentlich „alle Rechte vorbehalten"? — *What does "all rights reserved" actually mean?*
Ich habe Hunger, aber das heißt nicht, dass wir jetzt essen müssen. — *I'm hungry, but that doesn't mean we have to eat now.*
Das Hoftheater hieß nun Staatstheater. — *The Court Theater was now called the State Theater.*

das heißt (d.h.) *that is, that is to say (i.e.)*

Wir bleiben hier, das heißt Jörg, Emil und ich. — *We're staying here, that is to say, Jörg, Emil, and I.*
Nur dann kann die wichtigste Frage beantwortet werden, d.h. wie ist das Universum entstanden? — *Only then can the most important question be answered, i.e., how did the universe come to be?*

willkommen heißen *to bid welcome, welcome*

Der König hieß die Gäste herzlich willkommen. — *The king bade the guests a cordial welcome.*
Wir heißen Sie willkommen auf der Homepage der Gemeinde Oberstdorf. — *We welcome you to the homepage of the town of Oberstdorf.*

es heißt

Wie es im Sprichwort heißt: „Morgen, morgen nur nicht heute, sagen alle faulen Leute." — *As the proverb says, "Don't put off until tomorrow what you can do today."*
In dem Bericht heißt es, dass Nebenwirkungen entstehen können. — *In the report, it says that side effects can appear.*
Nun heißt es auf die Ergebnisse warten. — *Now it's time to wait for the results.*
Neuerdings heißt es, dass das Rathaus saniert wird. — *It's recently been rumored that city hall is to be renovated.*
Die Kirche habe, so hieß es abschließend, eine besondere Verantwortung für die Armen und Schwachen in der Welt. — *The church has, it was stated in closing, a special responsibility for the poor and weak in the world.*
In der Urteilsbegründung heißt es: „Kein Krieg ist in sich logisch." — *The court opinion states, "No war is in itself logical."*

IDIOMATIC EXPRESSIONS

Es will schon was heißen, wenn ein Hersteller seine eigenen Produkte nicht verwendet. — *It means something when a manufacturer doesn't use its own products.*
„Was hast du heute in der Schule gelernt?" — *"What did you learn in school today?"*
„Zeus und Poseidon und wie sie alle hießen." — *"Zeus and Poseidon and whatever all their names were."*
Was heißt und zu welchem Ende studiert man Universalgeschichte? (SCHILLER) — *What is and to what end does one study universal history?*
Das hieße dann, dass er jetzt auf die 60 geht. — *That would mean he's now approaching 60.*

PRESENT

ich heiße	wir heißen
du heißt	ihr heißt
Sie heißen	Sie heißen
er/sie/es heißt	sie heißen

SIMPLE PAST

ich hieß	wir hießen
du hießest	ihr hießt
Sie hießen	Sie hießen
er/sie/es hieß	sie hießen

FUTURE

ich werde	wir werden	heißen
du wirst	ihr werdet	
Sie werden	Sie werden	
er/sie/es wird	sie werden	

PRESENT SUBJUNCTIVE I

ich heiße	wir heißen
du heißest	ihr heißet
Sie heißen	Sie heißen
er/sie/es heiße	sie heißen

PRESENT SUBJUNCTIVE II

ich hieße	wir hießen
du hießest	ihr hießet
Sie hießen	Sie hießen
er/sie/es hieße	sie hießen

FUTURE SUBJUNCTIVE I

ich werde	wir werden	heißen
du werdest	ihr werdet	
Sie werden	Sie werden	
er/sie/es werde	sie werden	

FUTURE SUBJUNCTIVE II

ich würde	wir würden	heißen
du würdest	ihr würdet	
Sie würden	Sie würden	
er/sie/es würde	sie würden	

COMMANDS heiß(e)! heißt! heißen Sie!

PRESENT PARTICIPLE heißend

PRESENT PERFECT

ich habe	wir haben	geheißen
du hast	ihr habt	
Sie haben	Sie haben	
er/sie/es hat	sie haben	

PAST PERFECT

ich hatte	wir hatten	geheißen
du hattest	ihr hattet	
Sie hatten	Sie hatten	
er/sie/es hatte	sie hatten	

FUTURE PERFECT

ich werde	wir werden	geheißen haben
du wirst	ihr werdet	
Sie werden	Sie werden	
er/sie/es wird	sie werden	

PAST SUBJUNCTIVE I

ich habe	wir haben	geheißen
du habest	ihr habet	
Sie haben	Sie haben	
er/sie/es habe	sie haben	

PAST SUBJUNCTIVE II

ich hätte	wir hätten	geheißen
du hättest	ihr hättet	
Sie hätten	Sie hätten	
er/sie/es hätte	sie hätten	

FUTURE PERFECT SUBJUNCTIVE I

ich werde	wir werden	geheißen haben
du werdest	ihr werdet	
Sie werden	Sie werden	
er/sie/es werde	sie werden	

FUTURE PERFECT SUBJUNCTIVE II

ich würde	wir würden	geheißen haben
du würdest	ihr würdet	
Sie würden	Sie würden	
er/sie/es würde	sie würden	

Usage

Seine Schüler hießen Rudolf und Josef von Droste.	*His pupils were named Rudolf and Josef von Droste.*
Ihr Häuptling hieß Alkorak und er war ungemein stark.	*Their chief was called Alkorak and he was unusually strong.*
Wie heißt du mit Nachnamen?	*What is your last name?*
Mein Hund heißt Bernie.	*My dog is named Bernie.*
Sein Großvater hat Valentin geheißen.	*His grandfather was named Valentin.*
Wie heißt die Straße, in der Sie wohnen?	*What is the street called where you live?*
Unsere Gruppe heißt „Jugendliche gegen Atomkraft."	*Our group is called "Youth Against Nuclear Power."*
Wie heißen alle deutschen Bundeskanzler seit 1945?	*What are the names of all German chancellors since 1945?*
Mein Vater hieß Karl.	*My father was named Karl.*
Wie heißt das auf Japanisch?	*How do you say that in Japanese?*
Wie heißt der Film, den ihr gesehen habt?	*What's the name of the film you saw?*

RELATED VERBS gut·heißen, verheißen

240 heizen *to heat*

heizt · heizte · geheizt regular weak verb

PRESENT

ich heize	wir heizen
du heizt	ihr heizt
Sie heizen	Sie heizen
er/sie/es heizt	sie heizen

SIMPLE PAST

ich heizte	wir heizten
du heiztest	ihr heiztet
Sie heizten	Sie heizten
er/sie/es heizte	sie heizten

FUTURE

ich werde	wir werden	heizen
du wirst	ihr werdet	
Sie werden	Sie werden	
er/sie/es wird	sie werden	

PRESENT SUBJUNCTIVE I

ich heize	wir heizen
du heizest	ihr heizet
Sie heizen	Sie heizen
er/sie/es heize	sie heizen

PRESENT SUBJUNCTIVE II

ich heizte	wir heizten
du heiztest	ihr heiztet
Sie heizten	Sie heizten
er/sie/es heizte	sie heizten

FUTURE SUBJUNCTIVE I

ich werde	wir werden	heizen
du werdest	ihr werdet	
Sie werden	Sie werden	
er/sie/es werde	sie werden	

FUTURE SUBJUNCTIVE II

ich würde	wir würden	heizen
du würdest	ihr würdet	
Sie würden	Sie würden	
er/sie/es würde	sie würden	

PRESENT PERFECT

ich habe	wir haben	geheizt
du hast	ihr habt	
Sie haben	Sie haben	
er/sie/es hat	sie haben	

PAST PERFECT

ich hatte	wir hatten	geheizt
du hattest	ihr hattet	
Sie hatten	Sie hatten	
er/sie/es hatte	sie hatten	

FUTURE PERFECT

ich werde	wir werden	geheizt haben
du wirst	ihr werdet	
Sie werden	Sie werden	
er/sie/es wird	sie werden	

PAST SUBJUNCTIVE I

ich habe	wir haben	geheizt
du habest	ihr habet	
Sie haben	Sie haben	
er/sie/es habe	sie haben	

PAST SUBJUNCTIVE II

ich hätte	wir hätten	geheizt
du hättest	ihr hättet	
Sie hätten	Sie hätten	
er/sie/es hätte	sie hätten	

FUTURE PERFECT SUBJUNCTIVE I

ich werde	wir werden	geheizt haben
du werdest	ihr werdet	
Sie werden	Sie werden	
er/sie/es werde	sie werden	

FUTURE PERFECT SUBJUNCTIVE II

ich würde	wir würden	geheizt haben
du würdest	ihr würdet	
Sie würden	Sie würden	
er/sie/es würde	sie würden	

COMMANDS heiz(e)! heizt! heizen Sie!

PRESENT PARTICIPLE heizend

Usage

Dort muss man das Haus mit Holz heizen.	*There they have to heat the house with wood.*
Hier kann kaum mit Sonnenenergie geheizt werden.	*Here it is hardly possible to heat with solar energy.*
Heizt du nur das Wohnzimmer?	*Do you heat only the living room?*
Frau Eckerts Kachelofen heizte das ganze Haus.	*Mrs. Eckert's tiled stove heated her whole house.*
Im Süden der USA werden viele neue Häuser elektrisch geheizt.	*In the southern United States, many new homes have electric heat.*
Wo wird noch mit Kohle geheizt?	*Where do people still heat with coal?*
Heizen Sie den Ofen auf 200 Grad.	*Heat the oven to 200 degrees.*
Die alte Dorfkirche ist nicht geheizt.	*The old village church is not heated.*

sich heizen *to heat*

Das dritte Schlafzimmer heizt sich schlecht.	*The third bedroom heats poorly.*

RELATED VERBS an·heizen, beheizen, durch·heizen, ein·heizen, überheizen, verheizen, vor·heizen

strong verb (dative object) **hilft · half · geholfen**

PRESENT	
ich helfe	wir helfen
du hilfst	ihr helft
Sie helfen	Sie helfen
er/sie/es hilft	sie helfen

PRESENT PERFECT		
ich habe	wir haben	geholfen
du hast	ihr habt	
Sie haben	Sie haben	
er/sie/es hat	sie haben	

SIMPLE PAST	
ich half	wir halfen
du halfst	ihr halft
Sie halfen	Sie halfen
er/sie/es half	sie halfen

PAST PERFECT		
ich hatte	wir hatten	geholfen
du hattest	ihr hattet	
Sie hatten	Sie hatten	
er/sie/es hatte	sie hatten	

FUTURE		
ich werde	wir werden	helfen
du wirst	ihr werdet	
Sie werden	Sie werden	
er/sie/es wird	sie werden	

FUTURE PERFECT		
ich werde	wir werden	geholfen haben
du wirst	ihr werdet	
Sie werden	Sie werden	
er/sie/es wird	sie werden	

PRESENT SUBJUNCTIVE I	
ich helfe	wir helfen
du helfest	ihr helfet
Sie helfen	Sie helfen
er/sie/es helfe	sie helfen

PAST SUBJUNCTIVE I		
ich habe	wir haben	geholfen
du habest	ihr habet	
Sie haben	Sie haben	
er/sie/es habe	sie haben	

PRESENT SUBJUNCTIVE II	
ich hülfe/hälfe	wir hülfen/hälfen
du hülfest/hälfest	ihr hülfet/hälfet
Sie hülfen/hälfen	Sie hülfen/hälfen
er/sie/es hülfe/hälfe	sie hülfen/hälfen

PAST SUBJUNCTIVE II		
ich hätte	wir hätten	geholfen
du hättest	ihr hättet	
Sie hätten	Sie hätten	
er/sie/es hätte	sie hätten	

FUTURE SUBJUNCTIVE I		
ich werde	wir werden	helfen
du werdest	ihr werdet	
Sie werden	Sie werden	
er/sie/es werde	sie werden	

FUTURE PERFECT SUBJUNCTIVE I		
ich werde	wir werden	geholfen haben
du werdest	ihr werdet	
Sie werden	Sie werden	
er/sie/es werde	sie werden	

FUTURE SUBJUNCTIVE II		
ich würde	wir würden	helfen
du würdest	ihr würdet	
Sie würden	Sie würden	
er/sie/es würde	sie würden	

FUTURE PERFECT SUBJUNCTIVE II		
ich würde	wir würden	geholfen haben
du würdest	ihr würdet	
Sie würden	Sie würden	
er/sie/es würde	sie würden	

COMMANDS hilf! helft! helfen Sie!

PRESENT PARTICIPLE helfend

Usage

Wie können wir den Armen finanziell helfen?	*How can we assist the poor financially?*
Ich helfe Ihnen bei der Zimmersuche.	*I'll help you look for a room.*
Die Gemeinde hat versucht, der Familie zu helfen.	*The community tried to help the family.*
Die Polizisten halfen bei der Arbeit.	*The police helped with the work.*
Meine Eltern sind bereit zu helfen.	*My parents are prepared to help.*
Ihre Antwort hat gar nicht geholfen.	*Her answer didn't help at all.*
Kannst du mir helfen?	*Can you help me?*
Ihm konnte nicht geholfen werden.	*He could not be helped.*
Hat die Lehrerin euch geholfen?	*Did the teacher help you?*
Frau Jansen wollte ihrer Bekannten mit der Gartenarbeit helfen.	*Mrs. Jansen wanted to help her acquaintance with the garden work.*

RELATED VERBS ab·helfen, auf·helfen, aus·helfen, behelfen, durch·helfen, mit·helfen, nach·helfen, verhelfen, weiter·helfen

TOP 50 VERB ☞

helfen *to help, assist; support; remedy*

hilft · half · geholfen

strong verb

MORE USAGE SENTENCES WITH helfen

Er behauptet, dass sie ihm helfen würden. — *He claims that they are helping him.*
Hilfst du Oma ins Auto? — *Will you assist Grandma into the car?*
Ingrid war im Begriff, dem älteren Herrn aus dem Sessel zu helfen, als es an der Tür klopfte. — *Ingrid was just about to help the elderly gentleman from the chair when there was a knock at the door.*
Gerd hat seiner Schwester über die Runden geholfen. — *Gerd helped his sister make ends meet.*
Jammern hilft nicht. — *Complaining won't help.*
Wir müssen ihm helfen. — *We must help him.*
Drei Nachbarn kamen angelaufen, um zu helfen. — *Three neighbors came running up to help.*
Unser Ziel ist es, den Bedürftigen zu helfen. — *Our goal is to help the needy.*
Ihre Bereitschaft, anderen zu helfen, war klar ersichtlich. — *Her readiness to help others was clearly evident.*
Aus Mitleid hat sie ihrem Nachbarn geholfen. — *She helped her neighbor out of compassion.*
Ned Detwiler half uns jeden Sommer bei der Ernte. — *Ned Detwiler helped us with the harvest every summer.*
Wir sehen uns verpflichtet, Ihnen zu helfen. — *We feel obligated to assist you.*
Hätten Sie die Güte, uns mit den Unkosten zu helfen? — *Would you be so kind as to help us with the expenses?*
Vor ein paar Jahren hat mir Ernst aus einer heiklen Lage geholfen. — *A few years ago, Ernst helped me out of a difficult situation.*
Wir möchten helfen, wo immer wir es können. — *We'd like to help wherever we can.*
Kann ich Ihnen helfen? — *Can I be of assistance?*
Hilfst du mir die Koffer tragen? — *Will you help me carry the suitcases?*
Maria hat mir beim Umzug nach Kalifornien geholfen. — *Maria helped me move to California.*
Kerstin will schon mehrere Male geholfen haben. — *Kerstin claims to have helped many times already.*
Was hülfe es dem Menschen, wenn er die ganze Welt gewönne und nähme doch Schaden an seiner Seele? (MATTHÄUS 16,26) — *What is a man profited if he shall gain the whole world and lose his own soul?* (MATTHEW 16:26)
Das Beschuldigen von anderen hilft nichts. — *Placing the blame on others doesn't remedy anything.*

sich zu helfen wissen *to be able to help oneself, be able to cope*

Das Kind lebte allein, aber wusste sich immer zu helfen. — *The child lived alone, but could always fend for himself.*
Ich weiß mir nicht mehr zu helfen, mein Mann schnarcht wie eine Kettensäge. — *I'm at the end of my rope; my husband snores like a chainsaw.*

helfen gegen *to be a remedy for, be good for*

Was hilft gegen Kopfschmerzen? — *What's a remedy for headaches?*
Wermuttee hilft gegen Magenschmerzen. — *Wormwood tea is good for stomachaches.*

IDIOMATIC EXPRESSIONS

Dir werde ich helfen, dich über mich lustig zu machen, du Idiot! — *I'll teach you to make fun of me, you idiot!*
Oliver half ihr wieder auf die Beine. — *Oliver helped her back on her feet.*
Was hilft's? — *What's the use?*
Da hilft alles nichts. — *Nothing helps.*
Hilf dir selbst, so hilft dir Gott. (PROVERB) — *God helps those who help themselves.*
So wahr mir Gott helfe. (*formulaic*) — *So help me God.*
Wer das nicht versteht, dem ist nicht zu helfen. — *Whoever doesn't understand that is beyond help.*
Jost kann sich nicht helfen, er ist bulimisch. — *Jost can't help it—he's bulimic.*
Es hilft nichts, den Computer anzuschreien, wenn du selber schuld bist. — *It does no good to shout at the computer when you yourself are to blame.*

strong verb **kommt her · kam her · hergekommen**

PRESENT

ich komme	wir kommen	her
du kommst	ihr kommt	
Sie kommen	Sie kommen	
er/sie/es kommt	sie kommen	

SIMPLE PAST

ich kam	wir kamen	her
du kamst	ihr kamt	
Sie kamen	Sie kamen	
er/sie/es kam	sie kamen	

FUTURE

ich werde	wir werden	herkommen
du wirst	ihr werdet	
Sie werden	Sie werden	
er/sie/es wird	sie werden	

PRESENT SUBJUNCTIVE I

ich komme	wir kommen	her
du kommest	ihr kommet	
Sie kommen	Sie kommen	
er/sie/es komme	sie kommen	

PRESENT SUBJUNCTIVE II

ich käme	wir kämen	her
du kämest	ihr kämet	
Sie kämen	Sie kämen	
er/sie/es käme	sie kämen	

FUTURE SUBJUNCTIVE I

ich werde	wir werden	herkommen
du werdest	ihr werdet	
Sie werden	Sie werden	
er/sie/es werde	sie werden	

FUTURE SUBJUNCTIVE II

ich würde	wir würden	herkommen
du würdest	ihr würdet	
Sie würden	Sie würden	
er/sie/es würde	sie würden	

PRESENT PERFECT

ich bin	wir sind	hergekommen
du bist	ihr seid	
Sie sind	Sie sind	
er/sie/es ist	sie sind	

PAST PERFECT

ich war	wir waren	hergekommen
du warst	ihr wart	
Sie waren	Sie waren	
er/sie/es war	sie waren	

FUTURE PERFECT

ich werde	wir werden	hergekommen sein
du wirst	ihr werdet	
Sie werden	Sie werden	
er/sie/es wird	sie werden	

PAST SUBJUNCTIVE I

ich sei	wir seien	hergekommen
du seiest	ihr seiet	
Sie seien	Sie seien	
er/sie/es sei	sie seien	

PAST SUBJUNCTIVE II

ich wäre	wir wären	hergekommen
du wärest	ihr wäret	
Sie wären	Sie wären	
er/sie/es wäre	sie wären	

FUTURE PERFECT SUBJUNCTIVE I

ich werde	wir werden	hergekommen sein
du werdest	ihr werdet	
Sie werden	Sie werden	
er/sie/es werde	sie werden	

FUTURE PERFECT SUBJUNCTIVE II

ich würde	wir würden	hergekommen sein
du würdest	ihr würdet	
Sie würden	Sie würden	
er/sie/es würde	sie würden	

COMMANDS komm(e) her! kommt her! kommen Sie her!

PRESENT PARTICIPLE herkommend

Usage

Wir sind zum Studieren hergekommen.	*We've come here to study.*
Komm mal her!	*Come here!*
Die Katze kam zu mir her, setzte sich hin, und guckte mich an.	*The cat came up to me, sat down, and looked at me.*
Das Kreischen kam vom Baumgipfel her.	*The screeching emanated from the treetop.*
Auf die Frage, wo er herkomme, sagte er nur: „Daher“.	*In answer to the question about where he comes from, he said only, "From there."*
Wo kommen Sie her?	*Where do you come from?*
Das ist die Stadt, aus der ich hergekommen bin.	*That's the town I'm from.*
Mama, wo kommen Babys denn her?	*Mama, where do babies come from?*
Wo diese Sitte herkommt, weiß man nicht genau.	*People don't exactly know where this tradition originated.*
Katrin möchte feststellen, wo ihre irrationalen Ängste herkommen.	*Katrin would like to determine the source of her irrational fears.*

RELATED VERBS daher·kommen; *see also* **kommen** (265)

243 herrschen *to rule, reign; govern; dominate*

herrscht · herrschte · geherrscht regular weak verb

PRESENT

ich herrsche	wir herrschen
du herrschst	ihr herrscht
Sie herrschen	Sie herrschen
er/sie/es herrscht	sie herrschen

SIMPLE PAST

ich herrschte	wir herrschten
du herrschtest	ihr herrschtet
Sie herrschten	Sie herrschten
er/sie/es herrschte	sie herrschten

FUTURE

ich werde	wir werden	herrschen
du wirst	ihr werdet	
Sie werden	Sie werden	
er/sie/es wird	sie werden	

PRESENT SUBJUNCTIVE I

ich herrsche	wir herrschen
du herrschest	ihr herrschet
Sie herrschen	Sie herrschen
er/sie/es herrsche	sie herrschen

PRESENT SUBJUNCTIVE II

ich herrschte	wir herrschten
du herrschtest	ihr herrschtet
Sie herrschten	Sie herrschten
er/sie/es herrschte	sie herrschten

FUTURE SUBJUNCTIVE I

ich werde	wir werden	herrschen
du werdest	ihr werdet	
Sie werden	Sie werden	
er/sie/es werde	sie werden	

FUTURE SUBJUNCTIVE II

ich würde	wir würden	herrschen
du würdest	ihr würdet	
Sie würden	Sie würden	
er/sie/es würde	sie würden	

PRESENT PERFECT

ich habe	wir haben	geherrscht
du hast	ihr habt	
Sie haben	Sie haben	
er/sie/es hat	sie haben	

PAST PERFECT

ich hatte	wir hatten	geherrscht
du hattest	ihr hattet	
Sie hatten	Sie hatten	
er/sie/es hatte	sie hatten	

FUTURE PERFECT

ich werde	wir werden	geherrscht haben
du wirst	ihr werdet	
Sie werden	Sie werden	
er/sie/es wird	sie werden	

PAST SUBJUNCTIVE I

ich habe	wir haben	geherrscht
du habest	ihr habet	
Sie haben	Sie haben	
er/sie/es habe	sie haben	

PAST SUBJUNCTIVE II

ich hätte	wir hätten	geherrscht
du hättest	ihr hättet	
Sie hätten	Sie hätten	
er/sie/es hätte	sie hätten	

FUTURE PERFECT SUBJUNCTIVE I

ich werde	wir werden	geherrscht haben
du werdest	ihr werdet	
Sie werden	Sie werden	
er/sie/es werde	sie werden	

FUTURE PERFECT SUBJUNCTIVE II

ich würde	wir würden	geherrscht haben
du würdest	ihr würdet	
Sie würden	Sie würden	
er/sie/es würde	sie würden	

COMMANDS herrsch(e)! herrscht! herrschen Sie!

PRESENT PARTICIPLE herrschend

Usage

Ein Markgraf herrschte hier von 1350 bis 1353. — *A margrave ruled here from 1350 to 1353.*

Kaiser herrschten über das Heilige Römische Reich. — *Emperors reigned over the Holy Roman Empire.*

Wer hat denn das Recht zu herrschen? — *Who has the right to rule?*

Der neue Fürst herrscht mit der Unterstützung der Nachbarländer. — *The new prince is ruling with the support of neighboring countries.*

Dieses Adelsgeschlecht herrschte bis 1918. — *This aristocratic family ruled until 1918.*

Die Konservativen herrschen seit 20 Jahren. — *The conservatives have governed for 20 years.*

Nach dem Krieg herrschte Chaos im Lande. — *After the war, chaos dominated the country.*

In Washington herrscht eine andere Mentalität. — *In Washington, a different mentality predominates.*

Ein positiver Ton hat in den Diskussionen geherrscht. — *A positive tone prevailed in the discussions.*

Die friedliche Zusammenarbeit, die früher geherrscht hat, war produktiver als der jetzige Zustand. — *The peaceful cooperation that used to prevail was more productive than the current situation.*

Kühle Temperaturen herrschten den ganzen Sommer. — *Cool temperatures dominated the entire summer.*

RELATED VERBS an·herrschen, beherrschen, vor·herrschen

regular weak verb **stellt her · stellte her · hergestellt**

PRESENT			PRESENT PERFECT		
ich stelle	wir stellen	her	ich habe	wir haben	hergestellt
du stellst	ihr stellt		du hast	ihr habt	
Sie stellen	Sie stellen		Sie haben	Sie haben	
er/sie/es stellt	sie stellen		er/sie/es hat	sie haben	

SIMPLE PAST			PAST PERFECT		
ich stellte	wir stellten	her	ich hatte	wir hatten	hergestellt
du stelltest	ihr stelltet		du hattest	ihr hattet	
Sie stellten	Sie stellten		Sie hatten	Sie hatten	
er/sie/es stellte	sie stellten		er/sie/es hatte	sie hatten	

FUTURE			FUTURE PERFECT		
ich werde	wir werden	herstellen	ich werde	wir werden	hergestellt haben
du wirst	ihr werdet		du wirst	ihr werdet	
Sie werden	Sie werden		Sie werden	Sie werden	
er/sie/es wird	sie werden		er/sie/es wird	sie werden	

PRESENT SUBJUNCTIVE I			PAST SUBJUNCTIVE I		
ich stelle	wir stellen	her	ich habe	wir haben	hergestellt
du stellest	ihr stellet		du habest	ihr habet	
Sie stellen	Sie stellen		Sie haben	Sie haben	
er/sie/es stelle	sie stellen		er/sie/es habe	sie haben	

PRESENT SUBJUNCTIVE II			PAST SUBJUNCTIVE II		
ich stellte	wir stellten	her	ich hätte	wir hätten	hergestellt
du stelltest	ihr stelltet		du hättest	ihr hättet	
Sie stellten	Sie stellten		Sie hätten	Sie hätten	
er/sie/es stellte	sie stellten		er/sie/es hätte	sie hätten	

FUTURE SUBJUNCTIVE I			FUTURE PERFECT SUBJUNCTIVE I		
ich werde	wir werden	herstellen	ich werde	wir werden	hergestellt haben
du werdest	ihr werdet		du werdest	ihr werdet	
Sie werden	Sie werden		Sie werden	Sie werden	
er/sie/es werde	sie werden		er/sie/es werde	sie werden	

FUTURE SUBJUNCTIVE II			FUTURE PERFECT SUBJUNCTIVE II		
ich würde	wir würden	herstellen	ich würde	wir würden	hergestellt haben
du würdest	ihr würdet		du würdest	ihr würdet	
Sie würden	Sie würden		Sie würden	Sie würden	
er/sie/es würde	sie würden		er/sie/es würde	sie würden	

COMMANDS stell(e) her! stellt her! stellen Sie her!

PRESENT PARTICIPLE herstellend

Usage

Wo werden diese Geräte hergestellt?	*Where are these devices produced?*
Diese Fabrik stellt Waffen her.	*This factory manufactures weapons.*
Solche Produkte können in anderen Ländern billiger hergestellt werden.	*Such products can be made more cheaply in other countries.*
Die Marketingmanager möchten ein völlig neues Produkt herstellen.	*The marketing managers would like to create a completely new product.*
Die Firma stellt Designermöbel her.	*The company manufactures designer furniture.*
Wir planen umweltfreundliche Batterien herzustellen.	*We plan to produce environmentally friendly batteries.*
Der Politiker wollte einen Zusammenhang herstellen.	*The politician wanted to establish a link.*

sich herstellen *to arise, come to be*

Eine politische Verbindung stellte sich langsam her.	*A political connection gradually emerged.*

RELATED VERBS wiederher·stellen; *see also* **stellen** (426)

245 hinterlassen *to leave behind, bequeath*

hinterlässt · hinterließ · hinterlassen

strong verb

PRESENT

ich hinterlasse	wir hinterlassen
du hinterlässt	ihr hinterlasst
Sie hinterlassen	Sie hinterlassen
er/sie/es hinterlässt	sie hinterlassen

SIMPLE PAST

ich hinterließ	wir hinterließen
du hinterließest	ihr hinterließt
Sie hinterließen	Sie hinterließen
er/sie/es hinterließ	sie hinterließen

FUTURE

ich werde	wir werden	hinterlassen
du wirst	ihr werdet	
Sie werden	Sie werden	
er/sie/es wird	sie werden	

PRESENT SUBJUNCTIVE I

ich hinterlasse	wir hinterlassen
du hinterlassest	ihr hinterlasset
Sie hinterlassen	Sie hinterlassen
er/sie/es hinterlasse	sie hinterlassen

PRESENT SUBJUNCTIVE II

ich hinterließe	wir hinterließen
du hinterließest	ihr hinterließet
Sie hinterließen	Sie hinterließen
er/sie/es hinterließe	sie hinterließen

FUTURE SUBJUNCTIVE I

ich werde	wir werden	hinterlassen
du werdest	ihr werdet	
Sie werden	Sie werden	
er/sie/es werde	sie werden	

FUTURE SUBJUNCTIVE II

ich würde	wir würden	hinterlassen
du würdest	ihr würdet	
Sie würden	Sie würden	
er/sie/es würde	sie würden	

PRESENT PERFECT

ich habe	wir haben	hinterlassen
du hast	ihr habt	
Sie haben	Sie haben	
er/sie/es hat	sie haben	

PAST PERFECT

ich hatte	wir hatten	hinterlassen
du hattest	ihr hattet	
Sie hatten	Sie hatten	
er/sie/es hatte	sie hatten	

FUTURE PERFECT

ich werde	wir werden	hinterlassen haben
du wirst	ihr werdet	
Sie werden	Sie werden	
er/sie/es wird	sie werden	

PAST SUBJUNCTIVE I

ich habe	wir haben	hinterlassen
du habest	ihr habet	
Sie haben	Sie haben	
er/sie/es habe	sie haben	

PAST SUBJUNCTIVE II

ich hätte	wir hätten	hinterlassen
du hättest	ihr hättet	
Sie hätten	Sie hätten	
er/sie/es hätte	sie hätten	

FUTURE PERFECT SUBJUNCTIVE I

ich werde	wir werden	hinterlassen haben
du werdest	ihr werdet	
Sie werden	Sie werden	
er/sie/es werde	sie werden	

FUTURE PERFECT SUBJUNCTIVE II

ich würde	wir würden	hinterlassen haben
du würdest	ihr würdet	
Sie würden	Sie würden	
er/sie/es würde	sie würden	

COMMANDS hinterlass(e)! hinterlasst! hinterlassen Sie!

PRESENT PARTICIPLE hinterlassend

Usage

Herr Schmidt hinterlässt eine 73-jährige Frau und drei erwachsene Kinder.	*Mr. Schmidt leaves behind a 73-year-old wife and three grown children.*
Der Dieb hatte Fingerabdrücke an der Türklinke hinterlassen.	*The thief had left fingerprints on the door handle.*
Tsunami hinterlässt eine Spur der Verwüstung (NEWS HEADLINE)	*Tsunami leaves behind a wake of devastation*
Hinterlassen Sie bitte eine Nachricht nach dem Piepton.	*Please leave a message after the beep.*
Der Fuchs hinterließ Spuren im Schnee.	*The fox left tracks in the snow.*
Die Reise hat bei meiner Mutter bleibende Eindrücke hinterlassen.	*The trip has left lasting impressions on my mother.*
Das Bier hinterlässt einen komischen Nachgeschmack.	*The beer leaves a funny aftertaste.*
Du hast bei ihr einen guten Eindruck hinterlassen.	*You've made a good impression on her.*
Frau Escher hinterließ ihrem Mann ihr Vermögen.	*Mrs. Escher bequeathed her wealth to her husband.*
Ich hinterlasse meinen Kindern 100 000 Dollar und das Grundstück in Wisconsin.	*I bequeath to my children $100,000 and the property in Wisconsin.*

RELATED VERBS *see* **lassen** (280)

regular weak verb **hofft · hoffte · gehofft**

PRESENT			PRESENT PERFECT		
ich hoffe	wir hoffen		ich habe	wir haben	gehofft
du hoffst	ihr hofft		du hast	ihr habt	
Sie hoffen	Sie hoffen		Sie haben	Sie haben	
er/sie/es hofft	sie hoffen		er/sie/es hat	sie haben	
SIMPLE PAST			**PAST PERFECT**		
ich hoffte	wir hofften		ich hatte	wir hatten	gehofft
du hofftest	ihr hofftet		du hattest	ihr hattet	
Sie hofften	Sie hofften		Sie hatten	Sie hatten	
er/sie/es hoffte	sie hofften		er/sie/es hatte	sie hatten	
FUTURE			**FUTURE PERFECT**		
ich werde	wir werden	hoffen	ich werde	wir werden	gehofft haben
du wirst	ihr werdet		du wirst	ihr werdet	
Sie werden	Sie werden		Sie werden	Sie werden	
er/sie/es wird	sie werden		er/sie/es wird	sie werden	
PRESENT SUBJUNCTIVE I			**PAST SUBJUNCTIVE I**		
ich hoffe	wir hoffen		ich habe	wir haben	gehofft
du hoffest	ihr hoffet		du habest	ihr habet	
Sie hoffen	Sie hoffen		Sie haben	Sie haben	
er/sie/es hoffe	sie hoffen		er/sie/es habe	sie haben	
PRESENT SUBJUNCTIVE II			**PAST SUBJUNCTIVE II**		
ich hoffte	wir hofften		ich hätte	wir hätten	gehofft
du hofftest	ihr hofftet		du hättest	ihr hättet	
Sie hofften	Sie hofften		Sie hätten	Sie hätten	
er/sie/es hoffte	sie hofften		er/sie/es hätte	sie hätten	
FUTURE SUBJUNCTIVE I			**FUTURE PERFECT SUBJUNCTIVE I**		
ich werde	wir werden	hoffen	ich werde	wir werden	gehofft haben
du werdest	ihr werdet		du werdest	ihr werdet	
Sie werden	Sie werden		Sie werden	Sie werden	
er/sie/es werde	sie werden		er/sie/es werde	sie werden	
FUTURE SUBJUNCTIVE II			**FUTURE PERFECT SUBJUNCTIVE II**		
ich würde	wir würden	hoffen	ich würde	wir würden	gehofft haben
du würdest	ihr würdet		du würdest	ihr würdet	
Sie würden	Sie würden		Sie würden	Sie würden	
er/sie/es würde	sie würden		er/sie/es würde	sie würden	

COMMANDS hoff(e)! hofft! hoffen Sie!

PRESENT PARTICIPLE hoffend

Usage

Ich hoffe, dass sich der enorme Aufwand lohnt.	*I hope the enormous effort is worth it.*
Es ist zu hoffen, dass Politiker Stellung zu diesen Themen nehmen.	*It is hoped that politicians will take a position on these issues.*
Die ganze Familie hofft auf eine baldige Besserung.	*The entire family is hoping for a quick recovery.*
Hoffen Sie, Ihr Studium im nächsten Jahr abschließen zu können?	*Do you hope to be able to complete your studies in the next year?*
Wir hoffen auf ein Ende des Konflikts.	*We are hoping for an end to the conflict.*
Ich hoffe es gefällt dir.	*I hope you like it.*
Tante Irmgard hoffte insgeheim auf ein Wunder.	*Aunt Irmgard was secretly hoping for a miracle.*
Die Radler hatten auf gutes Wetter gehofft.	*The cyclists had hoped for good weather.*
Er hofft es.	*He hopes so.*
Ich wage es nicht zu hoffen.	*I dare not hope for it.*
Hoffen wir das Beste.	*Let's hope for the best.*

RELATED VERB erhoffen

247 holen *to get, go for, fetch*

holt · holte · geholt — regular weak verb

PRESENT

ich hole	wir holen
du holst	ihr holt
Sie holen	Sie holen
er/sie/es holt	sie holen

SIMPLE PAST

ich holte	wir holten
du holtest	ihr holtet
Sie holten	Sie holten
er/sie/es holte	sie holten

FUTURE

ich werde	wir werden	holen
du wirst	ihr werdet	
Sie werden	Sie werden	
er/sie/es wird	sie werden	

PRESENT SUBJUNCTIVE I

ich hole	wir holen
du holest	ihr holet
Sie holen	Sie holen
er/sie/es hole	sie holen

PRESENT SUBJUNCTIVE II

ich holte	wir holten
du holtest	ihr holtet
Sie holten	Sie holten
er/sie/es holte	sie holten

FUTURE SUBJUNCTIVE I

ich werde	wir werden	holen
du werdest	ihr werdet	
Sie werden	Sie werden	
er/sie/es werde	sie werden	

FUTURE SUBJUNCTIVE II

ich würde	wir würden	holen
du würdest	ihr würdet	
Sie würden	Sie würden	
er/sie/es würde	sie würden	

PRESENT PERFECT

ich habe	wir haben	geholt
du hast	ihr habt	
Sie haben	Sie haben	
er/sie/es hat	sie haben	

PAST PERFECT

ich hatte	wir hatten	geholt
du hattest	ihr hattet	
Sie hatten	Sie hatten	
er/sie/es hatte	sie hatten	

FUTURE PERFECT

ich werde	wir werden	geholt haben
du wirst	ihr werdet	
Sie werden	Sie werden	
er/sie/es wird	sie werden	

PAST SUBJUNCTIVE I

ich habe	wir haben	geholt
du habest	ihr habet	
Sie haben	Sie haben	
er/sie/es habe	sie haben	

PAST SUBJUNCTIVE II

ich hätte	wir hätten	geholt
du hättest	ihr hättet	
Sie hätten	Sie hätten	
er/sie/es hätte	sie hätten	

FUTURE PERFECT SUBJUNCTIVE I

ich werde	wir werden	geholt haben
du werdest	ihr werdet	
Sie werden	Sie werden	
er/sie/es werde	sie werden	

FUTURE PERFECT SUBJUNCTIVE II

ich würde	wir würden	geholt haben
du würdest	ihr würdet	
Sie würden	Sie würden	
er/sie/es würde	sie würden	

COMMANDS hol(e)! holt! holen Sie!

PRESENT PARTICIPLE holend

Usage

Ich muss Bargeld am Geldautomaten holen. — *I have to get some cash at the ATM.*
Anke, hol mir bitte ein Taschentuch. — *Anke, please get me a tissue.*
Wir wollten das Essen holen. — *We wanted to go get the food.*
Heinz ging die Post holen. — *Heinz went to get the mail.*
Da schickte der Vater einen der Knaben eilends zur Quelle, Taufwasser zu holen. (GRIMM) — *Then the father sent one of the lads quickly to the spring to fetch baptismal water.*
Holen Sie tief Luft. — *Take a deep breath.*
Holen Sie bitte die Polizei! — *Please get the police!*

sich etwas holen *to get/procure oneself something*

Holen Sie sich doch Rat bei einem Facharzt. — *Why don't you seek advice from a medical specialist?*

RELATED VERBS auf·holen, aus·holen, ein·holen, heim·holen, herbei·holen, nach·holen, nieder·holen, über·holen, zurück·holen, zusammen·holen; *see also* **ab·holen** (4), **erholen** (159), **überholen** (459), **wiederholen** (533)

PRESENT

ich höre	wir hören
du hörst	ihr hört
Sie hören	Sie hören
er/sie/es hört	sie hören

SIMPLE PAST

ich hörte	wir hörten
du hörtest	ihr hörtet
Sie hörten	Sie hörten
er/sie/es hörte	sie hörten

FUTURE

ich werde	wir werden	hören
du wirst	ihr werdet	
Sie werden	Sie werden	
er/sie/es wird	sie werden	

PRESENT SUBJUNCTIVE I

ich höre	wir hören
du hörest	ihr höret
Sie hören	Sie hören
er/sie/es höre	sie hören

PRESENT SUBJUNCTIVE II

ich hörte	wir hörten
du hörtest	ihr hörtet
Sie hörten	Sie hörten
er/sie/es hörte	sie hörten

FUTURE SUBJUNCTIVE I

ich werde	wir werden	hören
du werdest	ihr werdet	
Sie werden	Sie werden	
er/sie/es werde	sie werden	

FUTURE SUBJUNCTIVE II

ich würde	wir würden	hören
du würdest	ihr würdet	
Sie würden	Sie würden	
er/sie/es würde	sie würden	

PRESENT PERFECT

ich habe	wir haben	gehört
du hast	ihr habt	
Sie haben	Sie haben	
er/sie/es hat	sie haben	

PAST PERFECT

ich hatte	wir hatten	gehört
du hattest	ihr hattet	
Sie hatten	Sie hatten	
er/sie/es hatte	sie hatten	

FUTURE PERFECT

ich werde	wir werden	gehört haben
du wirst	ihr werdet	
Sie werden	Sie werden	
er/sie/es wird	sie werden	

PAST SUBJUNCTIVE I

ich habe	wir haben	gehört
du habest	ihr habet	
Sie haben	Sie haben	
er/sie/es habe	sie haben	

PAST SUBJUNCTIVE II

ich hätte	wir hätten	gehört
du hättest	ihr hättet	
Sie hätten	Sie hätten	
er/sie/es hätte	sie hätten	

FUTURE PERFECT SUBJUNCTIVE I

ich werde	wir werden	gehört haben
du werdest	ihr werdet	
Sie werden	Sie werden	
er/sie/es werde	sie werden	

FUTURE PERFECT SUBJUNCTIVE II

ich würde	wir würden	gehört haben
du würdest	ihr würdet	
Sie würden	Sie würden	
er/sie/es würde	sie würden	

COMMANDS hör(e)! hört! hören Sie!

PRESENT PARTICIPLE hörend

Usage

Herr Töpfer hört gern Bigband-Musik.	*Mr. Töpfer likes listening to big band music.*
Haben Sie mal die Lieder von Friedrich Silcher gehört?	*Have you heard the songs of Friedrich Silcher?*
Im Nebenzimmer war ein lautes Geräusch zu hören.	*A loud noise could be heard in the next room.*
Wir haben gesungen und Geistergeschichten gehört.	*We sang and listened to ghost stories.*
Hör mal, Jan, ich kann es nicht mehr machen!	*Listen, Jan, I can't do it anymore!*
Ich habe lange nichts von dir gehört.	*I haven't heard anything from you for a long time.*
Hörst du mich jetzt?	*Do you hear me now?*
In Bodos Stimme konnte ich Unsicherheit hören.	*I could hear insecurity in Bodo's voice.*
Alle Studentinnen und Studenten müssen die folgenden Vorlesungen gehört haben.	*All students must have attended the following lectures.*
Opa hört jeden Morgen Radio.	*Grandpa listens to the radio every morning.*

RELATED VERBS ab·hören, an·hören, durch·hören, erhören, mit·hören, schwarz·hören, überhören, um·hören, verhören; *see also* **auf·hören** (28), **gehören** (211), **zu·hören** (550)

hören *to hear, listen; attend*

hört · hörte · gehört regular weak verb

MORE USAGE SENTENCES WITH hören

Omi hört schwer. *Granny is hard of hearing.*
Live-Musik ist auf der Bühne zu hören. *Live music can be heard on stage.*
Sie hören jetzt einen Auszug aus einem Radiospiel. *You will now hear an excerpt from a radio play.*
Manni will einfach nicht hören. *Manni simply doesn't want to listen.*
Ich kann sein Meckern nicht mehr hören. *I can't listen to his whining anymore.*
Habt ihr den Donner gehört? *Did you hear the thunder?*
Plötzlich war die Musik nebenan nicht mehr zu hören. *Suddenly, the music next door could no longer be heard.*
Schumann soll Stimmen im Kopf gehört haben. *Schumann is supposed to have heard voices in his head.*

hören + infinitive

Hörst du sie den Flur entlangkommen? *Do you hear her coming down the hall?*
Die Eltern konnten ihre Kinder im Nebenzimmer lachen hören. *The parents could hear their children laughing in the next room.*
Ich habe sagen hören, dass die Vorstellung drei Stunden dauert. *I've heard it said that the presentation lasts three hours.*

hören an + dative *to tell by*

An seinem Atem hörte man, dass er schon eingeschlafen war. *You could tell by his breathing that he'd already fallen asleep.*

hören auf + accusative *to answer/respond to; heed, obey*

Der Hund hört auf den Namen Maxl. *The dog answers to the name Maxl.*
Hört auf mein Wort, ihr Nationen! (*archaic*) *Heed my word, ye nations!*
Alexis hörte auf den Rat ihrer Freunde, sich öfter zu entspannen. *Alexis heeded her friends' advice to relax more often.*
Ihr müsst nicht auf sie hören. *You don't have to do what they say.*

hören lassen *to be heard*

Ortwins Onkel ist nach Argentinien ausgewandert und hat nichts mehr von sich hören lassen. *Ortwin's uncle emigrated to Argentina and wasn't heard from again.*
Lasst mal von euch hören! (*when taking leave*) *You all keep in touch!*
Ich lasse von mir hören. (*when taking leave*) *I'll be in touch.*
Das lässt sich hören. *That sounds acceptable.*
In der Ferne ließ sich das Geblöke von Schafen hören. *In the distance you could hear the bleating of sheep.*

hören von *to hear from, hear of*

Ich habe von Inge gehört, dass die beiden heiraten. *I heard from Inge that the two are getting married.*
Haben Sie von dem Philosophen Rudolf Steiner gehört? *Have you heard of the philosopher Rudolf Steiner?*

IDIOMATIC EXPRESSIONS

Wer nicht hören will, muss fühlen! *If you don't do as you're told, you'll pay the consequences!*
Hören Sie mal! *Listen here now!*
Es war so laut, dass ich meine eigenen Worte nicht hören konnte. *It was so loud I couldn't hear myself speak.*
Ich kann mich an seiner Stimme nicht satt hören. *I can't get enough of his voice. / I love hearing his voice.*
Der Junge hat etwas von seiner Mutter zu hören bekommen. (*colloquial*) *The boy was scolded by his mother.*
Man höre und staune! (*formulaic*) *Will wonders never cease!*
Wenn ich das Wort schon höre, wird mir schlecht! *If I so much as hear that word, it makes me sick!*

regular weak verb **informiert · informierte · informiert**

PRESENT

ich informiere	wir informieren
du informierst	ihr informiert
Sie informieren	Sie informieren
er/sie/es informiert	sie informieren

SIMPLE PAST

ich informierte	wir informierten
du informiertest	ihr informiertet
Sie informierten	Sie informierten
er/sie/es informierte	sie informierten

FUTURE

ich werde	wir werden	informieren
du wirst	ihr werdet	
Sie werden	Sie werden	
er/sie/es wird	sie werden	

PRESENT SUBJUNCTIVE I

ich informiere	wir informieren
du informierest	ihr informieret
Sie informieren	Sie informieren
er/sie/es informiere	sie informieren

PRESENT SUBJUNCTIVE II

ich informierte	wir informierten
du informiertest	ihr informiertet
Sie informierten	Sie informierten
er/sie/es informierte	sie informierten

FUTURE SUBJUNCTIVE I

ich werde	wir werden	informieren
du werdest	ihr werdet	
Sie werden	Sie werden	
er/sie/es werde	sie werden	

FUTURE SUBJUNCTIVE II

ich würde	wir würden	informieren
du würdest	ihr würdet	
Sie würden	Sie würden	
er/sie/es würde	sie würden	

PRESENT PERFECT

ich habe	wir haben	informiert
du hast	ihr habt	
Sie haben	Sie haben	
er/sie/es hat	sie haben	

PAST PERFECT

ich hatte	wir hatten	informiert
du hattest	ihr hattet	
Sie hatten	Sie hatten	
er/sie/es hatte	sie hatten	

FUTURE PERFECT

ich werde	wir werden	informiert haben
du wirst	ihr werdet	
Sie werden	Sie werden	
er/sie/es wird	sie werden	

PAST SUBJUNCTIVE I

ich habe	wir haben	informiert
du habest	ihr habet	
Sie haben	Sie haben	
er/sie/es habe	sie haben	

PAST SUBJUNCTIVE II

ich hätte	wir hätten	informiert
du hättest	ihr hättet	
Sie hätten	Sie hätten	
er/sie/es hätte	sie hätten	

FUTURE PERFECT SUBJUNCTIVE I

ich werde	wir werden	informiert haben
du werdest	ihr werdet	
Sie werden	Sie werden	
er/sie/es werde	sie werden	

FUTURE PERFECT SUBJUNCTIVE II

ich würde	wir würden	informiert haben
du würdest	ihr würdet	
Sie würden	Sie würden	
er/sie/es würde	sie würden	

COMMANDS informier(e)! informiert! informieren Sie!

PRESENT PARTICIPLE informierend

Usage

Die Abgeordneten werden über die neuen Regelungen informieren. — *The representatives will provide information on the new regulations.*

Der Bewerber ist im Februar informiert worden. — *The applicant was notified in February.*

Wie könnte man die Teilnehmer über Zeitplanveränderungen informieren? — *How could the participants be advised of schedule changes?*

sich informieren *to inform oneself, learn*

Morgen haben Besucher die Möglichkeit, sich über die verschiedenen Studiengänge zu informieren. — *Tomorrow, visitors will have an opportunity to learn about the various fields of study.*

Wenn Sie Interesse haben, können Sie sich über unsere Website weiter informieren. — *If you are interested, you can learn more on our Web site.*

Warum informierst du dich nicht darüber? — *Why don't you inquire about that?*

Obwohl er sich zum Thema eingehend informiert hatte, wusste er keine Antworten auf unsere Fragen. — *Although he had thoroughly acquainted himself with the topic, he could not answer our questions.*

250 interessieren *to interest, hold interest for; get* (someone) *interested*

interessiert · interessierte · interessiert regular weak verb

PRESENT

ich interessiere	wir interessieren
du interessierst	ihr interessiert
Sie interessieren	Sie interessieren
er/sie/es interessiert	sie interessieren

SIMPLE PAST

ich interessierte	wir interessierten
du interessiertest	ihr interessiertet
Sie interessierten	Sie interessierten
er/sie/es interessierte	sie interessierten

FUTURE

ich werde	wir werden	interessieren
du wirst	ihr werdet	
Sie werden	Sie werden	
er/sie/es wird	sie werden	

PRESENT SUBJUNCTIVE I

ich interessiere	wir interessieren
du interessierest	ihr interessieret
Sie interessieren	Sie interessieren
er/sie/es interessiere	sie interessieren

PRESENT SUBJUNCTIVE II

ich interessierte	wir interessierten
du interessiertest	ihr interessiertet
Sie interessierten	Sie interessierten
er/sie/es interessierte	sie interessierten

FUTURE SUBJUNCTIVE I

ich werde	wir werden	interessieren
du werdest	ihr werdet	
Sie werden	Sie werden	
er/sie/es werde	sie werden	

FUTURE SUBJUNCTIVE II

ich würde	wir würden	interessieren
du würdest	ihr würdet	
Sie würden	Sie würden	
er/sie/es würde	sie würden	

PRESENT PERFECT

ich habe	wir haben	interessiert
du hast	ihr habt	
Sie haben	Sie haben	
er/sie/es hat	sie haben	

PAST PERFECT

ich hatte	wir hatten	interessiert
du hattest	ihr hattet	
Sie hatten	Sie hatten	
er/sie/es hatte	sie hatten	

FUTURE PERFECT

ich werde	wir werden	interessiert haben
du wirst	ihr werdet	
Sie werden	Sie werden	
er/sie/es wird	sie werden	

PAST SUBJUNCTIVE I

ich habe	wir haben	interessiert
du habest	ihr habet	
Sie haben	Sie haben	
er/sie/es habe	sie haben	

PAST SUBJUNCTIVE II

ich hätte	wir hätten	interessiert
du hättest	ihr hättet	
Sie hätten	Sie hätten	
er/sie/es hätte	sie hätten	

FUTURE PERFECT SUBJUNCTIVE I

ich werde	wir werden	interessiert haben
du werdest	ihr werdet	
Sie werden	Sie werden	
er/sie/es werde	sie werden	

FUTURE PERFECT SUBJUNCTIVE II

ich würde	wir würden	interessiert haben
du würdest	ihr würdet	
Sie würden	Sie würden	
er/sie/es würde	sie würden	

COMMANDS interessier(e)! interessiert! interessieren Sie!

PRESENT PARTICIPLE interessierend

Usage

Diese Frage begann den Wissenschaftler zu interessieren. — *This question began to hold the scientist's interest.*

Mark hat mich an Orchideen interessiert. — *Mark has gotten me interested in orchids.*

Mich würde interessieren, wie viele Besucher meine Website gehabt hat. — *I'd be interested in knowing how many visitors my Web site has had.*

Deine Probleme interessieren mich gar nicht! — *Your problems are of no interest to me whatsoever.*

„Sie interessieren mich sehr, Herr Maier", sagte der Detektiv. — *"You interest me greatly, Mr. Maier," said the detective.*

sich interessieren für *to be interested in*

Interessierst du dich für alte Stummfilme? — *Are you interested in old silent films?*

Ich habe mich früher für Meteorologie interessiert. — *I used to be interested in meteorology.*

Kai interessiert sich nicht für Mädchen. — *Kai is not interested in girls.*

Ihr interessiert euch bestimmt für Computerspiele, nicht wahr? — *You must surely be interested in computer games, aren't you?*

regular weak verb **interpretiert · interpretierte · interpretiert**

PRESENT

ich interpretiere	wir interpretieren
du interpretierst	ihr interpretiert
Sie interpretieren	Sie interpretieren
er/sie/es interpretiert	sie interpretieren

SIMPLE PAST

ich interpretierte	wir interpretierten
du interpretiertest	ihr interpretiertet
Sie interpretierten	Sie interpretierten
er/sie/es interpretierte	sie interpretierten

FUTURE

ich werde	wir werden	interpretieren
du wirst	ihr werdet	
Sie werden	Sie werden	
er/sie/es wird	sie werden	

PRESENT SUBJUNCTIVE I

ich interpretiere	wir interpretieren
du interpretierest	ihr interpretieret
Sie interpretieren	Sie interpretieren
er/sie/es interpretiere	sie interpretieren

PRESENT SUBJUNCTIVE II

ich interpretierte	wir interpretierten
du interpretiertest	ihr interpretiertet
Sie interpretierten	Sie interpretierten
er/sie/es interpretierte	sie interpretierten

FUTURE SUBJUNCTIVE I

ich werde	wir werden	interpretieren
du werdest	ihr werdet	
Sie werden	Sie werden	
er/sie/es werde	sie werden	

FUTURE SUBJUNCTIVE II

ich würde	wir würden	interpretieren
du würdest	ihr würdet	
Sie würden	Sie würden	
er/sie/es würde	sie würden	

PRESENT PERFECT

ich habe	wir haben	interpretiert
du hast	ihr habt	
Sie haben	Sie haben	
er/sie/es hat	sie haben	

PAST PERFECT

ich hatte	wir hatten	interpretiert
du hattest	ihr hattet	
Sie hatten	Sie hatten	
er/sie/es hatte	sie hatten	

FUTURE PERFECT

ich werde	wir werden	interpretiert haben
du wirst	ihr werdet	
Sie werden	Sie werden	
er/sie/es wird	sie werden	

PAST SUBJUNCTIVE I

ich habe	wir haben	interpretiert
du habest	ihr habet	
Sie haben	Sie haben	
er/sie/es habe	sie haben	

PAST SUBJUNCTIVE II

ich hätte	wir hätten	interpretiert
du hättest	ihr hättet	
Sie hätten	Sie hätten	
er/sie/es hätte	sie hätten	

FUTURE PERFECT SUBJUNCTIVE I

ich werde	wir werden	interpretiert haben
du werdest	ihr werdet	
Sie werden	Sie werden	
er/sie/es werde	sie werden	

FUTURE PERFECT SUBJUNCTIVE II

ich würde	wir würden	interpretiert haben
du würdest	ihr würdet	
Sie würden	Sie würden	
er/sie/es würde	sie würden	

COMMANDS interpretier(e)! interpretiert! interpretieren Sie!

PRESENT PARTICIPLE interpretierend

Usage

Wie ist Ernst Jandls Gedicht „schtzngrmm“ eigentlich zu interpretieren? — *How is Ernst Jandl's poem "schtzngrmm" to be interpreted, anyway?*

Jost Maier interpretiert diese Textstelle sogar als eine Anspielung auf Homer. — *Jost Maier even interprets this place in the text as an allusion to Homer.*

Das weltberühmte Ensemble interpretiert Bachs „Brandenburgische Konzerte“. — *The world-famous ensemble interprets Bach's "Brandenburg Concertos."*

Wenn man das Werk interpretiert, stellt man oft die Frage der Gattungszugehörigkeit. — *When one interprets the work, one often deals with the question of its genre.*

Das Gesetz wird von ihnen anders interpretiert. — *The law is interpreted differently by them.*

Ich habe seine Andeutungen falsch interpretiert. — *I incorrectly interpreted his intimations.*

Wie interpretiert man einen Film? — *How does one interpret a film?*

Wie interpretierst du diese Entwicklung? — *How do you explain this development?*

Interpretieren Sie das folgende Diagramm. — *Explain the following graph.*

252 kämpfen *to fight, battle, struggle*

kämpft · kämpfte · gekämpft regular weak verb

PRESENT

ich kämpfe	wir kämpfen
du kämpfst	ihr kämpft
Sie kämpfen	Sie kämpfen
er/sie/es kämpft	sie kämpfen

SIMPLE PAST

ich kämpfte	wir kämpften
du kämpftest	ihr kämpftet
Sie kämpften	Sie kämpften
er/sie/es kämpfte	sie kämpften

FUTURE

ich werde	wir werden	kämpfen
du wirst	ihr werdet	
Sie werden	Sie werden	
er/sie/es wird	sie werden	

PRESENT SUBJUNCTIVE I

ich kämpfe	wir kämpfen
du kämpfest	ihr kämpfet
Sie kämpfen	Sie kämpfen
er/sie/es kämpfe	sie kämpfen

PRESENT SUBJUNCTIVE II

ich kämpfte	wir kämpften
du kämpftest	ihr kämpftet
Sie kämpften	Sie kämpften
er/sie/es kämpfte	sie kämpften

FUTURE SUBJUNCTIVE I

ich werde	wir werden	kämpfen
du werdest	ihr werdet	
Sie werden	Sie werden	
er/sie/es werde	sie werden	

FUTURE SUBJUNCTIVE II

ich würde	wir würden	kämpfen
du würdest	ihr würdet	
Sie würden	Sie würden	
er/sie/es würde	sie würden	

PRESENT PERFECT

ich habe	wir haben	gekämpft
du hast	ihr habt	
Sie haben	Sie haben	
er/sie/es hat	sie haben	

PAST PERFECT

ich hatte	wir hatten	gekämpft
du hattest	ihr hattet	
Sie hatten	Sie hatten	
er/sie/es hatte	sie hatten	

FUTURE PERFECT

ich werde	wir werden	gekämpft haben
du wirst	ihr werdet	
Sie werden	Sie werden	
er/sie/es wird	sie werden	

PAST SUBJUNCTIVE I

ich habe	wir haben	gekämpft
du habest	ihr habet	
Sie haben	Sie haben	
er/sie/es habe	sie haben	

PAST SUBJUNCTIVE II

ich hätte	wir hätten	gekämpft
du hättest	ihr hättet	
Sie hätten	Sie hätten	
er/sie/es hätte	sie hätten	

FUTURE PERFECT SUBJUNCTIVE I

ich werde	wir werden	gekämpft haben
du werdest	ihr werdet	
Sie werden	Sie werden	
er/sie/es werde	sie werden	

FUTURE PERFECT SUBJUNCTIVE II

ich würde	wir würden	gekämpft haben
du würdest	ihr würdet	
Sie würden	Sie würden	
er/sie/es würde	sie würden	

COMMANDS kämpf(e)! kämpft! kämpfen Sie!

PRESENT PARTICIPLE kämpfend

Usage

Martin Luther King Jr. kämpfte für Gesetzesänderungen. *Martin Luther King, Jr. fought for changes in the law.*

Lester kämpft gegen seine Drogensucht. *Lester is struggling against his drug addiction.*

Die Österreicher und Franzosen kämpften 1800 bei Marengo in Italien. *The Austrians and the French battled near Marengo in Italy in 1800.*

Letztes Jahr wurde um den Weltpokal gekämpft. *Last year, they battled for the world cup.*

Nach der Hirnoperation musste Jörg um sein Leben kämpfen. *After the brain surgery, Jörg had to fight to live.*

Die Spieler haben bis zum Ende hart gekämpft. *The players fought hard to the end.*

Die beiden Prinzen kämpften um den Thron. *The two princes battled for the throne.*

sich kämpfen *to fight one's way*

Die Forscher kämpften sich durch den Dschungel. *The explorers fought their way through the jungle.*

RELATED VERBS ab·kämpfen, an·kämpfen, aus·kämpfen, bekämpfen, durch·kämpfen, erkämpfen, mit·kämpfen, nieder·kämpfen, vor·kämpfen, weiter·kämpfen

253 kaufen *to buy, purchase*

regular weak verb

kauft · kaufte · gekauft

PRESENT

ich kaufe	wir kaufen
du kaufst	ihr kauft
Sie kaufen	Sie kaufen
er/sie/es kauft	sie kaufen

SIMPLE PAST

ich kaufte	wir kauften
du kauftest	ihr kauftet
Sie kauften	Sie kauften
er/sie/es kaufte	sie kauften

FUTURE

ich werde	wir werden	kaufen
du wirst	ihr werdet	
Sie werden	Sie werden	
er/sie/es wird	sie werden	

PRESENT SUBJUNCTIVE I

ich kaufe	wir kaufen
du kaufest	ihr kaufet
Sie kaufen	Sie kaufen
er/sie/es kaufe	sie kaufen

PRESENT SUBJUNCTIVE II

ich kaufte	wir kauften
du kauftest	ihr kauftet
Sie kauften	Sie kauften
er/sie/es kaufte	sie kauften

FUTURE SUBJUNCTIVE I

ich werde	wir werden	kaufen
du werdest	ihr werdet	
Sie werden	Sie werden	
er/sie/es werde	sie werden	

FUTURE SUBJUNCTIVE II

ich würde	wir würden	kaufen
du würdest	ihr würdet	
Sie würden	Sie würden	
er/sie/es würde	sie würden	

PRESENT PERFECT

ich habe	wir haben	gekauft
du hast	ihr habt	
Sie haben	Sie haben	
er/sie/es hat	sie haben	

PAST PERFECT

ich hatte	wir hatten	gekauft
du hattest	ihr hattet	
Sie hatten	Sie hatten	
er/sie/es hatte	sie hatten	

FUTURE PERFECT

ich werde	wir werden	gekauft haben
du wirst	ihr werdet	
Sie werden	Sie werden	
er/sie/es wird	sie werden	

PAST SUBJUNCTIVE I

ich habe	wir haben	gekauft
du habest	ihr habet	
Sie haben	Sie haben	
er/sie/es habe	sie haben	

PAST SUBJUNCTIVE II

ich hätte	wir hätten	gekauft
du hättest	ihr hättet	
Sie hätten	Sie hätten	
er/sie/es hätte	sie hätten	

FUTURE PERFECT SUBJUNCTIVE I

ich werde	wir werden	gekauft haben
du werdest	ihr werdet	
Sie werden	Sie werden	
er/sie/es werde	sie werden	

FUTURE PERFECT SUBJUNCTIVE II

ich würde	wir würden	gekauft haben
du würdest	ihr würdet	
Sie würden	Sie würden	
er/sie/es würde	sie würden	

COMMANDS kauf(e)! kauft! kaufen Sie!

PRESENT PARTICIPLE kaufend

Usage

Am Flohmarkt werden allerlei interessante Sachen gekauft und verkauft.	*At the flea market, all sorts of interesting items are bought and sold.*
Er behauptet, man könne von ihm illegale Waffen kaufen.	*He maintains that you can purchase illegal weapons from him.*
Ich möchte eine mittelalterliche Handschrift kaufen.	*I would like to buy a medieval manuscript.*
Frau Backbesser kaufte immer Vanille aus Madagaskar.	*Mrs. Backbesser always bought vanilla from Madagascar.*
Wo kann man hier eine Zeitung kaufen?	*Where can you buy a newspaper here?*
Sollten wir kaufen oder mieten?	*Should we buy or rent?*
Diese Firma kauft Immobilien.	*This firm purchases real estate.*
Kaufst du mir dieses Buch?	*Are you going to buy me this book?*

RELATED VERBS ab·kaufen, an·kaufen, auf·kaufen, aus·kaufen, erkaufen, frei·kaufen, los·kaufen, nach·kaufen, zurück·kaufen; *see also* **ein·kaufen** (133), **verkaufen** (491)

TOP 50 VERB ☞

kaufen *to buy, purchase*

kauft · kaufte · gekauft regular weak verb

MORE USAGE SENTENCES WITH kaufen

Maria hat einen Pullover bei Hertie gekauft. *Maria bought a sweater at Hertie.*
Das Ding hast du zu teuer gekauft. *You paid too much for that thing.*
Ich hätte mir eine neue Sonnenbrille gekauft, nur ich bin pleite. *I would have bought myself new sunglasses, only I'm broke.*
Manni soll seinen neuen Porsche auf Kredit gekauft haben. *Manni is said to have purchased his new Porsche on credit.*
Wir zeigen Ihnen, wie Sie Ihr Auto billig kaufen können. *We'll show you how you can buy your car cheap.*
Möbelstücke, die auf Raten gekauft wurden, können gepfändet werden. *Furniture bought on installment can be repossessed.*
Parmesankäse hält länger, wenn man ihn am Stück kauft. *Parmesan cheese will keep longer if you buy it ungrated.*
Ich kaufe Brot immer am Stück, so verschimmelt es nicht so schnell. *I always buy bread unsliced; that way, it doesn't get moldy as quickly.*
Frau Immerschick kauft keine Kleidung von der Stange, sie lässt sie maßschneidern. *Mrs. Immerschick never buys clothes off the rack; she has them custom tailored.*
Man kann den Salat fertig kaufen, aber frisch zubereitet schmeckt er am besten. *You can buy the salad ready-made, but it will taste best when freshly prepared.*
Lars sagte, er hätte den Fernseher für 1200 Euro gekauft. *Lars said he bought the television for 1,200 euros.*
Kauft ihr Bio-Rindfleisch direkt vom Erzeuger? *Do you buy organic beef directly from the producer?*
Das Obst und Gemüse kaufe ich am Wochenmarkt, aber wir kaufen das Fleisch beim Metzger. *The fruit and vegetables I buy at the weekly market, but we buy our meat at the butcher's.*
Glück ist nicht zu kaufen. *Happiness can't be bought.*
Das schönste Papier ist gekauft, und wir nehmen uns vor, darauf zu zeichnen. (GOETHE) *The most beautiful paper has been bought, and we intend to do sketches on it.*
Mein Mann kauft alles Mögliche online: Bücher, CDs, alles! *My husband purchases all sorts of things online: books, CDs, everything!*
Mein Onkel hat kubanische Zigarren schwarz gekauft. *My uncle purchased some black market Cuban cigars.*
Renate kauft sich einen Gebrauchtwagen. *Renate is buying herself a used car.*
In Second-Hand-Läden kann man Kleidung zu günstigen Preisen kaufen. *In secondhand shops, you can buy clothing at reasonable prices.*
Robert möchte eine Eigentumswohnung kaufen. *Robert would like to purchase a condominium.*
Fritz kauft sich eine CD von seinem Taschengeld. *Fritz is buying himself a CD with his allowance.*
Vom Konsumrausch befallen, fühlt man sich gezwungen möglichst viel zu kaufen. *Overcome by consumption frenzy, one feels compelled to buy as much as possible.*
Wenn du ein spottbilliges Produkt kaufst, geschieht das auf Kosten der unterbezahlten Arbeiter, die das Produkt herstellten. *Whenever you buy a dirt cheap product, it is at the expense of the underpaid laborers who made that product.*

IDIOMATIC EXPRESSIONS

Das Videospiel wird viel gekauft. *The video game is selling well.*
Dafür kann ich mir nichts kaufen! *That does me no good!*
Ich habe den DVD-Spieler für einen Apfel und ein Ei gekauft. *I bought the DVD player for a song/for peanuts.*
Heinz hat das Auto aus erster Hand gekauft. *Heinz bought the car from the original owner.*
Kauf die Katze nicht im Sack. *Don't buy a pig in a poke.*
Wo bekommt man das zu kaufen? (*colloquial*) *Where can you buy that?*
Kaufen Sie nicht mehr bei Schmidt! *Don't shop at Schmidt's anymore!*

regular weak verb **kehrt · kehrte · gekehrt**

PRESENT		PRESENT PERFECT		
ich kehre	wir kehren	ich habe	wir haben	gekehrt
du kehrst	ihr kehrt	du hast	ihr habt	
Sie kehren	Sie kehren	Sie haben	Sie haben	
er/sie/es kehrt	sie kehren	er/sie/es hat	sie haben	

SIMPLE PAST		PAST PERFECT		
ich kehrte	wir kehrten	ich hatte	wir hatten	gekehrt
du kehrtest	ihr kehrtet	du hattest	ihr hattet	
Sie kehrten	Sie kehrten	Sie hatten	Sie hatten	
er/sie/es kehrte	sie kehrten	er/sie/es hatte	sie hatten	

FUTURE			FUTURE PERFECT		
ich werde	wir werden	kehren	ich werde	wir werden	gekehrt haben
du wirst	ihr werdet		du wirst	ihr werdet	
Sie werden	Sie werden		Sie werden	Sie werden	
er/sie/es wird	sie werden		er/sie/es wird	sie werden	

PRESENT SUBJUNCTIVE I		PAST SUBJUNCTIVE I		
ich kehre	wir kehren	ich habe	wir haben	gekehrt
du kehrest	ihr kehret	du habest	ihr habet	
Sie kehren	Sie kehren	Sie haben	Sie haben	
er/sie/es kehre	sie kehren	er/sie/es habe	sie haben	

PRESENT SUBJUNCTIVE II		PAST SUBJUNCTIVE II		
ich kehrte	wir kehrten	ich hätte	wir hätten	gekehrt
du kehrtest	ihr kehrtet	du hättest	ihr hättet	
Sie kehrten	Sie kehrten	Sie hätten	Sie hätten	
er/sie/es kehrte	sie kehrten	er/sie/es hätte	sie hätten	

FUTURE SUBJUNCTIVE I			FUTURE PERFECT SUBJUNCTIVE I		
ich werde	wir werden	kehren	ich werde	wir werden	gekehrt haben
du werdest	ihr werdet		du werdest	ihr werdet	
Sie werden	Sie werden		Sie werden	Sie werden	
er/sie/es werde	sie werden		er/sie/es werde	sie werden	

FUTURE SUBJUNCTIVE II			FUTURE PERFECT SUBJUNCTIVE II		
ich würde	wir würden	kehren	ich würde	wir würden	gekehrt haben
du würdest	ihr würdet		du würdest	ihr würdet	
Sie würden	Sie würden		Sie würden	Sie würden	
er/sie/es würde	sie würden		er/sie/es würde	sie würden	

COMMANDS kehr(e)! kehrt! kehren Sie!

PRESENT PARTICIPLE kehrend

Usage

Der 18-jährige Sohn eines Finanziers hat seiner Familie den Rücken gekehrt.	*The 18-year-old son of a financier has turned his back on his family.*
Sara kehrte die Innenseite des Mantels nach außen.	*Sara turned the coat inside out.*
Die Mannschaft hoffte, das Spiel kehren zu können.	*The team hoped to be able to turn the game around.*
Paul kehrt lieber mit einem Naturbesen.	*Paul prefers to sweep with a natural broom.*
Die Vorgesetzten kehrten das Problem einfach unter den Teppich. (*idiomatic*)	*The supervisors simply swept the problem under the rug.*

kehren (with sein) *to turn, return*

Sie waren voller Begeisterung nach Hause gekehrt.	*They had returned home full of enthusiasm.*

sich kehren *to turn (around)*

Der Diener kehrte sich und ging weg.	*The servant turned around and went away.*

RELATED VERBS ab·kehren, auf·kehren, aus·kehren, bekehren, ein·kehren, heim·kehren, um·kehren, verkehren, weg·kehren, wieder·kehren, zu·kehren, zurück·kehren

255 keimen *to germinate, sprout; arise*

keimt · keimte · gekeimt regular weak verb

PRESENT

ich keime	wir keimen
du keimst	ihr keimt
Sie keimen	Sie keimen
er/sie/es keimt	sie keimen

PRESENT PERFECT

ich habe	wir haben	gekeimt
du hast	ihr habt	
Sie haben	Sie haben	
er/sie/es hat	sie haben	

SIMPLE PAST

ich keimte	wir keimten
du keimtest	ihr keimtet
Sie keimten	Sie keimten
er/sie/es keimte	sie keimten

PAST PERFECT

ich hatte	wir hatten	gekeimt
du hattest	ihr hattet	
Sie hatten	Sie hatten	
er/sie/es hatte	sie hatten	

FUTURE

ich werde	wir werden	keimen
du wirst	ihr werdet	
Sie werden	Sie werden	
er/sie/es wird	sie werden	

FUTURE PERFECT

ich werde	wir werden	gekeimt haben
du wirst	ihr werdet	
Sie werden	Sie werden	
er/sie/es wird	sie werden	

PRESENT SUBJUNCTIVE I

ich keime	wir keimen
du keimest	ihr keimet
Sie keimen	Sie keimen
er/sie/es keime	sie keimen

PAST SUBJUNCTIVE I

ich habe	wir haben	gekeimt
du habest	ihr habet	
Sie haben	Sie haben	
er/sie/es habe	sie haben	

PRESENT SUBJUNCTIVE II

ich keimte	wir keimten
du keimtest	ihr keimtet
Sie keimten	Sie keimten
er/sie/es keimte	sie keimten

PAST SUBJUNCTIVE II

ich hätte	wir hätten	gekeimt
du hättest	ihr hättet	
Sie hätten	Sie hätten	
er/sie/es hätte	sie hätten	

FUTURE SUBJUNCTIVE I

ich werde	wir werden	keimen
du werdest	ihr werdet	
Sie werden	Sie werden	
er/sie/es werde	sie werden	

FUTURE PERFECT SUBJUNCTIVE I

ich werde	wir werden	gekeimt haben
du werdest	ihr werdet	
Sie werden	Sie werden	
er/sie/es werde	sie werden	

FUTURE SUBJUNCTIVE II

ich würde	wir würden	keimen
du würdest	ihr würdet	
Sie würden	Sie würden	
er/sie/es würde	sie würden	

FUTURE PERFECT SUBJUNCTIVE II

ich würde	wir würden	gekeimt haben
du würdest	ihr würdet	
Sie würden	Sie würden	
er/sie/es würde	sie würden	

COMMANDS keim(e)! keimt! keimen Sie!

PRESENT PARTICIPLE keimend

Usage

Der Samen keimt nach circa 60 Tagen.	*The seed germinates after about 60 days.*
Warum haben die Kartoffeln nicht gekeimt?	*Why haven't the potatoes sprouted?*
Eine Woche nachdem die Bohnen gekeimt haben, kann man sie ernten.	*One week after the beans have sprouted, you can harvest them.*
Du keimst, du blühst und du verwelkest auch! (Storm)	*You sprout, you blossom, and you wither as well!*
Die Knospen keimen schon.	*The buds are already sprouting.*
Die Blumen keimen und die Vögel zwitschern.	*The flowers are budding and the birds are twittering.*
Eine Freundschaft keimt zwischen ihnen.	*A friendship is budding between them.*
Ideen für mein nächstes Projekt keimen schon.	*Ideas for my next project are already germinating.*
In ihm keimte der Verdacht, dass seine neue Nachbarin ihn insgeheim beobachtete.	*The suspicion arose within him that his new neighbor was secretly watching him.*
Allmählich keimte in mir der Gedanke einer Reise nach Japan.	*Gradually, the thought of a trip to Japan took shape in my mind.*

RELATED VERBS auf·keimen, aus·keimen, entkeimen

mixed verb **kennt · kannte · gekannt**

PRESENT

ich kenne	wir kennen
du kennst	ihr kennt
Sie kennen	Sie kennen
er/sie/es kennt	sie kennen

PRESENT PERFECT

ich habe	wir haben	gekannt
du hast	ihr habt	
Sie haben	Sie haben	
er/sie/es hat	sie haben	

SIMPLE PAST

ich kannte	wir kannten
du kanntest	ihr kanntet
Sie kannten	Sie kannten
er/sie/es kannte	sie kannten

PAST PERFECT

ich hatte	wir hatten	gekannt
du hattest	ihr hattet	
Sie hatten	Sie hatten	
er/sie/es hatte	sie hatten	

FUTURE

ich werde	wir werden	kennen
du wirst	ihr werdet	
Sie werden	Sie werden	
er/sie/es wird	sie werden	

FUTURE PERFECT

ich werde	wir werden	gekannt haben
du wirst	ihr werdet	
Sie werden	Sie werden	
er/sie/es wird	sie werden	

PRESENT SUBJUNCTIVE I

ich kenne	wir kennen
du kennest	ihr kennet
Sie kennen	Sie kennen
er/sie/es kenne	sie kennen

PAST SUBJUNCTIVE I

ich habe	wir haben	gekannt
du habest	ihr habet	
Sie haben	Sie haben	
er/sie/es habe	sie haben	

PRESENT SUBJUNCTIVE II

ich kennte	wir kennten
du kenntest	ihr kenntet
Sie kennten	Sie kennten
er/sie/es kennte	sie kennten

PAST SUBJUNCTIVE II

ich hätte	wir hätten	gekannt
du hättest	ihr hättet	
Sie hätten	Sie hätten	
er/sie/es hätte	sie hätten	

FUTURE SUBJUNCTIVE I

ich werde	wir werden	kennen
du werdest	ihr werdet	
Sie werden	Sie werden	
er/sie/es werde	sie werden	

FUTURE PERFECT SUBJUNCTIVE I

ich werde	wir werden	gekannt haben
du werdest	ihr werdet	
Sie werden	Sie werden	
er/sie/es werde	sie werden	

FUTURE SUBJUNCTIVE II

ich würde	wir würden	kennen
du würdest	ihr würdet	
Sie würden	Sie würden	
er/sie/es würde	sie würden	

FUTURE PERFECT SUBJUNCTIVE II

ich würde	wir würden	gekannt haben
du würdest	ihr würdet	
Sie würden	Sie würden	
er/sie/es würde	sie würden	

COMMANDS kenn(e)! kennt! kennen Sie!

PRESENT PARTICIPLE kennend

Usage

Ich kenne ihn aus der Schule.	*I know him from school.*
Kennst du Deutschland?	*Are you familiar with Germany?*
Kennen Sie den Film „Matrix"?	*Do you know the film* Matrix*?*
Frau Schmidt wohnte dreißig Jahre in der Schorlemerstraße, aber kannte keinen ihrer Nachbarn.	*Mrs. Schmidt lived on Schorlemer Street for 30 years but wasn't acquainted with any of her neighbors.*
Man kennt sich nicht.	*We/They/You do not know one another.*
Als Kinder haben wir nur Rinderbraten und Brathähnchen gekannt; heute essen wir Tofu.	*As children, we knew only roast beef and fried chicken; today we're eating tofu.*
Sie scheinen mich nicht sehr gut zu kennen.	*You don't seem to know me very well.*
„Kennt ihr Friedrich Müller?"	*Do you know Friedrich Müller?*
„Wir kennen einen Manfred Müller."	*We know a Manfred Müller.*
Ich kenne den Namen, aber nicht seine Werke.	*I know the name but not his work.*

RELATED VERBS aus·kennen, bekennen, verkennen; *see also* **erkennen** (162)

TOP 50 VERB ☞

kennen *to know, be familiar with, be acquainted with*

kennt · kannte · gekannt mixed verb

MORE USAGE SENTENCES WITH kennen

Entschuldigung, wir kennen uns noch nicht. Ich bin Angela, die Tochter von Herrn Groß. — *Excuse me, we don't know each other yet. I'm Angela, Mr. Groß's daughter.*

Ich kenne ihn vom Sehen her, aber wir sprechen nicht miteinander. — *I've seen him around, but I haven't spoken with him.*

Kennen Sie Nägelis Kompositionen? — *Are you familiar with Nägeli's compositions?*

Kennst du die Romane von Hermann Hesse? — *Are you acquainted with the novels of Hermann Hesse?*

Wenn du das glaubst, dann kennst du mich aber schlecht, Antje! — *If you believe that, then you don't know me very well, Antje!*

Politik kennt keine Grenzen. — *Politics knows no limits.*

Ich habe meine junge Schwester nicht mehr gekannt. — *I didn't know my little sister anymore.*

Kennst du den Ausdruck „Schwein haben"? — *Do you know the expression "Schwein haben" (= to have good luck)?*

Auf dem Dorf kennt jeder jeden. — *In a village, everybody knows everybody.*

Maria und ich kennen uns seit 23 Jahren. — *Maria and I have known each other for 23 years.*

Ernst sagt, er kenne den Präsidenten persönlich. — *Ernst says he knows the president personally.*

Ursula? Ich kannte sie nur flüchtig vor ein paar Jahren. — *Ursula? I knew her only in passing a few years back.*

Kennt ihr eine gute Kneipe in der Gegend? — *Do you know a good pub in the area?*

kennen *to have/know (from experience)*

Die Völker auf der kleineren Insel haben keine Autos oder Fernseher gekannt. — *The people on the smaller island had no cars or televisions.*

Der Angeklagte kannte keine Schuld. — *The accused had no guilt.*

„Tut das nicht weh?"
„Nee, ein echter Mann kennt keinen Schmerz." — *"Doesn't that hurt?" "No, a real man knows no pain."*

„Trägst du denn keinen Helm beim Motorradfahren?"
„Nein, ein erfahrener Fahrer kennt keinen Helm." — *"Don't you wear a helmet when riding a motorcycle?" "No, an experienced rider doesn't need a helmet."*

Der Wagen steht immer in der Garage und kennt keinen Regen. — *The car is always in the garage and has never been rained on.*

kennen an + dative *to know/recognize by*

Ich kenne Steve an seinem Lachen. — *I know Steve by his laugh.*

kennen lernen *to meet, make the acquaintance of, get to know*

Mark und ich haben uns online kennen gelernt. — *Mark and I became acquainted online.*

Wir hatten letzte Woche Zeit, sie kennen zu lernen. — *We had time last week to get acquainted with them.*

Ich hatte schon die Ehre, Sie kennen zu lernen. — *I've already had the honor of meeting you.*

Es freut mich, Sie kennen zu lernen. — *It's a pleasure to meet you.*

IDIOMATIC EXPRESSIONS

Das kenne ich! — *I know what you mean!/You're telling me!*

Sie wissen nicht, dass sie benachteiligt sind, weil sie das gar nicht anders kennen. — *They don't know they're disadvantaged, because it's always been like that for them.*

Ich kannte ihn als freundlichen Kollegen. — *I knew him to be a friendly colleague.*

Es gibt mehrere Sorten, ich kenne sie nicht auseinander. — *There are several types—I can't distinguish one from another.*

Lars kennt seine Heimatstadt wie seine Hosentasche. — *Lars knows his hometown like the back of his hand.*

Ich kenne Göttingen in- und auswendig. — *I know Göttingen inside and out.*

Die Ausrede kenne ich schon. — *I've heard that excuse before.*

regular weak verb **klagt · klagte · geklagt**

PRESENT		PRESENT PERFECT		
ich klage	wir klagen	ich habe	wir haben	geklagt
du klagst	ihr klagt	du hast	ihr habt	
Sie klagen	Sie klagen	Sie haben	Sie haben	
er/sie/es klagt	sie klagen	er/sie/es hat	sie haben	

SIMPLE PAST		PAST PERFECT		
ich klagte	wir klagten	ich hatte	wir hatten	geklagt
du klagtest	ihr klagtet	du hattest	ihr hattet	
Sie klagten	Sie klagten	Sie hatten	Sie hatten	
er/sie/es klagte	sie klagten	er/sie/es hatte	sie hatten	

FUTURE			FUTURE PERFECT		
ich werde	wir werden	klagen	ich werde	wir werden	geklagt haben
du wirst	ihr werdet		du wirst	ihr werdet	
Sie werden	Sie werden		Sie werden	Sie werden	
er/sie/es wird	sie werden		er/sie/es wird	sie werden	

PRESENT SUBJUNCTIVE I		PAST SUBJUNCTIVE I		
ich klage	wir klagen	ich habe	wir haben	geklagt
du klagest	ihr klaget	du habest	ihr habet	
Sie klagen	Sie klagen	Sie haben	Sie haben	
er/sie/es klage	sie klagen	er/sie/es habe	sie haben	

PRESENT SUBJUNCTIVE II		PAST SUBJUNCTIVE II		
ich klagte	wir klagten	ich hätte	wir hätten	geklagt
du klagtest	ihr klagtet	du hättest	ihr hättet	
Sie klagten	Sie klagten	Sie hätten	Sie hätten	
er/sie/es klagte	sie klagten	er/sie/es hätte	sie hätten	

FUTURE SUBJUNCTIVE I			FUTURE PERFECT SUBJUNCTIVE I		
ich werde	wir werden	klagen	ich werde	wir werden	geklagt haben
du werdest	ihr werdet		du werdest	ihr werdet	
Sie werden	Sie werden		Sie werden	Sie werden	
er/sie/es werde	sie werden		er/sie/es werde	sie werden	

FUTURE SUBJUNCTIVE II			FUTURE PERFECT SUBJUNCTIVE II		
ich würde	wir würden	klagen	ich würde	wir würden	geklagt haben
du würdest	ihr würdet		du würdest	ihr würdet	
Sie würden	Sie würden		Sie würden	Sie würden	
er/sie/es würde	sie würden		er/sie/es würde	sie würden	

COMMANDS klag(e)! klagt! klagen Sie!

PRESENT PARTICIPLE klagend

Usage

Sara will nicht darüber klagen.	*Sara does not want to complain about it.*
Klagt nicht, handelt!	*Don't complain, act!*
Warum klagst du ständig über Zeitmangel?	*Why do you constantly complain about not having enough time?*
„Das ist zu laut!" klagte der Nachbar.	*"That's too loud!" complained the neighbor.*
Kurz danach hat er seinem älteren Bruder geklagt, dass er Hunger hatte.	*Shortly thereafter, he complained to his older brother that he was hungry.*
Ich hätte nicht über das Wetter klagen sollen.	*I shouldn't have complained about the weather.*
Ich kann nicht klagen.	*I can't complain.*
Frau Lindemann klagt den Verlust ihrer wertvollen japanischen Windorchidee.	*Mrs. Lindemann is bemoaning the loss of her valuable Japanese Wind Orchid.*
Die Computerfirma klagt gegen die EU wegen Lizenzrechte.	*The computer firm is suing the E.U. over licensing rights.*

RELATED VERBS an·klagen, aus·klagen, beklagen, ein·klagen, verklagen, wehklagen

258 klappen *to fold, tilt; work well, go without a hitch; bang, slam*

klappt · klappte · geklappt regular weak verb

PRESENT

ich klappe	wir klappen
du klappst	ihr klappt
Sie klappen	Sie klappen
er/sie/es klappt	sie klappen

SIMPLE PAST

ich klappte	wir klappten
du klapptest	ihr klapptet
Sie klappten	Sie klappten
er/sie/es klappte	sie klappten

FUTURE

ich werde	wir werden	klappen
du wirst	ihr werdet	
Sie werden	Sie werden	
er/sie/es wird	sie werden	

PRESENT SUBJUNCTIVE I

ich klappe	wir klappen
du klappest	ihr klappet
Sie klappen	Sie klappen
er/sie/es klappe	sie klappen

PRESENT SUBJUNCTIVE II

ich klappte	wir klappten
du klapptest	ihr klapptet
Sie klappten	Sie klappten
er/sie/es klappte	sie klappten

FUTURE SUBJUNCTIVE I

ich werde	wir werden	klappen
du werdest	ihr werdet	
Sie werden	Sie werden	
er/sie/es werde	sie werden	

FUTURE SUBJUNCTIVE II

ich würde	wir würden	klappen
du würdest	ihr würdet	
Sie würden	Sie würden	
er/sie/es würde	sie würden	

PRESENT PERFECT

ich habe	wir haben	geklappt
du hast	ihr habt	
Sie haben	Sie haben	
er/sie/es hat	sie haben	

PAST PERFECT

ich hatte	wir hatten	geklappt
du hattest	ihr hattet	
Sie hatten	Sie hatten	
er/sie/es hatte	sie hatten	

FUTURE PERFECT

ich werde	wir werden	geklappt haben
du wirst	ihr werdet	
Sie werden	Sie werden	
er/sie/es wird	sie werden	

PAST SUBJUNCTIVE I

ich habe	wir haben	geklappt
du habest	ihr habet	
Sie haben	Sie haben	
er/sie/es habe	sie haben	

PAST SUBJUNCTIVE II

ich hätte	wir hätten	geklappt
du hättest	ihr hättet	
Sie hätten	Sie hätten	
er/sie/es hätte	sie hätten	

FUTURE PERFECT SUBJUNCTIVE I

ich werde	wir werden	geklappt haben
du werdest	ihr werdet	
Sie werden	Sie werden	
er/sie/es werde	sie werden	

FUTURE PERFECT SUBJUNCTIVE II

ich würde	wir würden	geklappt haben
du würdest	ihr würdet	
Sie würden	Sie würden	
er/sie/es würde	sie würden	

COMMANDS klapp(e)! klappt! klappen Sie!

PRESENT PARTICIPLE klappend

Usage

Klapp mal den Deckel so.	*Fold the lid like this.*
Man kann die Tastatur auch höher klappen.	*You can also tilt the keyboard higher.*
Klappen Sie den Hemdkragen nach oben.	*Turn the shirt collar up.*
Wir hoffen, dass es beim nächsten Versuch klappt.	*We hope it works well on the next try.*
Wenn alles klappt, ist sie in guter Laune.	*When everything's going well, she's in a good mood.*
Ingrids Plan scheint zu klappen.	*Ingrid's plan seems to be proceeding without a hitch.*
Es wird bestimmt klappen.	*It will surely work out.*
Die Zusammenarbeit der vier Partner hat trotz einiger Probleme ziemlich gut geklappt.	*The cooperation among the four partners worked out fairly well despite a few problems.*
Wenn die neue Webpage angezeigt wird, dann muss der Upload geklappt haben.	*If the new Web page is displayed, then the upload must have been successful.*
In der Nacht hörten die Gäste Türen klappen und Fußschritte im Dachboden.	*During the night, the guests heard doors slamming and footsteps in the attic.*

RELATED VERBS ab·klappen, auf·klappen, hoch·klappen, um·klappen, zu·klappen, zusammen·klappen

regular weak verb **klebt · klebte · geklebt**

PRESENT

ich klebe	wir kleben
du klebst	ihr klebt
Sie kleben	Sie kleben
er/sie/es klebt	sie kleben

PRESENT PERFECT

ich habe	wir haben	geklebt
du hast	ihr habt	
Sie haben	Sie haben	
er/sie/es hat	sie haben	

SIMPLE PAST

ich klebte	wir klebten
du klebtest	ihr klebtet
Sie klebten	Sie klebten
er/sie/es klebte	sie klebten

PAST PERFECT

ich hatte	wir hatten	geklebt
du hattest	ihr hattet	
Sie hatten	Sie hatten	
er/sie/es hatte	sie hatten	

FUTURE

ich werde	wir werden	kleben
du wirst	ihr werdet	
Sie werden	Sie werden	
er/sie/es wird	sie werden	

FUTURE PERFECT

ich werde	wir werden	geklebt haben
du wirst	ihr werdet	
Sie werden	Sie werden	
er/sie/es wird	sie werden	

PRESENT SUBJUNCTIVE I

ich klebe	wir kleben
du klebest	ihr klebet
Sie kleben	Sie kleben
er/sie/es klebe	sie kleben

PAST SUBJUNCTIVE I

ich habe	wir haben	geklebt
du habest	ihr habet	
Sie haben	Sie haben	
er/sie/es habe	sie haben	

PRESENT SUBJUNCTIVE II

ich klebte	wir klebten
du klebtest	ihr klebtet
Sie klebten	Sie klebten
er/sie/es klebte	sie klebten

PAST SUBJUNCTIVE II

ich hätte	wir hätten	geklebt
du hättest	ihr hättet	
Sie hätten	Sie hätten	
er/sie/es hätte	sie hätten	

FUTURE SUBJUNCTIVE I

ich werde	wir werden	kleben
du werdest	ihr werdet	
Sie werden	Sie werden	
er/sie/es werde	sie werden	

FUTURE PERFECT SUBJUNCTIVE I

ich werde	wir werden	geklebt haben
du werdest	ihr werdet	
Sie werden	Sie werden	
er/sie/es werde	sie werden	

FUTURE SUBJUNCTIVE II

ich würde	wir würden	kleben
du würdest	ihr würdet	
Sie würden	Sie würden	
er/sie/es würde	sie würden	

FUTURE PERFECT SUBJUNCTIVE II

ich würde	wir würden	geklebt haben
du würdest	ihr würdet	
Sie würden	Sie würden	
er/sie/es würde	sie würden	

COMMANDS kleb(e)! klebt! kleben Sie!

PRESENT PARTICIPLE klebend

Usage

Anja und Ortwin haben Anti-Atom-Plakate überall auf dem Campus geklebt. — *Anja and Ortwin have posted anti-nuclear bills everywhere on campus.*

Meine Nichte Sandra könnte stundenlang basteln, schneiden, kleben und malen. — *My niece Sandra could do handicrafts, cut, paste, and paint for hours.*

Kleben Sie einen Zettel an die Tür. — *Stick a note on the door.*

Der alte Leim klebt nicht mehr. — *The old glue isn't sticking anymore.*

Wenn der Redner am Text klebt, wird die Rede langweilig. — *If a speaker just sticks to his script, the speech gets boring.*

Das Kaugummi klebte in ihren Haaren. — *The chewing gum was stuck in her hair.*

Eine tote Fliege klebte am Fenster. — *A dead fly was stuck to the window.*

Der Herr am Nebentisch wurde inne, dass Marmelade an seinem Bart klebte. — *The gentleman at the next table became aware of the marmalade stuck to his beard.*

Wie kann man Filme kleben? — *How can you splice film?*

RELATED VERBS an·kleben, auf·kleben, aus·kleben, bekleben, ein·kleben, fest·kleben, überkleben, verkleben, zu·kleben, zusammen·kleben

260 klettern *to climb*

klettert · kletterte · geklettert regular weak verb

PRESENT		PRESENT PERFECT		
ich klettere	wir klettern	ich bin	wir sind	geklettert
du kletterst	ihr klettert	du bist	ihr seid	
Sie klettern	Sie klettern	Sie sind	Sie sind	
er/sie/es klettert	sie klettern	er/sie/es ist	sie sind	

SIMPLE PAST		PAST PERFECT		
ich kletterte	wir kletterten	ich war	wir waren	geklettert
du klettertest	ihr klettertet	du warst	ihr wart	
Sie kletterten	Sie kletterten	Sie waren	Sie waren	
er/sie/es kletterte	sie kletterten	er/sie/es war	sie waren	

FUTURE			FUTURE PERFECT		
ich werde	wir werden	klettern	ich werde	wir werden	geklettert sein
du wirst	ihr werdet		du wirst	ihr werdet	
Sie werden	Sie werden		Sie werden	Sie werden	
er/sie/es wird	sie werden		er/sie/es wird	sie werden	

PRESENT SUBJUNCTIVE I		PAST SUBJUNCTIVE I		
ich klettere	wir klettern	ich sei	wir seien	geklettert
du kletterst	ihr klettert	du seiest	ihr seiet	
Sie klettern	Sie klettern	Sie seien	Sie seien	
er/sie/es klettere	sie klettern	er/sie/es sei	sie seien	

PRESENT SUBJUNCTIVE II		PAST SUBJUNCTIVE II		
ich kletterte	wir kletterten	ich wäre	wir wären	geklettert
du klettertest	ihr klettertet	du wärest	ihr wäret	
Sie kletterten	Sie kletterten	Sie wären	Sie wären	
er/sie/es kletterte	sie kletterten	er/sie/es wäre	sie wären	

FUTURE SUBJUNCTIVE I			FUTURE PERFECT SUBJUNCTIVE I		
ich werde	wir werden	klettern	ich werde	wir werden	geklettert sein
du werdest	ihr werdet		du werdest	ihr werdet	
Sie werden	Sie werden		Sie werden	Sie werden	
er/sie/es werde	sie werden		er/sie/es werde	sie werden	

FUTURE SUBJUNCTIVE II			FUTURE PERFECT SUBJUNCTIVE II		
ich würde	wir würden	klettern	ich würde	wir würden	geklettert sein
du würdest	ihr würdet		du würdest	ihr würdet	
Sie würden	Sie würden		Sie würden	Sie würden	
er/sie/es würde	sie würden		er/sie/es würde	sie würden	

COMMANDS klettere! klettert! klettern Sie!

PRESENT PARTICIPLE kletternd

Usage

Die Kinder sind heute auf den Hügel geklettert. — *The children climbed up the hill today.*

Im Sommer klettern die Temperaturen in die Höhe. — *In the summer, the temperatures climb upward.*

Das Eichhörnchen ist vor der Katze geflohen und auf einen Baum geklettert. — *The squirrel fled from the cat and climbed up a tree.*

Der Landstreicher kletterte über den steinernen Zaun und lief weiter. — *The vagabond climbed over the stone fence and walked on.*

Jost ist aus dem Fenster aufs Dach geklettert. — *Jost climbed out the window onto the roof.*

Das Tier war in den Schornstein geklettert. — *The animal had climbed into the chimney.*

Wir wollten in den Alpen wandern und klettern. — *We wanted to hike and climb in the Alps.*

Wolf, klettere doch bitte nicht höher! — *Wolf, please just don't climb any higher!*

klettern (with **haben**, when used with general reference to the activity) *to climb*

Früher habe ich gern geklettert. — *I used to like to go climbing.*

RELATED VERBS durch·klettern, empor·klettern, erklettern, überklettern strong verb **klingt · klang · geklungen**

PRESENT

ich klinge	wir klingen
du klingst	ihr klingt
Sie klingen	Sie klingen
er/sie/es klingt	sie klingen

SIMPLE PAST

ich klang	wir klangen
du klangst	ihr klangt
Sie klangen	Sie klangen
er/sie/es klang	sie klangen

FUTURE

ich werde	wir werden	klingen
du wirst	ihr werdet	
Sie werden	Sie werden	
er/sie/es wird	sie werden	

PRESENT SUBJUNCTIVE I

ich klinge	wir klingen
du klingest	ihr klinget
Sie klingen	Sie klingen
er/sie/es klinge	sie klingen

PRESENT SUBJUNCTIVE II

ich klänge	wir klängen
du klängest	ihr klänget
Sie klängen	Sie klängen
er/sie/es klänge	sie klängen

FUTURE SUBJUNCTIVE I

ich werde	wir werden	klingen
du werdest	ihr werdet	
Sie werden	Sie werden	
er/sie/es werde	sie werden	

FUTURE SUBJUNCTIVE II

ich würde	wir würden	klingen
du würdest	ihr würdet	
Sie würden	Sie würden	
er/sie/es würde	sie würden	

PRESENT PERFECT

ich habe	wir haben	geklungen
du hast	ihr habt	
Sie haben	Sie haben	
er/sie/es hat	sie haben	

PAST PERFECT

ich hatte	wir hatten	geklungen
du hattest	ihr hattet	
Sie hatten	Sie hatten	
er/sie/es hatte	sie hatten	

FUTURE PERFECT

ich werde	wir werden	geklungen haben
du wirst	ihr werdet	
Sie werden	Sie werden	
er/sie/es wird	sie werden	

PAST SUBJUNCTIVE I

ich habe	wir haben	geklungen
du habest	ihr habet	
Sie haben	Sie haben	
er/sie/es habe	sie haben	

PAST SUBJUNCTIVE II

ich hätte	wir hätten	geklungen
du hättest	ihr hättet	
Sie hätten	Sie hätten	
er/sie/es hätte	sie hätten	

FUTURE PERFECT SUBJUNCTIVE I

ich werde	wir werden	geklungen haben
du werdest	ihr werdet	
Sie werden	Sie werden	
er/sie/es werde	sie werden	

FUTURE PERFECT SUBJUNCTIVE II

ich würde	wir würden	geklungen haben
du würdest	ihr würdet	
Sie würden	Sie würden	
er/sie/es würde	sie würden	

COMMANDS kling(e)! klingt! klingen Sie!

PRESENT PARTICIPLE klingend

Usage

Es mag zynisch klingen, aber ich glaube ihm nicht mehr.	*It might sound cynical, but I don't believe him anymore.*
„Wollen wir essen gehen?"	*"Do we want to go eat?"*
„Ja, das klingt gut."	*"Yes, that sounds good."*
Das Stück klang wie eine Sonate von Mozart.	*The piece sounded like a sonata by Mozart.*
Seit hundertundfünfzig Jahren hat keine Axt hier geklungen. (Goethe)	*For 150 years, no ax has been heard here.*
Man sagt, dass meine Stimme heute etwas besser klänge.	*They say my voice is sounding somewhat better today.*
Du klingst deprimiert. Ist was?	*You sound depressed. Is something wrong?*
Die Musik klang noch in ihren Ohren.	*The music still rang in her ears.*
Die Glocken klangen im Dorf eine Stunde lang.	*The bells in the village chimed for an hour.*
Münzen klingen in seiner Tasche.	*Coins are jingling in his pocket.*

RELATED VERBS ab·klingen, an·klingen, auf·klingen, aus·klingen, durchklingen, durch·klingen, erklingen, mit·klingen, nach·klingen, verklingen, zusammen·klingen

262 klopfen *to beat, knock, pound; break; throb, pulsate*

klopft · klopfte · geklopft regular weak verb

PRESENT

ich klopfe	wir klopfen
du klopfst	ihr klopft
Sie klopfen	Sie klopfen
er/sie/es klopft	sie klopfen

SIMPLE PAST

ich klopfte	wir klopften
du klopftest	ihr klopftet
Sie klopften	Sie klopften
er/sie/es klopfte	sie klopften

FUTURE

ich werde	wir werden	klopfen
du wirst	ihr werdet	
Sie werden	Sie werden	
er/sie/es wird	sie werden	

PRESENT SUBJUNCTIVE I

ich klopfe	wir klopfen
du klopfest	ihr klopfet
Sie klopfen	Sie klopfen
er/sie/es klopfe	sie klopfen

PRESENT SUBJUNCTIVE II

ich klopfte	wir klopften
du klopftest	ihr klopftet
Sie klopften	Sie klopften
er/sie/es klopfte	sie klopften

FUTURE SUBJUNCTIVE I

ich werde	wir werden	klopfen
du werdest	ihr werdet	
Sie werden	Sie werden	
er/sie/es werde	sie werden	

FUTURE SUBJUNCTIVE II

ich würde	wir würden	klopfen
du würdest	ihr würdet	
Sie würden	Sie würden	
er/sie/es würde	sie würden	

PRESENT PERFECT

ich habe	wir haben	geklopft
du hast	ihr habt	
Sie haben	Sie haben	
er/sie/es hat	sie haben	

PAST PERFECT

ich hatte	wir hatten	geklopft
du hattest	ihr hattet	
Sie hatten	Sie hatten	
er/sie/es hatte	sie hatten	

FUTURE PERFECT

ich werde	wir werden	geklopft haben
du wirst	ihr werdet	
Sie werden	Sie werden	
er/sie/es wird	sie werden	

PAST SUBJUNCTIVE I

ich habe	wir haben	geklopft
du habest	ihr habet	
Sie haben	Sie haben	
er/sie/es habe	sie haben	

PAST SUBJUNCTIVE II

ich hätte	wir hätten	geklopft
du hättest	ihr hättet	
Sie hätten	Sie hätten	
er/sie/es hätte	sie hätten	

FUTURE PERFECT SUBJUNCTIVE I

ich werde	wir werden	geklopft haben
du werdest	ihr werdet	
Sie werden	Sie werden	
er/sie/es werde	sie werden	

FUTURE PERFECT SUBJUNCTIVE II

ich würde	wir würden	geklopft haben
du würdest	ihr würdet	
Sie würden	Sie würden	
er/sie/es würde	sie würden	

COMMANDS klopf(e)! klopft! klopfen Sie!

PRESENT PARTICIPLE klopfend

Usage

Wer klopft an die Tür?	*Who is knocking at the door?*
Der Motor klopft wegen schlechten Benzins.	*The engine is knocking because of bad gasoline.*
Nach einer guten Vorlesung wird auf die Tische Beifall geklopft.	*After a good lecture, people bang on the tables to show approval.*
Hört ihr, wie das Herz vom Baby klopft?	*Do you hear how the baby's heart is beating?*
Die Schnitzel klopfen, bis sie 8 mm dick sind. (RECIPE)	*Pound the cutlets until they are 8 mm thick.*
Leon klopfte sich den Schlamm von seinem Mantel und zog ihn an.	*Leon knocked the mud off his coat and put it on.*
Morgen muss Frau Saubermann die Teppiche klopfen.	*Tomorrow, Mrs. Saubermann has to beat the rugs.*
Die Arbeiter haben die Steine mit Hammer und Pickel geklopft.	*The laborers broke the stones with hammer and pick.*
Ich habe schwere Bauchschmerzen und hohes Fieber und mein Kopf klopft.	*I have a bad stomachache and high fever, and my head is throbbing.*

RELATED VERBS ab·klopfen, an·klopfen, auf·klopfen, aus·klopfen, beklopfen

PRESENT		PRESENT PERFECT		
ich knie	wir knien	ich habe	wir haben	gekniet
du kniest	ihr kniet	du hast	ihr habt	
Sie knien	Sie knien	Sie haben	Sie haben	
er/sie/es kniet	sie knien	er/sie/es hat	sie haben	

SIMPLE PAST		PAST PERFECT		
ich kniete	wir knieten	ich hatte	wir hatten	gekniet
du knietest	ihr knietet	du hattest	ihr hattet	
Sie knieten	Sie knieten	Sie hatten	Sie hatten	
er/sie/es kniete	sie knieten	er/sie/es hatte	sie hatten	

FUTURE			FUTURE PERFECT		
ich werde	wir werden	knien	ich werde	wir werden	gekniet haben
du wirst	ihr werdet		du wirst	ihr werdet	
Sie werden	Sie werden		Sie werden	Sie werden	
er/sie/es wird	sie werden		er/sie/es wird	sie werden	

PRESENT SUBJUNCTIVE I		PAST SUBJUNCTIVE I		
ich knie	wir knien	ich habe	wir haben	gekniet
du kniest	ihr kniet	du habest	ihr habet	
Sie knien	Sie knien	Sie haben	Sie haben	
er/sie/es knie	sie knien	er/sie/es habe	sie haben	

PRESENT SUBJUNCTIVE II		PAST SUBJUNCTIVE II		
ich kniete	wir knieten	ich hätte	wir hätten	gekniet
du knietest	ihr knietet	du hättest	ihr hättet	
Sie knieten	Sie knieten	Sie hätten	Sie hätten	
er/sie/es kniete	sie knieten	er/sie/es hätte	sie hätten	

FUTURE SUBJUNCTIVE I			FUTURE PERFECT SUBJUNCTIVE I		
ich werde	wir werden	knien	ich werde	wir werden	gekniet haben
du werdest	ihr werdet		du werdest	ihr werdet	
Sie werden	Sie werden		Sie werden	Sie werden	
er/sie/es werde	sie werden		er/sie/es werde	sie werden	

FUTURE SUBJUNCTIVE II			FUTURE PERFECT SUBJUNCTIVE II		
ich würde	wir würden	knien	ich würde	wir würden	gekniet haben
du würdest	ihr würdet		du würdest	ihr würdet	
Sie würden	Sie würden		Sie würden	Sie würden	
er/sie/es würde	sie würden		er/sie/es würde	sie würden	

COMMANDS knie! kniet! knien Sie!

PRESENT PARTICIPLE kniend

Usage

Am 7. Dezember 1970 kniete Willy Brandt vor dem Mahnmal des Warschauer Ghettos in Polen. — *On December 7, 1970, Willy Brandt knelt before the Warsaw Ghetto Monument in Poland.*

Ich knie Euch zu Füßen, mein König, und flehe dringend um Verzeihung. — *I kneel at your feet, my king, and plead urgently for forgiveness.*

Als Knab' und Jüngling kniet' er schon im Tempel vor der Göttin Thron. (GOETHE) — *Even as a boy and youth, he was kneeling in the temple before the goddess's throne.*

Der Priester kniete vor dem Altar. — *The priest genuflected before the altar.*

sich knien *to get onto one's knees, kneel down*

Lara kniete sich neben mich und betete. — *Lara got onto her knees beside me and prayed.*

Knien Sie sich auf die rutschfeste Yogaunterlage und heben Sie die Arme hoch. — *Kneel down on a nonslip yoga mat and raise your arms up.*

Knie dich in die Arbeit! (*idiomatic*) — *Buckle down and get to work! / Get involved in work!*

RELATED VERBS auf·knien, beknien, nieder·knien

kochen *to boil, cook; seethe*

kocht · kochte · gekocht regular weak verb

PRESENT

ich koche	wir kochen
du kochst	ihr kocht
Sie kochen	Sie kochen
er/sie/es kocht	sie kochen

SIMPLE PAST

ich kochte	wir kochten
du kochtest	ihr kochtet
Sie kochten	Sie kochten
er/sie/es kochte	sie kochten

FUTURE

ich werde	wir werden	kochen
du wirst	ihr werdet	
Sie werden	Sie werden	
er/sie/es wird	sie werden	

PRESENT SUBJUNCTIVE I

ich koche	wir kochen
du kochest	ihr kochet
Sie kochen	Sie kochen
er/sie/es koche	sie kochen

PRESENT SUBJUNCTIVE II

ich kochte	wir kochten
du kochtest	ihr kochtet
Sie kochten	Sie kochten
er/sie/es kochte	sie kochten

FUTURE SUBJUNCTIVE I

ich werde	wir werden	kochen
du werdest	ihr werdet	
Sie werden	Sie werden	
er/sie/es werde	sie werden	

FUTURE SUBJUNCTIVE II

ich würde	wir würden	kochen
du würdest	ihr würdet	
Sie würden	Sie würden	
er/sie/es würde	sie würden	

PRESENT PERFECT

ich habe	wir haben	gekocht
du hast	ihr habt	
Sie haben	Sie haben	
er/sie/es hat	sie haben	

PAST PERFECT

ich hatte	wir hatten	gekocht
du hattest	ihr hattet	
Sie hatten	Sie hatten	
er/sie/es hatte	sie hatten	

FUTURE PERFECT

ich werde	wir werden	gekocht haben
du wirst	ihr werdet	
Sie werden	Sie werden	
er/sie/es wird	sie werden	

PAST SUBJUNCTIVE I

ich habe	wir haben	gekocht
du habest	ihr habet	
Sie haben	Sie haben	
er/sie/es habe	sie haben	

PAST SUBJUNCTIVE II

ich hätte	wir hätten	gekocht
du hättest	ihr hättet	
Sie hätten	Sie hätten	
er/sie/es hätte	sie hätten	

FUTURE PERFECT SUBJUNCTIVE I

ich werde	wir werden	gekocht haben
du werdest	ihr werdet	
Sie werden	Sie werden	
er/sie/es werde	sie werden	

FUTURE PERFECT SUBJUNCTIVE II

ich würde	wir würden	gekocht haben
du würdest	ihr würdet	
Sie würden	Sie würden	
er/sie/es würde	sie würden	

COMMANDS koch(e)! kocht! kochen Sie!

PRESENT PARTICIPLE kochend

Usage

Kochen Sie gern?	*Do you like to cook?*
Die Bohnen zehn Minuten kochen, bis sie weich sind. (RECIPE)	*Cook the beans for ten minutes until they are tender.*
Ich kann nicht einmal Wasser kochen.	*I can't even boil water.*
Zu Hause kochen wir immer vegetarisch.	*At home, we always cook vegetarian.*
Da meine Mutter im Krankenhaus liegt, muss mein Vater kochen, putzen und Wäsche waschen.	*Since my mother is in the hospital, my father has to cook, clean, and do the laundry.*
Serena kocht nicht jeden Tag, sie isst oft in der Mensa.	*Serena doesn't cook every day; she often eats in the student cafeteria.*
Könntest du bitte das Mittagessen fertig kochen?	*Could you please finish cooking lunch?*
Die Kartoffeln in Salzwasser gar kochen. (RECIPE)	*Cook the potatoes in salted water until done.*
Ich koche uns einen Kaffee.	*I'll make us some coffee.*
Frau Ärgerbauch kochte innerlich.	*Mrs. Ärgerbauch was seething inside.*

RELATED VERBS ab·kochen, an·kochen, auf·kochen, aus·kochen, bekochen, durch·kochen, ein·kochen, über·kochen, verkochen, zerkochen

PRESENT

ich komme	wir kommen
du kommst	ihr kommt
Sie kommen	Sie kommen
er/sie/es kommt	sie kommen

SIMPLE PAST

ich kam	wir kamen
du kamst	ihr kamt
Sie kamen	Sie kamen
er/sie/es kam	sie kamen

FUTURE

ich werde	wir werden	kommen
du wirst	ihr werdet	
Sie werden	Sie werden	
er/sie/es wird	sie werden	

PRESENT SUBJUNCTIVE I

ich komme	wir kommen
du kommest	ihr kommet
Sie kommen	Sie kommen
er/sie/es komme	sie kommen

PRESENT SUBJUNCTIVE II

ich käme	wir kämen
du kämest	ihr kämet
Sie kämen	Sie kämen
er/sie/es käme	sie kämen

FUTURE SUBJUNCTIVE I

ich werde	wir werden	kommen
du werdest	ihr werdet	
Sie werden	Sie werden	
er/sie/es werde	sie werden	

FUTURE SUBJUNCTIVE II

ich würde	wir würden	kommen
du würdest	ihr würdet	
Sie würden	Sie würden	
er/sie/es würde	sie würden	

PRESENT PERFECT

ich bin	wir sind	gekommen
du bist	ihr seid	
Sie sind	Sie sind	
er/sie/es ist	sie sind	

PAST PERFECT

ich war	wir waren	gekommen
du warst	ihr wart	
Sie waren	Sie waren	
er/sie/es war	sie waren	

FUTURE PERFECT

ich werde	wir werden	gekommen sein
du wirst	ihr werdet	
Sie werden	Sie werden	
er/sie/es wird	sie werden	

PAST SUBJUNCTIVE I

ich sei	wir seien	gekommen
du seiest	ihr seiet	
Sie seien	Sie seien	
er/sie/es sei	sie seien	

PAST SUBJUNCTIVE II

ich wäre	wir wären	gekommen
du wärest	ihr wäret	
Sie wären	Sie wären	
er/sie/es wäre	sie wären	

FUTURE PERFECT SUBJUNCTIVE I

ich werde	wir werden	gekommen sein
du werdest	ihr werdet	
Sie werden	Sie werden	
er/sie/es werde	sie werden	

FUTURE PERFECT SUBJUNCTIVE II

ich würde	wir würden	gekommen sein
du würdest	ihr würdet	
Sie würden	Sie würden	
er/sie/es würde	sie würden	

COMMANDS komm(e)! kommt! kommen Sie!

PRESENT PARTICIPLE kommend

Usage

Dann kam Papa nach Hause.	*Then Papa came home.*
Daniel ist letzte Woche zu uns gekommen.	*Daniel came to our house last week.*
Patrick sagte, er käme aus Prag!	*Patrick said he comes from Prague!*
Onkel Herbert kommt in drei Wochen.	*Uncle Herbert is coming in three weeks.*
Das kommt von zu viel Koffein.	*That comes from too much caffeine.*
Gertruds Kollegin ist ihr zur Hilfe gekommen.	*Gertrud's colleague came to her aid.*
Herr Gruber ist beruflich weit gekommen.	*Mr. Gruber has come a long way with his career.*

RELATED VERBS ab·kommen, auf·kommen, aus·kommen, bei·kommen, dazwischen·kommen, durch·kommen, ein·kommen, empor·kommen, entgegen·kommen, entkommen, entlang·kommen, fort·kommen, frei·kommen, gleich·kommen, heim·kommen, los·kommen, mit·kommen, nach·kommen, überein·kommen, überkommen, über·kommen, um·kommen, unter·kommen, verkommen, vorbei·kommen, weg·kommen, weiter·kommen, wieder·kommen, zu·kommen, zurecht·kommen, zurück·kommen, zusammen·kommen; *see also* **an·kommen** (12), **bekommen** (66), **her·kommen** (242), **vor·kommen** (509)

TOP 50 VERB ☞

kommen *to come; go; get; happen*

kommt · kam · gekommen strong verb

MORE USAGE SENTENCES WITH kommen

Viele sind zur Ansicht gekommen, dass das Rentensystem reformiert werden muss. — *Many have come to the conclusion that the pension system must be reformed.*
Ich war wohl eine halbe Stunde weit gelaufen und ihm doch nicht näher gekommen. (BETTINA VON ARNIM) — *I had walked for probably half an hour and still hadn't come closer to him.*
Eine große Freude kam über ihn. — *A great joy came over him.*
Seine Gedanken kamen selten zum Ausdruck. — *His thoughts were rarely expressed.*
Wohin kommen die Handtücher? — *Where do the towels go?*
Wie kommt das Schiffchen in die Flasche? — *How does that little ship get into the bottle?*
Du kommst mir nicht aus dem Sinn. — *I cannot get you out of my mind.*
Wie komme ich zum Stadtarchiv? — *How do I get to the city archives?*
Wie ist es gekommen, dass Liesl kein Geld mehr hat? — *How did it happen that Liesl has no more money?*

kommen auf + accusative

Ich wäre nie auf diese Idee gekommen. — *That idea would never have occurred to me.*
Wie kommst du darauf? — *What gives you that idea?*
Lars war schon mal auf den Gedanken gekommen, Everest zu besteigen. — *Lars had already thought of climbing Everest.*

jemandem kommen *to be/act to/toward someone*

Komm mir bloß nicht so! — *Don't get that way with me!*
Bist du ihr vielleicht unfreundlich gekommen? — *Were you perhaps unfriendly to her?*
Ute wurde entlassen, aber das kam ihr gerade recht. — *Ute was laid off, but that suited her perfectly.*

kommen lassen *to send for, order*

Regina ließ einen Arzt kommen. — *Regina sent for a doctor.*
Wir haben ein Taxi kommen lassen. — *We called for a taxi.*

zu sich kommen *to gain consciousness, come to*

Der Verletzte kam wieder zu sich. — *The injured person regained consciousness.*
Man sagt, dass es eine Weile gedauert hat, bis ich zu mir kam. — *They say it was a while before I came to.*

um etwas kommen *to lose something, be deprived of something*

Die Familie war 1932 im Brand um Hab und Gut gekommen. — *The family lost all their possessions in a fire in 1932.*
Laut Berichten seien drei Insassen ums Leben gekommen. — *According to reports, three occupants lost their lives.*

kommen + past participle of motion

Es kam ein Mann aus dem Wald gegangen. — *A man came walking out of the forest.*
Eines Tages ist ein Prinz ins Dorf geritten gekommen. — *One day, a prince came riding into the village.*
Die Balletttänzerinnen kamen plötzlich ins Zimmer getanzt. — *The ballerinas suddenly came dancing into the room.*

IDIOMATIC EXPRESSIONS

Komm' ich heute nicht, komm' ich morgen. (PROVERB) — *I'll get there when I get there.*
Das kommt nicht in Frage! — *That's out of the question!*
Wir sind endlich hinter die Wahrheit gekommen. — *We've finally gotten at the truth.*
Kinder kommen mit sechs Jahren in die Schule. — *Children start school at age six.*
Wann komme ich an die Reihe? — *When will I get my turn?*
Heute bin ich zu nichts gekommen. — *I accomplished nothing today.*
Ingrid ist nicht zu Wort gekommen. — *Ingrid did not have a chance to speak.*
Alles kann ganz anders als erwartet kommen. — *Everything can turn out quite differently from what was expected.*

modal verb **kann · konnte · gekonnt**

PRESENT	
ich kann	wir können
du kannst	ihr könnt
Sie können	Sie können
er/sie/es kann	sie können

SIMPLE PAST	
ich konnte	wir konnten
du konntest	ihr konntet
Sie konnten	Sie konnten
er/sie/es konnte	sie konnten

FUTURE		
ich werde	wir werden	können
du wirst	ihr werdet	
Sie werden	Sie werden	
er/sie/es wird	sie werden	

PRESENT SUBJUNCTIVE I	
ich könne	wir können
du könnest	ihr könnet
Sie können	Sie können
er/sie/es könne	sie können

PRESENT SUBJUNCTIVE II	
ich könnte	wir könnten
du könntest	ihr könntet
Sie könnten	Sie könnten
er/sie/es könnte	sie könnten

FUTURE SUBJUNCTIVE I		
ich werde	wir werden	können
du werdest	ihr werdet	
Sie werden	Sie werden	
er/sie/es werde	sie werden	

FUTURE SUBJUNCTIVE II		
ich würde	wir würden	können
du würdest	ihr würdet	
Sie würden	Sie würden	
er/sie/es würde	sie würden	

PRESENT PERFECT		
ich habe	wir haben	gekonnt
du hast	ihr habt	
Sie haben	Sie haben	
er/sie/es hat	sie haben	

PAST PERFECT		
ich hatte	wir hatten	gekonnt
du hattest	ihr hattet	
Sie hatten	Sie hatten	
er/sie/es hatte	sie hatten	

FUTURE PERFECT		
ich werde	wir werden	gekonnt haben
du wirst	ihr werdet	
Sie werden	Sie werden	
er/sie/es wird	sie werden	

PAST SUBJUNCTIVE I		
ich habe	wir haben	gekonnt
du habest	ihr habet	
Sie haben	Sie haben	
er/sie/es habe	sie haben	

PAST SUBJUNCTIVE II		
ich hätte	wir hätten	gekonnt
du hättest	ihr hättet	
Sie hätten	Sie hätten	
er/sie/es hätte	sie hätten	

FUTURE PERFECT SUBJUNCTIVE I		
ich werde	wir werden	gekonnt haben
du werdest	ihr werdet	
Sie werden	Sie werden	
er/sie/es werde	sie werden	

FUTURE PERFECT SUBJUNCTIVE II		
ich würde	wir würden	gekonnt haben
du würdest	ihr würdet	
Sie würden	Sie würden	
er/sie/es würde	sie würden	

COMMANDS —

PRESENT PARTICIPLE können d

Usage

Sie können mit der Bahn bequem an Ihr Ziel kommen.	*You can get to your destination comfortably by train.*
Wie kannst du das sagen?	*How can you say that?*
Ich konnte ihn nicht verstehen.	*I was unable to understand him.*
Können Sie Englisch?	*Do you know how to speak English?*
Dieser Wagen kann nicht vermietet werden.	*This car cannot be rented.*
Könntest du mir bitte helfen?	*Could you please help me?*
Die Schüler konnten kaum glauben, dass der Schultag schon vorbei war.	*The students could hardly believe that the school day was already over.*
Reginald hat bis spät in die Nacht gearbeitet, damit er einen Tag früher in Urlaub fahren konnte.	*Reginald worked late into the night so he could start his vacation a day earlier.*
Kann ich auch in die Stadt fahren?	*May I also go into town?*

RELATED VERB umhin·können

TOP 50 VERB ☞

können *can, to be able to, know (how to); be allowed to*

kann · konnte · gekonnt — modal verb

MORE USAGE SENTENCES WITH können

Können Sie mir sagen, wo die Post ist?	*Can you tell me where the post office is?*
Ich tat, was ich konnte, aber das war nicht genug.	*I did what I could, but that wasn't enough.*
Am Samstag kann sich Liesl von der stressigen Woche erholen.	*On Saturday, Liesl can recover from the stressful week.*
Doch könntet Ihr selbst der Betrogne sein. (SCHILLER)	*But you yourself could be the one deceived.*
Man kann die Geschichte auf verschiedenen Ebenen interpretieren.	*The story can be interpreted on many levels.*
Ich wundere mich, dass du das gemacht hast. Ich hätte es nicht gekonnt.	*I'm amazed you did that; I couldn't have.*
Ich konnte meine Verwunderung nicht bergen.	*I was unable to hide my amazement.*
Norbert hat nicht kommen können.	*Norbert was unable to come.*
Zu viel Stress kann schädlich sein.	*Too much stress can be harmful.*
Ein Imker kann leicht gestochen werden.	*A beekeeper can easily be stung.*
Was du heute kannst besorgen, das verschiebe nicht auf morgen. (PROVERB)	*Don't put off until tomorrow what you can do today.*
Kannst du Klavier spielen?	*Can you play the piano?*

können *could, may, might, be* (subjective meaning to express supposition or speculation)

Das kann doch nicht sein!	*That just can't be!*
Das kann sein.	*That is possible.*
Es kann jeden Moment geschehen.	*It might happen at any moment.*
Es könnte gut sein, dass die Verhandlungen bis nächste Woche andauern.	*It might well be that the negotiations will last until next week.*
Manfred kann nicht auf der Party gewesen sein, er war bei mir.	*Manfred couldn't have been at the party; he was with me.*
Es hätte doch sein können, dass Frau Fritsch einfach keine Lust dazu hatte.	*It could have been that Mrs. Fritsch simply didn't feel like doing that.*
In der Zwischenzeit kann viel passiert sein.	*A lot may have happened in the meantime.*

IDIOMATIC EXPRESSIONS

Das kannst du laut sagen!	*You can say that again!*
Der Tank war leer und wir konnten nicht weiter.	*The tank was empty and we could go no farther.*
Du kannst mich mal! (*vulgar*)	*Up yours!/Shove it!*
Ernst konnte nicht anders, als das Spektakel anzusehen.	*Ernst couldn't help but watch the spectacle.*
Ich kann nicht mehr!	*I can't take it anymore!/I can't continue!/I can't go on!*
Ich kann nichts dafür, dass du anderer Meinung bist.	*I can't help it if you have a different opinion.*
„Kann Lars jonglieren?"	*"Can Lars juggle?"*
„Ja, er kann das gut."	*"Yes, he's good at it."*
Man kann hoffen, dass sich eine Lösung findet.	*It is to be hoped that a solution will be found.*
Man kann nie wissen.	*You never know.*
Mareike kann es nicht leiden, wenn ihre Nachbarin Trompete spielt.	*Mareike can't stand it when her neighbor plays the trumpet.*
Mein Sohn ist davon überzeugt, dass er nichts kann.	*My son is convinced he has no skill.*
Sie kann doch nichts dafür!	*It's not her fault!*
Wenn ihr die Stimme hört, dann rennt was ihr könnt!	*If you hear that voice, then run as fast as you can!*
Inge freute sich darüber, dass sie das Gedicht gut auswendig konnte.	*Inge was happy that she knew the poem well from memory.*

konzentrieren 267

to concentrate, focus

regular weak verb

konzentriert · konzentrierte · konzentriert

PRESENT

ich konzentriere	wir konzentrieren
du konzentrierst	ihr konzentriert
Sie konzentrieren	Sie konzentrieren
er/sie/es konzentriert	sie konzentrieren

SIMPLE PAST

ich konzentrierte	wir konzentrierten
du konzentriertest	ihr konzentriertet
Sie konzentrierten	Sie konzentrierten
er/sie/es konzentrierte	sie konzentrierten

FUTURE

ich werde	wir werden	konzentrieren
du wirst	ihr werdet	
Sie werden	Sie werden	
er/sie/es wird	sie werden	

PRESENT SUBJUNCTIVE I

ich konzentriere	wir konzentrieren
du konzentrierest	ihr konzentrieret
Sie konzentrieren	Sie konzentrieren
er/sie/es konzentriere	sie konzentrieren

PRESENT SUBJUNCTIVE II

ich konzentrierte	wir konzentrierten
du konzentriertest	ihr konzentriertet
Sie konzentrierten	Sie konzentrierten
er/sie/es konzentrierte	sie konzentrierten

FUTURE SUBJUNCTIVE I

ich werde	wir werden	konzentrieren
du werdest	ihr werdet	
Sie werden	Sie werden	
er/sie/es werde	sie werden	

FUTURE SUBJUNCTIVE II

ich würde	wir würden	konzentrieren
du würdest	ihr würdet	
Sie würden	Sie würden	
er/sie/es würde	sie würden	

PRESENT PERFECT

ich habe	wir haben	konzentriert
du hast	ihr habt	
Sie haben	Sie haben	
er/sie/es hat	sie haben	

PAST PERFECT

ich hatte	wir hatten	konzentriert
du hattest	ihr hattet	
Sie hatten	Sie hatten	
er/sie/es hatte	sie hatten	

FUTURE PERFECT

ich werde	wir werden	konzentriert haben
du wirst	ihr werdet	
Sie werden	Sie werden	
er/sie/es wird	sie werden	

PAST SUBJUNCTIVE I

ich habe	wir haben	konzentriert
du habest	ihr habet	
Sie haben	Sie haben	
er/sie/es habe	sie haben	

PAST SUBJUNCTIVE II

ich hätte	wir hätten	konzentriert
du hättest	ihr hättet	
Sie hätten	Sie hätten	
er/sie/es hätte	sie hätten	

FUTURE PERFECT SUBJUNCTIVE I

ich werde	wir werden	konzentriert haben
du werdest	ihr werdet	
Sie werden	Sie werden	
er/sie/es werde	sie werden	

FUTURE PERFECT SUBJUNCTIVE II

ich würde	wir würden	konzentriert haben
du würdest	ihr würdet	
Sie würden	Sie würden	
er/sie/es würde	sie würden	

COMMANDS konzentrier(e)! konzentriert! konzentrieren Sie!

PRESENT PARTICIPLE konzentrierend

Usage

Ab jetzt müssen wir all unsere Bemühungen auf eine Lösung konzentrieren. — *Henceforth, we must focus all our efforts on a solution.*

Eine Lösung aus Säure und Reinigungsmittel wird konzentriert und auf Reinheit überprüft. — *A solution of acid and cleaning fluid is concentrated and tested for purity.*

Die Firma konzentriert das Marketing auf regionale und überregionale Märkte. — *The firm is focusing marketing on regional and national markets.*

Man hat die Truppen an der Grenze konzentriert. — *The troops were concentrated on the border.*

sich konzentrieren *to concentrate, focus; be concentrated/focused*

Der Radler hat sich auf die letzte Stufe des Rennens konzentriert. — *The cyclist was focused on the last stage of the race.*

Hier gibt es zu viel Lärm; ich kann mich nicht konzentrieren. — *There is too much noise here—I can't concentrate.*

Der Plan konzentriert sich auf Länder der dritten Welt. — *The plan is focused on Third World countries.*

268 korrigieren *to rectify, correct; adjust, modify*

korrigiert · korrigierte · korrigiert

regular weak verb

PRESENT

ich korrigiere	wir korrigieren
du korrigierst	ihr korrigiert
Sie korrigieren	Sie korrigieren
er/sie/es korrigiert	sie korrigieren

SIMPLE PAST

ich korrigierte	wir korrigierten
du korrigiertest	ihr korrigiertet
Sie korrigierten	Sie korrigierten
er/sie/es korrigierte	sie korrigierten

FUTURE

ich werde	wir werden	korrigieren
du wirst	ihr werdet	
Sie werden	Sie werden	
er/sie/es wird	sie werden	

PRESENT SUBJUNCTIVE I

ich korrigiere	wir korrigieren
du korrigierest	ihr korrigieret
Sie korrigieren	Sie korrigieren
er/sie/es korrigiere	sie korrigieren

PRESENT SUBJUNCTIVE II

ich korrigierte	wir korrigierten
du korrigiertest	ihr korrigiertet
Sie korrigierten	Sie korrigierten
er/sie/es korrigierte	sie korrigierten

FUTURE SUBJUNCTIVE I

ich werde	wir werden	korrigieren
du werdest	ihr werdet	
Sie werden	Sie werden	
er/sie/es werde	sie werden	

FUTURE SUBJUNCTIVE II

ich würde	wir würden	korrigieren
du würdest	ihr würdet	
Sie würden	Sie würden	
er/sie/es würde	sie würden	

PRESENT PERFECT

ich habe	wir haben	korrigiert
du hast	ihr habt	
Sie haben	Sie haben	
er/sie/es hat	sie haben	

PAST PERFECT

ich hatte	wir hatten	korrigiert
du hattest	ihr hattet	
Sie hatten	Sie hatten	
er/sie/es hatte	sie hatten	

FUTURE PERFECT

ich werde	wir werden	korrigiert haben
du wirst	ihr werdet	
Sie werden	Sie werden	
er/sie/es wird	sie werden	

PAST SUBJUNCTIVE I

ich habe	wir haben	korrigiert
du habest	ihr habet	
Sie haben	Sie haben	
er/sie/es habe	sie haben	

PAST SUBJUNCTIVE II

ich hätte	wir hätten	korrigiert
du hättest	ihr hättet	
Sie hätten	Sie hätten	
er/sie/es hätte	sie hätten	

FUTURE PERFECT SUBJUNCTIVE I

ich werde	wir werden	korrigiert haben
du werdest	ihr werdet	
Sie werden	Sie werden	
er/sie/es werde	sie werden	

FUTURE PERFECT SUBJUNCTIVE II

ich würde	wir würden	korrigiert haben
du würdest	ihr würdet	
Sie würden	Sie würden	
er/sie/es würde	sie würden	

COMMANDS korrigier(e)! korrigiert! korrigieren Sie!

PRESENT PARTICIPLE korrigierend

Usage

Unser Deutschlehrer hat meine Aussprache von „Charakter“ korrigiert. — *Our German teacher corrected my pronunciation of "Charakter."*

Wir möchten, dass die Angelegenheit möglichst bald korrigiert wird. — *We would like for the matter to be rectified as soon as possible.*

Der Finanzminister korrigierte heute seine allzu optimistische Aussage von gestern. — *Today, the Minister of Finance corrected his overly optimistic statement of yesterday.*

Dieser Druckfehler ist noch nicht korrigiert worden. — *This printing error has not yet been corrected.*

„Warum korrigierst du mich ständig?“ — *"Why do you constantly correct me?"*

„Ich korrigiere dich nicht ständig, nur ab und zu.“ — *"I don't constantly correct you, only once in a while."*

Ich versuche, die roten Augen im Foto zu korrigieren. — *I'm trying to correct the red-eye in the photo.*

Die unrealistischen Erwartungen der Kursteilnehmer müssen nun korrigiert werden. — *The unrealistic expectations of the course participants must be modified.*

Korrigieren Sie die Zahlen und drucken Sie es noch mal. — *Adjust the numbers and print it again.*

regular weak verb

kostet · kostete · gekostet

PRESENT

ich koste	wir kosten
du kostest	ihr kostet
Sie kosten	Sie kosten
er/sie/es kostet	sie kosten

SIMPLE PAST

ich kostete	wir kosteten
du kostetest	ihr kostetet
Sie kosteten	Sie kosteten
er/sie/es kostete	sie kosteten

FUTURE

ich werde	wir werden	kosten
du wirst	ihr werdet	
Sie werden	Sie werden	
er/sie/es wird	sie werden	

PRESENT SUBJUNCTIVE I

ich koste	wir kosten
du kostest	ihr kostet
Sie kosten	Sie kosten
er/sie/es koste	sie kosten

PRESENT SUBJUNCTIVE II

ich kostete	wir kosteten
du kostetest	ihr kostetet
Sie kosteten	Sie kosteten
er/sie/es kostete	sie kosteten

FUTURE SUBJUNCTIVE I

ich werde	wir werden	kosten
du werdest	ihr werdet	
Sie werden	Sie werden	
er/sie/es werde	sie werden	

FUTURE SUBJUNCTIVE II

ich würde	wir würden	kosten
du würdest	ihr würdet	
Sie würden	Sie würden	
er/sie/es würde	sie würden	

PRESENT PERFECT

ich habe	wir haben	gekostet
du hast	ihr habt	
Sie haben	Sie haben	
er/sie/es hat	sie haben	

PAST PERFECT

ich hatte	wir hatten	gekostet
du hattest	ihr hattet	
Sie hatten	Sie hatten	
er/sie/es hatte	sie hatten	

FUTURE PERFECT

ich werde	wir werden	gekostet haben
du wirst	ihr werdet	
Sie werden	Sie werden	
er/sie/es wird	sie werden	

PAST SUBJUNCTIVE I

ich habe	wir haben	gekostet
du habest	ihr habet	
Sie haben	Sie haben	
er/sie/es habe	sie haben	

PAST SUBJUNCTIVE II

ich hätte	wir hätten	gekostet
du hättest	ihr hättet	
Sie hätten	Sie hätten	
er/sie/es hätte	sie hätten	

FUTURE PERFECT SUBJUNCTIVE I

ich werde	wir werden	gekostet haben
du werdest	ihr werdet	
Sie werden	Sie werden	
er/sie/es werde	sie werden	

FUTURE PERFECT SUBJUNCTIVE II

ich würde	wir würden	gekostet haben
du würdest	ihr würdet	
Sie würden	Sie würden	
er/sie/es würde	sie würden	

COMMANDS koste! kostet! kosten Sie!

PRESENT PARTICIPLE kostend

Usage

Dieser Skandal hat den Kandidaten die Wahl gekostet. — *This scandal cost the candidate the election.*
Wie viel kostet dieser Schal? — *How much does this scarf cost?*
Im 20. Jahrhundert kosteten Kriege mehr als 50 Millionen Menschenleben. — *In the 20th century, wars cost more than 50 million human lives.*
Die Eintrittskarte und das Essen kosten zusammen dreißig Dollar. — *The ticket and the meal cost 30 dollars altogether.*
Dem Bericht nach koste das Projekt zu viel Zeit und Geld. — *According to the report, the project costs too much time and money.*
Koste es, was es wolle, die Brücke wird gebaut! — *Cost what it may, the bridge will be built!*
Ein Doppelzimmer kostet mehr als ein Einzelzimmer. — *A double room costs more than a single room.*
Hast du die Schokoladentorte gekostet? — *Have you tasted the chocolate torte?*
Wir haben einen Diavortrag gesehen und von der mongolischen Küche gekostet. — *We saw a slide show and sampled Mongolian cuisine.*

RELATED VERBS aus·kosten, durch·kosten, durchkosten, vor·kosten

270 kreischen *to screech, shriek, creak, scream*

kreischt · kreischte · gekreischt regular weak verb

PRESENT

ich kreische	wir kreischen
du kreischst	ihr kreischt
Sie kreischen	Sie kreischen
er/sie/es kreischt	sie kreischen

SIMPLE PAST

ich kreischte	wir kreischten
du kreischtest	ihr kreischtet
Sie kreischten	Sie kreischten
er/sie/es kreischte	sie kreischten

FUTURE

ich werde	wir werden	kreischen
du wirst	ihr werdet	
Sie werden	Sie werden	
er/sie/es wird	sie werden	

PRESENT SUBJUNCTIVE I

ich kreische	wir kreischen
du kreischest	ihr kreischet
Sie kreischen	Sie kreischen
er/sie/es kreische	sie kreischen

PRESENT SUBJUNCTIVE II

ich kreischte	wir kreischten
du kreischtest	ihr kreischtet
Sie kreischten	Sie kreischten
er/sie/es kreischte	sie kreischten

FUTURE SUBJUNCTIVE I

ich werde	wir werden	kreischen
du werdest	ihr werdet	
Sie werden	Sie werden	
er/sie/es werde	sie werden	

FUTURE SUBJUNCTIVE II

ich würde	wir würden	kreischen
du würdest	ihr würdet	
Sie würden	Sie würden	
er/sie/es würde	sie würden	

PRESENT PERFECT

ich habe	wir haben	gekreischt
du hast	ihr habt	
Sie haben	Sie haben	
er/sie/es hat	sie haben	

PAST PERFECT

ich hatte	wir hatten	gekreischt
du hattest	ihr hattet	
Sie hatten	Sie hatten	
er/sie/es hatte	sie hatten	

FUTURE PERFECT

ich werde	wir werden	gekreischt haben
du wirst	ihr werdet	
Sie werden	Sie werden	
er/sie/es wird	sie werden	

PAST SUBJUNCTIVE I

ich habe	wir haben	gekreischt
du habest	ihr habet	
Sie haben	Sie haben	
er/sie/es habe	sie haben	

PAST SUBJUNCTIVE II

ich hätte	wir hätten	gekreischt
du hättest	ihr hättet	
Sie hätten	Sie hätten	
er/sie/es hätte	sie hätten	

FUTURE PERFECT SUBJUNCTIVE I

ich werde	wir werden	gekreischt haben
du werdest	ihr werdet	
Sie werden	Sie werden	
er/sie/es werde	sie werden	

FUTURE PERFECT SUBJUNCTIVE II

ich würde	wir würden	gekreischt haben
du würdest	ihr würdet	
Sie würden	Sie würden	
er/sie/es würde	sie würden	

COMMANDS kreisch(e)! kreischt! kreischen Sie!

PRESENT PARTICIPLE kreischend

NOTE The strong forms **krisch, gekrischen** are considered regional or archaic.

Usage

Hoch über uns hatte ein Adler gekreischt.	*High above us, an eagle had screeched.*
Hänsl kreischte vor Freude über den kleinen Hund.	*Hänsl squealed with joy over the little dog.*
Diese Tür kreischt und quietscht.	*This door creaks and squeaks.*
Die begeisterten Zuschauer kreischten und klatschten, als der Popstar auf die Bühne kam.	*The enthusiastic audience screamed and clapped as the pop star came onto the stage.*
Unser Papagei Max kreischt „Nein!", wenn ihm etwas nicht gefällt.	*Our parrot, Max, screeches "No!" when something doesn't please him.*
Wir hörten in der Ferne Bremsen kreischen.	*We heard brakes screeching in the distance.*
Wieso kreischst du, wenn du eine Spinne siehst?	*Why do you shriek when you see a spider?*
Er krisch und klagte und kroch in alle Winkel. (SIMROCK'S EDDA)	*He shrieked and complained and crept into the corners.*

RELATED VERB auf·kreischen

strong verb **kriecht · kroch · gekrochen**

PRESENT

ich krieche	wir kriechen
du kriechst	ihr kriecht
Sie kriechen	Sie kriechen
er/sie/es kriecht	sie kriechen

SIMPLE PAST

ich kroch	wir krochen
du krochst	ihr krocht
Sie krochen	Sie krochen
er/sie/es kroch	sie krochen

FUTURE

ich werde	wir werden	kriechen
du wirst	ihr werdet	
Sie werden	Sie werden	
er/sie/es wird	sie werden	

PRESENT SUBJUNCTIVE I

ich krieche	wir kriechen
du kriechest	ihr kriechet
Sie kriechen	Sie kriechen
er/sie/es krieche	sie kriechen

PRESENT SUBJUNCTIVE II

ich kröche	wir kröchen
du kröchest	ihr kröchet
Sie kröchen	Sie kröchen
er/sie/es kröche	sie kröchen

FUTURE SUBJUNCTIVE I

ich werde	wir werden	kriechen
du werdest	ihr werdet	
Sie werden	Sie werden	
er/sie/es werde	sie werden	

FUTURE SUBJUNCTIVE II

ich würde	wir würden	kriechen
du würdest	ihr würdet	
Sie würden	Sie würden	
er/sie/es würde	sie würden	

PRESENT PERFECT

ich bin	wir sind	gekrochen
du bist	ihr seid	
Sie sind	Sie sind	
er/sie/es ist	sie sind	

PAST PERFECT

ich war	wir waren	gekrochen
du warst	ihr wart	
Sie waren	Sie waren	
er/sie/es war	sie waren	

FUTURE PERFECT

ich werde	wir werden	gekrochen sein
du wirst	ihr werdet	
Sie werden	Sie werden	
er/sie/es wird	sie werden	

PAST SUBJUNCTIVE I

ich sei	wir seien	gekrochen
du seiest	ihr seiet	
Sie seien	Sie seien	
er/sie/es sei	sie seien	

PAST SUBJUNCTIVE II

ich wäre	wir wären	gekrochen
du wärest	ihr wäret	
Sie wären	Sie wären	
er/sie/es wäre	sie wären	

FUTURE PERFECT SUBJUNCTIVE I

ich werde	wir werden	gekrochen sein
du werdest	ihr werdet	
Sie werden	Sie werden	
er/sie/es werde	sie werden	

FUTURE PERFECT SUBJUNCTIVE II

ich würde	wir würden	gekrochen sein
du würdest	ihr würdet	
Sie würden	Sie würden	
er/sie/es würde	sie würden	

COMMANDS kriech(e)! kriecht! kriechen Sie!

PRESENT PARTICIPLE kriechend

Usage

Schaben krochen eilig über den hölzernen Fußboden. *Cockroaches crawled hurriedly across the wooden floor.*
Mäuse können durch unglaublich kleine Löcher kriechen. *Mice can crawl through unbelievably small holes.*
Die Schnecke ist aus dem Garten ins Haus gekrochen. *The snail crept out of the garden into the house.*
Kurz nach Mitternacht sind wir endlich ins Bett gekrochen und haben tief geschlafen. *Just after midnight, we finally crawled into bed and slept soundly.*
Die Katze kroch ängstlich hinter das Sofa. *The cat crawled fearfully behind the sofa.*
Der Efeu Gloire de Marengo kriecht über den Zaun in den Garten der Nachbarn. *The Gloire de Marengo ivy is creeping over the fence into the neighbors' yard.*
Manchmal wollte ich am liebsten in ein Loch kriechen. (*idiomatic*) *Sometimes, I just felt like crawling in a hole.*

kriechen (with **haben**) *to grovel, cringe*

Die Untertanen haben vor ihren Herrschern gekrochen. *The subjects groveled before their rulers.*

RELATED VERBS an·kriechen, aus·kriechen, durch·kriechen, durchkriechen, fort·kriechen, verkriechen

kriegen *to get*

kriegt · kriegte · gekriegt

regular weak verb

PRESENT

ich kriege	wir kriegen
du kriegst	ihr kriegt
Sie kriegen	Sie kriegen
er/sie/es kriegt	sie kriegen

SIMPLE PAST

ich kriegte	wir kriegten
du kriegtest	ihr kriegtet
Sie kriegten	Sie kriegten
er/sie/es kriegte	sie kriegten

FUTURE

ich werde	wir werden	kriegen
du wirst	ihr werdet	
Sie werden	Sie werden	
er/sie/es wird	sie werden	

PRESENT SUBJUNCTIVE I

ich kriege	wir kriegen
du kriegest	ihr krieget
Sie kriegen	Sie kriegen
er/sie/es kriege	sie kriegen

PRESENT SUBJUNCTIVE II

ich kriegte	wir kriegten
du kriegtest	ihr kriegtet
Sie kriegten	Sie kriegten
er/sie/es kriegte	sie kriegten

FUTURE SUBJUNCTIVE I

ich werde	wir werden	kriegen
du werdest	ihr werdet	
Sie werden	Sie werden	
er/sie/es werde	sie werden	

FUTURE SUBJUNCTIVE II

ich würde	wir würden	kriegen
du würdest	ihr würdet	
Sie würden	Sie würden	
er/sie/es würde	sie würden	

PRESENT PERFECT

ich habe	wir haben	gekriegt
du hast	ihr habt	
Sie haben	Sie haben	
er/sie/es hat	sie haben	

PAST PERFECT

ich hatte	wir hatten	gekriegt
du hattest	ihr hattet	
Sie hatten	Sie hatten	
er/sie/es hatte	sie hatten	

FUTURE PERFECT

ich werde	wir werden	gekriegt haben
du wirst	ihr werdet	
Sie werden	Sie werden	
er/sie/es wird	sie werden	

PAST SUBJUNCTIVE I

ich habe	wir haben	gekriegt
du habest	ihr habet	
Sie haben	Sie haben	
er/sie/es habe	sie haben	

PAST SUBJUNCTIVE II

ich hätte	wir hätten	gekriegt
du hättest	ihr hättet	
Sie hätten	Sie hätten	
er/sie/es hätte	sie hätten	

FUTURE PERFECT SUBJUNCTIVE I

ich werde	wir werden	gekriegt haben
du werdest	ihr werdet	
Sie werden	Sie werden	
er/sie/es werde	sie werden	

FUTURE PERFECT SUBJUNCTIVE II

ich würde	wir würden	gekriegt haben
du würdest	ihr würdet	
Sie würden	Sie würden	
er/sie/es würde	sie würden	

COMMANDS krieg(e)! kriegt! kriegen Sie!

PRESENT PARTICIPLE kriegend

NOTE The verb **kriegen** is very common in informal German, but generally considered too colloquial for formal use.

Usage

Wie viel kriegst du dafür? — *How much are you getting for that?*

Ich habe das alte Foto von meiner Tante gekriegt. — *I got the old photo from my aunt.*

Heiner kriegt eine E-Mail von seiner Freundin. — *Heiner is getting an e-mail from his girlfriend.*

Maria hat einen Schreck gekriegt. — *Maria got a scare.*

Erichs Frau sagte, sie hätte den Esstisch von Freunden geschenkt gekriegt. — *Erich's wife said she was given the dining table by friends.*

Wir kriegen das Buch nie fertig. — *We'll never get the book finished.*

Ihr kriegt heute Abend Besuch, nicht wahr? — *You're having company this evening, aren't you?*

Liesls Vater sucht seit Monaten eine Stelle in der Textilindustrie, aber er hat nichts gekriegt. — *Liesl's father has been looking for a job in the textile industry for months, but he hasn't gotten anything.*

Luise kriegt ein Kind. — *Luise is having a baby.*

RELATED VERBS ab·kriegen, hin·kriegen, klein·kriegen, los·kriegen, mit·kriegen, unter·kriegen, weg·kriegen

regular weak verb **kümmert · kümmerte · gekümmert**

PRESENT

ich kümmere	wir kümmern
du kümmerst	ihr kümmert
Sie kümmern	Sie kümmern
er/sie/es kümmert	sie kümmern

SIMPLE PAST

ich kümmerte	wir kümmerten
du kümmertest	ihr kümmertet
Sie kümmerten	Sie kümmerten
er/sie/es kümmerte	sie kümmerten

FUTURE

ich werde	wir werden	kümmern
du wirst	ihr werdet	
Sie werden	Sie werden	
er/sie/es wird	sie werden	

PRESENT SUBJUNCTIVE I

ich kümmere	wir kümmern
du kümmerst	ihr kümmert
Sie kümmern	Sie kümmern
er/sie/es kümmere	sie kümmern

PRESENT SUBJUNCTIVE II

ich kümmerte	wir kümmerten
du kümmertest	ihr kümmertet
Sie kümmerten	Sie kümmerten
er/sie/es kümmerte	sie kümmerten

FUTURE SUBJUNCTIVE I

ich werde	wir werden	kümmern
du werdest	ihr werdet	
Sie werden	Sie werden	
er/sie/es werde	sie werden	

FUTURE SUBJUNCTIVE II

ich würde	wir würden	kümmern
du würdest	ihr würdet	
Sie würden	Sie würden	
er/sie/es würde	sie würden	

PRESENT PERFECT

ich habe	wir haben	gekümmert
du hast	ihr habt	
Sie haben	Sie haben	
er/sie/es hat	sie haben	

PAST PERFECT

ich hatte	wir hatten	gekümmert
du hattest	ihr hattet	
Sie hatten	Sie hatten	
er/sie/es hatte	sie hatten	

FUTURE PERFECT

ich werde	wir werden	gekümmert haben
du wirst	ihr werdet	
Sie werden	Sie werden	
er/sie/es wird	sie werden	

PAST SUBJUNCTIVE I

ich habe	wir haben	gekümmert
du habest	ihr habet	
Sie haben	Sie haben	
er/sie/es habe	sie haben	

PAST SUBJUNCTIVE II

ich hätte	wir hätten	gekümmert
du hättest	ihr hättet	
Sie hätten	Sie hätten	
er/sie/es hätte	sie hätten	

FUTURE PERFECT SUBJUNCTIVE I

ich werde	wir werden	gekümmert haben
du werdest	ihr werdet	
Sie werden	Sie werden	
er/sie/es werde	sie werden	

FUTURE PERFECT SUBJUNCTIVE II

ich würde	wir würden	gekümmert haben
du würdest	ihr würdet	
Sie würden	Sie würden	
er/sie/es würde	sie würden	

COMMANDS kümmere! kümmert! kümmern Sie!

PRESENT PARTICIPLE kümmernd

Usage

Die Situation hat mich damals sehr gekümmert. — *The situation really worried me at the time.*

Es kümmerte ihn nicht, dass diese Gesetze gegen die Verfassung verstoßen. — *It didn't concern him that these laws violate the constitution.*

Umweltverschmutzung kümmert uns immer mehr. — *Environmental degradation worries us more and more.*

Der hohe Preis scheint dich nicht zu kümmern. — *The high price doesn't seem to bother you.*

Was kümmert mich das? — *What do I care?*

sich kümmern um *to be worried about; concern oneself with, take care of*

Herr Iwanowitsch wird sich um die praktischen Kleinigkeiten kümmern. — *Mr. Ivanovich will be concerned with the practical details.*

Angelika kümmert sich um ihren Vater. — *Angelika is worried about her father.*

Kümmere dich nicht um uns. — *Don't worry about us.*

Der Hirt kümmert sich um seine Schafe. — *The shepherd tends to his sheep.*

RELATED VERBS bekümmern, verkümmern

274 kündigen *to give notice, quit; recall, terminate, cancel*

kündigt · kündigte · gekündigt — regular weak verb

PRESENT

ich kündige	wir kündigen
du kündigst	ihr kündigt
Sie kündigen	Sie kündigen
er/sie/es kündigt	sie kündigen

SIMPLE PAST

ich kündigte	wir kündigten
du kündigtest	ihr kündigtet
Sie kündigten	Sie kündigten
er/sie/es kündigte	sie kündigten

FUTURE

ich werde	wir werden	kündigen
du wirst	ihr werdet	
Sie werden	Sie werden	
er/sie/es wird	sie werden	

PRESENT SUBJUNCTIVE I

ich kündige	wir kündigen
du kündigest	ihr kündiget
Sie kündigen	Sie kündigen
er/sie/es kündige	sie kündigen

PRESENT SUBJUNCTIVE II

ich kündigte	wir kündigten
du kündigtest	ihr kündigtet
Sie kündigten	Sie kündigten
er/sie/es kündigte	sie kündigten

FUTURE SUBJUNCTIVE I

ich werde	wir werden	kündigen
du werdest	ihr werdet	
Sie werden	Sie werden	
er/sie/es werde	sie werden	

FUTURE SUBJUNCTIVE II

ich würde	wir würden	kündigen
du würdest	ihr würdet	
Sie würden	Sie würden	
er/sie/es würde	sie würden	

PRESENT PERFECT

ich habe	wir haben	gekündigt
du hast	ihr habt	
Sie haben	Sie haben	
er/sie/es hat	sie haben	

PAST PERFECT

ich hatte	wir hatten	gekündigt
du hattest	ihr hattet	
Sie hatten	Sie hatten	
er/sie/es hatte	sie hatten	

FUTURE PERFECT

ich werde	wir werden	gekündigt haben
du wirst	ihr werdet	
Sie werden	Sie werden	
er/sie/es wird	sie werden	

PAST SUBJUNCTIVE I

ich habe	wir haben	gekündigt
du habest	ihr habet	
Sie haben	Sie haben	
er/sie/es habe	sie haben	

PAST SUBJUNCTIVE II

ich hätte	wir hätten	gekündigt
du hättest	ihr hättet	
Sie hätten	Sie hätten	
er/sie/es hätte	sie hätten	

FUTURE PERFECT SUBJUNCTIVE I

ich werde	wir werden	gekündigt haben
du werdest	ihr werdet	
Sie werden	Sie werden	
er/sie/es werde	sie werden	

FUTURE PERFECT SUBJUNCTIVE II

ich würde	wir würden	gekündigt haben
du würdest	ihr würdet	
Sie würden	Sie würden	
er/sie/es würde	sie würden	

COMMANDS kündig(e)! kündigt! kündigen Sie!

PRESENT PARTICIPLE kündigend

Usage

Ich kündige! — *I quit!*

Onkel Marston kündigt seine Stelle bei der Exportfirma und zieht nach Tahiti. — *Uncle Marston is quitting his job at the export company and moving to Tahiti.*

Warum kündigst du nicht? — *Why don't you give notice?*

Unserem Nachbarn ist die Wohnung zum 31. August gekündigt worden. — *Our neighbor has been given notice to vacate his apartment by August 31.*

Der Vertrag wird bis Ende des Jahres gekündigt. — *The contract will be terminated by the end of the year.*

Kirstens Chef hat ihr wegen Diebstahlverdacht kündigen müssen. — *Kirsten's boss had to terminate her on suspicion of theft.*

Ich möchte mein Abonnement kündigen. — *I would like to cancel my subscription.*

Meine Bank hat den Kredit gekündigt. — *My bank has recalled the loan.*

Gestern hat die Axt-Brigade die einseitige Waffenruhe gekündigt. — *Yesterday, the Ax-brigade called off the unilateral truce.*

RELATED VERBS ab·kündigen, an·kündigen, auf·kündigen, verkündigen

regular weak verb

kürzt · kürzte · gekürzt

PRESENT

ich kürze	wir kürzen
du kürzt	ihr kürzt
Sie kürzen	Sie kürzen
er/sie/es kürzt	sie kürzen

SIMPLE PAST

ich kürzte	wir kürzten
du kürztest	ihr kürztet
Sie kürzten	Sie kürzten
er/sie/es kürzte	sie kürzten

FUTURE

ich werde	wir werden	kürzen
du wirst	ihr werdet	
Sie werden	Sie werden	
er/sie/es wird	sie werden	

PRESENT SUBJUNCTIVE I

ich kürze	wir kürzen
du kürzest	ihr kürzet
Sie kürzen	Sie kürzen
er/sie/es kürze	sie kürzen

PRESENT SUBJUNCTIVE II

ich kürzte	wir kürzten
du kürztest	ihr kürztet
Sie kürzten	Sie kürzten
er/sie/es kürzte	sie kürzten

FUTURE SUBJUNCTIVE I

ich werde	wir werden	kürzen
du werdest	ihr werdet	
Sie werden	Sie werden	
er/sie/es werde	sie werden	

FUTURE SUBJUNCTIVE II

ich würde	wir würden	kürzen
du würdest	ihr würdet	
Sie würden	Sie würden	
er/sie/es würde	sie würden	

PRESENT PERFECT

ich habe	wir haben	gekürzt
du hast	ihr habt	
Sie haben	Sie haben	
er/sie/es hat	sie haben	

PAST PERFECT

ich hatte	wir hatten	gekürzt
du hattest	ihr hattet	
Sie hatten	Sie hatten	
er/sie/es hatte	sie hatten	

FUTURE PERFECT

ich werde	wir werden	gekürzt haben
du wirst	ihr werdet	
Sie werden	Sie werden	
er/sie/es wird	sie werden	

PAST SUBJUNCTIVE I

ich habe	wir haben	gekürzt
du habest	ihr habet	
Sie haben	Sie haben	
er/sie/es habe	sie haben	

PAST SUBJUNCTIVE II

ich hätte	wir hätten	gekürzt
du hättest	ihr hättet	
Sie hätten	Sie hätten	
er/sie/es hätte	sie hätten	

FUTURE PERFECT SUBJUNCTIVE I

ich werde	wir werden	gekürzt haben
du werdest	ihr werdet	
Sie werden	Sie werden	
er/sie/es werde	sie werden	

FUTURE PERFECT SUBJUNCTIVE II

ich würde	wir würden	gekürzt haben
du würdest	ihr würdet	
Sie würden	Sie würden	
er/sie/es würde	sie würden	

COMMANDS kürz(e)! kürzt! kürzen Sie!

PRESENT PARTICIPLE kürzend

Usage

So kann man die Fahrzeit um fünfzehn Minuten kürzen, ohne schneller zu fahren. — *In this way, you can shorten the drive time by 15 minutes without driving faster.*

Das Seil muss gekürzt werden. — *The rope must be shortened.*

Viktor hat den Roman gekürzt und übersetzt. — *Viktor abridged and translated the novel.*

Die Gehälter werden ab Juni um 2% gekürzt. — *Salaries are being cut by 2% beginning in June.*

Werden die Renten wirklich gekürzt? — *Are the pensions really being cut?*

Die Bundesregierung kürzt die Bildungsausgaben fast jedes Jahr. — *The federal government cuts education expenditures almost every year.*

Die Mitgliedsstädte kürzen ihre Zuschüsse. — *The member cities are curtailing their subsidies.*

Im vorigen Jahr waren viele Leistungen der Fürsorgeanstalt gekürzt worden. — *In the previous year, many services of the welfare institute had been reduced.*

Können Sie bitte diese Hosen um drei Zentimeter kürzen? — *Can you shorten these trousers by three centimeters, please?*

RELATED VERBS ab·kürzen, verkürzen

lächeln *to smile*

lächelt · lächelte · gelächelt regular weak verb

PRESENT

ich läch(e)le	wir lächeln
du lächelst	ihr lächelt
Sie lächeln	Sie lächeln
er/sie/es lächelt	sie lächeln

SIMPLE PAST

ich lächelte	wir lächelten
du lächeltest	ihr lächeltet
Sie lächelten	Sie lächelten
er/sie/es lächelte	sie lächelten

FUTURE

ich werde	wir werden	lächeln
du wirst	ihr werdet	
Sie werden	Sie werden	
er/sie/es wird	sie werden	

PRESENT SUBJUNCTIVE I

ich läch(e)le	wir lächeln
du lächelst	ihr lächelt
Sie lächeln	Sie lächeln
er/sie/es läch(e)le	sie lächeln

PRESENT SUBJUNCTIVE II

ich lächelte	wir lächelten
du lächeltest	ihr lächeltet
Sie lächelten	Sie lächelten
er/sie/es lächelte	sie lächelten

FUTURE SUBJUNCTIVE I

ich werde	wir werden	lächeln
du werdest	ihr werdet	
Sie werden	Sie werden	
er/sie/es werde	sie werden	

FUTURE SUBJUNCTIVE II

ich würde	wir würden	lächeln
du würdest	ihr würdet	
Sie würden	Sie würden	
er/sie/es würde	sie würden	

PRESENT PERFECT

ich habe	wir haben	gelächelt
du hast	ihr habt	
Sie haben	Sie haben	
er/sie/es hat	sie haben	

PAST PERFECT

ich hatte	wir hatten	gelächelt
du hattest	ihr hattet	
Sie hatten	Sie hatten	
er/sie/es hatte	sie hatten	

FUTURE PERFECT

ich werde	wir werden	gelächelt haben
du wirst	ihr werdet	
Sie werden	Sie werden	
er/sie/es wird	sie werden	

PAST SUBJUNCTIVE I

ich habe	wir haben	gelächelt
du habest	ihr habet	
Sie haben	Sie haben	
er/sie/es habe	sie haben	

PAST SUBJUNCTIVE II

ich hätte	wir hätten	gelächelt
du hättest	ihr hättet	
Sie hätten	Sie hätten	
er/sie/es hätte	sie hätten	

FUTURE PERFECT SUBJUNCTIVE I

ich werde	wir werden	gelächelt haben
du werdest	ihr werdet	
Sie werden	Sie werden	
er/sie/es werde	sie werden	

FUTURE PERFECT SUBJUNCTIVE II

ich würde	wir würden	gelächelt haben
du würdest	ihr würdet	
Sie würden	Sie würden	
er/sie/es würde	sie würden	

COMMANDS läch(e)le! lächelt! lächeln Sie!

PRESENT PARTICIPLE lächelnd

Usage

Der Mann lächelte belustigt und sagte dem Kind: „Das ist ja allerhand!“ — *The amused man smiled and said to the child, "That's really something!"*

Warum hat Heike über das Unglück ihrer Mitschülerinnen so gelächelt? — *Why did Heike smile like that about her schoolmates' misfortune?*

Sie lächelte verlegen und wurde rot. — *She smiled in embarrassment and blushed.*

Wenn du lächelst, lächele ich auch. — *When you smile, I smile too.*

Lächelt da Vincis Mona Lisa wirklich über einen Witz? — *Is da Vinci's Mona Lisa really smiling about a joke?*

In welchem Alter beginnt ein Baby zu lächeln? — *At what age does a baby begin smiling?*

Der Nachbarshund Boris sah gerade aus, als ob er lächeln würde. — *The neighbor's dog, Boris, just now looked as though he were smiling.*

Der Junge hatte gesagt, er wollte Schauspieler werden, und ich musste darüber lächeln. — *The boy had said he wanted to become an actor, and I had to smile at that.*

Wenn Vögel nur lächeln könnten! — *If only birds could smile!*

RELATED VERBS an·lächeln, belächeln, zu·lächeln

regular weak verb

lacht · lachte · gelacht

PRESENT

ich lache	wir lachen
du lachst	ihr lacht
Sie lachen	Sie lachen
er/sie/es lacht	sie lachen

SIMPLE PAST

ich lachte	wir lachten
du lachtest	ihr lachtet
Sie lachten	Sie lachten
er/sie/es lachte	sie lachten

FUTURE

ich werde	wir werden	lachen
du wirst	ihr werdet	
Sie werden	Sie werden	
er/sie/es wird	sie werden	

PRESENT SUBJUNCTIVE I

ich lache	wir lachen
du lachest	ihr lachet
Sie lachen	Sie lachen
er/sie/es lache	sie lachen

PRESENT SUBJUNCTIVE II

ich lachte	wir lachten
du lachtest	ihr lachtet
Sie lachten	Sie lachten
er/sie/es lachte	sie lachten

FUTURE SUBJUNCTIVE I

ich werde	wir werden	lachen
du werdest	ihr werdet	
Sie werden	Sie werden	
er/sie/es werde	sie werden	

FUTURE SUBJUNCTIVE II

ich würde	wir würden	lachen
du würdest	ihr würdet	
Sie würden	Sie würden	
er/sie/es würde	sie würden	

PRESENT PERFECT

ich habe	wir haben	gelacht
du hast	ihr habt	
Sie haben	Sie haben	
er/sie/es hat	sie haben	

PAST PERFECT

ich hatte	wir hatten	gelacht
du hattest	ihr hattet	
Sie hatten	Sie hatten	
er/sie/es hatte	sie hatten	

FUTURE PERFECT

ich werde	wir werden	gelacht haben
du wirst	ihr werdet	
Sie werden	Sie werden	
er/sie/es wird	sie werden	

PAST SUBJUNCTIVE I

ich habe	wir haben	gelacht
du habest	ihr habet	
Sie haben	Sie haben	
er/sie/es habe	sie haben	

PAST SUBJUNCTIVE II

ich hätte	wir hätten	gelacht
du hättest	ihr hättet	
Sie hätten	Sie hätten	
er/sie/es hätte	sie hätten	

FUTURE PERFECT SUBJUNCTIVE I

ich werde	wir werden	gelacht haben
du werdest	ihr werdet	
Sie werden	Sie werden	
er/sie/es werde	sie werden	

FUTURE PERFECT SUBJUNCTIVE II

ich würde	wir würden	gelacht haben
du würdest	ihr würdet	
Sie würden	Sie würden	
er/sie/es würde	sie würden	

COMMANDS lach(e)! lacht! lachen Sie!

PRESENT PARTICIPLE lachend

Usage

Chronisch kranke Kinder im Krankenhaus werden dazu angeregt öfter zu lachen. — *Chronically ill children in the hospital are encouraged to laugh more often.*

Je mehr ein Patient lacht, desto schneller genest er. — *The more a patient laughs, the faster he recovers.*

Es gibt nichts zu lachen. — *There's nothing to laugh about.*

Man muss über sich selbst lachen können. — *You have to be able to laugh at yourself.*

Die Zuschauer lachten und klatschten Beifall. — *The spectators laughed and clapped their approval.*

Es wurde bei der Party viel geredet und gelacht. — *There was a lot of talking and laughing at the party.*

Ich habe selten so gelacht wie über seine Witze. — *I have seldom laughed as I did at his jokes.*

Die Spielerei der Kinder machte den Herrn lachen. — *The children's play made the gentleman laugh.*

Warum lachen Sie? — *Why are you laughing?*

Wie oft lachst du völlig ungehemmt? — *How often do you really burst out laughing?*

Der Chef war um Worte verlegen, und ich lachte vor mich hin. — *The boss was at a loss for words, and I chuckled to myself.*

RELATED VERBS an·lachen, auf·lachen, aus·lachen, belachen, verlachen, zu·lachen

278 **laden** *to load, put, lay, charge; summon, subpoena*

lädt · lud · geladen strong verb

PRESENT

ich lade	wir laden
du lädst	ihr ladet
Sie laden	Sie laden
er/sie/es lädt	sie laden

SIMPLE PAST

ich lud	wir luden
du ludst	ihr ludet
Sie luden	Sie luden
er/sie/es lud	sie luden

FUTURE

ich werde	wir werden	laden
du wirst	ihr werdet	
Sie werden	Sie werden	
er/sie/es wird	sie werden	

PRESENT SUBJUNCTIVE I

ich lade	wir laden
du ladest	ihr ladet
Sie laden	Sie laden
er/sie/es lade	sie laden

PRESENT SUBJUNCTIVE II

ich lüde	wir lüden
du lüdest	ihr lüdet
Sie lüden	Sie lüden
er/sie/es lüde	sie lüden

FUTURE SUBJUNCTIVE I

ich werde	wir werden	laden
du werdest	ihr werdet	
Sie werden	Sie werden	
er/sie/es werde	sie werden	

FUTURE SUBJUNCTIVE II

ich würde	wir würden	laden
du würdest	ihr würdet	
Sie würden	Sie würden	
er/sie/es würde	sie würden	

PRESENT PERFECT

ich habe	wir haben	geladen
du hast	ihr habt	
Sie haben	Sie haben	
er/sie/es hat	sie haben	

PAST PERFECT

ich hatte	wir hatten	geladen
du hattest	ihr hattet	
Sie hatten	Sie hatten	
er/sie/es hatte	sie hatten	

FUTURE PERFECT

ich werde	wir werden	geladen haben
du wirst	ihr werdet	
Sie werden	Sie werden	
er/sie/es wird	sie werden	

PAST SUBJUNCTIVE I

ich habe	wir haben	geladen
du habest	ihr habet	
Sie haben	Sie haben	
er/sie/es habe	sie haben	

PAST SUBJUNCTIVE II

ich hätte	wir hätten	geladen
du hättest	ihr hättet	
Sie hätten	Sie hätten	
er/sie/es hätte	sie hätten	

FUTURE PERFECT SUBJUNCTIVE I

ich werde	wir werden	geladen haben
du werdest	ihr werdet	
Sie werden	Sie werden	
er/sie/es werde	sie werden	

FUTURE PERFECT SUBJUNCTIVE II

ich würde	wir würden	geladen haben
du würdest	ihr würdet	
Sie würden	Sie würden	
er/sie/es würde	sie würden	

COMMANDS lade! ladet! laden Sie!

PRESENT PARTICIPLE ladend

Usage

Die Arbeiter laden die Fracht aufs Schiff.	*The workers are loading the freight onto the ship.*
Der Bauersknecht lud die Milchkannen auf den Wagen.	*The farmhand loaded the milk cans onto the wagon.*
Hat er die Pistole mit Platzpatronen geladen?	*Did he load the pistol with blanks?*
Ich muss meinen Handy-Akku laden.	*I have to charge my cell phone battery.*
Wer lädt das Gepäck ins Auto?	*Who will load the luggage into the car?*
Das System lädt die neue Version der Software.	*The system is loading the new version of the software.*
Der Finanzminister lädt die Schuld für den Verlust auf das Parlament.	*The finance minister lays the blame for the shortfall on the parliament.*
Warum ladet ihr diese Verantwortung auf euch selbst?	*Why are you putting this responsibility on yourselves?*
Herr Bohnen wird als Zeuge vor Gericht geladen.	*Mr. Bohnen is being subpoenaed to court as a witness.*
Fürstbischof Friedrich Wilhelm von Westphalen lud Georg nach Hildesheim.	*Prince bishop Friedrich Wilhelm von Westphalen summoned Georg to Hildesheim.*

RELATED VERBS ab·laden, auf·laden, aus·laden, beladen, entladen, überladen, um·laden, verladen, vor·laden, zu·laden; *see also* **ein·laden** (134)

PRESENT		PRESENT PERFECT		
ich lande	wir landen	ich bin	wir sind	gelandet
du landest	ihr landet	du bist	ihr seid	
Sie landen	Sie landen	Sie sind	Sie sind	
er/sie/es landet	sie landen	er/sie/es ist	sie sind	

SIMPLE PAST		PAST PERFECT		
ich landete	wir landeten	ich war	wir waren	gelandet
du landetest	ihr landetet	du warst	ihr wart	
Sie landeten	Sie landeten	Sie waren	Sie waren	
er/sie/es landete	sie landeten	er/sie/es war	sie waren	

FUTURE			FUTURE PERFECT		
ich werde	wir werden	landen	ich werde	wir werden	gelandet sein
du wirst	ihr werdet		du wirst	ihr werdet	
Sie werden	Sie werden		Sie werden	Sie werden	
er/sie/es wird	sie werden		er/sie/es wird	sie werden	

PRESENT SUBJUNCTIVE I		PAST SUBJUNCTIVE I		
ich lande	wir landen	ich sei	wir seien	gelandet
du landest	ihr landet	du seiest	ihr seiet	
Sie landen	Sie landen	Sie seien	Sie seien	
er/sie/es lande	sie landen	er/sie/es sei	sie seien	

PRESENT SUBJUNCTIVE II		PAST SUBJUNCTIVE II		
ich landete	wir landeten	ich wäre	wir wären	gelandet
du landetest	ihr landetet	du wärest	ihr wäret	
Sie landeten	Sie landeten	Sie wären	Sie wären	
er/sie/es landete	sie landeten	er/sie/es wäre	sie wären	

FUTURE SUBJUNCTIVE I			FUTURE PERFECT SUBJUNCTIVE I		
ich werde	wir werden	landen	ich werde	wir werden	gelandet sein
du werdest	ihr werdet		du werdest	ihr werdet	
Sie werden	Sie werden		Sie werden	Sie werden	
er/sie/es werde	sie werden		er/sie/es werde	sie werden	

FUTURE SUBJUNCTIVE II			FUTURE PERFECT SUBJUNCTIVE II		
ich würde	wir würden	landen	ich würde	wir würden	gelandet sein
du würdest	ihr würdet		du würdest	ihr würdet	
Sie würden	Sie würden		Sie würden	Sie würden	
er/sie/es würde	sie würden		er/sie/es würde	sie würden	

COMMANDS lande! landet! landen Sie!

PRESENT PARTICIPLE landend

Usage

Die alliierten Truppen waren am 6. Juni 1944 in der Normandie gelandet. — *The Allied troops had landed in Normandy on June 6, 1944.*

Nach sieben Stunden ist Familie Fritsch endlich in Istanbul gelandet. — *After seven hours, the Fritsch family finally landed in Istanbul.*

Wann werden wir landen? — *When will we land?*

Das außerordentlich zähe Steak ist Therese plötzlich vom Teller gerutscht und auf dem Boden gelandet. — *The unusually tough steak suddenly slipped from Therese's plate and landed on the floor.*

Die meisten Leserbriefe landen im Papierkorb. — *Most letters to the editor end up in the wastebasket.*

landen (with haben) *to land*

Die erfahrene Pilotin hat das Flugzeug trotz des Wetters sicher gelandet. — *The experienced pilot safely landed the plane in spite of the weather.*

Wie kann man so einen Ballon landen? — *How can you land a balloon like that?*

RELATED VERBS not·landen, zwischen·landen

lassen *to let, allow, permit; leave; stop, put aside; relinquish, let go*

lässt · ließ · gelassen strong verb

MORE USAGE SENTENCES WITH lassen

Ihr wisst, dass er das Rauchen nicht lassen kann. — *You know he can't give up smoking.*
Lasst bitte eure Kommentare! — *Please put aside your comments!*
Lassen Sie die Katze bitte nicht ins Schlafzimmer. — *Please don't let the cat into the bedroom.*
Lass das bitte! — *Please stop that!*

lass(t) uns ... *let's ...*

Lass uns gehen. — *Let's go.*
Lasst uns hier bleiben. — *Let's stay here.*

lassen + adverb

Die gigantischen Wellen haben nichts übrig gelassen. — *The giant waves spared nothing.*
Der Stadtrat ließ die Frage der Kosten offen. — *The city council left open the question of costs.*

lassen + infinitive *to leave, let*

Ernst ließ das Auto vor der Schule stehen. — *Ernst left the car sitting in front of the school.*
Hans hat sein Buch fallen lassen. — *Hans dropped his book.*
Wie konnten Sie das geschehen lassen? — *How could you let that happen?*
Ich habe meinen Mantel liegen lassen. — *I left my coat behind.*
Wir wollten euch wissen lassen, dass wir an euch denken. — *We wanted to let you know we're thinking of you.*

NOTE The verb **lassen** can combine with other verbs and direct objects to express the notion of causing or permitting an action. Context must sometimes determine whether the sense is one of causation or permission.

(jemanden/etwas) (etwas) + infinitive + **lassen** *to have/get (something) done, have/let (someone) do (something)*

Hoffmann ließ 1804 seinen Namen ändern. — *Hoffmann had his name changed in 1804.*
Herr Holzbauer lässt das Fachwerkhaus sanieren. — *Mr. Holzbauer is having the half-timber house renovated.*
Birgit hat sich die Haare schneiden lassen. — *Birgit got her hair cut.*
Leben und leben lassen. (PROVERB) — *Live and let live.*
Manfred hat mich vorne sitzen lassen. — *Manfred let/had me sit up front.*
Renate hätte das Kind ihr Auto nicht fahren lassen. — *Renate would not have let the child drive her car.*
Ich lasse Fritz mein Auto waschen. — *I'm having Fritz wash my car.*
Ich lasse dich nicht mit uns spielen. — *I'm not letting you play with us.*
Max und Maria lassen sich scheiden. — *Max and Maria are getting divorced.*

NOTE The verb **lassen** can combine with a reflexive pronoun and another verb to express the notion of capacity or ability. In this structure, **lassen** acts much like an auxiliary verb in that no **zu** is required; it is frequently a substitute for the passive voice.

sich + infinitive + **lassen** *to be doable, be feasible to do*

Das lässt sich leicht lernen. — *That can easily be learned.*
Herbert meint, der Rotwein ließe sich nicht trinken. — *Herbert says the red wine isn't drinkable.*
Das lässt sich schon machen. — *That can be managed.*
Es lässt sich denken, dass Frau Kugel gar kein Geld hat. — *It's conceivable that Mrs. Kugel has no money at all.*

IDIOMATIC EXPRESSIONS

Das musst du dir nicht gefallen lassen. — *You don't have to put up with that.*
Man hat mir am Projekt freie Hand gelassen. — *I was given a free hand in the project.*
Lass von dir hören! — *Don't be a stranger!*
Lassen Sie es sich gut schmecken! — *Bon appétit!*

strong verb **lässt · ließ · gelassen**

PRESENT

ich lasse	wir lassen
du lässt	ihr lasst
Sie lassen	Sie lassen
er/sie/es lässt	sie lassen

SIMPLE PAST

ich ließ	wir ließen
du ließest	ihr ließt
Sie ließen	Sie ließen
er/sie/es ließ	sie ließen

FUTURE

ich werde	wir werden	lassen
du wirst	ihr werdet	
Sie werden	Sie werden	
er/sie/es wird	sie werden	

PRESENT SUBJUNCTIVE I

ich lasse	wir lassen
du lassest	ihr lasset
Sie lassen	Sie lassen
er/sie/es lasse	sie lassen

PRESENT SUBJUNCTIVE II

ich ließe	wir ließen
du ließest	ihr ließet
Sie ließen	Sie ließen
er/sie/es ließe	sie ließen

FUTURE SUBJUNCTIVE I

ich werde	wir werden	lassen
du werdest	ihr werdet	
Sie werden	Sie werden	
er/sie/es werde	sie werden	

FUTURE SUBJUNCTIVE II

ich würde	wir würden	lassen
du würdest	ihr würdet	
Sie würden	Sie würden	
er/sie/es würde	sie würden	

PRESENT PERFECT

ich habe	wir haben	gelassen
du hast	ihr habt	
Sie haben	Sie haben	
er/sie/es hat	sie haben	

PAST PERFECT

ich hatte	wir hatten	gelassen
du hattest	ihr hattet	
Sie hatten	Sie hatten	
er/sie/es hatte	sie hatten	

FUTURE PERFECT

ich werde	wir werden	gelassen haben
du wirst	ihr werdet	
Sie werden	Sie werden	
er/sie/es wird	sie werden	

PAST SUBJUNCTIVE I

ich habe	wir haben	gelassen
du habest	ihr habet	
Sie haben	Sie haben	
er/sie/es habe	sie haben	

PAST SUBJUNCTIVE II

ich hätte	wir hätten	gelassen
du hättest	ihr hättet	
Sie hätten	Sie hätten	
er/sie/es hätte	sie hätten	

FUTURE PERFECT SUBJUNCTIVE I

ich werde	wir werden	gelassen haben
du werdest	ihr werdet	
Sie werden	Sie werden	
er/sie/es werde	sie werden	

FUTURE PERFECT SUBJUNCTIVE II

ich würde	wir würden	gelassen haben
du würdest	ihr würdet	
Sie würden	Sie würden	
er/sie/es würde	sie würden	

COMMANDS lass(e)! lasst! lassen Sie!

PRESENT PARTICIPLE lassend

Usage

Ich lasse der älteren Frau den Vortritt. — *I am letting the older woman go first.*

Sie hatten sich nicht genügend Zeit gelassen. — *They hadn't allowed themselves sufficient time.*

Lassen Sie mich bitte zu Wort kommen. — *Please permit me to say a word.*

Erich hat sein Fahrrad zu Hause gelassen und ist zu Fuß zur Universität gegangen. — *Erich left his bicycle at home and walked to the university.*

Der Reiseleiter hat die Touristen im Stich gelassen. — *The tour guide left the tourists in the lurch.*

Das Theaterstück ist ein Fragment; der Autor ließ die Handlung unvollendet. — *The play is a fragment; the playwright left the plot incomplete.*

Das Ende der Geschichte lässt den Leser im Ungewissen über das Schicksal des Protagonisten. — *The end of the story leaves the reader not knowing the protagonist's fate.*

RELATED VERBS ab·lassen, an·lassen, auf·lassen, aus·lassen, belassen, durch·lassen, ein·lassen, erlassen, fort·lassen, frei·lassen, herab·lassen, los·lassen, nach·lassen, nieder·lassen, überlassen, unterlassen, vor·lassen, weg·lassen, zerlassen, zu·lassen, zurück·lassen, zusammen·lassen; *see also* **entlassen** (145), **hinterlassen** (245), **verlassen** (493)

laufen *to run, walk; work, function; extend*

läuft · lief · gelaufen strong verb

MORE USAGE SENTENCES WITH laufen

Beide Filme liefen nur zwei Wochen in den Kinos.	*Both films played in theaters for only two weeks.*
Die Anmeldefrist läuft bis Ende August.	*The enrollment period extends until the end of August.*
Marianne ließ die Badewanne voll laufen.	*Marianne let the bathtub run full.*
Kein Projekt läuft genau wie geplant.	*No project goes exactly as planned.*
Das Wasser war vom Dachgeschoss durch das ganze Haus gelaufen.	*The water had run from the attic through the whole house.*
Das Schiff soll Dienstagabend auf Grund gelaufen sein.	*The ship is said to have run aground Tuesday evening.*
Früher mussten Verbrecher Spießruten laufen.	*Criminals used to have to run a gauntlet.*
Kriegsvorbereitungen laufen auf Hochtouren.	*Preparations for war are running full speed ahead.*
Wie kann ich den Film rückwärts laufen lassen?	*How can I run the film backwards?*
Die beiden Veranstaltungen laufen parallel mit einander.	*The two events are running parallel with each other.*

laufen (with **haben**) *to run*

1964 lief Andrea Schmitz einen neuen Weltrekord.	*In 1964, Andrea Schmitz broke the world record.*
Hast du den Marathon zu Ende gelaufen?	*Did you run the marathon to the finish line?*

sich laufen *to run, walk*

Mit hohen Absätzen läuft es sich sehr unbequem.	*It's very uncomfortable to walk in high heels.*
Jost hat sich müde gelaufen.	*Jost got tired from walking.*

IDIOMATIC EXPRESSIONS

Lassen Sie den Motor 10 Minuten im Leerlauf laufen.	*Let the engine idle for 10 minutes.*
Umweltschutzorganisationen laufen Sturm gegen das geplante Einkaufszentrum.	*Environmental groups are up in arms about the planned shopping center.*
Die alten Heerstraßen laufen in Dinkelsburg auseinander.	*The old military roads diverge in Dinkelsburg.*
Ich wollte ihn anrufen, aber es ist heute vieles schief gelaufen und ich bin nicht dazu gekommen.	*I wanted to call him, but a lot has gone wrong today and I didn't get around to it.*
Das neue Modell ist Probe gelaufen.	*The new model has been tested.*
Alles ist gut gelaufen.	*Everything went well.*
Welch ein Gerücht läuft durch den Lagerplatz? (Kleist)	*What's the rumor going around the camp?*
In Whistler kann man Ski laufen und snowboarden.	*In Whistler, you can ski and snowboard.*
Patrick läuft gern Rollschuh.	*Patrick likes to roller skate.*
Andrea ist krank, ihre Nase läuft den ganzen Tag.	*Andrea is sick; her nose has been runny all day.*
Auf wessen Namen läuft das Abonnement?	*Whose name is the subscription under?*
Am letzten Tag meiner Europareise habe ich mir die Füße wund gelaufen.	*On the last day of my European vacation, I got blisters from walking so much.*
Die Sache ist gelaufen.	*It's all over. / The matter is settled. / It's too late now.*
Man läuft Gefahr, die wirklichen Ursachen zu übersehen.	*We're running the risk of overlooking the real causes.*
Mit der Patentierung lebendiger Wesen ist die Gentechnik Amok gelaufen.	*With the patenting of living beings, genetic engineering has run amok.*
Das läuft schon ins Geld, wenn du jeden Abend essen gehst, gell?	*That runs into some money if you go out to eat every evening, doesn't it?*
Das Prinzip läuft wider den gesunden Verstand.	*The principle goes against common sense.*
Sein erster Song war ein Hit, aber die anderen rangieren unter „ferner liefen".	*His first song was a hit, but the others were "also rans."*
Es lief ihm eiskalt über den Rücken.	*A chill ran down his spine.*
Bei Gisela läuft der Fernseher den ganzen Tag.	*At Gisela's house, the television is on all day long.*
Andreas ließ sich mit Schnapps und Bier voll laufen.	*Andreas got tanked up on schnapps and beer.*

strong verb **läuft · lief · gelaufen**

PRESENT

ich laufe	wir laufen
du läufst	ihr lauft
Sie laufen	Sie laufen
er/sie/es läuft	sie laufen

SIMPLE PAST

ich lief	wir liefen
du liefst	ihr lieft
Sie liefen	Sie liefen
er/sie/es lief	sie liefen

FUTURE

ich werde	wir werden	laufen
du wirst	ihr werdet	
Sie werden	Sie werden	
er/sie/es wird	sie werden	

PRESENT SUBJUNCTIVE I

ich laufe	wir laufen
du laufest	ihr laufet
Sie laufen	Sie laufen
er/sie/es laufe	sie laufen

PRESENT SUBJUNCTIVE II

ich liefe	wir liefen
du liefest	ihr liefet
Sie liefen	Sie liefen
er/sie/es liefe	sie liefen

FUTURE SUBJUNCTIVE I

ich werde	wir werden	laufen
du werdest	ihr werdet	
Sie werden	Sie werden	
er/sie/es werde	sie werden	

FUTURE SUBJUNCTIVE II

ich würde	wir würden	laufen
du würdest	ihr würdet	
Sie würden	Sie würden	
er/sie/es würde	sie würden	

PRESENT PERFECT

ich bin	wir sind	gelaufen
du bist	ihr seid	
Sie sind	Sie sind	
er/sie/es ist	sie sind	

PAST PERFECT

ich war	wir waren	gelaufen
du warst	ihr wart	
Sie waren	Sie waren	
er/sie/es war	sie waren	

FUTURE PERFECT

ich werde	wir werden	gelaufen sein
du wirst	ihr werdet	
Sie werden	Sie werden	
er/sie/es wird	sie werden	

PAST SUBJUNCTIVE I

ich sei	wir seien	gelaufen
du seiest	ihr seiet	
Sie seien	Sie seien	
er/sie/es sei	sie seien	

PAST SUBJUNCTIVE II

ich wäre	wir wären	gelaufen
du wärest	ihr wäret	
Sie wären	Sie wären	
er/sie/es wäre	sie wären	

FUTURE PERFECT SUBJUNCTIVE I

ich werde	wir werden	gelaufen sein
du werdest	ihr werdet	
Sie werden	Sie werden	
er/sie/es werde	sie werden	

FUTURE PERFECT SUBJUNCTIVE II

ich würde	wir würden	gelaufen sein
du würdest	ihr würdet	
Sie würden	Sie würden	
er/sie/es würde	sie würden	

COMMANDS lauf(e)! lauft! laufen Sie!

PRESENT PARTICIPLE laufend

Usage

Werner und Edwina laufen gern barfuß am Strand.	*Werner and Edwina like to run barefoot on the beach.*
Der Sportler läuft in die falsche Richtung.	*The athlete is running in the wrong direction.*
Jakob lernt gerade laufen.	*Jakob is just learning to walk.*
Die Kinder laufen mit einander um die Wette.	*The children are racing each other.*
Der Spieler war leider ins Abseits gelaufen.	*The player had unfortunately run out of bounds.*
Ich bin gestern zum ersten Mal auf Stelzen gelaufen.	*I walked on stilts for the first time yesterday.*
Der Motor lief immer heiß.	*The motor always ran hot.*
Mein Computer läuft nicht mehr so richtig.	*My computer isn't working quite right anymore.*
Vorbereitungen auf die Konferenz laufen nach Plan.	*Preparations for the conference are going according to plan.*

RELATED VERBS ab·laufen, an·laufen, auf·laufen, aus·laufen, belaufen, durch·laufen, durchlaufen, ein·laufen, entgegen·laufen, entlang·laufen, entlaufen, erlaufen, fest·laufen, fort·laufen, hinaus·laufen, mit·laufen, nach·laufen, über·laufen, überlaufen, um·laufen, umlaufen, unter·laufen, unterlaufen, verlaufen, vorbei·laufen, weg·laufen, weiter·laufen, zerlaufen, zu·laufen, zurück·laufen, zusammen·laufen, zuwider·laufen

leben *to live, exist, be living; dwell, reside*

lebt · lebte · gelebt regular weak verb

PRESENT		PRESENT PERFECT		
ich lebe	wir leben	ich habe	wir haben	gelebt
du lebst	ihr lebt	du hast	ihr habt	
Sie leben	Sie leben	Sie haben	Sie haben	
er/sie/es lebt	sie leben	er/sie/es hat	sie haben	

SIMPLE PAST		PAST PERFECT		
ich lebte	wir lebten	ich hatte	wir hatten	gelebt
du lebtest	ihr lebtet	du hattest	ihr hattet	
Sie lebten	Sie lebten	Sie hatten	Sie hatten	
er/sie/es lebte	sie lebten	er/sie/es hatte	sie hatten	

FUTURE			FUTURE PERFECT		
ich werde	wir werden	leben	ich werde	wir werden	gelebt haben
du wirst	ihr werdet		du wirst	ihr werdet	
Sie werden	Sie werden		Sie werden	Sie werden	
er/sie/es wird	sie werden		er/sie/es wird	sie werden	

PRESENT SUBJUNCTIVE I		PAST SUBJUNCTIVE I		
ich lebe	wir leben	ich habe	wir haben	gelebt
du lebest	ihr lebet	du habest	ihr habet	
Sie leben	Sie leben	Sie haben	Sie haben	
er/sie/es lebe	sie leben	er/sie/es habe	sie haben	

PRESENT SUBJUNCTIVE II		PAST SUBJUNCTIVE II		
ich lebte	wir lebten	ich hätte	wir hätten	gelebt
du lebtest	ihr lebtet	du hättest	ihr hättet	
Sie lebten	Sie lebten	Sie hätten	Sie hätten	
er/sie/es lebte	sie lebten	er/sie/es hätte	sie hätten	

FUTURE SUBJUNCTIVE I			FUTURE PERFECT SUBJUNCTIVE I		
ich werde	wir werden	leben	ich werde	wir werden	gelebt haben
du werdest	ihr werdet		du werdest	ihr werdet	
Sie werden	Sie werden		Sie werden	Sie werden	
er/sie/es werde	sie werden		er/sie/es werde	sie werden	

FUTURE SUBJUNCTIVE II			FUTURE PERFECT SUBJUNCTIVE II		
ich würde	wir würden	leben	ich würde	wir würden	gelebt haben
du würdest	ihr würdet		du würdest	ihr würdet	
Sie würden	Sie würden		Sie würden	Sie würden	
er/sie/es würde	sie würden		er/sie/es würde	sie würden	

COMMANDS leb(e)! lebt! leben Sie!

PRESENT PARTICIPLE lebend

Usage

Um das Jahr 1200 lebte man in einer Welt mitten in politischem Umbruch. — *Around the year 1200, people lived in a world in the midst of political upheaval.*

Mein Großvater Karl lebt nicht mehr. — *My grandfather Karl is not alive anymore.*

Mehr als eine Milliarde Menschen leben in Armut. — *More than one billion people live in poverty.*

Muss ich lernen, mit den Schmerzen zu leben? — *Must I learn to live with the pain?*

Eine lange Zeit lebte Bernal vom Redigieren. — *For a long time, Bernal made a living as an editor.*

Habt ihr jemals im Ausland gelebt? — *Have you ever lived abroad?*

Er hat einige Zeit in Nürnberg gearbeitet, aber er lebt jetzt in München. — *He worked in Nuremberg for a while, but he now resides in Munich.*

Hoffmann wurde am 24. Januar 1776 in Königsberg geboren, wo er bis 1796 lebte. — *Hoffmann was born on January 24, 1776 in Königsberg, where he lived until 1796.*

Sie leben auf einem Rittergut in Grafschaft Glatz. — *They currently live on a manor in County Glatz.*

RELATED VERBS auf·leben, aus·leben, beleben, durchleben, ein·leben, fort·leben, hoch·leben, nach·leben, überleben, verleben, vor·leben, wieder·beleben, zusammen·leben; *see also* **erleben** (165)

regular weak verb **legt · legte · gelegt**

PRESENT

ich lege	wir legen
du legst	ihr legt
Sie legen	Sie legen
er/sie/es legt	sie legen

SIMPLE PAST

ich legte	wir legten
du legtest	ihr legtet
Sie legten	Sie legten
er/sie/es legte	sie legten

FUTURE

ich werde	wir werden	legen
du wirst	ihr werdet	
Sie werden	Sie werden	
er/sie/es wird	sie werden	

PRESENT SUBJUNCTIVE I

ich lege	wir legen
du legest	ihr leget
Sie legen	Sie legen
er/sie/es lege	sie legen

PRESENT SUBJUNCTIVE II

ich legte	wir legten
du legtest	ihr legtet
Sie legten	Sie legten
er/sie/es legte	sie legten

FUTURE SUBJUNCTIVE I

ich werde	wir werden	legen
du werdest	ihr werdet	
Sie werden	Sie werden	
er/sie/es werde	sie werden	

FUTURE SUBJUNCTIVE II

ich würde	wir würden	legen
du würdest	ihr würdet	
Sie würden	Sie würden	
er/sie/es würde	sie würden	

PRESENT PERFECT

ich habe	wir haben	gelegt
du hast	ihr habt	
Sie haben	Sie haben	
er/sie/es hat	sie haben	

PAST PERFECT

ich hatte	wir hatten	gelegt
du hattest	ihr hattet	
Sie hatten	Sie hatten	
er/sie/es hatte	sie hatten	

FUTURE PERFECT

ich werde	wir werden	gelegt haben
du wirst	ihr werdet	
Sie werden	Sie werden	
er/sie/es wird	sie werden	

PAST SUBJUNCTIVE I

ich habe	wir haben	gelegt
du habest	ihr habet	
Sie haben	Sie haben	
er/sie/es habe	sie haben	

PAST SUBJUNCTIVE II

ich hätte	wir hätten	gelegt
du hättest	ihr hättet	
Sie hätten	Sie hätten	
er/sie/es hätte	sie hätten	

FUTURE PERFECT SUBJUNCTIVE I

ich werde	wir werden	gelegt haben
du werdest	ihr werdet	
Sie werden	Sie werden	
er/sie/es werde	sie werden	

FUTURE PERFECT SUBJUNCTIVE II

ich würde	wir würden	gelegt haben
du würdest	ihr würdet	
Sie würden	Sie würden	
er/sie/es würde	sie würden	

COMMANDS leg(e)! legt! legen Sie!

PRESENT PARTICIPLE legend

Usage

Mareike hat den Mantel auf das Sofa gelegt.	*Mareike laid the coat on the sofa.*
Frau Werner legt das Kind ins Bett.	*Mrs. Werner is laying the baby on the bed.*
Legen Sie das Gemüse bitte auf die Waage.	*Please put the vegetables on the scale.*
An der Sicherheitskontrolle mussten wir unser Handgepäck auf ein Fließband legen.	*At the security checkpoint, we had to place our carry-on luggage onto a conveyor belt.*
Er legte seine Hand auf ihren Kopf.	*He placed his hand on her head.*
Legen Sie bitte die Bücher nebeneinander.	*Please lay the books next to one another.*
Ich habe die Bretter aufeinander gelegt.	*I laid the boards one on top of the other.*

RELATED VERBS ab·legen, an·legen, auf·erlegen, auf·legen, aus·legen, bei·legen, belegen, bereit·legen, bloß·legen, brach·legen, dar·legen, ein·legen, erlegen, fest·legen, fort·legen, frei·legen, hin·legen, hinterlegen, nach·legen, nieder·legen, still·legen, trocken·legen, über·legen, um·legen, umlegen, unter·legen, unterlegen, verlegen, vor·legen, weg·legen, widerlegen, zerlegen, zu·legen, zurecht·legen, zurück·legen, zusammen·legen; *see also* **überlegen** (460)

TOP 50 VERB ☞

legen *to lay, put, place*

legt · legte · gelegt regular weak verb

MORE USAGE SENTENCES WITH legen

Claudio legte vier Asse auf den Tisch. *Claudio laid four aces on the table.*

Leg den Mantel beiseite und setz dich hierhin. *Push the coat out of the way and sit down here.*

Eine amerikanische Flagge wurde über den Sarg gelegt. *An American flag was draped across the casket.*

Jedes Huhn legt pro Jahr circa 300 Eier. *Each hen lays about 300 eggs per year.*

1884 wurde der Grundstein des Berliner Reichstags gelegt. *In 1884, the cornerstone of the Berlin Reichstag was laid.*

Onkel Dirk hat uns neue Teppiche gelegt. *Uncle Dirk laid new carpet for us.*

Glasfaserkabel wurde neulich bei uns in der Gegend gelegt. *Optical fiber cable was recently laid in our area.*

Es hieß, an diesem Tage habe Mergel zuerst Hand an sie gelegt. (Droste-Hülshoff) *It was said that Mergel first laid hands on her that day.*

Martin legt jeden Monat etwas Geld beiseite. *Martin puts a little money aside each month.*

sich legen *to lie down; abate, subside, die down*

Der bewaffnete Bankräuber sagte den Kunden, sie sollten sich auf den Boden legen. *The armed bank robber told the customers to lie down on the floor.*

Wir haben uns im Park ins Gras gelegt und geschlafen. *We lay down in the grass in the park and slept.*

Sobald sich die Aufregung gelegt hat, versuchen wir es noch mal. *As soon as the excitement has died down, we'll try it again.*

Endlich legte sich das Gewitter und wir schliefen ein. *Finally, the storm subsided and we fell asleep.*

Am Spätabend wird sich der Wind legen. *Late in the evening, the wind will die down.*

IDIOMATIC EXPRESSIONS

Der riesige Airbus 380 legte sich auf die rechte Seite, um den Anflug zu beginnen. *The giant Airbus 380 banked sharply to the right to begin its approach.*

Es wird versucht, diese Vorstellungen im Einzelnen auseinander zu legen. *An attempt will be made to analyze these ideas individually.*

Wenn du gleich alle Karten auf den Tisch legst, hast du die Oberhand verloren. *If you show all your cards at once, you've lost the upper hand.*

Herr Strenger legt großen Wert auf Formalitäten. *Mr. Strenger attaches great value to formalities.*

Die Geschäftsleitung legt besonderes Gewicht auf die Gesundheit der Mitarbeiter. *The management attaches special importance to the health of its employees.*

Ein Motorradfahrer muss sich in Kurven legen. *A motorcyclist must lean into turns.*

Ich hatte mich entschlossen, mich ein paar Minuten aufs Ohr zu legen. *I had decided to nap for a few minutes.*

Eine dichte Rauchwolke legte sich über das breite Tal. *A dense cloud of smoke settled over the wide valley.*

Laut Angaben sei er von den Soldaten in Fesseln gelegt und verprügelt worden. *According to reports, he was shackled and beaten by the soldiers.*

Das Buch war dermaßen spannend, dass ich es nicht aus der Hand legen konnte. *The book was so enthralling that I couldn't put it down.*

Der Kampfhund wurde an eine Kette gelegt, weil er Passanten angegriffen hatte. *The attack dog was chained up because he had attacked passersby.*

1945 wurde der Dom samt 300 Jahre alter Orgel in Asche gelegt. *In 1945, the cathedral, along with its 300-year-old organ, was reduced to ashes.*

Marlene legte die letzte Hand an die Dekorationen. *Marlene put the finishing touches on the decorations.*

Er hat mir ans Herz gelegt, dass seine Orchideen aufmerksam zu pflegen sind. *He impressed upon me that his orchids must be attentively cared for.*

Anja muss sich krumm legen, um die Miete zu zahlen. *Anja has to pinch and scrape to pay the rent.*

regular weak verb **lehnt · lehnte · gelehnt**

PRESENT

ich lehne	wir lehnen
du lehnst	ihr lehnt
Sie lehnen	Sie lehnen
er/sie/es lehnt	sie lehnen

SIMPLE PAST

ich lehnte	wir lehnten
du lehntest	ihr lehntet
Sie lehnten	Sie lehnten
er/sie/es lehnte	sie lehnten

FUTURE

ich werde	wir werden	lehnen
du wirst	ihr werdet	
Sie werden	Sie werden	
er/sie/es wird	sie werden	

PRESENT SUBJUNCTIVE I

ich lehne	wir lehnen
du lehnest	ihr lehnet
Sie lehnen	Sie lehnen
er/sie/es lehne	sie lehnen

PRESENT SUBJUNCTIVE II

ich lehnte	wir lehnten
du lehntest	ihr lehntet
Sie lehnten	Sie lehnten
er/sie/es lehnte	sie lehnten

FUTURE SUBJUNCTIVE I

ich werde	wir werden	lehnen
du werdest	ihr werdet	
Sie werden	Sie werden	
er/sie/es werde	sie werden	

FUTURE SUBJUNCTIVE II

ich würde	wir würden	lehnen
du würdest	ihr würdet	
Sie würden	Sie würden	
er/sie/es würde	sie würden	

PRESENT PERFECT

ich habe	wir haben	gelehnt
du hast	ihr habt	
Sie haben	Sie haben	
er/sie/es hat	sie haben	

PAST PERFECT

ich hatte	wir hatten	gelehnt
du hattest	ihr hattet	
Sie hatten	Sie hatten	
er/sie/es hatte	sie hatten	

FUTURE PERFECT

ich werde	wir werden	gelehnt haben
du wirst	ihr werdet	
Sie werden	Sie werden	
er/sie/es wird	sie werden	

PAST SUBJUNCTIVE I

ich habe	wir haben	gelehnt
du habest	ihr habet	
Sie haben	Sie haben	
er/sie/es habe	sie haben	

PAST SUBJUNCTIVE II

ich hätte	wir hätten	gelehnt
du hättest	ihr hättet	
Sie hätten	Sie hätten	
er/sie/es hätte	sie hätten	

FUTURE PERFECT SUBJUNCTIVE I

ich werde	wir werden	gelehnt haben
du werdest	ihr werdet	
Sie werden	Sie werden	
er/sie/es werde	sie werden	

FUTURE PERFECT SUBJUNCTIVE II

ich würde	wir würden	gelehnt haben
du würdest	ihr würdet	
Sie würden	Sie würden	
er/sie/es würde	sie würden	

COMMANDS lehn(e)! lehnt! lehnen Sie!

PRESENT PARTICIPLE lehnend

Usage

Serena lehnte ihren Kopf an ihn.	*Serena leaned her head against him.*
Lehn das Kochbuch an den Einkaufskorb.	*Prop the cookbook up against the shopping basket.*
Lehnen Sie den Oberkörper langsam nach rechts.	*Slowly lean your upper body to the right.*
Ein Foto war an eine Vase gelehnt worden.	*A photograph had been leaned against the vase.*
Ein Billardstock lehnt an der Wand.	*A billiard cue is propped against the wall.*
Das Mofa hat an einem Baum vor dem Haus gelehnt.	*The moped was leaning against a tree in front of the house.*
Sein rechter Arm lehnt am Tisch, ein Buch in der Hand.	*His right arm rests on the table, a book in his hand.*
Nicht über das Geländer lehnen! (SIGN)	*Do not lean over the railing!*

sich lehnen *to lean, prop, recline (oneself)*

Lehnen Sie sich auf diese großen Kissen.	*Prop yourself up on these big pillows.*
Ich habe mich an den Zaun gelehnt.	*I leaned against the fence.*

RELATED VERBS an·lehnen, auf·lehnen, hinaus·lehnen, vor·lehnen, zurück·lehnen; *see also* **ab·lehnen** (5)

285 lehren *to teach, instruct*

lehrt · lehrte · gelehrt regular weak verb

PRESENT

ich lehre	wir lehren
du lehrst	ihr lehrt
Sie lehren	Sie lehren
er/sie/es lehrt	sie lehren

PRESENT PERFECT

ich habe	wir haben	gelehrt
du hast	ihr habt	
Sie haben	Sie haben	
er/sie/es hat	sie haben	

SIMPLE PAST

ich lehrte	wir lehrten
du lehrtest	ihr lehrtet
Sie lehrten	Sie lehrten
er/sie/es lehrte	sie lehrten

PAST PERFECT

ich hatte	wir hatten	gelehrt
du hattest	ihr hattet	
Sie hatten	Sie hatten	
er/sie/es hatte	sie hatten	

FUTURE

ich werde	wir werden	lehren
du wirst	ihr werdet	
Sie werden	Sie werden	
er/sie/es wird	sie werden	

FUTURE PERFECT

ich werde	wir werden	gelehrt haben
du wirst	ihr werdet	
Sie werden	Sie werden	
er/sie/es wird	sie werden	

PRESENT SUBJUNCTIVE I

ich lehre	wir lehren
du lehrest	ihr lehret
Sie lehren	Sie lehren
er/sie/es lehre	sie lehren

PAST SUBJUNCTIVE I

ich habe	wir haben	gelehrt
du habest	ihr habet	
Sie haben	Sie haben	
er/sie/es habe	sie haben	

PRESENT SUBJUNCTIVE II

ich lehrte	wir lehrten
du lehrtest	ihr lehrtet
Sie lehrten	Sie lehrten
er/sie/es lehrte	sie lehrten

PAST SUBJUNCTIVE II

ich hätte	wir hätten	gelehrt
du hättest	ihr hättet	
Sie hätten	Sie hätten	
er/sie/es hätte	sie hätten	

FUTURE SUBJUNCTIVE I

ich werde	wir werden	lehren
du werdest	ihr werdet	
Sie werden	Sie werden	
er/sie/es werde	sie werden	

FUTURE PERFECT SUBJUNCTIVE I

ich werde	wir werden	gelehrt haben
du werdest	ihr werdet	
Sie werden	Sie werden	
er/sie/es werde	sie werden	

FUTURE SUBJUNCTIVE II

ich würde	wir würden	lehren
du würdest	ihr würdet	
Sie würden	Sie würden	
er/sie/es würde	sie würden	

FUTURE PERFECT SUBJUNCTIVE II

ich würde	wir würden	gelehrt haben
du würdest	ihr würdet	
Sie würden	Sie würden	
er/sie/es würde	sie würden	

COMMANDS lehr(e)! lehrt! lehren Sie!

PRESENT PARTICIPLE lehrend

Usage

Der Ägyptologe Heinrich Brugsch lehrte 1868–1870 an der Universität Göttingen. — *The Egyptologist Heinrich Brugsch taught at the University of Göttingen from 1868 to 1870.*

Jörg lehrt seit einem Jahr Tango. — *Jörg has been teaching tango for a year.*

Diese Bücher lehrten die Menschen, wie sie den Weg zu Gott finden. — *These books taught people how to find the way to God.*

Ich habe am Gymnasium Biologie gelehrt. — *I taught biology in high school.*

Hier lehrt man Theorie und Praxis. — *They teach theory and practice here.*

Eine spezielle Version der Software ist für Lehrende und Lernende lieferbar. — *A special version of the software is available for teachers and students.*

lehren + infinitive *to teach (how to)*

Sein Freund hatte ihn tanzen gelehrt. — *His friend had taught him how to dance.*

Ihre Schwester lehrt sie lesen. — *Her sister is teaching her to read.*

RELATED VERB belehren

strong verb **leidet · litt · gelitten**

PRESENT

ich leide	wir leiden
du leidest	ihr leidet
Sie leiden	Sie leiden
er/sie/es leidet	sie leiden

SIMPLE PAST

ich litt	wir litten
du littst	ihr littet
Sie litten	Sie litten
er/sie/es litt	sie litten

FUTURE

ich werde	wir werden	leiden
du wirst	ihr werdet	
Sie werden	Sie werden	
er/sie/es wird	sie werden	

PRESENT SUBJUNCTIVE I

ich leide	wir leiden
du leidest	ihr leidet
Sie leiden	Sie leiden
er/sie/es leide	sie leiden

PRESENT SUBJUNCTIVE II

ich litte	wir litten
du littest	ihr littet
Sie litten	Sie litten
er/sie/es litte	sie litten

FUTURE SUBJUNCTIVE I

ich werde	wir werden	leiden
du werdest	ihr werdet	
Sie werden	Sie werden	
er/sie/es werde	sie werden	

FUTURE SUBJUNCTIVE II

ich würde	wir würden	leiden
du würdest	ihr würdet	
Sie würden	Sie würden	
er/sie/es würde	sie würden	

COMMANDS leide! leidet! leiden Sie!

PRESENT PARTICIPLE leidend

PRESENT PERFECT

ich habe	wir haben	gelitten
du hast	ihr habt	
Sie haben	Sie haben	
er/sie/es hat	sie haben	

PAST PERFECT

ich hatte	wir hatten	gelitten
du hattest	ihr hattet	
Sie hatten	Sie hatten	
er/sie/es hatte	sie hatten	

FUTURE PERFECT

ich werde	wir werden	gelitten haben
du wirst	ihr werdet	
Sie werden	Sie werden	
er/sie/es wird	sie werden	

PAST SUBJUNCTIVE I

ich habe	wir haben	gelitten
du habest	ihr habet	
Sie haben	Sie haben	
er/sie/es habe	sie haben	

PAST SUBJUNCTIVE II

ich hätte	wir hätten	gelitten
du hättest	ihr hättet	
Sie hätten	Sie hätten	
er/sie/es hätte	sie hätten	

FUTURE PERFECT SUBJUNCTIVE I

ich werde	wir werden	gelitten haben
du werdest	ihr werdet	
Sie werden	Sie werden	
er/sie/es werde	sie werden	

FUTURE PERFECT SUBJUNCTIVE II

ich würde	wir würden	gelitten haben
du würdest	ihr würdet	
Sie würden	Sie würden	
er/sie/es würde	sie würden	

Usage

Du musst wirklich gelitten haben!	*You must have really suffered!*
Der Metzger leidet an Zuckerkrankheit.	*The butcher suffers from diabetes.*
Die Qualität der Tonaufnahme hat wegen des Studios gelitten.	*The quality of the sound recording suffered because of the studio.*
Gregs guter Ruf hatte daher stark gelitten.	*Greg's good reputation had suffered substantially as a result.*
Maria sagte, sie leide jetzt unter Ischiasschmerzen.	*Maria said she now suffers from sciatic pain.*
Beim Rugbyspiel wurde gestern Abend viel gelitten.	*There was a lot of suffering at the rugby match last night.*
Diese Fotos haben unter den hellen Lampen des Museums gelitten.	*These photographs deteriorated under the bright museum lights.*
Ingrid mag ihn gern leiden.	*Ingrid is fond of him.*
Bernd konnte seine Chefin nicht leiden.	*Bernd couldn't stand his boss.*
Die Angelegenheit leidet keinen Aufschub.	*The matter admits of no delay.*
Das wird hier nicht gelitten.	*That is not tolerated here.*

RELATED VERBS erleiden, mit·leiden

287 leihen *to lend, loan; borrow; rent*

leiht · lieh · geliehen strong verb

PRESENT

ich leihe	wir leihen
du leihst	ihr leiht
Sie leihen	Sie leihen
er/sie/es leiht	sie leihen

SIMPLE PAST

ich lieh	wir liehen
du liehst	ihr lieht
Sie liehen	Sie liehen
er/sie/es lieh	sie liehen

FUTURE

ich werde	wir werden	leihen
du wirst	ihr werdet	
Sie werden	Sie werden	
er/sie/es wird	sie werden	

PRESENT SUBJUNCTIVE I

ich leihe	wir leihen
du leihest	ihr leihet
Sie leihen	Sie leihen
er/sie/es leihe	sie leihen

PRESENT SUBJUNCTIVE II

ich liehe	wir liehen
du liehest	ihr liehet
Sie liehen	Sie liehen
er/sie/es liehe	sie liehen

FUTURE SUBJUNCTIVE I

ich werde	wir werden	leihen
du werdest	ihr werdet	
Sie werden	Sie werden	
er/sie/es werde	sie werden	

FUTURE SUBJUNCTIVE II

ich würde	wir würden	leihen
du würdest	ihr würdet	
Sie würden	Sie würden	
er/sie/es würde	sie würden	

PRESENT PERFECT

ich habe	wir haben	geliehen
du hast	ihr habt	
Sie haben	Sie haben	
er/sie/es hat	sie haben	

PAST PERFECT

ich hatte	wir hatten	geliehen
du hattest	ihr hattet	
Sie hatten	Sie hatten	
er/sie/es hatte	sie hatten	

FUTURE PERFECT

ich werde	wir werden	geliehen haben
du wirst	ihr werdet	
Sie werden	Sie werden	
er/sie/es wird	sie werden	

PAST SUBJUNCTIVE I

ich habe	wir haben	geliehen
du habest	ihr habet	
Sie haben	Sie haben	
er/sie/es habe	sie haben	

PAST SUBJUNCTIVE II

ich hätte	wir hätten	geliehen
du hättest	ihr hättet	
Sie hätten	Sie hätten	
er/sie/es hätte	sie hätten	

FUTURE PERFECT SUBJUNCTIVE I

ich werde	wir werden	geliehen haben
du werdest	ihr werdet	
Sie werden	Sie werden	
er/sie/es werde	sie werden	

FUTURE PERFECT SUBJUNCTIVE II

ich würde	wir würden	geliehen haben
du würdest	ihr würdet	
Sie würden	Sie würden	
er/sie/es würde	sie würden	

COMMANDS leih(e)! leiht! leihen Sie!

PRESENT PARTICIPLE leihend

Usage

Könntest du mir das Buch leihen, wenn du es fertig gelesen hast? — *Could you lend me the book when you've finished reading it?*

Ich leihe dir mein Video von dem Konzert. — *I'll lend you my video of the concert.*

Leihst du deinen Freunden Geld? — *Do you loan money to your friends?*

Annalies hatte einer Freundin ihr Auto geliehen. — *Annalies had lent her car to a friend.*

Stefan hat sich von Ingo Geld geliehen. — *Stefan borrowed money from Ingo.*

Du darfst von mir keine Bücher mehr leihen. — *You can't borrow any more books from me.*

Wir haben uns das Auto meines Onkels geliehen. — *We borrowed my uncle's car.*

Wer möchte die DVD von mir leihen? — *Who would like to borrow the DVD from me?*

Möchtet ihr für heute Abend eine DVD leihen? — *Would you like to rent a DVD for this evening?*

Wir haben ein Auto bei Hertz geliehen. — *We rented a car from Hertz.*

Leiht mir eure Ohren, und ich singe euch ein Lied. — *Lend me your ears, and I'll sing you a song.*

RELATED VERBS aus·leihen, beleihen, entleihen, verleihen

regular weak verb **leistet · leistete · geleistet**

PRESENT

ich leiste	wir leisten
du leistest	ihr leistet
Sie leisten	Sie leisten
er/sie/es leistet	sie leisten

SIMPLE PAST

ich leistete	wir leisteten
du leistetest	ihr leistetet
Sie leisteten	Sie leisteten
er/sie/es leistete	sie leisteten

FUTURE

ich werde	wir werden	leisten
du wirst	ihr werdet	
Sie werden	Sie werden	
er/sie/es wird	sie werden	

PRESENT SUBJUNCTIVE I

ich leiste	wir leisten
du leistest	ihr leistet
Sie leisten	Sie leisten
er/sie/es leiste	sie leisten

PRESENT SUBJUNCTIVE II

ich leistete	wir leisteten
du leistetest	ihr leistetet
Sie leisteten	Sie leisteten
er/sie/es leistete	sie leisteten

FUTURE SUBJUNCTIVE I

ich werde	wir werden	leisten
du werdest	ihr werdet	
Sie werden	Sie werden	
er/sie/es werde	sie werden	

FUTURE SUBJUNCTIVE II

ich würde	wir würden	leisten
du würdest	ihr würdet	
Sie würden	Sie würden	
er/sie/es würde	sie würden	

PRESENT PERFECT

ich habe	wir haben	geleistet
du hast	ihr habt	
Sie haben	Sie haben	
er/sie/es hat	sie haben	

PAST PERFECT

ich hatte	wir hatten	geleistet
du hattest	ihr hattet	
Sie hatten	Sie hatten	
er/sie/es hatte	sie hatten	

FUTURE PERFECT

ich werde	wir werden	geleistet haben
du wirst	ihr werdet	
Sie werden	Sie werden	
er/sie/es wird	sie werden	

PAST SUBJUNCTIVE I

ich habe	wir haben	geleistet
du habest	ihr habet	
Sie haben	Sie haben	
er/sie/es habe	sie haben	

PAST SUBJUNCTIVE II

ich hätte	wir hätten	geleistet
du hättest	ihr hättet	
Sie hätten	Sie hätten	
er/sie/es hätte	sie hätten	

FUTURE PERFECT SUBJUNCTIVE I

ich werde	wir werden	geleistet haben
du werdest	ihr werdet	
Sie werden	Sie werden	
er/sie/es werde	sie werden	

FUTURE PERFECT SUBJUNCTIVE II

ich würde	wir würden	geleistet haben
du würdest	ihr würdet	
Sie würden	Sie würden	
er/sie/es würde	sie würden	

COMMANDS leiste! leistet! leisten Sie!

PRESENT PARTICIPLE leistend

Usage

Wer kann diese schwere Aufgabe leisten?	*Who can accomplish this difficult task?*
Während der schwierigen Jahre leistete sie ihm Beistand.	*During the difficult years, she stood by him.*
Können Sie Erste Hilfe leisten?	*Can you perform first aid?*
Die Firma leistet ihren Beitrag an die Baukosten.	*The firm is contributing to construction costs.*
Voriges Jahr haben wir Erstaunliches geleistet.	*We achieved amazing things last year.*
Welche kirchlichen Gruppen leisteten Widerstand?	*Which church groups offered resistance?*
Unser neuester Kopierer leistet bis zu 30 Seiten pro Minute.	*Our newest copier outputs up to 30 pages a minute.*

sich etwas leisten *to treat oneself to something, allow oneself something*

Ich leiste mir heute ein Eis.	*I'll allow myself an ice cream today.*

sich etwas leisten können *to be able to afford something*

Ihre Eltern können sich ein Internat nicht leisten.	*Her parents cannot afford a boarding school.*

RELATED VERBS ab·leisten, gewährleisten

289 leiten *to direct, guide, conduct, lead, control*

leitet · leitete · geleitet regular weak verb

PRESENT

ich leite	wir leiten
du leitest	ihr leitet
Sie leiten	Sie leiten
er/sie/es leitet	sie leiten

SIMPLE PAST

ich leitete	wir leiteten
du leitetest	ihr leitetet
Sie leiteten	Sie leiteten
er/sie/es leitete	sie leiteten

FUTURE

ich werde	wir werden	leiten
du wirst	ihr werdet	
Sie werden	Sie werden	
er/sie/es wird	sie werden	

PRESENT SUBJUNCTIVE I

ich leite	wir leiten
du leitest	ihr leitet
Sie leiten	Sie leiten
er/sie/es leite	sie leiten

PRESENT SUBJUNCTIVE II

ich leitete	wir leiteten
du leitetest	ihr leitetet
Sie leiteten	Sie leiteten
er/sie/es leitete	sie leiteten

FUTURE SUBJUNCTIVE I

ich werde	wir werden	leiten
du werdest	ihr werdet	
Sie werden	Sie werden	
er/sie/es werde	sie werden	

FUTURE SUBJUNCTIVE II

ich würde	wir würden	leiten
du würdest	ihr würdet	
Sie würden	Sie würden	
er/sie/es würde	sie würden	

PRESENT PERFECT

ich habe	wir haben	geleitet
du hast	ihr habt	
Sie haben	Sie haben	
er/sie/es hat	sie haben	

PAST PERFECT

ich hatte	wir hatten	geleitet
du hattest	ihr hattet	
Sie hatten	Sie hatten	
er/sie/es hatte	sie hatten	

FUTURE PERFECT

ich werde	wir werden	geleitet haben
du wirst	ihr werdet	
Sie werden	Sie werden	
er/sie/es wird	sie werden	

PAST SUBJUNCTIVE I

ich habe	wir haben	geleitet
du habest	ihr habet	
Sie haben	Sie haben	
er/sie/es habe	sie haben	

PAST SUBJUNCTIVE II

ich hätte	wir hätten	geleitet
du hättest	ihr hättet	
Sie hätten	Sie hätten	
er/sie/es hätte	sie hätten	

FUTURE PERFECT SUBJUNCTIVE I

ich werde	wir werden	geleitet haben
du werdest	ihr werdet	
Sie werden	Sie werden	
er/sie/es werde	sie werden	

FUTURE PERFECT SUBJUNCTIVE II

ich würde	wir würden	geleitet haben
du würdest	ihr würdet	
Sie würden	Sie würden	
er/sie/es würde	sie würden	

COMMANDS leite! leitet! leiten Sie!

PRESENT PARTICIPLE leitend

Usage

Michael Uhrig leitet die Firma als Hauptgeschäftsführer.	*Michael Uhrig directs the firm as chief executive officer.*
Daniel Barenboim leitete das Chicago Symphony Orchestra.	*Daniel Barenboim conducted the Chicago Symphony Orchestra.*
Werner hat die Sitzung über Ortsgeschichte geleitet.	*Werner led the session on local history.*
Kann destilliertes Wasser Strom leiten?	*Can distilled water conduct electricity?*
Ein Schiedsrichter leitet das Spiel.	*A referee controls the game.*
Das Trinkwasser ist durch Kanäle geleitet worden.	*The drinking water has been channeled through canals.*
Wer möchte den Workshop leiten?	*Who would like to conduct the workshop?*
Ein gepflasterter Weg leitet Touristen zum Aussichtsturm.	*A paved path guides tourists to the observation tower.*
Herr Nägeli leitet den Männerchor seit 1965.	*Mr. Nägeli has directed the men's chorus since 1965.*
Diese Kampagne wurde von unserer eigenen Organisation geleitet.	*This campaign was led by our own organization.*

RELATED VERBS ab·leiten, an·leiten, ein·leiten, fehl·leiten, geleiten, her·leiten, irre·leiten, über·leiten, um·leiten, verleiten, weiter·leiten, zu·leiten, zurück·leiten

regular weak verb **lernt · lernte · gelernt**

PRESENT

ich lerne	wir lernen
du lernst	ihr lernt
Sie lernen	Sie lernen
er/sie/es lernt	sie lernen

SIMPLE PAST

ich lernte	wir lernten
du lerntest	ihr lerntet
Sie lernten	Sie lernten
er/sie/es lernte	sie lernten

FUTURE

ich werde	wir werden	lernen
du wirst	ihr werdet	
Sie werden	Sie werden	
er/sie/es wird	sie werden	

PRESENT SUBJUNCTIVE I

ich lerne	wir lernen
du lernest	ihr lernet
Sie lernen	Sie lernen
er/sie/es lerne	sie lernen

PRESENT SUBJUNCTIVE II

ich lernte	wir lernten
du lerntest	ihr lerntet
Sie lernten	Sie lernten
er/sie/es lernte	sie lernten

FUTURE SUBJUNCTIVE I

ich werde	wir werden	lernen
du werdest	ihr werdet	
Sie werden	Sie werden	
er/sie/es werde	sie werden	

FUTURE SUBJUNCTIVE II

ich würde	wir würden	lernen
du würdest	ihr würdet	
Sie würden	Sie würden	
er/sie/es würde	sie würden	

PRESENT PERFECT

ich habe	wir haben	gelernt
du hast	ihr habt	
Sie haben	Sie haben	
er/sie/es hat	sie haben	

PAST PERFECT

ich hatte	wir hatten	gelernt
du hattest	ihr hattet	
Sie hatten	Sie hatten	
er/sie/es hatte	sie hatten	

FUTURE PERFECT

ich werde	wir werden	gelernt haben
du wirst	ihr werdet	
Sie werden	Sie werden	
er/sie/es wird	sie werden	

PAST SUBJUNCTIVE I

ich habe	wir haben	gelernt
du habest	ihr habet	
Sie haben	Sie haben	
er/sie/es habe	sie haben	

PAST SUBJUNCTIVE II

ich hätte	wir hätten	gelernt
du hättest	ihr hättet	
Sie hätten	Sie hätten	
er/sie/es hätte	sie hätten	

FUTURE PERFECT SUBJUNCTIVE I

ich werde	wir werden	gelernt haben
du werdest	ihr werdet	
Sie werden	Sie werden	
er/sie/es werde	sie werden	

FUTURE PERFECT SUBJUNCTIVE II

ich würde	wir würden	gelernt haben
du würdest	ihr würdet	
Sie würden	Sie würden	
er/sie/es würde	sie würden	

COMMANDS lern(e)! lernt! lernen Sie!

PRESENT PARTICIPLE lernend

Usage

Hannelore lernt Bauchtanz.	*Hannelore is learning belly dancing.*
Heute Abend muss ich Vokabeln lernen.	*I have to study vocabulary this evening.*
Ein Kind lernt in diesem Alter, Verantwortung zu übernehmen.	*A child learns to take responsibility at this age.*
Er hat den Liedtext auswendig gelernt.	*He memorized the lyrics.*
Ich habe bei Fräulein Zwickel Algebra gelernt.	*I learned algebra from Miss Zwickel.*
Theodor lernt den Beruf Mechaniker seit einem Jahr.	*Theodor has been a mechanic's apprentice for a year.*

lernen + infinitive

Ich möchte Klavier spielen lernen.	*I'd like to learn to play the piano.*
Durch den Unfall hat er das Leben schätzen gelernt.	*From the accident, he's learned to appreciate life.*
In Berlin lernte er unter anderen Eichendorff und Brentano kennen.	*In Berlin, he became acquainted with Eichendorff and Brentano, among others.*

RELATED VERBS an·lernen, aus·lernen, ein·lernen, erlernen, um·lernen, verlernen

291 lesen *to read; gather, pick*

liest · las · gelesen strong verb

PRESENT

ich lese	wir lesen
du liest	ihr lest
Sie lesen	Sie lesen
er/sie/es liest	sie lesen

SIMPLE PAST

ich las	wir lasen
du lasest	ihr last
Sie lasen	Sie lasen
er/sie/es las	sie lasen

FUTURE

ich werde	wir werden	lesen
du wirst	ihr werdet	
Sie werden	Sie werden	
er/sie/es wird	sie werden	

PRESENT SUBJUNCTIVE I

ich lese	wir lesen
du lesest	ihr leset
Sie lesen	Sie lesen
er/sie/es lese	sie lesen

PRESENT SUBJUNCTIVE II

ich läse	wir läsen
du läsest	ihr läset
Sie läsen	Sie läsen
er/sie/es läse	sie läsen

FUTURE SUBJUNCTIVE I

ich werde	wir werden	lesen
du werdest	ihr werdet	
Sie werden	Sie werden	
er/sie/es werde	sie werden	

FUTURE SUBJUNCTIVE II

ich würde	wir würden	lesen
du würdest	ihr würdet	
Sie würden	Sie würden	
er/sie/es würde	sie würden	

PRESENT PERFECT

ich habe	wir haben	gelesen
du hast	ihr habt	
Sie haben	Sie haben	
er/sie/es hat	sie haben	

PAST PERFECT

ich hatte	wir hatten	gelesen
du hattest	ihr hattet	
Sie hatten	Sie hatten	
er/sie/es hatte	sie hatten	

FUTURE PERFECT

ich werde	wir werden	gelesen haben
du wirst	ihr werdet	
Sie werden	Sie werden	
er/sie/es wird	sie werden	

PAST SUBJUNCTIVE I

ich habe	wir haben	gelesen
du habest	ihr habet	
Sie haben	Sie haben	
er/sie/es habe	sie haben	

PAST SUBJUNCTIVE II

ich hätte	wir hätten	gelesen
du hättest	ihr hättet	
Sie hätten	Sie hätten	
er/sie/es hätte	sie hätten	

FUTURE PERFECT SUBJUNCTIVE I

ich werde	wir werden	gelesen haben
du werdest	ihr werdet	
Sie werden	Sie werden	
er/sie/es werde	sie werden	

FUTURE PERFECT SUBJUNCTIVE II

ich würde	wir würden	gelesen haben
du würdest	ihr würdet	
Sie würden	Sie würden	
er/sie/es würde	sie würden	

COMMANDS lies! lest! lesen Sie!

PRESENT PARTICIPLE lesend

Usage

Melanie und ihr Freund lasen gern Science Fiction. — *Melanie and her boyfriend liked to read science fiction.*
Hast du dieses Buch noch nicht fertig gelesen? — *Haven't you finished reading that book yet?*
Ich habe den Aufsatz gelesen aber nicht verstanden. — *I read the essay but didn't understand it.*
Er spielt fantastisch aber er liest keine Noten. — *He plays fantastically, but he doesn't read music.*
Diese Schrift ist ziemlich schwer zu lesen. — *This script is rather difficult to read.*
Ein polnischer Priester las die Messe. — *A Polish priest said mass.*
Wir werden bald Brombeeren lesen. — *We will soon be picking blackberries.*
Wie werden die Trauben für den Eiswein gelesen? — *How are the grapes picked for the ice wine?*

sich lesen *to read*

Seine Biografie liest sich wie ein Kriminalroman. — *His biography reads like a crime novel.*
Diese Kindergeschichte liest sich leicht. — *This children's story is easy to read.*

RELATED VERBS ab·lesen, an·lesen, auf·lesen, aus·lesen, durch·lesen, ein·lesen, erlesen, nach·lesen, überlesen, verlesen, vor·lesen, weiter·lesen, zusammen·lesen

regular weak verb **liebt · liebte · geliebt**

PRESENT

ich liebe	wir lieben
du liebst	ihr liebt
Sie lieben	Sie lieben
er/sie/es liebt	sie lieben

SIMPLE PAST

ich liebte	wir liebten
du liebtest	ihr liebtet
Sie liebten	Sie liebten
er/sie/es liebte	sie liebten

FUTURE

ich werde	wir werden	lieben
du wirst	ihr werdet	
Sie werden	Sie werden	
er/sie/es wird	sie werden	

PRESENT SUBJUNCTIVE I

ich liebe	wir lieben
du liebest	ihr liebet
Sie lieben	Sie lieben
er/sie/es liebe	sie lieben

PRESENT SUBJUNCTIVE II

ich liebte	wir liebten
du liebtest	ihr liebtet
Sie liebten	Sie liebten
er/sie/es liebte	sie liebten

FUTURE SUBJUNCTIVE I

ich werde	wir werden	lieben
du werdest	ihr werdet	
Sie werden	Sie werden	
er/sie/es werde	sie werden	

FUTURE SUBJUNCTIVE II

ich würde	wir würden	lieben
du würdest	ihr würdet	
Sie würden	Sie würden	
er/sie/es würde	sie würden	

PRESENT PERFECT

ich habe	wir haben	geliebt
du hast	ihr habt	
Sie haben	Sie haben	
er/sie/es hat	sie haben	

PAST PERFECT

ich hatte	wir hatten	geliebt
du hattest	ihr hattet	
Sie hatten	Sie hatten	
er/sie/es hatte	sie hatten	

FUTURE PERFECT

ich werde	wir werden	geliebt haben
du wirst	ihr werdet	
Sie werden	Sie werden	
er/sie/es wird	sie werden	

PAST SUBJUNCTIVE I

ich habe	wir haben	geliebt
du habest	ihr habet	
Sie haben	Sie haben	
er/sie/es habe	sie haben	

PAST SUBJUNCTIVE II

ich hätte	wir hätten	geliebt
du hättest	ihr hättet	
Sie hätten	Sie hätten	
er/sie/es hätte	sie hätten	

FUTURE PERFECT SUBJUNCTIVE I

ich werde	wir werden	geliebt haben
du werdest	ihr werdet	
Sie werden	Sie werden	
er/sie/es werde	sie werden	

FUTURE PERFECT SUBJUNCTIVE II

ich würde	wir würden	geliebt haben
du würdest	ihr würdet	
Sie würden	Sie würden	
er/sie/es würde	sie würden	

COMMANDS lieb(e)! liebt! lieben Sie!

PRESENT PARTICIPLE liebend

Usage

Erich liebte sie vom ganzen Herzen.	*Erich loved her with all his heart.*
Wir haben gelebt, geliebt und gelernt.	*We lived, loved, and learned.*
Sie lieben sich nicht mehr.	*They no longer love one another.*
Die Kinder lieben es, Karneval-Kostüme zu tragen.	*The children love wearing carnival costumes.*
Liebst du mich?	*Do you love me?*
Herbert liebt große Gesellschaften nicht besonders.	*Herbert is not particularly fond of large social gatherings.*
Mein Kater liebt die Wärme vor dem Kamin.	*My cat loves the warmth in front of the fireplace.*
Sie hatte ihn platonisch geliebt.	*She had loved him platonically.*
Herr Biedermann liebt sein Land.	*Mr. Biedermann loves his country.*
Unser Papagei liebt besonders Äpfel und Birnen.	*Our parrot especially loves apples and pears.*
Ich liebe alles an ihm.	*I love everything about him.*
Welch Glück, geliebt zu werden! (GOETHE)	*What happiness, to be loved!*

RELATED VERBS belieben; *see also* **verlieben** (495)

293 liefern *to deliver, furnish, supply, provide*

liefert · lieferte · geliefert regular weak verb

PRESENT

ich liefere	wir liefern
du lieferst	ihr liefert
Sie liefern	Sie liefern
er/sie/es liefert	sie liefern

SIMPLE PAST

ich lieferte	wir lieferten
du liefertest	ihr liefertet
Sie lieferten	Sie lieferten
er/sie/es lieferte	sie lieferten

FUTURE

ich werde	wir werden	liefern
du wirst	ihr werdet	
Sie werden	Sie werden	
er/sie/es wird	sie werden	

PRESENT SUBJUNCTIVE I

ich liefere	wir liefern
du lieferst	ihr liefert
Sie liefern	Sie liefern
er/sie/es liefere	sie liefern

PRESENT SUBJUNCTIVE II

ich lieferte	wir lieferten
du liefertest	ihr liefertet
Sie lieferten	Sie lieferten
er/sie/es lieferte	sie lieferten

FUTURE SUBJUNCTIVE I

ich werde	wir werden	liefern
du werdest	ihr werdet	
Sie werden	Sie werden	
er/sie/es werde	sie werden	

FUTURE SUBJUNCTIVE II

ich würde	wir würden	liefern
du würdest	ihr würdet	
Sie würden	Sie würden	
er/sie/es würde	sie würden	

PRESENT PERFECT

ich habe	wir haben	geliefert
du hast	ihr habt	
Sie haben	Sie haben	
er/sie/es hat	sie haben	

PAST PERFECT

ich hatte	wir hatten	geliefert
du hattest	ihr hattet	
Sie hatten	Sie hatten	
er/sie/es hatte	sie hatten	

FUTURE PERFECT

ich werde	wir werden	geliefert haben
du wirst	ihr werdet	
Sie werden	Sie werden	
er/sie/es wird	sie werden	

PAST SUBJUNCTIVE I

ich habe	wir haben	geliefert
du habest	ihr habet	
Sie haben	Sie haben	
er/sie/es habe	sie haben	

PAST SUBJUNCTIVE II

ich hätte	wir hätten	geliefert
du hättest	ihr hättet	
Sie hätten	Sie hätten	
er/sie/es hätte	sie hätten	

FUTURE PERFECT SUBJUNCTIVE I

ich werde	wir werden	geliefert haben
du werdest	ihr werdet	
Sie werden	Sie werden	
er/sie/es werde	sie werden	

FUTURE PERFECT SUBJUNCTIVE II

ich würde	wir würden	geliefert haben
du würdest	ihr würdet	
Sie würden	Sie würden	
er/sie/es würde	sie würden	

COMMANDS liefere! liefert! liefern Sie!

PRESENT PARTICIPLE liefernd

Usage

Frische Brötchen werden jeden Morgen geliefert.	*Fresh rolls are delivered every morning.*
Sechs Brunnen liefern circa 70 m³ Trinkwasser pro Tag.	*Six wells supply about 70 cubic meters of water per day.*
Die folgende Tabelle liefert spezifische Daten.	*The following table provides specific data.*
Clyde Tombaugh lieferte 1930 den Beweis für die Existenz von Pluto.	*Clyde Tombaugh furnished evidence for the existence of Pluto in 1930.*
Unsere 124 Kühe liefern die Milch für den Käse, den wir machen.	*Our 124 cows supply the milk for the cheese that we make.*
Ein Stück Kuchen liefert circa 400 Kalorien.	*A piece of cake supplies about 400 calories.*
Stefans Erlebnisse in Indien liefern den Stoff für den Roman.	*Stefan's experiences in India furnish the material for the novel.*
Dietrich Hombacher hat eine alternative Erklärung geliefert.	*Dietrich Hombacher has offered an alternative explanation.*
Wir versprechen, den Erstsatz termingemäß zu liefern.	*We promise to deliver the first proof on time.*

RELATED VERBS ab·liefern, an·liefern, auf·liefern, aus·liefern, beliefern, ein·liefern, nach·liefern, überliefern

strong verb **liegt · lag · gelegen**

PRESENT

ich liege	wir liegen
du liegst	ihr liegt
Sie liegen	Sie liegen
er/sie/es liegt	sie liegen

SIMPLE PAST

ich lag	wir lagen
du lagst	ihr lagt
Sie lagen	Sie lagen
er/sie/es lag	sie lagen

FUTURE

ich werde	wir werden	liegen
du wirst	ihr werdet	
Sie werden	Sie werden	
er/sie/es wird	sie werden	

PRESENT SUBJUNCTIVE I

ich liege	wir liegen
du liegest	ihr lieget
Sie liegen	Sie liegen
er/sie/es liege	sie liegen

PRESENT SUBJUNCTIVE II

ich läge	wir lägen
du lägest	ihr läget
Sie lägen	Sie lägen
er/sie/es läge	sie lägen

FUTURE SUBJUNCTIVE I

ich werde	wir werden	liegen
du werdest	ihr werdet	
Sie werden	Sie werden	
er/sie/es werde	sie werden	

FUTURE SUBJUNCTIVE II

ich würde	wir würden	liegen
du würdest	ihr würdet	
Sie würden	Sie würden	
er/sie/es würde	sie würden	

PRESENT PERFECT

ich habe	wir haben	gelegen
du hast	ihr habt	
Sie haben	Sie haben	
er/sie/es hat	sie haben	

PAST PERFECT

ich hatte	wir hatten	gelegen
du hattest	ihr hattet	
Sie hatten	Sie hatten	
er/sie/es hatte	sie hatten	

FUTURE PERFECT

ich werde	wir werden	gelegen haben
du wirst	ihr werdet	
Sie werden	Sie werden	
er/sie/es wird	sie werden	

PAST SUBJUNCTIVE I

ich habe	wir haben	gelegen
du habest	ihr habet	
Sie haben	Sie haben	
er/sie/es habe	sie haben	

PAST SUBJUNCTIVE II

ich hätte	wir hätten	gelegen
du hättest	ihr hättet	
Sie hätten	Sie hätten	
er/sie/es hätte	sie hätten	

FUTURE PERFECT SUBJUNCTIVE I

ich werde	wir werden	gelegen haben
du werdest	ihr werdet	
Sie werden	Sie werden	
er/sie/es werde	sie werden	

FUTURE PERFECT SUBJUNCTIVE II

ich würde	wir würden	gelegen haben
du würdest	ihr würdet	
Sie würden	Sie würden	
er/sie/es würde	sie würden	

COMMANDS lieg(e)! liegt! liegen Sie!

PRESENT PARTICIPLE liegend

Usage

Die wieder gefundenen Handschriften hatten seit 1832 in einem Schrank hinter Büchern gelegen.	*The rediscovered manuscripts had rested in a cabinet behind some books since 1832.*
Paul lag mit Fieber im Bett.	*Paul was lying in bed with a fever.*
Ich habe das Modellauto im Gebüsch liegen gefunden.	*I found the model car lying in the brush.*
Nein, bleib liegen. Du darfst noch nicht aus dem Bett.	*No, stay lying down. You can't get out of bed yet.*
Liegst du auf dem Bauch, wenn du schläfst?	*Do you lie on your stomach when you sleep?*
„Wo ist mein Pulli?" „Er liegt auf dem Sofa."	*"Where's my sweater?" "It's on the sofa."*
Unsere Wohnung liegt sehr günstig.	*Our apartment is conveniently located.*
Die Stadt Brünn liegt in der Provinz Mähren.	*The city of Brno is located in the province of Moravia.*
Ingrid hat viele alte Bücher auf dem Dachboden liegen.	*Ingrid has a lot of old books lying in the attic.*

RELATED VERBS ab·liegen, an·liegen, auf·liegen, aus·liegen, bei·liegen, bereit·liegen, bloß·liegen, brach·liegen, erliegen, fest·liegen, gegenüber·liegen, ob·liegen, obliegen, still·liegen, unterliegen, vor·liegen, zusammen·liegen

TOP 50 VERB ☞

liegen *to lie, be lying, rest; be located/situated*

liegt · lag · gelegen strong verb

MORE USAGE SENTENCES WITH liegen

Auch im Sommer liegt Schnee auf den höheren Gipfeln. *Even in the summer, there's snow on the higher summits.*
1972 lag die Wahlbeteiligung bei 91%. *In 1972, voter turnout was 91%.*
Mit diesem neuen Rekord liegt Mark jetzt auf Platz eins. *With this new record, Mark is now in first place.*
Gottseidank liegt das alles jetzt hinter uns. *Thank God that's all behind us now.*
Santa Fe liegt höher als Denver. *Santa Fe sits at a higher elevation than Denver.*
Das Wohnhaus liegt zentral, aber es ist doch auch ruhig. *The residence is centrally located, but it is also quiet.*
Bad Bentheim liegt nah an der niederländischen Grenze. *Bad Bentheim is situated close to the Dutch border.*

liegen an + dative *to lie near/on; be due to, depend on*

„Woran liegt das?" *"What's the reason for that?"*
„Es liegt an seinem Mangel an Erfahrung." *"It's due to his lack of experience."*
Die Stadt Dresden liegt an der Elbe. *The city of Dresden lies on the Elbe River.*
Fred sagt, das Problem liege an der Software. *Fred says the problem lies with the software.*
„Macht Lars mit?" „Tja, das liegt an dir." *"Is Lars participating?" "Well, that depends on you."*
An wem liegt es? An der Gesellschaft? Am Individuum? *Whose fault is it? Society's? The individual's?*
San Francisco liegt an der Pazifik-Küste. *San Francisco lies on the Pacific coast.*

jemandem daran gelegen sein *to be of concern for someone*

Es ist uns daran gelegen, einen gesunden Meinungsaustausch zu fördern. *We are anxious to promote a healthy exchange of opinions.*
Wenn es ihm wirklich daran gelegen wäre, den Mord zu klären, würde er sich freiwillig bei uns melden. *If he were really interested in solving the murder, he would contact us on his own.*

IDIOMATIC EXPRESSIONS

Es liegt mir nicht. *I don't care for it.*
Das Wort lag mir auf der Zunge. *The word was on the tip of my tongue.*
Wie die Sache momentan liegt, bekommen wir 50 000 Euro Entschädigung. *As matters currently stand, we'll receive 50,000 euros in restitution.*
Gerade da liegt der Hase im Pfeffer. *That is precisely the fly in the ointment.*
Der Akzent liegt auf der vorletzten Silbe. *The accent is on the penultimate syllable.*
Die Antwort auf unser Problem liegt ja auf der Hand. *The answer to our problem is quite obvious.*
Die breite, sonnige Terrasse liegt nach Süden. *The wide, sunny patio faces south.*
Nichts lag ihm ferner als der Gedanke, Priester zu werden. *Nothing was further from his mind than the thought of becoming a priest.*
Hast du dein Portemonnaie zu Hause liegen lassen? *Did you leave your wallet at home?*
Ich habe mein Heft liegen lassen. *I forgot my notebook.*
Das eine Fenster liegt zum Garten, das andere zur Straße. *The one window faces the yard, the other the street.*
Fastfood liegt mir immer schwer im Magen. *Fast food always sits heavy on my stomach.*
Bei Stephanie liegt die Tischdecke nie falsch. *At Stephanie's, the tablecloth is never crooked.*
Es liegt mir fern, Ihren Vorschlag zu kritisieren. *Far be it from me to criticize your suggestion.*
Die Frage liegt nahe, warum der Kanzler diese Meinung überhaupt vertritt. *The obvious question is why the chancellor holds this opinion at all.*
Ihr Schicksal liegt in Ihrer Hand. *Your destiny is in your hands.*
Da liegst du richtig. (*colloquial*) *You're right about that.*
Du liegst ganz falsch, wenn du das glaubst. (*colloquial*) *You are quite mistaken if you believe that.*
In der Kürze liegt die Würze! (PROVERB) *Brevity is the soul of wit!*
Im Wein liegt die Wahrheit. (PROVERB) *In wine there is truth.* / In vino veritas.

PRESENT

ich lobe	wir loben
du lobst	ihr lobt
Sie loben	Sie loben
er/sie/es lobt	sie loben

SIMPLE PAST

ich lobte	wir lobten
du lobtest	ihr lobtet
Sie lobten	Sie lobten
er/sie/es lobte	sie lobten

FUTURE

ich werde	wir werden	loben
du wirst	ihr werdet	
Sie werden	Sie werden	
er/sie/es wird	sie werden	

PRESENT SUBJUNCTIVE I

ich lobe	wir loben
du lobest	ihr lobet
Sie loben	Sie loben
er/sie/es lobe	sie loben

PRESENT SUBJUNCTIVE II

ich lobte	wir lobten
du lobtest	ihr lobtet
Sie lobten	Sie lobten
er/sie/es lobte	sie lobten

FUTURE SUBJUNCTIVE I

ich werde	wir werden	loben
du werdest	ihr werdet	
Sie werden	Sie werden	
er/sie/es werde	sie werden	

FUTURE SUBJUNCTIVE II

ich würde	wir würden	loben
du würdest	ihr würdet	
Sie würden	Sie würden	
er/sie/es würde	sie würden	

PRESENT PERFECT

ich habe	wir haben	gelobt
du hast	ihr habt	
Sie haben	Sie haben	
er/sie/es hat	sie haben	

PAST PERFECT

ich hatte	wir hatten	gelobt
du hattest	ihr hattet	
Sie hatten	Sie hatten	
er/sie/es hatte	sie hatten	

FUTURE PERFECT

ich werde	wir werden	gelobt haben
du wirst	ihr werdet	
Sie werden	Sie werden	
er/sie/es wird	sie werden	

PAST SUBJUNCTIVE I

ich habe	wir haben	gelobt
du habest	ihr habet	
Sie haben	Sie haben	
er/sie/es habe	sie haben	

PAST SUBJUNCTIVE II

ich hätte	wir hätten	gelobt
du hättest	ihr hättet	
Sie hätten	Sie hätten	
er/sie/es hätte	sie hätten	

FUTURE PERFECT SUBJUNCTIVE I

ich werde	wir werden	gelobt haben
du werdest	ihr werdet	
Sie werden	Sie werden	
er/sie/es werde	sie werden	

FUTURE PERFECT SUBJUNCTIVE II

ich würde	wir würden	gelobt haben
du würdest	ihr würdet	
Sie würden	Sie würden	
er/sie/es würde	sie würden	

COMMANDS lob(e)! lobt! loben Sie!

PRESENT PARTICIPLE lobend

Usage

Petersen lobt die Arbeit von Franken.	*Petersen praises Franken's work.*
Meiers lobte die Anstrengungen der Gemeinde.	*Meiers lauded the community's efforts.*
„Das klingt wunderschön, Maria!" lobte die Klavierlehrerin.	*"That sounds wonderful, Maria!" exulted the piano teacher.*
Gelobt sei Jesus Christus. (*formulaic*)	*Jesus Christ be praised.*
Loben und ermutigen Sie Ihre Kinder.	*Praise and encourage your children.*
Mein Englischlehrer lobt nie.	*My English teacher never gives praise.*
Die Rezensenten haben die neue Tolkien-Ausgabe von A. Smith gelobt.	*The reviewers have praised the new Tolkien edition by A. Smith.*
Ich wollte es weder tadeln noch loben.	*I didn't want to criticize or praise it.*
Werner konnte das Stück allerdings nicht uneingeschränkt loben.	*However, Werner was unable to offer unqualified praise for the piece.*
Man soll den Tag nicht vor dem Abend loben. (PROVERB)	*Don't count your chickens before they're hatched.*

RELATED VERBS an·geloben, entloben, geloben, verloben

296 lohnen *to reward, remunerate, compensate, pay*

lohnt · lohnte · gelohnt

regular weak verb

PRESENT

ich lohne	wir lohnen
du lohnst	ihr lohnt
Sie lohnen	Sie lohnen
er/sie/es lohnt	sie lohnen

SIMPLE PAST

ich lohnte	wir lohnten
du lohntest	ihr lohntet
Sie lohnten	Sie lohnten
er/sie/es lohnte	sie lohnten

FUTURE

ich werde	wir werden	lohnen
du wirst	ihr werdet	
Sie werden	Sie werden	
er/sie/es wird	sie werden	

PRESENT SUBJUNCTIVE I

ich lohne	wir lohnen
du lohnest	ihr lohnet
Sie lohnen	Sie lohnen
er/sie/es lohne	sie lohnen

PRESENT SUBJUNCTIVE II

ich lohnte	wir lohnten
du lohntest	ihr lohntet
Sie lohnten	Sie lohnten
er/sie/es lohnte	sie lohnten

FUTURE SUBJUNCTIVE I

ich werde	wir werden	lohnen
du werdest	ihr werdet	
Sie werden	Sie werden	
er/sie/es werde	sie werden	

FUTURE SUBJUNCTIVE II

ich würde	wir würden	lohnen
du würdest	ihr würdet	
Sie würden	Sie würden	
er/sie/es würde	sie würden	

PRESENT PERFECT

ich habe	wir haben	gelohnt
du hast	ihr habt	
Sie haben	Sie haben	
er/sie/es hat	sie haben	

PAST PERFECT

ich hatte	wir hatten	gelohnt
du hattest	ihr hattet	
Sie hatten	Sie hatten	
er/sie/es hatte	sie hatten	

FUTURE PERFECT

ich werde	wir werden	gelohnt haben
du wirst	ihr werdet	
Sie werden	Sie werden	
er/sie/es wird	sie werden	

PAST SUBJUNCTIVE I

ich habe	wir haben	gelohnt
du habest	ihr habet	
Sie haben	Sie haben	
er/sie/es habe	sie haben	

PAST SUBJUNCTIVE II

ich hätte	wir hätten	gelohnt
du hättest	ihr hättet	
Sie hätten	Sie hätten	
er/sie/es hätte	sie hätten	

FUTURE PERFECT SUBJUNCTIVE I

ich werde	wir werden	gelohnt haben
du werdest	ihr werdet	
Sie werden	Sie werden	
er/sie/es werde	sie werden	

FUTURE PERFECT SUBJUNCTIVE II

ich würde	wir würden	gelohnt haben
du würdest	ihr würdet	
Sie würden	Sie würden	
er/sie/es würde	sie würden	

COMMANDS lohn(e)! lohnt! lohnen Sie!

PRESENT PARTICIPLE lohnend

Usage

Lauter Beifall hat ihm seine Mühe gelohnt. — *Loud applause rewarded him for his trouble.*
Gott lohne es dir. — *May God reward you for it.*
Der König lohnte ihr die Rettung mit Goldmünzen. — *The king remunerated her for the rescue with gold coins.*
Die Mitglieder lohnten dem Mann seine Arbeit. — *The members compensated the man for his work.*
Lohnst du mir also für meine schlaflosen Nächte? (Schiller) — *Are you compensating me for my sleepless nights?*

sich lohnen *to be worthwhile, pay off*

Es hat sich nicht gelohnt, diesen Umweg zu fahren. — *It wasn't worth it to take this detour.*
Es lohnt sich nicht, Geld in jedem Land zu tauschen. — *It isn't worth it to exchange currency in every country.*
Der Aufwand lohnt sich in diesem Fall. — *The effort is worthwhile in this case.*
Diese Investition wird sich lohnen. — *This investment will pay off.*
Endlich haben sich meine Bemühungen gelohnt. — *Finally, my efforts have paid off.*

RELATED VERBS belohnen, entlohnen, verlohnen

297 löschen

to put out, extinguish; liquidate; delete, erase; quench

regular weak verb — **löscht · löschte · gelöscht**

PRESENT

ich lösche	wir löschen
du löschst	ihr löscht
Sie löschen	Sie löschen
er/sie/es löscht	sie löschen

SIMPLE PAST

ich löschte	wir löschten
du löschtest	ihr löschtet
Sie löschten	Sie löschten
er/sie/es löschte	sie löschten

FUTURE

ich werde	wir werden	löschen
du wirst	ihr werdet	
Sie werden	Sie werden	
er/sie/es wird	sie werden	

PRESENT SUBJUNCTIVE I

ich lösche	wir löschen
du löschest	ihr löschet
Sie löschen	Sie löschen
er/sie/es lösche	sie löschen

PRESENT SUBJUNCTIVE II

ich löschte	wir löschten
du löschtest	ihr löschtet
Sie löschten	Sie löschten
er/sie/es löschte	sie löschten

FUTURE SUBJUNCTIVE I

ich werde	wir werden	löschen
du werdest	ihr werdet	
Sie werden	Sie werden	
er/sie/es werde	sie werden	

FUTURE SUBJUNCTIVE II

ich würde	wir würden	löschen
du würdest	ihr würdet	
Sie würden	Sie würden	
er/sie/es würde	sie würden	

PRESENT PERFECT

ich habe	wir haben	gelöscht
du hast	ihr habt	
Sie haben	Sie haben	
er/sie/es hat	sie haben	

PAST PERFECT

ich hatte	wir hatten	gelöscht
du hattest	ihr hattet	
Sie hatten	Sie hatten	
er/sie/es hatte	sie hatten	

FUTURE PERFECT

ich werde	wir werden	gelöscht haben
du wirst	ihr werdet	
Sie werden	Sie werden	
er/sie/es wird	sie werden	

PAST SUBJUNCTIVE I

ich habe	wir haben	gelöscht
du habest	ihr habet	
Sie haben	Sie haben	
er/sie/es habe	sie haben	

PAST SUBJUNCTIVE II

ich hätte	wir hätten	gelöscht
du hättest	ihr hättet	
Sie hätten	Sie hätten	
er/sie/es hätte	sie hätten	

FUTURE PERFECT SUBJUNCTIVE I

ich werde	wir werden	gelöscht haben
du werdest	ihr werdet	
Sie werden	Sie werden	
er/sie/es werde	sie werden	

FUTURE PERFECT SUBJUNCTIVE II

ich würde	wir würden	gelöscht haben
du würdest	ihr würdet	
Sie würden	Sie würden	
er/sie/es würde	sie würden	

COMMANDS lösch(e)! löscht! löschen Sie!

PRESENT PARTICIPLE löschend

Usage

Der Brand konnte schnell gelöscht werden. — *They were able to put the fire out quickly.*

Nachdem Sie die Flamme gelöscht haben, lassen Sie den Wachs um den Docht abkühlen. — *After you have extinguished the flame, let the wax around the wick cool.*

Ich habe mein Konto löschen lassen. — *I had my account liquidated.*

Wolltest du die System-Dateien wirklich löschen? — *Did you really want to delete the system files?*

Jan hat seinen Durst mit einem Bier gelöscht. — *Jan quenched his thirst with a beer.*

NOTE When **löschen** means "to burn out, fizzle out, go out," it is typically strong and takes **sein** as its auxiliary: **lischt, losch, ist geloschen**. This usage is not common in modern German.

löschen (with sein) *to burn out, fizzle out, go out*

Das restliche Feuer losch und die Kälte kroch ihnen durch Mark und Bein. — *The remaining fire burned out and they were chilled to the bone.*

RELATED VERBS ab·löschen, aus·löschen, verlöschen; *see also* **erlöschen** (167)

298 lösen *to solve, resolve; loosen, release; break off; redeem*

löst · löste · gelöst

regular weak verb

PRESENT

ich löse	wir lösen
du löst	ihr löst
Sie lösen	Sie lösen
er/sie/es löst	sie lösen

SIMPLE PAST

ich löste	wir lösten
du löstest	ihr löstet
Sie lösten	Sie lösten
er/sie/es löste	sie lösten

FUTURE

ich werde	wir werden	lösen
du wirst	ihr werdet	
Sie werden	Sie werden	
er/sie/es wird	sie werden	

PRESENT SUBJUNCTIVE I

ich löse	wir lösen
du lösest	ihr löset
Sie lösen	Sie lösen
er/sie/es löse	sie lösen

PRESENT SUBJUNCTIVE II

ich löste	wir lösten
du löstest	ihr löstet
Sie lösten	Sie lösten
er/sie/es löste	sie lösten

FUTURE SUBJUNCTIVE I

ich werde	wir werden	lösen
du werdest	ihr werdet	
Sie werden	Sie werden	
er/sie/es werde	sie werden	

FUTURE SUBJUNCTIVE II

ich würde	wir würden	lösen
du würdest	ihr würdet	
Sie würden	Sie würden	
er/sie/es würde	sie würden	

PRESENT PERFECT

ich habe	wir haben	gelöst
du hast	ihr habt	
Sie haben	Sie haben	
er/sie/es hat	sie haben	

PAST PERFECT

ich hatte	wir hatten	gelöst
du hattest	ihr hattet	
Sie hatten	Sie hatten	
er/sie/es hatte	sie hatten	

FUTURE PERFECT

ich werde	wir werden	gelöst haben
du wirst	ihr werdet	
Sie werden	Sie werden	
er/sie/es wird	sie werden	

PAST SUBJUNCTIVE I

ich habe	wir haben	gelöst
du habest	ihr habet	
Sie haben	Sie haben	
er/sie/es habe	sie haben	

PAST SUBJUNCTIVE II

ich hätte	wir hätten	gelöst
du hättest	ihr hättet	
Sie hätten	Sie hätten	
er/sie/es hätte	sie hätten	

FUTURE PERFECT SUBJUNCTIVE I

ich werde	wir werden	gelöst haben
du werdest	ihr werdet	
Sie werden	Sie werden	
er/sie/es werde	sie werden	

FUTURE PERFECT SUBJUNCTIVE II

ich würde	wir würden	gelöst haben
du würdest	ihr würdet	
Sie würden	Sie würden	
er/sie/es würde	sie würden	

COMMANDS lös(e)! löst! lösen Sie!

PRESENT PARTICIPLE lösend

Usage

Das Theaterstück schildert ein Dilemma, das das Publikum selbst lösen muss. — *The play presents a dilemma that the audience itself must resolve.*

Ich will keine Rätsel mehr lösen müssen! — *I don't want to have to solve any more riddles!*

Kannst du diesen Knoten lösen? — *Can you loosen this knot?*

1802 löste er eine vierjährige Verlobung mit Minna Beck und heiratete Minnas Schwester Michaela. — *In 1802, he broke off a four-year engagement with Minna Beck and married Minna's sister Michaela.*

Wo kann man Pfandflaschen lösen? — *Where can you redeem deposit bottles?*

sich lösen *to come loose; dissolve*

Die Schuhriemen hatten sich im Laufe des Tages gelöst. — *The shoestrings had come loose in the course of the day.*

Ihre Beziehung löste sich nach einem Jahr. — *Their relationship fell apart after one year.*

Wie schnell löst sich Salz in Wasser? — *How quickly will salt dissolve in water?*

RELATED VERBS ab·lösen, auf·lösen, aus·lösen, ein·lösen, erlösen, los·lösen, nach·lösen

strong verb

lügt · log · gelogen

PRESENT

ich lüge	wir lügen
du lügst	ihr lügt
Sie lügen	Sie lügen
er/sie/es lügt	sie lügen

SIMPLE PAST

ich log	wir logen
du logst	ihr logt
Sie logen	Sie logen
er/sie/es log	sie logen

FUTURE

ich werde	wir werden	lügen
du wirst	ihr werdet	
Sie werden	Sie werden	
er/sie/es wird	sie werden	

PRESENT SUBJUNCTIVE I

ich lüge	wir lügen
du lügest	ihr lüget
Sie lügen	Sie lügen
er/sie/es lüge	sie lügen

PRESENT SUBJUNCTIVE II

ich löge	wir lögen
du lögest	ihr löget
Sie lögen	Sie lögen
er/sie/es löge	sie lögen

FUTURE SUBJUNCTIVE I

ich werde	wir werden	lügen
du werdest	ihr werdet	
Sie werden	Sie werden	
er/sie/es werde	sie werden	

FUTURE SUBJUNCTIVE II

ich würde	wir würden	lügen
du würdest	ihr würdet	
Sie würden	Sie würden	
er/sie/es würde	sie würden	

PRESENT PERFECT

ich habe	wir haben	gelogen
du hast	ihr habt	
Sie haben	Sie haben	
er/sie/es hat	sie haben	

PAST PERFECT

ich hatte	wir hatten	gelogen
du hattest	ihr hattet	
Sie hatten	Sie hatten	
er/sie/es hatte	sie hatten	

FUTURE PERFECT

ich werde	wir werden	gelogen haben
du wirst	ihr werdet	
Sie werden	Sie werden	
er/sie/es wird	sie werden	

PAST SUBJUNCTIVE I

ich habe	wir haben	gelogen
du habest	ihr habet	
Sie haben	Sie haben	
er/sie/es habe	sie haben	

PAST SUBJUNCTIVE II

ich hätte	wir hätten	gelogen
du hättest	ihr hättet	
Sie hätten	Sie hätten	
er/sie/es hätte	sie hätten	

FUTURE PERFECT SUBJUNCTIVE I

ich werde	wir werden	gelogen haben
du werdest	ihr werdet	
Sie werden	Sie werden	
er/sie/es werde	sie werden	

FUTURE PERFECT SUBJUNCTIVE II

ich würde	wir würden	gelogen haben
du würdest	ihr würdet	
Sie würden	Sie würden	
er/sie/es würde	sie würden	

COMMANDS lüg(e)! lügt! lügen Sie!

PRESENT PARTICIPLE lügend

Usage

Die Konzerne logen über ihre illegalen Investitionen. — *The companies lied about their illegal investments.*

„Warum hast du gelogen?" — *"Why did you lie?"*

„Ich musste lügen." — *"I had to lie."*

Es wurde viel gelogen und betrogen. — *There was a lot of lying and deception.*

Das Kind schaut die Frau an, als ob sie löge. — *The child is looking at the woman as if she were lying.*

Lügt ihr oder lügt er? — *Are you lying or is he lying?*

Nach dem Tod ihres Kindes hat sie immer öfter über ihre Gefühle gelogen. — *After the death of her child, she lied about her feelings more and more often.*

Herr Petersen lügt seit sieben Jahren darüber. — *Mr. Petersen has been lying for seven years about it.*

Martina log, um ihre Freundin nicht zu beleidigen. — *Martina lied in order not to insult her friend.*

Es wäre gelogen zu sagen, dass es mir nicht gefallen hat. — *It would be lying if I said I didn't like it.*

Wir glauben, der Politiker lügt nach Strich und Faden. — *We think the politician is lying through his teeth.*

Das ist gelogen! — *That's a lie!*

RELATED VERBS an·lügen, belügen, erlügen

machen *to make, do; construct; cause; constitute; come to*

macht · machte · gemacht regular weak verb

MORE USAGE SENTENCES WITH machen

Viel Arbeit macht hungrig. — *A lot of work makes you hungry.*
Frau Detmold hat es uns klar gemacht, dass wir bei ihr nicht rauchen dürfen. — *Mrs. Detmold made it clear to us that we can't smoke in her house.*
Am Samstag möchten wir einen Tagesausflug nach Potsdam machen. — *On Saturday, we'd like to make a day trip to Potsdam.*
Möchtet ihr einen Spaziergang machen? — *Would you like to go for a walk?*
Warum machst du so ein Gesicht? — *Why are you making such a face?*
Ich hatte mir darüber oft Gedanken gemacht. — *I'd often pondered that.*
Der Bericht hat uns bewusst gemacht, dass die Umwelt gefährdet ist. — *The report made us conscious of the fact that the environment is in peril.*
Die Reformatoren machten guten Gebrauch von traditionellen Genres. — *The reformers made good use of traditional genres.*
Der junge Student machte sich diese Auffassung zu eigen. — *The young student made this viewpoint his own.*
Das Buch heißt *Programmierung leicht gemacht.* — *The book is called* Programming Made Easy.
Herr Oeynhaim machte einen freundlichen Eindruck auf seine neuen Nachbarn. — *Mr. Oeynhaim made a friendly impression on his new neighbors.*
Das Kind sagte einfach: "Das mache ich nicht." — *The child said simply, "I won't do that."*
Was kann man machen? — *What's to do?*
Da kann man nichts machen. — *You can't do anything about it.*
Wie wird's gemacht? — *How is it done?*
Macht, dass ihr ins Bett kommt! — *See to it that you get to bed!*
Es gibt in einem kleinen Dorf nicht viel zu machen. — *There's not a lot to do in a small village.*
Die Handschuhe sind aus Rindsleder gemacht. — *The gloves are made from cow leather.*
„Was macht das zusammen?" — *"How much is it altogether?"*
„Das macht zehn Euro zwanzig." — *"That comes to 10 euros 20."*

sich machen + adjective *to make oneself/itself*

Ein seltsames Geräusch machte sich bemerkbar in der Ecke des Zimmers. — *A peculiar sound became noticeable in the corner of the room.*
Mach dich nicht so breit! — *Don't take up so much space!*
Mach dich fit! — *Get in shape! / Get fit!*

IDIOMATIC EXPRESSIONS

Macht das was? — *Does that matter?*
Das macht nichts. — *That doesn't matter. / That's all right.*
Es macht ihr nichts. — *She doesn't mind.*
Mit diesem diplomatischen Schritt wird Geschichte gemacht. — *With this diplomatic step, history is being made.*
Roberts Familie hat ihm Mut gemacht, im Ausland weiter zu studieren. — *Robert's family encouraged him to continue his university studies abroad.*
Erich hat nur Spaß gemacht. — *Erich was only joking.*
Surfen macht zwar Spaß, aber ich gehe lieber windsurfen. — *Surfing is fun, but I prefer to go windsurfing.*
Karl-Heinz hat die Arbeit schon fertig gemacht. — *Karl-Heinz has already finished the work.*
Der Verlag hat eine Tolkien-Ausgabe von A. Smith bekannt gemacht. — *The publisher has announced a Tolkien edition by A. Smith.*
Hans machte sich auf den Weg nach Hause. — *Hans set out for home.*
Liebe macht blind. (PROVERB) — *Love is blind.*

to make, do; construct; cause; constitute; come to **machen** 300

regular weak verb **macht · machte · gemacht**

PRESENT

ich mache	wir machen
du machst	ihr macht
Sie machen	Sie machen
er/sie/es macht	sie machen

SIMPLE PAST

ich machte	wir machten
du machtest	ihr machtet
Sie machten	Sie machten
er/sie/es machte	sie machten

FUTURE

ich werde	wir werden	machen
du wirst	ihr werdet	
Sie werden	Sie werden	
er/sie/es wird	sie werden	

PRESENT SUBJUNCTIVE I

ich mache	wir machen
du machest	ihr machet
Sie machen	Sie machen
er/sie/es mache	sie machen

PRESENT SUBJUNCTIVE II

ich machte	wir machten
du machtest	ihr machtet
Sie machten	Sie machten
er/sie/es machte	sie machten

FUTURE SUBJUNCTIVE I

ich werde	wir werden	machen
du werdest	ihr werdet	
Sie werden	Sie werden	
er/sie/es werde	sie werden	

FUTURE SUBJUNCTIVE II

ich würde	wir würden	machen
du würdest	ihr würdet	
Sie würden	Sie würden	
er/sie/es würde	sie würden	

COMMANDS mach(e)! macht! machen Sie!

PRESENT PARTICIPLE machend

PRESENT PERFECT

ich habe	wir haben	gemacht
du hast	ihr habt	
Sie haben	Sie haben	
er/sie/es hat	sie haben	

PAST PERFECT

ich hatte	wir hatten	gemacht
du hattest	ihr hattet	
Sie hatten	Sie hatten	
er/sie/es hatte	sie hatten	

FUTURE PERFECT

ich werde	wir werden	gemacht haben
du wirst	ihr werdet	
Sie werden	Sie werden	
er/sie/es wird	sie werden	

PAST SUBJUNCTIVE I

ich habe	wir haben	gemacht
du habest	ihr habet	
Sie haben	Sie haben	
er/sie/es habe	sie haben	

PAST SUBJUNCTIVE II

ich hätte	wir hätten	gemacht
du hättest	ihr hättet	
Sie hätten	Sie hätten	
er/sie/es hätte	sie hätten	

FUTURE PERFECT SUBJUNCTIVE I

ich werde	wir werden	gemacht haben
du werdest	ihr werdet	
Sie werden	Sie werden	
er/sie/es werde	sie werden	

FUTURE PERFECT SUBJUNCTIVE II

ich würde	wir würden	gemacht haben
du würdest	ihr würdet	
Sie würden	Sie würden	
er/sie/es würde	sie würden	

Usage

Ich mache diesmal eine Ausnahme.	*I'll make an exception this time.*
Die Bemerkungen des Präsidenten haben uns wütend gemacht.	*The president's comments made us furious.*
Lisa sagt, sie hätte bloß einen Fehler gemacht.	*Lisa says she just made a mistake.*
Mama macht die Betten jeden Tag.	*Mama makes the beds every day.*
Ihr Plan machte keinen Sinn.	*Her plan made no sense.*
Was macht ihr morgen Abend?	*What are you doing tomorrow evening?*
Was machen Sie beruflich?	*What do you do professionally?*
Wollen wir eine Pause machen?	*Do we want to take a break?*
Die Studentinnen und Studenten haben alle gute Erfahrungen gemacht.	*The students have all had good experiences.*

RELATED VERBS ab·machen, auf·machen, bereit·machen, ein·machen, fest·machen, frei·machen, gut·machen, irre·machen, kehrt·machen, mit·machen, mobil·machen, vermachen, zu·machen; *see also* **an·machen** (13), **aus·machen** (36)

301 mahlen *to grind, mill*

mahlt · mahlte · gemahlen

regular weak verb/strong verb

PRESENT

ich mahle	wir mahlen
du mahlst	ihr mahlt
Sie mahlen	Sie mahlen
er/sie/es mahlt	sie mahlen

SIMPLE PAST

ich mahlte	wir mahlten
du mahltest	ihr mahltet
Sie mahlten	Sie mahlten
er/sie/es mahlte	sie mahlten

FUTURE

ich werde	wir werden	mahlen
du wirst	ihr werdet	
Sie werden	Sie werden	
er/sie/es wird	sie werden	

PRESENT SUBJUNCTIVE I

ich mahle	wir mahlen
du mahlest	ihr mahlet
Sie mahlen	Sie mahlen
er/sie/es mahle	sie mahlen

PRESENT SUBJUNCTIVE II

ich mahlte	wir mahlten
du mahltest	ihr mahltet
Sie mahlten	Sie mahlten
er/sie/es mahlte	sie mahlten

FUTURE SUBJUNCTIVE I

ich werde	wir werden	mahlen
du werdest	ihr werdet	
Sie werden	Sie werden	
er/sie/es werde	sie werden	

FUTURE SUBJUNCTIVE II

ich würde	wir würden	mahlen
du würdest	ihr würdet	
Sie würden	Sie würden	
er/sie/es würde	sie würden	

PRESENT PERFECT

ich habe	wir haben	gemahlen
du hast	ihr habt	
Sie haben	Sie haben	
er/sie/es hat	sie haben	

PAST PERFECT

ich hatte	wir hatten	gemahlen
du hattest	ihr hattet	
Sie hatten	Sie hatten	
er/sie/es hatte	sie hatten	

FUTURE PERFECT

ich werde	wir werden	gemahlen haben
du wirst	ihr werdet	
Sie werden	Sie werden	
er/sie/es wird	sie werden	

PAST SUBJUNCTIVE I

ich habe	wir haben	gemahlen
du habest	ihr habet	
Sie haben	Sie haben	
er/sie/es habe	sie haben	

PAST SUBJUNCTIVE II

ich hätte	wir hätten	gemahlen
du hättest	ihr hättet	
Sie hätten	Sie hätten	
er/sie/es hätte	sie hätten	

FUTURE PERFECT SUBJUNCTIVE I

ich werde	wir werden	gemahlen haben
du werdest	ihr werdet	
Sie werden	Sie werden	
er/sie/es werde	sie werden	

FUTURE PERFECT SUBJUNCTIVE II

ich würde	wir würden	gemahlen haben
du würdest	ihr würdet	
Sie würden	Sie würden	
er/sie/es würde	sie würden	

COMMANDS mahl(e)! mahlt! mahlen Sie!

PRESENT PARTICIPLE mahlend

NOTE The verb **mahlen** is a regular weak verb but has a strong past participle.

Usage

Jeden Morgen mahlt er seine fair gehandelten Kaffeebohnen und kocht sich einen starken Kaffee.
Every morning, he grinds his Fair Trade coffee beans and makes himself a strong coffee.

Herr Müllermann mahlte Weizen- und Gerstenmehl.
Mr. Müllermann milled wheat and barley flour.

Mögen Sie frisch gemahlenen Pfeffer?
Do you like freshly ground pepper?

Getreide wurde in einer Wassermühle gemahlen.
Grain was ground in a watermill.

Den Stangenzimt zu Pulver mahlen und auf den gekochten Reis streuen. (RECIPE)
Grind the cinnamon stick to a powder and sprinkle it onto the cooked rice.

Kaufst du fertig gemahlenen Kaffee oder mahlst du die Bohnen selbst?
Do you buy pre-ground coffee or do you grind the beans yourself?

Wer zuerst kommt, mahlt zuerst. (PROVERB)
First come, first served.

Eine Mühle kann nicht mit dem Wasser von gestern mahlen. (PROVERB)
A mill cannot grind with water that has passed by.

RELATED VERBS aus·mahlen, durch·mahlen, zermahlen

regular weak verb **malt · malte · gemalt**

PRESENT

ich male	wir malen
du malst	ihr malt
Sie malen	Sie malen
er/sie/es malt	sie malen

SIMPLE PAST

ich malte	wir malten
du maltest	ihr maltet
Sie malten	Sie malten
er/sie/es malte	sie malten

FUTURE

ich werde	wir werden	malen
du wirst	ihr werdet	
Sie werden	Sie werden	
er/sie/es wird	sie werden	

PRESENT SUBJUNCTIVE I

ich male	wir malen
du malest	ihr malet
Sie malen	Sie malen
er/sie/es male	sie malen

PRESENT SUBJUNCTIVE II

ich malte	wir malten
du maltest	ihr maltet
Sie malten	Sie malten
er/sie/es malte	sie malten

FUTURE SUBJUNCTIVE I

ich werde	wir werden	malen
du werdest	ihr werdet	
Sie werden	Sie werden	
er/sie/es werde	sie werden	

FUTURE SUBJUNCTIVE II

ich würde	wir würden	malen
du würdest	ihr würdet	
Sie würden	Sie würden	
er/sie/es würde	sie würden	

PRESENT PERFECT

ich habe	wir haben	gemalt
du hast	ihr habt	
Sie haben	Sie haben	
er/sie/es hat	sie haben	

PAST PERFECT

ich hatte	wir hatten	gemalt
du hattest	ihr hattet	
Sie hatten	Sie hatten	
er/sie/es hatte	sie hatten	

FUTURE PERFECT

ich werde	wir werden	gemalt haben
du wirst	ihr werdet	
Sie werden	Sie werden	
er/sie/es wird	sie werden	

PAST SUBJUNCTIVE I

ich habe	wir haben	gemalt
du habest	ihr habet	
Sie haben	Sie haben	
er/sie/es habe	sie haben	

PAST SUBJUNCTIVE II

ich hätte	wir hätten	gemalt
du hättest	ihr hättet	
Sie hätten	Sie hätten	
er/sie/es hätte	sie hätten	

FUTURE PERFECT SUBJUNCTIVE I

ich werde	wir werden	gemalt haben
du werdest	ihr werdet	
Sie werden	Sie werden	
er/sie/es werde	sie werden	

FUTURE PERFECT SUBJUNCTIVE II

ich würde	wir würden	gemalt haben
du würdest	ihr würdet	
Sie würden	Sie würden	
er/sie/es würde	sie würden	

COMMANDS mal(e)! malt! malen Sie!

PRESENT PARTICIPLE malend

Usage

Als Kind malte sie Bilder von fantastischen Landschaften und exotischen Tieren. — *As a child, she painted pictures of fantastical landscapes and exotic animals.*

Wer hat dieses Porträt der Herzogin Helene Luise von Orleans gemalt? — *Who painted this portrait of Duchess Helen Louise of Orleans?*

Es macht ihm großen Spaß zu malen. — *Painting is great fun for him.*

Der Wissenschaftler malt ein schwarzes Bild der Zukunft. — *The scientist paints a gloomy picture of the future.*

Der Politiker weiß, komplexe Situationen schwarz-weiß zu malen. — *The politician knows how to depict complex situations in black and white.*

Malst du gern? — *Do you like to paint?*

sich malen *to be depicted/reflected*

In ihren Augen malte sich Angst. — *The very image of fear was reflected in her eyes.*

RELATED VERBS ab·malen, an·malen, auf·malen, aus·malen, bemalen, nach·malen, übermalen, untermalen, vermalen

303 **meiden** *to avoid, shun*

meidet · mied · gemieden strong verb

PRESENT

ich meide	wir meiden
du meidest	ihr meidet
Sie meiden	Sie meiden
er/sie/es meidet	sie meiden

SIMPLE PAST

ich mied	wir mieden
du miedst	ihr miedet
Sie mieden	Sie mieden
er/sie/es mied	sie mieden

FUTURE

ich werde	wir werden	meiden
du wirst	ihr werdet	
Sie werden	Sie werden	
er/sie/es wird	sie werden	

PRESENT SUBJUNCTIVE I

ich meide	wir meiden
du meidest	ihr meidet
Sie meiden	Sie meiden
er/sie/es meide	sie meiden

PRESENT SUBJUNCTIVE II

ich miede	wir mieden
du miedest	ihr miedet
Sie mieden	Sie mieden
er/sie/es miede	sie mieden

FUTURE SUBJUNCTIVE I

ich werde	wir werden	meiden
du werdest	ihr werdet	
Sie werden	Sie werden	
er/sie/es werde	sie werden	

FUTURE SUBJUNCTIVE II

ich würde	wir würden	meiden
du würdest	ihr würdet	
Sie würden	Sie würden	
er/sie/es würde	sie würden	

PRESENT PERFECT

ich habe	wir haben	gemieden
du hast	ihr habt	
Sie haben	Sie haben	
er/sie/es hat	sie haben	

PAST PERFECT

ich hatte	wir hatten	gemieden
du hattest	ihr hattet	
Sie hatten	Sie hatten	
er/sie/es hatte	sie hatten	

FUTURE PERFECT

ich werde	wir werden	gemieden haben
du wirst	ihr werdet	
Sie werden	Sie werden	
er/sie/es wird	sie werden	

PAST SUBJUNCTIVE I

ich habe	wir haben	gemieden
du habest	ihr habet	
Sie haben	Sie haben	
er/sie/es habe	sie haben	

PAST SUBJUNCTIVE II

ich hätte	wir hätten	gemieden
du hättest	ihr hättet	
Sie hätten	Sie hätten	
er/sie/es hätte	sie hätten	

FUTURE PERFECT SUBJUNCTIVE I

ich werde	wir werden	gemieden haben
du werdest	ihr werdet	
Sie werden	Sie werden	
er/sie/es werde	sie werden	

FUTURE PERFECT SUBJUNCTIVE II

ich würde	wir würden	gemieden haben
du würdest	ihr würdet	
Sie würden	Sie würden	
er/sie/es würde	sie würden	

COMMANDS meide! meidet! meiden Sie!

PRESENT PARTICIPLE meidend

Usage

Kalium und Phosphor müssen von Nierenkranken gemieden werden. — *Potassium and phosphorus must be avoided by those with kidney disease.*

Rolf meidet immer offenen Konflikt. — *Rolf always avoids open conflict.*

Der Ort, an dem er sich umbrachte, wird wie die Pest gemieden. — *The place where he committed suicide is avoided like the plague.*

Immer mehr Menschen meiden gentechnisch veränderte Organismen in Lebensmitteln. — *More and more people are staying away from genetically modified organisms in foods.*

Dieses Reiseziel sollte wegen des Krieges gemieden werden. — *This travel destination should be avoided because of the war.*

Andere Kinder mieden ihn. — *Other children shunned him.*

Warum meidest du mich? — *Why are you avoiding me?*

Es war Vollmond, und der Schlaf mied mich. — *There was a full moon, and sleep eluded me.*

Es liegt mir fern, das Licht der Öffentlichkeit zu meiden! — *Far be it from me to avoid the limelight!*

RELATED VERB vermeiden

regular weak verb **meint · meinte · gemeint**

PRESENT

ich meine	wir meinen
du meinst	ihr meint
Sie meinen	Sie meinen
er/sie/es meint	sie meinen

SIMPLE PAST

ich meinte	wir meinten
du meintest	ihr meintet
Sie meinten	Sie meinten
er/sie/es meinte	sie meinten

FUTURE

ich werde	wir werden	meinen
du wirst	ihr werdet	
Sie werden	Sie werden	
er/sie/es wird	sie werden	

PRESENT SUBJUNCTIVE I

ich meine	wir meinen
du meinest	ihr meinet
Sie meinen	Sie meinen
er/sie/es meine	sie meinen

PRESENT SUBJUNCTIVE II

ich meinte	wir meinten
du meintest	ihr meintet
Sie meinten	Sie meinten
er/sie/es meinte	sie meinten

FUTURE SUBJUNCTIVE I

ich werde	wir werden	meinen
du werdest	ihr werdet	
Sie werden	Sie werden	
er/sie/es werde	sie werden	

FUTURE SUBJUNCTIVE II

ich würde	wir würden	meinen
du würdest	ihr würdet	
Sie würden	Sie würden	
er/sie/es würde	sie würden	

PRESENT PERFECT

ich habe	wir haben	gemeint
du hast	ihr habt	
Sie haben	Sie haben	
er/sie/es hat	sie haben	

PAST PERFECT

ich hatte	wir hatten	gemeint
du hattest	ihr hattet	
Sie hatten	Sie hatten	
er/sie/es hatte	sie hatten	

FUTURE PERFECT

ich werde	wir werden	gemeint haben
du wirst	ihr werdet	
Sie werden	Sie werden	
er/sie/es wird	sie werden	

PAST SUBJUNCTIVE I

ich habe	wir haben	gemeint
du habest	ihr habet	
Sie haben	Sie haben	
er/sie/es habe	sie haben	

PAST SUBJUNCTIVE II

ich hätte	wir hätten	gemeint
du hättest	ihr hättet	
Sie hätten	Sie hätten	
er/sie/es hätte	sie hätten	

FUTURE PERFECT SUBJUNCTIVE I

ich werde	wir werden	gemeint haben
du werdest	ihr werdet	
Sie werden	Sie werden	
er/sie/es werde	sie werden	

FUTURE PERFECT SUBJUNCTIVE II

ich würde	wir würden	gemeint haben
du würdest	ihr würdet	
Sie würden	Sie würden	
er/sie/es würde	sie würden	

COMMANDS mein(e)! meint! meinen Sie!

PRESENT PARTICIPLE meinend

Usage

Was meinen Sie?	*What is your opinion?*
Was meinen Sie damit?	*What do you mean by that?*
Das habe ich nicht so gemeint.	*I didn't mean it that way.*
Die Behörden meinten, das alte Haus abreißen zu lassen.	*The authorities intended to have the old house demolished.*
Ingrid meint das ernst.	*Ingrid seriously means that.*
Ich meine, Sie sind wohl der ehrgeizigste von der Gruppe.	*I think you are probably the most ambitious of the group.*
Verstehst du was ich meine?	*Do you understand what I mean?*
Habt ihr mich gemeint?	*Did you mean me?*
Gregor meint, seine Bemerkung sei humorvoll gemeint, aber ich meine, es war sein Ernst.	*Gregor says his comment was meant to be humorous, but I think he was serious.*
„Wir werden sehen", meinte der Kobold grinsend.	*"We'll see," said the goblin with a grin.*

RELATED VERB vermeinen

305

melden *to report, announce, notify, recount*

meldet · meldete · gemeldet

regular weak verb

PRESENT

ich melde	wir melden
du meldest	ihr meldet
Sie melden	Sie melden
er/sie/es meldet	sie melden

SIMPLE PAST

ich meldete	wir meldeten
du meldetest	ihr meldetet
Sie meldeten	Sie meldeten
er/sie/es meldete	sie meldeten

FUTURE

ich werde	wir werden	melden
du wirst	ihr werdet	
Sie werden	Sie werden	
er/sie/es wird	sie werden	

PRESENT SUBJUNCTIVE I

ich melde	wir melden
du meldest	ihr meldet
Sie melden	Sie melden
er/sie/es melde	sie melden

PRESENT SUBJUNCTIVE II

ich meldete	wir meldeten
du meldetest	ihr meldetet
Sie meldeten	Sie meldeten
er/sie/es meldete	sie meldeten

FUTURE SUBJUNCTIVE I

ich werde	wir werden	melden
du werdest	ihr werdet	
Sie werden	Sie werden	
er/sie/es werde	sie werden	

FUTURE SUBJUNCTIVE II

ich würde	wir würden	melden
du würdest	ihr würdet	
Sie würden	Sie würden	
er/sie/es würde	sie würden	

PRESENT PERFECT

ich habe	wir haben	gemeldet
du hast	ihr habt	
Sie haben	Sie haben	
er/sie/es hat	sie haben	

PAST PERFECT

ich hatte	wir hatten	gemeldet
du hattest	ihr hattet	
Sie hatten	Sie hatten	
er/sie/es hatte	sie hatten	

FUTURE PERFECT

ich werde	wir werden	gemeldet haben
du wirst	ihr werdet	
Sie werden	Sie werden	
er/sie/es wird	sie werden	

PAST SUBJUNCTIVE I

ich habe	wir haben	gemeldet
du habest	ihr habet	
Sie haben	Sie haben	
er/sie/es habe	sie haben	

PAST SUBJUNCTIVE II

ich hätte	wir hätten	gemeldet
du hättest	ihr hättet	
Sie hätten	Sie hätten	
er/sie/es hätte	sie hätten	

FUTURE PERFECT SUBJUNCTIVE I

ich werde	wir werden	gemeldet haben
du werdest	ihr werdet	
Sie werden	Sie werden	
er/sie/es werde	sie werden	

FUTURE PERFECT SUBJUNCTIVE II

ich würde	wir würden	gemeldet haben
du würdest	ihr würdet	
Sie würden	Sie würden	
er/sie/es würde	sie würden	

COMMANDS melde! meldet! melden Sie!

PRESENT PARTICIPLE meldend

Usage

Ein Erdbeben wurde gerade im Fernsehen gemeldet.	*An earthquake was just reported on television.*
Der Wahlleiter meldet die Wahlergebnisse.	*The elections director is announcing the election results.*
Änderungen sind umgehend zu melden.	*Changes are to be reported immediately.*
Lutz meldete der Polizei, dass das Autoradio gestohlen worden sei.	*Lutz notified the police that the car radio had been stolen.*
Die Teilnehmer haben uns gemeldet, wie viel Spaß es gemacht hat.	*The participants recounted to us how much fun it was.*

sich melden *to come forward, volunteer; answer; announce oneself*

Die Lehrerin stellte eine Frage, aber keiner meldete sich.	*The teacher asked a question, but no one raised his hand.*
Werner hat sich nicht gemeldet.	*Werner didn't respond.*
„Hast du bei ihm telefoniert?"	*"Did you phone him?"*
„Ja, aber er meldet sich nicht."	*"Yes, but he doesn't answer."*

RELATED VERBS ab·melden, krank·melden, vermelden, zurück·melden; *see also* **an·melden** (14)

regular weak verb **merkt · merkte · gemerkt**

PRESENT			PRESENT PERFECT		
ich merke	wir merken		ich habe	wir haben	gemerkt
du merkst	ihr merkt		du hast	ihr habt	
Sie merken	Sie merken		Sie haben	Sie haben	
er/sie/es merkt	sie merken		er/sie/es hat	sie haben	
SIMPLE PAST			**PAST PERFECT**		
ich merkte	wir merkten		ich hatte	wir hatten	gemerkt
du merktest	ihr merktet		du hattest	ihr hattet	
Sie merkten	Sie merkten		Sie hatten	Sie hatten	
er/sie/es merkte	sie merkten		er/sie/es hatte	sie hatten	
FUTURE			**FUTURE PERFECT**		
ich werde	wir werden	merken	ich werde	wir werden	gemerkt haben
du wirst	ihr werdet		du wirst	ihr werdet	
Sie werden	Sie werden		Sie werden	Sie werden	
er/sie/es wird	sie werden		er/sie/es wird	sie werden	
PRESENT SUBJUNCTIVE I			**PAST SUBJUNCTIVE I**		
ich merke	wir merken		ich habe	wir haben	gemerkt
du merkest	ihr merket		du habest	ihr habet	
Sie merken	Sie merken		Sie haben	Sie haben	
er/sie/es merke	sie merken		er/sie/es habe	sie haben	
PRESENT SUBJUNCTIVE II			**PAST SUBJUNCTIVE II**		
ich merkte	wir merkten		ich hätte	wir hätten	gemerkt
du merktest	ihr merktet		du hättest	ihr hättet	
Sie merkten	Sie merkten		Sie hätten	Sie hätten	
er/sie/es merkte	sie merkten		er/sie/es hätte	sie hätten	
FUTURE SUBJUNCTIVE I			**FUTURE PERFECT SUBJUNCTIVE I**		
ich werde	wir werden	merken	ich werde	wir werden	gemerkt haben
du werdest	ihr werdet		du werdest	ihr werdet	
Sie werden	Sie werden		Sie werden	Sie werden	
er/sie/es werde	sie werden		er/sie/es werde	sie werden	
FUTURE SUBJUNCTIVE II			**FUTURE PERFECT SUBJUNCTIVE II**		
ich würde	wir würden	merken	ich würde	wir würden	gemerkt haben
du würdest	ihr würdet		du würdest	ihr würdet	
Sie würden	Sie würden		Sie würden	Sie würden	
er/sie/es würde	sie würden		er/sie/es würde	sie würden	

COMMANDS merk(e)! merkt! merken Sie!

PRESENT PARTICIPLE merkend

Usage

Smith merkt, dass keine überzeugende Theorie existiert. — *Smith observes that no convincing theory exists.*
Konrad merkte nicht, dass es regnete. — *Konrad didn't realize it was raining.*
Hier ist zu merken, dass der vorangehende Satz keine Ausklammerung aufweist. — *One should notice here that the preceding sentence shows no left detachment.*
Ich merkte, wie der starke Nordwind die trockenen Blätter mit sich trug. — *I observed how the strong north wind was carrying the dry leaves along.*
Merkst du ein seltsames Gefühl im Bauch? — *Do you sense an odd feeling in your stomach?*
An ihrem schlurfenden Gang merkt man, dass sie deprimiert ist. — *You can tell by the way she shuffles along that she's depressed.*

sich merken *to remember, keep in mind*

Ich muss mir die Telefonnummer merken. — *I'll have to remember the telephone number.*
Wer hat sich die meisten Namen gemerkt? — *Who remembered the most names?*

RELATED VERBS an·merken, auf·merken, vermerken, vor·merken; *see also* **bemerken** (69)

307 messen *to measure, gauge; compare*

misst · maß · gemessen — strong verb

PRESENT

ich messe	wir messen
du misst	ihr messt
Sie messen	Sie messen
er/sie/es misst	sie messen

PRESENT PERFECT

ich habe	wir haben	gemessen
du hast	ihr habt	
Sie haben	Sie haben	
er/sie/es hat	sie haben	

SIMPLE PAST

ich maß	wir maßen
du maßest	ihr maßt
Sie maßen	Sie maßen
er/sie/es maß	sie maßen

PAST PERFECT

ich hatte	wir hatten	gemessen
du hattest	ihr hattet	
Sie hatten	Sie hatten	
er/sie/es hatte	sie hatten	

FUTURE

ich werde	wir werden	messen
du wirst	ihr werdet	
Sie werden	Sie werden	
er/sie/es wird	sie werden	

FUTURE PERFECT

ich werde	wir werden	gemessen haben
du wirst	ihr werdet	
Sie werden	Sie werden	
er/sie/es wird	sie werden	

PRESENT SUBJUNCTIVE I

ich messe	wir messen
du messest	ihr messet
Sie messen	Sie messen
er/sie/es messe	sie messen

PAST SUBJUNCTIVE I

ich habe	wir haben	gemessen
du habest	ihr habet	
Sie haben	Sie haben	
er/sie/es habe	sie haben	

PRESENT SUBJUNCTIVE II

ich mäße	wir mäßen
du mäßest	ihr mäßet
Sie mäßen	Sie mäßen
er/sie/es mäße	sie mäßen

PAST SUBJUNCTIVE II

ich hätte	wir hätten	gemessen
du hättest	ihr hättet	
Sie hätten	Sie hätten	
er/sie/es hätte	sie hätten	

FUTURE SUBJUNCTIVE I

ich werde	wir werden	messen
du werdest	ihr werdet	
Sie werden	Sie werden	
er/sie/es werde	sie werden	

FUTURE PERFECT SUBJUNCTIVE I

ich werde	wir werden	gemessen haben
du werdest	ihr werdet	
Sie werden	Sie werden	
er/sie/es werde	sie werden	

FUTURE SUBJUNCTIVE II

ich würde	wir würden	messen
du würdest	ihr würdet	
Sie würden	Sie würden	
er/sie/es würde	sie würden	

FUTURE PERFECT SUBJUNCTIVE II

ich würde	wir würden	gemessen haben
du würdest	ihr würdet	
Sie würden	Sie würden	
er/sie/es würde	sie würden	

COMMANDS miss! messt! messen Sie!

PRESENT PARTICIPLE messend

Usage

Ein *yard* misst 0,9144 Meter.	*A yard measures 0.9144 meters.*
Früher hat man Bodenfläche in Morgen gemessen.	*People used to measure acreage in* morgen.
Ein Morgen maß zwischen 0,25 und 1,22 Hektar.	*A* morgen *measured between 0.25 and 1.22 hectares.*
Heute wird das Land in Hektar gemessen.	*Today land is measured in hectares.*
Wann ist die Luftqualität das letzte Mal gemessen worden?	*When was the air quality last measured?*
Wie lässt sich die Härte von Mineralien messen?	*How is the hardness of minerals gauged?*
Du sollst Laura an ihrer Zwillingsschwester nicht messen.	*You shouldn't compare Laura to her twin sister.*

sich messen (mit) *to compete (with), pit oneself (against)*

Sechs Mannschaften messen sich in Kaiserslautern.	*Six teams are competing in Kaiserslautern.*
Sebastian misst sich mit dem 21-jährigen Österreicher Jörg Huber.	*Sebastian is competing against the 21-year-old Austrian Jörg Huber.*

RELATED VERBS ab·messen, an·messen, aus·messen, bei·messen, bemessen, durchmessen, durch·messen, ermessen, nach·messen, vermessen, zu·messen

PRESENT

ich miete	wir mieten
du mietest	ihr mietet
Sie mieten	Sie mieten
er/sie/es mietet	sie mieten

SIMPLE PAST

ich mietete	wir mieteten
du mietetest	ihr mietetet
Sie mieteten	Sie mieteten
er/sie/es mietete	sie mieteten

FUTURE

ich werde	wir werden	mieten
du wirst	ihr werdet	
Sie werden	Sie werden	
er/sie/es wird	sie werden	

PRESENT SUBJUNCTIVE I

ich miete	wir mieten
du mietest	ihr mietet
Sie mieten	Sie mieten
er/sie/es miete	sie mieten

PRESENT SUBJUNCTIVE II

ich mietete	wir mieteten
du mietetest	ihr mietetet
Sie mieteten	Sie mieteten
er/sie/es mietete	sie mieteten

FUTURE SUBJUNCTIVE I

ich werde	wir werden	mieten
du werdest	ihr werdet	
Sie werden	Sie werden	
er/sie/es werde	sie werden	

FUTURE SUBJUNCTIVE II

ich würde	wir würden	mieten
du würdest	ihr würdet	
Sie würden	Sie würden	
er/sie/es würde	sie würden	

PRESENT PERFECT

ich habe	wir haben	gemietet
du hast	ihr habt	
Sie haben	Sie haben	
er/sie/es hat	sie haben	

PAST PERFECT

ich hatte	wir hatten	gemietet
du hattest	ihr hattet	
Sie hatten	Sie hatten	
er/sie/es hatte	sie hatten	

FUTURE PERFECT

ich werde	wir werden	gemietet haben
du wirst	ihr werdet	
Sie werden	Sie werden	
er/sie/es wird	sie werden	

PAST SUBJUNCTIVE I

ich habe	wir haben	gemietet
du habest	ihr habet	
Sie haben	Sie haben	
er/sie/es habe	sie haben	

PAST SUBJUNCTIVE II

ich hätte	wir hätten	gemietet
du hättest	ihr hättet	
Sie hätten	Sie hätten	
er/sie/es hätte	sie hätten	

FUTURE PERFECT SUBJUNCTIVE I

ich werde	wir werden	gemietet haben
du werdest	ihr werdet	
Sie werden	Sie werden	
er/sie/es werde	sie werden	

FUTURE PERFECT SUBJUNCTIVE II

ich würde	wir würden	gemietet haben
du würdest	ihr würdet	
Sie würden	Sie würden	
er/sie/es würde	sie würden	

COMMANDS miete! mietet! mieten Sie!

PRESENT PARTICIPLE mietend

Usage

In Mallorca haben wir uns eine Wohnung gemietet.	*In Mallorca, we rented an apartment for ourselves.*
Mietet ihr oder besitzt ihr das Haus?	*Do you rent or own the house?*
Am besten mieten Sie eine Limousine.	*It is best for you to hire a limousine.*
Für die Hochzeit mieten wir einen weitläufigen Raum im Schloss!	*For the wedding, we are renting a spacious room in the castle!*
Wo sind Fahrräder zu mieten?	*Where can bicycles be rented?*
Der Wagen muss in der Filiale zurückgegeben werden, in der er gemietet wurde.	*The car must be returned to the branch where it was rented.*
Kann der Saal gemietet werden?	*Can the room be rented?*
Ich miete den Computer und bekomme jedes Jahr ein neues Modell.	*I lease the computer and get a new model every year.*
Vor 1853 mietete Nicolaus Fricke die Mühle am Bitterbach.	*Before 1853, Nicolaus Fricke rented the mill on Bitter Creek.*

RELATED VERBS ab·vermieten, ein·mieten, untervermieten, vermieten, weiter·vermieten

309 misslingen *to fail, be unsuccessful*

misslingt · misslang · misslungen strong verb (dative object)

PRESENT		PRESENT PERFECT	
er/sie/es misslingt	sie misslingen	er/sie/es ist misslungen	sie sind misslungen
SIMPLE PAST		**PAST PERFECT**	
er/sie/es misslang	sie misslangen	er/sie/es war misslungen	sie waren misslungen
FUTURE		**FUTURE PERFECT**	
er/sie/es wird misslingen	sie werden misslingen	er/sie/es wird misslungen sein	sie werden misslungen sein
PRESENT SUBJUNCTIVE I		**PAST SUBJUNCTIVE I**	
er/sie/es misslinge	sie misslingen	er/sie/es sei misslungen	sie seien misslungen
PRESENT SUBJUNCTIVE II		**PAST SUBJUNCTIVE II**	
er/sie/es misslänge	sie misslängen	er/sie/es wäre misslungen	sie wären misslungen
FUTURE SUBJUNCTIVE I		**FUTURE PERFECT SUBJUNCTIVE I**	
er/sie/es werde misslingen	sie werden misslingen	er/sie/es werde misslungen sein	sie werden misslungen sein
FUTURE SUBJUNCTIVE II		**FUTURE PERFECT SUBJUNCTIVE II**	
er/sie/es würde misslingen	sie würden misslingen	er/sie/es würde misslungen sein	sie würden misslungen sein

COMMANDS —

PRESENT PARTICIPLE misslingend

NOTE Only impersonal forms are generally used.

Usage

Alle Versuche, die alte Windmühle zu reparieren, misslangen. — *All attempts to repair the old windmill were unsuccessful.*

Schneiders neues Buch ist aus mehreren Gründen misslungen. — *Schneider's new book failed for several reasons.*

Der Film wird Millionen einbringen, auch wenn der Schluss völlig misslingt. — *The film will bring in millions, even if the ending is a complete bust.*

Dem Jungen misslang ein Sprung über einen Graben und er verstauchte sich das Fußgelenk. — *The boy's attempt to jump across a ditch failed, and he sprained his ankle.*

Wenn der Versuch uns misslänge, müssten wir wieder von vorne anfangen. — *If our attempt should fail, we would have to start over from the beginning.*

Trotz noch eines misslungenen Versuchs gab der Wissenschaftler nicht auf. — *In spite of yet another failed attempt, the scientist did not give up.*

Im Jahr 1863 misslang ein Aufstand der Loyalisten des Tokugawa-Schogunats in Nara. — *In the year 1863, an uprising of the Tokugawa Shogunate loyalists in Nara was unsuccessful.*

RELATED VERB *see* **gelingen** (212)

regular weak verb **teilt mit · teilte mit · mitgeteilt**

PRESENT

ich teile	wir teilen	mit
du teilst	ihr teilt	
Sie teilen	Sie teilen	
er/sie/es teilt	sie teilen	

PRESENT PERFECT

ich habe	wir haben	mitgeteilt
du hast	ihr habt	
Sie haben	Sie haben	
er/sie/es hat	sie haben	

SIMPLE PAST

ich teilte	wir teilten	mit
du teiltest	ihr teiltet	
Sie teilten	Sie teilten	
er/sie/es teilte	sie teilten	

PAST PERFECT

ich hatte	wir hatten	mitgeteilt
du hattest	ihr hattet	
Sie hatten	Sie hatten	
er/sie/es hatte	sie hatten	

FUTURE

ich werde	wir werden	mitteilen
du wirst	ihr werdet	
Sie werden	Sie werden	
er/sie/es wird	sie werden	

FUTURE PERFECT

ich werde	wir werden	mitgeteilt haben
du wirst	ihr werdet	
Sie werden	Sie werden	
er/sie/es wird	sie werden	

PRESENT SUBJUNCTIVE I

ich teile	wir teilen	mit
du teilest	ihr teilet	
Sie teilen	Sie teilen	
er/sie/es teile	sie teilen	

PAST SUBJUNCTIVE I

ich habe	wir haben	mitgeteilt
du habest	ihr habet	
Sie haben	Sie haben	
er/sie/es habe	sie haben	

PRESENT SUBJUNCTIVE II

ich teilte	wir teilten	mit
du teiltest	ihr teiltet	
Sie teilten	Sie teilten	
er/sie/es teilte	sie teilten	

PAST SUBJUNCTIVE II

ich hätte	wir hätten	mitgeteilt
du hättest	ihr hättet	
Sie hätten	Sie hätten	
er/sie/es hätte	sie hätten	

FUTURE SUBJUNCTIVE I

ich werde	wir werden	mitteilen
du werdest	ihr werdet	
Sie werden	Sie werden	
er/sie/es werde	sie werden	

FUTURE PERFECT SUBJUNCTIVE I

ich werde	wir werden	mitgeteilt haben
du werdest	ihr werdet	
Sie werden	Sie werden	
er/sie/es werde	sie werden	

FUTURE SUBJUNCTIVE II

ich würde	wir würden	mitteilen
du würdest	ihr würdet	
Sie würden	Sie würden	
er/sie/es würde	sie würden	

FUTURE PERFECT SUBJUNCTIVE II

ich würde	wir würden	mitgeteilt haben
du würdest	ihr würdet	
Sie würden	Sie würden	
er/sie/es würde	sie würden	

COMMANDS teil(e) mit! teilt mit! teilen Sie mit!

PRESENT PARTICIPLE mitteilend

Usage

Ernst sagte, er hätte etwas Neues mitzuteilen. — *Ernst said he has something new to pass on.*

„Wir geben nicht auf“, teilte ein Polizeisprecher mit. — *“We're not giving up,” announced a police spokesperson.*

Der Vorsitzende hat dem Vorstand seinen sofortigen Rücktritt mitgeteilt. — *The chairman communicated his immediate resignation to the board.*

Teilen Sie uns alle Änderungen umgehend mit. — *Inform us of all changes immediately.*

Frederike möchte ihrem Mann ihr Vorhaben mitteilen. — *Frederike would like to tell her husband of her plan.*

Ich muss jetzt meine Bedenken mitteilen. — *I have to communicate my misgivings now.*

Seine Eltern haben ihm gestern mitgeteilt, er sei mit zwei Jahren adoptiert worden. — *His parents informed him yesterday that he had been adopted at the age of two.*

Prüfungsergebnisse werden Studierenden per Email mitgeteilt. — *Test results are now communicated to students via e-mail.*

sich mitteilen *to spread, catch on*

Sein Enthusiasmus teilte sich uns mit. — *His enthusiasm caught on with us.*

RELATED VERBS *see* **teilen** (443)

mögen *to like (to)*

mag · mochte · gemocht modal verb

MORE USAGE SENTENCES WITH mögen

Laura hat es nicht gemocht, dass wir nicht mehr miteinander telefonierten. — *Laura didn't like it that we no longer talked on the telephone.*

Manche mögen es scharf. — *Some like it spicy.*

mögen (in present subjunctive II) *would like, would like to* (polite request/desire); *to want (to)*

Florian möchte das Schnitzel. — *Florian would like the cutlet.*

Mein Kollege möchte ein Pils und ich möchte gern ein Glas Rotwein. — *My colleague would like a beer, and I'd like a glass of red wine.*

Möchtest du tanzen? — *Would you like to dance?*

Möchtet ihr Jazzmusik hören? — *Would you like to listen to some jazz?*

Ich möchte den Sonntag zu Hause verbringen. — *I'd like to spend Sunday at home.*

Lukas möchte keine Erdnüsse mehr. — *Lukas doesn't want any more peanuts.*

Ich möchte nicht missverstanden werden, aber Doris hat völlig Recht. — *I don't want to be misunderstood, but Doris is exactly right.*

Ich möchte Spinat mögen, denn er ist sehr gesund. — *I'd like to like spinach, because it's very healthy.*

Frau Spears möchte lieber bar bezahlen. — *Mrs. Spears would rather pay cash.*

Wenn Sie möchten, können Sie abends tanzen oder ins Theater gehen. — *If you wish, you can go dancing or to the theater in the evening.*

mögen + infinitive *can, to like to, want to*

Ich mag ihn nicht leiden. — *I cannot tolerate him.*

Herr Friedrichsen mag es nicht leiden, wenn seine Frau ihn „Hansel" nennt. — *Mr. Friedrichsen can't stand it when his wife calls him "Hansel."*

Magst du tanzen? — *Do you like to dance? / Are you fond of dancing?*

Ich mag nicht gehen, aber mein Mann ist müde. — *I don't want to go, but my husband is tired.*

Der Bote reichte ihr den Brief und sagte, sie möchte ihn selbst lesen. (*elevated style*) — *The messenger handed her the letter and said she should read it herself.*

mögen *may, might* (subjective meaning to express supposition or speculation)

Das mag sein, aber das ist nicht der Punkt. — *That may be, but that is not the point.*

Es mag aber wirklich sein, dass Sie die Absicht Ihrer Mutter falsch interpretiert haben. — *However, it might really be that you've misinterpreted your mother's intention.*

Wer mag der Mann sein? — *Who might that man be?*

Ein Grund dafür mag gewesen sein, dass er am Kurs gar nicht teilgenommen hatte. — *One reason for that might have been that he hadn't participated in the course at all.*

Es mochte wohl erst drei Uhr morgens sein, als das Telefon klingelte. — *It was perhaps only three o'clock in the morning when the telephone rang.*

IDIOMATIC EXPRESSIONS

Du magst tun was du willst. — *I'll let you do whatever you want. (I don't care.)*

Was er auch tun mochte, sie war nicht berechtigt ihm Vorwürfe zu machen. (ACHIM VON ARNIM) — *No matter what he did, she had no right to reproach him.*

Diese fürchterliche Situation bleibt immer dieselbe, was ich auch tun mag. — *This horrible situation always stays the same, no matter what I do.*

Wie dem auch sein mag, … — *Be that as it may, …*

Möge es euch wohl bekommen. — *May it do you much good.*

Möge es Ihnen gelingen. — *May you be successful.*

Mag kommen was will. — *Come what may.*

PRESENT

ich mag	wir mögen
du magst	ihr mögt
Sie mögen	Sie mögen
er/sie/es mag	sie mögen

SIMPLE PAST

ich mochte	wir mochten
du mochtest	ihr mochtet
Sie mochten	Sie mochten
er/sie/es mochte	sie mochten

FUTURE

ich werde	wir werden	mögen
du wirst	ihr werdet	
Sie werden	Sie werden	
er/sie/es wird	sie werden	

PRESENT SUBJUNCTIVE I

ich möge	wir mögen
du mögest	ihr möget
Sie mögen	Sie mögen
er/sie/es möge	sie mögen

PRESENT SUBJUNCTIVE II

ich möchte	wir möchten
du möchtest	ihr möchtet
Sie möchten	Sie möchten
er/sie/es möchte	sie möchten

FUTURE SUBJUNCTIVE I

ich werde	wir werden	mögen
du werdest	ihr werdet	
Sie werden	Sie werden	
er/sie/es werde	sie werden	

FUTURE SUBJUNCTIVE II

ich würde	wir würden	mögen
du würdest	ihr würdet	
Sie würden	Sie würden	
er/sie/es würde	sie würden	

PRESENT PERFECT

ich habe	wir haben	gemocht
du hast	ihr habt	
Sie haben	Sie haben	
er/sie/es hat	sie haben	

PAST PERFECT

ich hatte	wir hatten	gemocht
du hattest	ihr hattet	
Sie hatten	Sie hatten	
er/sie/es hatte	sie hatten	

FUTURE PERFECT

ich werde	wir werden	gemocht haben
du wirst	ihr werdet	
Sie werden	Sie werden	
er/sie/es wird	sie werden	

PAST SUBJUNCTIVE I

ich habe	wir haben	gemocht
du habest	ihr habet	
Sie haben	Sie haben	
er/sie/es habe	sie haben	

PAST SUBJUNCTIVE II

ich hätte	wir hätten	gemocht
du hättest	ihr hättet	
Sie hätten	Sie hätten	
er/sie/es hätte	sie hätten	

FUTURE PERFECT SUBJUNCTIVE I

ich werde	wir werden	gemocht haben
du werdest	ihr werdet	
Sie werden	Sie werden	
er/sie/es werde	sie werden	

FUTURE PERFECT SUBJUNCTIVE II

ich würde	wir würden	gemocht haben
du würdest	ihr würdet	
Sie würden	Sie würden	
er/sie/es würde	sie würden	

COMMANDS —

PRESENT PARTICIPLE mögend

Usage

Magst du Sushi?	*Do you like sushi?*
Sergej mag es nicht, wenn seine Eltern sich streiten.	*Sergei doesn't like it when his parents fight.*
Als Kind mochte Erwin keinen Blumenkohl.	*As a child, Erwin didn't like cauliflower.*
Wir haben die Spielplätze in Düsseldorf sehr gemocht.	*We really liked the playgrounds in Düsseldorf.*
Mögen Sie lieber französische Weißweine oder kalifornische?	*Do you like French or Californian white wines better?*
Mögt ihr klassische Musik?	*Do you like classical music?*
Ab und zu mögen wir ein Glas Wein zum Abendessen.	*Now and again, we like a glass of wine with dinner.*
Du musst dich selbst mögen, damit andere Menschen dich mögen.	*You must like yourself so that other people like you.*
Ich habe früher Jogurt gemocht, aber ich kann ihn nicht mehr essen.	*I used to be fond of yogurt, but I can't eat it anymore.*
Ortwin mag keine Schokolade.	*Ortwin doesn't like chocolate.*

RELATED VERB vermögen

müssen *must, to have to, be obliged to*

muss · musste · gemusst modal verb

MORE USAGE SENTENCES WITH müssen

Das muss man wissen.	*You need to know that.*
Die Kunst muss erlebt werden, sie darf nicht nur analysiert werden.	*Art must be experienced; it cannot merely be analyzed.*
In diesem Augenblick musste Karen die richtige Entscheidung treffen.	*At that moment, Karen had to make the right decision.*
Wir bedauern sehr, Ihnen mitteilen zu müssen, dass unser Vorstandsvorsitzender verstorben ist.	*We regret very much having to inform you that our chairman of the board has passed away.*
Man muss Fremdsprachen können, wenn man viel unterwegs im Ausland ist.	*You have to know foreign languages if you travel abroad a lot.*
Wie lange müssen wir warten?	*How long must we wait?*
Als sie das sagte, musste ich lachen.	*When she said that, I had to laugh.*
Die Trauben müssen sechs bis sieben Wochen in großen Behältnissen gären.	*The grapes have to ferment for six to seven weeks in large vats.*
Wir haben unsere unrealistischen Erwartungen zurückschrauben müssen.	*We have had to scale back our unrealistic expectations.*

nicht müssen *to not have to, not need to*

NOTE **Nicht müssen** does not mean "must not." "Must not" is rendered in German by **nicht dürfen.**

Du musst das nicht machen!	*You don't have to do that!*
Sie müssen sich nicht aufregen.	*You don't need to get excited.*

müssen *must, to have to, be obliged to* (used as a full verb, not as a modal)

Ich musste zu ihr.	*I had to go to her.*
Jörg muss ins Krankenhaus.	*Jörg has to go to the hospital.*
Die Tatsache ist, dass ich es einfach muss.	*The fact is that I simply must (do it).*
Müssen Sie schon weg?	*Do you have to leave already?*
Was Sie auch gemusst hätten, wenn der Graf noch lebte. (LESSING)	*Which you would have had to do if the count were still living.*
Um wie viel Uhr müsst ihr ins Bett?	*At what time do you have to go to bed?*

müssen *must, to have to, should, ought to* (subjective meaning to express supposition or speculation)

Die Journalistin muss aus Russland kommen, denn sie spricht Russisch.	*The journalist must be from Russia because she speaks Russian.*
Das muss Marta Becker gewesen sein, die gerade vorbeigefahren ist.	*That must have been Marta Becker who just drove past.*
Es ist schon sieben Uhr? Ja, Andreas müsste schon zu Hause sein.	*It's already seven o'clock? Yes, Andreas ought to be home by now.*
Das muss wirklich wehgetan haben!	*That must have really hurt!*
Es müsste einen Weg geben, die Dateien von der Festplatte auf eine CD zu übertragen.	*There should be a way to transfer the files from the hard drive to a CD.*
Das schöne Fachwerkhaus an der Ecke müsste vor 1500 gebaut worden sein.	*The beautiful half-timber house on the corner would have to have been built before 1500.*

IDIOMATIC EXPRESSIONS

Wenn es sein muss, kann ich mitkommen.	*If need be, I can come along.*
Muss das denn sein?	*Is that really necessary?*
Ich muss sagen, ich bin völlig überrascht worden.	*I must say, I was completely surprised.*
Mami, ich muss mal. (*children's language*)	*Mommy, I have to go potty.*

modal verb **muss · musste · gemusst**

PRESENT

ich muss	wir müssen
du musst	ihr müsst
Sie müssen	Sie müssen
er/sie/es muss	sie müssen

SIMPLE PAST

ich musste	wir mussten
du musstest	ihr musstet
Sie mussten	Sie mussten
er/sie/es musste	sie mussten

FUTURE

ich werde	wir werden	müssen
du wirst	ihr werdet	
Sie werden	Sie werden	
er/sie/es wird	sie werden	

PRESENT SUBJUNCTIVE I

ich müsse	wir müssen
du müssest	ihr müsset
Sie müssen	Sie müssen
er/sie/es müsse	sie müssen

PRESENT SUBJUNCTIVE II

ich müsste	wir müssten
du müsstest	ihr müsstet
Sie müssten	Sie müssten
er/sie/es müsste	sie müssten

FUTURE SUBJUNCTIVE I

ich werde	wir werden	müssen
du werdest	ihr werdet	
Sie werden	Sie werden	
er/sie/es werde	sie werden	

FUTURE SUBJUNCTIVE II

ich würde	wir würden	müssen
du würdest	ihr würdet	
Sie würden	Sie würden	
er/sie/es würde	sie würden	

PRESENT PERFECT

ich habe	wir haben	gemusst
du hast	ihr habt	
Sie haben	Sie haben	
er/sie/es hat	sie haben	

PAST PERFECT

ich hatte	wir hatten	gemusst
du hattest	ihr hattet	
Sie hatten	Sie hatten	
er/sie/es hatte	sie hatten	

FUTURE PERFECT

ich werde	wir werden	gemusst haben
du wirst	ihr werdet	
Sie werden	Sie werden	
er/sie/es wird	sie werden	

PAST SUBJUNCTIVE I

ich habe	wir haben	gemusst
du habest	ihr habet	
Sie haben	Sie haben	
er/sie/es habe	sie haben	

PAST SUBJUNCTIVE II

ich hätte	wir hätten	gemusst
du hättest	ihr hättet	
Sie hätten	Sie hätten	
er/sie/es hätte	sie hätten	

FUTURE PERFECT SUBJUNCTIVE I

ich werde	wir werden	gemusst haben
du werdest	ihr werdet	
Sie werden	Sie werden	
er/sie/es werde	sie werden	

FUTURE PERFECT SUBJUNCTIVE II

ich würde	wir würden	gemusst haben
du würdest	ihr würdet	
Sie würden	Sie würden	
er/sie/es würde	sie würden	

COMMANDS —

PRESENT PARTICIPLE müssend

Usage

Ich muss ein paar Bemerkungen vorbringen.	*I must put forward a few comments.*
In diesem Fall musste das Untersuchungsobjekt etwas genauer definiert werden.	*In this case, the object of study had to be more precisely defined.*
Alle Besucher müssen aktiv teilnehmen.	*All visitors are obliged to participate actively.*
Müssen Künstler sich der Welt entziehen, um eine künstlerische Sichtweise zu pflegen?	*Must artists withdraw from the world in order to cultivate an artistic point of view?*
Jetzt müssen die synchronischen Aspekte besprochen werden.	*The synchronic aspects must now be discussed.*
Der Patient meint, er müsse übernatürliche Kräfte verwenden, um aus der Klinik zu entkommen.	*The patient says he must use supernatural powers to escape from the clinic.*
Herr Erkermann wird als Zeuge vortreten müssen.	*Mr. Erkermann will have to come forward as a witness.*
Warum müsst ihr euch so benehmen?	*Why do you have to behave like that?*
Der Vertrag muss innerhalb einer Woche unterschrieben werden.	*The contract must be signed within one week.*

313 nach·denken *to reflect, meditate, ponder, mull (over)*

denkt nach · dachte nach · nachgedacht mixed verb

PRESENT

ich denke	wir denken	nach
du denkst	ihr denkt	
Sie denken	Sie denken	
er/sie/es denkt	sie denken	

PRESENT PERFECT

ich habe	wir haben	nachgedacht
du hast	ihr habt	
Sie haben	Sie haben	
er/sie/es hat	sie haben	

SIMPLE PAST

ich dachte	wir dachten	nach
du dachtest	ihr dachtet	
Sie dachten	Sie dachten	
er/sie/es dachte	sie dachten	

PAST PERFECT

ich hatte	wir hatten	nachgedacht
du hattest	ihr hattet	
Sie hatten	Sie hatten	
er/sie/es hatte	sie hatten	

FUTURE

ich werde	wir werden	nachdenken
du wirst	ihr werdet	
Sie werden	Sie werden	
er/sie/es wird	sie werden	

FUTURE PERFECT

ich werde	wir werden	nachgedacht haben
du wirst	ihr werdet	
Sie werden	Sie werden	
er/sie/es wird	sie werden	

PRESENT SUBJUNCTIVE I

ich denke	wir denken	nach
du denkest	ihr denket	
Sie denken	Sie denken	
er/sie/es denke	sie denken	

PAST SUBJUNCTIVE I

ich habe	wir haben	nachgedacht
du habest	ihr habet	
Sie haben	Sie haben	
er/sie/es habe	sie haben	

PRESENT SUBJUNCTIVE II

ich dächte	wir dächten	nach
du dächtest	ihr dächtet	
Sie dächten	Sie dächten	
er/sie/es dächte	sie dächten	

PAST SUBJUNCTIVE II

ich hätte	wir hätten	nachgedacht
du hättest	ihr hättet	
Sie hätten	Sie hätten	
er/sie/es hätte	sie hätten	

FUTURE SUBJUNCTIVE I

ich werde	wir werden	nachdenken
du werdest	ihr werdet	
Sie werden	Sie werden	
er/sie/es werde	sie werden	

FUTURE PERFECT SUBJUNCTIVE I

ich werde	wir werden	nachgedacht haben
du werdest	ihr werdet	
Sie werden	Sie werden	
er/sie/es werde	sie werden	

FUTURE SUBJUNCTIVE II

ich würde	wir würden	nachdenken
du würdest	ihr würdet	
Sie würden	Sie würden	
er/sie/es würde	sie würden	

FUTURE PERFECT SUBJUNCTIVE II

ich würde	wir würden	nachgedacht haben
du würdest	ihr würdet	
Sie würden	Sie würden	
er/sie/es würde	sie würden	

COMMANDS denk(e) nach! denkt nach! denken Sie nach!

PRESENT PARTICIPLE nachdenkend

Usage

Denken Sie sorgfältig darüber nach, ob diese Schönheitsoperation wirklich notwendig ist. — *Carefully consider whether this cosmetic surgery is really necessary.*

Zu selten wird über seine negativen Auswirkungen auf die Umwelt nachgedacht. — *Too seldom do people reflect over its negative effects on the environment.*

Er redete ohne erstmal nachzudenken und merkte seinen Fehler erst im Nachhinein. — *He spoke without thinking first and realized his mistake only in retrospect.*

Je länger Ute über Ingrids Worte nachdachte, desto böser wurde sie. — *The longer Ute reflected on Ingrid's words, the angrier she became.*

Nimm dir die Zeit, über Sachen nachzudenken. — *Take the time to mull things over.*

Ich dachte über meine Zukunft nach. — *I was pondering my future.*

Denk doch mal nach! — *Think about it!*

Über die Forderungen meiner Eltern muss ich viel nachdenken. — *I've got to do a lot of thinking about my parents' demands.*

RELATED VERBS *see* **denken** (122)

PRESENT

ich nehme	wir nehmen
du nimmst	ihr nehmt
Sie nehmen	Sie nehmen
er/sie/es nimmt	sie nehmen

SIMPLE PAST

ich nahm	wir nahmen
du nahmst	ihr nahmt
Sie nahmen	Sie nahmen
er/sie/es nahm	sie nahmen

FUTURE

ich werde	wir werden	nehmen
du wirst	ihr werdet	
Sie werden	Sie werden	
er/sie/es wird	sie werden	

PRESENT SUBJUNCTIVE I

ich nehme	wir nehmen
du nehmest	ihr nehmet
Sie nehmen	Sie nehmen
er/sie/es nehme	sie nehmen

PRESENT SUBJUNCTIVE II

ich nähme	wir nähmen
du nähmest	ihr nähmet
Sie nähmen	Sie nähmen
er/sie/es nähme	sie nähmen

FUTURE SUBJUNCTIVE I

ich werde	wir werden	nehmen
du werdest	ihr werdet	
Sie werden	Sie werden	
er/sie/es werde	sie werden	

FUTURE SUBJUNCTIVE II

ich würde	wir würden	nehmen
du würdest	ihr würdet	
Sie würden	Sie würden	
er/sie/es würde	sie würden	

PRESENT PERFECT

ich habe	wir haben	genommen
du hast	ihr habt	
Sie haben	Sie haben	
er/sie/es hat	sie haben	

PAST PERFECT

ich hatte	wir hatten	genommen
du hattest	ihr hattet	
Sie hatten	Sie hatten	
er/sie/es hatte	sie hatten	

FUTURE PERFECT

ich werde	wir werden	genommen haben
du wirst	ihr werdet	
Sie werden	Sie werden	
er/sie/es wird	sie werden	

PAST SUBJUNCTIVE I

ich habe	wir haben	genommen
du habest	ihr habet	
Sie haben	Sie haben	
er/sie/es habe	sie haben	

PAST SUBJUNCTIVE II

ich hätte	wir hätten	genommen
du hättest	ihr hättet	
Sie hätten	Sie hätten	
er/sie/es hätte	sie hätten	

FUTURE PERFECT SUBJUNCTIVE I

ich werde	wir werden	genommen haben
du werdest	ihr werdet	
Sie werden	Sie werden	
er/sie/es werde	sie werden	

FUTURE PERFECT SUBJUNCTIVE II

ich würde	wir würden	genommen haben
du würdest	ihr würdet	
Sie würden	Sie würden	
er/sie/es würde	sie würden	

COMMANDS nimm! nehmt! nehmen Sie!

PRESENT PARTICIPLE nehmend

Usage

Nehmen Sie bitte Platz.	*Please take a seat.*
Herr Hüttenbach nahm seinen Hut und eilte aus der Tür.	*Mr. Hüttenbach took his hat and hurried out the door.*
Wer hat mir meinen Bleistift genommen?	*Who took my pencil from me?*
Sie darf nichts gegen Kopfschmerzen nehmen.	*She is not allowed to take anything for headaches.*
Wir nehmen den Bus nach Simmelsdorf.	*We're taking the bus to Simmelsdorf.*
Um neun Uhr nahm der Professor Abschied von der Familie.	*The professor took leave of the family at nine o'clock.*
Hobbyfahrer werden nicht ernst genommen.	*Amateur drivers are not taken seriously.*

RELATED VERBS auf·nehmen, aus·nehmen, benehmen, durch·nehmen, ein·nehmen, entgegen·nehmen, entnehmen, fest·nehmen, fort·nehmen, frei·nehmen, hin·nehmen, mit·nehmen, nach·nehmen, über·nehmen, vernehmen, vor·nehmen, vorweg·nehmen, wahr·nehmen, weg·nehmen, zurücknehmen, zusammen·nehmen; *see also* **ab·nehmen** (6), **an·nehmen** (15), **teil·nehmen** (444), **übernehmen** (461), **unternehmen** (469), **zu·nehmen** (551)

TOP 50 VERB ☞

314 nehmen *to take*

nimmt · nahm · genommen strong verb

MORE USAGE SENTENCES WITH nehmen

Ich nehme mir die Zeit dafür. — *I'll take the time for that.*
Warum nehmt ihr nicht die A1 bis Münster? — *Why don't you take the A1 to Münster?*
Trina hat die Schuld dafür auf sich genommen. — *Trina has taken the blame for that.*
Drei Eier nehmen und sie zwei Minuten kochen. (RECIPE) — *Take three eggs and boil them for two minutes.*
Vom Flughafen kann man auch ein Taxi nehmen. — *From the airport, you can also take a taxi.*
Debora hat ihren alternden Vater zu sich nach Hause genommen. — *Debora took her aging father into her home.*
Man nehme zum Beispiel den Fall des irischen Kartoffelhungers im 19. Jahrhundert. — *Take, for example, the case of the Irish potato famine in the nineteenth century.*
Erich nahm Renate beiseite und erklärte ihr den Plan. — *Erich took Renate aside and explained the plan to her.*
Die Soldaten wurden gefangen genommen. — *The soldiers were taken prisoner.*
Nimm es mir bitte nicht übel, aber du bist naiv. — *Please don't take offense, but you're naive.*
Das Projekt nimmt viel Zeit in Anspruch. — *The project is taking a lot of time.*
Das Kind möchte kein Bad nehmen. — *The child doesn't want to take a bath.*
Warum nehmt ihr zum Thema nicht Stellung? — *Why aren't you taking a position on the matter?*
Man kann sie beim Wort nehmen. — *You can take her word for it.*
Ich nehme mir deinen Rat zu Herzen. — *I will take your advice to heart.*
Laut Angaben seien die Männer ohne rechtliche Basis in Haft genommen worden. — *According to reports, the men were taken into custody without just cause.*
Das gräfliche Heer nahm die Stadt ohne Gegenwehr. — *The count's army took the city without resistance.*
Du nimmst die Sache zu leicht! — *You're taking the matter too lightly!*
Nehmen Sie die Kursänderungen bitte zur Kenntnis. — *Please take note of the course changes.*

nehmen *to get, receive; charge*

Woher nimmst du die Inspiration für deine Kunst? — *Where do you get the inspiration for your art?*
Wie viel nehmen Sie für so ein Gerät? — *How much do you charge for a device like that?*

IDIOMATIC EXPRESSIONS

Das ist entweder positiv oder negativ, je nachdem wie man es nimmt. — *That's either positive or negative, depending on how you look at it.*
Der Vertrag nimmt Bezug auf Ratsbeschlüsse. — *The contract makes reference to city council decisions.*
Opa lässt es sich nicht nehmen, alleine Auto zu fahren. — *Grandpa won't be deprived of driving the car by himself.*
Dieser Betrieb hat an der Entwicklung des Produkts Anteil genommen. — *This plant had a part in the development of the product.*
Nimm doch etwas Vernünftiges zu dir. — *Why don't you eat something sensible?*
Sie können das Glossar auf Seite 233 zu Hilfe nehmen. — *You can use the glossary on page 233 as an aid.*
Man muss die negativen Folgen in Kauf nehmen. — *You have to accept the negative consequences.*
Lars ist im Grunde genommen ein netter Junge. — *Lars is basically a nice boy.*
Der Konflikt zwischen den beiden Ländern scheint kein Ende zu nehmen. — *The conflict between the two countries seems never to end.*
Die Notwendigkeit einer engeren Zusammenarbeit wird selten in den Blick genommen. — *The necessity of closer cooperation is rarely looked at.*
Von der Leistung her nehmen sich die beiden Modelle nichts. — *In terms of performance, one model is just as good as the other.*
Streng genommen ist die Tomate ein Obst. — *Strictly speaking, the tomato is a fruit.*
Nehmen Sie bitte etwas Rücksicht auf die Bedürfnisse anderer. — *Please show some consideration for the needs of others.*

PRESENT

ich nenne	wir nennen
du nennst	ihr nennt
Sie nennen	Sie nennen
er/sie/es nennt	sie nennen

SIMPLE PAST

ich nannte	wir nannten
du nanntest	ihr nanntet
Sie nannten	Sie nannten
er/sie/es nannte	sie nannten

FUTURE

ich werde	wir werden	nennen
du wirst	ihr werdet	
Sie werden	Sie werden	
er/sie/es wird	sie werden	

PRESENT SUBJUNCTIVE I

ich nenne	wir nennen
du nennest	ihr nennet
Sie nennen	Sie nennen
er/sie/es nenne	sie nennen

PRESENT SUBJUNCTIVE II

ich nennte	wir nennten
du nenntest	ihr nenntet
Sie nennten	Sie nennten
er/sie/es nennte	sie nennten

FUTURE SUBJUNCTIVE I

ich werde	wir werden	nennen
du werdest	ihr werdet	
Sie werden	Sie werden	
er/sie/es werde	sie werden	

FUTURE SUBJUNCTIVE II

ich würde	wir würden	nennen
du würdest	ihr würdet	
Sie würden	Sie würden	
er/sie/es würde	sie würden	

PRESENT PERFECT

ich habe	wir haben	genannt
du hast	ihr habt	
Sie haben	Sie haben	
er/sie/es hat	sie haben	

PAST PERFECT

ich hatte	wir hatten	genannt
du hattest	ihr hattet	
Sie hatten	Sie hatten	
er/sie/es hatte	sie hatten	

FUTURE PERFECT

ich werde	wir werden	genannt haben
du wirst	ihr werdet	
Sie werden	Sie werden	
er/sie/es wird	sie werden	

PAST SUBJUNCTIVE I

ich habe	wir haben	genannt
du habest	ihr habet	
Sie haben	Sie haben	
er/sie/es habe	sie haben	

PAST SUBJUNCTIVE II

ich hätte	wir hätten	genannt
du hättest	ihr hättet	
Sie hätten	Sie hätten	
er/sie/es hätte	sie hätten	

FUTURE PERFECT SUBJUNCTIVE I

ich werde	wir werden	genannt haben
du werdest	ihr werdet	
Sie werden	Sie werden	
er/sie/es werde	sie werden	

FUTURE PERFECT SUBJUNCTIVE II

ich würde	wir würden	genannt haben
du würdest	ihr würdet	
Sie würden	Sie würden	
er/sie/es würde	sie würden	

COMMANDS nenn(e)! nennt! nennen Sie!

PRESENT PARTICIPLE nennend

Usage

Sie nannten ihn „Kenji", denn er war der zweitgeborene Sohn. — *They named him "Kenji" because he was the second-born son.*
Dirk sagt, er wolle keine Namen nennen. — *Dirk says he doesn't want to name names.*
Nennt mich bei meinem Vornamen. — *Call me by my first name.*
Es fiel mir schwer, ihn einen festen Freund zu nennen. — *It was difficult for me to call him a close friend.*
Eichholz hatte mehrere Gründe genannt. — *Eichholz had mentioned several reasons.*
Die Partei hat ihren Kandidaten genannt. — *The party has nominated its candidate.*

sich nennen *to be named/called*

Die erste Band nannte sich „Übel im Trübel". — *The first band was named "Übel im Trübel."*
Wie nennt sich dieses Gerät? — *What is this device called?*

RELATED VERBS benennen, ernennen, um·benennen

316 **nutzen** *to use, make use of, exploit; benefit, be useful/advantageous*

nutzt · nutzte · genutzt regular weak verb

PRESENT

ich nutze	wir nutzen
du nutzt	ihr nutzt
Sie nutzen	Sie nutzen
er/sie/es nutzt	sie nutzen

PRESENT PERFECT

ich habe	wir haben	genutzt
du hast	ihr habt	
Sie haben	Sie haben	
er/sie/es hat	sie haben	

SIMPLE PAST

ich nutzte	wir nutzten
du nutztest	ihr nutztet
Sie nutzten	Sie nutzten
er/sie/es nutzte	sie nutzten

PAST PERFECT

ich hatte	wir hatten	genutzt
du hattest	ihr hattet	
Sie hatten	Sie hatten	
er/sie/es hatte	sie hatten	

FUTURE

ich werde	wir werden	nutzen
du wirst	ihr werdet	
Sie werden	Sie werden	
er/sie/es wird	sie werden	

FUTURE PERFECT

ich werde	wir werden	genutzt haben
du wirst	ihr werdet	
Sie werden	Sie werden	
er/sie/es wird	sie werden	

PRESENT SUBJUNCTIVE I

ich nutze	wir nutzen
du nutzest	ihr nutzet
Sie nutzen	Sie nutzen
er/sie/es nutze	sie nutzen

PAST SUBJUNCTIVE I

ich habe	wir haben	genutzt
du habest	ihr habet	
Sie haben	Sie haben	
er/sie/es habe	sie haben	

PRESENT SUBJUNCTIVE II

ich nutzte	wir nutzten
du nutztest	ihr nutztet
Sie nutzten	Sie nutzten
er/sie/es nutzte	sie nutzten

PAST SUBJUNCTIVE II

ich hätte	wir hätten	genutzt
du hättest	ihr hättet	
Sie hätten	Sie hätten	
er/sie/es hätte	sie hätten	

FUTURE SUBJUNCTIVE I

ich werde	wir werden	nutzen
du werdest	ihr werdet	
Sie werden	Sie werden	
er/sie/es werde	sie werden	

FUTURE PERFECT SUBJUNCTIVE I

ich werde	wir werden	genutzt haben
du werdest	ihr werdet	
Sie werden	Sie werden	
er/sie/es werde	sie werden	

FUTURE SUBJUNCTIVE II

ich würde	wir würden	nutzen
du würdest	ihr würdet	
Sie würden	Sie würden	
er/sie/es würde	sie würden	

FUTURE PERFECT SUBJUNCTIVE II

ich würde	wir würden	genutzt haben
du würdest	ihr würdet	
Sie würden	Sie würden	
er/sie/es würde	sie würden	

COMMANDS nutz(e)! nutzt! nutzen Sie!

PRESENT PARTICIPLE nutzend

NOTE The umlauted variant **nützen** is also common, especially in the south.

Usage

Nutzen Sie diese Möglichkeit, sich zu informieren.	*Use this opportunity to get informed.*
Diese Ressourcen dürfen nicht genutzt werden.	*These resources may not be used.*
Yvonne nutzt die Zeit zum Lesen.	*Yvonne uses the time to read.*
Nutzt eure Kenntnisse aus der Schule!	*Make use of what you learn in school!*
Man muss seine Stärken nutzen können.	*You have to be able to exploit your strengths.*
Du musst es sinnvoll nutzen lernen.	*You have to learn how to use it sensibly.*
Die Malerin darf dieses Zimmer mietfrei nutzen.	*The painter can use this room rent free.*
Wie wird das Areal jetzt genutzt?	*How will this land be used now?*
Es nutzt mir nichts, über Einstellungen zu reden, da ich noch keinen Drucker habe.	*It's of no benefit for me to talk about settings, since I don't have a printer yet.*
Die Demonstrationen haben nichts genutzt.	*The demonstrations were to no avail.*

RELATED VERBS ab·nutzen, aus·nutzen; *see also* **benutzen** (71)

regular weak verb **öffnet · öffnete · geöffnet**

PRESENT			PRESENT PERFECT		
ich öffne	wir öffnen		ich habe	wir haben	geöffnet
du öffnest	ihr öffnet		du hast	ihr habt	
Sie öffnen	Sie öffnen		Sie haben	Sie haben	
er/sie/es öffnet	sie öffnen		er/sie/es hat	sie haben	
SIMPLE PAST			**PAST PERFECT**		
ich öffnete	wir öffneten		ich hatte	wir hatten	geöffnet
du öffnetest	ihr öffnetet		du hattest	ihr hattet	
Sie öffneten	Sie öffneten		Sie hatten	Sie hatten	
er/sie/es öffnete	sie öffneten		er/sie/es hatte	sie hatten	
FUTURE			**FUTURE PERFECT**		
ich werde	wir werden	öffnen	ich werde	wir werden	geöffnet haben
du wirst	ihr werdet		du wirst	ihr werdet	
Sie werden	Sie werden		Sie werden	Sie werden	
er/sie/es wird	sie werden		er/sie/es wird	sie werden	
PRESENT SUBJUNCTIVE I			**PAST SUBJUNCTIVE I**		
ich öffne	wir öffnen		ich habe	wir haben	geöffnet
du öffnest	ihr öffnet		du habest	ihr habet	
Sie öffnen	Sie öffnen		Sie haben	Sie haben	
er/sie/es öffne	sie öffnen		er/sie/es habe	sie haben	
PRESENT SUBJUNCTIVE II			**PAST SUBJUNCTIVE II**		
ich öffnete	wir öffneten		ich hätte	wir hätten	geöffnet
du öffnetest	ihr öffnetet		du hättest	ihr hättet	
Sie öffneten	Sie öffneten		Sie hätten	Sie hätten	
er/sie/es öffnete	sie öffneten		er/sie/es hätte	sie hätten	
FUTURE SUBJUNCTIVE I			**FUTURE PERFECT SUBJUNCTIVE I**		
ich werde	wir werden	öffnen	ich werde	wir werden	geöffnet haben
du werdest	ihr werdet		du werdest	ihr werdet	
Sie werden	Sie werden		Sie werden	Sie werden	
er/sie/es werde	sie werden		er/sie/es werde	sie werden	
FUTURE SUBJUNCTIVE II			**FUTURE PERFECT SUBJUNCTIVE II**		
ich würde	wir würden	öffnen	ich würde	wir würden	geöffnet haben
du würdest	ihr würdet		du würdest	ihr würdet	
Sie würden	Sie würden		Sie würden	Sie würden	
er/sie/es würde	sie würden		er/sie/es würde	sie würden	

COMMANDS öffne! öffnet! öffnen Sie!

PRESENT PARTICIPLE öffnend

Usage

Sie wollte das Fenster öffnen. — *She wanted to open the window.*
Die Erfahrung hat mir neue Perspektiven geöffnet. — *This experience has opened up new perspectives for me.*
Öffnet euch die Augen. — *Open your eyes.*
Nach einiger Zeit wurden alle Geheimnisse geöffnet. — *After a while, all secrets were revealed.*
1989 öffnete man die Grenze zwischen der BRD und der DDR. — *In 1989, the border between the F.R.G. and the G.D.R. was opened.*
Seine Worte öffneten mir den Blick für eine andere Möglichkeit. — *His words opened my eyes to another possibility.*

sich öffnen *to open, unlock*

Sesam, öffne dich! — *Open, Sesame!*
Die Tür öffnete sich und ein Mann mit einem Cowboyhut trat herein. — *The door opened, and a man with a cowboy hat stepped in.*

RELATED VERBS *see* **eröffnen** (168)

318 ordnen *to order, arrange, file, classify, organize*

ordnet · ordnete · geordnet

regular weak verb

PRESENT

ich ordne	wir ordnen
du ordnest	ihr ordnet
Sie ordnen	Sie ordnen
er/sie/es ordnet	sie ordnen

SIMPLE PAST

ich ordnete	wir ordneten
du ordnetest	ihr ordnetet
Sie ordneten	Sie ordneten
er/sie/es ordnete	sie ordneten

FUTURE

ich werde	wir werden	ordnen
du wirst	ihr werdet	
Sie werden	Sie werden	
er/sie/es wird	sie werden	

PRESENT SUBJUNCTIVE I

ich ordne	wir ordnen
du ordnest	ihr ordnet
Sie ordnen	Sie ordnen
er/sie/es ordne	sie ordnen

PRESENT SUBJUNCTIVE II

ich ordnete	wir ordneten
du ordnetest	ihr ordnetet
Sie ordneten	Sie ordneten
er/sie/es ordnete	sie ordneten

FUTURE SUBJUNCTIVE I

ich werde	wir werden	ordnen
du werdest	ihr werdet	
Sie werden	Sie werden	
er/sie/es werde	sie werden	

FUTURE SUBJUNCTIVE II

ich würde	wir würden	ordnen
du würdest	ihr würdet	
Sie würden	Sie würden	
er/sie/es würde	sie würden	

PRESENT PERFECT

ich habe	wir haben	geordnet
du hast	ihr habt	
Sie haben	Sie haben	
er/sie/es hat	sie haben	

PAST PERFECT

ich hatte	wir hatten	geordnet
du hattest	ihr hattet	
Sie hatten	Sie hatten	
er/sie/es hatte	sie hatten	

FUTURE PERFECT

ich werde	wir werden	geordnet haben
du wirst	ihr werdet	
Sie werden	Sie werden	
er/sie/es wird	sie werden	

PAST SUBJUNCTIVE I

ich habe	wir haben	geordnet
du habest	ihr habet	
Sie haben	Sie haben	
er/sie/es habe	sie haben	

PAST SUBJUNCTIVE II

ich hätte	wir hätten	geordnet
du hättest	ihr hättet	
Sie hätten	Sie hätten	
er/sie/es hätte	sie hätten	

FUTURE PERFECT SUBJUNCTIVE I

ich werde	wir werden	geordnet haben
du werdest	ihr werdet	
Sie werden	Sie werden	
er/sie/es werde	sie werden	

FUTURE PERFECT SUBJUNCTIVE II

ich würde	wir würden	geordnet haben
du würdest	ihr würdet	
Sie würden	Sie würden	
er/sie/es würde	sie würden	

COMMANDS ordne! ordnet! ordnen Sie!

PRESENT PARTICIPLE ordnend

Usage

Larissa will die User-Dateien besser ordnen.	*Larissa wants to arrange the user files better.*
Ich ordnete Akten den ganzen Tag.	*I did filing all day long.*
Ordnen Sie die Ereignisse chronologisch.	*Put the events in chronological order.*
Die Gedichte sind nach Autoren geordnet.	*The poems are arranged by author.*
Franz versucht, seine Gedanken zu ordnen.	*Franz is trying to collect his thoughts.*
Die Firma steht vor der Aufgabe, den Vorstand neu ordnen zu müssen.	*The firm is faced with the task of having to reorganize the board.*
Diese Liste wird regelmäßig geordnet.	*This list is regularly organized.*
Sie ordnet die Chrysanthemen zu einem Herbststrauß.	*She is arranging the mums in an autumn bouquet.*

sich ordnen *to form, arrange*

Die Atome ordneten sich in eine kristallförmige Struktur.	*The atoms formed a crystalline structure.*

RELATED VERBS ab·ordnen, an·ordnen, bei·ordnen, ein·ordnen, über·ordnen, unter·ordnen, verordnen, zu·ordnen

regular weak verb **packt · packte · gepackt**

PRESENT

ich packe	wir packen
du packst	ihr packt
Sie packen	Sie packen
er/sie/es packt	sie packen

SIMPLE PAST

ich packte	wir packten
du packtest	ihr packtet
Sie packten	Sie packten
er/sie/es packte	sie packten

FUTURE

ich werde	wir werden	packen
du wirst	ihr werdet	
Sie werden	Sie werden	
er/sie/es wird	sie werden	

PRESENT SUBJUNCTIVE I

ich packe	wir packen
du packest	ihr packet
Sie packen	Sie packen
er/sie/es packe	sie packen

PRESENT SUBJUNCTIVE II

ich packte	wir packten
du packtest	ihr packtet
Sie packten	Sie packten
er/sie/es packte	sie packten

FUTURE SUBJUNCTIVE I

ich werde	wir werden	packen
du werdest	ihr werdet	
Sie werden	Sie werden	
er/sie/es werde	sie werden	

FUTURE SUBJUNCTIVE II

ich würde	wir würden	packen
du würdest	ihr würdet	
Sie würden	Sie würden	
er/sie/es würde	sie würden	

PRESENT PERFECT

ich habe	wir haben	gepackt
du hast	ihr habt	
Sie haben	Sie haben	
er/sie/es hat	sie haben	

PAST PERFECT

ich hatte	wir hatten	gepackt
du hattest	ihr hattet	
Sie hatten	Sie hatten	
er/sie/es hatte	sie hatten	

FUTURE PERFECT

ich werde	wir werden	gepackt haben
du wirst	ihr werdet	
Sie werden	Sie werden	
er/sie/es wird	sie werden	

PAST SUBJUNCTIVE I

ich habe	wir haben	gepackt
du habest	ihr habet	
Sie haben	Sie haben	
er/sie/es habe	sie haben	

PAST SUBJUNCTIVE II

ich hätte	wir hätten	gepackt
du hättest	ihr hättet	
Sie hätten	Sie hätten	
er/sie/es hätte	sie hätten	

FUTURE PERFECT SUBJUNCTIVE I

ich werde	wir werden	gepackt haben
du werdest	ihr werdet	
Sie werden	Sie werden	
er/sie/es werde	sie werden	

FUTURE PERFECT SUBJUNCTIVE II

ich würde	wir würden	gepackt haben
du würdest	ihr würdet	
Sie würden	Sie würden	
er/sie/es würde	sie würden	

COMMANDS pack(e)! packt! packen Sie!

PRESENT PARTICIPLE packend

Usage

Was packst du alles in deine Büchertasche?	*What all are you packing in your book bag?*
Maria hat noch nicht gepackt.	*Maria hasn't packed yet.*
Wir durften für die Reise keine Kleidung packen.	*We weren't allowed to pack any clothing for the trip.*
Jan packte drei große Koffer und ein Handgepäck.	*Jan packed three large suitcases and one carry-on bag.*
Packt ihr schon für den Umzug?	*Are you already packing for the move?*
Ich packe das Geschenk in buntes Papier.	*I'll wrap the present in colorful paper.*
Sie haben ihre Winterkleidung in den Schrank gepackt.	*They stowed their winter clothes in the cabinet.*
Ein Fremder packte sie am Arm aber sie entkam ihm.	*A stranger took hold of her arm, but she got away from him.*
Wir müssen diese Gelegenheit packen.	*We must seize this opportunity.*
Peter und Georg wurden plötzlich vom Reisefieber gepackt und sind vier Wochen nach Hawaii geflogen.	*Peter and Georg suddenly caught the travel bug and flew to Hawaii for four weeks.*

RELATED VERBS an·packen, auf·packen, aus·packen, bei·packen, bepacken, ein·packen, um·packen, verpacken, weg·packen, zu·packen, zusammen·packen

passieren *to happen, occur, come to pass*

passiert · passierte · passiert

regular weak verb

PRESENT

ich passiere	wir passieren
du passierst	ihr passiert
Sie passieren	Sie passieren
er/sie/es passiert	sie passieren

SIMPLE PAST

ich passierte	wir passierten
du passiertest	ihr passiertet
Sie passierten	Sie passierten
er/sie/es passierte	sie passierten

FUTURE

ich werde	wir werden	passieren
du wirst	ihr werdet	
Sie werden	Sie werden	
er/sie/es wird	sie werden	

PRESENT SUBJUNCTIVE I

ich passiere	wir passieren
du passierest	ihr passieret
Sie passieren	Sie passieren
er/sie/es passiere	sie passieren

PRESENT SUBJUNCTIVE II

ich passierte	wir passierten
du passiertest	ihr passiertet
Sie passierten	Sie passierten
er/sie/es passierte	sie passierten

FUTURE SUBJUNCTIVE I

ich werde	wir werden	passieren
du werdest	ihr werdet	
Sie werden	Sie werden	
er/sie/es werde	sie werden	

FUTURE SUBJUNCTIVE II

ich würde	wir würden	passieren
du würdest	ihr würdet	
Sie würden	Sie würden	
er/sie/es würde	sie würden	

PRESENT PERFECT

ich bin	wir sind	passiert
du bist	ihr seid	
Sie sind	Sie sind	
er/sie/es ist	sie sind	

PAST PERFECT

ich war	wir waren	passiert
du warst	ihr wart	
Sie waren	Sie waren	
er/sie/es war	sie waren	

FUTURE PERFECT

ich werde	wir werden	passiert sein
du wirst	ihr werdet	
Sie werden	Sie werden	
er/sie/es wird	sie werden	

PAST SUBJUNCTIVE I

ich sei	wir seien	passiert
du seiest	ihr seiet	
Sie seien	Sie seien	
er/sie/es sei	sie seien	

PAST SUBJUNCTIVE II

ich wäre	wir wären	passiert
du wärest	ihr wäret	
Sie wären	Sie wären	
er/sie/es wäre	sie wären	

FUTURE PERFECT SUBJUNCTIVE I

ich werde	wir werden	passiert sein
du werdest	ihr werdet	
Sie werden	Sie werden	
er/sie/es werde	sie werden	

FUTURE PERFECT SUBJUNCTIVE II

ich würde	wir würden	passiert sein
du würdest	ihr würdet	
Sie würden	Sie würden	
er/sie/es würde	sie würden	

COMMANDS passier(e)! passiert! passieren Sie!

PRESENT PARTICIPLE passierend

Usage

Was ist passiert? — *What happened?*
Ein Unfall war gerade passiert, als er vorbeifuhr. — *An accident had just occurred as he drove by.*
Grausame Dinge passierten ihm im Krieg. — *Horrible things happened to him in the war.*
Es war das Schlimmste, was passieren konnte. — *It was the worst thing that could happen.*
Was wäre, wenn die amerikanische Revolution nicht passiert wäre? — *What would it be like if the American Revolution had never happened?*
Keine Angst, dir passiert nichts! — *Don't be afraid, nothing will happen to you!*

passieren (with **haben**) *to pass (through), cross*

Die Beeren durch ein Sieb passieren, um die Kerne zu entfernen. (RECIPE) — *Strain the berries through a sieve to remove the seeds.*
Wo passieren wir den Zoll? — *Where do we pass through customs?*
Letztes Jahr haben 350 032 PKWs die Grenze bei Lichtstedt passiert. — *Last year, 350,032 vehicles crossed the border at Lichtstedt.*

strong verb

pfeift · pfiff · gepfiffen

PRESENT

ich pfeife	wir pfeifen
du pfeifst	ihr pfeift
Sie pfeifen	Sie pfeifen
er/sie/es pfeift	sie pfeifen

SIMPLE PAST

ich pfiff	wir pfiffen
du pfiffst	ihr pfifft
Sie pfiffen	Sie pfiffen
er/sie/es pfiff	sie pfiffen

FUTURE

ich werde	wir werden	pfeifen
du wirst	ihr werdet	
Sie werden	Sie werden	
er/sie/es wird	sie werden	

PRESENT SUBJUNCTIVE I

ich pfeife	wir pfeifen
du pfeifest	ihr pfeifet
Sie pfeifen	Sie pfeifen
er/sie/es pfeife	sie pfeifen

PRESENT SUBJUNCTIVE II

ich pfiffe	wir pfiffen
du pfiffest	ihr pfiffet
Sie pfiffen	Sie pfiffen
er/sie/es pfiffe	sie pfiffen

FUTURE SUBJUNCTIVE I

ich werde	wir werden	pfeifen
du werdest	ihr werdet	
Sie werden	Sie werden	
er/sie/es werde	sie werden	

FUTURE SUBJUNCTIVE II

ich würde	wir würden	pfeifen
du würdest	ihr würdet	
Sie würden	Sie würden	
er/sie/es würde	sie würden	

PRESENT PERFECT

ich habe	wir haben	gepfiffen
du hast	ihr habt	
Sie haben	Sie haben	
er/sie/es hat	sie haben	

PAST PERFECT

ich hatte	wir hatten	gepfiffen
du hattest	ihr hattet	
Sie hatten	Sie hatten	
er/sie/es hatte	sie hatten	

FUTURE PERFECT

ich werde	wir werden	gepfiffen haben
du wirst	ihr werdet	
Sie werden	Sie werden	
er/sie/es wird	sie werden	

PAST SUBJUNCTIVE I

ich habe	wir haben	gepfiffen
du habest	ihr habet	
Sie haben	Sie haben	
er/sie/es habe	sie haben	

PAST SUBJUNCTIVE II

ich hätte	wir hätten	gepfiffen
du hättest	ihr hättet	
Sie hätten	Sie hätten	
er/sie/es hätte	sie hätten	

FUTURE PERFECT SUBJUNCTIVE I

ich werde	wir werden	gepfiffen haben
du werdest	ihr werdet	
Sie werden	Sie werden	
er/sie/es werde	sie werden	

FUTURE PERFECT SUBJUNCTIVE II

ich würde	wir würden	gepfiffen haben
du würdest	ihr würdet	
Sie würden	Sie würden	
er/sie/es würde	sie würden	

COMMANDS pfeif(e)! pfeift! pfeifen Sie!

PRESENT PARTICIPLE pfeifend

Usage

Bernhard singt nicht in der Dusche, er pfeift.	*Bernhard doesn't sing in the shower, he whistles.*
Wenn er pfiff, kam der Hund.	*Whenever he whistled, the dog came.*
Der Schiedsrichter hatte zweimal gepfiffen, aber niemand hörte es.	*The referee had blown the whistle twice, but nobody heard it.*
Ich kann nicht gut pfeifen.	*I can't whistle well.*
Warum pfeifen die Vögel nicht mehr?	*Why aren't the birds singing anymore?*
Der unglückliche Schauspieler wurde noch mal von der Bühne gepfiffen.	*The unfortunate actor was again booed* (lit., *whistled*) *off stage.*
Hans pfeift diese Melodie, wenn er zufrieden ist.	*Hans whistles that tune when he's happy.*
Pfeift er immer nach dem Kellner so?	*Does he always whistle for the waiter like that?*
Herr Zebrand hofft, das Endspiel pfeifen zu können.	*Mr. Zebrand hopes to be able to referee the final game.*
Die Spatzen pfeifen es von den Dächern. (PROVERB)	*It's all over town. / It's common knowledge.* (lit., *The sparrows are whistling it from the rooftops.*)

RELATED VERBS aus·pfeifen, zurück·pfeifen

322 **pflegen** *to tend, care for; cultivate, foster*

pflegt · pflegte/pflog · gepflegt/gepflogen regular weak verb or strong verb

PRESENT

ich pflege	wir pflegen
du pflegst	ihr pflegt
Sie pflegen	Sie pflegen
er/sie/es pflegt	sie pflegen

SIMPLE PAST

ich pflegte/pflog	wir pflegten/pflogen
du pflegtest/pflogst	ihr pflegtet/pflogt
Sie pflegten/pflogen	Sie pflegten/pflogen
er/sie/es pflegte/pflog	sie pflegten/pflogen

FUTURE

ich werde	wir werden	pflegen
du wirst	ihr werdet	
Sie werden	Sie werden	
er/sie/es wird	sie werden	

PRESENT SUBJUNCTIVE I

ich pflege	wir pflegen
du pflegest	ihr pfleget
Sie pflegen	Sie pflegen
er/sie/es pflege	sie pflegen

PRESENT SUBJUNCTIVE II

ich pflegte/pflöge	wir pflegten/pflögen
du pflegtest/pflögest	ihr pflegtet/pflöget
Sie pflegten/pflögen	Sie pflegten/pflögen
er/sie/es pflegte/pflöge	sie pflegten/pflögen

FUTURE SUBJUNCTIVE I

ich werde	wir werden	pflegen
du werdest	ihr werdet	
Sie werden	Sie werden	
er/sie/es werde	sie werden	

FUTURE SUBJUNCTIVE II

ich würde	wir würden	pflegen
du würdest	ihr würdet	
Sie würden	Sie würden	
er/sie/es würde	sie würden	

PRESENT PERFECT

ich habe	wir haben	gepflegt/gepflogen
du hast	ihr habt	
Sie haben	Sie haben	
er/sie/es hat	sie haben	

PAST PERFECT

ich hatte	wir hatten	gepflegt/gepflogen
du hattest	ihr hattet	
Sie hatten	Sie hatten	
er/sie/es hatte	sie hatten	

FUTURE PERFECT

ich werde	wir werden	gepflegt haben OR gepflogen haben
du wirst	ihr werdet	
Sie werden	Sie werden	
er/sie/es wird	sie werden	

PAST SUBJUNCTIVE I

ich habe	wir haben	gepflegt/gepflogen
du habest	ihr habet	
Sie haben	Sie haben	
er/sie/es habe	sie haben	

PAST SUBJUNCTIVE II

ich hätte	wir hätten	gepflegt/gepflogen
du hättest	ihr hättet	
Sie hätten	Sie hätten	
er/sie/es hätte	sie hätten	

FUTURE PERFECT SUBJUNCTIVE I

ich werde	wir werden	gepflegt haben OR gepflogen haben
du werdest	ihr werdet	
Sie werden	Sie werden	
er/sie/es werde	sie werden	

FUTURE PERFECT SUBJUNCTIVE II

ich würde	wir würden	gepflegt haben OR gepflogen haben
du würdest	ihr würdet	
Sie würden	Sie würden	
er/sie/es würde	sie würden	

COMMANDS pfleg(e)! pflegt! pflegen Sie!

PRESENT PARTICIPLE pflegend

NOTE In modern German, the strong forms of **pflegen** occur in limited contexts.

Usage

Meine Mutter pflegt ihren kränklichen Mann. — *My mother is caring for her invalid husband.*

Im Sommer pflegte Herr Milek seinen Garten. — *In the summer, Mr. Milek tended his garden.*

Die beiden pflegten ihre Freundschaft bis zu seinem Tod. — *The two of them maintained their friendship until his death.*

Nur so kann eine Zusammenarbeit gepflegt werden. — *Only in this way can cooperation be cultivated.*

Wie können wir ein Klima der Versöhnung pflegen? — *How can we foster a climate of reconciliation?*

Sein Herr zum mindesten pflog lange Unterredungen mit ihm. (Ebner-Eschenbach) — *His master at least cultivated long conversations with him.*

pflegen + infinitive *to be accustomed to, be wont to*

Unser Kater pflegt hier vor dem Kamin zu schlafen. — *Our cat is accustomed to sleeping here in front of the hearth.*

Robert pflegte immer zu sagen: „Da bin ich überfragt." — *Robert was always wont to say, "I'm not the one to ask."*

RELATED VERB verpflegen

regular weak verb **plant · plante · geplant**

PRESENT		PRESENT PERFECT		
ich plane	wir planen	ich habe	wir haben	geplant
du planst	ihr plant	du hast	ihr habt	
Sie planen	Sie planen	Sie haben	Sie haben	
er/sie/es plant	sie planen	er/sie/es hat	sie haben	

SIMPLE PAST		PAST PERFECT		
ich plante	wir planten	ich hatte	wir hatten	geplant
du plantest	ihr plantet	du hattest	ihr hattet	
Sie planten	Sie planten	Sie hatten	Sie hatten	
er/sie/es plante	sie planten	er/sie/es hatte	sie hatten	

FUTURE			FUTURE PERFECT		
ich werde	wir werden	planen	ich werde	wir werden	geplant haben
du wirst	ihr werdet		du wirst	ihr werdet	
Sie werden	Sie werden		Sie werden	Sie werden	
er/sie/es wird	sie werden		er/sie/es wird	sie werden	

PRESENT SUBJUNCTIVE I		PAST SUBJUNCTIVE I		
ich plane	wir planen	ich habe	wir haben	geplant
du planest	ihr planet	du habest	ihr habet	
Sie planen	Sie planen	Sie haben	Sie haben	
er/sie/es plane	sie planen	er/sie/es habe	sie haben	

PRESENT SUBJUNCTIVE II		PAST SUBJUNCTIVE II		
ich plante	wir planten	ich hätte	wir hätten	geplant
du plantest	ihr plantet	du hättest	ihr hättet	
Sie planten	Sie planten	Sie hätten	Sie hätten	
er/sie/es plante	sie planten	er/sie/es hätte	sie hätten	

FUTURE SUBJUNCTIVE I			FUTURE PERFECT SUBJUNCTIVE I		
ich werde	wir werden	planen	ich werde	wir werden	geplant haben
du werdest	ihr werdet		du werdest	ihr werdet	
Sie werden	Sie werden		Sie werden	Sie werden	
er/sie/es werde	sie werden		er/sie/es werde	sie werden	

FUTURE SUBJUNCTIVE II			FUTURE PERFECT SUBJUNCTIVE II		
ich würde	wir würden	planen	ich würde	wir würden	geplant haben
du würdest	ihr würdet		du würdest	ihr würdet	
Sie würden	Sie würden		Sie würden	Sie würden	
er/sie/es würde	sie würden		er/sie/es würde	sie würden	

COMMANDS plan(e)! plant! planen Sie!

PRESENT PARTICIPLE planend

Usage

Der Lehrer plant den morgigen Unterricht.	*The teacher is planning tomorrow's class.*
Ich plane eine große Hochzeit.	*I am planning a big wedding.*
Die Firma plant einen Personalabbau.	*The company is planning a workforce reduction.*
Wir planen ein Haus zu kaufen.	*We plan to buy a house.*
Planen Sie schon Ihren Urlaub?	*Are you already planning your vacation?*
Ein Konzert und Feuerwerke werden für den Nationalfeiertag geplant.	*A concert and fireworks are being planned for the national holiday.*
Die USA planen einen militärischen Einsatz.	*The U.S. is planning a military engagement.*
Der Architekt Sven Teichler hat das Rathaus geplant.	*The architect Sven Teichler designed city hall.*
Ein Sprecher teilte mit, dass das Parlament einen neuen Personalausweis plane.	*A spokesperson reported that parliament is proposing a new personal identification card.*
Im Geheimen planten die Verschwörer gegen Hitler.	*The conspirators plotted secretly against Hitler.*
Der Angriff war von langer Hand geplant. (*idiomatic*)	*The attack had been in the works for a long time.*

RELATED VERBS ein·planen, verplanen

324 preisen *to praise, extol, laud*

preist · pries · gepriesen

strong verb

PRESENT

ich preise	wir preisen
du preist	ihr preist
Sie preisen	Sie preisen
er/sie/es preist	sie preisen

SIMPLE PAST

ich pries	wir priesen
du priesest	ihr priest
Sie priesen	Sie priesen
er/sie/es pries	sie priesen

FUTURE

ich werde	wir werden	preisen
du wirst	ihr werdet	
Sie werden	Sie werden	
er/sie/es wird	sie werden	

PRESENT SUBJUNCTIVE I

ich preise	wir preisen
du preisest	ihr preiset
Sie preisen	Sie preisen
er/sie/es preise	sie preisen

PRESENT SUBJUNCTIVE II

ich priese	wir priesen
du priesest	ihr prieset
Sie priesen	Sie priesen
er/sie/es priese	sie priesen

FUTURE SUBJUNCTIVE I

ich werde	wir werden	preisen
du werdest	ihr werdet	
Sie werden	Sie werden	
er/sie/es werde	sie werden	

FUTURE SUBJUNCTIVE II

ich würde	wir würden	preisen
du würdest	ihr würdet	
Sie würden	Sie würden	
er/sie/es würde	sie würden	

PRESENT PERFECT

ich habe	wir haben	gepriesen
du hast	ihr habt	
Sie haben	Sie haben	
er/sie/es hat	sie haben	

PAST PERFECT

ich hatte	wir hatten	gepriesen
du hattest	ihr hattet	
Sie hatten	Sie hatten	
er/sie/es hatte	sie hatten	

FUTURE PERFECT

ich werde	wir werden	gepriesen haben
du wirst	ihr werdet	
Sie werden	Sie werden	
er/sie/es wird	sie werden	

PAST SUBJUNCTIVE I

ich habe	wir haben	gepriesen
du habest	ihr habet	
Sie haben	Sie haben	
er/sie/es habe	sie haben	

PAST SUBJUNCTIVE II

ich hätte	wir hätten	gepriesen
du hättest	ihr hättet	
Sie hätten	Sie hätten	
er/sie/es hätte	sie hätten	

FUTURE PERFECT SUBJUNCTIVE I

ich werde	wir werden	gepriesen haben
du werdest	ihr werdet	
Sie werden	Sie werden	
er/sie/es werde	sie werden	

FUTURE PERFECT SUBJUNCTIVE II

ich würde	wir würden	gepriesen haben
du würdest	ihr würdet	
Sie würden	Sie würden	
er/sie/es würde	sie würden	

COMMANDS preis(e)! preist! preisen Sie!

PRESENT PARTICIPLE preisend

Usage

Der Präsident pries die Tapferkeit der im Krieg Gefallenen. — *The president paid tribute to the bravery of those who had fallen in battle.*

Die Schönheit dieses mittelalterlichen Dorfs wird von allen gepriesen. — *The beauty of this medieval village is extolled by all.*

Mein Großvater preist die Tüchtigkeit und den Fleiß seiner Frau. — *My grandfather praises his wife's efficiency and industriousness.*

Das Volk pries seine Vorfahren. — *The people praised their ancestors.*

Fridigerns Taten priesen die Goten in Liedern. (Grimm) — *The Goths praised Fridigern's deeds in songs.*

Müller pries die Predigten als „göttliche Poesie". — *Müller praised the sermons as "divine poetry."*

Das Produkt wird als Wunder gepriesen. — *The product is being trumpeted as a miracle.*

Ich preise mich glücklich, in Berkeley studieren zu können. — *I consider myself lucky to be able to study in Berkeley.*

RELATED VERBS an·preisen, lob(·)preisen

regular weak verb

probiert · probierte · probiert

PRESENT

ich probiere	wir probieren
du probierst	ihr probiert
Sie probieren	Sie probieren
er/sie/es probiert	sie probieren

SIMPLE PAST

ich probierte	wir probierten
du probiertest	ihr probiertet
Sie probierten	Sie probierten
er/sie/es probierte	sie probierten

FUTURE

ich werde	wir werden	probieren
du wirst	ihr werdet	
Sie werden	Sie werden	
er/sie/es wird	sie werden	

PRESENT SUBJUNCTIVE I

ich probiere	wir probieren
du probierest	ihr probieret
Sie probieren	Sie probieren
er/sie/es probiere	sie probieren

PRESENT SUBJUNCTIVE II

ich probierte	wir probierten
du probiertest	ihr probiertet
Sie probierten	Sie probierten
er/sie/es probierte	sie probierten

FUTURE SUBJUNCTIVE I

ich werde	wir werden	probieren
du werdest	ihr werdet	
Sie werden	Sie werden	
er/sie/es werde	sie werden	

FUTURE SUBJUNCTIVE II

ich würde	wir würden	probieren
du würdest	ihr würdet	
Sie würden	Sie würden	
er/sie/es würde	sie würden	

PRESENT PERFECT

ich habe	wir haben	probiert
du hast	ihr habt	
Sie haben	Sie haben	
er/sie/es hat	sie haben	

PAST PERFECT

ich hatte	wir hatten	probiert
du hattest	ihr hattet	
Sie hatten	Sie hatten	
er/sie/es hatte	sie hatten	

FUTURE PERFECT

ich werde	wir werden	probiert haben
du wirst	ihr werdet	
Sie werden	Sie werden	
er/sie/es wird	sie werden	

PAST SUBJUNCTIVE I

ich habe	wir haben	probiert
du habest	ihr habet	
Sie haben	Sie haben	
er/sie/es habe	sie haben	

PAST SUBJUNCTIVE II

ich hätte	wir hätten	probiert
du hättest	ihr hättet	
Sie hätten	Sie hätten	
er/sie/es hätte	sie hätten	

FUTURE PERFECT SUBJUNCTIVE I

ich werde	wir werden	probiert haben
du werdest	ihr werdet	
Sie werden	Sie werden	
er/sie/es werde	sie werden	

FUTURE PERFECT SUBJUNCTIVE II

ich würde	wir würden	probiert haben
du würdest	ihr würdet	
Sie würden	Sie würden	
er/sie/es würde	sie würden	

COMMANDS probier(e)! probiert! probieren Sie!

PRESENT PARTICIPLE probierend

Usage

Hast du den Kuchen probiert?	*Have you tasted the cake?*
Probieren Sie die Spezialitäten des Hauses!	*Try the specialties of the house!*
Wir haben nur ein bisschen probiert.	*We sampled just a little bit.*
Unser Papa möchte ein anderes Medikament probieren.	*Our papa would like to try a different medicine.*
Wie viele Jugendliche probieren illegale Drogen vor dem Alter von dreizehn Jahren?	*How many young people try illegal drugs before the age of 13 years?*
Man kann das Produkt kostenlos probieren.	*You can try the product free of charge.*
Probier mal den Met. Er schmeckt lecker.	*Taste the mead. It tastes delicious.*
Ich probiere erstmal von der Erdbeerkonfitüre, dann von der Loganbeere.	*First, I'll sample the strawberry preserves, then the loganberry.*
Was passiert, wenn du es noch mal probierst?	*What happens when you try it again?*
Okay, Kinder, probieren wir das Lied noch einmal.	*Okay, children, let's rehearse the song one more time.*
Probieren geht über Studieren. (PROVERB)	*The proof of the pudding is in the eating.*

RELATED VERBS an·probieren, auf·probieren, aus·probieren

326 protestieren *to protest, object (to)*

protestiert · protestierte · protestiert regular weak verb

PRESENT

ich protestiere	wir protestieren
du protestierst	ihr protestiert
Sie protestieren	Sie protestieren
er/sie/es protestiert	sie protestieren

SIMPLE PAST

ich protestierte	wir protestierten
du protestiertest	ihr protestiertet
Sie protestierten	Sie protestierten
er/sie/es protestierte	sie protestierten

FUTURE

ich werde	wir werden	protestieren
du wirst	ihr werdet	
Sie werden	Sie werden	
er/sie/es wird	sie werden	

PRESENT SUBJUNCTIVE I

ich protestiere	wir protestieren
du protestierest	ihr protestieret
Sie protestieren	Sie protestieren
er/sie/es protestiere	sie protestieren

PRESENT SUBJUNCTIVE II

ich protestierte	wir protestierten
du protestiertest	ihr protestiertet
Sie protestierten	Sie protestierten
er/sie/es protestierte	sie protestierten

FUTURE SUBJUNCTIVE I

ich werde	wir werden	protestieren
du werdest	ihr werdet	
Sie werden	Sie werden	
er/sie/es werde	sie werden	

FUTURE SUBJUNCTIVE II

ich würde	wir würden	protestieren
du würdest	ihr würdet	
Sie würden	Sie würden	
er/sie/es würde	sie würden	

PRESENT PERFECT

ich habe	wir haben	protestiert
du hast	ihr habt	
Sie haben	Sie haben	
er/sie/es hat	sie haben	

PAST PERFECT

ich hatte	wir hatten	protestiert
du hattest	ihr hattet	
Sie hatten	Sie hatten	
er/sie/es hatte	sie hatten	

FUTURE PERFECT

ich werde	wir werden	protestiert haben
du wirst	ihr werdet	
Sie werden	Sie werden	
er/sie/es wird	sie werden	

PAST SUBJUNCTIVE I

ich habe	wir haben	protestiert
du habest	ihr habet	
Sie haben	Sie haben	
er/sie/es habe	sie haben	

PAST SUBJUNCTIVE II

ich hätte	wir hätten	protestiert
du hättest	ihr hättet	
Sie hätten	Sie hätten	
er/sie/es hätte	sie hätten	

FUTURE PERFECT SUBJUNCTIVE I

ich werde	wir werden	protestiert haben
du werdest	ihr werdet	
Sie werden	Sie werden	
er/sie/es werde	sie werden	

FUTURE PERFECT SUBJUNCTIVE II

ich würde	wir würden	protestiert haben
du würdest	ihr würdet	
Sie würden	Sie würden	
er/sie/es würde	sie würden	

COMMANDS protestier(e)! protestiert! protestieren Sie!

PRESENT PARTICIPLE protestierend

Usage

Überall wurde demonstriert und protestiert. — *Everywhere there were demonstrations and protests.*

Anwohner protestieren heftig gegen das geplante Industriegebiet. — *Residents vehemently object to the proposed industrial park.*

Wir haben gegen den Krieg protestiert. — *We protested against the war.*

Ulrike protestiert gegen den Plan, gentechnisch veränderte Lebensmittel auf dem Markt zuzulassen. — *Ulrike objects to the plan to allow genetically modified foods onto the market.*

Die Sendung wurde aus dem Programm gestrichen, aber die Zuschauer haben protestiert. — *The program was cut from the schedule, but viewers protested.*

Bürger protestierten bei der Stadt gegen den Abbau der Subventionen. — *Citizens protested to the city against the cutback in subsidies.*

Warum protestierst du nicht dagegen? — *Why aren't you protesting that?*

Ihr protestiert gegen unsere Lösung, aber ihr bietet keine Alternative. — *You object to our solution, but you offer no alternative.*

Soll ich den Wechsel protestieren lassen? — *Should I dispute the bill?*

regular weak verb

prüft · prüfte · geprüft

PRESENT

ich prüfe	wir prüfen
du prüfst	ihr prüft
Sie prüfen	Sie prüfen
er/sie/es prüft	sie prüfen

SIMPLE PAST

ich prüfte	wir prüften
du prüftest	ihr prüftet
Sie prüften	Sie prüften
er/sie/es prüfte	sie prüften

FUTURE

ich werde	wir werden	prüfen
du wirst	ihr werdet	
Sie werden	Sie werden	
er/sie/es wird	sie werden	

PRESENT SUBJUNCTIVE I

ich prüfe	wir prüfen
du prüfest	ihr prüfet
Sie prüfen	Sie prüfen
er/sie/es prüfe	sie prüfen

PRESENT SUBJUNCTIVE II

ich prüfte	wir prüften
du prüftest	ihr prüftet
Sie prüften	Sie prüften
er/sie/es prüfte	sie prüften

FUTURE SUBJUNCTIVE I

ich werde	wir werden	prüfen
du werdest	ihr werdet	
Sie werden	Sie werden	
er/sie/es werde	sie werden	

FUTURE SUBJUNCTIVE II

ich würde	wir würden	prüfen
du würdest	ihr würdet	
Sie würden	Sie würden	
er/sie/es würde	sie würden	

PRESENT PERFECT

ich habe	wir haben	geprüft
du hast	ihr habt	
Sie haben	Sie haben	
er/sie/es hat	sie haben	

PAST PERFECT

ich hatte	wir hatten	geprüft
du hattest	ihr hattet	
Sie hatten	Sie hatten	
er/sie/es hatte	sie hatten	

FUTURE PERFECT

ich werde	wir werden	geprüft haben
du wirst	ihr werdet	
Sie werden	Sie werden	
er/sie/es wird	sie werden	

PAST SUBJUNCTIVE I

ich habe	wir haben	geprüft
du habest	ihr habet	
Sie haben	Sie haben	
er/sie/es habe	sie haben	

PAST SUBJUNCTIVE II

ich hätte	wir hätten	geprüft
du hättest	ihr hättet	
Sie hätten	Sie hätten	
er/sie/es hätte	sie hätten	

FUTURE PERFECT SUBJUNCTIVE I

ich werde	wir werden	geprüft haben
du werdest	ihr werdet	
Sie werden	Sie werden	
er/sie/es werde	sie werden	

FUTURE PERFECT SUBJUNCTIVE II

ich würde	wir würden	geprüft haben
du würdest	ihr würdet	
Sie würden	Sie würden	
er/sie/es würde	sie würden	

COMMANDS prüf(e)! prüft! prüfen Sie!

PRESENT PARTICIPLE prüfend

Usage

Prüfen Sie, ob eine Internetverbindung vorhanden ist. — *Check whether an Internet connection exists.*
Ich prüfe die Bremsen, ehe wir losfahren. — *I'll check the brakes before we set off.*
Dieses Skript prüft die Gültigkeit der Eingabe. — *This script checks the input for validity.*
Welche Themen wurden im Schlussexamen geprüft? — *What topics were tested in the final exam?*
Es ist zu prüfen, wie schnell die Batterien geladen werden können. — *The batteries must be tested to see how quickly they can be charged.*
Schüler werden in mehreren Fächern geprüft. — *Pupils are tested in several subjects.*
Das Rennauto muss vor dem Rennen auf Funktionstüchtigkeit geprüft werden. — *The racecar must be inspected for efficiency before the race.*
Das Komitee wird die Entscheidung prüfen. — *The committee will review the decision.*
Wie prüft man Hefe? — *How do you proof yeast?*
Wir prüften die Kandidaten auf Herz und Nieren. (*figurative*) — *We put the candidates through their paces.*

RELATED VERBS durch·prüfen, nach·prüfen, überprüfen

rächen *to avenge*

rächt · rächte · gerächt regular weak verb

PRESENT

ich räche	wir rächen
du rächst	ihr rächt
Sie rächen	Sie rächen
er/sie/es rächt	sie rächen

SIMPLE PAST

ich rächte	wir rächten
du rächtest	ihr rächtet
Sie rächten	Sie rächten
er/sie/es rächte	sie rächten

FUTURE

ich werde	wir werden	rächen
du wirst	ihr werdet	
Sie werden	Sie werden	
er/sie/es wird	sie werden	

PRESENT SUBJUNCTIVE I

ich räche	wir rächen
du rächest	ihr rächet
Sie rächen	Sie rächen
er/sie/es räche	sie rächen

PRESENT SUBJUNCTIVE II

ich rächte	wir rächten
du rächtest	ihr rächtet
Sie rächten	Sie rächten
er/sie/es rächte	sie rächten

FUTURE SUBJUNCTIVE I

ich werde	wir werden	rächen
du werdest	ihr werdet	
Sie werden	Sie werden	
er/sie/es werde	sie werden	

FUTURE SUBJUNCTIVE II

ich würde	wir würden	rächen
du würdest	ihr würdet	
Sie würden	Sie würden	
er/sie/es würde	sie würden	

PRESENT PERFECT

ich habe	wir haben	gerächt
du hast	ihr habt	
Sie haben	Sie haben	
er/sie/es hat	sie haben	

PAST PERFECT

ich hatte	wir hatten	gerächt
du hattest	ihr hattet	
Sie hatten	Sie hatten	
er/sie/es hatte	sie hatten	

FUTURE PERFECT

ich werde	wir werden	gerächt haben
du wirst	ihr werdet	
Sie werden	Sie werden	
er/sie/es wird	sie werden	

PAST SUBJUNCTIVE I

ich habe	wir haben	gerächt
du habest	ihr habet	
Sie haben	Sie haben	
er/sie/es habe	sie haben	

PAST SUBJUNCTIVE II

ich hätte	wir hätten	gerächt
du hättest	ihr hättet	
Sie hätten	Sie hätten	
er/sie/es hätte	sie hätten	

FUTURE PERFECT SUBJUNCTIVE I

ich werde	wir werden	gerächt haben
du werdest	ihr werdet	
Sie werden	Sie werden	
er/sie/es werde	sie werden	

FUTURE PERFECT SUBJUNCTIVE II

ich würde	wir würden	gerächt haben
du würdest	ihr würdet	
Sie würden	Sie würden	
er/sie/es würde	sie würden	

COMMANDS räch(e)! rächt! rächen Sie!

PRESENT PARTICIPLE rächend

Usage

Kriemhilde wollte Siegfried rächen. — *Kriemhilde wanted to avenge Siegfried.*

Ellen sagt, sie habe bloß eine Beleidigung gerächt. — *Ellen says she was merely avenging an insult.*

Der Bauersknecht rächte seine Schwester, indem er den Täter gründlich verprügelte. — *The farmhand avenged his sister by giving the culprit a thorough lashing.*

Versprich mir meinen Tod nicht zu rächen. — *Promise not to avenge my death.*

sich rächen *to get revenge, avenge oneself;* (impersonal) *be paid back in kind, take its/their toll*

Dietrich schwört seiner Frau, sich an Degenhard für den Mord ihrer Schwester zu rächen. — *Dietrich swears to his wife to get revenge on Degenhard for the murder of her sister.*

Wie grausam rächst du dich! (Wieland) — *How cruelly you avenge yourself!*

Rächt euch doch nicht. — *Don't take revenge.*

Trina hat beschlossen, sich zu rächen. — *Trina has decided to get revenge.*

Manfred rächte sich an dem Kellner für die Nichtachtung. — *Manfred got even with the waiter for ignoring him.*

Dein riskantes Benehmen rächt sich eines Tages. — *Your risky behavior will take its toll some day.*

strong verb **rät · riet · geraten**

PRESENT

ich rate	wir raten
du rätst	ihr ratet
Sie raten	Sie raten
er/sie/es rät	sie raten

SIMPLE PAST

ich riet	wir rieten
du rietst	ihr rietet
Sie rieten	Sie rieten
er/sie/es riet	sie rieten

FUTURE

ich werde	wir werden	raten
du wirst	ihr werdet	
Sie werden	Sie werden	
er/sie/es wird	sie werden	

PRESENT SUBJUNCTIVE I

ich rate	wir raten
du ratest	ihr ratet
Sie raten	Sie raten
er/sie/es rate	sie raten

PRESENT SUBJUNCTIVE II

ich riete	wir rieten
du rietest	ihr rietet
Sie rieten	Sie rieten
er/sie/es riete	sie rieten

FUTURE SUBJUNCTIVE I

ich werde	wir werden	raten
du werdest	ihr werdet	
Sie werden	Sie werden	
er/sie/es werde	sie werden	

FUTURE SUBJUNCTIVE II

ich würde	wir würden	raten
du würdest	ihr würdet	
Sie würden	Sie würden	
er/sie/es würde	sie würden	

PRESENT PERFECT

ich habe	wir haben	geraten
du hast	ihr habt	
Sie haben	Sie haben	
er/sie/es hat	sie haben	

PAST PERFECT

ich hatte	wir hatten	geraten
du hattest	ihr hattet	
Sie hatten	Sie hatten	
er/sie/es hatte	sie hatten	

FUTURE PERFECT

ich werde	wir werden	geraten haben
du wirst	ihr werdet	
Sie werden	Sie werden	
er/sie/es wird	sie werden	

PAST SUBJUNCTIVE I

ich habe	wir haben	geraten
du habest	ihr habet	
Sie haben	Sie haben	
er/sie/es habe	sie haben	

PAST SUBJUNCTIVE II

ich hätte	wir hätten	geraten
du hättest	ihr hättet	
Sie hätten	Sie hätten	
er/sie/es hätte	sie hätten	

FUTURE PERFECT SUBJUNCTIVE I

ich werde	wir werden	geraten haben
du werdest	ihr werdet	
Sie werden	Sie werden	
er/sie/es werde	sie werden	

FUTURE PERFECT SUBJUNCTIVE II

ich würde	wir würden	geraten haben
du würdest	ihr würdet	
Sie würden	Sie würden	
er/sie/es würde	sie würden	

COMMANDS rate! ratet! raten Sie!

PRESENT PARTICIPLE ratend

Usage

Meine Freunde raten mir, nicht mitzufahren.	*My friends advise me not to go along.*
Sie haben mir schlecht geraten.	*You gave me bad advice.*
Das Gesundheitsministerium rät zur Impfung.	*The health ministry advises immunization.*
Forscher raten Eltern, ihren Kindern mehr vorzulesen.	*Researchers advise parents to read to their children more.*
Meine Ärztin riet mir zur Operation.	*My doctor advised me to have an operation.*
Wir haben Heinz geraten, mit dem Rauchen aufzuhören.	*We've advised Heinz to give up smoking.*
Dr. Prawelski rät Männern, die mit Krebs leben.	*Dr. Prawelski counsels men living with cancer.*
Ich rate euch, mit dem Zug zu fahren.	*I advise you to go by train.*
Wem nicht zu raten ist, dem ist auch nicht zu helfen. (PROVERB)	*He who won't listen to counsel can't be helped.*
Rate mal, wem ich gerade begegnet bin!	*Guess whom I just met!*
Darf ich nochmal raten?	*May I guess again?*

RELATED VERBS ab·raten, an·raten, entraten, erraten, missraten, verraten, widerraten, zu·raten; *see also* **beraten** (73), **geraten** (216)

330 räumen *to clear (away/out), remove; quit, leave, give up, vacate, evacuate*

räumt · räumte · geräumt

regular weak verb

PRESENT

ich räume	wir räumen
du räumst	ihr räumt
Sie räumen	Sie räumen
er/sie/es räumt	sie räumen

SIMPLE PAST

ich räumte	wir räumten
du räumtest	ihr räumtet
Sie räumten	Sie räumten
er/sie/es räumte	sie räumten

FUTURE

ich werde	wir werden	räumen
du wirst	ihr werdet	
Sie werden	Sie werden	
er/sie/es wird	sie werden	

PRESENT SUBJUNCTIVE I

ich räume	wir räumen
du räumest	ihr räumet
Sie räumen	Sie räumen
er/sie/es räume	sie räumen

PRESENT SUBJUNCTIVE II

ich räumte	wir räumten
du räumtest	ihr räumtet
Sie räumten	Sie räumten
er/sie/es räumte	sie räumten

FUTURE SUBJUNCTIVE I

ich werde	wir werden	räumen
du werdest	ihr werdet	
Sie werden	Sie werden	
er/sie/es werde	sie werden	

FUTURE SUBJUNCTIVE II

ich würde	wir würden	räumen
du würdest	ihr würdet	
Sie würden	Sie würden	
er/sie/es würde	sie würden	

PRESENT PERFECT

ich habe	wir haben	geräumt
du hast	ihr habt	
Sie haben	Sie haben	
er/sie/es hat	sie haben	

PAST PERFECT

ich hatte	wir hatten	geräumt
du hattest	ihr hattet	
Sie hatten	Sie hatten	
er/sie/es hatte	sie hatten	

FUTURE PERFECT

ich werde	wir werden	geräumt haben
du wirst	ihr werdet	
Sie werden	Sie werden	
er/sie/es wird	sie werden	

PAST SUBJUNCTIVE I

ich habe	wir haben	geräumt
du habest	ihr habet	
Sie haben	Sie haben	
er/sie/es habe	sie haben	

PAST SUBJUNCTIVE II

ich hätte	wir hätten	geräumt
du hättest	ihr hättet	
Sie hätten	Sie hätten	
er/sie/es hätte	sie hätten	

FUTURE PERFECT SUBJUNCTIVE I

ich werde	wir werden	geräumt haben
du werdest	ihr werdet	
Sie werden	Sie werden	
er/sie/es werde	sie werden	

FUTURE PERFECT SUBJUNCTIVE II

ich würde	wir würden	geräumt haben
du würdest	ihr würdet	
Sie würden	Sie würden	
er/sie/es würde	sie würden	

COMMANDS räum(e)! räumt! räumen Sie!

PRESENT PARTICIPLE räumend

Usage

Wir mussten die Wohnung räumen.	*We had to vacate the apartment.*
Räumt bitte eure Spielzeuge aus dem Weg.	*Please clear your toys out of the way.*
Die Unfallstelle war immer noch nicht geräumt worden.	*The scene of the accident had still not been cleared.*
Der andere Fahrer wartet, bis das Auto die Kreuzung geräumt hat.	*The other driver is waiting until the car has cleared the intersection.*
Ich räume den Schnee vom Gehweg.	*I'm clearing the sidewalk of snow.*
Die Partei muss jetzt zwei Sitze im Parlament räumen.	*The party must now give up two seats in parliament.*
Der Saal wird bald geräumt werden.	*The room will soon be cleared.*
Nach der Reaktorkatastrophe mussten ganze Dörfer geräumt werden.	*After the reactor catastrophe, entire villages had to be evacuated.*
Räumst du bitte die Zeitungen vom Tisch?	*Would you please clear the newspapers from the table?*
Bitte Gerald, die Geschirrspülmaschine zu räumen.	*Ask Gerald to empty the dishwasher.*
Unser Sohn starb, als seine Kompanie Minen räumte.	*Our son died when his company was sweeping mines.*

RELATED VERBS ab·räumen, aus·räumen, ein·räumen, um·räumen, weg·räumen; *see also* **auf·räumen** (30)

regular weak verb **reagiert · reagierte · reagiert**

PRESENT

ich reagiere	wir reagieren
du reagierst	ihr reagiert
Sie reagieren	Sie reagieren
er/sie/es reagiert	sie reagieren

SIMPLE PAST

ich reagierte	wir reagierten
du reagiertest	ihr reagiertet
Sie reagierten	Sie reagierten
er/sie/es reagierte	sie reagierten

FUTURE

ich werde	wir werden	reagieren
du wirst	ihr werdet	
Sie werden	Sie werden	
er/sie/es wird	sie werden	

PRESENT SUBJUNCTIVE I

ich reagiere	wir reagieren
du reagierest	ihr reagieret
Sie reagieren	Sie reagieren
er/sie/es reagiere	sie reagieren

PRESENT SUBJUNCTIVE II

ich reagierte	wir reagierten
du reagiertest	ihr reagiertet
Sie reagierten	Sie reagierten
er/sie/es reagierte	sie reagierten

FUTURE SUBJUNCTIVE I

ich werde	wir werden	reagieren
du werdest	ihr werdet	
Sie werden	Sie werden	
er/sie/es werde	sie werden	

FUTURE SUBJUNCTIVE II

ich würde	wir würden	reagieren
du würdest	ihr würdet	
Sie würden	Sie würden	
er/sie/es würde	sie würden	

PRESENT PERFECT

ich habe	wir haben	reagiert
du hast	ihr habt	
Sie haben	Sie haben	
er/sie/es hat	sie haben	

PAST PERFECT

ich hatte	wir hatten	reagiert
du hattest	ihr hattet	
Sie hatten	Sie hatten	
er/sie/es hatte	sie hatten	

FUTURE PERFECT

ich werde	wir werden	reagiert haben
du wirst	ihr werdet	
Sie werden	Sie werden	
er/sie/es wird	sie werden	

PAST SUBJUNCTIVE I

ich habe	wir haben	reagiert
du habest	ihr habet	
Sie haben	Sie haben	
er/sie/es habe	sie haben	

PAST SUBJUNCTIVE II

ich hätte	wir hätten	reagiert
du hättest	ihr hättet	
Sie hätten	Sie hätten	
er/sie/es hätte	sie hätten	

FUTURE PERFECT SUBJUNCTIVE I

ich werde	wir werden	reagiert haben
du werdest	ihr werdet	
Sie werden	Sie werden	
er/sie/es werde	sie werden	

FUTURE PERFECT SUBJUNCTIVE II

ich würde	wir würden	reagiert haben
du würdest	ihr würdet	
Sie würden	Sie würden	
er/sie/es würde	sie würden	

COMMANDS reagier(e)! reagiert! reagieren Sie!

PRESENT PARTICIPLE reagierend

Usage

Meine Schwester hat nicht rational reagiert.	*My sister didn't react rationally.*
Nebenan spielt jemand Posaune. Wie reagieren Sie?	*Next door, someone is playing the trombone. How do you respond?*
Auf der Autobahn muss man schnell reagieren können.	*One must be able to react quickly on the autobahn.*
Ich wollte auf seine Kommentare nicht reagieren.	*I didn't want to react to his comments.*
Unsere Katze reagiert aggressiv auf Hunde.	*Our cat reacts aggressively to dogs.*
Die Kinder reagierten mit Wut.	*The children reacted with rage.*
Musst du immer auf ihn reagieren?	*Must you always give him a reaction?*
Andere Substanzen reagieren mit den T-Zellen.	*Other substances react with the T-cells.*
Eine Säure ist eine chemische Verbindung, die mit einer Base reagiert.	*An acid is a chemical compound that reacts with a base.*
Wie hat er auf deine Entscheidung reagiert?	*How did he react to your decision?*
Wir suchen einen Unterhändler, der schnell reagiert.	*We're looking for a negotiator who thinks on his feet.*

RELATED VERB ab·reagieren

332 rechnen *to reckon; estimate; take into account, do/make a calculation*

rechnet · rechnete · gerechnet

regular weak verb

PRESENT

ich rechne	wir rechnen
du rechnest	ihr rechnet
Sie rechnen	Sie rechnen
er/sie/es rechnet	sie rechnen

SIMPLE PAST

ich rechnete	wir rechneten
du rechnetest	ihr rechnetet
Sie rechneten	Sie rechneten
er/sie/es rechnete	sie rechneten

FUTURE

ich werde	wir werden	rechnen
du wirst	ihr werdet	
Sie werden	Sie werden	
er/sie/es wird	sie werden	

PRESENT SUBJUNCTIVE I

ich rechne	wir rechnen
du rechnest	ihr rechnet
Sie rechnen	Sie rechnen
er/sie/es rechne	sie rechnen

PRESENT SUBJUNCTIVE II

ich rechnete	wir rechneten
du rechnetest	ihr rechnetet
Sie rechneten	Sie rechneten
er/sie/es rechnete	sie rechneten

FUTURE SUBJUNCTIVE I

ich werde	wir werden	rechnen
du werdest	ihr werdet	
Sie werden	Sie werden	
er/sie/es werde	sie werden	

FUTURE SUBJUNCTIVE II

ich würde	wir würden	rechnen
du würdest	ihr würdet	
Sie würden	Sie würden	
er/sie/es würde	sie würden	

PRESENT PERFECT

ich habe	wir haben	gerechnet
du hast	ihr habt	
Sie haben	Sie haben	
er/sie/es hat	sie haben	

PAST PERFECT

ich hatte	wir hatten	gerechnet
du hattest	ihr hattet	
Sie hatten	Sie hatten	
er/sie/es hatte	sie hatten	

FUTURE PERFECT

ich werde	wir werden	gerechnet haben
du wirst	ihr werdet	
Sie werden	Sie werden	
er/sie/es wird	sie werden	

PAST SUBJUNCTIVE I

ich habe	wir haben	gerechnet
du habest	ihr habet	
Sie haben	Sie haben	
er/sie/es habe	sie haben	

PAST SUBJUNCTIVE II

ich hätte	wir hätten	gerechnet
du hättest	ihr hättet	
Sie hätten	Sie hätten	
er/sie/es hätte	sie hätten	

FUTURE PERFECT SUBJUNCTIVE I

ich werde	wir werden	gerechnet haben
du werdest	ihr werdet	
Sie werden	Sie werden	
er/sie/es werde	sie werden	

FUTURE PERFECT SUBJUNCTIVE II

ich würde	wir würden	gerechnet haben
du würdest	ihr würdet	
Sie würden	Sie würden	
er/sie/es würde	sie würden	

COMMANDS rechne! rechnet! rechnen Sie!

PRESENT PARTICIPLE rechnend

Usage

Du kannst damit rechnen, dass es jeden Tag regnet.	*You can count on it to rain every day.*
Wie rechnet man die Kosten dafür?	*How do you reckon costs for that?*
Die Behörden rechneten mit 4.500 Teilnehmern.	*Officials estimated 4,500 participants.*
Auf ihn ist zu rechnen.	*You can rely on him.*
Lars kann gut im Kopf rechnen.	*Lars is good at doing calculations in his head.*
Manche Anthropologen weigern sich, den Neandertaler zur Spezies *Homo sapiens* zu rechnen.	*Many anthropologists refuse to classify Neandertal man as* Homo sapiens.
Noam Chomsky wird zu den größten Intellektuellen unserer Zeit gerechnet.	*Noam Chomsky is one of the greatest intellectuals of our time.*
Rechnet nicht mit mir!	*Count me out!*
Die neue Chefin rechnet mit keinen Veränderungen.	*The new boss isn't figuring on any changes.*

RELATED VERBS ab·rechnen, an·rechnen, auf·rechnen, aus·rechnen, berechnen, durch·rechnen, ein·rechnen, errechnen, mit·rechnen, nach·rechnen, um·rechnen, verrechnen, voraus·berechnen, vorher·berechnen, vor·rechnen, zu·rechnen, zusammen·rechnen

regular weak verb

redet · redete · geredet

PRESENT

ich rede	wir reden
du redest	ihr redet
Sie reden	Sie reden
er/sie/es redet	sie reden

SIMPLE PAST

ich redete	wir redeten
du redetest	ihr redetet
Sie redeten	Sie redeten
er/sie/es redete	sie redeten

FUTURE

ich werde	wir werden	reden
du wirst	ihr werdet	
Sie werden	Sie werden	
er/sie/es wird	sie werden	

PRESENT SUBJUNCTIVE I

ich rede	wir reden
du redest	ihr redet
Sie reden	Sie reden
er/sie/es rede	sie reden

PRESENT SUBJUNCTIVE II

ich redete	wir redeten
du redetest	ihr redetet
Sie redeten	Sie redeten
er/sie/es redete	sie redeten

FUTURE SUBJUNCTIVE I

ich werde	wir werden	reden
du werdest	ihr werdet	
Sie werden	Sie werden	
er/sie/es werde	sie werden	

FUTURE SUBJUNCTIVE II

ich würde	wir würden	reden
du würdest	ihr würdet	
Sie würden	Sie würden	
er/sie/es würde	sie würden	

PRESENT PERFECT

ich habe	wir haben	geredet
du hast	ihr habt	
Sie haben	Sie haben	
er/sie/es hat	sie haben	

PAST PERFECT

ich hatte	wir hatten	geredet
du hattest	ihr hattet	
Sie hatten	Sie hatten	
er/sie/es hatte	sie hatten	

FUTURE PERFECT

ich werde	wir werden	geredet haben
du wirst	ihr werdet	
Sie werden	Sie werden	
er/sie/es wird	sie werden	

PAST SUBJUNCTIVE I

ich habe	wir haben	geredet
du habest	ihr habet	
Sie haben	Sie haben	
er/sie/es habe	sie haben	

PAST SUBJUNCTIVE II

ich hätte	wir hätten	geredet
du hättest	ihr hättet	
Sie hätten	Sie hätten	
er/sie/es hätte	sie hätten	

FUTURE PERFECT SUBJUNCTIVE I

ich werde	wir werden	geredet haben
du werdest	ihr werdet	
Sie werden	Sie werden	
er/sie/es werde	sie werden	

FUTURE PERFECT SUBJUNCTIVE II

ich würde	wir würden	geredet haben
du wurdest	ihr würdet	
Sie würden	Sie würden	
er/sie/es würde	sie würden	

COMMANDS rede! redet! reden Sie!

PRESENT PARTICIPLE redend

Usage

Der Präsident redet wieder Unsinn. — *The president is talking nonsense again.*

Sie möchte über das Ereignis reden. — *She would like to talk about the event.*

Hast du versucht, mit ihm über seine Probleme zu reden? — *Have you tried talking with him about his problems?*

Ja, wir haben drei Stunden darüber geredet. — *Yes, we talked about that for three hours.*

Die Hauptfigur im Spiel redet mit den anderen Figuren kaum. — *The main character in the play hardly speaks with the other characters.*

Der Prediger redete in einem persönlichen Stil, der den Zuhörer anlockt. — *The preacher spoke in a personal style that draws the listener in.*

Ich kann nicht vor einem Publikum reden. — *I can't speak in front of an audience.*

Karla meint es gut, aber sie redet wie ein Wasserfall. (*idiomatic*) — *Karla means well, but she talks nonstop.*

RELATED VERBS an·reden, auf·reden, aus·reden, bereden, daher·reden, dahin·reden, dazwischen·reden, einher·reden, ein·reden, hinein·reden, klug·reden, mit·reden, nach·reden, überreden, unterreden, verabreden, vorbei·reden, zu·reden

334 regeln *to regulate; settle, put in order; control*

regelt · regelte · geregelt regular weak verb

PRESENT

ich reg(e)le	wir regeln
du regelst	ihr regelt
Sie regeln	Sie regeln
er/sie/es regelt	sie regeln

SIMPLE PAST

ich regelte	wir regelten
du regeltest	ihr regeltet
Sie regelten	Sie regelten
er/sie/es regelte	sie regelten

FUTURE

ich werde	wir werden	regeln
du wirst	ihr werdet	
Sie werden	Sie werden	
er/sie/es wird	sie werden	

PRESENT SUBJUNCTIVE I

ich reg(e)le	wir regeln
du regelst	ihr regelt
Sie regeln	Sie regeln
er/sie/es reg(e)le	sie regeln

PRESENT SUBJUNCTIVE II

ich regelte	wir regelten
du regeltest	ihr regeltet
Sie regelten	Sie regelten
er/sie/es regelte	sie regelten

FUTURE SUBJUNCTIVE I

ich werde	wir werden	regeln
du werdest	ihr werdet	
Sie werden	Sie werden	
er/sie/es werde	sie werden	

FUTURE SUBJUNCTIVE II

ich würde	wir würden	regeln
du würdest	ihr würdet	
Sie würden	Sie würden	
er/sie/es würde	sie würden	

PRESENT PERFECT

ich habe	wir haben	geregelt
du hast	ihr habt	
Sie haben	Sie haben	
er/sie/es hat	sie haben	

PAST PERFECT

ich hatte	wir hatten	geregelt
du hattest	ihr hattet	
Sie hatten	Sie hatten	
er/sie/es hatte	sie hatten	

FUTURE PERFECT

ich werde	wir werden	geregelt haben
du wirst	ihr werdet	
Sie werden	Sie werden	
er/sie/es wird	sie werden	

PAST SUBJUNCTIVE I

ich habe	wir haben	geregelt
du habest	ihr habet	
Sie haben	Sie haben	
er/sie/es habe	sie haben	

PAST SUBJUNCTIVE II

ich hätte	wir hätten	geregelt
du hättest	ihr hättet	
Sie hätten	Sie hätten	
er/sie/es hätte	sie hätten	

FUTURE PERFECT SUBJUNCTIVE I

ich werde	wir werden	geregelt haben
du werdest	ihr werdet	
Sie werden	Sie werden	
er/sie/es werde	sie werden	

FUTURE PERFECT SUBJUNCTIVE II

ich würde	wir würden	geregelt haben
du würdest	ihr würdet	
Sie würden	Sie würden	
er/sie/es würde	sie würden	

COMMANDS reg(e)le! regelt! regeln Sie!

PRESENT PARTICIPLE regelnd

Usage

Diese Bereiche werden verträglich geregelt. — *These domains are regulated contractually.*
Ihre Tätigkeit wird nicht gesetzlich geregelt. — *Their activity is not regulated by law.*
Diese Technologie muss geregelt werden. — *This technology must be regulated.*
Leitlinien regeln den Umgang unter Teilnehmern. — *Guidelines determine how participants are to deal with one another.*

Ich regle es schon! — *I'll settle the matter!*
Eine Ampel regelt jetzt den Verkehr dort. — *A traffic light controls traffic there now.*
Diese Proteinsynthese wird wiederum durch ein Regulatorgen geregelt. — *This protein synthesis is in turn controlled by a regulator gene.*

sich regeln *to be regulated, be governed*

Geschäftsbedingungen regeln sich nach den gesetzlichen Vorschriften. — *Business terms are governed by regulatory laws.*

RELATED VERB maßregeln

PRESENT

ich regiere	wir regieren
du regierst	ihr regiert
Sie regieren	Sie regieren
er/sie/es regiert	sie regieren

SIMPLE PAST

ich regierte	wir regierten
du regiertest	ihr regiertet
Sie regierten	Sie regierten
er/sie/es regierte	sie regierten

FUTURE

ich werde	wir werden	regieren
du wirst	ihr werdet	
Sie werden	Sie werden	
er/sie/es wird	sie werden	

PRESENT SUBJUNCTIVE I

ich regiere	wir regieren
du regierest	ihr regieret
Sie regieren	Sie regieren
er/sie/es regiere	sie regieren

PRESENT SUBJUNCTIVE II

ich regierte	wir regierten
du regiertest	ihr regiertet
Sie regierten	Sie regierten
er/sie/es regierte	sie regierten

FUTURE SUBJUNCTIVE I

ich werde	wir werden	regieren
du werdest	ihr werdet	
Sie werden	Sie werden	
er/sie/es werde	sie werden	

FUTURE SUBJUNCTIVE II

ich würde	wir würden	regieren
du würdest	ihr würdet	
Sie würden	Sie würden	
er/sie/es würde	sie würden	

PRESENT PERFECT

ich habe	wir haben	regiert
du hast	ihr habt	
Sie haben	Sie haben	
er/sie/es hat	sie haben	

PAST PERFECT

ich hatte	wir hatten	regiert
du hattest	ihr hattet	
Sie hatten	Sie hatten	
er/sie/es hatte	sie hatten	

FUTURE PERFECT

ich werde	wir werden	regiert haben
du wirst	ihr werdet	
Sie werden	Sie werden	
er/sie/es wird	sie werden	

PAST SUBJUNCTIVE I

ich habe	wir haben	regiert
du habest	ihr habet	
Sie haben	Sie haben	
er/sie/es habe	sie haben	

PAST SUBJUNCTIVE II

ich hätte	wir hätten	regiert
du hättest	ihr hättet	
Sie hätten	Sie hätten	
er/sie/es hätte	sie hätten	

FUTURE PERFECT SUBJUNCTIVE I

ich werde	wir werden	regiert haben
du werdest	ihr werdet	
Sie werden	Sie werden	
er/sie/es werde	sie werden	

FUTURE PERFECT SUBJUNCTIVE II

ich würde	wir würden	regiert haben
du würdest	ihr würdet	
Sie würden	Sie würden	
er/sie/es würde	sie würden	

COMMANDS regier(e)! regiert! regieren Sie!

PRESENT PARTICIPLE regierend

Usage

Das Bistum Hildesheim wurde viele Jahre von Fürstbischöfen regiert.	*The Bishopric of Hildesheim was ruled by prince-bishops for many years.*
Welches Bundesland regieren die Sozialdemokraten?	*Which state do the Social Democrats govern?*
Dieses Land wird von einer Plutokratie regiert.	*This country is ruled by a plutocracy.*
Die Partei regiert mit absoluter Mehrheit.	*The party governs with an absolute majority.*
Welche Regierung die beste sei? Diejenige, die uns lehrt, uns selbst zu regieren. (GOETHE)	*Which government is the best? The one that teaches us to govern ourselves.*
Diktatoren regieren seit zwanzig Jahren dort.	*Dictators have ruled there for twenty years.*
Karl der Große regierte von 768 bis 814.	*Charlemagne reigned from 768 to 814.*
Der Hunger regiert in diesen Dörfern.	*Hunger holds sway in these villages.*
Ich habe eine Liste aller Verben, die den Genitiv regieren, angelegt.	*I've compiled a list of all the verbs that take the genitive.*
Geld regiert die Welt. (*idiomatic*)	*Money makes the world go round.*

RELATED VERB mit·regieren

336 regnen *to rain*

regnet · regnete · geregnet regular weak verb

PRESENT

ich regne	wir regnen
du regnest	ihr regnet
Sie regnen	Sie regnen
er/sie/es regnet	sie regnen

SIMPLE PAST

ich regnete	wir regneten
du regnetest	ihr regnetet
Sie regneten	Sie regneten
er/sie/es regnete	sie regneten

FUTURE

ich werde	wir werden	regnen
du wirst	ihr werdet	
Sie werden	Sie werden	
er/sie/es wird	sie werden	

PRESENT SUBJUNCTIVE I

ich regne	wir regnen
du regnest	ihr regnet
Sie regnen	Sie regnen
er/sie/es regne	sie regnen

PRESENT SUBJUNCTIVE II

ich regnete	wir regneten
du regnetest	ihr regnetet
Sie regneten	Sie regneten
er/sie/es regnete	sie regneten

FUTURE SUBJUNCTIVE I

ich werde	wir werden	regnen
du werdest	ihr werdet	
Sie werden	Sie werden	
er/sie/es werde	sie werden	

FUTURE SUBJUNCTIVE II

ich würde	wir würden	regnen
du würdest	ihr würdet	
Sie würden	Sie würden	
er/sie/es würde	sie würden	

PRESENT PERFECT

ich habe	wir haben	geregnet
du hast	ihr habt	
Sie haben	Sie haben	
er/sie/es hat	sie haben	

PAST PERFECT

ich hatte	wir hatten	geregnet
du hattest	ihr hattet	
Sie hatten	Sie hatten	
er/sie/es hatte	sie hatten	

FUTURE PERFECT

ich werde	wir werden	geregnet haben
du wirst	ihr werdet	
Sie werden	Sie werden	
er/sie/es wird	sie werden	

PAST SUBJUNCTIVE I

ich habe	wir haben	geregnet
du habest	ihr habet	
Sie haben	Sie haben	
er/sie/es habe	sie haben	

PAST SUBJUNCTIVE II

ich hätte	wir hätten	geregnet
du hättest	ihr hättet	
Sie hätten	Sie hätten	
er/sie/es hätte	sie hätten	

FUTURE PERFECT SUBJUNCTIVE I

ich werde	wir werden	geregnet haben
du werdest	ihr werdet	
Sie werden	Sie werden	
er/sie/es werde	sie werden	

FUTURE PERFECT SUBJUNCTIVE II

ich würde	wir würden	geregnet haben
du würdest	ihr würdet	
Sie würden	Sie würden	
er/sie/es würde	sie würden	

COMMANDS regne! regnet! regnen Sie!

PRESENT PARTICIPLE regnend

NOTE The first- and second-person forms of **regnen** are used poetically.

Usage

Es hat jeden Tag geregnet.	*It rained every day.*
Wie lange hat es geregnet?	*How long did it rain?*
Wenn es regnet, bleiben wir zu Hause.	*If it rains, we'll stay at home.*
Nach einigen Minuten begann es wieder zu regnen.	*After a few minutes, it began to rain again.*
Drei Stunden lang regnete es stark.	*For three hours it rained hard.*
Lass es regnen!	*Let it rain!*
Den ganzen Tag regnet es fein.	*It's been drizzling all day long.*
Es regnete Bindfäden, als wir uns die Treppen hinaufstürzten. (*idiomatic*)	*It was raining cats and dogs as we dashed up the steps.*

regnen (with **sein**) *to rain* (used figuratively)

Nach der Hochzeit regnete es Reis auf uns.	*After the wedding, rice rained down on us.*

RELATED VERBS aus·regnen, beregnen, durch·regnen, ein·regnen, herab·regnen, verregnen

PRESENT

ich reibe	wir reiben
du reibst	ihr reibt
Sie reiben	Sie reiben
er/sie/es reibt	sie reiben

SIMPLE PAST

ich rieb	wir rieben
du riebst	ihr riebt
Sie rieben	Sie rieben
er/sie/es rieb	sie rieben

FUTURE

ich werde	wir werden	reiben
du wirst	ihr werdet	
Sie werden	Sie werden	
er/sie/es wird	sie werden	

PRESENT SUBJUNCTIVE I

ich reibe	wir reiben
du reibest	ihr reibet
Sie reiben	Sie reiben
er/sie/es reibe	sie reiben

PRESENT SUBJUNCTIVE II

ich riebe	wir rieben
du riebest	ihr riebet
Sie rieben	Sie rieben
er/sie/es riebe	sie rieben

FUTURE SUBJUNCTIVE I

ich werde	wir werden	reiben
du werdest	ihr werdet	
Sie werden	Sie werden	
er/sie/es werde	sie werden	

FUTURE SUBJUNCTIVE II

ich würde	wir würden	reiben
du würdest	ihr würdet	
Sie würden	Sie würden	
er/sie/es würde	sie würden	

PRESENT PERFECT

ich habe	wir haben	gerieben
du hast	ihr habt	
Sie haben	Sie haben	
er/sie/es hat	sie haben	

PAST PERFECT

ich hatte	wir hatten	gerieben
du hattest	ihr hattet	
Sie hatten	Sie hatten	
er/sie/es hatte	sie hatten	

FUTURE PERFECT

ich werde	wir werden	gerieben haben
du wirst	ihr werdet	
Sie werden	Sie werden	
er/sie/es wird	sie werden	

PAST SUBJUNCTIVE I

ich habe	wir haben	gerieben
du habest	ihr habet	
Sie haben	Sie haben	
er/sie/es habe	sie haben	

PAST SUBJUNCTIVE II

ich hätte	wir hätten	gerieben
du hättest	ihr hättet	
Sie hätten	Sie hätten	
er/sie/es hätte	sie hätten	

FUTURE PERFECT SUBJUNCTIVE I

ich werde	wir werden	gerieben haben
du werdest	ihr werdet	
Sie werden	Sie werden	
er/sie/es werde	sie werden	

FUTURE PERFECT SUBJUNCTIVE II

ich würde	wir würden	gerieben haben
du würdest	ihr würdet	
Sie würden	Sie würden	
er/sie/es würde	sie würden	

COMMANDS reib(e)! reibt! reiben Sie!

PRESENT PARTICIPLE reibend

Usage

Sie rieb sich die Augen.	*She rubbed her eyes.*
Der DAX steigt an, die Börsenhändler reiben sich die Hände.	*The DAX is rising; stock traders are rubbing their hands with anticipation.*
Hast du Sonnencreme auf die Haut gerieben?	*Did you apply sunscreen to your skin?*
Die Schuhe reiben mir die Fersen.	*The shoes are rubbing against my heels.*
Der Hund reibt seine Schnauze an meinem Bein.	*The dog is rubbing his nose on my leg.*
Eine Birne in das Müsli reiben. (RECIPE)	*Grate a pear into the muesli.*
Ich mag frisch geriebenen Käse.	*I like freshly grated cheese.*
Musst du mir unter die Nase reiben, dass ich kein Griechisch kann? (*idiomatic*)	*Must you rub it in that I don't know Greek?*

sich reiben *to irritate, annoy*

Hans reibt sich mit seinen Kollegen.	*Hans irritates his colleagues.*

RELATED VERBS ab·reiben, auf·reiben, aus·reiben, ein·reiben, trocken·reiben, verreiben, zerreiben

338 **reichen** *to be enough; reach, pass, hand; extend*

reicht · reichte · gereicht — regular weak verb

PRESENT

ich reiche	wir reichen
du reichst	ihr reicht
Sie reichen	Sie reichen
er/sie/es reicht	sie reichen

SIMPLE PAST

ich reichte	wir reichten
du reichtest	ihr reichtet
Sie reichten	Sie reichten
er/sie/es reichte	sie reichten

FUTURE

ich werde	wir werden	reichen
du wirst	ihr werdet	
Sie werden	Sie werden	
er/sie/es wird	sie werden	

PRESENT SUBJUNCTIVE I

ich reiche	wir reichen
du reichest	ihr reichet
Sie reichen	Sie reichen
er/sie/es reiche	sie reichen

PRESENT SUBJUNCTIVE II

ich reichte	wir reichten
du reichtest	ihr reichtet
Sie reichten	Sie reichten
er/sie/es reichte	sie reichten

FUTURE SUBJUNCTIVE I

ich werde	wir werden	reichen
du werdest	ihr werdet	
Sie werden	Sie werden	
er/sie/es werde	sie werden	

FUTURE SUBJUNCTIVE II

ich würde	wir würden	reichen
du würdest	ihr würdet	
Sie würden	Sie würden	
er/sie/es würde	sie würden	

PRESENT PERFECT

ich habe	wir haben	gereicht
du hast	ihr habt	
Sie haben	Sie haben	
er/sie/es hat	sie haben	

PAST PERFECT

ich hatte	wir hatten	gereicht
du hattest	ihr hattet	
Sie hatten	Sie hatten	
er/sie/es hatte	sie hatten	

FUTURE PERFECT

ich werde	wir werden	gereicht haben
du wirst	ihr werdet	
Sie werden	Sie werden	
er/sie/es wird	sie werden	

PAST SUBJUNCTIVE I

ich habe	wir haben	gereicht
du habest	ihr habet	
Sie haben	Sie haben	
er/sie/es habe	sie haben	

PAST SUBJUNCTIVE II

ich hätte	wir hätten	gereicht
du hättest	ihr hättet	
Sie hätten	Sie hätten	
er/sie/es hätte	sie hätten	

FUTURE PERFECT SUBJUNCTIVE I

ich werde	wir werden	gereicht haben
du werdest	ihr werdet	
Sie werden	Sie werden	
er/sie/es werde	sie werden	

FUTURE PERFECT SUBJUNCTIVE II

ich würde	wir würden	gereicht haben
du würdest	ihr würdet	
Sie würden	Sie würden	
er/sie/es würde	sie würden	

COMMANDS reich(e)! reicht! reichen Sie!

PRESENT PARTICIPLE reichend

Usage

100 Dollar reichen nicht für den Abend.	*One hundred dollars is not enough for the evening.*
Das Geld reicht nicht, um das Gebäude zu sanieren.	*There is not enough money to renovate the building.*
Ich habe dir schon zehn Euro gegeben. Reicht das nicht?	*I already gave you ten euros. Isn't that enough?*
Reichst du mir bitte die Butter?	*Would you please pass me the butter?*
Erna hatte ihm einen Zettel gereicht.	*Erna had given him a slip of paper.*
Man hat sich die Hände gereicht und sich versöhnt.	*They shook hands and made up.*
Kaffee und Torten wurden gereicht.	*Coffee and tarts were passed around.*
Das Land der Hunnen reichte bis zur Wolga.	*The land of the Huns extended as far as the Volga.*
Lanas Haar reicht ihr bis zum Gürtel.	*Lana's hair goes down to her waist.*
Hoffentlich reichen wir mit der Milch bis Samstag.	*Hopefully, the milk will last us until Saturday.*
Nebenwirkungen reichen von Halsschmerzen bis hin zum Fieber.	*Side effects range from sore throat to fever.*

RELATED VERBS aus·reichen, durch·reichen, ein·reichen, gereichen, herum·reichen, hin·reichen, überreichen, verabreichen, zu·reichen, zurück·reichen; *see also* **erreichen** (169)

regular weak verb **reist · reiste · gereist**

PRESENT

ich reise	wir reisen
du reist	ihr reist
Sie reisen	Sie reisen
er/sie/es reist	sie reisen

SIMPLE PAST

ich reiste	wir reisten
du reistest	ihr reistet
Sie reisten	Sie reisten
er/sie/es reiste	sie reisten

FUTURE

ich werde	wir werden	reisen
du wirst	ihr werdet	
Sie werden	Sie werden	
er/sie/es wird	sie werden	

PRESENT SUBJUNCTIVE I

ich reise	wir reisen
du reisest	ihr reiset
Sie reisen	Sie reisen
er/sie/es reise	sie reisen

PRESENT SUBJUNCTIVE II

ich reiste	wir reisten
du reistest	ihr reistet
Sie reisten	Sie reisten
er/sie/es reiste	sie reisten

FUTURE SUBJUNCTIVE I

ich werde	wir werden	reisen
du werdest	ihr werdet	
Sie werden	Sie werden	
er/sie/es werde	sie werden	

FUTURE SUBJUNCTIVE II

ich würde	wir würden	reisen
du würdest	ihr würdet	
Sie würden	Sie würden	
er/sie/es würde	sie würden	

PRESENT PERFECT

ich bin	wir sind	gereist
du bist	ihr seid	
Sie sind	Sie sind	
er/sie/es ist	sie sind	

PAST PERFECT

ich war	wir waren	gereist
du warst	ihr wart	
Sie waren	Sie waren	
er/sie/es war	sie waren	

FUTURE PERFECT

ich werde	wir werden	gereist sein
du wirst	ihr werdet	
Sie werden	Sie werden	
er/sie/es wird	sie werden	

PAST SUBJUNCTIVE I

ich sei	wir seien	gereist
du seiest	ihr seiet	
Sie seien	Sie seien	
er/sie/es sei	sie seien	

PAST SUBJUNCTIVE II

ich wäre	wir wären	gereist
du wärest	ihr wäret	
Sie wären	Sie wären	
er/sie/es wäre	sie wären	

FUTURE PERFECT SUBJUNCTIVE I

ich werde	wir werden	gereist sein
du werdest	ihr werdet	
Sie werden	Sie werden	
er/sie/es werde	sie werden	

FUTURE PERFECT SUBJUNCTIVE II

ich würde	wir würden	gereist sein
du würdcst	ihr würdet	
Sie würden	Sie würden	
er/sie/es würde	sie würden	

COMMANDS reis(e)! reist! reisen Sie!

PRESENT PARTICIPLE reisend

Usage

Tante Amalie reist gern.	*Aunt Amalie likes to travel.*
1996 bin ich eine Woche nach Zürich gereist.	*In 1996, I traveled to Zurich for a week.*
Reist du oft in Amerika?	*Do you often travel in America?*
Wir möchten nach Yamaguchi in Japan reisen.	*We'd like to travel to Yamaguchi in Japan.*
Sven reist mit dem Motorrad nach Belgrad.	*Sven is traveling by motorcycle to Belgrade.*
Reisen Sie mit uns um die Welt!	*Travel around the world with us!*
Wohin würden Sie reisen, wenn Sie viel Zeit und Geld hätten?	*Where would you travel if you had a lot of time and money?*
Meine Mutter reist immer in der ersten Klasse.	*My mother always travels in first class.*
Nächste Woche muss mein Vater geschäftlich reisen.	*My father has to travel next week on business.*
Werner reist, um etwas zu tun zu haben.	*Werner travels in order to have something to do.*
Vor kurzem reisten meine Eltern aufs Land.	*My parents left for the country a little while ago.*

RELATED VERBS ab·reisen, an·reisen, aus·reisen, bereisen, durch·reisen, ein·reisen, fort·reisen, heim·reisen, mit·reisen, nach·reisen, umher·reisen, verreisen, weg·reisen, weiter·reisen, zurück·reisen

reißen *to tear, yank*

reißt · riss · gerissen strong verb

PRESENT

ich reiße	wir reißen
du reißt	ihr reißt
Sie reißen	Sie reißen
er/sie/es reißt	sie reißen

SIMPLE PAST

ich riss	wir rissen
du rissest	ihr risst
Sie rissen	Sie rissen
er/sie/es riss	sie rissen

FUTURE

ich werde	wir werden	reißen
du wirst	ihr werdet	
Sie werden	Sie werden	
er/sie/es wird	sie werden	

PRESENT SUBJUNCTIVE I

ich reiße	wir reißen
du reißest	ihr reißet
Sie reißen	Sie reißen
er/sie/es reiße	sie reißen

PRESENT SUBJUNCTIVE II

ich risse	wir rissen
du rissest	ihr risset
Sie rissen	Sie rissen
er/sie/es risse	sie rissen

FUTURE SUBJUNCTIVE I

ich werde	wir werden	reißen
du werdest	ihr werdet	
Sie werden	Sie werden	
er/sie/es werde	sie werden	

FUTURE SUBJUNCTIVE II

ich würde	wir würden	reißen
du würdest	ihr würdet	
Sie würden	Sie würden	
er/sie/es würde	sie würden	

PRESENT PERFECT

ich habe	wir haben	gerissen
du hast	ihr habt	
Sie haben	Sie haben	
er/sie/es hat	sie haben	

PAST PERFECT

ich hatte	wir hatten	gerissen
du hattest	ihr hattet	
Sie hatten	Sie hatten	
er/sie/es hatte	sie hatten	

FUTURE PERFECT

ich werde	wir werden	gerissen haben
du wirst	ihr werdet	
Sie werden	Sie werden	
er/sie/es wird	sie werden	

PAST SUBJUNCTIVE I

ich habe	wir haben	gerissen
du habest	ihr habet	
Sie haben	Sie haben	
er/sie/es habe	sie haben	

PAST SUBJUNCTIVE II

ich hätte	wir hätten	gerissen
du hättest	ihr hättet	
Sie hätten	Sie hätten	
er/sie/es hätte	sie hätten	

FUTURE PERFECT SUBJUNCTIVE I

ich werde	wir werden	gerissen haben
du werdest	ihr werdet	
Sie werden	Sie werden	
er/sie/es werde	sie werden	

FUTURE PERFECT SUBJUNCTIVE II

ich würde	wir würden	gerissen haben
du würdest	ihr würdet	
Sie würden	Sie würden	
er/sie/es würde	sie würden	

COMMANDS reiß(e)! reißt! reißen Sie!

PRESENT PARTICIPLE reißend

Usage

Du hast ein Loch in die Hose gerissen! — *You've torn a hole in your pants!*
Der Wind riss den Schornstein von dem Dach. — *The wind ripped the chimney off the roof.*
Warum reißen Sie mich aus dem Bett? — *Why are you yanking me out of bed?*
Das Bellen eines Hundes riss ihn aus dem Schlaf. — *The barking of a dog wrenched him from his sleep.*

reißen (with **sein**) *to tear, rip, snap*

Wenn Muskeln gerissen sind, dann tut es echt weh. — *If muscles have torn, then it really hurts.*
Der Riemen war gerissen und die Tasche zum Boden gefallen. — *The strap had snapped and the purse had fallen to the ground.*

sich reißen von etwas *to tear oneself from something*

Ich habe mich vom Sofa gerissen und bin ausgegangen. — *I tore myself from the sofa and went out.*

RELATED VERBS ab·reißen, an·reißen, auf·reißen, aus·reißen, durch·reißen, ein·reißen, entreißen, fort·reißen, hin·reißen, los·reißen, mit·reißen, nieder·reißen, um·reißen, umreißen, verreißen, weg·reißen, zerreißen strong verb **reitet · ritt · geritten**

PRESENT

ich reite	wir reiten
du reitest	ihr reitet
Sie reiten	Sie reiten
er/sie/es reitet	sie reiten

SIMPLE PAST

ich ritt	wir ritten
du ritt(e)st	ihr rittet
Sie ritten	Sie ritten
er/sie/es ritt	sie ritten

FUTURE

ich werde	wir werden	reiten
du wirst	ihr werdet	
Sie werden	Sie werden	
er/sie/es wird	sie werden	

PRESENT SUBJUNCTIVE I

ich reite	wir reiten
du reitest	ihr reitet
Sie reiten	Sie reiten
er/sie/es reite	sie reiten

PRESENT SUBJUNCTIVE II

ich ritte	wir ritten
du rittest	ihr rittet
Sie ritten	Sie ritten
er/sie/es ritte	sie ritten

FUTURE SUBJUNCTIVE I

ich werde	wir werden	reiten
du werdest	ihr werdet	
Sie werden	Sie werden	
er/sie/es werde	sie werden	

FUTURE SUBJUNCTIVE II

ich würde	wir würden	reiten
du würdest	ihr würdet	
Sie würden	Sie würden	
er/sie/es würde	sie würden	

PRESENT PERFECT

ich bin	wir sind	geritten
du bist	ihr seid	
Sie sind	Sie sind	
er/sie/es ist	sie sind	

PAST PERFECT

ich war	wir waren	geritten
du warst	ihr wart	
Sie waren	Sie waren	
er/sie/es war	sie waren	

FUTURE PERFECT

ich werde	wir werden	geritten sein
du wirst	ihr werdet	
Sie werden	Sie werden	
er/sie/es wird	sie werden	

PAST SUBJUNCTIVE I

ich sei	wir seien	geritten
du seiest	ihr seiet	
Sie seien	Sie seien	
er/sie/es sei	sie seien	

PAST SUBJUNCTIVE II

ich wäre	wir wären	geritten
du wärest	ihr wäret	
Sie wären	Sie wären	
er/sie/es wäre	sie wären	

FUTURE PERFECT SUBJUNCTIVE I

ich werde	wir werden	geritten sein
du werdest	ihr werdet	
Sie werden	Sie werden	
er/sie/es werde	sie werden	

FUTURE PERFECT SUBJUNCTIVE II

ich würde	wir würden	geritten sein
du würdest	ihr würdet	
Sie würden	Sie würden	
er/sie/es würde	sie würden	

COMMANDS reite! reitet! reiten Sie!

PRESENT PARTICIPLE reitend

Usage

Wer reitet so spät durch Nacht und Wind? (GOETHE) — *Who's riding so late through night and wind?*

Der alte Staatsmann pflegte, so oft wie möglich spazieren zu reiten. — *The old statesman used to go riding for pleasure as often as possible.*

Der Clown ritt auf einem Elefanten um die Zuschauer. — *The clown rode around the spectators on an elephant.*

Warum rittst du lieber allein als mit mir? — *Why did you prefer to ride alone than with me?*

Wir waren nur zehn Minuten geritten, als es zu regnen begann. — *We had ridden only ten minutes when it began to rain.*

reiten (with **haben**) *to ride*

Dürfen unsere Kinder diese Pferde reiten? — *May our children ride these horses?*

sich reiten *to ride* (impersonal)

Bei diesem fabelhaften Wetter reitet es sich sehr gut. — *This fabulous weather is great for riding.*

RELATED VERBS ab·reiten, an·reiten, auf·reiten, aus·reiten, durchreiten, durch·reiten, ein·reiten, fort·reiten, umreiten, um·reiten, vor·reiten, weg·reiten, zu·reiten

342 rennen *to run*

rennt · rannte · gerannt mixed verb

PRESENT		PRESENT PERFECT		
ich renne	wir rennen	ich bin	wir sind	gerannt
du rennst	ihr rennt	du bist	ihr seid	
Sie rennen	Sie rennen	Sie sind	Sie sind	
er/sie/es rennt	sie rennen	er/sie/es ist	sie sind	

SIMPLE PAST		PAST PERFECT		
ich rannte	wir rannten	ich war	wir waren	gerannt
du ranntest	ihr ranntet	du warst	ihr wart	
Sie rannten	Sie rannten	Sie waren	Sie waren	
er/sie/es rannte	sie rannten	er/sie/es war	sie waren	

FUTURE			FUTURE PERFECT		
ich werde	wir werden	rennen	ich werde	wir werden	gerannt sein
du wirst	ihr werdet		du wirst	ihr werdet	
Sie werden	Sie werden		Sie werden	Sie werden	
er/sie/es wird	sie werden		er/sie/es wird	sie werden	

PRESENT SUBJUNCTIVE I		PAST SUBJUNCTIVE I		
ich renne	wir rennen	ich sei	wir seien	gerannt
du rennest	ihr rennet	du seiest	ihr seiet	
Sie rennen	Sie rennen	Sie seien	Sie seien	
er/sie/es renne	sie rennen	er/sie/es sei	sie seien	

PRESENT SUBJUNCTIVE II		PAST SUBJUNCTIVE II		
ich rennte	wir rennten	ich wäre	wir wären	gerannt
du renntest	ihr renntet	du wärest	ihr wäret	
Sie rennten	Sie rennten	Sie wären	Sie wären	
er/sie/es rennte	sie rennten	er/sie/es wäre	sie wären	

FUTURE SUBJUNCTIVE I			FUTURE PERFECT SUBJUNCTIVE I		
ich werde	wir werden	rennen	ich werde	wir werden	gerannt sein
du werdest	ihr werdet		du werdest	ihr werdet	
Sie werden	Sie werden		Sie werden	Sie werden	
er/sie/es werde	sie werden		er/sie/es werde	sie werden	

FUTURE SUBJUNCTIVE II			FUTURE PERFECT SUBJUNCTIVE II		
ich würde	wir würden	rennen	ich würde	wir würden	gerannt sein
du würdest	ihr würdet		du würdest	ihr würdet	
Sie würden	Sie würden		Sie würden	Sie würden	
er/sie/es würde	sie würden		er/sie/es würde	sie würden	

COMMANDS renn(e)! rennt! rennen Sie!

PRESENT PARTICIPLE rennend

Usage

Die Sportlerin konnte nach dem Unfall nicht mehr rennen.	*After the accident, the athlete was no longer able to run.*
Silvia rannte um die Ecke und stoß auf ihn.	*Silvia ran around the corner and bumped into him.*
Die Kinder rennen um die Wette.	*The children are running competitively.*
Der Elch ist in den Wald gerannt.	*The elk ran into the forest.*
Nathan rannte ins Zimmer und fiel tot um.	*Nathan ran into the room and fell down dead.*
Eine Katze ist mir vors Auto gerannt und ich habe sie überfahren.	*A cat ran in front of my car and I ran over it.*
Ich kann schneller rennen als er.	*I can run faster than he can.*
Sammi rennt zu jedem Räumungsverkauf in der Stadt.	*Sammi goes to every clearance sale in town.*
Der Anstreicher ist mit dem Kopf gegen die Leiter gerannt.	*The painter bumped his head on the ladder.*

rennen (with **haben**) *to bang, ram*

Alex hat mir fast ein Loch in den Kopf gerannt.	*In the collision, Alex nearly opened a gash in my head.*

RELATED VERBS an·rennen, durch·rennen, durchrennen, ein·rennen, überrennen, um·rennen, weg·rennen

to reserve reservieren 343

regular weak verb

reserviert · reservierte · reserviert

PRESENT

ich reserviere	wir reservieren
du reservierst	ihr reserviert
Sie reservieren	Sie reservieren
er/sie/es reserviert	sie reservieren

PRESENT PERFECT

ich habe	wir haben	reserviert
du hast	ihr habt	
Sie haben	Sie haben	
er/sie/es hat	sie haben	

SIMPLE PAST

ich reservierte	wir reservierten
du reserviertest	ihr reserviertet
Sie reservierten	Sie reservierten
er/sie/es reservierte	sie reservierten

PAST PERFECT

ich hatte	wir hatten	reserviert
du hattest	ihr hattet	
Sie hatten	Sie hatten	
er/sie/es hatte	sie hatten	

FUTURE

ich werde	wir werden	reservieren
du wirst	ihr werdet	
Sie werden	Sie werden	
er/sie/es wird	sie werden	

FUTURE PERFECT

ich werde	wir werden	reserviert haben
du wirst	ihr werdet	
Sie werden	Sie werden	
er/sie/es wird	sie werden	

PRESENT SUBJUNCTIVE I

ich reserviere	wir reservieren
du reservierest	ihr reservieret
Sie reservieren	Sie reservieren
er/sie/es reserviere	sie reservieren

PAST SUBJUNCTIVE I

ich habe	wir haben	reserviert
du habest	ihr habet	
Sie haben	Sie haben	
er/sie/es habe	sie haben	

PRESENT SUBJUNCTIVE II

ich reservierte	wir reservierten
du reserviertest	ihr reserviertet
Sie reservierten	Sie reservierten
er/sie/es reservierte	sie reservierten

PAST SUBJUNCTIVE II

ich hätte	wir hätten	reserviert
du hättest	ihr hättet	
Sie hätten	Sie hätten	
er/sie/es hätte	sie hätten	

FUTURE SUBJUNCTIVE I

ich werde	wir werden	reservieren
du werdest	ihr werdet	
Sie werden	Sie werden	
er/sie/es werde	sie werden	

FUTURE PERFECT SUBJUNCTIVE I

ich werde	wir werden	reserviert haben
du werdest	ihr werdet	
Sie werden	Sie werden	
er/sie/es werde	sie werden	

FUTURE SUBJUNCTIVE II

ich würde	wir würden	reservieren
du würdest	ihr würdet	
Sie würden	Sie würden	
er/sie/es würde	sie würden	

FUTURE PERFECT SUBJUNCTIVE II

ich würde	wir würden	reserviert haben
du würdest	ihr würdet	
Sie würden	Sie würden	
er/sie/es würde	sie würden	

COMMANDS reservier(e)! reserviert! reservieren Sie!

PRESENT PARTICIPLE reservierend

Usage

Wir möchten ein Doppelzimmer mit Bad reservieren.	*We'd like to reserve a double room with bath.*
Wie kann man ein Zimmer im Voraus reservieren?	*How does one reserve a room in advance?*
Willst du für uns Plätze reservieren lassen?	*Do you want to have seats reserved for us?*
Dieser Parkplatz ist für Behinderte reserviert.	*This parking space is reserved for the handicapped.*
Tickets können telefonisch reserviert werden.	*Tickets can be reserved by phone.*
Marta hat für sechs Personen im Restaurant nebenan reserviert.	*Martha made a reservation for six people at the restaurant next door.*
Ich reserviere meinen Lieblingsplatz vor dem Kamin.	*I reserve my favorite spot in front of the fireplace.*
Habt ihr für vier reserviert?	*Did you make reservations for four?*
Gabriele hat vor, die Lifttickets zu reservieren.	*Gabriele is planning to order the lift tickets ahead.*
Hast du deinen Flug schon reserviert?	*Have you already booked your flight?*
Hat die Studentin das Buch ausgeliehen oder nur reserviert?	*Did the student check the book out or only put it on hold?*

retten *to save, rescue*

rettet · rettete · gerettet regular weak verb

PRESENT

ich rette	wir retten
du rettest	ihr rettet
Sie retten	Sie retten
er/sie/es rettet	sie retten

SIMPLE PAST

ich rettete	wir retteten
du rettetest	ihr rettetet
Sie retteten	Sie retteten
er/sie/es rettete	sie retteten

FUTURE

ich werde	wir werden	retten
du wirst	ihr werdet	
Sie werden	Sie werden	
er/sie/es wird	sie werden	

PRESENT SUBJUNCTIVE I

ich rette	wir retten
du rettest	ihr rettet
Sie retten	Sie retten
er/sie/es rette	sie retten

PRESENT SUBJUNCTIVE II

ich rettete	wir retteten
du rettetest	ihr rettetet
Sie retteten	Sie retteten
er/sie/es rettete	sie retteten

FUTURE SUBJUNCTIVE I

ich werde	wir werden	retten
du werdest	ihr werdet	
Sie werden	Sie werden	
er/sie/es werde	sie werden	

FUTURE SUBJUNCTIVE II

ich würde	wir würden	retten
du würdest	ihr würdet	
Sie würden	Sie würden	
er/sie/es würde	sie würden	

PRESENT PERFECT

ich habe	wir haben	gerettet
du hast	ihr habt	
Sie haben	Sie haben	
er/sie/es hat	sie haben	

PAST PERFECT

ich hatte	wir hatten	gerettet
du hattest	ihr hattet	
Sie hatten	Sie hatten	
er/sie/es hatte	sie hatten	

FUTURE PERFECT

ich werde	wir werden	gerettet haben
du wirst	ihr werdet	
Sie werden	Sie werden	
er/sie/es wird	sie werden	

PAST SUBJUNCTIVE I

ich habe	wir haben	gerettet
du habest	ihr habet	
Sie haben	Sie haben	
er/sie/es habe	sie haben	

PAST SUBJUNCTIVE II

ich hätte	wir hätten	gerettet
du hättest	ihr hättet	
Sie hätten	Sie hätten	
er/sie/es hätte	sie hätten	

FUTURE PERFECT SUBJUNCTIVE I

ich werde	wir werden	gerettet haben
du werdest	ihr werdet	
Sie werden	Sie werden	
er/sie/es werde	sie werden	

FUTURE PERFECT SUBJUNCTIVE II

ich würde	wir würden	gerettet haben
du würdest	ihr würdet	
Sie würden	Sie würden	
er/sie/es würde	sie würden	

COMMANDS rette! rettet! retten Sie!

PRESENT PARTICIPLE rettend

Usage

Die Schwimmer wurden gerettet.	*The swimmers were rescued.*
Die Feuerwehr hat meine Katze gerettet.	*The fire department rescued my cat.*
Der Held rettete die Prinzessin vor dem Drachen.	*The hero rescued the princess from the dragon.*
Der Vater war im Brand gestorben, um seinen Sohn retten zu können.	*The father had died in the fire in order to be able to save his son.*
Rund 10.000 alte Bücher wurden von Passanten gerettet.	*About 10,000 old books were saved by passersby.*
Der Surfer rettete das kleine Kind vor der Brandungsrückströmung.	*The surfer rescued the little child from the riptide.*
Du hast mir das Leben gerettet!	*You saved my life!*
Er ist nicht zu retten.	*He can't be helped.*
Die Eishockey-Saison ist nicht mehr zu retten.	*The ice hockey season can't be salvaged.*
Die Städter haben sich vor der Überschwemmung auf Behelfsflößen gerettet.	*The townspeople escaped the flood on makeshift rafts.*

RELATED VERB erretten

strong verb **riecht · roch · gerochen**

PRESENT

ich rieche	wir riechen
du riechst	ihr riecht
Sie riechen	Sie riechen
er/sie/es riecht	sie riechen

SIMPLE PAST

ich roch	wir rochen
du rochst	ihr rocht
Sie rochen	Sie rochen
er/sie/es roch	sie rochen

FUTURE

ich werde	wir werden	riechen
du wirst	ihr werdet	
Sie werden	Sie werden	
er/sie/es wird	sie werden	

PRESENT SUBJUNCTIVE I

ich rieche	wir riechen
du riechest	ihr riechet
Sie riechen	Sie riechen
er/sie/es rieche	sie riechen

PRESENT SUBJUNCTIVE II

ich röche	wir röchen
du röchest	ihr röchet
Sie röchen	Sie röchen
er/sie/es röche	sie röchen

FUTURE SUBJUNCTIVE I

ich werde	wir werden	riechen
du werdest	ihr werdet	
Sie werden	Sie werden	
er/sie/es werde	sie werden	

FUTURE SUBJUNCTIVE II

ich würde	wir würden	riechen
du würdest	ihr würdet	
Sie würden	Sie würden	
er/sie/es würde	sie würden	

PRESENT PERFECT

ich habe	wir haben	gerochen
du hast	ihr habt	
Sie haben	Sie haben	
er/sie/es hat	sie haben	

PAST PERFECT

ich hatte	wir hatten	gerochen
du hattest	ihr hattet	
Sie hatten	Sie hatten	
er/sie/es hatte	sie hatten	

FUTURE PERFECT

ich werde	wir werden	gerochen haben
du wirst	ihr werdet	
Sie werden	Sie werden	
er/sie/es wird	sie werden	

PAST SUBJUNCTIVE I

ich habe	wir haben	gerochen
du habest	ihr habet	
Sie haben	Sie haben	
er/sie/es habe	sie haben	

PAST SUBJUNCTIVE II

ich hätte	wir hätten	gerochen
du hättest	ihr hättet	
Sie hätten	Sie hätten	
er/sie/es hätte	sie hätten	

FUTURE PERFECT SUBJUNCTIVE I

ich werde	wir werden	gerochen haben
du werdest	ihr werdet	
Sie werden	Sie werden	
er/sie/es werde	sie werden	

FUTURE PERFECT SUBJUNCTIVE II

ich würde	wir würden	gerochen haben
du würdest	ihr würdet	
Sie würden	Sie würden	
er/sie/es würde	sie würden	

COMMANDS riech(e)! riecht! riechen Sie!

PRESENT PARTICIPLE riechend

Usage

Die Rosen riechen gut.	*The roses smell good.*
Hier riecht es nach Schweinen.	*It smells like pigs here.*
Ich rieche Fisch.	*I smell fish.*
Der Braten riecht lecker.	*The roast smells delicious.*
Der Mann roch nach Alkohol.	*The man reeked of alcohol.*
Die Kapstachelbeeren riechen nach Ananas.	*The ground cherries smell like pineapple.*
Euer Hund hat an der toten Maus gerochen.	*Your dog picked up the scent of the dead mouse.*
Im Kaufhaus muss meine Freundin an jeder Parfümflasche riechen.	*At the department store, my girlfriend has to sniff every bottle of perfume.*
Ein guter Detektiv hätte den Drogenhandel gerochen.	*A good detective would have sniffed out the drug trafficking.*
Brunhilda riecht aus dem Mund.	*Brunhilda has bad breath.*
Das riecht nach einem Hardwareproblem.	*That sounds like a hardware problem.*

RELATED VERBS an·riechen, beriechen

346 ringen *to wrestle, struggle, grapple, compete; wring*

ringt · rang · gerungen strong verb

PRESENT

ich ringe	wir ringen
du ringst	ihr ringt
Sie ringen	Sie ringen
er/sie/es ringt	sie ringen

SIMPLE PAST

ich rang	wir rangen
du rangst	ihr rangt
Sie rangen	Sie rangen
er/sie/es rang	sie rangen

FUTURE

ich werde	wir werden	ringen
du wirst	ihr werdet	
Sie werden	Sie werden	
er/sie/es wird	sie werden	

PRESENT SUBJUNCTIVE I

ich ringe	wir ringen
du ringest	ihr ringet
Sie ringen	Sie ringen
er/sie/es ringe	sie ringen

PRESENT SUBJUNCTIVE II

ich ränge	wir rängen
du rängest	ihr ränget
Sie rängen	Sie rängen
er/sie/es ränge	sie rängen

FUTURE SUBJUNCTIVE I

ich werde	wir werden	ringen
du werdest	ihr werdet	
Sie werden	Sie werden	
er/sie/es werde	sie werden	

FUTURE SUBJUNCTIVE II

ich würde	wir würden	ringen
du würdest	ihr würdet	
Sie würden	Sie würden	
er/sie/es würde	sie würden	

PRESENT PERFECT

ich habe	wir haben	gerungen
du hast	ihr habt	
Sie haben	Sie haben	
er/sie/es hat	sie haben	

PAST PERFECT

ich hatte	wir hatten	gerungen
du hattest	ihr hattet	
Sie hatten	Sie hatten	
er/sie/es hatte	sie hatten	

FUTURE PERFECT

ich werde	wir werden	gerungen haben
du wirst	ihr werdet	
Sie werden	Sie werden	
er/sie/es wird	sie werden	

PAST SUBJUNCTIVE I

ich habe	wir haben	gerungen
du habest	ihr habet	
Sie haben	Sie haben	
er/sie/es habe	sie haben	

PAST SUBJUNCTIVE II

ich hätte	wir hätten	gerungen
du hättest	ihr hättet	
Sie hätten	Sie hätten	
er/sie/es hätte	sie hätten	

FUTURE PERFECT SUBJUNCTIVE I

ich werde	wir werden	gerungen haben
du werdest	ihr werdet	
Sie werden	Sie werden	
er/sie/es werde	sie werden	

FUTURE PERFECT SUBJUNCTIVE II

ich würde	wir würden	gerungen haben
du würdest	ihr würdet	
Sie würden	Sie würden	
er/sie/es würde	sie würden	

COMMANDS ring(e)! ringt! ringen Sie!

PRESENT PARTICIPLE ringend

Usage

Die beiden österreichischen Sportler haben eine Stunde lang gerungen.	*The two Austrian athletes wrestled for an hour.*
Georg hat lange mit dem Tode gerungen.	*Georg wrestled with death for a long time.*
Du rangst doch auch mit ihm? (HEBBEL)	*You wrestled with him too?*
Du ringst mit den Wogen, versinkest im Sturm. (BRENTANO)	*You fight with the waves, sink in the storm.*
Der Surfer rang mit den großen Wellen.	*The surfer battled the huge waves.*
Es wird darum gerungen, ob Stammzellen verwendet werden dürfen.	*People are struggling with the notion of whether use of stem cells should be allowed.*
Ich ringe mit einer wichtigen Entscheidung.	*I'm grappling with an important decision.*
200 Bewerber ringen um eine Stelle.	*Two hundred applicants are competing for one position.*
Der Witwer rang nach Atem und schrie: „Weh mir!"	*The widower gasped for breath and cried, "Woe is me!"*
Warum ringen Sie die Hände?	*Why are you wringing your hands?*

RELATED VERBS ab·ringen, durch·ringen, entringen, erringen

strong verb **ruft · rief · gerufen**

PRESENT

ich rufe	wir rufen
du rufst	ihr ruft
Sie rufen	Sie rufen
er/sie/es ruft	sie rufen

SIMPLE PAST

ich rief	wir riefen
du riefst	ihr rieft
Sie riefen	Sie riefen
er/sie/es rief	sie riefen

FUTURE

ich werde	wir werden	rufen
du wirst	ihr werdet	
Sie werden	Sie werden	
er/sie/es wird	sie werden	

PRESENT SUBJUNCTIVE I

ich rufe	wir rufen
du rufest	ihr rufet
Sie rufen	Sie rufen
er/sie/es rufe	sie rufen

PRESENT SUBJUNCTIVE II

ich riefe	wir riefen
du riefest	ihr riefet
Sie riefen	Sie riefen
er/sie/es riefe	sie riefen

FUTURE SUBJUNCTIVE I

ich werde	wir werden	rufen
du werdest	ihr werdet	
Sie werden	Sie werden	
er/sie/es werde	sie werden	

FUTURE SUBJUNCTIVE II

ich würde	wir würden	rufen
du würdest	ihr würdet	
Sie würden	Sie würden	
er/sie/es würde	sie würden	

PRESENT PERFECT

ich habe	wir haben	gerufen
du hast	ihr habt	
Sie haben	Sie haben	
er/sie/es hat	sie haben	

PAST PERFECT

ich hatte	wir hatten	gerufen
du hattest	ihr hattet	
Sie hatten	Sie hatten	
er/sie/es hatte	sie hatten	

FUTURE PERFECT

ich werde	wir werden	gerufen haben
du wirst	ihr werdet	
Sie werden	Sie werden	
er/sie/es wird	sie werden	

PAST SUBJUNCTIVE I

ich habe	wir haben	gerufen
du habest	ihr habet	
Sie haben	Sie haben	
er/sie/es habe	sie haben	

PAST SUBJUNCTIVE II

ich hätte	wir hätten	gerufen
du hättest	ihr hättet	
Sie hätten	Sie hätten	
er/sie/es hätte	sie hätten	

FUTURE PERFECT SUBJUNCTIVE I

ich werde	wir werden	gerufen haben
du werdest	ihr werdet	
Sie werden	Sie werden	
er/sie/es werde	sie werden	

FUTURE PERFECT SUBJUNCTIVE II

ich würde	wir würden	gerufen haben
du würdest	ihr würdet	
Sie würden	Sie würden	
er/sie/es würde	sie würden	

COMMANDS ruf(e)! ruft! rufen Sie!

PRESENT PARTICIPLE rufend

Usage

Hast du mich gerufen?	*Did you call me?*
Die Geschichte rief meine Kindheit in Erinnerung.	*The story brought my childhood to mind.*
Man ruft nach einer Erneuerung der Partei.	*They're calling for a revival of the party.*
Wer hat ein Taxi gerufen?	*Who hailed a taxi?*
Der Diplomat wurde nach Berlin gerufen.	*The diplomat was summoned to Berlin.*
Ruft doch um Hilfe.	*Cry for help.*
Ich höre meinen Großvater rufen.	*I hear my grandfather calling.*
Rufen Sie nicht so laut!	*Don't shout so loud!*
Wir müssen einen Notarzt rufen.	*We have to call a doctor.*
Unser Nachbar lässt sich von Fremden beim Vornamen rufen.	*Our neighbor lets strangers call him by his first name.*
Ich möchte einen Buchklub ins Leben rufen.	*I'd like to start up a book club.*

RELATED VERBS ab·rufen, auf·rufen, aus·rufen, dazwischen·rufen, hervor·rufen, nach·rufen, wach·rufen, widerrufen, zurück·rufen, zu·rufen, zusammen·rufen; *see also* **an·rufen** (16), **berufen** (79)

348 ruhen *to rest, sleep; have stopped, be at a standstill*

ruht · ruhte · geruht regular weak verb

PRESENT

ich ruhe	wir ruhen
du ruhst	ihr ruht
Sie ruhen	Sie ruhen
er/sie/es ruht	sie ruhen

SIMPLE PAST

ich ruhte	wir ruhten
du ruhtest	ihr ruhtet
Sie ruhten	Sie ruhten
er/sie/es ruhte	sie ruhten

FUTURE

ich werde	wir werden	ruhen
du wirst	ihr werdet	
Sie werden	Sie werden	
er/sie/es wird	sie werden	

PRESENT SUBJUNCTIVE I

ich ruhe	wir ruhen
du ruhest	ihr ruhet
Sie ruhen	Sie ruhen
er/sie/es ruhe	sie ruhen

PRESENT SUBJUNCTIVE II

ich ruhte	wir ruhten
du ruhtest	ihr ruhtet
Sie ruhten	Sie ruhten
er/sie/es ruhte	sie ruhten

FUTURE SUBJUNCTIVE I

ich werde	wir werden	ruhen
du werdest	ihr werdet	
Sie werden	Sie werden	
er/sie/es werde	sie werden	

FUTURE SUBJUNCTIVE II

ich würde	wir würden	ruhen
du würdest	ihr würdet	
Sie würden	Sie würden	
er/sie/es würde	sie würden	

PRESENT PERFECT

ich habe	wir haben	geruht
du hast	ihr habt	
Sie haben	Sie haben	
er/sie/es hat	sie haben	

PAST PERFECT

ich hatte	wir hatten	geruht
du hattest	ihr hattet	
Sie hatten	Sie hatten	
er/sie/es hatte	sie hatten	

FUTURE PERFECT

ich werde	wir werden	geruht haben
du wirst	ihr werdet	
Sie werden	Sie werden	
er/sie/es wird	sie werden	

PAST SUBJUNCTIVE I

ich habe	wir haben	geruht
du habest	ihr habet	
Sie haben	Sie haben	
er/sie/es habe	sie haben	

PAST SUBJUNCTIVE II

ich hätte	wir hätten	geruht
du hättest	ihr hättet	
Sie hätten	Sie hätten	
er/sie/es hätte	sie hätten	

FUTURE PERFECT SUBJUNCTIVE I

ich werde	wir werden	geruht haben
du werdest	ihr werdet	
Sie werden	Sie werden	
er/sie/es werde	sie werden	

FUTURE PERFECT SUBJUNCTIVE II

ich würde	wir würden	geruht haben
du würdest	ihr würdet	
Sie würden	Sie würden	
er/sie/es würde	sie würden	

COMMANDS ruh(e)! ruht! ruhen Sie!

PRESENT PARTICIPLE ruhend

Usage

Unser Kater ruht gern vor dem Fernseher.	*Our cat likes to sleep in front of the television.*
Wann können wir endlich ruhen?	*When can we finally get some rest?*
Ruhen Sie auf diesen großen Kissen.	*Rest on these large pillows.*
Der Hund ruht unter einem Baum im Garten.	*The dog is resting under a tree in the garden.*
Alle Besucher müssen ruhen.	*All visitors must rest.*
Heute wird nicht geruht!	*There is no rest today!*
Ruhst du heute Abend?	*Are you resting this evening?*
Chronisch Kranke werden dazu angeregt öfter zu ruhen.	*Chronically sick people are encouraged to relax more often.*
Der Patient muss unbedingt ruhen.	*The patient simply must rest.*
Das Fließband ruht nur am Sonntag.	*The assembly line only stops on Sundays.*
Hier ruht Elisa Olberg, geb. Stern. (TOMBSTONE)	*Here lies Elisa Olberg, née Stern.*
Wir werden nicht ruhen noch rasten, bis der Mörder gefasst ist. (*idiomatic*)	*We won't rest until the murderer is caught.*

RELATED VERBS aus·ruhen, beruhen, geruhen

regular weak verb **rührt · rührte · gerührt**

PRESENT

ich rühre	wir rühren
du rührst	ihr rührt
Sie rühren	Sie rühren
er/sie/es rührt	sie rühren

SIMPLE PAST

ich rührte	wir rührten
du rührtest	ihr rührtet
Sie rührten	Sie rührten
er/sie/es rührte	sie rührten

FUTURE

ich werde	wir werden	rühren
du wirst	ihr werdet	
Sie werden	Sie werden	
er/sie/es wird	sie werden	

PRESENT SUBJUNCTIVE I

ich rühre	wir rühren
du rührest	ihr rühret
Sie rühren	Sie rühren
er/sie/es rühre	sie rühren

PRESENT SUBJUNCTIVE II

ich rührte	wir rührten
du rührtest	ihr rührtet
Sie rührten	Sie rührten
er/sie/es rührte	sie rührten

FUTURE SUBJUNCTIVE I

ich werde	wir werden	rühren
du werdest	ihr werdet	
Sie werden	Sie werden	
er/sie/es werde	sie werden	

FUTURE SUBJUNCTIVE II

ich würde	wir würden	rühren
du würdest	ihr würdet	
Sie würden	Sie würden	
er/sie/es würde	sie würden	

PRESENT PERFECT

ich habe	wir haben	gerührt
du hast	ihr habt	
Sie haben	Sie haben	
er/sie/es hat	sie haben	

PAST PERFECT

ich hatte	wir hatten	gerührt
du hattest	ihr hattet	
Sie hatten	Sie hatten	
er/sie/es hatte	sie hatten	

FUTURE PERFECT

ich werde	wir werden	gerührt haben
du wirst	ihr werdet	
Sie werden	Sie werden	
er/sie/es wird	sie werden	

PAST SUBJUNCTIVE I

ich habe	wir haben	gerührt
du habest	ihr habet	
Sie haben	Sie haben	
er/sie/es habe	sie haben	

PAST SUBJUNCTIVE II

ich hätte	wir hätten	gerührt
du hättest	ihr hättet	
Sie hätten	Sie hätten	
er/sie/es hätte	sie hätten	

FUTURE PERFECT SUBJUNCTIVE I

ich werde	wir werden	gerührt haben
du werdest	ihr werdet	
Sie werden	Sie werden	
er/sie/es werde	sie werden	

FUTURE PERFECT SUBJUNCTIVE II

ich würde	wir würden	gerührt haben
du würdest	ihr würdet	
Sie würden	Sie würden	
er/sie/es würde	sie würden	

COMMANDS rühr(e)! rührt! rühren Sie!

PRESENT PARTICIPLE rührend

Usage

Den Teig gut rühren. (RECIPE) — *Stir the batter thoroughly.*
Der Koch rührte die Suppe in der Schüssel. — *The cook stirred the soup in the bowl.*
Der Brei muss per Hand gerührt werden. — *The mash must be stirred by hand.*
Der Junge rührte mit den Fingern in den Erbsen. — *The boy stirred the peas with his fingers.*
Der schwache Hund konnte seinen Kopf nicht mehr rühren. — *The weak dog could no longer move his head.*
Das Publikum wurde von der Rede gerührt. — *The audience was moved by the speech.*
Die folgende Aussage rührte die Reisenden. — *The following statement moved the passengers.*
Meine Frau wurde von der romantischen Schlussszene gerührt. — *My wife was moved by the romantic closing scene.*
Der Bürgermeister rührte die Besucher mit seiner Ansprache. — *The mayor inspired the visitors with his address.*
Du rührst mich sehr. — *You really touch my heart.*

RELATED VERBS an·rühren, auf·rühren, berühren, durch·rühren, ein·rühren, um·rühren, verrühren

sagen *to say, mean, tell*

sagt · sagte · gesagt regular weak verb

MORE USAGE SENTENCES WITH sagen

Sagt dir das etwas? — *Does that mean anything to you?*
Was will der Autor mir sagen? — *What is the author trying to tell me?*
Was ich hier sage ist nichts Neues. — *What I'm saying here is nothing new.*
Silke hat nichts davon gesagt. — *Silke said nothing about that.*
Erich hat es sich nicht zweimal sagen lassen. — *Erich didn't have to be told twice.*
Wie sagt man „Ei" auf Japanisch? — *How do you say "egg" in Japanese?*
Wem sagen Sie das? — *You're telling* me?
Was sagen sie über ihn? — *What are they saying about him?*
Das sagt mir nichts. — *That tells me nothing.*
Was Sie nicht sagen! — *You don't say!*
Er scheint es nicht sagen zu wollen. — *He doesn't seem to want to say.*
Augenzeugen sagten viel über die Ereignisse des Tages. — *Eyewitnesses said a lot about the day's events.*
Es wurde gesagt, dass der Inhaber ermordet worden sei. — *It was said that the owner was murdered.*
Dennis hat etwas (dabei) zu sagen. — *Dennis has something to say (in the matter).*
Ich traue mich nicht, ihm das ins Gesicht zu sagen. — *I don't dare tell him that to his face.*
Ursula hat beiläufig gesagt, sie hätte ein neues Auto. — *Ursula said in passing that she has a new car.*
Hänsel sagte zu Gretel: „Wir werden den Weg schon finden." (GRIMM) — *Hansel said to Gretel, "We'll surely find the path."*
Es ist schwer zu sagen, wann er wiederkommt. — *It is difficult to say when he's coming again.*
Das ist genau, was ich gerade sagen wollte. — *That's exactly what I was about to say.*

sich sagen *to say/think to oneself*

Was sagen Sie sich dann? — *What do you say to yourself then?*
Nur noch ein paar Tage, sagte ich mir wiederholt. — *Just a few more days, I thought to myself over and over.*

IDIOMATIC EXPRESSIONS

Das hat nichts zu sagen. — *That is of no significance.*
Du hast mir nichts zu sagen. — *You can't tell me what to do.*
Seine Idee finde ich—mit Verlaub zu sagen—irrsinnig. — *I find his idea to be—with all due respect—ludicrous.*
Sagen Sie mir einen einzigen guten Grund. — *Give me one good reason.*
Mein Arzt hat mir durch die Blume gesagt, dass ich Hypochonder wäre. — *My doctor told me in a roundabout way that I'm a hypochondriac.*
Donald wollte ihr gehörig seine Meinung sagen. — *Donald wanted to give her a piece of his mind.*
Ich lasse ihr sagen, dass ich nicht kommen kann. — *I'm sending word to her that I can't come.*
Lasst euch das gesagt sein! — *Let that be a warning to you!*
Hans war eigensinnig, er ließ sich nichts sagen. — *Hans was hardheaded; he listened to no one.*
Unter uns gesagt: Herr Leitner prüft selten nach, ob man pünktlich da ist. — *Just between us, Mr. Leitner seldom checks to see if we're there on time.*
Dürer war, wie gesagt, ein äußerst produktiver Künstler. — *Dürer was, as I mentioned, an extremely prolific artist.*
Das ist nicht gesagt. — *That's not a sure thing.*
Gesagt, getan! (PROVERB) — *No sooner said than done!*

COLLOQUIAL EXPRESSIONS

Frank kann das sehr gut, das sag' ich dir! — *Frank is good at that, I'm telling you!*
Das ist einer dieser… na, wie sagt man? — *That's one of those … er, what's the word?*
Sag bloß, du willst schon wieder einen neuen Computer! — *Don't tell me you want a new computer again already!*
Sag mal, warst du nicht letzten Samstag auf der Fete? — *Say, weren't you at the party last Saturday?*
Ich sage dir, es war unglaublich. — *I tell you, it was incredible.*

regular weak verb **sagt · sagte · gesagt**

PRESENT

ich sage	wir sagen
du sagst	ihr sagt
Sie sagen	Sie sagen
er/sie/es sagt	sie sagen

SIMPLE PAST

ich sagte	wir sagten
du sagtest	ihr sagtet
Sie sagten	Sie sagten
er/sie/es sagte	sie sagten

FUTURE

ich werde	wir werden	sagen
du wirst	ihr werdet	
Sie werden	Sie werden	
er/sie/es wird	sie werden	

PRESENT SUBJUNCTIVE I

ich sage	wir sagen
du sagest	ihr saget
Sie sagen	Sie sagen
er/sie/es sage	sie sagen

PRESENT SUBJUNCTIVE II

ich sagte	wir sagten
du sagtest	ihr sagtet
Sie sagten	Sie sagten
er/sie/es sagte	sie sagten

FUTURE SUBJUNCTIVE I

ich werde	wir werden	sagen
du werdest	ihr werdet	
Sie werden	Sie werden	
er/sie/es werde	sie werden	

FUTURE SUBJUNCTIVE II

ich würde	wir würden	sagen
du würdest	ihr würdet	
Sie würden	Sie würden	
er/sie/es würde	sie würden	

COMMANDS sag(e)! sagt! sagen Sie!

PRESENT PARTICIPLE sagend

PRESENT PERFECT

ich habe	wir haben	gesagt
du hast	ihr habt	
Sie haben	Sie haben	
er/sie/es hat	sie haben	

PAST PERFECT

ich hatte	wir hatten	gesagt
du hattest	ihr hattet	
Sie hatten	Sie hatten	
er/sie/es hatte	sie hatten	

FUTURE PERFECT

ich werde	wir werden	gesagt haben
du wirst	ihr werdet	
Sie werden	Sie werden	
er/sie/es wird	sie werden	

PAST SUBJUNCTIVE I

ich habe	wir haben	gesagt
du habest	ihr habet	
Sie haben	Sie haben	
er/sie/es habe	sie haben	

PAST SUBJUNCTIVE II

ich hätte	wir hätten	gesagt
du hättest	ihr hättet	
Sie hätten	Sie hätten	
er/sie/es hätte	sie hätten	

FUTURE PERFECT SUBJUNCTIVE I

ich werde	wir werden	gesagt haben
du werdest	ihr werdet	
Sie werden	Sie werden	
er/sie/es werde	sie werden	

FUTURE PERFECT SUBJUNCTIVE II

ich würde	wir würden	gesagt haben
du würdest	ihr würdet	
Sie würden	Sie würden	
er/sie/es würde	sie würden	

Usage

Was hast du gesagt?	*What did you say?*
Sagen Sie es mir!	*Tell me!*
Sigrid kann nicht nein sagen, sie hilft jedem.	*Sigrid doesn't know how to say no; she helps everyone.*
Die Konzerne sagen nichts über ihre Investitionen.	*The companies keep mum about their investments.*
Das können Sie laut sagen!	*You can say that again!*
Das kann man leicht sagen.	*That's easy to say.*
Was wollt ihr damit sagen?	*What do you mean by that?*
Wenn Sie in einer Großstadt sind, sagen wir mal New York, da sind die Hotels viel teurer.	*If you're in a large city, let's say New York, hotels are much more expensive there.*

RELATED VERBS ab·sagen, an·sagen, auf·sagen, aus·sagen, besagen, dank·sagen, durch·sagen, entsagen, gut·sagen, nach·sagen, tot·sagen, untersagen, versagen, vorher·sagen, vor·sagen, wahr·sagen, weissagen, weiter·sagen, zu·sagen

351 **sammeln** *to collect, gather*

sammelt · sammelte · gesammelt regular weak verb

PRESENT

ich samm(e)le	wir sammeln
du sammelst	ihr sammelt
Sie sammeln	Sie sammeln
er/sie/es sammelt	sie sammeln

SIMPLE PAST

ich sammelte	wir sammelten
du sammeltest	ihr sammeltet
Sie sammelten	Sie sammelten
er/sie/es sammelte	sie sammelten

FUTURE

ich werde	wir werden	sammeln
du wirst	ihr werdet	
Sie werden	Sie werden	
er/sie/es wird	sie werden	

PRESENT SUBJUNCTIVE I

ich samm(e)le	wir sammeln
du sammelst	ihr sammelt
Sie sammeln	Sie sammeln
er/sie/es samm(e)le	sie sammeln

PRESENT SUBJUNCTIVE II

ich sammelte	wir sammelten
du sammeltest	ihr sammeltet
Sie sammelten	Sie sammelten
er/sie/es sammelte	sie sammelten

FUTURE SUBJUNCTIVE I

ich werde	wir werden	sammeln
du werdest	ihr werdet	
Sie werden	Sie werden	
er/sie/es werde	sie werden	

FUTURE SUBJUNCTIVE II

ich würde	wir würden	sammeln
du würdest	ihr würdet	
Sie würden	Sie würden	
er/sie/es würde	sie würden	

PRESENT PERFECT

ich habe	wir haben	gesammelt
du hast	ihr habt	
Sie haben	Sie haben	
er/sie/es hat	sie haben	

PAST PERFECT

ich hatte	wir hatten	gesammelt
du hattest	ihr hattet	
Sie hatten	Sie hatten	
er/sie/es hatte	sie hatten	

FUTURE PERFECT

ich werde	wir werden	gesammelt haben
du wirst	ihr werdet	
Sie werden	Sie werden	
er/sie/es wird	sie werden	

PAST SUBJUNCTIVE I

ich habe	wir haben	gesammelt
du habest	ihr habet	
Sie haben	Sie haben	
er/sie/es habe	sie haben	

PAST SUBJUNCTIVE II

ich hätte	wir hätten	gesammelt
du hättest	ihr hättet	
Sie hätten	Sie hätten	
er/sie/es hätte	sie hätten	

FUTURE PERFECT SUBJUNCTIVE I

ich werde	wir werden	gesammelt haben
du werdest	ihr werdet	
Sie werden	Sie werden	
er/sie/es werde	sie werden	

FUTURE PERFECT SUBJUNCTIVE II

ich würde	wir würden	gesammelt haben
du würdest	ihr würdet	
Sie würden	Sie würden	
er/sie/es würde	sie würden	

COMMANDS samm(e)le! sammelt! sammeln Sie!

PRESENT PARTICIPLE sammelnd

Usage

Ich sammle Briefmarken.	*I collect stamps.*
Sabine hat als Kind Steine gesammelt.	*Sabine collected rocks as a child.*
Wie sind die Daten gesammelt worden?	*How were the data collected?*
Warum sammelst du so viele Sachen?	*Why do you collect so many things?*
Kristin sammelt Kindergeschichten.	*Kristin collects children's stories.*
Ich sammle schon Ideen für mein nächstes Projekt.	*I'm already gathering ideas for my next project.*
Die Vögel in unserem Garten sammeln gern Hirsesamen.	*The birds in our yard like to hoard millet seed.*
Archäologen haben die alten Mauerreste gesammelt.	*Archeologists salvaged the remains of the old wall.*
Auf dieser Webseite wird alles Mögliche gesammelt.	*Everything imaginable is clumped on this Web page.*

sich sammeln *to collect, gather*

Die Gäste sammelten sich an der Eingangstür.	*The guests collected at the entryway.*
Die Snowboarder sammelten sich vor dem Restaurant.	*The snowboarders gathered in front of the restaurant.*

RELATED VERBS an·sammeln, auf·sammeln, ein·sammeln, versammeln

strong verb **säuft · soff · gesoffen**

PRESENT

ich saufe	wir saufen
du säufst	ihr sauft
Sie saufen	Sie saufen
er/sie/es säuft	sie saufen

SIMPLE PAST

ich soff	wir soffen
du soffst	ihr sofft
Sie soffen	Sie soffen
er/sie/es soff	sie soffen

FUTURE

ich werde	wir werden	saufen
du wirst	ihr werdet	
Sie werden	Sie werden	
er/sie/es wird	sie werden	

PRESENT SUBJUNCTIVE I

ich saufe	wir saufen
du saufest	ihr saufet
Sie saufen	Sie saufen
er/sie/es saufe	sie saufen

PRESENT SUBJUNCTIVE II

ich söffe	wir söffen
du söffest	ihr söffet
Sie söffen	Sie söffen
er/sie/es söffe	sie söffen

FUTURE SUBJUNCTIVE I

ich werde	wir werden	saufen
du werdest	ihr werdet	
Sie werden	Sie werden	
er/sie/es werde	sie werden	

FUTURE SUBJUNCTIVE II

ich würde	wir würden	saufen
du würdest	ihr würdet	
Sie würden	Sie würden	
er/sie/es würde	sie würden	

PRESENT PERFECT

ich habe	wir haben	gesoffen
du hast	ihr habt	
Sie haben	Sie haben	
er/sie/es hat	sie haben	

PAST PERFECT

ich hatte	wir hatten	gesoffen
du hattest	ihr hattet	
Sie hatten	Sie hatten	
er/sie/es hatte	sie hatten	

FUTURE PERFECT

ich werde	wir werden	gesoffen haben
du wirst	ihr werdet	
Sie werden	Sie werden	
er/sie/es wird	sie werden	

PAST SUBJUNCTIVE I

ich habe	wir haben	gesoffen
du habest	ihr habet	
Sie haben	Sie haben	
er/sie/es habe	sie haben	

PAST SUBJUNCTIVE II

ich hätte	wir hätten	gesoffen
du hättest	ihr hättet	
Sie hätten	Sie hätten	
er/sie/es hätte	sie hätten	

FUTURE PERFECT SUBJUNCTIVE I

ich werde	wir werden	gesoffen haben
du werdest	ihr werdet	
Sie werden	Sie werden	
er/sie/es werde	sie werden	

FUTURE PERFECT SUBJUNCTIVE II

ich würde	wir würden	gesoffen haben
du würdest	ihr würdet	
Sie würden	Sie würden	
er/sie/es würde	sie würden	

COMMANDS sauf(e)! sauft! saufen Sie!

PRESENT PARTICIPLE saufend

Usage

Sauf doch nicht so!	*Don't drink like that!*
Unsere Kuh säuft jeden Tag 30 Liter Wasser.	*Our cow drinks 30 liters of water per day.*
Sein Hund Maxl säuft lieber Apfelsaft als Wasser.	*His dog, Maxl, prefers drinking apple juice to water.*
Trina hat monatlich 300 Euro gesoffen.	*Trina drank 300 euros' worth of liquor a month.*
Mein Großvater Hans säuft nicht mehr.	*My grandfather Hans doesn't drink anymore.*
Herr Stolpermann säuft schon um zwölf Uhr.	*Mr. Stolpermann starts drinking at 12 o'clock.*
Herr Petersen säuft seit sieben Jahren.	*Mr. Petersen has been drinking for seven years.*
Viele Studenten saufen während der Spring Break.	*Many students drink during spring break.*
Der General soff regelmäßig mit seinen Truppen.	*The general drank regularly with his troops.*
Jahre lang soff Ingrid viel.	*For years Ingrid drank a lot.*
Der jüngste Sohn der Familie säuft.	*The youngest son in the family drinks.*
Es wurde gesagt, dass der pensionierte Soldat sich zu Tode gesoffen habe.	*It was said that the retired soldier drank himself to death.*

RELATED VERBS ab·saufen, aus·saufen, ersaufen, versaufen

353 saugen *to suck*

saugt · sog/saugte · gesogen/gesaugt — strong verb or regular weak verb

PRESENT

ich sauge	wir saugen
du saugst	ihr saugt
Sie saugen	Sie saugen
er/sie/es saugt	sie saugen

SIMPLE PAST

ich sog/saugte	wir sogen/saugten
du sogst/saugtest	ihr sogt/saugtet
Sie sogen/saugten	Sie sogen/saugten
er/sie/es sog/saugte	sie sogen/saugten

FUTURE

ich werde	wir werden	saugen
du wirst	ihr werdet	
Sie werden	Sie werden	
er/sie/es wird	sie werden	

PRESENT SUBJUNCTIVE I

ich sauge	wir saugen
du saugest	ihr sauget
Sie saugen	Sie saugen
er/sie/es sauge	sie saugen

PRESENT SUBJUNCTIVE II

ich söge/saugte	wir sögen/saugten
du sögest/saugtest	ihr söget/saugtet
Sie sögen/saugten	Sie sögen/saugten
er/sie/es söge/saugte	sie sögen/saugten

FUTURE SUBJUNCTIVE I

ich werde	wir werden	saugen
du werdest	ihr werdet	
Sie werden	Sie werden	
er/sie/es werde	sie werden	

FUTURE SUBJUNCTIVE II

ich würde	wir würden	saugen
du würdest	ihr würdet	
Sie würden	Sie würden	
er/sie/es würde	sie würden	

PRESENT PERFECT

ich habe	wir haben	gesogen/gesaugt
du hast	ihr habt	
Sie haben	Sie haben	
er/sie/es hat	sie haben	

PAST PERFECT

ich hatte	wir hatten	gesogen/gesaugt
du hattest	ihr hattet	
Sie hatten	Sie hatten	
er/sie/es hatte	sie hatten	

FUTURE PERFECT

ich werde	wir werden	gesogen haben
du wirst	ihr werdet	OR
Sie werden	Sie werden	gesaugt haben
er/sie/es wird	sie werden	

PAST SUBJUNCTIVE I

ich habe	wir haben	gesogen/gesaugt
du habest	ihr habet	
Sie haben	Sie haben	
er/sie/es habe	sie haben	

PAST SUBJUNCTIVE II

ich hätte	wir hätten	gesogen/gesaugt
du hättest	ihr hättet	
Sie hätten	Sie hätten	
er/sie/es hätte	sie hätten	

FUTURE PERFECT SUBJUNCTIVE I

ich werde	wir werden	gesogen haben
du werdest	ihr werdet	OR
Sie werden	Sie werden	gesaugt haben
er/sie/es werde	sie werden	

FUTURE PERFECT SUBJUNCTIVE II

ich würde	wir würden	gesogen haben
du würdest	ihr würdet	OR
Sie würden	Sie würden	gesaugt haben
er/sie/es würde	sie würden	

COMMANDS saug(e)! saugt! saugen Sie!

PRESENT PARTICIPLE saugend

Usage

Vampire sogen Blut von ihren Opfern. — *Vampires sucked the blood of their victims.*
Luft wird vom Vergaser durch einen Filter gesaugt. — *Air is suctioned through a filter by the carburetor.*
Jost wurde vom Wirbelwind aus dem Haus gesaugt. — *Jost was sucked from the house by a tornado.*
Die Zecke saugt Blut. — *The tick sucks blood.*
Grete hat die Brotkrümel vom Teller gesogen. — *Grete sucked the bread crumbs from the plate.*
Saugte er wirklich die Zahnpasta aus der Tube? — *Did he really suck toothpaste from the tube?*
Wasser wird durch ein Rohr gesaugt. — *Water is suctioned through a pipe.*
Die Flüssigkeiten werden durch einen Strohhalm gesaugt. — *The fluids are sucked through a straw.*
Der Knabe saugte sich eine Antwort aus den Fingern. (*idiomatic*) — *The boy made up an answer.*

sich saugen *to absorb, suck up*

Die Binde saugte sich voll mit Blut. — *The bandage absorbed the blood completely.*

RELATED VERBS ab·saugen, an·saugen, auf·saugen, aus·saugen, ein·saugen, staubsaugen

regular weak verb (dative object) **schadet · schadete · geschadet**

PRESENT

ich schade	wir schaden
du schadest	ihr schadet
Sie schaden	Sie schaden
er/sie/es schadet	sie schaden

SIMPLE PAST

ich schadete	wir schadeten
du schadetest	ihr schadetet
Sie schadeten	Sie schadeten
er/sie/es schadete	sie schadeten

FUTURE

ich werde	wir werden	schaden
du wirst	ihr werdet	
Sie werden	Sie werden	
er/sie/es wird	sie werden	

PRESENT SUBJUNCTIVE I

ich schade	wir schaden
du schadest	ihr schadet
Sie schaden	Sie schaden
er/sie/es schade	sie schaden

PRESENT SUBJUNCTIVE II

ich schadete	wir schadeten
du schadetest	ihr schadetet
Sie schadeten	Sie schadeten
er/sie/es schadete	sie schadeten

FUTURE SUBJUNCTIVE I

ich werde	wir werden	schaden
du werdest	ihr werdet	
Sie werden	Sie werden	
er/sie/es werde	sie werden	

FUTURE SUBJUNCTIVE II

ich würde	wir würden	schaden
du würdest	ihr würdet	
Sie würden	Sie würden	
er/sie/es würde	sie würden	

PRESENT PERFECT

ich habe	wir haben	geschadet
du hast	ihr habt	
Sie haben	Sie haben	
er/sie/es hat	sie haben	

PAST PERFECT

ich hatte	wir hatten	geschadet
du hattest	ihr hattet	
Sie hatten	Sie hatten	
er/sie/es hatte	sie hatten	

FUTURE PERFECT

ich werde	wir werden	geschadet haben
du wirst	ihr werdet	
Sie werden	Sie werden	
er/sie/es wird	sie werden	

PAST SUBJUNCTIVE I

ich habe	wir haben	geschadet
du habest	ihr habet	
Sie haben	Sie haben	
er/sie/es habe	sie haben	

PAST SUBJUNCTIVE II

ich hätte	wir hätten	geschadet
du hättest	ihr hättet	
Sie hätten	Sie hätten	
er/sie/es hätte	sie hätten	

FUTURE PERFECT SUBJUNCTIVE I

ich werde	wir werden	geschadet haben
du werdest	ihr werdet	
Sie werden	Sie werden	
er/sie/es werde	sie werden	

FUTURE PERFECT SUBJUNCTIVE II

ich würde	wir würden	geschadet haben
du würdest	ihr würdet	
Sie würden	Sie würden	
er/sie/es würde	sie würden	

COMMANDS schad(e)! schadet! schaden Sie!

PRESENT PARTICIPLE schadend

Usage

Das schadet nichts.	*No damage is done. / That doesn't matter.*
Was kann eine Email schaden?	*What can an e-mail hurt?*
Zu viel sprechen schadet der Stimme.	*Too much talking damages your voice.*
UK-Wellen werden dem Gerät nicht schaden.	*VHF waves will not damage the device.*
Stress schadet der Gesundheit.	*Stress is harmful to your health.*
Solches Benehmen schadet ihnen nicht.	*Such behavior will not harm them.*
Ein Mangel an Erfolg schadet der Moral.	*A lack of success hurts morale.*
Ihre Antwort hat gar nichts geschadet.	*Her answer did no harm.*
Ich wollte dir nicht schaden.	*I didn't want to harm you.*
Ich hoffe es schadet euch nicht.	*I hope it doesn't hurt you.*
Die Sonne hat seinen Augen geschadet.	*The sun injured his eyes.*
Die Kritik hat ihm geschadet.	*The criticism did him some harm.*
Der Krieg hat ihm auf sein ganzes Leben emotionell geschadet.	*The war caused him emotional trauma for the rest of his life.*

355 schaffen *to create; manage (to do), work*

schafft · schaffte/schuf · geschafft/geschaffen regular weak verb or strong verb

PRESENT

ich schaffe	wir schaffen
du schaffst	ihr schafft
Sie schaffen	Sie schaffen
er/sie/es schafft	sie schaffen

SIMPLE PAST

ich schaffte/schuf	wir schafften/schufen
du schafftest/schufst	ihr schafftet/schuft
Sie schafften/schufen	Sie schafften/schufen
er/sie/es schaffte/schuf	sie schafften/schufen

FUTURE

ich werde	wir werden	schaffen
du wirst	ihr werdet	
Sie werden	Sie werden	
er/sie/es wird	sie werden	

PRESENT SUBJUNCTIVE I

ich schaffe	wir schaffen
du schaffest	ihr schaffet
Sie schaffen	Sie schaffen
er/sie/es schaffe	sie schaffen

PRESENT SUBJUNCTIVE II

ich schaffte/schüfe	wir schafften/schüfen
du schafftest/schüfest	ihr schafftet/schüfet
Sie schafften/schüfen	Sie schafften/schüfen
er/sie/es schaffte/schüfe	sie schafften/schüfen

FUTURE SUBJUNCTIVE I

ich werde	wir werden	schaffen
du werdest	ihr werdet	
Sie werden	Sie werden	
er/sie/es werde	sie werden	

FUTURE SUBJUNCTIVE II

ich würde	wir würden	schaffen
du würdest	ihr würdet	
Sie würden	Sie würden	
er/sie/es würde	sie würden	

PRESENT PERFECT

ich habe	wir haben	geschafft/geschaffen
du hast	ihr habt	
Sie haben	Sie haben	
er/sie/es hat	sie haben	

PAST PERFECT

ich hatte	wir hatten	geschafft/geschaffen
du hattest	ihr hattet	
Sie hatten	Sie hatten	
er/sie/es hatte	sie hatten	

FUTURE PERFECT

ich werde	wir werden	geschafft haben
du wirst	ihr werdet	OR
Sie werden	Sie werden	geschaffen haben
er/sie/es wird	sie werden	

PAST SUBJUNCTIVE I

ich habe	wir haben	geschafft/geschaffen
du habest	ihr habet	
Sie haben	Sie haben	
er/sie/es habe	sie haben	

PAST SUBJUNCTIVE II

ich hätte	wir hätten	geschafft/geschaffen
du hättest	ihr hättet	
Sie hätten	Sie hätten	
er/sie/es hätte	sie hätten	

FUTURE PERFECT SUBJUNCTIVE I

ich werde	wir werden	geschafft haben
du werdest	ihr werdet	OR
Sie werden	Sie werden	geschaffen haben
er/sie/es werde	sie werden	

FUTURE PERFECT SUBJUNCTIVE II

ich würde	wir würden	geschafft haben
du würdest	ihr würdet	OR
Sie würden	Sie würden	geschaffen haben
er/sie/es würde	sie würden	

COMMANDS schaff(e)! schafft! schaffen Sie!

PRESENT PARTICIPLE schaffend

Usage

Wir schaffen es noch!	*We'll succeed yet!*
Yoga schafft Wohlbefinden.	*Yoga brings about a sense of well-being.*
Wie soll das geschafft werden?	*How is that to be accomplished?*
Wie kann man Filme schaffen?	*How does one make films?*
Lindemann schuf 1912 dieses Kunstwerk.	*Lindemann created this work of art in 1912.*
Kannst du das schaffen?	*Can you do that?*
Die Frauen schufen einen Korb aus Stroh.	*The women created a basket from straw.*
Der Junge hat einen Gehstock aus einem Zweig geschaffen.	*The boy fashioned a walking stick from a twig.*
Das schaffe ich nicht.	*I won't get that done.*

sich schaffen *to accomplish*

Mit diesem Programm schafft es sich leichter.	*It is easier to accomplish with this program.*

RELATED VERBS ab·schaffen, an·schaffen, beschaffen, erschaffen, fort·schaffen, verschaffen, weg·schaffen

strong verb/regular weak verb **schallt · scholl/schallte · geschallt**

PRESENT

ich schalle	wir schallen
du schallst	ihr schallt
Sie schallen	Sie schallen
er/sie/es schallt	sie schallen

SIMPLE PAST

ich scholl/schallte	wir schollen/schallten
du schollst/schalltest	ihr schollt/schalltet
Sie schollen/schallten	Sie schollen/schallten
er/sie/es scholl/schallte	sie schollen/schallten

FUTURE

ich werde	wir werden	schallen
du wirst	ihr werdet	
Sie werden	Sie werden	
er/sie/es wird	sie werden	

PRESENT SUBJUNCTIVE I

ich schalle	wir schallen
du schallest	ihr schallet
Sie schallen	Sie schallen
er/sie/es schalle	sie schallen

PRESENT SUBJUNCTIVE II

ich schölle/schallte	wir schöllen/schallten
du schöllest/schalltest	ihr schöllet/schalltet
Sie schöllen/schallten	Sie schöllen/schallten
er/sie/es schölle/schallte	sie schöllen/schallten

FUTURE SUBJUNCTIVE I

ich werde	wir werden	schallen
du werdest	ihr werdet	
Sie werden	Sie werden	
er/sie/es werde	sie werden	

FUTURE SUBJUNCTIVE II

ich würde	wir würden	schallen
du würdest	ihr würdet	
Sie würden	Sie würden	
er/sie/es würde	sie würden	

PRESENT PERFECT

ich habe	wir haben	geschallt
du hast	ihr habt	
Sie haben	Sie haben	
er/sie/es hat	sie haben	

PAST PERFECT

ich hatte	wir hatten	geschallt
du hattest	ihr hattet	
Sie hatten	Sie hatten	
er/sie/es hatte	sie hatten	

FUTURE PERFECT

ich werde	wir werden	geschallt haben
du wirst	ihr werdet	
Sie werden	Sie werden	
er/sie/es wird	sie werden	

PAST SUBJUNCTIVE I

ich habe	wir haben	geschallt
du habest	ihr habet	
Sie haben	Sie haben	
er/sie/es habe	sie haben	

PAST SUBJUNCTIVE II

ich hätte	wir hätten	geschallt
du hättest	ihr hättet	
Sie hätten	Sie hätten	
er/sie/es hätte	sie hätten	

FUTURE PERFECT SUBJUNCTIVE I

ich werde	wir werden	geschallt haben
du werdest	ihr werdet	
Sie werden	Sie werden	
er/sie/es werde	sie werden	

FUTURE PERFECT SUBJUNCTIVE II

ich würde	wir würden	geschallt haben
du würdest	ihr würdet	
Sie würden	Sie würden	
er/sie/es würde	sie würden	

COMMANDS schall(e)! schallt! schallen Sie!

PRESENT PARTICIPLE schallend

Usage

Zwei Schüsse schallten aus der Ferne.	*Two shots rang out in the distance.*
Ihre Stimme schallte durch den Korridor.	*Her voice echoed through the corridor.*
Habt ihr die Hörner schallen gehört?	*Did you hear the horns playing?*
Ein großer Aufruhr schallte.	*There was the rumbling of a great uprising.*
Die Trompeten schollen und die Soldaten rückten vor.	*The trumpets sounded and the soldiers advanced.*
Die Musik schallt noch in ihren Ohren.	*The music still echoes in their ears.*
Der Motor schallt ziemlich laut.	*The motor sounds rather loud.*
Das Gelächter schallte durch den Hörsaal.	*The laughter echoed through the auditorium.*
Das Bellen eines Hundes schallte über die Wiese.	*The barking of a dog resounded across the meadow.*
Buhrufe schallten vom Publikum.	*Boos rang out from the audience.*
Als die Glocken schallten, kamen die Mädchen in die Kirche.	*As the bells pealed, the girls entered the church.*
Es wurde per Echokardiogramm auf hypertrophe Cardiomyopathie geschallt.	*They used an echocardiogram to check for hypertrophic cardiomyopathy.*

RELATED VERBS beschallen, durch·schallen, erschallen

357 schalten *to switch, connect; change*

schaltet · schaltete · geschaltet — regular weak verb

PRESENT

ich schalte	wir schalten
du schaltest	ihr schaltet
Sie schalten	Sie schalten
er/sie/es schaltet	sie schalten

SIMPLE PAST

ich schaltete	wir schalteten
du schaltetest	ihr schaltetet
Sie schalteten	Sie schalteten
er/sie/es schaltete	sie schalteten

FUTURE

ich werde	wir werden	schalten
du wirst	ihr werdet	
Sie werden	Sie werden	
er/sie/es wird	sie werden	

PRESENT SUBJUNCTIVE I

ich schalte	wir schalten
du schaltest	ihr schaltet
Sie schalten	Sie schalten
er/sie/es schalte	sie schalten

PRESENT SUBJUNCTIVE II

ich schaltete	wir schalteten
du schaltetest	ihr schaltetet
Sie schalteten	Sie schalteten
er/sie/es schaltete	sie schalteten

FUTURE SUBJUNCTIVE I

ich werde	wir werden	schalten
du werdest	ihr werdet	
Sie werden	Sie werden	
er/sie/es werde	sie werden	

FUTURE SUBJUNCTIVE II

ich würde	wir würden	schalten
du würdest	ihr würdet	
Sie würden	Sie würden	
er/sie/es würde	sie würden	

PRESENT PERFECT

ich habe	wir haben	geschaltet
du hast	ihr habt	
Sie haben	Sie haben	
er/sie/es hat	sie haben	

PAST PERFECT

ich hatte	wir hatten	geschaltet
du hattest	ihr hattet	
Sie hatten	Sie hatten	
er/sie/es hatte	sie hatten	

FUTURE PERFECT

ich werde	wir werden	geschaltet haben
du wirst	ihr werdet	
Sie werden	Sie werden	
er/sie/es wird	sie werden	

PAST SUBJUNCTIVE I

ich habe	wir haben	geschaltet
du habest	ihr habet	
Sie haben	Sie haben	
er/sie/es habe	sie haben	

PAST SUBJUNCTIVE II

ich hätte	wir hätten	geschaltet
du hättest	ihr hättet	
Sie hätten	Sie hätten	
er/sie/es hätte	sie hätten	

FUTURE PERFECT SUBJUNCTIVE I

ich werde	wir werden	geschaltet haben
du werdest	ihr werdet	
Sie werden	Sie werden	
er/sie/es werde	sie werden	

FUTURE PERFECT SUBJUNCTIVE II

ich würde	wir würden	geschaltet haben
du würdest	ihr würdet	
Sie würden	Sie würden	
er/sie/es würde	sie würden	

COMMANDS schalte! schaltet! schalten Sie!

PRESENT PARTICIPLE schaltend

Usage

Wie schaltet sich dieses Gerät?	*How does this device switch gears?*
Mein Auto lässt sich nicht schalten.	*My car won't shift (gears).*
Du schaltest zu früh.	*You are shifting too soon.*
Er will schon geschaltet haben.	*He claims to have already shifted.*
Kann man den Fernseher per Fernbedienung in den Schlafmodus schalten?	*Can you switch the television to sleep mode using the remote control?*
Ich musste mein Handy auf Stumm schalten.	*I had to switch my cell phone to silent.*
Ein Motor schaltet die Klappe nach oben.	*A motor turns the lid upwards.*
Ich konnte das Gerät nicht auf Automatik schalten.	*I was unable to switch the device to automatic.*
Sie werden ihr Computersystem noch nicht auf Euro geschalten haben können.	*They won't yet have been able to change their computer system to euros.*
Die Ampel schaltet auf Grün.	*The light is turning green.*

RELATED VERBS ab·schalten, an·schalten, gleich·schalten, um·schalten; *see also* **aus·schalten** (37), **ein·schalten** (136)

regular weak verb

schätzt · schätzte · geschätzt

PRESENT

ich schätze	wir schätzen
du schätzt	ihr schätzt
Sie schätzen	Sie schätzen
er/sie/es schätzt	sie schätzen

SIMPLE PAST

ich schätzte	wir schätzten
du schätztest	ihr schätztet
Sie schätzten	Sie schätzten
er/sie/es schätzte	sie schätzten

FUTURE

ich werde	wir werden	schätzen
du wirst	ihr werdet	
Sie werden	Sie werden	
er/sie/es wird	sie werden	

PRESENT SUBJUNCTIVE I

ich schätze	wir schätzen
du schätzest	ihr schätzet
Sie schätzen	Sie schätzen
er/sie/es schätze	sie schätzen

PRESENT SUBJUNCTIVE II

ich schätzte	wir schätzten
du schätztest	ihr schätztet
Sie schätzten	Sie schätzten
er/sie/es schätzte	sie schätzten

FUTURE SUBJUNCTIVE I

ich werde	wir werden	schätzen
du werdest	ihr werdet	
Sie werden	Sie werden	
er/sie/es werde	sie werden	

FUTURE SUBJUNCTIVE II

ich würde	wir würden	schätzen
du würdest	ihr würdet	
Sie würden	Sie würden	
er/sie/es würde	sie würden	

PRESENT PERFECT

ich habe	wir haben	geschätzt
du hast	ihr habt	
Sie haben	Sie haben	
er/sie/es hat	sie haben	

PAST PERFECT

ich hatte	wir hatten	geschätzt
du hattest	ihr hattet	
Sie hatten	Sie hatten	
er/sie/es hatte	sie hatten	

FUTURE PERFECT

ich werde	wir werden	geschätzt haben
du wirst	ihr werdet	
Sie werden	Sie werden	
er/sie/es wird	sie werden	

PAST SUBJUNCTIVE I

ich habe	wir haben	geschätzt
du habest	ihr habet	
Sie haben	Sie haben	
er/sie/es habe	sie haben	

PAST SUBJUNCTIVE II

ich hätte	wir hätten	geschätzt
du hättest	ihr hättet	
Sie hätten	Sie hätten	
er/sie/es hätte	sie hätten	

FUTURE PERFECT SUBJUNCTIVE I

ich werde	wir werden	geschätzt haben
du werdest	ihr werdet	
Sie werden	Sie werden	
er/sie/es werde	sie werden	

FUTURE PERFECT SUBJUNCTIVE II

ich würde	wir würden	geschätzt haben
du würdest	ihr würdet	
Sie würden	Sie würden	
er/sie/es würde	sie würden	

COMMANDS schätz(e)! schätzt! schätzen Sie!

PRESENT PARTICIPLE schätzend

Usage

Ich kann nicht gut schätzen.	*I'm not very good at estimating.*
Wie hoch schätzt du den Betrag?	*How high do you reckon the amount to be?*
Worauf schätzt du dieses Buch?	*How much do you think this book is worth?*
Yvonne schätzt die Abendzeit zum Lesen.	*Yvonne values her time in the evening for reading.*
Andere Kinder schätzen ihn.	*Other children appreciate him.*
Schätzen sie solche Fähigkeiten bei dieser Bank?	*Do they value such skills at this bank?*
Schätzt du meine Teilnahme nicht mehr?	*Do you no longer value my participation?*
Wer kann das schon schätzen?	*Who can even guess that?*
Sie haben aber schlecht geschätzt.	*You've guessed badly.*
Schätzen Sie mal!	*Guess!*
Oliver hat den Preis richtig geschätzt.	*Oliver guessed the price correctly.*
Ich möchte schätzen.	*I'd like to guess.*
Dürfen wir nochmal schätzen?	*May we guess again?*

RELATED VERBS ab·schätzen, ein·schätzen, überschätzen, unterschätzen, verschätzen

359 schauen *to look (at), watch*

schaut · schaute · geschaut — regular weak verb

PRESENT

ich schaue	wir schauen
du schaust	ihr schaut
Sie schauen	Sie schauen
er/sie/es schaut	sie schauen

SIMPLE PAST

ich schaute	wir schauten
du schautest	ihr schautet
Sie schauten	Sie schauten
er/sie/es schaute	sie schauten

FUTURE

ich werde	wir werden	schauen
du wirst	ihr werdet	
Sie werden	Sie werden	
er/sie/es wird	sie werden	

PRESENT SUBJUNCTIVE I

ich schaue	wir schauen
du schauest	ihr schauet
Sie schauen	Sie schauen
er/sie/es schaue	sie schauen

PRESENT SUBJUNCTIVE II

ich schaute	wir schauten
du schautest	ihr schautet
Sie schauten	Sie schauten
er/sie/es schaute	sie schauten

FUTURE SUBJUNCTIVE I

ich werde	wir werden	schauen
du werdest	ihr werdet	
Sie werden	Sie werden	
er/sie/es werde	sie werden	

FUTURE SUBJUNCTIVE II

ich würde	wir würden	schauen
du würdest	ihr würdet	
Sie würden	Sie würden	
er/sie/es würde	sie würden	

PRESENT PERFECT

ich habe	wir haben	geschaut
du hast	ihr habt	
Sie haben	Sie haben	
er/sie/es hat	sie haben	

PAST PERFECT

ich hatte	wir hatten	geschaut
du hattest	ihr hattet	
Sie hatten	Sie hatten	
er/sie/es hatte	sie hatten	

FUTURE PERFECT

ich werde	wir werden	geschaut haben
du wirst	ihr werdet	
Sie werden	Sie werden	
er/sie/es wird	sie werden	

PAST SUBJUNCTIVE I

ich habe	wir haben	geschaut
du habest	ihr habet	
Sie haben	Sie haben	
er/sie/es habe	sie haben	

PAST SUBJUNCTIVE II

ich hätte	wir hätten	geschaut
du hättest	ihr hättet	
Sie hätten	Sie hätten	
er/sie/es hätte	sie hätten	

FUTURE PERFECT SUBJUNCTIVE I

ich werde	wir werden	geschaut haben
du werdest	ihr werdet	
Sie werden	Sie werden	
er/sie/es werde	sie werden	

FUTURE PERFECT SUBJUNCTIVE II

ich würde	wir würden	geschaut haben
du würdest	ihr würdet	
Sie würden	Sie würden	
er/sie/es würde	sie würden	

COMMANDS schau(e)! schaut! schauen Sie!

PRESENT PARTICIPLE schauend

Usage

Schau mal!	*Look!*
Wir wollen mal schauen, wie es geht.	*We want to see how it goes.*
Wo kann man Filme schauen?	*Where can you watch films?*
Wer möchte die DVD von mir schauen?	*Who would like to watch the DVD of me?*
Was schaut ihr morgen Abend?	*What are you watching tomorrow evening?*
Sollten wir nach dem Weg schauen?	*Should we look for directions?*
Lasst uns schauen.	*Let's have a look.*
Ich schaue Akten den ganzen Tag.	*I look at files all day long.*
Es gibt nicht viel zu schauen.	*There's not much to look at.*
Schaust du gern Fußball?	*Do you like to watch soccer?*
Saul schaute seiner Mutter fest in die Augen.	*Saul looked his mother straight in the eye.*
Du flehst … mich zu schauen. (GOETHE)	*You plead to see me.*

RELATED VERBS aus·schauen, durchschauen, voraus·schauen; *see also* **an·schauen** (17)

scheiden *to separate, divide* 360

strong verb

scheidet · schied · geschieden

PRESENT

ich scheide	wir scheiden
du scheidest	ihr scheidet
Sie scheiden	Sie scheiden
er/sie/es scheidet	sie scheiden

SIMPLE PAST

ich schied	wir schieden
du schiedst	ihr schiedet
Sie schieden	Sie schieden
er/sie/es schied	sie schieden

FUTURE

ich werde	wir werden	scheiden
du wirst	ihr werdet	
Sie werden	Sie werden	
er/sie/es wird	sie werden	

PRESENT SUBJUNCTIVE I

ich scheide	wir scheiden
du scheidest	ihr scheidet
Sie scheiden	Sie scheiden
er/sie/es scheide	sie scheiden

PRESENT SUBJUNCTIVE II

ich schiede	wir schieden
du schiedest	ihr schiedet
Sie schieden	Sie schieden
er/sie/es schiede	sie schieden

FUTURE SUBJUNCTIVE I

ich werde	wir werden	scheiden
du werdest	ihr werdet	
Sie werden	Sie werden	
er/sie/es werde	sie werden	

FUTURE SUBJUNCTIVE II

ich würde	wir würden	scheiden
du würdest	ihr würdet	
Sie würden	Sie würden	
er/sie/es würde	sie würden	

PRESENT PERFECT

ich habe	wir haben	geschieden
du hast	ihr habt	
Sie haben	Sie haben	
er/sie/es hat	sie haben	

PAST PERFECT

ich hatte	wir hatten	geschieden
du hattest	ihr hattet	
Sie hatten	Sie hatten	
er/sie/es hatte	sie hatten	

FUTURE PERFECT

ich werde	wir werden	geschieden haben
du wirst	ihr werdet	
Sie werden	Sie werden	
er/sie/es wird	sie werden	

PAST SUBJUNCTIVE I

ich habe	wir haben	geschieden
du habest	ihr habet	
Sie haben	Sie haben	
er/sie/es habe	sie haben	

PAST SUBJUNCTIVE II

ich hätte	wir hätten	geschieden
du hättest	ihr hättet	
Sie hätten	Sie hätten	
er/sie/es hätte	sie hätten	

FUTURE PERFECT SUBJUNCTIVE I

ich werde	wir werden	geschieden haben
du werdest	ihr werdet	
Sie werden	Sie werden	
er/sie/es werde	sie werden	

FUTURE PERFECT SUBJUNCTIVE II

ich würde	wir würden	geschieden haben
du würdest	ihr würdet	
Sie würden	Sie würden	
er/sie/es würde	sie würden	

COMMANDS scheide! scheidet! scheiden Sie!

PRESENT PARTICIPLE scheidend

Usage

Wir sind zusammen, bis uns der Tod scheidet.	*We are together until death separates us.*
Wie können wir sie scheiden?	*How can we separate them?*
Sollten wir die Kandidaten nach ihrer Erfahrung scheiden?	*Should we separate out the candidates based on their experience?*

sich scheiden *to divorce, separate, divide*

Meine Eltern sind bereit sich scheiden zu lassen.	*My parents are ready to get divorced.*
Wir wollen uns nicht scheiden.	*We don't want to part ways.*
Hier scheiden sich Theorie und Praxis.	*Theory and practice go separate ways here.*
Die Meinungen scheiden sich, ob das der wirkliche Grund ist.	*Opinions differ as to what the real reason is.*

scheiden (with **sein**) *to leave, part*

Er ist aus dem Leben geschieden.	*He has departed this life.*

RELATED VERBS ab·scheiden, aus·scheiden, bescheiden, verscheiden; *see also* **entscheiden** (146), **unterscheiden** (471)

361 scheinen *to shine; seem, appear*

scheint · schien · geschienen strong verb

PRESENT

ich scheine	wir scheinen
du scheinst	ihr scheint
Sie scheinen	Sie scheinen
er/sie/es scheint	sie scheinen

SIMPLE PAST

ich schien	wir schienen
du schienst	ihr schient
Sie schienen	Sie schienen
er/sie/es schien	sie schienen

FUTURE

ich werde	wir werden	scheinen
du wirst	ihr werdet	
Sie werden	Sie werden	
er/sie/es wird	sie werden	

PRESENT SUBJUNCTIVE I

ich scheine	wir scheinen
du scheinest	ihr scheinet
Sie scheinen	Sie scheinen
er/sie/es scheine	sie scheinen

PRESENT SUBJUNCTIVE II

ich schiene	wir schienen
du schienest	ihr schienet
Sie schienen	Sie schienen
er/sie/es schiene	sie schienen

FUTURE SUBJUNCTIVE I

ich werde	wir werden	scheinen
du werdest	ihr werdet	
Sie werden	Sie werden	
er/sie/es werde	sie werden	

FUTURE SUBJUNCTIVE II

ich würde	wir würden	scheinen
du würdest	ihr würdet	
Sie würden	Sie würden	
er/sie/es würde	sie würden	

PRESENT PERFECT

ich habe	wir haben	geschienen
du hast	ihr habt	
Sie haben	Sie haben	
er/sie/es hat	sie haben	

PAST PERFECT

ich hatte	wir hatten	geschienen
du hattest	ihr hattet	
Sie hatten	Sie hatten	
er/sie/es hatte	sie hatten	

FUTURE PERFECT

ich werde	wir werden	geschienen haben
du wirst	ihr werdet	
Sie werden	Sie werden	
er/sie/es wird	sie werden	

PAST SUBJUNCTIVE I

ich habe	wir haben	geschienen
du habest	ihr habet	
Sie haben	Sie haben	
er/sie/es habe	sie haben	

PAST SUBJUNCTIVE II

ich hätte	wir hätten	geschienen
du hättest	ihr hättet	
Sie hätten	Sie hätten	
er/sie/es hätte	sie hätten	

FUTURE PERFECT SUBJUNCTIVE I

ich werde	wir werden	geschienen haben
du werdest	ihr werdet	
Sie werden	Sie werden	
er/sie/es werde	sie werden	

FUTURE PERFECT SUBJUNCTIVE II

ich würde	wir würden	geschienen haben
du würdest	ihr würdet	
Sie würden	Sie würden	
er/sie/es würde	sie würden	

COMMANDS schein(e)! scheint! scheinen Sie!

PRESENT PARTICIPLE scheinend

Usage

Die Sonne scheint und die Vögel zwitschern.	*The sun is shining and the birds are chirping.*
Vor dem Urknall schienen keine Sterne.	*Before the Big Bang, no stars were shining.*
Das Licht scheint ihm ins Gesicht.	*The light is shining in his face.*
Er scheint nicht verstanden zu haben.	*He seems not to have understood.*
WAP-fähige Handys scheinen populär zu sein.	*WAP-enabled cell phones seem to be popular.*
Aschenputtel scheint ihre Stiefmutter nicht zu lieben.	*Cinderella doesn't seem to love her stepmother.*
Ich scheine der einzige zu sein, der das will.	*I seem to be the only one who wants that.*
Das Werk schien immer noch problematisch für Literaturwissenschaftler zu sein.	*The work still appeared to be problematic for literary scholars.*
Das System scheint wieder zu funktionieren.	*The system seems to be working again.*
Das Kind scheint Angst zu haben.	*The child seems to be afraid.*
Das Hemd schien zu passen.	*The shirt seemed to fit.*
Das Bier scheint einen komischen Nachgeschmack zu haben.	*The beer seems to have a funny aftertaste.*

RELATED VERBS auf·scheinen, bescheinen, durch·scheinen, durchscheinen; see also **erscheinen** (170)

regular weak verb **scheitert · scheiterte · gescheitert**

PRESENT

ich scheitere	wir scheitern
du scheiterst	ihr scheitert
Sie scheitern	Sie scheitern
er/sie/es scheitert	sie scheitern

SIMPLE PAST

ich scheiterte	wir scheiterten
du scheitertest	ihr scheitertet
Sie scheiterten	Sie scheiterten
er/sie/es scheiterte	sie scheiterten

FUTURE

ich werde	wir werden	scheitern
du wirst	ihr werdet	
Sie werden	Sie werden	
er/sie/es wird	sie werden	

PRESENT SUBJUNCTIVE I

ich scheitere	wir scheitern
du scheiterst	ihr scheitert
Sie scheitern	Sie scheitern
er/sie/es scheitere	sie scheitern

PRESENT SUBJUNCTIVE II

ich scheiterte	wir scheiterten
du scheitertest	ihr scheitertet
Sie scheiterten	Sie scheiterten
er/sie/es scheiterte	sie scheiterten

FUTURE SUBJUNCTIVE I

ich werde	wir werden	scheitern
du werdest	ihr werdet	
Sie werden	Sie werden	
er/sie/es werde	sie werden	

FUTURE SUBJUNCTIVE II

ich würde	wir würden	scheitern
du würdest	ihr würdet	
Sie würden	Sie würden	
er/sie/es würde	sie würden	

PRESENT PERFECT

ich bin	wir sind	gescheitert
du bist	ihr seid	
Sie sind	Sie sind	
er/sie/es ist	sie sind	

PAST PERFECT

ich war	wir waren	gescheitert
du warst	ihr wart	
Sie waren	Sie waren	
er/sie/es war	sie waren	

FUTURE PERFECT

ich werde	wir werden	gescheitert sein
du wirst	ihr werdet	
Sie werden	Sie werden	
er/sie/es wird	sie werden	

PAST SUBJUNCTIVE I

ich sei	wir seien	gescheitert
du seiest	ihr seiet	
Sie seien	Sie seien	
er/sie/es sei	sie seien	

PAST SUBJUNCTIVE II

ich wäre	wir wären	gescheitert
du wärest	ihr wäret	
Sie wären	Sie wären	
er/sie/es wäre	sie wären	

FUTURE PERFECT SUBJUNCTIVE I

ich werde	wir werden	gescheitert sein
du werdest	ihr werdet	
Sie werden	Sie werden	
er/sie/es werde	sie werden	

FUTURE PERFECT SUBJUNCTIVE II

ich würde	wir würden	gescheitert sein
du würdest	ihr würdet	
Sie würden	Sie würden	
er/sie/es würde	sie würden	

COMMANDS scheitere! scheitert! scheitern Sie!

PRESENT PARTICIPLE scheiternd

Usage

Das Boot scheiterte auf einem Felsen und sank.	*The boat foundered on a rock and sank.*
1972 scheiterte die Partei bei der Bundestagswahl.	*The party was defeated in the federal election in 1972.*
Warum bist du an der Prüfung gescheitert?	*Why did you fail the test?*
Sein neues Buch war leider gescheitert.	*His new book had unfortunately bombed.*
Sara will nicht gescheitert sein.	*Sara claims not to have failed.*
Nach einem Jahr sind sie gescheitert.	*After one year, they failed.*
Maria ist trotz einer hervorragenden Leistung gescheitert.	*Maria failed in spite of an outstanding performance.*
Lars wird im Viertelfinale wohl gescheitert sein.	*Lars will have been eliminated in the quarterfinals.*
Ich konnte ihn nicht scheitern lassen.	*I couldn't let him fail.*
Der Versuch scheint gescheitert zu sein.	*The attempt appears to have come to nothing.*
Der Film ist wegen schlechten Marketings gescheitert.	*The film was a flop because of poor marketing.*
Das Produkt wird bestimmt scheitern.	*The product will surely fail.*
Der Versuch scheiterte wegen Geldmangel.	*The attempt was frustrated by a lack of money.*
Unser Projekt scheiterte am Tod des Verwalters.	*Our project fell through because of the manager's death.*

363 schelten *to moan, complain; scold; call; reprimand*

schilt · schalt · gescholten strong verb

PRESENT

ich schelte	wir schelten
du schiltst	ihr scheltet
Sie schelten	Sie schelten
er/sie/es schilt	sie schelten

SIMPLE PAST

ich schalt	wir schalten
du schaltst	ihr schaltet
Sie schalten	Sie schalten
er/sie/es schalt	sie schalten

FUTURE

ich werde	wir werden	schelten
du wirst	ihr werdet	
Sie werden	Sie werden	
er/sie/es wird	sie werden	

PRESENT SUBJUNCTIVE I

ich schelte	wir schelten
du scheltest	ihr scheltet
Sie schelten	Sie schelten
er/sie/es schelte	sie schelten

PRESENT SUBJUNCTIVE II

ich schölte	wir schölten
du schöltest	ihr schöltet
Sie schölten	Sie schölten
er/sie/es schölte	sie schölten

FUTURE SUBJUNCTIVE I

ich werde	wir werden	schelten
du werdest	ihr werdet	
Sie werden	Sie werden	
er/sie/es werde	sie werden	

FUTURE SUBJUNCTIVE II

ich würde	wir würden	schelten
du würdest	ihr würdet	
Sie würden	Sie würden	
er/sie/es würde	sie würden	

PRESENT PERFECT

ich habe	wir haben	gescholten
du hast	ihr habt	
Sie haben	Sie haben	
er/sie/es hat	sie haben	

PAST PERFECT

ich hatte	wir hatten	gescholten
du hattest	ihr hattet	
Sie hatten	Sie hatten	
er/sie/es hatte	sie hatten	

FUTURE PERFECT

ich werde	wir werden	gescholten haben
du wirst	ihr werdet	
Sie werden	Sie werden	
er/sie/es wird	sie werden	

PAST SUBJUNCTIVE I

ich habe	wir haben	gescholten
du habest	ihr habet	
Sie haben	Sie haben	
er/sie/es habe	sie haben	

PAST SUBJUNCTIVE II

ich hätte	wir hätten	gescholten
du hättest	ihr hättet	
Sie hätten	Sie hätten	
er/sie/es hätte	sie hätten	

FUTURE PERFECT SUBJUNCTIVE I

ich werde	wir werden	gescholten haben
du werdest	ihr werdet	
Sie werden	Sie werden	
er/sie/es werde	sie werden	

FUTURE PERFECT SUBJUNCTIVE II

ich würde	wir würden	gescholten haben
du würdest	ihr würdet	
Sie würden	Sie würden	
er/sie/es würde	sie würden	

COMMANDS schilt! scheltet! schelten Sie!

PRESENT PARTICIPLE scheltend

Usage

Warum schiltst du so?	*Why are you complaining like that?*
Der Nachbar schilt uns wegen des Lärms.	*The neighbor is complaining to us because of the noise.*
Anwohner schalten die Politiker über das geplante Einkaufszentrum.	*Residents complained to the politicians about the planned shopping center.*
Warum scheltet ihr mich?	*Why are you scolding me?*
Die Stiefmutter schilt Aschenputtel täglich.	*The stepmother scolds Cinderella on a daily basis.*
Der Vater schalt seinen Sohn.	*The father read his son the riot act.*
Dass ich ihn schelte ist nichts Neues.	*That I am scolding him is nothing new.*
Anton hatte sie immer gescholten.	*Anton had always berated her.*
Unser Papagei schilt uns, wenn er Hunger hat.	*Our parrot calls us when he's hungry.*
Dominik schilt seine Katze, wenn sie sich nicht benimmt.	*Dominik reprimands his cat when it doesn't behave.*
Der Lehrer hat Max und Moritz gescholten.	*The teacher reprimanded Max and Moritz.*
Der Bischof schalt den Stadtrat.	*The bishop reprimanded the city council.*

RELATED VERB aus·schelten

regular weak verb

schenkt · schenkte · geschenkt

PRESENT

ich schenke	wir schenken
du schenkst	ihr schenkt
Sie schenken	Sie schenken
er/sie/es schenkt	sie schenken

SIMPLE PAST

ich schenkte	wir schenkten
du schenktest	ihr schenktet
Sie schenkten	Sie schenkten
er/sie/es schenkte	sie schenkten

FUTURE

ich werde	wir werden	schenken
du wirst	ihr werdet	
Sie werden	Sie werden	
er/sie/es wird	sie werden	

PRESENT SUBJUNCTIVE I

ich schenke	wir schenken
du schenkest	ihr schenket
Sie schenken	Sie schenken
er/sie/es schenke	sie schenken

PRESENT SUBJUNCTIVE II

ich schenkte	wir schenkten
du schenktest	ihr schenktet
Sie schenkten	Sie schenkten
er/sie/es schenkte	sie schenkten

FUTURE SUBJUNCTIVE I

ich werde	wir werden	schenken
du werdest	ihr werdet	
Sie werden	Sie werden	
er/sie/es werde	sie werden	

FUTURE SUBJUNCTIVE II

ich würde	wir würden	schenken
du würdest	ihr würdet	
Sie würden	Sie würden	
er/sie/es würde	sie würden	

PRESENT PERFECT

ich habe	wir haben	geschenkt
du hast	ihr habt	
Sie haben	Sie haben	
er/sie/es hat	sie haben	

PAST PERFECT

ich hatte	wir hatten	geschenkt
du hattest	ihr hattet	
Sie hatten	Sie hatten	
er/sie/es hatte	sie hatten	

FUTURE PERFECT

ich werde	wir werden	geschenkt haben
du wirst	ihr werdet	
Sie werden	Sie werden	
er/sie/es wird	sie werden	

PAST SUBJUNCTIVE I

ich habe	wir haben	geschenkt
du habest	ihr habet	
Sie haben	Sie haben	
er/sie/es habe	sie haben	

PAST SUBJUNCTIVE II

ich hätte	wir hätten	geschenkt
du hättest	ihr hättet	
Sie hätten	Sie hätten	
er/sie/es hätte	sie hätten	

FUTURE PERFECT SUBJUNCTIVE I

ich werde	wir werden	geschenkt haben
du werdest	ihr werdet	
Sie werden	Sie werden	
er/sie/es werde	sie werden	

FUTURE PERFECT SUBJUNCTIVE II

ich würde	wir würden	geschenkt haben
du würdest	ihr würdet	
Sie würden	Sie würden	
er/sie/es würde	sie würden	

COMMANDS schenk(e)! schenkt! schenken Sie!

PRESENT PARTICIPLE schenkend

Usage

Was schenkst du deiner Mutter zum Geburtstag?	*What are you giving your mother for her birthday?*
Was können wir ihnen schenken?	*What can we give them?*
Schenkt ihnen doch eine CD.	*Give them a CD.*
Jedes Jahr schenkt Tante Bärbel einen Adventkranz aus Tannenzweigen.	*Every year, Aunt Bärbel gives an advent wreath made of fir branches.*
Ich habe meinem Mann eine Kamera geschenkt.	*I've given my husband a camera.*
Frau Escher schenkte ihrem Mann ihr Vermögen.	*Mrs. Escher gave her fortune to her husband.*
Es gibt nichts zu schenken.	*There's nothing to give.*
Den Frauen wurden Körbe geschenkt.	*The women were given baskets.*
Am besten schenken Sie eine Limousinenfahrt.	*The best thing is for you to give a limousine ride.*
Schenkst du deinen Freunden Geld?	*Do you give your friends money?*
Bitte schenken Sie mir Ihre ganze Aufmerksamkeit.	*Please give me your undivided attention.*
Der Drogenhändler schenkte dem Polizeispitzel das Leben.	*The drug dealer spared the police informer's life.*

RELATED VERBS aus·schenken, beschenken, ein·schenken, nach·schenken, verschenken

365 **schicken** *to send*

schickt · schickte · geschickt

regular weak verb

PRESENT

ich schicke	wir schicken
du schickst	ihr schickt
Sie schicken	Sie schicken
er/sie/es schickt	sie schicken

SIMPLE PAST

ich schickte	wir schickten
du schicktest	ihr schicktet
Sie schickten	Sie schickten
er/sie/es schickte	sie schickten

FUTURE

ich werde	wir werden	schicken
du wirst	ihr werdet	
Sie werden	Sie werden	
er/sie/es wird	sie werden	

PRESENT SUBJUNCTIVE I

ich schicke	wir schicken
du schickest	ihr schicket
Sie schicken	Sie schicken
er/sie/es schicke	sie schicken

PRESENT SUBJUNCTIVE II

ich schickte	wir schickten
du schicktest	ihr schicktet
Sie schickten	Sie schickten
er/sie/es schickte	sie schickten

FUTURE SUBJUNCTIVE I

ich werde	wir werden	schicken
du werdest	ihr werdet	
Sie werden	Sie werden	
er/sie/es werde	sie werden	

FUTURE SUBJUNCTIVE II

ich würde	wir würden	schicken
du würdest	ihr würdet	
Sie würden	Sie würden	
er/sie/es würde	sie würden	

PRESENT PERFECT

ich habe	wir haben	geschickt
du hast	ihr habt	
Sie haben	Sie haben	
er/sie/es hat	sie haben	

PAST PERFECT

ich hatte	wir hatten	geschickt
du hattest	ihr hattet	
Sie hatten	Sie hatten	
er/sie/es hatte	sie hatten	

FUTURE PERFECT

ich werde	wir werden	geschickt haben
du wirst	ihr werdet	
Sie werden	Sie werden	
er/sie/es wird	sie werden	

PAST SUBJUNCTIVE I

ich habe	wir haben	geschickt
du habest	ihr habet	
Sie haben	Sie haben	
er/sie/es habe	sie haben	

PAST SUBJUNCTIVE II

ich hätte	wir hätten	geschickt
du hättest	ihr hättet	
Sie hätten	Sie hätten	
er/sie/es hätte	sie hätten	

FUTURE PERFECT SUBJUNCTIVE I

ich werde	wir werden	geschickt haben
du werdest	ihr werdet	
Sie werden	Sie werden	
er/sie/es werde	sie werden	

FUTURE PERFECT SUBJUNCTIVE II

ich würde	wir würden	geschickt haben
du würdest	ihr würdet	
Sie würden	Sie würden	
er/sie/es würde	sie würden	

COMMANDS schick(e)! schickt! schicken Sie!

PRESENT PARTICIPLE schickend

Usage

Maria hat mir eine tolle Ansichtskarte aus Lettland geschickt.	*Maria sent me a cool postcard from Latvia.*
Ich wurde nach Hause geschickt.	*I was sent home.*
Der Befehlshaber schickte mehr als 1 000 Menschen in den Tod.	*The commander sent more than 1,000 people to their deaths.*
Ab und zu schickt Mirna mir eine Flasche Rotwein aus Sizilien.	*Once in a while, Mirna sends me a bottle of red wine from Sicily.*
Schickt bitte eure Kommentare!	*Send your comments.*
Sollten wir nicht nach Hilfe schicken?	*Hadn't we better send for help?*

sich schicken *to be appropriate/suitable/proper*

Seine Worte schicken sich nicht in dieser Situation.	*His words are not appropriate in this situation.*

RELATED VERBS ab·schicken, an·schicken, aus·schicken, beschicken, ein·schicken, fort·schicken, hin·schicken, mit·schicken, nach·schicken, verschicken, voraus·schicken, weg·schicken, weiter·schicken, zurück·schicken, zu·schicken strong verb **schiebt · schob · geschoben**

PRESENT		PRESENT PERFECT		
ich schiebe	wir schieben	ich habe	wir haben	geschoben
du schiebst	ihr schiebt	du hast	ihr habt	
Sie schieben	Sie schieben	Sie haben	Sie haben	
er/sie/es schiebt	sie schieben	er/sie/es hat	sie haben	

SIMPLE PAST		PAST PERFECT		
ich schob	wir schoben	ich hatte	wir hatten	geschoben
du schobst	ihr schobt	du hattest	ihr hattet	
Sie schoben	Sie schoben	Sie hatten	Sie hatten	
er/sie/es schob	sie schoben	er/sie/es hatte	sie hatten	

FUTURE			FUTURE PERFECT		
ich werde	wir werden	schieben	ich werde	wir werden	geschoben haben
du wirst	ihr werdet		du wirst	ihr werdet	
Sie werden	Sie werden		Sie werden	Sie werden	
er/sie/es wird	sie werden		er/sie/es wird	sie werden	

PRESENT SUBJUNCTIVE I		PAST SUBJUNCTIVE I		
ich schiebe	wir schieben	ich habe	wir haben	geschoben
du schiebest	ihr schiebet	du habest	ihr habet	
Sie schieben	Sie schieben	Sie haben	Sie haben	
er/sie/es schiebe	sie schieben	er/sie/es habe	sie haben	

PRESENT SUBJUNCTIVE II		PAST SUBJUNCTIVE II		
ich schöbe	wir schöben	ich hätte	wir hätten	geschoben
du schöbest	ihr schöbet	du hättest	ihr hättet	
Sie schöben	Sie schöben	Sie hätten	Sie hätten	
er/sie/es schöbe	sie schöben	er/sie/es hätte	sie hätten	

FUTURE SUBJUNCTIVE I			FUTURE PERFECT SUBJUNCTIVE I		
ich werde	wir werden	schieben	ich werde	wir werden	geschoben haben
du werdest	ihr werdet		du werdest	ihr werdet	
Sie werden	Sie werden		Sie werden	Sie werden	
er/sie/es werde	sie werden		er/sie/es werde	sie werden	

FUTURE SUBJUNCTIVE II			FUTURE PERFECT SUBJUNCTIVE II		
ich würde	wir würden	schieben	ich würde	wir würden	geschoben haben
du würdest	ihr würdet		du würdest	ihr würdet	
Sie würden	Sie würden		Sie würden	Sie würden	
er/sie/es würde	sie würden		er/sie/es würde	sie würden	

COMMANDS schieb(e)! schiebt! schieben Sie!

PRESENT PARTICIPLE schiebend

Usage

Die Frauen schoben einen Karren. — *The women were pushing a cart.*
Die alten Männer schieben einander. — *The old men are shoving one another.*
Der Passant wurde aus dem Weg geschoben. — *The passerby was pushed aside.*
Der Junge hat seine Socken in die Schublade geschoben. — *The boy shoved his socks into the drawer.*
Der alte Bauer schob das tote Tier in eine Klamm. — *The old farmer pushed the dead animal into a ravine.*
Der Lehrer schob die Schuld auf meinen Bruder. — *The teacher placed the blame on my brother.*
In der Sitzung wurden mehrere Projekte auf die lange Bank geschoben. (*figurative*) — *At the meeting, several projects were shelved/postponed.*

sich schieben *to move; force, push one's way*

1722 schob sich die Grenze nach Norden. — *The border moved northward in 1722.*
Die Polizistin hat sich durch die Demonstranten geschoben. — *The policewoman pushed her way through the protesters.*

RELATED VERBS ab·schieben, an·schieben, auf·schieben, durch·schieben, ein·schieben, unterschieben, unter·schieben, verschieben, vor·schieben, weg·schieben, zurück·schieben, zu·schieben

367 schießen *to shoot, fire*

schießt · schoss · geschossen strong verb

PRESENT

ich schieße	wir schießen
du schießt	ihr schießt
Sie schießen	Sie schießen
er/sie/es schießt	sie schießen

SIMPLE PAST

ich schoss	wir schossen
du schossest	ihr schosst
Sie schossen	Sie schossen
er/sie/es schoss	sie schossen

FUTURE

ich werde	wir werden	schießen
du wirst	ihr werdet	
Sie werden	Sie werden	
er/sie/es wird	sie werden	

PRESENT SUBJUNCTIVE I

ich schieße	wir schießen
du schießest	ihr schießet
Sie schießen	Sie schießen
er/sie/es schieße	sie schießen

PRESENT SUBJUNCTIVE II

ich schösse	wir schössen
du schössest	ihr schösset
Sie schössen	Sie schössen
er/sie/es schösse	sie schössen

FUTURE SUBJUNCTIVE I

ich werde	wir werden	schießen
du werdest	ihr werdet	
Sie werden	Sie werden	
er/sie/es werde	sie werden	

FUTURE SUBJUNCTIVE II

ich würde	wir würden	schießen
du würdest	ihr würdet	
Sie würden	Sie würden	
er/sie/es würde	sie würden	

PRESENT PERFECT

ich habe	wir haben	geschossen
du hast	ihr habt	
Sie haben	Sie haben	
er/sie/es hat	sie haben	

PAST PERFECT

ich hatte	wir hatten	geschossen
du hattest	ihr hattet	
Sie hatten	Sie hatten	
er/sie/es hatte	sie hatten	

FUTURE PERFECT

ich werde	wir werden	geschossen haben
du wirst	ihr werdet	
Sie werden	Sie werden	
er/sie/es wird	sie werden	

PAST SUBJUNCTIVE I

ich habe	wir haben	geschossen
du habest	ihr habet	
Sie haben	Sie haben	
er/sie/es habe	sie haben	

PAST SUBJUNCTIVE II

ich hätte	wir hätten	geschossen
du hättest	ihr hättet	
Sie hätten	Sie hätten	
er/sie/es hätte	sie hätten	

FUTURE PERFECT SUBJUNCTIVE I

ich werde	wir werden	geschossen haben
du werdest	ihr werdet	
Sie werden	Sie werden	
er/sie/es werde	sie werden	

FUTURE PERFECT SUBJUNCTIVE II

ich würde	wir würden	geschossen haben
du würdest	ihr würdet	
Sie würden	Sie würden	
er/sie/es würde	sie würden	

COMMANDS schieß(e)! schießt! schießen Sie!

PRESENT PARTICIPLE schießend

Usage

Wie oft gehst du schießen?	*How often do you go shooting?*
Sasha wollte durch das Fenster schießen.	*Sasha wanted to fire the gun through the window.*
Gestern Abend wurde bei uns geschossen.	*There was shooting last night at our place.*
Die Soldaten schießen nicht mehr.	*The soldiers are not shooting anymore.*
Auf der Demonstration ist nicht geschossen worden.	*There were no shots fired at the demonstration.*
Der Räuber stolperte und schoss sich ins Bein.	*The robber tripped and shot himself in the leg.*

schießen (with sein) *to gush, rush*

Die Rakete ist in die Luft geschossen.	*The rocket whooshed into the air.*
Die Katze ist ängstlich hinter das Sofa geschossen.	*The cat shot behind the sofa, terrified.*
Maria schießt um die Ecke.	*Maria rushes around the corner.*

RELATED VERBS ab·schießen, an·schießen, beschießen, durchschießen, durch·schießen, ein·schießen, erschießen, hoch·schießen, nieder·schießen, überschießen, über·schießen, verschießen, vorbei·schießen, zerschießen, zurück·schießen, zu·schießen

regular weak verb **schimpft · schimpfte · geschimpft**

PRESENT

ich schimpfe	wir schimpfen
du schimpfst	ihr schimpft
Sie schimpfen	Sie schimpfen
er/sie/es schimpft	sie schimpfen

SIMPLE PAST

ich schimpfte	wir schimpften
du schimpftest	ihr schimpftet
Sie schimpften	Sie schimpften
er/sie/es schimpfte	sie schimpften

FUTURE

ich werde	wir werden	schimpfen
du wirst	ihr werdet	
Sie werden	Sie werden	
er/sie/es wird	sie werden	

PRESENT SUBJUNCTIVE I

ich schimpfe	wir schimpfen
du schimpfest	ihr schimpfet
Sie schimpfen	Sie schimpfen
er/sie/es schimpfe	sie schimpfen

PRESENT SUBJUNCTIVE II

ich schimpfte	wir schimpften
du schimpftest	ihr schimpftet
Sie schimpften	Sie schimpften
er/sie/es schimpfte	sie schimpften

FUTURE SUBJUNCTIVE I

ich werde	wir werden	schimpfen
du werdest	ihr werdet	
Sie werden	Sie werden	
er/sie/es werde	sie werden	

FUTURE SUBJUNCTIVE II

ich würde	wir würden	schimpfen
du würdest	ihr würdet	
Sie würden	Sie würden	
er/sie/es würde	sie würden	

PRESENT PERFECT

ich habe	wir haben	geschimpft
du hast	ihr habt	
Sie haben	Sie haben	
er/sie/es hat	sie haben	

PAST PERFECT

ich hatte	wir hatten	geschimpft
du hattest	ihr hattet	
Sie hatten	Sie hatten	
er/sie/es hatte	sie hatten	

FUTURE PERFECT

ich werde	wir werden	geschimpft haben
du wirst	ihr werdet	
Sie werden	Sie werden	
er/sie/es wird	sie werden	

PAST SUBJUNCTIVE I

ich habe	wir haben	geschimpft
du habest	ihr habet	
Sie haben	Sie haben	
er/sie/es habe	sie haben	

PAST SUBJUNCTIVE II

ich hätte	wir hätten	geschimpft
du hättest	ihr hättet	
Sie hätten	Sie hätten	
er/sie/es hätte	sie hätten	

FUTURE PERFECT SUBJUNCTIVE I

ich werde	wir werden	geschimpft haben
du werdest	ihr werdet	
Sie werden	Sie werden	
er/sie/es werde	sie werden	

FUTURE PERFECT SUBJUNCTIVE II

ich würde	wir würden	geschimpft haben
du würdest	ihr würdet	
Sie würden	Sie würden	
er/sie/es würde	sie würden	

COMMANDS schimpf(e)! schimpft! schimpfen Sie!

PRESENT PARTICIPLE schimpfend

Usage

Mein Mann schimpft, weil das Abendessen noch nicht fertig ist.	*My husband is grumbling because dinner isn't ready yet.*
Oma Josephine hat früher immer geschimpft.	*Grandma Josephine always used to swear.*
Die Spieler haben bis zum Ende geschimpft.	*The players groused to the end.*
Der Skifahrer schimpft über den Schneemangel.	*The skier is complaining about the lack of snow.*
Die Konservativen schimpfen seit 20 Jahren.	*The conservatives have complained for 20 years.*
Die Computerfirma schimpft mit der EU.	*The computer firm is airing its grievance to the E.U.*
Opa schimpft über Steuerhinterzieher.	*Grandpa is griping about tax dodgers.*
Die Außenminister schimpfen über den Konflikt.	*The foreign ministers are grumbling about the conflict.*
Die Näherinnen schimpfen über die Arbeitsbedingungen.	*The seamstresses are bemoaning the working conditions.*
Die Abgeordneten werden über die neuen Regelungen schimpfen.	*The representatives will complain about the new regulations.*
Das Eichhörnchen schimpft mit der Katze, die es anguckt.	*The squirrel is scolding the cat that's watching it.*

RELATED VERBS aus·schimpfen, beschimpfen

369 **schinden** *to skin, flay; mistreat, ill-treat, overwork*

schindet · schindete/schund · geschunden regular weak verb/strong verb

PRESENT

ich schinde	wir schinden
du schindest	ihr schindet
Sie schinden	Sie schinden
er/sie/es schindet	sie schinden

SIMPLE PAST

ich schindete/schund	wir schindeten/schunden
du schindetest/schund(e)st	ihr schindetet/schundet
Sie schindeten/schunden	Sie schindeten/schunden
er/sie/es schindete/schund	sie schindeten/schunden

FUTURE

ich werde	wir werden	schinden
du wirst	ihr werdet	
Sie werden	Sie werden	
er/sie/es wird	sie werden	

PRESENT SUBJUNCTIVE I

ich schinde	wir schinden
du schindest	ihr schindet
Sie schinden	Sie schinden
er/sie/es schinde	sie schinden

PRESENT SUBJUNCTIVE II

ich schindete/schünde	wir schindeten/schünden
du schindetest/schündest	ihr schindetet/schündet
Sie schindeten/schünden	Sie schindeten/schünden
er/sie/es schindete/schünde	sie schindeten/schünden

FUTURE SUBJUNCTIVE I

ich werde	wir werden	schinden
du werdest	ihr werdet	
Sie werden	Sie werden	
er/sie/es werde	sie werden	

FUTURE SUBJUNCTIVE II

ich würde	wir würden	schinden
du würdest	ihr würdet	
Sie würden	Sie würden	
er/sie/es würde	sie würden	

PRESENT PERFECT

ich habe	wir haben	geschunden
du hast	ihr habt	
Sie haben	Sie haben	
er/sie/es hat	sie haben	

PAST PERFECT

ich hatte	wir hatten	geschunden
du hattest	ihr hattet	
Sie hatten	Sie hatten	
er/sie/es hatte	sie hatten	

FUTURE PERFECT

ich werde	wir werden	geschunden haben
du wirst	ihr werdet	
Sie werden	Sie werden	
er/sie/es wird	sie werden	

PAST SUBJUNCTIVE I

ich habe	wir haben	geschunden
du habest	ihr habet	
Sie haben	Sie haben	
er/sie/es habe	sie haben	

PAST SUBJUNCTIVE II

ich hätte	wir hätten	geschunden
du hättest	ihr hättet	
Sie hätten	Sie hätten	
er/sie/es hätte	sie hätten	

FUTURE PERFECT SUBJUNCTIVE I

ich werde	wir werden	geschunden haben
du werdest	ihr werdet	
Sie werden	Sie werden	
er/sie/es werde	sie werden	

FUTURE PERFECT SUBJUNCTIVE II

ich würde	wir würden	geschunden haben
du würdest	ihr würdet	
Sie würden	Sie würden	
er/sie/es würde	sie würden	

COMMANDS schinde! schindet! schinden Sie!

PRESENT PARTICIPLE schindend

NOTE The simple tenses of **schinden** are typically regular weak in modern German.

Usage

Das Tier wurde lebendig geschunden.	*The animal was skinned alive.*
Ich habe die Studenten und Studentinnen geschunden.	*I worked the students like slaves.*
Der Herrscher schund das Bauernvolk.	*The ruler treated the peasantry badly.*
In manchen Ländern werden Kinder zu Tode geschunden.	*In some countries, children are worked to death.*
Die Sklaven wurden regelmäßig geschunden.	*The slaves were regularly overworked.*
Der Hauptgeschäftsführer schindete alle Mitarbeiter in der Firma gleichermaßen.	*The CEO overworked all company employees equally.*

sich schinden *to overwork (oneself)*

Manfred schindet sich für seine Familie.	*Manfred slaves away for his family.*
Der Bauersknecht schund sich jeden Tag.	*The hired hand worked himself to exhaustion every day.*
Besonders die Armen müssen sich schinden.	*Especially the poor have to work themselves to death.*

RELATED VERB ab·schinden

strong verb **schläft · schlief · geschlafen**

PRESENT

ich schlafe	wir schlafen
du schläfst	ihr schlaft
Sie schlafen	Sie schlafen
er/sie/es schläft	sie schlafen

SIMPLE PAST

ich schlief	wir schliefen
du schliefst	ihr schlieft
Sie schliefen	Sie schliefen
er/sie/es schlief	sie schliefen

FUTURE

ich werde	wir werden	schlafen
du wirst	ihr werdet	
Sie werden	Sie werden	
er/sie/es wird	sie werden	

PRESENT SUBJUNCTIVE I

ich schlafe	wir schlafen
du schlafest	ihr schlafet
Sie schlafen	Sie schlafen
er/sie/es schlafe	sie schlafen

PRESENT SUBJUNCTIVE II

ich schliefe	wir schliefen
du schliefest	ihr schliefet
Sie schliefen	Sie schliefen
er/sie/es schliefe	sie schliefen

FUTURE SUBJUNCTIVE I

ich werde	wir werden	schlafen
du werdest	ihr werdet	
Sie werden	Sie werden	
er/sie/es werde	sie werden	

FUTURE SUBJUNCTIVE II

ich würde	wir würden	schlafen
du würdest	ihr würdet	
Sie würden	Sie würden	
er/sie/es würde	sie würden	

PRESENT PERFECT

ich habe	wir haben	geschlafen
du hast	ihr habt	
Sie haben	Sie haben	
er/sie/es hat	sie haben	

PAST PERFECT

ich hatte	wir hatten	geschlafen
du hattest	ihr hattet	
Sie hatten	Sie hatten	
er/sie/es hatte	sie hatten	

FUTURE PERFECT

ich werde	wir werden	geschlafen haben
du wirst	ihr werdet	
Sie werden	Sie werden	
er/sie/es wird	sie werden	

PAST SUBJUNCTIVE I

ich habe	wir haben	geschlafen
du habest	ihr habet	
Sie haben	Sie haben	
er/sie/es habe	sie haben	

PAST SUBJUNCTIVE II

ich hätte	wir hätten	geschlafen
du hättest	ihr hättet	
Sie hätten	Sie hätten	
er/sie/es hätte	sie hätten	

FUTURE PERFECT SUBJUNCTIVE I

ich werde	wir werden	geschlafen haben
du werdest	ihr werdet	
Sie werden	Sie werden	
er/sie/es werde	sie werden	

FUTURE PERFECT SUBJUNCTIVE II

ich würde	wir würden	geschlafen haben
du würdest	ihr würdet	
Sie würden	Sie würden	
er/sie/es würde	sie würden	

COMMANDS schlaf(e)! schlaft! schlafen Sie!

PRESENT PARTICIPLE schlafend

Usage

Könnt ihr bitte etwas leiser sein, das Baby schläft.	*Can you please be quieter? The baby is asleep.*
Opa nimmt Tabletten, damit er schlafen kann.	*Grandpa takes medicine so he can sleep.*
Unser Kater Dominik schläft den ganzen Tag.	*Our tomcat, Dominik, sleeps the whole day.*
Der Hund hat die ganze Nacht geschlafen.	*The dog slept the whole night.*
Schlafen Fische?	*Do fish sleep?*
Maria scheint zu schlafen.	*Maria appears to be asleep.*
Grete hat den schlafenden Hund nicht gesehen.	*Grete didn't see the sleeping dog.*
Bernd wollte nicht schlafen.	*Bernd didn't want to sleep.*
Alle Dorfbewohner schliefen, als der Wolf aus dem Wald kam.	*All the village residents were sleeping when the wolf came out of the forest.*
Uwe sagt, er hätte die ganze Nacht nicht schlafen können.	*Uwe says he couldn't sleep the whole night.*
Schläft Maria noch?	*Is Maria still asleep?*

RELATED VERBS aus·schlafen, bei·schlafen, durch·schlafen, durchschlafen, ein·schlafen, entschlafen, überschlafen, verschlafen, weiter·schlafen

TOP 50 VERB ☞

schlafen *to sleep, be asleep*

schläft · schlief · geschlafen strong verb

schlafen + preposition

Ein Nachtwächter darf nicht bei der Arbeit schlafen. *A night watchman can't sleep on the job.*
Das Kind schläft noch bei den Eltern. *The child still sleeps with its parents.*
Schlaft ihr bei Freunden oder in Hotels? *Are you staying with friends or in hotels?*
Er hat bei ihr geschlafen. *He slept at her place / in her room.*
Sie hat mit ihm geschlafen. *She slept with him. / She had sex with him.*
Sonntags schlafe ich bis zehn Uhr. *On Sundays, I sleep until 10 o'clock.*
Heiko schlief um zwanzig Uhr ein und schlief bis acht Uhr morgens. *Heiko fell asleep at 8 P.M. and slept until 8 in the morning.*
Peter schläft seit drei Stunden, ist er krank? *Peter has been asleep for three hours; is he ill?*
Ich schlafe jetzt seit mehreren Monaten auf einem Futon. *I've been sleeping on a futon for several months now.*
Meine Mutter schläft von 23 Uhr bis 7 Uhr. *My mother sleeps from 11 P.M. to 7 A.M.*

schlafen + adverb

Dierdre ist es gewöhnt, kalt zu schlafen. *Dierdre is accustomed to sleeping in an unheated room.*
Was du nicht sagst! Wie lange schlafen die beiden denn miteinander? *You don't say! How long have the two of them been sleeping together?*
Das Ehepaar schläft seit zehn Jahren getrennt. *The married couple has slept separately for ten years.*
Nach einigen Minuten schliefen wir alle fest. *After a few minutes, we were all fast asleep.*
Am Sonntagmorgen hat Kurt lange geschlafen. *On Sunday morning, Kurt slept in.*
Franz-Josef schläft tief. *Franz-Josef sleeps soundly.*
Dirk schlief noch halb, als das Telefon klingelte. *Dirk was still half asleep when the phone rang.*
Schlaf gut! *Sleep well!*
Der kränkliche Mann schläft viel. *The sickly man sleeps a lot.*
Schläfst du schon wieder? *Are you sleeping again?*
Herr Seefeldt pflegt sehr wenig zu schlafen. *Mr. Seefeldt tends to sleep very little.*

schlafen + verb

Ich lege das Kind schlafen und bin gleich wieder da. *I'll put the child to bed and be right back.*
Um Mitternacht haben wir uns schlafen gelegt. *At midnight, we went to bed.*
Katerina ist noch nicht schlafen gegangen. *Katerina hasn't gone to bed yet.*
Lasst uns schlafen gehen. *Let's go to bed.*
Onkel Heinz geht mit den Hühnern schlafen. (*idiomatic*) *Uncle Heinz goes to bed with the chickens* (that is, *very early*).

es schläft sich (impersonal) *sleeping is/to sleep is*

Schläft es sich gut auf deinem Wasserbett? *Is your waterbed good to sleep on?*
An der frischen Luft schläft es sich am Besten! *Sleeping outdoors is the best!*

IDIOMATIC EXPRESSIONS

Ich muss erst einmal darüber schlafen. *I have to sleep on it first* (that is, *think it over*).
Irmgard sagt, Norbert hätte wie ein Murmeltier geschlafen. *Irmgard says Norbert slept like a log.*
Jost soll bis in die Puppen geschlafen haben. *Jost is said to have slept till all hours.*
Hast du zu lange geschlafen? *Did you oversleep?*
Wir hoffen, dass der Vulkan noch ein paar Jahre schläft. *We hope the volcano remains dormant for a few more years.*

Tief unter dem Berg schlief ein uralter Drachen namens Forhtatior. *Deep under the mountain slumbered the ancient dragon called Forhtatior.*
Du hast wohl mit offenen Augen geschlafen. *You were probably daydreaming* (that is, *not paying attention*).

strong verb

schlägt · schlug · geschlagen

PRESENT

ich schlage	wir schlagen
du schlägst	ihr schlagt
Sie schlagen	Sie schlagen
er/sie/es schlägt	sie schlagen

SIMPLE PAST

ich schlug	wir schlugen
du schlugst	ihr schlugt
Sie schlugen	Sie schlugen
er/sie/es schlug	sie schlugen

FUTURE

ich werde	wir werden	schlagen
du wirst	ihr werdet	
Sie werden	Sie werden	
er/sie/es wird	sie werden	

PRESENT SUBJUNCTIVE I

ich schlage	wir schlagen
du schlagest	ihr schlaget
Sie schlagen	Sie schlagen
er/sie/es schlage	sie schlagen

PRESENT SUBJUNCTIVE II

ich schlüge	wir schlügen
du schlügest	ihr schlüget
Sie schlügen	Sie schlügen
er/sie/es schlüge	sie schlügen

FUTURE SUBJUNCTIVE I

ich werde	wir werden	schlagen
du werdest	ihr werdet	
Sie werden	Sie werden	
er/sie/es werde	sie werden	

FUTURE SUBJUNCTIVE II

ich würde	wir würden	schlagen
du würdest	ihr würdet	
Sie würden	Sie würden	
er/sie/es würde	sie würden	

PRESENT PERFECT

ich habe	wir haben	geschlagen
du hast	ihr habt	
Sie haben	Sie haben	
er/sie/es hat	sie haben	

PAST PERFECT

ich hatte	wir hatten	geschlagen
du hattest	ihr hattet	
Sie hatten	Sie hatten	
er/sie/es hatte	sie hatten	

FUTURE PERFECT

ich werde	wir werden	geschlagen haben
du wirst	ihr werdet	
Sie werden	Sie werden	
er/sie/es wird	sie werden	

PAST SUBJUNCTIVE I

ich habe	wir haben	geschlagen
du habest	ihr habet	
Sie haben	Sie haben	
er/sie/es habe	sie haben	

PAST SUBJUNCTIVE II

ich hätte	wir hätten	geschlagen
du hättest	ihr hättet	
Sie hätten	Sie hätten	
er/sie/es hätte	sie hätten	

FUTURE PERFECT SUBJUNCTIVE I

ich werde	wir werden	geschlagen haben
du werdest	ihr werdet	
Sie werden	Sie werden	
er/sie/es werde	sie werden	

FUTURE PERFECT SUBJUNCTIVE II

ich würde	wir würden	geschlagen haben
du würdest	ihr würdet	
Sie würden	Sie würden	
er/sie/es würde	sie würden	

COMMANDS schlag(e)! schlagt! schlagen Sie!

PRESENT PARTICIPLE schlagend

Usage

Zwölf Gefangene werden geschlagen.	*Twelve prisoners are being beaten.*
Mein Herz schlägt für dich.	*My heart beats for you.*
Die Eier dreißig Sekunden schlagen. (RECIPE)	*Beat the eggs for 30 seconds.*
Warum hast du ihn mit der Faust geschlagen?	*Why did you punch him?*
Die Uhr hatte gerade zwölf geschlagen.	*The clock had just struck 12.*
Als das Feuer ausbrach, schlug Peter an unsere Tür.	*When the fire broke out, Peter pounded on our door.*
Schlagen Sie den Ball mit der linken Hand.	*Hit the ball with your left hand.*
Tante Inges Standuhr schlägt die Stunden.	*Aunt Inge's grandfather clock strikes the hours.*

RELATED VERBS ab·schlagen, an·schlagen, auf·schlagen, aus·schlagen, beschlagen, durchschlagen, durch·schlagen, ein·schlagen, entschlagen, erschlagen, fehl·schlagen, nach·schlagen, nieder·schlagen, tot·schlagen, über·schlagen, überschlagen, um·schlagen, unter·schlagen, unterschlagen, verschlagen, vorbei·schlagen, zerschlagen, zurück·schlagen, zusammen·schlagen; *see also* **vor·schlagen** (510)

TOP 50 VERB ☞

schlagen *to hit, beat, strike, punch, slap*

schlägt · schlug · geschlagen strong verb

MORE USAGE SENTENCES WITH schlagen

Der Kandidat hat seinen Gegner geschlagen. *The candidate has defeated his opponent.*
Schlagen Sie den linken Arm nach hinten. *Throw your left arm back.*
Die Sahne schlagen, bis sie steif ist. (RECIPE) *Whip the cream until it is stiff.*
Ute hat ihm die Zigarette aus der Hand geschlagen. *Ute knocked the cigarette from his hand.*
Der Dicke schlug Hans zu Boden. *The fat man knocked Hans to the floor.*
Der Kolibri schlägt sehr schnell mit den Flügeln. *The hummingbird flaps its wings very rapidly.*

sich schlagen *to fight; take sides; slip; hold one's own*

Hänsl schlägt sich mit seinem Kumpel Ortwin. *Hänsl fights with his buddy Ortwin.*
Die Firmen schlagen sich um die Kunden. *The firms are fighting over the customers.*
Die Bauern schlugen sich zu den Aufständischen. *The farmers took sides with the rebels.*
Manni schlägt sich auf die Seite der Deutschen. *Manni is siding with the Germans.*
Der Täter schlug sich ungesehen in den Wald. *The perpetrator slipped unseen into the woods.*
Du hast dich in der Debatte ganz gut geschlagen. *You held your own quite well in the debate.*

schlagen (with **sein**) *to hit, strike, bang; shoot; break; take (after)*

Ich war mit dem Kopf gegen ein Regal geschlagen. *I had banged my head against a bookcase.*
Flammen sind aus dem Dach geschlagen. *Flames shot from the roof.*
Die Wellen schlagen an den Strand. *The waves are breaking on the beach.*
Dietrich ist nach seinem Vater geschlagen. *Dietrich takes after his father.*

IDIOMATIC EXPRESSIONS

So werden zwei Fliegen mit einer Klappe geschlagen. *That way we can kill two birds with one stone.*
Jetzt schlägt es aber dreizehn! *Now things have gone too far!*
Kannst du einen Wirbel schlagen? *Can you do a drumroll?*
Ich schlage das Flugblatt mit Nägeln an die Wand. *I'll nail the flyer on the wall.*
Mein Fuß schlug den Takt der Musik. *My foot kept time with the music.*
Der Regenwald wird kahl geschlagen. *The rain forest is being clear-cut.*
Das Schiff hat leck geschlagen. *The ship has sprung a leak.*
Man schlägt jetzt Alarm wegen GMOs. *People are now sounding the alarm about GMOs.*
Schlagen Sie die Arme ineinander. *Fold your arms together.*
Schlagen Sie die Beine übereinander. *Cross your legs.*
Wir wollen Brücken zwischen Kulturen schlagen. *We want to establish ties between cultures.*
Man wollte aus seinen Fehlern Kapital schlagen. *People wanted to capitalize on his mistakes.*
Schlag dir das aus dem Kopf. *Put that out of your mind. / Forget about that.*
Der Baum schlug Wurzel und wuchs schnell. *The tree took root and grew quickly.*
Wurde Mick Jagger zum Ritter geschlagen? *Was Mick Jagger knighted?*
Das Gewissen schlug Heidi, sie schlief kaum. *Heidi's conscience bothered her; she hardly slept.*
Soll ich mein Leben in die Schanze schlagen? *Should I risk my life?*
Asta schlug die Augen zu Boden und schwieg. *Asta cast down her eyes and fell silent.*
Die Zinsen werden zum Kapital geschlagen. *The interest is compounded to the principal.*
Rauchen schlägt aufs Gehirn. *Smoking affects the brain.*
Dieter wurde einmal vom Blitz geschlagen. *Dieter was once struck by lightning.*
Schlagt einen Kreis mit dem Zirkel. *Trace a circle with the compass.*
Schlagen Sie Ihre Sorgen in den Wind! *Throw your worries to the wind!*
Willis Puls schlug schneller, als er ihn erblickte. *Willi's pulse quickened when he caught sight of him.*
Wir haben die Nacht um die Ohren geschlagen. *We partied the whole night through.*

strong verb **schleicht · schlich · geschlichen**

PRESENT

ich schleiche	wir schleichen
du schleichst	ihr schleicht
Sie schleichen	Sie schleichen
er/sie/es schleicht	sie schleichen

PRESENT PERFECT

ich bin	wir sind	geschlichen
du bist	ihr seid	
Sie sind	Sie sind	
er/sie/es ist	sie sind	

SIMPLE PAST

ich schlich	wir schlichen
du schlichst	ihr schlicht
Sie schlichen	Sie schlichen
er/sie/es schlich	sie schlichen

PAST PERFECT

ich war	wir waren	geschlichen
du warst	ihr wart	
Sie waren	Sie waren	
er/sie/es war	sie waren	

FUTURE

ich werde	wir werden	schleichen
du wirst	ihr werdet	
Sie werden	Sie werden	
er/sie/es wird	sie werden	

FUTURE PERFECT

ich werde	wir werden	geschlichen sein
du wirst	ihr werdet	
Sie werden	Sie werden	
er/sie/es wird	sie werden	

PRESENT SUBJUNCTIVE I

ich schleiche	wir schleichen
du schleichest	ihr schleichet
Sie schleichen	Sie schleichen
er/sie/es schleiche	sie schleichen

PAST SUBJUNCTIVE I

ich sei	wir seien	geschlichen
du seiest	ihr seiet	
Sie seien	Sie seien	
er/sie/es sei	sie seien	

PRESENT SUBJUNCTIVE II

ich schliche	wir schlichen
du schlichest	ihr schlichet
Sie schlichen	Sie schlichen
er/sie/es schliche	sie schlichen

PAST SUBJUNCTIVE II

ich wäre	wir wären	geschlichen
du wärest	ihr wäret	
Sie wären	Sie wären	
er/sie/es wäre	sie wären	

FUTURE SUBJUNCTIVE I

ich werde	wir werden	schleichen
du werdest	ihr werdet	
Sie werden	Sie werden	
er/sie/es werde	sie werden	

FUTURE PERFECT SUBJUNCTIVE I

ich werde	wir werden	geschlichen sein
du werdest	ihr werdet	
Sie werden	Sie werden	
er/sie/es werde	sie werden	

FUTURE SUBJUNCTIVE II

ich würde	wir würden	schleichen
du würdest	ihr würdet	
Sie würden	Sie würden	
er/sie/es würde	sie würden	

FUTURE PERFECT SUBJUNCTIVE II

ich würde	wir würden	geschlichen sein
du würdest	ihr würdet	
Sie würden	Sie würden	
er/sie/es würde	sie würden	

COMMANDS schleich(e)! schleicht! schleichen Sie!

PRESENT PARTICIPLE schleichend

Usage

Sie schlichen betrunken nach Hause.	*They crawled home drunk.*
Maximilian ist vorzeitig aus dem Unterricht geschlichen.	*Maximilian sneaked out of class early.*
Eine Maus ist durch das kleine Loch geschlichen.	*A mouse stole through the tiny hole.*
Ein päpstliches Heer war in Thüringen geschlichen.	*A papal army had stolen into Thuringia.*
Die Regenwürmer schlichen durch die verfaulten Blätter.	*The earthworms crawled through the decayed leaves.*
Die Kinder waren aus dem Haus geschlichen um zu spielen.	*The children had sneaked outside to play.*
Die Katze schlich leise ins Schlafzimmer.	*The cat crept quietly into the bedroom.*
Der Dieb schleicht um das Haus.	*The thief is skulking around the house.*
Er ist nachts ins Auto geschlichen und weggefahren.	*He sneaked into the car at night and drove away.*

sich schleichen (with **haben**) *to sneak*

500 Menschen haben sich ins Grenzgebiet geschlichen.	*Five hundred people have slipped into the border region.*

RELATED VERBS an·schleichen, beschleichen, durch·schleichen, ein·schleichen, erschleichen, nach·schleichen, umschleichen, vorbei·schleichen, weg·schleichen

373 schleifen *to sharpen, grind; polish*

schleift · schliff · geschliffen strong verb

PRESENT

ich schleife	wir schleifen
du schleifst	ihr schleift
Sie schleifen	Sie schleifen
er/sie/es schleift	sie schleifen

SIMPLE PAST

ich schliff	wir schliffen
du schliffst	ihr schlifft
Sie schliffen	Sie schliffen
er/sie/es schliff	sie schliffen

FUTURE

ich werde	wir werden	schleifen
du wirst	ihr werdet	
Sie werden	Sie werden	
er/sie/es wird	sie werden	

PRESENT SUBJUNCTIVE I

ich schleife	wir schleifen
du schleifest	ihr schleifet
Sie schleifen	Sie schleifen
er/sie/es schleife	sie schleifen

PRESENT SUBJUNCTIVE II

ich schliffe	wir schliffen
du schliffest	ihr schliffet
Sie schliffen	Sie schliffen
er/sie/es schliffe	sie schliffen

FUTURE SUBJUNCTIVE I

ich werde	wir werden	schleifen
du werdest	ihr werdet	
Sie werden	Sie werden	
er/sie/es werde	sie werden	

FUTURE SUBJUNCTIVE II

ich würde	wir würden	schleifen
du würdest	ihr würdet	
Sie würden	Sie würden	
er/sie/es würde	sie würden	

PRESENT PERFECT

ich habe	wir haben	geschliffen
du hast	ihr habt	
Sie haben	Sie haben	
er/sie/es hat	sie haben	

PAST PERFECT

ich hatte	wir hatten	geschliffen
du hattest	ihr hattet	
Sie hatten	Sie hatten	
er/sie/es hatte	sie hatten	

FUTURE PERFECT

ich werde	wir werden	geschliffen haben
du wirst	ihr werdet	
Sie werden	Sie werden	
er/sie/es wird	sie werden	

PAST SUBJUNCTIVE I

ich habe	wir haben	geschliffen
du habest	ihr habet	
Sie haben	Sie haben	
er/sie/es habe	sie haben	

PAST SUBJUNCTIVE II

ich hätte	wir hätten	geschliffen
du hättest	ihr hättet	
Sie hätten	Sie hätten	
er/sie/es hätte	sie hätten	

FUTURE PERFECT SUBJUNCTIVE I

ich werde	wir werden	geschliffen haben
du werdest	ihr werdet	
Sie werden	Sie werden	
er/sie/es werde	sie werden	

FUTURE PERFECT SUBJUNCTIVE II

ich würde	wir würden	geschliffen haben
du würdest	ihr würdet	
Sie würden	Sie würden	
er/sie/es würde	sie würden	

COMMANDS schleif(e)! schleift! schleifen Sie!

PRESENT PARTICIPLE schleifend

Usage

Der Bauernknecht schliff das Messer. — *The hired hand sharpened the knife.*
In uralten Zeiten wurden Nadeln aus Knochen geschliffen. — *In ancient times, needles were ground out of bones.*
Du hättest das nicht schleifen sollen. — *You shouldn't have sharpened that.*
Heute musste mir der Zahnarzt die Zähne schleifen. — *Today the dentist had to polish my teeth.*

schleifen (regular weak verb) *to drag; raze, tear down*

Doris schleifte eine alte Kiste über den Dachboden. — *Doris dragged an old crate across the attic floor.*
Der Dieb ist hinter einem Pferd geschleift worden. — *The thief was dragged behind a horse.*
Das alte Gebäude wurde letzte Woche geschleift. — *The old building was demolished last week.*
Wer hat denn meine Sandburg geschleift? — *Now who tore down my sand castle?*
Im Mittelalter wurde die römische Stadtmauer geschleift. — *In the Middle Ages, the Roman city wall was razed.*
Die alte Dorfkirche ist nicht geschleift worden. — *The old village church was not razed.*
Dort muss man das Haus schleifen. — *The house there has to be torn down.*

RELATED VERBS ab·schleifen, an·schleifen, aus·schleifen, ein·schleifen regular weak verb or strong verb **schleißt · schleißte/schliss · geschleißt/geschlissen**

PRESENT

ich schleiße	wir schleißen
du schleißt	ihr schleißt
Sie schleißen	Sie schleißen
er/sie/es schleißt	sie schleißen

SIMPLE PAST

ich schleißte/schliss	wir schleißten/schlissen
du schleißtest/schlissest	ihr schleißtet/schlisst
Sie schleißten/schlissen	Sie schleißten/schlissen
er/sie/es schleißte/schliss	sie schleißten/schlissen

FUTURE

ich werde	wir werden	schleißen
du wirst	ihr werdet	
Sie werden	Sie werden	
er/sie/es wird	sie werden	

PRESENT SUBJUNCTIVE I

ich schleiße	wir schleißen
du schleißest	ihr schleißet
Sie schleißen	Sie schleißen
er/sie/es schleiße	sie schleißen

PRESENT SUBJUNCTIVE II

ich schleißte/schlisse	wir schleißten/schlissen
du schleißtest/schlissest	ihr schleißtet/schlisset
Sie schleißten/schlissen	Sie schleißten/schlissen
er/sie/es schleißte/schlisse	sie schleißten/schlissen

FUTURE SUBJUNCTIVE I

ich werde	wir werden	schleißen
du werdest	ihr werdet	
Sie werden	Sie werden	
er/sie/es werde	sie werden	

FUTURE SUBJUNCTIVE II

ich würde	wir würden	schleißen
du würdest	ihr würdet	
Sie würden	Sie würden	
er/sie/es würde	sie würden	

PRESENT PERFECT

ich habe	wir haben	geschleißt/ geschlissen
du hast	ihr habt	
Sie haben	Sie haben	
er/sie/es hat	sie haben	

PAST PERFECT

ich hatte	wir hatten	geschleißt/ geschlissen
du hattest	ihr hattet	
Sie hatten	Sie hatten	
er/sie/es hatte	sie hatten	

FUTURE PERFECT

ich werde	wir werden	geschleißt haben OR geschlissen haben
du wirst	ihr werdet	
Sie werden	Sie werden	
er/sie/es wird	sie werden	

PAST SUBJUNCTIVE I

ich habe	wir haben	geschleißt/ geschlissen
du habest	ihr habet	
Sie haben	Sie haben	
er/sie/es habe	sie haben	

PAST SUBJUNCTIVE II

ich hätte	wir hätten	geschleißt/ geschlissen
du hättest	ihr hättet	
Sie hätten	Sie hätten	
er/sie/es hätte	sie hätten	

FUTURE PERFECT SUBJUNCTIVE I

ich werde	wir werden	geschleißt haben OR geschlissen haben
du werdest	ihr werdet	
Sie werden	Sie werden	
er/sie/es werde	sie werden	

FUTURE PERFECT SUBJUNCTIVE II

ich würde	wir würden	geschleißt haben OR geschlissen haben
du würdest	ihr würdet	
Sie würden	Sie würden	
er/sie/es würde	sie würden	

COMMANDS schleiß(e)! schleißt! schleißen Sie!

PRESENT PARTICIPLE schleißend

NOTE The verb **schleißen** is usually conjugated as a regular weak verb in modern German.

Usage

Als Kind hat mein Vater jeden Morgen Scheite geschlissen. *As a child, my father split firewood every morning.*
Womit schleißen Sie das Holz? *What do you use to split wood?*
Schlissest du Scheite, als der Oheim starb? *Were you splitting wood when Uncle died?*
Früher hat man Vogelfedern geschleißt, um Schreibfedern zu machen. *People used to strip quills in order to make writing instruments.*
Diese Feder ist ziemlich schwer zu schleißen. *This quill is rather hard to strip.*
Kaum hat er gegessen einen Bissen, hat er drei Haufen Scheite geschleißt und geschlissen. (TONGUE TWISTER) *He had hardly eaten a single bite, when he had already split three piles of firewood.*

schleißen (with sein) *to wear out*

Nach einigen Jahren war der Mantel geschlissen. *After some years, the coat had worn out.*

RELATED VERB verschleißen

375 schließen *to close, shut; turn off; fasten; conclude*

schließt · schloss · geschlossen strong verb

PRESENT

ich schließe	wir schließen
du schließt	ihr schließt
Sie schließen	Sie schließen
er/sie/es schließt	sie schließen

SIMPLE PAST

ich schloss	wir schlossen
du schlossest	ihr schlosst
Sie schlossen	Sie schlossen
er/sie/es schloss	sie schlossen

FUTURE

ich werde	wir werden	schließen
du wirst	ihr werdet	
Sie werden	Sie werden	
er/sie/es wird	sie werden	

PRESENT SUBJUNCTIVE I

ich schließe	wir schließen
du schließest	ihr schließet
Sie schließen	Sie schließen
er/sie/es schließe	sie schließen

PRESENT SUBJUNCTIVE II

ich schlösse	wir schlössen
du schlössest	ihr schlösset
Sie schlössen	Sie schlössen
er/sie/es schlösse	sie schlössen

FUTURE SUBJUNCTIVE I

ich werde	wir werden	schließen
du werdest	ihr werdet	
Sie werden	Sie werden	
er/sie/es werde	sie werden	

FUTURE SUBJUNCTIVE II

ich würde	wir würden	schließen
du würdest	ihr würdet	
Sie würden	Sie würden	
er/sie/es würde	sie würden	

PRESENT PERFECT

ich habe	wir haben	geschlossen
du hast	ihr habt	
Sie haben	Sie haben	
er/sie/es hat	sie haben	

PAST PERFECT

ich hatte	wir hatten	geschlossen
du hattest	ihr hattet	
Sie hatten	Sie hatten	
er/sie/es hatte	sie hatten	

FUTURE PERFECT

ich werde	wir werden	geschlossen haben
du wirst	ihr werdet	
Sie werden	Sie werden	
er/sie/es wird	sie werden	

PAST SUBJUNCTIVE I

ich habe	wir haben	geschlossen
du habest	ihr habet	
Sie haben	Sie haben	
er/sie/es habe	sie haben	

PAST SUBJUNCTIVE II

ich hätte	wir hätten	geschlossen
du hättest	ihr hättet	
Sie hätten	Sie hätten	
er/sie/es hätte	sie hätten	

FUTURE PERFECT SUBJUNCTIVE I

ich werde	wir werden	geschlossen haben
du werdest	ihr werdet	
Sie werden	Sie werden	
er/sie/es werde	sie werden	

FUTURE PERFECT SUBJUNCTIVE II

ich würde	wir würden	geschlossen haben
du würdest	ihr würdet	
Sie würden	Sie würden	
er/sie/es würde	sie würden	

COMMANDS schließ(e)! schließt! schließen Sie!

PRESENT PARTICIPLE schließend

Usage

Wir mussten den Laden schließen.	*We had to close the shop.*
Unser Papagei kann seine Käfigtür selbst schließen.	*Our parrot can close the cage door himself.*
Die Regierung hat die Grenzen geschlossen.	*The government has sealed the borders.*
Dieses Fenster ist schwer zu schließen.	*This window is hard to close.*
Die Stadtbibliothek darf nicht geschlossen werden!	*The city library cannot be closed!*
1985 wurde das Theater geschlossen.	*In 1985, the theater was closed.*
Wir schlossen einen Vertrag zur weltweiten Lizenzierung.	*We entered into a contract for global licensing.*
Die jetzige Situation schließt in sich die Gefahr eines sich ausbreitenden Radikalismus.	*The current situation entails the danger of a spreading radicalism.*

sich schließen *to close*

Das Fenster schließt sich, aber das Programm beendet sich nicht.	*The window closes, but the program doesn't end.*

RELATED VERBS ab·schließen, an·schließen, auf·schließen, ein·schließen, erschließen, kurz·schließen, umschließen, verschließen, weg·schließen, zusammen·schließen; *see also* **aus·schließen** (38), **beschließen** (83), **entschließen** (147)

strong verb

schlingt · schlang · geschlungen

PRESENT

ich schlinge	wir schlingen
du schlingst	ihr schlingt
Sie schlingen	Sie schlingen
er/sie/es schlingt	sie schlingen

SIMPLE PAST

ich schlang	wir schlangen
du schlangst	ihr schlangt
Sie schlangen	Sie schlangen
er/sie/es schlang	sie schlangen

FUTURE

ich werde	wir werden	schlingen
du wirst	ihr werdet	
Sie werden	Sie werden	
er/sie/es wird	sie werden	

PRESENT SUBJUNCTIVE I

ich schlinge	wir schlingen
du schlingest	ihr schlinget
Sie schlingen	Sie schlingen
er/sie/es schlinge	sie schlingen

PRESENT SUBJUNCTIVE II

ich schlänge	wir schlängen
du schlängest	ihr schlänget
Sie schlängen	Sie schlängen
er/sie/es schlänge	sie schlängen

FUTURE SUBJUNCTIVE I

ich werde	wir werden	schlingen
du werdest	ihr werdet	
Sie werden	Sie werden	
er/sie/es werde	sie werden	

FUTURE SUBJUNCTIVE II

ich würde	wir würden	schlingen
du würdest	ihr würdet	
Sie würden	Sie würden	
er/sie/es würde	sie würden	

PRESENT PERFECT

ich habe	wir haben	geschlungen
du hast	ihr habt	
Sie haben	Sie haben	
er/sie/es hat	sie haben	

PAST PERFECT

ich hatte	wir hatten	geschlungen
du hattest	ihr hattet	
Sie hatten	Sie hatten	
er/sie/es hatte	sie hatten	

FUTURE PERFECT

ich werde	wir werden	geschlungen haben
du wirst	ihr werdet	
Sie werden	Sie werden	
er/sie/es wird	sie werden	

PAST SUBJUNCTIVE I

ich habe	wir haben	geschlungen
du habest	ihr habet	
Sie haben	Sie haben	
er/sie/es habe	sie haben	

PAST SUBJUNCTIVE II

ich hätte	wir hätten	geschlungen
du hättest	ihr hättet	
Sie hätten	Sie hätten	
er/sie/es hätte	sie hätten	

FUTURE PERFECT SUBJUNCTIVE I

ich werde	wir werden	geschlungen haben
du werdest	ihr werdet	
Sie werden	Sie werden	
er/sie/es werde	sie werden	

FUTURE PERFECT SUBJUNCTIVE II

ich würde	wir würden	geschlungen haben
du würdest	ihr würdet	
Sie würden	Sie würden	
er/sie/es würde	sie würden	

COMMANDS schling(e)! schlingt! schlingen Sie!

PRESENT PARTICIPLE schlingend

Usage

Sie haben ihm ein Seil um den Hals geschlungen. — *They wound a rope around his neck.*
Der schüchterne Knabe schlang seine Arme um seine Mutter. — *The shy boy wrapped his arms around his mother.*
Schlingen Sie ein Band um den Knoten. — *Tie a ribbon around the knot.*
Wie schlingt man so einen Knoten? — *How do you tie a knot like that?*
Ich habe den Kuchen geschlungen. — *I wolfed down the cake.*
Das Ferkel hat die Melone geschlungen. — *The piglet gulped down the melon.*
Der Hund schlang das Steak, ohne zu kauen. — *The dog devoured the steak without chewing.*

sich schlingen *to wind, coil*

Die Schlange schlingt sich um die Maus. — *The snake is coiled around the mouse.*
Liebend schlingen sich die Reben an dem Baum, den sie umgeben. (WILHELM GOTTLIEB BECKER) — *The vines wind lovingly around the tree they embrace.*

RELATED VERBS umschlingen, um·schlingen, verschlingen

377 schmecken *to taste (good); sample*

schmeckt · schmeckte · geschmeckt regular weak verb

PRESENT

ich schmecke	wir schmecken
du schmeckst	ihr schmeckt
Sie schmecken	Sie schmecken
er/sie/es schmeckt	sie schmecken

SIMPLE PAST

ich schmeckte	wir schmeckten
du schmecktest	ihr schmecktet
Sie schmeckten	Sie schmeckten
er/sie/es schmeckte	sie schmeckten

FUTURE

ich werde	wir werden	schmecken
du wirst	ihr werdet	
Sie werden	Sie werden	
er/sie/es wird	sie werden	

PRESENT SUBJUNCTIVE I

ich schmecke	wir schmecken
du schmeckest	ihr schmecket
Sie schmecken	Sie schmecken
er/sie/es schmecke	sie schmecken

PRESENT SUBJUNCTIVE II

ich schmeckte	wir schmeckten
du schmecktest	ihr schmecktet
Sie schmeckten	Sie schmeckten
er/sie/es schmeckte	sie schmeckten

FUTURE SUBJUNCTIVE I

ich werde	wir werden	schmecken
du werdest	ihr werdet	
Sie werden	Sie werden	
er/sie/es werde	sie werden	

FUTURE SUBJUNCTIVE II

ich würde	wir würden	schmecken
du würdest	ihr würdet	
Sie würden	Sie würden	
er/sie/es würde	sie würden	

PRESENT PERFECT

ich habe	wir haben	geschmeckt
du hast	ihr habt	
Sie haben	Sie haben	
er/sie/es hat	sie haben	

PAST PERFECT

ich hatte	wir hatten	geschmeckt
du hattest	ihr hattet	
Sie hatten	Sie hatten	
er/sie/es hatte	sie hatten	

FUTURE PERFECT

ich werde	wir werden	geschmeckt haben
du wirst	ihr werdet	
Sie werden	Sie werden	
er/sie/es wird	sie werden	

PAST SUBJUNCTIVE I

ich habe	wir haben	geschmeckt
du habest	ihr habet	
Sie haben	Sie haben	
er/sie/es habe	sie haben	

PAST SUBJUNCTIVE II

ich hätte	wir hätten	geschmeckt
du hättest	ihr hättet	
Sie hätten	Sie hätten	
er/sie/es hätte	sie hätten	

FUTURE PERFECT SUBJUNCTIVE I

ich werde	wir werden	geschmeckt haben
du werdest	ihr werdet	
Sie werden	Sie werden	
er/sie/es werde	sie werden	

FUTURE PERFECT SUBJUNCTIVE II

ich würde	wir würden	geschmeckt haben
du würdest	ihr würdet	
Sie würden	Sie würden	
er/sie/es würde	sie würden	

COMMANDS schmeck(e)! schmeckt! schmecken Sie!

PRESENT PARTICIPLE schmeckend

Usage

Das Goldbeergelee schmeckt etwas sauer.	*The ground cherry jelly tastes rather sour.*
Aber Zitronen schmecken noch saurer.	*But lemons taste even more sour.*
Wie haben euch die Pralinen geschmeckt?	*How did you like the pralines?*
Schmeckt deutsches Bier besser als amerikanisches?	*Does German beer taste better than American?*
Eine kubanische Zigarre schmeckt am besten.	*A Cuban cigar tastes the best.*
Die Brötchen schmecken himmlisch.	*The rolls taste heavenly.*
Dem Hund schmeckt das Katzenfutter besser.	*The dog likes the taste of the cat food better.*
Das Schnitzel schmeckte ihm nicht, aber den Braten aß er.	*He didn't like the taste of the cutlet, but he ate the roast.*
Das Kaugummi schmeckt nach Bananen.	*The chewing gum tastes like bananas.*
Das Essen muss gut schmecken, sonst isst Oma nichts.	*The food has to taste good, else Grandma won't eat anything.*
Wir haben den Auflauf geschmeckt.	*We sampled the casserole.*
Das schmeckt nach Sabotage.	*That smacks of sabotage.*

RELATED VERBS ab·schmecken, durch·schmecken, nach·schmecken, vor·schmecken

strong verb **schmeißt · schmiss · geschmissen**

PRESENT

ich schmeiße	wir schmeißen
du schmeißt	ihr schmeißt
Sie schmeißen	Sie schmeißen
er/sie/es schmeißt	sie schmeißen

SIMPLE PAST

ich schmiss	wir schmissen
du schmissest	ihr schmisst
Sie schmissen	Sie schmissen
er/sie/es schmiss	sie schmissen

FUTURE

ich werde	wir werden	schmeißen
du wirst	ihr werdet	
Sie werden	Sie werden	
er/sie/es wird	sie werden	

PRESENT SUBJUNCTIVE I

ich schmeiße	wir schmeißen
du schmeißest	ihr schmeißet
Sie schmeißen	Sie schmeißen
er/sie/es schmeiße	sie schmeißen

PRESENT SUBJUNCTIVE II

ich schmisse	wir schmissen
du schmissest	ihr schmisset
Sie schmissen	Sie schmissen
er/sie/es schmisse	sie schmissen

FUTURE SUBJUNCTIVE I

ich werde	wir werden	schmeißen
du werdest	ihr werdet	
Sie werden	Sie werden	
er/sie/es werde	sie werden	

FUTURE SUBJUNCTIVE II

ich würde	wir würden	schmeißen
du würdest	ihr würdet	
Sie würden	Sie würden	
er/sie/es würde	sie würden	

PRESENT PERFECT

ich habe	wir haben	geschmissen
du hast	ihr habt	
Sie haben	Sie haben	
er/sie/es hat	sie haben	

PAST PERFECT

ich hatte	wir hatten	geschmissen
du hattest	ihr hattet	
Sie hatten	Sie hatten	
er/sie/es hatte	sie hatten	

FUTURE PERFECT

ich werde	wir werden	geschmissen haben
du wirst	ihr werdet	
Sie werden	Sie werden	
er/sie/es wird	sie werden	

PAST SUBJUNCTIVE I

ich habe	wir haben	geschmissen
du habest	ihr habet	
Sie haben	Sie haben	
er/sie/es habe	sie haben	

PAST SUBJUNCTIVE II

ich hätte	wir hätten	geschmissen
du hättest	ihr hättet	
Sie hätten	Sie hätten	
er/sie/es hätte	sie hätten	

FUTURE PERFECT SUBJUNCTIVE I

ich werde	wir werden	geschmissen haben
du werdest	ihr werdet	
Sie werden	Sie werden	
er/sie/es werde	sie werden	

FUTURE PERFECT SUBJUNCTIVE II

ich würde	wir würden	geschmissen haben
du würdest	ihr würdet	
Sie würden	Sie würden	
er/sie/es würde	sie würden	

COMMANDS schmeiß(e)! schmeißt! schmeißen Sie!

PRESENT PARTICIPLE schmeißend

Usage

Wer hat den Baseball durchs Fenster geschmissen? — *Who threw the baseball through the window?*
Unser Papagei schmeißt gern Obststücke gegen den Spiegel. — *Our parrot likes to fling pieces of fruit against the mirror.*

Ingrid wollte ein Glas gegen die Wand schmeißen. — *Ingrid wanted to hurl a glass against the wall.*
Die Zuschauer haben Tomaten geschmissen. — *The spectators threw tomatoes.*
Der Mann wurde von seiner Frau aus dem Haus geschmissen. — *The man was thrown out of the house by his wife.*
Ich habe die Ausbildung als Bäcker geschmissen. — *I've given up training to be a baker.*
Vanessa hat ihren Freund Gregor geschmissen. — *Vanessa has dumped her boyfriend, Gregor.*

sich schmeißen *to dress; hurl oneself*

Liesl hat sich in einen schicken Rock geschmissen. — *Liesl dressed in a chic skirt.*
Yvonne hat sich aufs Sofa geschmissen. — *Yvonne threw herself onto the sofa.*
Der verzweifelte Schauspieler schmiss sich in den Fluss. — *The desperate actor hurled himself into the river.*

RELATED VERBS beschmeißen, ein·schmeißen, um·schmeißen, weg·schmeißen

379 schmelzen *to melt, dissolve*

schmilzt · schmolz · geschmolzen strong verb

PRESENT		PRESENT PERFECT		
ich schmelze	wir schmelzen	ich bin	wir sind	geschmolzen
du schmilzt	ihr schmelzt	du bist	ihr seid	
Sie schmelzen	Sie schmelzen	Sie sind	Sie sind	
er/sie/es schmilzt	sie schmelzen	er/sie/es ist	sie sind	

SIMPLE PAST		PAST PERFECT		
ich schmolz	wir schmolzen	ich war	wir waren	geschmolzen
du schmolzest	ihr schmolzt	du warst	ihr wart	
Sie schmolzen	Sie schmolzen	Sie waren	Sie waren	
er/sie/es schmolz	sie schmolzen	er/sie/es war	sie waren	

FUTURE			FUTURE PERFECT		
ich werde	wir werden	schmelzen	ich werde	wir werden	geschmolzen sein
du wirst	ihr werdet		du wirst	ihr werdet	
Sie werden	Sie werden		Sie werden	Sie werden	
er/sie/es wird	sie werden		er/sie/es wird	sie werden	

PRESENT SUBJUNCTIVE I		PAST SUBJUNCTIVE I		
ich schmelze	wir schmelzen	ich sei	wir seien	geschmolzen
du schmelzest	ihr schmelzet	du seiest	ihr seiet	
Sie schmelzen	Sie schmelzen	Sie seien	Sie seien	
er/sie/es schmelze	sie schmelzen	er/sie/es sei	sie seien	

PRESENT SUBJUNCTIVE II		PAST SUBJUNCTIVE II		
ich schmölze	wir schmölzen	ich wäre	wir wären	geschmolzen
du schmölzest	ihr schmölzet	du wärest	ihr wäret	
Sie schmölzen	Sie schmölzen	Sie wären	Sie wären	
er/sie/es schmölze	sie schmölzen	er/sie/es wäre	sie wären	

FUTURE SUBJUNCTIVE I			FUTURE PERFECT SUBJUNCTIVE I		
ich werde	wir werden	schmelzen	ich werde	wir werden	geschmolzen sein
du werdest	ihr werdet		du werdest	ihr werdet	
Sie werden	Sie werden		Sie werden	Sie werden	
er/sie/es werde	sie werden		er/sie/es werde	sie werden	

FUTURE SUBJUNCTIVE II			FUTURE PERFECT SUBJUNCTIVE II		
ich würde	wir würden	schmelzen	ich würde	wir würden	geschmolzen sein
du würdest	ihr würdet		du würdest	ihr würdet	
Sie würden	Sie würden		Sie würden	Sie würden	
er/sie/es würde	sie würden		er/sie/es würde	sie würden	

COMMANDS schmilz! schmelzt! schmelzen Sie!

PRESENT PARTICIPLE schmelzend

Usage

Das Eis ist bei der Hitze schnell geschmolzen.	*The ice cream quickly melted in the heat.*
Ingrids Makeup scheint zu schmelzen.	*Ingrid's makeup seems to be melting away.*
Dieses Metall schmilzt bei niedriger Temperatur.	*This metal fuses at a low temperature.*
Die wertvolle Skulptur soll im Brand geschmolzen sein.	*The valuable sculpture is supposed to have melted in a fire.*
Die Pralinen sind leider geschmolzen.	*The pralines melted, unfortunately.*
Der Zinnsoldat schmolz im Ofen.	*The tin soldier melted in the furnace.*
Beim Stromausfall ist das Eis in unserem Kühlschrank geschmolzen.	*During the power outage, the ice cream in our refrigerator melted.*

schmelzen (with haben) *to melt, dissolve*

Wie wird das Eisen geschmolzen?	*How is the iron fused?*
Man hat das Besteck geschmolzen und das Silber verkauft.	*They melted down the cutlery and sold the silver.*
Zucker in Wasser in einer Pfanne schmelzen. (RECIPE)	*Dissolve the sugar in a pan of water.*

RELATED VERBS ab·schmelzen, auf·schmelzen, aus·schmelzen, ein·schmelzen, um·schmelzen, verschmelzen, zerschmelzen, zusammen·schmelzen regular weak verb or strong verb

schnaubt · schnaubte/schnob · geschnaubt/geschnoben

PRESENT

ich schnaube	wir schnauben
du schnaubst	ihr schnaubt
Sie schnauben	Sie schnauben
er/sie/es schnaubt	sie schnauben

SIMPLE PAST

ich schnaubte/schnob	wir schnaubten/schnoben
du schnaubtest/schnobst	ihr schnaubtet/schnobt
Sie schnaubten/schnoben	Sie schnaubten/schnoben
er/sie/es schnaubte/schnob	sie schnaubten/schnoben

FUTURE

ich werde	wir werden	schnauben
du wirst	ihr werdet	
Sie werden	Sie werden	
er/sie/es wird	sie werden	

PRESENT SUBJUNCTIVE I

ich schnaube	wir schnauben
du schnaubest	ihr schnaubet
Sie schnauben	Sie schnauben
er/sie/es schnaube	sie schnauben

PRESENT SUBJUNCTIVE II

ich schnaubte/schnöbe	wir schnaubten/schnöben
du schnaubtest/schnöbest	ihr schnaubtet/schnöbet
Sie schnaubten/schnöben	Sie schnaubten/schnöben
er/sie/es schnaubte/schnöbe	sie schnaubten/schnöben

FUTURE SUBJUNCTIVE I

ich werde	wir werden	schnauben
du werdest	ihr werdet	
Sie werden	Sie werden	
er/sie/es werde	sie werden	

FUTURE SUBJUNCTIVE II

ich würde	wir würden	schnauben
du würdest	ihr würdet	
Sie würden	Sie würden	
er/sie/es würde	sie würden	

PRESENT PERFECT

ich habe	wir haben	geschnaubt/ geschnoben
du hast	ihr habt	
Sie haben	Sie haben	
er/sie/es hat	sie haben	

PAST PERFECT

ich hatte	wir hatten	geschnaubt/ geschnoben
du hattest	ihr hattet	
Sie hatten	Sie hatten	
er/sie/es hatte	sie hatten	

FUTURE PERFECT

ich werde	wir werden	geschnaubt haben OR geschnoben haben
du wirst	ihr werdet	
Sie werden	Sie werden	
er/sie/es wird	sie werden	

PAST SUBJUNCTIVE I

ich habe	wir haben	geschnaubt/ geschnoben
du habest	ihr habet	
Sie haben	Sie haben	
er/sie/es habe	sie haben	

PAST SUBJUNCTIVE II

ich hätte	wir hätten	geschnaubt/ geschnoben
du hättest	ihr hättet	
Sie hätten	Sie hätten	
er/sie/es hätte	sie hätten	

FUTURE PERFECT SUBJUNCTIVE I

ich werde	wir werden	geschnaubt haben OR geschnoben haben
du werdest	ihr werdet	
Sie werden	Sie werden	
er/sie/es werde	sie werden	

FUTURE PERFECT SUBJUNCTIVE II

ich würde	wir würden	geschnaubt haben OR geschnoben haben
du würdest	ihr würdet	
Sie würden	Sie würden	
er/sie/es würde	sie würden	

COMMANDS schnaub(e)! schnaubt! schnauben Sie!

PRESENT PARTICIPLE schnaubend

NOTE The strong forms of **schnauben** are older.

Usage

Warum schnauben Sie den Rauch in diese Richtung?	*Why are you blowing the smoke in this direction?*
Manni schnaubte eine Ausrede.	*Manni grunted an excuse.*
Lars schnaubte vor Wut.	*Lars was fuming with rage.*
Hänsl schnaubte außer Atem.	*Hänsl panted to catch his breath.*
Die Pferde wieherten und schnoben im Stall.	*The horses neighed and snorted in the stall.*
Das Mädchen schnaubte in Verlegenheit: „Das kann nicht sein!“	*The girl snorted in embarrassment, “That can't be!”*
„Das ist zu laut!“ schnaubte der Nachbar.	*“That's too loud!” snarled the neighbor.*
Dann schnob die ängstliche Kuh und lief weg.	*Then the frightened cow snorted and ran away.*
Warum hast du geschnaubt?	*Why did you snort?*
Herbert schnaubte laut und die anderen schwiegen.	*Herbert snorted loudly and the others fell silent.*

RELATED VERB aus·schnauben

381 schneiden *to cut*

schneidet · schnitt · geschnitten — strong verb

PRESENT

ich schneide	wir schneiden
du schneidest	ihr schneidet
Sie schneiden	Sie schneiden
er/sie/es schneidet	sie schneiden

SIMPLE PAST

ich schnitt	wir schnitten
du schnittst	ihr schnittet
Sie schnitten	Sie schnitten
er/sie/es schnitt	sie schnitten

FUTURE

ich werde	wir werden	schneiden
du wirst	ihr werdet	
Sie werden	Sie werden	
er/sie/es wird	sie werden	

PRESENT SUBJUNCTIVE I

ich schneide	wir schneiden
du schneidest	ihr schneidet
Sie schneiden	Sie schneiden
er/sie/es schneide	sie schneiden

PRESENT SUBJUNCTIVE II

ich schnitte	wir schnitten
du schnittest	ihr schnittet
Sie schnitten	Sie schnitten
er/sie/es schnitte	sie schnitten

FUTURE SUBJUNCTIVE I

ich werde	wir werden	schneiden
du werdest	ihr werdet	
Sie werden	Sie werden	
er/sie/es werde	sie werden	

FUTURE SUBJUNCTIVE II

ich würde	wir würden	schneiden
du würdest	ihr würdet	
Sie würden	Sie würden	
er/sie/es würde	sie würden	

PRESENT PERFECT

ich habe	wir haben	geschnitten
du hast	ihr habt	
Sie haben	Sie haben	
er/sie/es hat	sie haben	

PAST PERFECT

ich hatte	wir hatten	geschnitten
du hattest	ihr hattet	
Sie hatten	Sie hatten	
er/sie/es hatte	sie hatten	

FUTURE PERFECT

ich werde	wir werden	geschnitten haben
du wirst	ihr werdet	
Sie werden	Sie werden	
er/sie/es wird	sie werden	

PAST SUBJUNCTIVE I

ich habe	wir haben	geschnitten
du habest	ihr habet	
Sie haben	Sie haben	
er/sie/es habe	sie haben	

PAST SUBJUNCTIVE II

ich hätte	wir hätten	geschnitten
du hättest	ihr hättet	
Sie hätten	Sie hätten	
er/sie/es hätte	sie hätten	

FUTURE PERFECT SUBJUNCTIVE I

ich werde	wir werden	geschnitten haben
du werdest	ihr werdet	
Sie werden	Sie werden	
er/sie/es werde	sie werden	

FUTURE PERFECT SUBJUNCTIVE II

ich würde	wir würden	geschnitten haben
du würdest	ihr würdet	
Sie würden	Sie würden	
er/sie/es würde	sie würden	

COMMANDS schneide! schneidet! schneiden Sie!

PRESENT PARTICIPLE schneidend

Usage

Mark hat sich den Finger geschnitten.	*Mark cut his finger.*
Amalie hat sich am Arm geschnitten.	*Amalie has cut her arm.*
Die gekochten Eier klein schneiden. (RECIPE)	*Finely dice the boiled eggs.*
Das Seil muss geschnitten werden.	*The rope must be cut.*
Das kann ich nicht schneiden.	*I can't cut that.*
Schneide den Deckel so.	*Cut the lid like this.*
Maria hat das Kaugummi aus ihrem Haar schneiden müssen.	*Maria had to cut the chewing gum out of her hair.*
Diese Motorsäge schneidet viele verschiedene Materialien.	*This electric saw cuts many different materials.*
Schneidest du dir selbst die Haare?	*Do you cut your own hair?*
Aluminium ist leicht zu schneiden.	*Aluminum is easy to cut.*
Schneiden Sie bitte das Gemüse.	*Please cut the vegetables.*

RELATED VERBS ab·schneiden, an·schneiden, auf·schneiden, aus·schneiden, beschneiden, durch·schneiden, durchschneiden, ein·schneiden, überschneiden, verschneiden, vor·schneiden, weg·schneiden, zerschneiden, zu·schneiden regular weak verb **schneit · schneite · geschneit**

PRESENT

ich schneie	wir schneien
du schneist	ihr schneit
Sie schneien	Sie schneien
er/sie/es schneit	sie schneien

SIMPLE PAST

ich schneite	wir schneiten
du schneitest	ihr schneitet
Sie schneiten	Sie schneiten
er/sie/es schneite	sie schneiten

FUTURE

ich werde	wir werden	schneien
du wirst	ihr werdet	
Sie werden	Sie werden	
er/sie/es wird	sie werden	

PRESENT SUBJUNCTIVE I

ich schneie	wir schneien
du schneiest	ihr schneiet
Sie schneien	Sie schneien
er/sie/es schneie	sie schneien

PRESENT SUBJUNCTIVE II

ich schneite	wir schneiten
du schneitest	ihr schneitet
Sie schneiten	Sie schneiten
er/sie/es schneite	sie schneiten

FUTURE SUBJUNCTIVE I

ich werde	wir werden	schneien
du werdest	ihr werdet	
Sie werden	Sie werden	
er/sie/es werde	sie werden	

FUTURE SUBJUNCTIVE II

ich würde	wir würden	schneien
du würdest	ihr würdet	
Sie würden	Sie würden	
er/sie/es würde	sie würden	

PRESENT PERFECT

ich habe	wir haben	geschneit
du hast	ihr habt	
Sie haben	Sie haben	
er/sie/es hat	sie haben	

PAST PERFECT

ich hatte	wir hatten	geschneit
du hattest	ihr hattet	
Sie hatten	Sie hatten	
er/sie/es hatte	sie hatten	

FUTURE PERFECT

ich werde	wir werden	geschneit haben
du wirst	ihr werdet	
Sie werden	Sie werden	
er/sie/es wird	sie werden	

PAST SUBJUNCTIVE I

ich habe	wir haben	geschneit
du habest	ihr habet	
Sie haben	Sie haben	
er/sie/es habe	sie haben	

PAST SUBJUNCTIVE II

ich hätte	wir hätten	geschneit
du hättest	ihr hättet	
Sie hätten	Sie hätten	
er/sie/es hätte	sie hätten	

FUTURE PERFECT SUBJUNCTIVE I

ich werde	wir werden	geschneit haben
du werdest	ihr werdet	
Sie werden	Sie werden	
er/sie/es werde	sie werden	

FUTURE PERFECT SUBJUNCTIVE II

ich würde	wir würden	geschneit haben
du würdest	ihr würdet	
Sie würden	Sie würden	
er/sie/es würde	sie würden	

COMMANDS schnei(e)! schneit! schneien Sie!

PRESENT PARTICIPLE schneiend

NOTE The first- and second-person forms of **schneien** are rare, except in poetry.

Usage

Letztes Jahr hat es in Seattle viermal geschneit.	*It snowed four times last year in Seattle.*
Am nächsten Tag schneite es in Yosemite.	*The next day, it snowed in Yosemite.*
In der Zwischenzeit wird es wohl viel mehr geschneit haben.	*In the meantime, it will likely have snowed a lot more.*
Voriges Jahr hat es erstaunlich oft geschneit.	*Last year, it snowed unusually often.*
Um wie viel Uhr begann es zu schneien?	*At what time did it begin snowing?*
In Alaska schneit es von Oktober bis Mai.	*In Alaska, it snows from October to May.*
Ab und zu schneit es auch in San Francisco.	*Once in a while, it snows in San Francisco, too.*
Beim Rugbyspiel hat es gestern Abend viel geschneit.	*It snowed a lot at the rugby game last night.*
Im Süden der USA schneit es selten.	*In the American South, it seldom snows.*

schneien (with **sein**) (used figuratively) *to fall like snow*

Blumen sind auf uns geschneit.	*Flowers fell like snow on us.*

RELATED VERBS ein·schneien, verschneien, zu·schneien

schrauben *to screw*

schraubt · schraubte · geschraubt

regular weak verb

PRESENT

ich schraube	wir schrauben
du schraubst	ihr schraubt
Sie schrauben	Sie schrauben
er/sie/es schraubt	sie schrauben

SIMPLE PAST

ich schraubte	wir schraubten
du schraubtest	ihr schraubtet
Sie schraubten	Sie schraubten
er/sie/es schraubte	sie schraubten

FUTURE

ich werde	wir werden	schrauben
du wirst	ihr werdet	
Sie werden	Sie werden	
er/sie/es wird	sie werden	

PRESENT SUBJUNCTIVE I

ich schraube	wir schrauben
du schraubest	ihr schraubet
Sie schrauben	Sie schrauben
er/sie/es schraube	sie schrauben

PRESENT SUBJUNCTIVE II

ich schraubte	wir schraubten
du schraubtest	ihr schraubtet
Sie schraubten	Sie schraubten
er/sie/es schraubte	sie schraubten

FUTURE SUBJUNCTIVE I

ich werde	wir werden	schrauben
du werdest	ihr werdet	
Sie werden	Sie werden	
er/sie/es werde	sie werden	

FUTURE SUBJUNCTIVE II

ich würde	wir würden	schrauben
du würdest	ihr würdet	
Sie würden	Sie würden	
er/sie/es würde	sie würden	

PRESENT PERFECT

ich habe	wir haben	geschraubt
du hast	ihr habt	
Sie haben	Sie haben	
er/sie/es hat	sie haben	

PAST PERFECT

ich hatte	wir hatten	geschraubt
du hattest	ihr hattet	
Sie hatten	Sie hatten	
er/sie/es hatte	sie hatten	

FUTURE PERFECT

ich werde	wir werden	geschraubt haben
du wirst	ihr werdet	
Sie werden	Sie werden	
er/sie/es wird	sie werden	

PAST SUBJUNCTIVE I

ich habe	wir haben	geschraubt
du habest	ihr habet	
Sie haben	Sie haben	
er/sie/es habe	sie haben	

PAST SUBJUNCTIVE II

ich hätte	wir hätten	geschraubt
du hättest	ihr hättet	
Sie hätten	Sie hätten	
er/sie/es hätte	sie hätten	

FUTURE PERFECT SUBJUNCTIVE I

ich werde	wir werden	geschraubt haben
du werdest	ihr werdet	
Sie werden	Sie werden	
er/sie/es werde	sie werden	

FUTURE PERFECT SUBJUNCTIVE II

ich würde	wir würden	geschraubt haben
du würdest	ihr würdet	
Sie würden	Sie würden	
er/sie/es würde	sie würden	

COMMANDS schraub(e)! schraubt! schrauben Sie!

PRESENT PARTICIPLE schraubend

Usage

Man muss einen Griff an den Deckel schrauben. — *A handle must be screwed onto the lid.*
Bücherregale werden wegen Erdbeben an die Wand geschraubt. — *Bookcases are screwed to the wall because of earthquakes.*

höher/niedriger schrauben *to raise/lower*

Die Preise werden immer höher geschraubt. — *The prices are being pushed higher and higher.*
Wir müssen die Erwartungen etwas niedriger schrauben. — *We must lower the expectations somewhat.*

sich schrauben *to spin, spiral*

Die Molekeln schrauben sich in eine neue Struktur. — *The molecules spin into a new structure.*
Die Rauchwolke schraubte sich in den Himmel. — *The cloud of smoke spiraled into the sky.*
Im Sommer schrauben sich die Temperaturen in die Höhe. — *In the summer, the temperatures spiral upwards.*

RELATED VERBS ab·schrauben, an·schrauben, auf·schrauben, aus·schrauben, ein·schrauben, fest·schrauben, hoch·schrauben, verschrauben, zurück·schrauben, zusammen·schrauben, zu·schrauben regular weak verb or strong verb

schreckt/schrickt · schreckte/schrak · geschreckt/geschrocken

PRESENT

ich schrecke	wir schrecken
du schreckst/schrickst	ihr schreckt
Sie schrecken	Sie schrecken
er/sie/es schreckt/schrickt	sie schrecken

SIMPLE PAST

ich schreckte/schrak	wir schreckten/schraken
du schrecktest/schrakst	ihr schrecktet/schrakt
Sie schreckten/schraken	Sie schreckten/schraken
er/sie/es schreckte/schrak	sie schreckten/schraken

FUTURE

ich werde	wir werden	schrecken
du wirst	ihr werdet	
Sie werden	Sie werden	
er/sie/es wird	sie werden	

PRESENT SUBJUNCTIVE I

ich schrecke	wir schrecken
du schreckest	ihr schrecket
Sie schrecken	Sie schrecken
er/sie/es schrecke	sie schrecken

PRESENT SUBJUNCTIVE II

ich schreckte/schräke	wir schreckten/schräken
du schrecktest/schräkest	ihr schrecktet/schräket
Sie schreckten/schräken	Sie schreckten/schräken
er/sie/es schreckte/schräke	sie schreckten/schräken

FUTURE SUBJUNCTIVE I

ich werde	wir werden	schrecken
du werdest	ihr werdet	
Sie werden	Sie werden	
er/sie/es werde	sie werden	

FUTURE SUBJUNCTIVE II

ich würde	wir würden	schrecken
du würdest	ihr würdet	
Sie würden	Sie würden	
er/sie/es würde	sie würden	

PRESENT PERFECT

ich bin	wir sind	geschreckt/ geschrocken
du bist	ihr seid	
Sie sind	Sie sind	
er/sie/es ist	sie sind	

PAST PERFECT

ich war	wir waren	geschreckt/ geschrocken
du warst	ihr wart	
Sie waren	Sie waren	
er/sie/es war	sie waren	

FUTURE PERFECT

ich werde	wir werden	geschreckt sein OR geschrocken sein
du wirst	ihr werdet	
Sie werden	Sie werden	
er/sie/es wird	sie werden	

PAST SUBJUNCTIVE I

ich sei	wir seien	geschreckt/ geschrocken
du seiest	ihr seiet	
Sie seien	Sie seien	
er/sie/es sei	sie seien	

PAST SUBJUNCTIVE II

ich wäre	wir wären	geschreckt/ geschrocken
du wärest	ihr wäret	
Sie wären	Sie wären	
er/sie/es wäre	sie wären	

FUTURE PERFECT SUBJUNCTIVE I

ich werde	wir werden	geschreckt sein OR geschrocken sein
du werdest	ihr werdet	
Sie werden	Sie werden	
er/sie/es werde	sie werden	

FUTURE PERFECT SUBJUNCTIVE II

ich würde	wir würden	geschreckt sein OR geschrocken sein
du würdest	ihr würdet	
Sie würden	Sie würden	
er/sie/es würde	sie würden	

COMMANDS schreck(e)!/schrick! schreckt! schrecken Sie!

PRESENT PARTICIPLE schreckend

NOTE The archaic strong past participle **geschrocken** is extremely rare, whereas the strong simple tenses are more common.

Usage

Erich ist aus tiefem Schlaf geschreckt.	*Erich was startled from a deep sleep.*
Die Bürger werden über die neuen Regelungen schrecken.	*The citizens will be frightened by the new laws.*
Der Hund schrak und lief weg.	*The dog got scared and ran away.*

schrecken (when transitive, all forms are always regular weak with **haben**) *to frighten, scare, startle*

Schreck mich nicht so.	*Don't startle me like that.*
Meine neue Chefin schreckt mich.	*My new boss scares me.*
Karen möchte uns nicht schrecken.	*Karen doesn't want to frighten us.*
Hat der Film dich nicht geschreckt?	*Did the film not scare you?*
Die politischen Ereignisse schrecken uns.	*The political events are alarming us.*
Der Bauersknecht schreckte den Hasen.	*The hired hand startled the hare.*

RELATED VERBS ab·schrecken, auf·schrecken, hoch·schrecken, zurück·schrecken; *see also* **erschrecken** (171)

385 schreiben *to write; spell*

schreibt · schrieb · geschrieben

strong verb

PRESENT

ich schreibe	wir schreiben
du schreibst	ihr schreibt
Sie schreiben	Sie schreiben
er/sie/es schreibt	sie schreiben

SIMPLE PAST

ich schrieb	wir schrieben
du schriebst	ihr schriebt
Sie schrieben	Sie schrieben
er/sie/es schrieb	sie schrieben

FUTURE

ich werde	wir werden	schreiben
du wirst	ihr werdet	
Sie werden	Sie werden	
er/sie/es wird	sie werden	

PRESENT SUBJUNCTIVE I

ich schreibe	wir schreiben
du schreibest	ihr schreibet
Sie schreiben	Sie schreiben
er/sie/es schreibe	sie schreiben

PRESENT SUBJUNCTIVE II

ich schriebe	wir schrieben
du schriebest	ihr schriebet
Sie schrieben	Sie schrieben
er/sie/es schriebe	sie schrieben

FUTURE SUBJUNCTIVE I

ich werde	wir werden	schreiben
du werdest	ihr werdet	
Sie werden	Sie werden	
er/sie/es werde	sie werden	

FUTURE SUBJUNCTIVE II

ich würde	wir würden	schreiben
du würdest	ihr würdet	
Sie würden	Sie würden	
er/sie/es würde	sie würden	

PRESENT PERFECT

ich habe	wir haben	geschrieben
du hast	ihr habt	
Sie haben	Sie haben	
er/sie/es hat	sie haben	

PAST PERFECT

ich hatte	wir hatten	geschrieben
du hattest	ihr hattet	
Sie hatten	Sie hatten	
er/sie/es hatte	sie hatten	

FUTURE PERFECT

ich werde	wir werden	geschrieben haben
du wirst	ihr werdet	
Sie werden	Sie werden	
er/sie/es wird	sie werden	

PAST SUBJUNCTIVE I

ich habe	wir haben	geschrieben
du habest	ihr habet	
Sie haben	Sie haben	
er/sie/es habe	sie haben	

PAST SUBJUNCTIVE II

ich hätte	wir hätten	geschrieben
du hättest	ihr hättet	
Sie hätten	Sie hätten	
er/sie/es hätte	sie hätten	

FUTURE PERFECT SUBJUNCTIVE I

ich werde	wir werden	geschrieben haben
du werdest	ihr werdet	
Sie werden	Sie werden	
er/sie/es werde	sie werden	

FUTURE PERFECT SUBJUNCTIVE II

ich würde	wir würden	geschrieben haben
du würdest	ihr würdet	
Sie würden	Sie würden	
er/sie/es würde	sie würden	

COMMANDS schreib(e)! schreibt! schreiben Sie!

PRESENT PARTICIPLE schreibend

Usage

Ich muss meiner Mutter jetzt schreiben.	*I have to write my mother now.*
Dieses Gedicht müsste vor 1500 geschrieben worden sein.	*This poem must have been written before 1500.*
Die alten Männer schreiben einander regelmäßig.	*The old men write to one another regularly.*
Schreibt man das Wort „Leid“ groß oder klein?	*Do you write the word “Leid” in upper case or lower case?*
Hast du den Aufsatz schon geschrieben?	*Have you already written the essay?*
Frank Schröter wollte den Liedtext geschrieben haben.	*Frank Schröter claimed to have written the lyrics.*
Diese Geschichte wurde 1959 geschrieben.	*This story was written in 1959.*

sich schreiben *to write; be spelled*

Mit diesem Stift schreibt es sich leicht.	*It's easy to write with this pen.*
Schreibt sich das Wort „Ruhm“ mit oder ohne „h“?	*Is the word “Ruhm” spelled with or without an “h”?*

RELATED VERBS ab·schreiben, an·schreiben, auf·schreiben, aus·schreiben, durch·schreiben, ein·schreiben, gut·schreiben, krank·schreiben, mit·schreiben, nach·schreiben, nieder·schreiben, schön·schreiben, überschreiben, um·schreiben, umschreiben, verschreiben, vor·schreiben, zurück·schreiben, zusammen·schreiben, zu·schreiben; *see also* **beschreiben** (84), **unterschreiben** (472)

PRESENT

ich schreie	wir schreien
du schreist	ihr schreit
Sie schreien	Sie schreien
er/sie/es schreit	sie schreien

SIMPLE PAST

ich schrie	wir schrien
du schriest	ihr schriet
Sie schrien	Sie schrien
er/sie/es schrie	sie schrien

FUTURE

ich werde	wir werden	schreien
du wirst	ihr werdet	
Sie werden	Sie werden	
er/sie/es wird	sie werden	

PRESENT SUBJUNCTIVE I

ich schreie	wir schreien
du schreiest	ihr schreiet
Sie schreien	Sie schreien
er/sie/es schreie	sie schreien

PRESENT SUBJUNCTIVE II

ich schrie	wir schrien
du schriest	ihr schriet
Sie schrien	Sie schrien
er/sie/es schrie	sie schrien

FUTURE SUBJUNCTIVE I

ich werde	wir werden	schreien
du werdest	ihr werdet	
Sie werden	Sie werden	
er/sie/es werde	sie werden	

FUTURE SUBJUNCTIVE II

ich würde	wir würden	schreien
du würdest	ihr würdet	
Sie würden	Sie würden	
er/sie/es würde	sie würden	

PRESENT PERFECT

ich habe	wir haben	geschrien
du hast	ihr habt	
Sie haben	Sie haben	
er/sie/es hat	sie haben	

PAST PERFECT

ich hatte	wir hatten	geschrien
du hattest	ihr hattet	
Sie hatten	Sie hatten	
er/sie/es hatte	sie hatten	

FUTURE PERFECT

ich werde	wir werden	geschrien haben
du wirst	ihr werdet	
Sie werden	Sie werden	
er/sie/es wird	sie werden	

PAST SUBJUNCTIVE I

ich habe	wir haben	geschrien
du habest	ihr habet	
Sie haben	Sie haben	
er/sie/es habe	sie haben	

PAST SUBJUNCTIVE II

ich hätte	wir hätten	geschrien
du hättest	ihr hättet	
Sie hätten	Sie hätten	
er/sie/es hätte	sie hätten	

FUTURE PERFECT SUBJUNCTIVE I

ich werde	wir werden	geschrien haben
du werdest	ihr werdet	
Sie werden	Sie werden	
er/sie/es werde	sie werden	

FUTURE PERFECT SUBJUNCTIVE II

ich würde	wir würden	geschrien haben
du würdest	ihr würdet	
Sie würden	Sie würden	
er/sie/es würde	sie würden	

COMMANDS schrei(e)! schreit! schreien Sie!

PRESENT PARTICIPLE schreiend

Usage

Wir hörten in der Ferne ein Baby schreien.	*We heard a baby crying in the distance.*
Wegen des Lärms musste der Flugbegleiter fast schreien.	*Because of the noise, the flight attendant almost had to scream.*
Warum hast du geschrien?	*Why did you yell?*
Unser Papagei schreit: „Süßer", wenn er etwas will.	*Our parrot cries "Darling" when he wants something.*
Stefan schrie um Hilfe, aber keiner kam.	*Stefan cried for help, but no one came.*
Schreien Sie bitte nicht am Telefon.	*Please don't yell on the telephone.*
In meinem Alptraum hat ein Eichhörnchen wie ein Affe geschrien.	*In my nightmare, a squirrel was screeching like an ape.*
Ich wollte schreien, aber ich musste stillschweigen.	*I wanted to scream but had to remain silent.*
Hast du schon mal ein Kaninchen schreien gehört?	*Have you ever heard a rabbit scream?*
Du hättest auch geschrien, wenn es dir passiert wäre.	*You would have screamed too, if it had happened to you.*
Die Fußballfans schrien bis zum Ende des Spiels.	*The soccer fans yelled until the end of the game.*

RELATED VERBS an·schreien, auf·schreien, aus·schreien, beschreien, nach·schreien, überschreien, zu·schreien

387 schreiten *to step; walk; stride, march; progress, proceed, advance*

schreitet · schritt · geschritten strong verb

PRESENT

ich schreite	wir schreiten
du schreitest	ihr schreitet
Sie schreiten	Sie schreiten
er/sie/es schreitet	sie schreiten

SIMPLE PAST

ich schritt	wir schritten
du schrittst	ihr schrittet
Sie schritten	Sie schritten
er/sie/es schritt	sie schritten

FUTURE

ich werde	wir werden	schreiten
du wirst	ihr werdet	
Sie werden	Sie werden	
er/sie/es wird	sie werden	

PRESENT SUBJUNCTIVE I

ich schreite	wir schreiten
du schreitest	ihr schreitet
Sie schreiten	Sie schreiten
er/sie/es schreite	sie schreiten

PRESENT SUBJUNCTIVE II

ich schritte	wir schritten
du schrittest	ihr schrittet
Sie schritten	Sie schritten
er/sie/es schritte	sie schritten

FUTURE SUBJUNCTIVE I

ich werde	wir werden	schreiten
du werdest	ihr werdet	
Sie werden	Sie werden	
er/sie/es werde	sie werden	

FUTURE SUBJUNCTIVE II

ich würde	wir würden	schreiten
du würdest	ihr würdet	
Sie würden	Sie würden	
er/sie/es würde	sie würden	

PRESENT PERFECT

ich bin	wir sind	geschritten
du bist	ihr seid	
Sie sind	Sie sind	
er/sie/es ist	sie sind	

PAST PERFECT

ich war	wir waren	geschritten
du warst	ihr wart	
Sie waren	Sie waren	
er/sie/es war	sie waren	

FUTURE PERFECT

ich werde	wir werden	geschritten sein
du wirst	ihr werdet	
Sie werden	Sie werden	
er/sie/es wird	sie werden	

PAST SUBJUNCTIVE I

ich sei	wir seien	geschritten
du seiest	ihr seiet	
Sie seien	Sie seien	
er/sie/es sei	sie seien	

PAST SUBJUNCTIVE II

ich wäre	wir wären	geschritten
du wärest	ihr wäret	
Sie wären	Sie wären	
er/sie/es wäre	sie wären	

FUTURE PERFECT SUBJUNCTIVE I

ich werde	wir werden	geschritten sein
du werdest	ihr werdet	
Sie werden	Sie werden	
er/sie/es werde	sie werden	

FUTURE PERFECT SUBJUNCTIVE II

ich würde	wir würden	geschritten sein
du würdest	ihr würdet	
Sie würden	Sie würden	
er/sie/es würde	sie würden	

COMMANDS schreite! schreitet! schreiten Sie!

PRESENT PARTICIPLE schreitend

Usage

Wir wollten nur mal kurz über die Grenze schreiten. — *We just wanted to step across the border briefly.*

Die Kinder schritten vorsichtig auf den zugefrorenen Teich. — *The children stepped slowly onto the frozen pond.*

Ich küsste diese Schwelle, über die sie so oft geschritten ist. (Bettine von Arnim) — *I kissed the threshold over which she so often passed.*

Traurig schritt er nach Hause. — *He walked home sadly.*

Die Studenten schritten langsam in den Hörsaal. — *The students strode slowly into the auditorium.*

Die Armee schreitet vorwärts ins Grenzgebiet. — *The army is marching into the border region.*

Sie wollen zu pragmatischer Politik schreiten. — *They want to proceed to pragmatic politics.*

Nach kurzer Debatte schritt das Parlament zur Aufhebung des kontroversen Gesetzes. — *After a short debate, the parliament proceeded to rescind the controversial law.*

Muss man vorwärts schreiten. — *One must move forward.*

Man ist zu drastischen Maßnahmen geschritten. — *They've taken to drastic measures.*

RELATED VERBS ab·schreiten, aus·schreiten, beschreiten, durchschreiten, ein·schreiten, fort·schreiten, überschreiten, unterschreiten, vor·schreiten, weiter·schreiten

PRESENT

ich schütze	wir schützen
du schützt	ihr schützt
Sie schützen	Sie schützen
er/sie/es schützt	sie schützen

SIMPLE PAST

ich schützte	wir schützten
du schütztest	ihr schütztet
Sie schützten	Sie schützten
er/sie/es schützte	sie schützten

FUTURE

ich werde	wir werden	schützen
du wirst	ihr werdet	
Sie werden	Sie werden	
er/sie/es wird	sie werden	

PRESENT SUBJUNCTIVE I

ich schütze	wir schützen
du schützest	ihr schützet
Sie schützen	Sie schützen
er/sie/es schütze	sie schützen

PRESENT SUBJUNCTIVE II

ich schützte	wir schützten
du schütztest	ihr schütztet
Sie schützten	Sie schützten
er/sie/es schützte	sie schützten

FUTURE SUBJUNCTIVE I

ich werde	wir werden	schützen
du werdest	ihr werdet	
Sie werden	Sie werden	
er/sie/es werde	sie werden	

FUTURE SUBJUNCTIVE II

ich würde	wir würden	schützen
du würdest	ihr würdet	
Sie würden	Sie würden	
er/sie/es würde	sie würden	

PRESENT PERFECT

ich habe	wir haben	geschützt
du hast	ihr habt	
Sie haben	Sie haben	
er/sie/es hat	sie haben	

PAST PERFECT

ich hatte	wir hatten	geschützt
du hattest	ihr hattet	
Sie hatten	Sie hatten	
er/sie/es hatte	sie hatten	

FUTURE PERFECT

ich werde	wir werden	geschützt haben
du wirst	ihr werdet	
Sie werden	Sie werden	
er/sie/es wird	sie werden	

PAST SUBJUNCTIVE I

ich habe	wir haben	geschützt
du habest	ihr habet	
Sie haben	Sie haben	
er/sie/es habe	sie haben	

PAST SUBJUNCTIVE II

ich hätte	wir hätten	geschützt
du hättest	ihr hättet	
Sie hätten	Sie hätten	
er/sie/es hätte	sie hätten	

FUTURE PERFECT SUBJUNCTIVE I

ich werde	wir werden	geschützt haben
du werdest	ihr werdet	
Sie werden	Sie werden	
er/sie/es werde	sie werden	

FUTURE PERFECT SUBJUNCTIVE II

ich würde	wir würden	geschützt haben
du würdest	ihr würdet	
Sie würden	Sie würden	
er/sie/es würde	sie würden	

COMMANDS schütz(e)! schützt! schützen Sie!

PRESENT PARTICIPLE schützend

Usage

Vitamine schützen die Gesundheit. — *Vitamins protect your health.*
Sie sollten das Baby vor der Hitze schützen. — *You should protect the baby from the heat.*
Sep versuchte seinen Kopf zu schützen. — *Sep tried to protect his head.*
Kannst du die Kinder vor dem Hund schützen? — *Can you protect the children from the dog?*
In den Nationalparks werden die Wunder der Natur geschützt. — *In the national parks, wonders of nature are protected.*
Hans meint, der Wolf wäre missverstanden worden; er habe Rotkäppchen eigentlich schützen wollen. — *Hans thinks the wolf was misunderstood; he actually only wanted to protect Red Riding Hood.*
Du musst dich jetzt schützen. — *You must protect yourself now.*
Die warmen Temperaturen haben das Obst geschützt. — *The warm temperatures protected the fruit.*
Die Feuerwehr schützte die Tiere. — *The fire department protected the animals.*
Der große Baum hat uns vor dem Regenschauer geschützt. — *The large tree sheltered us from the rain shower.*
Andere Kinder schützen ihn. — *Other children are protective of him.*

RELATED VERBS beschützen, vor·schützen

389 schweben *to hover, hang; float*

schwebt · schwebte · geschwebt regular weak verb

PRESENT

ich schwebe	wir schweben
du schwebst	ihr schwebt
Sie schweben	Sie schweben
er/sie/es schwebt	sie schweben

SIMPLE PAST

ich schwebte	wir schwebten
du schwebtest	ihr schwebtet
Sie schwebten	Sie schwebten
er/sie/es schwebte	sie schwebten

FUTURE

ich werde	wir werden	schweben
du wirst	ihr werdet	
Sie werden	Sie werden	
er/sie/es wird	sie werden	

PRESENT SUBJUNCTIVE I

ich schwebe	wir schweben
du schwebest	ihr schwebet
Sie schweben	Sie schweben
er/sie/es schwebe	sie schweben

PRESENT SUBJUNCTIVE II

ich schwebte	wir schwebten
du schwebtest	ihr schwebtet
Sie schwebten	Sie schwebten
er/sie/es schwebte	sie schwebten

FUTURE SUBJUNCTIVE I

ich werde	wir werden	schweben
du werdest	ihr werdet	
Sie werden	Sie werden	
er/sie/es werde	sie werden	

FUTURE SUBJUNCTIVE II

ich würde	wir würden	schweben
du würdest	ihr würdet	
Sie würden	Sie würden	
er/sie/es würde	sie würden	

PRESENT PERFECT

ich habe	wir haben	geschwebt
du hast	ihr habt	
Sie haben	Sie haben	
er/sie/es hat	sie haben	

PAST PERFECT

ich hatte	wir hatten	geschwebt
du hattest	ihr hattet	
Sie hatten	Sie hatten	
er/sie/es hatte	sie hatten	

FUTURE PERFECT

ich werde	wir werden	geschwebt haben
du wirst	ihr werdet	
Sie werden	Sie werden	
er/sie/es wird	•sie werden	

PAST SUBJUNCTIVE I

ich habe	wir haben	geschwebt
du habest	ihr habet	
Sie haben	Sie haben	
er/sie/es habe	sie haben	

PAST SUBJUNCTIVE II

ich hätte	wir hätten	geschwebt
du hättest	ihr hättet	
Sie hätten	Sie hätten	
er/sie/es hätte	sie hätten	

FUTURE PERFECT SUBJUNCTIVE I

ich werde	wir werden	geschwebt haben
du werdest	ihr werdet	
Sie werden	Sie werden	
er/sie/es werde	sie werden	

FUTURE PERFECT SUBJUNCTIVE II

ich würde	wir würden	geschwebt haben
du würdest	ihr würdet	
Sie würden	Sie würden	
er/sie/es würde	sie würden	

COMMANDS schweb(e)! schwebt! schweben Sie!

PRESENT PARTICIPLE schwebend

Usage

Fantastische Figuren schwebten in seinen Träumen. — *Fantastical figures hovered in his dreams.*
Hoch über uns schwebte ein Geier. — *High above us, a vulture hovered.*
Eine Schlinge schwebte über dem verurteilten Mann. — *A noose hung above the condemned man.*
Der Mann schwebt zwischen Leben und Tod. — *The man is hovering between life and death.*
Um das Jahr 2000 schwebte man in einer Welt mitten in politischem Umbruch. — *Around the year 2000, people were suspended in a world in the midst of political upheaval.*
Ein Hubschrauber schwebte über dem Dach. — *A helicopter hovered above the roof.*
Eine Aschenwolke schwebt heute über dem Vulkan. — *A cloud of ash hangs above the volcano today.*

schweben (with **sein**) *to float, soar, flit*

Ein Schmetterling ist durch die Tür geschwebt. — *A butterfly flitted through the door.*
Die Hexe schwebte durch die Luft auf ihrem Naturbesen. — *The witch soared through the air on her natural broom.*
Harfenmusik schwebte aus dem Konzerthaus. — *Harp music wafted from the concert hall.*

RELATED VERBS entschweben, umschweben, vor·schweben

390 schweigen

to remain silent, say nothing; stop

strong verb

schweigt · schwieg · geschwiegen

PRESENT

ich schweige	wir schweigen
du schweigst	ihr schweigt
Sie schweigen	Sie schweigen
er/sie/es schweigt	sie schweigen

SIMPLE PAST

ich schwieg	wir schwiegen
du schwiegst	ihr schwiegt
Sie schwiegen	Sie schwiegen
er/sie/es schwieg	sie schwiegen

FUTURE

ich werde	wir werden	schweigen
du wirst	ihr werdet	
Sie werden	Sie werden	
er/sie/es wird	sie werden	

PRESENT SUBJUNCTIVE I

ich schweige	wir schweigen
du schweigest	ihr schweiget
Sie schweigen	Sie schweigen
er/sie/es schweige	sie schweigen

PRESENT SUBJUNCTIVE II

ich schwiege	wir schwiegen
du schwiegest	ihr schwieget
Sie schwiegen	Sie schwiegen
er/sie/es schwiege	sie schwiegen

FUTURE SUBJUNCTIVE I

ich werde	wir werden	schweigen
du werdest	ihr werdet	
Sie werden	Sie werden	
er/sie/es werde	sie werden	

FUTURE SUBJUNCTIVE II

ich würde	wir würden	schweigen
du würdest	ihr würdet	
Sie würden	Sie würden	
er/sie/es würde	sie würden	

PRESENT PERFECT

ich habe	wir haben	geschwiegen
du hast	ihr habt	
Sie haben	Sie haben	
er/sie/es hat	sie haben	

PAST PERFECT

ich hatte	wir hatten	geschwiegen
du hattest	ihr hattet	
Sie hatten	Sie hatten	
er/sie/es hatte	sie hatten	

FUTURE PERFECT

ich werde	wir werden	geschwiegen haben
du wirst	ihr werdet	
Sie werden	Sie werden	
er/sie/es wird	sie werden	

PAST SUBJUNCTIVE I

ich habe	wir haben	geschwiegen
du habest	ihr habet	
Sie haben	Sie haben	
er/sie/es habe	sie haben	

PAST SUBJUNCTIVE II

ich hätte	wir hätten	geschwiegen
du hättest	ihr hättet	
Sie hätten	Sie hätten	
er/sie/es hätte	sie hätten	

FUTURE PERFECT SUBJUNCTIVE I

ich werde	wir werden	geschwiegen haben
du werdest	ihr werdet	
Sie werden	Sie werden	
er/sie/es werde	sie werden	

FUTURE PERFECT SUBJUNCTIVE II

ich würde	wir würden	geschwiegen haben
du würdest	ihr würdet	
Sie würden	Sie würden	
er/sie/es würde	sie würden	

COMMANDS schweig(e)! schweigt! schweigen Sie!

PRESENT PARTICIPLE schweigend

Usage

Augenzeugen schweigen über die Ereignisse des Tages.	*Eyewitnesses remain silent about the day's events.*
Warum schweigen eure Gäste?	*Why are your guests not talking?*
Lars schweigt über seine Lage.	*Lars is saying nothing about his situation.*
Jörg schweigt seit einem Jahr darüber.	*Jörg has been quiet about that for a year.*
Der Politiker schwieg auf die Frage, weil er keine Antwort wusste.	*The politician didn't comment on the question, because he had no answer.*
Unser Papagei schweigt, nur wenn er schläft.	*Our parrot is quiet only when he is asleep.*
Auf einem Mal schwieg der Hund, der mehrere Stunden gebellt hatte.	*All at once, the dog that had barked for several hours was quiet.*
Er scheint nicht schweigen zu wollen.	*He doesn't seem to want to be quiet.*
Die Regierung schweigt zum Thema der Katastrophe.	*The government is silent on the topic of the catastrophe.*
Warum hast du geschwiegen?	*Why did you say nothing?*
Schweig!	*Shut up!*

RELATED VERBS aus·schweigen, still·schweigen, tot·schweigen, verschweigen

391 schwellen *to swell, become swollen*

schwillt · schwoll · geschwollen strong verb

PRESENT

ich schwelle	wir schwellen
du schwillst	ihr schwellt
Sie schwellen	Sie schwellen
er/sie/es schwillt	sie schwellen

SIMPLE PAST

ich schwoll	wir schwollen
du schwollst	ihr schwollt
Sie schwollen	Sie schwollen
er/sie/es schwoll	sie schwollen

FUTURE

ich werde	wir werden	schwellen
du wirst	ihr werdet	
Sie werden	Sie werden	
er/sie/es wird	sie werden	

PRESENT SUBJUNCTIVE I

ich schwelle	wir schwellen
du schwellest	ihr schwellet
Sie schwellen	Sie schwellen
er/sie/es schwelle	sie schwellen

PRESENT SUBJUNCTIVE II

ich schwölle	wir schwöllen
du schwöllest	ihr schwöllet
Sie schwöllen	Sie schwöllen
er/sie/es schwölle	sie schwöllen

FUTURE SUBJUNCTIVE I

ich werde	wir werden	schwellen
du werdest	ihr werdet	
Sie werden	Sie werden	
er/sie/es werde	sie werden	

FUTURE SUBJUNCTIVE II

ich würde	wir würden	schwellen
du würdest	ihr würdet	
Sie würden	Sie würden	
er/sie/es würde	sie würden	

PRESENT PERFECT

ich bin	wir sind	geschwollen
du bist	ihr seid	
Sie sind	Sie sind	
er/sie/es ist	sie sind	

PAST PERFECT

ich war	wir waren	geschwollen
du warst	ihr wart	
Sie waren	Sie waren	
er/sie/es war	sie waren	

FUTURE PERFECT

ich werde	wir werden	geschwollen sein
du wirst	ihr werdet	
Sie werden	Sie werden	
er/sie/es wird	sie werden	

PAST SUBJUNCTIVE I

ich sei	wir seien	geschwollen
du seiest	ihr seiet	
Sie seien	Sie seien	
er/sie/es sei	sie seien	

PAST SUBJUNCTIVE II

ich wäre	wir wären	geschwollen
du wärest	ihr wäret	
Sie wären	Sie wären	
er/sie/es wäre	sie wären	

FUTURE PERFECT SUBJUNCTIVE I

ich werde	wir werden	geschwollen sein
du werdest	ihr werdet	
Sie werden	Sie werden	
er/sie/es werde	sie werden	

FUTURE PERFECT SUBJUNCTIVE II

ich würde	wir würden	geschwollen sein
du würdest	ihr würdet	
Sie würden	Sie würden	
er/sie/es würde	sie würden	

COMMANDS schwill! schwellt! schwellen Sie!

PRESENT PARTICIPLE schwellend

Usage

Seine Augen waren rot und geschwollen.	*His eyes were red and swollen.*
Nach der Operation waren die Füße geschwollen.	*After the operation, the feet became swollen.*
Nach dem Schlangenbiss schwoll ihr die Hand.	*After the snake bite, her hand became swollen.*
Mark liegt mit geschwollenen Backen im Bett. Könnte das der Mumps sein?	*Mark is lying in bed with swollen cheeks. Could it be the mumps?*
Ingrids Nase schwillt.	*Ingrid's nose is swelling.*
Ihre Hände waren geschwollen, so dass die Handschuhe nicht mehr passten.	*Her hands had swollen so that the gloves no longer fit.*
Dem Soldaten schwoll die Brust vor Stolz bei den Worten der Nationalhymne.	*The soldier's chest swelled with pride at the words of the national anthem.*

schwellen (when transitive, all forms are always regular weak with **haben**) *to swell*

Eine leichte Brise hatte das Segel geschwellt.	*A light breeze had billowed the sail.*

RELATED VERBS ab·schwellen, an·schwellen, auf·schwellen

strong verb **schwimmt · schwamm · geschwommen**

PRESENT

ich schwimme	wir schwimmen
du schwimmst	ihr schwimmt
Sie schwimmen	Sie schwimmen
er/sie/es schwimmt	sie schwimmen

SIMPLE PAST

ich schwamm	wir schwammen
du schwammst	ihr schwammt
Sie schwammen	Sie schwammen
er/sie/es schwamm	sie schwammen

FUTURE

ich werde	wir werden	schwimmen
du wirst	ihr werdet	
Sie werden	Sie werden	
er/sie/es wird	sie werden	

PRESENT SUBJUNCTIVE I

ich schwimme	wir schwimmen
du schwimmest	ihr schwimmet
Sie schwimmen	Sie schwimmen
er/sie/es schwimme	sie schwimmen

PRESENT SUBJUNCTIVE II

ich schwömme/schwämme	wir schwömmen/schwämmen
du schwömmest/schwämmest	ihr schwömmet/schwämmet
Sie schwömmen/schwämmen	Sie schwömmen/schwämmen
er/sie/es schwömme/schwämme	sie schwömmen/schwämmen

FUTURE SUBJUNCTIVE I

ich werde	wir werden	schwimmen
du werdest	ihr werdet	
Sie werden	Sie werden	
er/sie/es werde	sie werden	

FUTURE SUBJUNCTIVE II

ich würde	wir würden	schwimmen
du würdest	ihr würdet	
Sie würden	Sie würden	
er/sie/es würde	sie würden	

PRESENT PERFECT

ich bin	wir sind	geschwommen
du bist	ihr seid	
Sie sind	Sie sind	
er/sie/es ist	sie sind	

PAST PERFECT

ich war	wir waren	geschwommen
du warst	ihr wart	
Sie waren	Sie waren	
er/sie/es war	sie waren	

FUTURE PERFECT

ich werde	wir werden	geschwommen sein
du wirst	ihr werdet	
Sie werden	Sie werden	
er/sie/es wird	sie werden	

PAST SUBJUNCTIVE I

ich sei	wir seien	geschwommen
du seiest	ihr seiet	
Sie seien	Sie seien	
er/sie/es sei	sie seien	

PAST SUBJUNCTIVE II

ich wäre	wir wären	geschwommen
du wärest	ihr wäret	
Sie wären	Sie wären	
er/sie/es wäre	sie wären	

FUTURE PERFECT SUBJUNCTIVE I

ich werde	wir werden	geschwommen sein
du werdest	ihr werdet	
Sie werden	Sie werden	
er/sie/es werde	sie werden	

FUTURE PERFECT SUBJUNCTIVE II

ich würde	wir würden	geschwommen sein
du würdest	ihr würdet	
Sie würden	Sie würden	
er/sie/es würde	sie würden	

COMMANDS schwimm(e)! schwimmt! schwimmen Sie!

PRESENT PARTICIPLE schwimmend

Usage

Weiße Schwäne schwimmen über den stillen Teich.	*White swans swim across the silent pond.*
Seid ihr jemals im Rhein geschwommen?	*Have you ever gone swimming in the Rhine?*
Schwimmt ihr jeden Tag?	*Do you swim every day?*
Kannst du gut schwimmen?	*Can you swim well?*
Es macht ihm großen Spaß zu schwimmen.	*Swimming is great fun for him.*
Er scheint nicht schwimmen zu wollen.	*He doesn't seem to want to swim.*
Um wie viel Uhr wird geschwommen?	*At what time is there swimming?*
Kannst du auf dem Rücken schwimmen?	*Can you do the backstroke?*
Blaugrüne Algen schwimmen im warmen Wasser.	*Blue-green algae are floating in the warm water.*

schwimmen (with **haben**) *to swim*

Er hatte Jahre lang in Schulden geschwommen.	*He had been swimming in debt for many years.*

RELATED VERBS ab·schwimmen, an·schwimmen, auf·schwimmen, durchschwimmen, durch·schwimmen, fort·schwimmen, herum·schwimmen, hinaus·schwimmen, verschwimmen, weg·schwimmen

393 schwinden *to fade, run out, dwindle; lessen; disappear*

schwindet · schwand · geschwunden strong verb

PRESENT

ich schwinde	wir schwinden
du schwindest	ihr schwindet
Sie schwinden	Sie schwinden
er/sie/es schwindet	sie schwinden

SIMPLE PAST

ich schwand	wir schwanden
du schwandst	ihr schwandet
Sie schwanden	Sie schwanden
er/sie/es schwand	sie schwanden

FUTURE

ich werde	wir werden	schwinden
du wirst	ihr werdet	
Sie werden	Sie werden	
er/sie/es wird	sie werden	

PRESENT SUBJUNCTIVE I

ich schwinde	wir schwinden
du schwindest	ihr schwindet
Sie schwinden	Sie schwinden
er/sie/es schwinde	sie schwinden

PRESENT SUBJUNCTIVE II

ich schwände	wir schwänden
du schwändest	ihr schwändet
Sie schwänden	Sie schwänden
er/sie/es schwände	sie schwänden

FUTURE SUBJUNCTIVE I

ich werde	wir werden	schwinden
du werdest	ihr werdet	
Sie werden	Sie werden	
er/sie/es werde	sie werden	

FUTURE SUBJUNCTIVE II

ich würde	wir würden	schwinden
du würdest	ihr würdet	
Sie würden	Sie würden	
er/sie/es würde	sie würden	

PRESENT PERFECT

ich bin	wir sind	geschwunden
du bist	ihr seid	
Sie sind	Sie sind	
er/sie/es ist	sie sind	

PAST PERFECT

ich war	wir waren	geschwunden
du warst	ihr wart	
Sie waren	Sie waren	
er/sie/es war	sie waren	

FUTURE PERFECT

ich werde	wir werden	geschwunden sein
du wirst	ihr werdet	
Sie werden	Sie werden	
er/sie/es wird	sie werden	

PAST SUBJUNCTIVE I

ich sei	wir seien	geschwunden
du seiest	ihr seiet	
Sie seien	Sie seien	
er/sie/es sei	sie seien	

PAST SUBJUNCTIVE II

ich wäre	wir wären	geschwunden
du wärest	ihr wäret	
Sie wären	Sie wären	
er/sie/es wäre	sie wären	

FUTURE PERFECT SUBJUNCTIVE I

ich werde	wir werden	geschwunden sein
du werdest	ihr werdet	
Sie werden	Sie werden	
er/sie/es werde	sie werden	

FUTURE PERFECT SUBJUNCTIVE II

ich würde	wir würden	geschwunden sein
du würdest	ihr würdet	
Sie würden	Sie würden	
er/sie/es würde	sie würden	

COMMANDS schwinde! schwindet! schwinden Sie!

PRESENT PARTICIPLE schwindend

Usage

Sein Ruf schwindet auch im Ausland.	*Even abroad, his reputation is fading.*
Ihre sprachliche Kompetenz schwand langsam, nachdem sie ausgewandert waren.	*Their linguistic competence slowly declined after they had emigrated.*
Seine Investition ist schnell geschwunden.	*His investment quickly dwindled.*
Meine Leidenschaft für Science-Fiction ist schon lange geschwunden.	*My passion for science fiction ran out a long time ago.*
Onkel Johanns Kraft schwand und er aß nichts mehr.	*Uncle Johann's strength eroded and he ate nothing more.*
Der Mond verbirgt sein Licht, die Lampe schwindet! (Goethe)	*The moon is hiding its light, the light is fading!*
Svens Traum einer Eigentumswohnung schwindet dieses Jahr.	*Sven's dream of owning a home will fade this year.*
Der Vorrat an Lebensmitteln schwindet beträchtlich.	*The supply of food is dwindling significantly.*
Deine Probleme schwinden gar nicht!	*Your problems will not just go away.*
Der Schnee war geschwunden und der Frühling gekommen.	*The snow had disappeared, and spring had arrived.*

RELATED VERBS entschwinden, verschwinden

strong verb **schwingt · schwang · geschwungen**

PRESENT

ich schwinge	wir schwingen
du schwingst	ihr schwingt
Sie schwingen	Sie schwingen
er/sie/es schwingt	sie schwingen

SIMPLE PAST

ich schwang	wir schwangen
du schwangst	ihr schwangt
Sie schwangen	Sie schwangen
er/sie/es schwang	sie schwangen

FUTURE

ich werde	wir werden	schwingen
du wirst	ihr werdet	
Sie werden	Sie werden	
er/sie/es wird	sie werden	

PRESENT SUBJUNCTIVE I

ich schwinge	wir schwingen
du schwingest	ihr schwinget
Sie schwingen	Sie schwingen
er/sie/es schwinge	sie schwingen

PRESENT SUBJUNCTIVE II

ich schwänge	wir schwängen
du schwängest	ihr schwänget
Sie schwängen	Sie schwängen
er/sie/es schwänge	sie schwängen

FUTURE SUBJUNCTIVE I

ich werde	wir werden	schwingen
du werdest	ihr werdet	
Sie werden	Sie werden	
er/sie/es werde	sie werden	

FUTURE SUBJUNCTIVE II

ich würde	wir würden	schwingen
du würdest	ihr würdet	
Sie würden	Sie würden	
er/sie/es würde	sie würden	

PRESENT PERFECT

ich habe	wir haben	geschwungen
du hast	ihr habt	
Sie haben	Sie haben	
er/sie/es hat	sie haben	

PAST PERFECT

ich hatte	wir hatten	geschwungen
du hattest	ihr hattet	
Sie hatten	Sie hatten	
er/sie/es hatte	sie hatten	

FUTURE PERFECT

ich werde	wir werden	geschwungen haben
du wirst	ihr werdet	
Sie werden	Sie werden	
er/sie/es wird	sie werden	

PAST SUBJUNCTIVE I

ich habe	wir haben	geschwungen
du habest	ihr habet	
Sie haben	Sie haben	
er/sie/es habe	sie haben	

PAST SUBJUNCTIVE II

ich hätte	wir hätten	geschwungen
du hättest	ihr hättet	
Sie hätten	Sie hätten	
er/sie/es hätte	sie hätten	

FUTURE PERFECT SUBJUNCTIVE I

ich werde	wir werden	geschwungen haben
du werdest	ihr werdet	
Sie werden	Sie werden	
er/sie/es werde	sie werden	

FUTURE PERFECT SUBJUNCTIVE II

ich würde	wir würden	geschwungen haben
du würdest	ihr würdet	
Sie würden	Sie würden	
er/sie/es würde	sie würden	

COMMANDS schwing(e)! schwingt! schwingen Sie!

PRESENT PARTICIPLE schwingend

Usage

Der Ritter schwang sich in den Sattel.	*The knight swung himself into the saddle.*
Sabina konnte den großen Hammer nicht schwingen.	*Sabine was unable to swing the large hammer.*
Der Förster hat seine Axt ein Mal zu viel geschwungen.	*The woodsman swung his ax one too many times.*
Der Degen schwang ein Schwert über seinem Kopf.	*The warrior brandished a sword above his head.*
Papa schwingt das Baby durch die Luft.	*Papa is swinging the baby through the air.*
Der Ton entsteht dadurch, dass die Saite schwingt.	*The sound arises from the vibration of the string.*
Auf der Gitarre schwingt die A-Saite mit einer Frequenz von 440 Hz.	*The A string on the guitar vibrates at a frequency of 440 Hz.*

schwingen (with **sein**) *to swing, soar*

Beim Erdbeben ist die Lampe hin und her geschwungen.	*During the earthquake, the lamp swung back and forth.*
Der Affe schwang an einem Seil.	*The ape swung on a rope.*
Die Schwalben schwangen in den blauen Himmel.	*The swallows soared into the blue sky.*

RELATED VERBS ab·schwingen, auf·schwingen, aus·schwingen, erschwingen, mit·schwingen

395 schwitzen *to sweat; steam up*

schwitzt · schwitzte · geschwitzt regular weak verb

PRESENT

ich schwitze	wir schwitzen
du schwitzt	ihr schwitzt
Sie schwitzen	Sie schwitzen
er/sie/es schwitzt	sie schwitzen

SIMPLE PAST

ich schwitzte	wir schwitzten
du schwitztest	ihr schwitztet
Sie schwitzten	Sie schwitzten
er/sie/es schwitzte	sie schwitzten

FUTURE

ich werde	wir werden	schwitzen
du wirst	ihr werdet	
Sie werden	Sie werden	
er/sie/es wird	sie werden	

PRESENT SUBJUNCTIVE I

ich schwitze	wir schwitzen
du schwitzest	ihr schwitzet
Sie schwitzen	Sie schwitzen
er/sie/es schwitze	sie schwitzen

PRESENT SUBJUNCTIVE II

ich schwitzte	wir schwitzten
du schwitztest	ihr schwitztet
Sie schwitzten	Sie schwitzten
er/sie/es schwitzte	sie schwitzten

FUTURE SUBJUNCTIVE I

ich werde	wir werden	schwitzen
du werdest	ihr werdet	
Sie werden	Sie werden	
er/sie/es werde	sie werden	

FUTURE SUBJUNCTIVE II

ich würde	wir würden	schwitzen
du würdest	ihr würdet	
Sie würden	Sie würden	
er/sie/es würde	sie würden	

PRESENT PERFECT

ich habe	wir haben	geschwitzt
du hast	ihr habt	
Sie haben	Sie haben	
er/sie/es hat	sie haben	

PAST PERFECT

ich hatte	wir hatten	geschwitzt
du hattest	ihr hattet	
Sie hatten	Sie hatten	
er/sie/es hatte	sie hatten	

FUTURE PERFECT

ich werde	wir werden	geschwitzt haben
du wirst	ihr werdet	
Sie werden	Sie werden	
er/sie/es wird	sie werden	

PAST SUBJUNCTIVE I

ich habe	wir haben	geschwitzt
du habest	ihr habet	
Sie haben	Sie haben	
er/sie/es habe	sie haben	

PAST SUBJUNCTIVE II

ich hätte	wir hätten	geschwitzt
du hättest	ihr hättet	
Sie hätten	Sie hätten	
er/sie/es hätte	sie hätten	

FUTURE PERFECT SUBJUNCTIVE I

ich werde	wir werden	geschwitzt haben
du werdest	ihr werdet	
Sie werden	Sie werden	
er/sie/es werde	sie werden	

FUTURE PERFECT SUBJUNCTIVE II

ich würde	wir würden	geschwitzt haben
du würdest	ihr würdet	
Sie würden	Sie würden	
er/sie/es würde	sie würden	

COMMANDS schwitz(e)! schwitzt! schwitzen Sie!

PRESENT PARTICIPLE schwitzend

Usage

Die Snowboarder schwitzten trotz der Temperatur.	*The snowboarders were sweating in spite of the temperature.*
Der professionelle Sportler schwitzt mehr als der normale Mensch.	*The professional athlete sweats more than the average person.*
Im Hörsaal schwitzten die Studenten vor Angst.	*In the lecture hall, the students were sweating from anxiety.*
Warum schwitzt du so?	*Why are you sweating like that?*
Die Näherinnen schwitzen bei der Arbeit.	*The seamstresses are sweating at work.*
Paul liegt mit Fieber im Bett und schwitzt.	*Paul is lying in bed with a fever and is sweaty.*
Herr Tolzmann schwitzt immer viel.	*Mr. Tolzmann always sweats a lot.*
Frau Immerkühl schwitzt nicht gern.	*Mrs. Immerkühl doesn't like to perspire.*
Ich schwitze nicht mehr unter den Armen mit Hilfe des neuen Deos.	*I don't perspire under the arms anymore, thanks to the new deodorant.*
Molly schwitzte Blut und Wasser, als der Polizist näher kam. (*figurative*)	*Molly broke out in a cold sweat as the policeman approached.*

RELATED VERBS ab·schwitzen, aus·schwitzen, durchschwitzen, durch·schwitzen, verschwitzen

strong verb **schwört · schwor/schwur · geschworen**

PRESENT		PRESENT PERFECT		
ich schwöre	wir schwören	ich habe	wir haben	geschworen
du schwörst	ihr schwört	du hast	ihr habt	
Sie schwören	Sie schwören	Sie haben	Sie haben	
er/sie/es schwört	sie schwören	er/sie/es hat	sie haben	

SIMPLE PAST		PAST PERFECT		
ich schwor/schwur	wir schworen/schwuren	ich hatte	wir hatten	geschworen
du schworst/schwurst	ihr schwort/schwurt	du hattest	ihr hattet	
Sie schworen/schwuren	Sie schworen/schwuren	Sie hatten	Sie hatten	
er/sie/es schwor/schwur	sie schworen/schwuren	er/sie/es hatte	sie hatten	

FUTURE			FUTURE PERFECT		
ich werde	wir werden	schwören	ich werde	wir werden	geschworen haben
du wirst	ihr werdet		du wirst	ihr werdet	
Sie werden	Sie werden		Sie werden	Sie werden	
er/sie/es wird	sie werden		er/sie/es wird	sie werden	

PRESENT SUBJUNCTIVE I		PAST SUBJUNCTIVE I		
ich schwöre	wir schwören	ich habe	wir haben	geschworen
du schwörest	ihr schwöret	du habest	ihr habet	
Sie schwören	Sie schwören	Sie haben	Sie haben	
er/sie/es schwöre	sie schwören	er/sie/es habe	sie haben	

PRESENT SUBJUNCTIVE II		PAST SUBJUNCTIVE II		
ich schwöre/schwüre	wir schwören/schwüren	ich hätte	wir hätten	geschworen
du schwörest/schwürest	ihr schwöret/schwüret	du hättest	ihr hättet	
Sie schwören/schwüren	Sie schwören/schwüren	Sie hätten	Sie hätten	
er/sie/es schwöre/schwüre	sie schwören/schwüren	er/sie/es hätte	sie hätten	

FUTURE SUBJUNCTIVE I			FUTURE PERFECT SUBJUNCTIVE I		
ich werde	wir werden	schwören	ich werde	wir werden	geschworen haben
du werdest	ihr werdet		du werdest	ihr werdet	
Sie werden	Sie werden		Sie werden	Sie werden	
er/sie/es werde	sie werden		er/sie/es werde	sie werden	

FUTURE SUBJUNCTIVE II			FUTURE PERFECT SUBJUNCTIVE II		
ich würde	wir würden	schwören	ich würde	wir würden	geschworen haben
du würdest	ihr würdet		du würdest	ihr würdet	
Sie würden	Sie würden		Sie würden	Sie würden	
er/sie/es würde	sie würden		er/sie/es würde	sie würden	

COMMANDS schwör(e)! schwört! schwören Sie!

PRESENT PARTICIPLE schwörend

Usage

Sara schwört auf dieses Heilmittel.	*Sara swears by this medicine.*
Früher schwor man manchmal auf Latein.	*People used to take oaths in Latin.*
Die Familien haben sich Feindschaft geschworen.	*The families have sworn hostility to one another.*
Der König schwor die Waisen zu retten.	*The king pledged to save the orphans.*
Augenzeugen schwören, dass er die Tat begangen hat.	*Eyewitnesses swear that he committed the act.*
Der Prinz schwor seinem Gegner Rache.	*The prince vowed vengeance against his opponent.*
Der Protagonist des Romans musste bei Gott schwören.	*The protagonist of the novel had to swear to God.*
Ein Soldat muss zur Fahne schwören.	*A soldier must take a military oath.*
Die Untertanen schwören ihrem König Treue.	*The subjects swear loyalty to their king.*
Ich war's nicht, ich schwöre es dir.	*It wasn't me, I swear to you.*
„Schwürest du bei Gott und seinen Heiligen", sagte sie, „so schwürest du falsch." (C. F. Meyer)	*"If you were to swear to God and the saints," she said, "then you would be perjuring yourself."*
Der Zeuge hat Meineid geschworen.	*The witness has committed perjury.*

RELATED VERBS ab·schwören, beschwören, ein·schwören, herauf·beschwören, verschwören

397 **sehen** *to see, look; watch*

sieht · sah · gesehen — strong verb

MORE USAGE SENTENCES WITH sehen

Max und Moritz konnten den Lehrer nicht sehen.	*Max and Moritz couldn't see the teacher.*
Und siehe, da war ein Mensch, der hatte eine verdorrte Hand. (MATTHÄUS 12,10) (*archaic*)	*And behold, there was a man who had his hand withered.* (MATTHEW 12:10)
Siehe Seite 120. / Siehe oben. (*reference in a book*)	*See page 120. / See above.*
Fast sollte man denken, du sähest sie mit andern Augen. (GOETHE)	*One would almost think you were seeing them through different eyes.*

sich sehen *to see oneself*

Ein Vampir kann sich nicht im Spiegel sehen.	*A vampire can't see himself in the mirror.*
Trent sieht sich als Held.	*Trent sees himself as a hero.*
Fritz sah sich außerstande, seinem Freund zu helfen.	*Fritz felt unable to help his friend.*
Ich sehe mich genötigt, die Gelder zu kürzen.	*I am compelled to reduce the funds.*
Wir sehen uns nächste Woche, nicht?	*We'll see each other next week, right?*

sich sehen lassen *to show oneself, appear*

Ihr habt euch lange nicht sehen lassen.	*You haven't been around for a while.*
Das Endprodukt konnte sich nicht sehen lassen.	*The final product was not presentable.*

sehen + preposition

Lars sieht auf Pünktlichkeit.	*He sets great store in punctuality.*
Das Fenster sieht auf einen wunderschönen Garten.	*The window faces a beautiful garden.*
Nur seine Flosse sah aus dem Wasser.	*Only its fin showed above the water.*
An seiner Miene sah man, dass er es schon wusste.	*You could see by his expression that he already knew.*
Was siehst du in ihr?	*What do you see in her?*
Wieso siehst du ständig nach der Uhr?	*How come you're constantly looking at your watch?*
Ich wollte kurz nach Maria sehen.	*I wanted to look in on Maria briefly.*

IDIOMATIC EXPRESSIONS

Erich hat es kommen sehen.	*Erich knew it would happen. / Erich saw it coming.*
Das sieht dir ähnlich!	*That's just like you! / That's what I'd expect of you!*
Sara sieht ihrer Tante Inge sehr ähnlich.	*Sara greatly resembles her Aunt Inge.*
Wenn ich das schon sehe, wird mir schlecht.	*If I so much as see that, it makes me sick.*
Herr Klett sieht es nicht gern, dass sein Sohn trinkt.	*Mr. Klett doesn't approve of his son's drinking.*
Bei uns sind Sie immer gern gesehen.	*You are always a welcome guest in our home.*
Opa sieht schlecht.	*Grandpa has poor eyesight.*
Wir konnten uns an dem Blick nie satt sehen.	*We could never tire of looking at the view.*
Na, siehst du?	*You see now? / I told you so.*
Mal sehen.	*We'll (wait and) see.*
Lass mal sehen!	*Let me see! / Show me!*
Siehe da! (*archaic*)	*Lo and behold!*
Sehen Sie mal!	*Look here!*
Ich habe den Bären nur flüchtig gesehen.	*I just caught a glimpse of the bear.*
Die Werke von Rembrandt sind jetzt zu sehen.	*The works of Rembrandt are now on exhibition.*
Hoppla! Deine Unterhose ist zu sehen!	*Oops! Your underwear is showing.*
Weit und breit war keiner zu sehen.	*There wasn't a soul in sight.*
Das kann ich nicht sehen.	*I can't bear the sight of that.*
Man muss sehen, dass die Vorstellung pünktlich beginnt.	*You have to see to it that the performance begins promptly.*
Geschichtlich gesehen ist diese Anschauung verständlich.	*Seen from a historical perspective, this view is comprehensible.*

PRESENT

ich sehe	wir sehen
du siehst	ihr seht
Sie sehen	Sie sehen
er/sie/es sieht	sie sehen

PRESENT PERFECT

ich habe	wir haben	gesehen
du hast	ihr habt	
Sie haben	Sie haben	
er/sie/es hat	sie haben	

SIMPLE PAST

ich sah	wir sahen
du sahst	ihr saht
Sie sahen	Sie sahen
er/sie/es sah	sie sahen

PAST PERFECT

ich hatte	wir hatten	gesehen
du hattest	ihr hattet	
Sie hatten	Sie hatten	
er/sie/es hatte	sie hatten	

FUTURE

ich werde	wir werden	sehen
du wirst	ihr werdet	
Sie werden	Sie werden	
er/sie/es wird	sie werden	

FUTURE PERFECT

ich werde	wir werden	gesehen haben
du wirst	ihr werdet	
Sie werden	Sie werden	
er/sie/es wird	sie werden	

PRESENT SUBJUNCTIVE I

ich sehe	wir sehen
du sehest	ihr sehet
Sie sehen	Sie sehen
er/sie/es sehe	sie sehen

PAST SUBJUNCTIVE I

ich habe	wir haben	gesehen
du habest	ihr habet	
Sie haben	Sie haben	
er/sie/es habe	sie haben	

PRESENT SUBJUNCTIVE II

ich sähe	wir sähen
du sähest	ihr sähet
Sie sähen	Sie sähen
er/sie/es sähe	sie sähen

PAST SUBJUNCTIVE II

ich hätte	wir hätten	gesehen
du hättest	ihr hättet	
Sie hätten	Sie hätten	
er/sie/es hätte	sie hätten	

FUTURE SUBJUNCTIVE I

ich werde	wir werden	sehen
du werdest	ihr werdet	
Sie werden	Sie werden	
er/sie/es werde	sie werden	

FUTURE PERFECT SUBJUNCTIVE I

ich werde	wir werden	gesehen haben
du werdest	ihr werdet	
Sie werden	Sie werden	
er/sie/es werde	sie werden	

FUTURE SUBJUNCTIVE II

ich würde	wir würden	sehen
du würdest	ihr würdet	
Sie würden	Sie würden	
er/sie/es würde	sie würden	

FUTURE PERFECT SUBJUNCTIVE II

ich würde	wir würden	gesehen haben
du würdest	ihr würdet	
Sie würden	Sie würden	
er/sie/es würde	sie würden	

COMMANDS sieh! seht! sehen Sie!

PRESENT PARTICIPLE sehend

Usage

War der Verbrecher schon gesehen worden?	*Had the criminal already been seen?*
Die Minister sehen den Angriff als einen Fehler.	*The ministers see the attack as a mistake.*
Voriges Jahr haben wir Erstaunliches gesehen.	*Last year, we saw amazing things.*
Wer hat meine Schlüssel gesehen?	*Who has seen my keys?*
Ich habe einen Papagei mit einer Sonnenbrille gesehen.	*I saw a parrot with sunglasses.*
Was ist hier zu sehen?	*What's there to see here?*
Darwin hat ungewöhnliche Tiere in den Galápagos gesehen.	*Darwin saw unusual animals in the Galápagos.*
Cecilie hat das Handtuch am Haken gesehen.	*Cecilie saw the towel on the hook.*
Das Mofa wurde vor dem Buchladen gesehen.	*The moped was seen in front of the bookstore.*
Traurig sah die Prinzessin aus dem Schloss.	*The princess looked out sadly from the castle.*
Oliver sagt, dass er den Präsidenten gesehen habe.	*Oliver says he saw the president.*

RELATED VERBS ab·sehen, auf·sehen, besehen, durch·sehen, ein·sehen, entgegen·sehen, ersehen, fern·sehen, gegenüber·sehen, nach·sehen, schwarz·sehen, übersehen, um·sehen, versehen, vorher·sehen, weg·sehen, wieder·sehen, zurück·sehen, zu·sehen; *see also* **an·sehen** (18), **aus·sehen** (39)

sein *to be, exist*

ist · war · gewesen irregular verb (perfect auxiliary)

MORE USAGE SENTENCES WITH sein

Sei es heute oder nächsten Monat, wir schaffen es noch!	*Whether it be today or next month, we will get it done!*
Ich bin froh, dass die Prüfung vorbei ist.	*I'm glad the exam is over.*
Renate ist sich der Sache bewusst.	*Renate is aware of the matter.*
Sein oder Nichtsein, das ist hier die Frage. (Shakespeare)	*To be or not to be, that is the question.*
Wie viel Zeit wird dazu nötig sein?	*How much time will that require?*
Es ist zu hoffen, dass unsere Tochter täglich Biologie lernt.	*It is to be hoped that our daughter will study biology every day.*
Lass dir das eine Lehre sein!	*Let that be a lesson to you!*

sein + dative

Mir ist es zu warm hier.	*I'm too warm here.*
Ist es dir recht, wenn ich das Fenster aufmache?	*Is it okay with you if I open the window?*
Es ist mir egal.	*It makes no difference to me.*
Ihm war plötzlich schlecht.	*He was suddenly ill.*

sein + genitive

Uwe war der Ansicht, dass alle Mitglieder anwesend sein müssen.	*Uwe held the view that all members have to be present.*
Ich bin anderer Meinung.	*I am of a different opinion.*

IDIOMATIC EXPRESSIONS

Berta war außer sich vor Freude.	*Berta was beside herself with joy.*
Ich lasse ihn hier, es sei denn, dass du mitkommst.	*I'll leave him here, unless you're coming along.*
Y sei 23. (*mathematics*)	*Let y equal 23.*
Die Gefahr ist jetzt vorüber.	*The danger has now passed.*
Danke, das wär's. (*in a store*)	*Thanks, that's all.*
Die Zeit ist um.	*Time is up.*
Was hin ist, ist hin.	*When it's gone, it's gone.*
Es war einmal…	*Once upon a time, there was …*
Was nicht ist, kann noch werden. (proverb)	*What isn't yet may well still come to be.*
Mein Hut ist ab! (*congratulatory*)	*Hats off!*
Ich bin nicht in der Lage mitzuhelfen.	*I'm not able to help out.*
Jost war gerade dabei, die Garage zu räumen.	*Jost was just about to clean the garage.*
Mir ist nach Singen zumute.	*I'm in the mood for singing.*
Es sollte ein Kompliment sein.	*I meant it as a compliment.*
Wie wäre es mit einem Sprachkurs in Österreich?	*How about a language course in Austria?*
Günter ist gern für sich.	*Günter likes to be alone.*

COLLOQUIAL/INFORMAL EXPRESSIONS

Was ist los?	*What's up? / What's the matter?*
Der Fernseher ist an.	*The television is on.*
Das Fenster ist auf.	*The window is open.*
Ist die Tür zu?	*Is the door closed?*
Es war noch Kuchen über.	*There was still some cake left.*
Mit ihm ist es aus!	*It's all over for/with him.*
Das Feuer ist noch nicht aus.	*The fire isn't out yet.*
Jost ist auf Erfolg aus.	*Jost is out to succeed.*
Der Typ ist schon wer.	*That guy's a big shot / VIP.*
Das Buch ist fort.	*The book's gone.*
Der Hamster ist los!	*The hamster is loose.*
Wir sind das Problem endlich los.	*We're finally rid of the problem.*

to be, exist **sein** 398

irregular verb (perfect auxiliary) **ist · war · gewesen**

PRESENT

ich bin	wir sind
du bist	ihr seid
Sie sind	Sie sind
er/sie/es ist	sie sind

SIMPLE PAST

ich war	wir waren
du warst	ihr wart
Sie waren	Sie waren
er/sie/es war	sie waren

FUTURE

ich werde	wir werden	sein
du wirst	ihr werdet	
Sie werden	Sie werden	
er/sie/es wird	sie werden	

PRESENT SUBJUNCTIVE I

ich sei	wir seien
du seiest	ihr seiet
Sie seien	Sie seien
er/sie/es sei	sie seien

PRESENT SUBJUNCTIVE II

ich wäre	wir wären
du wärest	ihr wäret
Sie wären	Sie wären
er/sie/es wäre	sie wären

FUTURE SUBJUNCTIVE I

ich werde	wir werden	sein
du werdest	ihr werdet	
Sie werden	Sie werden	
er/sie/es werde	sie werden	

FUTURE SUBJUNCTIVE II

ich würde	wir würden	sein
du würdest	ihr würdet	
Sie würden	Sie würden	
er/sie/es würde	sie würden	

PRESENT PERFECT

ich bin	wir sind	gewesen
du bist	ihr seid	
Sie sind	Sie sind	
er/sie/es ist	sie sind	

PAST PERFECT

ich war	wir waren	gewesen
du warst	ihr wart	
Sie waren	Sie waren	
er/sie/es war	sie waren	

FUTURE PERFECT

ich werde	wir werden	gewesen sein
du wirst	ihr werdet	
Sie werden	Sie werden	
er/sie/es wird	sie werden	

PAST SUBJUNCTIVE I

ich sei	wir seien	gewesen
du seiest	ihr seiet	
Sie seien	Sie seien	
er/sie/es sei	sie seien	

PAST SUBJUNCTIVE II

ich wäre	wir wären	gewesen
du wärest	ihr wäret	
Sie wären	Sie wären	
er/sie/es wäre	sie wären	

FUTURE PERFECT SUBJUNCTIVE I

ich werde	wir werden	gewesen sein
du werdest	ihr werdet	
Sie werden	Sie werden	
er/sie/es werde	sie werden	

FUTURE PERFECT SUBJUNCTIVE II

ich würde	wir würden	gewesen sein
du würdest	ihr würdet	
Sie würden	Sie würden	
er/sie/es würde	sie würden	

COMMANDS sei! seid! seien Sie!

PRESENT PARTICIPLE seiend

Usage

„Warst du das?“	*“Was that you?”*
„Ich war es nicht.“	*“It wasn’t me.”*
Wo ist der Arzt?	*Where is the doctor?*
Was sind die Ursachen des Terrorismus?	*What are the causes of terrorism?*
Unser Wagen ist neu.	*Our car is new.*
Das Kleid ist teuer.	*The dress is expensive.*
Dieser Mann ist Herr Littner.	*This man is Mr. Littner.*
Diese CD von Anne Sophie-Mutter ist fantastisch.	*This CD by Anne Sophie-Mutter is fantastic.*
Theodor ist Mechaniker.	*Theodor is a mechanic.*
Auf dem Eis ist es besonders kalt.	*On the ice, it is especially cold.*
Die Brötchen sind lecker.	*The rolls are delicious.*
„Bist du heute Abend zu Hause?“	*“Will you be at home this evening?”*
„Nein, ich bin bei der Arbeit.“	*“No, I’ll be at work.”*
Zwei mal drei ist sechs.	*Two times three is six.*

399

senden *to send; broadcast, transmit*

sendet · sandte/sendete · gesandt/gesendet mixed verb or regular weak verb

PRESENT

ich sende	wir senden
du sendest	ihr sendet
Sie senden	Sie senden
er/sie/es sendet	sie senden

SIMPLE PAST

ich sandte/sendete	wir sandten/sendeten
du sandtest/sendetest	ihr sandtet/sendetet
Sie sandten/sendeten	Sie sandten/sendeten
er/sie/es sandte/sendete	sie sandten/sendeten

FUTURE

ich werde	wir werden	senden
du wirst	ihr werdet	
Sie werden	Sie werden	
er/sie/es wird	sie werden	

PRESENT SUBJUNCTIVE I

ich sende	wir senden
du sendest	ihr sendet
Sie senden	Sie senden
er/sie/es sende	sie senden

PRESENT SUBJUNCTIVE II

ich sendete	wir sendeten
du sendetest	ihr sendetet
Sie sendeten	Sie sendeten
er/sie/es sendete	sie sendeten

FUTURE SUBJUNCTIVE I

ich werde	wir werden	senden
du werdest	ihr werdet	
Sie werden	Sie werden	
er/sie/es werde	sie werden	

FUTURE SUBJUNCTIVE II

ich würde	wir würden	senden
du würdest	ihr würdet	
Sie würden	Sie würden	
er/sie/es würde	sie würden	

PRESENT PERFECT

ich habe	wir haben	gesandt/gesendet
du hast	ihr habt	
Sie haben	Sie haben	
er/sie/es hat	sie haben	

PAST PERFECT

ich hatte	wir hatten	gesandt/gesendet
du hattest	ihr hattet	
Sie hatten	Sie hatten	
er/sie/es hatte	sie hatten	

FUTURE PERFECT

ich werde	wir werden	gesandt haben OR gesendet haben
du wirst	ihr werdet	
Sie werden	Sie werden	
er/sie/es wird	sie werden	

PAST SUBJUNCTIVE I

ich habe	wir haben	gesandt/gesendet
du habest	ihr habet	
Sie haben	Sie haben	
er/sie/es habe	sie haben	

PAST SUBJUNCTIVE II

ich hätte	wir hätten	gesandt/gesendet
du hättest	ihr hättet	
Sie hätten	Sie hätten	
er/sie/es hätte	sie hätten	

FUTURE PERFECT SUBJUNCTIVE I

ich werde	wir werden	gesandt haben OR gesendet haben
du werdest	ihr werdet	
Sie werden	Sie werden	
er/sie/es werde	sie werden	

FUTURE PERFECT SUBJUNCTIVE II

ich würde	wir würden	gesandt haben OR gesendet haben
du würdest	ihr würdet	
Sie würden	Sie würden	
er/sie/es würde	sie würden	

COMMANDS sende! sendet! senden Sie!

PRESENT PARTICIPLE sendend

NOTE When **senden** means "to broadcast," it is regular weak: **sendete, gesendet**.

Usage

Larissa will uns die User-Dateien senden.	*Larissa wants to send us the user files.*
Wohin kann man Pfandflaschen senden?	*Where can we send the return bottles?*
Der Notarzt wurde gesandt.	*The doctor was sent.*
Hiermit senden wir die Waren.	*We are sending the goods herewith.*
Voriges Jahr sandte ihn der Minister ins Ausland.	*Last year, the minister sent him abroad.*
Senden Sie die Abbildung bitte per Fax.	*Please send the illustration by fax.*
Herbert ist letzte Woche zu uns gesandt worden.	*Herbert was dispatched to us last week.*
Hast du das Buch schon gesandt?	*Have you already sent the book?*
Du kannst mir eine SMS-Nachricht per Email senden.	*You can send me a text message via e-mail.*
Diese Rundfunkstation sendet Musik rund um die Uhr.	*This radio station broadcasts music around the clock.*

RELATED VERBS ab·senden, aus·senden, ein·senden, entsenden, nach·senden, übersenden, versenden, zurück·senden, zu·senden regular weak verb **setzt · setzte · gesetzt**

PRESENT		PRESENT PERFECT		
ich setze	wir setzen	ich habe	wir haben	gesetzt
du setzt	ihr setzt	du hast	ihr habt	
Sie setzen	Sie setzen	Sie haben	Sie haben	
er/sie/es setzt	sie setzen	er/sie/es hat	sie haben	

SIMPLE PAST		PAST PERFECT		
ich setzte	wir setzten	ich hatte	wir hatten	gesetzt
du setztest	ihr setztet	du hattest	ihr hattet	
Sie setzten	Sie setzten	Sie hatten	Sie hatten	
er/sie/es setzte	sie setzten	er/sie/es hatte	sie hatten	

FUTURE			FUTURE PERFECT		
ich werde	wir werden	setzen	ich werde	wir werden	gesetzt haben
du wirst	ihr werdet		du wirst	ihr werdet	
Sie werden	Sie werden		Sie werden	Sie werden	
er/sie/es wird	sie werden		er/sie/es wird	sie werden	

PRESENT SUBJUNCTIVE I		PAST SUBJUNCTIVE I		
ich setze	wir setzen	ich habe	wir haben	gesetzt
du setzest	ihr setzet	du habest	ihr habet	
Sie setzen	Sie setzen	Sie haben	Sie haben	
er/sie/es setze	sie setzen	er/sie/es habe	sie haben	

PRESENT SUBJUNCTIVE II		PAST SUBJUNCTIVE II		
ich setzte	wir setzten	ich hätte	wir hätten	gesetzt
du setztest	ihr setztet	du hättest	ihr hättet	
Sie setzten	Sie setzten	Sie hätten	Sie hätten	
er/sie/es setzte	sie setzten	er/sie/es hätte	sie hätten	

FUTURE SUBJUNCTIVE I			FUTURE PERFECT SUBJUNCTIVE I		
ich werde	wir werden	setzen	ich werde	wir werden	gesetzt haben
du werdest	ihr werdet		du werdest	ihr werdet	
Sie werden	Sie werden		Sie werden	Sie werden	
er/sie/es werde	sie werden		er/sie/es werde	sie werden	

FUTURE SUBJUNCTIVE II			FUTURE PERFECT SUBJUNCTIVE II		
ich würde	wir würden	setzen	ich würde	wir würden	gesetzt haben
du würdest	ihr würdet		du würdest	ihr würdet	
Sie würden	Sie würden		Sie würden	Sie würden	
er/sie/es würde	sie würden		er/sie/es würde	sie würden	

COMMANDS setz(e)! setzt! setzen Sie!

PRESENT PARTICIPLE setzend

Usage

Die Frist wurde vom Gericht gesetzt.	*The deadline was set by the court.*
Hast du die Option Papiergröße A4 gesetzt?	*Did you set the paper size option to A4?*
Euer Vater muss euch immer Grenzen gesetzt haben.	*Your father must have always set limits for you.*
Otto II. wurde 976 auf den Thron gesetzt.	*Otto II was placed on the throne in 976.*
Ich setze keinen Fuß mehr über die Schwelle ihrer Wohnung.	*I won't set foot in her house again.*
Ich setze heute keinen Fuß vor die Tür, es ist zu kalt!	*I'm not setting foot outside today; it's too cold!*
Drei Knaben hatten die alte Scheune in Brand gesetzt.	*Three lads had set fire to the old barn.*
Frank setzt seine Hoffnungen auf eine neuere Technologie.	*Frank is placing his hopes on a newer technology.*

RELATED VERBS ab·setzen, an·setzen, auf·setzen, aus·setzen, bei·setzen, besetzen, durchsetzen, durch·setzen, entgegen·setzen, entsetzen, ersetzen, fest·setzen, fort·setzen, frei·setzen, gleich·setzen, herab·setzen, hin·setzen, nach·setzen, nieder·setzen, strafversetzen, über·setzen, um·besetzen, um·setzen, untersetzen, unter·setzen, versetzen, voraus·setzen, vor·setzen, weg·setzen, widersetzen, zersetzen, zurecht·setzen, zurück·setzen, zurück·versetzen, zusammen·setzen, zu·setzen; *see also* **ein·setzen** (137), **übersetzen** (463)

TOP 50 VERB ☞

setzen *to set, place, put; sit* (someone) *(down); plant; wager; compose*

setzt · setzte · gesetzt regular weak verb

MORE USAGE SENTENCES WITH setzen

Somit werden verschiedene psychische Mechanismen in Gang gesetzt. — *Thus a variety of psychic mechanisms is set in motion.*
Am 18. September 1502 setzte Columbus wieder an Land. — *On September 18, 1502, Columbus put ashore again.*
Der König wird durch dieses Manöver matt gesetzt. (*chess game*) — *The king is put in check with this maneuver.*
John Hancock war der erste, der seine Unterschrift unter das Dokument setzte. — *John Hancock was the first to affix his signature to the document.*
Setzen Sie ein Komma vor dem Wort „um". — *Place a comma before the word "um."*
Wer hat meinen Namen auf die Liste gesetzt? — *Who put my name on the list?*
Das Gedicht wurde von Samuel Barber in Musik gesetzt. — *The poem was set to music by Samuel Barber.*
Mareike hat das Baby auf das Sofa gesetzt. — *Mareike sat the baby on the sofa.*
Pfingstrosen sollte man nicht zu tief in den Boden setzen. — *Peonies shouldn't be planted too deeply in the ground.*
Heinz hat auf das richtige Pferd gesetzt und gewonnen. — *Heinz wagered on the right horse and won.*
Wird dieser Text in einer von Hermann Zapf entworfenen Schrift gesetzt werden? — *Will this text be set in a typeface designed by Hermann Zapf?*
Die Sonate wurde für Fagott und Klavier gesetzt. — *The sonata was composed for bassoon and piano.*

sich setzen *to sit (down), seat oneself; settle*

Zwölf Personen haben sich an den Tisch gesetzt. — *Twelve people sat down at the table.*
Der Mann hatte die Arme ausgestreckt, als ob er sich auf den Boden setzen wollte. — *The man had stretched out his arms as though he wanted to sit down on the ground.*
Setzt euch zu uns. — *Sit down with us.*
Christian setzte sich ihr gegenüber. — *Christian sat down across from her.*
Herr Milek setzte sich im Garten und beobachtete die Spatzen. — *Mr. Milek sat down in the garden and watched the sparrows.*
Feiner Staub setzte sich in die Poren der Oberfläche. — *Fine dust settled into the surface pores.*
Feuchtigkeit setzt sich in die Wände und führt zu Schimmel. — *Moisture settles in the walls and causes mold to form.*

setzen (with **sein**) *to jump, leap, cross*

Der Dobermann ist aus dem Stand über den Zaun gesetzt. — *The Doberman jumped over the fence in a single bound.*
Wir sind mit einem Nachen über den Fluss gesetzt. — *We crossed the river on a dinghy.*

IDIOMATIC EXPRESSIONS

Nach zehn Minuten setzte sich Weigand an die Spitze. — *Weigand took the lead after 10 minutes.*
Herr Eichholz wird sich mit Ihnen in Verbindung setzen. — *Mr. Eichholz will get in touch with you.*
Der Geldautomat wurde außer Betrieb gesetzt. — *The automatic teller machine was taken out of service.*
Gesetzt den Fall, Sie wären Präsident. Was würden Sie tun? — *Suppose you were president. What would you do?*
Man hat mir eine letzte Frist gesetzt. — *I've been given a final deadline.*
Die Kosten können auf meine Rechnung gesetzt werden. — *The expenses can be charged to my account.*
Tucholsky setzte sein gesamtes Vermögen aufs Spiel. — *Tucholsky risked his entire fortune.*
Ich setze mein Leben daran! — *I'll stake my life on it!*
Er sagte, er würde alles daran setzen, euch zu helfen. — *He said he would do his utmost to help you.*
Die Regelung wurde vom Ministerium außer Kraft gesetzt. — *The regulation was repealed by the ministry.*
Die Dorfbewohner setzten sich zur Wehr gegen den Feind. — *The village residents took a stand against the enemy.*
Im Juni wurde Lars als Assistent an die Stelle von Pawel gesetzt. — *In June, Lars replaced Pawel as assistant.*

regular weak verb **sichert · sicherte · gesichert**

PRESENT

ich sichere	wir sichern
du sicherst	ihr sichert
Sie sichern	Sie sichern
er/sie/es sichert	sie sichern

PRESENT PERFECT

ich habe	wir haben	gesichert
du hast	ihr habt	
Sie haben	Sie haben	
er/sie/es hat	sie haben	

SIMPLE PAST

ich sicherte	wir sicherten
du sichertest	ihr sichertet
Sie sicherten	Sie sicherten
er/sie/es sicherte	sie sicherten

PAST PERFECT

ich hatte	wir hatten	gesichert
du hattest	ihr hattet	
Sie hatten	Sie hatten	
er/sie/es hatte	sie hatten	

FUTURE

ich werde	wir werden	sichern
du wirst	ihr werdet	
Sie werden	Sie werden	
er/sie/es wird	sie werden	

FUTURE PERFECT

ich werde	wir werden	gesichert haben
du wirst	ihr werdet	
Sie werden	Sie werden	
er/sie/es wird	sie werden	

PRESENT SUBJUNCTIVE I

ich sichere	wir sichern
du sicherst	ihr sichert
Sie sichern	Sie sichern
er/sie/es sichere	sie sichern

PAST SUBJUNCTIVE I

ich habe	wir haben	gesichert
du habest	ihr habet	
Sie haben	Sie haben	
er/sie/es habe	sie haben	

PRESENT SUBJUNCTIVE II

ich sicherte	wir sicherten
du sichertest	ihr sichertet
Sie sicherten	Sie sicherten
er/sie/es sicherte	sie sicherten

PAST SUBJUNCTIVE II

ich hätte	wir hätten	gesichert
du hättest	ihr hättet	
Sie hätten	Sie hätten	
er/sie/es hätte	sie hätten	

FUTURE SUBJUNCTIVE I

ich werde	wir werden	sichern
du werdest	ihr werdet	
Sie werden	Sie werden	
er/sie/es werde	sie werden	

FUTURE PERFECT SUBJUNCTIVE I

ich werde	wir werden	gesichert haben
du werdest	ihr werdet	
Sie werden	Sie werden	
er/sie/es werde	sie werden	

FUTURE SUBJUNCTIVE II

ich würde	wir würden	sichern
du würdest	ihr würdet	
Sie würden	Sie würden	
er/sie/es würde	sie würden	

FUTURE PERFECT SUBJUNCTIVE II

ich würde	wir würden	gesichert haben
du würdest	ihr würdet	
Sie würden	Sie würden	
er/sie/es würde	sie würden	

COMMANDS sichere! sichert! sichern Sie!

PRESENT PARTICIPLE sichernd

Usage

Wie sind die Daten gesichert worden?	*How was the data protected?*
Wann wurde das Areal endlich gesichert?	*When was the area finally made secure?*
Soll er die Pistole nicht gesichert haben?	*Isn't he supposed to have put the pistol on "safe"?*
Das Fundament wurde vorgestern gesichert.	*The foundation was secured two days ago.*
Bürgermeister von Schnurbusch sichert Unterstützung für seine Pläne.	*Mayor von Schnurbusch is lining up support for his plans.*
War die Tür schon gesichert worden?	*Had the door already been secured?*
Der jüngere Detektiv sichert die Fingerabdrücke.	*The younger detective is obtaining the fingerprints.*
Die Arbeiter sichern die Fracht auf dem Schiff.	*The workers are securing the cargo on the ship.*
Das Geld sichert uns eine gute Zukunft.	*The money will ensure a good future for us.*
Eine ambivalente Wirklichkeit sichert dem Dichter schöpferische Kraft.	*An ambivalent reality ensures the poet creative energy.*
Nur eine Biopsie kann die Diagnose des Karzinoms sichern.	*Only a biopsy can confirm the cancer diagnosis.*

RELATED VERBS ab·sichern, entsichern, rückversichern, zu·sichern; *see also* **versichern** (499)

402 sieden *to boil, seethe*

siedet · siedete/sott · gesiedet/gesotten — regular weak verb or strong verb

PRESENT

ich siede	wir sieden
du siedest	ihr siedet
Sie sieden	Sie sieden
er/sie/es siedet	sie sieden

SIMPLE PAST

ich siedete/sott	wir siedeten/sotten
du siedetest/sottest	ihr siedetet/sottet
Sie siedeten/sotten	Sie siedeten/sotten
er/sie/es siedete/sott	sie siedeten/sotten

FUTURE

ich werde	wir werden	sieden
du wirst	ihr werdet	
Sie werden	Sie werden	
er/sie/es wird	sie werden	

PRESENT SUBJUNCTIVE I

ich siede	wir sieden
du siedest	ihr siedet
Sie sieden	Sie sieden
er/sie/es siede	sie sieden

PRESENT SUBJUNCTIVE II

ich siedete/sötte	wir siedeten/sötten
du siedetest/söttest	ihr siedetet/söttet
Sie siedeten/sötten	Sie siedeten/sötten
er/sie/es siedete/sötte	sie siedeten/sötten

FUTURE SUBJUNCTIVE I

ich werde	wir werden	sieden
du werdest	ihr werdet	
Sie werden	Sie werden	
er/sie/es werde	sie werden	

FUTURE SUBJUNCTIVE II

ich würde	wir würden	sieden
du würdest	ihr würdet	
Sie würden	Sie würden	
er/sie/es würde	sie würden	

PRESENT PERFECT

ich habe	wir haben	gesiedet/gesotten
du hast	ihr habt	
Sie haben	Sie haben	
er/sie/es hat	sie haben	

PAST PERFECT

ich hatte	wir hatten	gesiedet/gesotten
du hattest	ihr hattet	
Sie hatten	Sie hatten	
er/sie/es hatte	sie hatten	

FUTURE PERFECT

ich werde	wir werden	gesiedet haben
du wirst	ihr werdet	OR
Sie werden	Sie werden	gesotten haben
er/sie/es wird	sie werden	

PAST SUBJUNCTIVE I

ich habe	wir haben	gesiedet/gesotten
du habest	ihr habet	
Sie haben	Sie haben	
er/sie/es habe	sie haben	

PAST SUBJUNCTIVE II

ich hätte	wir hätten	gesiedet/gesotten
du hättest	ihr hättet	
Sie hätten	Sie hätten	
er/sie/es hätte	sie hätten	

FUTURE PERFECT SUBJUNCTIVE I

ich werde	wir werden	gesiedet haben
du werdest	ihr werdet	OR
Sie werden	Sie werden	gesotten haben
er/sie/es werde	sie werden	

FUTURE PERFECT SUBJUNCTIVE II

ich würde	wir würden	gesiedet haben
du würdest	ihr würdet	OR
Sie würden	Sie würden	gesotten haben
er/sie/es würde	sie würden	

COMMANDS siede! siedet! sieden Sie!

PRESENT PARTICIPLE siedend

NOTE Both strong and regular weak forms of **sieden** are correct, although the strong forms tend to be older.

Usage

Bei welcher Temperatur siedet dieser Stoff?	*At what temperature does this compound boil?*
Die Sonne hat ihn gesotten. (HEYM)	*The sun boiled it.*
Wasser siedet bei 100 Grad Celsius.	*Water boils at 100 degrees Celsius.*
Wasser mit Zucker sieden lassen. (RECIPE)	*Let the water and sugar come to a boil.*
Siedet die Flüssigkeit im Kühler?	*Is the fluid in the radiator boiling?*
Sein Blut siedete.	*His blood boiled.*
… als sötte besagter Lehrherr weiche Eier. (E.T.A. HOFFMANN)	*… as though aforesaid master were soft-boiling eggs.*
Das Wasser in diesem Hotel ist entweder siedend heiß oder eiskalt.	*The water at this hotel is either boiling hot or ice cold.*
Der Ritter siedete vor Wut.	*The knight seethed with rage.*
Warum hat der Dirigent immer vor Zorn gesiedet?	*Why was the conductor always fuming with anger?*

RELATED VERB über·sieden

strong verb **singt · sang · gesungen**

PRESENT

ich singe	wir singen
du singst	ihr singt
Sie singen	Sie singen
er/sie/es singt	sie singen

PRESENT PERFECT

ich habe	wir haben	gesungen
du hast	ihr habt	
Sie haben	Sie haben	
er/sie/es hat	sie haben	

SIMPLE PAST

ich sang	wir sangen
du sangst	ihr sangt
Sie sangen	Sie sangen
er/sie/es sang	sie sangen

PAST PERFECT

ich hatte	wir hatten	gesungen
du hattest	ihr hattet	
Sie hatten	Sie hatten	
er/sie/es hatte	sie hatten	

FUTURE

ich werde	wir werden	singen
du wirst	ihr werdet	
Sie werden	Sie werden	
er/sie/es wird	sie werden	

FUTURE PERFECT

ich werde	wir werden	gesungen haben
du wirst	ihr werdet	
Sie werden	Sie werden	
er/sie/es wird	sie werden	

PRESENT SUBJUNCTIVE I

ich singe	wir singen
du singest	ihr singet
Sie singen	Sie singen
er/sie/es singe	sie singen

PAST SUBJUNCTIVE I

ich habe	wir haben	gesungen
du habest	ihr habet	
Sie haben	Sie haben	
er/sie/es habe	sie haben	

PRESENT SUBJUNCTIVE II

ich sänge	wir sängen
du sängest	ihr sänget
Sie sängen	Sie sängen
er/sie/es sänge	sie sängen

PAST SUBJUNCTIVE II

ich hätte	wir hätten	gesungen
du hättest	ihr hättet	
Sie hätten	Sie hätten	
er/sie/es hätte	sie hätten	

FUTURE SUBJUNCTIVE I

ich werde	wir werden	singen
du werdest	ihr werdet	
Sie werden	Sie werden	
er/sie/es werde	sie werden	

FUTURE PERFECT SUBJUNCTIVE I

ich werde	wir werden	gesungen haben
du werdest	ihr werdet	
Sie werden	Sie werden	
er/sie/es werde	sie werden	

FUTURE SUBJUNCTIVE II

ich würde	wir würden	singen
du würdest	ihr würdet	
Sie würden	Sie würden	
er/sie/es würde	sie würden	

FUTURE PERFECT SUBJUNCTIVE II

ich würde	wir würden	gesungen haben
du würdest	ihr würdet	
Sie würden	Sie würden	
er/sie/es würde	sie würden	

COMMANDS sing(e)! singt! singen Sie!

PRESENT PARTICIPLE singend

Usage

Sie will in dieser Oper gesungen haben.	*She claims to have sung in that opera.*
Lasst uns singen!	*Let us sing!*
Könntest du bitte nicht singen?	*Could you please not sing?*
Die Mutter hat ihren Kindern ein Lied gesungen.	*The mother sang her children a song.*
Ihr Herz sang vor Freude.	*Her heart sang with joy.*
Werner und Edwina singen gern in der Dusche.	*Werner and Edwina like singing in the shower.*
In der Kneipe haben die Männer laut gesungen.	*In the pub, the men sang loudly.*
Früher sang man viel mehr auf Latein.	*People used to sing more in Latin.*
Es machte ihr viel Spaß, im Chor zu singen.	*She had great fun singing in the choir.*
Mein Hauptgrund zu singen war das schöne Wetter.	*My main reason for singing was the beautiful weather.*
Mein Bruder fängt immer frühmorgens an zu singen.	*My brother always breaks into song early in the morning.*
Habt ihr mit Tante Irene singen können?	*Were you able to sing with Aunt Irene?*
Rudolf singt immer sein eigenes Lob. (*figurative*)	*Rudolf is always tooting his own horn.*

RELATED VERBS ab·singen, an·singen, aus·singen, besingen, ein·singen, lob(·)singen, mit·singen, vor·singen

404 sinken *to sink, go down, descend, fall*

sinkt · sank · gesunken strong verb

PRESENT

ich sinke	wir sinken
du sinkst	ihr sinkt
Sie sinken	Sie sinken
er/sie/es sinkt	sie sinken

SIMPLE PAST

ich sank	wir sanken
du sankst	ihr sankt
Sie sanken	Sie sanken
er/sie/es sank	sie sanken

FUTURE

ich werde	wir werden	sinken
du wirst	ihr werdet	
Sie werden	Sie werden	
er/sie/es wird	sie werden	

PRESENT SUBJUNCTIVE I

ich sinke	wir sinken
du sinkest	ihr sinket
Sie sinken	Sie sinken
er/sie/es sinke	sie sinken

PRESENT SUBJUNCTIVE II

ich sänke	wir sänken
du sänkest	ihr sänket
Sie sänken	Sie sänken
er/sie/es sänke	sie sänken

FUTURE SUBJUNCTIVE I

ich werde	wir werden	sinken
du werdest	ihr werdet	
Sie werden	Sie werden	
er/sie/es werde	sie werden	

FUTURE SUBJUNCTIVE II

ich würde	wir würden	sinken
du würdest	ihr würdet	
Sie würden	Sie würden	
er/sie/es würde	sie würden	

PRESENT PERFECT

ich bin	wir sind	gesunken
du bist	ihr seid	
Sie sind	Sie sind	
er/sie/es ist	sie sind	

PAST PERFECT

ich war	wir waren	gesunken
du warst	ihr wart	
Sie waren	Sie waren	
er/sie/es war	sie waren	

FUTURE PERFECT

ich werde	wir werden	gesunken sein
du wirst	ihr werdet	
Sie werden	Sie werden	
er/sie/es wird	sie werden	

PAST SUBJUNCTIVE I

ich sei	wir seien	gesunken
du seiest	ihr seiet	
Sie seien	Sie seien	
er/sie/es sei	sie seien	

PAST SUBJUNCTIVE II

ich wäre	wir wären	gesunken
du wärest	ihr wäret	
Sie wären	Sie wären	
er/sie/es wäre	sie wären	

FUTURE PERFECT SUBJUNCTIVE I

ich werde	wir werden	gesunken sein
du werdest	ihr werdet	
Sie werden	Sie werden	
er/sie/es werde	sie werden	

FUTURE PERFECT SUBJUNCTIVE II

ich würde	wir würden	gesunken sein
du würdest	ihr würdet	
Sie würden	Sie würden	
er/sie/es würde	sie würden	

COMMANDS sink(e)! sinkt! sinken Sie!

PRESENT PARTICIPLE sinkend

Usage

Venedig sinkt ins Meer. — *Venice is sinking into the sea.*
Katrin ist ins Sofa gesunken und eingeschlafen. — *Katrin sank into the sofa and fell asleep.*
Die Küstenwache konnte die Taucher retten, deren Boot gesunken war. — *The coast guard rescued the divers whose boat had sunk.*
Die Leiche des Opfers sank samt Auto in den See. — *The victim's body sank with the car into the lake.*
Die Sonne sank am Horizont. — *The sun went down over the horizon.*
Die *Titanic* rammte einen Eisberg und sank. — *The* Titanic *rammed an iceberg and sank.*
Warum sinkt der Schwamm? — *Why is the sponge sinking?*
Der unerfahrene Snowboarder sank in den tiefen Schnee. — *The inexperienced snowboarder sank into the deep snow.*
Der Luftballon sank zu Boden. — *The air balloon descended to the ground.*
Wann werden die Benzinpreise endlich sinken? — *When will gasoline prices finally fall?*
Die Qualität der Produkte ist im letzten Jahr gesunken. — *The quality of the products has gone down in the last year.*

RELATED VERBS ab·sinken, ein·sinken, entsinken, nieder·sinken, um·sinken, unter·sinken, versinken, zurück·sinken, zusammen·sinken strong verb **sinnt · sann · gesonnen**

PRESENT

ich sinne	wir sinnen
du sinnst	ihr sinnt
Sie sinnen	Sie sinnen
er/sie/es sinnt	sie sinnen

SIMPLE PAST

ich sann	wir sannen
du sannst	ihr sannt
Sie sannen	Sie sannen
er/sie/es sann	sie sannen

FUTURE

ich werde	wir werden	sinnen
du wirst	ihr werdet	
Sie werden	Sie werden	
er/sie/es wird	sie werden	

PRESENT SUBJUNCTIVE I

ich sinne	wir sinnen
du sinnest	ihr sinnet
Sie sinnen	Sie sinnen
er/sie/es sinne	sie sinnen

PRESENT SUBJUNCTIVE II

ich sänne/sönne	wir sännen/sönnen
du sännest/sönnest	ihr sännet/sönnet
Sie sännen/sönnen	Sie sännen/sönnen
er/sie/es sänne/sönne	sie sännen/sönnen

FUTURE SUBJUNCTIVE I

ich werde	wir werden	sinnen
du werdest	ihr werdet	
Sie werden	Sie werden	
er/sie/es werde	sie werden	

FUTURE SUBJUNCTIVE II

ich würde	wir würden	sinnen
du würdest	ihr würdet	
Sie würden	Sie würden	
er/sie/es würde	sie würden	

PRESENT PERFECT

ich habe	wir haben	gesonnen
du hast	ihr habt	
Sie haben	Sie haben	
er/sie/es hat	sie haben	

PAST PERFECT

ich hatte	wir hatten	gesonnen
du hattest	ihr hattet	
Sie hatten	Sie hatten	
er/sie/es hatte	sie hatten	

FUTURE PERFECT

ich werde	wir werden	gesonnen haben
du wirst	ihr werdet	
Sie werden	Sie werden	
er/sie/es wird	sie werden	

PAST SUBJUNCTIVE I

ich habe	wir haben	gesonnen
du habest	ihr habet	
Sie haben	Sie haben	
er/sie/es habe	sie haben	

PAST SUBJUNCTIVE II

ich hätte	wir hätten	gesonnen
du hättest	ihr hättet	
Sie hätten	Sie hätten	
er/sie/es hätte	sie hätten	

FUTURE PERFECT SUBJUNCTIVE I

ich werde	wir werden	gesonnen haben
du werdest	ihr werdet	
Sie werden	Sie werden	
er/sie/es werde	sie werden	

FUTURE PERFECT SUBJUNCTIVE II

ich würde	wir würden	gesonnen haben
du würdest	ihr würdet	
Sie würden	Sie würden	
er/sie/es würde	sie würden	

COMMANDS sinn(e)! sinnt! sinnen Sie!

PRESENT PARTICIPLE sinnend

NOTE The present subjunctive II forms **sönne**, etc. are archaic.

Usage

Die Vorstandsmitglieder sinnen auf eine Lösung.	*The members of the board are deliberating a solution.*
Der Protagonist des Romans sann auf Mord.	*The protagonist of the novel was contemplating murder.*
Das Paar sinnt auf Hochzeit.	*The couple is thinking about a wedding.*
Die Konzerne sinnen auf weitere Investitionen.	*The companies are weighing further investments.*
Alle Kandidaten sinnen, wie die Wahl zu gewinnen ist.	*All candidates are studying how to win the election.*
Sinnen die Frauen auf Rache?	*Are the women plotting revenge?*
Die Bauern sannen auf einen Plan.	*The peasants were thinking up a plan.*
Der Bürgermeister hat auf eine Reise nach Waltham Abbey gesonnen.	*The mayor considered a trip to Waltham Abbey.*
Herr Petersen sinnt seit sieben Jahren darauf.	*Mr. Petersen has been reflecting on that for seven years.*
Der Präsident war nicht gesonnen, sich mit den Umweltschützern zu unterhalten.	*The president wasn't inclined to dialog with the environmentalists.*

RELATED VERBS besinnen, entsinnen, ersinnen, nach·sinnen

sitzen *to be sitting/seated, be situated; be in session*

sitzt · saß · gesessen strong verb

MORE USAGE SENTENCES WITH sitzen

Samuel sitzt auf dem Balkon und raucht eine Zigarette. *Samuel is sitting on the balcony smoking a cigarette.*
Heiner sitzt am Computer und schreibt Emails. *Heiner is sitting at the computer and writing e-mails.*
An der Grenze mussten die Touristen zwei Stunden im Bus sitzen. *At the border, the tourists had to sit on the bus for two hours.*
Sitz doch gerade! *Sit up straight!*
Wir mussten im Bus dicht aufeinander sitzen. *We had to sit really close together on the bus.*
Am Lagerfeuer haben wir beieinander gesessen und Geschichten erzählt. *We sat around the campfire together and told stories.*
Ich will vorne sitzen, du hast gestern vorne gesessen. *I want to sit up front; you sat up front yesterday.*
Norbert sitzt im Ausschuss für Landwirtschaft. *Norbert is on the agriculture committee.*
Franz-Josef sitzt seit 2002 im Gemeinderat. *Franz-Josef has had a seat on the town council since 2002.*
BMW sitzt in München. *BMW is based in Munich.*
Das Parlament sitzt von Oktober bis Juni. *The parliament is in session from October to June.*

sitzen bleiben *to remain seated*

Bleiben Sie bitte sitzen, bis die Maschine zum Stillstand gekommen ist. *Please remain seated until the aircraft has come to a complete stop.*
Wir mussten drei Stunden sitzen bleiben. *We had to stay seated for three hours.*

es sitzt sich (impersonal) *sitting is*

Hier sitzt es sich bequem. *This seat is comfortable. / I am comfortable sitting here.*
Ach, schau mal, hier sitzt es sich gut in der dritten Reihe! *Oh, look, here are some good seats in the third row!*

sitzen *to fit* (of clothing)

Ingrid freute sich, dass ihre neue Bluse perfekt saß. *Ingrid was happy that her new blouse fit perfectly.*
Der Mantel steht dir gut, aber der Hut sitzt nicht. *The coat looks good on you, but the hat isn't on straight.*
Die Uniform sitzt ihm wie angegossen. *The uniform fits him like a glove.*

IDIOMATIC EXPRESSIONS

Die Truppen saßen im Kessel. *The troops were surrounded.*
Greenpeace sitzt den Ölkonzernen auf dem Nacken. *Greenpeace is a pain in the neck to the oil companies.*
Die Familie saß bei Tisch und redete miteinander. *The family sat at the table eating and talking.*
Der Schmerz saß noch tief. *The pain was still deep-seated.*
Die Angst hatte ihm eine lange Zeit in den Knochen gesessen. *The fear had gripped him to the marrow for a long time.*
Billy the Kid saß einige Zeit in Lincoln County/New Mexiko im Gefängnis. *Billy the Kid served some time in prison in Lincoln County, New Mexico.*
Hans und Ingrid hatten sich verlobt, aber er ließ sie sitzen und fand eine andere. *Hans and Ingrid had gotten engaged, but he walked out on her and hooked up with another woman.*
Der Trainer übt mit dem Hund, bis das erwünschte Verhalten sitzt. *The trainer practices with the dog until the desired behavior becomes ingrained.*
Erich sitzt den ganzen Tag über seinen Büchern. *Erich pores over his books all day long.*
Jost sitzt zwischen Baum und Borke. *Jost is stuck between a rock and a hard place.*
Willi sitzt in der Klemme und ich will ihm helfen. *Willi is in a tight spot, and I want to help him.*
Im Augenblick sitzen die Politiker zwischen zwei Stühlen. *For the time being, the politicians will sit on the fence.*
Zum größten Teil führen wir heutzutage eine sitzende Lebensweise. *For the most part, we lead sedentary lives nowadays.*

strong verb **sitzt · saß · gesessen**

PRESENT		PRESENT PERFECT		
ich sitze	wir sitzen	ich habe	wir haben	gesessen
du sitzt	ihr sitzt	du hast	ihr habt	
Sie sitzen	Sie sitzen	Sie haben	Sie haben	
er/sie/es sitzt	sie sitzen	er/sie/es hat	sie haben	

SIMPLE PAST		PAST PERFECT		
ich saß	wir saßen	ich hatte	wir hatten	gesessen
du saßest	ihr saßt	du hattest	ihr hattet	
Sie saßen	Sie saßen	Sie hatten	Sie hatten	
er/sie/es saß	sie saßen	er/sie/es hatte	sie hatten	

FUTURE			FUTURE PERFECT		
ich werde	wir werden	sitzen	ich werde	wir werden	gesessen haben
du wirst	ihr werdet		du wirst	ihr werdet	
Sie werden	Sie werden		Sie werden	Sie werden	
er/sie/es wird	sie werden		er/sie/es wird	sie werden	

PRESENT SUBJUNCTIVE I		PAST SUBJUNCTIVE I		
ich sitze	wir sitzen	ich habe	wir haben	gesessen
du sitzest	ihr sitzet	du habest	ihr habet	
Sie sitzen	Sie sitzen	Sie haben	Sie haben	
er/sie/es sitze	sie sitzen	er/sie/es habe	sie haben	

PRESENT SUBJUNCTIVE II		PAST SUBJUNCTIVE II		
ich säße	wir säßen	ich hätte	wir hätten	gesessen
du säßest	ihr säßet	du hättest	ihr hättet	
Sie säßen	Sie säßen	Sie hätten	Sie hätten	
er/sie/es säße	sie säßen	er/sie/es hätte	sie hätten	

FUTURE SUBJUNCTIVE I			FUTURE PERFECT SUBJUNCTIVE I		
ich werde	wir werden	sitzen	ich werde	wir werden	gesessen haben
du werdest	ihr werdet		du werdest	ihr werdet	
Sie werden	Sie werden		Sie werden	Sie werden	
er/sie/es werde	sie werden		er/sie/es werde	sie werden	

FUTURE SUBJUNCTIVE II			FUTURE PERFECT SUBJUNCTIVE II		
ich würde	wir würden	sitzen	ich würde	wir würden	gesessen haben
du würdest	ihr würdet		du würdest	ihr würdet	
Sie würden	Sie würden		Sie würden	Sie würden	
er/sie/es würde	sie würden		er/sie/es würde	sie würden	

COMMANDS sitz(e)! sitzt! sitzen Sie!

PRESENT PARTICIPLE sitzend

Usage

Kai sitzt schon im Auto und wartet. — *Kai is already sitting in the car waiting.*

Die Katze sitzt ängstlich hinter dem Sofa. — *The frightened cat is sitting behind the sofa.*

Im Hörsaal saßen über 500 Studentinnen und Studenten. — *Over 500 students were seated in the auditorium.*

Lola wollte immer auf einem Zauberteppich sitzen. — *Lola always wanted to sit on a magic carpet.*

Die Snowboarder sitzen in der Kneipe, weil es keinen Schnee gibt. — *The snowboarders are sitting in the pub because there's no snow.*

Wie lange wirst du vor dem Fernseher sitzen? — *How long are you going to sit in front of the television?*

Frau Werner saß im Bett und las einen Liebesroman. — *Mrs. Werner sat in bed and read a romance novel.*

Mein Kater sitzt gern vor dem Kamin. — *My cat likes to sit in front of the fireplace.*

Das Passagierschiff *Borussia* sitzt seit 1879 vor der Küste Spaniens auf dem Meeresboden. — *The passenger ship* Borussia *has been sitting on the ocean floor off the coast of Spain since 1879.*

RELATED VERBS ab·sitzen, auf·sitzen, aus·sitzen, dabei·sitzen, da·sitzen, durch·sitzen, ein·sitzen, fest·sitzen, gegenüber·sitzen, herum·sitzen, nach·sitzen, still·sitzen, vor·sitzen, zusammen·sitzen; *see also* **besitzen** (87)

407 sollen *should, to be supposed to*

soll · sollte · gesollt modal verb

PRESENT		PRESENT PERFECT		
ich soll	wir sollen	ich habe	wir haben	gesollt
du sollst	ihr sollt	du hast	ihr habt	
Sie sollen	Sie sollen	Sie haben	Sie haben	
er/sie/es soll	sie sollen	er/sie/es hat	sie haben	

SIMPLE PAST		PAST PERFECT		
ich sollte	wir sollten	ich hatte	wir hatten	gesollt
du solltest	ihr solltet	du hattest	ihr hattet	
Sie sollten	Sie sollten	Sie hatten	Sie hatten	
er/sie/es sollte	sie sollten	er/sie/es hatte	sie hatten	

FUTURE			FUTURE PERFECT		
ich werde	wir werden	sollen	ich werde	wir werden	gesollt haben
du wirst	ihr werdet		du wirst	ihr werdet	
Sie werden	Sie werden		Sie werden	Sie werden	
er/sie/es wird	sie werden		er/sie/es wird	sie werden	

PRESENT SUBJUNCTIVE I		PAST SUBJUNCTIVE I		
ich solle	wir sollen	ich habe	wir haben	gesollt
du sollest	ihr sollet	du habest	ihr habet	
Sie sollen	Sie sollen	Sie haben	Sie haben	
er/sie/es solle	sie sollen	er/sie/es habe	sie haben	

PRESENT SUBJUNCTIVE II		PAST SUBJUNCTIVE II		
ich sollte	wir sollten	ich hätte	wir hätten	gesollt
du solltest	ihr solltet	du hättest	ihr hättet	
Sie sollten	Sie sollten	Sie hätten	Sie hätten	
er/sie/es sollte	sie sollten	er/sie/es hätte	sie hätten	

FUTURE SUBJUNCTIVE I			FUTURE PERFECT SUBJUNCTIVE I		
ich werde	wir werden	sollen	ich werde	wir werden	gesollt haben
du werdest	ihr werdet		du werdest	ihr werdet	
Sie werden	Sie werden		Sie werden	Sie werden	
er/sie/es werde	sie werden		er/sie/es werde	sie werden	

FUTURE SUBJUNCTIVE II			FUTURE PERFECT SUBJUNCTIVE II		
ich würde	wir würden	sollen	ich würde	wir würden	gesollt haben
du würdest	ihr würdet		du würdest	ihr würdet	
Sie würden	Sie würden		Sie würden	Sie würden	
er/sie/es würde	sie würden		er/sie/es würde	sie würden	

COMMANDS —

PRESENT PARTICIPLE sollend

Usage

Wir sollten um acht Uhr da sein.	*We were supposed to be there at eight o'clock.*
Das Schiff sollte am 13. Dezember in New York eintreffen.	*The ship was supposed to arrive in New York on December 13.*
Basilikum soll gut in Töpfen wachsen.	*Basil is supposed to grow well in pots.*
Pläne für eine Implementierung sollen schon besprochen worden sein.	*Implementation plans are supposed to have been already discussed.*
Diese Substanzen sollen schnell wirken.	*These substances are supposed to work quickly.*
Augenzeugen sollen über die Ereignisse berichten.	*Eyewitnesses are supposed to report on the events.*
Mama sagt, du sollst den Tisch decken.	*Mama says you should set the table.*
Heiner soll seiner Frau eine Email schicken.	*Heiner is supposed to send his wife an e-mail.*
Sie sollten sich mehr bewegen!	*You should get more exercise!*
Drogemeyer soll letzte Woche 500 Mitarbeiter entlassen haben.	*Drogemeyer is said to have laid off 500 employees last week.*

RELATED VERBS mit·sollen, weiter·sollen, zurück·sollen

PRESENT

ich sorge	wir sorgen
du sorgst	ihr sorgt
Sie sorgen	Sie sorgen
er/sie/es sorgt	sie sorgen

SIMPLE PAST

ich sorgte	wir sorgten
du sorgtest	ihr sorgtet
Sie sorgten	Sie sorgten
er/sie/es sorgte	sie sorgten

FUTURE

ich werde	wir werden	sorgen
du wirst	ihr werdet	
Sie werden	Sie werden	
er/sie/es wird	sie werden	

PRESENT SUBJUNCTIVE I

ich sorge	wir sorgen
du sorgest	ihr sorget
Sie sorgen	Sie sorgen
er/sie/es sorge	sie sorgen

PRESENT SUBJUNCTIVE II

ich sorgte	wir sorgten
du sorgtest	ihr sorgtet
Sie sorgten	Sie sorgten
er/sie/es sorgte	sie sorgten

FUTURE SUBJUNCTIVE I

ich werde	wir werden	sorgen
du werdest	ihr werdet	
Sie werden	Sie werden	
er/sie/es werde	sie werden	

FUTURE SUBJUNCTIVE II

ich würde	wir würden	sorgen
du würdest	ihr würdet	
Sie würden	Sie würden	
er/sie/es würde	sie würden	

PRESENT PERFECT

ich habe	wir haben	gesorgt
du hast	ihr habt	
Sie haben	Sie haben	
er/sie/es hat	sie haben	

PAST PERFECT

ich hatte	wir hatten	gesorgt
du hattest	ihr hattet	
Sie hatten	Sie hatten	
er/sie/es hatte	sie hatten	

FUTURE PERFECT

ich werde	wir werden	gesorgt haben
du wirst	ihr werdet	
Sie werden	Sie werden	
er/sie/es wird	sie werden	

PAST SUBJUNCTIVE I

ich habe	wir haben	gesorgt
du habest	ihr habet	
Sie haben	Sie haben	
er/sie/es habe	sie haben	

PAST SUBJUNCTIVE II

ich hätte	wir hätten	gesorgt
du hättest	ihr hättet	
Sie hätten	Sie hätten	
er/sie/es hätte	sie hätten	

FUTURE PERFECT SUBJUNCTIVE I

ich werde	wir werden	gesorgt haben
du werdest	ihr werdet	
Sie werden	Sie werden	
er/sie/es werde	sie werden	

FUTURE PERFECT SUBJUNCTIVE II

ich würde	wir würden	gesorgt haben
du würdest	ihr würdet	
Sie würden	Sie würden	
er/sie/es würde	sie würden	

COMMANDS sorg(e)! sorgt! sorgen Sie!

PRESENT PARTICIPLE sorgend

Usage

Manni sorgt für die Altbauwohnung in der Innenstadt. — *Manni is looking after the old apartment in the inner city.*
Man muss für sich selbst sorgen können. — *One must be able to provide for oneself.*
Meine Mutter sorgt für ihren kränklichen Mann. — *My mother is taking care of her sick husband.*
Mark hat für seine Tante im Altersheim gesorgt. — *Mark took care of his aunt in the nursing home.*
Tante Rosies Besuch sorgte für allgemeine Freude unter den Kindern. — *Aunt Rosie's visit made the children happy all around.*
Dieses Skript sorgt für die Gültigkeit der Eingabe. — *This script ensures that the entry is valid.*

sich sorgen um *to worry about, be worried about*

Die Studenten sorgen sich um die Schlussexamen. — *The students are worrying about final exams.*
Der Bauer sorgt sich um seine kranke Kuh. — *The farmer is worried about his sick cow.*
Herr Petersen sorgt sich seit mehreren Jahren darum. — *Mr. Petersen has been worried about that for several years.*
Leslie sorgt sich um die Drogensucht ihres Sohnes. — *Leslie is worried about her son's drug addiction.*

RELATED VERBS befürsorgen, umsorgen, versorgen, vor·sorgen; *see also* **besorgen** (88)

409 spalten *to split, break down, crack*

spaltet · spaltete · gespalten/gespaltet regular weak verb/strong verb

PRESENT

ich spalte	wir spalten
du spaltest	ihr spaltet
Sie spalten	Sie spalten
er/sie/es spaltet	sie spalten

SIMPLE PAST

ich spaltete	wir spalteten
du spaltetest	ihr spaltetet
Sie spalteten	Sie spalteten
er/sie/es spaltete	sie spalteten

FUTURE

ich werde	wir werden	spalten
du wirst	ihr werdet	
Sie werden	Sie werden	
er/sie/es wird	sie werden	

PRESENT SUBJUNCTIVE I

ich spalte	wir spalten
du spaltest	ihr spaltet
Sie spalten	Sie spalten
er/sie/es spalte	sie spalten

PRESENT SUBJUNCTIVE II

ich spaltete	wir spalteten
du spaltetest	ihr spaltetet
Sie spalteten	Sie spalteten
er/sie/es spaltete	sie spalteten

FUTURE SUBJUNCTIVE I

ich werde	wir werden	spalten
du werdest	ihr werdet	
Sie werden	Sie werden	
er/sie/es werde	sie werden	

FUTURE SUBJUNCTIVE II

ich würde	wir würden	spalten
du würdest	ihr würdet	
Sie würden	Sie würden	
er/sie/es würde	sie würden	

PRESENT PERFECT

ich habe	wir haben	gespalten/gespaltet
du hast	ihr habt	
Sie haben	Sie haben	
er/sie/es hat	sie haben	

PAST PERFECT

ich hatte	wir hatten	gespalten/gespaltet
du hattest	ihr hattet	
Sie hatten	Sie hatten	
er/sie/es hatte	sie hatten	

FUTURE PERFECT

ich werde	wir werden	gespalten haben
du wirst	ihr werdet	OR
Sie werden	Sie werden	gespaltet haben
er/sie/es wird	sie werden	

PAST SUBJUNCTIVE I

ich habe	wir haben	gespalten/gespaltet
du habest	ihr habet	
Sie haben	Sie haben	
er/sie/es habe	sie haben	

PAST SUBJUNCTIVE II

ich hätte	wir hätten	gespalten/gespaltet
du hättest	ihr hättet	
Sie hätten	Sie hätten	
er/sie/es hätte	sie hätten	

FUTURE PERFECT SUBJUNCTIVE I

ich werde	wir werden	gespalten haben
du werdest	ihr werdet	OR
Sie werden	Sie werden	gespaltet haben
er/sie/es werde	sie werden	

FUTURE PERFECT SUBJUNCTIVE II

ich würde	wir würden	gespalten haben
du würdest	ihr würdet	OR
Sie würden	Sie würden	gespaltet haben
er/sie/es würde	sie würden	

COMMANDS spalte! spaltet! spalten Sie!

PRESENT PARTICIPLE spaltend

NOTE The past participle is more commonly **gespalten**, although **gespaltet** is not incorrect.

Usage

Serena hat die Kokosnuss mit einem Hammer gespalten.	*Serena cracked the coconut open with a hammer.*
Der Archäologe hat den alten Schenkelknochen versehentlich gespalten.	*The archeologist accidentally fractured the old femur.*
Das ultraviolette Licht spaltet die Moleküle.	*The ultraviolet light splits the molecules.*
Diese Frage begann die Wissenschaftler in zwei Lager zu spalten.	*This question began to divide the scientists into two camps.*
Das Fundament wurde vom Erdbeben gespalten.	*The foundation was cracked by an earthquake.*
Der Porzellantopf wurde von der Hitze gespalten.	*The porcelain pot was cracked by the heat.*
Die Antikörper spalten diese Substanzen.	*The antibodies are breaking down these substances.*

sich spalten *to split, break down, crack*

Die verstärkte Mauer spaltete sich, aber fiel nicht zusammen.	*The reinforced wall cracked but didn't collapse.*

RELATED VERBS ab·spalten, auf·spalten, zerspalten

regular weak verb

spart · sparte · gespart

PRESENT

ich spare	wir sparen
du sparst	ihr spart
Sie sparen	Sie sparen
er/sie/es spart	sie sparen

SIMPLE PAST

ich sparte	wir sparten
du spartest	ihr spartet
Sie sparten	Sie sparten
er/sie/es sparte	sie sparten

FUTURE

ich werde	wir werden	sparen
du wirst	ihr werdet	
Sie werden	Sie werden	
er/sie/es wird	sie werden	

PRESENT SUBJUNCTIVE I

ich spare	wir sparen
du sparest	ihr sparet
Sie sparen	Sie sparen
er/sie/es spare	sie sparen

PRESENT SUBJUNCTIVE II

ich sparte	wir sparten
du spartest	ihr spartet
Sie sparten	Sie sparten
er/sie/es sparte	sie sparten

FUTURE SUBJUNCTIVE I

ich werde	wir werden	sparen
du werdest	ihr werdet	
Sie werden	Sie werden	
er/sie/es werde	sie werden	

FUTURE SUBJUNCTIVE II

ich würde	wir würden	sparen
du würdest	ihr würdet	
Sie würden	Sie würden	
er/sie/es würde	sie würden	

PRESENT PERFECT

ich habe	wir haben	gespart
du hast	ihr habt	
Sie haben	Sie haben	
er/sie/es hat	sie haben	

PAST PERFECT

ich hatte	wir hatten	gespart
du hattest	ihr hattet	
Sie hatten	Sie hatten	
er/sie/es hatte	sie hatten	

FUTURE PERFECT

ich werde	wir werden	gespart haben
du wirst	ihr werdet	
Sie werden	Sie werden	
er/sie/es wird	sie werden	

PAST SUBJUNCTIVE I

ich habe	wir haben	gespart
du habest	ihr habet	
Sie haben	Sie haben	
er/sie/es habe	sie haben	

PAST SUBJUNCTIVE II

ich hätte	wir hätten	gespart
du hättest	ihr hättet	
Sie hätten	Sie hätten	
er/sie/es hätte	sie hätten	

FUTURE PERFECT SUBJUNCTIVE I

ich werde	wir werden	gespart haben
du werdest	ihr werdet	
Sie werden	Sie werden	
er/sie/es werde	sie werden	

FUTURE PERFECT SUBJUNCTIVE II

ich würde	wir würden	gespart haben
du würdest	ihr würdet	
Sie würden	Sie würden	
er/sie/es würde	sie würden	

COMMANDS spar(e)! spart! sparen Sie!

PRESENT PARTICIPLE sparend

Usage

Willi spart auf eine zweiäugige Spiegelreflexkamera.	*Willi is saving for a double-lens reflex camera.*
Warum spart ihr nicht?	*Why don't you economize?*
Du musst ab jetzt sparen.	*You have to be on a budget from now on.*
Ich kann nicht gut sparen.	*I'm not good at saving.*
Herr und Frau Kleist möchten auf eine Eigentumswohnung in Ansbach sparen.	*Mr. and Mrs. Kleist would like to save for a home in Ansbach.*
Norbert findet es leicht zu sparen.	*Norbert finds it easy to be thrifty.*
Das Geld wird für einen guten Zweck gespart.	*The money is being saved for a good purpose.*
Wir sparen seit einem Jahr auf eine neue Waschmaschine.	*We've been saving for a year for a new washing machine.*
Lieschen hat 45 Euro gespart.	*Lieschen has saved 45 euros.*
Diese Lösung hat mir viel Mühe gespart.	*This solution has saved me a lot of trouble.*
Um Kosten zu sparen, teilen wir ein Hotelzimmer.	*To save expenses, we're sharing a hotel room.*
Spar nicht am braunen Zucker!	*Don't skimp on the brown sugar!*

RELATED VERBS ab·sparen, auf·sparen, aus·sparen, ein·sparen, ersparen

411 spazieren *to stroll, go for a walk/ride*

spaziert · spazierte · spaziert — regular weak verb

PRESENT

ich spaziere	wir spazieren
du spazierst	ihr spaziert
Sie spazieren	Sie spazieren
er/sie/es spaziert	sie spazieren

SIMPLE PAST

ich spazierte	wir spazierten
du spaziertest	ihr spaziertet
Sie spazierten	Sie spazierten
er/sie/es spazierte	sie spazierten

FUTURE

ich werde	wir werden	spazieren
du wirst	ihr werdet	
Sie werden	Sie werden	
er/sie/es wird	sie werden	

PRESENT SUBJUNCTIVE I

ich spaziere	wir spazieren
du spazierest	ihr spazieret
Sie spazieren	Sie spazieren
er/sie/es spaziere	sie spazieren

PRESENT SUBJUNCTIVE II

ich spazierte	wir spazierten
du spaziertest	ihr spaziertet
Sie spazierten	Sie spazierten
er/sie/es spazierte	sie spazierten

FUTURE SUBJUNCTIVE I

ich werde	wir werden	spazieren
du werdest	ihr werdet	
Sie werden	Sie werden	
er/sie/es werde	sie werden	

FUTURE SUBJUNCTIVE II

ich würde	wir würden	spazieren
du würdest	ihr würdet	
Sie würden	Sie würden	
er/sie/es würde	sie würden	

PRESENT PERFECT

ich bin	wir sind	spaziert
du bist	ihr seid	
Sie sind	Sie sind	
er/sie/es ist	sie sind	

PAST PERFECT

ich war	wir waren	spaziert
du warst	ihr wart	
Sie waren	Sie waren	
er/sie/es war	sie waren	

FUTURE PERFECT

ich werde	wir werden	spaziert sein
du wirst	ihr werdet	
Sie werden	Sie werden	
er/sie/es wird	sie werden	

PAST SUBJUNCTIVE I

ich sei	wir seien	spaziert
du seiest	ihr seiet	
Sie seien	Sie seien	
er/sie/es sei	sie seien	

PAST SUBJUNCTIVE II

ich wäre	wir wären	spaziert
du wärest	ihr wäret	
Sie wären	Sie wären	
er/sie/es wäre	sie wären	

FUTURE PERFECT SUBJUNCTIVE I

ich werde	wir werden	spaziert sein
du werdest	ihr werdet	
Sie werden	Sie werden	
er/sie/es werde	sie werden	

FUTURE PERFECT SUBJUNCTIVE II

ich würde	wir würden	spaziert sein
du würdest	ihr würdet	
Sie würden	Sie würden	
er/sie/es würde	sie würden	

COMMANDS spazier(e)! spaziert! spazieren Sie!

PRESENT PARTICIPLE spazierend

NOTE In modern German, **spazieren** is typically combined with another verb of motion, such as **gehen** or **fahren**.

Usage

Wenn ich im Urlaub bin, gehe ich nachmittags am Strand spazieren.	*When I'm on vacation, I take walks on the beach in the afternoon.*
Rotkäppchen spazierte durch den Wald.	*Red Riding Hood went for a walk through the forest.*
Es macht Ingrid großen Spaß spazieren zu gehen.	*Ingrid has great fun going for walks.*
Annalies ist mit dem Auto einer Freundin spazieren gefahren.	*Annalies went for a spin in her friend's car.*
An diesem Morgen ritt Nicolaus Fricke am Bach spazieren.	*On this particular morning, Nicolaus Fricke took a leisurely ride along the stream.*

spazieren (with haben) *to take for a stroll/walk/ride*

Wo kann ich meinen Hund spazieren führen?	*Where can I take my dog for a walk?*
Darrell hat seine Freundin mit seinem Motorrad spazieren gefahren.	*Darrell took his girlfriend for a ride on his motorcycle.*

PRESENT

ich speie	wir speien
du speist	ihr speit
Sie speien	Sie speien
er/sie/es speit	sie speien

SIMPLE PAST

ich spie	wir spien
du spiest	ihr spiet
Sie spien	Sie spien
er/sie/es spie	sie spien

FUTURE

ich werde	wir werden	speien
du wirst	ihr werdet	
Sie werden	Sie werden	
er/sie/es wird	sie werden	

PRESENT SUBJUNCTIVE I

ich speie	wir speien
du speiest	ihr speiet
Sie speien	Sie speien
er/sie/es speie	sie speien

PRESENT SUBJUNCTIVE II

ich spie	wir spien
du spiest	ihr spiet
Sie spien	Sie spien
er/sie/es spie	sie spien

FUTURE SUBJUNCTIVE I

ich werde	wir werden	speien
du werdest	ihr werdet	
Sie werden	Sie werden	
er/sie/es werde	sie werden	

FUTURE SUBJUNCTIVE II

ich würde	wir würden	speien
du würdest	ihr würdet	
Sie würden	Sie würden	
er/sie/es würde	sie würden	

PRESENT PERFECT

ich habe	wir haben	gespien
du hast	ihr habt	
Sie haben	Sie haben	
er/sie/es hat	sie haben	

PAST PERFECT

ich hatte	wir hatten	gespien
du hattest	ihr hattet	
Sie hatten	Sie hatten	
er/sie/es hatte	sie hatten	

FUTURE PERFECT

ich werde	wir werden	gespien haben
du wirst	ihr werdet	
Sie werden	Sie werden	
er/sie/es wird	sie werden	

PAST SUBJUNCTIVE I

ich habe	wir haben	gespien
du habest	ihr habet	
Sie haben	Sie haben	
er/sie/es habe	sie haben	

PAST SUBJUNCTIVE II

ich hätte	wir hätten	gespien
du hättest	ihr hättet	
Sie hätten	Sie hätten	
er/sie/es hätte	sie hätten	

FUTURE PERFECT SUBJUNCTIVE I

ich werde	wir werden	gespien haben
du werdest	ihr werdet	
Sie werden	Sie werden	
er/sie/es werde	sie werden	

FUTURE PERFECT SUBJUNCTIVE II

ich würde	wir würden	gespien haben
du würdest	ihr würdet	
Sie würden	Sie würden	
er/sie/es würde	sie würden	

COMMANDS spei(e)! speit! speien Sie!

PRESENT PARTICIPLE speiend

Usage

Marmorne Pferde speien Wasser in die Luft.	*Marble horses spout water into the air.*
Ihr Mund spie Wut.	*Her mouth spewed rage.*
Ein Drache speit Feuer aus seinem Maul.	*A dragon spits fire from his mouth.*
Der Wal spie Jona aufs Land.	*The whale spit Jonah onto land.*
Der Vulkan hat Asche und Lava gespien.	*The volcano belched ash and lava.*
Der schwer verletzte Soldat lag auf dem Boden und spie Blut.	*The seriously injured soldier lay on the ground and spit blood.*
Der Narren Mund speit eitel Narrheit. (SPRÜCHE 15,2)	*The mouth of fools poureth out foolishness.* (PROVERBS 15:2)
„Du Schweinehund!“, spie der Mann.	*“You dirty dog!” spat the man.*
Frau Lotte Haesli spie Gift und Galle, wenn man nur an sie tippte. (HUGO BALL) (*figurative*)	*Mrs. Lotte Haesli vented her rage when someone so much as touched her.*
Es ist zum Speien! (*slang*)	*It makes me wanna puke!*

RELATED VERBS an·speien, bespeien

spielen *to play, act, perform*

spielt · spielte · gespielt regular weak verb

MORE USAGE SENTENCES WITH spielen

Ihr habt hoch gespielt und viel Geld verloren!	*You played for high stakes and lost a lot of money!*
Wir haben bis zwei Uhr morgens Schach gespielt.	*We played chess until two in the morning.*
Jetzt wird nicht mehr gespielt sondern gelernt!	*Playtime is over; now it's time to study!*
Josts Vater spielt gern am Spielautomaten.	*Jost's father likes to play the slot machine.*
Mein Kater spielt mit einer toten Maus.	*My cat is playing with a dead mouse.*
Unser Hund pflegt hier vor dem Kamin zu spielen.	*Our dog tends to play here in front of the fireplace.*
Schillers *Die Räuber* wird oft in Weimar gespielt.	*Schiller's* Die Räuber *is performed often in Weimar.*
Im seinem nächsten Film spielt der Schauspieler einen schizophrenen Geodät.	*In his next film, the actor will play a schizophrenic geodesist.*
Peter Lorre spielte die Rolle von einem Kindermörder.	*Peter Lorre played the part of a child murderer.*
Ich möchte Gitarre spielen lernen.	*I'd like to learn to play guitar.*
Kannst du wirklich Klavier spielen?	*Can you really play the piano?*
Du hast falsch gespielt, das ist ja ein Fis.	*You played a wrong note; that's an F sharp.*
Mozart konnte nach Gehör spielen und komponieren.	*Mozart could play and compose by ear.*
Die Marschkapelle spielte eine bewegende Version der Nationalhymne.	*The marching band played a moving rendition of the national anthem.*
Im letzten Konzert hat man Beethovens 7. gespielt.	*In the last concert, they played Beethoven's 7th.*
Inflation spielt hier keine Rolle.	*Inflation plays no part in this.*
Die Zahl drei spielt eine Rolle in der Handlung.	*The number three figures in the plot.*
Mutti ist heute nicht da, ich spiele Koch!	*Mom isn't here today; I'm playing cook!*
Frau Esterhazy spielt immer den Unschuldigen.	*Mrs. Esterhazy always acts innocent.*
Ralf hat seiner Schwester einen Streich gespielt.	*Ralf played a trick on his sister.*
Somit spielt er seinen Gegnern nur in die Hände.	*By doing this, he's only playing into his opponents' hands.*

sich spielen *to play until one reaches a certain state/condition*

Ich habe mich vor dem Spiel warm gespielt.	*I warmed up before the game.*
Die Kinder haben sich hungrig gespielt.	*The children worked up an appetite playing.*

IDIOMATIC EXPRESSIONS

Das Stück spielt in England im 16. Jahrhundert.	*The play is set in sixteenth-century England.*
Die Jacke spielt ins Grüne.	*The jacket has a greenish tinge.*
Erwin hat wieder angefangen, um Geld zu spielen.	*Erwin has started gambling again.*
Ortfrid spielt gern mit Worten.	*Ortfrid likes to make puns.*
Den kannst du ignorieren, der spielt immer den großen Herrn.	*You can ignore that guy; he's always blowing his own horn.*
Es ist schwierig vom Blatt zu spielen.	*It's difficult to sight-read music.*
Wir haben mit dem Gedanken gespielt, nach Kanada umzuziehen.	*We've toyed with the idea of moving to Canada.*
Bei ihnen wird allzu oft mit verdeckten Karten gespielt.	*They all too often deal in an underhanded manner.*
Ich werde meine Beziehungen für dich spielen lassen.	*I'll pull some strings for you.*
Dirk klagt, dass er neben Lars ständig zweite Geige spielen muss.	*Dirk complains he constantly has to take a back seat to Lars.*
Erich lässt die Muskeln spielen.	*Erich is flexing his muscles.*
Sie sagte, sie hätte den Orgasmus gespielt.	*She said she faked the orgasm.*
Der Politiker spielte ein doppeltes Spiel, solang es ihm nützlich war.	*The politician played both sides of the fence as long as it was useful to him.*
Dortmund hat gegen Bremen unentschieden gespielt.	*Dortmund tied Bremen.*

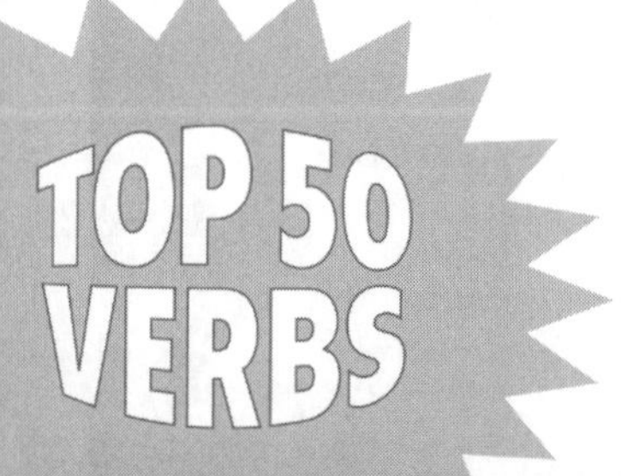

regular weak verb **spielt · spielte · gespielt**

PRESENT	
ich spiele	wir spielen
du spielst	ihr spielt
Sie spielen	Sie spielen
er/sie/es spielt	sie spielen

SIMPLE PAST	
ich spielte	wir spielten
du spieltest	ihr spieltet
Sie spielten	Sie spielten
er/sie/es spielte	sie spielten

FUTURE		
ich werde	wir werden	spielen
du wirst	ihr werdet	
Sie werden	Sie werden	
er/sie/es wird	sie werden	

PRESENT SUBJUNCTIVE I	
ich spiele	wir spielen
du spielest	ihr spielet
Sie spielen	Sie spielen
er/sie/es spiele	sie spielen

PRESENT SUBJUNCTIVE II	
ich spielte	wir spielten
du spieltest	ihr spieltet
Sie spielten	Sie spielten
er/sie/es spielte	sie spielten

FUTURE SUBJUNCTIVE I		
ich werde	wir werden	spielen
du werdest	ihr werdet	
Sie werden	Sie werden	
er/sie/es werde	sie werden	

FUTURE SUBJUNCTIVE II		
ich würde	wir würden	spielen
du würdest	ihr würdet	
Sie würden	Sie würden	
er/sie/es würde	sie würden	

PRESENT PERFECT		
ich habe	wir haben	gespielt
du hast	ihr habt	
Sie haben	Sie haben	
er/sie/es hat	sie haben	

PAST PERFECT		
ich hatte	wir hatten	gespielt
du hattest	ihr hattet	
Sie hatten	Sie hatten	
er/sie/es hatte	sie hatten	

FUTURE PERFECT		
ich werde	wir werden	gespielt haben
du wirst	ihr werdet	
Sie werden	Sie werden	
er/sie/es wird	sie werden	

PAST SUBJUNCTIVE I		
ich habe	wir haben	gespielt
du habest	ihr habet	
Sie haben	Sie haben	
er/sie/es habe	sie haben	

PAST SUBJUNCTIVE II		
ich hätte	wir hätten	gespielt
du hättest	ihr hättet	
Sie hätten	Sie hätten	
er/sie/es hätte	sie hätten	

FUTURE PERFECT SUBJUNCTIVE I		
ich werde	wir werden	gespielt haben
du werdest	ihr werdet	
Sie werden	Sie werden	
er/sie/es werde	sie werden	

FUTURE PERFECT SUBJUNCTIVE II		
ich würde	wir würden	gespielt haben
du würdest	ihr würdet	
Sie würden	Sie würden	
er/sie/es würde	sie würden	

COMMANDS spiel(e)! spielt! spielen Sie!

PRESENT PARTICIPLE spielend

Usage

Die Tormänner haben heute gut gespielt.	*The goalkeepers played well today.*
Bei wem spielt jetzt Hansel?	*Who is Hansel playing for now?*
Die Bulls spielten am Samstag gegen die Hawks in Chicago.	*The Bulls played the Hawks in Chicago on Saturday.*
Wir spielen heute um die Meisterschaft.	*We're playing for the championship today.*
Die Kinder spielen mit einem Ball.	*The children are playing with a ball.*
He, du spielst unfair!	*Hey, you're not playing fairly!*
Regina spielt seit zwei Stunden im Garten.	*Regina has been playing in the yard for the last two hours.*
Man kann das Spiel auch online spielen.	*You can play the game online, too.*
Kinder, wollt ihr Fangen spielen?	*Children, do you want to play tag?*
Wie spielt man Skat?	*How is Skat played?*
Wollen wir Karten spielen?	*Should we play cards?*

RELATED VERBS ab·spielen, an·spielen, auf·spielen, aus·spielen, durch·spielen, ein·spielen, mit·spielen, nach·spielen, überspielen, verspielen, vor·spielen, weiter·spielen, zusammen·spielen, zu·spielen

414 spinnen *to spin; plot, think up*

spinnt · spann · gesponnen strong verb

PRESENT

ich spinne	wir spinnen
du spinnst	ihr spinnt
Sie spinnen	Sie spinnen
er/sie/es spinnt	sie spinnen

SIMPLE PAST

ich spann	wir spannen
du spannst	ihr spannt
Sie spannen	Sie spannen
er/sie/es spann	sie spannen

FUTURE

ich werde	wir werden	spinnen
du wirst	ihr werdet	
Sie werden	Sie werden	
er/sie/es wird	sie werden	

PRESENT SUBJUNCTIVE I

ich spinne	wir spinnen
du spinnest	ihr spinnet
Sie spinnen	Sie spinnen
er/sie/es spinne	sie spinnen

PRESENT SUBJUNCTIVE II

ich spönne/spänne	wir spönnen/spännen
du spönnest/spännest	ihr spönnet/spännet
Sie spönnen/spännen	Sie spönnen/spännen
er/sie/es spönne/spänne	sie spönnen/spännen

FUTURE SUBJUNCTIVE I

ich werde	wir werden	spinnen
du werdest	ihr werdet	
Sie werden	Sie werden	
er/sie/es werde	sie werden	

FUTURE SUBJUNCTIVE II

ich würde	wir würden	spinnen
du würdest	ihr würdet	
Sie würden	Sie würden	
er/sie/es würde	sie würden	

PRESENT PERFECT

ich habe	wir haben	gesponnen
du hast	ihr habt	
Sie haben	Sie haben	
er/sie/es hat	sie haben	

PAST PERFECT

ich hatte	wir hatten	gesponnen
du hattest	ihr hattet	
Sie hatten	Sie hatten	
er/sie/es hatte	sie hatten	

FUTURE PERFECT

ich werde	wir werden	gesponnen haben
du wirst	ihr werdet	
Sie werden	Sie werden	
er/sie/es wird	sie werden	

PAST SUBJUNCTIVE I

ich habe	wir haben	gesponnen
du habest	ihr habet	
Sie haben	Sie haben	
er/sie/es habe	sie haben	

PAST SUBJUNCTIVE II

ich hätte	wir hätten	gesponnen
du hättest	ihr hättet	
Sie hätten	Sie hätten	
er/sie/es hätte	sie hätten	

FUTURE PERFECT SUBJUNCTIVE I

ich werde	wir werden	gesponnen haben
du werdest	ihr werdet	
Sie werden	Sie werden	
er/sie/es werde	sie werden	

FUTURE PERFECT SUBJUNCTIVE II

ich würde	wir würden	gesponnen haben
du würdest	ihr würdet	
Sie würden	Sie würden	
er/sie/es würde	sie würden	

COMMANDS spinn(e)! spinnt! spinnen Sie!

PRESENT PARTICIPLE spinnend

Usage

Im August muss die Wolle gesponnen werden. — *In August, the wool must be spun.*

Wie hätte ich mich losreißen können, wenn der dauerhafte Faden nicht gesponnen wäre? (GOETHE) — *How could I have broken free, if the lasting thread had not been spun?*

Oma saß vor dem Kamin und spann. — *Grandma was sitting in front of the fire spinning.*

Rumpelstilzchen soll Stroh zu Gold gesponnen haben. — *Rumpelstilzchen is said to have spun straw into gold.*

Die Larve spinnt einen Kokon. — *The larva spins a cocoon.*

„Spinnen wir es nächste Woche", sagte Tante Marie. — *"Let's spin it next week," said Aunt Marie.*

Stimmt es, dass Flachs zu Leinen gesponnen wird? — *Is it true that flax is spun into linen?*

Können Sie Garn spinnen? — *Can you spin yarn?*

Die Weiber spannen und woben den Flachs und die Wolle. (ENGELS) — *The weavers spun and wove the flax and wool.*

Die Propagandisten spinnen immer mehr Lügen. — *The propagandists are forever thinking up more lies.*

Du spinnst! (*slang*) — *You're wacko!*

RELATED VERBS an·spinnen, aus·spinnen, ein·spinnen, umspinnen, verspinnen

415 sprechen

to speak, talk; recite; pronounce

strong verb

spricht · sprach · gesprochen

PRESENT

ich spreche	wir sprechen
du sprichst	ihr sprecht
Sie sprechen	Sie sprechen
er/sie/es spricht	sie sprechen

SIMPLE PAST

ich sprach	wir sprachen
du sprachst	ihr spracht
Sie sprachen	Sie sprachen
er/sie/es sprach	sie sprachen

FUTURE

ich werde	wir werden	sprechen
du wirst	ihr werdet	
Sie werden	Sie werden	
er/sie/es wird	sie werden	

PRESENT SUBJUNCTIVE I

ich spreche	wir sprechen
du sprechest	ihr sprechet
Sie sprechen	Sie sprechen
er/sie/es spreche	sie sprechen

PRESENT SUBJUNCTIVE II

ich spräche	wir sprächen
du sprächest	ihr sprächet
Sie sprächen	Sie sprächen
er/sie/es spräche	sie sprächen

FUTURE SUBJUNCTIVE I

ich werde	wir werden	sprechen
du werdest	ihr werdet	
Sie werden	Sie werden	
er/sie/es werde	sie werden	

FUTURE SUBJUNCTIVE II

ich würde	wir würden	sprechen
du würdest	ihr würdet	
Sie würden	Sie würden	
er/sie/es würde	sie würden	

PRESENT PERFECT

ich habe	wir haben	gesprochen
du hast	ihr habt	
Sie haben	Sie haben	
er/sie/es hat	sie haben	

PAST PERFECT

ich hatte	wir hatten	gesprochen
du hattest	ihr hattet	
Sie hatten	Sie hatten	
er/sie/es hatte	sie hatten	

FUTURE PERFECT

ich werde	wir werden	gesprochen haben
du wirst	ihr werdet	
Sie werden	Sie werden	
er/sie/es wird	sie werden	

PAST SUBJUNCTIVE I

ich habe	wir haben	gesprochen
du habest	ihr habet	
Sie haben	Sie haben	
er/sie/es habe	sie haben	

PAST SUBJUNCTIVE II

ich hätte	wir hätten	gesprochen
du hättest	ihr hättet	
Sie hätten	Sie hätten	
er/sie/es hätte	sie hätten	

FUTURE PERFECT SUBJUNCTIVE I

ich werde	wir werden	gesprochen haben
du werdest	ihr werdet	
Sie werden	Sie werden	
er/sie/es werde	sie werden	

FUTURE PERFECT SUBJUNCTIVE II

ich würde	wir würden	gesprochen haben
du würdest	ihr würdet	
Sie würden	Sie würden	
er/sie/es würde	sie würden	

COMMANDS sprich! sprecht! sprechen Sie!

PRESENT PARTICIPLE sprechend

Usage

Hast du mit ihm darüber gesprochen?	*Have you spoken with him about it?*
Wer spricht?	*Who's speaking?*
Der Popstar spricht oft mit seinem Astrologen.	*The pop star talks frequently with his astrologer.*
Lars will Finnisch sprechen können.	*Lars claims to be able to speak Finnish.*
Sprechen Sie Englisch?	*Do you speak English?*
Komisch, du sprichst mit einem französischen Akzent, aber du bist aus den USA!	*Funny, you talk with a French accent, but you're from the U.S.!*
Opa sprach nur Dialekt, aber wir verstanden ihn.	*Grandpa spoke only dialect, but we understood him.*
„Sprichst du Italienisch?" „Ja, aber nicht fließend."	*"Do you speak Italian?" "Yes, but not fluently."*
Die Häftlinge sprachen von Tortur.	*The prisoners have spoken of torture.*

RELATED VERBS ab·sprechen, an·sprechen, besprechen, durch·sprechen, ein·sprechen, frei·sprechen, herum·sprechen, hohn·sprechen, los·sprechen, mit·sprechen, nach·sprechen, übersprechen, vor·sprechen, weiter·sprechen, zu·sprechen; *see also* **aus·sprechen** (40), **entsprechen** (149), **versprechen** (500), **widersprechen** (531)

TOP 50 VERB ☞

sprechen *to speak, talk; recite; pronounce*

spricht · sprach · gesprochen

strong verb

MORE USAGE SENTENCES WITH sprechen

Susanne spricht mit Sofie am Telefon. *Susanne is talking with Sofie on the telephone.*
Sprechen Sie bitte über Ihre Erfahrungen im Ausland. *Please talk about your experiences abroad.*
Nach der Hirnoperation konnte Gerd nur langsam sprechen. *After the brain surgery, Gerd was only able to speak slowly.*
Der Bube hatte den Mund aufgemacht, als ob er sprechen wollte. *The boy had opened his mouth as though he wanted to speak.*
Mein Vater hat nicht viel über seine Kindheit gesprochen. *My father hasn't spoken much about his childhood.*
„Also!" sprach Zarathustra. *"So!" said Zoroaster.*
In welchem Alter lernt ein Kind sprechen? *At what age does a child learn to speak?*
Es tut mir Leid, aber Herr Hüppe ist momentan nicht zu sprechen. *I'm sorry, but Mr. Hüppe is not available to speak with anyone at the moment.*
In lockerer Atmosphäre sprach Herr Schmit über seine persönliche Beziehung zum Vorstandsvorsitzenden. *In a relaxed atmosphere, Mr. Schmit spoke about his relationship with the chairman of the board.*
Wie lange hat der Redner gesprochen? *How long did the speaker talk?*
Das Wetter ist immer ein sicheres Thema, sprich mit ihr über das Wetter! *The weather is always a safe subject; talk with her about the weather!*
Sprichst du mit dir selbst? *Do you talk to yourself?*
Guten Morgen, ich möchte Herrn Doktor Meier sprechen. *Good morning, I'd like to speak to Doctor Meier.*
Die Ergebnisse sprechen für sich selbst. *The results speak for themselves.*
So sprichst du nicht mit deiner Mutter. *That's no way to talk to your mother.*
Lars spricht schlecht von seinem Zimmerkollegen. *Lars speaks ill of his roommate.*
Heute haben wir zum Thema Ausländerfeindlichkeit gesprochen. *Today we spoke on the topic of xenophobia.*
Irgendwie sind wir auf das Thema Schule zu sprechen gekommen und die Zeit verging schnell. *We somehow got started talking about school, and time passed quickly.*
Franziska hat während der Versammlung ein schönes Gedicht gesprochen. *Franziska recited a nice poem during the assembly.*
Der Richter hat ein Urteil gesprochen, das meines Erachtens ungerecht ist. *The judge has pronounced a judgment that is, in my estimation, unjust.*
Jesus sprach zu ihnen: „Wahrlich, wahrlich, ich sage euch." (Johannes 8,34) *(archaic)* *Jesus spake unto them, "Verily, verily, I say unto you."* (John 8:34)

IDIOMATIC EXPRESSIONS

Im Jahr 1235 wurde Elisabeth heilig gesprochen. *Elisabeth was canonized in the year 1235.*
Ernst ist vor dem Gericht mündig gesprochen worden. *Ernst has been declared of legal age before the court.*
2003 hat man Mutter Teresa selig gesprochen. *In 2003, Mother Teresa was beatified.*
Wir haben nicht genügende Ressourcen, sprich Geld. *We don't have sufficient resources, that is to say, money.*
Aus ihrem Gesicht sprach ein auffallendes Selbstbewusstsein. *Remarkable self-confidence was written on her face.*
Bernd hat für die Maßnahme gesprochen, ich bin aber dagegen. *Bernd spoke in favor of the measure, but I'm against it.*
Alles spricht dafür, dass die Wirtschaft bald wieder schneller wächst. *There is every indication that the economy will soon grow more quickly once again.*
Ich bin auf ihn nicht mehr gut zu sprechen. *I don't take kindly to him anymore.*
Lassen Sie Diamanten sprechen! *Say it with diamonds!*
Marga lässt ihr Herz sprechen. *Marga follows her heart.*
Unter uns gesprochen, ich finde seine Idee unrealistisch. *Between us, I think his idea is unrealistic.*
Sprechen wir von etwas anderem. *Let's change the subject.*

strong verb **sprießt · spross · gesprossen**

PRESENT

ich sprieße	wir sprießen
du sprießt	ihr sprießt
Sie sprießen	Sie sprießen
er/sie/es sprießt	sie sprießen

SIMPLE PAST

ich spross	wir sprossen
du sprossest	ihr sprosst
Sie sprossen	Sie sprossen
er/sie/es spross	sie sprossen

FUTURE

ich werde	wir werden	sprießen
du wirst	ihr werdet	
Sie werden	Sie werden	
er/sie/es wird	sie werden	

PRESENT SUBJUNCTIVE I

ich sprieße	wir sprießen
du sprießest	ihr sprießet
Sie sprießen	Sie sprießen
er/sie/es sprieße	sie sprießen

PRESENT SUBJUNCTIVE II

ich sprösse	wir sprössen
du sprössest	ihr sprösset
Sie sprössen	Sie sprössen
er/sie/es sprösse	sie sprössen

FUTURE SUBJUNCTIVE I

ich werde	wir werden	sprießen
du werdest	ihr werdet	
Sie werden	Sie werden	
er/sie/es werde	sie werden	

FUTURE SUBJUNCTIVE II

ich würde	wir würden	sprießen
du würdest	ihr würdet	
Sie würden	Sie würden	
er/sie/es würde	sie würden	

PRESENT PERFECT

ich bin	wir sind	gesprossen
du bist	ihr seid	
Sie sind	Sie sind	
er/sie/es ist	sie sind	

PAST PERFECT

ich war	wir waren	gesprossen
du warst	ihr wart	
Sie waren	Sie waren	
er/sie/es war	sie waren	

FUTURE PERFECT

ich werde	wir werden	gesprossen sein
du wirst	ihr werdet	
Sie werden	Sie werden	
er/sie/es wird	sie werden	

PAST SUBJUNCTIVE I

ich sei	wir seien	gesprossen
du seiest	ihr seiet	
Sie seien	Sie seien	
er/sie/es sei	sie seien	

PAST SUBJUNCTIVE II

ich wäre	wir wären	gesprossen
du wärest	ihr wäret	
Sie wären	Sie wären	
er/sie/es wäre	sie wären	

FUTURE PERFECT SUBJUNCTIVE I

ich werde	wir werden	gesprossen sein
du werdest	ihr werdet	
Sie werden	Sie werden	
er/sie/es werde	sie werden	

FUTURE PERFECT SUBJUNCTIVE II

ich würde	wir würden	gesprossen sein
du würdest	ihr würdet	
Sie würden	Sie würden	
er/sie/es würde	sie würden	

COMMANDS sprieß(e)! sprießt! sprießen Sie!

PRESENT PARTICIPLE sprießend

Usage

Sogar Zitronenbäume sprossen auf dieser Insel.	*Even lemon trees sprang up on this island.*
Die Blüten sprossen schon im Februar.	*The blossoms were already opening in February.*
Hunderte Pilze sind am nächsten Tag gesprossen.	*Hundreds of mushrooms shot up the next day.*
Rolands Bart sprießt wieder.	*Roland's growing a beard again.*
Viele neue Häuser sind wie Pilze aus dem Boden gesprossen.	*Many new houses sprang up out of the ground like mushrooms.*
Nur ein einziges Blatt ist gesprossen.	*Only a single leaf sprouted.*
Wie soll das sprießen?	*How is that supposed to germinate?*
Neue Blätter sprießen aus dem Wurzelstock.	*New leaves are sprouting from the trunk.*
Nach einigen Tagen werden die Bohnen sprießen.	*After a few days, the beans will sprout.*
Graue Haare sprießen schon!	*Gray hairs are already popping up!*
Hirsesamen sprießen im Garten.	*Millet seed is sprouting in the yard.*
Wieder sprießen dir nützliche Körner? (Hebbel)	*Are useful seeds sprouting once again?*

RELATED VERB entsprießen

417 **springen** *to jump, leap, spring; dive; bound*

springt · sprang · gesprungen strong verb

PRESENT

ich springe	wir springen
du springst	ihr springt
Sie springen	Sie springen
er/sie/es springt	sie springen

SIMPLE PAST

ich sprang	wir sprangen
du sprangst	ihr sprangt
Sie sprangen	Sie sprangen
er/sie/es sprang	sie sprangen

FUTURE

ich werde	wir werden	springen
du wirst	ihr werdet	
Sie werden	Sie werden	
er/sie/es wird	sie werden	

PRESENT SUBJUNCTIVE I

ich springe	wir springen
du springest	ihr springet
Sie springen	Sie springen
er/sie/es springe	sie springen

PRESENT SUBJUNCTIVE II

ich spränge	wir sprängen
du sprängest	ihr spränget
Sie sprängen	Sie sprängen
er/sie/es spränge	sie sprängen

FUTURE SUBJUNCTIVE I

ich werde	wir werden	springen
du werdest	ihr werdet	
Sie werden	Sie werden	
er/sie/es werde	sie werden	

FUTURE SUBJUNCTIVE II

ich würde	wir würden	springen
du würdest	ihr würdet	
Sie würden	Sie würden	
er/sie/es würde	sie würden	

PRESENT PERFECT

ich bin	wir sind	gesprungen
du bist	ihr seid	
Sie sind	Sie sind	
er/sie/es ist	sie sind	

PAST PERFECT

ich war	wir waren	gesprungen
du warst	ihr wart	
Sie waren	Sie waren	
er/sie/es war	sie waren	

FUTURE PERFECT

ich werde	wir werden	gesprungen sein
du wirst	ihr werdet	
Sie werden	Sie werden	
er/sie/es wird	sie werden	

PAST SUBJUNCTIVE I

ich sei	wir seien	gesprungen
du seiest	ihr seiet	
Sie seien	Sie seien	
er/sie/es sei	sie seien	

PAST SUBJUNCTIVE II

ich wäre	wir wären	gesprungen
du wärest	ihr wäret	
Sie wären	Sie wären	
er/sie/es wäre	sie wären	

FUTURE PERFECT SUBJUNCTIVE I

ich werde	wir werden	gesprungen sein
du werdest	ihr werdet	
Sie werden	Sie werden	
er/sie/es werde	sie werden	

FUTURE PERFECT SUBJUNCTIVE II

ich würde	wir würden	gesprungen sein
du würdest	ihr würdet	
Sie würden	Sie würden	
er/sie/es würde	sie würden	

COMMANDS spring(e)! springt! springen Sie!

PRESENT PARTICIPLE springend

Usage

Der Fußballstar sprang über seinen Gegner. — *The soccer star leapt over his opponent.*
Der Sportler sprang in die falsche Richtung. — *The athlete jumped in the wrong direction.*
Wie hoch kannst du springen? — *How high can you jump?*
Jörg hatte die Arme ausgestreckt, als ob er springen wollte. — *Jörg had stretched his arms out as though he wanted to jump.*
Ingrid will über den zwei Meter hohen Zaun gesprungen sein. — *Ingrid claims to have jumped over the two-meter-high fence.*
Er ist über den Kanal gesprungen und in den Wald gelaufen. — *He leapt over the canal and ran into the forest.*
Die Katze springt ängstlich hinter die Kommode. — *The cat dives nervously behind the cabinet.*
Der Junge sprang in den Teich. — *The boy dived into the pond.*
Unser Hund Maximilian sprang auf das Sofa und leckte dem Kind das Gesicht. — *Our dog, Maximilian, bounded onto the sofa and licked the child's face.*

RELATED VERBS ab·springen, an·springen, auf·springen, ein·springen, entspringen, überspringen, über·springen, um·springen, vor·springen, zu·springen

regular weak verb

spült · spülte · gespült

PRESENT

ich spüle	wir spülen
du spülst	ihr spült
Sie spülen	Sie spülen
er/sie/es spült	sie spülen

SIMPLE PAST

ich spülte	wir spülten
du spültest	ihr spültet
Sie spülten	Sie spülten
er/sie/es spülte	sie spülten

FUTURE

ich werde	wir werden	spülen
du wirst	ihr werdet	
Sie werden	Sie werden	
er/sie/es wird	sie werden	

PRESENT SUBJUNCTIVE I

ich spüle	wir spülen
du spülest	ihr spület
Sie spülen	Sie spülen
er/sie/es spüle	sie spülen

PRESENT SUBJUNCTIVE II

ich spülte	wir spülten
du spültest	ihr spültet
Sie spülten	Sie spülten
er/sie/es spülte	sie spülten

FUTURE SUBJUNCTIVE I

ich werde	wir werden	spülen
du werdest	ihr werdet	
Sie werden	Sie werden	
er/sie/es werde	sie werden	

FUTURE SUBJUNCTIVE II

ich würde	wir würden	spülen
du würdest	ihr würdet	
Sie würden	Sie würden	
er/sie/es würde	sie würden	

PRESENT PERFECT

ich habe	wir haben	gespült
du hast	ihr habt	
Sie haben	Sie haben	
er/sie/es hat	sie haben	

PAST PERFECT

ich hatte	wir hatten	gespült
du hattest	ihr hattet	
Sie hatten	Sie hatten	
er/sie/es hatte	sie hatten	

FUTURE PERFECT

ich werde	wir werden	gespült haben
du wirst	ihr werdet	
Sie werden	Sie werden	
er/sie/es wird	sie werden	

PAST SUBJUNCTIVE I

ich habe	wir haben	gespült
du habest	ihr habet	
Sie haben	Sie haben	
er/sie/es habe	sie haben	

PAST SUBJUNCTIVE II

ich hätte	wir hätten	gespült
du hättest	ihr hättet	
Sie hätten	Sie hätten	
er/sie/es hätte	sie hätten	

FUTURE PERFECT SUBJUNCTIVE I

ich werde	wir werden	gespült haben
du werdest	ihr werdet	
Sie werden	Sie werden	
er/sie/es werde	sie werden	

FUTURE PERFECT SUBJUNCTIVE II

ich würde	wir würden	gespült haben
du würdest	ihr würdet	
Sie würden	Sie würden	
er/sie/es würde	sie würden	

COMMANDS spül(e)! spült! spülen Sie!

PRESENT PARTICIPLE spülend

Usage

Wir mussten den Pullover mit kaltem Wasser spülen.	*We had to rinse the sweater in cold water.*
Das Gerät scheint wieder zu spülen.	*The device seems to be rinsing again.*
Spül bitte das Glas.	*Please rinse the glass.*
Die Flaschen werden gespült und wieder gefüllt.	*The bottles are rinsed and refilled.*
Roland spült sich das Shampoo aus dem Haar.	*Roland is rinsing the shampoo from his hair.*
Monika hat schon heute Morgen gespült.	*Monika already washed dishes this morning.*
Darf man diese Weingläser in die Geschirrspülmaschine tun, oder muss man sie per Hand spülen?	*Can you put these wine glasses in the dishwasher, or do you have to wash them by hand?*
Spült die Waschmaschine schon?	*Is the washing machine already on rinse?*
Das Geschirr wurde dreimal gespült.	*The dishes were washed three times.*
Ich spüle und du trocknest, okay?	*I'll wash and you dry, okay?*
Hast du keine Zeit zu spülen?	*Do you not have time to wash dishes?*
Hast du die Toilette gerade gespült?	*Did you just flush the toilet?*

RELATED VERBS ab·spülen, aus·spülen, durch·spülen, unterspülen, weg·spülen

419 starten *to start, launch, begin*

startet · startete · gestartet

regular weak verb

PRESENT

ich starte	wir starten
du startest	ihr startet
Sie starten	Sie starten
er/sie/es startet	sie starten

SIMPLE PAST

ich startete	wir starteten
du startetest	ihr startetet
Sie starteten	Sie starteten
er/sie/es startete	sie starteten

FUTURE

ich werde	wir werden	starten
du wirst	ihr werdet	
Sie werden	Sie werden	
er/sie/es wird	sie werden	

PRESENT SUBJUNCTIVE I

ich starte	wir starten
du startest	ihr startet
Sie starten	Sie starten
er/sie/es starte	sie starten

PRESENT SUBJUNCTIVE II

ich startete	wir starteten
du startetest	ihr startetet
Sie starteten	Sie starteten
er/sie/es startete	sie starteten

FUTURE SUBJUNCTIVE I

ich werde	wir werden	starten
du werdest	ihr werdet	
Sie werden	Sie werden	
er/sie/es werde	sie werden	

FUTURE SUBJUNCTIVE II

ich würde	wir würden	starten
du würdest	ihr würdet	
Sie würden	Sie würden	
er/sie/es würde	sie würden	

PRESENT PERFECT

ich habe	wir haben	gestartet
du hast	ihr habt	
Sie haben	Sie haben	
er/sie/es hat	sie haben	

PAST PERFECT

ich hatte	wir hatten	gestartet
du hattest	ihr hattet	
Sie hatten	Sie hatten	
er/sie/es hatte	sie hatten	

FUTURE PERFECT

ich werde	wir werden	gestartet haben
du wirst	ihr werdet	
Sie werden	Sie werden	
er/sie/es wird	sie werden	

PAST SUBJUNCTIVE I

ich habe	wir haben	gestartet
du habest	ihr habet	
Sie haben	Sie haben	
er/sie/es habe	sie haben	

PAST SUBJUNCTIVE II

ich hätte	wir hätten	gestartet
du hättest	ihr hättet	
Sie hätten	Sie hätten	
er/sie/es hätte	sie hätten	

FUTURE PERFECT SUBJUNCTIVE I

ich werde	wir werden	gestartet haben
du werdest	ihr werdet	
Sie werden	Sie werden	
er/sie/es werde	sie werden	

FUTURE PERFECT SUBJUNCTIVE II

ich würde	wir würden	gestartet haben
du würdest	ihr würdet	
Sie würden	Sie würden	
er/sie/es würde	sie würden	

COMMANDS starte! startet! starten Sie!

PRESENT PARTICIPLE startend

Usage

Herberts altes Auto ist nicht leicht zu starten.	*Herbert's old car is not easy to start.*
Hast du den Motor nicht starten können?	*Were you not able to start the engine?*
Ein Knopfdruck startet das Spiel.	*A push of the button starts the game.*
Man kann die Videokamera per Fernbedienung starten.	*You can start the video camera by remote control.*
Um zwölf Uhr startete man das Wettrennen.	*At 12 o'clock, they started the race.*
Mit welchem Befehl startet man diesen Prozess?	*What command do you use to activate this process?*
Die Firma startet eine neue Werbekampagne.	*The company is launching a new ad campaign.*

starten (with **sein**) *to depart, take off, launch*

Um halb acht startet der nächste Bus nach Steinbrück.	*At 7:30, the next bus for Steinbrück departs.*
Ist der Flug pünktlich gestartet?	*Did the flight take off on time?*
Die Rakete startet morgen Abend.	*The rocket launches tomorrow evening.*
Nach der Installation der Software müssen Sie den Computer neu starten.	*After the software installation, you have to restart the computer.*
Vier dramatische Filme starten bald in den Kinos.	*Four dramatic movies will open soon in theaters.*

strong verb **findet statt · fand statt · stattgefunden**

PRESENT

ich finde	wir finden	statt
du findest	ihr findet	
Sie finden	Sie finden	
er/sie/es findet	sie finden	

SIMPLE PAST

ich fand	wir fanden	statt
du fandst	ihr fandet	
Sie fanden	Sie fanden	
er/sie/es fand	sie fanden	

FUTURE

ich werde	wir werden	stattfinden
du wirst	ihr werdet	
Sie werden	Sie werden	
er/sie/es wird	sie werden	

PRESENT SUBJUNCTIVE I

ich finde	wir finden	statt
du findest	ihr findet	
Sie finden	Sie finden	
er/sie/es finde	sie finden	

PRESENT SUBJUNCTIVE II

ich fände	wir fänden	statt
du fändest	ihr fändet	
Sie fänden	Sie fänden	
er/sie/es fände	sie fänden	

FUTURE SUBJUNCTIVE I

ich werde	wir werden	stattfinden
du werdest	ihr werdet	
Sie werden	Sie werden	
er/sie/es werde	sie werden	

FUTURE SUBJUNCTIVE II

ich würde	wir würden	stattfinden
du würdest	ihr würdet	
Sie würden	Sie würden	
er/sie/es würde	sie würden	

PRESENT PERFECT

ich habe	wir haben	stattgefunden
du hast	ihr habt	
Sie haben	Sie haben	
er/sie/es hat	sie haben	

PAST PERFECT

ich hatte	wir hatten	stattgefunden
du hattest	ihr hattet	
Sie hatten	Sie hatten	
er/sie/es hatte	sie hatten	

FUTURE PERFECT

ich werde	wir werden	stattgefunden haben
du wirst	ihr werdet	
Sie werden	Sie werden	
er/sie/es wird	sie werden	

PAST SUBJUNCTIVE I

ich habe	wir haben	stattgefunden
du habest	ihr habet	
Sie haben	Sie haben	
er/sie/es habe	sie haben	

PAST SUBJUNCTIVE II

ich hätte	wir hätten	stattgefunden
du hättest	ihr hättet	
Sie hätten	Sie hätten	
er/sie/es hätte	sie hätten	

FUTURE PERFECT SUBJUNCTIVE I

ich werde	wir werden	stattgefunden haben
du werdest	ihr werdet	
Sie werden	Sie werden	
er/sie/es werde	sie werden	

FUTURE PERFECT SUBJUNCTIVE II

ich würde	wir würden	stattgefunden haben
du würdest	ihr würdet	
Sie würden	Sie würden	
er/sie/es würde	sie würden	

COMMANDS finde statt! findet statt! finden Sie statt!

PRESENT PARTICIPLE stattfindend

NOTE First- and second-person forms of **stattfinden** occur only in figurative or poetic use.

Usage

Wo hat das Weltmeisterschaftsspiel stattgefunden?	*Where did the world championship game take place?*
Die Hochzeit hat auf einer ehemaligen Zuckerplantage auf Hawaii stattgefunden.	*The wedding took place on a former sugar plantation in Hawaii.*
Wann findet die Hannover Messe statt?	*When does the Hannover Fair take place?*
Der Chef verspricht, dass ein Personalabbau stattfindet.	*The boss promises a personnel cut will happen.*
Die ganze dritte Szene findet in einer Kneipe statt.	*The entire third scene takes place in a pub.*
Ihr erstes Treffen muss in den 60er Jahren stattgefunden haben.	*Their first meeting must have taken place in the 1960s.*
Die Veranstaltung fand trotz des Wetters statt.	*The event took place in spite of the weather.*
Das Verhör findet im Hörsaal statt.	*The hearing will take place in the auditorium.*
Alle zwei Jahre wird eine Kommunalwahl stattfinden.	*Every two years, a local election will be held.*

RELATED VERBS *see* **finden** (186)

stechen *to prick, sting, bite; stab*

sticht · stach · gestochen strong verb

PRESENT

ich steche	wir stechen
du stichst	ihr stecht
Sie stechen	Sie stechen
er/sie/es sticht	sie stechen

SIMPLE PAST

ich stach	wir stachen
du stachst	ihr stacht
Sie stachen	Sie stachen
er/sie/es stach	sie stachen

FUTURE

ich werde	wir werden	stechen
du wirst	ihr werdet	
Sie werden	Sie werden	
er/sie/es wird	sie werden	

PRESENT SUBJUNCTIVE I

ich steche	wir stechen
du stechest	ihr stechet
Sie stechen	Sie stechen
er/sie/es steche	sie stechen

PRESENT SUBJUNCTIVE II

ich stäche	wir stächen
du stächest	ihr stächet
Sie stächen	Sie stächen
er/sie/es stäche	sie stächen

FUTURE SUBJUNCTIVE I

ich werde	wir werden	stechen
du werdest	ihr werdet	
Sie werden	Sie werden	
er/sie/es werde	sie werden	

FUTURE SUBJUNCTIVE II

ich würde	wir würden	stechen
du würdest	ihr würdet	
Sie würden	Sie würden	
er/sie/es würde	sie würden	

PRESENT PERFECT

ich habe	wir haben	gestochen
du hast	ihr habt	
Sie haben	Sie haben	
er/sie/es hat	sie haben	

PAST PERFECT

ich hatte	wir hatten	gestochen
du hattest	ihr hattet	
Sie hatten	Sie hatten	
er/sie/es hatte	sie hatten	

FUTURE PERFECT

ich werde	wir werden	gestochen haben
du wirst	ihr werdet	
Sie werden	Sie werden	
er/sie/es wird	sie werden	

PAST SUBJUNCTIVE I

ich habe	wir haben	gestochen
du habest	ihr habet	
Sie haben	Sie haben	
er/sie/es habe	sie haben	

PAST SUBJUNCTIVE II

ich hätte	wir hätten	gestochen
du hättest	ihr hättet	
Sie hätten	Sie hätten	
er/sie/es hätte	sie hätten	

FUTURE PERFECT SUBJUNCTIVE I

ich werde	wir werden	gestochen haben
du werdest	ihr werdet	
Sie werden	Sie werden	
er/sie/es werde	sie werden	

FUTURE PERFECT SUBJUNCTIVE II

ich würde	wir würden	gestochen haben
du würdest	ihr würdet	
Sie würden	Sie würden	
er/sie/es würde	sie würden	

COMMANDS stich! stecht! stechen Sie!

PRESENT PARTICIPLE stechend

Usage

Sticht die Raupe?	*Will the caterpillar bite?*
Röslein sprach: Ich steche dich, daß du ewig denkst an mich. (GOETHE)	*The little rose said, "I'll prick you so you'll always remember me."*
Leon ist von einer Mücke gestochen worden.	*Leon has been bitten by a mosquito.*
Ich habe mich an einem Dorn gestochen.	*I've pricked myself on a thorn.*
Hast du dir die Ohren stechen lassen?	*Did you have your ears pierced?*
Die Kuh hat sich an einem Nagel gestochen.	*The cow jabbed itself on a nail.*
Die Biene stach ihm ins Gesicht.	*The bee stung him in the face.*
Der Junge sticht mit einer Nadel in den Luftballon.	*The boy is puncturing the balloon with a needle.*
Sophie hat sich die Hand am Angelhaken gestochen.	*Sophie has pricked her hand on the fishhook.*
Frau Unruh wurde mit einem Dolch gestochen.	*Mrs. Unruh was stabbed with a dagger.*
Melanie will Uwe mit einem Messer gestochen haben.	*Melanie claims to have stabbed Uwe with a knife.*

RELATED VERBS ab·stechen, an·stechen, auf·stechen, aus·stechen, bestechen, durchstechen, durch·stechen, ein·stechen, erstechen, überstechen, zerstechen, zu·stechen

PRESENT

ich stecke	wir stecken
du steckst	ihr steckt
Sie stecken	Sie stecken
er/sie/es steckt	sie stecken

PRESENT PERFECT

ich habe	wir haben	gesteckt
du hast	ihr habt	
Sie haben	Sie haben	
er/sie/es hat	sie haben	

SIMPLE PAST

ich steckte (stak)	wir steckten (staken)
du stecktest (stakst)	ihr stecktet (stakt)
Sie steckten (staken)	Sie steckten (staken)
er/sie/es steckte (stak)	sie steckten (staken)

PAST PERFECT

ich hatte	wir hatten	gesteckt
du hattest	ihr hattet	
Sie hatten	Sie hatten	
er/sie/es hatte	sie hatten	

FUTURE

ich werde	wir werden	stecken
du wirst	ihr werdet	
Sie werden	Sie werden	
er/sie/es wird	sie werden	

FUTURE PERFECT

ich werde	wir werden	gesteckt haben
du wirst	ihr werdet	
Sie werden	Sie werden	
er/sie/es wird	sie werden	

PRESENT SUBJUNCTIVE I

ich stecke	wir stecken
du steckest	ihr stecket
Sie stecken	Sie stecken
er/sie/es stecke	sie stecken

PAST SUBJUNCTIVE I

ich habe	wir haben	gesteckt
du habest	ihr habet	
Sie haben	Sie haben	
er/sie/es habe	sie haben	

PRESENT SUBJUNCTIVE II

ich steckte (stäke)	wir steckten (stäken)
du stecktest (stäkest)	ihr stecktet (stäket)
Sie steckten (stäken)	Sie steckten (stäken)
er/sie/es steckte (stäke)	sie steckten (stäken)

PAST SUBJUNCTIVE II

ich hätte	wir hätten	gesteckt
du hättest	ihr hättet	
Sie hätten	Sie hätten	
er/sie/es hätte	sie hätten	

FUTURE SUBJUNCTIVE I

ich werde	wir werden	stecken
du werdest	ihr werdet	
Sie werden	Sie werden	
er/sie/es werde	sie werden	

FUTURE PERFECT SUBJUNCTIVE I

ich werde	wir werden	gesteckt haben
du werdest	ihr werdet	
Sie werden	Sie werden	
er/sie/es werde	sie werden	

FUTURE SUBJUNCTIVE II

ich würde	wir würden	stecken
du würdest	ihr würdet	
Sie würden	Sie würden	
er/sie/es würde	sie würden	

FUTURE PERFECT SUBJUNCTIVE II

ich würde	wir würden	gesteckt haben
du würdest	ihr würdet	
Sie würden	Sie würden	
er/sie/es würde	sie würden	

COMMANDS steck(e)! steckt! stecken Sie!

PRESENT PARTICIPLE steckend

NOTE When **stecken** is intransitive, the strong simple past is sometimes used: **stak**.

Usage

Reinhard hat sich die Hände in die Taschen gesteckt.	*Reinhard stuck his hands in his pockets.*
Unser Papagei steckte eine Münze in den Schnabel.	*Our parrot stuck a coin in his beak.*
Der Wagen ist im Schlamm stecken geblieben.	*The car got stuck in the mud.*
Der Luftballon steckt in der Eiche.	*The balloon is stuck in the oak tree.*
Die Arme in den Hosen drein; im Ärmel stak gezwängt das Bein. (E.T.A. HOFFMANN)	*His arms were in the pant legs; his leg stuck tight in the sleeves.*
Die Regierung steckte 5 Millionen in das Projekt.	*The government put five million into the project.*
Mareike hat den Mantel in die Kommode gesteckt.	*Mareike put the coat in the chest of drawers.*
Herr Reich steckt sein ganzes Geld in das Geschäft.	*Mr. Reich puts all his money into the business.*
Wo steckt der Schlüssel?	*Where is the key?*
Steckt bitte eure Spielzeuge unter das Bett.	*Please put your toys under the bed.*
Sie hat sich eine Blume ins Haar gesteckt.	*She pinned a flower in her hair.*

RELATED VERBS ab·stecken, an·stecken, auf·stecken, aus·stecken, ein·stecken, verstecken

stehen *to stand, be situated; be*

steht · stand · gestanden strong verb

MORE USAGE SENTENCES WITH stehen

Die Stadt stand drei Tage lang unter Wasser. — *The city was under water for three days.*
Vater möchte, dass das Auto in der Garage steht. — *Father wants the car to be in the garage.*
Der relevante Ort steht nicht auf der Landkarte. — *The location in question is not on the map.*

stehen *to be (printed, written)*

Sein Name wird im Bericht stehen. — *His name will be (mentioned) in the report.*
Wo steht diese Regelung geschrieben? — *Where is that regulation in writing?*
Stand das wirklich in der Zeitung? — *Was that really (printed) in the newspaper?*
Die Antwort steht auf Seite 255. — *The answer is on page 255.*

stehen für *to stand for, represent*

Wofür steht die Farbe Gold in diesem Märchen? — *What does the color gold stand for in this fairy tale?*

stehen vor *to stand in front of; be faced with*

Luca stand vor dem Haus und winkte uns zu. — *Luca stood in front of the house and waved to us.*
Wir stehen vor einer schwierigen Entscheidung. — *We are faced with a difficult decision.*

stehen zu *to stand by, support*

Mark hat in den schweren Zeiten zu mir gestanden. — *Mark stood by me during the difficult times.*

stehen + dative *to suit, look, become*

Das gelbe Kleid steht dir viel besser als das blaue. — *The yellow dress suits you much better than the blue one.*
Ein Bart würde Felix gut stehen. — *Felix would look good with a beard.*
„Der Tod steht ihr gut" (FILM TITLE) — *"Death Becomes Her"*

stehen + verb

Jonas ging drei Schritte und blieb stehen. — *Jonas took three steps and stood still.*
Wir sind in Kapitel 3 stehen geblieben. — *We left off in Chapter 3.*
Oma und Opa hatten früher ein Regal in der Ecke stehen. — *Grandma and Grandpa used to have a bookcase standing in the corner.*

IDIOMATIC EXPRESSIONS

Wir haben bis zwei Uhr Schlange gestanden. — *We stood in line until two o'clock.*
Wie steht das Spiel? — *What's the score? / What's the status of the game?*
Wie steht's bei der Arbeit? — *How are things at work?*
Fehler werden uns teuer zu stehen kommen. — *We will have to pay dearly for any mistakes.*
Mir stehen die Haare zu Berge. — *My hair is standing on end.*
Die Aufgabe steht mir bis zum Hals! — *I'm fed up with / sick and tired of this assignment!*
Meine Aktien stehen heute gut. — *My stock shares are up today.*
Die Wanduhr steht schon wieder! — *The wall clock has stopped again!*
Mark steht auf Orchideen. (*colloquial*) — *Mark is into / really likes orchids.*
Das Ölkonzern musste dem Publikum Rede und Antwort stehen. — *The oil company had to justify its actions to the public.*
Warum steht die Tür offen? — *Why is the door ajar?*
Alles steht auf dem Spiel. — *Everything is at stake.*
Lena steht im Verdacht des Missbrauchs von Geldern. — *Lena is under suspicion for misusing funds.*
Ich stehe Ihnen zur Verfügung. — *I am at your disposal.*
Unbegrenzte Ressourcen standen uns zur Verfügung. — *We had access to unlimited resources.*
Franz steht sich sehr gut mit seinem Chef. — *Franz is on very good terms with his boss.*

PRESENT

ich stehe	wir stehen
du stehst	ihr steht
Sie stehen	Sie stehen
er/sie/es steht	sie stehen

PRESENT PERFECT

ich habe	wir haben	gestanden
du hast	ihr habt	
Sie haben	Sie haben	
er/sie/es hat	sie haben	

SIMPLE PAST

ich stand	wir standen
du standst	ihr standet
Sie standen	Sie standen
er/sie/es stand	sie standen

PAST PERFECT

ich hatte	wir hatten	gestanden
du hattest	ihr hattet	
Sie hatten	Sie hatten	
er/sie/es hatte	sie hatten	

FUTURE

ich werde	wir werden	stehen
du wirst	ihr werdet	
Sie werden	Sie werden	
er/sie/es wird	sie werden	

FUTURE PERFECT

ich werde	wir werden	gestanden haben
du wirst	ihr werdet	
Sie werden	Sie werden	
er/sie/es wird	sie werden	

PRESENT SUBJUNCTIVE I

ich stehe	wir stehen
du stehest	ihr stehet
Sie stehen	Sie stehen
er/sie/es stehe	sie stehen

PAST SUBJUNCTIVE I

ich habe	wir haben	gestanden
du habest	ihr habet	
Sie haben	Sie haben	
er/sie/es habe	sie haben	

PRESENT SUBJUNCTIVE II

ich stünde/stände	wir stünden/ständen
du stündest/ständest	ihr stündet/ständet
Sie stünden/ständen	Sie stünden/ständen
er/sie/es stünde/stände	sie stünden/ständen

PAST SUBJUNCTIVE II

ich hätte	wir hätten	gestanden
du hättest	ihr hättet	
Sie hätten	Sie hätten	
er/sie/es hätte	sie hätten	

FUTURE SUBJUNCTIVE I

ich werde	wir werden	stehen
du werdest	ihr werdet	
Sie werden	Sie werden	
er/sie/es werde	sie werden	

FUTURE PERFECT SUBJUNCTIVE I

ich werde	wir werden	gestanden haben
du werdest	ihr werdet	
Sie werden	Sie werden	
er/sie/es werde	sie werden	

FUTURE SUBJUNCTIVE II

ich würde	wir würden	stehen
du würdest	ihr würdet	
Sie würden	Sie würden	
er/sie/es würde	sie würden	

FUTURE PERFECT SUBJUNCTIVE II

ich würde	wir würden	gestanden haben
du würdest	ihr würdet	
Sie würden	Sie würden	
er/sie/es würde	sie würden	

COMMANDS steh(e)! steht! stehen Sie!

PRESENT PARTICIPLE stehend

Usage

Warum steht Tim auf dem Dach?	*Why is Tim standing on the roof?*
Herr Fischer stand in seinem Garten, als das Auto vorbeifuhr.	*Mr. Fischer was standing in his garden when the car drove by.*
Die Patientin versuchte vergeblich zu stehen.	*The patient tried unsuccessfully to stand.*
Die Katze steht hinter dem Sofa.	*The cat is standing behind the sofa.*
Die beiden Brüder stehen neben einander in der Ecke.	*The two brothers are standing next to one another in the corner.*
Der Tannenbaum steht nicht gerade.	*The Christmas tree isn't standing straight.*
Das große Haus, das an der Ecke stand, gehörte dem Apotheker Schmidthammer.	*The big house that stood on the corner belonged to the pharmacist Schmidthammer.*

RELATED VERBS ab·stehen, an·stehen, auf·erstehen, aus·stehen, bei·stehen, bereit·stehen, bevor·stehen, da·stehen, ein·gestehen, ein·stehen, entgegen·stehen, erstehen, fest·stehen, frei·stehen, gegenüber·stehen, gerade·stehen, gestehen, gleich·stehen, hervor·stehen, nach·stehen, still·stehen, überstehen, unterstehen, unter·stehen, vor·stehen, widerstehen, zu·gestehen, zurück·stehen, zu·stehen; *see also* **auf·stehen** (32), **bestehen** (90), **entstehen** (150), **verstehen** (501)

424 stehlen *to steal*

stiehlt · stahl · gestohlen strong verb

PRESENT

ich stehle	wir stehlen
du stiehlst	ihr stehlt
Sie stehlen	Sie stehlen
er/sie/es stiehlt	sie stehlen

PRESENT PERFECT

ich habe	wir haben	gestohlen
du hast	ihr habt	
Sie haben	Sie haben	
er/sie/es hat	sie haben	

SIMPLE PAST

ich stahl	wir stahlen
du stahlst	ihr stahlt
Sie stahlen	Sie stahlen
er/sie/es stahl	sie stahlen

PAST PERFECT

ich hatte	wir hatten	gestohlen
du hattest	ihr hattet	
Sie hatten	Sie hatten	
er/sie/es hatte	sie hatten	

FUTURE

ich werde	wir werden	stehlen
du wirst	ihr werdet	
Sie werden	Sie werden	
er/sie/es wird	sie werden	

FUTURE PERFECT

ich werde	wir werden	gestohlen haben
du wirst	ihr werdet	
Sie werden	Sie werden	
er/sie/es wird	sie werden	

PRESENT SUBJUNCTIVE I

ich stehle	wir stehlen
du stehlest	ihr stehlet
Sie stehlen	Sie stehlen
er/sie/es stehle	sie stehlen

PAST SUBJUNCTIVE I

ich habe	wir haben	gestohlen
du habest	ihr habet	
Sie haben	Sie haben	
er/sie/es habe	sie haben	

PRESENT SUBJUNCTIVE II

ich stähle/stöhle	wir stählen/stöhlen
du stählest/stöhlest	ihr stählet/stöhlet
Sie stählen/stöhlen	Sie stählen/stöhlen
er/sie/es stähle/stöhle	sie stählen/stöhlen

PAST SUBJUNCTIVE II

ich hätte	wir hätten	gestohlen
du hättest	ihr hättet	
Sie hätten	Sie hätten	
er/sie/es hätte	sie hätten	

FUTURE SUBJUNCTIVE I

ich werde	wir werden	stehlen
du werdest	ihr werdet	
Sie werden	Sie werden	
er/sie/es werde	sie werden	

FUTURE PERFECT SUBJUNCTIVE I

ich werde	wir werden	gestohlen haben
du werdest	ihr werdet	
Sie werden	Sie werden	
er/sie/es werde	sie werden	

FUTURE SUBJUNCTIVE II

ich würde	wir würden	stehlen
du würdest	ihr würdet	
Sie würden	Sie würden	
er/sie/es würde	sie würden	

FUTURE PERFECT SUBJUNCTIVE II

ich würde	wir würden	gestohlen haben
du würdest	ihr würdet	
Sie würden	Sie würden	
er/sie/es würde	sie würden	

COMMANDS stiehl! stehlt! stehlen Sie!

PRESENT PARTICIPLE stehlend

Usage

Zum Glück war nichts gestohlen worden.	*Luckily, nothing had been stolen.*
Sein Hund Maxl stiehlt immer das Katzenfutter.	*His dog, Maxl, always steals the cat food.*
Er sagte, dass Davids neuer DVD-Spieler vor einigen Tagen gestohlen worden sei.	*He said that David's new DVD player was stolen a few days ago.*
In Münster werden viele Fahrräder vom Bahnhof gestohlen.	*In Münster, many bicycles are stolen from the train station.*
Du sollst nicht stehlen. (2. Mose 20,15)	*Thou shalt not steal.* (Exodus 20:15)
Im Banküberfall wurden 5 Millionen gestohlen.	*Five million was stolen in the bank robbery.*
Robin Hood stahl von den Reichen und gab den Armen.	*Robin Hood stole from the rich and gave to the poor.*
Der Dieb hatte ein Auto bei Hertz gestohlen.	*The thief had stolen a car at Hertz.*

sich stehlen *to slink, steal*

Maximilian stahl sich hinter den Baum.	*Maximilian stole behind the tree.*

RELATED VERBS bestehlen, weg·stehlen

strong verb **steigt · stieg · gestiegen**

PRESENT

ich steige	wir steigen
du steigst	ihr steigt
Sie steigen	Sie steigen
er/sie/es steigt	sie steigen

SIMPLE PAST

ich stieg	wir stiegen
du stiegst	ihr stiegt
Sie stiegen	Sie stiegen
er/sie/es stieg	sie stiegen

FUTURE

ich werde	wir werden	steigen
du wirst	ihr werdet	
Sie werden	Sie werden	
er/sie/es wird	sie werden	

PRESENT SUBJUNCTIVE I

ich steige	wir steigen
du steigest	ihr steiget
Sie steigen	Sie steigen
er/sie/es steige	sie steigen

PRESENT SUBJUNCTIVE II

ich stiege	wir stiegen
du stiegest	ihr stieget
Sie stiegen	Sie stiegen
er/sie/es stiege	sie stiegen

FUTURE SUBJUNCTIVE I

ich werde	wir werden	steigen
du werdest	ihr werdet	
Sie werden	Sie werden	
er/sie/es werde	sie werden	

FUTURE SUBJUNCTIVE II

ich würde	wir würden	steigen
du würdest	ihr würdet	
Sie würden	Sie würden	
er/sie/es würde	sie würden	

PRESENT PERFECT

ich bin	wir sind	gestiegen
du bist	ihr seid	
Sie sind	Sie sind	
er/sie/es ist	sie sind	

PAST PERFECT

ich war	wir waren	gestiegen
du warst	ihr wart	
Sie waren	Sie waren	
er/sie/es war	sie waren	

FUTURE PERFECT

ich werde	wir werden	gestiegen sein
du wirst	ihr werdet	
Sie werden	Sie werden	
er/sie/es wird	sie werden	

PAST SUBJUNCTIVE I

ich sei	wir seien	gestiegen
du seiest	ihr seiet	
Sie seien	Sie seien	
er/sie/es sei	sie seien	

PAST SUBJUNCTIVE II

ich wäre	wir wären	gestiegen
du wärest	ihr wäret	
Sie wären	Sie wären	
er/sie/es wäre	sie wären	

FUTURE PERFECT SUBJUNCTIVE I

ich werde	wir werden	gestiegen sein
du werdest	ihr werdet	
Sie werden	Sie werden	
er/sie/es werde	sie werden	

FUTURE PERFECT SUBJUNCTIVE II

ich würde	wir würden	gestiegen sein
du würdest	ihr würdet	
Sie würden	Sie würden	
er/sie/es würde	sie würden	

COMMANDS steig(e)! steigt! steigen Sie!

PRESENT PARTICIPLE steigend

Usage

Warum wollte Lea aus dem Fenster steigen?	*Why did Lea want to climb out the window?*
Ein abscheulicher Geruch stieg mir in die Nase.	*A disgusting smell rose to my nose.*
Der Wasserpegel steigt immer weiter.	*The water level is rising higher and higher.*
Wir durften nicht auf den Turm steigen.	*We weren't allowed to climb up the tower.*
Wir sind über den Zaun gestiegen und weiter gelaufen.	*We climbed over the fence and ran farther.*
Am nächsten Tag sind wir auf den Half-Dome gestiegen.	*The next day, we climbed Half Dome.*
Der kleine Dackel konnte nicht aufs Sofa steigen.	*The little dachshund couldn't climb onto the sofa.*
Die Ballons stiegen langsam in die Luft.	*The balloons ascended slowly in the air.*
Ölpreise steigen.	*Oil prices are rising.*
Im Sommer steigen die Temperaturen in die Höhe.	*In the summer, the temperatures climb.*
Die Opferzahl steigt jetzt auf 63.	*The number of victims has now increased to 63.*
Wann dürfen wir ins Flugzeug steigen?	*When can we board the plane?*

RELATED VERBS ab·steigen, an·steigen, auf·steigen, aus·steigen, besteigen, ersteigen, um·steigen; *see also* **ein·steigen** (138)

stellen *to put, place; stand; set*

stellt · stellte · gestellt regular weak verb

MORE USAGE SENTENCES WITH stellen

An der Sicherheitskontrolle mussten wir unsere Schuhe auf ein Fließband stellen.	*At the security checkpoint, we had to place our shoes on a conveyor belt.*
Kannst du die Stange wieder gerade stellen?	*Can you put the rod straight again?*
Muss man auch die H-Milch nicht kalt stellen?	*Don't you have to put ultra-pasteurized milk in the fridge, too?*
Stell die Musik bitte etwas lauter.	*Please turn the music a bit louder.*
Sie haben die Lampe in den Schrank gestellt.	*They stood the lamp in the closet.*
Könntest du die Uhr bitte richtig stellen?	*Could you please reset the clock to the correct time?*

sich stellen *to put/place oneself, stand; pretend to be, feign, act*

Der Täter soll sich der Polizei drei Tage danach gestellt haben.	*The perpetrator is said to have given himself up to the police three days later.*
Stellen Sie sich bitte neben Frau Lehmann!	*Please stand next to Mrs. Lehmann!*
Frau Krause musste sich dem Gericht stellen.	*Mrs. Krause had to appear in court.*
Wieso stellt sich Harry ständig gegen sie?	*How come Harry is taking an antagonistic attitude toward her?*
Der tapfere junge Kämpfer stellte sich seinem erfahreneren Gegner.	*The brave young warrior faced his more experienced adversary.*
Katharina stellt sich unfähig, um der Verantwortung auszuweichen.	*Katharina feigns incompetence to avoid responsibility.*
Ist der Präsident wirklich naiv oder stellt er sich nur so?	*Is the president really naive, or is he only putting on an act?*
Der Hund kann sich tot stellen.	*The dog can play dead.*

IDIOMATIC EXPRESSIONS

Manchmal stellen Kinder komische Fragen an Erwachsene.	*Sometimes, children ask adults funny questions.*
Christoph hat seine Fähigkeiten mehrmals unter Beweis gestellt.	*Christoph has proved his abilities several times.*
Leons Absichten werden jetzt in Frage gestellt.	*Leon's intentions are now being questioned.*
Ich möchte das Projekt so bald wie möglich fertig stellen.	*I'd like to finish the project as soon as possible.*
Der Junge stellte ihr ein Bein und sie ist hingefallen.	*The boy tripped her and she fell.*
Die Chefin stellt immer mehr Forderungen.	*The boss is making more and more demands.*
Die Regierung hat die Wahrheit auf den Kopf gestellt.	*The government has distorted the truth* (lit., *turned truth on its head*).
Tim ist ganz auf sich selbst gestellt.	*Tim is entirely dependent on his own resources.*
Reinhard ist ziemlich schlecht gestellt.	*Reinhard is pretty bad off.*
Die alte Dorfkirche wurde unter Denkmalschutz gestellt.	*The old village church was protected as a historical monument.*
Die geplante Parkanlage ist zur Diskussion gestellt worden.	*The planned parkway has been brought up for discussion.*
Die Postgebühren werden Ihnen in Rechnung gestellt.	*The postage will be charged to your account.*
Ernst hat uns seinen Diaprojektor zur Verfügung gestellt.	*Ernst has put his slide projector at our disposal.*
Frau Dormagen wollte einen Antrag auf Genehmigung stellen.	*Mrs. Dormagen wanted to submit an application for authorization.*
Sein Wissen wird in der Debatte endlich auf die Probe gestellt.	*His knowledge is finally being put to the test in the debate.*

regular weak verb **stellt · stellte · gestellt**

PRESENT

ich stelle	wir stellen
du stellst	ihr stellt
Sie stellen	Sie stellen
er/sie/es stellt	sie stellen

SIMPLE PAST

ich stellte	wir stellten
du stelltest	ihr stelltet
Sie stellten	Sie stellten
er/sie/es stellte	sie stellten

FUTURE

ich werde	wir werden	stellen
du wirst	ihr werdet	
Sie werden	Sie werden	
er/sie/es wird	sie werden	

PRESENT SUBJUNCTIVE I

ich stelle	wir stellen
du stellest	ihr stellet
Sie stellen	Sie stellen
er/sie/es stelle	sie stellen

PRESENT SUBJUNCTIVE II

ich stellte	wir stellten
du stelltest	ihr stelltet
Sie stellten	Sie stellten
er/sie/es stellte	sie stellten

FUTURE SUBJUNCTIVE I

ich werde	wir werden	stellen
du werdest	ihr werdet	
Sie werden	Sie werden	
er/sie/es werde	sie werden	

FUTURE SUBJUNCTIVE II

ich würde	wir würden	stellen
du würdest	ihr würdet	
Sie würden	Sie würden	
er/sie/es würde	sie würden	

PRESENT PERFECT

ich habe	wir haben	gestellt
du hast	ihr habt	
Sie haben	Sie haben	
er/sie/es hat	sie haben	

PAST PERFECT

ich hatte	wir hatten	gestellt
du hattest	ihr hattet	
Sie hatten	Sie hatten	
er/sie/es hatte	sie hatten	

FUTURE PERFECT

ich werde	wir werden	gestellt haben
du wirst	ihr werdet	
Sie werden	Sie werden	
er/sie/es wird	sie werden	

PAST SUBJUNCTIVE I

ich habe	wir haben	gestellt
du habest	ihr habet	
Sie haben	Sie haben	
er/sie/es habe	sie haben	

PAST SUBJUNCTIVE II

ich hätte	wir hätten	gestellt
du hättest	ihr hättet	
Sie hätten	Sie hätten	
er/sie/es hätte	sie hätten	

FUTURE PERFECT SUBJUNCTIVE I

ich werde	wir werden	gestellt haben
du werdest	ihr werdet	
Sie werden	Sie werden	
er/sie/es werde	sie werden	

FUTURE PERFECT SUBJUNCTIVE II

ich würde	wir würden	gestellt haben
du würdest	ihr würdet	
Sie würden	Sie würden	
er/sie/es würde	sie würden	

COMMANDS stell(e)! stellt! stellen Sie!

PRESENT PARTICIPLE stellend

Usage

Wohin stellt man die Pfandflaschen?	*Where do you put the deposit bottles?*
Stellen Sie das Buch bitte ins Bücherregal.	*Please put the book on the bookshelf.*
Man kann die Tastatur auch höher stellen.	*You can also position the keyboard higher.*
Die Tondachziegel werden in einen großen Ofen gestellt.	*The clay tile shingles are placed in a large oven.*
Wohin sind Fahrräder zu stellen?	*Where do you put the bicycles?*
Wer stellt das Gepäck ins Auto?	*Who will put the luggage in the car?*
Was stellst du alles in deine Büchertasche?	*What all are you putting in your book bag?*
Geliebter, du stellst mich zur schrecklichsten Wahl. (GOTTFRIED BÜRGER)	*Beloved, you present me with a most terrible choice.*

RELATED VERBS ab·stellen, an·stellen, auf·stellen, bereit·stellen, bloß·stellen, dar·stellen, durch·stellen, entgegen·stellen, entstellen, erstellen, frei·stellen, gleich·stellen, hin·stellen, hoch·stellen, kalt·stellen, klar·stellen, nach·stellen, sicher·stellen, um·stellen, unterstellen, unter·stellen, verstellen, voran·stellen, weg·stellen, zurecht·stellen, zurück·stellen, zusammen·stellen, zu·stellen; *see also* **aus·stellen** (41), **bestellen** (91), **ein·stellen** (139), **fest·stellen** (185), **her·stellen** (244), **vor·stellen** (511)

sterben *to die, perish*

stirbt · starb · gestorben strong verb

MORE USAGE SENTENCES WITH sterben

Laut Aussage der Polizei seien zwölf Gefangene gestorben. — *According to police statements, 12 prisoners have died.*

Tante Mae ist im Alter von 98 eines natürlichen Todes gestorben. — *Aunt Mae died of natural causes at the age of 98.*

Der Präsident starb durch einen Gewehrschuss in den Kopf. — *The president died of a rifle shot to the head.*

Kerstins Zwillingsschwester ist jung gestorben. — *Kerstin's twin sister died young.*

Die ganze Familie starb in den Flammen. — *The whole family perished in the flames.*

Jan Hus starb 1415 den Martyrertod, als er auf dem Scheiterhaufen verbrannt wurde. — *Jan Hus died a martyr's death in 1415, when he was burned at the stake.*

Was sollte dann aus mir werden, wenn du stürbest? (Karl Immermann) — *What would then become of me if you were to die?*

Ein drittes Kind war ihr gestorben. — *She had lost a third child to death.*

Clemens Huber starb in der Schlacht bei Marengo in Italien. — *Clemens Huber died in the Battle of Marengo in Italy.*

Die junge Mutter starb an Komplikationen der Niederkunft. — *The young mother died from complications of childbirth.*

Der General wollte lieber sterben als vor dem Feind kapitulieren. — *The general would rather have died than surrender to the enemy.*

Eher will ich sterben als... — *I'd rather die than ...*

Jedes Jahr sterben in Deutschland über 100 000 Menschen an den Folgen des Rauchens. — *Every year, over 100,000 people die in Germany as a result of smoking.*

Wenn man ertrinkt, stirbt man durch Mangel an Sauerstoff. — *When you drown, you die of a lack of oxygen.*

Laut dem Staatschef seien die Soldaten nicht umsonst gestorben. — *According to the head of state, the soldiers did not die in vain.*

Ist John Wayne an Krebs gestorben? — *Did John Wayne die of cancer?*

Mitte des 14. Jahrhunderts starb ein Drittel der gesamten Bevölkerung Mitteleuropas an der Pest. — *In the mid-fourteenth century, a third of the entire population of central Europe died of the plague.*

Blaugrüne Algen sterben in kaltem Wasser. — *Blue-green algae die in cold water.*

Der Wald stirbt wegen sauren Regens. — *The forest is dying because of acid rain.*

Wie sind meine Finger so grün / Blumen hab' ich zerrissen / sie wollten für mich blühn / und haben sterben müssen. (Droste-Hülshoff) — *How green my fingers are, I was pulling up flowers, they wanted to bloom for me but had to perish.*

IDIOMATIC EXPRESSIONS

Und wenn sie nicht gestorben sind, dann leben sie noch heute. (*formulaic end of a fairy tale*) — *And they lived happily ever after.* (lit., *And if they haven't died, they're still alive today.*)

Ich bin tausende Tode gestorben. — *I died a thousand deaths / a thousand times over.*

Sie ist für mich gestorben. — *She doesn't exist as far as I'm concerned. / I'm finished with her.*

Ich sterbe vor Durst! — *I'm dying of thirst!*

Ich sterbe vor Angst! — *I'm scared to death!*

Gestorben! (*film director jargon, said when a take is completed*) — *Cut! / In the can!*

Auf dem Schlachtfeld starben die Soldaten wie Fliegen. — *The soldiers were dropping like flies on the battlefield.*

Davon stirbt man nicht gleich! — *It won't kill you!*

strong verb **stirbt · starb · gestorben**

PRESENT

ich sterbe	wir sterben
du stirbst	ihr sterbt
Sie sterben	Sie sterben
er/sie/es stirbt	sie sterben

PRESENT PERFECT

ich bin	wir sind	gestorben
du bist	ihr seid	
Sie sind	Sie sind	
er/sie/es ist	sie sind	

SIMPLE PAST

ich starb	wir starben
du starbst	ihr starbt
Sie starben	Sie starben
er/sie/es starb	sie starben

PAST PERFECT

ich war	wir waren	gestorben
du warst	ihr wart	
Sie waren	Sie waren	
er/sie/es war	sie waren	

FUTURE

ich werde	wir werden	sterben
du wirst	ihr werdet	
Sie werden	Sie werden	
er/sie/es wird	sie werden	

FUTURE PERFECT

ich werde	wir werden	gestorben sein
du wirst	ihr werdet	
Sie werden	Sie werden	
er/sie/es wird	sie werden	

PRESENT SUBJUNCTIVE I

ich sterbe	wir sterben
du sterbest	ihr sterbet
Sie sterben	Sie sterben
er/sie/es sterbe	sie sterben

PAST SUBJUNCTIVE I

ich sei	wir seien	gestorben
du seiest	ihr seiet	
Sie seien	Sie seien	
er/sie/es sei	sie seien	

PRESENT SUBJUNCTIVE II

ich stürbe	wir stürben
du stürbest	ihr stürbet
Sie stürben	Sie stürben
er/sie/es stürbe	sie stürben

PAST SUBJUNCTIVE II

ich wäre	wir wären	gestorben
du wärest	ihr wäret	
Sie wären	Sie wären	
er/sie/es wäre	sie wären	

FUTURE SUBJUNCTIVE I

ich werde	wir werden	sterben
du werdest	ihr werdet	
Sie werden	Sie werden	
er/sie/es werde	sie werden	

FUTURE PERFECT SUBJUNCTIVE I

ich werde	wir werden	gestorben sein
du werdest	ihr werdet	
Sie werden	Sie werden	
er/sie/es werde	sie werden	

FUTURE SUBJUNCTIVE II

ich würde	wir würden	sterben
du würdest	ihr würdet	
Sie würden	Sie würden	
er/sie/es würde	sie würden	

FUTURE PERFECT SUBJUNCTIVE II

ich würde	wir würden	gestorben sein
du würdest	ihr würdet	
Sie würden	Sie würden	
er/sie/es würde	sie würden	

COMMANDS stirb! sterbt! sterben Sie!

PRESENT PARTICIPLE sterbend

Usage

Früher starb man schon oft mit 40 Jahren.	*People often used to die as early as 40 years of age.*
Wie viele sind im Krieg gestorben?	*How many have died in the war?*
Die Opfer sterben nach nur einigen Tagen.	*The victims die after only a few days.*
Plötzlich starb die Prinzessin an Trauer um ihren verstorbenen Geliebten.	*Suddenly, the princess died of sorrow over her departed beloved.*
Manfred ist aber noch nicht gestorben!	*But Manfred hasn't died yet!*
Der Milliardär stirbt auf seiner Insel im Pazifik.	*The billionaire is dying on his island in the Pacific.*
Etwa 4 000 Personen sollen den Hungertod gestorben sein.	*About 4,000 people are said to have died of starvation.*
Der alte König wollte eines sanften Todes sterben.	*The old king wanted to die in peace.*
Der Musiker starb im Jahr 1832 umgeben von Freunden und Anhängern.	*The musician died in the year 1832, surrounded by friends and followers.*
Ernst war genau an diesem Ort gestorben.	*Ernst had died at this very spot.*

RELATED VERBS ab·sterben, aus·sterben, ersterben, versterben, weg·sterben

428 stimmen *to be right/correct; vote; make; tune*

stimmt · stimmte · gestimmt regular weak verb

PRESENT

ich stimme	wir stimmen
du stimmst	ihr stimmt
Sie stimmen	Sie stimmen
er/sie/es stimmt	sie stimmen

SIMPLE PAST

ich stimmte	wir stimmten
du stimmtest	ihr stimmtet
Sie stimmten	Sie stimmten
er/sie/es stimmte	sie stimmten

FUTURE

ich werde	wir werden	stimmen
du wirst	ihr werdet	
Sie werden	Sie werden	
er/sie/es wird	sie werden	

PRESENT SUBJUNCTIVE I

ich stimme	wir stimmen
du stimmest	ihr stimmet
Sie stimmen	Sie stimmen
er/sie/es stimme	sie stimmen

PRESENT SUBJUNCTIVE II

ich stimmte	wir stimmten
du stimmtest	ihr stimmtet
Sie stimmten	Sie stimmten
er/sie/es stimmte	sie stimmten

FUTURE SUBJUNCTIVE I

ich werde	wir werden	stimmen
du werdest	ihr werdet	
Sie werden	Sie werden	
er/sie/es werde	sie werden	

FUTURE SUBJUNCTIVE II

ich würde	wir würden	stimmen
du würdest	ihr würdet	
Sie würden	Sie würden	
er/sie/es würde	sie würden	

PRESENT PERFECT

ich habe	wir haben	gestimmt
du hast	ihr habt	
Sie haben	Sie haben	
er/sie/es hat	sie haben	

PAST PERFECT

ich hatte	wir hatten	gestimmt
du hattest	ihr hattet	
Sie hatten	Sie hatten	
er/sie/es hatte	sie hatten	

FUTURE PERFECT

ich werde	wir werden	gestimmt haben
du wirst	ihr werdet	
Sie werden	Sie werden	
er/sie/es wird	sie werden	

PAST SUBJUNCTIVE I

ich habe	wir haben	gestimmt
du habest	ihr habet	
Sie haben	Sie haben	
er/sie/es habe	sie haben	

PAST SUBJUNCTIVE II

ich hätte	wir hätten	gestimmt
du hättest	ihr hättet	
Sie hätten	Sie hätten	
er/sie/es hätte	sie hätten	

FUTURE PERFECT SUBJUNCTIVE I

ich werde	wir werden	gestimmt haben
du werdest	ihr werdet	
Sie werden	Sie werden	
er/sie/es werde	sie werden	

FUTURE PERFECT SUBJUNCTIVE II

ich würde	wir würden	gestimmt haben
du würdest	ihr würdet	
Sie würden	Sie würden	
er/sie/es würde	sie würden	

COMMANDS stimm(e)! stimmt! stimmen Sie!

PRESENT PARTICIPLE stimmend

Usage

Hier stimmt etwas nicht.	*Something's not right here.*
Stimmt so. (*to a waiter, taxi driver, etc.*)	*Keep the change.*
Ihre Antwort stimmte nur teilweise.	*Her answer was only partly correct.*
Hast du keine Zeit zu stimmen?	*Don't you have time to vote?*
Der Vorstand stimmt über eine Etatkürzung.	*The board is voting on a budget cut.*
Nicht nur Stadtbewohner dürfen stimmen.	*Not just city dwellers are permitted to vote.*
Ich würde nicht für ihn stimmen, er ist zu konservativ.	*I wouldn't vote for him; he's too conservative.*
Jeder Mitarbeiter muss als Firmenvertreter stimmen können.	*Every employee must be able to vote as a company representative.*
Wir haben gegen den Krieg gestimmt.	*We voted against the war.*
Sein Tod hat mich traurig gestimmt.	*His death has made me sad.*
Das alte Klavier war nicht leicht zu stimmen.	*The old piano was not easy to tune.*

RELATED VERBS ab·stimmen, überein·stimmen, um·stimmen, verstimmen, zu·stimmen; see *also* **bestimmen** (92)

PRESENT

ich stinke	wir stinken
du stinkst	ihr stinkt
Sie stinken	Sie stinken
er/sie/es stinkt	sie stinken

SIMPLE PAST

ich stank	wir stanken
du stankst	ihr stankt
Sie stanken	Sie stanken
er/sie/es stank	sie stanken

FUTURE

ich werde	wir werden	stinken
du wirst	ihr werdet	
Sie werden	Sie werden	
er/sie/es wird	sie werden	

PRESENT SUBJUNCTIVE I

ich stinke	wir stinken
du stinkest	ihr stinket
Sie stinken	Sie stinken
er/sie/es stinke	sie stinken

PRESENT SUBJUNCTIVE II

ich stänke	wir stänken
du stänkest	ihr stänket
Sie stänken	Sie stänken
er/sie/es stänke	sie stänken

FUTURE SUBJUNCTIVE I

ich werde	wir werden	stinken
du werdest	ihr werdet	
Sie werden	Sie werden	
er/sie/es werde	sie werden	

FUTURE SUBJUNCTIVE II

ich würde	wir würden	stinken
du würdest	ihr würdet	
Sie würden	Sie würden	
er/sie/es würde	sie würden	

PRESENT PERFECT

ich habe	wir haben	gestunken
du hast	ihr habt	
Sie haben	Sie haben	
er/sie/es hat	sie haben	

PAST PERFECT

ich hatte	wir hatten	gestunken
du hattest	ihr hattet	
Sie hatten	Sie hatten	
er/sie/es hatte	sie hatten	

FUTURE PERFECT

ich werde	wir werden	gestunken haben
du wirst	ihr werdet	
Sie werden	Sie werden	
er/sie/es wird	sie werden	

PAST SUBJUNCTIVE I

ich habe	wir haben	gestunken
du habest	ihr habet	
Sie haben	Sie haben	
er/sie/es habe	sie haben	

PAST SUBJUNCTIVE II

ich hätte	wir hätten	gestunken
du hättest	ihr hättet	
Sie hätten	Sie hätten	
er/sie/es hätte	sie hätten	

FUTURE PERFECT SUBJUNCTIVE I

ich werde	wir werden	gestunken haben
du werdest	ihr werdet	
Sie werden	Sie werden	
er/sie/es werde	sie werden	

FUTURE PERFECT SUBJUNCTIVE II

ich würde	wir würden	gestunken haben
du würdest	ihr würdet	
Sie würden	Sie würden	
er/sie/es würde	sie würden	

COMMANDS stink(e)! stinkt! stinken Sie!

PRESENT PARTICIPLE stinkend

Usage

Mein Hund stinkt.	*My dog smells.*
Warum stinkt ein Stinktier?	*Why does a skunk smell?*
Im Kuhstall stinkt es nach Jauche.	*It smells like manure in the cow stall.*
Der Fisch stank entsetzlich, aber die Katze fraß ihn auf.	*The fish stank horribly, but the cat ate it up.*
Das esse ich nicht, es stinkt!	*I won't eat that; it stinks!*
Stinken die roten Socken mehr als die gelben?	*Do the red socks smell worse then the yellow ones?*
„Du stinkst nach Knoblauch!" rief die jüngere Schwester.	*"You smell like garlic!" cried the younger sister.*
Warum haben die Kartoffeln so gestunken?	*Why did the potatoes smell like that?*
Die Schuhe haben sehr gestunken.	*The shoes smelled bad.*
Die Luft stinkt nach Abgasen.	*The air smells like exhaust.*
Nach zehn Tagen wird es im Zimmer bestimmt stinken.	*After 10 days, the room will surely smell.*
Die ranzigen Bohnen haben mir schlecht gestunken.	*The rancid beans smelled bad to me.*
Der Nachbarjunge stinkt vor Faulheit. (*colloquial*)	*The neighbor boy is downright lazy.*
Das Ganze stinkt mir nach Betrug. (*figurative*)	*To me, the whole thing reeks of fraud.*

430 stoppen *to stop*

stoppt · stoppte · gestoppt regular weak verb

PRESENT

ich stoppe	wir stoppen
du stoppst	ihr stoppt
Sie stoppen	Sie stoppen
er/sie/es stoppt	sie stoppen

SIMPLE PAST

ich stoppte	wir stoppten
du stopptest	ihr stopptet
Sie stoppten	Sie stoppten
er/sie/es stoppte	sie stoppten

FUTURE

ich werde	wir werden	stoppen
du wirst	ihr werdet	
Sie werden	Sie werden	
er/sie/es wird	sie werden	

PRESENT SUBJUNCTIVE I

ich stoppe	wir stoppen
du stoppest	ihr stoppet
Sie stoppen	Sie stoppen
er/sie/es stoppe	sie stoppen

PRESENT SUBJUNCTIVE II

ich stoppte	wir stoppten
du stopptest	ihr stopptet
Sie stoppten	Sie stoppten
er/sie/es stoppte	sie stoppten

FUTURE SUBJUNCTIVE I

ich werde	wir werden	stoppen
du werdest	ihr werdet	
Sie werden	Sie werden	
er/sie/es werde	sie werden	

FUTURE SUBJUNCTIVE II

ich würde	wir würden	stoppen
du würdest	ihr würdet	
Sie würden	Sie würden	
er/sie/es würde	sie würden	

PRESENT PERFECT

ich habe	wir haben	gestoppt
du hast	ihr habt	
Sie haben	Sie haben	
er/sie/es hat	sie haben	

PAST PERFECT

ich hatte	wir hatten	gestoppt
du hattest	ihr hattet	
Sie hatten	Sie hatten	
er/sie/es hatte	sie hatten	

FUTURE PERFECT

ich werde	wir werden	gestoppt haben
du wirst	ihr werdet	
Sie werden	Sie werden	
er/sie/es wird	sie werden	

PAST SUBJUNCTIVE I

ich habe	wir haben	gestoppt
du habest	ihr habet	
Sie haben	Sie haben	
er/sie/es habe	sie haben	

PAST SUBJUNCTIVE II

ich hätte	wir hätten	gestoppt
du hättest	ihr hättet	
Sie hätten	Sie hätten	
er/sie/es hätte	sie hätten	

FUTURE PERFECT SUBJUNCTIVE I

ich werde	wir werden	gestoppt haben
du werdest	ihr werdet	
Sie werden	Sie werden	
er/sie/es werde	sie werden	

FUTURE PERFECT SUBJUNCTIVE II

ich würde	wir würden	gestoppt haben
du würdest	ihr würdet	
Sie würden	Sie würden	
er/sie/es würde	sie würden	

COMMANDS stopp(e)! stoppt! stoppen Sie!

PRESENT PARTICIPLE stoppend

Usage

Diese Werbekampagne wurde von unserer eigenen Organisation gestoppt.	*This ad campaign was stopped by our own organization.*
Der Fußballspieler muss seinen Gegner stoppen.	*The soccer player must stop his opponent.*
Wir müssen Atomkraft stoppen!	*We must put a halt to nuclear energy!*
Das Gericht stoppte die Einführung genetisch modifizierter Organismen.	*The court halted the introduction of genetically modified organisms.*
In der Weimarer Republik der 20er Jahre war die Inflation nicht zu stoppen.	*In the 1920s Weimar Republic, inflation was unstoppable.*
Wie stoppt man ein Skateboard?	*How do you stop a skateboard?*
Wir wollten den Krieg stoppen.	*We wanted to end the war.*
Der Zug konnte nicht gestoppt werden.	*The train couldn't be stopped.*
Die unethischen Aktivitäten wurden gestoppt.	*The unethical activities were stopped.*
Im 100-m-Rennen wurde Veronika mit 11,4 Sekunden gestoppt.	*Veronika ran the 100-meter race in 11.4 seconds.*

RELATED VERB ab·stoppen

regular weak verb **stört · störte · gestört**

PRESENT

ich störe	wir stören
du störst	ihr stört
Sie stören	Sie stören
er/sie/es stört	sie stören

SIMPLE PAST

ich störte	wir störten
du störtest	ihr störtet
Sie störten	Sie störten
er/sie/es störte	sie störten

FUTURE

ich werde	wir werden	stören
du wirst	ihr werdet	
Sie werden	Sie werden	
er/sie/es wird	sie werden	

PRESENT SUBJUNCTIVE I

ich störe	wir stören
du störest	ihr störet
Sie stören	Sie stören
er/sie/es störe	sie stören

PRESENT SUBJUNCTIVE II

ich störte	wir störten
du störtest	ihr störtet
Sie störten	Sie störten
er/sie/es störte	sie störten

FUTURE SUBJUNCTIVE I

ich werde	wir werden	stören
du werdest	ihr werdet	
Sie werden	Sie werden	
er/sie/es werde	sie werden	

FUTURE SUBJUNCTIVE II

ich würde	wir würden	stören
du würdest	ihr würdet	
Sie würden	Sie würden	
er/sie/es würde	sie würden	

PRESENT PERFECT

ich habe	wir haben	gestört
du hast	ihr habt	
Sie haben	Sie haben	
er/sie/es hat	sie haben	

PAST PERFECT

ich hatte	wir hatten	gestört
du hattest	ihr hattet	
Sie hatten	Sie hatten	
er/sie/es hatte	sie hatten	

FUTURE PERFECT

ich werde	wir werden	gestört haben
du wirst	ihr werdet	
Sie werden	Sie werden	
er/sie/es wird	sie werden	

PAST SUBJUNCTIVE I

ich habe	wir haben	gestört
du habest	ihr habet	
Sie haben	Sie haben	
er/sie/es habe	sie haben	

PAST SUBJUNCTIVE II

ich hätte	wir hätten	gestört
du hättest	ihr hättet	
Sie hätten	Sie hätten	
er/sie/es hätte	sie hätten	

FUTURE PERFECT SUBJUNCTIVE I

ich werde	wir werden	gestört haben
du werdest	ihr werdet	
Sie werden	Sie werden	
er/sie/es werde	sie werden	

FUTURE PERFECT SUBJUNCTIVE II

ich würde	wir würden	gestört haben
du würdest	ihr würdet	
Sie würden	Sie würden	
er/sie/es würde	sie würden	

COMMANDS stör(e)! stört! stören Sie!

PRESENT PARTICIPLE störend

Usage

Entschuldigung, ich muss mal kurz stören.	*Excuse me, I have to interrupt a second.*
Stört Sie die Musik?	*Does the music disturb you?*
Ich würde dich nicht stören.	*I wouldn't disturb you.*
Der Hund störte den Nachbarn.	*The dog annoyed the neighbor.*
Das dumpfe Geräusch störte sie und sie konnte nicht schlafen.	*The muffled sound disturbed her and she couldn't sleep.*
Wir wollen die Kühe nicht stören.	*We don't want to agitate the cows.*
Ihre Einstellung störte mich.	*Her attitude perturbed me.*
Jens hat seine Freundin mit seiner Äußerung gestört.	*Jens disturbed his girlfriend with his comment.*
Der Quartalumsatz hat Investoren gestört.	*The quarterly revenue figures disturbed investors.*
Ich hoffe, es stört euch nicht, wenn ich mitkomme.	*I hope it won't bother you if I come along.*
Das grelle Licht störte ihn.	*The harsh lighting bothered him.*
Die Katze lässt sich von der Türklingel nicht stören.	*The cat is not bothered by the doorbell.*

RELATED VERBS auf·stören, verstören; *see also* **zerstören** (548)

432 stoßen *to punch, kick; plunge, thrust; knock, bang; push*

stößt · stieß · gestoßen strong verb

PRESENT

ich stoße	wir stoßen
du stößt	ihr stoßt
Sie stoßen	Sie stoßen
er/sie/es stößt	sie stoßen

SIMPLE PAST

ich stieß	wir stießen
du stießest	ihr stießt
Sie stießen	Sie stießen
er/sie/es stieß	sie stießen

FUTURE

ich werde	wir werden	stoßen
du wirst	ihr werdet	
Sie werden	Sie werden	
er/sie/es wird	sie werden	

PRESENT SUBJUNCTIVE I

ich stoße	wir stoßen
du stoßest	ihr stoßet
Sie stoßen	Sie stoßen
er/sie/es stoße	sie stoßen

PRESENT SUBJUNCTIVE II

ich stieße	wir stießen
du stießest	ihr stießet
Sie stießen	Sie stießen
er/sie/es stieße	sie stießen

FUTURE SUBJUNCTIVE I

ich werde	wir werden	stoßen
du werdest	ihr werdet	
Sie werden	Sie werden	
er/sie/es werde	sie werden	

FUTURE SUBJUNCTIVE II

ich würde	wir würden	stoßen
du würdest	ihr würdet	
Sie würden	Sie würden	
er/sie/es würde	sie würden	

PRESENT PERFECT

ich habe	wir haben	gestoßen
du hast	ihr habt	
Sie haben	Sie haben	
er/sie/es hat	sie haben	

PAST PERFECT

ich hatte	wir hatten	gestoßen
du hattest	ihr hattet	
Sie hatten	Sie hatten	
er/sie/es hatte	sie hatten	

FUTURE PERFECT

ich werde	wir werden	gestoßen haben
du wirst	ihr werdet	
Sie werden	Sie werden	
er/sie/es wird	sie werden	

PAST SUBJUNCTIVE I

ich habe	wir haben	gestoßen
du habest	ihr habet	
Sie haben	Sie haben	
er/sie/es habe	sie haben	

PAST SUBJUNCTIVE II

ich hätte	wir hätten	gestoßen
du hättest	ihr hättet	
Sie hätten	Sie hätten	
er/sie/es hätte	sie hätten	

FUTURE PERFECT SUBJUNCTIVE I

ich werde	wir werden	gestoßen haben
du werdest	ihr werdet	
Sie werden	Sie werden	
er/sie/es werde	sie werden	

FUTURE PERFECT SUBJUNCTIVE II

ich würde	wir würden	gestoßen haben
du würdest	ihr würdet	
Sie würden	Sie würden	
er/sie/es würde	sie würden	

COMMANDS stoß(e)! stoßt! stoßen Sie!

PRESENT PARTICIPLE stoßend

Usage

Warum hast du den Rowdy nicht mit der Faust gestoßen?	*Why didn't you punch the hoodlum with your fist?*
Er hat sie mit dem Ellbogen gestoßen.	*He jabbed her with his elbow.*
Man muss dem Vampir einen Pfahl ins Herz stoßen.	*You have to drive a stake in the vampire's heart.*
Der Bulle stößt mit seinen Hörnern.	*The bull is butting with his horns.*

stoßen (with sein) *to push, shove, strike, bump; meet with*

Markus will auf Gold gestoßen sein.	*Markus claims to have struck it rich.*
Das Kind war mit dem Kopf gegen einen Stuhl gestoßen.	*The child had bumped his head on a chair.*
Am Markt bin ich auf Thorsten gestoßen.	*At the market, I bumped into Thorsten.*
Maria ist auf Widerstand gestoßen.	*Maria has met with resistance.*
Die Mitglieder stießen immer wieder auf Ablehnung.	*The members met with disapproval again and again.*
Auf dem Dachboden sind sie auf alte Urkunden gestoßen.	*In the attic, they came across some old documents.*

RELATED VERBS ab·stoßen, an·stoßen, auf·stoßen, ein·stoßen, um·stoßen, verstoßen, vor·stoßen, zurück·stoßen, zusammen·stoßen, zu·stoßen

regular weak verb **strahlt · strahlte · gestrahlt**

PRESENT

ich strahle	wir strahlen
du strahlst	ihr strahlt
Sie strahlen	Sie strahlen
er/sie/es strahlt	sie strahlen

SIMPLE PAST

ich strahlte	wir strahlten
du strahltest	ihr strahltet
Sie strahlten	Sie strahlten
er/sie/es strahlte	sie strahlten

FUTURE

ich werde	wir werden	strahlen
du wirst	ihr werdet	
Sie werden	Sie werden	
er/sie/es wird	sie werden	

PRESENT SUBJUNCTIVE I

ich strahle	wir strahlen
du strahlest	ihr strahlet
Sie strahlen	Sie strahlen
er/sie/es strahle	sie strahlen

PRESENT SUBJUNCTIVE II

ich strahlte	wir strahlten
du strahltest	ihr strahltet
Sie strahlten	Sie strahlten
er/sie/es strahlte	sie strahlten

FUTURE SUBJUNCTIVE I

ich werde	wir werden	strahlen
du werdest	ihr werdet	
Sie werden	Sie werden	
er/sie/es werde	sie werden	

FUTURE SUBJUNCTIVE II

ich würde	wir würden	strahlen
du würdest	ihr würdet	
Sie würden	Sie würden	
er/sie/es würde	sie würden	

PRESENT PERFECT

ich habe	wir haben	gestrahlt
du hast	ihr habt	
Sie haben	Sie haben	
er/sie/es hat	sie haben	

PAST PERFECT

ich hatte	wir hatten	gestrahlt
du hattest	ihr hattet	
Sie hatten	Sie hatten	
er/sie/es hatte	sie hatten	

FUTURE PERFECT

ich werde	wir werden	gestrahlt haben
du wirst	ihr werdet	
Sie werden	Sie werden	
er/sie/es wird	sie werden	

PAST SUBJUNCTIVE I

ich habe	wir haben	gestrahlt
du habest	ihr habet	
Sie haben	Sie haben	
er/sie/es habe	sie haben	

PAST SUBJUNCTIVE II

ich hätte	wir hätten	gestrahlt
du hättest	ihr hättet	
Sie hätten	Sie hätten	
er/sie/es hätte	sie hätten	

FUTURE PERFECT SUBJUNCTIVE I

ich werde	wir werden	gestrahlt haben
du werdest	ihr werdet	
Sie werden	Sie werden	
er/sie/es werde	sie werden	

FUTURE PERFECT SUBJUNCTIVE II

ich würde	wir würden	gestrahlt haben
du würdest	ihr würdet	
Sie würden	Sie würden	
er/sie/es würde	sie würden	

COMMANDS strahl(e)! strahlt! strahlen Sie!

PRESENT PARTICIPLE strahlend

Usage

Die Morgensonne strahlt durch das Küchenfenster.	*The morning sun is shining through the kitchen window.*
Die Sonne strahlte durch die Ritzen der alten Waldhütte.	*The sun shone through the cracks in the old cabin.*
Die Sterne strahlen hell am Himmel.	*The stars shine brightly in the sky.*
Wenn man das Silberbesteck regelmäßig putzt, strahlt es wie neu.	*If you clean the silver cutlery regularly, it will sparkle like new.*
Die Diamanten strahlten im Licht.	*The diamonds sparkled in the light.*
Matthias' neues Auto strahlte.	*Matthias's new car sparkled.*
Mit diesem Spülmittel wird das Geschirr strahlen.	*With this detergent, the dishes will sparkle.*
Die neue Mutter strahlte vor Freude.	*The new mother beamed with joy.*
„Das ist ja fantastisch!" strahlte der Knabe.	*"That's fantastic!" beamed the boy.*
Die Wärme strahlte bis in das Schlafzimmer.	*The warmth radiated as far as the bedroom.*
Plutonium strahlt radioaktiv.	*Plutonium emits radioactive rays.*
Die Chi-Energie strahlt durch alle Räume des Hauses.	*The chi energy radiates through all rooms of the house.*

RELATED VERBS aus·strahlen, bestrahlen, ein·strahlen, verstrahlen

434 streben *to strive*

strebt · strebte · gestrebt regular weak verb

PRESENT

ich strebe	wir streben
du strebst	ihr strebt
Sie streben	Sie streben
er/sie/es strebt	sie streben

PRESENT PERFECT

ich habe	wir haben	gestrebt
du hast	ihr habt	
Sie haben	Sie haben	
er/sie/es hat	sie haben	

SIMPLE PAST

ich strebte	wir strebten
du strebtest	ihr strebtet
Sie strebten	Sie strebten
er/sie/es strebte	sie strebten

PAST PERFECT

ich hatte	wir hatten	gestrebt
du hattest	ihr hattet	
Sie hatten	Sie hatten	
er/sie/es hatte	sie hatten	

FUTURE

ich werde	wir werden	streben
du wirst	ihr werdet	
Sie werden	Sie werden	
er/sie/es wird	sie werden	

FUTURE PERFECT

ich werde	wir werden	gestrebt haben
du wirst	ihr werdet	
Sie werden	Sie werden	
er/sie/es wird	sie werden	

PRESENT SUBJUNCTIVE I

ich strebe	wir streben
du strebest	ihr strebet
Sie streben	Sie streben
er/sie/es strebe	sie streben

PAST SUBJUNCTIVE I

ich habe	wir haben	gestrebt
du habest	ihr habet	
Sie haben	Sie haben	
er/sie/es habe	sie haben	

PRESENT SUBJUNCTIVE II

ich strebte	wir strebten
du strebtest	ihr strebtet
Sie strebten	Sie strebten
er/sie/es strebte	sie strebten

PAST SUBJUNCTIVE II

ich hätte	wir hätten	gestrebt
du hättest	ihr hättet	
Sie hätten	Sie hätten	
er/sie/es hätte	sie hätten	

FUTURE SUBJUNCTIVE I

ich werde	wir werden	streben
du werdest	ihr werdet	
Sie werden	Sie werden	
er/sie/es werde	sie werden	

FUTURE PERFECT SUBJUNCTIVE I

ich werde	wir werden	gestrebt haben
du werdest	ihr werdet	
Sie werden	Sie werden	
er/sie/es werde	sie werden	

FUTURE SUBJUNCTIVE II

ich würde	wir würden	streben
du würdest	ihr würdet	
Sie würden	Sie würden	
er/sie/es würde	sie würden	

FUTURE PERFECT SUBJUNCTIVE II

ich würde	wir würden	gestrebt haben
du würdest	ihr würdet	
Sie würden	Sie würden	
er/sie/es würde	sie würden	

COMMANDS streb(e)! strebt! streben Sie!

PRESENT PARTICIPLE strebend

Usage

Der Mensch strebt nach Gott. — *Humans seek God.*
Politiker streben nach einem einfacheren Steuersystem. — *Politicians are pressing for a simpler tax system.*
Die Kurzsichtigen streben nur nach höherem Gewinn. — *The shortsighted strive only for greater profit.*
Wonach streben Sie? — *What are you trying to achieve?*
Liesl strebt nach einem neuen Weltrekord. — *Liesl is aiming for a new world record.*
Man strebt nach Gleichberechtigung. — *People struggle for equal rights.*
Die Bibliothek hat danach gestrebt, eine mittelalterliche Handschrift zu kaufen. — *The library endeavored to buy a medieval manuscript.*
Die beiden Prinzen strebten nach dem Thron. — *Both princes aspired to the throne.*

streben (with sein) *to make one's way briskly*

Der Hund stand auf und strebte zur Tür. — *The dog stood up and quickly made its way to the door.*
Nach dem Konzert streben sie nach Hause. — *They make their way home briskly after the concert.*

RELATED VERBS an·streben, auf·streben, bestreben, erstreben, widerstreben, zu·streben

strong verb

streicht · strich · gestrichen

PRESENT

ich streiche	wir streichen
du streichst	ihr streicht
Sie streichen	Sie streichen
er/sie/es streicht	sie streichen

SIMPLE PAST

ich strich	wir strichen
du strichst	ihr stricht
Sie strichen	Sie strichen
er/sie/es strich	sie strichen

FUTURE

ich werde	wir werden	streichen
du wirst	ihr werdet	
Sie werden	Sie werden	
er/sie/es wird	sie werden	

PRESENT SUBJUNCTIVE I

ich streiche	wir streichen
du streichest	ihr streichet
Sie streichen	Sie streichen
er/sie/es streiche	sie streichen

PRESENT SUBJUNCTIVE II

ich striche	wir strichen
du strichest	ihr strichet
Sie strichen	Sie strichen
er/sie/es striche	sie strichen

FUTURE SUBJUNCTIVE I

ich werde	wir werden	streichen
du werdest	ihr werdet	
Sie werden	Sie werden	
er/sie/es werde	sie werden	

FUTURE SUBJUNCTIVE II

ich würde	wir würden	streichen
du würdest	ihr würdet	
Sie würden	Sie würden	
er/sie/es würde	sie würden	

PRESENT PERFECT

ich habe	wir haben	gestrichen
du hast	ihr habt	
Sie haben	Sie haben	
er/sie/es hat	sie haben	

PAST PERFECT

ich hatte	wir hatten	gestrichen
du hattest	ihr hattet	
Sie hatten	Sie hatten	
er/sie/es hatte	sie hatten	

FUTURE PERFECT

ich werde	wir werden	gestrichen haben
du wirst	ihr werdet	
Sie werden	Sie werden	
er/sie/es wird	sie werden	

PAST SUBJUNCTIVE I

ich habe	wir haben	gestrichen
du habest	ihr habet	
Sie haben	Sie haben	
er/sie/es habe	sie haben	

PAST SUBJUNCTIVE II

ich hätte	wir hätten	gestrichen
du hättest	ihr hättet	
Sie hätten	Sie hätten	
er/sie/es hätte	sie hätten	

FUTURE PERFECT SUBJUNCTIVE I

ich werde	wir werden	gestrichen haben
du werdest	ihr werdet	
Sie werden	Sie werden	
er/sie/es werde	sie werden	

FUTURE PERFECT SUBJUNCTIVE II

ich würde	wir würden	gestrichen haben
du würdest	ihr würdet	
Sie würden	Sie würden	
er/sie/es würde	sie würden	

COMMANDS streich(e)! streicht! streichen Sie!

PRESENT PARTICIPLE streichend

Usage

Sie strich dem Kind über die Stirn.	*She stroked the child's forehead.*
Die Wände werden jetzt gestrichen.	*The walls are being painted now.*
Frisch gestrichen (SIGN)	*Wet Paint*
Petra strich Butter und Marmelade aufs Brot.	*Petra spread butter and marmalade on the bread.*
Die Pläne für den Kernreaktor wurden gestrichen.	*The plans for the nuclear reactor were cancelled.*
Nichtzutreffendes bitte streichen.	*Please delete anything that doesn't apply.*
2.000 Arbeitsplätze wurden gestern gestrichen.	*Two thousand jobs were cut yesterday.*
Streichen Sie meinen Namen von der Liste.	*Remove my name from the list.*

streichen (with **sein**) *to roam, stroll, prowl*

Jan strich durch das Land aber wusste nicht wohin.	*Jan roamed through the country but didn't know where to go.*
Ein Wolf strich durch den Wald.	*A wolf was prowling through the forest.*

RELATED VERBS ab·streichen, an·streichen, auf·streichen, aus·streichen, bestreichen, durch·streichen, ein·streichen, überstreichen, über·streichen, unterstreichen, verstreichen, weg·streichen, zurück·streichen

436 streiten *to quarrel, argue, squabble*

streitet · stritt · gestritten

strong verb

PRESENT

ich streite	wir streiten
du streitest	ihr streitet
Sie streiten	Sie streiten
er/sie/es streitet	sie streiten

SIMPLE PAST

ich stritt	wir stritten
du strittst	ihr strittet
Sie stritten	Sie stritten
er/sie/es stritt	sie stritten

FUTURE

ich werde	wir werden	streiten
du wirst	ihr werdet	
Sie werden	Sie werden	
er/sie/es wird	sie werden	

PRESENT SUBJUNCTIVE I

ich streite	wir streiten
du streitest	ihr streitet
Sie streiten	Sie streiten
er/sie/es streite	sie streiten

PRESENT SUBJUNCTIVE II

ich stritte	wir stritten
du strittest	ihr strittet
Sie stritten	Sie stritten
er/sie/es stritte	sie stritten

FUTURE SUBJUNCTIVE I

ich werde	wir werden	streiten
du werdest	ihr werdet	
Sie werden	Sie werden	
er/sie/es werde	sie werden	

FUTURE SUBJUNCTIVE II

ich würde	wir würden	streiten
du würdest	ihr würdet	
Sie würden	Sie würden	
er/sie/es würde	sie würden	

PRESENT PERFECT

ich habe	wir haben	gestritten
du hast	ihr habt	
Sie haben	Sie haben	
er/sie/es hat	sie haben	

PAST PERFECT

ich hatte	wir hatten	gestritten
du hattest	ihr hattet	
Sie hatten	Sie hatten	
er/sie/es hatte	sie hatten	

FUTURE PERFECT

ich werde	wir werden	gestritten haben
du wirst	ihr werdet	
Sie werden	Sie werden	
er/sie/es wird	sie werden	

PAST SUBJUNCTIVE I

ich habe	wir haben	gestritten
du habest	ihr habet	
Sie haben	Sie haben	
er/sie/es habe	sie haben	

PAST SUBJUNCTIVE II

ich hätte	wir hätten	gestritten
du hättest	ihr hättet	
Sie hätten	Sie hätten	
er/sie/es hätte	sie hätten	

FUTURE PERFECT SUBJUNCTIVE I

ich werde	wir werden	gestritten haben
du werdest	ihr werdet	
Sie werden	Sie werden	
er/sie/es werde	sie werden	

FUTURE PERFECT SUBJUNCTIVE II

ich würde	wir würden	gestritten haben
du würdest	ihr würdet	
Sie würden	Sie würden	
er/sie/es würde	sie würden	

COMMANDS streite! streitet! streiten Sie!

PRESENT PARTICIPLE streitend

Usage

Sie hat sich mit ihren Schwestern gestritten.	*She squabbled with her sisters.*
Die Mitgliedsstädte streiten über Zuschüsse.	*The member cities are arguing over subsidies.*
Die Katzen streiten sich wieder!	*The cats are quarreling again!*
Warum streitet ihr darüber?	*Why are you quarreling over that?*
Sie streiten sich nicht mehr.	*They aren't squabbling any longer.*
Bei der Planung stritten wir über die Notwendigkeit einer neuen Perspektive.	*During the planning, we argued over the necessity of a new perspective.*
Ich will nicht streiten.	*I don't want to quarrel.*
Nach einem Jahr hat man immer noch gestritten.	*After one year, they were still quarreling.*
Die beiden Nachfolger streiten sich um den Thron.	*The two successors are fighting over the throne.*
Die Abgeordneten werden über die neuen Regelungen streiten.	*The representatives will debate the new regulations.*
Über Geschmack lässt sich nicht streiten. (PROVERB)	*There's no accounting for taste.*

RELATED VERBS ab·streiten, bestreiten, erstreiten, widerstreiten

regular weak verb **studiert · studierte · studiert**

PRESENT

ich studiere	wir studieren
du studierst	ihr studiert
Sie studieren	Sie studieren
er/sie/es studiert	sie studieren

SIMPLE PAST

ich studierte	wir studierten
du studiertest	ihr studiertet
Sie studierten	Sie studierten
er/sie/es studierte	sie studierten

FUTURE

ich werde	wir werden	studieren
du wirst	ihr werdet	
Sie werden	Sie werden	
er/sie/es wird	sie werden	

PRESENT SUBJUNCTIVE I

ich studiere	wir studieren
du studierest	ihr studieret
Sie studieren	Sie studieren
er/sie/es studiere	sie studieren

PRESENT SUBJUNCTIVE II

ich studierte	wir studierten
du studiertest	ihr studiertet
Sie studierten	Sie studierten
er/sie/es studierte	sie studierten

FUTURE SUBJUNCTIVE I

ich werde	wir werden	studieren
du werdest	ihr werdet	
Sie werden	Sie werden	
er/sie/es werde	sie werden	

FUTURE SUBJUNCTIVE II

ich würde	wir würden	studieren
du würdest	ihr würdet	
Sie würden	Sie würden	
er/sie/es würde	sie würden	

PRESENT PERFECT

ich habe	wir haben	studiert
du hast	ihr habt	
Sie haben	Sie haben	
er/sie/es hat	sie haben	

PAST PERFECT

ich hatte	wir hatten	studiert
du hattest	ihr hattet	
Sie hatten	Sie hatten	
er/sie/es hatte	sie hatten	

FUTURE PERFECT

ich werde	wir werden	studiert haben
du wirst	ihr werdet	
Sie werden	Sie werden	
er/sie/es wird	sie werden	

PAST SUBJUNCTIVE I

ich habe	wir haben	studiert
du habest	ihr habet	
Sie haben	Sie haben	
er/sie/es habe	sie haben	

PAST SUBJUNCTIVE II

ich hätte	wir hätten	studiert
du hättest	ihr hättet	
Sie hätten	Sie hätten	
er/sie/es hätte	sie hätten	

FUTURE PERFECT SUBJUNCTIVE I

ich werde	wir werden	studiert haben
du werdest	ihr werdet	
Sie werden	Sie werden	
er/sie/es werde	sie werden	

FUTURE PERFECT SUBJUNCTIVE II

ich würde	wir würden	studiert haben
du würdest	ihr würdet	
Sie würden	Sie würden	
er/sie/es würde	sie würden	

COMMANDS studier(e)! studiert! studieren Sie!

PRESENT PARTICIPLE studierend

Usage

„Studierst du?“ — *“Are you going to college?”*
„Ja, ich studiere Andragogik.“ — *“Yes, I'm majoring in adult education.”*

Meine Mutter möchte, dass ich Medizin studiere. — *My mother wants me to study medicine.*

Franz hat in Göttingen und Hohenheim studiert. — *Franz went to college in Göttingen and Hohenheim.*

Mein Neffe studiert Zoologie an der Uni Bochum. — *My nephew is studying zoology at the university in Bochum.*

Grimm studierte Jura und wurde Germanistikprofessor in Göttingen. — *Grimm studied law and became a professor of German in Göttingen.*

Mahler studierte am Konservatorium in Wien. — *Mahler studied at the conservatory in Vienna.*

Seine Tochter studiert jetzt im dritten Semester. — *His daughter is now a sophomore in college.*

Heutzutage studieren immer mehr junge Leute. — *Nowadays, more and more young people are going to college.*

Wirst du studieren oder ein Handwerk lernen? — *Are you going to college or will you learn a trade?*

Früher haben wenige Frauen studieren dürfen. — *In the past, few women were permitted to go to college.*

Probieren geht über studieren. (PROVERB) — *Experiencing something is better than studying it.*

RELATED VERB ein·studieren

438 stürzen *to fall, plunge, plummet, tumble, collapse*

stürzt · stürzte · gestürzt regular weak verb

PRESENT

ich stürze	wir stürzen
du stürzt	ihr stürzt
Sie stürzen	Sie stürzen
er/sie/es stürzt	sie stürzen

SIMPLE PAST

ich stürzte	wir stürzten
du stürztest	ihr stürztet
Sie stürzten	Sie stürzten
er/sie/es stürzte	sie stürzten

FUTURE

ich werde	wir werden	stürzen
du wirst	ihr werdet	
Sie werden	Sie werden	
er/sie/es wird	sie werden	

PRESENT SUBJUNCTIVE I

ich stürze	wir stürzen
du stürzest	ihr stürzet
Sie stürzen	Sie stürzen
er/sie/es stürze	sie stürzen

PRESENT SUBJUNCTIVE II

ich stürzte	wir stürzten
du stürztest	ihr stürztet
Sie stürzten	Sie stürzten
er/sie/es stürzte	sie stürzten

FUTURE SUBJUNCTIVE I

ich werde	wir werden	stürzen
du werdest	ihr werdet	
Sie werden	Sie werden	
er/sie/es werde	sie werden	

FUTURE SUBJUNCTIVE II

ich würde	wir würden	stürzen
du würdest	ihr würdet	
Sie würden	Sie würden	
er/sie/es würde	sie würden	

PRESENT PERFECT

ich bin	wir sind	gestürzt
du bist	ihr seid	
Sie sind	Sie sind	
er/sie/es ist	sie sind	

PAST PERFECT

ich war	wir waren	gestürzt
du warst	ihr wart	
Sie waren	Sie waren	
er/sie/es war	sie waren	

FUTURE PERFECT

ich werde	wir werden	gestürzt sein
du wirst	ihr werdet	
Sie werden	Sie werden	
er/sie/es wird	sie werden	

PAST SUBJUNCTIVE I

ich sei	wir seien	gestürzt
du seiest	ihr seiet	
Sie seien	Sie seien	
er/sie/es sei	sie seien	

PAST SUBJUNCTIVE II

ich wäre	wir wären	gestürzt
du wärest	ihr wäret	
Sie wären	Sie wären	
er/sie/es wäre	sie wären	

FUTURE PERFECT SUBJUNCTIVE I

ich werde	wir werden	gestürzt sein
du werdest	ihr werdet	
Sie werden	Sie werden	
er/sie/es werde	sie werden	

FUTURE PERFECT SUBJUNCTIVE II

ich würde	wir würden	gestürzt sein
du würdest	ihr würdet	
Sie würden	Sie würden	
er/sie/es würde	sie würden	

COMMANDS stürz(e)! stürzt! stürzen Sie!

PRESENT PARTICIPLE stürzend

Usage

Katja ist ins Wasser gestürzt und ertrunken. — *Katja fell into the water and drowned.*
Mutti ist auf den Boden gestürzt. — *Mom tumbled onto the ground.*
Das Land stürzt in den Abgrund. — *The country is plunging to its ruin.*
Die Preise stürzen und die Banken werden geschlossen. — *Prices are plummeting and banks are closing.*
Ein Kampfhubschrauber war in der Nacht auf ein Hotel gestürzt. — *A military helicopter had crashed into a hotel during the night.*
Um drei sind die Männer aus der Kneipe gestürzt. — *At three o'clock, the men tumbled out of the pub.*

stürzen (with **haben**) *to overthrow, topple, pounce*

Die Untertanen stürzten ihren König. — *The subjects have toppled their king.*
Der Mann hat sich von einer Brücke gestürzt. — *The man threw himself off the bridge.*
Der Anwalt stürzte sich auf die Aussage des Zeugen. — *The lawyer pounced on the witness's testimony.*

RELATED VERBS ab·stürzen, an·stürzen, bestürzen, ein·stürzen, nieder·stürzen, um·stürzen, zusammen·stürzen, zu·stürzen

regular weak verb **stützt · stützte · gestützt**

PRESENT

ich stütze	wir stützen
du stützt	ihr stützt
Sie stützen	Sie stützen
er/sie/es stützt	sie stützen

SIMPLE PAST

ich stützte	wir stützten
du stütztest	ihr stütztet
Sie stützten	Sie stützten
er/sie/es stützte	sie stützten

FUTURE

ich werde	wir werden	stützen
du wirst	ihr werdet	
Sie werden	Sie werden	
er/sie/es wird	sie werden	

PRESENT SUBJUNCTIVE I

ich stütze	wir stützen
du stützest	ihr stützet
Sie stützen	Sie stützen
er/sie/es stütze	sie stützen

PRESENT SUBJUNCTIVE II

ich stützte	wir stützten
du stütztest	ihr stütztet
Sie stützten	Sie stützten
er/sie/es stützte	sie stützten

FUTURE SUBJUNCTIVE I

ich werde	wir werden	stützen
du werdest	ihr werdet	
Sie werden	Sie werden	
er/sie/es werde	sie werden	

FUTURE SUBJUNCTIVE II

ich würde	wir würden	stützen
du würdest	ihr würdet	
Sie würden	Sie würden	
er/sie/es würde	sie würden	

PRESENT PERFECT

ich habe	wir haben	gestützt
du hast	ihr habt	
Sie haben	Sie haben	
er/sie/es hat	sie haben	

PAST PERFECT

ich hatte	wir hatten	gestützt
du hattest	ihr hattet	
Sie hatten	Sie hatten	
er/sie/es hatte	sie hatten	

FUTURE PERFECT

ich werde	wir werden	gestützt haben
du wirst	ihr werdet	
Sie werden	Sie werden	
er/sie/es wird	sie werden	

PAST SUBJUNCTIVE I

ich habe	wir haben	gestützt
du habest	ihr habet	
Sie haben	Sie haben	
er/sie/es habe	sie haben	

PAST SUBJUNCTIVE II

ich hätte	wir hätten	gestützt
du hättest	ihr hättet	
Sie hätten	Sie hätten	
er/sie/es hätte	sie hätten	

FUTURE PERFECT SUBJUNCTIVE I

ich werde	wir werden	gestützt haben
du werdest	ihr werdet	
Sie werden	Sie werden	
er/sie/es werde	sie werden	

FUTURE PERFECT SUBJUNCTIVE II

ich würde	wir würden	gestützt haben
du würdest	ihr würdet	
Sie würden	Sie würden	
er/sie/es würde	sie würden	

COMMANDS stütz(e)! stützt! stützen Sie!

PRESENT PARTICIPLE stützend

Usage

Womit wurde die alte Stadtmauer gestützt? — *How was the old city wall supported?*
Sandsäcke stützen den sonst festen Deich. — *Sandbags shore up the otherwise stable dike.*
Gute Schuhe stützen den Körper. — *Good shoes support the body.*
Ich stützte meinen Kopf in meine Hände. — *I rested my head in my hands.*
Milchpreise werden staatlich gestützt. — *The government provides price supports for milk.*
Man will den argentinischen Peso stützen. — *They want to prop up the Argentinian peso.*

sich stützen *to support oneself, be supported*

Der ältere Herr stützte sich auf einen Stock. — *The elderly gentleman supported himself with a cane.*
Das Konzept stützt sich auf drei Faktoren. — *The concept depends on three factors.*
Seine Meinung stützt sich auf subjektive Eindrücke. — *His opinion is based on subjective impressions.*
Sammi freute sich, dass er sich auf seine Freunde stützen konnte. — *Sammi was happy that he could count on his friends.*

RELATED VERBS ab·stützen, auf·stützen, unter·stützen; *see also* **unterstützen** (473)

suchen *to look/search for, seek*

sucht · suchte · gesucht

regular weak verb

PRESENT

ich suche	wir suchen
du suchst	ihr sucht
Sie suchen	Sie suchen
er/sie/es sucht	sie suchen

SIMPLE PAST

ich suchte	wir suchten
du suchtest	ihr suchtet
Sie suchten	Sie suchten
er/sie/es suchte	sie suchten

FUTURE

ich werde	wir werden	suchen
du wirst	ihr werdet	
Sie werden	Sie werden	
er/sie/es wird	sie werden	

PRESENT SUBJUNCTIVE I

ich suche	wir suchen
du suchest	ihr suchet
Sie suchen	Sie suchen
er/sie/es suche	sie suchen

PRESENT SUBJUNCTIVE II

ich suchte	wir suchten
du suchtest	ihr suchtet
Sie suchten	Sie suchten
er/sie/es suchte	sie suchten

FUTURE SUBJUNCTIVE I

ich werde	wir werden	suchen
du werdest	ihr werdet	
Sie werden	Sie werden	
er/sie/es werde	sie werden	

FUTURE SUBJUNCTIVE II

ich würde	wir würden	suchen
du würdest	ihr würdet	
Sie würden	Sie würden	
er/sie/es würde	sie würden	

PRESENT PERFECT

ich habe	wir haben	gesucht
du hast	ihr habt	
Sie haben	Sie haben	
er/sie/es hat	sie haben	

PAST PERFECT

ich hatte	wir hatten	gesucht
du hattest	ihr hattet	
Sie hatten	Sie hatten	
er/sie/es hatte	sie hatten	

FUTURE PERFECT

ich werde	wir werden	gesucht haben
du wirst	ihr werdet	
Sie werden	Sie werden	
er/sie/es wird	sie werden	

PAST SUBJUNCTIVE I

ich habe	wir haben	gesucht
du habest	ihr habet	
Sie haben	Sie haben	
er/sie/es habe	sie haben	

PAST SUBJUNCTIVE II

ich hätte	wir hätten	gesucht
du hättest	ihr hättet	
Sie hätten	Sie hätten	
er/sie/es hätte	sie hätten	

FUTURE PERFECT SUBJUNCTIVE I

ich werde	wir werden	gesucht haben
du werdest	ihr werdet	
Sie werden	Sie werden	
er/sie/es werde	sie werden	

FUTURE PERFECT SUBJUNCTIVE II

ich würde	wir würden	gesucht haben
du würdest	ihr würdet	
Sie würden	Sie würden	
er/sie/es würde	sie würden	

COMMANDS such(e)! sucht! suchen Sie!

PRESENT PARTICIPLE suchend

Usage

Inge sucht das Dorf Kleischa. — *Inge is looking for the village of Kleischa.*

Seit drei Jahren sucht sie ihren leiblichen Vater. — *For three years, she has been searching for her biological father.*

Manfred und seine Frau suchen eine Wohnung in der Innenstadt. — *Manfred and his wife are looking for an apartment downtown.*

Wir suchen eine Erklärung der Umstände. — *We seek an explanation of the circumstances.*

Was suchen Sie in Ihrer Büchertasche? — *What are you looking for in your book bag?*

Ich habe die Zeitung gesucht aber nicht gefunden. — *I looked for the newspaper but didn't find it.*

Kann man in diesem Katalog nach Erstausgaben suchen? — *Can you search for first editions in this catalog?*

Oliver suchte vergeblich seine Schlüssel. — *Oliver looked for his keys in vain.*

Debora sucht ein vegetarisches Restaurant. — *Debora is looking for a vegetarian restaurant.*

Larry wird von der Polizei gesucht. — *Larry is wanted by the police.*

RELATED VERBS ab·suchen, an·suchen, auf·suchen, aus·suchen, durchsuchen, durch·suchen, ersuchen, heim·suchen, untersuchen; *see also* **besuchen** (93), **versuchen** (502)

regular weak verb

tankt · tankte · getankt

PRESENT

ich tanke	wir tanken
du tankst	ihr tankt
Sie tanken	Sie tanken
er/sie/es tankt	sie tanken

SIMPLE PAST

ich tankte	wir tankten
du tanktest	ihr tanktet
Sie tankten	Sie tankten
er/sie/es tankte	sie tankten

FUTURE

ich werde	wir werden	tanken
du wirst	ihr werdet	
Sie werden	Sie werden	
er/sie/es wird	sie werden	

PRESENT SUBJUNCTIVE I

ich tanke	wir tanken
du tankest	ihr tanket
Sie tanken	Sie tanken
er/sie/es tanke	sie tanken

PRESENT SUBJUNCTIVE II

ich tankte	wir tankten
du tanktest	ihr tanktet
Sie tankten	Sie tankten
er/sie/es tankte	sie tankten

FUTURE SUBJUNCTIVE I

ich werde	wir werden	tanken
du werdest	ihr werdet	
Sie werden	Sie werden	
er/sie/es werde	sie werden	

FUTURE SUBJUNCTIVE II

ich würde	wir würden	tanken
du würdest	ihr würdet	
Sie würden	Sie würden	
er/sie/es würde	sie würden	

PRESENT PERFECT

ich habe	wir haben	getankt
du hast	ihr habt	
Sie haben	Sie haben	
er/sie/es hat	sie haben	

PAST PERFECT

ich hatte	wir hatten	getankt
du hattest	ihr hattet	
Sie hatten	Sie hatten	
er/sie/es hatte	sie hatten	

FUTURE PERFECT

ich werde	wir werden	getankt haben
du wirst	ihr werdet	
Sie werden	Sie werden	
er/sie/es wird	sie werden	

PAST SUBJUNCTIVE I

ich habe	wir haben	getankt
du habest	ihr habet	
Sie haben	Sie haben	
er/sie/es habe	sie haben	

PAST SUBJUNCTIVE II

ich hätte	wir hätten	getankt
du hättest	ihr hättet	
Sie hätten	Sie hätten	
er/sie/es hätte	sie hätten	

FUTURE PERFECT SUBJUNCTIVE I

ich werde	wir werden	getankt haben
du werdest	ihr werdet	
Sie werden	Sie werden	
er/sie/es werde	sie werden	

FUTURE PERFECT SUBJUNCTIVE II

ich würde	wir würden	getankt haben
du würdest	ihr würdet	
Sie würden	Sie würden	
er/sie/es würde	sie würden	

COMMANDS tank(e)! tankt! tanken Sie!

PRESENT PARTICIPLE tankend

Usage

Hast du zufällig Diesel getankt?	*Did you accidentally fill up with diesel?*
Wir mussten das Mietauto selbst tanken.	*We had to fill up the rental car ourselves.*
Ich muss Benzin tanken.	*I have to get gas.*
Wo kann man denn um zwei Uhr morgens tanken?	*Where can you fill up at two in the morning?*
Wir wollen noch nicht tanken.	*We don't want to fill up yet.*
In Oregon durften wir nicht selbst tanken.	*In Oregon, we weren't allowed to pump the gas ourselves.*
Ich habe gerade 20 Liter getankt.	*I just pumped 20 liters of gasoline.*
Wann hast du das letzte Mal getankt?	*When did you last fill up?*
Hier kannst du billiger tanken.	*You can fill up here more cheaply.*
Einmal im Monat muss ich voll tanken.	*Once a month, I fill the tank.*
Nach der stressigen Woche wollte ich Schlaf tanken.	*After a stressful week, I wanted to catch up on sleep.*
Ich muss meinen Handy-Akku tanken.	*I have to recharge my cell phone battery.*
Im Urlaub habe ich Sonne und Energie getankt.	*On vacation, I replenished my supply of sun and energy.*

RELATED VERB auf·tanken

442 tanzen *to dance*

tanzt · tanzte · getanzt regular weak verb

PRESENT

ich tanze	wir tanzen
du tanzt	ihr tanzt
Sie tanzen	Sie tanzen
er/sie/es tanzt	sie tanzen

SIMPLE PAST

ich tanzte	wir tanzten
du tanztest	ihr tanztet
Sie tanzten	Sie tanzten
er/sie/es tanzte	sie tanzten

FUTURE

ich werde	wir werden	tanzen
du wirst	ihr werdet	
Sie werden	Sie werden	
er/sie/es wird	sie werden	

PRESENT SUBJUNCTIVE I

ich tanze	wir tanzen
du tanzest	ihr tanzet
Sie tanzen	Sie tanzen
er/sie/es tanze	sie tanzen

PRESENT SUBJUNCTIVE II

ich tanzte	wir tanzten
du tanztest	ihr tanztet
Sie tanzten	Sie tanzten
er/sie/es tanzte	sie tanzten

FUTURE SUBJUNCTIVE I

ich werde	wir werden	tanzen
du werdest	ihr werdet	
Sie werden	Sie werden	
er/sie/es werde	sie werden	

FUTURE SUBJUNCTIVE II

ich würde	wir würden	tanzen
du würdest	ihr würdet	
Sie würden	Sie würden	
er/sie/es würde	sie würden	

PRESENT PERFECT

ich habe	wir haben	getanzt
du hast	ihr habt	
Sie haben	Sie haben	
er/sie/es hat	sie haben	

PAST PERFECT

ich hatte	wir hatten	getanzt
du hattest	ihr hattet	
Sie hatten	Sie hatten	
er/sie/es hatte	sie hatten	

FUTURE PERFECT

ich werde	wir werden	getanzt haben
du wirst	ihr werdet	
Sie werden	Sie werden	
er/sie/es wird	sie werden	

PAST SUBJUNCTIVE I

ich habe	wir haben	getanzt
du habest	ihr habet	
Sie haben	Sie haben	
er/sie/es habe	sie haben	

PAST SUBJUNCTIVE II

ich hätte	wir hätten	getanzt
du hättest	ihr hättet	
Sie hätten	Sie hätten	
er/sie/es hätte	sie hätten	

FUTURE PERFECT SUBJUNCTIVE I

ich werde	wir werden	getanzt haben
du werdest	ihr werdet	
Sie werden	Sie werden	
er/sie/es werde	sie werden	

FUTURE PERFECT SUBJUNCTIVE II

ich würde	wir würden	getanzt haben
du würdest	ihr würdet	
Sie würden	Sie würden	
er/sie/es würde	sie würden	

COMMANDS tanz(e)! tanzt! tanzen Sie!

PRESENT PARTICIPLE tanzend

Usage

Wir haben bis zwei Uhr morgens getanzt.	*We danced until two in the morning.*
Kannst du den Ententanz tanzen?	*Can you dance the funky chicken?*
Susanne tanzt mit Sofie.	*Susanne is dancing with Sofie.*
Kleine Figuren tanzten vor seinen Augen.	*Little figures danced before his eyes.*
Wann hast du tanzen gelernt?	*When did you learn to dance?*
Stefan und Nicole tanzen gern am Strand.	*Stefan and Nicole like to dance on the beach.*
Ihr tanzt schon seit einer Stunde!	*You've been dancing for an hour already!*
Wenn die Katze aus dem Haus ist, tanzen die Mäuse. (PROVERB)	*When the cat's away, the mice will play.*
Jeden Tag bei Arbeit muss Tess auf dem Seil tanzen. (*figurative*)	*Every day at work, Tess has to walk the tightrope.*
Alfred tanzt immer nach Cassandras Pfeife. (*figurative*)	*Alfred always does Cassandra's bidding.*

tanzen (with **sein**) *to dance*

Das Paar ist durch den Saal getanzt.	*The couple danced across the room.*

RELATED VERBS an·tanzen, durchtanzen, durch·tanzen, umtanzen, vor·tanzen

regular weak verb **teilt · teilte · geteilt**

PRESENT

ich teile	wir teilen
du teilst	ihr teilt
Sie teilen	Sie teilen
er/sie/es teilt	sie teilen

SIMPLE PAST

ich teilte	wir teilten
du teiltest	ihr teiltet
Sie teilten	Sie teilten
er/sie/es teilte	sie teilten

FUTURE

ich werde	wir werden	teilen
du wirst	ihr werdet	
Sie werden	Sie werden	
er/sie/es wird	sie werden	

PRESENT SUBJUNCTIVE I

ich teile	wir teilen
du teilest	ihr teilet
Sie teilen	Sie teilen
er/sie/es teile	sie teilen

PRESENT SUBJUNCTIVE II

ich teilte	wir teilten
du teiltest	ihr teiltet
Sie teilten	Sie teilten
er/sie/es teilte	sie teilten

FUTURE SUBJUNCTIVE I

ich werde	wir werden	teilen
du werdest	ihr werdet	
Sie werden	Sie werden	
er/sie/es werde	sie werden	

FUTURE SUBJUNCTIVE II

ich würde	wir würden	teilen
du würdest	ihr würdet	
Sie würden	Sie würden	
er/sie/es würde	sie würden	

PRESENT PERFECT

ich habe	wir haben	geteilt
du hast	ihr habt	
Sie haben	Sie haben	
er/sie/es hat	sie haben	

PAST PERFECT

ich hatte	wir hatten	geteilt
du hattest	ihr hattet	
Sie hatten	Sie hatten	
er/sie/es hatte	sie hatten	

FUTURE PERFECT

ich werde	wir werden	geteilt haben
du wirst	ihr werdet	
Sie werden	Sie werden	
er/sie/es wird	sie werden	

PAST SUBJUNCTIVE I

ich habe	wir haben	geteilt
du habest	ihr habet	
Sie haben	Sie haben	
er/sie/es habe	sie haben	

PAST SUBJUNCTIVE II

ich hätte	wir hätten	geteilt
du hättest	ihr hättet	
Sie hätten	Sie hätten	
er/sie/es hätte	sie hätten	

FUTURE PERFECT SUBJUNCTIVE I

ich werde	wir werden	geteilt haben
du werdest	ihr werdet	
Sie werden	Sie werden	
er/sie/es werde	sie werden	

FUTURE PERFECT SUBJUNCTIVE II

ich würde	wir würden	geteilt haben
du würdest	ihr würdet	
Sie würden	Sie würden	
er/sie/es würde	sie würden	

COMMANDS teil(e)! teilt! teilen Sie!

PRESENT PARTICIPLE teilend

Usage

Nach dem Zweiten Weltkrieg wurde Deutschland in Besatzungszonen geteilt.	*After World War II, Germany was divided into occupation zones.*
Kleinkinder müssen teilen lernen.	*Small children must learn to share.*
Wir haben das Boot mit vier anderen Personen geteilt.	*We shared the boat with four other people.*
Die Zahnärztin teilt die Praxis mit einem Kollegen.	*The dentist shares the office with a colleague.*
Ich teile meine Suppe mit dir, wenn du Hunger hast.	*I'll share my soup with you if you're hungry.*
Ich teile das Zimmer mit einem Freund von mir, der auch Student ist.	*I'm sharing the room with a friend of mine who is also a student.*
Wir teilen den Gewinn 50:50.	*We are splitting the profit 50-50.*
Frau Klepsch teilte ihr Vermögen mit ihrer Schwägerin.	*Mrs. Klepsch shared her wealth with her sister-in-law.*

sich teilen *to be divided, differ, diverge*

Darüber teilen sich ihre Ansichten.	*Their viewpoints differ on that matter.*

RELATED VERBS ab·teilen, auf·teilen, aus·teilen, beurteilen, ein·teilen, erteilen, unterteilen, urteilen, verurteilen, zerteilen, zu·teilen; *see also* **mit·teilen** (310), **verteilen** (503)

444 teil·nehmen *to attend, take part; share*

nimmt teil · nahm teil · teilgenommen strong verb

PRESENT

ich nehme	wir nehmen	teil
du nimmst	ihr nehmt	
Sie nehmen	Sie nehmen	
er/sie/es nimmt	sie nehmen	

SIMPLE PAST

ich nahm	wir nahmen	teil
du nahmst	ihr nahmt	
Sie nahmen	Sie nahmen	
er/sie/es nahm	sie nahmen	

FUTURE

ich werde	wir werden	teilnehmen
du wirst	ihr werdet	
Sie werden	Sie werden	
er/sie/es wird	sie werden	

PRESENT SUBJUNCTIVE I

ich nehme	wir nehmen	teil
du nehmest	ihr nehmet	
Sie nehmen	Sie nehmen	
er/sie/es nehme	sie nehmen	

PRESENT SUBJUNCTIVE II

ich nähme	wir nähmen	teil
du nähmest	ihr nähmet	
Sie nähmen	Sie nähmen	
er/sie/es nähme	sie nähmen	

FUTURE SUBJUNCTIVE I

ich werde	wir werden	teilnehmen
du werdest	ihr werdet	
Sie werden	Sie werden	
er/sie/es werde	sie werden	

FUTURE SUBJUNCTIVE II

ich würde	wir würden	teilnehmen
du würdest	ihr würdet	
Sie würden	Sie würden	
er/sie/es würde	sie würden	

PRESENT PERFECT

ich habe	wir haben	teilgenommen
du hast	ihr habt	
Sie haben	Sie haben	
er/sie/es hat	sie haben	

PAST PERFECT

ich hatte	wir hatten	teilgenommen
du hattest	ihr hattet	
Sie hatten	Sie hatten	
er/sie/es hatte	sie hatten	

FUTURE PERFECT

ich werde	wir werden	teilgenommen haben
du wirst	ihr werdet	
Sie werden	Sie werden	
er/sie/es wird	sie werden	

PAST SUBJUNCTIVE I

ich habe	wir haben	teilgenommen
du habest	ihr habet	
Sie haben	Sie haben	
er/sie/es habe	sie haben	

PAST SUBJUNCTIVE II

ich hätte	wir hätten	teilgenommen
du hättest	ihr hättet	
Sie hätten	Sie hätten	
er/sie/es hätte	sie hätten	

FUTURE PERFECT SUBJUNCTIVE I

ich werde	wir werden	teilgenommen haben
du werdest	ihr werdet	
Sie werden	Sie werden	
er/sie/es werde	sie werden	

FUTURE PERFECT SUBJUNCTIVE II

ich würde	wir würden	teilgenommen haben
du würdest	ihr würdet	
Sie würden	Sie würden	
er/sie/es würde	sie würden	

COMMANDS nimm teil! nehmt teil! nehmen Sie teil!

PRESENT PARTICIPLE teilnehmend

Usage

Letztes Jahr habe ich an einem Webdesign-Workshop teilgenommen.	*Last year, I attended a Web design workshop.*
Studierende nehmen an internationalen Austauschprogrammen teil.	*Students take part in international exchange programs.*
Sogar die Loyalisten sollen am Aufstand teilgenommen haben.	*Even the loyalists are said to have joined in the uprising.*
Wir haben an einer Friedensdemonstration teilgenommen.	*We took part in a peace demonstration.*
Herr Hartmann nahm an diesem Mord nicht teil.	*Mr. Hartmann wasn't involved in this murder.*
Hättet ihr an der Wahl teilgenommen?	*Would you have participated in the election?*
Etwa 3 500 Personen haben daran teilgenommen.	*About 3,500 people took part.*
14 000 Soldaten nahmen am militärischen Einsatz teil.	*Fourteen thousand soldiers took part in the military intervention.*
Die ganze Familie nimmt am Projekt teil.	*The whole family is collaborating on the project.*

RELATED VERBS *see* **nehmen** (314)

regular weak verb **tötet · tötete · getötet**

PRESENT

ich töte	wir töten
du tötest	ihr tötet
Sie töten	Sie töten
er/sie/es tötet	sie töten

SIMPLE PAST

ich tötete	wir töteten
du tötetest	ihr tötetet
Sie töteten	Sie töteten
er/sie/es tötete	sie töteten

FUTURE

ich werde	wir werden	töten
du wirst	ihr werdet	
Sie werden	Sie werden	
er/sie/es wird	sie werden	

PRESENT SUBJUNCTIVE I

ich töte	wir töten
du tötest	ihr tötet
Sie töten	Sie töten
er/sie/es töte	sie töten

PRESENT SUBJUNCTIVE II

ich tötete	wir töteten
du tötetest	ihr tötetet
Sie töteten	Sie töteten
er/sie/es tötete	sie töteten

FUTURE SUBJUNCTIVE I

ich werde	wir werden	töten
du werdest	ihr werdet	
Sie werden	Sie werden	
er/sie/es werde	sie werden	

FUTURE SUBJUNCTIVE II

ich würde	wir würden	töten
du würdest	ihr würdet	
Sie würden	Sie würden	
er/sie/es würde	sie würden	

PRESENT PERFECT

ich habe	wir haben	getötet
du hast	ihr habt	
Sie haben	Sie haben	
er/sie/es hat	sie haben	

PAST PERFECT

ich hatte	wir hatten	getötet
du hattest	ihr hattet	
Sie hatten	Sie hatten	
er/sie/es hatte	sie hatten	

FUTURE PERFECT

ich werde	wir werden	getötet haben
du wirst	ihr werdet	
Sie werden	Sie werden	
er/sie/es wird	sie werden	

PAST SUBJUNCTIVE I

ich habe	wir haben	getötet
du habest	ihr habet	
Sie haben	Sie haben	
er/sie/es habe	sie haben	

PAST SUBJUNCTIVE II

ich hätte	wir hätten	getötet
du hättest	ihr hättet	
Sie hätten	Sie hätten	
er/sie/es hätte	sie hätten	

FUTURE PERFECT SUBJUNCTIVE I

ich werde	wir werden	getötet haben
du werdest	ihr werdet	
Sie werden	Sie werden	
er/sie/es werde	sie werden	

FUTURE PERFECT SUBJUNCTIVE II

ich würde	wir würden	getötet haben
du würdest	ihr würdet	
Sie würden	Sie würden	
er/sie/es würde	sie würden	

COMMANDS töte! tötet! töten Sie!

PRESENT PARTICIPLE tötend

Usage

Elefanten werden für ihr Elfenbein illegal getötet.	*Elephants are illegally killed for their ivory.*
Der Massenmörder tötete insgesamt 17 Menschen.	*The mass murderer killed a total of 17 people.*
Werther tötete sich mit einer Pistole.	*Werther killed himself with a pistol.*
Freiherr Alderbusch wollte seine Frau töten.	*Baron Alderbusch wanted to kill his wife.*
Der tapfere Ritter tötete den Drachen.	*The brave knight slew the dragon.*
Du sollst nicht töten. (2. Mose 20,13)	*Thou shalt not kill.* (Exodus 20:13)
Unser Kater hat gerade eine Maus getötet.	*Our cat just killed a mouse.*
Im Krieg musste der Soldat töten lernen.	*In the war, the soldier had to learn to kill.*
Drei Gefangene wurden heute getötet.	*Three prisoners were put to death today.*
Der Nachbarshund soll ein 4-jähriges Mädchen getötet haben.	*The neighbor's dog is supposed to have killed a four-year-old girl.*
Wenn jemand einen Menschen tötet, so soll es sein, als hätte er die ganze Menschheit getötet. (Koran 5,33)	*If someone kills a person, it is as if he has killed all of humanity.* (Koran 5:33)

RELATED VERB ab·töten

tragen *to carry, hold; wear; bear, endure*

trägt · trug · getragen — strong verb

MORE USAGE SENTENCES WITH tragen

Trägst du deinen Laptop bei dir überall, wo du hingehst? — *Do you take your laptop with you everywhere you go?*
Sie haben ihre Winterkleidung getragen. — *They were wearing their winter clothes.*
Tante Inge trägt gern Diamanten. — *Aunt Inge likes wearing diamonds.*
Kim hat ihr Haar im Sommer gern kurz getragen. — *Kim liked to wear her hair short in the summer.*
Oma trug früher immer einen Dutt. — *Grandma used to always wear her hair in a bun.*
Ich trage selten eine Krawatte. — *I seldom wear a tie.*
Der Käufer muss die Versandkosten tragen. — *The buyer must bear the shipping costs.*
Das Ensemble trug den Namen „Lorelei". — *The ensemble went by the name "Lorelei."*
Mein Konto trägt Zinsen. — *My account is interest-bearing.*
Oliver muss diese Last alleine tragen. — *Oliver must bear this burden alone.*
Ich trage die Verantwortung für den Inhalt des Films. — *I bear the responsibility for the film's content.*
Der Darlehensvertrag trägt die Unterschriften aller drei Geschwister. — *The mortgage contract bears the signatures of all three siblings.*
Die Firma trägt alle Kosten. — *The company will bear all the costs.*
Der Bauer musste den Verlust seiner Lieblingskuh Bessie tragen. — *The farmer had to bear the loss of his pet cow, Bessie.*
Luka hat ein schweres Los zu tragen. — *Luka has to endure a difficult fate.*
Es wäre vernünftig, du ehrtest die Götter und trügest geduldig die Last des Elends. (HEINE) — *It would be sensible if you honored the gods and bore patiently the burden of your misery.*

sich tragen (impersonal) *to carry*

Ein Klavier trägt sich sehr schwer. — *Carrying a piano is very difficult.*
Der Fernseher trägt sich leichter zu zweit. — *Two can carry the television more easily.*

sich tragen mit *to contemplate*

Annalies trägt sich mit Heiratsgedanken. — *Annalies is contemplating marriage.*
Frau Dinkelgruber trug sich mit dem Gedanken, Tulpen anstatt Dahlien zu pflanzen. — *Mrs. Dinkelgruber was toying with the idea of planting tulips instead of dahlias.*
Norbert trägt sich mit der Absicht, für den Stadtrat zu kandidieren. — *Norbert intends to run for city council.*

IDIOMATIC EXPRESSIONS

Unser Kirschbaum trägt nicht. — *Our cherry tree is not producing.*
Ich werde alle Gebühren tragen. — *I'll cover all fees.*
Wir hoffen, dass die Zusammenarbeit Früchte trägt. — *We hope the cooperative undertaking will be productive.*
Die vornehme Dame trug ihre Juwelen zur Schau. — *The wealthy lady flaunted her jewelry.*
Man muss den Meinungen anderer Teilnehmer Rechnung tragen. — *One must take into account the opinions of other participants.*
Ich trage Bedenken wegen seines Vorschlags. — *I have some doubts about his suggestion.*
Wenn du das machst, musst du die Folgen tragen. — *If you do that, you'll have to accept the consequences.*
Dirk trägt das Herz auf der Zunge. — *Dirk wears his heart on his sleeve* (lit., *on his tongue*).
Wer trägt die Schuld dafür? — *Who will take the blame for that?*
Die Gemeindeblaskapelle trägt sich über Mitgliedsbeiträge. — *The community band is self-supporting through membership dues.*
Die Überdachung wird von metallenen Säulen getragen. — *The roof is supported by metal columns.*
Erich hat die Folgen mit Fassung getragen. — *Erich took the consequences in stride.*
Eulen nach Athen tragen. (PROVERB) — *To carry coals to Newcastle.* (lit., *To transport owls to Athens.*)

PRESENT

ich trage	wir tragen
du trägst	ihr tragt
Sie tragen	Sie tragen
er/sie/es trägt	sie tragen

SIMPLE PAST

ich trug	wir trugen
du trugst	ihr trugt
Sie trugen	Sie trugen
er/sie/es trug	sie trugen

FUTURE

ich werde	wir werden	tragen
du wirst	ihr werdet	
Sie werden	Sie werden	
er/sie/es wird	sie werden	

PRESENT SUBJUNCTIVE I

ich trage	wir tragen
du tragest	ihr traget
Sie tragen	Sie tragen
er/sie/es trage	sie tragen

PRESENT SUBJUNCTIVE II

ich trüge	wir trügen
du trügest	ihr trüget
Sie trügen	Sie trügen
er/sie/es trüge	sie trügen

FUTURE SUBJUNCTIVE I

ich werde	wir werden	tragen
du werdest	ihr werdet	
Sie werden	Sie werden	
er/sie/es werde	sie werden	

FUTURE SUBJUNCTIVE II

ich würde	wir würden	tragen
du würdest	ihr würdet	
Sie würden	Sie würden	
er/sie/es würde	sie würden	

PRESENT PERFECT

ich habe	wir haben	getragen
du hast	ihr habt	
Sie haben	Sie haben	
er/sie/es hat	sie haben	

PAST PERFECT

ich hatte	wir hatten	getragen
du hattest	ihr hattet	
Sie hatten	Sie hatten	
er/sie/es hatte	sie hatten	

FUTURE PERFECT

ich werde	wir werden	getragen haben
du wirst	ihr werdet	
Sie werden	Sie werden	
er/sie/es wird	sie werden	

PAST SUBJUNCTIVE I

ich habe	wir haben	getragen
du habest	ihr habet	
Sie haben	Sie haben	
er/sie/es habe	sie haben	

PAST SUBJUNCTIVE II

ich hätte	wir hätten	getragen
du hättest	ihr hättet	
Sie hätten	Sie hätten	
er/sie/es hätte	sie hätten	

FUTURE PERFECT SUBJUNCTIVE I

ich werde	wir werden	getragen haben
du werdest	ihr werdet	
Sie werden	Sie werden	
er/sie/es werde	sie werden	

FUTURE PERFECT SUBJUNCTIVE II

ich würde	wir würden	getragen haben
du würdest	ihr würdet	
Sie würden	Sie würden	
er/sie/es würde	sie würden	

COMMANDS trag(e)! tragt! tragen Sie!

PRESENT PARTICIPLE tragend

Usage

Aluminium ist leichter als Blei zu tragen.	*Aluminum is easier to carry than lead.*
Grete hat den kranken Hund zum Tierarzt getragen.	*Grete carried the sick dog to the veterinarian.*
Der Cowboy hat eine Pistole bei sich getragen.	*The cowboy carried a pistol.*
Die Kuh trägt ein Kalb.	*The cow is carrying a calf.*
Bernhards tiefe Stimme trug gut durch die kalte nächtliche Luft.	*Bernhard's deep voice carried well through the cold night air.*
Die Katze trug eine Maus im Maul.	*The cat was holding a mouse in its mouth.*
Er trägt einen Ball in der linken Hand.	*He's holding a ball in his left hand.*
Der Hund Maxl lässt sich nicht tragen.	*The dog, Maxl, won't let you hold him.*
Pass auf, diese Leiter trägt dich nicht, du bist zu schwer!	*Watch out, this ladder won't hold you; you're too heavy!*
Trägst du gern T-Shirts?	*Do you like to wear T-shirts?*

RELATED VERBS ab·tragen, an·tragen, auf·tragen, aus·tragen, bei·tragen, durch·tragen, ein·tragen, ertragen, heran·tragen, nach·tragen, übertragen, vertragen, vor·tragen, weg·tragen, zurück·tragen, zusammen·tragen, zu·tragen; *see also* **betragen** (97)

447 trauen *to trust; marry*

traut · traute · getraut

regular weak verb

PRESENT

ich traue	wir trauen
du traust	ihr traut
Sie trauen	Sie trauen
er/sie/es traut	sie trauen

SIMPLE PAST

ich traute	wir trauten
du trautest	ihr trautet
Sie trauten	Sie trauten
er/sie/es traute	sie trauten

FUTURE

ich werde	wir werden	trauen
du wirst	ihr werdet	
Sie werden	Sie werden	
er/sie/es wird	sie werden	

PRESENT SUBJUNCTIVE I

ich traue	wir trauen
du trauest	ihr trauet
Sie trauen	Sie trauen
er/sie/es traue	sie trauen

PRESENT SUBJUNCTIVE II

ich traute	wir trauten
du trautest	ihr trautet
Sie trauten	Sie trauten
er/sie/es traute	sie trauten

FUTURE SUBJUNCTIVE I

ich werde	wir werden	trauen
du werdest	ihr werdet	
Sie werden	Sie werden	
er/sie/es werde	sie werden	

FUTURE SUBJUNCTIVE II

ich würde	wir würden	trauen
du würdest	ihr würdet	
Sie würden	Sie würden	
er/sie/es würde	sie würden	

PRESENT PERFECT

ich habe	wir haben	getraut
du hast	ihr habt	
Sie haben	Sie haben	
er/sie/es hat	sie haben	

PAST PERFECT

ich hatte	wir hatten	getraut
du hattest	ihr hattet	
Sie hatten	Sie hatten	
er/sie/es hatte	sie hatten	

FUTURE PERFECT

ich werde	wir werden	getraut haben
du wirst	ihr werdet	
Sie werden	Sie werden	
er/sie/es wird	sie werden	

PAST SUBJUNCTIVE I

ich habe	wir haben	getraut
du habest	ihr habet	
Sie haben	Sie haben	
er/sie/es habe	sie haben	

PAST SUBJUNCTIVE II

ich hätte	wir hätten	getraut
du hättest	ihr hättet	
Sie hätten	Sie hätten	
er/sie/es hätte	sie hätten	

FUTURE PERFECT SUBJUNCTIVE I

ich werde	wir werden	getraut haben
du werdest	ihr werdet	
Sie werden	Sie werden	
er/sie/es werde	sie werden	

FUTURE PERFECT SUBJUNCTIVE II

ich würde	wir würden	getraut haben
du würdest	ihr würdet	
Sie würden	Sie würden	
er/sie/es würde	sie würden	

COMMANDS trau(e)! traut! trauen Sie!

PRESENT PARTICIPLE trauend

Usage

Traust du dem Präsidenten noch?	*Do you still trust the president?*
Trau niemandem über 30!	*Don't trust anyone over 30!*
Maria hat seinen Worten nicht getraut.	*Maria didn't trust his words.*
Ich kann ihm nicht mehr trauen.	*I can no longer trust him.*
Man kann den Sinnen nicht immer trauen.	*One can't always trust one's senses.*
Du kannst mir trauen!	*You can trust me!*
Grete konnte ihren Augen kaum trauen.	*Grete could hardly believe her eyes.*
Pfarrer Eberhard hat meine Eltern getraut.	*Pastor Eberhard married my parents.*

sich trauen *to dare, venture, risk*

Wir trauen uns nicht, unsere Gefühle auszudrücken.	*We don't dare express our feelings.*
Der Schizophrene traute sich nicht aus dem Haus.	*The schizophrenic did not venture from the house.*
Serena traute sich nicht.	*Serena had no courage.*

RELATED VERBS an·trauen, betrauen, getrauen, misstrauen, zu·trauen; *see also* **vertrauen** (504)

regular weak verb

träumt · träumte · geträumt

PRESENT

ich träume	wir träumen
du träumst	ihr träumt
Sie träumen	Sie träumen
er/sie/es träumt	sie träumen

SIMPLE PAST

ich träumte	wir träumten
du träumtest	ihr träumtet
Sie träumten	Sie träumten
er/sie/es träumte	sie träumten

FUTURE

ich werde	wir werden	träumen
du wirst	ihr werdet	
Sie werden	Sie werden	
er/sie/es wird	sie werden	

PRESENT SUBJUNCTIVE I

ich träume	wir träumen
du träumest	ihr träumet
Sie träumen	Sie träumen
er/sie/es träume	sie träumen

PRESENT SUBJUNCTIVE II

ich träumte	wir träumten
du träumtest	ihr träumtet
Sie träumten	Sie träumten
er/sie/es träumte	sie träumten

FUTURE SUBJUNCTIVE I

ich werde	wir werden	träumen
du werdest	ihr werdet	
Sie werden	Sie werden	
er/sie/es werde	sie werden	

FUTURE SUBJUNCTIVE II

ich würde	wir würden	träumen
du würdest	ihr würdet	
Sie würden	Sie würden	
er/sie/es würde	sie würden	

PRESENT PERFECT

ich habe	wir haben	geträumt
du hast	ihr habt	
Sie haben	Sie haben	
er/sie/es hat	sie haben	

PAST PERFECT

ich hatte	wir hatten	geträumt
du hattest	ihr hattet	
Sie hatten	Sie hatten	
er/sie/es hatte	sie hatten	

FUTURE PERFECT

ich werde	wir werden	geträumt haben
du wirst	ihr werdet	
Sie werden	Sie werden	
er/sie/es wird	sie werden	

PAST SUBJUNCTIVE I

ich habe	wir haben	geträumt
du habest	ihr habet	
Sie haben	Sie haben	
er/sie/es habe	sie haben	

PAST SUBJUNCTIVE II

ich hätte	wir hätten	geträumt
du hättest	ihr hättet	
Sie hätten	Sie hätten	
er/sie/es hätte	sie hätten	

FUTURE PERFECT SUBJUNCTIVE I

ich werde	wir werden	geträumt haben
du werdest	ihr werdet	
Sie werden	Sie werden	
er/sie/es werde	sie werden	

FUTURE PERFECT SUBJUNCTIVE II

ich würde	wir würden	geträumt haben
du würdest	ihr würdet	
Sie würden	Sie würden	
er/sie/es würde	sie würden	

COMMANDS träum(e)! träumt! träumen Sie!

PRESENT PARTICIPLE träumend

Usage

Wir träumen von einer Eigentumswohnung. — *We dream of owning our own home.*
Träumt Gregor nur oder ist er wirklich ein Käfer? — *Is Gregor just imagining or is he really a bug?*
Theodor träumt davon, Astronaut zu werden. — *Theodor dreams of becoming an astronaut.*
Meine Eltern träumten von einer Weltreise. — *My parents dreamed of a trip around the world.*
Klaus träumte von Reichtum und Glück. — *Klaus dreamed of wealth and fortune.*
Ich habe von lilafarbenen Goldfischen geträumt. — *I was dreaming of purple goldfish.*
Das Kind muss schlecht geträumt haben. — *The child must have had a bad dream.*
Hast du wieder geträumt? — *Were you daydreaming again?*
Guck mal, der Hund träumt gerade. — *Look, the dog is dreaming.*
Die Prinzessin träumte von dem schönen Jüngling. — *The princess dreamed of the handsome youth.*
Träum süß! — *Sweet dreams!*
Wer Träume verwirklichen will, muss wacher sein und tiefer träumen als andere. (Karl Foerster) — *Whoever wants to make his dreams come true, has to be more awake and dream more intensely than others.*

RELATED VERBS aus·träumen, erträumen, verträumen

treffen *to hit, strike; hurt, affect; meet*

trifft · traf · getroffen strong verb

MORE USAGE SENTENCES WITH **treffen**

Die alten Männer treffen einander jeden Samstagabend in der Kneipe.	*The old men get together every Saturday evening at the pub.*
Ich habe Anke zufällig in der Innenstadt getroffen.	*I just happened to run into Anke downtown today.*

sich treffen (mit) *to meet (with)*

Wo trefft ihr euch?	*Where are you meeting?*
Wissenschaftler aus aller Welt treffen sich heute in Rom, um Globalerwärmung zu besprechen.	*Scientists from around the world are meeting today in Rome to discuss global warming.*
Die Chorsänger treffen sich jede Woche zur Probe.	*The choir singers meet each week to practice.*
Parallele Linien treffen sich theoretisch nirgends.	*Theoretically, parallel lines never meet.*
Ein Punkt ist ein Ort, an dem sich zwei Linien treffen.	*A point is a locus where two lines intersect.*
Zu Weihnachten treffen wir uns bei meinen Eltern und singen Weihnachtslieder.	*At Christmas, we'll meet at my parents' house and sing Christmas carols.*
Wir treffen uns morgen mit dem Anwalt.	*We are meeting with the lawyer tomorrow.*
Ich habe mich heute mit Sonja getroffen.	*I met with Sonja today.*
Ist das nicht die Frau, mit der du dich treffen wolltest?	*Isn't that the woman you wanted to meet with?*
Wo treffen sich die jungen Leute heutzutage?	*Where do young people congregate nowadays?*
Wir haben uns im Internet kennen gelernt und treffen uns noch regelmäßig in Chats.	*We met on the Internet and still meet regularly in chat rooms.*

treffen auf (with **sein**) *to come upon, go up against*

Im Supermarkt bin ich auf einen alten Freund getroffen.	*At the supermarket, I bumped into an old friend.*
In Dinkelsbach sind wir auf Widerstand getroffen.	*In Dinkelsbach, we came up against some resistance.*
Die Mannschaft trifft erneut auf den Erzgegner.	*The team is going up against its archrival again.*

es trifft sich (impersonal) *it is, it happens*

Es trifft sich gut, dass er heute nicht gekommen ist.	*It's a good thing he didn't come today.*
Es traf sich, dass Dirk sie am nächsten Tag wiedersah.	*It so happened that Dirk saw her the next day.*
Es traf sich glücklicherweise, dass dort noch niemals eine gesehen war. (GRIMM)	*Luckily, not a single one had ever been seen there.*

IDIOMATIC EXPRESSIONS

Daniel fühlt sich nicht getroffen.	*Daniel doesn't consider himself to be the target. / Daniel doesn't think it applies to him.*
Warum hast du eine Wahl getroffen, ohne uns zu berücksichtigen?	*Why did you make a choice without taking us into consideration?*
Habt ihr denn immer noch keine klare Entscheidung treffen können?	*Haven't you been able to make a final decision yet?*
In seiner Rede hat der Kanzler den richtigen Ton getroffen.	*The chancellor set the right tone in his speech.*
Warum trifft es immer mich?	*Why is it always me? / Why do these things always happen to me?*
Du hast ins Schwarze getroffen.	*You've hit the bull's-eye.*
Ihre Worte haben ihm ins Herz getroffen.	*Her words hurt him deeply.*
Wieder mal hast du den Nagel auf den Kopf getroffen.	*Once again, you've hit the nail on the head.*
Die Regierung hat neue Maßnahmen gegen Terrorismus getroffen.	*The government has taken new measures against terrorism.*
Der Schlag soll dich treffen! (*slang*)	*Drop dead!*
Diese Regelung trifft dich nicht, da du Ausländerin bist.	*This regulation doesn't apply to you since you're a foreigner.*

strong verb **trifft · traf · getroffen**

PRESENT

ich treffe	wir treffen
du triffst	ihr trefft
Sie treffen	Sie treffen
er/sie/es trifft	sie treffen

SIMPLE PAST

ich traf	wir trafen
du trafst	ihr traft
Sie trafen	Sie trafen
er/sie/es traf	sie trafen

FUTURE

ich werde	wir werden	treffen
du wirst	ihr werdet	
Sie werden	Sie werden	
er/sie/es wird	sie werden	

PRESENT SUBJUNCTIVE I

ich treffe	wir treffen
du treffest	ihr treffet
Sie treffen	Sie treffen
er/sie/es treffe	sie treffen

PRESENT SUBJUNCTIVE II

ich träfe	wir träfen
du träfest	ihr träfet
Sie träfen	Sie träfen
er/sie/es träfe	sie träfen

FUTURE SUBJUNCTIVE I

ich werde	wir werden	treffen
du werdest	ihr werdet	
Sie werden	Sie werden	
er/sie/es werde	sie werden	

FUTURE SUBJUNCTIVE II

ich würde	wir würden	treffen
du würdest	ihr würdet	
Sie würden	Sie würden	
er/sie/es würde	sie würden	

PRESENT PERFECT

ich habe	wir haben	getroffen
du hast	ihr habt	
Sie haben	Sie haben	
er/sie/es hat	sie haben	

PAST PERFECT

ich hatte	wir hatten	getroffen
du hattest	ihr hattet	
Sie hatten	Sie hatten	
er/sie/es hatte	sie hatten	

FUTURE PERFECT

ich werde	wir werden	getroffen haben
du wirst	ihr werdet	
Sie werden	Sie werden	
er/sie/es wird	sie werden	

PAST SUBJUNCTIVE I

ich habe	wir haben	getroffen
du habest	ihr habet	
Sie haben	Sie haben	
er/sie/es habe	sie haben	

PAST SUBJUNCTIVE II

ich hätte	wir hätten	getroffen
du hättest	ihr hättet	
Sie hätten	Sie hätten	
er/sie/es hätte	sie hätten	

FUTURE PERFECT SUBJUNCTIVE I

ich werde	wir werden	getroffen haben
du werdest	ihr werdet	
Sie werden	Sie werden	
er/sie/es werde	sie werden	

FUTURE PERFECT SUBJUNCTIVE II

ich würde	wir würden	getroffen haben
du würdest	ihr würdet	
Sie würden	Sie würden	
er/sie/es würde	sie würden	

COMMANDS triff! trefft! treffen Sie!

PRESENT PARTICIPLE treffend

Usage

Der Stein traf ihn am Kopf.	*The rock hit him on the head.*
Die Nachricht hat uns schwer getroffen.	*The news hit us hard.*
Nur eine von fünf Bomben treffen das Ziel.	*Only one in five bombs hits the target.*
Die Kugel traf den Reh in die Schulter.	*The bullet struck the deer in the shoulder.*
Der Baum wurde vom Blitz getroffen.	*The tree was struck by lightning.*
Lincoln wurde von einem Gewehrschuss getroffen und starb kurz darauf.	*Lincoln was struck by a gunshot and died shortly thereafter.*
Der Steuerskandal hat den Kandidaten hart getroffen.	*The tax scandal has seriously hurt the candidate.*
Der Sturm hat uns nicht getroffen.	*The storm did not affect us.*
Aber am tiefsten trafst du doch mich, den Freund, der im Arm dich hält. (GOETHE)	*But it was I whom you most deeply affected, the friend who holds you in his arm.*
Franz-Josef hat mich am Bahnhof in Rheine getroffen.	*Franz-Josef met me at the train station in Rheine.*

RELATED VERBS an·betreffen, an·treffen, auf·treffen, betreffen, ein·treffen, übertreffen, zusammen·treffen, zu·treffen

450 treiben *to drive; force; carry on, pursue; take too far*

treibt · trieb · getrieben — strong verb

PRESENT		PRESENT PERFECT		
ich treibe	wir treiben	ich habe	wir haben	getrieben
du treibst	ihr treibt	du hast	ihr habt	
Sie treiben	Sie treiben	Sie haben	Sie haben	
er/sie/es treibt	sie treiben	er/sie/es hat	sie haben	

SIMPLE PAST		PAST PERFECT		
ich trieb	wir trieben	ich hatte	wir hatten	getrieben
du triebst	ihr triebt	du hattest	ihr hattet	
Sie trieben	Sie trieben	Sie hatten	Sie hatten	
er/sie/es trieb	sie trieben	er/sie/es hatte	sie hatten	

FUTURE			FUTURE PERFECT		
ich werde	wir werden	treiben	ich werde	wir werden	getrieben haben
du wirst	ihr werdet		du wirst	ihr werdet	
Sie werden	Sie werden		Sie werden	Sie werden	
er/sie/es wird	sie werden		er/sie/es wird	sie werden	

PRESENT SUBJUNCTIVE I		PAST SUBJUNCTIVE I		
ich treibe	wir treiben	ich habe	wir haben	getrieben
du treibest	ihr treibet	du habest	ihr habet	
Sie treiben	Sie treiben	Sie haben	Sie haben	
er/sie/es treibe	sie treiben	er/sie/es habe	sie haben	

PRESENT SUBJUNCTIVE II		PAST SUBJUNCTIVE II		
ich triebe	wir trieben	ich hätte	wir hätten	getrieben
du triebest	ihr triebet	du hättest	ihr hättet	
Sie trieben	Sie trieben	Sie hätten	Sie hätten	
er/sie/es triebe	sie trieben	er/sie/es hätte	sie hätten	

FUTURE SUBJUNCTIVE I			FUTURE PERFECT SUBJUNCTIVE I		
ich werde	wir werden	treiben	ich werde	wir werden	getrieben haben
du werdest	ihr werdet		du werdest	ihr werdet	
Sie werden	Sie werden		Sie werden	Sie werden	
er/sie/es werde	sie werden		er/sie/es werde	sie werden	

FUTURE SUBJUNCTIVE II			FUTURE PERFECT SUBJUNCTIVE II		
ich würde	wir würden	treiben	ich würde	wir würden	getrieben haben
du würdest	ihr würdet		du würdest	ihr würdet	
Sie würden	Sie würden		Sie würden	Sie würden	
er/sie/es würde	sie würden		er/sie/es würde	sie würden	

COMMANDS treib(e)! treibt! treiben Sie!

PRESENT PARTICIPLE treibend

Usage

Sep nahm einen Stock und trieb die Kuh aus dem Stall.	*Sep took a stick and drove the cow from the stall.*
Er meint, seine Eltern hätten ihn in den Alkoholismus getrieben.	*He thinks his parents drove him to alcoholism.*
Über 50 000 Menschen wurden über die Grenze getrieben.	*Over 50,000 people were driven across the border.*
Der Preis wird in die Höhe getrieben.	*The price is being forced up.*
Moritz fühlte sich in die Enge getrieben.	*Moritz felt cornered.*
Was treibst du so? (*idiomatic*)	*What are you up to?*
Lars hat die Sache auf die Spitze getrieben.	*Lars pushed the matter to extremes.*
Freude, Freude treibt die Räder in der großen Weltenuhr. (SCHILLER)	*Joy, joy moves the wheels in the universal time machine.*

treiben (with **sein**) *to drift, be driven, be forced*

Das Boot ist ans Land getrieben.	*The boat drifted ashore.*

RELATED VERBS ab·treiben, an·treiben, auf·treiben, aus·treiben, betreiben, durch·treiben, ein·treiben, fort·treiben, hoch·treiben, übertreiben, vertreiben, voran·treiben, vor·treiben, weg·treiben, zurück·treiben, zusammen·treiben, zu·treiben

regular weak verb **trennt · trennte · getrennt**

PRESENT		PRESENT PERFECT		
ich trenne	wir trennen	ich habe	wir haben	getrennt
du trennst	ihr trennt	du hast	ihr habt	
Sie trennen	Sie trennen	Sie haben	Sie haben	
er/sie/es trennt	sie trennen	er/sie/es hat	sie haben	

SIMPLE PAST		PAST PERFECT		
ich trennte	wir trennten	ich hatte	wir hatten	getrennt
du trenntest	ihr trenntet	du hattest	ihr hattet	
Sie trennten	Sie trennten	Sie hatten	Sie hatten	
er/sie/es trennte	sie trennten	er/sie/es hatte	sie hatten	

FUTURE			FUTURE PERFECT		
ich werde	wir werden	trennen	ich werde	wir werden	getrennt haben
du wirst	ihr werdet		du wirst	ihr werdet	
Sie werden	Sie werden		Sie werden	Sie werden	
er/sie/es wird	sie werden		er/sie/es wird	sie werden	

PRESENT SUBJUNCTIVE I		PAST SUBJUNCTIVE I		
ich trenne	wir trennen	ich habe	wir haben	getrennt
du trennest	ihr trennet	du habest	ihr habet	
Sie trennen	Sie trennen	Sie haben	Sie haben	
er/sie/es trenne	sie trennen	er/sie/es habe	sie haben	

PRESENT SUBJUNCTIVE II		PAST SUBJUNCTIVE II		
ich trennte	wir trennten	ich hätte	wir hätten	getrennt
du trenntest	ihr trenntet	du hättest	ihr hättet	
Sie trennten	Sie trennten	Sie hätten	Sie hätten	
er/sie/es trennte	sie trennten	er/sie/es hätte	sie hätten	

FUTURE SUBJUNCTIVE I			FUTURE PERFECT SUBJUNCTIVE I		
ich werde	wir werden	trennen	ich werde	wir werden	getrennt haben
du werdest	ihr werdet		du werdest	ihr werdet	
Sie werden	Sie werden		Sie werden	Sie werden	
er/sie/es werde	sie werden		er/sie/es werde	sie werden	

FUTURE SUBJUNCTIVE II			FUTURE PERFECT SUBJUNCTIVE II		
ich würde	wir würden	trennen	ich würde	wir würden	getrennt haben
du würdest	ihr würdet		du würdest	ihr würdet	
Sie würden	Sie würden		Sie würden	Sie würden	
er/sie/es würde	sie würden		er/sie/es würde	sie würden	

COMMANDS trenn(e)! trennt! trennen Sie!

PRESENT PARTICIPLE trennend

Usage

Man muss den Müll trennen. — *You have to sort the trash for recycling.*
Im Autounfall wurde das linke Bein vom Rumpf getrennt. — *In the auto accident, the left leg was severed from the torso.*
Wie trennt man das Eiweiß von dem Eigelb? — *How do you separate the egg white from the yolk?*
Ein Bach trennt die Grundstücke. — *A brook separates the parcels of land.*
Bürgerkrieg hatte das Land getrennt. — *Civil war had divided the country.*
Wie trennt man das Wort „sitzen"? — *Where do you divide the word "sitzen"?*
Die beiden Systeme müssen klar voneinander getrennt werden. — *The two systems must be clearly differentiated from one another.*

sich trennen *to separate*

Das Ehepaar trennte sich nach sieben Monaten. — *The married couple split up after seven months.*
Anton trennte sich von seinem Sohn und zog nach Zürich. — *Anton left his son and moved to Zurich.*

RELATED VERBS ab·trennen, auf·trennen, aus·trennen, durchtrennen, zertrennen

452 treten *to step, go, come*

tritt · trat · getreten strong verb

PRESENT		PRESENT PERFECT		
ich trete	wir treten	ich bin	wir sind	getreten
du trittst	ihr tretet	du bist	ihr seid	
Sie treten	Sie treten	Sie sind	Sie sind	
er/sie/es tritt	sie treten	er/sie/es ist	sie sind	

SIMPLE PAST		PAST PERFECT		
ich trat	wir traten	ich war	wir waren	getreten
du tratst	ihr tratet	du warst	ihr wart	
Sie traten	Sie traten	Sie waren	Sie waren	
er/sie/es trat	sie traten	er/sie/es war	sie waren	

FUTURE			FUTURE PERFECT		
ich werde	wir werden	treten	ich werde	wir werden	getreten sein
du wirst	ihr werdet		du wirst	ihr werdet	
Sie werden	Sie werden		Sie werden	Sie werden	
er/sie/es wird	sie werden		er/sie/es wird	sie werden	

PRESENT SUBJUNCTIVE I		PAST SUBJUNCTIVE I		
ich trete	wir treten	ich sei	wir seien	getreten
du tretest	ihr tretet	du seiest	ihr seiet	
Sie treten	Sie treten	Sie seien	Sie seien	
er/sie/es trete	sie treten	er/sie/es sei	sie seien	

PRESENT SUBJUNCTIVE II		PAST SUBJUNCTIVE II		
ich träte	wir träten	ich wäre	wir wären	getreten
du trätest	ihr trätet	du wärest	ihr wäret	
Sie träten	Sie träten	Sie wären	Sie wären	
er/sie/es träte	sie träten	er/sie/es wäre	sie wären	

FUTURE SUBJUNCTIVE I			FUTURE PERFECT SUBJUNCTIVE I		
ich werde	wir werden	treten	ich werde	wir werden	getreten sein
du werdest	ihr werdet		du werdest	ihr werdet	
Sie werden	Sie werden		Sie werden	Sie werden	
er/sie/es werde	sie werden		er/sie/es werde	sie werden	

FUTURE SUBJUNCTIVE II			FUTURE PERFECT SUBJUNCTIVE II		
ich würde	wir würden	treten	ich würde	wir würden	getreten sein
du würdest	ihr würdet		du würdest	ihr würdet	
Sie würden	Sie würden		Sie würden	Sie würden	
er/sie/es würde	sie würden		er/sie/es würde	sie würden	

COMMANDS tritt! tretet! treten Sie!

PRESENT PARTICIPLE tretend

Usage

Treten Sie bitte nach vorn! — *Please step forward.*
Der Mississippi war über die Ufer getreten. — *The Mississippi had overflowed its banks.*
Der Bischof will aus dem Dienst treten. — *The bishop wants to retire from service.*
Das Gesetz tritt nie in Kraft. — *The law will never go into effect.*
Seit dem Vorfall ist er in den Vordergrund getreten. — *After the incident, he came into prominence.*
Neuigkeiten sind ans Licht getreten. — *New information has come to light.*
Sigrid ist auf meine Seite getreten. — *Sigrid sided with me.*

treten (with haben) *to tread on, kick, beat; pedal*

Trete mich nicht. — *Don't tread on me.*
Wenn er Geige spielt, tritt er den Takt. — *When he plays the violin, he keeps time with his foot.*
Tritt doch langsamer! — *Why don't you pedal more slowly!*

RELATED VERBS ab·treten, an·treten, auf·treten, aus·treten, bei·treten, betreten, durch·treten, ein·treten, entgegen·treten, fest·treten, gegenüber·treten, nieder·treten, übertreten, über·treten, vertreten, vor·treten, weg·treten, zertreten, zurück·treten, zusammen·treten, zu·treten

strong verb

trieft · troff · getroffen

PRESENT

ich triefe	wir triefen
du triefst	ihr trieft
Sie triefen	Sie triefen
er/sie/es trieft	sie triefen

PRESENT PERFECT

ich bin	wir sind	getroffen
du bist	ihr seid	
Sie sind	Sie sind	
er/sie/es ist	sie sind	

SIMPLE PAST

ich troff	wir troffen
du troffst	ihr trofft
Sie troffen	Sie troffen
er/sie/es troff	sie troffen

PAST PERFECT

ich war	wir waren	getroffen
du warst	ihr wart	
Sie waren	Sie waren	
er/sie/es war	sie waren	

FUTURE

ich werde	wir werden	triefen
du wirst	ihr werdet	
Sie werden	Sie werden	
er/sie/es wird	sie werden	

FUTURE PERFECT

ich werde	wir werden	getroffen sein
du wirst	ihr werdet	
Sie werden	Sie werden	
er/sie/es wird	sie werden	

PRESENT SUBJUNCTIVE I

ich triefe	wir triefen
du triefest	ihr triefet
Sie triefen	Sie triefen
er/sie/es triefe	sie triefen

PAST SUBJUNCTIVE I

ich sei	wir seien	getroffen
du seiest	ihr seiet	
Sie seien	Sie seien	
er/sie/es sei	sie seien	

PRESENT SUBJUNCTIVE II

ich tröffe	wir tröffen
du tröffest	ihr tröffet
Sie tröffen	Sie tröffen
er/sie/es tröffe	sie tröffen

PAST SUBJUNCTIVE II

ich wäre	wir wären	getroffen
du wärest	ihr wäret	
Sie wären	Sie wären	
er/sie/es wäre	sie wären	

FUTURE SUBJUNCTIVE I

ich werde	wir werden	triefen
du werdest	ihr werdet	
Sie werden	Sie werden	
er/sie/es werde	sie werden	

FUTURE PERFECT SUBJUNCTIVE I

ich werde	wir werden	getroffen sein
du werdest	ihr werdet	
Sie werden	Sie werden	
er/sie/es werde	sie werden	

FUTURE SUBJUNCTIVE II

ich würde	wir würden	triefen
du würdest	ihr würdet	
Sie würden	Sie würden	
er/sie/es würde	sie würden	

FUTURE PERFECT SUBJUNCTIVE II

ich würde	wir würden	getroffen sein
du würdest	ihr würdet	
Sie würden	Sie würden	
er/sie/es würde	sie würden	

COMMANDS trief(e)! trieft! triefen Sie!

PRESENT PARTICIPLE triefend

NOTE Regular weak forms of **triefen** are also common in modern German: **triefte, ist/hat getrieft**.

Usage

Blut troff ihr aus dem Mund.	*Blood trickled from her mouth.*
Wasser ist von der Decke getroffen.	*Water dripped from the ceiling.*
Der Regen trieft durch die Löcher.	*The rain is trickling through the holes.*
Honig troff aus der Bienenwabe.	*Honey was dripping from the honeycomb.*

triefen (with **haben**) *to drip, run, water, be soaked*

Die Augen troffen ihm.	*His eyes were watering.*
Mir trieft die Nase wegen Pollenallergien.	*My nose is runny from pollen allergies.*
Sein Hut troff vor Nässe.	*His hat was soaking wet.*
Lars trieft von Hass.	*Lars is overflowing with hate.*
Martials Gedichte triefen vor Satire und Sarkasmus.	*Martial's poems ooze with satire and sarcasm.*

454 trinken *to drink*

trinkt · trank · getrunken strong verb

PRESENT

ich trinke	wir trinken
du trinkst	ihr trinkt
Sie trinken	Sie trinken
er/sie/es trinkt	sie trinken

SIMPLE PAST

ich trank	wir tranken
du trankst	ihr trankt
Sie tranken	Sie tranken
er/sie/es trank	sie tranken

FUTURE

ich werde	wir werden	trinken
du wirst	ihr werdet	
Sie werden	Sie werden	
er/sie/es wird	sie werden	

PRESENT SUBJUNCTIVE I

ich trinke	wir trinken
du trinkest	ihr trinket
Sie trinken	Sie trinken
er/sie/es trinke	sie trinken

PRESENT SUBJUNCTIVE II

ich tränke	wir tränken
du tränkest	ihr tränket
Sie tränken	Sie tränken
er/sie/es tränke	sie tränken

FUTURE SUBJUNCTIVE I

ich werde	wir werden	trinken
du werdest	ihr werdet	
Sie werden	Sie werden	
er/sie/es werde	sie werden	

FUTURE SUBJUNCTIVE II

ich würde	wir würden	trinken
du würdest	ihr würdet	
Sie würden	Sie würden	
er/sie/es würde	sie würden	

PRESENT PERFECT

ich habe	wir haben	getrunken
du hast	ihr habt	
Sie haben	Sie haben	
er/sie/es hat	sie haben	

PAST PERFECT

ich hatte	wir hatten	getrunken
du hattest	ihr hattet	
Sie hatten	Sie hatten	
er/sie/es hatte	sie hatten	

FUTURE PERFECT

ich werde	wir werden	getrunken haben
du wirst	ihr werdet	
Sie werden	Sie werden	
er/sie/es wird	sie werden	

PAST SUBJUNCTIVE I

ich habe	wir haben	getrunken
du habest	ihr habet	
Sie haben	Sie haben	
er/sie/es habe	sie haben	

PAST SUBJUNCTIVE II

ich hätte	wir hätten	getrunken
du hättest	ihr hättet	
Sie hätten	Sie hätten	
er/sie/es hätte	sie hätten	

FUTURE PERFECT SUBJUNCTIVE I

ich werde	wir werden	getrunken haben
du werdest	ihr werdet	
Sie werden	Sie werden	
er/sie/es werde	sie werden	

FUTURE PERFECT SUBJUNCTIVE II

ich würde	wir würden	getrunken haben
du würdest	ihr würdet	
Sie würden	Sie würden	
er/sie/es würde	sie würden	

COMMANDS trink(e)! trinkt! trinken Sie!

PRESENT PARTICIPLE trinkend

Usage

Ich trinke keinen Kaffee mehr.	*I don't drink coffee anymore.*
Werner hat keinen Alkohol getrunken.	*Werner didn't drink any alcohol.*
Lola trank den letzten Schluck und stand auf.	*Lola drank the last sip and stood up.*
Trinken wir einen!	*Let's have a drink!*
Möchten die Kinder vielleicht Apfelsaft trinken?	*Would the children perhaps like to drink apple juice?*
Wie viel Wasser trinkt eine Kuh pro Tag?	*How much water does a cow drink per day?*
Holger trinkt nie aus der Dose.	*Holger never drinks from a can.*
Hast du das Glas leer getrunken?	*Did you drink the whole glass?*
Meinhard will zwei Liter Wasser in einem Zug getrunken haben.	*Meinhard claims to have drunk two liters of water in one gulp.*
Sie atmete langsam und tief, als tränke sie … die letzten Tropfen aus dem Becher der Zeit. (Hedwig Dohm)	*She breathed slowly and deeply, as though she were drinking … the last drops from the cup of time.*
Dieses Bier lässt sich trinken.	*This beer is good.*

RELATED VERBS ab·trinken, an·trinken, aus·trinken, betrinken, ertrinken, vertrinken, zu·trinken

regular weak verb **tröstet · tröstete · getröstet**

PRESENT

ich tröste	wir trösten
du tröstest	ihr tröstet
Sie trösten	Sie trösten
er/sie/es tröstet	sie trösten

PRESENT PERFECT

ich habe	wir haben	getröstet
du hast	ihr habt	
Sie haben	Sie haben	
er/sie/es hat	sie haben	

SIMPLE PAST

ich tröstete	wir trösteten
du tröstetest	ihr tröstetet
Sie trösteten	Sie trösteten
er/sie/es tröstete	sie trösteten

PAST PERFECT

ich hatte	wir hatten	getröstet
du hattest	ihr hattet	
Sie hatten	Sie hatten	
er/sie/es hatte	sie hatten	

FUTURE

ich werde	wir werden	trösten
du wirst	ihr werdet	
Sie werden	Sie werden	
er/sie/es wird	sie werden	

FUTURE PERFECT

ich werde	wir werden	getröstet haben
du wirst	ihr werdet	
Sie werden	Sie werden	
er/sie/es wird	sie werden	

PRESENT SUBJUNCTIVE I

ich tröste	wir trösten
du tröstest	ihr tröstet
Sie trösten	Sie trösten
er/sie/es tröste	sie trösten

PAST SUBJUNCTIVE I

ich habe	wir haben	getröstet
du habest	ihr habet	
Sie haben	Sie haben	
er/sie/es habe	sie haben	

PRESENT SUBJUNCTIVE II

ich tröstete	wir trösteten
du tröstetest	ihr tröstetet
Sie trösteten	Sie trösteten
er/sie/es tröstete	sie trösteten

PAST SUBJUNCTIVE II

ich hätte	wir hätten	getröstet
du hättest	ihr hättet	
Sie hätten	Sie hätten	
er/sie/es hätte	sie hätten	

FUTURE SUBJUNCTIVE I

ich werde	wir werden	trösten
du werdest	ihr werdet	
Sie werden	Sie werden	
er/sie/es werde	sie werden	

FUTURE PERFECT SUBJUNCTIVE I

ich werde	wir werden	getröstet haben
du werdest	ihr werdet	
Sie werden	Sie werden	
er/sie/es werde	sie werden	

FUTURE SUBJUNCTIVE II

ich würde	wir würden	trösten
du würdest	ihr würdet	
Sie würden	Sie würden	
er/sie/es würde	sie würden	

FUTURE PERFECT SUBJUNCTIVE II

ich würde	wir würden	getröstet haben
du würdest	ihr würdet	
Sie würden	Sie würden	
er/sie/es würde	sie würden	

COMMANDS tröste! tröstet! trösten Sie!

PRESENT PARTICIPLE tröstend

Usage

Heike tröstete ihre Mitschülerinnen.	*Heike consoled her schoolmates.*
Die Mutter tröstet das weinende Kind.	*The mother comforts the crying child.*
Kannst du die Kinder trösten?	*Can you console the children?*
Manni hatte seine Freundin getröstet.	*Manni had comforted his girlfriend.*
Ich hoffe, es tröstet dich ein wenig.	*I hope it comforts you a little.*
Nach dem Tod seiner Mutter hat ihn Maria getröstet.	*After his mother's death, Maria comforted him.*
Tröste mich, Lämpchen ... (GOETHE)	*Comfort me, little lamp ...*
Danke, dass ihr mich getröstet habt.	*Thanks for comforting me.*

sich trösten (mit) *to find consolation in, take comfort in*

Tante Ute tröstet sich mit Essen.	*Aunt Ute finds comfort in eating.*
Wie tröstest du dich damit?	*How do you find consolation in that?*
Dirk lässt sich nicht trösten.	*Dirk is inconsolable.*
Ich tröste mich damit, dass sie nicht länger leidet.	*I take comfort in the fact that she's not suffering anymore.*

RELATED VERB vertrösten

456 trügen *to deceive, be deceptive; be a delusion*

trügt · trog · getrogen strong verb

PRESENT

ich trüge	wir trügen
du trügst	ihr trügt
Sie trügen	Sie trügen
er/sie/es trügt	sie trügen

SIMPLE PAST

ich trog	wir trogen
du trogst	ihr trogt
Sie trogen	Sie trogen
er/sie/es trog	sie trogen

FUTURE

ich werde	wir werden	trügen
du wirst	ihr werdet	
Sie werden	Sie werden	
er/sie/es wird	sie werden	

PRESENT SUBJUNCTIVE I

ich trüge	wir trügen
du trügest	ihr trüget
Sie trügen	Sie trügen
er/sie/es trüge	sie trügen

PRESENT SUBJUNCTIVE II

ich tröge	wir trögen
du trögest	ihr tröget
Sie trögen	Sie trögen
er/sie/es tröge	sie trögen

FUTURE SUBJUNCTIVE I

ich werde	wir werden	trügen
du werdest	ihr werdet	
Sie werden	Sie werden	
er/sie/es werde	sie werden	

FUTURE SUBJUNCTIVE II

ich würde	wir würden	trügen
du würdest	ihr würdet	
Sie würden	Sie würden	
er/sie/es würde	sie würden	

PRESENT PERFECT

ich habe	wir haben	getrogen
du hast	ihr habt	
Sie haben	Sie haben	
er/sie/es hat	sie haben	

PAST PERFECT

ich hatte	wir hatten	getrogen
du hattest	ihr hattet	
Sie hatten	Sie hatten	
er/sie/es hatte	sie hatten	

FUTURE PERFECT

ich werde	wir werden	getrogen haben
du wirst	ihr werdet	
Sie werden	Sie werden	
er/sie/es wird	sie werden	

PAST SUBJUNCTIVE I

ich habe	wir haben	getrogen
du habest	ihr habet	
Sie haben	Sie haben	
er/sie/es habe	sie haben	

PAST SUBJUNCTIVE II

ich hätte	wir hätten	getrogen
du hättest	ihr hättet	
Sie hätten	Sie hätten	
er/sie/es hätte	sie hätten	

FUTURE PERFECT SUBJUNCTIVE I

ich werde	wir werden	getrogen haben
du werdest	ihr werdet	
Sie werden	Sie werden	
er/sie/es werde	sie werden	

FUTURE PERFECT SUBJUNCTIVE II

ich würde	wir würden	getrogen haben
du würdest	ihr würdet	
Sie würden	Sie würden	
er/sie/es würde	sie würden	

COMMANDS trüg(e)! trügt! trügen Sie!

PRESENT PARTICIPLE trügend

Usage

Jetzt trügen mich die Augen. — *Now my eyes deceive me.*

Der Geruch trügt; das Essen schmeckt himmlisch. — *The smell is deceiving; the food tastes heavenly.*

Der Eindruck hat uns nicht getrogen. — *Our impression was correct.*

Das Bild trügt, denn sie ist eigentlich 60 Jahre alt. — *The picture is deceptive, because she is actually 60 years old.*

Wenn mich meine Erinnerung nicht trügt, hat er drei Brüder und eine Schwester. — *If memory serves, he has three brothers and one sister.*

Die Stille trügt; der Sturm ist noch nicht vorbei. — *The silence is deceiving; the storm is not over.*

Dir scheint es möglich, weil der Wunsch dich trügt. (GOETHE) — *For you, it seems possible because desire deceives you.*

Der Schein trügt. (PROVERB) — *Appearances are deceptive.*

Sein Gedächtnis hat ihn getrogen. — *His memory misled him.*

Manchmal trügen die Sinne. — *Sometimes the senses are deceiving.*

Mein Gefühl trog mich nicht. — *The feeling I had was not a delusion.*

RELATED VERBS *see* **betrügen** (98)

irregular verb **tut · tat · getan**

PRESENT

ich tue	wir tun
du tust	ihr tut
Sie tun	Sie tun
er/sie/es tut	sie tun

SIMPLE PAST

ich tat	wir taten
du tat(e)st	ihr tatet
Sie taten	Sie taten
er/sie/es tat	sie taten

FUTURE

ich werde	wir werden	tun
du wirst	ihr werdet	
Sie werden	Sie werden	
er/sie/es wird	sie werden	

PRESENT SUBJUNCTIVE I

ich tue	wir tuen
du tuest	ihr tuet
Sie tuen	Sie tuen
er/sie/es tue	sie tuen

PRESENT SUBJUNCTIVE II

ich täte	wir täten
du tätest	ihr tätet
Sie täten	Sie täten
er/sie/es täte	sie täten

FUTURE SUBJUNCTIVE I

ich werde	wir werden	tun
du werdest	ihr werdet	
Sie werden	Sie werden	
er/sie/es werde	sie werden	

FUTURE SUBJUNCTIVE II

ich würde	wir würden	tun
du würdest	ihr würdet	
Sie würden	Sie würden	
er/sie/es würde	sie würden	

PRESENT PERFECT

ich habe	wir haben	getan
du hast	ihr habt	
Sie haben	Sie haben	
er/sie/es hat	sie haben	

PAST PERFECT

ich hatte	wir hatten	getan
du hattest	ihr hattet	
Sie hatten	Sie hatten	
er/sie/es hatte	sie hatten	

FUTURE PERFECT

ich werde	wir werden	getan haben
du wirst	ihr werdet	
Sie werden	Sie werden	
er/sie/es wird	sie werden	

PAST SUBJUNCTIVE I

ich habe	wir haben	getan
du habest	ihr habet	
Sie haben	Sie haben	
er/sie/es habe	sie haben	

PAST SUBJUNCTIVE II

ich hätte	wir hätten	getan
du hättest	ihr hättet	
Sie hätten	Sie hätten	
er/sie/es hätte	sie hätten	

FUTURE PERFECT SUBJUNCTIVE I

ich werde	wir werden	getan haben
du werdest	ihr werdet	
Sie werden	Sie werden	
er/sie/es werde	sie werden	

FUTURE PERFECT SUBJUNCTIVE II

ich würde	wir würden	getan haben
du würdest	ihr würdet	
Sie würden	Sie würden	
er/sie/es würde	sie würden	

COMMANDS tu(e)! tut! tun Sie!

PRESENT PARTICIPLE tuend

Usage

Was ist hier zu tun?	*What is to be done here?*
Einiges kann noch getan werden.	*Several things can still be done.*
Was darf ich für Sie tun?	*What can I do for you?*
Das kann ich nicht tun.	*I can't do that.*
Verstehst du, was zu tun ist?	*Do you understand what needs to be done?*
Maria hat nichts getan.	*Maria did nothing.*
Meine Eltern sind bereit, alles zu tun, was sie können.	*My parents are prepared to do everything they can.*
Das tue ich nicht!	*I won't do that!*
Ich habe nichts zu tun.	*I've got nothing to do.*
Lars kann das nicht getan haben, denn er war zu Hause.	*Lars can't have done that, since he was at home.*
Tu was!	*Do something!*
Ingrid hätte das nicht tun sollen.	*Ingrid shouldn't have done that.*

RELATED VERBS ab·tun, an·tun, auf·tun, dar·tun, genug·tun, gleich·tun, groß·tun, kund·tun, vertun, weg·tun, weh·tun, zusammen·tun, zu·tun, zuvor·tun

TOP 50 VERB ☞

tun *to do; work, perform*

tut · tat · getan irregular verb

MORE USAGE SENTENCES WITH tun

Herr Westermann geht manchmal ins Kasino, aber er tut es heimlich. — *Mr. Westermann sometimes goes to the casino, but he does it secretly.*
In der Sauna zu sitzen tut wohl. — *It does one good to sit in the sauna.*
Lars tat den ganzen Tag nichts als schlafen. — *Lars did nothing all day but sleep.*
„Ich tue dir nichts", sagte Ernst zu der Katze. — *"I won't do anything to you," said Ernst to the cat.*
Ich tue, was ich kann. — *I'll do what I can.*
Jost hat das Thema Geld wieder angesprochen, aber die Sache hat nichts mit Geld zu tun. — *Jost brought up the topic of money again, but the issue has nothing to do with money.*
Herr Schleier hat das mit Recht getan. — *Mr. Schleier was within his rights to do that.*
Erich sollte mithelfen, aber das tat er nicht. — *Erich was supposed to help out, but he didn't do that.*
Kannst du mir einen Gefallen tun? — *Can you do me a favor?*
Oliver tut weniger als Ingrid, aber er bekommt ein höheres Gehalt. — *Oliver does less than Ingrid, but he receives a higher salary.*
„Was macht Herr Kolowsky?" — *"What's Mr. Kolowsky doing?"*
„Er tut momentan nichts." — *"He's not working at the moment."*
Meine Chefin hat mit beschränkten Mitteln Wunder getan. — *My boss worked miracles with limited resources.*

sich tun *to happen*

In der Zwischenzeit hat sich doch viel getan. — *A lot has actually happened in the meantime.*
Im Dorf Kleinheim tat sich sehr wenig. — *Very little happened in the village of Kleinheim.*

IDIOMATIC EXPRESSIONS

Es tut mir wirklich Leid! — *I'm really sorry!*
Ich habe zu tun. — *I have things to do. / I'm busy.*
Politische Bildung tut Not. — *There is a need for political education.*
Frau Schmidt tut das Ihrige dazu, den jungen Kindern zu helfen. — *Mrs. Schmidt is playing her part in helping the young children.*
Was tun? — *What is to be done? / What should we do?*
Nur mit Planen ist es noch lange nicht getan. — *Simply planning it is far from finishing it.*
Dirk hat mit sich selbst zu tun. — *Dirk has his own issues to deal with.*
Ich hatte nichts mit Herrn Thaler zu tun. — *I've not been involved with Mr. Thaler. / I haven't had anything to do with Mr. Thaler.*

Was tut das schon, wenn ich ihn liebe? — *What does it matter, if I love him?*
Der Hund tut nichts. — *The dog won't bite.*
Erna tat immer freundlich, war es aber nicht. — *Erna always pretended to be happy, but wasn't.*
Werner tut so, als ob er alles verstehen würde. — *Werner is pretending to understand everything.*
Es war ihm darum zu tun, seine Anhänger zu erziehen. — *It was important for him to educate his followers.*
Maria tut keine halben Dinge. — *Maria does nothing halfway.*
Ich habe in der letzten Zeit alle Hände voll zu tun. — *I've had my hands full recently.*
Ich habe Wichtigeres zu tun. — *I've got bigger fish to fry.*
Wenn du ihm ein wenig freundlich tätest, wenn du wolltest, er heiratete dich noch. (GOETHE) — *If you were to act a little bit friendly toward him, if you wanted he would marry you yet.*
Du wirst es mit mir zu tun haben! (*threat*) — *You'll have to deal with me! / You'll have to answer to me!*
Ralf tut sich schwer mit dem Computer. (*colloquial*) — *Ralf is having a tough time with the computer.*
Ich fürchte, dass unser alter Computer nicht mehr tut. (*colloquial*) — *I'm afraid that our old computer is kaputt.*

PRESENT		
ich kann	wir können	tun
du kannst	ihr könnt	
Sie können	Sie können	
er/sie/es kann	sie können	

SIMPLE PAST		
ich konnte	wir konnten	tun
du konntest	ihr konntet	
Sie konnten	Sie konnten	
er/sie/es konnte	sie konnten	

FUTURE		
ich werde	wir werden	tun können
du wirst	ihr werdet	
Sie werden	Sie werden	
er/sie/es wird	sie werden	

PRESENT SUBJUNCTIVE I		
ich könne	wir können	tun
du könnest	ihr könnet	
Sie können	Sie können	
er/sie/es könne	sie können	

PRESENT SUBJUNCTIVE II		
ich könnte	wir könnten	tun
du könntest	ihr könntet	
Sie könnten	Sie könnten	
er/sie/es könnte	sie könnten	

FUTURE SUBJUNCTIVE I		
ich werde	wir werden	tun können
du werdest	ihr werdet	
Sie werden	Sie werden	
er/sie/es werde	sie werden	

FUTURE SUBJUNCTIVE II		
ich würde	wir würden	tun können
du würdest	ihr würdet	
Sie würden	Sie würden	
er/sie/es würde	sie würden	

PRESENT PERFECT		
ich habe	wir haben	tun können
du hast	ihr habt	
Sie haben	Sie haben	
er/sie/es hat	sie haben	

PAST PERFECT		
ich hatte	wir hatten	tun können
du hattest	ihr hattet	
Sie hatten	Sie hatten	
er/sie/es hatte	sie hatten	

FUTURE PERFECT		
ich werde	wir werden	haben tun können OR getan haben können
du wirst	ihr werdet	
Sie werden	Sie werden	
er/sie/es wird	sie werden	

PAST SUBJUNCTIVE I		
ich habe	wir haben	tun können
du habest	ihr habet	
Sie haben	Sie haben	
er/sie/es habe	sie haben	

PAST SUBJUNCTIVE II		
ich hätte	wir hätten	tun können
du hättest	ihr hättet	
Sie hätten	Sie hätten	
er/sie/es hätte	sie hätten	

FUTURE PERFECT SUBJUNCTIVE I		
ich werde	wir werden	haben tun können OR getan haben können
du werdest	ihr werdet	
Sie werden	Sie werden	
er/sie/es werde	sie werden	

FUTURE PERFECT SUBJUNCTIVE II		
ich würde	wir würden	haben tun können OR getan haben können
du würdest	ihr würdet	
Sie würden	Sie würden	
er/sie/es würde	sie würden	

COMMANDS —

PRESENT PARTICIPLE tun könnend

Usage (showing examples of complex constructions involving a modal verb coupled with a main verb)

Es ist jetzt klar, dass die Öffentlichkeit nicht von der Sitzung hätte ausgeschlossen werden dürfen.	*It is now clear that the public shouldn't have been excluded from the meeting.*
Manfred wird bis morgen Abend den Roman noch nicht fertig gelesen haben können.	*Manfred won't yet have been able to finish reading the novel by tomorrow evening.*
Michaela hätte ein Visum bekommen können, wenn sie sich beeilt hätte.	*Michaela could have gotten a visa if she had hurried.*
Der Angeklagte behauptete, er habe das Geld nur ausleihen wollen.	*The defendant claimed that he only wanted to borrow the money.*
Die Flüchtlinge berichteten, dass sie ihre Heimat nächstes Jahr würden verlassen müssen.	*The refugees reported that they will have to leave their homeland next year.*
Mit dem Lottogewinn wird sich Frau Schmidt ein Auto kaufen können.	*With the lottery winnings, Mrs. Schmidt will be able to buy herself a car.*
Herr Peters teilte dem Rat mit, dass Herr Riegler ein neues Haus habe bauen lassen wollen.	*Mr. Peters informed the council that Mr. Riegler wanted to have a new house built.*

459 überholen *to pass, overtake; surpass; overhaul*

überholt · überholte · überholt regular weak verb

PRESENT

ich überhole	wir überholen
du überholst	ihr überholt
Sie überholen	Sie überholen
er/sie/es überholt	sie überholen

PRESENT PERFECT

ich habe	wir haben	überholt
du hast	ihr habt	
Sie haben	Sie haben	
er/sie/es hat	sie haben	

SIMPLE PAST

ich überholte	wir überholten
du überholtest	ihr überholtet
Sie überholten	Sie überholten
er/sie/es überholte	sie überholten

PAST PERFECT

ich hatte	wir hatten	überholt
du hattest	ihr hattet	
Sie hatten	Sie hatten	
er/sie/es hatte	sie hatten	

FUTURE

ich werde	wir werden	überholen
du wirst	ihr werdet	
Sie werden	Sie werden	
er/sie/es wird	sie werden	

FUTURE PERFECT

ich werde	wir werden	überholt haben
du wirst	ihr werdet	
Sie werden	Sie werden	
er/sie/es wird	sie werden	

PRESENT SUBJUNCTIVE I

ich überhole	wir überholen
du überholest	ihr überholet
Sie überholen	Sie überholen
er/sie/es überhole	sie überholen

PAST SUBJUNCTIVE I

ich habe	wir haben	überholt
du habest	ihr habet	
Sie haben	Sie haben	
er/sie/es habe	sie haben	

PRESENT SUBJUNCTIVE II

ich überholte	wir überholten
du überholtest	ihr überholtet
Sie überholten	Sie überholten
er/sie/es überholte	sie überholten

PAST SUBJUNCTIVE II

ich hätte	wir hätten	überholt
du hättest	ihr hättet	
Sie hätten	Sie hätten	
er/sie/es hätte	sie hätten	

FUTURE SUBJUNCTIVE I

ich werde	wir werden	überholen
du werdest	ihr werdet	
Sie werden	Sie werden	
er/sie/es werde	sie werden	

FUTURE PERFECT SUBJUNCTIVE I

ich werde	wir werden	überholt haben
du werdest	ihr werdet	
Sie werden	Sie werden	
er/sie/es werde	sie werden	

FUTURE SUBJUNCTIVE II

ich würde	wir würden	überholen
du würdest	ihr würdet	
Sie würden	Sie würden	
er/sie/es würde	sie würden	

FUTURE PERFECT SUBJUNCTIVE II

ich würde	wir würden	überholt haben
du würdest	ihr würdet	
Sie würden	Sie würden	
er/sie/es würde	sie würden	

COMMANDS überhol(e)! überholt! überholen Sie!

PRESENT PARTICIPLE überholend

Usage

Lisa ist so schnell gelaufen, dass sie sogar einen Fahrradfahrer überholt hat.	*Lisa ran so quickly that she even overtook a bicyclist.*
Überhol ihn doch mal!	*Why don't you pass him!*
Nachdem Heinz den Opel überholt hatte, hatte er eine Reifenpanne.	*After Heinz had passed the Opel, he had a flat tire.*
Langsam fahrende Autos werden oft überholt.	*Slow-moving cars are often overtaken.*
In Deutschland muss man links überholen.	*In Germany, you have to pass on the left.*
Der Mercedes überholte das Motorrad.	*The Mercedes overtook the motorcycle.*
Auf der Autobahn überhole ich nicht gern.	*On the autobahn, I don't like to pass.*
Kanada hatte Deutschland in Außenhandel überholt.	*Canada had surpassed Germany in foreign trade.*
Herr Klemp hat alle seine Kollegen schnell überholt.	*Mr. Klemp quickly got ahead of his colleagues.*
Der Motor wurde letztes Jahr überholt.	*The motor was overhauled last year.*
Das Gerät muss überholt werden.	*The device must be reconditioned.*

RELATED VERBS *see* **holen** (247)

regular weak verb **überlegt · überlegte · überlegt**

PRESENT

ich überlege	wir überlegen
du überlegst	ihr überlegt
Sie überlegen	Sie überlegen
er/sie/es überlegt	sie überlegen

PRESENT PERFECT

ich habe	wir haben	überlegt
du hast	ihr habt	
Sie haben	Sie haben	
er/sie/es hat	sie haben	

SIMPLE PAST

ich überlegte	wir überlegten
du überlegtest	ihr überlegtet
Sie überlegten	Sie überlegten
er/sie/es überlegte	sie überlegten

PAST PERFECT

ich hatte	wir hatten	überlegt
du hattest	ihr hattet	
Sie hatten	Sie hatten	
er/sie/es hatte	sie hatten	

FUTURE

ich werde	wir werden	überlegen
du wirst	ihr werdet	
Sie werden	Sie werden	
er/sie/es wird	sie werden	

FUTURE PERFECT

ich werde	wir werden	überlegt haben
du wirst	ihr werdet	
Sie werden	Sie werden	
er/sie/es wird	sie werden	

PRESENT SUBJUNCTIVE I

ich überlege	wir überlegen
du überlegest	ihr überleget
Sie überlegen	Sie überlegen
er/sie/es überlege	sie überlegen

PAST SUBJUNCTIVE I

ich habe	wir haben	überlegt
du habest	ihr habet	
Sie haben	Sie haben	
er/sie/es habe	sie haben	

PRESENT SUBJUNCTIVE II

ich überlegte	wir überlegten
du überlegtest	ihr überlegtet
Sie überlegten	Sie überlegten
er/sie/es überlegte	sie überlegten

PAST SUBJUNCTIVE II

ich hätte	wir hätten	überlegt
du hättest	ihr hättet	
Sie hätten	Sie hätten	
er/sie/es hätte	sie hätten	

FUTURE SUBJUNCTIVE I

ich werde	wir werden	überlegen
du werdest	ihr werdet	
Sie werden	Sie werden	
er/sie/es werde	sie werden	

FUTURE PERFECT SUBJUNCTIVE I

ich werde	wir werden	überlegt haben
du werdest	ihr werdet	
Sie werden	Sie werden	
er/sie/es werde	sie werden	

FUTURE SUBJUNCTIVE II

ich würde	wir würden	überlegen
du würdest	ihr würdet	
Sie würden	Sie würden	
er/sie/es würde	sie würden	

FUTURE PERFECT SUBJUNCTIVE II

ich würde	wir würden	überlegt haben
du würdest	ihr würdet	
Sie würden	Sie würden	
er/sie/es würde	sie würden	

COMMANDS überleg(e)! überlegt! überlegen Sie!

PRESENT PARTICIPLE überlegend

Usage

Der Fußballspieler überlegt, ob er seine Karriere beenden soll.	*The soccer player is considering retiring.*
Habt ihr es euch überlegt?	*Have you thought it over?*
Überlegt euch den Plan noch einmal.	*Reconsider the plan.*
Stefanie möchte sich ihre Lage neu überlegen.	*Stefanie would like to reconsider her situation.*
Überlegen Sie doch mal, was die Folgen sind.	*Just consider what the consequences are.*
Die Regierung überlegt neue Maßnahmen.	*The government is considering new measures.*
Manfred überlegt sich, ob er ins Ausland gehen soll.	*Manfred is considering whether he should go abroad.*
Ich möchte es mir überlegen.	*I'd like to reflect on it.*
Die Sache muss genau überlegt werden.	*The matter must be carefully considered.*
Ich habe es mir anders überlegt.	*I've changed my mind.*
„Was kann das sein?" überlegte sich Grete.	*"What can that be?" wondered Grete.*
Niklas überlegte lange hin und her, bevor er dem Vorschlag zustimmte.	*Niklas vacillated for a long time before he said yes to the proposal.*

RELATED VERBS *see* **legen** (283)

461 **übernehmen** *to take delivery of, receive; undertake; take over, borrow*

übernimmt · übernahm · übernommen strong verb

PRESENT

ich übernehme	wir übernehmen
du übernimmst	ihr übernehmt
Sie übernehmen	Sie übernehmen
er/sie/es übernimmt	sie übernehmen

SIMPLE PAST

ich übernahm	wir übernahmen
du übernahmst	ihr übernahmt
Sie übernahmen	Sie übernahmen
er/sie/es übernahm	sie übernahmen

FUTURE

ich werde	wir werden	übernehmen
du wirst	ihr werdet	
Sie werden	Sie werden	
er/sie/es wird	sie werden	

PRESENT SUBJUNCTIVE I

ich übernehme	wir übernehmen
du übernehmest	ihr übernehmet
Sie übernehmen	Sie übernehmen
er/sie/es übernehme	sie übernehmen

PRESENT SUBJUNCTIVE II

ich übernähme	wir übernähmen
du übernähmest	ihr übernähmet
Sie übernähmen	Sie übernähmen
er/sie/es übernähme	sie übernähmen

FUTURE SUBJUNCTIVE I

ich werde	wir werden	übernehmen
du werdest	ihr werdet	
Sie werden	Sie werden	
er/sie/es werde	sie werden	

FUTURE SUBJUNCTIVE II

ich würde	wir würden	übernehmen
du würdest	ihr würdet	
Sie würden	Sie würden	
er/sie/es würde	sie würden	

PRESENT PERFECT

ich habe	wir haben	übernommen
du hast	ihr habt	
Sie haben	Sie haben	
er/sie/es hat	sie haben	

PAST PERFECT

ich hatte	wir hatten	übernommen
du hattest	ihr hattet	
Sie hatten	Sie hatten	
er/sie/es hatte	sie hatten	

FUTURE PERFECT

ich werde	wir werden	übernommen haben
du wirst	ihr werdet	
Sie werden	Sie werden	
er/sie/es wird	sie werden	

PAST SUBJUNCTIVE I

ich habe	wir haben	übernommen
du habest	ihr habet	
Sie haben	Sie haben	
er/sie/es habe	sie haben	

PAST SUBJUNCTIVE II

ich hätte	wir hätten	übernommen
du hättest	ihr hättet	
Sie hätten	Sie hätten	
er/sie/es hätte	sie hätten	

FUTURE PERFECT SUBJUNCTIVE I

ich werde	wir werden	übernommen haben
du werdest	ihr werdet	
Sie werden	Sie werden	
er/sie/es werde	sie werden	

FUTURE PERFECT SUBJUNCTIVE II

ich würde	wir würden	übernommen haben
du würdest	ihr würdet	
Sie würden	Sie würden	
er/sie/es würde	sie würden	

COMMANDS übernimm! übernehmt! übernehmen Sie!

PRESENT PARTICIPLE übernehmend

Usage

Wann haben Sie die Waren übernommen?	*When did you take delivery of the goods?*
Der Spion sollte die Aktentasche am Marktplatz übernehmen.	*The spy was supposed to receive the briefcase at the market square.*
Das Training wurde von Klaus Becker übernommen.	*The training was undertaken by Klaus Becker.*
Die Arbeit wird von einer anderen Stelle übernommen.	*The work is being taken on by another office.*
Wir werden die Verantwortung übernehmen.	*We will assume responsibility.*
Die Stadt übernimmt Bürgschaft für das Konzern.	*The city is standing security for the company.*
Firma Z übernimmt Firma Y.	*Company X is taking over company Y.*
Wer kann das Projekt jetzt übernehmen?	*Who can take charge of the project?*
1355 übernahm Herzog Wilhelm das Gebiet.	*In 1355, Duke Wilhelm took over the region.*
Vivian hat das Haus und das Grundstück übernommen.	*Vivian has taken over the house and the property.*
Der erste Teil meines Berichts wurde aus einem Zeitungsartikel übernommen.	*The first part of my report was borrowed from a newspaper article.*

RELATED VERBS *see* **nehmen** (314)

PRESENT

ich überrasche	wir überraschen
du überraschst	ihr überrascht
Sie überraschen	Sie überraschen
er/sie/es überrascht	sie überraschen

SIMPLE PAST

ich überraschte	wir überraschten
du überraschtest	ihr überraschtet
Sie überraschten	Sie überraschten
er/sie/es überraschte	sie überraschten

FUTURE

ich werde	wir werden	überraschen
du wirst	ihr werdet	
Sie werden	Sie werden	
er/sie/es wird	sie werden	

PRESENT SUBJUNCTIVE I

ich überrasche	wir überraschen
du überraschest	ihr überraschet
Sie überraschen	Sie überraschen
er/sie/es überrasche	sie überraschen

PRESENT SUBJUNCTIVE II

ich überraschte	wir überraschten
du überraschtest	ihr überraschtet
Sie überraschten	Sie überraschten
er/sie/es überraschte	sie überraschten

FUTURE SUBJUNCTIVE I

ich werde	wir werden	überraschen
du werdest	ihr werdet	
Sie werden	Sie werden	
er/sie/es werde	sie werden	

FUTURE SUBJUNCTIVE II

ich würde	wir würden	überraschen
du würdest	ihr würdet	
Sie würden	Sie würden	
er/sie/es würde	sie würden	

PRESENT PERFECT

ich habe	wir haben	überrascht
du hast	ihr habt	
Sie haben	Sie haben	
er/sie/es hat	sie haben	

PAST PERFECT

ich hatte	wir hatten	überrascht
du hattest	ihr hattet	
Sie hatten	Sie hatten	
er/sie/es hatte	sie hatten	

FUTURE PERFECT

ich werde	wir werden	überrascht haben
du wirst	ihr werdet	
Sie werden	Sie werden	
er/sie/es wird	sie werden	

PAST SUBJUNCTIVE I

ich habe	wir haben	überrascht
du habest	ihr habet	
Sie haben	Sie haben	
er/sie/es habe	sie haben	

PAST SUBJUNCTIVE II

ich hätte	wir hätten	überrascht
du hättest	ihr hättet	
Sie hätten	Sie hätten	
er/sie/es hätte	sie hätten	

FUTURE PERFECT SUBJUNCTIVE I

ich werde	wir werden	überrascht haben
du werdest	ihr werdet	
Sie werden	Sie werden	
er/sie/es werde	sie werden	

FUTURE PERFECT SUBJUNCTIVE II

ich würde	wir würden	überrascht haben
du würdest	ihr würdet	
Sie würden	Sie würden	
er/sie/es würde	sie würden	

COMMANDS überrasch(e)! überrascht! überraschen Sie!

PRESENT PARTICIPLE überraschend

Usage

Überraschen Sie mich doch nicht so! — *Don't surprise me like that!*

Du überraschst mich immer wieder, Monika! — *You always surprise me, Monika!*

Wir wollen Maria überraschen. — *We want to surprise Maria.*

Ihre feindselige Einstellung überraschte uns alle. — *Her hostile attitude surprised us all.*

Die Kleiderpreise in Berlin haben uns überrascht. — *The clothing prices in Berlin surprised us.*

Die Öffentlichkeit wird von der Arroganz des Präsidenten nicht mehr überrascht. — *The public is no longer surprised at the president's arrogance.*

Ein Vulkanausbruch überraschte die Einwohner der Insel. — *A volcanic eruption caught the island's inhabitants off guard.*

Mein Mann hat mich mit Schokolade und Sekt überrascht. — *My husband surprised me with chocolate and champagne.*

Kannst du die Kinder bitte überraschen? — *Can you please spring a surprise on the children?*

Der Dieb wurde von der Polizei überrascht. — *The thief was caught unawares by the police.*

Hat dich ihre Ankunft nicht überrascht? — *Did her arrival catch you unawares?*

463 übersetzen *to translate*

übersetzt · übersetzte · übersetzt regular weak verb

PRESENT

ich übersetze	wir übersetzen
du übersetzt	ihr übersetzt
Sie übersetzen	Sie übersetzen
er/sie/es übersetzt	sie übersetzen

SIMPLE PAST

ich übersetzte	wir übersetzten
du übersetztest	ihr übersetztet
Sie übersetzten	Sie übersetzten
er/sie/es übersetzte	sie übersetzten

FUTURE

ich werde	wir werden	übersetzen
du wirst	ihr werdet	
Sie werden	Sie werden	
er/sie/es wird	sie werden	

PRESENT SUBJUNCTIVE I

ich übersetze	wir übersetzen
du übersetzest	ihr übersetzet
Sie übersetzen	Sie übersetzen
er/sie/es übersetze	sie übersetzen

PRESENT SUBJUNCTIVE II

ich übersetzte	wir übersetzten
du übersetztest	ihr übersetztet
Sie übersetzten	Sie übersetzten
er/sie/es übersetzte	sie übersetzten

FUTURE SUBJUNCTIVE I

ich werde	wir werden	übersetzen
du werdest	ihr werdet	
Sie werden	Sie werden	
er/sie/es werde	sie werden	

FUTURE SUBJUNCTIVE II

ich würde	wir würden	übersetzen
du würdest	ihr würdet	
Sie würden	Sie würden	
er/sie/es würde	sie würden	

PRESENT PERFECT

ich habe	wir haben	übersetzt
du hast	ihr habt	
Sie haben	Sie haben	
er/sie/es hat	sie haben	

PAST PERFECT

ich hatte	wir hatten	übersetzt
du hattest	ihr hattet	
Sie hatten	Sie hatten	
er/sie/es hatte	sie hatten	

FUTURE PERFECT

ich werde	wir werden	übersetzt haben
du wirst	ihr werdet	
Sie werden	Sie werden	
er/sie/es wird	sie werden	

PAST SUBJUNCTIVE I

ich habe	wir haben	übersetzt
du habest	ihr habet	
Sie haben	Sie haben	
er/sie/es habe	sie haben	

PAST SUBJUNCTIVE II

ich hätte	wir hätten	übersetzt
du hättest	ihr hättet	
Sie hätten	Sie hätten	
er/sie/es hätte	sie hätten	

FUTURE PERFECT SUBJUNCTIVE I

ich werde	wir werden	übersetzt haben
du werdest	ihr werdet	
Sie werden	Sie werden	
er/sie/es werde	sie werden	

FUTURE PERFECT SUBJUNCTIVE II

ich würde	wir würden	übersetzt haben
du würdest	ihr würdet	
Sie würden	Sie würden	
er/sie/es würde	sie würden	

COMMANDS übersetz(e)! übersetzt! übersetzen Sie!

PRESENT PARTICIPLE übersetzend

Usage

Übersetzen Sie ins Englische. — *Translate into English.*

Ich musste den Brief für meine Tante übersetzen. — *I had to translate the letter for my aunt.*

Die Software übersetzt aus mehreren Sprachen. — *The software translates from several languages.*

Der Mann an der Rezeption hat für uns übersetzt. — *The man at the front desk translated for us.*

Der Roman ist aus dem Englischen ins Deutsche neu übersetzt worden. — *The novel was retranslated from English into German.*

Manni übersetzte seiner Freundin den Ausdruck wörtlich und sie lachte sich tot. — *Manni translated the expression literally for his girlfriend and she died laughing.*

Namen kann man oft nicht übersetzen. — *Names often cannot be translated.*

Das Wort „Gemütlichkeit" kann man nur schwer übersetzen. — *The word "Gemütlichkeit" is difficult to translate.*

Der Text wurde frei übersetzt. — *The text was loosely translated.*

Er versucht seine Gefühle in Bilder zu übersetzen. — *He tries to translate his feelings into images.*

RELATED VERBS *see* **setzen** (400)

strong verb **überweist · überwies · überwiesen**

PRESENT

ich überweise	wir überweisen
du überweist	ihr überweist
Sie überweisen	Sie überweisen
er/sie/es überweist	sie überweisen

SIMPLE PAST

ich überwies	wir überwiesen
du überwiesest	ihr überwiest
Sie überwiesen	Sie überwiesen
er/sie/es überwies	sie überwiesen

FUTURE

ich werde	wir werden	überweisen
du wirst	ihr werdet	
Sie werden	Sie werden	
er/sie/es wird	sie werden	

PRESENT SUBJUNCTIVE I

ich überweise	wir überweisen
du überweisest	ihr überweiset
Sie überweisen	Sie überweisen
er/sie/es überweise	sie überweisen

PRESENT SUBJUNCTIVE II

ich überwiese	wir überwiesen
du überwiesest	ihr überwieset
Sie überwiesen	Sie überwiesen
er/sie/es überwiese	sie überwiesen

FUTURE SUBJUNCTIVE I

ich werde	wir werden	überweisen
du werdest	ihr werdet	
Sie werden	Sie werden	
er/sie/es werde	sie werden	

FUTURE SUBJUNCTIVE II

ich würde	wir würden	überweisen
du würdest	ihr würdet	
Sie würden	Sie würden	
er/sie/es würde	sie würden	

PRESENT PERFECT

ich habe	wir haben	überwiesen
du hast	ihr habt	
Sie haben	Sie haben	
er/sie/es hat	sie haben	

PAST PERFECT

ich hatte	wir hatten	überwiesen
du hattest	ihr hattet	
Sie hatten	Sie hatten	
er/sie/es hatte	sie hatten	

FUTURE PERFECT

ich werde	wir werden	überwiesen haben
du wirst	ihr werdet	
Sie werden	Sie werden	
er/sie/es wird	sie werden	

PAST SUBJUNCTIVE I

ich habe	wir haben	überwiesen
du habest	ihr habet	
Sie haben	Sie haben	
er/sie/es habe	sie haben	

PAST SUBJUNCTIVE II

ich hätte	wir hätten	überwiesen
du hättest	ihr hättet	
Sie hätten	Sie hätten	
er/sie/es hätte	sie hätten	

FUTURE PERFECT SUBJUNCTIVE I

ich werde	wir werden	überwiesen haben
du werdest	ihr werdet	
Sie werden	Sie werden	
er/sie/es werde	sie werden	

FUTURE PERFECT SUBJUNCTIVE II

ich würde	wir würden	überwiesen haben
du würdest	ihr würdet	
Sie würden	Sie würden	
er/sie/es würde	sie würden	

COMMANDS überweis(e)! überweist! überweisen Sie!

PRESENT PARTICIPLE überweisend

Usage

Warum überweist du es nicht bei der Post?	*Why don't you make the transfer at the post office?*
Wann werden Sie es überweisen?	*When will you transfer it?*
Sabine überweist monatlich über 3 000 Euro an ihre Eltern.	*Sabine transfers over 3,000 euros to her parents every month.*
Man kann die Zahlung auch online überweisen.	*You can make the transfer online, too.*
Kann man Geld per Handy überweisen?	*Can you make the transfer via cell phone?*
Ist der Betrag schon überwiesen worden?	*Has the amount already been transferred?*
Ich möchte 250 Dollar in die USA überweisen.	*I'd like to transfer 250 dollars to the U.S.*
Haben Sie die 100 Euro schon überwiesen?	*Have you already transferred the 100 euros?*
Er hat keine Zeit, die 50 Euro zu überweisen.	*He has no time to transfer the 50 euros.*
Das Hotel überweist die Rückzahlung auf unser Bankkonto.	*The hotel is transferring the refund into our bank account.*
Die Sache wird an das Komitee überwiesen werden.	*The matter will be referred to the committee.*

RELATED VERBS *see* **weisen** (526)

465 überwinden *to overcome, surmount, conquer; get past*

überwindet · überwand · überwunden strong verb

PRESENT

ich überwinde	wir überwinden
du überwindest	ihr überwindet
Sie überwinden	Sie überwinden
er/sie/es überwindet	sie überwinden

SIMPLE PAST

ich überwand	wir überwanden
du überwandest	ihr überwandet
Sie überwanden	Sie überwanden
er/sie/es überwand	sie überwanden

FUTURE

ich werde	wir werden	überwinden
du wirst	ihr werdet	
Sie werden	Sie werden	
er/sie/es wird	sie werden	

PRESENT SUBJUNCTIVE I

ich überwinde	wir überwinden
du überwindest	ihr überwindet
Sie überwinden	Sie überwinden
er/sie/es überwinde	sie überwinden

PRESENT SUBJUNCTIVE II

ich überwände	wir überwänden
du überwändest	ihr überwändet
Sie überwänden	Sie überwänden
er/sie/es überwände	sie überwänden

FUTURE SUBJUNCTIVE I

ich werde	wir werden	überwinden
du werdest	ihr werdet	
Sie werden	Sie werden	
er/sie/es werde	sie werden	

FUTURE SUBJUNCTIVE II

ich würde	wir würden	überwinden
du würdest	ihr würdet	
Sie würden	Sie würden	
er/sie/es würde	sie würden	

PRESENT PERFECT

ich habe	wir haben	überwunden
du hast	ihr habt	
Sie haben	Sie haben	
er/sie/es hat	sie haben	

PAST PERFECT

ich hatte	wir hatten	überwunden
du hattest	ihr hattet	
Sie hatten	Sie hatten	
er/sie/es hatte	sie hatten	

FUTURE PERFECT

ich werde	wir werden	überwunden haben
du wirst	ihr werdet	
Sie werden	Sie werden	
er/sie/es wird	sie werden	

PAST SUBJUNCTIVE I

ich habe	wir haben	überwunden
du habest	ihr habet	
Sie haben	Sie haben	
er/sie/es habe	sie haben	

PAST SUBJUNCTIVE II

ich hätte	wir hätten	überwunden
du hättest	ihr hättet	
Sie hätten	Sie hätten	
er/sie/es hätte	sie hätten	

FUTURE PERFECT SUBJUNCTIVE I

ich werde	wir werden	überwunden haben
du werdest	ihr werdet	
Sie werden	Sie werden	
er/sie/es werde	sie werden	

FUTURE PERFECT SUBJUNCTIVE II

ich würde	wir würden	überwunden haben
du würdest	ihr würdet	
Sie würden	Sie würden	
er/sie/es würde	sie würden	

COMMANDS überwinde! überwindet! überwinden Sie!

PRESENT PARTICIPLE überwindend

Usage

Lena musste eine schwere Krankheit überwinden.	*Lena had to overcome a serious illness.*
Sabines Vorschlag überwindet etliche Schwierigkeiten.	*Sabine's suggestion overcomes several difficulties.*
Man muss die eigenen Schwächen überwinden können.	*You have to be able to overcome your own weaknesses.*
Andreas scheint die Hindernisse überwunden zu haben.	*Andreas seems to have surmounted the obstacles.*
Wie können die emotionalen Barrieren überwunden werden?	*How can the emotional barriers be hurdled?*
Viele meinen, die Krise sei nicht zu überwinden.	*Many people think the crisis cannot be reined in.*
Nachdem er Malaria überwunden hatte, ist er an Krebs gestorben.	*After he had conquered malaria, he died of cancer.*
Der Kämpfer überwand seinen Gegner.	*The combatant triumphed over his opponent.*
Wie überwindet das Kind seine Angst vor der Dunkelheit?	*How does a child overcome fear of the dark?*
Herr Kästner hat den Tod seiner Frau nie wirklich überwunden.	*Mr. Kästner has never really gotten over the death of his wife.*
Bald hatte Birgit ihre Probleme überwunden.	*Soon Birgit had overcome her problems.*

RELATED VERBS *see* **winden** (535)

regular weak verb

überzeugt · überzeugte · überzeugt

PRESENT

ich überzeuge	wir überzeugen
du überzeugst	ihr überzeugt
Sie überzeugen	Sie überzeugen
er/sie/es überzeugt	sie überzeugen

SIMPLE PAST

ich überzeugte	wir überzeugten
du überzeugtest	ihr überzeugtet
Sie überzeugten	Sie überzeugten
er/sie/es überzeugte	sie überzeugten

FUTURE

ich werde	wir werden	überzeugen
du wirst	ihr werdet	
Sie werden	Sie werden	
er/sie/es wird	sie werden	

PRESENT SUBJUNCTIVE I

ich überzeuge	wir überzeugen
du überzeugest	ihr überzeuget
Sie überzeugen	Sie überzeugen
er/sie/es überzeuge	sie überzeugen

PRESENT SUBJUNCTIVE II

ich überzeugte	wir überzeugten
du überzeugtest	ihr überzeugtet
Sie überzeugten	Sie überzeugten
er/sie/es überzeugte	sie überzeugten

FUTURE SUBJUNCTIVE I

ich werde	wir werden	überzeugen
du werdest	ihr werdet	
Sie werden	Sie werden	
er/sie/es werde	sie werden	

FUTURE SUBJUNCTIVE II

ich würde	wir würden	überzeugen
du würdest	ihr würdet	
Sie würden	Sie würden	
er/sie/es würde	sie würden	

PRESENT PERFECT

ich habe	wir haben	überzeugt
du hast	ihr habt	
Sie haben	Sie haben	
er/sie/es hat	sie haben	

PAST PERFECT

ich hatte	wir hatten	überzeugt
du hattest	ihr hattet	
Sie hatten	Sie hatten	
er/sie/es hatte	sie hatten	

FUTURE PERFECT

ich werde	wir werden	überzeugt haben
du wirst	ihr werdet	
Sie werden	Sie werden	
er/sie/es wird	sie werden	

PAST SUBJUNCTIVE I

ich habe	wir haben	überzeugt
du habest	ihr habet	
Sie haben	Sie haben	
er/sie/es habe	sie haben	

PAST SUBJUNCTIVE II

ich hätte	wir hätten	überzeugt
du hättest	ihr hättet	
Sie hätten	Sie hätten	
er/sie/es hätte	sie hätten	

FUTURE PERFECT SUBJUNCTIVE I

ich werde	wir werden	überzeugt haben
du werdest	ihr werdet	
Sie werden	Sie werden	
er/sie/es werde	sie werden	

FUTURE PERFECT SUBJUNCTIVE II

ich würde	wir würden	überzeugt haben
du würdest	ihr würdet	
Sie würden	Sie würden	
er/sie/es würde	sie würden	

COMMANDS überzeug(e)! überzeugt! überzeugen Sie!

PRESENT PARTICIPLE überzeugend

Usage

Der Vortrag überzeugte den Großteil des Publikums. — *The presentation convinced a large portion of the audience.*

Was hat dich so tief davon überzeugt, dass Manfred Recht hat? — *What has so deeply convinced you that Manfred is right?*

Kannst du die Kinder überzeugen, zu Hause zu bleiben? — *Can you persuade the children to stay home?*

Ich wollte mich mit eigenen Augen überzeugen. — *I wanted to see for myself/with my own eyes.*

Der Dokumentarfilm hat sie von der Ernsthaftigkeit der Sache überzeugt. — *The documentary film convinced her of the seriousness of the matter.*

Die einfühlsame Interpretation des Pianisten überzeugte ganz. — *The pianist's sympathetic interpretation was full of conviction.*

Ich bin davon überzeugt, dass das Geschäft rentabel ist. — *I am convinced that the business is profitable.*

Karen möchte uns davon überzeugen, nach Tasmanien zu fliegen. — *Karen wants to persuade us to fly to Tasmania.*

Lasst euch nicht überzeugen! — *Don't let yourself be persuaded!*

RELATED VERB zeugen

467 unterbrechen *to interrupt, break; terminate*

unterbricht · unterbrach · unterbrochen strong verb

PRESENT

ich unterbreche	wir unterbrechen
du unterbrichst	ihr unterbrecht
Sie unterbrechen	Sie unterbrechen
er/sie/es unterbricht	sie unterbrechen

SIMPLE PAST

ich unterbrach	wir unterbrachen
du unterbrachst	ihr unterbracht
Sie unterbrachen	Sie unterbrachen
er/sie/es unterbrach	sie unterbrachen

FUTURE

ich werde	wir werden	unterbrechen
du wirst	ihr werdet	
Sie werden	Sie werden	
er/sie/es wird	sie werden	

PRESENT SUBJUNCTIVE I

ich unterbreche	wir unterbrechen
du unterbrechest	ihr unterbrechet
Sie unterbrechen	Sie unterbrechen
er/sie/es unterbreche	sie unterbrechen

PRESENT SUBJUNCTIVE II

ich unterbräche	wir unterbrächen
du unterbrächest	ihr unterbrächet
Sie unterbrächen	Sie unterbrächen
er/sie/es unterbräche	sie unterbrächen

FUTURE SUBJUNCTIVE I

ich werde	wir werden	unterbrechen
du werdest	ihr werdet	
Sie werden	Sie werden	
er/sie/es werde	sie werden	

FUTURE SUBJUNCTIVE II

ich würde	wir würden	unterbrechen
du würdest	ihr würdet	
Sie würden	Sie würden	
er/sie/es würde	sie würden	

PRESENT PERFECT

ich habe	wir haben	unterbrochen
du hast	ihr habt	
Sie haben	Sie haben	
er/sie/es hat	sie haben	

PAST PERFECT

ich hatte	wir hatten	unterbrochen
du hattest	ihr hattet	
Sie hatten	Sie hatten	
er/sie/es hatte	sie hatten	

FUTURE PERFECT

ich werde	wir werden	unterbrochen haben
du wirst	ihr werdet	
Sie werden	Sie werden	
er/sie/es wird	sie werden	

PAST SUBJUNCTIVE I

ich habe	wir haben	unterbrochen
du habest	ihr habet	
Sie haben	Sie haben	
er/sie/es habe	sie haben	

PAST SUBJUNCTIVE II

ich hätte	wir hätten	unterbrochen
du hättest	ihr hättet	
Sie hätten	Sie hätten	
er/sie/es hätte	sie hätten	

FUTURE PERFECT SUBJUNCTIVE I

ich werde	wir werden	unterbrochen haben
du werdest	ihr werdet	
Sie werden	Sie werden	
er/sie/es werde	sie werden	

FUTURE PERFECT SUBJUNCTIVE II

ich würde	wir würden	unterbrochen haben
du würdest	ihr würdet	
Sie würden	Sie würden	
er/sie/es würde	sie würden	

COMMANDS unterbrich! unterbrecht! unterbrechen Sie!

PRESENT PARTICIPLE unterbrechend

Usage

Das Wetter hat das Fußballspiel unterbrochen. — *The weather interrupted the soccer game.*

Fernsehsendungen werden von Werbungen unterbrochen. — *Television broadcasts are interrupted by commercials.*

Schallendes Gelächter unterbrach die Professorin. — *Peals of laughter interrupted the professor.*

Max und Moritz wollten den Lehrer nicht unterbrochen haben. — *Max and Moritz claimed not to have interrupted the teacher.*

Darf ich kurz unterbrechen? — *May I interrupt briefly?*

Lara hat ihr Studium unterbrochen, um eine Weltreise zu machen. — *Lara took a break from her studies to take a trip around the world.*

Dissonante Töne unterbrechen die Melodie an drei Stellen in diesem Stück. — *Dissonant notes disrupt the melody in three places in this piece.*

Die Sitzung wurde um drei Uhr unterbrochen. — *The session was adjourned at three o'clock.*

Karoline möchte die Schwangerschaft nicht unterbrechen. — *Karoline doesn't want to terminate the pregnancy.*

Leider mussten wir unseren Urlaub unterbrechen. — *Unfortunately, we had to cut our vacation short.*

RELATED VERBS *see* **brechen** (116)

strong verb **unterhält · unterhielt · unterhalten**

PRESENT

ich unterhalte	wir unterhalten
du unterhältst	ihr unterhaltet
Sie unterhalten	Sie unterhalten
er/sie/es unterhält	sie unterhalten

SIMPLE PAST

ich unterhielt	wir unterhielten
du unterhieltst	ihr unterhieltet
Sie unterhielten	Sie unterhielten
er/sie/es unterhielt	sie unterhielten

FUTURE

ich werde	wir werden	unterhalten
du wirst	ihr werdet	
Sie werden	Sie werden	
er/sie/es wird	sie werden	

PRESENT SUBJUNCTIVE I

ich unterhalte	wir unterhalten
du unterhaltest	ihr unterhaltet
Sie unterhalten	Sie unterhalten
er/sie/es unterhalte	sie unterhalten

PRESENT SUBJUNCTIVE II

ich unterhielte	wir unterhielten
du unterhieltest	ihr unterhieltet
Sie unterhielten	Sie unterhielten
er/sie/es unterhielte	sie unterhielten

FUTURE SUBJUNCTIVE I

ich werde	wir werden	unterhalten
du werdest	ihr werdet	
Sie werden	Sie werden	
er/sie/es werde	sie werden	

FUTURE SUBJUNCTIVE II

ich würde	wir würden	unterhalten
du würdest	ihr würdet	
Sie würden	Sie würden	
er/sie/es würde	sie würden	

PRESENT PERFECT

ich habe	wir haben	unterhalten
du hast	ihr habt	
Sie haben	Sie haben	
er/sie/es hat	sie haben	

PAST PERFECT

ich hatte	wir hatten	unterhalten
du hattest	ihr hattet	
Sie hatten	Sie hatten	
er/sie/es hatte	sie hatten	

FUTURE PERFECT

ich werde	wir werden	unterhalten haben
du wirst	ihr werdet	
Sie werden	Sie werden	
er/sie/es wird	sie werden	

PAST SUBJUNCTIVE I

ich habe	wir haben	unterhalten
du habest	ihr habet	
Sie haben	Sie haben	
er/sie/es habe	sie haben	

PAST SUBJUNCTIVE II

ich hätte	wir hätten	unterhalten
du hättest	ihr hättet	
Sie hätten	Sie hätten	
er/sie/es hätte	sie hätten	

FUTURE PERFECT SUBJUNCTIVE I

ich werde	wir werden	unterhalten haben
du werdest	ihr werdet	
Sie werden	Sie werden	
er/sie/es werde	sie werden	

FUTURE PERFECT SUBJUNCTIVE II

ich würde	wir würden	unterhalten haben
du würdest	ihr würdet	
Sie würden	Sie würden	
er/sie/es würde	sie würden	

COMMANDS unterhalte! unterhaltet! unterhalten Sie!

PRESENT PARTICIPLE unterhaltend

Usage

Wie ist eine 8-köpfige Familie zu unterhalten?	*How can a family of eight be supported?*
Ich unterhalte gute Beziehungen zu ihnen.	*I maintain good relations with them.*
Der Verein unterhält eine kleine Gaststätte am See.	*The club runs a small inn on the lake.*
Könnt ihr das Lagerfeuer bitte unterhalten?	*Could you please keep the campfire going?*
Wie unterhaltet ihr eure Gäste?	*How do you entertain your guests?*
Lars unterhielt seine Gäste mit Zaubertricks.	*Lars entertained his guests with magic tricks.*

sich unterhalten *to converse; enjoy oneself*

Karen möchte sich mit uns unterhalten.	*Karen would like to converse with us.*
Habt ihr euch mit Tante Bärbel unterhalten?	*Did you chat with Aunt Bärbel?*
Ich habe mich drei Stunden mit ihr unterhalten.	*I conversed with her for three hours.*
Hast du dich gut unterhalten?	*Did you have a nice time?*
Als Kind unterhielt ich mich mit Kreuzworträtseln.	*As a child, I enjoyed working crossword puzzles.*

RELATED VERBS *see* **halten** (231)

469

unternehmen *to undertake, do*

unternimmt · unternahm · unternommen strong verb

PRESENT

ich unternehme	wir unternehmen
du unternimmst	ihr unternehmt
Sie unternehmen	Sie unternehmen
er/sie/es unternimmt	sie unternehmen

SIMPLE PAST

ich unternahm	wir unternahmen
du unternahmst	ihr unternahmt
Sie unternahmen	Sie unternahmen
er/sie/es unternahm	sie unternahmen

FUTURE

ich werde	wir werden	unternehmen
du wirst	ihr werdet	
Sie werden	Sie werden	
er/sie/es wird	sie werden	

PRESENT SUBJUNCTIVE I

ich unternehme	wir unternehmen
du unternehmest	ihr unternehmet
Sie unternehmen	Sie unternehmen
er/sie/es unternehme	sie unternehmen

PRESENT SUBJUNCTIVE II

ich unternähme	wir unternähmen
du unternähmest	ihr unternähmet
Sie unternähmen	Sie unternähmen
er/sie/es unternähme	sie unternähmen

FUTURE SUBJUNCTIVE I

ich werde	wir werden	unternehmen
du werdest	ihr werdet	
Sie werden	Sie werden	
er/sie/es werde	sie werden	

FUTURE SUBJUNCTIVE II

ich würde	wir würden	unternehmen
du würdest	ihr würdet	
Sie würden	Sie würden	
er/sie/es würde	sie würden	

PRESENT PERFECT

ich habe	wir haben	unternommen
du hast	ihr habt	
Sie haben	Sie haben	
er/sie/es hat	sie haben	

PAST PERFECT

ich hatte	wir hatten	unternommen
du hattest	ihr hattet	
Sie hatten	Sie hatten	
er/sie/es hatte	sie hatten	

FUTURE PERFECT

ich werde	wir werden	unternommen haben
du wirst	ihr werdet	
Sie werden	Sie werden	
er/sie/es wird	sie werden	

PAST SUBJUNCTIVE I

ich habe	wir haben	unternommen
du habest	ihr habet	
Sie haben	Sie haben	
er/sie/es habe	sie haben	

PAST SUBJUNCTIVE II

ich hätte	wir hätten	unternommen
du hättest	ihr hättet	
Sie hätten	Sie hätten	
er/sie/es hätte	sie hätten	

FUTURE PERFECT SUBJUNCTIVE I

ich werde	wir werden	unternommen haben
du werdest	ihr werdet	
Sie werden	Sie werden	
er/sie/es werde	sie werden	

FUTURE PERFECT SUBJUNCTIVE II

ich würde	wir würden	unternommen haben
du würdest	ihr würdet	
Sie würden	Sie würden	
er/sie/es würde	sie würden	

COMMANDS unternimm! unternehmt! unternehmen Sie!

PRESENT PARTICIPLE unternehmend

Usage

Was unternehmt ihr dieses Wochenende?	*What are you doing this weekend?*
Bei dem Wetter konnten wir nichts unternehmen; wir saßen einfach im Zelt und spielten Karten.	*In that weather we couldn't do anything; we just sat in our tent and played cards.*
Unternehmen Sie bitte die Vorbereitungen auf die Konferenz.	*Please get busy with the preparations for the conference.*
Die Archäologen unternehmen Ausgrabungen in der Nähe von Athen.	*The archeologists are undertaking excavations in the vicinity of Athens.*
Diese Arbeit unternimmt den Versuch, den wirtschaftlichen Aufschwung zu erklären.	*This paper attempts to explain the economic boom.*
Die Stadt unternahm weitgreifende Maßnahmen.	*The city undertook far-reaching measures.*
Professor Unger und seine Frau unternehmen eine Reise nach Korfu.	*Professor Unger and his wife are taking a trip to Corfu.*
An deiner Stelle würde ich keinen Spaziergang unternehmen.	*If I were you, I wouldn't go for a walk.*

RELATED VERBS *see* **nehmen** (314)

to teach; inform **unterrichten** 470

regular weak verb

unterrichtet · unterrichtete · unterrichtet

PRESENT

ich unterrichte	wir unterrichten
du unterrichtest	ihr unterrichtet
Sie unterrichten	Sie unterrichten
er/sie/es unterrichtet	sie unterrichten

SIMPLE PAST

ich unterrichtete	wir unterrichteten
du unterrichtetest	ihr unterrichtetet
Sie unterrichteten	Sie unterrichteten
er/sie/es unterrichtete	sie unterrichteten

FUTURE

ich werde	wir werden	unterrichten
du wirst	ihr werdet	
Sie werden	Sie werden	
er/sie/es wird	sie werden	

PRESENT SUBJUNCTIVE I

ich unterrichte	wir unterrichten
du unterrichtest	ihr unterrichtet
Sie unterrichten	Sie unterrichten
er/sie/es unterrichte	sie unterrichten

PRESENT SUBJUNCTIVE II

ich unterrichtete	wir unterrichteten
du unterrichtetest	ihr unterrichtetet
Sie unterrichteten	Sie unterrichteten
er/sie/es unterrichtete	sie unterrichteten

FUTURE SUBJUNCTIVE I

ich werde	wir werden	unterrichten
du werdest	ihr werdet	
Sie werden	Sie werden	
er/sie/es werde	sie werden	

FUTURE SUBJUNCTIVE II

ich würde	wir würden	unterrichten
du würdest	ihr würdet	
Sie würden	Sie würden	
er/sie/es würde	sie würden	

PRESENT PERFECT

ich habe	wir haben	unterrichtet
du hast	ihr habt	
Sie haben	Sie haben	
er/sie/es hat	sie haben	

PAST PERFECT

ich hatte	wir hatten	unterrichtet
du hattest	ihr hattet	
Sie hatten	Sie hatten	
er/sie/es hatte	sie hatten	

FUTURE PERFECT

ich werde	wir werden	unterrichtet haben
du wirst	ihr werdet	
Sie werden	Sie werden	
er/sie/es wird	sie werden	

PAST SUBJUNCTIVE I

ich habe	wir haben	unterrichtet
du habest	ihr habet	
Sie haben	Sie haben	
er/sie/es habe	sie haben	

PAST SUBJUNCTIVE II

ich hätte	wir hätten	unterrichtet
du hättest	ihr hättet	
Sie hätten	Sie hätten	
er/sie/es hätte	sie hätten	

FUTURE PERFECT SUBJUNCTIVE I

ich werde	wir werden	unterrichtet haben
du werdest	ihr werdet	
Sie werden	Sie werden	
er/sie/es werde	sie werden	

FUTURE PERFECT SUBJUNCTIVE II

ich würde	wir würden	unterrichtet haben
du würdest	ihr würdet	
Sie würden	Sie würden	
er/sie/es würde	sie würden	

COMMANDS unterrichte! unterrichtet! unterrichten Sie!

PRESENT PARTICIPLE unterrichtend

Usage

Tante Inge unterrichtet seit zwanzig Jahren an der Grundschule. — *Aunt Inge has been teaching elementary school for 20 years.*

Ludmilla unterrichtet russische Kinder in ihrer Muttersprache. — *Ludmilla instructs Russian children in their mother tongue.*

„Wo ist Ingrid?“ „Sie unterrichtet gerade.“ — *“Where is Ingrid?” “She’s teaching at the moment.”*

Haben Sie Deutsch für die Mittelstufe unterrichtet? — *Have you taught intermediate German?*

Albrechtsberger unterrichtete Beethoven und viele andere berühmte Musiker. — *Albrechtsberger taught Beethoven and many other famous musicians.*

In welcher Stufe wird Ethik unterrichtet? — *In which grade is ethics taught?*

Dara unterrichtete in einem Sommerprogramm für ausländische Studierende. — *Dara taught in a summer program for foreign students.*

Herr Gunnarson unterrichtet über die politische Lage in seinem Land. — *Mr. Gunnarson is providing information on the political situation in his country.*

RELATED VERBS richten; *see also* **berichten** (76), **ein·richten** (135)

471 unterscheiden *to distinguish, differentiate*

unterscheidet · unterschied · unterschieden — strong verb

PRESENT

ich unterscheide	wir unterscheiden
du unterscheidest	ihr unterscheidet
Sie unterscheiden	Sie unterscheiden
er/sie/es unterscheidet	sie unterscheiden

SIMPLE PAST

ich unterschied	wir unterschieden
du unterschiedst	ihr unterschiedet
Sie unterschieden	Sie unterschieden
er/sie/es unterschied	sie unterschieden

FUTURE

ich werde	wir werden	unterscheiden
du wirst	ihr werdet	
Sie werden	Sie werden	
er/sie/es wird	sie werden	

PRESENT SUBJUNCTIVE I

ich unterscheide	wir unterscheiden
du unterscheidest	ihr unterscheidet
Sie unterscheiden	Sie unterscheiden
er/sie/es unterscheide	sie unterscheiden

PRESENT SUBJUNCTIVE II

ich unterschiede	wir unterschieden
du unterschiedest	ihr unterschiedet
Sie unterschieden	Sie unterschieden
er/sie/es unterschiede	sie unterschieden

FUTURE SUBJUNCTIVE I

ich werde	wir werden	unterscheiden
du werdest	ihr werdet	
Sie werden	Sie werden	
er/sie/es werde	sie werden	

FUTURE SUBJUNCTIVE II

ich würde	wir würden	unterscheiden
du würdest	ihr würdet	
Sie würden	Sie würden	
er/sie/es würde	sie würden	

PRESENT PERFECT

ich habe	wir haben	unterschieden
du hast	ihr habt	
Sie haben	Sie haben	
er/sie/es hat	sie haben	

PAST PERFECT

ich hatte	wir hatten	unterschieden
du hattest	ihr hattet	
Sie hatten	Sie hatten	
er/sie/es hatte	sie hatten	

FUTURE PERFECT

ich werde	wir werden	unterschieden haben
du wirst	ihr werdet	
Sie werden	Sie werden	
er/sie/es wird	sie werden	

PAST SUBJUNCTIVE I

ich habe	wir haben	unterschieden
du habest	ihr habet	
Sie haben	Sie haben	
er/sie/es habe	sie haben	

PAST SUBJUNCTIVE II

ich hätte	wir hätten	unterschieden
du hättest	ihr hättet	
Sie hätten	Sie hätten	
er/sie/es hätte	sie hätten	

FUTURE PERFECT SUBJUNCTIVE I

ich werde	wir werden	unterschieden haben
du werdest	ihr werdet	
Sie werden	Sie werden	
er/sie/es werde	sie werden	

FUTURE PERFECT SUBJUNCTIVE II

ich würde	wir würden	unterschieden haben
du würdest	ihr würdet	
Sie würden	Sie würden	
er/sie/es würde	sie würden	

COMMANDS unterscheide! unterscheidet! unterscheiden Sie!

PRESENT PARTICIPLE unterscheidend

Usage

Er konnte Makisushi von Nigirisushi nicht unterscheiden. — *He could not differentiate maki sushi from nigiri sushi.*

Man kann drei Arten von Haarausfall unterscheiden. — *Three types of hair loss can be distinguished.*

Der Philosoph hat den anaphorischen Bezug von dem kataphorischen unterschieden. — *The philosopher made a distinction between anaphoric and cataphoric reference.*

Diese Eigentümlichkeit unterscheidet ihn vom Rest der Familie. — *This peculiarity sets him apart from the rest of the family.*

sich unterscheiden *to differ, be different*

Die neue Ausgabe unterscheidet sich nicht radikal von der alten. — *The new edition does not differ radically from the old one.*

Die Autos unterscheiden sich kaum. — *There is hardly any difference between the cars.*

Unterscheidet sich die *Prunus insistitia L.* von der *Prunus domestica L.*? — *Does* Prunus insistitia L. *differ from* Prunus domestica L.*?*

RELATED VERBS *see* **scheiden** (360)

strong verb **unterschreibt · unterschrieb · unterschrieben**

PRESENT

ich unterschreibe	wir unterschreiben
du unterschreibst	ihr unterschreibt
Sie unterschreiben	Sie unterschreiben
er/sie/es unterschreibt	sie unterschreiben

SIMPLE PAST

ich unterschrieb	wir unterschrieben
du unterschriebst	ihr unterschriebt
Sie unterschrieben	Sie unterschrieben
er/sie/es unterschrieb	sie unterschrieben

FUTURE

ich werde	wir werden	unterschreiben
du wirst	ihr werdet	
Sie werden	Sie werden	
er/sie/es wird	sie werden	

PRESENT SUBJUNCTIVE I

ich unterschreibe	wir unterschreiben
du unterschreibest	ihr unterschreibet
Sie unterschreiben	Sie unterschreiben
er/sie/es unterschreibe	sie unterschreiben

PRESENT SUBJUNCTIVE II

ich unterschriebe	wir unterschrieben
du unterschriebest	ihr unterschriebet
Sie unterschrieben	Sie unterschrieben
er/sie/es unterschriebe	sie unterschrieben

FUTURE SUBJUNCTIVE I

ich werde	wir werden	unterschreiben
du werdest	ihr werdet	
Sie werden	Sie werden	
er/sie/es werde	sie werden	

FUTURE SUBJUNCTIVE II

ich würde	wir würden	unterschreiben
du würdest	ihr würdet	
Sie würden	Sie würden	
er/sie/es würde	sie würden	

PRESENT PERFECT

ich habe	wir haben	unterschrieben
du hast	ihr habt	
Sie haben	Sie haben	
er/sie/es hat	sie haben	

PAST PERFECT

ich hatte	wir hatten	unterschrieben
du hattest	ihr hattet	
Sie hatten	Sie hatten	
er/sie/es hatte	sie hatten	

FUTURE PERFECT

ich werde	wir werden	unterschrieben haben
du wirst	ihr werdet	
Sie werden	Sie werden	
er/sie/es wird	sie werden	

PAST SUBJUNCTIVE I

ich habe	wir haben	unterschrieben
du habest	ihr habet	
Sie haben	Sie haben	
er/sie/es habe	sie haben	

PAST SUBJUNCTIVE II

ich hätte	wir hätten	unterschrieben
du hättest	ihr hättet	
Sie hätten	Sie hätten	
er/sie/es hätte	sie hätten	

FUTURE PERFECT SUBJUNCTIVE I

ich werde	wir werden	unterschrieben haben
du werdest	ihr werdet	
Sie werden	Sie werden	
er/sie/es werde	sie werden	

FUTURE PERFECT SUBJUNCTIVE II

ich würde	wir würden	unterschrieben haben
du würdest	ihr würdet	
Sie würden	Sie würden	
er/sie/es würde	sie würden	

COMMANDS unterschreib(e)! unterschreibt! unterschreiben Sie!

PRESENT PARTICIPLE unterschreibend

Usage

Karen will nicht unterschreiben.	*Karen does not want to sign.*
Der Vertrag wurde mit Blut unterschrieben.	*The contract was signed in blood.*
Tante Inge unterschrieb den Brief mit meinem Namen.	*Aunt Inge signed the letter using my name.*
Unterschreiben Sie bitte hier.	*Please sign here.*
Amtliche Dokumente können elektronisch unterschrieben werden.	*Official documents can be signed electronically.*
Ein Kind hätte das nicht unterschreiben dürfen.	*A child should not have signed that.*
Der Präsident hat ein neues Gesetz unterschrieben.	*The president signed a new law.*
Ein Elternteil muss das Formular unterschrieben haben.	*A parent must have signed the form.*
Die Erklärung war nicht unterschrieben.	*The declaration was not signed.*
Der Gefangene wurde genötigt, ein Geständnis zu unterschreiben.	*The prisoner was forced to sign a confession.*
Ich kann diese Aussage nicht unterschreiben.	*I can't subscribe to this statement.*

RELATED VERBS *see* **schreiben** (385)

473 unterstützen *to support*

unterstützt · unterstützte · unterstützt regular weak verb

PRESENT

ich unterstütze	wir unterstützen
du unterstützt	ihr unterstützt
Sie unterstützen	Sie unterstützen
er/sie/es unterstützt	sie unterstützen

SIMPLE PAST

ich unterstützte	wir unterstützten
du unterstütztest	ihr unterstütztet
Sie unterstützten	Sie unterstützten
er/sie/es unterstützte	sie unterstützten

FUTURE

ich werde	wir werden	unterstützen
du wirst	ihr werdet	
Sie werden	Sie werden	
er/sie/es wird	sie werden	

PRESENT SUBJUNCTIVE I

ich unterstütze	wir unterstützen
du unterstützest	ihr unterstützet
Sie unterstützen	Sie unterstützen
er/sie/es unterstütze	sie unterstützen

PRESENT SUBJUNCTIVE II

ich unterstützte	wir unterstützten
du unterstütztest	ihr unterstütztet
Sie unterstützten	Sie unterstützten
er/sie/es unterstützte	sie unterstützten

FUTURE SUBJUNCTIVE I

ich werde	wir werden	unterstützen
du werdest	ihr werdet	
Sie werden	Sie werden	
er/sie/es werde	sie werden	

FUTURE SUBJUNCTIVE II

ich würde	wir würden	unterstützen
du würdest	ihr würdet	
Sie würden	Sie würden	
er/sie/es würde	sie würden	

PRESENT PERFECT

ich habe	wir haben	unterstützt
du hast	ihr habt	
Sie haben	Sie haben	
er/sie/es hat	sie haben	

PAST PERFECT

ich hatte	wir hatten	unterstützt
du hattest	ihr hattet	
Sie hatten	Sie hatten	
er/sie/es hatte	sie hatten	

FUTURE PERFECT

ich werde	wir werden	unterstützt haben
du wirst	ihr werdet	
Sie werden	Sie werden	
er/sie/es wird	sie werden	

PAST SUBJUNCTIVE I

ich habe	wir haben	unterstützt
du habest	ihr habet	
Sie haben	Sie haben	
er/sie/es habe	sie haben	

PAST SUBJUNCTIVE II

ich hätte	wir hätten	unterstützt
du hättest	ihr hättet	
Sie hätten	Sie hätten	
er/sie/es hätte	sie hätten	

FUTURE PERFECT SUBJUNCTIVE I

ich werde	wir werden	unterstützt haben
du werdest	ihr werdet	
Sie werden	Sie werden	
er/sie/es werde	sie werden	

FUTURE PERFECT SUBJUNCTIVE II

ich würde	wir würden	unterstützt haben
du würdest	ihr würdet	
Sie würden	Sie würden	
er/sie/es würde	sie würden	

COMMANDS unterstütz(e)! unterstützt! unterstützen Sie!

PRESENT PARTICIPLE unterstützend

Usage

Die Anwohner unterstützen die geplante Verkehrsregelung. — *The residents support the proposed traffic regulation.*
Unterstützt du meine These? — *Do you support my thesis?*
Die Maßnahmen werden von der SPD unterstützt. — *The measures are backed by the S.P.D.*
Die Vorstandsmitglieder unterstützten unsere Entscheidung. — *The board members supported our decision.*
Welchen Kandidaten unterstützen Sie? — *Which candidate do you support?*
Ich kann Ihre Methoden nicht unterstützen. — *I cannot sanction your methods.*
Von wem wird euer Projekt unterstützt? — *By whom is your project endorsed?*
Die Politiker unterstützen ein Waffenembargo. — *The politicians support an arms embargo.*
Dietrich Hombacher hat eine alternative Erklärung unterstützt. — *Dietrich Hombacher supported an alternate explanation.*
Die USA unterstützen einen militärischen Einsatz. — *The U.S. supports military intervention.*
Anja hat ihren Freund finanziell unterstützt. — *Anja supported her friend financially.*
Der Antrag wurde unterstützt und angenommen. — *The motion was seconded and approved.*

RELATED VERBS *see* **stützen** (439)

regular weak verb **verabschiedet · verabschiedete · verabschiedet**

PRESENT

ich verabschiede	wir verabschieden
du verabschiedest	ihr verabschiedet
Sie verabschieden	Sie verabschieden
er/sie/es verabschiedet	sie verabschieden

SIMPLE PAST

ich verabschiedete	wir verabschiedeten
du verabschiedetest	ihr verabschiedetet
Sie verabschiedeten	Sie verabschiedeten
er/sie/es verabschiedete	sie verabschiedeten

FUTURE

ich werde	wir werden	verabschieden
du wirst	ihr werdet	
Sie werden	Sie werden	
er/sie/es wird	sie werden	

PRESENT SUBJUNCTIVE I

ich verabschiede	wir verabschieden
du verabschiedest	ihr verabschiedet
Sie verabschieden	Sie verabschieden
er/sie/es verabschiede	sie verabschieden

PRESENT SUBJUNCTIVE II

ich verabschiedete	wir verabschiedeten
du verabschiedetest	ihr verabschiedetet
Sie verabschiedeten	Sie verabschiedeten
er/sie/es verabschiedete	sie verabschiedeten

FUTURE SUBJUNCTIVE I

ich werde	wir werden	verabschieden
du werdest	ihr werdet	
Sie werden	Sie werden	
er/sie/es werde	sie werden	

FUTURE SUBJUNCTIVE II

ich würde	wir würden	verabschieden
du würdest	ihr würdet	
Sie würden	Sie würden	
er/sie/es würde	sie würden	

PRESENT PERFECT

ich habe	wir haben	verabschiedet
du hast	ihr habt	
Sie haben	Sie haben	
er/sie/es hat	sie haben	

PAST PERFECT

ich hatte	wir hatten	verabschiedet
du hattest	ihr hattet	
Sie hatten	Sie hatten	
er/sie/es hatte	sie hatten	

FUTURE PERFECT

ich werde	wir werden	verabschiedet haben
du wirst	ihr werdet	
Sie werden	Sie werden	
er/sie/es wird	sie werden	

PAST SUBJUNCTIVE I

ich habe	wir haben	verabschiedet
du habest	ihr habet	
Sie haben	Sie haben	
er/sie/es habe	sie haben	

PAST SUBJUNCTIVE II

ich hätte	wir hätten	verabschiedet
du hättest	ihr hättet	
Sie hätten	Sie hätten	
er/sie/es hätte	sie hätten	

FUTURE PERFECT SUBJUNCTIVE I

ich werde	wir werden	verabschiedet haben
du werdest	ihr werdet	
Sie werden	Sie werden	
er/sie/es werde	sie werden	

FUTURE PERFECT SUBJUNCTIVE II

ich würde	wir würden	verabschiedet haben
du würdest	ihr würdet	
Sie würden	Sie würden	
er/sie/es würde	sie würden	

COMMANDS verabschiede! verabschiedet! verabschieden Sie!

PRESENT PARTICIPLE verabschiedend

Usage

Die Truppen werden bald verabschiedet.	*The troops will soon be disbanded.*
Der Offizier wurde gestern verabschiedet.	*The officer was discharged yesterday.*
Nach einer langen Debatte verabschiedete das Parlament eine Änderung des Gesetzes.	*After a long debate, the parliament adopted a change to the law.*
Der Kongress verabschiedete gestern ein ähnliches Gesetz.	*Congress passed a similar law yesterday.*

sich verabschieden *to take leave, say good-bye*

Opa Schmidt verabschiedete sich von seinen Kindern und starb wenige Minuten später.	*Grandpa Schmidt said good-bye to his children and died a few minutes later.*
Traurig verabschiedete er sich von seiner Familie und fuhr los.	*Sadly, he took leave of his family and drove away.*
Susanne und Sofie verabschiedeten sich voneinander mit einer Umarmung.	*Susanne and Sofie said good-bye with a hug.*
Verabschiedet ihr euch heute Abend schon?	*Are you going to say good-bye tonight already?*
Sara hatte ihre Freundinnen verlassen, ohne sich zu verabschieden.	*Sara had left her friends without saying good-bye.*

475 verändern *to change, modify, alter*

verändert · veränderte · verändert

regular weak verb

PRESENT

ich verändere	wir verändern
du veränderst	ihr verändert
Sie verändern	Sie verändern
er/sie/es verändert	sie verändern

PRESENT PERFECT

ich habe	wir haben	verändert
du hast	ihr habt	
Sie haben	Sie haben	
er/sie/es hat	sie haben	

SIMPLE PAST

ich veränderte	wir veränderten
du verändertest	ihr verändertet
Sie veränderten	Sie veränderten
er/sie/es veränderte	sie veränderten

PAST PERFECT

ich hatte	wir hatten	verändert
du hattest	ihr hattet	
Sie hatten	Sie hatten	
er/sie/es hatte	sie hatten	

FUTURE

ich werde	wir werden	verändern
du wirst	ihr werdet	
Sie werden	Sie werden	
er/sie/es wird	sie werden	

FUTURE PERFECT

ich werde	wir werden	verändert haben
du wirst	ihr werdet	
Sie werden	Sie werden	
er/sie/es wird	sie werden	

PRESENT SUBJUNCTIVE I

ich verändere	wir verändern
du veränderst	ihr verändert
Sie verändern	Sie verändern
er/sie/es verändere	sie verändern

PAST SUBJUNCTIVE I

ich habe	wir haben	verändert
du habest	ihr habet	
Sie haben	Sie haben	
er/sie/es habe	sie haben	

PRESENT SUBJUNCTIVE II

ich veränderte	wir veränderten
du verändertest	ihr verändertet
Sie veränderten	Sie veränderten
er/sie/es veränderte	sie veränderten

PAST SUBJUNCTIVE II

ich hätte	wir hätten	verändert
du hättest	ihr hättet	
Sie hätten	Sie hätten	
er/sie/es hätte	sie hätten	

FUTURE SUBJUNCTIVE I

ich werde	wir werden	verändern
du werdest	ihr werdet	
Sie werden	Sie werden	
er/sie/es werde	sie werden	

FUTURE PERFECT SUBJUNCTIVE I

ich werde	wir werden	verändert haben
du werdest	ihr werdet	
Sie werden	Sie werden	
er/sie/es werde	sie werden	

FUTURE SUBJUNCTIVE II

ich würde	wir würden	verändern
du würdest	ihr würdet	
Sie würden	Sie würden	
er/sie/es würde	sie würden	

FUTURE PERFECT SUBJUNCTIVE II

ich würde	wir würden	verändert haben
du würdest	ihr würdet	
Sie würden	Sie würden	
er/sie/es würde	sie würden	

COMMANDS verändere! verändert! verändern Sie!

PRESENT PARTICIPLE verändernd

Usage

Die Vergangenheit kann nicht verändert werden. — *The past cannot be altered.*
Immer mehr Organismen werden genetisch verändert. — *More and more organisms are being genetically modified.*
Wir wollen die Mentalität der Menschen verändern. — *We want to change people's mentality.*
Die Erfahrungen im Ausland haben uns verändert. — *The experience abroad changed us.*

sich verändern *to change*

Die Hafenstadt veränderte sich im Laufe der Jahre. — *The harbor city changed over the years.*
Die Bakterien haben sich genetisch verändert. — *The bacteria have mutated.*
Seit dem Fall der Berliner Mauer hat sich viel verändert. — *Since the fall of the Berlin Wall, a lot has changed.*
Ich habe mich zu meinem Vorteil verändert. — *I've changed for the better.*
In der Zwischenzeit kann sich viel verändert haben. — *A lot could have changed in the meantime.*
Michelle hat sich beruflich verändert. — *Michelle has changed careers.*

RELATED VERBS *see* ändern (9)

regular weak verb **verbessert · verbesserte · verbessert**

PRESENT		PRESENT PERFECT		
ich verbessere	wir verbessern	ich habe	wir haben	verbessert
du verbesserst	ihr verbessert	du hast	ihr habt	
Sie verbessern	Sie verbessern	Sie haben	Sie haben	
er/sie/es verbessert	sie verbessern	er/sie/es hat	sie haben	

SIMPLE PAST		PAST PERFECT		
ich verbesserte	wir verbesserten	ich hatte	wir hatten	verbessert
du verbessertest	ihr verbessertet	du hattest	ihr hattet	
Sie verbesserten	Sie verbesserten	Sie hatten	Sie hatten	
er/sie/es verbesserte	sie verbesserten	er/sie/es hatte	sie hatten	

FUTURE			FUTURE PERFECT		
ich werde	wir werden	verbessern	ich werde	wir werden	verbessert haben
du wirst	ihr werdet		du wirst	ihr werdet	
Sie werden	Sie werden		Sie werden	Sie werden	
er/sie/es wird	sie werden		er/sie/es wird	sie werden	

PRESENT SUBJUNCTIVE I		PAST SUBJUNCTIVE I		
ich verbessere	wir verbessern	ich habe	wir haben	verbessert
du verbesserst	ihr verbessert	du habest	ihr habet	
Sie verbessern	Sie verbessern	Sie haben	Sie haben	
er/sie/es verbessere	sie verbessern	er/sie/es habe	sie haben	

PRESENT SUBJUNCTIVE II		PAST SUBJUNCTIVE II		
ich verbesserte	wir verbesserten	ich hätte	wir hätten	verbessert
du verbessertest	ihr verbessertet	du hättest	ihr hättet	
Sie verbesserten	Sie verbesserten	Sie hätten	Sie hätten	
er/sie/es verbesserte	sie verbesserten	er/sie/es hätte	sie hätten	

FUTURE SUBJUNCTIVE I			FUTURE PERFECT SUBJUNCTIVE I		
ich werde	wir werden	verbessern	ich werde	wir werden	verbessert haben
du werdest	ihr werdet		du werdest	ihr werdet	
Sie werden	Sie werden		Sie werden	Sie werden	
er/sie/es werde	sie werden		er/sie/es werde	sie werden	

FUTURE SUBJUNCTIVE II			FUTURE PERFECT SUBJUNCTIVE II		
ich würde	wir würden	verbessern	ich würde	wir würden	verbessert haben
du würdest	ihr würdet		du würdest	ihr würdet	
Sie würden	Sie würden		Sie würden	Sie würden	
er/sie/es würde	sie würden		er/sie/es würde	sie würden	

COMMANDS verbessere! verbessert! verbessern Sie!

PRESENT PARTICIPLE verbessernd

Usage

Die Version 3.0 der Software ist verbessert worden. — *Version 3.0 of the software has been improved.*
Jörg möchte sein Aussehen verbessern. — *Jörg would like to improve his appearance.*
Die Produkte müssen verbessert werden. — *The products must be improved.*
Inwiefern haben Sie das Kuchenrezept verbessert? — *To what extent have you improved the recipe?*
Der Athlet trainiert, um seine Kondition zu verbessern. — *The athlete is working out to get in better shape.*
Der Lehrer verbesserte meine Aussprache. — *The teacher corrected my pronunciation.*
Verbessere mich bitte, wenn ich falsch liege. — *Please correct me if I'm wrong.*

sich verbessern *to improve, better/correct oneself*

Endlich hat sich das Wetter verbessert. — *Finally, the weather has improved.*
Die wirtschaftliche Lage hat sich beträchtlich verbessert. — *The economic situation has improved considerably.*
Der Wein verbessert sich jedes Jahr. — *The wine gets better every year.*
Erich hat sich beruflich verbessert. — *Erich has bettered himself in his career.*

RELATED VERB bessern

477 verbieten *to prohibit, forbid*

verbietet · verbot · verboten

strong verb

PRESENT

ich verbiete	wir verbieten
du verbietest	ihr verbietet
Sie verbieten	Sie verbieten
er/sie/es verbietet	sie verbieten

SIMPLE PAST

ich verbot	wir verboten
du verbot(e)st	ihr verbotet
Sie verboten	Sie verboten
er/sie/es verbot	sie verboten

FUTURE

ich werde	wir werden	verbieten
du wirst	ihr werdet	
Sie werden	Sie werden	
er/sie/es wird	sie werden	

PRESENT SUBJUNCTIVE I

ich verbiete	wir verbieten
du verbietest	ihr verbietet
Sie verbieten	Sie verbieten
er/sie/es verbiete	sie verbieten

PRESENT SUBJUNCTIVE II

ich verböte	wir verböten
du verbötest	ihr verbötet
Sie verböten	Sie verböten
er/sie/es verböte	sie verböten

FUTURE SUBJUNCTIVE I

ich werde	wir werden	verbieten
du werdest	ihr werdet	
Sie werden	Sie werden	
er/sie/es werde	sie werden	

FUTURE SUBJUNCTIVE II

ich würde	wir würden	verbieten
du würdest	ihr würdet	
Sie würden	Sie würden	
er/sie/es würde	sie würden	

PRESENT PERFECT

ich habe	wir haben	verboten
du hast	ihr habt	
Sie haben	Sie haben	
er/sie/es hat	sie haben	

PAST PERFECT

ich hatte	wir hatten	verboten
du hattest	ihr hattet	
Sie hatten	Sie hatten	
er/sie/es hatte	sie hatten	

FUTURE PERFECT

ich werde	wir werden	verboten haben
du wirst	ihr werdet	
Sie werden	Sie werden	
er/sie/es wird	sie werden	

PAST SUBJUNCTIVE I

ich habe	wir haben	verboten
du habest	ihr habet	
Sie haben	Sie haben	
er/sie/es habe	sie haben	

PAST SUBJUNCTIVE II

ich hätte	wir hätten	verboten
du hättest	ihr hättet	
Sie hätten	Sie hätten	
er/sie/es hätte	sie hätten	

FUTURE PERFECT SUBJUNCTIVE I

ich werde	wir werden	verboten haben
du werdest	ihr werdet	
Sie werden	Sie werden	
er/sie/es werde	sie werden	

FUTURE PERFECT SUBJUNCTIVE II

ich würde	wir würden	verboten haben
du würdest	ihr würdet	
Sie würden	Sie würden	
er/sie/es würde	sie würden	

COMMANDS verbiete! verbietet! verbieten Sie!

PRESENT PARTICIPLE verbietend

Usage

Nicht-christliche Rituale waren von den Missionären verboten worden. — *Non-Christian rituals had been prohibited by the missionaries.*

Frau Escher verbietet ihrer Tochter den Umgang mit Christian. — *Mrs. Escher forbids her daughter to have anything to do with Christian.*

Es ist doch verboten, den Rasen zu betreten! — *But it's forbidden to walk on the grass!*

Der König verbot den Handel mit katholischen Ländern. — *The king forbade trade with Catholic countries.*

Die Regierung hat gentechnisch modifizierte Organismen verboten. — *The government has banned genetically engineered organisms.*

Das Buch wurde in den USA verboten. — *The book was banned in the U.S.*

Kinderarbeit ist in den meisten Ländern verboten. — *Child labor is prohibited in most countries.*

Die kontroverse Szene wurde in Singapur von Zensoren verboten. — *The controversial scene was proscribed by censors in Singapore.*

Bei uns in der Schule ist es verboten, im Unterricht zu essen. — *In our school, eating in class is not allowed.*

RELATED VERBS *see* **bieten** (107)

478 verbinden

to bind, join, connect, combine; bandage

strong verb

verbindet · verband · verbunden

PRESENT

ich verbinde	wir verbinden
du verbindest	ihr verbindet
Sie verbinden	Sie verbinden
er/sie/es verbindet	sie verbinden

SIMPLE PAST

ich verband	wir verbanden
du verband(e)st	ihr verbandet
Sie verbanden	Sie verbanden
er/sie/es verband	sie verbanden

FUTURE

ich werde	wir werden	verbinden
du wirst	ihr werdet	
Sie werden	Sie werden	
er/sie/es wird	sie werden	

PRESENT SUBJUNCTIVE I

ich verbinde	wir verbinden
du verbindest	ihr verbindet
Sie verbinden	Sie verbinden
er/sie/es verbinde	sie verbinden

PRESENT SUBJUNCTIVE II

ich verbände	wir verbänden
du verbändest	ihr verbändet
Sie verbänden	Sie verbänden
er/sie/es verbände	sie verbänden

FUTURE SUBJUNCTIVE I

ich werde	wir werden	verbinden
du werdest	ihr werdet	
Sie werden	Sie werden	
er/sie/es werde	sie werden	

FUTURE SUBJUNCTIVE II

ich würde	wir würden	verbinden
du würdest	ihr würdet	
Sie würden	Sie würden	
er/sie/es würde	sie würden	

PRESENT PERFECT

ich habe	wir haben	verbunden
du hast	ihr habt	
Sie haben	Sie haben	
er/sie/es hat	sie haben	

PAST PERFECT

ich hatte	wir hatten	verbunden
du hattest	ihr hattet	
Sie hatten	Sie hatten	
er/sie/es hatte	sie hatten	

FUTURE PERFECT

ich werde	wir werden	verbunden haben
du wirst	ihr werdet	
Sie werden	Sie werden	
er/sie/es wird	sie werden	

PAST SUBJUNCTIVE I

ich habe	wir haben	verbunden
du habest	ihr habet	
Sie haben	Sie haben	
er/sie/es habe	sie haben	

PAST SUBJUNCTIVE II

ich hätte	wir hätten	verbunden
du hättest	ihr hättet	
Sie hätten	Sie hätten	
er/sie/es hätte	sie hätten	

FUTURE PERFECT SUBJUNCTIVE I

ich werde	wir werden	verbunden haben
du werdest	ihr werdet	
Sie werden	Sie werden	
er/sie/es werde	sie werden	

FUTURE PERFECT SUBJUNCTIVE II

ich würde	wir würden	verbunden haben
du würdest	ihr würdet	
Sie würden	Sie würden	
er/sie/es würde	sie würden	

COMMANDS verbinde! verbindet! verbinden Sie!

PRESENT PARTICIPLE verbindend

Usage

Man hat die Flüsse durch einen Kanal verbunden.	*The rivers were connected by a canal.*
Eine große Liebe verband sie mit ihrem Mann.	*A great love bound her to her husband.*
Das Programm verbindet die neue Software mit der alten Hardware.	*The program combines the new software with the old hardware.*
Wie kann ich die Computer miteinander verbinden?	*How can I connect the computers to one another?*
„Was verbinden Sie mit der Schweiz?"	*"What do you associate with Switzerland?"*
„Schokolade, natürlich!"	*"Chocolate, of course!"*
Verbinden Sie mich bitte mit Herrn Lefler.	*Please connect me with Mr. Lefler.*
Das Buch verbindet viele verschiedene Themen.	*The book combines many different topics.*
Der Waldpfad verbindet sich mit dem Fußweg hinter unserem Haus.	*The forest path joins with the footpath behind our house.*
Die Ärztin verband ihr den Kopf.	*The doctor bandaged her head.*

RELATED VERBS *see* **binden** (108)

479 **verbrauchen** *to use, consume; use up; wear out*

verbraucht · verbrauchte · verbraucht — regular weak verb

PRESENT

ich verbrauche	wir verbrauchen
du verbrauchst	ihr verbraucht
Sie verbrauchen	Sie verbrauchen
er/sie/es verbraucht	sie verbrauchen

SIMPLE PAST

ich verbrauchte	wir verbrauchten
du verbrauchtest	ihr verbrauchtet
Sie verbrauchten	Sie verbrauchten
er/sie/es verbrauchte	sie verbrauchten

FUTURE

ich werde	wir werden	verbrauchen
du wirst	ihr werdet	
Sie werden	Sie werden	
er/sie/es wird	sie werden	

PRESENT SUBJUNCTIVE I

ich verbrauche	wir verbrauchen
du verbrauchest	ihr verbrauchet
Sie verbrauchen	Sie verbrauchen
er/sie/es verbrauche	sie verbrauchen

PRESENT SUBJUNCTIVE II

ich verbrauchte	wir verbrauchten
du verbrauchtest	ihr verbrauchtet
Sie verbrauchten	Sie verbrauchten
er/sie/es verbrauchte	sie verbrauchten

FUTURE SUBJUNCTIVE I

ich werde	wir werden	verbrauchen
du werdest	ihr werdet	
Sie werden	Sie werden	
er/sie/es werde	sie werden	

FUTURE SUBJUNCTIVE II

ich würde	wir würden	verbrauchen
du würdest	ihr würdet	
Sie würden	Sie würden	
er/sie/es würde	sie würden	

PRESENT PERFECT

ich habe	wir haben	verbraucht
du hast	ihr habt	
Sie haben	Sie haben	
er/sie/es hat	sie haben	

PAST PERFECT

ich hatte	wir hatten	verbraucht
du hattest	ihr hattet	
Sie hatten	Sie hatten	
er/sie/es hatte	sie hatten	

FUTURE PERFECT

ich werde	wir werden	verbraucht haben
du wirst	ihr werdet	
Sie werden	Sie werden	
er/sie/es wird	sie werden	

PAST SUBJUNCTIVE I

ich habe	wir haben	verbraucht
du habest	ihr habet	
Sie haben	Sie haben	
er/sie/es habe	sie haben	

PAST SUBJUNCTIVE II

ich hätte	wir hätten	verbraucht
du hättest	ihr hättet	
Sie hätten	Sie hätten	
er/sie/es hätte	sie hätten	

FUTURE PERFECT SUBJUNCTIVE I

ich werde	wir werden	verbraucht haben
du werdest	ihr werdet	
Sie werden	Sie werden	
er/sie/es werde	sie werden	

FUTURE PERFECT SUBJUNCTIVE II

ich würde	wir würden	verbraucht haben
du würdest	ihr würdet	
Sie würden	Sie würden	
er/sie/es würde	sie würden	

COMMANDS verbrauch(e)! verbraucht! verbrauchen Sie!

PRESENT PARTICIPLE verbrauchend

Usage

Verbrauchen Sie bitte weniger Wasser beim Duschen.	*Please use less water when showering.*
In Deutschland wird mehr Diesel verbraucht als in den USA.	*In Germany, more diesel is used than in the U.S.*
Das ist ein Prozess, der nicht viel Energie verbraucht.	*That is a process that doesn't use much energy.*
Ich verbrauche mehr Jogurt als Käse.	*I consume more yogurt than cheese.*
Wie viel Benzin verbraucht Ihr PKW?	*How much fuel does your vehicle use?*
Der Mensch verbraucht jeden Tag 10 000 Liter Luft.	*A human being breathes in 10,000 liters of air every day.*
Der durchschnittliche Nordamerikaner verbraucht 650 Pfund Papier in einem Jahr.	*The average North American uses 650 pounds of paper a year.*
In Nordamerika werden täglich 50 000 000 Einwegwindeln verbraucht.	*In North America, 50,000,000 disposable diapers are used every day.*
Die Produkte im Lagerraum sind schon verbraucht worden.	*The products in the storage room have already been used up.*

RELATED VERBS *see* **brauchen** (115)

PRESENT

ich verbringe	wir verbringen
du verbringst	ihr verbringt
Sie verbringen	Sie verbringen
er/sie/es verbringt	sie verbringen

SIMPLE PAST

ich verbrachte	wir verbrachten
du verbrachtest	ihr verbrachtet
Sie verbrachten	Sie verbrachten
er/sie/es verbrachte	sie verbrachten

FUTURE

ich werde	wir werden	verbringen
du wirst	ihr werdet	
Sie werden	Sie werden	
er/sie/es wird	sie werden	

PRESENT SUBJUNCTIVE I

ich verbringe	wir verbringen
du verbringest	ihr verbringet
Sie verbringen	Sie verbringen
er/sie/es verbringe	sie verbringen

PRESENT SUBJUNCTIVE II

ich verbrächte	wir verbrächten
du verbrächtest	ihr verbrächtet
Sie verbrächten	Sie verbrächten
er/sie/es verbrächte	sie verbrächten

FUTURE SUBJUNCTIVE I

ich werde	wir werden	verbringen
du werdest	ihr werdet	
Sie werden	Sie werden	
er/sie/es werde	sie werden	

FUTURE SUBJUNCTIVE II

ich würde	wir würden	verbringen
du würdest	ihr würdet	
Sie würden	Sie würden	
er/sie/es würde	sie würden	

PRESENT PERFECT

ich habe	wir haben	verbracht
du hast	ihr habt	
Sie haben	Sie haben	
er/sie/es hat	sie haben	

PAST PERFECT

ich hatte	wir hatten	verbracht
du hattest	ihr hattet	
Sie hatten	Sie hatten	
er/sie/es hatte	sie hatten	

FUTURE PERFECT

ich werde	wir werden	verbracht haben
du wirst	ihr werdet	
Sie werden	Sie werden	
er/sie/es wird	sie werden	

PAST SUBJUNCTIVE I

ich habe	wir haben	verbracht
du habest	ihr habet	
Sie haben	Sie haben	
er/sie/es habe	sie haben	

PAST SUBJUNCTIVE II

ich hätte	wir hätten	verbracht
du hättest	ihr hättet	
Sie hätten	Sie hätten	
er/sie/es hätte	sie hätten	

FUTURE PERFECT SUBJUNCTIVE I

ich werde	wir werden	verbracht haben
du werdest	ihr werdet	
Sie werden	Sie werden	
er/sie/es werde	sie werden	

FUTURE PERFECT SUBJUNCTIVE II

ich würde	wir würden	verbracht haben
du würdest	ihr würdet	
Sie würden	Sie würden	
er/sie/es würde	sie würden	

COMMANDS verbring(e)! verbringt! verbringen Sie!

PRESENT PARTICIPLE verbringend

Usage

Wie verbringst du Weihnachten?	*How do you spend Christmas?*
Schmidts verbringen drei Wochen auf einer ehemaligen Zuckerplantage auf Hawaii.	*The Schmidts are spending three weeks on an old sugar plantation in Hawaii.*
Wir werden die Woche in Istanbul verbringen.	*We will spend the week in Istanbul.*
Ich verbringe den Sommer auf einem Bauernhof in der Nähe von Münster.	*I'm spending the summer on a farm near Münster.*
Wer von euch hat seine Kindheit auf dem Lande verbracht?	*Which one of you spent his childhood in the country?*
Herr und Frau Fricke möchten ihren Urlaub in Regensburg verbringen.	*Mr. and Mrs. Fricke would like to vacation in Regensburg.*
Dirk und Sara haben ihre Flitterwochen in Spanien verbracht.	*Dirk and Sara spent their honeymoon in Spain.*
Christian behauptet, zwei Jahre bei der Bundeswehr verbracht zu haben.	*Christian claims to have spent two years in the army.*
Lola verbrachte den Abend in der Kneipe.	*Lola spent the evening at the pub.*

RELATED VERBS *see* **bringen** (118)

481 verderben *to go bad, spoil*

verdirbt · verdarb · verdorben strong verb

PRESENT

ich verderbe	wir verderben
du verdirbst	ihr verderbt
Sie verderben	Sie verderben
er/sie/es verdirbt	sie verderben

SIMPLE PAST

ich verdarb	wir verdarben
du verdarbst	ihr verdarbt
Sie verdarben	Sie verdarben
er/sie/es verdarb	sie verdarben

FUTURE

ich werde	wir werden	verderben
du wirst	ihr werdet	
Sie werden	Sie werden	
er/sie/es wird	sie werden	

PRESENT SUBJUNCTIVE I

ich verderbe	wir verderben
du verderbest	ihr verderbet
Sie verderben	Sie verderben
er/sie/es verderbe	sie verderben

PRESENT SUBJUNCTIVE II

ich verdürbe	wir verdürben
du verdürbest	ihr verdürbet
Sie verdürben	Sie verdürben
er/sie/es verdürbe	sie verdürben

FUTURE SUBJUNCTIVE I

ich werde	wir werden	verderben
du werdest	ihr werdet	
Sie werden	Sie werden	
er/sie/es werde	sie werden	

FUTURE SUBJUNCTIVE II

ich würde	wir würden	verderben
du würdest	ihr würdet	
Sie würden	Sie würden	
er/sie/es würde	sie würden	

PRESENT PERFECT

ich bin	wir sind	verdorben
du bist	ihr seid	
Sie sind	Sie sind	
er/sie/es ist	sie sind	

PAST PERFECT

ich war	wir waren	verdorben
du warst	ihr wart	
Sie waren	Sie waren	
er/sie/es war	sie waren	

FUTURE PERFECT

ich werde	wir werden	verdorben sein
du wirst	ihr werdet	
Sie werden	Sie werden	
er/sie/es wird	sie werden	

PAST SUBJUNCTIVE I

ich sei	wir seien	verdorben
du seiest	ihr seiet	
Sie seien	Sie seien	
er/sie/es sei	sie seien	

PAST SUBJUNCTIVE II

ich wäre	wir wären	verdorben
du wärest	ihr wäret	
Sie wären	Sie wären	
er/sie/es wäre	sie wären	

FUTURE PERFECT SUBJUNCTIVE I

ich werde	wir werden	verdorben sein
du werdest	ihr werdet	
Sie werden	Sie werden	
er/sie/es werde	sie werden	

FUTURE PERFECT SUBJUNCTIVE II

ich würde	wir würden	verdorben sein
du würdest	ihr würdet	
Sie würden	Sie würden	
er/sie/es würde	sie würden	

COMMANDS verdirb! verderbt! verderben Sie!

PRESENT PARTICIPLE verderbend

Usage

Ist der Thunfisch schon verdorben?	*Has the tuna already gone bad?*
Die Birnen verdarben schneller als die Äpfel.	*The pears went bad more quickly than the apples.*
Nachdem das Wasser durch Industrieabfälle verdorben war, hatten sie nichts zu trinken.	*After the water had been contaminated with industrial waste, they had nothing to drink.*
H-Milch verdirbt nicht so schnell wie Rohmilch.	*Ultra-pasteurized milk doesn't spoil as quickly as raw milk.*
Fleisch verdirbt bei Zimmertemperatur.	*Meat spoils at room temperature.*
Die Torte ist verdorben.	*The cake has gone bad.*

verderben (with **haben**) *to spoil, ruin, upset; corrupt, deprave*

Du hast uns den Abend verdorben!	*You've spoiled our evening!*
Viele Köche verderben den Brei. (PROVERB)	*Too many cooks spoil the broth.*
Ein fauler Apfel macht zehn. (PROVERB)	*One bad apple spoils the whole bunch.*
Ein abscheulicher Geruch verdarb ihm den Appetit.	*A disgusting smell ruined his appetite.*
Das Eiswasser hat ihm den Magen verdorben.	*The ice water upset his stomach.*
Die heutige Jugend wird verdorben.	*Today's youth are being corrupted.*

regular weak verb **verdient · verdiente · verdient**

PRESENT

ich verdiene	wir verdienen
du verdienst	ihr verdient
Sie verdienen	Sie verdienen
er/sie/es verdient	sie verdienen

SIMPLE PAST

ich verdiente	wir verdienten
du verdientest	ihr verdientet
Sie verdienten	Sie verdienten
er/sie/es verdiente	sie verdienten

FUTURE

ich werde	wir werden	verdienen
du wirst	ihr werdet	
Sie werden	Sie werden	
er/sie/es wird	sie werden	

PRESENT SUBJUNCTIVE I

ich verdiene	wir verdienen
du verdienest	ihr verdienet
Sie verdienen	Sie verdienen
er/sie/es verdiene	sie verdienen

PRESENT SUBJUNCTIVE II

ich verdiente	wir verdienten
du verdientest	ihr verdientet
Sie verdienten	Sie verdienten
er/sie/es verdiente	sie verdienten

FUTURE SUBJUNCTIVE I

ich werde	wir werden	verdienen
du werdest	ihr werdet	
Sie werden	Sie werden	
er/sie/es werde	sie werden	

FUTURE SUBJUNCTIVE II

ich würde	wir würden	verdienen
du würdest	ihr würdet	
Sie würden	Sie würden	
er/sie/es würde	sie würden	

PRESENT PERFECT

ich habe	wir haben	verdient
du hast	ihr habt	
Sie haben	Sie haben	
er/sie/es hat	sie haben	

PAST PERFECT

ich hatte	wir hatten	verdient
du hattest	ihr hattet	
Sie hatten	Sie hatten	
er/sie/es hatte	sie hatten	

FUTURE PERFECT

ich werde	wir werden	verdient haben
du wirst	ihr werdet	
Sie werden	Sie werden	
er/sie/es wird	sie werden	

PAST SUBJUNCTIVE I

ich habe	wir haben	verdient
du habest	ihr habet	
Sie haben	Sie haben	
er/sie/es habe	sie haben	

PAST SUBJUNCTIVE II

ich hätte	wir hätten	verdient
du hättest	ihr hättet	
Sie hätten	Sie hätten	
er/sie/es hätte	sie hätten	

FUTURE PERFECT SUBJUNCTIVE I

ich werde	wir werden	verdient haben
du werdest	ihr werdet	
Sie werden	Sie werden	
er/sie/es werde	sie werden	

FUTURE PERFECT SUBJUNCTIVE II

ich würde	wir würden	verdient haben
du würdest	ihr würdet	
Sie würden	Sie würden	
er/sie/es würde	sie würden	

COMMANDS verdien(e)! verdient! verdienen Sie!

PRESENT PARTICIPLE verdienend

Usage

Unsere Mannschaft hat den Titel verdient.	*Our team earned the title.*
Nach einem Jahr hatte Maria über 725 000 Euro verdient.	*After a year, Maria had earned over 725,000 euros.*
Ich habe diesen Urlaub verdient.	*I've earned this vacation.*
In meinem Job als Tellerwäscher habe ich 1,85 Dollar die Stunde verdient.	*In my job as dishwasher, I earned $1.85 per hour.*
Früher habe ich mehr als jetzt verdient.	*I used to make more money than I do now.*
Stefan und Thomas verdienten Mitleid vom Publikum.	*Stefan and Thomas won the public's sympathy.*
Kann man als Klempner viel verdienen?	*Can you earn a lot as a plumber?*
Die Arbeiter verdienen ab Juli 2 % weniger als im Vorjahr.	*Beginning in July, the laborers will earn 2% less than last year.*
„Das habe ich mir verdient", sagte Jörg.	*"I've earned it for myself," said Jörg.*
Der Schauspieler hatte die Buhrufe wirklich verdient.	*The actor had really deserved the boos.*
Das Komitee hat unseren Respekt verdient.	*The committee deserves our respect.*

RELATED VERBS *see* **dienen** (123)

483 verdrießen *to irritate, annoy*

verdrießt · verdross · verdrossen strong verb

PRESENT

ich verdrieße	wir verdrießen
du verdrießt	ihr verdrießt
Sie verdrießen	Sie verdrießen
er/sie/es verdrießt	sie verdrießen

SIMPLE PAST

ich verdross	wir verdrossen
du verdrossest	ihr verdrosst
Sie verdrossen	Sie verdrossen
er/sie/es verdross	sie verdrossen

FUTURE

ich werde	wir werden	verdrießen
du wirst	ihr werdet	
Sie werden	Sie werden	
er/sie/es wird	sie werden	

PRESENT SUBJUNCTIVE I

ich verdrieße	wir verdrießen
du verdrießest	ihr verdrießet
Sie verdrießen	Sie verdrießen
er/sie/es verdrieße	sie verdrießen

PRESENT SUBJUNCTIVE II

ich verdrösse	wir verdrössen
du verdrössest	ihr verdrösset
Sie verdrössen	Sie verdrössen
er/sie/es verdrösse	sie verdrössen

FUTURE SUBJUNCTIVE I

ich werde	wir werden	verdrießen
du werdest	ihr werdet	
Sie werden	Sie werden	
er/sie/es werde	sie werden	

FUTURE SUBJUNCTIVE II

ich würde	wir würden	verdrießen
du würdest	ihr würdet	
Sie würden	Sie würden	
er/sie/es würde	sie würden	

PRESENT PERFECT

ich habe	wir haben	verdrossen
du hast	ihr habt	
Sie haben	Sie haben	
er/sie/es hat	sie haben	

PAST PERFECT

ich hatte	wir hatten	verdrossen
du hattest	ihr hattet	
Sie hatten	Sie hatten	
er/sie/es hatte	sie hatten	

FUTURE PERFECT

ich werde	wir werden	verdrossen haben
du wirst	ihr werdet	
Sie werden	Sie werden	
er/sie/es wird	sie werden	

PAST SUBJUNCTIVE I

ich habe	wir haben	verdrossen
du habest	ihr habet	
Sie haben	Sie haben	
er/sie/es habe	sie haben	

PAST SUBJUNCTIVE II

ich hätte	wir hätten	verdrossen
du hättest	ihr hättet	
Sie hätten	Sie hätten	
er/sie/es hätte	sie hätten	

FUTURE PERFECT SUBJUNCTIVE I

ich werde	wir werden	verdrossen haben
du werdest	ihr werdet	
Sie werden	Sie werden	
er/sie/es werde	sie werden	

FUTURE PERFECT SUBJUNCTIVE II

ich würde	wir würden	verdrossen haben
du würdest	ihr würdet	
Sie würden	Sie würden	
er/sie/es würde	sie würden	

COMMANDS verdrieß(e)! verdrießt! verdrießen Sie!

PRESENT PARTICIPLE verdrießend

Usage

Lass es dir nicht verdrießen.	*Don't be discouraged by it.*
Die Politik verdrießt mich.	*Politics irritates me.*
Reineken aber, den Dieb, verdross es, dass wir in Frieden glückliche Tage verlebten … (GOETHE)	*But Reineke the thief was annoyed that we lived happy days in peace …*
Es verdrießt mich, dass Uwe den wirklichen Grund nicht versteht.	*It aggravates me that Uwe doesn't understand the real reason.*
Es verdrießt mich an ihnen, dass sie sich wider dich setzen. (PSALMEN 139,21b)	*I am grieved with those who rise up against thee.* (PSALMS 139:21b)
Deine Gleichgültigkeit verdrießt deine Mutter.	*Your indifference displeases your mother.*
Das hat sie sehr verdrossen.	*That has irritated her greatly.*
Es verdross ihn, dass sein Nachbar ein neues Auto besaß.	*It annoyed him that his neighbor owned a new car.*
Lass dich die Mühe nicht verdrießen.	*Spare no effort.*
Vergib stets deinen Feinden, nichts verdrießt sie so. (PROVERB)	*Always forgive your enemies; nothing annoys them so much.*

strong verb

vergisst · vergaß · vergessen

PRESENT

ich vergesse	wir vergessen
du vergisst	ihr vergesst
Sie vergessen	Sie vergessen
er/sie/es vergisst	sie vergessen

SIMPLE PAST

ich vergaß	wir vergaßen
du vergaßest	ihr vergaßt
Sie vergaßen	Sie vergaßen
er/sie/es vergaß	sie vergaßen

FUTURE

ich werde	wir werden	vergessen
du wirst	ihr werdet	
Sie werden	Sie werden	
er/sie/es wird	sie werden	

PRESENT SUBJUNCTIVE I

ich vergesse	wir vergessen
du vergessest	ihr vergesset
Sie vergessen	Sie vergessen
er/sie/es vergesse	sie vergessen

PRESENT SUBJUNCTIVE II

ich vergäße	wir vergäßen
du vergäßest	ihr vergäßet
Sie vergäßen	Sie vergäßen
er/sie/es vergäße	sie vergäßen

FUTURE SUBJUNCTIVE I

ich werde	wir werden	vergessen
du werdest	ihr werdet	
Sie werden	Sie werden	
er/sie/es werde	sie werden	

FUTURE SUBJUNCTIVE II

ich würde	wir würden	vergessen
du würdest	ihr würdet	
Sie würden	Sie würden	
er/sie/es würde	sie würden	

PRESENT PERFECT

ich habe	wir haben	vergessen
du hast	ihr habt	
Sie haben	Sie haben	
er/sie/es hat	sie haben	

PAST PERFECT

ich hatte	wir hatten	vergessen
du hattest	ihr hattet	
Sie hatten	Sie hatten	
er/sie/es hatte	sie hatten	

FUTURE PERFECT

ich werde	wir werden	vergessen haben
du wirst	ihr werdet	
Sie werden	Sie werden	
er/sie/es wird	sie werden	

PAST SUBJUNCTIVE I

ich habe	wir haben	vergessen
du habest	ihr habet	
Sie haben	Sie haben	
er/sie/es habe	sie haben	

PAST SUBJUNCTIVE II

ich hätte	wir hätten	vergessen
du hättest	ihr hättet	
Sie hätten	Sie hätten	
er/sie/es hätte	sie hätten	

FUTURE PERFECT SUBJUNCTIVE I

ich werde	wir werden	vergessen haben
du werdest	ihr werdet	
Sie werden	Sie werden	
er/sie/es werde	sie werden	

FUTURE PERFECT SUBJUNCTIVE II

ich würde	wir würden	vergessen haben
du würdest	ihr würdet	
Sie würden	Sie würden	
er/sie/es würde	sie würden	

COMMANDS vergiss! vergesst! vergessen Sie!

PRESENT PARTICIPLE vergessend

Usage

Ingrid scheint den Termin vergessen zu haben.	*Ingrid seems to have forgotten the appointment.*
Georg will die Telefonnummer vergessen haben.	*Georg claims to have forgotten the telephone number.*
Ich werde die Erlebnisse nie vergessen.	*I will never forget the experiences.*
Das Kind hat seine Angst vergessen und stundenlang gespielt.	*The child forgot his fear and played for hours.*
Nach einem Monat hatte man ihn völlig vergessen.	*After one month, they had completely forgotten him.*
Vergiss es!	*Forget it!*
Ich habe den Aufsatz verloren aber nicht vergessen.	*I've lost the essay but not forgotten it.*
Papa hat Mamas Geburtstag vergessen.	*Papa forgot Mama's birthday.*
Kurt pflegt immer zu sagen: „Hab's vergessen."	*Kurt is always wont to say, "It slipped my mind."*
Ach du lieber, wir haben die Kinder vergessen!	*Oh dear, we've left the children behind!*
Den neuen Film kann man getrost vergessen.	*You can safely ignore the new film.*
Alte Kuh gar leicht vergisst, dass sie ein Kalb gewesen ist. (PROVERB)	*We easily forget that we were young once.*

485 vergleichen *to compare*

vergleicht · verglich · verglichen strong verb

PRESENT			PRESENT PERFECT		
ich vergleiche	wir vergleichen		ich habe	wir haben	verglichen
du vergleichst	ihr vergleicht		du hast	ihr habt	
Sie vergleichen	Sie vergleichen		Sie haben	Sie haben	
er/sie/es vergleicht	sie vergleichen		er/sie/es hat	sie haben	

SIMPLE PAST			PAST PERFECT		
ich verglich	wir verglichen		ich hatte	wir hatten	verglichen
du verglichst	ihr verglicht		du hattest	ihr hattet	
Sie verglichen	Sie verglichen		Sie hatten	Sie hatten	
er/sie/es verglich	sie verglichen		er/sie/es hatte	sie hatten	

FUTURE			FUTURE PERFECT		
ich werde	wir werden	vergleichen	ich werde	wir werden	verglichen haben
du wirst	ihr werdet		du wirst	ihr werdet	
Sie werden	Sie werden		Sie werden	Sie werden	
er/sie/es wird	sie werden		er/sie/es wird	sie werden	

PRESENT SUBJUNCTIVE I			PAST SUBJUNCTIVE I		
ich vergleiche	wir vergleichen		ich habe	wir haben	verglichen
du vergleichest	ihr vergleichet		du habest	ihr habet	
Sie vergleichen	Sie vergleichen		Sie haben	Sie haben	
er/sie/es vergleiche	sie vergleichen		er/sie/es habe	sie haben	

PRESENT SUBJUNCTIVE II			PAST SUBJUNCTIVE II		
ich vergliche	wir verglichen		ich hätte	wir hätten	verglichen
du verglichest	ihr verglichet		du hättest	ihr hättet	
Sie verglichen	Sie verglichen		Sie hätten	Sie hätten	
er/sie/es vergliche	sie verglichen		er/sie/es hätte	sie hätten	

FUTURE SUBJUNCTIVE I			FUTURE PERFECT SUBJUNCTIVE I		
ich werde	wir werden	vergleichen	ich werde	wir werden	verglichen haben
du werdest	ihr werdet		du werdest	ihr werdet	
Sie werden	Sie werden		Sie werden	Sie werden	
er/sie/es werde	sie werden		er/sie/es werde	sie werden	

FUTURE SUBJUNCTIVE II			FUTURE PERFECT SUBJUNCTIVE II		
ich würde	wir würden	vergleichen	ich würde	wir würden	verglichen haben
du würdest	ihr würdet		du würdest	ihr würdet	
Sie würden	Sie würden		Sie würden	Sie würden	
er/sie/es würde	sie würden		er/sie/es würde	sie würden	

COMMANDS vergleich(e)! vergleicht! vergleichen Sie!

PRESENT PARTICIPLE vergleichend

Usage

Warum vergleichst du mich mit deiner Exfrau?	*Why are you comparing me with your ex-wife?*
Die Flughäfen sind nicht zu vergleichen.	*The airports are not comparable.*
Der Detektiv vergleicht die Fingerabdrücke.	*The detective is comparing the fingerprints.*
Vor Bestellung vergleichen wir die Kaffeesorten.	*Before we order, let's compare the types of coffee.*
Vergleichen Sie die Preise.	*Compare prices. / Shop around.*
Vergleicht das Motiv Rache im *Nibelungenlied* mit dem Begriff Gerechtigkeit.	*Compare the motif of vengeance in the* Lay of the Nibelung *with the concept of justice.*
Wir haben 12 Autos miteinander verglichen.	*We compared 12 cars with one other.*
Du darfst die Kinder nicht vergleichen.	*You can't compare the children.*
Man soll nicht Äpfel mit Birnen vergleichen. (*figurative*)	*You shouldn't compare apples and oranges.*

sich vergleichen *to compete; settle*

Der Sportler verglich sich mit seinem Gegner.	*The athlete competed against his opponent.*
Die Beteiligten haben sich vor Gericht verglichen.	*The parties settled in court.*

RELATED VERBS *see* **gleichen** (222)

regular weak verb **verhaftet · verhaftete · verhaftet**

PRESENT

ich verhafte	wir verhaften
du verhaftest	ihr verhaftet
Sie verhaften	Sie verhaften
er/sie/es verhaftet	sie verhaften

PRESENT PERFECT

ich habe	wir haben	verhaftet
du hast	ihr habt	
Sie haben	Sie haben	
er/sie/es hat	sie haben	

SIMPLE PAST

ich verhaftete	wir verhafteten
du verhaftetest	ihr verhaftetet
Sie verhafteten	Sie verhafteten
er/sie/es verhaftete	sie verhafteten

PAST PERFECT

ich hatte	wir hatten	verhaftet
du hattest	ihr hattet	
Sie hatten	Sie hatten	
er/sie/es hatte	sie hatten	

FUTURE

ich werde	wir werden	verhaften
du wirst	ihr werdet	
Sie werden	Sie werden	
er/sie/es wird	sie werden	

FUTURE PERFECT

ich werde	wir werden	verhaftet haben
du wirst	ihr werdet	
Sie werden	Sie werden	
er/sie/es wird	sie werden	

PRESENT SUBJUNCTIVE I

ich verhafte	wir verhaften
du verhaftest	ihr verhaftet
Sie verhaften	Sie verhaften
er/sie/es verhafte	sie verhaften

PAST SUBJUNCTIVE I

ich habe	wir haben	verhaftet
du habest	ihr habet	
Sie haben	Sie haben	
er/sie/es habe	sie haben	

PRESENT SUBJUNCTIVE II

ich verhaftete	wir verhafteten
du verhaftetest	ihr verhaftetet
Sie verhafteten	Sie verhafteten
er/sie/es verhaftete	sie verhafteten

PAST SUBJUNCTIVE II

ich hätte	wir hätten	verhaftet
du hättest	ihr hättet	
Sie hätten	Sie hätten	
er/sie/es hätte	sie hätten	

FUTURE SUBJUNCTIVE I

ich werde	wir werden	verhaften
du werdest	ihr werdet	
Sie werden	Sie werden	
er/sie/es werde	sie werden	

FUTURE PERFECT SUBJUNCTIVE I

ich werde	wir werden	verhaftet haben
du werdest	ihr werdet	
Sie werden	Sie werden	
er/sie/es werde	sie werden	

FUTURE SUBJUNCTIVE II

ich würde	wir würden	verhaften
du würdest	ihr würdet	
Sie würden	Sie würden	
er/sie/es würde	sie würden	

FUTURE PERFECT SUBJUNCTIVE II

ich würde	wir würden	verhaftet haben
du würdest	ihr würdet	
Sie würden	Sie würden	
er/sie/es würde	sie würden	

COMMANDS verhafte! verhaftet! verhaften Sie!

PRESENT PARTICIPLE verhaftend

Usage

Herr Iwanowitsch wird wegen Mordverdacht verhaftet.	*Mr. Ivanovich is being arrested on suspicion of murder.*
Die Täter sind noch nicht verhaftet worden.	*The perpetrators have not yet been apprehended.*
Die Polizei verhaftete zwei italienische Journalisten.	*The police arrested two Italian journalists.*
Unser Nachbar wurde wegen Drogenhandel verhaftet.	*Our neighbor was busted for dealing drugs.*
Der König ließ die Prinzessin verhaften.	*The king had the princess placed in confinement.*
Wurden Bonnie und Clyde endlich verhaftet?	*Were Bonnie and Clyde finally arrested?*
Dank Ihrer Arbeit wurden die Terroristen verhaftet.	*Thanks to your work, the terrorists were apprehended.*
Nach Pearl Harbor wurden über 100 000 Amerikaner verhaftet, weil sie japanischer Herkunft waren.	*After Pearl Harbor, more than 100,000 Americans were taken into custody because they were of Japanese heritage.*
Herr Sayyed ist ohne Grund verhaftet und ins Gefängnis gesteckt worden.	*Mr. Sayyed was arrested without reason and imprisoned.*
Ursula war der Idee verhaftet, dass holländische Tomaten besser schmecken. (*figurative*)	*Ursula was obsessed with the idea that Dutch tomatoes taste better.*

RELATED VERB haften

487 verhalten *to hold back, restrain*

verhält · verhielt · verhalten strong verb

PRESENT

ich verhalte	wir verhalten
du verhältst	ihr verhaltet
Sie verhalten	Sie verhalten
er/sie/es verhält	sie verhalten

SIMPLE PAST

ich verhielt	wir verhielten
du verhieltst	ihr verhieltet
Sie verhielten	Sie verhielten
er/sie/es verhielt	sie verhielten

FUTURE

ich werde	wir werden	verhalten
du wirst	ihr werdet	
Sie werden	Sie werden	
er/sie/es wird	sie werden	

PRESENT SUBJUNCTIVE I

ich verhalte	wir verhalten
du verhaltest	ihr verhaltet
Sie verhalten	Sie verhalten
er/sie/es verhalte	sie verhalten

PRESENT SUBJUNCTIVE II

ich verhielte	wir verhielten
du verhieltest	ihr verhieltet
Sie verhielten	Sie verhielten
er/sie/es verhielte	sie verhielten

FUTURE SUBJUNCTIVE I

ich werde	wir werden	verhalten
du werdest	ihr werdet	
Sie werden	Sie werden	
er/sie/es werde	sie werden	

FUTURE SUBJUNCTIVE II

ich würde	wir würden	verhalten
du würdest	ihr würdet	
Sie würden	Sie würden	
er/sie/es würde	sie würden	

PRESENT PERFECT

ich habe	wir haben	verhalten
du hast	ihr habt	
Sie haben	Sie haben	
er/sie/es hat	sie haben	

PAST PERFECT

ich hatte	wir hatten	verhalten
du hattest	ihr hattet	
Sie hatten	Sie hatten	
er/sie/es hatte	sie hatten	

FUTURE PERFECT

ich werde	wir werden	verhalten haben
du wirst	ihr werdet	
Sie werden	Sie werden	
er/sie/es wird	sie werden	

PAST SUBJUNCTIVE I

ich habe	wir haben	verhalten
du habest	ihr habet	
Sie haben	Sie haben	
er/sie/es habe	sie haben	

PAST SUBJUNCTIVE II

ich hätte	wir hätten	verhalten
du hättest	ihr hättet	
Sie hätten	Sie hätten	
er/sie/es hätte	sie hätten	

FUTURE PERFECT SUBJUNCTIVE I

ich werde	wir werden	verhalten haben
du werdest	ihr werdet	
Sie werden	Sie werden	
er/sie/es werde	sie werden	

FUTURE PERFECT SUBJUNCTIVE II

ich würde	wir würden	verhalten haben
du würdest	ihr würdet	
Sie würden	Sie würden	
er/sie/es würde	sie würden	

COMMANDS verhalte! verhaltet! verhalten Sie!

PRESENT PARTICIPLE verhaltend

Usage

Ich musste das Lachen verhalten.	*I had to stifle my laughter.*
Können Sie den Zorn verhalten?	*Can you contain your anger?*

sich verhalten *to behave, react, act*

Verhältst du dich immer so?	*So you always behave like this?*
Sie hat sich ihm gegenüber fair verhalten.	*She treated him fairly.*
Wie verhält sich euer Hund in Gesellschaft anderer Hunde?	*How does your dog behave in the presence of other dogs?*
Viele Patienten verhalten sich wesentlich anders.	*Many patients behave substantially differently.*
Die Kinder verhielten sich relativ ruhig.	*The children reacted relatively calmly.*
Mein Sohn verhält sich so, als ob er mich gar nicht kennen würde.	*My son acts as though he doesn't even know me.*
X verhält sich zu *Y* wie π zu 3.	X *is to* Y *as* π *is to 3.*

RELATED VERBS *see* **halten** (231)

regular weak verb **verhandelt · verhandelte · verhandelt**

PRESENT

ich verhand(e)le	wir verhandeln
du verhandelst	ihr verhandelt
Sie verhandeln	Sie verhandeln
er/sie/es verhandelt	sie verhandeln

PRESENT PERFECT

ich habe	wir haben	verhandelt
du hast	ihr habt	
Sie haben	Sie haben	
er/sie/es hat	sie haben	

SIMPLE PAST

ich verhandelte	wir verhandelten
du verhandeltest	ihr verhandeltet
Sie verhandelten	Sie verhandelten
er/sie/es verhandelte	sie verhandelten

PAST PERFECT

ich hatte	wir hatten	verhandelt
du hattest	ihr hattet	
Sie hatten	Sie hatten	
er/sie/es hatte	sie hatten	

FUTURE

ich werde	wir werden	verhandeln
du wirst	ihr werdet	
Sie werden	Sie werden	
er/sie/es wird	sie werden	

FUTURE PERFECT

ich werde	wir werden	verhandelt haben
du wirst	ihr werdet	
Sie werden	Sie werden	
er/sie/es wird	sie werden	

PRESENT SUBJUNCTIVE I

ich verhand(e)le	wir verhandeln
du verhandelst	ihr verhandelt
Sie verhandeln	Sie verhandeln
er/sie/es verhand(e)le	sie verhandeln

PAST SUBJUNCTIVE I

ich habe	wir haben	verhandelt
du habest	ihr habet	
Sie haben	Sie haben	
er/sie/es habe	sie haben	

PRESENT SUBJUNCTIVE II

ich verhandelte	wir verhandelten
du verhandeltest	ihr verhandeltet
Sie verhandelten	Sie verhandelten
er/sie/es verhandelte	sie verhandelten

PAST SUBJUNCTIVE II

ich hätte	wir hätten	verhandelt
du hättest	ihr hättet	
Sie hätten	Sie hätten	
er/sie/es hätte	sie hätten	

FUTURE SUBJUNCTIVE I

ich werde	wir werden	verhandeln
du werdest	ihr werdet	
Sie werden	Sie werden	
er/sie/es werde	sie werden	

FUTURE PERFECT SUBJUNCTIVE I

ich werde	wir werden	verhandelt haben
du werdest	ihr werdet	
Sie werden	Sie werden	
er/sie/es werde	sie werden	

FUTURE SUBJUNCTIVE II

ich würde	wir würden	verhandeln
du würdest	ihr würdet	
Sie würden	Sie würden	
er/sie/es würde	sie würden	

FUTURE PERFECT SUBJUNCTIVE II

ich würde	wir würden	verhandelt haben
du würdest	ihr würdet	
Sie würden	Sie würden	
er/sie/es würde	sie würden	

COMMANDS verhand(e)le! verhandelt! verhandeln Sie!

PRESENT PARTICIPLE verhandelnd

Usage

Die Außenminister verhandelten über ein Ende des Konflikts. — *The foreign ministers were negotiating an end to the conflict.*

Ich verhandele nicht gern. — *I don't like to negotiate.*

Die Firmen sollen über eine Fusion verhandelt haben. — *The companies are supposed to have negotiated a merger.*

Der Vorsitzende hat mit dem Vorstand über seinen Rücktritt verhandelt. — *The chairman negotiated his resignation with the board.*

Der Schriftsteller verhandelt mit einem Verlag. — *The writer is negotiating with a publisher.*

Die Opfer verhandeln mit der Regierung über Schadenersatz. — *The victims are negotiating with the government over compensatory damages.*

Wir verhandeln fair mit Ihnen. — *We will treat you fairly.*

Auf dem Flohmarkt kann man über den Preis verhandeln. — *At the flea market, you can haggle over price.*

Gegen Frau Pritschow wird wegen Steuerhinterziehung verhandelt. — *Mrs. Pritchov is being tried for tax evasion.*

RELATED VERBS *see* **handeln** (232)

489 sich verheiraten *to marry, get married*

verheiratet sich · verheiratete sich · sich verheiratet regular weak verb

PRESENT

ich verheirate mich	wir verheiraten uns
du verheiratest dich	ihr verheiratet euch
Sie verheiraten sich	Sie verheiraten sich
er/sie/es verheiratet sich	sie verheiraten sich

PRESENT PERFECT

ich habe mich	wir haben uns	verheiratet
du hast dich	ihr habt euch	
Sie haben sich	Sie haben sich	
er/sie/es hat sich	sie haben sich	

SIMPLE PAST

ich verheiratete mich	wir verheirateten uns
du verheiratetest dich	ihr verheiratetet euch
Sie verheirateten sich	Sie verheirateten sich
er/sie/es verheiratete sich	sie verheirateten sich

PAST PERFECT

ich hatte mich	wir hatten uns	verheiratet
du hattest dich	ihr hattet euch	
Sie hatten sich	Sie hatten sich	
er/sie/es hatte sich	sie hatten sich	

FUTURE

ich werde mich	wir werden uns	verheiraten
du wirst dich	ihr werdet euch	
Sie werden sich	Sie werden sich	
er/sie/es wird sich	sie werden sich	

FUTURE PERFECT

ich werde mich	wir werden uns	verheiratet haben
du wirst dich	ihr werdet euch	
Sie werden sich	Sie werden sich	
er/sie/es wird sich	sie werden sich	

PRESENT SUBJUNCTIVE I

ich verheirate mich	wir verheiraten uns
du verheiratest dich	ihr verheiratet euch
Sie verheiraten sich	Sie verheiraten sich
er/sie/es verheirate sich	sie verheiraten sich

PAST SUBJUNCTIVE I

ich habe mich	wir haben uns	verheiratet
du habest dich	ihr habet euch	
Sie haben sich	Sie haben sich	
er/sie/es habe sich	sie haben sich	

PRESENT SUBJUNCTIVE II

ich verheiratete mich	wir verheirateten uns
du verheiratetest dich	ihr verheiratetet euch
Sie verheirateten sich	Sie verheirateten sich
er/sie/es verheiratete sich	sie verheirateten sich

PAST SUBJUNCTIVE II

ich hätte mich	wir hätten uns	verheiratet
du hättest dich	ihr hättet euch	
Sie hätten sich	Sie hätten sich	
er/sie/es hätte sich	sie hätten sich	

FUTURE SUBJUNCTIVE I

ich werde mich	wir werden uns	verheiraten
du werdest dich	ihr werdet euch	
Sie werden sich	Sie werden sich	
er/sie/es werde sich	sie werden sich	

FUTURE PERFECT SUBJUNCTIVE I

ich werde mich	wir werden uns	verheiratet haben
du werdest dich	ihr werdet euch	
Sie werden sich	Sie werden sich	
er/sie/es werde sich	sie werden sich	

FUTURE SUBJUNCTIVE II

ich würde mich	wir würden uns	verheiraten
du würdest dich	ihr würdet euch	
Sie würden sich	Sie würden sich	
er/sie/es würde sich	sie würden sich	

FUTURE PERFECT SUBJUNCTIVE II

ich würde mich	wir würden uns	verheiratet haben
du würdest dich	ihr würdet euch	
Sie würden sich	Sie würden sich	
er/sie/es würde sich	sie würden sich	

COMMANDS verheirate dich! verheiratet euch! verheiraten Sie sich!

PRESENT PARTICIPLE sich verheiratend

Usage

Lars Wolfrum verheiratete sich mit Elisabeth Becker aus Donaueschingen. — *Lars Wolfrum married Elisabeth Becker from Donaueschingen.*

Annalies hat sich mit einem Engländer verheiratet. — *Annalies married an Englishman.*

„Hat sie geheiratet?“ — *“Has she married?”*

„Nein, sie ist immer noch nicht verheiratet.“ — *“No, she's still not married.”*

Bernd ist mit seinem Beruf verheiratet. (*figurative*) — *Bernd is married to his career.*

Frisch verheiratet. — *Just married.*

Du verheiratest dich doch so bald nicht. (Goethe) — *But you won't be getting married that soon.*

Die junge Witwe verheiratete sich 1995 wieder. — *The young widow remarried in 1995.*

verheiraten *to give in marriage*

Jost Jäger verheiratete seine Tochter Amalie an einen wohlhabenden Bürger aus Aschersleben. — *Jost Jäger gave his daughter Amalie in marriage to a wealthy citizen from Aschersleben.*

RELATED VERBS *see* **heiraten** (238)

regular weak verb **verhindert · verhinderte · verhindert**

PRESENT		PRESENT PERFECT		
ich verhindere	wir verhindern	ich habe	wir haben	verhindert
du verhinderst	ihr verhindert	du hast	ihr habt	
Sie verhindern	Sie verhindern	Sie haben	Sie haben	
er/sie/es verhindert	sie verhindern	er/sie/es hat	sie haben	

SIMPLE PAST		PAST PERFECT		
ich verhinderte	wir verhinderten	ich hatte	wir hatten	verhindert
du verhindertest	ihr verhindertet	du hattest	ihr hattet	
Sie verhinderten	Sie verhinderten	Sie hatten	Sie hatten	
er/sie/es verhinderte	sie verhinderten	er/sie/es hatte	sie hatten	

FUTURE			FUTURE PERFECT		
ich werde	wir werden	verhindern	ich werde	wir werden	verhindert haben
du wirst	ihr werdet		du wirst	ihr werdet	
Sie werden	Sie werden		Sie werden	Sie werden	
er/sie/es wird	sie werden		er/sie/es wird	sie werden	

PRESENT SUBJUNCTIVE I		PAST SUBJUNCTIVE I		
ich verhindere	wir verhindern	ich habe	wir haben	verhindert
du verhinderst	ihr verhindert	du habest	ihr habet	
Sie verhindern	Sie verhindern	Sie haben	Sie haben	
er/sie/es verhindere	sie verhindern	er/sie/es habe	sie haben	

PRESENT SUBJUNCTIVE II		PAST SUBJUNCTIVE II		
ich verhinderte	wir verhinderten	ich hätte	wir hätten	verhindert
du verhindertest	ihr verhindertet	du hättest	ihr hättet	
Sie verhinderten	Sie verhinderten	Sie hätten	Sie hätten	
er/sie/es verhinderte	sie verhinderten	er/sie/es hätte	sie hätten	

FUTURE SUBJUNCTIVE I			FUTURE PERFECT SUBJUNCTIVE I		
ich werde	wir werden	verhindern	ich werde	wir werden	verhindert haben
du werdest	ihr werdet		du werdest	ihr werdet	
Sie werden	Sie werden		Sie werden	Sie werden	
er/sie/es werde	sie werden		er/sie/es werde	sie werden	

FUTURE SUBJUNCTIVE II			FUTURE PERFECT SUBJUNCTIVE II		
ich würde	wir würden	verhindern	ich würde	wir würden	verhindert haben
du würdest	ihr würdet		du würdest	ihr würdet	
Sie würden	Sie würden		Sie würden	Sie würden	
er/sie/es würde	sie würden		er/sie/es würde	sie würden	

COMMANDS verhindere! verhindert! verhindern Sie!

PRESENT PARTICIPLE verhindernd

Usage

Die neue Regelung hat offene Diskussionen verhindert.	*The new rule has hampered open discussions.*
Der Bau des Denkmals wurde kurzfristig verhindert.	*Construction of the monument was stopped momentarily.*
Wie hätte Krieg verhindert werden können?	*How could war have been averted?*
Bürgerproteste könnten sein Vorhaben verhindert haben.	*Citizen protests could have frustrated his plan.*
Ich konnte ihn nicht verhindern.	*I was unable to stop him.*
Wir wollen verhindern, dass Zivilisten getötet werden.	*We want to prevent civilians from being killed.*
Dank seiner Aufmerksamkeit wurde ein zweiter Mord verhindert.	*Thanks to his attentiveness, a second murder was averted.*
Durch die heutige Lösung wird ein offener Konflikt verhindert.	*Today's solution heads off an open conflict.*
Neue Maßnahmen sollen weitere Anschläge verhindern.	*New measures are supposed to prevent further attacks.*
Es lässt sich nicht mehr verhindern, dass er selbst hingeht.	*He can no longer be prevented from going there himself.*
Das verhindert Missbrauch Ihres Kennworts durch Dritte.	*This prevents misuse of your password by third parties.*

RELATED VERBS hindern; *see also* **behindern** (64)

491 verkaufen *to sell*

verkauft · verkaufte · verkauft regular weak verb

PRESENT		PRESENT PERFECT		
ich verkaufe	wir verkaufen	ich habe	wir haben	verkauft
du verkaufst	ihr verkauft	du hast	ihr habt	
Sie verkaufen	Sie verkaufen	Sie haben	Sie haben	
er/sie/es verkauft	sie verkaufen	er/sie/es hat	sie haben	

SIMPLE PAST		PAST PERFECT		
ich verkaufte	wir verkauften	ich hatte	wir hatten	verkauft
du verkauftest	ihr verkauftet	du hattest	ihr hattet	
Sie verkauften	Sie verkauften	Sie hatten	Sie hatten	
er/sie/es verkaufte	sie verkauften	er/sie/es hatte	sie hatten	

FUTURE			FUTURE PERFECT		
ich werde	wir werden	verkaufen	ich werde	wir werden	verkauft haben
du wirst	ihr werdet		du wirst	ihr werdet	
Sie werden	Sie werden		Sie werden	Sie werden	
er/sie/es wird	sie werden		er/sie/es wird	sie werden	

PRESENT SUBJUNCTIVE I		PAST SUBJUNCTIVE I		
ich verkaufe	wir verkaufen	ich habe	wir haben	verkauft
du verkaufest	ihr verkaufet	du habest	ihr habet	
Sie verkaufen	Sie verkaufen	Sie haben	Sie haben	
er/sie/es verkaufe	sie verkaufen	er/sie/es habe	sie haben	

PRESENT SUBJUNCTIVE II		PAST SUBJUNCTIVE II		
ich verkaufte	wir verkauften	ich hätte	wir hätten	verkauft
du verkauftest	ihr verkauftet	du hättest	ihr hättet	
Sie verkauften	Sie verkauften	Sie hätten	Sie hätten	
er/sie/es verkaufte	sie verkauften	er/sie/es hätte	sie hätten	

FUTURE SUBJUNCTIVE I			FUTURE PERFECT SUBJUNCTIVE I		
ich werde	wir werden	verkaufen	ich werde	wir werden	verkauft haben
du werdest	ihr werdet		du werdest	ihr werdet	
Sie werden	Sie werden		Sie werden	Sie werden	
er/sie/es werde	sie werden		er/sie/es werde	sie werden	

FUTURE SUBJUNCTIVE II			FUTURE PERFECT SUBJUNCTIVE II		
ich würde	wir würden	verkaufen	ich würde	wir würden	verkauft haben
du würdest	ihr würdet		du würdest	ihr würdet	
Sie würden	Sie würden		Sie würden	Sie würden	
er/sie/es würde	sie würden		er/sie/es würde	sie würden	

COMMANDS verkauf(e)! verkauft! verkaufen Sie!

PRESENT PARTICIPLE verkaufend

Usage

Wir verkaufen zu günstigen Preisen.	*We sell at reasonable prices.*
Firma Rössler verkauft Autozubehör.	*The Rössler Company sells auto accessories.*
Er will seinem Nachbarn eine Lokomotive verkauft haben!	*He claims to have sold his neighbor a locomotive!*
Friedrich hat seinen ersten Roman an einen Verlag verkauft.	*Friedrich has sold his first novel to a publisher.*
Onkel Heinz verkauft seinen alten Mercedes.	*Uncle Heinz is selling his old Mercedes.*
Die Eigentümer wollten das Grundstück für 250 000 Euro verkaufen.	*The owners wanted to sell the property for 250,000 euros.*
Verkaufst du mir deine Bücher?	*Will you sell me your books?*
Werner wird seine Aktien nicht verkaufen.	*Werner will not dispose of his shares.*
Damals wurden Frauen und Kinder in die Sklaverei verkauft.	*Back then, women and children were sold into slavery.*
Das neue Modell verkauft sich sehr gut.	*The new model is selling very well.*
Ich musste meinen alten Computer für ein Butterbrot verkaufen.	*I had to sell my old computer for next to nothing* (lit., *for buttered bread*).

RELATED VERBS aus·verkaufen, weiter·verkaufen; *see also* **kaufen** (253)

regular weak verb **verlangt · verlangte · verlangt**

PRESENT

ich verlange	wir verlangen
du verlangst	ihr verlangt
Sie verlangen	Sie verlangen
er/sie/es verlangt	sie verlangen

SIMPLE PAST

ich verlangte	wir verlangten
du verlangtest	ihr verlangtet
Sie verlangten	Sie verlangten
er/sie/es verlangte	sie verlangten

FUTURE

ich werde	wir werden	verlangen
du wirst	ihr werdet	
Sie werden	Sie werden	
er/sie/es wird	sie werden	

PRESENT SUBJUNCTIVE I

ich verlange	wir verlangen
du verlangest	ihr verlanget
Sie verlangen	Sie verlangen
er/sie/es verlange	sie verlangen

PRESENT SUBJUNCTIVE II

ich verlangte	wir verlangten
du verlangtest	ihr verlangtet
Sie verlangten	Sie verlangten
er/sie/es verlangte	sie verlangten

FUTURE SUBJUNCTIVE I

ich werde	wir werden	verlangen
du werdest	ihr werdet	
Sie werden	Sie werden	
er/sie/es werde	sie werden	

FUTURE SUBJUNCTIVE II

ich würde	wir würden	verlangen
du würdest	ihr würdet	
Sie würden	Sie würden	
er/sie/es würde	sie würden	

PRESENT PERFECT

ich habe	wir haben	verlangt
du hast	ihr habt	
Sie haben	Sie haben	
er/sie/es hat	sie haben	

PAST PERFECT

ich hatte	wir hatten	verlangt
du hattest	ihr hattet	
Sie hatten	Sie hatten	
er/sie/es hatte	sie hatten	

FUTURE PERFECT

ich werde	wir werden	verlangt haben
du wirst	ihr werdet	
Sie werden	Sie werden	
er/sie/es wird	sie werden	

PAST SUBJUNCTIVE I

ich habe	wir haben	verlangt
du habest	ihr habet	
Sie haben	Sie haben	
er/sie/es habe	sie haben	

PAST SUBJUNCTIVE II

ich hätte	wir hätten	verlangt
du hättest	ihr hättet	
Sie hätten	Sie hätten	
er/sie/es hätte	sie hätten	

FUTURE PERFECT SUBJUNCTIVE I

ich werde	wir werden	verlangt haben
du werdest	ihr werdet	
Sie werden	Sie werden	
er/sie/es werde	sie werden	

FUTURE PERFECT SUBJUNCTIVE II

ich würde	wir würden	verlangt haben
du würdest	ihr würdet	
Sie würden	Sie würden	
er/sie/es würde	sie würden	

COMMANDS verlang(e)! verlangt! verlangen Sie!

PRESENT PARTICIPLE verlangend

Usage

Was verlangen Sie von mir?	*What do you want from me?*
Der Vorstand verlangt den Rücktritt des Vorsitzenden.	*The board is demanding the resignation of the chairman.*
Das Volk verlangt ein gerechteres Steuersystem.	*The people want a more just tax system.*
Auf dem Bauernhof wurde ziemlich viel Arbeit von mir verlangt.	*On the farm, quite a bit of work was required of me.*
Darf mein Vermieter verlangen, dass ich ein neues Dach bezahle?	*Can my landlord require me to pay for a new roof?*
Der Anwalt verlangt 200 Euro die Stunde.	*The lawyer charges 200 euros an hour.*
Gabis Friseur verlangt 15 Euro für einen Haarschnitt.	*Gabi's hairdresser charges 15 euros for a haircut.*
Das ist zu viel verlangt.	*That's asking too much.*
Mehr kann man nicht verlangen!	*You can't ask for more than that!*
Der Fahrer des verunglückten Fahrzeuges verlangt Schadenersatz.	*The driver of the wrecked vehicle is seeking damages.*

RELATED VERBS ab·verlangen, langen, zurück·verlangen

493 verlassen *to leave, forsake, abandon*

verlässt · verließ · verlassen strong verb

PRESENT

ich verlasse	wir verlassen
du verlässt	ihr verlasst
Sie verlassen	Sie verlassen
er/sie/es verlässt	sie verlassen

SIMPLE PAST

ich verließ	wir verließen
du verließest	ihr verließt
Sie verließen	Sie verließen
er/sie/es verließ	sie verließen

FUTURE

ich werde	wir werden	verlassen
du wirst	ihr werdet	
Sie werden	Sie werden	
er/sie/es wird	sie werden	

PRESENT SUBJUNCTIVE I

ich verlasse	wir verlassen
du verlassest	ihr verlasset
Sie verlassen	Sie verlassen
er/sie/es verlasse	sie verlassen

PRESENT SUBJUNCTIVE II

ich verließe	wir verließen
du verließest	ihr verließet
Sie verließen	Sie verließen
er/sie/es verließe	sie verließen

FUTURE SUBJUNCTIVE I

ich werde	wir werden	verlassen
du werdest	ihr werdet	
Sie werden	Sie werden	
er/sie/es werde	sie werden	

FUTURE SUBJUNCTIVE II

ich würde	wir würden	verlassen
du würdest	ihr würdet	
Sie würden	Sie würden	
er/sie/es würde	sie würden	

PRESENT PERFECT

ich habe	wir haben	verlassen
du hast	ihr habt	
Sie haben	Sie haben	
er/sie/es hat	sie haben	

PAST PERFECT

ich hatte	wir hatten	verlassen
du hattest	ihr hattet	
Sie hatten	Sie hatten	
er/sie/es hatte	sie hatten	

FUTURE PERFECT

ich werde	wir werden	verlassen haben
du wirst	ihr werdet	
Sie werden	Sie werden	
er/sie/es wird	sie werden	

PAST SUBJUNCTIVE I

ich habe	wir haben	verlassen
du habest	ihr habet	
Sie haben	Sie haben	
er/sie/es habe	sie haben	

PAST SUBJUNCTIVE II

ich hätte	wir hätten	verlassen
du hättest	ihr hättet	
Sie hätten	Sie hätten	
er/sie/es hätte	sie hätten	

FUTURE PERFECT SUBJUNCTIVE I

ich werde	wir werden	verlassen haben
du werdest	ihr werdet	
Sie werden	Sie werden	
er/sie/es werde	sie werden	

FUTURE PERFECT SUBJUNCTIVE II

ich würde	wir würden	verlassen haben
du würdest	ihr würdet	
Sie würden	Sie würden	
er/sie/es würde	sie würden	

COMMANDS verlass(e)! verlasst! verlassen Sie!

PRESENT PARTICIPLE verlassend

Usage

Hast du deine Frau verlassen? — *Did you leave your wife?*
Wir mussten wegen eines Unfalls die Autobahn verlassen. — *We had to get off the autobahn because of an accident.*
Viele Intellektuellen verließen Deutschland nach der Machtergreifung der Nationalsozialisten. — *Many intellectuals left Germany after the National Socialists seized power.*
Nach dem Krieg wurden die deutschen Einwohner aufgefordert, das Sudetenland zu verlassen. — *After the war, the German inhabitants were ordered to leave the Sudeten region.*
Bodo verlässt seine Wohnung jeden Morgen um sieben. — *Bodo leaves his apartment every morning at seven.*

sich verlassen *to rely, depend*

Ich verlasse mich auf dich! — *I'm relying on you!*
Besonders kleine Kinder verlassen sich auf ihre Eltern. — *Small children, especially, rely on their parents.*
Darauf können Sie sich verlassen. — *You can count on that.*
Verlasst euch nicht auf Gewalt. (Psalmen 62,10) — *Trust not in oppression.* (Psalms 62:10)

RELATED VERBS *see* **lassen (280)**

regular weak verb **verletzt · verletzte · verletzt**

PRESENT

ich verletze	wir verletzen
du verletzt	ihr verletzt
Sie verletzen	Sie verletzen
er/sie/es verletzt	sie verletzen

PRESENT PERFECT

ich habe	wir haben	verletzt
du hast	ihr habt	
Sie haben	Sie haben	
er/sie/es hat	sie haben	

SIMPLE PAST

ich verletzte	wir verletzten
du verletztest	ihr verletztet
Sie verletzten	Sie verletzten
er/sie/es verletzte	sie verletzten

PAST PERFECT

ich hatte	wir hatten	verletzt
du hattest	ihr hattet	
Sie hatten	Sie hatten	
er/sie/es hatte	sie hatten	

FUTURE

ich werde	wir werden	verletzen
du wirst	ihr werdet	
Sie werden	Sie werden	
er/sie/es wird	sie werden	

FUTURE PERFECT

ich werde	wir werden	verletzt haben
du wirst	ihr werdet	
Sie werden	Sie werden	
er/sie/es wird	sie werden	

PRESENT SUBJUNCTIVE I

ich verletze	wir verletzen
du verletzest	ihr verletzet
Sie verletzen	Sie verletzen
er/sie/es verletze	sie verletzen

PAST SUBJUNCTIVE I

ich habe	wir haben	verletzt
du habest	ihr habet	
Sie haben	Sie haben	
er/sie/es habe	sie haben	

PRESENT SUBJUNCTIVE II

ich verletzte	wir verletzten
du verletztest	ihr verletztet
Sie verletzten	Sie verletzten
er/sie/es verletzte	sie verletzten

PAST SUBJUNCTIVE II

ich hätte	wir hätten	verletzt
du hättest	ihr hättet	
Sie hätten	Sie hätten	
er/sie/es hätte	sie hätten	

FUTURE SUBJUNCTIVE I

ich werde	wir werden	verletzen
du werdest	ihr werdet	
Sie werden	Sie werden	
er/sie/es werde	sie werden	

FUTURE PERFECT SUBJUNCTIVE I

ich werde	wir werden	verletzt haben
du werdest	ihr werdet	
Sie werden	Sie werden	
er/sie/es werde	sie werden	

FUTURE SUBJUNCTIVE II

ich würde	wir würden	verletzen
du würdest	ihr würdet	
Sie würden	Sie würden	
er/sie/es würde	sie würden	

FUTURE PERFECT SUBJUNCTIVE II

ich würde	wir würden	verletzt haben
du würdest	ihr würdet	
Sie würden	Sie würden	
er/sie/es würde	sie würden	

COMMANDS verletz(e)! verletzt! verletzen Sie!

PRESENT PARTICIPLE verletzend

Usage

Renates Sohn ist von einem Kampfhund verletzt worden.	*Renate's son was injured by an attack dog.*
Beim Spielen hat sich Christian den Arm verletzt.	*Christian injured his arm while playing.*
Ihre Worte haben mich verletzt.	*Your words cut me to the quick.*
Zwei Insassen wurden schwer verletzt.	*Two passengers were severely injured.*
Sara verletzt sich oft.	*Sara often injures herself.*
Du hast seinen Stolz verletzt.	*You've wounded his pride.*
Wie verhält sich ein Kind, wenn seine persönlichen Grenzen verletzt werden?	*How does a child behave when his personal limits are violated?*
Das Kunstwerk verletzt den guten Geschmack.	*The work of art violates good taste.*
Habe ich ein Gesetz verletzt?	*Have I violated a law?*
Mindestens zwölf Regeln wurden dabei verletzt.	*At least 12 rules were broken in the process.*
Jeder Passagier, der die Sicherheitsbestimmungen verletzt, wird verhaftet.	*Every passenger who breaches security will be detained.*

RELATED VERB letzen

495 sich verlieben *to fall in love*

verliebt sich · verliebte sich · sich verliebt regular weak verb

PRESENT

ich verliebe mich	wir verlieben uns
du verliebst dich	ihr verliebt euch
Sie verlieben sich	Sie verlieben sich
er/sie/es verliebt sich	sie verlieben sich

PRESENT PERFECT

ich habe mich	wir haben uns	verliebt
du hast dich	ihr habt euch	
Sie haben sich	Sie haben sich	
er/sie/es hat sich	sie haben sich	

SIMPLE PAST

ich verliebte mich	wir verliebten uns
du verliebtest dich	ihr verliebtet euch
Sie verliebten sich	Sie verliebten sich
er/sie/es verliebte sich	sie verliebten sich

PAST PERFECT

ich hatte mich	wir hatten uns	verliebt
du hattest dich	ihr hattet euch	
Sie hatten sich	Sie hatten sich	
er/sie/es hatte sich	sie hatten sich	

FUTURE

ich werde mich	wir werden uns	verlieben
du wirst dich	ihr werdet euch	
Sie werden sich	Sie werden sich	
er/sie/es wird sich	sie werden sich	

FUTURE PERFECT

ich werde mich	wir werden uns	verliebt haben
du wirst dich	ihr werdet euch	
Sie werden sich	Sie werden sich	
er/sie/es wird sich	sie werden sich	

PRESENT SUBJUNCTIVE I

ich verliebe mich	wir verlieben uns
du verliebest dich	ihr verliebet euch
Sie verlieben sich	Sie verlieben sich
er/sie/es verliebe sich	sie verlieben sich

PAST SUBJUNCTIVE I

ich habe mich	wir haben uns	verliebt
du habest dich	ihr habet euch	
Sie haben sich	Sie haben sich	
er/sie/es habe sich	sie haben sich	

PRESENT SUBJUNCTIVE II

ich verliebte mich	wir verliebten uns
du verliebtest dich	ihr verliebtet euch
Sie verliebten sich	Sie verliebten sich
er/sie/es verliebte sich	sie verliebten sich

PAST SUBJUNCTIVE II

ich hätte mich	wir hätten uns	verliebt
du hättest dich	ihr hättet euch	
Sie hätten sich	Sie hätten sich	
er/sie/es hätte sich	sie hätten sich	

FUTURE SUBJUNCTIVE I

ich werde mich	wir werden uns	verlieben
du werdest dich	ihr werdet euch	
Sie werden sich	Sie werden sich	
er/sie/es werde sich	sie werden sich	

FUTURE PERFECT SUBJUNCTIVE I

ich werde mich	wir werden uns	verliebt haben
du werdest dich	ihr werdet euch	
Sie werden sich	Sie werden sich	
er/sie/es werde sich	sie werden sich	

FUTURE SUBJUNCTIVE II

ich würde mich	wir würden uns	verlieben
du würdest dich	ihr würdet euch	
Sie würden sich	Sie würden sich	
er/sie/es würde sich	sie würden sich	

FUTURE PERFECT SUBJUNCTIVE II

ich würde mich	wir würden uns	verliebt haben
du würdest dich	ihr würdet euch	
Sie würden sich	Sie würden sich	
er/sie/es würde sich	sie würden sich	

COMMANDS verlieb(e) dich! verliebt euch! verlieben Sie sich!

PRESENT PARTICIPLE sich verliebend

Usage

Erich verliebte sich in ihre grünen Augen.	*Erich fell in love with her green eyes.*
Hast du dich schon mal verliebt?	*Have you ever fallen in love?*
Ich verliebe mich gern.	*I like falling in love.*
Die Prinzessin verliebte sich sofort in den schönen Jüngling.	*The princess immediately fell in love with the handsome youth.*
Der Schriftsteller verliebte sich in eine Figur aus seinem Roman.	*The writer fell in love with a character from his novel.*
Aaron hatte sich in die Musik von Beethoven verliebt.	*Aaron had fallen in love with the music of Beethoven.*
Onkel Bert hat sich in das neue Auto verliebt.	*Uncle Bert fell in love with the new car.*
Das Paar verliebte sich ineinander und heiratete bald danach.	*The couple fell in love and married soon thereafter.*
In wen hat sich Jörg jetzt verliebt?	*Who has Jörg fallen in love with now?*
Dorian hat sich in sich selbst verliebt.	*Dorian has fallen in love with himself.*

RELATED VERBS *see* **lieben** (292)

PRESENT

ich verliere	wir verlieren
du verlierst	ihr verliert
Sie verlieren	Sie verlieren
er/sie/es verliert	sie verlieren

SIMPLE PAST

ich verlor	wir verloren
du verlorst	ihr verlort
Sie verloren	Sie verloren
er/sie/es verlor	sie verloren

FUTURE

ich werde	wir werden	verlieren
du wirst	ihr werdet	
Sie werden	Sie werden	
er/sie/es wird	sie werden	

PRESENT SUBJUNCTIVE I

ich verliere	wir verlieren
du verlierest	ihr verlieret
Sie verlieren	Sie verlieren
er/sie/es verliere	sie verlieren

PRESENT SUBJUNCTIVE II

ich verlöre	wir verlören
du verlörest	ihr verlöret
Sie verlören	Sie verlören
er/sie/es verlöre	sie verlören

FUTURE SUBJUNCTIVE I

ich werde	wir werden	verlieren
du werdest	ihr werdet	
Sie werden	Sie werden	
er/sie/es werde	sie werden	

FUTURE SUBJUNCTIVE II

ich würde	wir würden	verlieren
du würdest	ihr würdet	
Sie würden	Sie würden	
er/sie/es würde	sie würden	

PRESENT PERFECT

ich habe	wir haben	verloren
du hast	ihr habt	
Sie haben	Sie haben	
er/sie/es hat	sie haben	

PAST PERFECT

ich hatte	wir hatten	verloren
du hattest	ihr hattet	
Sie hatten	Sie hatten	
er/sie/es hatte	sie hatten	

FUTURE PERFECT

ich werde	wir werden	verloren haben
du wirst	ihr werdet	
Sie werden	Sie werden	
er/sie/es wird	sie werden	

PAST SUBJUNCTIVE I

ich habe	wir haben	verloren
du habest	ihr habet	
Sie haben	Sie haben	
er/sie/es habe	sie haben	

PAST SUBJUNCTIVE II

ich hätte	wir hätten	verloren
du hättest	ihr hättet	
Sie hätten	Sie hätten	
er/sie/es hätte	sie hätten	

FUTURE PERFECT SUBJUNCTIVE I

ich werde	wir werden	verloren haben
du werdest	ihr werdet	
Sie werden	Sie werden	
er/sie/es werde	sie werden	

FUTURE PERFECT SUBJUNCTIVE II

ich würde	wir würden	verloren haben
du würdest	ihr würdet	
Sie würden	Sie würden	
er/sie/es würde	sie würden	

COMMANDS verlier(e)! verliert! verlieren Sie!

PRESENT PARTICIPLE verlierend

Usage

Der US-Dollar hat zum Euro an Wert verloren.	*The U.S. dollar has declined in value against the euro.*
Verlieren Sie nicht die Hoffnung!	*Don't lose hope!*
Letzten Monat hat Bernd 10 000 Euro in einem Spielkasino verloren.	*Last month, Bernd lost 10,000 euros at a casino.*
FC Köln hat 1:0 verloren.	*FC Cologne lost 1 to 0.*
Er scheint das Spiel verlieren zu wollen.	*He seems to want to lose the game.*
1944 verlor sie ihren Mann und dann ihren Sohn.	*In 1944, she lost her husband and then her son.*
Wo wurde das Mountainbike verloren?	*Where was the mountain bike lost?*
Ich habe das alte Foto von meiner Tante verloren.	*I've lost the old photo of my aunt.*
Der Wolf verliert die Haare im Frühling.	*The wolf sheds its coat in the spring.*

sich verlieren *to subside, vanish; lose oneself, get lost*

Der Pfad verlor sich im Wald.	*The path vanished into the forest.*
Werther verlor sich in seinen Gedanken.	*Werther lost himself in his thoughts.*
Das Buch verliert sich in Nebensächlichkeiten.	*The book gets lost in trivialities.*

497 vermuten *to suspect, conjecture*

vermutet · vermutete · vermutet regular weak verb

PRESENT

ich vermute	wir vermuten
du vermutest	ihr vermutet
Sie vermuten	Sie vermuten
er/sie/es vermutet	sie vermuten

SIMPLE PAST

ich vermutete	wir vermuteten
du vermutetest	ihr vermutetet
Sie vermuteten	Sie vermuteten
er/sie/es vermutete	sie vermuteten

FUTURE

ich werde	wir werden	vermuten
du wirst	ihr werdet	
Sie werden	Sie werden	
er/sie/es wird	sie werden	

PRESENT SUBJUNCTIVE I

ich vermute	wir vermuten
du vermutest	ihr vermutet
Sie vermuten	Sie vermuten
er/sie/es vermute	sie vermuten

PRESENT SUBJUNCTIVE II

ich vermutete	wir vermuteten
du vermutetest	ihr vermutetet
Sie vermuteten	Sie vermuteten
er/sie/es vermutete	sie vermuteten

FUTURE SUBJUNCTIVE I

ich werde	wir werden	vermuten
du werdest	ihr werdet	
Sie werden	Sie werden	
er/sie/es werde	sie werden	

FUTURE SUBJUNCTIVE II

ich würde	wir würden	vermuten
du würdest	ihr würdet	
Sie würden	Sie würden	
er/sie/es würde	sie würden	

PRESENT PERFECT

ich habe	wir haben	vermutet
du hast	ihr habt	
Sie haben	Sie haben	
er/sie/es hat	sie haben	

PAST PERFECT

ich hatte	wir hatten	vermutet
du hattest	ihr hattet	
Sie hatten	Sie hatten	
er/sie/es hatte	sie hatten	

FUTURE PERFECT

ich werde	wir werden	vermutet haben
du wirst	ihr werdet	
Sie werden	Sie werden	
er/sie/es wird	sie werden	

PAST SUBJUNCTIVE I

ich habe	wir haben	vermutet
du habest	ihr habet	
Sie haben	Sie haben	
er/sie/es habe	sie haben	

PAST SUBJUNCTIVE II

ich hätte	wir hätten	vermutet
du hättest	ihr hättet	
Sie hätten	Sie hätten	
er/sie/es hätte	sie hätten	

FUTURE PERFECT SUBJUNCTIVE I

ich werde	wir werden	vermutet haben
du werdest	ihr werdet	
Sie werden	Sie werden	
er/sie/es werde	sie werden	

FUTURE PERFECT SUBJUNCTIVE II

ich würde	wir würden	vermutet haben
du würdest	ihr würdet	
Sie würden	Sie würden	
er/sie/es würde	sie würden	

COMMANDS vermute! vermutet! vermuten Sie!

PRESENT PARTICIPLE vermutend

Usage

Es lässt sich vermuten, dass der Autor selbst an Krebs litt.	*One might suspect that the author himself suffered from cancer.*
Ich vermute, dass er zu Hause ist.	*I guess he's at home.*
Der Vermisste wird in Bonn vermutet.	*The missing man is presumed to be in Bonn.*
Archäologen vermuten, dass das Fundament der Kirche etwas älter ist.	*Archeologists conjecture that the church's foundation is somewhat older.*
Nach einem Jahr wurde der Mann als tot vermutet.	*After one year, the man was presumed dead.*
Mord wird in diesem Fall nicht vermutet.	*Murder is not suspected in this case.*
Ein weiterer Planet wird von Astronomen vermutet.	*An additional planet is suspected by astronomers.*
Herr Thyssen vermutet Atlantis im Mittelmeerraum.	*Mr. Thyssen conjectures that Atlantis is in the Mediterranean region.*
Es wurde vermutet, dass ihr Sohn ein photographisches Gedächtnis besaß.	*It was assumed that their son possessed a photographic memory.*

RELATED VERB muten

regular weak verb **veröffentlicht · veröffentlichte · veröffentlicht**

PRESENT

ich veröffentliche	wir veröffentlichen
du veröffentlichst	ihr veröffentlicht
Sie veröffentlichen	Sie veröffentlichen
er/sie/es veröffentlicht	sie veröffentlichen

SIMPLE PAST

ich veröffentlichte	wir veröffentlichten
du veröffentlichtest	ihr veröffentlichtet
Sie veröffentlichten	Sie veröffentlichten
er/sie/es veröffentlichte	sie veröffentlichten

FUTURE

ich werde	wir werden	veröffentlichen
du wirst	ihr werdet	
Sie werden	Sie werden	
er/sie/es wird	sie werden	

PRESENT SUBJUNCTIVE I

ich veröffentliche	wir veröffentlichen
du veröffentlichest	ihr veröffentlichet
Sie veröffentlichen	Sie veröffentlichen
er/sie/es veröffentliche	sie veröffentlichen

PRESENT SUBJUNCTIVE II

ich veröffentlichte	wir veröffentlichten
du veröffentlichtest	ihr veröffentlichtet
Sie veröffentlichten	Sie veröffentlichten
er/sie/es veröffentlichte	sie veröffentlichten

FUTURE SUBJUNCTIVE I

ich werde	wir werden	veröffentlichen
du werdest	ihr werdet	
Sie werden	Sie werden	
er/sie/es werde	sie werden	

FUTURE SUBJUNCTIVE II

ich würde	wir würden	veröffentlichen
du würdest	ihr würdet	
Sie würden	Sie würden	
er/sie/es würde	sie würden	

PRESENT PERFECT

ich habe	wir haben	veröffentlicht
du hast	ihr habt	
Sie haben	Sie haben	
er/sie/es hat	sie haben	

PAST PERFECT

ich hatte	wir hatten	veröffentlicht
du hattest	ihr hattet	
Sie hatten	Sie hatten	
er/sie/es hatte	sie hatten	

FUTURE PERFECT

ich werde	wir werden	veröffentlicht haben
du wirst	ihr werdet	
Sie werden	Sie werden	
er/sie/es wird	sie werden	

PAST SUBJUNCTIVE I

ich habe	wir haben	veröffentlicht
du habest	ihr habet	
Sie haben	Sie haben	
er/sie/es habe	sie haben	

PAST SUBJUNCTIVE II

ich hätte	wir hätten	veröffentlicht
du hättest	ihr hättet	
Sie hätten	Sie hätten	
er/sie/es hätte	sie hätten	

FUTURE PERFECT SUBJUNCTIVE I

ich werde	wir werden	veröffentlicht haben
du werdest	ihr werdet	
Sie werden	Sie werden	
er/sie/es werde	sie werden	

FUTURE PERFECT SUBJUNCTIVE II

ich würde	wir würden	veröffentlicht haben
du würdest	ihr würdet	
Sie würden	Sie würden	
er/sie/es würde	sie würden	

COMMANDS veröffentlich(e)! veröffentlicht! veröffentlichen Sie!

PRESENT PARTICIPLE veröffentlichend

Usage

Haben Sie neulich etwas über den amerikanischen Bürgerkrieg veröffentlicht?	*Have you published anything on the American Civil War recently?*
Goethes Werke werden in vielen Sprachen veröffentlicht.	*Goethe's works are published in many languages.*
1994 ist der Artikel endlich veröffentlicht worden.	*In 1994, the article was finally published.*
Der Finanzminister veröffentlicht heute eine verbesserte Prognose fürs kommende Jahr.	*The finance minister will make public today an improved forecast for the coming year.*
Im frühen Mittelalter wurden viele offizielle Texte auf Latein veröffentlicht.	*In the early Middle Ages, many official texts were published in Latin.*
Veröffentlichen Sie demnächst ein Kochbuch?	*Are you publishing a cookbook soon?*
Die Rede des Politikers hat man früher veröffentlicht.	*The politician's speech was released earlier.*
Wir möchten die Forschungsergebnisse erst nächste Woche veröffentlichen.	*We'd like to wait until next week to publish the research results.*
David hofft, limitierte Auflagen ihrer Gedichte zu veröffentlichen.	*David hopes to publish limited editions of her poetry.*

499 versichern *to assert, affirm, assure, attest; insure*

versichert · versichert e · versichert

regular weak verb

PRESENT

ich versichere	wir versichern
du versicherst	ihr versichert
Sie versichern	Sie versichern
er/sie/es versichert	sie versichern

SIMPLE PAST

ich versicherte	wir versicherten
du versichertest	ihr versichertet
Sie versicherten	Sie versicherten
er/sie/es versicherte	sie versicherten

FUTURE

ich werde	wir werden	versichern
du wirst	ihr werdet	
Sie werden	Sie werden	
er/sie/es wird	sie werden	

PRESENT SUBJUNCTIVE I

ich versichere	wir versichern
du versicherst	ihr versichert
Sie versichern	Sie versichern
er/sie/es versichere	sie versichern

PRESENT SUBJUNCTIVE II

ich versicherte	wir versicherten
du versichertest	ihr versichertet
Sie versicherten	Sie versicherten
er/sie/es versicherte	sie versicherten

FUTURE SUBJUNCTIVE I

ich werde	wir werden	versichern
du werdest	ihr werdet	
Sie werden	Sie werden	
er/sie/es werde	sie werden	

FUTURE SUBJUNCTIVE II

ich würde	wir würden	versichern
du würdest	ihr würdet	
Sie würden	Sie würden	
er/sie/es würde	sie würden	

PRESENT PERFECT

ich habe	wir haben	versichert
du hast	ihr habt	
Sie haben	Sie haben	
er/sie/es hat	sie haben	

PAST PERFECT

ich hatte	wir hatten	versichert
du hattest	ihr hattet	
Sie hatten	Sie hatten	
er/sie/es hatte	sie hatten	

FUTURE PERFECT

ich werde	wir werden	versichert haben
du wirst	ihr werdet	
Sie werden	Sie werden	
er/sie/es wird	sie werden	

PAST SUBJUNCTIVE I

ich habe	wir haben	versichert
du habest	ihr habet	
Sie haben	Sie haben	
er/sie/es habe	sie haben	

PAST SUBJUNCTIVE II

ich hätte	wir hätten	versichert
du hättest	ihr hättet	
Sie hätten	Sie hätten	
er/sie/es hätte	sie hätten	

FUTURE PERFECT SUBJUNCTIVE I

ich werde	wir werden	versichert haben
du werdest	ihr werdet	
Sie werden	Sie werden	
er/sie/es werde	sie werden	

FUTURE PERFECT SUBJUNCTIVE II

ich würde	wir würden	versichert haben
du würdest	ihr würdet	
Sie würden	Sie würden	
er/sie/es würde	sie würden	

COMMANDS versichere! versichert! versichern Sie!

PRESENT PARTICIPLE versichernd

Usage

Das Gesundheitsministerium versicherte heute, dass die Epidemie unter Kontrolle ist. — *The Ministry of Health affirmed today that the epidemic is under control.*

Lassen Sie sich versichern, dass Ihr Geld gut angelegt wird. — *Be assured that your money is being well invested.*

Das kann ich dir nicht versichern. — *I can't assure you of that.*

Man soll das kostbare Kunstwerk nicht gegen Diebstahl versichert haben! — *The precious work of art is said not to have been insured against theft!*

Stefan hat sein Motorrad gut versichert. — *Stefan has insured his motorcycle well.*

sich versichern *to make sure, assure oneself; insure oneself*

Ich wollte mich versichern, dass sie das Geld überwiesen hat. — *I wanted to make sure that she has transferred the money.*

Hast du dich gegen Berufsunfähigkeit versichert? — *Have you insured yourself against occupational disability?*

RELATED VERBS *see* **sichern** (401)

strong verb **verspricht · versprach · versprochen**

PRESENT		PRESENT PERFECT		
ich verspreche	wir versprechen	ich habe	wir haben	versprochen
du versprichst	ihr versprecht	du hast	ihr habt	
Sie versprechen	Sie versprechen	Sie haben	Sie haben	
er/sie/es verspricht	sie versprechen	er/sie/es hat	sie haben	

SIMPLE PAST		PAST PERFECT		
ich versprach	wir versprachen	ich hatte	wir hatten	versprochen
du versprachst	ihr verspracht	du hattest	ihr hattet	
Sie versprachen	Sie versprachen	Sie hatten	Sie hatten	
er/sie/es versprach	sie versprachen	er/sie/es hatte	sie hatten	

FUTURE			FUTURE PERFECT		
ich werde	wir werden	versprechen	ich werde	wir werden	versprochen haben
du wirst	ihr werdet		du wirst	ihr werdet	
Sie werden	Sie werden		Sie werden	Sie werden	
er/sie/es wird	sie werden		er/sie/es wird	sie werden	

PRESENT SUBJUNCTIVE I		PAST SUBJUNCTIVE I		
ich verspreche	wir versprechen	ich habe	wir haben	versprochen
du versprechest	ihr versprechet	du habest	ihr habet	
Sie versprechen	Sie versprechen	Sie haben	Sie haben	
er/sie/es verspreche	sie versprechen	er/sie/es habe	sie haben	

PRESENT SUBJUNCTIVE II		PAST SUBJUNCTIVE II		
ich verspräche	wir versprächen	ich hätte	wir hätten	versprochen
du versprächest	ihr verspprächet	du hättest	ihr hättet	
Sie versprächen	Sie versprächen	Sie hätten	Sie hätten	
er/sie/es verspräche	sie versprächen	er/sie/es hätte	sie hätten	

FUTURE SUBJUNCTIVE I			FUTURE PERFECT SUBJUNCTIVE I		
ich werde	wir werden	versprechen	ich werde	wir werden	versprochen haben
du werdest	ihr werdet		du werdest	ihr werdet	
Sie werden	Sie werden		Sie werden	Sie werden	
er/sie/es werde	sie werden		er/sie/es werde	sie werden	

FUTURE SUBJUNCTIVE II			FUTURE PERFECT SUBJUNCTIVE II		
ich würde	wir würden	versprechen	ich würde	wir würden	versprochen haben
du würdest	ihr würdet		du würdest	ihr würdet	
Sie würden	Sie würden		Sie würden	Sie würden	
er/sie/es würde	sie würden		er/sie/es würde	sie würden	

COMMANDS versprich! versprecht! versprechen Sie!

PRESENT PARTICIPLE versprechend

Usage

Versprichst du mir das?	*Do you promise me that?*
Ich kann dir nicht versprechen, dass der Kuchen schmeckt, denn ich habe ihn gebacken!	*I can't promise you that the cake tastes good, because I baked it!*
Der Tag verspricht Spaß und Spannung.	*The day promises fun and excitement.*
Der Abend versprach interessant zu werden.	*The evening promised to be interesting.*
Wir haben den Kindern ein Eis versprochen.	*We've promised the children some ice cream.*
Wie Lars immer sagt: „Politiker versprechen alles, tun aber nichts."	*As Lars always says, "Politicians promise everything, but do nothing."*
Ein klarer Himmel versprach gutes Wetter für das Picknick.	*A clear sky promised good weather for the picnic.*
Stefan und Thomas versprechen ihre Hilfe.	*Stefan and Thomas are pledging their help.*
Sie versprachen seine Forderung nächstens zu befriedigen. (GOETHE)	*They promised to meet his demand right away.*
Amalie ist dem Hans versprochen. (*archaic*)	*Amalie is promised to Hans in marriage.*

RELATED VERBS *see* **sprechen** (415)

501 verstehen *to understand; make out; know how to*

versteht · verstand · verstanden strong verb

PRESENT

ich verstehe	wir verstehen
du verstehst	ihr versteht
Sie verstehen	Sie verstehen
er/sie/es versteht	sie verstehen

SIMPLE PAST

ich verstand	wir verstanden
du verstandst	ihr verstandet
Sie verstanden	Sie verstanden
er/sie/es verstand	sie verstanden

FUTURE

ich werde	wir werden	verstehen
du wirst	ihr werdet	
Sie werden	Sie werden	
er/sie/es wird	sie werden	

PRESENT SUBJUNCTIVE I

ich verstehe	wir verstehen
du verstehest	ihr verstehet
Sie verstehen	Sie verstehen
er/sie/es verstehe	sie verstehen

PRESENT SUBJUNCTIVE II

ich verstünde/verstände	wir verstünden/verständen
du verstündest/verständest	ihr verstündet/verständet
Sie verstünden/verständen	Sie verstünden/verständen
er/sie/es verstünde/verstände	sie verstünden/verständen

FUTURE SUBJUNCTIVE I

ich werde	wir werden	verstehen
du werdest	ihr werdet	
Sie werden	Sie werden	
er/sie/es werde	sie werden	

FUTURE SUBJUNCTIVE II

ich würde	wir würden	verstehen
du würdest	ihr würdet	
Sie würden	Sie würden	
er/sie/es würde	sie würden	

PRESENT PERFECT

ich habe	wir haben	verstanden
du hast	ihr habt	
Sie haben	Sie haben	
er/sie/es hat	sie haben	

PAST PERFECT

ich hatte	wir hatten	verstanden
du hattest	ihr hattet	
Sie hatten	Sie hatten	
er/sie/es hatte	sie hatten	

FUTURE PERFECT

ich werde	wir werden	verstanden haben
du wirst	ihr werdet	
Sie werden	Sie werden	
er/sie/es wird	sie werden	

PAST SUBJUNCTIVE I

ich habe	wir haben	verstanden
du habest	ihr habet	
Sie haben	Sie haben	
er/sie/es habe	sie haben	

PAST SUBJUNCTIVE II

ich hätte	wir hätten	verstanden
du hättest	ihr hättet	
Sie hätten	Sie hätten	
er/sie/es hätte	sie hätten	

FUTURE PERFECT SUBJUNCTIVE I

ich werde	wir werden	verstanden haben
du werdest	ihr werdet	
Sie werden	Sie werden	
er/sie/es werde	sie werden	

FUTURE PERFECT SUBJUNCTIVE II

ich würde	wir würden	verstanden haben
du würdest	ihr würdet	
Sie würden	Sie würden	
er/sie/es würde	sie würden	

COMMANDS versteh(e)! versteht! verstehen Sie!

PRESENT PARTICIPLE verstehend

Usage

Verstehst du Russisch?	*Do you understand Russian?*
Meine Mutter versteht mich nicht.	*My mother doesn't understand me.*
Können Affen menschliche Sprache verstehen?	*Can apes understand human language?*
Sorry, ich habe dich falsch verstanden.	*Sorry, I misunderstood you.*
Frau Fritsch konnte kein einziges Wort verstehen.	*Mrs. Fritsch couldn't make out a single word.*
Dirk verstand es, andere zu manipulieren.	*Dirk knew how to manipulate others.*
Ich hatte Ihnen zu verstehen gegeben, dass ich nicht mitmache.	*I had intimated to you that I won't participate.*

sich verstehen *to understand oneself/one another; be in agreement; be understood, be self-evident*

Die beiden verstehen sich nicht mehr.	*The two no longer understand each other.*
Manfred versteht sich nicht als Partner sondern als Gegner.	*Manfred understands himself to be not a partner, but an adversary.*
Es versteht sich von selbst, dass Streiks politisch sind.	*It is self-evident that strikes are political.*

RELATED VERBS missverstehen; *see also* **stehen** (423)

regular weak verb **versucht · versuchte · versucht**

PRESENT			PRESENT PERFECT		
ich versuche	wir versuchen		ich habe	wir haben	versucht
du versuchst	ihr versucht		du hast	ihr habt	
Sie versuchen	Sie versuchen		Sie haben	Sie haben	
er/sie/es versucht	sie versuchen		er/sie/es hat	sie haben	
SIMPLE PAST			**PAST PERFECT**		
ich versuchte	wir versuchten		ich hatte	wir hatten	versucht
du versuchtest	ihr versuchtet		du hattest	ihr hattet	
Sie versuchten	Sie versuchten		Sie hatten	Sie hatten	
er/sie/es versuchte	sie versuchten		er/sie/es hatte	sie hatten	
FUTURE			**FUTURE PERFECT**		
ich werde	wir werden	versuchen	ich werde	wir werden	versucht haben
du wirst	ihr werdet		du wirst	ihr werdet	
Sie werden	Sie werden		Sie werden	Sie werden	
er/sie/es wird	sie werden		er/sie/es wird	sie werden	
PRESENT SUBJUNCTIVE I			**PAST SUBJUNCTIVE I**		
ich versuche	wir versuchen		ich habe	wir haben	versucht
du versuchest	ihr versuchet		du habest	ihr habet	
Sie versuchen	Sie versuchen		Sie haben	Sie haben	
er/sie/es versuche	sie versuchen		er/sie/es habe	sie haben	
PRESENT SUBJUNCTIVE II			**PAST SUBJUNCTIVE II**		
ich versuchte	wir versuchten		ich hätte	wir hätten	versucht
du versuchtest	ihr versuchtet		du hättest	ihr hättet	
Sie versuchten	Sie versuchten		Sie hätten	Sie hätten	
er/sie/es versuchte	sie versuchten		er/sie/es hätte	sie hätten	
FUTURE SUBJUNCTIVE I			**FUTURE PERFECT SUBJUNCTIVE I**		
ich werde	wir werden	versuchen	ich werde	wir werden	versucht haben
du werdest	ihr werdet		du werdest	ihr werdet	
Sie werden	Sie werden		Sie werden	Sie werden	
er/sie/es werde	sie werden		er/sie/es werde	sie werden	
FUTURE SUBJUNCTIVE II			**FUTURE PERFECT SUBJUNCTIVE II**		
ich würde	wir würden	versuchen	ich würde	wir würden	versucht haben
du würdest	ihr würdet		du würdest	ihr würdet	
Sie würden	Sie würden		Sie würden	Sie würden	
er/sie/es würde	sie würden		er/sie/es würde	sie würden	

COMMANDS versuch(e)! versucht! versuchen Sie!

PRESENT PARTICIPLE versuchend

Usage

Ute versuchte ein anderes Medikament gegen Akne. — *Ute tried a different medication for acne.*
Sie versuchen sich immer zu rechtfertigen. — *You always try to vindicate yourself.*
Versuchen Sie den Griff festzuhalten. — *Try to hold the handle tight.*
Das Schwein hat versucht aus dem Stall herauszukommen. — *The pig tried to come out of the stall.*
Liesl möchte Schauspielerin werden und versucht ihr Glück in Hollywood. — *Liesl wants to become an actor and is trying her luck in Hollywood.*
Herr Müllermann versucht den Emmer anzubauen. — *Mr. Müllermann is attempting to cultivate emmer.*
Dreimal hatte Berta Selbstmord versucht. — *Three times, Berta attempted suicide.*
Da wurde Jesus vom Geist in die Wüste geführt, damit er von dem Teufel versucht würde. (MATTHÄUS 4,1) — *Then was Jesus led up by the Spirit into the wilderness to be tempted by the devil.* (MATTHEW 4:1)

sich versuchen *to try one's hand*

Maximilian versucht sich am Banjo. — *Maximilian is trying his hand at the banjo.*

RELATED VERBS *see* **suchen** (440)

503 verteilen *to distribute, hand out; spread*

verteilt · verteilte · verteilt regular weak verb

PRESENT

ich verteile	wir verteilen
du verteilst	ihr verteilt
Sie verteilen	Sie verteilen
er/sie/es verteilt	sie verteilen

SIMPLE PAST

ich verteilte	wir verteilten
du verteiltest	ihr verteiltet
Sie verteilten	Sie verteilten
er/sie/es verteilte	sie verteilten

FUTURE

ich werde	wir werden	verteilen
du wirst	ihr werdet	
Sie werden	Sie werden	
er/sie/es wird	sie werden	

PRESENT SUBJUNCTIVE I

ich verteile	wir verteilen
du verteilest	ihr verteilet
Sie verteilen	Sie verteilen
er/sie/es verteile	sie verteilen

PRESENT SUBJUNCTIVE II

ich verteilte	wir verteilten
du verteiltest	ihr verteiltet
Sie verteilten	Sie verteilten
er/sie/es verteilte	sie verteilten

FUTURE SUBJUNCTIVE I

ich werde	wir werden	verteilen
du werdest	ihr werdet	
Sie werden	Sie werden	
er/sie/es werde	sie werden	

FUTURE SUBJUNCTIVE II

ich würde	wir würden	verteilen
du würdest	ihr würdet	
Sie würden	Sie würden	
er/sie/es würde	sie würden	

PRESENT PERFECT

ich habe	wir haben	verteilt
du hast	ihr habt	
Sie haben	Sie haben	
er/sie/es hat	sie haben	

PAST PERFECT

ich hatte	wir hatten	verteilt
du hattest	ihr hattet	
Sie hatten	Sie hatten	
er/sie/es hatte	sie hatten	

FUTURE PERFECT

ich werde	wir werden	verteilt haben
du wirst	ihr werdet	
Sie werden	Sie werden	
er/sie/es wird	sie werden	

PAST SUBJUNCTIVE I

ich habe	wir haben	verteilt
du habest	ihr habet	
Sie haben	Sie haben	
er/sie/es habe	sie haben	

PAST SUBJUNCTIVE II

ich hätte	wir hätten	verteilt
du hättest	ihr hättet	
Sie hätten	Sie hätten	
er/sie/es hätte	sie hätten	

FUTURE PERFECT SUBJUNCTIVE I

ich werde	wir werden	verteilt haben
du werdest	ihr werdet	
Sie werden	Sie werden	
er/sie/es werde	sie werden	

FUTURE PERFECT SUBJUNCTIVE II

ich würde	wir würden	verteilt haben
du würdest	ihr würdet	
Sie würden	Sie würden	
er/sie/es würde	sie würden	

COMMANDS verteil(e)! verteilt! verteilen Sie!

PRESENT PARTICIPLE verteilend

Usage

Nicht alle Leserbriefe werden verteilt. — *Not all letters to the editor are being distributed.*
Heute muss ich die Rechnungen verteilen. — *Today I have to distribute the invoices.*
Ortwin hat gestern Flugblätter verteilt. — *Ortwin handed out flyers yesterday.*
Wir verteilen die Arbeit an andere Mitarbeiter. — *We are allocating the work to other employees.*
Der Lehrer verteilte die Übungsblätter. — *The teacher handed out the worksheets.*
Ich möchte die Heizölkosten auf das ganze Jahr verteilen. — *I'd like to spread the heating oil costs over the whole year.*

sich verteilen *to disperse, deploy; be distributed, be spread out*

Rizinusöl verteilt sich im Wasser. — *Castor oil disperses in water.*
Die österreichischen Truppen verteilten sich im Dorf und im umliegenden Tal. — *The Austrian troops deployed in the village and in the surrounding valley.*
Seine Analyse verteilt sich auf vier Bände. — *His analysis is spread across four volumes.*
Die Sandkörner verteilten sich über den Fußboden. — *The grains of sand were scattered across the floor.*

RELATED VERBS *see* **teilen** (443)

regular weak verb

vertraut · vertraute · vertraut

PRESENT

ich vertraue	wir vertrauen
du vertraust	ihr vertraut
Sie vertrauen	Sie vertrauen
er/sie/es vertraut	sie vertrauen

SIMPLE PAST

ich vertraute	wir vertrauten
du vertrautest	ihr vertrautet
Sie vertrauten	Sie vertrauten
er/sie/es vertraute	sie vertrauten

FUTURE

ich werde	wir werden	vertrauen
du wirst	ihr werdet	
Sie werden	Sie werden	
er/sie/es wird	sie werden	

PRESENT SUBJUNCTIVE I

ich vertraue	wir vertrauen
du vertrauest	ihr vertrauet
Sie vertrauen	Sie vertrauen
er/sie/es vertraue	sie vertrauen

PRESENT SUBJUNCTIVE II

ich vertraute	wir vertrauten
du vertrautest	ihr vertrautet
Sie vertrauten	Sie vertrauten
er/sie/es vertraute	sie vertrauten

FUTURE SUBJUNCTIVE I

ich werde	wir werden	vertrauen
du werdest	ihr werdet	
Sie werden	Sie werden	
er/sie/es werde	sie werden	

FUTURE SUBJUNCTIVE II

ich würde	wir würden	vertrauen
du würdest	ihr würdet	
Sie würden	Sie würden	
er/sie/es würde	sie würden	

PRESENT PERFECT

ich habe	wir haben	vertraut
du hast	ihr habt	
Sie haben	Sie haben	
er/sie/es hat	sie haben	

PAST PERFECT

ich hatte	wir hatten	vertraut
du hattest	ihr hattet	
Sie hatten	Sie hatten	
er/sie/es hatte	sie hatten	

FUTURE PERFECT

ich werde	wir werden	vertraut haben
du wirst	ihr werdet	
Sie werden	Sie werden	
er/sie/es wird	sie werden	

PAST SUBJUNCTIVE I

ich habe	wir haben	vertraut
du habest	ihr habet	
Sie haben	Sie haben	
er/sie/es habe	sie haben	

PAST SUBJUNCTIVE II

ich hätte	wir hätten	vertraut
du hättest	ihr hättet	
Sie hätten	Sie hätten	
er/sie/es hätte	sie hätten	

FUTURE PERFECT SUBJUNCTIVE I

ich werde	wir werden	vertraut haben
du werdest	ihr werdet	
Sie werden	Sie werden	
er/sie/es werde	sie werden	

FUTURE PERFECT SUBJUNCTIVE II

ich würde	wir würden	vertraut haben
du würdest	ihr würdet	
Sie würden	Sie würden	
er/sie/es würde	sie würden	

COMMANDS vertrau(e)! vertraut! vertrauen Sie!

PRESENT PARTICIPLE vertrauend

Usage

Vertraust du mir?	*Do you trust me?*
Ihren Verwandten vertraute sie kaum, einem Fremden noch weniger.	*She barely trusted her relatives, much less a stranger.*
Frau Engelbrecht vertraute ihrer Bekannten Frau Riegler.	*Mrs. Engelbrecht confided in her friend Mrs. Riegler.*
Wer dem Zufall vertraut, kann sich schwer Ziele setzen.	*He who trusts to chance is hard pressed to set goals.*
Ein Blinder muss seinem Führhund vertrauen können.	*A blind person must be able to trust his guide dog.*
Die Lehrerin hätte Max nicht vertrauen sollen.	*The teacher shouldn't have trusted Max.*
Der Regisseur vertraute dem Urteil der Kritiker.	*The director trusted the critics' judgment.*
Mein Mann und ich vertrauen einander.	*My husband and I trust each other.*
Wir haben deinem Wort vertraut.	*We took you at your word.*
Kann man ihm vertrauen?	*Can he be trusted?*
Und wenn sie dem Frieden zugeneigt sind, dann seid auch ihr ihm zugeneigt und vertraut auf Gott. (Koran 8,61)	*And if they incline toward peace, do you also incline toward it and trust in Allah.*

RELATED VERBS an·vertrauen; *see also* **trauen** (447)

505 verwenden *to use; spend*

verwendet · verwendete/verwandte · verwendet/verwandt — regular weak verb/mixed verb

PRESENT

ich verwende	wir verwenden
du verwendest	ihr verwendet
Sie verwenden	Sie verwenden
er/sie/es verwendet	sie verwenden

SIMPLE PAST

ich verwendete/verwandte	wir verwendeten/verwandten
du verwendetest/verwandtest	ihr verwendetet/verwandtet
Sie verwendeten/verwandten	Sie verwendeten/verwandten
er/sie/es verwendete/verwandte	sie verwendeten/verwandten

FUTURE

ich werde	wir werden	verwenden
du wirst	ihr werdet	
Sie werden	Sie werden	
er/sie/es wird	sie werden	

PRESENT SUBJUNCTIVE I

ich verwende	wir verwenden
du verwendest	ihr verwendet
Sie verwenden	Sie verwenden
er/sie/es verwende	sie verwenden

PRESENT SUBJUNCTIVE II

ich verwendete	wir verwendeten
du verwendetest	ihr verwendetet
Sie verwendeten	Sie verwendeten
er/sie/es verwendete	sie verwendeten

FUTURE SUBJUNCTIVE I

ich werde	wir werden	verwenden
du werdest	ihr werdet	
Sie werden	Sie werden	
er/sie/es werde	sie werden	

FUTURE SUBJUNCTIVE II

ich würde	wir würden	verwenden
du würdest	ihr würdet	
Sie würden	Sie würden	
er/sie/es würde	sie würden	

PRESENT PERFECT

ich habe	wir haben	verwendet/verwandt
du hast	ihr habt	
Sie haben	Sie haben	
er/sie/es hat	sie haben	

PAST PERFECT

ich hatte	wir hatten	verwendet/verwandt
du hattest	ihr hattet	
Sie hatten	Sie hatten	
er/sie/es hatte	sie hatten	

FUTURE PERFECT

ich werde	wir werden	verwendet haben OR verwandt haben
du wirst	ihr werdet	
Sie werden	Sie werden	
er/sie/es wird	sie werden	

PAST SUBJUNCTIVE I

ich habe	wir haben	verwendet/verwandt
du habest	ihr habet	
Sie haben	Sie haben	
er/sie/es habe	sie haben	

PAST SUBJUNCTIVE II

ich hätte	wir hätten	verwendet/verwandt
du hättest	ihr hättet	
Sie hätten	Sie hätten	
er/sie/es hätte	sie hätten	

FUTURE PERFECT SUBJUNCTIVE I

ich werde	wir werden	verwendet haben OR verwandt haben
du werdest	ihr werdet	
Sie werden	Sie werden	
er/sie/es werde	sie werden	

FUTURE PERFECT SUBJUNCTIVE II

ich würde	wir würden	verwendet haben OR verwandt haben
du würdest	ihr würdet	
Sie würden	Sie würden	
er/sie/es würde	sie würden	

COMMANDS verwende! verwendet! verwenden Sie!

PRESENT PARTICIPLE verwendend

Usage

Wie oft verwendest du das Passwort?	*How often do you use the password?*
Am besten verwendet man einen normalen Kugelschreiber.	*It is best to use a normal ballpoint pen.*
Das System verwendet die neue Version der Software.	*The system uses the new version of the software.*
Rembrandt verwandte häufig einen Hell-Dunkel-Kontrast.	*Rembrandt frequently used a light-dark contrast.*
Die unscharfen Bilder konnten nicht verwendet werden.	*The blurry pictures could not be used.*
Gerlinde hat den Gruß „Adele" gern verwendet.	*Gerlinde liked to use the greeting "Adele."*
Verwenden Sie das folgende Diagramm und beantworten Sie die Fragen.	*Use the following diagram and answer the questions.*
Ab und zu verwende ich Olivenöl anstatt Butter.	*Once in a while, I use olive oil instead of butter.*
Erich verwendet Grafiktablett und Stift anstatt einer Maus.	*Erich uses a graphic pad and stylus instead of a mouse.*
Muss ein Teleskop verwendet werden, um den Mars zu beobachten?	*Must a telescope be used to view Mars?*
Wofür wird das Geld verwendet?	*How is the money being spent?*

RELATED VERBS *see* **wenden** (527)

regular weak verb

verwirrt · verwirrte · verwirrt

PRESENT

ich verwirre	wir verwirren
du verwirrst	ihr verwirrt
Sie verwirren	Sie verwirren
er/sie/es verwirrt	sie verwirren

SIMPLE PAST

ich verwirrte	wir verwirrten
du verwirrtest	ihr verwirrtet
Sie verwirrten	Sie verwirrten
er/sie/es verwirrte	sie verwirrten

FUTURE

ich werde	wir werden	verwirren
du wirst	ihr werdet	
Sie werden	Sie werden	
er/sie/es wird	sie werden	

PRESENT SUBJUNCTIVE I

ich verwirre	wir verwirren
du verwirrest	ihr verwirret
Sie verwirren	Sie verwirren
er/sie/es verwirre	sie verwirren

PRESENT SUBJUNCTIVE II

ich verwirrte	wir verwirrten
du verwirrtest	ihr verwirrtet
Sie verwirrten	Sie verwirrten
er/sie/es verwirrte	sie verwirrten

FUTURE SUBJUNCTIVE I

ich werde	wir werden	verwirren
du werdest	ihr werdet	
Sie werden	Sie werden	
er/sie/es werde	sie werden	

FUTURE SUBJUNCTIVE II

ich würde	wir würden	verwirren
du würdest	ihr würdet	
Sie würden	Sie würden	
er/sie/es würde	sie würden	

PRESENT PERFECT

ich habe	wir haben	verwirrt
du hast	ihr habt	
Sie haben	Sie haben	
er/sie/es hat	sie haben	

PAST PERFECT

ich hatte	wir hatten	verwirrt
du hattest	ihr hattet	
Sie hatten	Sie hatten	
er/sie/es hatte	sie hatten	

FUTURE PERFECT

ich werde	wir werden	verwirrt haben
du wirst	ihr werdet	
Sie werden	Sie werden	
er/sie/es wird	sie werden	

PAST SUBJUNCTIVE I

ich habe	wir haben	verwirrt
du habest	ihr habet	
Sie haben	Sie haben	
er/sie/es habe	sie haben	

PAST SUBJUNCTIVE II

ich hätte	wir hätten	verwirrt
du hättest	ihr hättet	
Sie hätten	Sie hätten	
er/sie/es hätte	sie hätten	

FUTURE PERFECT SUBJUNCTIVE I

ich werde	wir werden	verwirrt haben
du werdest	ihr werdet	
Sie werden	Sie werden	
er/sie/es werde	sie werden	

FUTURE PERFECT SUBJUNCTIVE II

ich würde	wir würden	verwirrt haben
du würdest	ihr würdet	
Sie würden	Sie würden	
er/sie/es würde	sie würden	

COMMANDS verwirr(e)! verwirrt! verwirren Sie!

PRESENT PARTICIPLE verwirrend

Usage

Die Katze hatte die lange Telefonschnur vollkommen verwirrt. — *The cat had gotten the long telephone cord all tangled up.*

Der Wind verwirrte ihr Haar. — *The wind tousled her hair.*

Der Physikprofessor verwirrte seine Studenten mit seinen Überlegungen zum Thema Relativität. — *The physics professor confused his students with his thoughts on the topic of relativity.*

Diese Gedanken verwirrten ihn zutiefst. — *These thoughts confused him profoundly.*

Seine Erklärung hat mich eher verwirrt als erleuchtet. — *His explanation perplexed rather than enlightened me.*

Am Anfang wurde das Publikum offenkundig verwirrt. — *In the beginning, the public was obviously bewildered.*

Kleine Kinder sind leicht zu verwirren. — *Small children are easily confused.*

sich verwirren *to become entangled/confused*

Die Situation verwirrte sich weiter, als sich Manfred eine neue Ausrede einfallen ließ. — *The situation became further confused when Manfred came up with a new excuse.*

RELATED VERB wirren

507 verzeihen *to forgive; excuse*

verzeiht · verzieh · verziehen

strong verb

PRESENT

ich verzeihe	wir verzeihen
du verzeihst	ihr verzeiht
Sie verzeihen	Sie verzeihen
er/sie/es verzeiht	sie verzeihen

SIMPLE PAST

ich verzieh	wir verziehen
du verziehst	ihr verzieht
Sie verziehen	Sie verziehen
er/sie/es verzieh	sie verziehen

FUTURE

ich werde	wir werden	verzeihen
du wirst	ihr werdet	
Sie werden	Sie werden	
er/sie/es wird	sie werden	

PRESENT SUBJUNCTIVE I

ich verzeihe	wir verzeihen
du verzeihest	ihr verzeihet
Sie verzeihen	Sie verzeihen
er/sie/es verzeihe	sie verzeihen

PRESENT SUBJUNCTIVE II

ich verziehe	wir verziehen
du verziehest	ihr verziehet
Sie verziehen	Sie verziehen
er/sie/es verziehe	sie verziehen

FUTURE SUBJUNCTIVE I

ich werde	wir werden	verzeihen
du werdest	ihr werdet	
Sie werden	Sie werden	
er/sie/es werde	sie werden	

FUTURE SUBJUNCTIVE II

ich würde	wir würden	verzeihen
du würdest	ihr würdet	
Sie würden	Sie würden	
er/sie/es würde	sie würden	

PRESENT PERFECT

ich habe	wir haben	verziehen
du hast	ihr habt	
Sie haben	Sie haben	
er/sie/es hat	sie haben	

PAST PERFECT

ich hatte	wir hatten	verziehen
du hattest	ihr hattet	
Sie hatten	Sie hatten	
er/sie/es hatte	sie hatten	

FUTURE PERFECT

ich werde	wir werden	verziehen haben
du wirst	ihr werdet	
Sie werden	Sie werden	
er/sie/es wird	sie werden	

PAST SUBJUNCTIVE I

ich habe	wir haben	verziehen
du habest	ihr habet	
Sie haben	Sie haben	
er/sie/es habe	sie haben	

PAST SUBJUNCTIVE II

ich hätte	wir hätten	verziehen
du hättest	ihr hättet	
Sie hätten	Sie hätten	
er/sie/es hätte	sie hätten	

FUTURE PERFECT SUBJUNCTIVE I

ich werde	wir werden	verziehen haben
du werdest	ihr werdet	
Sie werden	Sie werden	
er/sie/es werde	sie werden	

FUTURE PERFECT SUBJUNCTIVE II

ich würde	wir würden	verziehen haben
du würdest	ihr würdet	
Sie würden	Sie würden	
er/sie/es würde	sie würden	

COMMANDS verzeih(e)! verzeiht! verzeihen Sie!

PRESENT PARTICIPLE verzeihend

Usage

Frau Strauss soll ihrem Mörder verziehen haben, kurz bevor er sie erschoss.	*Mrs. Strauss is said to have forgiven her murderer just before he shot her.*
Im Sterbebett hat sie ihrer Tochter endlich verziehen.	*On her deathbed, she finally forgave her daughter.*
Wie kann das Opfer dem Täter verzeihen?	*How can the victim forgive the perpetrator?*
Seine Missetaten sind längst verziehen worden.	*His misdeeds have long been forgiven.*
Bernd hat Frau Dormagen den Unfall verziehen.	*Bernd forgave Mrs. Dormagen for the accident.*
Elisabeth verzieh ihrem Bruder nie, dass er keinen Kontakt mit ihr haben wollte.	*Elisabeth never forgave her brother for not wanting contact with her.*
Ihm wurden selbst die kleinsten Fehler nicht verziehen.	*He wasn't forgiven for even the smallest mistakes.*
Die Tat ist nicht zu verzeihen.	*The deed is inexcusable.*
Verzeihen Sie, können Sie mir die Uhrzeit sagen?	*Excuse me, can you tell me the time?*
Verzeihen Sie die Störung, ich brauche mal Ihren Rat.	*Pardon the interruption, but I need your advice.*
Verzeihen Sie meine Ausdrucksweise.	*Pardon my French* (lit., *my way of expressing myself*).

RELATED VERB zeihen

regular weak verb **bereitet vor · bereitete vor · vorbereitet**

PRESENT			PRESENT PERFECT		
ich bereite	wir bereiten	vor	ich habe	wir haben	vorbereitet
du bereitest	ihr bereitet		du hast	ihr habt	
Sie bereiten	Sie bereiten		Sie haben	Sie haben	
er/sie/es bereitet	sie bereiten		er/sie/es hat	sie haben	

SIMPLE PAST			PAST PERFECT		
ich bereitete	wir bereiteten	vor	ich hatte	wir hatten	vorbereitet
du bereitetest	ihr bereitetet		du hattest	ihr hattet	
Sie bereiteten	Sie bereiteten		Sie hatten	Sie hatten	
er/sie/es bereitete	sie bereiteten		er/sie/es hatte	sie hatten	

FUTURE			FUTURE PERFECT		
ich werde	wir werden	vorbereiten	ich werde	wir werden	vorbereitet haben
du wirst	ihr werdet		du wirst	ihr werdet	
Sie werden	Sie werden		Sie werden	Sie werden	
er/sie/es wird	sie werden		er/sie/es wird	sie werden	

PRESENT SUBJUNCTIVE I			PAST SUBJUNCTIVE I		
ich bereite	wir bereiten	vor	ich habe	wir haben	vorbereitet
du bereitest	ihr bereitet		du habest	ihr habet	
Sie bereiten	Sie bereiten		Sie haben	Sie haben	
er/sie/es bereite	sie bereiten		er/sie/es habe	sie haben	

PRESENT SUBJUNCTIVE II			PAST SUBJUNCTIVE II		
ich bereitete	wir bereiteten	vor	ich hätte	wir hätten	vorbereitet
du bereitetest	ihr bereitetet		du hättest	ihr hättet	
Sie bereiteten	Sie bereiteten		Sie hätten	Sie hätten	
er/sie/es bereitete	sie bereiteten		er/sie/es hätte	sie hätten	

FUTURE SUBJUNCTIVE I			FUTURE PERFECT SUBJUNCTIVE I		
ich werde	wir werden	vorbereiten	ich werde	wir werden	vorbereitet haben
du werdest	ihr werdet		du werdest	ihr werdet	
Sie werden	Sie werden		Sie werden	Sie werden	
er/sie/es werde	sie werden		er/sie/es werde	sie werden	

FUTURE SUBJUNCTIVE II			FUTURE PERFECT SUBJUNCTIVE II		
ich würde	wir würden	vorbereiten	ich würde	wir würden	vorbereitet haben
du würdest	ihr würdet		du würdest	ihr würdet	
Sie würden	Sie würden		Sie würden	Sie würden	
er/sie/es würde	sie würden		er/sie/es würde	sie würden	

COMMANDS bereite vor! bereitet vor! bereiten Sie vor!

PRESENT PARTICIPLE vorbereitend

Usage

Inge bereitet die Kinder auf die Reise vor.	*Inge is preparing the children for the trip.*
Nicht alle Sushi-Sorten werden mit Fisch vorbereitet.	*Not all types of sushi are prepared with fish.*
Ilona bereitete uns ein wunderschönes Abendessen vor.	*Ilona was preparing a wonderful dinner for us.*
Der Kandidat hatte keine Rede vorbereitet.	*The candidate had not prepared a speech.*
Diese Kampagne wurde von unserer eigenen Organisation vorbereitet.	*This campaign was prepared by our own organization.*
Heute muss der Saal vorbereitet werden.	*Today the room must be set up.*
Der Anwalt bereitete den Angeklagten auf das Verhör vor.	*The lawyer prepared the defendant for the hearing.*

sich vorbereiten auf *to prepare (oneself) for*

Die Studierenden hatten sich auf das Examen vorbereitet.	*The students had prepared for the exam.*
Bereiten Sie sich schon auf Ihren Urlaub?	*Are you already making preparations for your vacation?*
Hast du dich darauf vorbereitet?	*Have you prepared for that?*

RELATED VERBS *see* **bereiten** (74)

509 vor·kommen *to happen, occur; appear, seem*

kommt vor · kam vor · vorgekommen strong verb

PRESENT

ich komme	wir kommen	vor
du kommst	ihr kommt	
Sie kommen	Sie kommen	
er/sie/es kommt	sie kommen	

SIMPLE PAST

ich kam	wir kamen	vor
du kamst	ihr kamt	
Sie kamen	Sie kamen	
er/sie/es kam	sie kamen	

FUTURE

ich werde	wir werden	vorkommen
du wirst	ihr werdet	
Sie werden	Sie werden	
er/sie/es wird	sie werden	

PRESENT SUBJUNCTIVE I

ich komme	wir kommen	vor
du kommest	ihr kommet	
Sie kommen	Sie kommen	
er/sie/es komme	sie kommen	

PRESENT SUBJUNCTIVE II

ich käme	wir kämen	vor
du kämest	ihr kämet	
Sie kämen	Sie kämen	
er/sie/es käme	sie kämen	

FUTURE SUBJUNCTIVE I

ich werde	wir werden	vorkommen
du werdest	ihr werdet	
Sie werden	Sie werden	
er/sie/es werde	sie werden	

FUTURE SUBJUNCTIVE II

ich würde	wir würden	vorkommen
du würdest	ihr würdet	
Sie würden	Sie würden	
er/sie/es würde	sie würden	

PRESENT PERFECT

ich bin	wir sind	vorgekommen
du bist	ihr seid	
Sie sind	Sie sind	
er/sie/es ist	sie sind	

PAST PERFECT

ich war	wir waren	vorgekommen
du warst	ihr wart	
Sie waren	Sie waren	
er/sie/es war	sie waren	

FUTURE PERFECT

ich werde	wir werden	vorgekommen sein
du wirst	ihr werdet	
Sie werden	Sie werden	
er/sie/es wird	sie werden	

PAST SUBJUNCTIVE I

ich sei	wir seien	vorgekommen
du seiest	ihr seiet	
Sie seien	Sie seien	
er/sie/es sei	sie seien	

PAST SUBJUNCTIVE II

ich wäre	wir wären	vorgekommen
du wärest	ihr wäret	
Sie wären	Sie wären	
er/sie/es wäre	sie wären	

FUTURE PERFECT SUBJUNCTIVE I

ich werde	wir werden	vorgekommen sein
du werdest	ihr werdet	
Sie werden	Sie werden	
er/sie/es werde	sie werden	

FUTURE PERFECT SUBJUNCTIVE II

ich würde	wir würden	vorgekommen sein
du würdest	ihr würdet	
Sie würden	Sie würden	
er/sie/es würde	sie würden	

COMMANDS komm(e) vor! kommt vor! kommen Sie vor!

PRESENT PARTICIPLE vorkommend

Usage

So etwas ist noch nie vorgekommen.	*Nothing like that has ever happened.*
Was ist eigentlich vorgekommen?	*What actually happened?*
Grausame Dinge kommen im Krieg vor.	*Horrible things happen in war.*
Es kann vorkommen, dass keiner da ist.	*It might turn out that nobody is there.*
Diese Gelegenheit kommt relativ selten vor.	*This opportunity comes along relatively seldom.*
Seine Erklärung kommt mir plausibel vor.	*His explanation seems plausible to me.*
Die Themen Liebe und Leid kamen in der Poesie des Mittelalters oft vor.	*The topics of love and suffering appeared often in medieval poetry.*
Lenes Großvater kam uns stets als missmutig vor.	*Lene's grandfather always seemed ill humored to us.*
Michael Jensen kommt diese Textstelle als eine Anspielung auf Milton vor.	*This place in the text appears to Michael Jensen to be an allusion to Milton.*
Der Name Weigl kommt im Register nicht vor.	*The name Weigl does not appear in the index.*
Es ist uns vorgekommen, als würde der Hund das Auto fahren.	*It looked to us like the dog was driving the car.*

RELATED VERBS zuvor·kommen; *see also* **kommen** (265)

strong verb **schlägt vor · schlug vor · vorgeschlagen**

PRESENT

ich schlage	wir schlagen	vor
du schlägst	ihr schlagt	
Sie schlagen	Sie schlagen	
er/sie/es schlägt	sie schlagen	

SIMPLE PAST

ich schlug	wir schlugen	vor
du schlugst	ihr schlugt	
Sie schlugen	Sie schlugen	
er/sie/es schlug	sie schlugen	

FUTURE

ich werde	wir werden	vorschlagen
du wirst	ihr werdet	
Sie werden	Sie werden	
er/sie/es wird	sie werden	

PRESENT SUBJUNCTIVE I

ich schlage	wir schlagen	vor
du schlagest	ihr schlaget	
Sie schlagen	Sie schlagen	
er/sie/es schlage	sie schlagen	

PRESENT SUBJUNCTIVE II

ich schlüge	wir schlügen	vor
du schlügest	ihr schlüget	
Sie schlügen	Sie schlügen	
er/sie/es schlüge	sie schlügen	

FUTURE SUBJUNCTIVE I

ich werde	wir werden	vorschlagen
du werdest	ihr werdet	
Sie werden	Sie werden	
er/sie/es werde	sie werden	

FUTURE SUBJUNCTIVE II

ich würde	wir würden	vorschlagen
du würdest	ihr würdet	
Sie würden	Sie würden	
er/sie/es würde	sie würden	

PRESENT PERFECT

ich habe	wir haben	vorgeschlagen
du hast	ihr habt	
Sie haben	Sie haben	
er/sie/es hat	sie haben	

PAST PERFECT

ich hatte	wir hatten	vorgeschlagen
du hattest	ihr hattet	
Sie hatten	Sie hatten	
er/sie/es hatte	sie hatten	

FUTURE PERFECT

ich werde	wir werden	vorgeschlagen haben
du wirst	ihr werdet	
Sie werden	Sie werden	
er/sie/es wird	sie werden	

PAST SUBJUNCTIVE I

ich habe	wir haben	vorgeschlagen
du habest	ihr habet	
Sie haben	Sie haben	
er/sie/es habe	sie haben	

PAST SUBJUNCTIVE II

ich hätte	wir hätten	vorgeschlagen
du hättest	ihr hättet	
Sie hätten	Sie hätten	
er/sie/es hätte	sie hätten	

FUTURE PERFECT SUBJUNCTIVE I

ich werde	wir werden	vorgeschlagen haben
du werdest	ihr werdet	
Sie werden	Sie werden	
er/sie/es werde	sie werden	

FUTURE PERFECT SUBJUNCTIVE II

ich würde	wir würden	vorgeschlagen haben
du würdest	ihr würdet	
Sie würden	Sie würden	
er/sie/es würde	sie würden	

COMMANDS schlag(e) vor! schlagt vor! schlagen Sie vor!

PRESENT PARTICIPLE vorschlagend

Usage

Haben Sie etwas vorzuschlagen?	*Do you have anything to suggest?*
Ich würde vorschlagen, dass du mit ihm über das Problem redest.	*I'd recommend that you talk with him about the problem.*
Ich schlage vor, dass wir uns am Marktplatz treffen.	*I suggest we meet at the market square.*
Mike schlägt eine andere Methode vor.	*Mike is proposing another method.*
Inge hat vorgeschlagen, ich sollte das Auto in die Werkstatt bringen.	*Inge suggested that I take the car to a mechanic.*
Bernds Idee war schon von anderen vorgeschlagen worden.	*Bernd's idea had already been suggested by other people.*
Daraufhin schlug der Graf einen Waffenstillstand vor.	*Consequently, the count proposed a cease-fire.*
Bei der Planung haben wir eine neue Perspektive vorgeschlagen.	*At the planning stage, we proposed a new perspective.*
1847 wurde Constantin als neuer Bischof vorgeschlagen.	*In 1847, Constantin was nominated as the new bishop.*
Herders Schrift wurde für einen Preis vorgeschlagen.	*Herder's writing was nominated for a prize.*

RELATED VERBS *see* **schlagen** (371)

511 vor·stellen *to introduce, present; put/move forward*

stellt vor · stellte vor · vorgestellt regular weak verb

PRESENT

ich stelle	wir stellen	vor
du stellst	ihr stellt	
Sie stellen	Sie stellen	
er/sie/es stellt	sie stellen	

PRESENT PERFECT

ich habe	wir haben	vorgestellt
du hast	ihr habt	
Sie haben	Sie haben	
er/sie/es hat	sie haben	

SIMPLE PAST

ich stellte	wir stellten	vor
du stelltest	ihr stelltet	
Sie stellten	Sie stellten	
er/sie/es stellte	sie stellten	

PAST PERFECT

ich hatte	wir hatten	vorgestellt
du hattest	ihr hattet	
Sie hatten	Sie hatten	
er/sie/es hatte	sie hatten	

FUTURE

ich werde	wir werden	vorstellen
du wirst	ihr werdet	
Sie werden	Sie werden	
er/sie/es wird	sie werden	

FUTURE PERFECT

ich werde	wir werden	vorgestellt haben
du wirst	ihr werdet	
Sie werden	Sie werden	
er/sie/es wird	sie werden	

PRESENT SUBJUNCTIVE I

ich stelle	wir stellen	vor
du stellest	ihr stellet	
Sie stellen	Sie stellen	
er/sie/es stelle	sie stellen	

PAST SUBJUNCTIVE I

ich habe	wir haben	vorgestellt
du habest	ihr habet	
Sie haben	Sie haben	
er/sie/es habe	sie haben	

PRESENT SUBJUNCTIVE II

ich stellte	wir stellten	vor
du stelltest	ihr stelltet	
Sie stellten	Sie stellten	
er/sie/es stellte	sie stellten	

PAST SUBJUNCTIVE II

ich hätte	wir hätten	vorgestellt
du hättest	ihr hättet	
Sie hätten	Sie hätten	
er/sie/es hätte	sie hätten	

FUTURE SUBJUNCTIVE I

ich werde	wir werden	vorstellen
du werdest	ihr werdet	
Sie werden	Sie werden	
er/sie/es werde	sie werden	

FUTURE PERFECT SUBJUNCTIVE I

ich werde	wir werden	vorgestellt haben
du werdest	ihr werdet	
Sie werden	Sie werden	
er/sie/es werde	sie werden	

FUTURE SUBJUNCTIVE II

ich würde	wir würden	vorstellen
du würdest	ihr würdet	
Sie würden	Sie würden	
er/sie/es würde	sie würden	

FUTURE PERFECT SUBJUNCTIVE II

ich würde	wir würden	vorgestellt haben
du würdest	ihr würdet	
Sie würden	Sie würden	
er/sie/es würde	sie würden	

COMMANDS stell(e) vor! stellt vor! stellen Sie vor!

PRESENT PARTICIPLE vorstellend

Usage

Darf ich vorstellen? Das ist Max Brinkmann, ein Kollege von mir. — *May I introduce someone? This is Max Brinkmann, a colleague of mine.*

Ich möchte meine Kollegin Vera vorstellen. — *I'd like to present my colleague Vera.*

Annalies hatte ihn ihrer Freundin 1994 vorgestellt. — *Annalies had introduced him to her girlfriend in 1994.*

Heute müssen wir die Uhr um eine Stunde vorstellen. — *Today we have to set the clock forward by one hour.*

sich vorstellen *to introduce oneself; interview* (for a position)

Markus stellte sich den anderen Studenten vor. — *Markus introduced himself to the other students.*

Lars hat sich letzte Woche bei der Firma vorgestellt. — *Lars interviewed with the firm last week.*

sich etwas vorstellen *to imagine/visualize something*

Georg kann sich nicht vorstellen, wie seine Schwägerin mit zehn Kindern zurechtkommt. — *Georg can't imagine how his sister-in-law copes with 10 children.*

Wie stellst du dir eine Reise nach Tibet vor? — *What do you imagine a trip to Tibet to be like?*

RELATED VERBS *see* **stellen** (426)

strong verb **wächst · wuchs · gewachsen**

PRESENT

ich wachse	wir wachsen
du wächst	ihr wachst
Sie wachsen	Sie wachsen
er/sie/es wächst	sie wachsen

SIMPLE PAST

ich wuchs	wir wuchsen
du wuchsest	ihr wuchst
Sie wuchsen	Sie wuchsen
er/sie/es wuchs	sie wuchsen

FUTURE

ich werde	wir werden	wachsen
du wirst	ihr werdet	
Sie werden	Sie werden	
er/sie/es wird	sie werden	

PRESENT SUBJUNCTIVE I

ich wachse	wir wachsen
du wachsest	ihr wachset
Sie wachsen	Sie wachsen
er/sie/es wachse	sie wachsen

PRESENT SUBJUNCTIVE II

ich wüchse	wir wüchsen
du wüchsest	ihr wüchset
Sie wüchsen	Sie wüchsen
er/sie/es wüchse	sie wüchsen

FUTURE SUBJUNCTIVE I

ich werde	wir werden	wachsen
du werdest	ihr werdet	
Sie werden	Sie werden	
er/sie/es werde	sie werden	

FUTURE SUBJUNCTIVE II

ich würde	wir würden	wachsen
du würdest	ihr würdet	
Sie würden	Sie würden	
er/sie/es würde	sie würden	

PRESENT PERFECT

ich bin	wir sind	gewachsen
du bist	ihr seid	
Sie sind	Sie sind	
er/sie/es ist	sie sind	

PAST PERFECT

ich war	wir waren	gewachsen
du warst	ihr wart	
Sie waren	Sie waren	
er/sie/es war	sie waren	

FUTURE PERFECT

ich werde	wir werden	gewachsen sein
du wirst	ihr werdet	
Sie werden	Sie werden	
er/sie/es wird	sie werden	

PAST SUBJUNCTIVE I

ich sei	wir seien	gewachsen
du seiest	ihr seiet	
Sie seien	Sie seien	
er/sie/es sei	sie seien	

PAST SUBJUNCTIVE II

ich wäre	wir wären	gewachsen
du wärest	ihr wäret	
Sie wären	Sie wären	
er/sie/es wäre	sie wären	

FUTURE PERFECT SUBJUNCTIVE I

ich werde	wir werden	gewachsen sein
du werdest	ihr werdet	
Sie werden	Sie werden	
er/sie/es werde	sie werden	

FUTURE PERFECT SUBJUNCTIVE II

ich würde	wir würden	gewachsen sein
du würdest	ihr würdet	
Sie würden	Sie würden	
er/sie/es würde	sie würden	

COMMANDS wachs(e)! wachst! wachsen Sie!

PRESENT PARTICIPLE wachsend

Usage

Der Apfelbaum vor dem Haus war rasch gewachsen. — *The apple tree in front of the house had grown quickly.*
Wachsen blaugrüne Algen im warmen Wasser? — *Do blue-green algae grow in the warm water?*
In einem Topf wächst ein Rosenbusch nicht sehr gut. — *A rosebush doesn't grow very well in a pot.*
Ich lasse mir die Haare wachsen. — *I'm letting my hair grow.*
Dietrich ist wieder ein Bart gewachsen. — *Dietrich's beard has grown out again.*
Die Kinder wachsen aber schnell! — *My, how the children are growing!*
Du wächst in die falsche Richtung! (*colloquial*) — *You're putting on weight!* (lit., *You're growing in the wrong direction!*)

Unerwartet wuchs eine gegenseitige Sympathie. — *Unexpectedly, a mutual fondness developed.*
Klaus ist der Verantwortung nicht gewachsen. — *Klaus can't cope with the responsibility.*
Arbeitslosigkeit wächst von Jahr zu Jahr. — *Unemployment is rising from year to year.*
Religiöse Bräuche wachsen im Laufe der Zeit. — *Religious traditions evolve over the course of time.*

RELATED VERBS auf·wachsen, aus·wachsen, erwachsen, heran·wachsen, nach·wachsen, umwachsen, verwachsen, zusammen·wachsen, zu·wachsen

513 wagen *to risk, dare*

wagt · wagte · gewagt regular weak verb

PRESENT		PRESENT PERFECT		
ich wage	wir wagen	ich habe	wir haben	gewagt
du wagst	ihr wagt	du hast	ihr habt	
Sie wagen	Sie wagen	Sie haben	Sie haben	
er/sie/es wagt	sie wagen	er/sie/es hat	sie haben	

SIMPLE PAST		PAST PERFECT		
ich wagte	wir wagten	ich hatte	wir hatten	gewagt
du wagtest	ihr wagtet	du hattest	ihr hattet	
Sie wagten	Sie wagten	Sie hatten	Sie hatten	
er/sie/es wagte	sie wagten	er/sie/es hatte	sie hatten	

FUTURE			FUTURE PERFECT		
ich werde	wir werden	wagen	ich werde	wir werden	gewagt haben
du wirst	ihr werdet		du wirst	ihr werdet	
Sie werden	Sie werden		Sie werden	Sie werden	
er/sie/es wird	sie werden		er/sie/es wird	sie werden	

PRESENT SUBJUNCTIVE I		PAST SUBJUNCTIVE I		
ich wage	wir wagen	ich habe	wir haben	gewagt
du wagest	ihr waget	du habest	ihr habet	
Sie wagen	Sie wagen	Sie haben	Sie haben	
er/sie/es wage	sie wagen	er/sie/es habe	sie haben	

PRESENT SUBJUNCTIVE II		PAST SUBJUNCTIVE II		
ich wagte	wir wagten	ich hätte	wir hätten	gewagt
du wagtest	ihr wagtet	du hättest	ihr hättet	
Sie wagten	Sie wagten	Sie hätten	Sie hätten	
er/sie/es wagte	sie wagten	er/sie/es hätte	sie hätten	

FUTURE SUBJUNCTIVE I			FUTURE PERFECT SUBJUNCTIVE I		
ich werde	wir werden	wagen	ich werde	wir werden	gewagt haben
du werdest	ihr werdet		du werdest	ihr werdet	
Sie werden	Sie werden		Sie werden	Sie werden	
er/sie/es werde	sie werden		er/sie/es werde	sie werden	

FUTURE SUBJUNCTIVE II			FUTURE PERFECT SUBJUNCTIVE II		
ich würde	wir würden	wagen	ich würde	wir würden	gewagt haben
du würdest	ihr würdet		du würdest	ihr würdet	
Sie würden	Sie würden		Sie würden	Sie würden	
er/sie/es würde	sie würden		er/sie/es würde	sie würden	

COMMANDS wag(e)! wagt! wagen Sie!

PRESENT PARTICIPLE wagend

Usage

An deiner Stelle würde ich den Flug noch nicht wagen. — *If I were you, I wouldn't risk the flight yet.*
Die kaiserlichen Truppen wagten einen Angriff. — *The imperial troops attempted an attack.*
Er hat sein Leben gewagt. — *He risked his life.*
Vor fünfzig Jahren hätte man nie gewagt zu glauben, dass Organismen gentechnisch verändert werden könnten. — *Fifty years ago, you would never have dared believe that organisms could be genetically engineered.*
Man wagte es nicht, gegen die Regierung zu sprechen. — *People didn't dare speak against the government.*
Ich wage es nicht, daran zu denken. — *I don't dare think about it.*
Nichts gewagt, nichts gewonnen. (PROVERB) — *Nothing ventured, nothing gained.*

sich wagen *to venture*

Trotz des Wetters wagte sie sich zögerlich aus dem Haus, um Lebensmitteln zu beschaffen. — *In spite of the weather, she ventured hesitantly from the house to get some food.*
Der ängstliche Hund wagt sich nicht vor die Tür. — *The frightened dog will not go to the door.*

RELATED VERBS heraus·wagen, hinaus·wagen, vor·wagen

PRESENT

ich wäge	wir wägen
du wägst	ihr wägt
Sie wägen	Sie wägen
er/sie/es wägt	sie wägen

SIMPLE PAST

ich wog/wägte	wir wogen/wägten
du wogst/wägtest	ihr wogt/wägtet
Sie wogen/wägten	Sie wogen/wägten
er/sie/es wog/wägte	sie wogen/wägten

FUTURE

ich werde	wir werden	wägen
du wirst	ihr werdet	
Sie werden	Sie werden	
er/sie/es wird	sie werden	

PRESENT SUBJUNCTIVE I

ich wäge	wir wägen
du wägest	ihr wäget
Sie wägen	Sie wägen
er/sie/es wäge	sie wägen

PRESENT SUBJUNCTIVE II

ich wöge/wägte	wir wögen/wägten
du wögest/wägtest	ihr wöget/wägtet
Sie wögen/wägten	Sie wögen/wägten
er/sie/es wöge/wägte	sie wögen/wägten

FUTURE SUBJUNCTIVE I

ich werde	wir werden	wägen
du werdest	ihr werdet	
Sie werden	Sie werden	
er/sie/es werde	sie werden	

FUTURE SUBJUNCTIVE II

ich würde	wir würden	wägen
du würdest	ihr würdet	
Sie würden	Sie würden	
er/sie/es würde	sie würden	

PRESENT PERFECT

ich habe	wir haben	gewogen/gewägt
du hast	ihr habt	
Sie haben	Sie haben	
er/sie/es hat	sie haben	

PAST PERFECT

ich hatte	wir hatten	gewogen/gewägt
du hattest	ihr hattet	
Sie hatten	Sie hatten	
er/sie/es hatte	sie hatten	

FUTURE PERFECT

ich werde	wir werden	gewogen haben OR gewägt haben
du wirst	ihr werdet	
Sie werden	Sie werden	
er/sie/es wird	sie werden	

PAST SUBJUNCTIVE I

ich habe	wir haben	gewogen/gewägt
du habest	ihr habet	
Sie haben	Sie haben	
er/sie/es habe	sie haben	

PAST SUBJUNCTIVE II

ich hätte	wir hätten	gewogen/gewägt
du hättest	ihr hättet	
Sie hätten	Sie hätten	
er/sie/es hätte	sie hätten	

FUTURE PERFECT SUBJUNCTIVE I

ich werde	wir werden	gewogen haben OR gewägt haben
du werdest	ihr werdet	
Sie werden	Sie werden	
er/sie/es werde	sie werden	

FUTURE PERFECT SUBJUNCTIVE II

ich würde	wir würden	gewogen haben OR gewägt haben
du würdest	ihr würdet	
Sie würden	Sie würden	
er/sie/es würde	sie würden	

COMMANDS wäg(e)! wägt! wägen Sie!

PRESENT PARTICIPLE wägend

Usage

Man muss die Informationen in den Berichten sehr genau wägen.	*One must very carefully consider the information in the reports.*
Ihm war bald was zu kurz, zu lang, wägte alles gar bedächtig. (GOETHE)	*For him, things were too short or too long; he considered everything with circumspection.*
Das Bündnis wolle sorgfältig wägen, ob ein militärischer Einsatz nötig ist, so der Pressesprecher.	*The alliance wants to ponder carefully whether military intervention is necessary, according to the spokesman.*
Die Fakten müssen gewägt werden.	*The facts must be considered.*
Man sollte ihre Worte wohl wägen.	*You should carefully weigh what she says.*
Spezialfahrzeuge mit mehr als vier Achsen sind an dieser Stelle zu wägen.	*Special vehicles with more than four axles are to be weighed at this location.*
Man soll die Stimmen wägen und nicht zählen. (SCHILLER)	*The votes should be weighed and not counted.*
Erst wägen, dann wagen. (PROVERB)	*Look before you leap.*

RELATED VERBS ab·wägen, erwägen

515 wählen *to choose, select; elect; vote (for); dial*

wählt · wählte · gewählt regular weak verb

PRESENT

ich wähle	wir wählen
du wählst	ihr wählt
Sie wählen	Sie wählen
er/sie/es wählt	sie wählen

PRESENT PERFECT

ich habe	wir haben	gewählt
du hast	ihr habt	
Sie haben	Sie haben	
er/sie/es hat	sie haben	

SIMPLE PAST

ich wählte	wir wählten
du wähltest	ihr wähltet
Sie wählten	Sie wählten
er/sie/es wählte	sie wählten

PAST PERFECT

ich hatte	wir hatten	gewählt
du hattest	ihr hattet	
Sie hatten	Sie hatten	
er/sie/es hatte	sie hatten	

FUTURE

ich werde	wir werden	wählen
du wirst	ihr werdet	
Sie werden	Sie werden	
er/sie/es wird	sie werden	

FUTURE PERFECT

ich werde	wir werden	gewählt haben
du wirst	ihr werdet	
Sie werden	Sie werden	
er/sie/es wird	sie werden	

PRESENT SUBJUNCTIVE I

ich wähle	wir wählen
du wählest	ihr wählet
Sie wählen	Sie wählen
er/sie/es wähle	sie wählen

PAST SUBJUNCTIVE I

ich habe	wir haben	gewählt
du habest	ihr habet	
Sie haben	Sie haben	
er/sie/es habe	sie haben	

PRESENT SUBJUNCTIVE II

ich wählte	wir wählten
du wähltest	ihr wähltet
Sie wählten	Sie wählten
er/sie/es wählte	sie wählten

PAST SUBJUNCTIVE II

ich hätte	wir hätten	gewählt
du hättest	ihr hättet	
Sie hätten	Sie hätten	
er/sie/es hätte	sie hätten	

FUTURE SUBJUNCTIVE I

ich werde	wir werden	wählen
du werdest	ihr werdet	
Sie werden	Sie werden	
er/sie/es werde	sie werden	

FUTURE PERFECT SUBJUNCTIVE I

ich werde	wir werden	gewählt haben
du werdest	ihr werdet	
Sie werden	Sie werden	
er/sie/es werde	sie werden	

FUTURE SUBJUNCTIVE II

ich würde	wir würden	wählen
du würdest	ihr würdet	
Sie würden	Sie würden	
er/sie/es würde	sie würden	

FUTURE PERFECT SUBJUNCTIVE II

ich würde	wir würden	gewählt haben
du würdest	ihr würdet	
Sie würden	Sie würden	
er/sie/es würde	sie würden	

COMMANDS wähl(e)! wählt! wählen Sie!

PRESENT PARTICIPLE wählend

Usage

Hast du schon ein Hauptfach gewählt?	*Have you already chosen a major?*
Beatrices Buch über Tee ist aus vielen Gründen gewählt worden.	*Beatrice's book on tea was selected for many reasons.*
Ungewöhnliche Methoden wurden vom Komitee gewählt.	*Unusual methods were chosen by the committee.*
Habt ihr Stoff- oder Einwegwindeln gewählt?	*Did you opt for cotton diapers or disposable ones?*
Ernst hat den Ort gewählt.	*Ernst picked the location.*
Nächstes Jahr wird ein neuer Bundespräsident gewählt.	*Next year, a new federal president is being elected.*
Lothar Muldenhauer wurde zum Stadtrat gewählt.	*Lothar Muldenhauer was elected to the city council.*
Frau Schmidt wählt immer SPD.	*Mrs. Schmidt always votes for the Social Democrats.*
Kann man per Internet wählen?	*Can you vote via the Internet?*
In den USA darf man mit achtzehn Jahren wählen.	*In the U.S., you can vote at the age of 18.*
Wenn ich dich von hier aus anrufe, muss ich die Vorwahl nicht wählen.	*If I call you from here, I don't have to dial the area code.*

RELATED VERBS aus·erwählen, aus·wählen, erwählen, verwählen, wieder·wählen

regular weak verb **wandert · wanderte · gewandert**

PRESENT		PRESENT PERFECT		
ich wandere	wir wandern	ich bin	wir sind	gewandert
du wanderst	ihr wandert	du bist	ihr seid	
Sie wandern	Sie wandern	Sie sind	Sie sind	
er/sie/es wandert	sie wandern	er/sie/es ist	sie sind	

SIMPLE PAST		PAST PERFECT		
ich wanderte	wir wanderten	ich war	wir waren	gewandert
du wandertest	ihr wandertet	du warst	ihr wart	
Sie wanderten	Sie wanderten	Sie waren	Sie waren	
er/sie/es wanderte	sie wanderten	er/sie/es war	sie waren	

FUTURE			FUTURE PERFECT		
ich werde	wir werden	wandern	ich werde	wir werden	gewandert sein
du wirst	ihr werdet		du wirst	ihr werdet	
Sie werden	Sie werden		Sie werden	Sie werden	
er/sie/es wird	sie werden		er/sie/es wird	sie werden	

PRESENT SUBJUNCTIVE I		PAST SUBJUNCTIVE I		
ich wandere	wir wandern	ich sei	wir seien	gewandert
du wanderst	ihr wandert	du seiest	ihr seiet	
Sie wandern	Sie wandern	Sie seien	Sie seien	
er/sie/es wandere	sie wandern	er/sie/es sei	sie seien	

PRESENT SUBJUNCTIVE II		PAST SUBJUNCTIVE II		
ich wanderte	wir wanderten	ich wäre	wir wären	gewandert
du wandertest	ihr wandertet	du wärest	ihr wäret	
Sie wanderten	Sie wanderten	Sie wären	Sie wären	
er/sie/es wanderte	sie wanderten	er/sie/es wäre	sie wären	

FUTURE SUBJUNCTIVE I			FUTURE PERFECT SUBJUNCTIVE I		
ich werde	wir werden	wandern	ich werde	wir werden	gewandert sein
du werdest	ihr werdet		du werdest	ihr werdet	
Sie werden	Sie werden		Sie werden	Sie werden	
er/sie/es werde	sie werden		er/sie/es werde	sie werden	

FUTURE SUBJUNCTIVE II			FUTURE PERFECT SUBJUNCTIVE II		
ich würde	wir würden	wandern	ich würde	wir würden	gewandert sein
du würdest	ihr würdet		du würdest	ihr würdet	
Sie würden	Sie würden		Sie würden	Sie würden	
er/sie/es würde	sie würden		er/sie/es würde	sie würden	

COMMANDS wandere! wandert! wandern Sie!

PRESENT PARTICIPLE wandernd

Usage

Klaus und Dirk sind um den Berg gewandert.	*Klaus and Dirk hiked around the mountain.*
Ihr müsst wirklich weit gewandert sein.	*You must have really hiked a considerable distance.*
Der Bison wandert im Mai in sein Sommergebiet.	*The bison roams into its summer range in May.*
Sein Blick wanderte von Jörg zu den anderen.	*His eyes wandered from Jörg to the others.*
Anton ist jeden Sommer durch das Berner Oberland gewandert.	*Anton hiked through the Bernese Uplands every summer.*
Beduinen wandern von Ort zu Ort.	*Bedouins lead a nomadic life.*
An einem unfreundlichen Novembertage wanderte ein armes Schneiderlein auf der Landstraße nach Goldach. (KELLER)	*One unpleasant November day, a poor tailor was traveling on the country road to Goldach.*
Viele Arme sind im 20. Jahrhundert in die Städte gewandert.	*Many poor people migrated to the cities in the twentieth century.*

RELATED VERBS ab·wandern, aus·wandern, durchwandern, durch·wandern, ein·wandern, erwandern, umwandern, unterwandern, zu·wandern

517 **warnen** *to warn, caution*

warnt · warnte · gewarnt regular weak verb

PRESENT

ich warne	wir warnen
du warnst	ihr warnt
Sie warnen	Sie warnen
er/sie/es warnt	sie warnen

SIMPLE PAST

ich warnte	wir warnten
du warntest	ihr warntet
Sie warnten	Sie warnten
er/sie/es warnte	sie warnten

FUTURE

ich werde	wir werden	warnen
du wirst	ihr werdet	
Sie werden	Sie werden	
er/sie/es wird	sie werden	

PRESENT SUBJUNCTIVE I

ich warne	wir warnen
du warnest	ihr warnet
Sie warnen	Sie warnen
er/sie/es warne	sie warnen

PRESENT SUBJUNCTIVE II

ich warnte	wir warnten
du warntest	ihr warntet
Sie warnten	Sie warnten
er/sie/es warnte	sie warnten

FUTURE SUBJUNCTIVE I

ich werde	wir werden	warnen
du werdest	ihr werdet	
Sie werden	Sie werden	
er/sie/es werde	sie werden	

FUTURE SUBJUNCTIVE II

ich würde	wir würden	warnen
du würdest	ihr würdet	
Sie würden	Sie würden	
er/sie/es würde	sie würden	

PRESENT PERFECT

ich habe	wir haben	gewarnt
du hast	ihr habt	
Sie haben	Sie haben	
er/sie/es hat	sie haben	

PAST PERFECT

ich hatte	wir hatten	gewarnt
du hattest	ihr hattet	
Sie hatten	Sie hatten	
er/sie/es hatte	sie hatten	

FUTURE PERFECT

ich werde	wir werden	gewarnt haben
du wirst	ihr werdet	
Sie werden	Sie werden	
er/sie/es wird	sie werden	

PAST SUBJUNCTIVE I

ich habe	wir haben	gewarnt
du habest	ihr habet	
Sie haben	Sie haben	
er/sie/es habe	sie haben	

PAST SUBJUNCTIVE II

ich hätte	wir hätten	gewarnt
du hättest	ihr hättet	
Sie hätten	Sie hätten	
er/sie/es hätte	sie hätten	

FUTURE PERFECT SUBJUNCTIVE I

ich werde	wir werden	gewarnt haben
du werdest	ihr werdet	
Sie werden	Sie werden	
er/sie/es werde	sie werden	

FUTURE PERFECT SUBJUNCTIVE II

ich würde	wir würden	gewarnt haben
du würdest	ihr würdet	
Sie würden	Sie würden	
er/sie/es würde	sie würden	

COMMANDS warn(e)! warnt! warnen Sie!

PRESENT PARTICIPLE warnend

Usage

Wissenschaftler warnen vor den Folgen der Erderwärmung.	*Scientists warn of the consequences of global warming.*
Die Küstenwache hatte sie gewarnt.	*The coast guard had warned them.*
Man wurde vor dem Glatteis gewarnt.	*People were warned about the slippery ice.*
Der Computeranwender wird durch eine Fehlermeldung gewarnt.	*The computer user is warned via an error message.*
Die Weltgesundheitsorganisation warnt vor einer Pocken-Epidemie.	*The World Health Organization is issuing a warning about a smallpox epidemic.*
Fußgänger werden visuell und akustisch davor gewarnt, dass ein Auto kommt.	*Pedestrians are alerted visually and aurally that a car is coming.*
In einem Fernsehinterview warnte der CEO vor einer voreiligen Entscheidung.	*In a television interview, the CEO cautioned against a hasty decision.*
Hat die Lehrerin dich nicht gewarnt?	*Didn't the teacher warn you?*
„Davor habe ich euch doch gewarnt", sagte der Junge.	*"I warned you about that," said the boy.*

RELATED VERBS entwarnen, verwarnen, vor·warnen

PRESENT

ich warte	wir warten
du wartest	ihr wartet
Sie warten	Sie warten
er/sie/es wartet	sie warten

PRESENT PERFECT

ich habe	wir haben	gewartet
du hast	ihr habt	
Sie haben	Sie haben	
er/sie/es hat	sie haben	

SIMPLE PAST

ich wartete	wir warteten
du wartetest	ihr wartetet
Sie warteten	Sie warteten
er/sie/es wartete	sie warteten

PAST PERFECT

ich hatte	wir hatten	gewartet
du hattest	ihr hattet	
Sie hatten	Sie hatten	
er/sie/es hatte	sie hatten	

FUTURE

ich werde	wir werden	warten
du wirst	ihr werdet	
Sie werden	Sie werden	
er/sie/es wird	sie werden	

FUTURE PERFECT

ich werde	wir werden	gewartet haben
du wirst	ihr werdet	
Sie werden	Sie werden	
er/sie/es wird	sie werden	

PRESENT SUBJUNCTIVE I

ich warte	wir warten
du wartest	ihr wartet
Sie warten	Sie warten
er/sie/es warte	sie warten

PAST SUBJUNCTIVE I

ich habe	wir haben	gewartet
du habest	ihr habet	
Sie haben	Sie haben	
er/sie/es habe	sie haben	

PRESENT SUBJUNCTIVE II

ich wartete	wir warteten
du wartetest	ihr wartetet
Sie warteten	Sie warteten
er/sie/es wartete	sie warteten

PAST SUBJUNCTIVE II

ich hätte	wir hätten	gewartet
du hättest	ihr hättet	
Sie hätten	Sie hätten	
er/sie/es hätte	sie hätten	

FUTURE SUBJUNCTIVE I

ich werde	wir werden	warten
du werdest	ihr werdet	
Sie werden	Sie werden	
er/sie/es werde	sie werden	

FUTURE PERFECT SUBJUNCTIVE I

ich werde	wir werden	gewartet haben
du werdest	ihr werdet	
Sie werden	Sie werden	
er/sie/es werde	sie werden	

FUTURE SUBJUNCTIVE II

ich würde	wir würden	warten
du würdest	ihr würdet	
Sie würden	Sie würden	
er/sie/es würde	sie würden	

FUTURE PERFECT SUBJUNCTIVE II

ich würde	wir würden	gewartet haben
du würdest	ihr würdet	
Sie würden	Sie würden	
er/sie/es würde	sie würden	

COMMANDS warte! wartet! warten Sie!

PRESENT PARTICIPLE wartend

Usage

Worauf warten Sie?	*What are you waiting for?*
Klaus will dreißig Minuten vor der Tür gewartet haben.	*Klaus claims to have waited 30 minutes at the door.*
Wartest du zu Hause oder im Büro?	*Are you waiting at home or at the office?*
Wer wartete an der Tür?	*Who was waiting at the door?*
Ich kann nicht länger warten.	*I can't wait any longer.*
Wir wollten mit dem Essen auf ihn warten.	*We wanted to hold dinner for him.*
Lars ließ Sabine drei Stunden auf ihn warten.	*Lars kept Sabine waiting for him for three hours.*
Ich möchte nicht warten.	*I don't want to wait.*
Warte auf mich!	*Wait for me!*
Adrian wartet auf einen Studienplatz an der Uni in Münster.	*Adrian is waiting to study at the university in Münster.*
Meine Schwester hat lange mit der Heirat gewartet.	*My sister waited a long time to get married.*
Ein Fahrzeug muss regelmäßig gewartet werden.	*A vehicle must be serviced regularly.*

RELATED VERBS ab·warten, auf·warten, zu·warten; *see also* **erwarten** (173)

519 **waschen** *to wash; do the washing*

wäscht · wusch · gewaschen strong verb

PRESENT

ich wasche	wir waschen
du wäschst	ihr wascht
Sie waschen	Sie waschen
er/sie/es wäscht	sie waschen

PRESENT PERFECT

ich habe	wir haben	gewaschen
du hast	ihr habt	
Sie haben	Sie haben	
er/sie/es hat	sie haben	

SIMPLE PAST

ich wusch	wir wuschen
du wuschest	ihr wuscht
Sie wuschen	Sie wuschen
er/sie/es wusch	sie wuschen

PAST PERFECT

ich hatte	wir hatten	gewaschen
du hattest	ihr hattet	
Sie hatten	Sie hatten	
er/sie/es hatte	sie hatten	

FUTURE

ich werde	wir werden	waschen
du wirst	ihr werdet	
Sie werden	Sie werden	
er/sie/es wird	sie werden	

FUTURE PERFECT

ich werde	wir werden	gewaschen haben
du wirst	ihr werdet	
Sie werden	Sie werden	
er/sie/es wird	sie werden	

PRESENT SUBJUNCTIVE I

ich wasche	wir waschen
du waschest	ihr waschet
Sie waschen	Sie waschen
er/sie/es wasche	sie waschen

PAST SUBJUNCTIVE I

ich habe	wir haben	gewaschen
du habest	ihr habet	
Sie haben	Sie haben	
er/sie/es habe	sie haben	

PRESENT SUBJUNCTIVE II

ich wüsche	wir wüschen
du wüschest	ihr wüschet
Sie wüschen	Sie wüschen
er/sie/es wüsche	sie wüschen

PAST SUBJUNCTIVE II

ich hätte	wir hätten	gewaschen
du hättest	ihr hättet	
Sie hätten	Sie hätten	
er/sie/es hätte	sie hätten	

FUTURE SUBJUNCTIVE I

ich werde	wir werden	waschen
du werdest	ihr werdet	
Sie werden	Sie werden	
er/sie/es werde	sie werden	

FUTURE PERFECT SUBJUNCTIVE I

ich werde	wir werden	gewaschen haben
du werdest	ihr werdet	
Sie werden	Sie werden	
er/sie/es werde	sie werden	

FUTURE SUBJUNCTIVE II

ich würde	wir würden	waschen
du würdest	ihr würdet	
Sie würden	Sie würden	
er/sie/es würde	sie würden	

FUTURE PERFECT SUBJUNCTIVE II

ich würde	wir würden	gewaschen haben
du würdest	ihr würdet	
Sie würden	Sie würden	
er/sie/es würde	sie würden	

COMMANDS wasch(e)! wascht! waschen Sie!

PRESENT PARTICIPLE waschend

Usage

Haben Sie die Bettdecken schon gewaschen?	*Have you already washed the bedspreads?*
Herr Kreiens wäscht seinen Porsche jeden Samstag.	*Mr. Kreiens washes his Porsche every Saturday.*
Wann wird der Patient gewaschen?	*When is the patient to be bathed?*
Wasch dein Fahrrad bitte nicht im Wohnzimmer!	*Please don't wash your bicycle in the living room!*
Sigrid, könntest du die Windeln bitte waschen?	*Sigrid, could you please wash the diapers?*
Früher wusch Oma die Wäsche per Hand.	*Grandma used to do laundry by hand.*
Wäschst du immer samstags?	*Do you always do the washing on Saturday?*
Die Bank soll Drogengeld gewaschen haben. (*figurative*)	*The bank is said to have laundered drug money.*
Eine Hand wäscht die andere. (PROVERB)	*One good turn deserves another.*

sich waschen *to wash up, wash oneself*

Wo kann ich mich waschen?	*Where can I wash up?*
Lena wäscht sich das Haar zweimal am Tag.	*Lena washes her hair twice a day.*

RELATED VERBS ab·waschen, auf·waschen, rein·waschen, weg·waschen

regular weak verb or strong verb **webt · webte/wob · gewebt/gewoben**

PRESENT		PRESENT PERFECT		
ich webe	wir weben	ich habe	wir haben	gewebt/gewoben
du webst	ihr webt	du hast	ihr habt	
Sie weben	Sie weben	Sie haben	Sie haben	
er/sie/es webt	sie weben	er/sie/es hat	sie haben	

SIMPLE PAST		PAST PERFECT		
ich webte/wob	wir webten/woben	ich hatte	wir hatten	gewebt/gewoben
du webtest/wobst	ihr webtet/wobt	du hattest	ihr hattet	
Sie webten/woben	Sie webten/woben	Sie hatten	Sie hatten	
er/sie/es webte/wob	sie webten/woben	er/sie/es hatte	sie hatten	

FUTURE			FUTURE PERFECT		
ich werde	wir werden	weben	ich werde	wir werden	gewebt haben OR gewoben haben
du wirst	ihr werdet		du wirst	ihr werdet	
Sie werden	Sie werden		Sie werden	Sie werden	
er/sie/es wird	sie werden		er/sie/es wird	sie werden	

PRESENT SUBJUNCTIVE I		PAST SUBJUNCTIVE I		
ich webe	wir weben	ich habe	wir haben	gewebt/gewoben
du webest	ihr webet	du habest	ihr habet	
Sie weben	Sie weben	Sie haben	Sie haben	
er/sie/es webe	sie weben	er/sie/es habe	sie haben	

PRESENT SUBJUNCTIVE II		PAST SUBJUNCTIVE II		
ich webte/wöbe	wir webten/wöben	ich hätte	wir hätten	gewebt/gewoben
du webtest/wöbest	ihr webtet/wöbet	du hättest	ihr hättet	
Sie webten/wöben	Sie webten/wöben	Sie hätten	Sie hätten	
er/sie/es webte/wöbe	sie webten/wöben	er/sie/es hätte	sie hätten	

FUTURE SUBJUNCTIVE I			FUTURE PERFECT SUBJUNCTIVE I		
ich werde	wir werden	weben	ich werde	wir werden	gewebt haben OR gewoben haben
du werdest	ihr werdet		du werdest	ihr werdet	
Sie werden	Sie werden		Sie werden	Sie werden	
er/sie/es werde	sie werden		er/sie/es werde	sie werden	

FUTURE SUBJUNCTIVE II			FUTURE PERFECT SUBJUNCTIVE II		
ich würde	wir würden	weben	ich würde	wir würden	gewebt haben OR gewoben haben
du würdest	ihr würdet		du würdest	ihr würdet	
Sie würden	Sie würden		Sie würden	Sie würden	
er/sie/es würde	sie würden		er/sie/es würde	sie würden	

COMMANDS web(e)! webt! weben Sie!

PRESENT PARTICIPLE webend

NOTE The verb **weben** is typically strong when used figuratively.

Usage

Diese Wolldecken werden in Schottland gewebt.	*These woolen blankets are woven in Scotland.*
Die Inselbewohner woben Leinen aus Flachs.	*The island inhabitants wove linen from flax.*
Über Nacht hatte eine Spinne ein riesiges Netz gewebt.	*Overnight a spider had woven a gigantic web.*
Luskana webte einen Teppich aus Stroh.	*Luskana wove a rug from straw.*
Ihre Schwester lehrte sie weben.	*Her sister taught her to weave.*
Diamanten wurden durch ihre Haare gewebt.	*Diamonds were woven into her hair.*
Die einheimischen Völker haben diese Sagen vor Jahrhunderten gewoben.	*The native peoples weaved these legends centuries ago.*
In seinem ersten Roman wob der Autor einen Teppich aus Liebe und Eifersucht.	*In his first novel, the author weaved a tapestry of love and jealousy.*
Glühend webst du über deinem Grabe, Genius! (GOETHE)	*Fiery you float over your grave, spirit!*

RELATED VERBS durchweben, ein·weben, verweben

521 wechseln *to change; exchange*

wechselt · wechselte · gewechselt regular weak verb

PRESENT

ich wechs(e)le	wir wechseln
du wechselst	ihr wechselt
Sie wechseln	Sie wechseln
er/sie/es wechselt	sie wechseln

SIMPLE PAST

ich wechselte	wir wechselten
du wechseltest	ihr wechseltet
Sie wechselten	Sie wechselten
er/sie/es wechselte	sie wechselten

FUTURE

ich werde	wir werden	wechseln
du wirst	ihr werdet	
Sie werden	Sie werden	
er/sie/es wird	sie werden	

PRESENT SUBJUNCTIVE I

ich wechs(e)le	wir wechseln
du wechselst	ihr wechselt
Sie wechseln	Sie wechseln
er/sie/es wechs(e)le	sie wechseln

PRESENT SUBJUNCTIVE II

ich wechselte	wir wechselten
du wechseltest	ihr wechseltet
Sie wechselten	Sie wechselten
er/sie/es wechselte	sie wechselten

FUTURE SUBJUNCTIVE I

ich werde	wir werden	wechseln
du werdest	ihr werdet	
Sie werden	Sie werden	
er/sie/es werde	sie werden	

FUTURE SUBJUNCTIVE II

ich würde	wir würden	wechseln
du würdest	ihr würdet	
Sie würden	Sie würden	
er/sie/es würde	sie würden	

PRESENT PERFECT

ich habe	wir haben	gewechselt
du hast	ihr habt	
Sie haben	Sie haben	
er/sie/es hat	sie haben	

PAST PERFECT

ich hatte	wir hatten	gewechselt
du hattest	ihr hattet	
Sie hatten	Sie hatten	
er/sie/es hatte	sie hatten	

FUTURE PERFECT

ich werde	wir werden	gewechselt haben
du wirst	ihr werdet	
Sie werden	Sie werden	
er/sie/es wird	sie werden	

PAST SUBJUNCTIVE I

ich habe	wir haben	gewechselt
du habest	ihr habet	
Sie haben	Sie haben	
er/sie/es habe	sie haben	

PAST SUBJUNCTIVE II

ich hätte	wir hätten	gewechselt
du hättest	ihr hättet	
Sie hätten	Sie hätten	
er/sie/es hätte	sie hätten	

FUTURE PERFECT SUBJUNCTIVE I

ich werde	wir werden	gewechselt haben
du werdest	ihr werdet	
Sie werden	Sie werden	
er/sie/es werde	sie werden	

FUTURE PERFECT SUBJUNCTIVE II

ich würde	wir würden	gewechselt haben
du würdest	ihr würdet	
Sie würden	Sie würden	
er/sie/es würde	sie würden	

COMMANDS wechs(e)le! wechselt! wechseln Sie!

PRESENT PARTICIPLE wechselnd

Usage

Ich muss den Reifen wechseln.	*I have to change the tire.*
Könnten Sie einen Fünfdollarschein in Münzen wechseln?	*Could you change a five-dollar bill for coins?*
Jetzt muss ich seine Windel wechseln.	*Now I have to change his diaper.*
Ihr habt das Thema wieder gewechselt!	*You've changed the topic again!*
Mit diesem Schritt wird er seine Ziele gewechselt haben.	*With this step, he will have changed his goals.*
Mama wechselt die Bettlaken jeden Tag.	*Mama changes the bedsheets every day.*
Wenn Sie den Wohnsitz gewechselt haben, müssen Sie dieses Formular ausfüllen.	*If you have moved, you have to fill out this form.*
Hoffentlich wechselt das Wetter wieder.	*Let's hope the weather changes again.*
Wir können am Flughafen Euro gegen Dollar wechseln.	*We can exchange euros for dollars at the airport.*

wechseln (with **sein**) *to move*

Katrin ist von einer Stelle zur anderen gewechselt.	*Katrin has moved from one job to another.*

RELATED VERBS ab·wechseln, aus·wechseln, ein·wechseln, über·wechseln, um·wechseln, verwechseln

PRESENT		
ich wecke	wir wecken	
du weckst	ihr weckt	
Sie wecken	Sie wecken	
er/sie/es weckt	sie wecken	

SIMPLE PAST		
ich weckte	wir weckten	
du wecktest	ihr wecktet	
Sie weckten	Sie weckten	
er/sie/es weckte	sie weckten	

FUTURE		
ich werde	wir werden	wecken
du wirst	ihr werdet	
Sie werden	Sie werden	
er/sie/es wird	sie werden	

PRESENT SUBJUNCTIVE I		
ich wecke	wir wecken	
du weckest	ihr wecket	
Sie wecken	Sie wecken	
er/sie/es wecke	sie wecken	

PRESENT SUBJUNCTIVE II		
ich weckte	wir weckten	
du wecktest	ihr wecktet	
Sie weckten	Sie weckten	
er/sie/es weckte	sie weckten	

FUTURE SUBJUNCTIVE I		
ich werde	wir werden	wecken
du werdest	ihr werdet	
Sie werden	Sie werden	
er/sie/es werde	sie werden	

FUTURE SUBJUNCTIVE II		
ich würde	wir würden	wecken
du würdest	ihr würdet	
Sie würden	Sie würden	
er/sie/es würde	sie würden	

PRESENT PERFECT		
ich habe	wir haben	geweckt
du hast	ihr habt	
Sie haben	Sie haben	
er/sie/es hat	sie haben	

PAST PERFECT		
ich hatte	wir hatten	geweckt
du hattest	ihr hattet	
Sie hatten	Sie hatten	
er/sie/es hatte	sie hatten	

FUTURE PERFECT		
ich werde	wir werden	geweckt haben
du wirst	ihr werdet	
Sie werden	Sie werden	
er/sie/es wird	sie werden	

PAST SUBJUNCTIVE I		
ich habe	wir haben	geweckt
du habest	ihr habet	
Sie haben	Sie haben	
er/sie/es habe	sie haben	

PAST SUBJUNCTIVE II		
ich hätte	wir hätten	geweckt
du hättest	ihr hättet	
Sie hätten	Sie hätten	
er/sie/es hätte	sie hätten	

FUTURE PERFECT SUBJUNCTIVE I		
ich werde	wir werden	geweckt haben
du werdest	ihr werdet	
Sie werden	Sie werden	
er/sie/es werde	sie werden	

FUTURE PERFECT SUBJUNCTIVE II		
ich würde	wir würden	geweckt haben
du würdest	ihr würdet	
Sie würden	Sie würden	
er/sie/es würde	sie würden	

COMMANDS weck(e)! weckt! wecken Sie!

PRESENT PARTICIPLE weckend

Usage

Wollten Sie mich wecken?	*Did you intend to wake me?*
Weck die Kinder bitte nicht.	*Please don't wake the children.*
Schlafwandler sind schwer zu wecken.	*Sleepwalkers are hard to wake.*
Ludwig weckte seinen Vater um zwei Uhr.	*Ludwig woke his father at two o'clock.*
Ich mag nicht geweckt werden.	*I don't like to be waked up.*
Ein vorbeifahrender LKW hat die Katze geweckt.	*A passing truck woke the cat.*
Der Papagei hat uns um zehn Uhr geweckt.	*The parrot woke us at 10 o'clock.*
Der Notarzt wurde aus tiefem Schlaf geweckt.	*The emergency physician was awakened from a deep sleep.*
Bist du schon mal von einem überlauten Wecker geweckt worden?	*Have you ever been woken by an extra-loud alarm clock?*
Sie weckte in mir den Wunsch, unserer Familiengeschichte nachzugehen.	*She aroused in me the desire to pursue our family history.*
Schlafende Hunde soll man nicht wecken. (PROVERB)	*Let sleeping dogs lie.*

RELATED VERBS auf·wecken, erwecken

523 wehren *to fight against, restrain, prevent*

wehrt · wehrte · gewehrt regular weak verb

PRESENT

ich wehre	wir wehren
du wehrst	ihr wehrt
Sie wehren	Sie wehren
er/sie/es wehrt	sie wehren

SIMPLE PAST

ich wehrte	wir wehrten
du wehrtest	ihr wehrtet
Sie wehrten	Sie wehrten
er/sie/es wehrte	sie wehrten

FUTURE

ich werde	wir werden	wehren
du wirst	ihr werdet	
Sie werden	Sie werden	
er/sie/es wird	sie werden	

PRESENT SUBJUNCTIVE I

ich wehre	wir wehren
du wehrest	ihr wehret
Sie wehren	Sie wehren
er/sie/es wehre	sie wehren

PRESENT SUBJUNCTIVE II

ich wehrte	wir wehrten
du wehrtest	ihr wehrtet
Sie wehrten	Sie wehrten
er/sie/es wehrte	sie wehrten

FUTURE SUBJUNCTIVE I

ich werde	wir werden	wehren
du werdest	ihr werdet	
Sie werden	Sie werden	
er/sie/es werde	sie werden	

FUTURE SUBJUNCTIVE II

ich würde	wir würden	wehren
du würdest	ihr würdet	
Sie würden	Sie würden	
er/sie/es würde	sie würden	

PRESENT PERFECT

ich habe	wir haben	gewehrt
du hast	ihr habt	
Sie haben	Sie haben	
er/sie/es hat	sie haben	

PAST PERFECT

ich hatte	wir hatten	gewehrt
du hattest	ihr hattet	
Sie hatten	Sie hatten	
er/sie/es hatte	sie hatten	

FUTURE PERFECT

ich werde	wir werden	gewehrt haben
du wirst	ihr werdet	
Sie werden	Sie werden	
er/sie/es wird	sie werden	

PAST SUBJUNCTIVE I

ich habe	wir haben	gewehrt
du habest	ihr habet	
Sie haben	Sie haben	
er/sie/es habe	sie haben	

PAST SUBJUNCTIVE II

ich hätte	wir hätten	gewehrt
du hättest	ihr hättet	
Sie hätten	Sie hätten	
er/sie/es hätte	sie hätten	

FUTURE PERFECT SUBJUNCTIVE I

ich werde	wir werden	gewehrt haben
du werdest	ihr werdet	
Sie werden	Sie werden	
er/sie/es werde	sie werden	

FUTURE PERFECT SUBJUNCTIVE II

ich würde	wir würden	gewehrt haben
du würdest	ihr würdet	
Sie würden	Sie würden	
er/sie/es würde	sie würden	

COMMANDS wehr(e)! wehrt! wehren Sie!

PRESENT PARTICIPLE wehrend

Usage

Wir müssen dieser Gefahr wehren. — *We must confront this danger aggressively.*

Willst du's ihm wehren? (Nietzsche) — *Do you intend to prevent him from doing that?*

sich wehren *to defend oneself, put up a fight, resist, fight*

Der Manager wehrt sich gegen die Vorwürfe der Steuerhinterziehung. — *The manager is defending himself against charges of tax evasion.*

Die Progressiven wehren sich gegen die Angriffe der Rechtsradikalen. — *The progressives are countering the attacks of the right-wing radicals.*

Der Junge hat sich mit einem Stock gewehrt. — *The boy defended himself with a stick.*

Die Gefangenen versuchten sich gegen Misshandlung zu wehren. — *The prisoners tried to defend themselves against mistreatment.*

Wehrt euch! — *Defend yourselves!*

Man fragt immer, warum ich mich nicht gewehrt hätte. — *People always ask why I didn't put up a fight.*

RELATED VERBS ab·wehren, bewehren, erwehren, verwehren

strong verb **weicht · wich · gewichen**

PRESENT		PRESENT PERFECT		
ich weiche	wir weichen	ich bin	wir sind	gewichen
du weichst	ihr weicht	du bist	ihr seid	
Sie weichen	Sie weichen	Sie sind	Sie sind	
er/sie/es weicht	sie weichen	er/sie/es ist	sie sind	

SIMPLE PAST		PAST PERFECT		
ich wich	wir wichen	ich war	wir waren	gewichen
du wichst	ihr wicht	du warst	ihr wart	
Sie wichen	Sie wichen	Sie waren	Sie waren	
er/sie/es wich	sie wichen	er/sie/es war	sie waren	

FUTURE			FUTURE PERFECT		
ich werde	wir werden	weichen	ich werde	wir werden	gewichen sein
du wirst	ihr werdet		du wirst	ihr werdet	
Sie werden	Sie werden		Sie werden	Sie werden	
er/sie/es wird	sie werden		er/sie/es wird	sie werden	

PRESENT SUBJUNCTIVE I		PAST SUBJUNCTIVE I		
ich weiche	wir weichen	ich sei	wir seien	gewichen
du weichest	ihr weichet	du seiest	ihr seiet	
Sie weichen	Sie weichen	Sie seien	Sie seien	
er/sie/es weiche	sie weichen	er/sie/es sei	sie seien	

PRESENT SUBJUNCTIVE II		PAST SUBJUNCTIVE II		
ich wiche	wir wichen	ich wäre	wir wären	gewichen
du wichest	ihr wichet	du wärest	ihr wäret	
Sie wichen	Sie wichen	Sie wären	Sie wären	
er/sie/es wiche	sie wichen	er/sie/es wäre	sie wären	

FUTURE SUBJUNCTIVE I			FUTURE PERFECT SUBJUNCTIVE I		
ich werde	wir werden	weichen	ich werde	wir werden	gewichen sein
du werdest	ihr werdet		du werdest	ihr werdet	
Sie werden	Sie werden		Sie werden	Sie werden	
er/sie/es werde	sie werden		er/sie/es werde	sie werden	

FUTURE SUBJUNCTIVE II			FUTURE PERFECT SUBJUNCTIVE II		
ich würde	wir würden	weichen	ich würde	wir würden	gewichen sein
du würdest	ihr würdet		du würdest	ihr würdet	
Sie würden	Sie würden		Sie würden	Sie würden	
er/sie/es würde	sie würden		er/sie/es würde	sie würden	

COMMANDS weich(e)! weicht! weichen Sie!

PRESENT PARTICIPLE weichend

NOTE When **weichen** means "to soften," it is regular weak: **weichte, hat geweicht**.

Usage

Lene wich nicht von der Stelle.	*Lene didn't budge an inch.*
Der gesunde Menschenverstand weicht einem paranoiden Wahnsinn.	*Good sense is giving way to paranoid mania.*
Wir werden ihnen nicht weichen.	*We will not give in to them.*
Der Hund war den ganzen Tag nicht von seiner Seite gewichen.	*The dog hadn't left his side the whole day.*
Seine Kraft ist von ihm gewichen.	*His strength has deserted him.*
Das kleinere Heer ist den kaiserlichen Truppen gewichen.	*The smaller army retreated before the imperial troops.*
Das Hochwasser war gewichen und wir kehrten heim.	*The floodwaters had receded and we returned home.*
Der Traum wich der kahlen Realität, in der wir uns befanden.	*The dream gave way to the stark reality in which we found ourselves.*

RELATED VERBS ab·weichen, aus·weichen, entweichen, zurück·weichen

weinen *to cry, weep*

weint · weinte · geweint regular weak verb

PRESENT

ich weine	wir weinen
du weinst	ihr weint
Sie weinen	Sie weinen
er/sie/es weint	sie weinen

SIMPLE PAST

ich weinte	wir weinten
du weintest	ihr weintet
Sie weinten	Sie weinten
er/sie/es weinte	sie weinten

FUTURE

ich werde	wir werden	weinen
du wirst	ihr werdet	
Sie werden	Sie werden	
er/sie/es wird	sie werden	

PRESENT SUBJUNCTIVE I

ich weine	wir weinen
du weinest	ihr weinet
Sie weinen	Sie weinen
er/sie/es weine	sie weinen

PRESENT SUBJUNCTIVE II

ich weinte	wir weinten
du weintest	ihr weintet
Sie weinten	Sie weinten
er/sie/es weinte	sie weinten

FUTURE SUBJUNCTIVE I

ich werde	wir werden	weinen
du werdest	ihr werdet	
Sie werden	Sie werden	
er/sie/es werde	sie werden	

FUTURE SUBJUNCTIVE II

ich würde	wir würden	weinen
du würdest	ihr würdet	
Sie würden	Sie würden	
er/sie/es würde	sie würden	

PRESENT PERFECT

ich habe	wir haben	geweint
du hast	ihr habt	
Sie haben	Sie haben	
er/sie/es hat	sie haben	

PAST PERFECT

ich hatte	wir hatten	geweint
du hattest	ihr hattet	
Sie hatten	Sie hatten	
er/sie/es hatte	sie hatten	

FUTURE PERFECT

ich werde	wir werden	geweint haben
du wirst	ihr werdet	
Sie werden	Sie werden	
er/sie/es wird	sie werden	

PAST SUBJUNCTIVE I

ich habe	wir haben	geweint
du habest	ihr habet	
Sie haben	Sie haben	
er/sie/es habe	sie haben	

PAST SUBJUNCTIVE II

ich hätte	wir hätten	geweint
du hättest	ihr hättet	
Sie hätten	Sie hätten	
er/sie/es hätte	sie hätten	

FUTURE PERFECT SUBJUNCTIVE I

ich werde	wir werden	geweint haben
du werdest	ihr werdet	
Sie werden	Sie werden	
er/sie/es werde	sie werden	

FUTURE PERFECT SUBJUNCTIVE II

ich würde	wir würden	geweint haben
du würdest	ihr würdet	
Sie würden	Sie würden	
er/sie/es würde	sie würden	

COMMANDS wein(e)! weint! weinen Sie!

PRESENT PARTICIPLE weinend

Usage

Das Baby weint nach seinem Vater.	*The baby is crying for its father.*
Yvonne hat die ganze Zeit geweint.	*Yvonne cried the entire time.*
Mutti, warum weint die Omi?	*Mommy, why is Grammy crying?*
Können Tiere weinen?	*Can animals cry?*
Sara weint, wenn sie an Lars denkt.	*Sara cries when she thinks of Lars.*
Ich möchte nicht mehr weinen.	*I don't want to cry anymore.*
Grete weinte um ihren verstorbenen Bruder.	*Grete shed tears over her deceased brother.*
Es wurde geweint und gelacht.	*There was crying and laughing.*
Es war das erste Mal, dass Kurt ungehemmt geweint hatte.	*It was the first time Kurt had cried without inhibition.*
Das Kind war sensibel und weinte häufig.	*The child was sensitive and cried frequently.*
Maria hat vor Freude über das Arbeitsangebot geweint.	*Maria wept for joy over the job offer.*
Barbara weinte bitterlich und fühlte sich allein.	*Barbara wept bitterly and felt alone.*
Nach dem Streit weinte sich Laura in den Schlaf.	*After the argument, Laura cried herself to sleep.*

RELATED VERBS auf·weinen, aus·weinen, beweinen

strong verb **weist · wies · gewiesen**

PRESENT

ich weise	wir weisen
du weist	ihr weist
Sie weisen	Sie weisen
er/sie/es weist	sie weisen

SIMPLE PAST

ich wies	wir wiesen
du wiesest	ihr wiest
Sie wiesen	Sie wiesen
er/sie/es wies	sie wiesen

FUTURE

ich werde	wir werden	weisen
du wirst	ihr werdet	
Sie werden	Sie werden	
er/sie/es wird	sie werden	

PRESENT SUBJUNCTIVE I

ich weise	wir weisen
du weisest	ihr weiset
Sie weisen	Sie weisen
er/sie/es weise	sie weisen

PRESENT SUBJUNCTIVE II

ich wiese	wir wiesen
du wiesest	ihr wieset
Sie wiesen	Sie wiesen
er/sie/es wiese	sie wiesen

FUTURE SUBJUNCTIVE I

ich werde	wir werden	weisen
du werdest	ihr werdet	
Sie werden	Sie werden	
er/sie/es werde	sie werden	

FUTURE SUBJUNCTIVE II

ich würde	wir würden	weisen
du würdest	ihr würdet	
Sie würden	Sie würden	
er/sie/es würde	sie würden	

PRESENT PERFECT

ich habe	wir haben	gewiesen
du hast	ihr habt	
Sie haben	Sie haben	
er/sie/es hat	sie haben	

PAST PERFECT

ich hatte	wir hatten	gewiesen
du hattest	ihr hattet	
Sie hatten	Sie hatten	
er/sie/es hatte	sie hatten	

FUTURE PERFECT

ich werde	wir werden	gewiesen haben
du wirst	ihr werdet	
Sie werden	Sie werden	
er/sie/es wird	sie werden	

PAST SUBJUNCTIVE I

ich habe	wir haben	gewiesen
du habest	ihr habet	
Sie haben	Sie haben	
er/sie/es habe	sie haben	

PAST SUBJUNCTIVE II

ich hätte	wir hätten	gewiesen
du hättest	ihr hättet	
Sie hätten	Sie hätten	
er/sie/es hätte	sie hätten	

FUTURE PERFECT SUBJUNCTIVE I

ich werde	wir werden	gewiesen haben
du werdest	ihr werdet	
Sie werden	Sie werden	
er/sie/es werde	sie werden	

FUTURE PERFECT SUBJUNCTIVE II

ich würde	wir würden	gewiesen haben
du würdest	ihr würdet	
Sie würden	Sie würden	
er/sie/es würde	sie würden	

COMMANDS weis(e)! weist! weisen Sie!

PRESENT PARTICIPLE weisend

Usage

Lara stand auf und wies dem Mann die Tür.	*Lara stood up and showed the man the door.*
Sabines Aufsatz weist auf ein schwerwiegendes Problem im familiären Bereich.	*Sabine's essay refers to a serious problem within the family.*
Ein Kompass weist den Weg.	*A compass points the way.*
Der Mitarbeiter wurde aus dem Zimmer gewiesen.	*The employee was sent from the room.*
Papa hat den Hund aus dem Haus gewiesen.	*Papa sent the dog out of the house.*
Wir wurden über die Grenze gewiesen.	*We were sent across the border.*
Viele wurden aus ihrer Heimat gewiesen.	*Many people were expelled from their homeland.*
Hat die Lehrerin euch von der Schule gewiesen?	*Did the teacher expel you from school?*
Der ehemalige Präsident hat den Vorwurf von sich gewiesen.	*The former president rejected the accusation.*
Dreimal wiesest du den Fürsten von dir. (SCHILLER)	*Three times you rejected the prince.*

RELATED VERBS ab·weisen, an·weisen, auf·weisen, aus·weisen, ein·weisen, erweisen, hin·weisen, nach·weisen, unterweisen, verweisen, vor·weisen, zurecht·weisen, zurück·verweisen, zurück·weisen, zu·weisen; *see also* **beweisen** (101), **überweisen** (464)

527 wenden *to turn; spend*

wendet · wandte/wendete · gewandt/gewendet mixed verb or regular weak verb

PRESENT

ich wende	wir wenden
du wendest	ihr wendet
Sie wenden	Sie wenden
er/sie/es wendet	sie wenden

SIMPLE PAST

ich wandte/wendete	wir wandten/wendeten
du wandtest/wendetest	ihr wandtet/wendetet
Sie wandten/wendeten	Sie wandten/wendeten
er/sie/es wandte/wendete	sie wandten/wendeten

FUTURE

ich werde	wir werden	wenden
du wirst	ihr werdet	
Sie werden	Sie werden	
er/sie/es wird	sie werden	

PRESENT SUBJUNCTIVE I

ich wende	wir wenden
du wendest	ihr wendet
Sie wenden	Sie wenden
er/sie/es wende	sie wenden

PRESENT SUBJUNCTIVE II

ich wendete	wir wendeten
du wendetest	ihr wendetet
Sie wendeten	Sie wendeten
er/sie/es wendete	sie wendeten

FUTURE SUBJUNCTIVE I

ich werde	wir werden	wenden
du werdest	ihr werdet	
Sie werden	Sie werden	
er/sie/es werde	sie werden	

FUTURE SUBJUNCTIVE II

ich würde	wir würden	wenden
du würdest	ihr würdet	
Sie würden	Sie würden	
er/sie/es würde	sie würden	

PRESENT PERFECT

ich habe	wir haben	gewandt/gewendet
du hast	ihr habt	
Sie haben	Sie haben	
er/sie/es hat	sie haben	

PAST PERFECT

ich hatte	wir hatten	gewandt/gewendet
du hattest	ihr hattet	
Sie hatten	Sie hatten	
er/sie/es hatte	sie hatten	

FUTURE PERFECT

ich werde	wir werden	gewandt haben
du wirst	ihr werdet	OR
Sie werden	Sie werden	gewendet haben
er/sie/es wird	sie werden	

PAST SUBJUNCTIVE I

ich habe	wir haben	gewandt/gewendet
du habest	ihr habet	
Sie haben	Sie haben	
er/sie/es habe	sie haben	

PAST SUBJUNCTIVE II

ich hätte	wir hätten	gewandt/gewendet
du hättest	ihr hättet	
Sie hätten	Sie hätten	
er/sie/es hätte	sie hätten	

FUTURE PERFECT SUBJUNCTIVE I

ich werde	wir werden	gewandt haben
du werdest	ihr werdet	OR
Sie werden	Sie werden	gewendet haben
er/sie/es werde	sie werden	

FUTURE PERFECT SUBJUNCTIVE II

ich würde	wir würden	gewandt haben
du würdest	ihr würdet	OR
Sie würden	Sie würden	gewendet haben
er/sie/es würde	sie würden	

COMMANDS wende! wendet! wenden Sie!

PRESENT PARTICIPLE wendend

Usage

Klara wandte den Kopf und sah mich an. — *Klara turned her head and looked at me.*
Jörgs Tor hat das Spiel gewendet. — *Jörg's goal turned the game around.*
Hier darf nicht gewendet werden. — *It is not permissible to make a U-turn here.*
Den Pfannkuchen nach 2–3 Minuten wenden. (RECIPE) — *Turn the pancake after 2–3 minutes.*
Ralf wendet viel Zeit an seiner Dissertation. — *Ralf is spending a lot of time on his dissertation.*

sich wenden *to turn; be intended*

Die Situation hat sich zum Schlechten gewendet. — *The situation has taken a turn for the worse.*
Amalies Glück hat sich endlich gewendet. — *Amalie's luck has finally turned around.*
Die Fernsehsendung wendet sich an Erwachsene. — *The television broadcast is intended for adults.*

sich wenden an jemanden *to turn to someone, see someone*

Gertrud hat sich an einen Psychiater gewandt. — *Gertrud has begun seeing a psychiatrist.*
Wenden Sie sich bitte an Herrn Nägeli. — *Please see Mr. Nägeli.*

RELATED VERBS ab·wenden, an·wenden, auf·wenden, ein·wenden, entwenden, zu·wenden; *see also* **verwenden** (505)

strong verb **wirbt · warb · geworben**

PRESENT

ich werbe	wir werben
du wirbst	ihr werbt
Sie werben	Sie werben
er/sie/es wirbt	sie werben

SIMPLE PAST

ich warb	wir warben
du warbst	ihr warbt
Sie warben	Sie warben
er/sie/es warb	sie warben

FUTURE

ich werde	wir werden	werben
du wirst	ihr werdet	
Sie werden	Sie werden	
er/sie/es wird	sie werden	

PRESENT SUBJUNCTIVE I

ich werbe	wir werben
du werbest	ihr werbet
Sie werben	Sie werben
er/sie/es werbe	sie werben

PRESENT SUBJUNCTIVE II

ich würbe	wir würben
du würbest	ihr würbet
Sie würben	Sie würben
er/sie/es würbe	sie würben

FUTURE SUBJUNCTIVE I

ich werde	wir werden	werben
du werdest	ihr werdet	
Sie werden	Sie werden	
er/sie/es werde	sie werden	

FUTURE SUBJUNCTIVE II

ich würde	wir würden	werben
du würdest	ihr würdet	
Sie würden	Sie würden	
er/sie/es würde	sie würden	

PRESENT PERFECT

ich habe	wir haben	geworben
du hast	ihr habt	
Sie haben	Sie haben	
er/sie/es hat	sie haben	

PAST PERFECT

ich hatte	wir hatten	geworben
du hattest	ihr hattet	
Sie hatten	Sie hatten	
er/sie/es hatte	sie hatten	

FUTURE PERFECT

ich werde	wir werden	geworben haben
du wirst	ihr werdet	
Sie werden	Sie werden	
er/sie/es wird	sie werden	

PAST SUBJUNCTIVE I

ich habe	wir haben	geworben
du habest	ihr habet	
Sie haben	Sie haben	
er/sie/es habe	sie haben	

PAST SUBJUNCTIVE II

ich hätte	wir hätten	geworben
du hättest	ihr hättet	
Sie hätten	Sie hätten	
er/sie/es hätte	sie hätten	

FUTURE PERFECT SUBJUNCTIVE I

ich werde	wir werden	geworben haben
du werdest	ihr werdet	
Sie werden	Sie werden	
er/sie/es werde	sie werden	

FUTURE PERFECT SUBJUNCTIVE II

ich würde	wir würden	geworben haben
du würdest	ihr würdet	
Sie würden	Sie würden	
er/sie/es würde	sie würden	

COMMANDS wirb! werbt! werben Sie!

PRESENT PARTICIPLE werbend

Usage

Die Firma wirbt in Regionalzeitungen. — *The firm advertises in regional newspapers.*

Auf dieser Webseite wird dafür geworben. — *This Web page publicizes that.*

Die Regierung will um Arbeitskräfte aus anderen Ländern werben. — *The government wants to woo workers from other countries.*

Er warb um des Königs Tochter. (Heine) — *He courted the king's daughter.*

Wir wollen mehr Kunden werben. — *We want to attract more customers.*

Umweltfreunde werben für umweltfreundlichere Autos. — *Environmentalists are pushing for more environmentally friendly cars.*

Politiker werben für eine Erhöhung der Studiengebühren. — *Politicians are pushing for an increase in student tuition.*

Manfred wirbt für die Sozialisten. — *Manfred is canvassing for the socialists.*

Der Verein hat viele neue Mitglieder geworben. — *The association has enlisted many new members.*

RELATED VERBS ab·werben, an·werben, erwerben, umwerben; *see also* **bewerben** (102)

529 **werden** *to become, get, turn, grow; come into existence*

wird · wurde · geworden irregular verb (future auxiliary) (passive auxiliary)

MORE USAGE SENTENCES WITH **werden**

Lars wurde böse. — *Lars got angry.*
Marga wurde immer dicker. — *Marga grew fatter and fatter.*
Dana ist in den letzten paar Jahren anders geworden. — *Dana has changed over the last few years.*
Wenn man alt wird, kann man Vieles nicht mehr machen. — *When one grows old, there are many things one can't do anymore.*

Im Sommer wird es in Norwegen schon um drei Uhr morgens hell. — *In the summer in Norway, it gets light already at three in the morning.*
Aus Trauer wurde Freude. — *Sadness turned to joy.*
Das Eis wird zu Wasser. — *The ice is melting.*
Die Arbeit wurde ihm zum Spiel. — *The work became a game for him.*
Mir wird schwindelig. — *I'm getting dizzy.*
Zahlung wird am 20. fällig. — *Payment comes due on the twentieth.*
Dem kleinen Hund wurde bange. — *The little dog became afraid.*
Papa ist krank geworden und muss zu Hause bleiben. — *Daddy has gotten sick and has to stay home.*
Was soll aus ihm werden, wenn seine Stelle gestrichen wird? — *What will become of him if his position is cut?*
Das wird schon werden. — *That will turn out okay.*
Nach einer Woche wurde Ernst wieder gesund. — *After one week, Ernst got well again.*
Hans ist seiner Schwäche nicht gewahr geworden. — *Hans hasn't become aware of his weakness.*
Weil sie aber so große Zähne hatte, ward ihm angst, und es wollte fortlaufen. (GRIMM) (*archaic form*) — *But because it had such big teeth, she became afraid and wanted to run away.*
Maximilian ist durch eine Pfütze gelaufen und schon wieder nass geworden. — *Maximilian has run through a puddle and gotten wet again.*
Es wurde Licht. (1. MOSE 1,3) — *There was light. / Light came into existence.* (GENESIS 1:3)

IDIOMATIC EXPRESSIONS

Axel schrie Ingrid ein Mal zu viel an und sie wurde wütend. — *Axel screamed at Ingrid one too many times and she lost her temper.*
Aus Sepp wird nichts. — *Sepp won't amount to anything. / Sepp will come to no good.*

Aus nichts wird nichts. — *Nothing comes from nothing. /* De nihilo nihil.
Aus seinen Plänen wird nichts. — *Nothing will come of his plans.*
Ach, meine Träume werden jetzt wahr! — *Oh, my dreams are now coming true!*
Das Kind ist immer noch nicht satt geworden. — *The child still hasn't eaten his fill.*
Es wird Zeit, etwas dagegen zu tun. — *Now's the time to do something about that. / It's about time to do something about that.*

Ich werde verrückt! — *I'm going crazy!*
Ich wurde um 4.30 Uhr wach und konnte nicht mehr schlafen. — *I awoke at 4:30 and couldn't sleep anymore.*

Wird's bald? — *Will you hurry up? / Is it finished yet?*
Wir wurden uns einig, dass die Sitzung am Mittwoch stattfindet. — *We agreed that the session will take place on Wednesday.*
Ich werde bald Onkel. — *I'm going to be an uncle soon.*
Als es Tag wurde, musste der Vampir wieder in den Sarg. — *As day broke, the vampire had to return to the coffin.*
Gregor wurde im Alter von 55 blind. — *Gregor went blind at the age of 55.*
Ich bin in Sarajewo mit ihm bekannt geworden. — *I made his acquaintance in Sarajevo.*
Was ist aus Craig geworden? — *Whatever became of Craig? / What's Craig doing these days?*

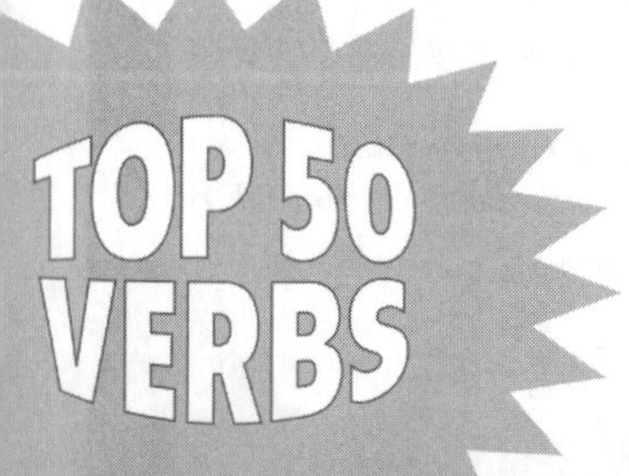

irregular verb (future auxiliary) (passive auxiliary) **wird · wurde · geworden**

PRESENT

ich werde	wir werden
du wirst	ihr werdet
Sie werden	Sie werden
er/sie/es wird	sie werden

SIMPLE PAST

ich wurde	wir wurden
du wurdest	ihr wurdet
Sie wurden	Sie wurden
er/sie/es wurde	sie wurden

FUTURE

ich werde	wir werden	werden
du wirst	ihr werdet	
Sie werden	Sie werden	
er/sie/es wird	sie werden	

PRESENT SUBJUNCTIVE I

ich werde	wir werden
du werdest	ihr werdet
Sie werden	Sie werden
er/sie/es werde	sie werden

PRESENT SUBJUNCTIVE II

ich würde	wir würden
du würdest	ihr würdet
Sie würden	Sie würden
er/sie/es würde	sie würden

FUTURE SUBJUNCTIVE I

ich werde	wir werden	werden
du werdest	ihr werdet	
Sie werden	Sie werden	
er/sie/es werde	sie werden	

FUTURE SUBJUNCTIVE II

ich würde	wir würden	werden
du würdest	ihr würdet	
Sie würden	Sie würden	
er/sie/es würde	sie würden	

PRESENT PERFECT

ich bin	wir sind	geworden
du bist	ihr seid	
Sie sind	Sie sind	
er/sie/es ist	sie sind	

PAST PERFECT

ich war	wir waren	geworden
du warst	ihr wart	
Sie waren	Sie waren	
er/sie/es war	sie waren	

FUTURE PERFECT

ich werde	wir werden	geworden sein
du wirst	ihr werdet	
Sie werden	Sie werden	
er/sie/es wird	sie werden	

PAST SUBJUNCTIVE I

ich sei	wir seien	geworden
du seiest	ihr seiet	
Sie seien	Sie seien	
er/sie/es sei	sie seien	

PAST SUBJUNCTIVE II

ich wäre	wir wären	geworden
du wärest	ihr wäret	
Sie wären	Sie wären	
er/sie/es wäre	sie wären	

FUTURE PERFECT SUBJUNCTIVE I

ich werde	wir werden	geworden sein
du werdest	ihr werdet	
Sie werden	Sie werden	
er/sie/es werde	sie werden	

FUTURE PERFECT SUBJUNCTIVE II

ich würde	wir würden	geworden sein
du würdest	ihr würdet	
Sie würden	Sie würden	
er/sie/es würde	sie würden	

COMMANDS werde! werdet! werden Sie!

PRESENT PARTICIPLE werdend

NOTE The past participle of the passive auxiliary is **worden**.

Usage

Mir wird schlecht.	*I'm getting sick.*
Ich bin letzte Woche einundzwanzig geworden.	*I turned 21 last week.*
Paul wird Architekt.	*Paul is becoming an architect.*
Er wollte nicht hysterisch werden.	*He didn't want to become hysterical.*
Was wurde eigentlich aus Klaus?	*Whatever became of Klaus?*
Im Laufe der Jahre wurde der Schriftsteller überall bekannt.	*Over the course of years, the writer became famous everywhere.*
Es wurde uns klar, dass er nicht ernst war.	*It became clear to us that he wasn't serious.*
Was möchtest du werden?	*What do you want to be/become?*
Gregor wurde ein Käfer.	*Gregor turned into a bug.*
Es wurde Tag für Tag kälter.	*It was getting colder day by day.*

RELATED VERBS inne·werden, irre·werden, kund·werden, los·werden

530 werfen *to throw, fling, cast, pitch, drop*

wirft · warf · geworfen

strong verb

PRESENT

ich werfe	wir werfen
du wirfst	ihr werft
Sie werfen	Sie werfen
er/sie/es wirft	sie werfen

SIMPLE PAST

ich warf	wir warfen
du warfst	ihr warft
Sie warfen	Sie warfen
er/sie/es warf	sie warfen

FUTURE

ich werde	wir werden	werfen
du wirst	ihr werdet	
Sie werden	Sie werden	
er/sie/es wird	sie werden	

PRESENT SUBJUNCTIVE I

ich werfe	wir werfen
du werfest	ihr werfet
Sie werfen	Sie werfen
er/sie/es werfe	sie werfen

PRESENT SUBJUNCTIVE II

ich würfe	wir würfen
du würfest	ihr würfet
Sie würfen	Sie würfen
er/sie/es würfe	sie würfen

FUTURE SUBJUNCTIVE I

ich werde	wir werden	werfen
du werdest	ihr werdet	
Sie werden	Sie werden	
er/sie/es werde	sie werden	

FUTURE SUBJUNCTIVE II

ich würde	wir würden	werfen
du würdest	ihr würdet	
Sie würden	Sie würden	
er/sie/es würde	sie würden	

PRESENT PERFECT

ich habe	wir haben	geworfen
du hast	ihr habt	
Sie haben	Sie haben	
er/sie/es hat	sie haben	

PAST PERFECT

ich hatte	wir hatten	geworfen
du hattest	ihr hattet	
Sie hatten	Sie hatten	
er/sie/es hatte	sie hatten	

FUTURE PERFECT

ich werde	wir werden	geworfen haben
du wirst	ihr werdet	
Sie werden	Sie werden	
er/sie/es wird	sie werden	

PAST SUBJUNCTIVE I

ich habe	wir haben	geworfen
du habest	ihr habet	
Sie haben	Sie haben	
er/sie/es habe	sie haben	

PAST SUBJUNCTIVE II

ich hätte	wir hätten	geworfen
du hättest	ihr hättet	
Sie hätten	Sie hätten	
er/sie/es hätte	sie hätten	

FUTURE PERFECT SUBJUNCTIVE I

ich werde	wir werden	geworfen haben
du werdest	ihr werdet	
Sie werden	Sie werden	
er/sie/es werde	sie werden	

FUTURE PERFECT SUBJUNCTIVE II

ich würde	wir würden	geworfen haben
du würdest	ihr würdet	
Sie würden	Sie würden	
er/sie/es würde	sie würden	

COMMANDS wirf! werft! werfen Sie!

PRESENT PARTICIPLE werfend

Usage

Wirf mir den Ball!	*Throw me the ball!*
Beim Unfall wurde Jens aus dem Auto geworfen.	*In the accident, Jens was thrown from the car.*
Das Kind warf die Schüssel auf den Boden.	*The child flung the bowl onto the floor.*
Die Bäume warfen lange Schatten in der Abendsonne.	*The trees cast long shadows in the evening sun.*
Beim Ringen wirft man seinen Gegner so schnell wie möglich.	*In wrestling, you throw your opponent as quickly as possible.*
Ingrid warf einen Blick ins Wohnzimmer.	*Ingrid cast a glance into the living room.*
Die Amerikaner haben zwei Atombomben auf Japan geworfen.	*The Americans dropped two atom bombs on Japan.*

sich werfen *to warp*

Grünes Holz wirft sich leicht.	*Green wood warps easily.*

RELATED VERBS ab·werfen, auf·werfen, aus·werfen, bewerfen, ein·werfen, entwerfen, nieder·werfen, überwerfen, über·werfen, um·werfen, unterwerfen, verwerfen, vor·werfen, weg·werfen, zurück·werfen, zusammen·werfen

strong verb (dative object) **widerspricht · widersprach · widersprochen**

PRESENT

ich widerspreche	wir widersprechen
du widersprichst	ihr widersprecht
Sie widersprechen	Sie widersprechen
er/sie/es widerspricht	sie widersprechen

SIMPLE PAST

ich widersprach	wir widersprachen
du widersprachst	ihr widerspracht
Sie widersprachen	Sie widersprachen
er/sie/es widersprach	sie widersprachen

FUTURE

ich werde	wir werden	widersprechen
du wirst	ihr werdet	
Sie werden	Sie werden	
er/sie/es wird	sie werden	

PRESENT SUBJUNCTIVE I

ich widerspreche	wir widersprechen
du widersprechest	ihr widersprechet
Sie widersprechen	Sie widersprechen
er/sie/es widerspreche	sie widersprechen

PRESENT SUBJUNCTIVE II

ich widerspräche	wir widersprächen
du widersprächest	ihr widersprächet
Sie widersprächen	Sie widersprächen
er/sie/es widerspräche	sie widersprächen

FUTURE SUBJUNCTIVE I

ich werde	wir werden	widersprechen
du werdest	ihr werdet	
Sie werden	Sie werden	
er/sie/es werde	sie werden	

FUTURE SUBJUNCTIVE II

ich würde	wir würden	widersprechen
du würdest	ihr würdet	
Sie würden	Sie würden	
er/sie/es würde	sie würden	

PRESENT PERFECT

ich habe	wir haben	widersprochen
du hast	ihr habt	
Sie haben	Sie haben	
er/sie/es hat	sie haben	

PAST PERFECT

ich hatte	wir hatten	widersprochen
du hattest	ihr hattet	
Sie hatten	Sie hatten	
er/sie/es hatte	sie hatten	

FUTURE PERFECT

ich werde	wir werden	widersprochen haben
du wirst	ihr werdet	
Sie werden	Sie werden	
er/sie/es wird	sie werden	

PAST SUBJUNCTIVE I

ich habe	wir haben	widersprochen
du habest	ihr habet	
Sie haben	Sie haben	
er/sie/es habe	sie haben	

PAST SUBJUNCTIVE II

ich hätte	wir hätten	widersprochen
du hättest	ihr hättet	
Sie hätten	Sie hätten	
er/sie/es hätte	sie hätten	

FUTURE PERFECT SUBJUNCTIVE I

ich werde	wir werden	widersprochen haben
du werdest	ihr werdet	
Sie werden	Sie werden	
er/sie/es werde	sie werden	

FUTURE PERFECT SUBJUNCTIVE II

ich würde	wir würden	widersprochen haben
du würdest	ihr würdet	
Sie würden	Sie würden	
er/sie/es würde	sie würden	

COMMANDS widersprich! widersprecht! widersprechen Sie!

PRESENT PARTICIPLE widersprechend

Usage

Warum widersprichst du mir ständig?	*Why do you constantly contradict me?*
Seine Thesen widersprechen einander indirekt.	*His theses are indirectly inconsistent with each other.*
Mit ihrer heutigen Antwort hat sich die Pressesprecherin widersprochen.	*With her answer today, the spokeswoman contradicted herself.*
Herrn Leitners Bemerkungen widersprechen den offiziellen Aussagen der Regierung.	*Mr. Leitner's comments contradict the government's official statements.*
Augenzeugen widersprachen sich in ihren Aussagen.	*Eyewitnesses contradicted each other in their statements.*
Ich muss deiner Behauptung widersprechen.	*I must contradict your claim.*
Der Politiker widerspricht sich selbst wieder.	*The politician is contradicting himself again.*
Das geplante System widerspricht dem Grundgesetz.	*The system being planned is in conflict with the constitution.*
„Nein, er war nicht dabei", widersprach Thorsten.	*"No, he wasn't there," countered Thorsten.*
Der einfache Bauer wagte es nicht, der Obrigkeit zu widersprechen.	*The simple peasant dared not oppose the ruling authorities.*

RELATED VERBS *see* **sprechen** (415)

widmen *to dedicate, devote; attend to*

widmet · widmete · gewidmet

regular weak verb

PRESENT

ich widme	wir widmen
du widmest	ihr widmet
Sie widmen	Sie widmen
er/sie/es widmet	sie widmen

SIMPLE PAST

ich widmete	wir widmeten
du widmetest	ihr widmetet
Sie widmeten	Sie widmeten
er/sie/es widmete	sie widmeten

FUTURE

ich werde	wir werden	widmen
du wirst	ihr werdet	
Sie werden	Sie werden	
er/sie/es wird	sie werden	

PRESENT SUBJUNCTIVE I

ich widme	wir widmen
du widmest	ihr widmet
Sie widmen	Sie widmen
er/sie/es widme	sie widmen

PRESENT SUBJUNCTIVE II

ich widmete	wir widmeten
du widmetest	ihr widmetet
Sie widmeten	Sie widmeten
er/sie/es widmete	sie widmeten

FUTURE SUBJUNCTIVE I

ich werde	wir werden	widmen
du werdest	ihr werdet	
Sie werden	Sie werden	
er/sie/es werde	sie werden	

FUTURE SUBJUNCTIVE II

ich würde	wir würden	widmen
du würdest	ihr würdet	
Sie würden	Sie würden	
er/sie/es würde	sie würden	

PRESENT PERFECT

ich habe	wir haben	gewidmet
du hast	ihr habt	
Sie haben	Sie haben	
er/sie/es hat	sie haben	

PAST PERFECT

ich hatte	wir hatten	gewidmet
du hattest	ihr hattet	
Sie hatten	Sie hatten	
er/sie/es hatte	sie hatten	

FUTURE PERFECT

ich werde	wir werden	gewidmet haben
du wirst	ihr werdet	
Sie werden	Sie werden	
er/sie/es wird	sie werden	

PAST SUBJUNCTIVE I

ich habe	wir haben	gewidmet
du habest	ihr habet	
Sie haben	Sie haben	
er/sie/es habe	sie haben	

PAST SUBJUNCTIVE II

ich hätte	wir hätten	gewidmet
du hättest	ihr hättet	
Sie hätten	Sie hätten	
er/sie/es hätte	sie hätten	

FUTURE PERFECT SUBJUNCTIVE I

ich werde	wir werden	gewidmet haben
du werdest	ihr werdet	
Sie werden	Sie werden	
er/sie/es werde	sie werden	

FUTURE PERFECT SUBJUNCTIVE II

ich würde	wir würden	gewidmet haben
du würdest	ihr würdet	
Sie würden	Sie würden	
er/sie/es würde	sie würden	

COMMANDS widme! widmet! widmen Sie!

PRESENT PARTICIPLE widmend

Usage

Die erste Woche des Kurses ist den Grundlagen gewidmet. — *The first week of the course is devoted to the basics.*

Das Geschichtsbuch wurde den im Krieg Gefallenen gewidmet. — *The history book was dedicated to those who died in war.*

Wann werden Sie sich diesem Projekt voll widmen können? — *When will you be able to commit yourself fully to this project?*

Christian hat der Bundeswehr zwei Jahre gewidmet. — *Christian spent two years in the army.*

Ich möchte meinen Eltern das Buch widmen. — *I'd like to dedicate this book to my parents.*

Seine nächste Sonate widmete er Ludwig van Beethoven. — *He dedicated his next sonata to Ludwig van Beethoven.*

Die Heilige Elisabeth hatte ihr Leben den Armen gewidmet. — *St. Elizabeth had devoted her life to the poor.*

Roland widmet ihr jetzt mehr Zeit. — *Roland is spending more time with her now.*

Liesl hat ihrem Mann ihren ersten Roman gewidmet. — *Liesl dedicated her first novel to her husband.*

Widmen Sie dieser Sache Ihre Aufmerksamkeit. — *Give your attention to this matter.*

RELATED VERB um·widmen

regular weak verb **wiederholt · wiederholte · wiederholt**

PRESENT

ich wiederhole	wir wiederholen
du wiederholst	ihr wiederholt
Sie wiederholen	Sie wiederholen
er/sie/es wiederholt	sie wiederholen

SIMPLE PAST

ich wiederholte	wir wiederholten
du wiederholtest	ihr wiederholtet
Sie wiederholten	Sie wiederholten
er/sie/es wiederholte	sie wiederholten

FUTURE

ich werde	wir werden	wiederholen
du wirst	ihr werdet	
Sie werden	Sie werden	
er/sie/es wird	sie werden	

PRESENT SUBJUNCTIVE I

ich wiederhole	wir wiederholen
du wiederholest	ihr wiederholet
Sie wiederholen	Sie wiederholen
er/sie/es wiederhole	sie wiederholen

PRESENT SUBJUNCTIVE II

ich wiederholte	wir wiederholten
du wiederholtest	ihr wiederholtet
Sie wiederholten	Sie wiederholten
er/sie/es wiederholte	sie wiederholten

FUTURE SUBJUNCTIVE I

ich werde	wir werden	wiederholen
du werdest	ihr werdet	
Sie werden	Sie werden	
er/sie/es werde	sie werden	

FUTURE SUBJUNCTIVE II

ich würde	wir würden	wiederholen
du würdest	ihr würdet	
Sie würden	Sie würden	
er/sie/es würde	sie würden	

PRESENT PERFECT

ich habe	wir haben	wiederholt
du hast	ihr habt	
Sie haben	Sie haben	
er/sie/es hat	sie haben	

PAST PERFECT

ich hatte	wir hatten	wiederholt
du hattest	ihr hattet	
Sie hatten	Sie hatten	
er/sie/es hatte	sie hatten	

FUTURE PERFECT

ich werde	wir werden	wiederholt haben
du wirst	ihr werdet	
Sie werden	Sie werden	
er/sie/es wird	sie werden	

PAST SUBJUNCTIVE I

ich habe	wir haben	wiederholt
du habest	ihr habet	
Sie haben	Sie haben	
er/sie/es habe	sie haben	

PAST SUBJUNCTIVE II

ich hätte	wir hätten	wiederholt
du hättest	ihr hättet	
Sie hätten	Sie hätten	
er/sie/es hätte	sie hätten	

FUTURE PERFECT SUBJUNCTIVE I

ich werde	wir werden	wiederholt haben
du werdest	ihr werdet	
Sie werden	Sie werden	
er/sie/es werde	sie werden	

FUTURE PERFECT SUBJUNCTIVE II

ich würde	wir würden	wiederholt haben
du würdest	ihr würdet	
Sie würden	Sie würden	
er/sie/es würde	sie würden	

COMMANDS wiederhol(e)! wiederholt! wiederholen Sie!

PRESENT PARTICIPLE wiederholend

NOTE When **wiederholen** means "to retrieve," its prefix is separable: **Der Junge holt den Ball wieder.**

Usage

Letztes Semester habe ich den Kurs wiederholt.	*Last semester, I repeated the course.*
Könnten Sie die Frage wiederholen?	*Could you repeat the question?*
Ich wiederhole: Der Zug aus Ulm verspätet sich um 30 Minuten.	*I repeat: The train from Ulm is delayed 30 minutes.*
Man fragte sie wieder und sie wiederholte ihre Antwort.	*They asked her again, and she gave them the same answer.*
Am nächsten Tag wurde die Warnung wiederholt.	*The next day, the warning was reiterated.*
Wiederholen wir jetzt den Konjunktiv.	*Let's review the subjunctive now.*

sich wiederholen *to repeat oneself, be repeated, recur*

Herr Biedermann wiederholt sich nicht gern.	*Mr. Biedermann doesn't like to repeat himself.*
Die Szene wiederholt sich am Ende des Films.	*The scene is repeated at the end of the film.*
Das Phänomen wiederholt sich jedes Jahr.	*The phenomenon recurs every year.*

RELATED VERBS *see* **holen** (247)

534 wiegen *to weigh*

wiegt · wog · gewogen — strong verb

PRESENT

ich wiege	wir wiegen
du wiegst	ihr wiegt
Sie wiegen	Sie wiegen
er/sie/es wiegt	sie wiegen

SIMPLE PAST

ich wog	wir wogen
du wogst	ihr wogt
Sie wogen	Sie wogen
er/sie/es wog	sie wogen

FUTURE

ich werde	wir werden	wiegen
du wirst	ihr werdet	
Sie werden	Sie werden	
er/sie/es wird	sie werden	

PRESENT SUBJUNCTIVE I

ich wiege	wir wiegen
du wiegest	ihr wieget
Sie wiegen	Sie wiegen
er/sie/es wiege	sie wiegen

PRESENT SUBJUNCTIVE II

ich wöge	wir wögen
du wögest	ihr wöget
Sie wögen	Sie wögen
er/sie/es wöge	sie wögen

FUTURE SUBJUNCTIVE I

ich werde	wir werden	wiegen
du werdest	ihr werdet	
Sie werden	Sie werden	
er/sie/es werde	sie werden	

FUTURE SUBJUNCTIVE II

ich würde	wir würden	wiegen
du würdest	ihr würdet	
Sie würden	Sie würden	
er/sie/es würde	sie würden	

PRESENT PERFECT

ich habe	wir haben	gewogen
du hast	ihr habt	
Sie haben	Sie haben	
er/sie/es hat	sie haben	

PAST PERFECT

ich hatte	wir hatten	gewogen
du hattest	ihr hattet	
Sie hatten	Sie hatten	
er/sie/es hatte	sie hatten	

FUTURE PERFECT

ich werde	wir werden	gewogen haben
du wirst	ihr werdet	
Sie werden	Sie werden	
er/sie/es wird	sie werden	

PAST SUBJUNCTIVE I

ich habe	wir haben	gewogen
du habest	ihr habet	
Sie haben	Sie haben	
er/sie/es habe	sie haben	

PAST SUBJUNCTIVE II

ich hätte	wir hätten	gewogen
du hättest	ihr hättet	
Sie hätten	Sie hätten	
er/sie/es hätte	sie hätten	

FUTURE PERFECT SUBJUNCTIVE I

ich werde	wir werden	gewogen haben
du werdest	ihr werdet	
Sie werden	Sie werden	
er/sie/es werde	sie werden	

FUTURE PERFECT SUBJUNCTIVE II

ich würde	wir würden	gewogen haben
du würdest	ihr würdet	
Sie würden	Sie würden	
er/sie/es würde	sie würden	

COMMANDS wieg(e)! wiegt! wiegen Sie!

PRESENT PARTICIPLE wiegend

Usage

Warum wiegst du die Katze? — *Why are you weighing the cat?*
Wie viel wiegen Sie? — *How much do you weigh?*
Bis 2001 hat Erich 95 Kilo gewogen. — *Until 2001, Erich weighed 95 kilos.*
Frau Escher wiegt sich jeden Morgen. — *Mrs. Escher weighs herself every morning.*
Bei der Geburt wog sie nur zwei Kilo. — *At birth, she weighed only two kilos.*
Vor seiner Krankheit hat Opa gut 100 Kilo gewogen. — *Before his illness, Grandpa weighed at least 100 kilos.*
Der kleine Jakob wiegt jetzt 10 Kilo. — *Little Jakob weighs 10 kilos now.*
Die neue Waage wiegt nicht richtig. — *The new scale doesn't weigh accurately.*
Auf dem Mond wiegt man nicht so viel wie auf der Erde. — *On the moon, you don't weigh as much as on earth.*
Ihre Tasche wiegt mehr als Ihr großer Koffer! — *Your purse weighs more than your big suitcase!*
Deine Worte wiegen schwer. — *Your words carry weight.*
Die langfristigen Folgen wiegen schwerer als die wirtschaftlichen Vorteile. — *The long-term consequences outweigh the economic benefits.*

RELATED VERBS ab·wiegen, auf·wiegen, aus·wiegen, nach·wiegen, überwiegen, verwiegen, vor·wiegen

PRESENT

ich winde	wir winden
du windest	ihr windet
Sie winden	Sie winden
er/sie/es windet	sie winden

SIMPLE PAST

ich wand	wir wanden
du wandest	ihr wandet
Sie wanden	Sie wanden
er/sie/es wand	sie wanden

FUTURE

ich werde	wir werden	winden
du wirst	ihr werdet	
Sie werden	Sie werden	
er/sie/es wird	sie werden	

PRESENT SUBJUNCTIVE I

ich winde	wir winden
du windest	ihr windet
Sie winden	Sie winden
er/sie/es winde	sie winden

PRESENT SUBJUNCTIVE II

ich wände	wir wänden
du wändest	ihr wändet
Sie wänden	Sie wänden
er/sie/es wände	sie wänden

FUTURE SUBJUNCTIVE I

ich werde	wir werden	winden
du werdest	ihr werdet	
Sie werden	Sie werden	
er/sie/es werde	sie werden	

FUTURE SUBJUNCTIVE II

ich würde	wir würden	winden
du würdest	ihr würdet	
Sie würden	Sie würden	
er/sie/es würde	sie würden	

PRESENT PERFECT

ich habe	wir haben	gewunden
du hast	ihr habt	
Sie haben	Sie haben	
er/sie/es hat	sie haben	

PAST PERFECT

ich hatte	wir hatten	gewunden
du hattest	ihr hattet	
Sie hatten	Sie hatten	
er/sie/es hatte	sie hatten	

FUTURE PERFECT

ich werde	wir werden	gewunden haben
du wirst	ihr werdet	
Sie werden	Sie werden	
er/sie/es wird	sie werden	

PAST SUBJUNCTIVE I

ich habe	wir haben	gewunden
du habest	ihr habet	
Sie haben	Sie haben	
er/sie/es habe	sie haben	

PAST SUBJUNCTIVE II

ich hätte	wir hätten	gewunden
du hättest	ihr hättet	
Sie hätten	Sie hätten	
er/sie/es hätte	sie hätten	

FUTURE PERFECT SUBJUNCTIVE I

ich werde	wir werden	gewunden haben
du werdest	ihr werdet	
Sie werden	Sie werden	
er/sie/es werde	sie werden	

FUTURE PERFECT SUBJUNCTIVE II

ich würde	wir würden	gewunden haben
du würdest	ihr würdet	
Sie würden	Sie würden	
er/sie/es würde	sie würden	

COMMANDS winde! windet! winden Sie!

PRESENT PARTICIPLE windend

Usage

Windest du eine Girlande um den Kranz? — *Are you winding a garland around the wreath?*

Sie hat mir eine Halskette aus Blumen um den Hals gewunden. — *She wound a necklace of flowers around my neck.*

Da griff ich zu den Blumen, die du siehst, und wand ihr Kränze meiner hohen Herrin. (GRILLPARZER) — *Then I picked the flowers that you see and bound them into wreaths for my mistress.*

Das Messer wurde dem Einbrecher aus der Hand gewunden. — *The knife was wrested from the intruder's hand.*

sich winden *to wind oneself; writhe, wriggle; meander*

Die riesige Schlange wand sich um den Hals des Mannes. — *The huge snake coiled itself around the man's neck.*

Im Entbindungszimmer hat sich eine Frau vor Schmerzen gewunden. — *A woman in the delivery room writhed in pain.*

Das Bitterbach windet sich durch die Wiesen des breiten Tals. — *Bitter Creek meanders through the meadows of the wide valley.*

RELATED VERBS auf·winden, durch·winden, entwinden, hoch·winden, umwinden; *see also* **überwinden** (465)

536 wirken *to have an effect, take effect; make an impression; appear; function*

wirkt · wirkte · gewirkt

regular weak verb

PRESENT

ich wirke	wir wirken
du wirkst	ihr wirkt
Sie wirken	Sie wirken
er/sie/es wirkt	sie wirken

SIMPLE PAST

ich wirkte	wir wirkten
du wirktest	ihr wirktet
Sie wirkten	Sie wirkten
er/sie/es wirkte	sie wirkten

FUTURE

ich werde	wir werden	wirken
du wirst	ihr werdet	
Sie werden	Sie werden	
er/sie/es wird	sie werden	

PRESENT SUBJUNCTIVE I

ich wirke	wir wirken
du wirkest	ihr wirket
Sie wirken	Sie wirken
er/sie/es wirke	sie wirken

PRESENT SUBJUNCTIVE II

ich wirkte	wir wirkten
du wirktest	ihr wirktet
Sie wirkten	Sie wirkten
er/sie/es wirkte	sie wirkten

FUTURE SUBJUNCTIVE I

ich werde	wir werden	wirken
du werdest	ihr werdet	
Sie werden	Sie werden	
er/sie/es werde	sie werden	

FUTURE SUBJUNCTIVE II

ich würde	wir würden	wirken
du würdest	ihr würdet	
Sie würden	Sie würden	
er/sie/es würde	sie würden	

PRESENT PERFECT

ich habe	wir haben	gewirkt
du hast	ihr habt	
Sie haben	Sie haben	
er/sie/es hat	sie haben	

PAST PERFECT

ich hatte	wir hatten	gewirkt
du hattest	ihr hattet	
Sie hatten	Sie hatten	
er/sie/es hatte	sie hatten	

FUTURE PERFECT

ich werde	wir werden	gewirkt haben
du wirst	ihr werdet	
Sie werden	Sie werden	
er/sie/es wird	sie werden	

PAST SUBJUNCTIVE I

ich habe	wir haben	gewirkt
du habest	ihr habet	
Sie haben	Sie haben	
er/sie/es habe	sie haben	

PAST SUBJUNCTIVE II

ich hätte	wir hätten	gewirkt
du hättest	ihr hättet	
Sie hätten	Sie hätten	
er/sie/es hätte	sie hätten	

FUTURE PERFECT SUBJUNCTIVE I

ich werde	wir werden	gewirkt haben
du werdest	ihr werdet	
Sie werden	Sie werden	
er/sie/es werde	sie werden	

FUTURE PERFECT SUBJUNCTIVE II

ich würde	wir würden	gewirkt haben
du würdest	ihr würdet	
Sie würden	Sie würden	
er/sie/es würde	sie würden	

COMMANDS wirk(e)! wirkt! wirken Sie!

PRESENT PARTICIPLE wirkend

Usage

Das Stück wirkt wie eine Sonate von Mozart.	*The piece has the effect of a Mozart sonata.*
Die zerbombten Häuser wirkten gespenstisch auf uns.	*The bombed-out houses had a spooky effect on us.*
Das Medikament wirkt nach zwei Minuten.	*The medicine takes effect in two minutes.*
Wie hat er auf dich gewirkt?	*How did he impress you?*
Du wirkst nervös. Was ist los?	*You seem nervous. What's the matter?*
Kräutertee wirkt Wunder gegen Stress.	*Herbal tea works wonders for stress.*
Die Heiligen wirkten Wunder.	*The saints performed miracles.*
Der heilige Nikolaus wirkte als Bischof in der Türkei.	*St. Nicolaus functioned as a bishop in Turkey.*
Dagmar durfte in der Kunstakademie nicht wirken.	*Dagmar wasn't allowed to work at the art academy.*
Julia wirkte für den Widerstand bis zum letzten Atemzug.	*Julia worked for the Resistance to her dying breath.*
Herr Wartensee wirkt seit 1994 als Chorleiter.	*Mr. Wartensee has been serving as choir director since 1994.*

RELATED VERBS aus·wirken, bewirken, ein·wirken, entgegen·wirken, erwirken, mit·wirken, nach·wirken, zusammen·wirken

PRESENT

ich weiß	wir wissen
du weißt	ihr wisst
Sie wissen	Sie wissen
er/sie/es weiß	sie wissen

SIMPLE PAST

ich wusste	wir wussten
du wusstest	ihr wusstet
Sie wussten	Sie wussten
er/sie/es wusste	sie wussten

FUTURE

ich werde	wir werden	wissen
du wirst	ihr werdet	
Sie werden	Sie werden	
er/sie/es wird	sie werden	

PRESENT SUBJUNCTIVE I

ich wisse	wir wissen
du wissest	ihr wisset
Sie wissen	Sie wissen
er/sie/es wisse	sie wissen

PRESENT SUBJUNCTIVE II

ich wüsste	wir wüssten
du wüsstest	ihr wüsstet
Sie wüssten	Sie wüssten
er/sie/es wüsste	sie wüssten

FUTURE SUBJUNCTIVE I

ich werde	wir werden	wissen
du werdest	ihr werdet	
Sie werden	Sie werden	
er/sie/es werde	sie werden	

FUTURE SUBJUNCTIVE II

ich würde	wir würden	wissen
du würdest	ihr würdet	
Sie würden	Sie würden	
er/sie/es würde	sie würden	

COMMANDS wisse! wisst! wissen Sie!

PRESENT PARTICIPLE wissend

PRESENT PERFECT

ich habe	wir haben	gewusst
du hast	ihr habt	
Sie haben	Sie haben	
er/sie/es hat	sie haben	

PAST PERFECT

ich hatte	wir hatten	gewusst
du hattest	ihr hattet	
Sie hatten	Sie hatten	
er/sie/es hatte	sie hatten	

FUTURE PERFECT

ich werde	wir werden	gewusst haben
du wirst	ihr werdet	
Sie werden	Sie werden	
er/sie/es wird	sie werden	

PAST SUBJUNCTIVE I

ich habe	wir haben	gewusst
du habest	ihr habet	
Sie haben	Sie haben	
er/sie/es habe	sie haben	

PAST SUBJUNCTIVE II

ich hätte	wir hätten	gewusst
du hättest	ihr hättet	
Sie hätten	Sie hätten	
er/sie/es hätte	sie hätten	

FUTURE PERFECT SUBJUNCTIVE I

ich werde	wir werden	gewusst haben
du werdest	ihr werdet	
Sie werden	Sie werden	
er/sie/es werde	sie werden	

FUTURE PERFECT SUBJUNCTIVE II

ich würde	wir würden	gewusst haben
du würdest	ihr würdet	
Sie würden	Sie würden	
er/sie/es würde	sie würden	

Usage

Das habe ich gewusst.	*I knew that.*
Anna darf die Wahrheit nicht wissen.	*Anna can't know the truth.*
Marta kommt morgen wieder, so weit ich weiß.	*Marta is returning tomorrow, as far as I know.*
Entschuldigung, wüssten Sie zufällig, wo hier eine Toilette ist?	*Pardon me, would you happen to know where a restroom is?*
Renate wusste genau, dass die Tür abgeschlossen war, als sie wegging.	*Renate was certain that the door was locked when she left.*
Woher soll ich wissen, wo Werner ist?	*How should I know where Werner is?*
Lass Ingrid wissen, dass ihr Bruder angerufen hat.	*Let Ingrid know that her brother called.*
Die Polizei wusste die Frau in Sicherheit.	*The police knew the woman to be safe.*
Was denken und wissen Tiere?	*What do animals think and know?*
Jost weiß, was er will.	*Jost knows what he wants.*
Wenn ich das damals nur gewusst hätte!	*If only I'd known that then!*

RELATED VERB voraus·wissen

TOP 50 VERB ☞

MORE USAGE SENTENCES WITH wissen

Tante Irmgard will nicht gewusst haben, dass ich weg war.	*Aunt Irmgard claims not to have known that I was gone.*
Mama wird die Antwort bestimmt wissen.	*Mama will surely know the answer.*
Was möchten Sie wissen?	*What would you like to know?*
Stefanie scheint den Grund zu wissen.	*Stefanie seems to know the reason.*
Ihr habt mein Alter gar nicht gewusst.	*You didn't even know my age.*
Wisse, dass mir sehr missfällt, wenn so viele singen und reden! (Goethe)	*Know that it greatly displeases me when so many sing and talk!*

wissen zu + infinitive *to be able to, know how to*

Der Vorsitzende wusste mitzuteilen, dass die Jahresgewinne leicht angestiegen waren.	*The chairman was able to report that annual earnings had risen slightly.*
Glücklicherweise weiß Oma sich weiterzuhelfen.	*Luckily, Grandma is able to look after herself.*
Unser Hund weiß sich unter anderen Hunden zu benehmen.	*Our dog knows how to behave when he's around other dogs.*
Ich wusste mich nicht zu fassen.	*I couldn't compose myself.*

wissen von *to be informed of, have knowledge of, be acquainted with*

Serena weiß von nichts.	*Serena has no knowledge (of it).*
Ich weiß nichts von der Angelegenheit.	*I am not acquainted with the issue.*

wissen über + accusative *to know about*

Du weißt doch ziemlich viel darüber.	*You know rather a lot about that.*
„Was wissen Sie über einen Herrn Gruber?" fragte der Detektiv.	*"What do you know about a Mr. Gruber?" asked the detective.*

wissen um *to understand, know well*

Die alte Frau wusste um Schmerzen und Leiden.	*The old woman knew all about pain and suffering.*

IDIOMATIC EXPRESSIONS

Weißt du noch, als wir in der Schule waren?	*Do you remember when we were in school?*
Der Film war gut, aber ich weiß den Titel nicht mehr.	*The film was good, but I can't remember the title.*
Weiß Gott!	*God only knows!*
Ich wusste nicht aus noch ein.	*I had no clue what to do.*
„Ist Lars krank?"	*"Is Lars ill?"*
„Nicht dass ich wüsste."	*"Not that I'm aware of."*
Trina will nichts mehr von ihm wissen.	*Trina doesn't want to have anything more to do with him.*
Wir standen da und wussten nicht weiter.	*We stood there not knowing what to do next.*
Tja, man kann nie wissen.	*Well, you can never tell.*
Es hätte wer weiß was passieren können. (*colloquial*)	*Who knows what might have happened.*
Wissen Sie was, ich mache es morgen. In Ordnung? (*colloquial*)	*I tell you what, I'll do it tomorrow. Okay?*
Was ich nicht weiß, macht mich nicht heiß. (PROVERB)	*What I don't know, won't hurt me.*
Wer nichts weiß, muss alles glauben. (PROVERB)	*He who knows nothing must believe everything.*
Claudio weiß Bescheid über technische Sachen.	*Claudio is well acquainted with technical matters.*
Ich wusste nichts mit mir anzufangen.	*I didn't know what to do with myself. / I was bored.*
Manni wusste keine Ausrede mehr.	*Manni could think of no more excuses.*
Meine Tante weiß immer alles besser.	*My aunt is a know-it-all.*

regular weak verb **wohnt · wohnte · gewohnt**

PRESENT

ich wohne	wir wohnen
du wohnst	ihr wohnt
Sie wohnen	Sie wohnen
er/sie/es wohnt	sie wohnen

SIMPLE PAST

ich wohnte	wir wohnten
du wohntest	ihr wohntet
Sie wohnten	Sie wohnten
er/sie/es wohnte	sie wohnten

FUTURE

ich werde	wir werden	wohnen
du wirst	ihr werdet	
Sie werden	Sie werden	
er/sie/es wird	sie werden	

PRESENT SUBJUNCTIVE I

ich wohne	wir wohnen
du wohnest	ihr wohnet
Sie wohnen	Sie wohnen
er/sie/es wohne	sie wohnen

PRESENT SUBJUNCTIVE II

ich wohnte	wir wohnten
du wohntest	ihr wohntet
Sie wohnten	Sie wohnten
er/sie/es wohnte	sie wohnten

FUTURE SUBJUNCTIVE I

ich werde	wir werden	wohnen
du werdest	ihr werdet	
Sie werden	Sie werden	
er/sie/es werde	sie werden	

FUTURE SUBJUNCTIVE II

ich würde	wir würden	wohnen
du würdest	ihr würdet	
Sie würden	Sie würden	
er/sie/es würde	sie würden	

PRESENT PERFECT

ich habe	wir haben	gewohnt
du hast	ihr habt	
Sie haben	Sie haben	
er/sie/es hat	sie haben	

PAST PERFECT

ich hatte	wir hatten	gewohnt
du hattest	ihr hattet	
Sie hatten	Sie hatten	
er/sie/es hatte	sie hatten	

FUTURE PERFECT

ich werde	wir werden	gewohnt haben
du wirst	ihr werdet	
Sie werden	Sie werden	
er/sie/es wird	sie werden	

PAST SUBJUNCTIVE I

ich habe	wir haben	gewohnt
du habest	ihr habet	
Sie haben	Sie haben	
er/sie/es habe	sie haben	

PAST SUBJUNCTIVE II

ich hätte	wir hätten	gewohnt
du hättest	ihr hättet	
Sie hätten	Sie hätten	
er/sie/es hätte	sie hätten	

FUTURE PERFECT SUBJUNCTIVE I

ich werde	wir werden	gewohnt haben
du werdest	ihr werdet	
Sie werden	Sie werden	
er/sie/es werde	sie werden	

FUTURE PERFECT SUBJUNCTIVE II

ich würde	wir würden	gewohnt haben
du würdest	ihr würdet	
Sie würden	Sie würden	
er/sie/es würde	sie würden	

COMMANDS wohn(e)! wohnt! wohnen Sie!

PRESENT PARTICIPLE wohnend

Usage

Maria wohnt im dritten Stock. — *Maria lives on the fourth floor.*

Paul und Mark wohnen im Erdgeschoss. — *Paul and Mark live on the ground floor.*

Im großen Haus an der Ecke wohnte früher der Apotheker Schmidthammer. — *The pharmacist Schmidthammer used to live in the big house on the corner.*

In Wien wohnte Beethoven zuerst im Palais des Fürsten Lichnowsky. — *In Vienna, Beethoven first lived in the palace of Prince Lichnowsky.*

Die Kinder haben in Göttingen in einer Jugendherberge gewohnt. — *The children stayed at a youth hostel in Göttingen.*

Wo möchtest du am liebsten wohnen? — *Where would you most like to live?*

Wir wohnen lieber in einem Vorort als in der Stadt. — *We'd rather live in a suburb than in town.*

Als Kind wohnte ich auf einem Bauernhof. — *As a child, I lived on a farm.*

Vor dem Fall der Berliner Mauer habe ich in Pankow gewohnt. — *Before the fall of the Berlin Wall, I lived in Pankow.*

RELATED VERBS ab·wohnen, bei·wohnen, bewohnen, inne·wohnen

TOP 50 VERB ☞

538 wohnen *to live, stay, dwell*

wohnt · wohnte · gewohnt regular weak verb

MORE USAGE SENTENCES WITH wohnen

Astrid wohnt außerhalb Frankfurt und pendelt jeden Tag 50 Kilometer zur Arbeit. — *Astrid lives outside Frankfurt and commutes 50 kilometers to work every day.*

Wenn man unter dem Dach wohnt, kann es im Sommer sehr warm werden. — *When you live directly under the roof, it can get really warm in the summer.*

Mein Freund Kai wohnt in einem Fachwerkhaus in der Innenstadt. — *My friend Kai lives in a half-timbered house in the city center.*

Joseph wohnte im Haus des Hofkapellmeisters. — *Joseph lived in the home of the court conductor.*

Franz Liste wohnte in der Kirchenstraße in Moritzberg. — *Franz Liste lived on Kirchenstraße in Moritzberg.*

Heiko wohnt seit mehreren Jahren in Hamburg. — *Heiko has lived in Hamburg for several years.*

Nun muss sich zeigen, ob etwas Menschliches in der Nähe wohnt! (Goethe) — *Now it will be seen whether any humanity dwells nearby!*

Habt ihr in Hotels oder bei Freunden gewohnt? — *Did you stay in hotels or with friends?*

Du hast Glück, dass du nur fünf Minuten vom Büro wohnst. — *You're lucky to live only five minutes from the office.*

Wohnen Sie lieber in der Stadt oder auf dem Land? — *Do you prefer living in the city or the country?*

Ich komme aus Istanbul, aber zur Zeit wohne ich in Mannheim. — *I'm from Istanbul, but at present I'm staying in Mannheim.*

„Wo wohnst du?“ — *“Where do you live?”*

„Gleich um die Ecke!“ — *“Just around the corner! / Not far from here!”*

Liesl wohnt nicht gern allein. — *Liesl doesn't like living alone.*

Werden Menschen eines Tages auf dem Mond wohnen? — *Will people live on the moon some day?*

Ich wohne etwas außerhalb. — *I live a ways out of town.*

Wir wohnen seit einem Jahr in Washington. — *We've been living in Washington for a year.*

Jost und sein Freund wohnen weit auseinander. — *Jost and his friend live far apart.*

Bob, wie lange wohnst du schon in Cincinnati? — *Bob, how long have you lived in Cincinnati?*

Als Student in Göttingen habe ich in einem Studentenwohnheim gewohnt. — *As a student in Göttingen, I lived in a dormitory.*

Wenn man auf dem Dorf wohnt, kennt jeder jeden. — *When you live in a small town, everyone knows everyone.*

In unserem Haus wohnen drei Generationen. — *Three generations live in our house.*

wohnen mit *to live with, cohabitate with, share a dwelling with*

Lars wohnt mit zwei anderen Studenten in einer Wohngemeinschaft. — *Lars lives with two other students in a cooperative.*

Ich wohne mit meiner Freundin Anja in einem Neubau in Leipzig. — *I live with my girlfriend, Anja, in a new building in Leipzig.*

wohnen bei *to live/stay with, live/stay at (the home of)*

Irmgard wohnt noch bei ihrer Mutter. — *Irmgard still lives with her mother.*

Ich wohne bei Lea, solange ich in Leipzig bin. — *I'll be staying at Lea's as long as I'm in Leipzig.*

IDIOMATIC EXPRESSIONS

Herr Drechsler wohnt seit 2003 dort zur Miete. — *Mr. Drechsler has been a lodger there since 2003.*

Mensch, du wohnst aber sehr zentral! — *Man, your home is really centrally located!*

Ihr wohnt ziemlich entlegen, nicht wahr? — *You live rather out of the way, don't you?*

Wenn Menschen Tür an Tür wohnen, lernen sie sich gut kennen. — *When people live next door to each other, they get to know each other well.*

Steve wohnt mit Blick auf die Golden Gate Brücke. — *Steve's apartment has a view of the Golden Gate Bridge.*

PRESENT

ich will	wir wollen
du willst	ihr wollt
Sie wollen	Sie wollen
er/sie/es will	sie wollen

SIMPLE PAST

ich wollte	wir wollten
du wolltest	ihr wolltet
Sie wollten	Sie wollten
er/sie/es wollte	sie wollten

FUTURE

ich werde	wir werden	wollen
du wirst	ihr werdet	
Sie werden	Sie werden	
er/sie/es wird	sie werden	

PRESENT SUBJUNCTIVE I

ich wolle	wir wollen
du wollest	ihr wollet
Sie wollen	Sie wollen
er/sie/es wolle	sie wollen

PRESENT SUBJUNCTIVE II

ich wollte	wir wollten
du wolltest	ihr wolltet
Sie wollten	Sie wollten
er/sie/es wollte	sie wollten

FUTURE SUBJUNCTIVE I

ich werde	wir werden	wollen
du werdest	ihr werdet	
Sie werden	Sie werden	
er/sie/es werde	sie werden	

FUTURE SUBJUNCTIVE II

ich würde	wir würden	wollen
du würdest	ihr würdet	
Sie würden	Sie würden	
er/sie/es würde	sie würden	

PRESENT PERFECT

ich habe	wir haben	gewollt
du hast	ihr habt	
Sie haben	Sie haben	
er/sie/es hat	sie haben	

PAST PERFECT

ich hatte	wir hatten	gewollt
du hattest	ihr hattet	
Sie hatten	Sie hatten	
er/sie/es hatte	sie hatten	

FUTURE PERFECT

ich werde	wir werden	gewollt haben
du wirst	ihr werdet	
Sie werden	Sie werden	
er/sie/es wird	sie werden	

PAST SUBJUNCTIVE I

ich habe	wir haben	gewollt
du habest	ihr habet	
Sie haben	Sie haben	
er/sie/es habe	sie haben	

PAST SUBJUNCTIVE II

ich hätte	wir hätten	gewollt
du hättest	ihr hättet	
Sie hätten	Sie hätten	
er/sie/es hätte	sie hätten	

FUTURE PERFECT SUBJUNCTIVE I

ich werde	wir werden	gewollt haben
du werdest	ihr werdet	
Sie werden	Sie werden	
er/sie/es werde	sie werden	

FUTURE PERFECT SUBJUNCTIVE II

ich würde	wir würden	gewollt haben
du würdest	ihr würdet	
Sie würden	Sie würden	
er/sie/es würde	sie würden	

COMMANDS wolle! wollt! wollen Sie!

PRESENT PARTICIPLE wollend

Usage

Ich wollte wandern gehen, aber es begann zu regnen.	*I wanted to go hiking, but it began to rain.*
Wir wollen den Namen geheim halten.	*We want to keep the name secret.*
Heute Abend wollen wir ins Kino gehen.	*This evening, we want to go to the movies.*
Sigrid scheint uns nicht helfen zu wollen.	*Sigrid doesn't seem to want to help us.*
Herbert fasste ihn am Hals, als ob er ihn erwürgen wollte.	*Herbert grabbed him by the throat as though he wanted to strangle him.*
Warum willst du nicht daran erinnert werden?	*Why don't you want to be reminded of that?*
Du musst viel üben, wenn du Klavier spielen willst.	*You have to practice a lot if you want to play the piano.*
Wolltet ihr nicht mitkommen?	*Didn't you want to come along?*
Ich will keine Fragen mehr beantworten müssen!	*I don't want to have to answer any more questions!*
Frederike will, dass Christian ihr einen Ring kauft.	*Frederike wants Christian to buy her a ring.*
Behandeln Sie sie genau so wie Sie von ihnen behandelt werden wollen.	*Treat them exactly as you want to be treated by them.*

RELATED VERBS fort·wollen, weg·wollen, weiter·wollen, zurück·wollen

TOP 50 VERB ☞

539 wollen *to want (to); intend to*

will · wollte · gewollt modal verb

MORE USAGE SENTENCES WITH **wollen**

Wolltet ihr, dass ich mitkomme? — *Did you want me to come along?*
Was wollen Sie denn von mir? — *What do you want of me? / What do you expect from me?*
Was willst du mit einer Kettensäge? — *What do you want a chainsaw for? / What are you going to do with a chainsaw?*

Meinetwegen kannst du machen, was du willst. — *As far as I'm concerned, you can do what you want.*
Ich will dir nichts verheimlichen. — *I don't intend to keep secrets from you.*

wollen *to claim to* (subjective meaning to relate someone's claim with skepticism)

Frau Schmitz will telekinetisch begabt sein. — *Mrs. Schmitz claims to be telekinetically gifted.*
Ernst will den ganzen Roman schon gelesen haben. — *Ernst claims to have read the entire novel already.*
Sandra will ein großes Grundstück in New York City besitzen. — *Sandra claims she owns a large piece of property in New York City.*
Opa wollte das Attentat auf J. F. Kennedy persönlich gesehen haben. — *Grandpa claimed he saw the assassination of J. F. Kennedy in person.*

wollen (with a verb of motion implied; colloquial)

Wohin wollt ihr? — *Where are you headed?*
Marta will schon nach Hause. — *Marta already wants to go home.*
Wir wollen weg. — *We want to get away.*

IDIOMATIC EXPRESSIONS

Der Hund will unbedingt mitkommen. — *The dog insists on coming along.*
„Was wollen Sie damit sagen?" fragte Stefanie. — *"What do you mean by that?" asked Stefanie.*
Ich will hoffen, dass Sie Ihre Brille dabei haben. — *I do hope you have your glasses with you.*
Ich will nichts gesagt haben. — *I take back what I said.*
Das will ich nicht gehört haben. — *Be careful what you say. / I'll pretend I didn't hear that.*
Ich habe meine Festplatte gelöscht, ohne es zu wollen. — *I unintentionally erased my hard drive.*
Der Fernseher will nicht mehr. — *The television stopped working.*
Ich habe keine andere Wahl, ich mag wollen oder nicht. — *I have no other choice, whether I like it or not.*
Wollen wir mal? (*colloquial*) — *Shall we (go / do it)?*
Das will ich auch meinen. (*colloquial*) — *I completely agree.*
Geduld will gelernt sein. — *Patience must be learned.*
Der erste Computer war—wenn man so will—der Abakus. — *The first computer was—if you like—the abacus.*
Erich will lieber ins Kino gehen. — *Erich would rather go to the movies.*
Ehrlich gesagt will Tim es nicht anders. — *Truthfully, Tim wouldn't have it any other way.*
Wir wollten gerade losfahren. — *We were just about to leave.*
Es will Nacht werden. — *Night is just about to fall.*
Das will nicht viel heißen, jeder kann das. (*colloquial*) — *That's nothing to write home about; anybody can do that.*
Geschehe, was da wolle. — *Come what may.*
Doch dem sei, wie ihm wolle. — *But be that as it may.*
Wie Sie wollen, mein Herr. — *As you wish, sire.*
Wie du willst! — *Suit yourself!*
Da ist nichts zu wollen. — *Nothing can be done about that.*
Koste es, was es wolle, das Konzerthaus wird gebaut! — *Cost what it will, the concert hall is being built!*
Irgendjemand muss ihr übel gewollt haben. — *Somebody must have wished her ill.*
Mit Birgit ist nichts zu wollen. — *There's nothing to be done with Birgit. / Birgit is a hopeless case.*

regular weak verb **wühlt · wühlte · gewühlt**

PRESENT

ich wühle	wir wühlen
du wühlst	ihr wühlt
Sie wühlen	Sie wühlen
er/sie/es wühlt	sie wühlen

SIMPLE PAST

ich wühlte	wir wühlten
du wühltest	ihr wühltet
Sie wühlten	Sie wühlten
er/sie/es wühlte	sie wühlten

FUTURE

ich werde	wir werden	wühlen
du wirst	ihr werdet	
Sie werden	Sie werden	
er/sie/es wird	sie werden	

PRESENT SUBJUNCTIVE I

ich wühle	wir wühlen
du wühlest	ihr wühlet
Sie wühlen	Sie wühlen
er/sie/es wühle	sie wühlen

PRESENT SUBJUNCTIVE II

ich wühlte	wir wühlten
du wühltest	ihr wühltet
Sie wühlten	Sie wühlten
er/sie/es wühlte	sie wühlten

FUTURE SUBJUNCTIVE I

ich werde	wir werden	wühlen
du werdest	ihr werdet	
Sie werden	Sie werden	
er/sie/es werde	sie werden	

FUTURE SUBJUNCTIVE II

ich würde	wir würden	wühlen
du würdest	ihr würdet	
Sie würden	Sie würden	
er/sie/es würde	sie würden	

PRESENT PERFECT

ich habe	wir haben	gewühlt
du hast	ihr habt	
Sie haben	Sie haben	
er/sie/es hat	sie haben	

PAST PERFECT

ich hatte	wir hatten	gewühlt
du hattest	ihr hattet	
Sie hatten	Sie hatten	
er/sie/es hatte	sie hatten	

FUTURE PERFECT

ich werde	wir werden	gewühlt haben
du wirst	ihr werdet	
Sie werden	Sie werden	
er/sie/es wird	sie werden	

PAST SUBJUNCTIVE I

ich habe	wir haben	gewühlt
du habest	ihr habet	
Sie haben	Sie haben	
er/sie/es habe	sie haben	

PAST SUBJUNCTIVE II

ich hätte	wir hätten	gewühlt
du hättest	ihr hättet	
Sie hätten	Sie hätten	
er/sie/es hätte	sie hätten	

FUTURE PERFECT SUBJUNCTIVE I

ich werde	wir werden	gewühlt haben
du werdest	ihr werdet	
Sie werden	Sie werden	
er/sie/es werde	sie werden	

FUTURE PERFECT SUBJUNCTIVE II

ich würde	wir würden	gewühlt haben
du würdest	ihr würdet	
Sie würden	Sie würden	
er/sie/es würde	sie würden	

COMMANDS wühl(e)! wühlt! wühlen Sie!

PRESENT PARTICIPLE wühlend

Usage

Nicht nur Schweine wühlen nach Trüffeln, Hunde auch!	*Not only pigs root for truffles, dogs do too!*
Das hungrige Huhn wühlte im Stroh.	*The hungry hen grubbed in the straw.*
Jürgen wühlt in der Schublade nach einer Kneifzange.	*Jürgen is rummaging in the drawer for a pair of pliers.*
Neid und Zorn wühlten in ihr.	*Envy and wrath rankled in her heart.*
Herr Fuchs wühlt in Geld, seitdem er das Lotto gewonnen hat.	*Mr. Fuchs has been wallowing in money ever since he won the lottery.*
Ich möchte ja nicht in die Wunde wühlen, aber… (*idiomatic*)	*I don't mean to pour salt on the wound, but …*

sich wühlen *to burrow, dig oneself*

Die Hunde wühlten sich unter den Zaun.	*The dogs burrowed under the fence.*
Unser LKW wühlte sich durch den Schnee, bis wir unser Ziel erreicht hatten.	*Our truck sludged its way through the snow until we had reached our destination.*

RELATED VERBS auf-wühlen, um-wühlen

541 wundern *to surprise, astonish*

wundert · wunderte · gewundert regular weak verb

PRESENT

ich wundere	wir wundern
du wunderst	ihr wundert
Sie wundern	Sie wundern
er/sie/es wundert	sie wundern

PRESENT PERFECT

ich habe	wir haben	gewundert
du hast	ihr habt	
Sie haben	Sie haben	
er/sie/es hat	sie haben	

SIMPLE PAST

ich wunderte	wir wunderten
du wundertest	ihr wundertet
Sie wunderten	Sie wunderten
er/sie/es wunderte	sie wunderten

PAST PERFECT

ich hatte	wir hatten	gewundert
du hattest	ihr hattet	
Sie hatten	Sie hatten	
er/sie/es hatte	sie hatten	

FUTURE

ich werde	wir werden	wundern
du wirst	ihr werdet	
Sie werden	Sie werden	
er/sie/es wird	sie werden	

FUTURE PERFECT

ich werde	wir werden	gewundert haben
du wirst	ihr werdet	
Sie werden	Sie werden	
er/sie/es wird	sie werden	

PRESENT SUBJUNCTIVE I

ich wundere	wir wundern
du wunderst	ihr wundert
Sie wundern	Sie wundern
er/sie/es wundere	sie wundern

PAST SUBJUNCTIVE I

ich habe	wir haben	gewundert
du habest	ihr habet	
Sie haben	Sie haben	
er/sie/es habe	sie haben	

PRESENT SUBJUNCTIVE II

ich wunderte	wir wunderten
du wundertest	ihr wundertet
Sie wunderten	Sie wunderten
er/sie/es wunderte	sie wunderten

PAST SUBJUNCTIVE II

ich hätte	wir hätten	gewundert
du hättest	ihr hättet	
Sie hätten	Sie hätten	
er/sie/es hätte	sie hätten	

FUTURE SUBJUNCTIVE I

ich werde	wir werden	wundern
du werdest	ihr werdet	
Sie werden	Sie werden	
er/sie/es werde	sie werden	

FUTURE PERFECT SUBJUNCTIVE I

ich werde	wir werden	gewundert haben
du werdest	ihr werdet	
Sie werden	Sie werden	
er/sie/es werde	sie werden	

FUTURE SUBJUNCTIVE II

ich würde	wir würden	wundern
du würdest	ihr würdet	
Sie würden	Sie würden	
er/sie/es würde	sie würden	

FUTURE PERFECT SUBJUNCTIVE II

ich würde	wir würden	gewundert haben
du würdest	ihr würdet	
Sie würden	Sie würden	
er/sie/es würde	sie würden	

COMMANDS wundere! wundert! wundern Sie!

PRESENT PARTICIPLE wundernd

Usage

Wundert es euch nicht, dass er nicht anruft?	*Doesn't it surprise you that he doesn't call?*
Sabines Vorschlag wunderte ihre Mitbewohner.	*Sabine's suggestion astonished her roommates.*
Hat ihre Ankunft dich nicht gewundert?	*Did their arrival not surprise you?*
Sein Kommentar hat uns gewundert.	*His comment took us by surprise.*
Seine Einstellung mir gegenüber wunderte mich, da wir uns sehr gut verstanden hatten.	*His attitude toward me was surprising, since we had gotten along very well together.*
Es wundert mich, dass Ingrid das gesagt hat.	*It amazes me that Ingrid said that.*

sich wundern *to be surprised, be astonished*

Man wundert sich sehr über die Politik der Regierung.	*People are flabbergasted at the government's policies.*
Jans Eltern wundern sich über seine Berufspläne.	*Jan's parents are surprised at his career plans.*
Ich muss mich über dich wundern!	*I'm surprised at you!*
„Wirklich?" wunderte er sich.	*"Really?" he asked, surprised.*

RELATED VERBS bewundern, verwundern

regular weak verb **wünscht · wünschte · gewünscht**

PRESENT

ich wünsche	wir wünschen
du wünschst	ihr wünscht
Sie wünschen	Sie wünschen
er/sie/es wünscht	sie wünschen

PRESENT PERFECT

ich habe	wir haben	gewünscht
du hast	ihr habt	
Sie haben	Sie haben	
er/sie/es hat	sie haben	

SIMPLE PAST

ich wünschte	wir wünschten
du wünschtest	ihr wünschtet
Sie wünschten	Sie wünschten
er/sie/es wünschte	sie wünschten

PAST PERFECT

ich hatte	wir hatten	gewünscht
du hattest	ihr hattet	
Sie hatten	Sie hatten	
er/sie/es hatte	sie hatten	

FUTURE

ich werde	wir werden	wünschen
du wirst	ihr werdet	
Sie werden	Sie werden	
er/sie/es wird	sie werden	

FUTURE PERFECT

ich werde	wir werden	gewünscht haben
du wirst	ihr werdet	
Sie werden	Sie werden	
er/sie/es wird	sie werden	

PRESENT SUBJUNCTIVE I

ich wünsche	wir wünschen
du wünschest	ihr wünschet
Sie wünschen	Sie wünschen
er/sie/es wünsche	sie wünschen

PAST SUBJUNCTIVE I

ich habe	wir haben	gewünscht
du habest	ihr habet	
Sie haben	Sie haben	
er/sie/es habe	sie haben	

PRESENT SUBJUNCTIVE II

ich wünschte	wir wünschten
du wünschtest	ihr wünschtet
Sie wünschten	Sie wünschten
er/sie/es wünschte	sie wünschten

PAST SUBJUNCTIVE II

ich hätte	wir hätten	gewünscht
du hättest	ihr hättet	
Sie hätten	Sie hätten	
er/sie/es hätte	sie hätten	

FUTURE SUBJUNCTIVE I

ich werde	wir werden	wünschen
du werdest	ihr werdet	
Sie werden	Sie werden	
er/sie/es werde	sie werden	

FUTURE PERFECT SUBJUNCTIVE I

ich werde	wir werden	gewünscht haben
du werdest	ihr werdet	
Sie werden	Sie werden	
er/sie/es werde	sie werden	

FUTURE SUBJUNCTIVE II

ich würde	wir würden	wünschen
du würdest	ihr würdet	
Sie würden	Sie würden	
er/sie/es würde	sie würden	

FUTURE PERFECT SUBJUNCTIVE II

ich würde	wir würden	gewünscht haben
du würdest	ihr würdet	
Sie würden	Sie würden	
er/sie/es würde	sie würden	

COMMANDS wünsch(e)! wünscht! wünschen Sie!

PRESENT PARTICIPLE wünschend

Usage

Wir wünschen euch ein frohes Weihnachtsfest.	*We wish you a Merry Christmas.*
Was wünschen Sie?	*What is your wish? / What would you like?*
Wie Sie wünschen.	*As you wish.*
Ich wünschte, wir hätten mehr Zeit.	*I wished we had more time.*
Die Radler hatten sich gutes Wetter gewünscht.	*The cyclists had longed for good weather.*
Ich wünsche dir alles Gute.	*I wish you all the best.*
Sage ihr, ich wünsche die neue Schöpfung zu sehen. (Goethe)	*Tell her I wish to see the new creation.*
Wünsch Papa mal gute Nacht.	*Wish Daddy good night.*
Sein Plan lässt viel zu wünschen übrig.	*His plan leaves a lot to be desired.*
Was wünschst du dir zum Geburtstag?	*What do you want for your birthday?*
Ich wünsche mir meine Mutter als Ärztin.	*I wish my mother was a doctor.*
Ältere Browser stellen Bilder nicht wie gewünscht dar.	*Older browsers don't display graphics the way you'd like.*

RELATED VERBS beglückwünschen, verwünschen

543 zahlen *to pay; pay for*

zahlt · zahlte · gezahlt regular weak verb

PRESENT

ich zahle	wir zahlen
du zahlst	ihr zahlt
Sie zahlen	Sie zahlen
er/sie/es zahlt	sie zahlen

PRESENT PERFECT

ich habe	wir haben	gezahlt
du hast	ihr habt	
Sie haben	Sie haben	
er/sie/es hat	sie haben	

SIMPLE PAST

ich zahlte	wir zahlten
du zahltest	ihr zahltet
Sie zahlten	Sie zahlten
er/sie/es zahlte	sie zahlten

PAST PERFECT

ich hatte	wir hatten	gezahlt
du hattest	ihr hattet	
Sie hatten	Sie hatten	
er/sie/es hatte	sie hatten	

FUTURE

ich werde	wir werden	zahlen
du wirst	ihr werdet	
Sie werden	Sie werden	
er/sie/es wird	sie werden	

FUTURE PERFECT

ich werde	wir werden	gezahlt haben
du wirst	ihr werdet	
Sie werden	Sie werden	
er/sie/es wird	sie werden	

PRESENT SUBJUNCTIVE I

ich zahle	wir zahlen
du zahlest	ihr zahlet
Sie zahlen	Sie zahlen
er/sie/es zahle	sie zahlen

PAST SUBJUNCTIVE I

ich habe	wir haben	gezahlt
du habest	ihr habet	
Sie haben	Sie haben	
er/sie/es habe	sie haben	

PRESENT SUBJUNCTIVE II

ich zahlte	wir zahlten
du zahltest	ihr zahltet
Sie zahlten	Sie zahlten
er/sie/es zahlte	sie zahlten

PAST SUBJUNCTIVE II

ich hätte	wir hätten	gezahlt
du hättest	ihr hättet	
Sie hätten	Sie hätten	
er/sie/es hätte	sie hätten	

FUTURE SUBJUNCTIVE I

ich werde	wir werden	zahlen
du werdest	ihr werdet	
Sie werden	Sie werden	
er/sie/es werde	sie werden	

FUTURE PERFECT SUBJUNCTIVE I

ich werde	wir werden	gezahlt haben
du werdest	ihr werdet	
Sie werden	Sie werden	
er/sie/es werde	sie werden	

FUTURE SUBJUNCTIVE II

ich würde	wir würden	zahlen
du würdest	ihr würdet	
Sie würden	Sie würden	
er/sie/es würde	sie würden	

FUTURE PERFECT SUBJUNCTIVE II

ich würde	wir würden	gezahlt haben
du würdest	ihr würdet	
Sie würden	Sie würden	
er/sie/es würde	sie würden	

COMMANDS zahl(e)! zahlt! zahlen Sie!

PRESENT PARTICIPLE zahlend

Usage

In Europa zahlt man häufig per Überweisung.	*In Europe, people frequently pay via bank transfer.*
Ich kann das Essen nicht zahlen, mein Portemonnaie ist weg!	*I can't pay for the meal; my wallet is gone!*
Ute meinte, Lukas hätte über 250 Euro gezahlt.	*Ute said Lukas paid over 250 euros.*
Ich zahle nicht mehr als 80 Euro.	*I'll pay no more than 80 euros.*
Ich zahle dir 50 Dollar, wenn du mir hilfst.	*I'll pay you 50 dollars if you help me.*
Die Rückerstattung wurde an den Käufer gezahlt.	*The refund was paid to the purchaser.*
Wenn man bar zahlt, bekommt man einen Preisnachlass.	*If you pay cash, you receive a discount.*
Zahlst du oft mit Kreditkarte?	*Do you often pay by credit card?*
Zahlen Sie bitte am nächsten Schalter.	*Please pay at the next window.*
Max und Alex zahlen immer noch an den Motorrädern.	*Max and Alex are still making payments on their motorcycles.*
Wir möchten zahlen. (*in a restaurant*)	*Check, please.*

RELATED VERBS ab·zahlen, an·zahlen, aus·zahlen, ein·zahlen, nach·zahlen, zurück·zahlen, zu·zahlen; *see also* **bezahlen** (103)

PRESENT		PRESENT PERFECT		
ich zähle	wir zählen	ich habe	wir haben	gezählt
du zählst	ihr zählt	du hast	ihr habt	
Sie zählen	Sie zählen	Sie haben	Sie haben	
er/sie/es zählt	sie zählen	er/sie/es hat	sie haben	

SIMPLE PAST		PAST PERFECT		
ich zählte	wir zählten	ich hatte	wir hatten	gezählt
du zähltest	ihr zähltet	du hattest	ihr hattet	
Sie zählten	Sie zählten	Sie hatten	Sie hatten	
er/sie/es zählte	sie zählten	er/sie/es hatte	sie hatten	

FUTURE			FUTURE PERFECT		
ich werde	wir werden	zählen	ich werde	wir werden	gezählt haben
du wirst	ihr werdet		du wirst	ihr werdet	
Sie werden	Sie werden		Sie werden	Sie werden	
er/sie/es wird	sie werden		er/sie/es wird	sie werden	

PRESENT SUBJUNCTIVE I		PAST SUBJUNCTIVE I		
ich zähle	wir zählen	ich habe	wir haben	gezählt
du zählest	ihr zählet	du habest	ihr habet	
Sie zählen	Sie zählen	Sie haben	Sie haben	
er/sie/es zähle	sie zählen	er/sie/es habe	sie haben	

PRESENT SUBJUNCTIVE II		PAST SUBJUNCTIVE II		
ich zählte	wir zählten	ich hätte	wir hätten	gezählt
du zähltest	ihr zähltet	du hättest	ihr hättet	
Sie zählten	Sie zählten	Sie hätten	Sie hätten	
er/sie/es zählte	sie zählten	er/sie/es hätte	sie hätten	

FUTURE SUBJUNCTIVE I			FUTURE PERFECT SUBJUNCTIVE I		
ich werde	wir werden	zählen	ich werde	wir werden	gezählt haben
du werdest	ihr werdet		du werdest	ihr werdet	
Sie werden	Sie werden		Sie werden	Sie werden	
er/sie/es werde	sie werden		er/sie/es werde	sie werden	

FUTURE SUBJUNCTIVE II			FUTURE PERFECT SUBJUNCTIVE II		
ich würde	wir würden	zählen	ich würde	wir würden	gezählt haben
du würdest	ihr würdet		du würdest	ihr würdet	
Sie würden	Sie würden		Sie würden	Sie würden	
er/sie/es würde	sie würden		er/sie/es würde	sie würden	

COMMANDS zähl(e)! zählt! zählen Sie!

PRESENT PARTICIPLE zählend

Usage

Er hat das Geld in seinem Sparschwein täglich gezählt. *He counted the money in his piggy bank daily.*

Als Kind hat die kleine Sara Steine vom Hof gesammelt und gezählt. *As a child, little Sara gathered rocks from the courtyard and counted them.*

Der 4-jährige kann bis 1000 zählen. *The four-year-old can count to 1,000.*

Du kannst auf mich zählen. *You can count on me.*

Im Jahr 2005 zählte die Weltbevölkerung circa 6,5 Milliarden. *In the year 2005, the world population totaled about 6.5 billion.*

Zu seinen Schülern zählten Gräfin Anna Maria von Zichy und Ludwig van Beethoven. *Reckoned among his students were Countess Anna Maria von Zichy and Ludwig van Beethoven.*

Der Koloss von Rhodos zählt zu den sieben Wundern der antiken Welt. *The Colossus of Rhodes is considered one of the Seven Wonders of the Ancient World.*

Der Junge zählte acht Jahre, als seine Eltern starben. *The boy was eight years old when his parents died.*

RELATED VERBS ab·zählen, auf·zählen, aus·zählen, durch·zählen, mit·zählen, nach·zählen; *see also* **erzählen** (174)

545 zeichnen *to draw, portray; sign*

zeichnet · zeichnete · gezeichnet regular weak verb

PRESENT

ich zeichne	wir zeichnen
du zeichnest	ihr zeichnet
Sie zeichnen	Sie zeichnen
er/sie/es zeichnet	sie zeichnen

SIMPLE PAST

ich zeichnete	wir zeichneten
du zeichnetest	ihr zeichnetet
Sie zeichneten	Sie zeichneten
er/sie/es zeichnete	sie zeichneten

FUTURE

ich werde	wir werden	zeichnen
du wirst	ihr werdet	
Sie werden	Sie werden	
er/sie/es wird	sie werden	

PRESENT SUBJUNCTIVE I

ich zeichne	wir zeichnen
du zeichnest	ihr zeichnet
Sie zeichnen	Sie zeichnen
er/sie/es zeichne	sie zeichnen

PRESENT SUBJUNCTIVE II

ich zeichnete	wir zeichneten
du zeichnetest	ihr zeichnetet
Sie zeichneten	Sie zeichneten
er/sie/es zeichnete	sie zeichneten

FUTURE SUBJUNCTIVE I

ich werde	wir werden	zeichnen
du werdest	ihr werdet	
Sie werden	Sie werden	
er/sie/es werde	sie werden	

FUTURE SUBJUNCTIVE II

ich würde	wir würden	zeichnen
du würdest	ihr würdet	
Sie würden	Sie würden	
er/sie/es würde	sie würden	

PRESENT PERFECT

ich habe	wir haben	gezeichnet
du hast	ihr habt	
Sie haben	Sie haben	
er/sie/es hat	sie haben	

PAST PERFECT

ich hatte	wir hatten	gezeichnet
du hattest	ihr hattet	
Sie hatten	Sie hatten	
er/sie/es hatte	sie hatten	

FUTURE PERFECT

ich werde	wir werden	gezeichnet haben
du wirst	ihr werdet	
Sie werden	Sie werden	
er/sie/es wird	sie werden	

PAST SUBJUNCTIVE I

ich habe	wir haben	gezeichnet
du habest	ihr habet	
Sie haben	Sie haben	
er/sie/es habe	sie haben	

PAST SUBJUNCTIVE II

ich hätte	wir hätten	gezeichnet
du hättest	ihr hättet	
Sie hätten	Sie hätten	
er/sie/es hätte	sie hätten	

FUTURE PERFECT SUBJUNCTIVE I

ich werde	wir werden	gezeichnet haben
du werdest	ihr werdet	
Sie werden	Sie werden	
er/sie/es werde	sie werden	

FUTURE PERFECT SUBJUNCTIVE II

ich würde	wir würden	gezeichnet haben
du würdest	ihr würdet	
Sie würden	Sie würden	
er/sie/es würde	sie würden	

COMMANDS zeichne! zeichnet! zeichnen Sie!

PRESENT PARTICIPLE zeichnend

Usage

Als Kind zeichnete sie gern Bilder von exotischen Tieren.	*As a child, she liked to draw pictures of exotic animals.*
Zeichnest du gerne?	*Do you like to draw?*
Paul zeichnet lieber mit einem Filzstift.	*Paul prefers drawing with a felt-tip marker.*
Die Skizze links wurde 1924 von Franken gezeichnet.	*The sketch on the left was made in 1924 by Franken.*
Wer hat das Porträt der Prinzessin Helene gezeichnet?	*Who sketched the portrait of Princess Helene?*
Jan Teichler soll das Bild gezeichnet haben.	*Jan Teichler is said to have drawn the picture.*
Ich möchte zeichnen lernen.	*I'd like to learn to draw.*
Hast du sie wirklich aus freier Hand gezeichnet?	*Did you really draw them freehand?*
Der Architekt Daniel Libeskind hat die Pläne gezeichnet.	*The architect Daniel Libeskind drew the plans.*
Beim Computer kann man leichter maßstäblich zeichnen.	*It's easier to draw to scale on a computer.*
Zehn Länder werden den Vertrag zeichnen.	*Ten countries will sign the treaty.*
Heute muss ich die Rechnungen zeichnen.	*Today I have to sign the invoices.*

RELATED VERBS ab·zeichnen, an·zeichnen, auf·zeichnen, aus·zeichnen, ein·zeichnen, kennzeichnen, nach·zeichnen, um·zeichnen, unterzeichnen, verzeichnen; *see also* **bezeichnen** (104)

regular weak verb **zeigt · zeigte · gezeigt**

PRESENT

ich zeige	wir zeigen
du zeigst	ihr zeigt
Sie zeigen	Sie zeigen
er/sie/es zeigt	sie zeigen

SIMPLE PAST

ich zeigte	wir zeigten
du zeigtest	ihr zeigtet
Sie zeigten	Sie zeigten
er/sie/es zeigte	sie zeigten

FUTURE

ich werde	wir werden	zeigen
du wirst	ihr werdet	
Sie werden	Sie werden	
er/sie/es wird	sie werden	

PRESENT SUBJUNCTIVE I

ich zeige	wir zeigen
du zeigest	ihr zeiget
Sie zeigen	Sie zeigen
er/sie/es zeige	sie zeigen

PRESENT SUBJUNCTIVE II

ich zeigte	wir zeigten
du zeigtest	ihr zeigtet
Sie zeigten	Sie zeigten
er/sie/es zeigte	sie zeigten

FUTURE SUBJUNCTIVE I

ich werde	wir werden	zeigen
du werdest	ihr werdet	
Sie werden	Sie werden	
er/sie/es werde	sie werden	

FUTURE SUBJUNCTIVE II

ich würde	wir würden	zeigen
du würdest	ihr würdet	
Sie würden	Sie würden	
er/sie/es würde	sie würden	

PRESENT PERFECT

ich habe	wir haben	gezeigt
du hast	ihr habt	
Sie haben	Sie haben	
er/sie/es hat	sie haben	

PAST PERFECT

ich hatte	wir hatten	gezeigt
du hattest	ihr hattet	
Sie hatten	Sie hatten	
er/sie/es hatte	sie hatten	

FUTURE PERFECT

ich werde	wir werden	gezeigt haben
du wirst	ihr werdet	
Sie werden	Sie werden	
er/sie/es wird	sie werden	

PAST SUBJUNCTIVE I

ich habe	wir haben	gezeigt
du habest	ihr habet	
Sie haben	Sie haben	
er/sie/es habe	sie haben	

PAST SUBJUNCTIVE II

ich hätte	wir hätten	gezeigt
du hättest	ihr hättet	
Sie hätten	Sie hätten	
er/sie/es hätte	sie hätten	

FUTURE PERFECT SUBJUNCTIVE I

ich werde	wir werden	gezeigt haben
du werdest	ihr werdet	
Sie werden	Sie werden	
er/sie/es werde	sie werden	

FUTURE PERFECT SUBJUNCTIVE II

ich würde	wir würden	gezeigt haben
du würdest	ihr würdet	
Sie würden	Sie würden	
er/sie/es würde	sie würden	

COMMANDS zeig(e)! zeigt! zeigen Sie!

PRESENT PARTICIPLE zeigend

Usage

Georg zeigte auf seine Armbanduhr und schlich aus der Hintertür. — *Georg pointed to his watch and sneaked out the back door.*
Worauf zeigen Sie? — *What are you pointing at?*
Könnten Sie mir den Weg zeigen? — *Could you show me the way?*
Zeig mir deinen schicken Pullover! — *Show me your chic sweater!*
Ein schweres Erdbeben wurde gerade im Fernsehen gezeigt. — *A severe earthquake was just shown on television.*
Dann zeigte ihr der Juwelenverkäufer eine Perlenkette. — *Then the jewelry salesman showed her a pearl necklace.*
Darf ich euch die Stadt zeigen? — *May I show you the city?*

sich zeigen *to show oneself, show up, emerge, become apparent*

Die Symptome zeigen sich innerhalb zehn Tagen. — *The symptoms show up within 10 days.*
Diese Tendenzen haben sich erst 2004 gezeigt. — *These tendencies became apparent only in 2004.*
Es wird sich zeigen, ob das Produkt sich gut verkauft. — *Time will tell whether the product sells well.*

RELATED VERBS an·zeigen, auf·zeigen, erzeigen, vor·zeigen

547 zerstieben *to scatter, disperse, vanish*

zerstiebt · zerstiebte/zerstob · zerstiebt/zerstoben regular weak verb or strong verb

PRESENT

ich zerstiebe	wir zerstieben
du zerstiebst	ihr zerstiebt
Sie zerstieben	Sie zerstieben
er/sie/es zerstiebt	sie zerstieben

PRESENT PERFECT

ich bin	wir sind	zerstoben/zerstiebt
du bist	ihr seid	
Sie sind	Sie sind	
er/sie/es ist	sie sind	

SIMPLE PAST

ich zerstiebte/zerstob	wir zerstiebten/zerstoben
du zerstiebtest/zerstobst	ihr zerstiebtet/zerstobt
Sie zerstiebten/zerstoben	Sie zerstiebten/zerstoben
er/sie/es zerstiebte/zerstob	sie zerstiebten/zerstoben

PAST PERFECT

ich war	wir waren	zerstoben/zerstiebt
du warst	ihr wart	
Sie waren	Sie waren	
er/sie/es war	sie waren	

FUTURE

ich werde	wir werden	zerstieben
du wirst	ihr werdet	
Sie werden	Sie werden	
er/sie/es wird	sie werden	

FUTURE PERFECT

ich werde	wir werden	zerstoben sein OR zerstiebt sein
du wirst	ihr werdet	
Sie werden	Sie werden	
er/sie/es wird	sie werden	

PRESENT SUBJUNCTIVE I

ich zerstiebe	wir zerstieben
du zerstiebest	ihr zerstiebet
Sie zerstieben	Sie zerstieben
er/sie/es zerstiebe	sie zerstieben

PAST SUBJUNCTIVE I

ich sei	wir seien	zerstoben/zerstiebt
du seiest	ihr seiet	
Sie seien	Sie seien	
er/sie/es sei	sie seien	

PRESENT SUBJUNCTIVE II

ich zerstiebte/zerstöbe	wir zerstiebten/zerstöben
du zerstiebtest/zerstöbest	ihr zerstiebtet/zerstöbet
Sie zerstiebten/zerstöben	Sie zerstiebten/zerstöben
er/sie/es zerstiebte/zerstöbe	sie zerstiebten/zerstöben

PAST SUBJUNCTIVE II

ich wäre	wir wären	zerstoben/zerstiebt
du wärest	ihr wäret	
Sie wären	Sie wären	
er/sie/es wäre	sie wären	

FUTURE SUBJUNCTIVE I

ich werde	wir werden	zerstieben
du werdest	ihr werdet	
Sie werden	Sie werden	
er/sie/es werde	sie werden	

FUTURE PERFECT SUBJUNCTIVE I

ich werde	wir werden	zerstoben sein OR zerstiebt sein
du werdest	ihr werdet	
Sie werden	Sie werden	
er/sie/es werde	sie werden	

FUTURE SUBJUNCTIVE II

ich würde	wir würden	zerstieben
du würdest	ihr würdet	
Sie würden	Sie würden	
er/sie/es würde	sie würden	

FUTURE PERFECT SUBJUNCTIVE II

ich würde	wir würden	zerstoben sein OR zerstiebt sein
du würdest	ihr würdet	
Sie würden	Sie würden	
er/sie/es würde	sie würden	

COMMANDS zerstieb(e)! zerstiebt! zerstieben Sie!

PRESENT PARTICIPLE zerstiebend

NOTE The simple tenses of **zerstieben** are commonly regular weak in modern standard German; the past participle is less frequently so.

Usage

Zerstoben ist das freundliche Gedränge. (Goethe)	*The friendly crowd has scattered.*
Was ich gesammelt, ist im Wind zerstoben. (Grillparzer)	*What I've collected has vanished in the wind.*
Ein Schwarm Möwen folgte dem Boot hinterher und zerstob bald darauf.	*A flock of seagulls followed the boat and dispersed soon after.*
Die Wellen zerstieben an den Felsen.	*The waves scatter on the rocks.*
Die Menschenmenge zerstob nach knapp zwei Stunden.	*The crowd of people dispersed after barely two hours.*
Der Traum ist längst zerstoben.	*The dream has long since vanished.*
Bald erschien ein Wolf und die ängstlichen Schafe zerstoben in alle Winde.	*Soon a wolf appeared, and the frightened sheep scattered in all directions.*

RELATED VERB stieben

regular weak verb **zerstört · zerstörte · zerstört**

PRESENT

ich zerstöre	wir zerstören
du zerstörst	ihr zerstört
Sie zerstören	Sie zerstören
er/sie/es zerstört	sie zerstören

PRESENT PERFECT

ich habe	wir haben	zerstört
du hast	ihr habt	
Sie haben	Sie haben	
er/sie/es hat	sie haben	

SIMPLE PAST

ich zerstörte	wir zerstörten
du zerstörtest	ihr zerstörtet
Sie zerstörten	Sie zerstörten
er/sie/es zerstörte	sie zerstörten

PAST PERFECT

ich hatte	wir hatten	zerstört
du hattest	ihr hattet	
Sie hatten	Sie hatten	
er/sie/es hatte	sie hatten	

FUTURE

ich werde	wir werden	zerstören
du wirst	ihr werdet	
Sie werden	Sie werden	
er/sie/es wird	sie werden	

FUTURE PERFECT

ich werde	wir werden	zerstört haben
du wirst	ihr werdet	
Sie werden	Sie werden	
er/sie/es wird	sie werden	

PRESENT SUBJUNCTIVE I

ich zerstöre	wir zerstören
du zerstörest	ihr zerstöret
Sie zerstören	Sie zerstören
er/sie/es zerstöre	sie zerstören

PAST SUBJUNCTIVE I

ich habe	wir haben	zerstört
du habest	ihr habet	
Sie haben	Sie haben	
er/sie/es habe	sie haben	

PRESENT SUBJUNCTIVE II

ich zerstörte	wir zerstörten
du zerstörtest	ihr zerstörtet
Sie zerstörten	Sie zerstörten
er/sie/es zerstörte	sie zerstörten

PAST SUBJUNCTIVE II

ich hätte	wir hätten	zerstört
du hättest	ihr hättet	
Sie hätten	Sie hätten	
er/sie/es hätte	sie hätten	

FUTURE SUBJUNCTIVE I

ich werde	wir werden	zerstören
du werdest	ihr werdet	
Sie werden	Sie werden	
er/sie/es werde	sie werden	

FUTURE PERFECT SUBJUNCTIVE I

ich werde	wir werden	zerstört haben
du werdest	ihr werdet	
Sie werden	Sie werden	
er/sie/es werde	sie werden	

FUTURE SUBJUNCTIVE II

ich würde	wir würden	zerstören
du würdest	ihr würdet	
Sie würden	Sie würden	
er/sie/es würde	sie würden	

FUTURE PERFECT SUBJUNCTIVE II

ich würde	wir würden	zerstört haben
du würdest	ihr würdet	
Sie würden	Sie würden	
er/sie/es würde	sie würden	

COMMANDS zerstör(e)! zerstört! zerstören Sie!

PRESENT PARTICIPLE zerstörend

Usage

Das hat den letzten Funken Hoffnung zerstört.	*That destroyed the last ray of hope.*
Der Tornado hat das ganze Dorf zerstört.	*The tornado wiped out the entire village.*
Das Virus zerstört Nervenzellen im Gehirn.	*The virus destroys nerve cells in the brain.*
Durch Luftangriffe der Alliierten wurde Dresden bis zu 80% zerstört.	*Through Allied air attacks, up to 80% of Dresden was destroyed.*
1883 zerstörte ein Vulkanausbruch Teile der Insel.	*In 1883, a volcanic eruption destroyed parts of the island.*
Die Leber ist durch Krebs zerstört worden.	*The liver has been destroyed by cancer.*
Ein Brand in der Bibliothek hat 30 000 wertvolle Bücher zerstört.	*A fire in the library destroyed 30,000 valuable books.*
Die Flammen zerstörten sofort die hölzerne Hütte.	*The flames destroyed the wooden hut in an instant.*
Der Koloss von Rhodos wurde durch ein Erdbeben zerstört.	*The Colossus of Rhodes was ruined by an earthquake.*
Der PKW wurde bei dem Unfall total zerstört.	*The car was completely wrecked in the accident.*

RELATED VERBS *see* **stören** (431)

549 **ziehen** *to draw, pull; extract; attract*

zieht · zog · gezogen strong verb

MORE USAGE SENTENCES WITH ziehen

Zieh sie am Ärmel, dann sieht sie dich.	*Tug at her shirtsleeve, then she'll see you.*
ZIEHEN (SIGN ON A DOOR)	*PULL*
Lars lässt sich einen Zahn ziehen.	*Lars is having a tooth extracted.*
Die Firma hat die Aufmerksamkeit auf sich gezogen.	*The firm has attracted attention to itself.*
Diese Splitterpartei hat bei der Wahl wenige Stimmen gezogen.	*This splinter party attracted few votes in the election.*

sich ziehen *to stretch, extend*

An dem Tag zog sich ein dichter Nebel über den Sumpf.	*On that day, a thick fog stretched across the swamp.*
Eine 1.500 Kilometer lange Straße zieht sich durch die Wüste.	*A 1,500-kilometer-long road runs across the desert.*
Das Projekt zieht sich in die Länge.	*The project is dragging on.*

ziehen (with **sein**) *to move, advance, pass, go*

Im Juni zieht Pawel nach München.	*In June, Pawel is moving to Munich.*
Wir möchten auf eine Insel ziehen.	*We'd like to move to an island to live.*
Dirk ist zu seinem Freund Thorsten gezogen.	*Dirk moved in with his boyfriend, Thorsten.*
1349 zog das kaiserliche Heer in das Fürstentum.	*In 1349, the imperial army advanced into the princedom.*
Der Sturm ist nach Osten gezogen.	*The storm has passed to the east.*
Das Land ist ohne guten Grund in den Krieg gezogen.	*The country has gone to war for no good reason.*

IDIOMATIC EXPRESSIONS

Diese Funktion zieht die Quadratwurzel aus einem Wert.	*This function extracts the square root of a value.*
Maximilians Vater wurde in der Presse durch den Schmutz gezogen.	*Maximilian's father was disparaged in the press.*
Wieso ziehst du ein Gesicht?	*How come you're making a face?*
Das Urheberrecht zieht klare Grenzen.	*Copyright law sets clear limits.*
Man muss die Nachteile auch in Betracht ziehen.	*You also have to take the disadvantages into consideration.*
Sonnenblumen sind leicht aus Samen zu ziehen.	*Sunflowers are easy to cultivate from seed.*
Das zieht bei mir nicht.	*I don't find that convincing.*
Den Tee drei Minuten ziehen lassen. (RECIPE)	*Let the tea steep for three minutes.*
Die Bremsen ziehen nicht richtig.	*The brakes aren't grabbing properly.*
Der Detektiv zog an seiner Zigarette und schaute sie an.	*The detective took a puff off his cigarette and looked at her.*
Es zieht.	*There's a draft (in the room).*
Ich habe Klaus mit diesem Vorschlag auf meine Seite gezogen.	*I've won Klaus over to my side with this suggestion.*
Habt ihr daraus eine Lehre ziehen können, Kinder?	*Were you able to learn a lesson from that, children?*
Er zieht Nutzen aus den Fehlern anderer.	*He capitalizes on other people's mistakes.*
Sara konnte noch den Kopf rechtzeitig aus der Schlinge ziehen.	*Sara was able to make her escape just in time.*
Herr Jansen wird wegen Diebstahl vor Gericht gezogen.	*Mr. Jansen is being arraigned for theft.*
Ich ziehe immer den kürzeren.	*I always get the short end of the stick.*
Diese Therapie kann Komplikationen nach sich ziehen.	*This therapy can result in complications.*
Sie ziehen Ihren Sohn doch ins Geheimnis? (SCHILLER)	*You're making your son privy to the secret?*

PRESENT	
ich ziehe	wir ziehen
du ziehst	ihr zieht
Sie ziehen	Sie ziehen
er/sie/es zieht	sie ziehen

PRESENT PERFECT		
ich habe	wir haben	gezogen
du hast	ihr habt	
Sie haben	Sie haben	
er/sie/es hat	sie haben	

SIMPLE PAST	
ich zog	wir zogen
du zogst	ihr zogt
Sie zogen	Sie zogen
er/sie/es zog	sie zogen

PAST PERFECT		
ich hatte	wir hatten	gezogen
du hattest	ihr hattet	
Sie hatten	Sie hatten	
er/sie/es hatte	sie hatten	

FUTURE		
ich werde	wir werden	ziehen
du wirst	ihr werdet	
Sie werden	Sie werden	
er/sie/es wird	sie werden	

FUTURE PERFECT		
ich werde	wir werden	gezogen haben
du wirst	ihr werdet	
Sie werden	Sie werden	
er/sie/es wird	sie werden	

PRESENT SUBJUNCTIVE I	
ich ziehe	wir ziehen
du ziehest	ihr ziehet
Sie ziehen	Sie ziehen
er/sie/es ziehe	sie ziehen

PAST SUBJUNCTIVE I		
ich habe	wir haben	gezogen
du habest	ihr habet	
Sie haben	Sie haben	
er/sie/es habe	sie haben	

PRESENT SUBJUNCTIVE II	
ich zöge	wir zögen
du zögest	ihr zöget
Sie zögen	Sie zögen
er/sie/es zöge	sie zögen

PAST SUBJUNCTIVE II		
ich hätte	wir hätten	gezogen
du hättest	ihr hättet	
Sie hätten	Sie hätten	
er/sie/es hätte	sie hätten	

FUTURE SUBJUNCTIVE I		
ich werde	wir werden	ziehen
du werdest	ihr werdet	
Sie werden	Sie werden	
er/sie/es werde	sie werden	

FUTURE PERFECT SUBJUNCTIVE I		
ich werde	wir werden	gezogen haben
du werdest	ihr werdet	
Sie werden	Sie werden	
er/sie/es werde	sie werden	

FUTURE SUBJUNCTIVE II		
ich würde	wir würden	ziehen
du würdest	ihr würdet	
Sie würden	Sie würden	
er/sie/es würde	sie würden	

FUTURE PERFECT SUBJUNCTIVE II		
ich würde	wir würden	gezogen haben
du würdest	ihr würdet	
Sie würden	Sie würden	
er/sie/es würde	sie würden	

COMMANDS zieh(e)! zieht! ziehen Sie!

PRESENT PARTICIPLE ziehend

Usage

Wenn man das Herzass zieht, gewinnt man das Kartenspiel.	*If you draw the ace of hearts, you win the card game.*
Typische Kutschen wurden von zwei Pferden gezogen.	*Typical carriages were drawn by two horses.*
Romeo zog Julia an sich und küsste sie.	*Romeo drew Juliet to himself and kissed her.*
Auf der Feier hat sie mich auf die Seite gezogen und alles erklärt.	*She took me aside at the party and explained everything.*
So könnte man wohl falsche Schlüsse ziehen.	*One might thus draw false conclusions.*
Ziehen Sie das Seil straff.	*Pull the rope taut.*
Anja hatte Angst und zog sich die Decke über den Kopf.	*Anja was afraid and pulled the blanket over her head.*
Max hat Sara an den Haaren gezogen.	*Max pulled Sara's hair.*

RELATED VERBS ab·ziehen, auf·ziehen, durchziehen, durch·ziehen, entziehen, erziehen, groß·ziehen, hinterziehen, nach·vollziehen, überziehen, über·ziehen, umher·ziehen, umziehen, um·ziehen, unterziehen, unter·ziehen, verziehen, vorüber·ziehen, vor·ziehen, weg·ziehen, weiter·ziehen, zurück·ziehen, zusammen·ziehen, zu·ziehen; *see also* **an·ziehen** (20), **aus·ziehen** (42), **beziehen** (105), **ein·ziehen** (140)

550 zu·hören *to listen to*

hört zu · hörte zu · zugehört — regular weak verb (dative object)

PRESENT

ich höre	wir hören	zu
du hörst	ihr hört	
Sie hören	Sie hören	
er/sie/es hört	sie hören	

SIMPLE PAST

ich hörte	wir hörten	zu
du hörtest	ihr hörtet	
Sie hörten	Sie hörten	
er/sie/es hörte	sie hörten	

FUTURE

ich werde	wir werden	zuhören
du wirst	ihr werdet	
Sie werden	Sie werden	
er/sie/es wird	sie werden	

PRESENT SUBJUNCTIVE I

ich höre	wir hören	zu
du hörest	ihr höret	
Sie hören	Sie hören	
er/sie/es höre	sie hören	

PRESENT SUBJUNCTIVE II

ich hörte	wir hörten	zu
du hörtest	ihr hörtet	
Sie hörten	Sie hörten	
er/sie/es hörte	sie hörten	

FUTURE SUBJUNCTIVE I

ich werde	wir werden	zuhören
du werdest	ihr werdet	
Sie werden	Sie werden	
er/sie/es werde	sie werden	

FUTURE SUBJUNCTIVE II

ich würde	wir würden	zuhören
du würdest	ihr würdet	
Sie würden	Sie würden	
er/sie/es würde	sie würden	

PRESENT PERFECT

ich habe	wir haben	zugehört
du hast	ihr habt	
Sie haben	Sie haben	
er/sie/es hat	sie haben	

PAST PERFECT

ich hatte	wir hatten	zugehört
du hattest	ihr hattet	
Sie hatten	Sie hatten	
er/sie/es hatte	sie hatten	

FUTURE PERFECT

ich werde	wir werden	zugehört haben
du wirst	ihr werdet	
Sie werden	Sie werden	
er/sie/es wird	sie werden	

PAST SUBJUNCTIVE I

ich habe	wir haben	zugehört
du habest	ihr habet	
Sie haben	Sie haben	
er/sie/es habe	sie haben	

PAST SUBJUNCTIVE II

ich hätte	wir hätten	zugehört
du hättest	ihr hättet	
Sie hätten	Sie hätten	
er/sie/es hätte	sie hätten	

FUTURE PERFECT SUBJUNCTIVE I

ich werde	wir werden	zugehört haben
du werdest	ihr werdet	
Sie werden	Sie werden	
er/sie/es werde	sie werden	

FUTURE PERFECT SUBJUNCTIVE II

ich würde	wir würden	zugehört haben
du würdest	ihr würdet	
Sie würden	Sie würden	
er/sie/es würde	sie würden	

COMMANDS hör(e) zu! hört zu! hören Sie zu!

PRESENT PARTICIPLE zuhörend

Usage

Nicolaus will unserem Gespräch zugehört haben. — *Nicolaus claims to have been listening to our discussion.*
Nach einer Stunde konnte man ihm nicht mehr zuhören. — *After an hour, people couldn't listen to him anymore.*
Momo kann gut zuhören. — *Momo is a good listener.*
Du darfst nicht zuhören. — *You can't listen. / You're not allowed to listen.*
In Nebenzimmer hörte Oma Schmitz aufmerksam zu. — *In the next room, Grandma Schmitz listened attentively.*

Er scheint nicht zuhören zu wollen. — *He doesn't seem to want to listen.*
Ich habe höflich zugehört, obwohl die Rede langweilig war. — *I listened politely even though the speech was boring.*
Amalie hat gar nicht zugehört. — *Amalie wasn't even listening.*
Wie kann der Mensch seinen eigenen Gedanken zuhören? — *How can a person listen to his own thoughts?*
Wer wird ihnen zuhören? — *Who will listen to them?*
Die Vereinsmitglieder hörten dem Vortrag interessiert zu. — *The club members listened to the presentation with interest.*

RELATED VERBS *see* **hören** (248)

strong verb **nimmt zu · nahm zu · zugenommen**

PRESENT

ich nehme	wir nehmen	zu
du nimmst	ihr nehmt	
Sie nehmen	Sie nehmen	
er/sie/es nimmt	sie nehmen	

PRESENT PERFECT

ich habe	wir haben	zugenommen
du hast	ihr habt	
Sie haben	Sie haben	
er/sie/es hat	sie haben	

SIMPLE PAST

ich nahm	wir nahmen	zu
du nahmst	ihr nahmt	
Sie nahmen	Sie nahmen	
er/sie/es nahm	sie nahmen	

PAST PERFECT

ich hatte	wir hatten	zugenommen
du hattest	ihr hattet	
Sie hatten	Sie hatten	
er/sie/es hatte	sie hatten	

FUTURE

ich werde	wir werden	zunehmen
du wirst	ihr werdet	
Sie werden	Sie werden	
er/sie/es wird	sie werden	

FUTURE PERFECT

ich werde	wir werden	zugenommen haben
du wirst	ihr werdet	
Sie werden	Sie werden	
er/sie/es wird	sie werden	

PRESENT SUBJUNCTIVE I

ich nehme	wir nehmen	zu
du nehmest	ihr nehmet	
Sie nehmen	Sie nehmen	
er/sie/es nehme	sie nehmen	

PAST SUBJUNCTIVE I

ich habe	wir haben	zugenommen
du habest	ihr habet	
Sie haben	Sie haben	
er/sie/es habe	sie haben	

PRESENT SUBJUNCTIVE II

ich nähme	wir nähmen	zu
du nähmest	ihr nähmet	
Sie nähmen	Sie nähmen	
er/sie/es nähme	sie nähmen	

PAST SUBJUNCTIVE II

ich hätte	wir hätten	zugenommen
du hättest	ihr hättet	
Sie hätten	Sie hätten	
er/sie/es hätte	sie hätten	

FUTURE SUBJUNCTIVE I

ich werde	wir werden	zunehmen
du werdest	ihr werdet	
Sie werden	Sie werden	
er/sie/es werde	sie werden	

FUTURE PERFECT SUBJUNCTIVE I

ich werde	wir werden	zugenommen haben
du werdest	ihr werdet	
Sie werden	Sie werden	
er/sie/es werde	sie werden	

FUTURE SUBJUNCTIVE II

ich würde	wir würden	zunehmen
du würdest	ihr würdet	
Sie würden	Sie würden	
er/sie/es würde	sie würden	

FUTURE PERFECT SUBJUNCTIVE II

ich würde	wir würden	zugenommen haben
du würdest	ihr würdet	
Sie würden	Sie würden	
er/sie/es würde	sie würden	

COMMANDS nimm zu! nehmt zu! nehmen Sie zu!

PRESENT PARTICIPLE zunehmend

Usage

Ihre Angst nahm nur noch zu, als der Hund sie anbellte. — *Her fear only increased when the dog barked at her.*

Der Weißkopf-Seeadler hat in den letzten Jahren an Zahl zugenommen. — *The bald eagle has increased in number in the last few years.*

Wert *x* nimmt im selben Maße zu, wie *y* zunimmt. — *Value* x *increases to the same degree that* y *increases.*

Die Anzahl der Studierenden nimmt jedes Jahr beträchtlich zu. — *The number of students increases considerably every year.*

Der Enthusiasmus für Bio-Lebensmittel scheint immer mehr zuzunehmen. — *Enthusiasm for organic foods seems to be ever on the rise.*

Da seine Schmerzen täglich zunahmen, probierte er ein anderes Medikament. — *Since his pain was intensifying daily, he tried a different medication.*

Ich habe letztes Jahr 10 Kilo zugenommen. — *I gained 10 kilos last year.*

Hast du zugenommen? — *Have you put on weight?*

Der Mond nimmt zu und er nimmt ab. — *The moon waxes and wanes.*

RELATED VERBS *see* **nehmen** (314)

552 zusammen·arbeiten *to cooperate, work together, collaborate*

arbeitet zusammen · arbeitete zusammen · zusammengearbeitet regular weak verb

PRESENT

ich arbeite	wir arbeiten	zusammen
du arbeitest	ihr arbeitet	
Sie arbeiten	Sie arbeiten	
er/sie/es arbeitet	sie arbeiten	

PRESENT PERFECT

ich habe	wir haben	zusammengearbeitet
du hast	ihr habt	
Sie haben	Sie haben	
er/sie/es hat	sie haben	

SIMPLE PAST

ich arbeitete	wir arbeiteten	zusammen
du arbeitetest	ihr arbeitetet	
Sie arbeiteten	Sie arbeiteten	
er/sie/es arbeitete	sie arbeiteten	

PAST PERFECT

ich hatte	wir hatten	zusammengearbeitet
du hattest	ihr hattet	
Sie hatten	Sie hatten	
er/sie/es hatte	sie hatten	

FUTURE

ich werde	wir werden	zusammenarbeiten
du wirst	ihr werdet	
Sie werden	Sie werden	
er/sie/es wird	sie werden	

FUTURE PERFECT

ich werde	wir werden	zusammengearbeitet haben
du wirst	ihr werdet	
Sie werden	Sie werden	
er/sie/es wird	sie werden	

PRESENT SUBJUNCTIVE I

ich arbeite	wir arbeiten	zusammen
du arbeitest	ihr arbeitet	
Sie arbeiten	Sie arbeiten	
er/sie/es arbeite	sie arbeiten	

PAST SUBJUNCTIVE I

ich habe	wir haben	zusammengearbeitet
du habest	ihr habet	
Sie haben	Sie haben	
er/sie/es habe	sie haben	

PRESENT SUBJUNCTIVE II

ich arbeitete	wir arbeiteten	zusammen
du arbeitetest	ihr arbeitetet	
Sie arbeiteten	Sie arbeiteten	
er/sie/es arbeitete	sie arbeiteten	

PAST SUBJUNCTIVE II

ich hätte	wir hätten	zusammengearbeitet
du hättest	ihr hättet	
Sie hätten	Sie hätten	
er/sie/es hätte	sie hätten	

FUTURE SUBJUNCTIVE I

ich werde	wir werden	zusammenarbeiten
du werdest	ihr werdet	
Sie werden	Sie werden	
er/sie/es werde	sie werden	

FUTURE PERFECT SUBJUNCTIVE I

ich werde	wir werden	zusammengearbeitet haben
du werdest	ihr werdet	
Sie werden	Sie werden	
er/sie/es werde	sie werden	

FUTURE SUBJUNCTIVE II

ich würde	wir würden	zusammenarbeiten
du würdest	ihr würdet	
Sie würden	Sie würden	
er/sie/es würde	sie würden	

FUTURE PERFECT SUBJUNCTIVE II

ich würde	wir würden	zusammengearbeitet haben
du würdest	ihr würdet	
Sie würden	Sie würden	
er/sie/es würde	sie würden	

COMMANDS arbeite zusammen! arbeitet zusammen! arbeiten Sie zusammen!

PRESENT PARTICIPLE zusammenarbeitend

Usage

Die Studenten arbeiten an einem Projekt zusammen. — *The students are working together on a project.*

Drei Komponisten haben an dem Stück zusammengearbeitet. — *Three composers collaborated on the piece.*

Hier wird zu wenig zusammengearbeitet! — *There is too little cooperation here!*

Er wird bestimmt mit uns zusammenarbeiten wollen. — *He will definitely want to work with us.*

Ich habe niemals wissentlich mit ausländischen Geheimdiensten zusammengearbeitet. — *I have never knowingly cooperated with foreign secret service.*

Pawel arbeitete mit Georg Polacky als Assistent zusammen. — *Pawel worked with Georg Polacky as an assistant.*

Sieben freiberufliche Software-Entwickler arbeiten jetzt an dem Programm zusammen. — *Seven freelance software developers are collaborating on the program now.*

Ab jetzt müssen wir alle an einer Lösung zusammenarbeiten. — *Henceforth, we must all work together on a solution.*

Möglicherweise arbeiten wir an einem Buch über Heimarbeit zusammen. — *We may collaborate on a book about working at home.*

RELATED VERBS *see* **arbeiten** (22)

regular weak verb **fasst zusammen · fasste zusammen · zusammengefasst**

PRESENT

ich fasse	wir fassen	zusammen
du fasst	ihr fasst	
Sie fassen	Sie fassen	
er/sie/es fasst	sie fassen	

PRESENT PERFECT

ich habe	wir haben	zusammengefasst
du hast	ihr habt	
Sie haben	Sie haben	
er/sie/es hat	sie haben	

SIMPLE PAST

ich fasste	wir fassten	zusammen
du fasstest	ihr fasstet	
Sie fassten	Sie fassten	
er/sie/es fasste	sie fassten	

PAST PERFECT

ich hatte	wir hatten	zusammengefasst
du hattest	ihr hattet	
Sie hatten	Sie hatten	
er/sie/es hatte	sie hatten	

FUTURE

ich werde	wir werden	zusammenfassen
du wirst	ihr werdet	
Sie werden	Sie werden	
er/sie/es wird	sie werden	

FUTURE PERFECT

ich werde	wir werden	zusammengefasst haben
du wirst	ihr werdet	
Sie werden	Sie werden	
er/sie/es wird	sie werden	

PRESENT SUBJUNCTIVE I

ich fasse	wir fassen	zusammen
du fassest	ihr fasset	
Sie fassen	Sie fassen	
er/sie/es fasse	sie fassen	

PAST SUBJUNCTIVE I

ich habe	wir haben	zusammengefasst
du habest	ihr habet	
Sie haben	Sie haben	
er/sie/es habe	sie haben	

PRESENT SUBJUNCTIVE II

ich fasste	wir fassten	zusammen
du fasstest	ihr fasstet	
Sie fassten	Sie fassten	
er/sie/es fasste	sie fassten	

PAST SUBJUNCTIVE II

ich hätte	wir hätten	zusammengefasst
du hättest	ihr hättet	
Sie hätten	Sie hätten	
er/sie/es hätte	sie hätten	

FUTURE SUBJUNCTIVE I

ich werde	wir werden	zusammenfassen
du werdest	ihr werdet	
Sie werden	Sie werden	
er/sie/es werde	sie werden	

FUTURE PERFECT SUBJUNCTIVE I

ich werde	wir werden	zusammengefasst haben
du werdest	ihr werdet	
Sie werden	Sie werden	
er/sie/es werde	sie werden	

FUTURE SUBJUNCTIVE II

ich würde	wir würden	zusammenfassen
du würdest	ihr würdet	
Sie würden	Sie würden	
er/sie/es würde	sie würden	

FUTURE PERFECT SUBJUNCTIVE II

ich würde	wir würden	zusammengefasst haben
du würdest	ihr würdet	
Sie würden	Sie würden	
er/sie/es würde	sie würden	

COMMANDS fass(e) zusammen! fasst zusammen! fassen Sie zusammen!

PRESENT PARTICIPLE zusammenfassend

Usage

Ich fasse jetzt zusammen.	*I will now sum up.*
Marga hat unsere Kommentare kurz zusammengefasst.	*Marga briefly summarized our comments.*
Der Lehrer fasste die Handlung des Films zusammen.	*The teacher summarized the film's plot.*
Fassen Sie den Zeitungsartikel in zehn Sätzen zusammen.	*Summarize the newspaper article in 10 sentences.*
Der Vorsitzende möchte seine Strategie zusammenfassen.	*The chairperson would like to recapitulate his strategy.*
Kleinere Beträge können eventuell in einer Summe zusammengefasst werden.	*Smaller amounts can possibly be combined into one grand total.*
Der Kurs fasst sechs Einheiten zusammen.	*The course comprises six units.*
Wenn wir unsere Ressourcen zusammenfassen, können wir viel mehr leisten.	*If we pool our resources, we can accomplish much more.*
Der neue Plan fasst rund siebzig bestehende Umweltprojekte zusammen.	*The new plan combines about 70 existing environmental projects.*
Kann diese Software Text und Bilder zusammenfassen?	*Can this software integrate text and graphics?*

RELATED VERBS *see* **fassen** (180)

554 zweifeln *to doubt*

zweifelt · zweifelte · gezweifelt regular weak verb

PRESENT

ich zweif(e)le	wir zweifeln
du zweifelst	ihr zweifelt
Sie zweifeln	Sie zweifeln
er/sie/es zweifelt	sie zweifeln

SIMPLE PAST

ich zweifelte	wir zweifelten
du zweifeltest	ihr zweifeltet
Sie zweifelten	Sie zweifelten
er/sie/es zweifelte	sie zweifelten

FUTURE

ich werde	wir werden	zweifeln
du wirst	ihr werdet	
Sie werden	Sie werden	
er/sie/es wird	sie werden	

PRESENT SUBJUNCTIVE I

ich zweif(e)le	wir zweifeln
du zweifelst	ihr zweifelt
Sie zweifeln	Sie zweifeln
er/sie/es zweif(e)le	sie zweifeln

PRESENT SUBJUNCTIVE II

ich zweifelte	wir zweifelten
du zweifeltest	ihr zweifeltet
Sie zweifelten	Sie zweifelten
er/sie/es zweifelte	sie zweifelten

FUTURE SUBJUNCTIVE I

ich werde	wir werden	zweifeln
du werdest	ihr werdet	
Sie werden	Sie werden	
er/sie/es werde	sie werden	

FUTURE SUBJUNCTIVE II

ich würde	wir würden	zweifeln
du würdest	ihr würdet	
Sie würden	Sie würden	
er/sie/es würde	sie würden	

PRESENT PERFECT

ich habe	wir haben	gezweifelt
du hast	ihr habt	
Sie haben	Sie haben	
er/sie/es hat	sie haben	

PAST PERFECT

ich hatte	wir hatten	gezweifelt
du hattest	ihr hattet	
Sie hatten	Sie hatten	
er/sie/es hatte	sie hatten	

FUTURE PERFECT

ich werde	wir werden	gezweifelt haben
du wirst	ihr werdet	
Sie werden	Sie werden	
er/sie/es wird	sie werden	

PAST SUBJUNCTIVE I

ich habe	wir haben	gezweifelt
du habest	ihr habet	
Sie haben	Sie haben	
er/sie/es habe	sie haben	

PAST SUBJUNCTIVE II

ich hätte	wir hätten	gezweifelt
du hättest	ihr hättet	
Sie hätten	Sie hätten	
er/sie/es hätte	sie hätten	

FUTURE PERFECT SUBJUNCTIVE I

ich werde	wir werden	gezweifelt haben
du werdest	ihr werdet	
Sie werden	Sie werden	
er/sie/es werde	sie werden	

FUTURE PERFECT SUBJUNCTIVE II

ich würde	wir würden	gezweifelt haben
du würdest	ihr würdet	
Sie würden	Sie würden	
er/sie/es würde	sie würden	

COMMANDS zweif(e)le! zweifelt! zweifeln Sie!

PRESENT PARTICIPLE zweifelnd

Usage

Warum zweifeln Sie?	*Why do you doubt?*
Literaturwissenschaftler zweifeln daran, dass Goethe den Text geschrieben hat.	*Literary scholars doubt that Goethe wrote that text.*
Es ist nicht zu zweifeln, dass die Maus durch das Loch unter der Kommode gekrochen sein könnte.	*There is no doubt that the mouse could have crawled through the hole under the chest of drawers.*
Monikas Benehmen lässt mich neuerdings an ihrer Ehrlichkeit zweifeln.	*Monika's behavior lately makes me doubt her sincerity.*
Zweifelt ihr auch etwa daran, dass die Erde eine Kugel ist?	*Do you also by any chance doubt that the earth is round?*
Ich zweifele an seinem Wissen.	*I have doubts about his knowledge.*
Leider muss ich an dir zweifeln.	*Unfortunately, I have to doubt you.*
Die Wähler haben keinen Grund, daran zu zweifeln, dass ihre Wahl richtig war.	*The voters have no reason to doubt that their choice was correct.*

RELATED VERBS an·zweifeln, bezweifeln, verzweifeln

strong verb

zwingt · zwang · gezwungen

PRESENT

ich zwinge	wir zwingen
du zwingst	ihr zwingt
Sie zwingen	Sie zwingen
er/sie/es zwingt	sie zwingen

SIMPLE PAST

ich zwang	wir zwangen
du zwangst	ihr zwangt
Sie zwangen	Sie zwangen
er/sie/es zwang	sie zwangen

FUTURE

ich werde	wir werden	zwingen
du wirst	ihr werdet	
Sie werden	Sie werden	
er/sie/es wird	sie werden	

PRESENT SUBJUNCTIVE I

ich zwinge	wir zwingen
du zwingest	ihr zwinget
Sie zwingen	Sie zwingen
er/sie/es zwinge	sie zwingen

PRESENT SUBJUNCTIVE II

ich zwänge	wir zwängen
du zwängest	ihr zwänget
Sie zwängen	Sie zwängen
er/sie/es zwänge	sie zwängen

FUTURE SUBJUNCTIVE I

ich werde	wir werden	zwingen
du werdest	ihr werdet	
Sie werden	Sie werden	
er/sie/es werde	sie werden	

FUTURE SUBJUNCTIVE II

ich würde	wir würden	zwingen
du würdest	ihr würdet	
Sie würden	Sie würden	
er/sie/es würde	sie würden	

PRESENT PERFECT

ich habe	wir haben	gezwungen
du hast	ihr habt	
Sie haben	Sie haben	
er/sie/es hat	sie haben	

PAST PERFECT

ich hatte	wir hatten	gezwungen
du hattest	ihr hattet	
Sie hatten	Sie hatten	
er/sie/es hatte	sie hatten	

FUTURE PERFECT

ich werde	wir werden	gezwungen haben
du wirst	ihr werdet	
Sie werden	Sie werden	
er/sie/es wird	sie werden	

PAST SUBJUNCTIVE I

ich habe	wir haben	gezwungen
du habest	ihr habet	
Sie haben	Sie haben	
er/sie/es habe	sie haben	

PAST SUBJUNCTIVE II

ich hätte	wir hätten	gezwungen
du hättest	ihr hättet	
Sie hätten	Sie hätten	
er/sie/es hätte	sie hätten	

FUTURE PERFECT SUBJUNCTIVE I

ich werde	wir werden	gezwungen haben
du werdest	ihr werdet	
Sie werden	Sie werden	
er/sie/es werde	sie werden	

FUTURE PERFECT SUBJUNCTIVE II

ich würde	wir würden	gezwungen haben
du würdest	ihr würdet	
Sie würden	Sie würden	
er/sie/es würde	sie würden	

COMMANDS zwing(e)! zwingt! zwingen Sie!

PRESENT PARTICIPLE zwingend

Usage

1941 zwangen ihn die politischen Verhältnisse ins Ausland zu emigrieren. — *In 1941, the political circumstances forced him to emigrate abroad.*

Der Vorsteher sagte, dass die Umstände ihn zum Rücktritt gezwungen hätten. — *The director said the situation has forced his resignation.*

Andauernde Dürren zwangen viele Landwirte, ihre Betriebe zu verlassen. — *Persistent droughts forced many farmers to abandon their farms.*

Die Gefangenen wurden gezwungen, auf dem Boden zu schlafen. — *The prisoners were forced to sleep on the ground.*

Die Kreativität lässt sich nicht zwingen. — *Creativity can't be forced.*

Heiner fühlte sich damals gezwungen, politisch aktiv zu sein. — *Heiner felt compelled in those days to be politically active.*

Rund 50 000 Flüchtlinge wurden während des Kriegs ins Grenzgebiet gezwungen. — *Around 50,000 refugees were forced into the border region during the war.*

RELATED VERBS ab·zwingen, auf·zwingen, erzwingen, nieder·zwingen

Exercises

- Answers to exercises are on page 650.

A *Write the correct form of each verb in the* ***present*** *tense to complete the sentences.*

MODEL Frank kauft ein Wörterbuch. Es kostet 15 Euro. (kaufen, kosten)

1. Ich ________ mich mit Yoga und Aerobik. ________ du Sport? (erholen, treiben)
2. Ulrich ________ keinen Spinat, aber er ________ gern Brokkoli. (mögen, essen)
3. Wir ________ nach Vancouver. Wohin ________ ihr? (fahren, gehen)
4. „Was ________ du von dieser Idee?“ „Ich ________ sie wunderbar.“ (halten, finden)
5. „Was ________ Sie von Beruf?“ „Ich ________ Pilot.“ (sein, sein)
6. „________ du einen Vorschlag?“ „Nein, ich ________ keine Ahnung.“ (haben, haben)
7. „Anke ________ einen Flug nach Rom.“ „________ Ute mitkommen?“ (buchen, können)
8. Ich ________ gern. ________ du auch gern? (reisen, reisen)
9. Tobias ________ gern Krimis. Er ________ Schriftsteller. (lesen, werden)
10. „________ du, wie viel Uhr es ist?“ „Nein, ich ________ es leider nicht.“ (wissen, wissen)
11. Heute ________ ich einkaufen. Ich ________ ein paar Sachen. (müssen, brauchen)
12. Ich ________, wir ________ genug zu tun. (denken, haben)

B *On separate paper, rewrite the sentences in Exercise A in the* ***present perfect*** *tense.*

MODEL Frank hat ein Wörterbuch gekauft. Es hat 15 Euro gekostet.

C *On separate paper, write complete sentences from the elements below, using the correct form of the prefixed verb in the* ***present*** *tense. Caution: Some prefixes are separable, while others are not!*

MODEL Wolfgang / aufstehen / um 8 Uhr → Wolfgang steht um 8 Uhr auf.

1. wir / abbiegen / hier
2. ich / besuchen / Anja
3. Michael / abnehmen
4. die Straße / aufhören / hier
5. das Kind / einsteigen / ins Auto
6. Alex / erwarten / uns
7. ich / nachdenken / darüber
8. die Firma / herstellen / Motoren
9. mein Chef / vorschlagen / etwas
10. das Auto / überholen / das Motorrad

D *On separate paper, rewrite the sentences in Exercise C in the* ***present perfect*** *tense.*

MODEL Wolfgang ist um 8 Uhr aufgestanden.

E *Write the correct form of each verb in the* ***simple past*** *tense to complete the sentences.*

MODEL Es __war__ einmal eine Königin. (sein)

1. Die Königin ___________ eine Tochter. (haben)
2. Ihre Tochter ___________ sehr schön. (sein)
3. Sie ___________ Schneewittchen. (heißen)
4. Die Königin ___________ eines Tages. (sterben)
5. Der König ___________ eine andere Dame. (heiraten)
6. Schneewittchens Stiefmutter ___________ sie. (hassen)
7. Die Stiefmutter ___________ Schneewittchen in den Wald. (schicken)
8. Schneewittchen ___________ sieben Zwerge im Wald. (finden)
9. Sie ___________ bei den Zwergen. (wohnen)
10. Schneewittchen putzte und ___________ für sie. (kochen)
11. Die Stiefmutter ___________ mit dem Spiegel. (sprechen)
12. Sie ___________, dass Schneewittchen noch ___________. (erfahren, leben)
13. Die Stiefmutter ___________ zu Schneewittchen. (kommen)
14. Sie ___________ ihr einen giftigen Apfel zu essen. (geben)
15. Schneewittchen ___________ den Apfel und starb darauf. (essen)
16. Die Zwerge ___________ Schneewittchen in einen Sarg aus Glas. (legen)
17. Ein Prinz ___________ Schneewittchen und ___________ sich. (sehen, verlieben)
18. Er küsste Schneewittchen und sie ___________. (aufwachen)

F *On separate paper, rewrite each sentence in the* ***future*** *tense using the auxiliary* werden.

MODEL Sandra singt im Chor. → Sandra wird im Chor singen.

1. Stefan leiht seinem Freund sein Auto.
2. Tobias kauft eine Lederjacke.
3. Am Samstag bin ich zu Hause.
4. Liest du den Roman?
5. Ich kann das nicht schaffen.
6. Ihr wisst die Antwort wohl.
7. Man verwendet keine Chemikalien.
8. Es ist sehr warm.
9. Es macht viel Spaß.
10. Dürfen wir eine Pause machen?
11. Wann findet die Sammlung statt?
12. Der Anzug sieht gut aus.
13. Es wird kalt und regnerisch.
14. Sprichst du mit ihm?

G *On separate paper, rewrite each sentence with the modal verb and tense indicated in parentheses.*

MODEL Susanne kauft heute ein. (müssen; *present*) → Susanne muss heute einkaufen.

1. Stefan leiht seinem Freund sein Auto. (wollen; *simple past*)
2. Tobias kauft keine Lederjacke. (dürfen; *present*)
3. Am Sonntag bleibe ich zu Hause. (sollen; *present*)
4. Arbeitest du am Wochenende? (müssen; *simple past*)
5. Frau Maier nimmt am Workshop teil. (wollen; *present perfect*)
6. Ich beeinflusse den Ausgang nicht. (können; *simple past*)
7. Martin geht ins Büro. (wollen; *present*)
8. Claudia lacht über den Vorfall. (müssen; *present perfect*)
9. Ich weiß es nicht. (müssen; *simple past*)

H *On separate paper, render the following sentences into German using the dative verb and tense indicated in parentheses.*

MODEL He doesn't answer her. (antworten, *present*) → Er antwortet ihr nicht.

1. Stefan met her yesterday. (begegnen, *simple past*)
2. I thank you for the wine. (danken, *present*)
3. I miss you. (fehlen, *present*) (*Hint: The subject is* Du.)
4. The wolf followed her. (folgen, *simple past*)
5. I like the shirt. (gefallen, present) (*Hint: The subject is* Das Hemd.)
6. She is not successful. (gelingen, *present*) (*Hint: The subject is* Es.)
7. Maria helped me. (helfen, *present perfect*)
8. Who does the book belong to? (gehören, *present*)
9. She is contradicting her answer. (widersprechen, *present*)

I *On separate paper, rewrite the following active sentences in the passive voice. If the active sentence has* man *as the subject, omit it in the passive sentence. All sentences are in the present tense.*

MODELS Der Präsident hält eine Rede. → Eine Rede wird vom Präsidenten gehalten.
Man bezahlt das Essen an der Kasse. → Das Essen wird an der Kasse bezahlt.

1. Tante Karin kocht das Essen.
2. Man befreit endlich die Gefangenen.
3. Man verbraucht zu viel Energie.
4. Herr Leitner veröffentlicht das Buch.
5. Der Autor liest das Gedicht vor.
6. Ein Affe fährt das Fahrrad durch die Stadt.
7. Man zündet Kerzen an und bereitet alles vor.
8. Frau Schlau unterrichtet Englisch.
9. Man spült das Geschirr per Hand.
10. Die Kinder singen ein Volkslied.

J *On separate paper, write commands in all three forms of the second-person imperative. Watch out for separable prefix verbs!*

MODEL träumen / süß → Träum(e) süß. Träumt süß. Träumen Sie süß.

1. helfen / mir
2. aufräumen / das Zimmer
3. kommen / zu mir
4. essen / nicht so schnell
5. geben / mir einen Kuss
6. überraschen / mich
7. vergessen / uns nicht
8. aufstehen / sofort

K *Write the correct form of each verb in the* ***present subjunctive II***, ***past subjunctive II***, *or* ***future subjunctive II*** *tense to complete the sentences.*

MODEL Lara tut, als ob sie die Antwort wüsste. (wissen, *present subjunctive II*)

1. Was ________ ________, wenn die Firmen es aber nicht ________?
   (passieren, *future subjunctive II*; tun, *present subjunctive II*)
2. Es ________ mir besser, wenn ich mehr Geld ________.
   (gehen, *present subjunctive II*; haben, *present subjunctive II*)
3. Wenn ich ihn ________ ________, ________ wir uns jetzt besser ________.
   (besuchen, *past subjunctive II*; kennen, *future subjunctive II*)
4. Er sah so aus, als ob er gerade von der Arbeit ________ ________.
   (kommen, *past subjunctive II*)
5. Wenn es ________ ________, ________ wir Regenschirme haben.
   (regnen, *future subjunctive II*; müssen, *present subjunctive II*)

L *Complete each sentence in indirect speech using the correct form of the* ***subjunctive I*** *or* ***subjunctive II***, *whichever is correct for standard German. (For a review of the rules, refer to pages 17–18, 20, 25, 26, 27, and 28.)*

MODEL Laut dem Bericht habe der Chef keinen Grund genannt. (haben)

1. Nach Polizeiangaben ________ die Männer unbekannt. (sein)
2. Der Sprecher behauptete, Herr Wolf ________ nicht dafür zuständig. (sein)
3. Die Zeugen berichteten, die Jugendlichen ________ Baseballmützen getragen. (haben)
4. Laut dem Bericht ________ die Bürgermeisterin die Antwort nicht genau. (wissen)
5. Nach Angaben ________ die Demonstranten aus Köln. (kommen)

Answers to Exercises

A

1. erhole, treibst 2. mag, isst 3. fahren, geht 4. hältst, finde 5. sind, bin 6. Hast, habe 7. bucht, Kann 8. reise, Reist 9. liest, wird 10. Weißt, weiß 11. muss, brauche 12. denke, haben

B

1. Ich habe mich mit Yoga und Aerobik erholt. Hast du Sport getrieben? 2. Ulrich hat keinen Spinat gemocht, aber er hat gern Brokkoli gegessen. 3. Wir sind nach Vancouver gefahren. Wohin seid ihr gegangen? 4. „Was hast du von dieser Idee gehalten?" „Ich habe sie wunderbar gefunden." 5. „Was sind Sie von Beruf gewesen?" „Ich bin Pilot gewesen." 6. „Hast du einen Vorschlag gehabt?" „Nein, ich habe keine Ahnung gehabt." 7. „Anke hat einen Flug nach Rom gebucht." „Hat Ute mitkommen können?" 8. Ich bin gern gereist. Bist du auch gern gereist? 9. Tobias hat gern Krimis gelesen. Er ist Schriftsteller geworden. 10. „Hast du gewusst, wie viel Uhr es ist?" „Nein, ich habe es leider nicht gewusst." 11. Heute habe ich einkaufen müssen. Ich habe ein paar Sachen gebraucht. 12. Ich habe gedacht, wir haben genug zu tun gehabt.

C

1. Wir biegen hier ab. 2. Ich besuche Anja. 3. Michael nimmt ab. 4. Die Straße hört hier auf. 5. Das Kind steigt ins Auto ein. 6. Alex erwartet uns. 7. Ich denke darüber nach. 8. Die Firma stellt Motoren her. 9. Mein Chef schlägt etwas vor. 10. Das Auto überholt das Motorrad.

D

1. Wir sind hier abgebogen. 2. Ich habe Anja besucht. 3. Michael hat abgenommen. 4. Die Straße hat hier aufgehört. 5. Das Kind ist ins Auto eingestiegen. 6. Alex hat uns erwartet. 7. Ich habe darüber nachgedacht. 8. Die Firma hat Motoren hergestellt. 9. Mein Chef hat etwas vorgeschlagen. 10. Das Auto hat das Motorrad überholt.

E

1. hatte 2. war 3. hieß 4. starb 5. heiratete 6. hasste 7. schickte 8. fand 9. wohnte 10. kochte 11. sprach 12. erfuhr, lebte 13. kam 14. gab 15. aß 16. legten 17. sah, verliebte 18. wachte auf

F

1. Stefan wird seinem Freund sein Auto leihen. 2. Tobias wird eine Lederjacke kaufen. 3. Am Samstag werde ich zu Hause sein. 4. Wirst du den Roman lesen? 5. Ich werde das nicht schaffen können. 6. Ihr werdet die Antwort wohl wissen. 7. Man wird keine Chemikalien verwenden. 8. Es wird sehr warm sein. 9. Es wird viel Spaß machen. 10. Werden wir eine Pause machen dürfen? 11. Wann wird die Sammlung stattfinden? 12. Der Anzug wird gut aussehen. 13. Es wird kalt und regnerisch werden. 14. Wirst du mit ihm sprechen?

G

1. Stefan wollte seinem Freund sein Auto leihen. 2. Tobias darf keine Lederjacke kaufen. 3. Am Sonntag soll ich zu Hause bleiben. 4. Musstest du am Wochenende arbeiten? 5. Frau Maier hat am Workshop teilnehmen wollen. 6. Ich konnte den Ausgang nicht beeinflussen. 7. Martin will ins Büro gehen. 8. Claudia hat über den Vorfall lachen müssen. 9. Ich musste es nicht wissen.

H

1. Stefan begegnete ihr gestern. 2. Ich danke dir [*or* Ihnen *or* euch] für den Wein. 3. Du fehlst mir. 4. Der Wolf folgte ihr. 5. Das Hemd gefällt mir. 6. Es gelingt ihr nicht. 7. Maria hat mir geholfen. 8. Wem gehört das Buch? 9. Sie widerspricht ihrer Antwort.

I

1. Das Essen wird von Tante Karin gekocht. 2. Die Gefangenen werden endlich befreit. 3. Zu viel Energie wird verbraucht. 4. Das Buch wird von Herrn Leitner veröffentlicht. 5. Das Gedicht wird vom Autor vorgelesen. 6. Das Fahrrad wird von einem Affen durch die Stadt gefahren. 7. Kerzen werden angezündet und alles wird vorbereitet. 8. Englisch wird von Frau Schlau unterrichtet. 9. Das Geschirr wird per Hand gespült. 10. Ein Volkslied wird von den Kindern gesungen.

J

1. Hilf mir. Helft mir. Helfen Sie mir. 2. Räum(e) das Zimmer auf. Räumt das Zimmer auf. Räumen Sie das Zimmer auf. 3. Komm(e) zu mir. Kommt zu mir. Kommen Sie zu mir. 4. Iss nicht so schnell. Esst nicht so schnell. Essen Sie nicht so schnell. 5. Gib mir einen Kuss. Gebt mir einen Kuss. Geben Sie mir einen Kuss. 6. Überrasch(e) mich. Überrascht mich. Überraschen Sie mich. 7. Vergiss uns nicht. Vergesst uns nicht. Vergessen Sie uns nicht. 8. Steh(e) sofort auf. Steht sofort auf. Stehen Sie sofort auf.

K

1. würde passieren, täten 2. ginge, hätte 3. besucht hätte, würden … kennen 4. gekommen wäre 5. regnen würde, müssten

L

1. seien 2. sei 3. hätten 4. wisse 5. kämen

English-German Verb Index

Use this index to look up the corresponding German verb conjugation chart by the English meaning. Some English verbs have more than one German equivalent; the semantic range of the meanings in a verb's conjugation banner, as well as the accompanying Usage sentences, will help you determine if you have located the appropriate German verb. Because this index references only the 555 verbs conjugated in this book, it is not to be used as a general dictionary of verbs.

A

B

C

D

S

Irregular Verb Form Index

It can sometimes be difficult to derive the infinitive of a particularly irregular verb form. This index guides you from an irregular form that you encounter to the appropriate model verb in this book. In this way, you can see irregular forms as part of the complete conjugation program.

T

U

V

W

Z

German Verb Index

This index contains 4,200 German verbs, listed alphabetically by present active infinitive. Included in each verb's entry are the third-person forms of the simple past tense and the present perfect tense (with the auxiliary verb), an English gloss, and a cross reference to one of the 555 model verbs in this book that has the same conjugation pattern in the simple tenses.

The 555 model verbs appear in bold type. A centerline dot in the infinitive form indicates that the prefix before the dot is separable when the verb is conjugated in a main clause and/or when it is in its past participle form. Slashes separate alternate forms, either of which may be correct, depending on the meaning intended. Prefixed forms that can be separable or inseparable with no difference in meaning are given in square brackets. The English glosses have been kept as concise as possible and often do not cover all meanings of the verb.

A

ab·ändern (änderte ab, hat abgeändert) *modify* 9
ab·arbeiten (arbeitete ab, hat abgearbeitet) *work off* 22
ab·backen (backte/buk ab, hat abgebacken) *bake off* 43
ab·bauen (baute ab, hat abgebaut) *dismantle* 45
ab·behalten (behielt ab, hat abbehalten) *keep off* 61
ab·bekommen (bekam ab, hat abbekommen) *receive a share of* 66
ab·berufen (berief ab, hat abberufen) *call away* 79
ab·bestellen (bestellte ab, hat abbestellt) *cancel* 91
ab·bezahlen (bezahlte ab, hat abbezahlt) *pay off* 103
ab·biegen (bog ab, hat/ist abgebogen) *turn (off); bend* 1
ab·bilden (bildete ab, hat abgebildet) *depict* 14
ab·binden (band ab, hat abgebunden) *untie; tie off* 108
ab·bitten (bat ab, hat abgebeten) *apologize* 109
ab·blasen (blies ab, hat abgeblasen) *blow off* 110
ab·bleichen (bleichte ab, ist abgebleicht) *grow pale* 112
ab·blühen (blühte ab, hat/ist abgeblüht) *stop blooming* 113
ab·brauchen (brauchte ab, hat abgebraucht) *wear out* 115
ab·brechen (brach ab, hat/ist abgebrochen) *break off* 116
ab·brennen (brannte ab, hat/ist abgebrannt) *burn off* 117
ab·bringen (brachte ab, hat abgebracht) *dissuade* 118
ab·danken (dankte ab, hat abgedankt) *abdicate* 120
ab·drehen (drehte ab, hat/ist abgedreht) *twist off* 125
ab·drucken (druckte ab, hat abgedruckt) *publish* 128
ab·drücken (drückte ab, hat abgedrückt) *pull the trigger* 129
ab·erkennen (erkannte ab [aberkannte], hat aberkannt) *discredit* 162
ab·essen (aß ab, hat abgegessen) *eat off* 175
ab·fahren (fuhr ab, hat/ist abgefahren) *depart* 2
ab·fallen (fiel ab, ist abgefallen) *fall off* 178
ab·fangen (fing ab, hat abgefangen) *intercept* 179
ab·fassen (fasste ab, hat abgefasst) *write out* 180
ab·finden (fand ab, hat abgefunden) *come to terms* 186
ab·fliegen (flog ab, hat/ist abgeflogen) *fly off* 188
ab·fließen (floss ab, ist abgeflossen) *flow off* 190
ab·fordern (forderte ab, hat abgefordert) *recall* 193
ab·fragen (fragte ab, hat abgefragt) *question* 194
ab·fressen (fraß ab, hat abgefressen) *graze on* 195
ab·frieren (fror ab, hat/ist abgefroren) *freeze off* 197
ab·fühlen (fühlte ab, hat abgefühlt) *palpate* 199
ab·führen (führte ab, hat abgeführt) *carry off* 200
ab·füllen (füllte ab, hat abgefüllt) *decant* 201
ab·geben (gab ab, hat abgegeben) *hand in; fire* 3
ab·gehen (ging ab, ist abgegangen) *go off* 210
ab·gelten (galt ab, hat abgegolten) *satisfy* 213
ab·gewinnen (gewann ab, hat abgewonnen) *extract* 218
ab·gewöhnen (gewöhnte ab, hat abgewöhnt) *disaccustom, break of* 219
ab·gießen (goss ab, hat abgegossen) *pour off* 220
ab·gleichen (glich ab, hat abgeglichen) *equalize* 222
ab·gleiten (glitt ab, ist abgeglitten) *slip off* 223
ab·graben (grub ab, hat abgegraben) *dig off* 225
ab·greifen (griff ab, hat abgegriffen) *wear out* 226
ab·gucken (guckte ab, hat abgeguckt) *copy* 229
ab·haben (hatte ab, hat abgehabt) *have off* 230
ab·halten (hielt ab, hat abgehalten) *deter* 231
ab·handeln (handelte ab, hat abgehandelt) *transact* 232
ab·hängen (hing ab, hat abgehangen) *hang down* 233
ab·hängen (hängte ab, hat abgehängt) *take down* 234
ab·hauen (haute/hieb ab, hat/ist abgehauen) *split* 236
ab·heben (hob ab, hat abgehoben) *lift off* 237
ab·helfen (half ab, hat abgeholfen) *redress* 241
ab·holen (holte ab, hat abgeholt) *fetch, pick up* 4
ab·holzen (holzte ab, hat abgeholzt) *deforest* 275
ab·hören (hörte ab, hat abgehört) *tap* (phone) 248
ab·kämpfen (kämpfte ab, hat abgekämpft) *fight off* 252
ab·kaufen (kaufte ab, hat abgekauft) *buy from* 253
ab·kehren (kehrte ab, hat abgekehrt) *avert* 254
ab·klappen (klappte ab, hat abgeklappt) *flip down* 258
ab·klemmen (klemmte ab, hat abgeklemmt) *pinch off* 428
ab·klingen (klang ab, ist abgeklungen) *fade away* 261
ab·klopfen (klopfte ab, hat abgeklopft) *knock off* 262
ab·kneifen (kniff ab, hat abgekniffen) *pinch off* 321
ab·kochen (kochte ab, hat abgekocht) *scald* 264
ab·kommen (kam ab, ist abgekommen) *come off* 265
ab·kriegen (kriegte ab, hat abgekriegt) *get off* 272
ab·kündigen (kündigte ab, hat abgekündigt) *proclaim* 274
ab·kürzen (kürzte ab, hat abgekürzt) *abridge* 275
ab·laden (lud ab, hat abgeladen) *dump* 278
ab·lassen (ließ ab, hat abgelassen) *let off* 280
ab·laufen (lief ab, hat/ist abgelaufen) *run off* 281
ab·legen (legte ab, hat abgelegt) *cast off* 283
ab·lehnen (lehnte ab, hat abgelehnt) *decline, refuse* 5
ab·leisten (leistete ab, hat abgeleistet) *serve out* 288
ab·leiten (leitete ab, hat abgeleitet) *derive* 289
ab·lenken (lenkte ab, hat abgelenkt) *distract* 364
ab·lesen (las ab, hat abgelesen) *read off* 291
ab·lichten (lichtete ab, hat abgelichtet) *photocopy* 76
ab·liefern (lieferte ab, hat abgeliefert) *deliver* 293
ab·liegen (lag ab, hat abgelegen) *be remote* 294

B

C

D

F

L

M

N

O

P

Q

R

S

T

U

V

W

Z